Table of Descriptive Catego

PRIMARY

African (Afr.)
American (Am.)
Ancient
Arab
Argentinian (Arg.)
Arthurian (Arth.)
Asian
Australian
Austrian (Aust.)
Babylonian
(Babyl.)
Belgian (Belg.)
British (Br.)
Buddhist
Canadian (Can.)
Chinese
Christian
Classical (Class.)
Czechoslovakian
(Czech.)
Danish (Dan.)
Dutch
Eastern
Egyptian (Egypt.)
European (Eur.)
Flemish (Flem.)
French (Fr.)
German (Ger.)
Greek (Gk.)
Hindu
Hungarian (Hung.)
Indian (Ind.)
Iranian
Irish
Islamic
Israeli

Italian (Ital.)
Japanese (Jpn.)
Jewish
Medieval
Mexican (Mex.)
Middle Eastern
(Middle East.)
Native American
(Native Am.)
Norse
Norwegian (Nor.)
Persian (Pers.)
Phoenician
Polish
Popular (Pop.)
Portuguese (Port.)
Renaissance (Ren.)
Roman Catholic
(Rom. Catholic)
Roman (Rom.)
Russian (Russ.)
Scottish (Scot.)
Sikh
Spanish (Span.)
Swedish (Swed.)
Swiss
Taoist
Tibetan
Traditional (Trad.)
Turkish
Welsh
Western
Yiddish

S

Animal Symbolism
Apocrypha
Architecture
Art
Astrology
Astronomy
Aviation
Ballad
Buddhism
Business
Children's Litera-
ture (Children's
Lit.)
Christianity
Comics
Cuisine
Culture
Dance
Entertainment
Fairy Tale
Film
Flower Symbolism
Folklore
Folktale
Gem Symbolism
Geography
Government
Graphic Novels
Hagiography
(Hagiog.)
Hinduism
History (Hist.)
Iconography
(Iconog.)
Islam
Journalism (Jour.)

Legend
Literature (Lit.)
Miscellaneous
(Misc.)
Music
Musical
Mythology (Myth.)
New Testament
(N.T.)
Nursery Rhyme
(Nurs. Rhyme)
Old Testament
(O.T.)
Opera
Philosophy (Phil.)
Physics
Plant Symbolism
Politics
Publishing
Radio
Religion (Rel.)
Science
Sports
Symbolism
Technology
Television (TV)
Theater
Theology (Theol.)
Trademarks
Tradition (Trad.)
Tree Symbolism
Usage

Ruffner's Allusions

Ruffner's Allusions

CULTURAL, LITERARY, BIBLICAL, AND HISTORICAL: A THEMATIC DICTIONARY

THIRD EDITION

By Frederick G. Ruffner, Jr.,
and Laurence Urdang

Edited by Laurie Lanzen Harris and Sharon R. Gunton

Omnigraphics

P.O. Box 31-1640
Detroit, MI 48231

Omnigraphics, Inc.

By Frederick G. Ruffner, Jr., and Laurence Urdang
Laurie Lanzen Harris, Sharon R. Gunton, and Amy Marcaccio Keyzer, *Editors*
Cherie D. Abbey, *Managing Editor*

Peter E. Ruffner, *Publisher*
Matthew P. Barbour, *Senior Vice President*

Elizabeth Collins, *Research and Permissions Coordinator*
Kevin M. Hayes, *Operations Manager*
Allison A. Beckett and Mary Butler, *Research Staff*
Cherry Stockdale, *Permissions Assistant*
Shirley Amore, Martha Johns, and Kirk Kauffmann, *Administrative Staff*

Copyright © 2009 Omnigraphics, Inc.
ISBN 978-0-7808-1122-5

Special thanks to Frederick G. Ruffner, Jr., for creating this publication.

Library of Congress Cataloging-in-Publication Data

Allusions--cultural, literary, biblical, and historical
Ruffner's allusions--cultural, literary, religious, and historical : a thematic dictionary / by Frederick G. Ruffner, Jr. and Laurence Urdang. -- 3rd ed.
    p. cm.
Includes bibliographical references and index.
    Summary: "A thematic dictionary, with almost 13,000 allusion entries organized under 730 thematic categories. Thematic categories are presented in alphabetical order; each thematic category is followed a list of allusions, including definitions, origins (nationality and genre), and sources. Includes a bibliography and index"--Provided by publisher.
    ISBN 978-0-7808-1122-5 (hardcover : alk. paper) 1. Allusions--Dictionaries. I. Ruffner, Frederick G. II. Urdang, Laurence. III. Title.
    PN43.A4 2009
    081--dc22

                               2009021711

Contents

Dedicated to the Memory of
Laurence Urdang
March 21, 1927 - August 21, 2008

Larry Urdang was one of the greatest lexicographers of the modern era. His prodigious output included more than 100 books, including the first *Random House Unabridged Dictionary*, as well as many volumes on language and usage published by Gale Research and other companies. It was a pleasure and privilege to work with Larry for over 40 years, from his early books for Gale, including the first and second editions of the *Allusions Dictionary*, to his final work, *The Last Word*, a fascinating account of the current state of the English language, published by OmniData in 2008. His wit and erudition informed everything he wrote; the world has lost a staunch defender of the best in clarity and precision, and we have lost a colleague of surpassing gifts.

Frederick G. Ruffner, Jr.
Publisher, OmniData, Inc.

Preface to the Third Edition

As this Third Edition of the *Allusions Dictionary* went to press, we heard of the passing of the work's first co-editor, lexicographer extraordinaire Laurence Urdang. It was an honor for me to edit Larry's final work on language, *The Last Word*, published by OmniData in 2008, and a pleasure to edit this Third Edition of what is now known as *Ruffner's Allusions*, named for the work's other co-editor, reference publisher Frederick G. Ruffner, Jr. It is difficult to exaggerate the influence of Fred Ruffner on me, and on a generation of reference editors and publishers who have learned so much from him, while he was publisher first at Gale Research, then at Omnigraphics, and now at OmniData. My co-editors on this volume, Sharon R. Gunton and Amy Marcaccio Keyzer, are also Gale alumnae, and it is our hope that our combined years of editorial experience at Gale and Omnigraphics are evident in this new edition.

Our task, as outlined by Fred Ruffner, was to update *Allusions*. The Second Edition contained 712 thematic categories—for example, AMBITION, FRIENDSHIP, and SLANDER. Under theses thematic categories, a total of 8,700 allusions were listed—references to such varied sources as literature, classical mythology, history, the arts, industry, and much more. Each allusion entry also included information on the source in which it appeared as well as its nationality and genre.

To create the Third Edition, we had several key goals in mind. First, we increased the number of entries, from 8,700 in the Second Edition, to nearly 13,000 in the Third. In compiling the entries, we focused on several areas: real people, a category avoided in earlier editions; technology and media, especially the profound influence of computers and the Internet; allusions pertinent to popular culture, especially television, film, and music; broadening the scope of non-Biblical religious allusions to include other faiths, especially Islam, Buddhism, and Hinduism; extending entries on children's literature, including characters and titles; and covering the past 50 years in politics and world history, a time of profound change that has brought with it concepts, and allusions, that are truly global in scope. We realize that we may have not covered key areas of interest to our users, and, as with earlier editions, we invite readers to write to us at Omnigraphics for suggestions for subsequent editions.

A note on sources: we did not change the bibliographic source information for allusions from previous editions, because, in most cases, the references are to standard reference sources, such as the *Encyclopedia Britannica* or *The New Columbia Encyclopedia*. We believed that a reader would be able to find the allusion in multiple editions of that source. For the allusions new to this edition, the source listed refers to the most recent edition of a source available to the reader, either in print or online. Because so many readers use on-line editions of reference sources cited here, we have not included page numbers in the source citations.

We look forward to hearing your thoughts. Please write to us with any suggestions you might have for improving future editions.

Laurie Lanzen Harris
Omnigraphics, Inc.
155 West Congress
Detroit, MI 48226
editorial@omnigraphics.com

Preface to the Second Edition

When *Allusions* was first published, in 1982, it was generally well received, providing sufficient encouragement for the preparation of this Second Edition, containing more than 8,700 entries, an increase of nearly 25 percent over the First Edition.

As with many books that attempt to break new ground, the First Edition contained a number of flaws, which we have sought to correct in this Second Edition. Among them, alas, was my failure to make it clear that we generally avoided the inclusion of real people unless they were felt to epitomize a particular characteristic that appears as a Thematic Category. The reason for that decision lay in the fact that it is impossible to list all of the **POETS, ARTISTS,** etc. who might be deemed worthy of entry, because they are considered proverbially great (like Milton), because they are an important referent for a certain style of poem (like Meredith, for "shaped" poetry), or for any other reason. A few have been retained (**Leonardo** under **INVENTIVENESS** and **VERSATILITY,** for example), though only those with specific attributes—for instance, Michelangelo does not appear.

A number of people have written to us with suggestions for additions, deletions, and shifts of entries from one category to another, and we have taken all of these offerings under serious consideration. Because of the enormous diversity of interests and expertness among contributors, we have received many suggestions that the editors felt to be too specialized for a work of general reference; in other cases, we have felt embarrassed at having missed some of the more obvious allusions. Sometimes, though a suggested entry may have been quite valid, its referent was far too general to allow its inclusion: for example, an attribute of a character who is not named in a work of fiction or whose name is extremely unlikely to be known and therefore cannot be classified into the present structure of the book has been eliminated from consideration. In other cases, the attribute or attributes of a character are too vague to admit entry. Also omitted are characters that are relatively obscure or, though prominent, appear in relatively obscure works of literature, even though those works might have been created by well-known authors.

In short, as we wrote in the First Edition,

Not everything is here, of course. There are probably hundreds of thousands of allusions.... Any reader of this book can find inclusions that may not be to his taste and omissions that he considers heinously unforgivable. We have attempted a broad coverage of a subject so vast and so mercurial that it is doubtful its documentation can ever be complete.

Those statements are still valid, and they are likely to remain so regardless of the number of editions of this book that might follow.

Some comment has focused on the presentation of the source material, both at the entry and in the Bibliography, chiefly at the decision to use a modern edition as a source. The decision to use secondary sources and modern editions was taken deliberately, for they are the sources most conveniently and most readily found on the shelves of libraries. Thus, reference is made, for example, to a 1970 edition of the Old Testament published by Oxford University Press, to a 1947 edition, also by O.U.P., of *Hamlet*, and to a 1965 Atheneum edition of *Golden Boy*, by Clifford Odets. Moreover, there are many references to secondary sources, like *The Reader's Encyclopedia*, by William Rose Benét (Crowell, 1965), *The New Columbia Encyclopedia* (Columbia U.P., 1975), and the *Encyclopaedia Britannica* (EB, 1977). It seemed obvious to the editors that secondary sources, recognized as such, would be more readily available than the original documents and other original sources on which they were based and, likewise, that no reasoning user of *Allusions* would think that we were suggesting that Old Testament, *Hamlet*, and *Golden Boy* were originally published in, respectively, 1970, 1947, and 1965.

The idea that, where practical, original publication dates be included somewhere in the Bibliography or at each entry is a good one, and we may be able to include them in a Third Edition; but there was not sufficient time to include them in the Second, and users will have to rely on other bibliographical sources for that information, which is easily found in many library catalogues.

We have been fortunate in obtaining the editorial expertise of David M. Glixon, who added more than 1,500 new entries and did considerable housekeeping on existing material. Paul Falla has provided valuable insight in his analysis of the First Edition and his suggestions for additions to the Second. And we are grateful to Elizabeth Chapman Hewitt, who has culled a great number of sources to provide suggestions for new entries. As always, however, the responsibility for the results rests on the editors, who, in their own wisdom (or lack of it) must assume that burden.

Laurence Urdang
Essex, Connecticut
March 1986

Preface to the First Edition

If language can be considered a fabric, then the warp are its words, the weft its grammar. There are plain-weave fabrics with little color and elaborate tapestries that are works of art. Much of literary language falls into the latter category. Yet we cannot ignore the poetry and the rhetorical devices used by those of us who are not poets. Language is by nature metaphoric.

With a few exceptions, dictionaries persist in ignoring the most productive, evocative, emotive, descriptive aspects of language. They pay scant attention to the creative genius of its users, whether they be poets or peasants. Rather, they are concerned with a sterile distillate which robs the lexicon of its intimations of creativity. Lexicographers by tradition or discipline ignore the innate ability of speakers to perceive relationships between the realities of life and the symbolism of myth, literature, culture, and language. The rationale is that dictionaries record denotation, not connotation. Even cursory examination of any desk (or larger) dictionary will show that such a claim is errant, arrant nonsense: one need only read through a few longer entries like *take, run,* or *set* to see how false that position is, how many metaphoric senses are listed.

Lexicographers, it must be acknowledged, are (almost) human, too: no matter how disciplined the mind, it cannot avoid metaphor or allusion. Language is not a plain weave, an ecru fustian; it is a colorful tapestry. Depending on the weaver, it may not always turn out to be a panoramic work of art, but colorful it often is, frequently realistic in some areas and abstract in others. Even the "scientific" lexicographer succumbs to its magic, unable to separate his work from his nature: there can be no objectivity in the description of one's own language.

Nevertheless, that does not keep lexicographers from trying to be objective, chiefly by the arbitrary elimination of certain classes of words and meanings and the inclusion—just as arbitrary—of others. We may ask why, for example, the word *Superman* (in reference to the comic-strip character) is omitted: surely, it has not only denotative meaning but also a host of useful connotations and metaphoric senses that are far more familiar to (American) English speakers than are the kinds of obscure entries that one customarily finds in dictionaries.

There are thousands of such references that constantly occur in our language. Some may be drawn from the comic strips, as in the case of *Superman*; many are drawn from literature (*Babbitt, Scrooge*), from legend or mythology (*Midas, Hercules, Paul Bunyan*), from brand names (*Edsel, Coca-Cola [Coke]*), from symbols (*closed book, yin-yang*), from real people (*Shakespeare, Rockefeller*-on a formula like, "He's a regular Rockefeller"), from events (*Watergate, Boston Tea Party*), from the names of places, buildings, or the like (*Loch Ness,*

Empire State Building), from music and the other arts (*Star-Spangled Banner, Mona Lisa*), from animals (*dolphin, leopard, mule, rabbit*--all have their attributes), and from every other classification of information associated with culture. By what criteria may such references be omitted from a dictionary that purports to contain "all of the common words and meanings of English"? Even so-called "unabridged" dictionaries don't list them.

These lexical items cannot be omitted on the grounds of lack of frequency: they are often more frequent than the words that are listed. They cannot be omitted because "everyone already knows them"; a (general) dictionary is supposed to be "a description of the lexicon, or word stock of a language," and they clearly are a part of the lexicon. Many words, now spelled with small letters, were once allusive referents-*thersitical, pander*. Some are listed in dictionaries with capitals-*Midas, Jonah, Adam, Gargantuan*.

Capitalization is an empty criterion if we consider language as primarily spoken, with any distinction between capital and small letters obviously inaudible. (It may be true that some proper names and adjectives are identifiable from their syntactic relationships, even in oral discourse, but it is not true of all: we speak of *Shakespeare*, "the" *George Washington Bridge*, and so on; but how can one analyze a *Shakespeare* 'a genius,' or a *Scrooge* 'a miser,' or a *Rockefeller* 'a wealthy man' as distinct from the senses for which they are equivalents? These are preceded by indefinite articles, hence are used metaphorically.)

Because we feel these words should be documented in their metaphoric senses, we have compiled this book. *Allusions—Cultural, Literary, Biblical, and Historical: A Thematic Dictionary*, contains more than 7,000 such references: to the Bible, Shakespeare, Dickens; to Greek, Roman, Scandinavian, and other mythologies; to American, European, Eastern, and other legends; to music, the arts, industry, comics, motion pictures, television, radio—in fact, to all of the diverse elements that make up what we classify under the general rubric of culture. These are our familiar, everyday references, the things we talk about and the things we use when we speak English, the veritable fabric of our lives, gathered in a single work for easy reference. Not everything is here, of course. There are probably hundreds of allusions (if they could all be counted), always arriving, always departing. Any reader of this book can find inclusions that may not be to his taste and omissions that he considers heinously unforgivable. We have attempted a broad coverage of a subject so vast and so mercurial that it is doubtful its documentation can ever be complete. We should be grateful for readers' comments, addenda, and corrigenda.

Laurence Urdang
Essex, Connecticut
August 1981

How to Use This Book

Ruffner's Allusions is a thematic dictionary, with almost 13,000 allusion entries organized under more than 730 thematic categories. These thematic categories are presented in the text in alphabetical order by the name of the category heading, for example, AMBITION, FRIENDSHIP, SLANDER. (A complete list, including cross references, is given in the Table of Thematic Categories, page xvii.) Under each thematic category, one or more—sometimes many more—appropriate entries for allusions are listed.

When seeking a set of allusions that deal with a particular theme, say ANGER, the reader will find it in the text as thematic category no. 24. Under that category number and name will be a list of allusions arranged alphabetically and numbered, as in the following example, which shows just a few of the listings under this category:

24
The thematic category number, used for ease of reference in the Index.

ANGER
The thematic category, listed in alphabetical order, with more than 730 throughout the book.

(See also EXASPERATION, IRASCIBILITY, RANTING.)
Cross references point to other related thematic terms.

arrow
Each allusion is given in alphabetical order in bold face type.

Islamic symbol for Allah's rage
A brief definition of the allusion is given after its name.

24. ANGER (See also EXASPERATION, IRASCIBILITY, RANTING.)
1. **Achilles** Greek warrior whose ire is noted in the opening line of *The Iliad*: "Sing, goddess, of the anger of Achilles." [Gk. Myth: *ODA*]
5. **arrow** Islamic symbol for Allah's rage. [Islam: *CEOS&S*, 208]
7. **Bernardo** enraged that member of a rival street-gang is making advances to his sister. [Am. Musical: *West Side Story*]
9. **Elmer Fudd** hapless man seethes over Bugs Bunny's antics. [Comics: "Bugs Bunny" in Horn, 140]
11. **Fawlty, Basil** temperamental proprietor of Fawlty Towers, from the TV show of the same name, hilariously acted by John Cleese. [Br. TV: *ODA*]
13. **Herod** angry at Wise Men's disobedience, orders slaughter of male infants. [N.T.: Matthew 2:16–17]
14. **Hulk, The Incredible** one of Marvel Comics' most popular superheroes; Dr. Banner—exposed to gamma radiation—turns into the super-strong Hulk when angry or under stress; made into popular TV show and films. [Am. Comics and TV: *SJEPC*]
18. **Othello** smothers wife, Desdemona, in paroxysm of rage over her suspected adultery. [Br. Lit.: *Othello*]
19. **Rumpelstiltskin** stamps ground in rage over lass's discovery of his name. [Ger. Fairy Tale: *Rumpelstiltskin*]

Ger. Fairy Tale
Descriptive categories (here, German Fairy Tale) provide more information about the origin of the allusion, generally nationality and genre (see the Table of Descriptive Categories, page xv).

Rumpelstiltskin
Source references (a primary or secondary source) provide further information about the background of the allusion; sources are identified in the Bibliography (see the Bibliography, page 819).

Table of Descriptive Categories (with Abbreviations)

Each of the almost 13,000 allusion entries in *Ruffner's Allusions* includes descriptive categories, which are listed below. These descriptive categories provide more information about the origin of the allusion, generally nationality and genre.

PRIMARY

African (Afr.)
American (Am.)
Ancient
Arab
Argentinian (Arg.)
Arthurian (Arth.)
Asian
Australian
Austrian (Aust.)
Babylonian (Babyl.)
Belgian (Belg.)
British (Br.)
Buddhist
Canadian (Can.)
Chinese
Christian
Classical (Class.)
Czechoslovakian (Czech.)
Danish (Dan.)
Dutch
Eastern
Egyptian (Egypt.)
European (Eur.)
Flemish (Flem.)
French (Fr.)
German (Ger.)
Greek (Gk.)
Hindu
Hungarian (Hung.)
Indian (Ind.)
Iranian
Irish
Islamic
Israeli
Italian (Ital.)
Japanese (Jpn.)

Jewish
Medieval
Mexican (Mex.)
Middle Eastern (Middle East.)
Native American (Native Am.)
Norse
Norwegian (Nor.)
Persian (Pers.)
Phoenician
Polish
Popular (Pop.)
Portuguese (Port.)
Renaissance (Ren.)
Roman Catholic (Rom. Catholic)
Roman (Rom.)
Russian (Russ.)
Scottish (Scot.)
Sikh
Spanish (Span.)
Swedish (Swed.)
Swiss
Taoist
Tibetan
Traditional (Trad.)
Turkish
Welsh
Western
Yiddish

SECONDARY

Animal Symbolism
Apocrypha
Architecture
Art
Astrology
Astronomy
Aviation

Ballad
Buddhism
Business
Children's Literature (Children's Lit.)
Christianity
Comics
Cuisine
Culture
Dance
Entertainment
Fairy Tale
Film
Flower Symbolism
Folklore
Folktale
Gem Symbolism
Geography
Government
Graphic Novels
Hagiography (Hagiog.)
Hinduism
History (Hist.)
Iconography (Iconog.)
Islam
Journalism (Jour.)
Judaism
Law

Legend
Literature (Lit.)
Miscellaneous (Misc.)
Music
Musical
Mythology (Myth.)
New Testament (N.T.)
Nursery Rhyme (Nurs. Rhyme)
Old Testament (O.T.)
Opera
Philosophy (Phil.)
Physics
Plant Symbolism
Politics
Publishing
Radio
Religion (Rel.)
Science
Sports
Symbolism
Technology
Television (TV)
Theater
Theology (Theol.)
Trademarks
Tradition (Trad.)
Tree Symbolism
Usage

Table of Thematic Categories

In *Ruffner's Allusions*, allusion entries are organized under more than 730 thematic categories, listed below. The thematic categories are arranged alphabetically, from ABANDONMENT to ZODIAC, with cross references that point to other related terms.

Artlessness (See INNOCENCE, NAÏVETÉ.)

42. ASCENSION
43. ASCETICISM (See also DISCI-PLINE.)
44. ASS
45. ASSASSINATION (See also MURDER.)
46. ASTROLOGY (See also ZODIAC.)
47. ASTRONOMY
48. ATHEISM
49. ATHLETICISM (See also SPORTS.)

Austerity (See ASCETICISM, DISCIPLINE, HARSHNESS.)

50. AUTHORITY

Autobiography (See BIOGRAPHY and AUTOBIOGRAPHY.)

51. AUTOMOBILE
52. AUTUMN
53. AVIATION (See also BALLOONING, SPACE TRAVEL.)

Award (See PRIZE.)

54. AWKWARDNESS (See also INEPTITUDE.)
55. BACHELOR

Bachelorette (See SINGLE WOMAN.)

Badness (See EVIL.)

56. BALDNESS
57. BALLOONING (See also AVIATION.)
58. BANISHMENT
59. BANKRUPTCY (See also POVERTY.)
60. BAPTISM
61. BARRENNESS
62. BARRIER
63. BASEBALL

Bashfulness (See TIMIDITY.)

64. BASKETBALL
65. BATTLE (See also WAR.)
66. BEAUTY
67. BEAUTY, FEMININE (See also BEAUTY, SENSUAL.)
68. BEAUTY, MASCULINE
69. BEAUTY, RUSTIC
70. BEAUTY, SENSUAL (See also BEAUTY, FEMININE; BEAUTY, MASCULINE; SEX SYMBOL.)
71. BESTIALITY (See also PERVERSION.)
72. BETRAYAL (See also TREACHERY, TREASON.)
73. BIGOTRY (See also ANTI-SEMITISM.)
74. BIOGRAPHY and AUTOBIOGRAPHY
75. BIRD

Birth (See CHILDBIRTH).

76. BIRTHSTONE
77. BLACKMAIL (See also BRIBERY.)

Blasphemy (See APOSTASY.)

78. BLINDNESS
79. BOASTFULNESS (See also ARROGANCE, CONCEIT, EGOTISM.)
80. BOHEMIANISM
81. BOREDOM (See also DESPAIR, FUTILITY.)
82. BORESOMENESS
83. BOXING
84. BRAVERY (See also FORTITUDE, HERO.)
85. BRAWNINESS (See also STRENGTH.)
86. BREVITY
87. BRIBERY (See also BLACKMAIL.)
88. BRIDGE
89. BRIGHTNESS
90. BRITAIN
91. BROADCASTING (See also JOURNALISM, TELEVISION.)
92. BRUTALITY (See also CRUELTY, GENOCIDE, MUTILATION, RUTHLESSNESS, TYRANNY.)
93. BUDDHISM (See also ENLIGHTENMENT, RELIGION.)
94. BULL
95. BULLYING
96. BUREAUCRACY
97. BURIAL ALIVE
98. BURIAL GROUND
99. BUSINESS
100. BUTLER (See also SERVANT.)
101. BUXOMNESS (See also SEX SYMBOL.)
102. CANNIBALISM

153. COURTESY (See also HOSPITALI-
TY.)
154. COURTESY, EXCESSIVE
Covetousness (See GREED.)
155. COWARDICE (See also TIMIDITY.)
156. CRAFTSMANSHIP
157. CREATION
Creativity (See INVENTIVENESS.)
158. CRIME FIGHTING (See also DE-
TECTIVE.)
159. CRIMINAL (See also GANGSTER-
ISM, OUTLAW.)
160. CRITICISM
161. CROSS-DRESSER
162. CRUELTY (See also BRUTALITY,
HEARTLESSNESS, MUTILATION,
TYRANNY.)
163. CRYING
164. CUCKOLDRY (See also ADUL-
TERY, FAITHLESSNESS.)
165. CULTISM
166. CUNNING (See also TRICKERY,
UNSCRUPULOUSNESS.)
167. CURIOSITY (See also EAVES-
DROPPING, VOYEURISM.)
168. CURMUDGEON
169. CURSE
170. CUTENESS
171. CYNICISM (See also PESSIMISM,
SKEPTICISM.)
172. DANCE
173. DANGER
Darkness (See NIGHT.)
174. DAWN
175. DEADLINESS
176. DEAFNESS
177. DEATH
178. DEATH, ACCIDENTAL (See also
DEATH, PREMATURE.)
179. DEATH, PREMATURE (See also
DEATH, ACCIDENTAL; LOVE,
TRAGIC; VICTIMS.)
Debauchery (See DISSIPATION, LI-
CENTIOUSNESS, PROMISCUITY.)
Debt (See BANKRUPTCY, POVER-
TY.)
180. DECADENCE
181. DECAPITATION (See also
HEADLESSNESS.)

182. DECEIT (See also FRAUDU-
LENCE, UNSCRUPULOUSNESS.)
183. DEFEAT
184. DEFENDER
185. DEFIANCE (See also REBEL-
LIOUSNESS.)
186. DEFORMITY
187. DELIVERANCE (See also FREE-
DOM.)
188. DELUSION
189. DEMAGOGUERY
190. DEMON (See also DEVIL.)
191. DESPAIR (See also BOREDOM,
FUTILITY, SUICIDE.)
Destiny (See FATE.)
192. DESTRUCTION
193. DETECTIVE (See also CRIME
FIGHTING, MYSTERY.)
194. DETERMINATION (See also
PERSERVERANCE.)
195. DEVIL (See also DEMON.)
Devotion (See FAITHLFULNESS.)
196. DICTION, FAULTY
197. DIGNITY (See also NOBLEMIND-
EDNESS.)
198. DILEMMA
199. DIMWITTEDNESS (See also IG-
NORANCE, STUPIDITY.)
200. DIRTINESS
201. DISAPPEARANCE (See also AB-
DUCTION.)
202. DISASTER (See also SHIPWRECK.)
203. DISCIPLINE (See also ASCETI-
CISM.)
204. DISCORD (See also CONFUSION.)
205. DISCOVERY
Discrimination (See ANTI-SEMI-
TISM, BIGOTRY, RACISM.)
206. DISEASE
207. DISGUISE
Dishonesty (See DECEIT.)
208. DISILLUSIONMENT
209. DISOBEDIENCE
Disorder (See CONFUSION.)
210. DISSIPATION (See also LICEN-
TIOUSNESS, PROMISCUITY.)
Divination (See OMEN.)
211. DOG

341. HEALING (See also HEALTH, MEDICINE.)
342. HEALTH (See also HEALING, MEDICINE.)
343. HEARTLESSNESS (See also CRUELTY, RUTHLESSNESS.)
344. HEAVEN (See also PARADISE.)
     Height (See GIANT, TALLNESS.)
345. HELL (See also UNDERWORLD.)
346. HELPFULNESS (See also AID, ORGANIZATIONAL; GENEROSITY; KINDNESS.)
347. HENPECKED HUSBAND
348. HERESY (See also APOSTASY, SACRILEGE.)
349. HERO (See also BRAVERY.)
350. HIGHSPIRITEDNESS (See also MISCHIEVOUSNESS.)
351. HIGHWAYMAN (See also OUTLAW, THIEF.)
352. HINDUISM (See also RELIGION.)
353. HOAX (See also FORGERY, FRAUDULENCE.)
354. HOCKEY
355. HOLY DAY and PERIOD
356. HOMECOMING
357. HOMOSEXUALITY (See also RIGHTS, GAY.)
358. HONESTY (See also NOBLEMINDEDNESS, RIGHTEOUSNESS, VIRTUOUSNESS.)
359. HOPE (See also OPTIMISM.)
360. HORROR
361. HORSE (See also RACING, HORSE.)
362. HOSPITALITY (See also COURTESY.)
363. HOUSE, FATEFUL
     Hugeness (See GIANT.)
364. HUMILITY (See also MODESTY.)
     Humorousness (See WITTINESS.)
365. HUNGER
366. HUNTING
367. HYPOCRISY (See also PRETENSION.)
368. IDEALISM
369. IDENTIFICATION
370. IDOLATRY

371. IGNORANCE (See also DIMWITTEDNESS, STUPIDITY.)
372. ILLEGITIMACY
373. ILLUSION (See also APPEARANCES, DECEIVING.)
374. IMAGINATION
375. IMMORTALITY (See also AGELESSNESS.)
376. IMPERIALISM
377. IMPERSONATION
378. IMPERTINENCE
     Impetuousness (See RASHNESS.)
     Impossibility (See UNATTAINABILITY.)
379. IMPRISONMENT (See also ISOLATION.)
380. INCEST
     Incompetence (See INEPTITUDE.)
381. INCOMPLETENESS
     Incorruptibility (See HONESTY.)
382. INDECISION
383. INDEPENDENCE
384. INDIFFERENCE
385. INDIVIDUALISM (See also EGOTISM.)
386. INDUCEMENT
387. INDUSTRIOUSNESS
388. INEPTITUDE
389. INEXPENSIVENESS
390. INEXPERIENCE (See also INNOCENCE, NAÏVETÉ.)
391. INFANTICIDE
     Infertility (See BARRENNESS.)
     Infidelity (See ADULTERY, CUCKOLDRY, FAITHLESSNESS.)
392. INFORMER
393. INGRATITUDE
394. INJUSTICE
395. INNOCENCE (See also INEXPERIENCE, NAÏVETÉ.)
396. INNOVATION (See also INVENTIVENESS.)
     Inquisitiveness (See CURIOSITY.)
     Insanity (See MADNESS.)
397. INSECURITY (See also ANXIETY.)
     Inseparability (See FRIENDSHIP.)
     Insolence (See ARROGANCE.)
398. INSPIRATION

651. SUN (See also LIGHT.)
652. SURPRISE
653. SURVIVAL (See also EN-
     DURANCE.)
654. SUSTENANCE
655. SWIFTNESS
656. SWIMMING
657. SWORD
     Sycophancy (See FLATTERY.)
658. TACITURNITY
659. TALKATIVENESS
660. TALLNESS (See also GIANT.)
     Tastlessness (See COARSENESS.)
661. TEACHING (See also EDUCA-
     TION.)
     Technology (See INTERNET.)
     Teenager (See ADOLESCENCE.)
662. TELEVISION (See also BROAD-
     CASTING.)
663. TEMPERANCE
664. TEMPTATION
665. TENNIS
     Terror (See HORROR.)
666. TERRORISM
667. TEST
668. THANKSGIVING
669. THEATER
670. THIEF (See also GANGSTERISM,
     HIGHWAYMAN, OUTLAW.)
671. THINNESS
672. THUNDER (See also LIGHT-
     NING.)
673. TIME
674. TIME TRAVEL
     Timelessness (See AGELESSNESS,
     IMMORTALITY.)
675. TIMIDITY (See also COWARDICE,
     WEAKNESS .)
676. TOTALITARIANISM
677. TRANSFORMATION
678. TRAVEL (See also JOURNEY.)
679. TREACHERY (See also BETRAYAL,
     TREASON.)
680. TREASON
681. TREASURE
682. TREE
683. TRICKERY (See also CUNNING,
     DECEIT, UNSCRUPULOUSNESS.)

684. TRINITY
     Truth (See HONESTY.)
685. TURNING POINT
686. TWINS (See also DOUBLES.)
687. TYRANNY (See also BRUTALITY,
     CRUELTY.)
688. UBIQUITY (See also OMNIPRES-
     ENCE.)
689. UGLINESS
690. UNATTAINABILITY
691. UNDERWORLD (See also HELL.)
     Unfaithfulness (See FAITHLESS-
     NESS.)
     Ungratefulness (See INGRATI-
     TUDE.)
     Unkindness (See CRUELTY.)
692. UNSCRUPULOUSNESS (See also
     CUNNING, DECEIT, FRAUDU-
     LENCE, TRICKERY.)
693. UNSOPHISTICATION (See also
     COARSENESS, NAÏVETÉ, RUS-
     TICITY, TASTELESSNESS.)
     Unworldliness (See ASCETICISM.)
     Uselessness (See FUTILITY.)
694. USURPATION
695. USURY
696. UTOPIA (See also PARADISE,
     WONDERLAND.)
     Valor (See BRAVERY.)
697. VANITY (See also CONCEIT, EGO-
     TISM.)
698. VENGEANCE
699. VICTIM (See also ASSASSINA-
     TION.)
700. VICTORY
701. VILLAIN (See also EVIL,
     WICKEDNESS.)
     Vindictiveness (See VENGEANCE.)
702. VIOLENCE (See also BRUTALITY,
     CRUELTY.)
703. VIRGINITY (See also CHASTITY,
     PURITY.)
     Virility (See MASCULINITY.)
704. VIRTUOUSNESS (See also DIGNI-
     TY, HONESTY, NOBLEMINDED-
     NESS, RIGHTEOUSNESS.)
     Voluptuousness (See BEAUTY,
     FEMININE; BUXOMNESS; SEX
     SYMBOLS.)

Ruffner's Allusions

A

1. ABANDONMENT (See also ORPHAN.)

1. **Ariadne** deserted by her lover Theseus at Naxos. [Gk. Myth.: Benét 48]

2. **Auburn** agricultural village which loses inhabitants with onslaught of industry. [Br. Lit.: "The Deserted Village" in *Traveller*]

3. **Cio-Cio San** deserted by family for renouncing her religion. [Ital. Opera: Puccini, *Madama Butterfly*, Westerman, 357]

4. **E.T.** alien character in 1982 film; accidently abandoned on earth, longs for home. [Am. Film: *E.T.*]

5. **Hauser, Caspar** foundling, in solitary confinement till sixteen, then thrown into the world, claimed as a royal scion, and assassinated. [Ger. Lit.: Wasserman *Caspar Hauser* in Benét, 446]

6. **Helmer, Nora** deserts family to find "whole woman" identity. [Nor. Lit.: *A Doll's House*]

7. **Henchard-Newson, Susan** Michael Henchard's deserted wife. [Br. Lit.: *The Mayor of Casterbridge*, Magill I, 571–573]

8. *Mary Celeste* brigantine found drifting with no hands aboard. [Br. Folklore: Leach, 683]

9. **Meeber, Carrie** deserted by her first lover, she deserts her second. [Am. Lit.: *Sister Carrie* in Magill I, 895]

10. **open city** a city abandoned, as Rome and Paris in World War II. [Western Culture: *FOF, MOD*]

11. **Paddington Bear** abandoned bear from Darkest Peru found sitting on suitcase in London's Paddington Station and so named by the family that adopts him; his bumbling brings a series of misadventures; from series of books by Michael Bond. [Br. Children's Lit.: Jones]

12. *Patna* ship, carrying Muslim pilgrims, abandoned by captain and crew in a storm. [Br. Lit.: Joseph Conrad, *Lord Jim*]

13. **Perdita** abandoned as an infant by the king, her father, secretly raised by a shepherd. [Br. Drama: Shakespeare *The Winter's Tale*]

14. **Philoctetes** Greek hero abandoned for ten years by his comrades because of the smell of his wound. [Gk. Drama: Sophocles *Philoctetes* in Benét, 783]

15. **Santuzza** deserted by Turiddu after yielding to his advances. [Ital. Opera: Mascagni, *Cavalleria Rusticana*, Westerman, 338–339]

16. **Smike** boy deserted and forgotten at Dotheboys Hall. [Br. Lit.: *Nicholas Nickleby*]

17. **Snow White** deserted in forest; found by seven dwarfs. [Ger. Fairy Tale: Grimm, 184]

18. **Tatiana** gives her love to Onegin, who scorns it and leaves her. [Russ. Lit.: *Eugene Onegin*]

19. **Thursday, Margaret** left on church doorstep as baby. [Children's Lit.: *Margaret Thursday*, Fisher, 199–200]

2. ABDUCTION

1. **Balfour, David** expecting inheritance, kidnapped by uncle. [Br. Lit.: *Kidnapped*]

2. **Bertram, Henry** kidnapped at age five; taken from Scotland. [Br. Lit.: *Guy Mannering*]

3. **Bonnard, Sylvestre** to save an orphan girl from cruel treatment, removes her from school by trickery and becomes her guardian. [Fr. Lit.: France *The Crime of Sylvestre Bonnard* in Magill II, 196]

4. **Cephalus** carried off in lusting Aurora's chariot. [Rom. Myth.: Hall, 36]

5. **Conway, Hugh** kidnapped to the lamasery called Shangri-la. [Br. Lit.: *Lost Horizon*]

6. **Europa** maiden carried off to Crete by Zeus in the form of a white bull. [Gk. Myth.: Benét, 327]

7. **Gilda** abducted by Duke of Mantua's courtiers. [Ital. Opera: Verdi, *Rigoletto*, Westerman, 299–300]

8. **Hearst, Patti (1954–)** granddaughter of William Randolph Hearst, was abducted by the Symbionese Liberation Army for two months; took part in bank robbery as "Tania." [Am. Hist.: *EB*]

9. **Helen** carried off by Paris, thus precipitating Trojan war. [Gk. Lit.: *Iliad*, Hall, 147]

10. **Hylas** boy beloved by Hercules is carried off by the nymphs after he draws water from the fountain. [Gk. Myth.: Brewer, *Dictionary*, 476]

11. **Lindbergh kidnapping** in 1932, the infant son of famous aviator Charles Lindbergh abducted and murdered; the ensuing investigation, trial, and execution of Bruno Hauptmann attracted worldwide attention. [Am. Hist.: *EB*]

12. **Lyudmilla** princess carried off on her wedding night by the wizard Chernomor. [Russ. Poetry: *Ruslan and Lyudmilla* in Haydn & Fuller, 653]

13. ***Prisoner of Zenda, The*** King of Ruritania is held captive in castle of Zenda. [Br. Lit.: *The Prisoner of Zenda*]

14. **Proserpina (Gk. Persephone)** whisked away by lustful Pluto in chariot. [Rom. Lit.: *Metamorphoses; Fasti;;* Art: Hall, 260]

15. **Raid of Ruthven** James VI kidnapped for ten months by Protestant nobles (1582–1583). [Scot. Hist.: Grun, 258]

16. **Resurrection Men** 1800s "body snatchers"; supplied cadavers for dissection. [Br. Hist.: Brewer *Note-Book*, 756]

17. **Sabine Women** menfolk absent, Romans carry off women for wives. [Rom. Hist.: Brewer *Dictionary*, 948; Flem. Art: Rubens, "Rape of the Sabine Women"]

18. **UFOs (Unidentified Flying Objects)** since the 1940s, Americans have periodically claimed to have sighted saucer-like flying objects and were convinced they were extraterrestrial spaceships; some have attested to abduction by aliens for observation. [Am. Pop. Culture: *SJEPC*]

19. **virgins of Jabesh-gilead** abducted by Israelites while dancing at Shiloh. [O.T.: Judges 21:12–24]

3. ABUNDANCE (See also FERTILITY.)

1. **Amalthea's horn** horn of Zeus's nurse-goat which became a cornucopia. [Gk. Myth.: Walsh *Classical*, 19]

2. **Copia** goddess of abundance. [Rom. Myth.: Kravitz, 65]

3. **cornucopia** conical receptacle which symbolizes abundance. [Rom. Myth.: Kravitz, 65]

4. **Cubbins, Bartholomew** head sports abundant supply of hats. [Children's Lit.: *The Five Hundred Hats of Bartholomew Cubbins*]

5. **Dagon (Dagan)** fish-corn god symbolizing fertility and abundance. [Babyl. Myth.: Parrinder, 72; Jobes, 410]

6. **Daikoku** god has inexhaustible sack of useful articles. [Jap. Myth.: *LLEI*, I: 325]

7. **Dhisana** Vedic goddess of abundance. [Hinduism: Jobes, 410]

8. **Doritis** epithet of Aphrodite, meaning "bountiful." [Gk. Myth.: Zimmerman, 25]

9. **Goshen** Egyptian fertile land; salvation for Jacob's family. [O.T.: Genesis 46:28]

10. **honey** linked with the gods; symbol of purity, inspiration, and plenty. [Symbolism: *CEOS&S*]

11. **horn of plenty** another term for cornucopia, horn-shaped bowl full of bounty of the harvest [Am. Culture: Misc.]

12. **land of milk and honey** land of fertility and abundance. [O.T.: Exodus 3:8, 33:3; Jeremiah 11:5]

13. **pumpkin** in China, symbol of prosperity and abundance. [Symbolism: *CEOS&S*]

14. **Sukkot** Jewish holiday celebrating the abundance of the fruit harvest. [Jewish Trad.: *HolSymb*]

15. **Thanksgiving Day** American holiday celebrating abundant harvest; observed by Pilgrims (1621). [Am. Culture: *NCE*, 2726]

16. **wheat ears, garland of** symbol of agricultural abundance and peace. [Western Folklore: Jobes, 374]

4. ACTING

1. **Barrymore** family name of several generations of American actors, from Lionel (1878–1959) to Drew (1975–); a "Barrymore" is an actor. [Am. Theater: *FOF, MOD*]

2. **Berma** great actress, whom the narrator sees in her prime and in her decline. [Fr. Lit.: Proust *Remembrance of Things Past*, in Benét, 99]

3. **Bernhardt, Sarah (1844–1923)** great French actress known for dramatic excess, called "The Divine Sarah"; a "Sarah Bernhardt" is someone who is overacting. [Theater: *FOF, MOD*]

4. **Meeber, Carrie** small-town girl finds work on chorus line and matures into successful actress. [Am. Lit.: *Sister Carrie* in Magill I, 895]

5. **method acting** school of acting based on theories of Russian director Konstantine Stanislavsky in which the actor delves into the psychological background of a character; famous practitioners include Marlon Brando. [Am. Theater: *FOF, MOD*]

6. **Olivier, Sir Laurence (1907–1989)** one of the most acclaimed actors of all times; first producer/director of Shakespearean films; an "Olivier" is a great actor. [Br. Theater: *SJEPC*]

7. **Players, the** acting troupe employed by Hamlet. [Br. Drama: Shakespeare, *Hamlet*]

8. **Thespis** first individual Greek performer; whence *thespain*. [Gk. Drama: Espy, 46]

9. **Trelawny, Rose** young actress sees married life as dull and returns to the stage. [Br. Drama: Arthur Wing Pinero *Trelawny of the "Wells"* in Benét, 1022]

10. **Vitus, Saint** patron saint of actors [Christian Hagiog.: Brewster, 291]

11. **Woffington, Peg** married and unmarried men admire her stage talents and fall in love with her. [Br. Lit.: *Peg Woffington* in Magill I, 724]

5. ACTIVISM (See also RIGHTS, CIVIL; RIGHTS, GAY; RIGHTS, WOMEN'S; SOCIAL PROTEST.)

1. **AARP (American Association of Retired Persons)** organization for Americans age 50 and older known for strong lobbying efforts to preserve Medicare and Social Security. [Am. Hist.: *SJEPC*]

2. **Addams, Jane (1860–1935)** social activist advocated causes of the urban poor and women; founded Hull House in Chicago. [Am. Hist.: *SJEPC*]

3. **Anthony, Susan B. (1820–1906)** along with Elizabeth Cady Stanton, fought for women's legal rights and suffrage; also abolitionist. [Am. Politics: Schenken, 37]

4. **Ashe, Arthur (1943–1993)** respected African-American tennis champion fought racism in America and South Africa; later became an AIDS activist, helping to de-stigmatize the disease. [Am. Sports: *SJEPC*]

5. **Baez, Joan (1941–)** folk singer commited to social and political causes from the 1960s into the 21st century. [Am. Music and Politics: *SJEPC*]

6. **Bethune, Mary McLeod (1875–1955)** African-American educator and Civil Rights activist; advocated for minorities and women. [Am. Hist.: *BBAAL1*]

7. **Buck, Pearl S. (1892–1973)** activist author supported progressive causes and sociopolitical change, speaking out against racial and gender discrimination, segregation, poverty, and armament. [Am. Lit.: *SJEPC*]

8. **Bunche, Ralph (1903–1971)** African-American statesman and Civil Rights leader; first person of color to win the Nobel Prize for Peace. [Am. Hist.: *BBAAL1*]

9. **Calvin, John (1509–1564)** French Protestest reformer, leader of the Protestent Reformation [Christianity *ODA*]

10. **Chavez, Cesar (1927–1993)** Hispanic labor leader and founder of the United Farm Workers, led successful boycott of California produce in the 1960s. [Am. Hist.: *BT1993*]

11. ***Consumer Reports*** independent, ad-free periodical provides unbiased information on products and services for consumers' benefit. [Am. Jour.: *SJEPC*]

12. **Douglass, Frederick (1818?-1895)** African-American abolitionist, editor, and orator; "The Father of the Civil Rights Movement." [Am. Hist.: *BBAAL1*]

13. **Du Bois, W. E. B. (1868–1963)** African-American historian and Civil Rights leader; a founder of the NAACP, important intellectual of the movement. [Am. Hist.: *BBAAL1*]

14. **Friedan, Betty (1921–2006)** considered founder of women's liberation movement in America and one of founders of National Organization for Women (NOW) [Am. Politics: *WB2*, 532]

15. **Garvey, Marcus (1887–1940)** black activist preached racial pride, unity, and the importance of African heritage in early 20th century; founded United Negro Improvement Assocation (UNIA) in

1914 and inspired future generations of African-American leaders. [Am. Hist.: *SJEPC*]

16. **Ghandi, Mohandas (1869–1948)** also Mahatma Ghandi; spiritual and political leader of India during its fight for independence from England; preaching reistance through nonviolence, he freed his country from oppressive taxation and foreign dominance. [Ind. Hist.: *WB2*]

17. **Gregory, Dick (1932–)** trailblazing African-American comedian won national, mainstream acclaim using his humor to highlight social and political issues such as racism and the Vietnam War in 1960s; continues to advance progressive social agenda. [Am. Entertainment: *SJEPC*]

18. **Jackson, Jesse (1941–)** African-American political and social activist; founder of the Rainbow/PUSH Coalition. [Am. Hist.: *BBAAL1*]

19. **Kennicott, Carol** idealist of social reform, especially village improvement. [Am. Lit.: *Main Street*]

20. **King, Coretta Scott (1927–2006)** African-American Civil Rights leader; founder of the King Center, to honor her husband, Martin Luther King Jr. [Am. Hist.: *BBAAL1*]

21. **King, Martin Luther, Jr. (1929–1968)** most significant leader of the Civil Rights movement in the 20th century, also a noted religious leader and winner of the Nobel Prize for Peace. [Am. Hist.: *BBAAL1*]

22. **Kuhn, Maggie (1905–1995)** social activist founded Gray Panthers in 1970 when forced to retire at age 65; fought ageism and promoted social and economic justice. [Am. Hist.: *SJEPC*]

23. **Malcolm X (1925–1965)** African-American political and religious leader and activist. [Am. Hist.: *BBAAL1*]

24. **Mandela, Nelson (1918–)** former president of South Africa who spent 27 years in prison; anti-apartheid activist and leader of African National Congress; awarded 1993 Nobel Peace Prize. [African Hist.: *WB2*]

25. **Marshall, Thurgood (1908–1993)** prominent African-American lawyer and jurist, argued Brown v. Board of Education on behalf of the NAACP; first African-American on the Supreme Court. [Am. Hist.: *BBAAL1*]

26. **McDaniel, Hattie (1895–1952)** African-American actor; formed Fair Play Committee to fight bigotry in Hollywood. [Am Film: *SJEPC*]

27. **McQueen, Butterfly (1911–1995)** African-American actor; fought racial stereotypes in Hollywood. [Am. Film: *SJEPC*]

28. **Mott, Lucretia Coffin (1793–1880)** leader of abolitionist and women's rights movements in US; organized Seneca Falls Convention. [Am. Politics: *WB2*, 880]

29. **NAACP** National Association for the Advancement of Colored People, founded in 1909 to fight racial injustice. [Am. Hist.: *BBAAL1*]

30. **Nader, Ralph (1934–)** famous advocate for safety and consumer protection. [Am. Law: *SJEPC*]

31. **National Right to Life** pro-life organization uses its clout to advocate for the unborn human embryo and fetus. [Am. Politics: *SJEPC*; Dudley, 166]

32. **New Left** emerging in the 1960s as an international movement against ineffectual liberalism; in US major opponent of Vietnam War. [Politics: *SJEPC*]

33. **NOW (National Organization for Women)** activist association begun in 1966 to promote women's "full partnership in American society" [Am. Politics: *SJEPC*]

34. **Pankhurst, Emmeline (1858–1928)** British suffragist who founded Women's Social and Political Union, using civil disobedience and vandalism to fight for suffrage [Br. Politics: *WB2*, 131]

35. **Parks, Rosa (1913–2005)** her refusal to give her bus seat to a white man was first step in her involvement in Civil Rights Movement. [Am. Hist.: *SJEPC*]

36. **Planned Parenthood** world's largest and oldest pro-choice organization advocates on behalf of women's reproductive rights, including the right to contraception and abortion. [Medicine and Politics: Keyzer, 475]

37. **Robeson, Paul (1898–1976)** known for his baritone rendition of "Ol' Man River" and outstanding oratorical acting talent; active proponent of leftist causes and opponent of racism. [Am. Theater: *SJEPC*]

38. **Sanger, Margaret (1883–1966)** early 20th-century birth control advocate faced obscenity charges and jail time for her ideas, publications, and activism in support of women's reproductive rights. [Am. Hist.: *SJEPC*; Brakeman, 316]

39. **Schlafly, Phyllis (1924–)** conservative leader oppposed to state and federal Equal Rights Amendments; founder of Stop ERA and Eagle Forum. [Am. Politics: Schenken, 601]

40. **Sinclair, Upton (1878–1968)** his 1906 novel *The Jungle* about the meat-packing industry brought about changes in the quality and cleanliness of processing; other socially-conscious novels followed. [Am. Lit.: *SJEPC*]

41. **Smits, Jimmy (1945–)** prominent Hispanic actor; cofounder of the National Hispanic Foundation for the Arts to help Hispanics find jobs in entertainment. [Am. Entertainment: *SJEPC*]

42. **Springsteen, Bruce (1949–)** hugely successful rock and roll singer/songwriter whose blue-collar background informs his music, as does his political and social ideology; has spearheaded several concerts to raise funds for social causes. [Am. Music: *SJEPC*]

43. **Stanton, Elizabeth Cady (1815–1902)** early women's rights advocate; also primary advocate for suffrage and organizer of Seneca Falls Convention. [Am. Politics: *WB2*, 839]

44. **Steinbeck, John (1902–1968)** writer of fiction, especially dealing with the sorry plight of itinerant farm workers; *Grapes of Wrath* is his classic Depression-era novel on that theme. [Am. Lit.: *SJEPC*]

45. **Steinem, Gloria (1934–)** feminist activist and media leader, co-founded *Ms. Magazine* and campaigned for women's rights. [Am. Politics: *WB2*, 886]

46. **Truth, Sojourner (1797?-1883)** African-American abolitionist and activist. [Am. Hist.: *BBAAL1*]

47. **Tubman, Harriet (1820–1913)** African-American abolitionist and activist; conductor of the Underground Railroad. [Am. Hist.: *BBAAL1*]

48. **Tutu, Desmond (1931–)** South African Anglican bishop and Nobel laureate who has devoted his life to fighting injustice through non-violence and bringing peace to all nations. [South African Rel.: *ODA*]

49. **Walesa, Lech (1943–)** anti-communist trade union and human rights advocate who later became the president of the Republic of Poland (1990–1995); leader of Solidarity trade union federation, first independent labor union in Soviet bloc; won Nobel Peace Prize in 1983. [Polish Hist.: *WB2*]

50. **Washington, Booker T. (1856–1915)** African-American educator, political leader, and founder of the Tuskegee Institute. [Am. Hist.: *BBAAL1*]

6. ADDICTION (See also ALCOHOLISM.)

1. **Belushi, John (1949–1982)** talented, energetic comedian and actor given to excess; was addicted to cocaine and heroin and died of drug overdose. [Am. Entertainment: *SJEPC*]

2. **Bruce, Lenny (1925–1966)** radical stand-up comic during conservative 1950s and 1960s was addicted to drugs and died of a morphine overdose. [Am. Entertainment: *SJEPC*]

3. **Burroughs, William S. (1914–1997)** morphine-addicted writer penned *Junky: Confessions of an Unredeemed Drug Addict* (1953) and *Naked Lunch* (1959). [Am. Lit.: *SJEPC*]

4. *Confessions of an English Opium-Eater* Thomas de Quincy tells of his opium addiction, his nightmarish experiences, and the sufferings of withdrawal. [Br. Lit.: Haydn & Fuller, 155]

5. **crack baby** infant born addicted to crack cocaine, exposed in utero to drugs through mother's use. [Usage: *SJEPC*]

6. **Garland, Judy (1922–1969)** legendary singer and film actress with relentless schedule and frail emotional health became addicted to diet and sleeping pills at a young age; died of drug overdose at age 47. [Am. Film and Music: *SJEPC*]

7. **Holmes, Sherlock** the famous sleuth, addicted to cocaine. [Br. Lit.: Benét, 473]

8. **Joplin, Janis (1943–1970)** considered greatest while female blues singer; highly passionate style and powerful, gritty voice; excessive in her performances and personal life; died young of heroin overdose. [Am. Music: *SJEPC*]

9. *Man with the Golden Arm, The* Chicagoan Frankie Machine, a failure, takes to morphine, murders his supplier, and hangs himself. [Am. Lit.: Benét, 632]

10. **Morrison, Jim (1943–1971)** lead singer of The Doors struggled with drug and alcohol abuse and appeared stoned onstage; died prematurely of probable overdose. [Am. Music: *SJEPC*]

11. *Naked Lunch* nightmarish stream-of-consciousness novel satirizing post-World War II America written by William S. Burroughs while under the influence of morphine (1959). [Am. Lit.: *SJEPC*; Henderson, 37]

12. **Parker, Charlie (1920–1955)** alto saxophonist and brilliant jazz improvisationist whose addiction to drugs and alcohol contributed to an early death. [Am. Music: *SJEPC*]

13. **Presley, Elvis (1935–1977)** famous rock 'n' roll singer whose drug use led to poor health and early death. [Am. Music: *SJEPC*]

14. **Pryor, Richard (1940–2005)** famous African-American comedian who used his racial background to create material that was often raunchy but hilarious; battled substance abuse throughout much of his career. [Am. Entertainment and Film: *SJEPC*]

15. **Tyrone, Mary** addicted to morphine after childbirth, thanks to her husband's choice of a quack doctor. [Am. Lit.: O'Neill *Long Day's Journey into Night* in Sobel, 431]

16. *Valley of the Dolls* portrays self-destruction of drug-addicted starlets. [Am. Lit.: *Valley of the Dolls*]

11

7. ADOLESCENCE

1. *Ah, Wilderness!* high-school senior has problems with girls and his father. [Am. Drama: O'Neill *Ah, Wilderness!* in Sobel, 15]

2. **Aldrich, Henry** teenaged film character of the 1940s. [Am. Film: Halliwell, 337]

3. *American Bandstand* durable and popular TV show; teenagers are featured performers. [TV: Terrace, I, 52]

4. *American Graffiti* George Lucas's 1973 film about teenagers on the brink of adulthood, set in California in 1962; launched the careers of Ron Howard, Richard Dreyfus, and Harrison Ford. [Am. Film: *SJEPC*]

5. **Archie** the eternal comic-book teenager. [Comics: Horn, 87]

6. **Avalon, Frankie (1939–)** clean-cut teen idol of the 1950s and 1960s starrred in beach party films with Annette Funicello. [Am. Entertainment: *SJEPC*]

7. **Baxter, William Sylvanus** adolescent in the throes of first love. [Am. Lit.: Booth Tarkington *Seventeen* in Benét, 918]

8. **Beach Boys, The** band with close-harmony style vocals epitomized 1960s Southern California youth culture. [Am. Music: *SJEPC*]

9. *Beavis and Butthead* irreverent MTV show featuring two crude, hormone-driven adolescents appealed to teens in the 1990s. [Am. TV: *SJEPC*]

10. *Beverly Hills 90210* teen drama of 1990s set in posh Beverly Hills focused on group of fashion-conscious, upper-class high school students. [Am. TV: *SJEPC*]

11. **Blutarsky, Bluto** outrageous, binge-drinking "party animal" college student portrayed by John Belushi. [Am. Film: *SJEPC*]

12. **bobby soxer** teenage girls in the 1940s who swooned over idol Frank Sinatra wore short socks. [Am. Culture: *SJEPC*]

13. **Brat Pack** group of actors in 1980s played angst-ridden, middle-class teenagers. [Am. Film: *SJEPC*]

14. **bubblegum rock** commercial rock music marketed to preteens arose in the 1960s with such bands as The Archies. [Am. Music: *SJEPC*]

15. *Bye, Bye Birdie* 1960 Broadway musical about small-town teenage fans of an Elvis-type rock star named Conrad Birdie; they become involved in his appearance on the Ed Sullivan TV show prior to Birdie's stint in the military. [Am. Theater: Misc.]

16. **Cassidy, David (1950–)** teenage heartthrob played part of Keith in 1970s hit musical TV comedy *The Partridge Family*. [Am. TV: *SJEPC*]

17. *Catcher in the Rye* in J.D. Salinger's only novel, alienated, disillusioned 16–year-old Holden Caulfield distinctively narrates his three-day adolescent adventure in New York City. [Am. Lit.: *SJEPC*; Harris *Characters*, 347–48]

18. **Caulfield, Holden** sensitive, troubled teenager who narrates J. D. Salinger's 1951 groundbreaking novel. [Am. Lit.: *Catcher in the Rye*]

19. **Clark, Dick (1929–)** known as "America's oldest living teenager." [Am. Music and TV: *SJEPC*]

20. *Dawson's Creek* popular TV show featuring angst and young love among teenagers in a mythical coastal town. [TV: Misc.]

21. **Dedalus, Stephen** undergoes all the trials, troubles, fears, and embarrassments of a teenager. [Irish. Lit.: Joyce *Portrait of the Artist as a Young Man*]

22. **Drew, Nancy** blonde teenaged detective in series of Stratemeyer Syndicate books for young readers beginning in 1930; bravely solves cases often given to her by her father, a criminal lawyer. [Am. Children's Lit.: Jones]

23. **drive-in theater** automobile-fueled teenage haven known for sexual encounters, illicit activities, and adolescent pranks, particularly in the 1940s-70s. [Am. Entertainment: *SJEPC*]

24. **Fabares, Shelley (1944–)** portrayed perky teenager Mary Stone on *The Donna Reed Show* (1958–63); recorded "Johnny Angel" (1962), starred with teen idol Fabian in *Ride the Wild Surf* (1964). [Am. Entertainment: *SJEPC*]

25. **Fabian (1943–)** 1950s-60s teen idol with more good looks than talent soared to top of music charts with singles like "I'm a Man" and appeared on screen in such movies as *North to Alaska*. [Am. Music and Film: *SJEPC*]

26. **Francis, Connie (1938–)** "America's Sweetheart" was teen idol and popular singer in late 1950s-60s. [Am. Music: *SJEPC*]

27. **Funicello, Annette (1942–)** sweet, wholesome actress became pioneering member of Disney's Mickey Mouse Club (1955–59) at age of 12; starred in beach movies with fellow teen idol Frankie Avalon in 1960s. [Am. TV and Film: *SJEPC*]

28. **Gidget** archetypal teenage girl. [TV: Terrace, I, 311–312]

29. **Gillis, Dobie** teenager struggled to postpone adulthood in popular TV show (1959–1963). [TV: "The Many Loves of Dobie Gillis" in Terrace, II, 64–66]

30. **Hardy, Andy** teenaged son of a "typical family" in a small midwestern town. [Am. Film: Halliwell, 323]

31. **Joe Camel** cartoon-like character not only promoted Camel cigarettes, but was controversially viewed as targeting youth and luring teenagers into the smoking habit. [Am. Business: Misc.]

32. **prom** high school dance held each year with rituals that includes formal dress, limosines, corsages, and such. [Am. Pop. Culture: *SJEPC*]

33. *Rebel without a Cause* 1955 Nicholas Ray film starring James Dean as youth who is as sweet as he is troubled, disaffected, and searching for meaning in life. [Am. Film: *SJEPC*; *FOF, MOD*]

34. *Sassy* 1988 magazine that approached teenaged females with information about sexual activity unlike other magazines of the time. [Am. Jour.: *SJEPC*]

35. *Seventeen* magazine first published in 1944; first magazine totally devoted to teen girls; extemely successful at focusing on topics relevant to its audience. [Am. Jour.: *SJEPC*]

36. *Seventeenth Summer* innocent, touching young adult romance novel by Maureen Daly that swept the U.S. when published in 1942; tells story of summer romance that ends when girl goes off to college, certain her first love has changed her forever. [Am. Children's Lit.: Gillespie and Naden]

37. *Soul Train* first mainstream American TV show to feature soul and rhythm and blues artists; the black *American Bandstand* showed teenaged guests decked out in the latest fashions dancing before the camera (1970–). [Am. TV: *SJEPC*]

38. **Spider-Man** first comic superhero who was a teen; first appeared in Marvel Comics in 1962; Peter Parker gets powers after bite from radioactive spider; fed fantasies and anxieties of adolescent readers; successful film versions followed. [Am. Comics and Films: *SJEPC*]

39. *Spring Awakening* alt-rock musical based on a banned German play; focuses on German teenagers in the late 1800s dealing with issues such as masturbation, rape, abortion, and suicide. [Am. Theater: Misc.]

40. **Wolfman Jack (1938–1995)** radio disc jockey with gravelly voice and signature growl ruled the airwaves in the 1960s and brought rock 'n' roll (especially rhythm and blues music of black artists) into the homes of his many teenage fans in America. [Am. Radio: *SJEPC*]

8. ADULTERY (See also CUCKOLDRY, FAITHLESSNESS.)

1. **Alcmena** unknowingly commits adultery when Jupiter impersonates her husband. [Rom. Lit.: *Amphitryon*]

2. **Alison** betrays old husband amusingly with her lodger, Nicholas. [Br. Lit.: *Canterbury Tales*, "Miller's Tale"]

3. **Almaviva, Count** plots to seduce the maid Susannah, betrothed to Figaro, as his right; foiled by Figaro, becomes contrite before the Countess. [Opera: Mozart *The Marriage of Figaro*]

4. **Andermatt, Christiane** eventually has child by lover, not husband. [Fr. Lit.: *Mont-Oriol*, Magill I, 618–620]

5. **Bathsheba** pressured by David to commit adultery during husband's absence. [O.T.: II Samuel 11:14]

6. **Bloom, Molly** sensual wife of Leopold has an affair with Blazes Boylan. [Irish Lit.: Joyce *Ulysses* in Magill I, 1040]

7. **Bovary, Emma** acquires lovers to find rapture marriage lacks. [Fr. Lit.: *Madame Bovary*, Magill I, 618–620]

8. **Brant, Capt. Adam** fatefully falls for general's wife. [Am. Lit.: *Mourning Becomes Electra*]

9. *Bridges of Madison County, The* maudlin story of passion and regret featuring an illicit, discreet love affair between a middle-aged married mother and a world-travelling photographer in a small Iowa town (1992). [Am. Lit.: *SJEPC*]

10. **Buchanan, Tom** even with Daisy's knowledge, deliberately has affairs. [Am. Lit.: *The Great Gatsby*]

11. **Chatterley, Connie** takes the gameskeeper of her impotent husband as her lover. [Br. Lit.: D.H. Lawrence *Lady Chatterley's Lover* in Benét, 559]

12. **Clytemnestra** takes Aegisthus as paramour. [Gk. Lit.: *Orestes*]

13. *Couples* group of ten husbands sleep with each others' wives. [Am. Lit.: Weiss, 108]

14. **Cunizza** amours with Sordello while married to first husband. [Br. Lit.: *Sordello*]

15. **currant** symbol of infidelity. [Flower Symbolism: Jobes, 398]

16. **de Lamare, Julien** Jeanne's young philandering husband, who has affairs with her foster-sister and their neighbor's wife. [Fr. Lit.: Maupassant *A Woman's Life* in Magill I, 1127]

17. **Dimmesdale, Rev. Arthur** Puritan minister who commits adultery. [Am. Lit.: Hawthorne *The Scarlet Letter*]

18. *Double Indemnity* adulterous love affair between insurance agent Walter Neff and seductive client Phyllis leads to murder of her husband to collect on the policy (novel, 1935; film, 1944). [Am. Film and Lit.: *SJEPC*]

19. **Guinevere** King Arthur's unfaithful wife. [Br. Lit.: *Le Morte d'Arthur*]

20. **Herzog** insatiable husband plays the field. [Am. Lit.: *Herzog*]

21. **Julia, Donna** Alfonso's wife; gives herself to Don Juan. [Br. Lit.: "Don Juan" in Magill I, 217–219]

22. **Karenina, Anna** commits adultery with Count Vronsky; scandalizes Russian society. [Russ. Lit.: *Anna Karenina*]

23. **Lancelot** enters into an adulterous relationship with Guinevere. [Br. Lit.: Malory *Le Morte d'Arthur*]

24. **Mannon, Christine** conspires with lover to poison husband; discovered, commits suicide. [Am. Lit.: *Mourning Becomes Electra*]

25. **Moechus** personification of adultery. [Br. Lit.: *The Purple Island*, Brewer *Handbook*, 715]

26. **Pozdnishef, Madame** bored with husband, acquires Trukhashevsky as lover. [Russ. Lit.: *The Kreutzer Sonata*, Magill I, 481–483]

27. **Prynne, Hester** adulterous woman in Puritan New England; condemned to wear a scarlet letter. [Am. Lit.: Gillespie and Naden]

28. *Scarlet Letter, The* Nathaniel Hawthorne's 1850 novel about intolerance and hypocristy in the Puritan community in Boston of 1642; young Hester Prynne is punished for adultery by public humiliation; she is made to wear a scarlet A on her dress, which she defiantly embroiders. [Am. Lit.: Gillespie and Naden]

29. **Tonio** after Nedda's repulsion, tells husband of her infidelities. [Ital. Opera: Leoncavallo, *Pagliacci*, Westerman, 341–342]

30. **Wicked Bible** misprint gives Commandment: "Thou shalt commit adultery." [*sic*] [Br. Hist.: Brewer *Dictionary*, 108]

9. ADVENTUROUSNESS (See also JOURNEY, QUEST, WANDERING.)

1. **Adverse, Anthony** leads adventurous and romantic life in Italy, France, and America in the Napoleonic era. [Am. Lit.: Haydn & Fuller, 36]

2. **Baggins, Bilbo** hobbit-protagonist; has adventures with dwarfs and other creatures of Middle Earth; finds the One Ring. [Br. Lit.: *The Hobbit*]

3. **Benjamin Bunny** Peter Rabbit's thrill-seeking cousin. [Children's Lit.: *The Tale of Benjamin Bunny*]

4. **Blas, Gil** picaresque victimizer and victim who encounters all the social classes of 18th-century Spain. [Fr. Lit.: *Gil Blas, Benét, 395]

5. **Bond, James** secret agent 007, whose exploits feature futuristic technology. [Br. Lit.: Herman, 27]

6. **Clarke, Micah** helps in Monmouth's unsuccessful attempt to wrest the throne from King James. [Br. Lit.: Doyle *Micah Clarke* in Magill I, 585]

7. **Crusoe, Robinson** experiences adventures among pirates, cannibals, and slavers. [Br. Lit.: Defoe *Robinson Crusoe*]

8. **Deadwood Dick** hero of Wild West dime novels. [Am. Folklore: Walsh *Modern*, 115]

9. **del Dongo, Fabrizio** partisan of Napoleon, involved in love, intrigue, a duel, and ends up as a Carthusian monk. [Fr. Lit.: Stendhal *The Charterhouse of Parma* in Magill I, 135]

10. **Eulenspiegel, Till** wanders the Low Countries, living by his wits and avenging the evil deeds of King Philip. [Belg. Lit.: Benét, 325]

11. **Fabio** 19th-century young runaway becomes gaucho; Argentinian Huckleberry Finn. [Arg. Lit.: *Don Segundo Sombra*]

12. **Finn, Huckleberry** 19th-century picaresque teenager travels down the Mississippi on a raft. [Am. Lit.: *Huckleberry Finn*]

13. **Flanders, Moll** amoral adventuress of many liasons. [Br. Lit.: Defoe *Moll Flanders* in Benét, 678]

14. **flappers** daring, sexually spirited young women of 1920s America rejected traditional values and exuberantly embraced new trends and behaviors, like wearing shorter skirts, dancing to jazz, and smoking cigarettes. [Am. Hist.: *SJEPC*]

15. **Fogg, Phileas** gentleman undertakes world trip on wager. [Fr. Lit.: *Around the World in Eighty Days*]

16. **Gilliatt** battles storms, disaster, and a giant octopus in order to salvage a ship's engine and win a bride. [Fr. Lit.: *Toilers of the Sea* in Magill II, 1037]

17. **Gordon, Flash** contantly launches into apparently hopeless adventures to combat evil powers. [Comics: Berger, 133]

18. **Gulliver, Lemuel** 17th-century hero travels to fanciful lands on extraordinary voyages. [Br. Lit.: *Gulliver's Travels*]

19. **Hajji Baba** shrewd rascal travels around Persia. [Fr. Lit. *Hajji Baba of Ispahan* in Magill I, 343]

20. **Hannay, Richard** tracked and hounded by enemies of England, has several narrow escapes. [Br. Lit. and Cinema: Buchan *The 39 Steps* in Magill I, 972]

21. **Hawkins, Jim** character from R.L. Stevenson's *Treasure Island*; after taking possession of a treasure map, sets out to sea with a rough crew to find the treasure. [Br. Children's Lit.: Jones]

22. **Hornblower, Horatio** gallant warship captain in Napoleonic era. [Br. Lit.: *Captain Horatio Hornblower*]

23. **Huon of Bordeaux** as penance for killing a prince, submits to perilous journey to the East. [Ger. Lit.: Benét, 487; German Opera: *Oberon*]

24. **Jason** leader of the Argonauts in successful quest for the Golden Fleece. [Gk. Legend: Brewer *Dictionary*, 500]

25. **Jones, Indiana** professor-archaeologist-adventurer played by Harrison Ford in film trilogy set in 1930s travels the world over to recover treasures, battling evil forces (1980s); older and wiser

17

chracter returns to adventuring once again in subsequent sequel (2008). [Am. Film: *SJEPC*; Misc.]

26. *Kidnapped* influential 1886 novel for young readers by R.L. Stevenson tells adventures of David Balfour in 1751 when he is kidnapped, shipwrecked, and becomes involved with Jacobites. [Scot. Children's Lit.: *OCCL*]

27. **Kim** orphan wanders streets of India with lama. [Br. Lit.: *Kim*]

28. **Kirk, Captain** adventurous captain of the starship Enterprise, "boldy goes where no man has gone before." [TV: *Star Trek*]

29. *Kon Tiki* tale of trip taken on primitive raft by Thor Heyerdahl to cross from Peru to the Tuamotu Islands (1947). [World Hist.: *Kon Tiki;; NCE, 1238–1239*]

30. **Krull, Felix** has adventures in Germany, France, and Portugal under a succession of names and professions. [Ger. Lit.: Mann *The Confessions of Felix Krull* in Magill III, 218]

31. **Lawrence of Arabia** T. E. Lawrence (1888–1935), legendary hero, led Arab revolt against Turkey. [Br. Hist.: Benét, 572]

32. *Lazarillo de Tormes* 16th-century picaresque novel about a run-away youth who lives by his wits, serving, in succession, a blind beggar and several unworthy ecclesiastics. [Span. Lit.: Haydn & Fuller, 415]

33. **Lismahago, Lieutenant Obadiah** 19th-century sportsman with quixotic tales. [Br. Lit.: *Humphry Clinker*, Magill I, 394–397]

34. **McFly, Marty** central character of the successful *Back to the Future* films, he embodies youthful adventurousness as he travels through time. [Am. Film: *Back to the Future*]

35. **McNutt, Boob** schlemiel has wild adventures among fabulous beasts on tropical isles. [Comics: Horn, 125]

36. **Mowgli** infant lost in the Indian forest is brought up by a wolf pack; from Rudyard Kipling's series for young readers, *The Jungle Books* (1894–1895). [Br. Children's Lit.: Jones]

37. **Munchausen, Baron** picaresqe traveler and teller of tall tales. [Ger. Lit.: *Baron Munchausen*]

38. *Nautilus* submarine in which its builder, Captain Nemo, cruises around the world. [Fr. Lit.: Jules Verne *Twenty Thousand Leagues Under the Sea*]

39. **Nemo, Captain** travels throughout the world in the *Nautilus*, a submarine of his own invention. [Fr. Lit.: Jules Verne *Twenty Thousand Leagues Under the Sea*]

40. **Odysseus** varied adventures after the Trojan War kept him away from Ithaca for ten years. [Gk. Myth.: *Odyssey*]

41. **Pickle, Peregrine** young rogue experiences escapades in England and on the Continent. [Br. Lit.: *Peregrine Pickle* in Magill I, 731–4]

42. **Polo, Marco (1254–1324)** 13th-Century Venetian traveler in central Asia and China; brought wonders of Orient to Europe. [World Hist.: *WB*, 15: 572–573;; Ital. Lit.: *Travels of Marco Polo*]

43. **Pym, Arthur Gordon** journeys include mutiny, shipwreck, savages, and the supernatural. [Am. Lit.: Poe, "The Narrative of Arthur Gordon Pym" in Magill I, 640–643]

44. **Quatermain, Allan** undertakes a dangerous African expedition in search of a lost diamond mine. [Br. Lit.: H. Rider Haggard *King Solomon's Mines* in Magill I, 475]

45. **Random, Roderick** exiled for killing in a duel, goes to sea, endures shipwreck and battles, and discovers his wealthy father. [Br. Lit.: *Roderick Random*, Haydn & Fuller, 644]

46. **Route 66** planned to meander, connecting the main streets of the U.S. from Chicago to Los Angeles; came to symbolize the joys of driving on the open road. [Am. Culture: *SJEPC*]

47. **Ruslan** undergoes many adventures to regain his abducted bride. [Russ. Poetry: *Rusland and Lyudmilla* in Haydn & Fuller, 653]

48. **Sawyer, Tom** classic 19th-century adventuresome, all-American boy. [Am. Lit.: *Tom Sawyer*]

49. *Simplicissimus* from callowness to audacity on 17th-century battlefields. [Ger. Lit.: *Simplicissimus*]

50. **Sinbad the Sailor** has scores of adventures in the course of seven voyages. [Arab Lit.: *Arabian Nights*]

51. **Skywalker, Luke** the adventurous hero of the *Star Wars* saga, son of Darth Vader and Padme, sister of Leia, becomes a Jedi knight imbued with the Force. [Am. Film: *Star Wars*]

52. **Solo, Han** character in Star Wars saga; witty spice smuggler who gets caught up in the Rebel Alliance and is soon fighting against the evil Galactic Empire. [Am. Film: Misc.]

53. **Tartarin** 19th-century French Quixote acts out his dreams of travel. [Fr. Lit.: *Tartarin de Tarascon*]

54. **Tarzan** jungle man leads adventurous life. [Am. Lit.: *Tarzan of the Apes*]

55. *Time Machine, The* H.G. Wells novel published in 1895; tells of inventor who travels into future; sees degeneration of life. [Br. Lit.: *The Time Machine*]

56. *Tom Jones* picaresque novel of a young man in 18th-century England. [Br. Lit.: Haydn & Fuller, 745]

57. *Treasure Island* first adventure story for young readers (published in 1883); written by R.L.Stevenson; set in mid-eighteenth

century, rousing tale of buried treasure and a young boy's adventures with the pirates who are seaching for the loot. [Scot. Children's Lit.: *OCCL*]

Adversity (See FAILURE.)

Advice (See COUNSEL.)

Advocacy (See ACTIVISM.)

Aeronautics (See AVIATION, SPACE TRAVEL.)

Affectation (See PRETENSION.)

Affliction (See SUFFERING.)

10. AGE, OLD

1. **AARP (American Association of Retired Persons)** nonprofit membership organization addresses the needs and interests of people 50 and older. [Am. Hist.: *SJPEC*]

2. **Alberich** 500 years old, but still child-sized. [Ger. Legend: Walsh, *Classical*, 13]

3. **Chuffey** old clerk. [Br. Lit.: *Martin Chuzzlewit*]

4. **Cumaean sibyl** was granted long life by Apollo; when she rejected his love, he withheld eternal youth and she withered away. [Gk. Myth.: *Metamorphoses*, 14]

5. **Darby and Joan** happily settled elderly couple. [Br. Ballad: Brewer *Dictionary*, 300]

6. **Elli** personification of Old Age, he out-wrestled Thor. [Norse Myth.: Edith Hamilton, *Mythology*]

7. **Ezekiel** portrayed with flowing white beard. [Art: Hall, 118]

8. **Father Time** personification of the old year. [Folklore: Misc.]

9. **Geritol** in the late 20th century, leading brand of tonic for geriatric health; symbol of old age. [Trademarks: Crowley *Trade*, 230]

10. *Golden Girls, The* four widowed or divorced older women share a household in Florida, navigating their post-menopausal years with supportive friendship and humor (NBC, 1985–92). [Am. TV: *SJEPC*]

11. **Gray Panthers** intergenerational activist organization advocates change to improve the lives of older Americans and end age discrimination; founded in 1970 by 65–year-old retiree Maggie Kuhn. [Am. Hist.: *SJEPC*; Misc.]

12. **Matlock, Lucinda** vigorous old woman dies at 96, scorning the degeneracy around her. [Am. Poetry: Masters *Spoon River Anthology*]

13. **"Memory"** popular song from musical *Cats* (1981) in which old, faded beauty Grizabella relates youthful days of glory. [Br. Music: *SJEPC*]

14. **Methuselah** oldest man mentioned in Bible. [O.T.: Genesis 5:27]

15. *Modern Maturity* magazine mailed to members of American Association of Retired Persons (AARP) [Am. Jour.: *SJEPC*]

16. **Noah** biblical patriarch lived to age 950, second only to Methuselah. [O.T.: Genesis 9:29]

17. **Parr, Thomas** husbandman; lived through reigns of ten sovreigns. [Br. Hist.: Brewer *Dictionary*]

18. **Philemon and Baucis** fabled aged couple. [Rom. Lit.: *Metamorphoses*]

19. **"Rabbi Ben Ezra"** Browning's poem about old age. [Br. Poetry: Benét, 836]

20. **Storks' Law** obliged children to maintain their needy parents in old age. [Rom. Hist.: Brewer *Dictionary*, 862]

21. *Superannuated Man, The* Charles Lamb's essay on his growing infirmities and subsequent retirement. [Br. Lit.: Lamb, Charles in Benét, 563]

22. **Tithonus** granted immortality but not eternal youth; continually got older. [Gk. Myth.: Kravitz]

11. AGELESSNESS (See also IMMORTALITY.)

1. **Clark, Dick (1929–)** perennially young TV host of rock 'n' roll music programs such as *American Bandstand* and *New Year's Rockin' Eve*. [Am. Music and TV: *SJEPC*]

2. **Endymion** man kept immortally youthful through eternal sleep. [Gk. Myth.: Howe, 91; Br. Lit.: "Endymion" in Harvey, 271]

3. **Gray, Dorian** artist Basil Hallward's "ideal of youth" remains young as his portrait ages. [Br. Lit.: *The Picture of Dorian Gray*, Magill I, 746–748]

4. **Grecian urn** lovers depicted on it will be forever young. [Br. Poetry: Keats "Ode on a Grecian Urn"]

Aggressiveness (See CONQUEST.)

12. AID, GOVERNMENTAL

1. **Berlin Airlift** free world's circumvention of Soviet blockade (1948–1949). [Eur. Hist.: Van Doren, 519]

2. **Fair Deal** federal program promoted by Pres. Harry Truman to increase aid to disadvantaged Americans. [Am. Hist.: Misc.]

3. **G.I. Bill** WWII U.S. veteran's educational subsidy by government. [Am. Hist.: Van Doren, 499]

4. **Great Society** governmental aid program created by Lyndon Johnson in 1964, to end poverty, improve education, health, and race relations. [Am. Hist. Misc.]

5. **Lend-Lease Act** provision of American material to beleaugured Allies in WWII. [Am. Hist.: Van Doren, 480]

6. **Marshall Plan** U.S.-led project to rebuild post-WWII Europe. [Eur. Hist.: Van Doren, 515]

7. **Medicaid** U.S. program of health insurance for the poor. [Am. Hist.: *EB*]

8. **Medicare** U.S. governmental program to provide health insurance for Americans age 65 and older. [Am. Hist.: Misc.]

9. **New Deal** federal program established in the 1930s by President Franklin Roosevelt to help the country out of the Great Depression. [Am. Hist.: Misc.]

10. **New Frontier** President John F. Kennedy's legislative program, encompassing such areas as civil rights, the economy, and foreign relations. [Am. Hist.: *WB*, K:212]

11. **Peace Corps** U.S. agency devoted to assisting underdeveloped nations. [Am. Hist.: Van Doren, 575–576]

12. **Social Security Act** U.S. legislation providing for old-age benefits financed by payroll taxes; later expanded to include more extensive coverage. [Am. Hist.: *EB*, IX: 314]

13. **VISTA** (Volunteers in Service to America), government agency which fights poverty in the U.S. [Am. Hist.: *WB*, I:27]

14. **WPA (1935–43)** provided work for unemployed construction and theater workers, artists, writers, and youth. [Am. Hist.: *NCE*, 3006]

13. AID, ORGANIZATIONAL (See also GENEROSITY.)

1. **American Legion** service organization dedicated to charitable causes. [Am. Culture: Misc.]

2. **B'nai B'rith** oldest and largest Jewish charitable organization. [Jewish Culture: Bowker]

3. **Boy Scouts** organization of boys dedicated to community service and character building. [Am. and Br. Hist.: *NCE*, 350]

4. **CARE** agency devoted to channeling relief to needy people abroad. [Am. Hist.: *NCE*, 456]

5. **Doctors Without Borders/Medecins Sans Frontieres** independent humanitarian organization created in 1971 to aid people threatened by "violence, negligence, or catastrophe." [World Hist.: *EB*]

6. **Farm Aid** organization spearheaded by country music legend Willie Nelson provides services and financial assistance to struggling American family farmers and lobbies for agricultural policy

change; funded by concerts featuring popular artists (1985–). [Am. Music: *SJEPC*]

7. **Girl Scouts** service organization for girls; builds character and life skills. [Am. and Br. Hist.: *NCE*, 1089]

8. **Hull House** settlement house providing services for poor immigrants founded in Chicago by social activist Jane Addams in early 20th century. [Am. Hist.: *SJEPC*]

9. **Kiwanis** international organization founded in 1915; dedicated to community service. [Culture: *SJEPC*]

10. **National Guard** military reserve units frequently help in civil disturbances and natural disasters. [Am. Hist.: *NCE*, 1885]

11. **Red Crescent** international disaster and wartime relief organization in predominantly Muslim societies affiliated with the Red Cross. [Islamic Hist. *UIMT*, 227]

12. **Red Cross** international philanthropic organization devoted to the alleviation of human suffering. [World Hist.: *NCE*, 2288]

13. **Salvation Army** Christian organization for philanthropic and evangelical work. [World Hist.: *NCE*, 2408–2409]

14. **Save the Children** independent organization that brings disaster and long-term relief to children worldwide. [World Hist.: *EB*]

15. **St. Vincent de Paul** charitable organization named after saint who worked and gave prodigiously of himself to poor. [Christian Hagiog.: Attwater, 337]

16. **UNICEF** United Nations International Children's Emergency Fund provides programs promoting health, nutrition, education, and the welfare of children worldwide. [World Hist.: *EB*]

17. **UNRRA (1943–1949)** supplied funds and personnel to areas freed from the Axis. [Eur. Hist.: *NCE*, 2832]

Aimlessness (See WANDERING.)

14. AIR

1. **Aeolus** god of the winds. [Gk. Myth.: Zimmerman, 9]

2. **Aether** god of whole atmosphere. [Gk. Myth.: Jobes, 42]

3. **Aurae** winged nymphs of breezes. [Rom. Myth.: *LLEI*, I: 323]

4. **Juno** in allegories of elements, personification of air. [Art: Hall, 128]

5. **sylph** spirit inhabiting atmosphere in Rosicrucian philosophy. [Medieval Hist.: Brewer, *Dictionary*, 1055]

15. ALCOHOLISM

1. **Alcoholics Anonymous (AA)** society of ex-alcoholics who help alcoholics to stop drinking. [Am. Hist.: Flexner, 356]

2. **Bowery, the** area in New York City known for its destitute and drunken population. [Am. Culture: Misc.]

3. **Brick** dipsomaniac; drinks until he feels a "click." [Am. Lit.: *Cat on a Hot Tin Roof*]

4. *Days of Wine and Roses* 1962 film; follows an American couple who slowly become alcoholics, suffer setbacks due to their addiction, and eventually try to overcome it. [Am. Film: Misc.]

5. **Eighteenth Amendment** amendment to the U.S. Constitution that prohibited the sale and transportation of alcohol; began Prohibition. [Am. Hist.: Misc.]

6. **Emery, Stan** drinking as only means to adjust to world. [Am. Lit.: *The Manhattan Transfer*]

7. **English, Julian** aristocratic drunkard mistreats his beloved wife, quarrels with everyone, and kills himself after a drunken bout. [Am. Lit.: *Appointment in Samarra*]

8. **Flyte, Sebastian** drinks to escape from his family, most of whom he detests. [Br. Lit.: Evelyn Waugh *Brideshead Revisited* in Magill I, 83]

9. *Iceman Cometh, The* portrayal of Harry Hope's rundown saloon which harbors alcoholics. [Am. Lit.: *The Iceman Cometh*]

10. *L'Assommoir* study of the demoralizing effects of alcohol. [Fr. Lit.: *L'Assommoir*]

11. *Leaving Las Vegas* 1995 film; focuses on the relationship between an alcoholic who has decided to drink himself to death after losing his job and a Las Vegas prostitute. [Am. Film: Misc.]

12. *Lost Weekend, The* study of Don Birman, an unsuccessful writer who drinks too much. [Am. Lit.: *The Lost Weekend*, Magill I, 531–532]

13. **Prohibition** era from 1920–1933, initiated by the 18th Amendment, during which the sale of alcohol was banned, in an effort to curb alcoholism. [Am. Hist.: Misc.]

14. **skid row** a run-down area frequented by alcoholics. [Am. Culture: Misc.]

16. ALIENATION

1. **Antonioni, Michelangelo (1912–2007)** Italian filmmaker noted for his bleak, alienated characters and atmosphere. [Ital. Film: *FOF, MOD*]

2. **Bergman, Ingmar (1918–2007)** Swedish filmmaker noted for his tragic, isolated world view. [Swed. Film: *FOF, MOD*]

3. **Brecht, Bertolt (1989–1956)** German playwright whose concept of "epic theater" purposely creates alienation, not identification, between actors and audience. [Ger. Theater: *FOF, MOD*]

4. **Hopper, Edward (1882–1967)** American painter, whose subject was often lonely, alienated people. [Am. Art: *ODA*]

5. **Kafka, Franz (1883–1924)** Czech novelist who wrote in German and whose works express the alienation, strangeness, and nightmarish quality of modern life. [Ger. Lit.: *The Trial*]

6. **Munch, Edvard (1863–1944)** Norwegian painter best known for his evocative work "The Scream," now a symbol of the horrors of modern life. [Eur. Art: *FOF, MOD*]

Allurement (See TEMPTATION.)

17. ALOOFNESS

1. **Bartleby** refuses to associate with others or even to mingle with other employees. [Am. Lit.: Melville *Bartleby the Scrivener*]

2. **Chapin, Joseph** successful attorney blinded by his emotional coldness and his need for propriety and respectability. [Am. Lit.: John O'Hara *Ten North Frederick* in Benét, 732]

3. **de Coverly, Major** so aloof that nobody dares to ask him his first name. [Am. Lit.: *Catch-22*]

4. **Garbo, Greta (1905–1990)** beautiful Swedish actress known for her reclusive ways and the phrase, "I vant to be alone." [Pop. Cult. Misc.]

5. **Gatsby, Jay** enigmatic and aloof from intimacy; addressed others as "old sport." [Am. Lit.: *The Great Gatsby*]

6. **Hatteras, Captain** paranoid sea captain remains incognito for half a voyage. [Fr. Lit.: *Captain Hatteras*]

7. **Havisham, Miss** eccentric lady who resents men; maintains a detached attitude toward Pip. [Br. Lit.: *Great Expectations*]

8. **Miriam** mysteriously reluctuant to reveal her past. [Am. Lit.: *The Marble Faun*]

9. **Morgan, Captain** officious officer; will not talk with enlisted men. [Am. Lit.: *Mister Roberts*, Magill I, 605–607]

10. **Trot, Dame** "not troubled with other folks' strife." [Nurs. Rhyme: *Mother Goose*, 13]

11. **Winterbourne** distant from even his own feelings about Daisy. [Am. Lit.: *Daisy Miller*]

18. AMBIGUITY

1. **Antonioni, Michelangelo (1912–2007)** Italian filmmaker who created films noted for their ambiguity, mystery, and despairing tone. [Ital. Film: *FOF, MOD*]

2. **Delphic oracle** ultimate authority in ancient Greece; often speaks in ambiguous terms. [Gk. Hist.: Leach, 305]

3. **Iseult's vow** pledge to husband has double meaning. [Arth. Legend: *Tristan*]

4. **Loxias** epithet of Apollo, meaning "ambiguous" in reference to his practically uninterpretable oracles. [Gk. Myth.: Zimmerman, 26]

5. **Pinter, Harold (1930–2008)** British dramatist and Nobel laureate, creator of plays noted for their ambiguous, menacing atmosphere. [Br. Theater: *FOF, MOD*]

6. **Pooh-Bah** different opinion for every one of his offices. [Br. Opera: *The Mikado*, Magill I, 591–592]

7. *Roshomon* Akira Kurosawa film (1950) depicting a rape and murder from different points of view: the victim, her husband, the criminal, and a witness; "Roshomon" is an allusion to the ambiguous nature of truth. [Jpn. Film: *FOF, MOD*]

19. AMBITION

1. **Alger, Horatio** author of a series of rags-to-riches stories. [Am. Lit.: *Ragged Dick*]

2. **Bart, Lily** sacrifices her principles and her chance for love in schemes to climb the social ladder. [Am. Lit.: *The House of Mirth* in Hart, 385]

3. **Chardon, Lucien (de Rubemprè)** young writer determined to achieve fame and wealth. [Fr. Lit.: Balzac *Lost Illusions* in Magill II, 595]

4. **Claudius** murders to gain throne; plots to keep it. [Br. Lit.: *Hamlet*]

5. **Constance** ambitioius for her son Arthur. [Br. Lit.: *King John*]

6. **Faustus, Doctor** makes a pact with the devil to further his own ambitions. [Br. Lit.: *The Tragical History of Doctor Faustus*]

7. **Golden Boy** talented young violinist gives up musical career for the sake of wealth and fame as a boxer. [Am. Lit.: Odets *Golden Boy* in Magill III, 422]

8. **hollyhock** traditional symbol of ambition. [Flower Symbolism: *Flora Symbolica*, 174]

9. **John, King** aspiring, self-assertive king of mediocre character. [Br. Lit.: *King John*]

10. **Macbeth** aspires to political power. [Br. Lit.: *Macbeth*]

11. **Macbeth, Lady** stops at nothing to gain political power for husband. [Br. Lit.: *Macbeth*]

12. **mountain laurel** traditional symbol of ambition. [Flower Symbolism: *Flora Symbolica*, 175]

13. **Ragged Dick** hero of a Horatio Alger rags-to-riches story. [Am. Lit,: *Ragged Dick*]

14. **Roxana** sleeps with the rich to get ahead in world. [Br. Lit.: *Roxana, The Fortunate Mistress*]

15. **Sejanus** chief minister of Emperor Tiberius uses seduction, conspiracy, and poisoning to gain the throne. [Br. Drama: Benét, 912]

16. **Slope, Rev. Obadiah** vainly strives to advance himself in objectionable ways. [Br. Lit.: Trollope *Barchester Towers* in Magill I, 55]

17. **Sutpen, Thomas** from poor origins, tries to gain aristocratic status. [Am. Lit.: Faulkner *Absalom, Absalom* in Magill I, 5]

18. **Tamburlaine** Scythian bandit becomes king of Persia and ruler of Turkey and Babylon. [Br. Drama: *Tamburlaine the Great* in Magill I, 950]

19. *What Makes Sammy Run* a dynamic but vicious opportunist attains success. [Am. Lit.: *What Makes Sammy Run*]

20. AMERICA

1. **apple pie** iconic, wholesome American dessert. [Am. Culture: Flexner, 68]

2. **bald eagle** national bird of the U.S.; native only to North America. [Am. Culture: *EB*, I: 753]

3. **baseball** traditional American sport and pastime. [Am. Sports: *EB*, I: 850]

4. **Berlin, Irving (1888–1989)** Russian-born composer's popular patriotic songs reflect 20th-century American life. [Am. Music: *SJEPC*]

5. **Big Apple** nickname for New York City, America's biggest and best-known metropolis. [Am. Culture: *SJEPC*]

6. **blue states** states with generally liberal voting patterns favoring the Democratic Party; contrast with "red states"; from the colored maps used by TV journalists during presidential elections. [Am. Politics: Misc.]

7. **Boy Scouts** youth organization's values include service to God and country. [Am. Hist.: *SJEPC*]

8. **Brother Jonathan** the original Uncle Sam. [Am. Hist.: Hart, 110]

9. **Coca-Cola** advertising uniting images of Coke with American life and culture, along with American servicemen's preference for the drink during World War II, helped cement the brand's status as an American icon. [Am. Business and Culture: *SJEPC*]

10. **Crossing of the Delaware** Washington's beleagured army attacks Trenton; famous event in American history (1776). [Am. Hist.: Jameson, 138]

11. **e pluribus unum** motto of the U.S.: Latin 'one out of many.' [Am. Culture: *RHD*, 481]

12. **Empire State Building** architectural symbol of America located in Manhattan was tallest building in the world from 1931 to 1971;

quintessential skyscraper's image used in many products and films. [Am. Architecture: *SJEPC*]

13. **Founding Fathers** refers to the leaders of the Revolutionary War and early America: Washington, Adams, Jefferson, Franklin, etc. [Am. Hist.: Misc.]

14. **Fourth of July** Independence Day; traditonal U.S. holiday; anniversary of adoption of Declaration of Independence (July 4, 1776). [Am. Culture: *EB*, V: 326]

15. **"God Bless America"** iconic patriotic song written by Irving Berlin during World War I; premiered by singer Kate Smith in 1938. [Am. Music: *SJEPC*]

16. **Jefferson, Thomas (1743–1826)** third president of the U.S. and principal author of the Declaration of Independence; "Jeffersonian Democracy" refers to a political philosophy promoting state's rights, natural rights, freedom of religion. [Am. Hist.: Misc.]

17. **Liberty Bell** symbol of American freedom; at Independence Hall, Philadelphia. [Am. Hist.: Jameson, 284]

18. **Mayflower** ship that brought the Pilgrims (1620). [Am. Hist.: Jameson, 313]

19. **melting pot** America as the home of many races and cultures. [Am. Pop. Culture: Misc.]

20. **Memorial Day** formerly Decoration Day, the fourth Monday of May, set aside to commemorate Americans who died in military service to the nation. [Am. Hist.: *HolFestDict*]

21. **Minute Man** heroic citizen-soldier of the American Revolution helped defeat the British and secure independence and liberty for the people. [Am. Hist.: *SJEPC*]

22. *Old Ironsides* the frigate *Constitution*, symbol of U.S. success in War of 1812, now preserved as a museum. [Am. Hist.: Bénet, 733]

23. **Peoria** typical mid-America town. [Am. Culture: Misc.]

24. **Pledge of Allegiance** statement of loyalty to the U. S., inaugurated in 1892 upon 400th anniversary of the discovery of America. [Am. Hist.: *WB*, P: 508]

25. **Plymouth Rock** site of Pilgrim landing in Massachusetts (1620). [Am. Hist.: Jameson, 395–396]

26. **pumpkin pie** traditional dish, especially at Thanksgiving. [Am. Culture: Flexner, 68]

27. **red states** states with generally conservative voting patterns favoring the Republican Party; contrast with "blue states"; from the colored maps used by TV journalists during presidential elections. [Am. Politics: Misc.]

28. **Red, White, and Blue** the colors of the U. S. flag, used in reference to the flag itself and ideals of patriotism. [Am. Hist.: Misc.]

29. **Sandburg, Carl (1878–1967)** distinguished poet whose diction reflected ordinary speech and captured America's national identity; famed biographer of Abraham Lincoln. [Am. Lit.: *SJEPC*]

30. *Saturday Evening Post, The* known as *The Post*; dominated American magazine readership for first thirty years of twentieth century; characterized by common-sense conservatism and middle-class values. [Am Jour.: *SJEPC*]

31. **Silent Majority** average Americans of middle class. [Am. Culture: Flexner, 375]

32. **Sousa, John Philip (1854–1932)** composer of over 100 rousing marches and leader of world-renowned concert band; devoted to making people proud of America, bringing him great popularity and a host of honors. [Am. Music: *SJEPC*]

33. **Stars and Stripes** nickname for the U.S. flag. [Am. Hist.: Brewer *Dictionary*, 8567]

34. **"Star-Spangled Banner, The"** U.S. national anthem. [Am. Hist.: *EB*, IX: 532]

35. **Statue of Liberty** great symbolic structure in New York harbor. [Am. Hist.: Jameson, 284]

36. **Thanksgiving** annual U.S. holiday celebrating harvest and yearly blessings; associated with Pilgrims (1621). [Am. Culture: *EB*, IX: 922]

37. **"This Land Is Your Land"** iconic American folk song by Woody Guthrie celebrates America from coast to coast (1940). [Am. Music: *SJEPC*]

38. **Uncle Sam** personifies people or government of the United States. [Am. Hist.: Hart, 870–871]

39. **Vespucci, Amerigo (1454–1512)** Italian navigator-explorer from whose name *America* is derived. [Am. Hist.: *EB*, X: 410]

40. **Washington, D.C.** nation's capital, center of of U.S. government, policies, etc. [Am. Hist.: Hart, 899]

41. **Washington, George (1732–1799)** "the Father of our country"; first U.S. President (1789–1797). [Am. Hist.: Jameson, 535–536]

42. **White House** official residence of the president of the U.S. in Washington, D.C. [Am. Culture: *EB*, X: 656]

43. **Yankee** to an American, a New Englander; to a Southern American, any Northerner; to a foreigner, any American. [Am. Hist.: Hart, 953]

21. AMERICA, SMALL-TOWN

1. *Blue Velvet* David Lynch film exposes seedy side of idyllic Lumbertown (1986). [Am. Film: *SJEPC*]

2. **Grover's Corners** the setting for Thornton Wilder's *Our Town*; by extension, the proto-typical small American town. [Am. Theater: *FOF, MOD*]

3. **Keillor, Garrison (1942–)** humorist whose writings depict small-town Midwest living at its most charming and sentimental; a devotee of radio, his extremely successful *Prarie Home Companion* show (debut, 1974) combines music performances and take-offs of old radio shows and ads. [Am. Lit. and Radio: *SJEPC*]

4. **Mayberry** fictional small Southern town in *The Andy Griffith Show* where life was slower, simpler, and friendlier. [Am. TV: *SJEPC*]

5. *Our Town* Thornton Wilder's 1938 play celebrating the extraordinary in ordinary small town life. [Am. Theater: Thornton Wilder *Our Town*]

6. **Podunk** a small town, especially one with narrow-minded inhabitants and limited expectations. [Am. Culture *FOF, MOD*]

7. **Price, Homer** protagonist of 1943 children's book by Robert McCloskey which satirizes small-town life in America; young Homer becomes involved in comical and memorable incidents, like the gross overproduction of donuts by a machine gone amok. [Am. Children's Lit.: *OCCL*]

8. **Rockwell, Norman (1894–1978)** best known for his illustrations for the cover of *Saturday Evening Post*; created folksy, traditional depictions of America. [Am. Art: *SJEPC*]

9. *Twin Peaks* created by filmmaker David Lynch; short-lived 1900s TV show had over 100 characters and intricate plots, all revolving around murder of a small-town beauty queen. [Am. TV: *SJEPC*]

22. ANDROGYNY

1. **Hermaphroditus** half-man, half-woman; offspring of Hermes and Aphrodite. [Gk. Myth.: Hall, 153]

2. **Iphis** Cretan maiden reared as boy because father ordered all daughters killed. [Gk. Myth.: Howe, 143]

3. *Orlando* 1928 semi-autobiographical novel by Virginia Woolf about her friend Vita Sackville-West; Orlando, a young man in England during Elizabeth I's reign, avoids aging and goes through the ages as a young man, but one day wakes up as a woman. [Br. Lit.: Misc.]

4. **Tiresias** prophet who lived as man and a woman. [Gk. Myth.: Zimmerman, 255–256]

5. *Victor Victoria* gender-bending Blake Edwards comedy (1982) featuring a woman who plays a male female impersonator: a woman, playing a man, playing a woman. [Am. Film: *EB*]

23. ANGEL

1. **Abaddon** angel in charge of Sheol's bottomless pit. [N.T.: Revelation 9:11; 20:1–3]

2. **Abdiel** faithful seraph who withstood Satan when urged to revolt. [Br. Lit.: *Paradise Lost*]

3. **Arcade** acquires knowledge of science, loses faith in God, and conspires to take over Heaven for Satan. [Fr. Lit.: *The Revolt of the Angels* in Magill I, 821]

4. **Azrael** watches over the dying and takes the soul; will himself be the last to die. [Islamic Myth.: Brewer *Dictionary*, 60]

5. **cherubim** four-winged, four-faced angels inspired Ezekiel to carry God's message to the people. [O.T.: Ezek. 1:15]

6. **City of Angels** moniker for Los Angeles, California. [Misc.: *SJEPC*]

7. **Gabriel** angel of the annunciation; tells Mary she will bear Christ child. [N.T.: Luke 1:26–38]

8. **guardian angel** believed to protect a particular person. [Folklore: Misc.]

9. **jinn** good and bad spirits, often attached to particular places in nature, with magical powers. [Islamic Folklore: *UIMT*, 184–85, 431]

10. **Jordan, Mr.** heavenly messenger has to find a new body for a boxer who died before his earthly time was up. [Am. Drama and Cinema: *Here Comes Mr. Jordan*]

11. **Lucifer** archangel; Satan's name before his fall from Heaven. [Christian Hagiog.: *Collier's*, XII, 143]

12. **Michael** leader of angels against Satan. [N.T.: Revelation 12:7–9; Br. Lit.: *Paradise Lost*]

13. **Raphael** God's healer and helper in Book of Tobit. [Apocrypha: Tobit]

14. **seraphim** six-winged angels of the highest order, distinguished by their zeal and love. [O.T.: Isaiah 6:2; Benét, 915]

15. **Uriel** sent by God to instruct prophet Esdras. [Apocrypha: II Esdras 4]

16. **Zadkiel** angel of the planet Jupiter. [Jewish Myth.: Brewer *Handbook*, 1237]

24. ANGER (See also EXASPERATION, IRASCIBILITY, RANTING.)

1. **Achilles** Greek warrior whose ire is noted in the opening line of *The Iliad*: "Sing, goddess, of the anger of Achilles." [Gk. Myth: *ODA*]

31

2. **Agamemmnon** King of Mycenae; his quarrel with Achilles brings disastrous consequences. [Gk. Myth: *ODA*]

3. **Allecto** one of the Three Furies, vengeful deities who punish evil-doers. [Gk. Myth.: Zimmerman, 274]

4. **Almeira** scorned woman like whom "hell hath no fury." [Br. Drama: *The Mourning Bride*]

5. **arrow** Islamic symbol for Allah's rage. [Islam: *CEOS&S*, 208]

6. **Belinda** furious over loss of lock of hair. [Br. Lit.: *Rape of the Lock*]

7. **Bernardo** enraged that member of a rival street-gang is making advances to his sister. [Am. Musical: *West Side Story*]

8. **Brunhild** furiously vengeful concerning Kriemhild's accusations of promiscuity. [Ger. Lit.: *Nibelungenlied*]

9. **Elmer Fudd** hapless man seethes over Bugs Bunny's antics. [Comics: "Bugs Bunny" in Horn, 140]

10. **Erinyes (the Furies)** angry and avenging deities who pursue evil-doers. [Gk Myth.: Leach, 347]

11. **Fawlty, Basil** tempermental proprietor of Fawlty Towers, from the TV show of the same name, hilariously acted by John Cleese. [Br. TV: *ODA*]

12. **Hera (Rom. Juno)** angry at Zeus's illicit sexual pleasure. [Gk Myth.: Leach, 563]

13. **Herod** angry at Wise Men's disobedience, orders slaughter of male infants. [N.T.: Matthew 2:16–17]

14. **Hulk, The Incredible** one of Marvel Comics' most popular superheroes; Dr. Banner—exposed to gamma radiation—turns into the super-strong Hulk when angry or under stress; made into popular TV show and films. [Am. Comics and TV: *SJEPC*]

15. **Megaera** one of the three Furies, vengeful deities who punish evil-doers. [Gk. Myth.: Zimmerman, 274]

16. **Nemesis** goddess of vengeance. [Gk. Myth.: Zimmerman, 173]

17. **Oronte** takes offense at Alceste's criticism of sonnet. [Fr. Lit.: *The Misanthrope*]

18. **Othello** smothers wife, Desdemona, in paroxysm of rage over her suspected adultery. [Br. Lit.: *Othello*]

19. **Rumpelstiltskin** stamps ground in rage over lass's discovery of his name. [Ger. Fairy Tale: *Rumpelstiltskin*]

20. **Tisiphone** one of the three Furies, vengeful deities who punish evil-doers. [Gk. Myth.: Zimmerman, 274]

21. **Volumnia** "in anger, Junolike." [Br. Lit.: *Coriolanus*]

22. **whin** indicates fury. [Flower Symbolism: *Flora Symbolica*, 178]

Angst (See ANXIETY, INSECURITY.)

25. ANNUNCIATION

1. **Ave Maria** invocation to Mary, mother of Jesus. [Christian Rel.: Bowker]
2. **dove and lily** pictured with Virgin and Gabriel. [Christian Iconography: Brewer *Dictionary*, 645]
3. **Elizabeth** Mary's old cousin; bears John the Baptist. [N.T.: Luke 1:36–80]
4. **Gabriel** messenger angel; tells Mary she will bear Christ child. [N.T.: Luke 1:26–38]
5. **Hail, Mary** prayer adapted from the words of Gabriel to Mary announcing the coming birth of Christ. [N.T.: Luke 1:26–36]
6. **Magnificat** Virgin Mary's song of praise: "My soul doth magnify the Lord." [Christian Rel.: Bowker]

26. ANTI-HEROISM

1. **Bloom, Leopold** his ineffectual wandering about Dublin is contrasted with Ulysses' epic adventures. [Irish Lit.: James Joyce *Ulysses* in Magill I, 1040]
2. **Bluntschli, Capt.** Swiss officer prefers eating chocolates and making love to fighting. [Br. Drama: Shaw *Arms and the Man* in Benét, 51]
3. **Brown, Charlie** bumbling boy with low self-esteem. [Comics: "Peanuts" in Horn, 542–543]
4. **Cooke, Ebenezer** his every move denies all things heroic. [Am. Lit.: *The Sot-Weed Factor*]
5. **Estragon** with Vladimir, one of two tramps, and anti-heroes, of Samuel Beckett's *Waiting for Godot* [Fr. Lit.: *Waiting for Godot*]
6. **Hoover, Dwayne** materially successful car dealer whose only friend is his dog. [Am. Lit.: *Breakfast of Champions*]
7. **Meursault** the 20th-century indifferent man to whom things happen because he allows them to. [Fr. Lit.: Camus *The Stranger* in Weiss, 445]
8. **Pechorin** alienated anti-hero and "superfluous man" of Mikhail Lermontov's *A Hero of Our Time* (1840). [Rus. Lit.: EB]
9. **Rosewater, Eliot** unemployed heir who spends all day buying drinks for volunteer firemen. [Am. Lit.: *God Bless You, Mr. Rosewater*]
10. **Spade, Sam** semi-literate, tough-talking private-eye; lacks culture. [Am. Lit.: *The Maltese Falcon*]

27. ANTIQUARIAN

1. **Clutterbuck, Cuthbert** retired captain, devoted to study of antiquities. [Br. Lit.: *The Monastery*]

2. **Oldbuck, Jonathan** learned and garrulous antiquary. [Br. Lit.: *The Antiquary*]

3. **Teufelsdroeckh, Herr** eccentric German philospher and professor. [Br. Lit.: *Sartor Resartus;*; Brewer *Handbook*, 1088]

28. ANTI-SEMITISM (See also BIGOTRY, GENOCIDE.)

1. **Agobard (799–840)** Lyonnais archbishop, father of medieval anti-Jewish racism. [Fr. Hist.: Wigoder, 15]

2. **Anti-Defamation League** B'nai B'rith organization which fights anti-Semitism. [Am. Hist.: Wigoder, 33]

3. **Armleder** medieval bands; ravaged Alsatian Jewish communities. [Ger. Hist.: Wigoder, 41]

4. **Ashkenazi, Simcha and Jacob** discover the tenuousness of their position when anti-Semitism spreads in Poland. [Yiddish Lit.: *Brothers Ashkenazi*]

5. **Babi Yar** Russian site of WWII German massacre of the Jews. [Russ. Hist.: Wigoder, 56]

6. **Bernheim Petition** 1933 petition exposed Nazi treatment of Jews. [Jew. Hist.: Wigoder, 83]

7. **Black Death pogroms** plague blamed on Jews who were later murdered. [Jew. Hist.: Bishop, 382]

8. **Black Hundreds** early 20th-century armed squads ravaged Jews. [Russ. Hist.: Wigoder, 92]

9. **blood libel** trials of Jews who allegedly murdered non-Jews for Passover blood. [Jew. Hist.: Wigoder, 95]

10. **Bok, Yakov** victim of Russian anti-Semitism; falsely accused of murder. [Am. Lit.: *The Fixer*]

11. **Dreyfus, Captain Alfred (1859–1935)** Jewish French miliary officer, victim of anti-semitism, falsely accused, imprisoned, then exonerated through the efforts of Emile Zola. [Fr. Hist.: *FOF, MOD*]

12. **Final Solution** Nazi plan to exterminate Jewish race. [Ger. Hist.: *Hitler*, 1037–1061]

13. **Frank, Anne (1929–1945)** young Dutch girl found and killed by Nazis after years in hiding. [Dutch Lit.: *Diary of Anne Frank*]

14. *Gentleman's Agreement* indictment of anti-Semitism. [Am. Lit.: *Gentleman's Agreement*]

15. **Goebbels, Joseph (1897–1945)** Hitler's infamous minister of propaganda; symbol of lying and deceit. [Ger. Hist.: *ODA*]

16. **Haman** convinces king to issue decree for Jewish extermination. [O.T.: Esther 3:1–11]

17. **Hep Hep Riots** Jewish pogroms in Germany (1819). [Ger. Hist.: Wigoder, 251]

18. **Hitler, Adolf (1889–1945)** Nazi dictator of Germany; eclipsed all predecessors' hatred for Jews. [World Hist.: *Hitler*]

19. *Jacobowsky and the Colonel* anti-Semitic Polish colonel refuses to recognize his rescuer because he is Jewish. [Ger. Lit.: *Jacobowsky and the Colonel*]

20. **Kishinev** Moldavian city; scene of pogroms and WWII genocide. [Jew. Hist.: Wigoder, 344]

21. **Kristallnacht** destruction of Jews' property anticipated later atrocities (November 9–10, 1938). [Ger. Hist.: *Hitler*, 689–694]

22. *Mein Kampf* Adolf Hitler's autobiography, including his theories on treatment of the Jews. [Ger. Hist.: *Mein Kampf*]

23. **Nazi** *Nazionalsozialist*; rabid anti-Semite member of Hitler's party. [Ger. Hist.: Shirer]

24. **New Order** partially fulfilled Nazification of Europe. [Eur. Hist.: *Hitler*, 935, 1055]

25. **Nuremberg Laws** stripped Jews of citizenship and civil rights (1935). [Ger. Hist.: Wigoder, 458]

26. *Protocols of the Elders of Zion* forged tract revealing Jewish conspiracy to control world. [Jew. Hist.: Wigoder, 170]

27. *Schindler's List* 1993 film by Steven Spielberg; story of Catholic German who saves over 1000 Poles from Nazi camps; filmed on location in black and white with mostly hand-held cameras. [Am. Film: *SJEPC*]

28. **swastika** symbol of German anti-Semitism since 1918; became emblem of Nazi party. [Ger. Hist.: *Collier's*, XVIII, 78]

29. **Torquemada, Tomás de (1420–1498)** head of Spanish Inquisition; instrumental in expelling Jews from Spain (1492). [Span. Hist.: Wigoder, 600]

30. **Untermenschen** subhumans; Nazi conception of Jews and Slavs. [Ger. Hist.: Shirer, 1223]

31. **Volkischer Beobachter** Nazi party organ featuring Jew-baiting articles. [Ger. Hist.: Shirer, 75–78]

32. **Wiesel, Elie (1928–)** Romanian Jewish writer and Holocaust survivor who has devoted his life to remembering and understanding the horrors of Nazism. [World Hist.: *EB*]

29. ANTISLAVERY

1. **Abolitionists** activist group working to free slaves. [Am. Hist.: Jameson, 1]

2. **Douglass, Frederick (1818?-1895)** African-American abolitionist, editor, and orator, "Father of the Civil Rights Movement." [Am. Hist.: *BBAAL1*]

3. **Emancipation Proclamation** edict issued by Abraham Lincoln freeing the slaves (1863). [Am. Hist.: *EB*, III: 869]

4. **Free Soil Party** Abolitionist political party before Civil War. [Am. Hist.: Flexner, 3]

5. **Jayhawkers** antislavery guerillas fighting on the Union side in Civil War. [Am. Hist.: Jameson, 256]

6. **"Laus Deo!"** poem written to celebrate emancipation of slaves. [Am. Lit.: "Laus Deo!" in Hart, 460]

7. *Liberator* William Lloyd Garrison's virulently Abolitionist newspaper. [Am. Hist.: Van Doren, 142]

8. **Lincoln, Abraham (1809–1865)** sixteenth U.S. president; issued Emancipation Proclamation, freeing the slaves. [Am. Hist.: Jameson, 286–287]

9. *North Star* newspaper supporting emancipation founded by Frederick Douglass. [Am. Hist.: Hart, 607]

10. *Roots* novel by Alex Haley about several generations of his mother's family, brought to the US from Africa as slaves; drew wide audiences in 1977 as TV minseries. [Am. Lit. and TV: *SJEPC*]

11. **Shelby, George** vows to devote self to freeing slaves. [Am. Lit.: *Uncle Tom's Cabin*]

12. **Stowe, Harriet Beecher (1811–1896)** author of *Uncle Tom's Cabin*, influential Abolitionist novel. [Am. Hist.: Jameson, 481]

13. **Truth, Sojourner (1797?-1883)** African-American abolitionist and activist. [Am. Hist.: *BBAAL1*]

14. **Tubman, Harriet (1820?-1913)** African-American abolitionist, activist, and conductor of the Underground Railroad. [Am. Hist.: *BBAAL1*]

15. *Uncle Tom's Cabin* highly effective, sentimental Abolitionist novel. [Am. Lit.: Jameson, 513]

16. **Underground Railroad** system of roads and safehouses that helped slaves to escape to the North. [Am. Hist.: *EB*, X: 255]

17. **Wilberforce, William (1759–1833)** British statesman and abolitionist, led the cause to abolish slavery in British colonies. [Br. Hist.: *EB*]

30. ANTIWAR (See also PEACE, PEACEMAKING.)

1. **"Alice's Restaurant"** 1967 antiwar song written by folksinger Arlo Guthrie featured 18 minutes of storytelling to a blues beat and became basis of 1969 movie. [Am. Music: *SJEPC*]

2. *All Quiet on the Western Front* 1928 novel first published in German; Erich Maria Remarque takes a vehemently antiwar stance in this work set in the German army during WWI; the horrifying

events are told in first person by nineteen-year-old recruit Paul Baumer. [Ger. Lit.: Gillespie and Naden]

3. **Arjuna** called upon by duty to be a warrior, he refuses to join the fratricidal battle. [Hindu Lit.: *The Bhagavad-Gita* in Benét, 103]

4. *Arms and the Man* satirizes romantic view of war. [Br. Lit.: *Arms and the Man*]

5. **"Blowin' in the Wind"** Bob Dylan's 1963 song protesting war and racial injustice in a series of questions was popularized by folk trio Peter, Paul and Mary. [Am. Music: *SJEPC*]

6. *Farewell to Arms, A* novel of lovers who flee from war's horrors. [Am. Lit.: *A Farewell to Arms*]

7. **flower power** slogan of the antiwar movement during the U.S. involvement in Vietnam War (1960s and 70s). [Am. Hist.: Misc.]

8. **hippies** antiwar youth of the 1960s and 1970s, espousing counterculture beliefs. [Pop. Cult.: Misc.]

9. **Quakers** known for service to peace. [Am. Hist.: *EB*, 7: 743–745]

10. **Sherston, George** refuses to continue taking part in a war being wrongfully prolonged. [Br. Lit.: *Memoirs of an Infantry Officer* in Magill I, 579]

31. ANXIETY (See also INSECURITY.)

1. **Allen, Woody (1935–)** neurotic auteur whose personal and professional lives are closely related; often stars in his own films. [Am. Film: *SJEPC*]

2. **Morissette, Alanis (1974–)** anger and unhappiness find their way into all of her rock songs. [Can. Music: *SJEPC*]

3. **Pinter, Harold (1930–2008)** British dramatist and Nobel Laureate whose plays have an anxious, menacing tone. [Br. Theater: *FOF, MOD*]

4. **Prozac** antidepressant medication with wide-spread use; the one billion prescriptions worldwide have some concerned that we are dulling normal human emotions. [Medicine: *SJEPC*]

5. **Valium** used to curb anxiety and depression; concern rose over abuse and addiction with millions of prescriptions being written, mainly for middle-aged, middle-class women. [Am. Medicine: *SJEPC*]

32. APHRODISIAC

1. **cestus** Aphrodite's girdle made by Hephaestus; magically induces passion. [Gk. Myth.: Benét, 183]

2. **ginseng** induces passion. [Plant Symbolism: *EB*, IV: 549]

3. **lupin** leguminous plant; arouses passion. [Plant Folklore: Boland, 9]

4. **mandrake** a narcotic that arouses passion. [Western Folklore: Boland, 13]

5. **marjoram** used on bedsheets; Venus used it with Ascanius. [Rom. Myth.: Boland, 11–12]

6. **periwinkle, worms, and houseleek** combination produces passion. [Plant Folklore: Boland, 9]

7. **raw oysters** food consumed as a love potion. [Popular Folklore: Misc.]

8. **Spanish fly** preparation made of green blister beetles and used to incite cattle to mate. [Insect Symbolism: *EB*, IX: 399]

9. **willow seeds** taken in water, produce only sons. [Western Folklore: Boland, 11]

33. APOCALYPSE

1. **behemoth** king of animals whose flesh will provide feast for chosen when Messiah comes. [Jew. Tradition: Leach, 132]

2. *Cat's Cradle* Kurt Vonnegut's 1963 science fiction novel about end of the world through bizarre science project that creates substance that can immediately freeze the oceans; novel probes the search for meaning in life through science and religion. [Am. Lit.: Gillespie and Naden]

3. **"Fire and Ice"** from a Robert Frost poem speculating on the end of the world: in fire or ice. [Am. Lit.: *FOF; MOD*]

4. **Four Horsemen of the Apocalypse** four riders symbolizing pestilence, war, famine, and death. [N.T.: Revelation 6:1–8]

5. **Goetterdammerung** "twilight of the gods"; the end of the world, brought on by the final battle between the good and evil gods; a byword for the apocalypse. [Ger. Folklore: Leach, 461]

6. **Gog and Magog** giant leaders in ultimate battle against God's people. [N.T.: Revelation 20:8]

7. **"Helter Skelter"** based on song by Paul McCartney, Charles Manson's prophesy of devastating racial war, leaving him as ruler of ravaged world [Am. Hist.: *SJEPC*]

8. **Leviathan** sea monster; symbol of apocalypse. [Jew. Tradition: Leach, 67]

9. **mushroom cloud** the radiation cloud emanating from a nuclear explosion; a symbol of the end of the world. [Am. Hist.: Misc.]

10. **Revelation** final book of the New Testament discussing the coming of the world's end. [N.T.: Revelation]

34. APOSTASY (See also HERESY, SACRILEGE.)

1. **Aholah and Aholibah** symbolize Samaria's and Jerusalem's abandonment to idols. [O.T.: Ezekiel 23:4]

2. **Jansenism** unorthodox Roman Catholic movement of the 17th and 18th centuries led by Cornelius Jansen. [Christian Hist.: *EB*, V: 515]

3. **Julian the Apostate (331–363)** Roman emperor, educated as a Christian but renounced Christianity when he became emperor. [Rom. Hist.: Benét, 533]

35. APPEARANCE, DECEIVING (See also ILLUSION.)

1. **Baldwin, George** "good" lawyer having affair with client's wife. [Am. Lit.: *The Manhattan Transfer*]

2. *City Lights* Charlie Chaplin's finest silent film centers on the sentimental love story of a blind woman who sells flowers and mistakes the smitten Little Tramp for a millionaire (1931). [Am. Film: *SJEPC*]

3. **Clinker, Humphry** admirable character concealed by shabby exterior. [Br. Lit.: *Humphry Clinker*]

4. **Cory, Richard** man "with everything" commits suicide. [Am. Lit.: "Richard Cory" in Hart, 711]

5. **Cowardly Lion** character in L. Frank Baum's Oz series who believes he is a coward, until the Wizard makes him see he has been brave all along. [Br. Children's Lit.: Jones]

6. **daffodil** beautiful, but narcotic. [Plant Symbolism: *Flora Symbolica*, 168]

7. **Gray, Dorian** his portrait becomes the record of his life. [Br. Lit.: *The Picture of Dorian Gray*]

8. *Hannah Montana* Disney TV show premiered in 2006; teenage girl functions as average high schooler by day and works as famous pop singer at night, a fact known only to her family and close friends. [Am. TV: Misc.]

9. **Little Buttercup** apparently dumpy woman, once "young and charming." [Br. Opera: *H.M.S. Pinafore*]

10. **Phaedra** pretends unkindness to Hippolytus to hide her passion for him. [Fr. Drama: *Phaedra*, Magill I, 741–742]

11. **Scarecrow** character in L. Frank Baum's Oz series who believes he has no brain, until the Wizard makes him see he is intelligent, just uneducated. [Br. Children's Lit.: Jones]

12. **Snape, Severus** character from J.K. Rowling's Harry Potter series for young readers (1997–2007); unpopular, snide teacher at Hogwarts who appears to be a foe, but turns out to be loyal to Dumbledore and protective of Harry; the complexity of his motivations is revealed at the end of the series. [Br. Children's Lit.: Misc.]

13. **Tchitchikoff** swindler-adventurer, outwardly a philanthropist. [Russ. Lit.: *Dead Souls*]

14. **Tin Woodsman** character in L. Frank Baum's Oz series who believe he has no heart, until the Wizard makes him see he is very caring. [Br. Children's Lit.: Jones]

15. **Valancourt** his gambling not a vice but attempt to secure money to aid friends. [Br. Lit.: *The Mysteries of Udolpho*, Magill I, 635–638]

16. **Venus's-flytrap** lures insects with sweet odor. [Flower Symbolism: *Flora Symbolica*, 178]

17. **Wizard of Oz** character in L. Frank Baum's Oz series; although he appears to be a powerful wizard, he is just a man behind a curtain creating an image of power; he proves to be wise, though, in his advice to Dorothy and her friends. [Br. Children's Lit.: Jones]

36. APPLE

1. **Adam and Eve** original couple tempted to eat forbidden fruit. [O.T.: Genesis 2:17]

2. **Apple Annie** nickname for women who sold apples on street corners during the Depression. [Am. Culture: Flexner, 11]

3. **Appleseed, Johnny (John Chapman, 1774–1845)** missionary nurseryman who supplied apple seeds to pioneers. [Am. Folklore: *EB*, II: 746]

4. **Big Apple** nickname for New York City. [Am. Folklore: Misc.]

5. **forbidden fruit** fruit that God forbade Adam and Eve to eat; byword for tempting object. [O.T.: Genesis 3:1–6]

6. **golden apples** given by Venus to Hippomenes to distract Atalanta and win his race with her. [Class. Myth.: *Metamorphoses*]

7. *Golden Apples, The* highly-regarded short story collection by Eudora Welty, depicting the mythical in the everyday lives of small-town Southerners. [Am. Lit.: *EB*]

8. **golden apples of the Hesperides** a wedding gift to Hera; Hercules stole some in the course of his labors. [Gk. Myth.: Brewer *Dictionary*, 451]

9. **Newton, Isaac (1642–1727)** English mathematician whose observation of apple's fall led to treatise on gravitation. [Br. Hist.: *EB*, 13: 16–21]

10. **Tell, William** Swiss Folk hero condemned to shoot apple from atop son's head. [Swiss Folklore: *EB*, IX: 872]

Architect (See ARCHITECTURE)

37. ARCHITECTURE

1. **Alberti (1404–1472)** Italian scholar and architect; developed Renaissance art theory, and major exponent of those theories in works like the church of San Andrea. [Ital. Architecture: *EB*]

2. **baroque** in an ornate style, from the period of the late Renaissance (17th-18th centuries). [Eur. Architecture *FOF, MOD*]

3. **Bauhaus** influential German school of architecture, noted for simple, clean lines, philosophy of: "form follows function." [Eur. Architecture *FOF, MOD*]

4. **Bernini (1598–1680)** Italian sculptor and architect of the Baroque era; he fused the two disciplines in such masterpieces as the baldachin over Peter's tomb at St. Peter's Basilica and the Triton fountain in Rome. [Ital. Architecture: *EB*]

5. **Bramante, Donato (1444–1514)** Italian architect of the High Renaissance, chief architect of St. Peter's Basilica and designer of the city of Rome. [Ital. Architecture: *EB*]

6. **Brunelleschi (1377–1446)** Italian architect of the early Renaissance; his major work includes the Dome of the Cathedral of Santa Maria del Fiore [Ital. Architecture: *EB*]

7. **Chrysler Building** prime example of 1920s Art Deco-style architecture, in New York City. [Am. Architecture: *SJEPC*]

8. **Corbusier, Le (1887–1965)** Swiss architect and proponent of the International School of architecture; created city plans and buildings noted for their spare, functional design. [Eur. Architecture: *EB*]

9. **Daedalus** mythical Greek architect said to have built the labyrinth for King Minos of Crete. [Gk. Myth.: *EB*, III: 342]

10. **Dymaxion house** revolutionary round house constructed of lightweight materials designed in 1929 by Buckminster Fuller; vision of a mass-produced version to ease post-World War II housing crunch never materialized. [Am. Architecture: *SJEPC*]

11. **Empire State Building** architectural symbol of America located in Manhattan was tallest building in the world from 1931 to 1971; quintessential skyscraper's image used in many products and films. [Am. Architecture: *SJEPC*]

12. **Fuller, Buckminster (1895–1983)** visionary architect with "more for less" philosophy designed the Dymaxion house (1929); unveiled his most-recognized work, a 76–meter-wide, plastic-tiled geodistic dome, at Expo '67 in Montreal. [Am. Architecture: *SJEPC*]

13. **Gehry, Frank (1929–)** American architect noted for using nontraditional materials and unusual forms, as in the Guggenheim Museum in Bilbao, Spain. [Am. Architecture: *EB*]

14. **Geodistic Dome** revolutionary structure made of lightweight materials patented by Buckminster Fuller in 1949 can be erected anywhere for temporary shelter; 76–meter-wide, plastic-tiled version immortalized at Expo '67 in Montreal. [Am. Architecture: *SJEPC*]

15. **gothic** style of architecture prominent in medieval Europe characterized by soaring interiors supported by flying buttresses; examples include Notre Dame in Paris. [Eur. Architecture *FOF, MOD*]

16. **Gropius, Walter (1883–1969)** German-born American architect and founder of the Bauhaus school, whose philosophy of "form follows function" inspired a generation of architects. [Architecture: *EB*]

17. **Johnson, Philip (1906–2005)** American architect and founder of the International School; designed the famous Glass House. [Am. Architecture: *EB*]

18. **Kahn, Louis (1901–1974)** American architect who broke with the International School to develop buildings of powerful, massive design, including the Salk Institute. [Am. Architecture: *EB*]

19. **L'Enfant, Pierre-Charles (1754–1825)** French-born American architect and engineer who designed the plan for Washington, D.C. [Am. Architecture: *EB*]

20. **Mies van der Rohe, Ludwig (1886–1969)** German-born American architect, influential practioner of the International Style, noted for skyscrapers made of steel and glass, including the Seagrams Building (NYC). [Am. Architecture: *EB*]

21. **Pei, I.M. (1917–)** Chinese-born American architect noted for elegant, large designs, including JFK Int'l Airport, the East bldg of the National Gallery, and the glass pyramid at the Louvre (Paris). [Am. Architecture: *EB*]

22. **Roark, Howard** central character in Ayn Rand's famous novel, symbol of egocentric individualism. [Am. Lit.: Ayn Rand *The Fountainhead*]

23. **Roecus** architect of the early temple of Hera at Samos. [Architecture: *NCE*, 1799]

24. **Saarinen, Eero (1910–1961)** Finnish-born American architect known for use of sculptural form designed the landmark arch in St. Louis, Missouri, and General Motors Technical Center in Warren, Michigan; son of architect Eliel Saarinen. [Architecture: *WB2*]

25. **Saarinen, Eliel (1873–1950)** internationally famous Finnish-born American architect designed Helsinki railroad station and buildings for Cranbrook Academy of Art in Bloomfield Hills, Michigan; father of architect Eero Saarinen. [Architecture: *WB2*]

26. **skyscrapers** extremely tall commercial buildings were a uniquely American design in late nineteenth century; now a presence in large cities worldwide, reflecting commerce and technological advances. [Architecture: *SJEPC*]

27. **Sullivan, Louis (1856–1924)** American architect noted for his development of the skyscraper and his influence on modern American architecture. [Am. Architecture: *EB*]

28. **Thomas, Saint** patron saint of architects. [Christian Hagiog.: *Saints and Festivals*, 30]

29. **White, Stanford (1853–1906)** famous architect killed by jealous husband of his mistress in 1906; seduced numerous women with invitation to "come up and see my etchings," the now stock pickup line he coined. [Am. Architecture: *SJEPC*]

30. **Wren, Sir Christoper (1632–1723)** British architect, considered the greatest of his era; his works include St. Paul's Cathedral (London). [Brit. Architecture: *EB*]

31. **Wright, Frank Lloyd (1867–1959)** American architect, most famous and influential of his era, whose "Prairie style" homes influenced home building design for generations. [Am. Architecture: *EB*]

38. ARGUMENTATIVENESS

1. **Absolute, Sir Anthony** warm-hearted but testy; always blames others. [Br. Drama: *The Rivals*]

2. *Bickersons, The* classic radio comedy starring Don Ameche and Frances Langford as a constantly battling couple. [Am. Radio: Misc.]

3. **Caterpillar** peevishly disputes with Alice. [Br. Lit.: *Alice's Adventures in Wonderland*]

4. **devil's advocate** a contrarian; one who takes the opposing side of an argument. [Gen. *ODA*]

5. **Lessways, Hilda** husband Edwin could never agree with her. [Br. Lit.: *The Clayhanger Trilogy*]

6. **McEnroe, John (1959–)** brilliant performances as a tennis player were coupled with spoiled-brat antics. [Am. Sports: *SJEPC*]

7. **Naggleton, Mr. and Mrs.** contentious and fault-finding couple. [Br. Lit.: *Punch*, 1864–1865; Brewer *Handbook*, 742]

8. **Steinbrenner, George (1930–)** owner of the New York Yankees baseball team beginning in 1973; often in the news for making critical comments about his team and embroiled in arguments with his managers. [Am. Sports: *SJEPC*]

9. **Vidal, Gore (1925–)** famous writer and media wit known for 1968 story of a transsexual, *Myra Breckinridge*, his iconoclastic political views, and his well-publicized fights (most notably with William F. Buckley, Jr.). [Am. Lit.: *SJEPC*]

39. ARISTOCRACY

1. **Almanach de Gotha** German social register. [Ger. Lit.: Benét, 26]

2. **Beaucaire, Monsieur** portrays English aristocracy as shallow, inept snobs. [Am. Lit.: *Monsieur Beaucaire*, Magill I, 616–617]

3. **blue blood** said to flow in the veins of the nobility. [Western Cult.: Brewer *Dictionary*]

4. **Brahmin** appellation accorded members of old, "aristocratic" New England families. [Am. Hist.: *EB*, II: 226]

5. *Cabala, The* portrays wealthy esoterics, mysteriously influential in governmental affairs. [Am. Lit.: *The Cabala*]

6. **First Families of Virginia** elite families of prestigious rank. [Am. Usage: Misc.]

7. **Four Hundred, the** social elite; the number of people Mrs. Astor could accommodate in her ballroom. [Am. Usage: Misc.]

8. **gold on white** symbol of elite class. [Chinese Art: Jobes, 357]

9. **Junkers** Prussian elite. [Ger. Hist.: *Hitler*, 387]

10. *Social Register* book listing names and addresses of social elite. [Am. Usage: Misc.]

11. **St. Aubert, Emily** young French woman of wealth and position. [Br. Lit.: *The Mysteries of Udolpho*, Magill I, 635–638]

40. ARROGANCE (See also BOASTFULNESS, CONCEIT, EGOTISM.)

1. **amber** traditional symbol of arrogance. [Gem Symbolism: Jobes, 81]

2. **Arachne** presumptuously challenges Athena to weaving contest; transformed into spider. [Gk. Myth.: Leach, 69]

3. **Citizen Kane** rich and powerful man drives away friends by use of power. [Am. Cinema: Halliwell, 149]

4. **Coriolanus** class-conscious and contemptuous leader. [Br. Lit.: *Coriolanus*]

5. **Darcy, Fitz William** proud of superior station. [Br. Lit.: *Pride and Prejudice*]

6. **de Bourgh, Lady Catherine** arrogant, vulgar woman. [Br. Lit.: *Pride and Prejudice*]

7. **Donald Duck** overbearing comic strip character with a chip on his shoulder. [Comics: Horn, 216–217]

8. **Dundreary, Lord** his aristocratic haughtiness a trademark. [Br. Lit.: *Our American Cousin*]

9. **Ferrara, Duke of** has had his wife murdered for too little appreciation of her place. [Br. Poetry: Browning *My Last Duchess* in Magill IV, 247]

10. **Humpty Dumpty** arbitrarily gives his own meanings to words, and tolerates no objections. [Br. Lit.: Lewis Carroll *Through the Looking-Glass*]

11. **Louis XIV (1638–1715)** the Sun King, arrogant and powerful. [Fr. Hist.: *ODA*]

12. **Lucifer** rebel archangel who challenged God's supremacy. [Christian Hagiog.: *Collier's*, XII, 143]

13. **Lucy** know-it-all cartoon character gives advice to other children. [Comics: "Peanuts" in Horn, 543]

14. **Miss Piggy** vain, egotistical Muppet known for self-confidence bordering on arrogance. [Am. TV: *The Muppet Show*]

15. **Niobe** for boasting of superiority, her children are killed. [Gk. Myth.: Hall, 224; Rom. Lit.: *Metamorphoses*]

16. **prima donna** operatic singer, usually a soprano, who is arrongant, demanding, and proud. [Western Music *FOF, MOD*]

17. **radical chic** term coined by Tom Wolfe to describe members of New York Society courting political radicals. [Am. Pop. Culture: Tom Wolfe *Radical Chic and Mau-Mauing the Flak Catchers*]

18. **rue** traditional symbol of arrogance. [Flower Symbolism: *Flora Symbolica*]

19. **tall sunflower** indicates haughtiness. [Flower Symbolism: *Flora Symbolica*]

20. **Uzziah** king of Judah assumed priests' function of burning incense; punished with leprosy. [O.T.: II Chronicles 26:16–19]

21. **veni, vidi, vici** Caesar's dispatch describing his subjugation of Pharnaces (47 B.C.). [Rom. Hist.: Brewer *Notebook*, 923]

22. **Volumnia** magisterial mother of Coriolanus; molds his character. [Br. Lit.: *Coriolanus*]

23. **White Rabbit** displays traits of snobbish, pampered upper class; from Lewis Carroll's *Alice's Adventures in Wonderland*. [Br. Children's Lit.: Jones]

24. **yellow carnation** traditional symbol of arrogance. [Flower Symbolism: Jobes, 291]

25. **yellow sultan** traditional symbol of arrogant contempt. [Flower Symbolism: *Flora Symbolica*]

41. ART

1. **Abstract Expressionism** highly subjective American art form originating in mid-20th-century New York focuses on the painter's creative experience and expression; brush strokes and color are typically spontaneously dripped or applied without regard for objective standards of art. [Am. Art: *SJEPC*]

2. **Armory Show** International Exhibition of Modern Art of 1913 introduced Modernism to the American public. [Art: *SJEPC*]

3. **Ashcan School** first specifically modern art style in America presented gritty urban subjects in a realistic manner. [Am. Art: *SJEPC*]

4. **Blake, William (1757–1827)** English artist and poet; creator of watercolors and engravings, often on Biblical and classical themes. [Br. Art: *ODA*]

5. **Botticelli, Sandro (1445–1510)** Italian painter known for his *Birth of Venus*, whose central female figure became a symbol of beauty. [Ital. Art: *ODA*]

6. **Bruegel, Pieter (c.1525–1569)** Flemish painter, known as Pieter Bruegel the Elder, famous for renderings of lives of peasants. [Flem. Art: *ODA*]

7. **Byzantium** ancient city, also known as Constantinople and Istanbul, noted for highly decorative style of art and iconography. [Art: *FOF, MOD*]

8. **Caravaggio, Michaelangelo (1571–1610)** Italian painter known for his use of *chiaroscuro*, the contrast of light and shade. [Ital. Art: *ODA*]

9. **Chagall, Marc (1887–1985)** Russian painter noted for dreamlike landscapes and characters, many drawn from Jewish and Russian folklore. [Rus. Art: *FOF, MOD*]

10. **Christo (1935–)** Bulgarian-born American environmental artist whose large-scale projects involve wrapping bridges, buildings, and vast acres of land all over the world. [Art: *SJEPC*]

11. **conceptual art** postmodernist movement originating in 1960s focuses on the political, social, and cultural ideas behind the art's creation rather than the art itself. [Art: *SJEPC*]

12. **Correggio, Antonio (1494–1534)** Italian Renaissance painter, noted for depictions of joyful cherubs. [Ital. Art: *ODA*]

13. **Dali, Salvador (1904–1989)** Spanish Surrealist painter; creator of works imbued with fantastic, dreamlike images. [Eur. Art: *ODA*]

14. **Degas, Edward (1834–1917)** French painter and sculptor of the Impressionist school, known for depicting dancers. [Fr. Art: *ODA*]

15. **di Bondone, Giotto (c.1267–1337)** Italian painter, brought greater naturalism to art; famous works include frescoes for Arena Chapel in Padua. [Ital. Art: *ODA*]

16. **Eisner, Will (1917–2005)** influential comic book artist internationally recognized as master of sequential art and father of the graphic novel. [Am. Comics: *SJEPC*; Misc.]

17. **Escher, M.C. (1902–1972)** Dutch artist known for prints featuring complex, paradoxical forms and structures. [Art *ODA*]

18. **Expressionism** art movement begun in Europe in the 19th century that emphasized nonrepresentative, exaggerated, emotionally charged style. [Art: Misc.]

19. **Greco, El (1541–1614)** Greek-born Spanish painter (Domenikos Theotokopoulos), known for religious-themed works, elongated human figures. [Span. Art: *ODA*]

20. **Hogarth, William (1697–1764)** English painter and engraver; known for satires on English society, i.e. *The Rake's Progress*. [Br. Art.: *ODA*]

21. **Hopper, Edward (1882–1967)** American painter whose subjects were often ordinary people, depicted as bleak and lonely. [Am. Art: *ODA*]

22. **Impressionism** art movement from mid-19th century Europe emphasizing the effects of light in nature. [Art: *FOF, MOD*]

23. **Johns, Jasper (1930–)** modern artist whose innovative approach to common icons (flags, targets, letters and numbers, etc.) ushered in era of American Pop Art in late 1950s; influential to minimalist and conceptual artists. [Am. Art: *SJPEC*]

24. **Lichtenstein, Roy (1923–1997)** created pop art canvases that duplicated huge comic strips and depicted gender stereotypes and trends in art history. [Art: *SJEPC*]

25. **Magritte, Rene (1898–1967)** Belgian surrealist painter whose works use common objects to create strange effects. [Belgian Art: *FOF, MOD*]

26. **Matisse, Henri (1869–1954)** French painter whose creations celebrated color and life; also known for paper cutouts and stained glass creations. [Fr. Art: *FOF, MOD*]

27. **Michelangelo (1475–1564)** Italian sculptor, painter, architect, and greatest artist of the Italian Renaissance; greatest works include statue of David, frescoes of the Sistine Chapel. [Ital. Art: *ODA*]

28. **Minerva** Roman goddess of arts and crafts; she corresponds to the Greek goddess Athena. [Rom. Myth: *ODA*]

29. **Monet, Claude (1840–1926)** French Impressionist painter who explored the effects of light in scenes of cities, buildings, and gardens. [Fr. Art: *FOF, MOD*]

30. **Myron** Greek sculptor (5th century B.C.) of Discobolus and other works acclaimed for extraordinary lifelikeness. [Gk. Art: *NCE*, 1870]

31. **Op Art** works that used optical perception in depictions of designs that seemed to move and change color. [Art: *SJEPC*]

32. **performance art** art form of the 1970s; artist uses act of performance, rather than the finished work, to relay meaning. [Art: *SJEPC*]

33. **Phidias** Greek sculptor (468–432 B.C.), epitome of classical art. [Gk. Art: Benét]

34. **Picasso, Pablo (1881–1974)** Spanish painter and sculptor, most influential artist of the 20th century; his work includes several different styles, including his "blue" and "rose" periods and Cubism. [Eur. Art: *ODA*]

35. **Pollock, Jackson (1912–1956)** his "action painting" technique of flinging and dripping paint onto canvas emphasized the creation of the work over the work itself; became preeminent among the abstract expressionists. [Am. Art: *SJEPC*]

36. **Pop Art** movement of the 1960s; bold and stylized works used everyday objects and consumer goods as subjects [Am. Art: *SJEPC*]

37. **Pre-Raphaelite** an art movement from 19th century England founded by Dante Gabriel Rosetti, John Everett Millais, and Holman Hunt; they celebrated the style and themes of pre-Renaissance masters. [Br. Art: *ODA*]

38. **Pygmalion** carved so beautiful and lifelike a statue that he fell in love with it. [Gk. Myth.: Benét]

39. **Raphael (1483–1520)** Italian painter of the high Renaissance known for *The School of Athens*, celebrating classical themes, and beautiful female figures. [Ital. Art: *FOF, MOD*]

40. **Rembrandt van Rijn (1606–1669)** Great Dutch painter of the 17th century, noted for portraits and self-portraits and use of light; a catchword for a great artist. [Dutch Art: *ODA*]

41. **Remington, Frederic (1861–1909)** his drawings, paintings, and bronze sculptures are energetic depictions of cowboys and Native Americans of the Western frontier. [Am. Art: *SJEPC*]

42. **Rockwell, Norman (1894–1978)** best known for his illustrations for the cover of the *Saturday Evening Post*; created folksy, traditional depictions of America. [Am. Art: *SJEPC*]

43. **Rubens, Peter Paul (1577–1640)** Flemish painter noted for his full-figured female nudes. [Flem. Art: *FOF, MOD*]

44. **Toulouse-Lautrec, Henri (1864–1901)** French painter of the Parisian demi-monde; he produced a famous series of posters for the Moulin Rouge. [Fr. Art: *ODA*]

45. **Turner, J. M. W. (1775–1851)** English painter whose works reflect his fascination with the quality of light. [Br. Art: *ODA*]

46. **Van Gogh, Vincent (1853–1890)** Dutch painter of the post-Impressionist era; his vibrant landscapes and sunflowers radiate his passionate intensity; he died a suicide. [Dutch Art: *ODA*]

47. **Warhol, Andy (1928–1987)** renowned Pop artist who used everyday objects— most notably, Campbell soup cans—as inspiration;

his outrageous behavior and pursuit of celebrity oftentimes over-shadowed his work as an artist. [Am. Art: *SJEPC*]

48. **Wyeth, Andrew (1917–2009)** austere New England subjects in earth tones and precise line, but tremendous depth of feeling; first living artist to have his work exhibited at National Gallery (1987) and first living artist to have retrospective at Metropolitan Museum of Art (1976). [Am. Art: *SJEPC*]

49. **Wyeth, N. C. (1882–1945)** painter and world-famous illustrator of classic adventure books and stories in periodicals of early twentieth century. [Am. Art: *SJEPC*]

50. **Zeuxis** Greek artist (420–390 B.C.) so skilled that birds reputedly flew to his painting of a bunch of grapes. [Gk. Art: *EB* (1963)]

Artist (See ART.)

Artistic Skill (See ART.)

Artlessness (See INNOCENCE, NAÏVETÉ.)

42. ASCENSION

1. **Assumption of Virgin Mary** belief that Mary was assumed bodily into heaven. [Christian Tradition: *NCE*, 1709]

2. **crescent moon** Mary often depicted standing on or above moon. [Christian Iconog.: Brewer *Dictionary*, 726]

3. **Elijah** transported to Heaven in a fiery chariot. [O.T.: II Kings 2:11]

4. **Helen of Troy** soars away into the air from the cave in which Menelaus left her. [Gk. Drama: Euripedes *Helen*]

5. **Jacob's ladder** from the Biblical story of Jacob, who dreamed of a ladder from earth to heaven, with angels ascending and descending. [O.T.: Genesis 28: 12]

6. **Jesus Christ** 40 days after Resurrection, ascended into heaven. [N.T.: Acts 1:1–11]

7. **Marguerite** borne to heaven by angels. [Fr. Opera: *Faust*, Westerman, 183–185]

8. **mi'raj** Muhammad's night journey to paradise. [Islam: Leach, 731]

9. **Romulus** taken to the heavens by Mars in a fiery chariot. [Rom. Myth.: Brewer *Dictionary*, 775]

10. **stars, garland of** emblem associated with the Assumption of the Virgin Mary. [Christian Iconog.: Jobes, 374]

43. ASCETICISM (See also DISCIPLINE.)

1. **Albigenses** heretical and ascetic Christian sect in France in 12th and 13th centuries. [Christian Hist.: *EB*, I: 201]

2. **Alexis, Saint** patron saint of beggars and hermits. [Christian Hagiog.: Brewer *Dictionary*, 22]

3. **Amish** conservative Christian group in North America noted for its simple, orderly life and nonconformist dress. [Am. Hist.: *EB*, I: 316]

4. **Anthony, Saint** founder of monasticism. [Christian Hagiog.: Attwater, 49]

5. **Bèguines** 12th-century French mendicant order. [Fr. Hist.: Espy, 98–99]

6. **Calvin, John (1509–1564)** French Protestant reformer; leader of Protestant Reformation; known for his harsh, punitive moral principles. [Christianity: *ODA*]

7. **Cathari** heretical and ascetic Christian sect in Europe in 12th and 13th centuries. [Christian Hist.: *EB*, II: 639]

8. **Cistercians** Roman Catholic monastic order observing strict asceticism, founded in 1098. [Christian Hist.: *EB*, II: 948]

9. **Clare, Saint** founder of mendicant Order of Poor Clares. [Christian Hagiog.: Hall, 69]

10. **Crazy Ivar** lived in hole on side of river bed. [Am. Lit.: *O Pioneers!*, Magill I, 663–665]

11. **Diogenes (412–323 B.C.)** despised worldly possessions; made his home in a tub. [Gk. Hist.: Hall, 104]

12. **Fakirs** fanatical mendicant sects found primarily in India. [Asian Hist.: Brewer *Note-Book*, 310]

13. **Franciscans** 13th-century religious order whose members lived in poverty. [Christian Hist.: *EB*, IV: 273]

14. **Gandhi, Mohandas K. (1869–1948)** Indian spiritual leader; embodied Hindu abstemiousness. [Indian Hist.: *NCE*, 1042]

15. **Jerome, Saint** Christian monastic leader who searched for peace as hermit in desert. [Christian Hist.: *EB*, V: 545]

16. **Knox, John (1505–1572)** Scottish Protestant reformer; founder of Scottish Presbyterian Church; noted for harsh moral ideas. [Christianity: *ODA*]

17. **Manichaean Sabbath** Manichaean observance of Sunday, demanding abstinence from food and sex. [Christian Hist.: *EB*, VIII: 746]

18. **Paul of Thebes, Saint** first Christian hermit; cave-dweller most of life. [Christian Hagiog.: Attwater, 268]

19. **Priscillianism** rigorously ascetic Christian sect found in Europe until the 6th century. [Christian Hist.: *EB*, VIII: 219]

20. **Puritanism** 16th- and 17th-century religious reform movement noted for moral earnestness and austerity. [Br. and Am. Hist.: *EB*, VIII, 309]

21. **Shakers** celibate religious sect flourishing in 19th-century U.S. [Am. Hist.: *EB*, IX: 105]

22. **Stoicism** philosophical school in Greco-Roman antiquity advocating rationality and austerity. [Gk. Hist.: *EB*, VIII: 746]

23. **Stylites, Saint Simeon** Christian monk whose philosophy was so ascetic that he dwelt atop a column to meditate. [Christian Hist.: *EB*, IX: 216]

24. **Timon of Athens** lost wealth, lived frugally; became misanthropic when deserted by friends. [Br. Lit.: *Timon of Athens*]

25. **Trappist monks** order with austere lifestyle. [Rom. Cath. Hist.: *NCE*, 2779]

26. **Waldenses** members of 12th-century French religious movement living in poverty. [Christian Hist.: *EB*, X: 519]

27. **Xenocrates** temperate philosopher, noted for contempt of wealth. [Gk. Hist.: Brewer *Dictionary*, 1169]

44. ASS

1. **Balaam's ass** ass which rebukes Balaam who then blesses the Israelites. [O.T.: Numbers 22:22–35]

2. **Bottom, Nick** oaf upon whom Puck fixes ass's head. [Br. Lit.: *Midsummer's Night Dream*]

3. **Dapple** Sancho's ass. [Span. Lit.: *Don Quixote*]

4. **donkey** symbol of Democratic Party in U.S. politics. [Am. Culture: Misc.]

5. *Golden Ass, The* Lucius, transformed into donkey, observes foibles of mankind. [Rom. Lit.: Benét, 44]

6. **Midas** for judging Pan winner of flute contest, his ears are changed to ass's ears. [Gk. Myth.: Leach, 83]

7. **Pinocchio and Lampwick** naughtiness causes them to sprout donkey's ears and tails; from C. Collodi's classic children's tale *The Adventures of Pinocchio* (1883). [Ital. Children's Lit.: Jones]

45. ASSASSINATION (See also MURDER.)

1. **Archduke Francis Ferdinand (1863–1914)** his assassination in 1914 was the catalyst for World War I. [Eur. Hist.: *EB*]

2. **assassins** Fanatical Moslem sect that smoked hashish and murdered Crusaders (11th-12th centuries). [Islamic Hist.: Brewer *Note-Book*, 52]

3. **Brutus** conspirator and assassin of Julius Caesar. [Br. Lit.: *Julius Caesar*]

4. **Caesar, Julius (102–44 B.C.)** murdered by conspirators. [Br. Lit.: *Julius Caesar*]

5. *Day of the Jackal* Frederick Forsyth's 1971 best-selling novel out-lined in authentic, chilling detail the inner workings of an assassi-nation plot against French president Charles de Gaulle. [Br. Lit.: *SJEPC*]

6. **Gorboduc** king killed by the people, who were horrified at his murderous family. [Br. Legend and Lit.: Benét, 410]

7. **Harmodius** assassinated Hipparchus, brother of the tyrant Hip-pias. [Gk. Hist.: *EB* (1963) XI: 198]

8. **hired gun** someone hired to kill; by extension, someone hired to do a nasty job. [Am. Culture: *FOF MOD*]

9. **hit list** from organized crime, a list of victims to be murdered; by extension, a list of people slated for firing, other bad news. [Am. Culture: *FOF, MOD*]

10. **Ides of March** Caesar killed by opposing factions (44 B.C.). [Rom. Hist.: *EB*, 3: 575–580]

11. *JFK* 1991 film by Oliver Stone; contends there was conspiracy to assassinate President John F. Kennedy; some critics feel it is histo-ry rewritten, others laud thoughtful portrayal of volatile subject. [Am. Film: *SJEPC*]

12. **Kennedy assassination** on November 22, 1963, U.S. President John F. Kennedy was shot as his car drove in a motorcade through Dallas, Texas; suspected killer, Lee Harvey Oswald was murdered within days, leading some to suspect a conspiracy. [Am. Hist.: *SJEPC*]

13. **Kennedy, Robert F. (1925–1968)** killed while campaigning for the Democratic presidential nomination. [Am. Hist.: *EB*]

14. **King, Martin Luther, Jr. (1929–1968)** considered the preeminent leader of Civil Rights movement for African Americans, was as-sassinated April 4, 1968, by James Earl Ray. [Am. Hist.: *SJEPC*]

15. **Lincoln, Abraham (1809–1865)** 16th President, assassinated by John Wilkes Booth at the Ford Theater, April 14, 1965. [Am. Hist.: *EB*]

46. ASTROLOGY (See also ZODIAC.)

1. **Chaldea** ancient Mesopotamian land where study of astrology developed. [Ancient Hist.: *NCE*, 499]

2. **Ecclitico** manipulator and false astrologer; dupes Buonafede. [Ger. Opera: Haydn, *The World of the Moon*, Westermark, 68–69]

3. **Mannering, Guy** cast fateful horoscope for young Bertram. [Br. Lit.: *Guy Mannering*]

4. **Nostradamus (1503–1566)** French astrologer/seer; wrote *Centuries* (1555), famous book of prognostications. [Fr. Hist.: *NCE*, 1969]

5. **Urania** muse of astrology. [Gk. Myth.: Brewer *Dictionary*, 1119]

47. ASTRONOMY

1. **Aristarchus of Samos (fl. c.270 B.C.)** Greek astronomer; first to maintain that Earth rotates and revolves around Sun. [Gk. Hist.: *EB*, I: 514]

2. **Copernicus, Nicolas (1453–1543)** Polish astronomer; author of the Copernican theory that planets orbit the sun. [Polish Hist.: *NCE*, 652]

3. **Galileo (1564–1642)** Italian mathematician, astronomer, and physicist. [Ital. Hist.: *EB*, IV: 388]

4. **Halley, Edmond (1656–1742)** British mathematician and astronomer; calculated orbit of comet named after him. [Br. Hist.: *EB*, IV: 860]

5. **Hipparchus (fl. 146–127 B.C.)** astronomer who calculated the year and discovered the precession of the equinoxes. [Turkish Hist.: *EB*, V: 55]

6. **Ptolemy (85–165)** eminent Greek astronomer. [Gk. Hist.: Hall, 255]

7. **Sagan, Carl (1934–1996)** his 1980 *COSMOS* and subsequent PBS broadcasts made articulate scientist a household name; instrumental in choosing samples of Earth's culture sent with Voyager's spacecraft into deep space. [Am. Science: *SJEPC*]

8. **Urania** muse of astronomy. [Gk. Myth.: Jobes, 374]

48. ATHEISM

1. **Dawkins, Richard (1941–)** British scientist, atheist, and critic of religion; author of the best-selling and controversial *The God Delusion*. [Br. Sci.: Misc.]

2. **Fountainhead, The** novel by Ayn Rand; based on her Objectivist philosophy. [Am. Lit.: *SJEPC*]

3. **Murray v. Curlett** 1963 Supreme Court decision in a case brought by atheist Madalyn Murray O'Hair banned prayer in the public schools. [Am. Hist.: Misc.]

4. **Objectivism** political philosophy of Ayn Rand; calls for libertarian individualism and atheism. [Am. Phil.: *SJEPC*]

5. **Rand, Ayn (1905–1982)** famous writer of philosophical novels about individuals rejecting societal and governmental restrictions [Am. Lit.: *SJEPC*]

49. ATHLETICISM (See also SPORTS.)

1. **Adidas** footwear and clothing associated with athletes, both Olympic and professional. [Business: *SJEPC*]

2. **Ali, Muhammad (1942–)** three-time heavyweight champion of the world; considered one of the greatest athletes of the 20th century. [Am. Sports: *BBAAL1*]

3. **Armstrong, Lance (1971–)** American cyclist, seven-time winner of the Tour de France; considered one of the finest athletes of all time. [Am. Sports: *BT2002*]

4. **Didrickson, Babe (1911–1956)** named Female Athlete of the Half Century by the Associated Press in 1950, she broke records, overcame gender barriers, and excelled in golf, basketball, track and field, swimming, and more. [Am. Sports: *SJEPC*]

5. **Evert, Chris (1954–)** disciplined, gracious tennis champion voted Greatest Woman Athlete of the Last 25 Years (Women's Sports Foundation, 1985); unanimously elected to International Tennis Hall of Fame (1995). [Am. Sport: *SJEPC*]

6. **Ironman Triathlon** competition includes 2.4 mile swim, 112 mile bike, and 26–mile run; one of the most grueling athletic contests in the world. [Sports: Misc.]

7. **Joyner-Kersee, Jackie (1962–)** world-class athlete in several sports and winner of six Olympic medals; excelled in the heptathlon, long jump; named Greatest Female Athlete of the 20th Century. [Am. Sports: *BBAAL1*]

8. **Leander** swims the mile-wide Hellespont every night to court Hero. [Gk. Myth.: Hamilton, 432]

9. **marathon** modern races, more than 26 miles, commemorate feat of Pheidippides. [World Sports: Benét, 633]

10. **Pheidippides** ran over 20 miles to Athens to announce victory at Marathon in 490 B.C., then died of exhaustion. [Gk. Legend: *Collier's*, XIII, 369]

11. **Thorpe, Jim (1888–1953)** gold medal winner of both pentathlon and decathlon in 1912 Olympics; medals later confiscated because of brief professional baseball career; went on to play professional baseball and football with great skill, winning numerous awards, many posthumously. [Am. Sports: *SJEPC*]

12. **Tour de France** world's largest annual sporting event, held nearly every year since 1903; grueling three-week, nearly 2500–mile bike race through France. [Sports: *SJEPC*]

13. ***Wide World of Sports*** TV show that began in the 1960s covering variety of sports; opening narration about "the thrill of victory and the agony of defeat" became famous. [Am. TV: *SJEPC*]

Austerity (See ASCETICISM, DISCIPLINE, HARSHNESS.)

50. AUTHORITY

1. **axe** worldwide symbol of power and authority. [Symbolism: *CEOS&S*]

2. **cathedra** throne indicative of religious power. [Folklore: Jobes, 307]

3. **CNN (Cable News Network)** viewed as the most authoritative source for major, breaking news worldwide. [Am. TV: *SJEPC*]

4. *Consumer Reports* considered unbiased, trustworthy source of consumer product information. [Am. Jour.: *SJEPC*]

5. **Cronkite, Walter (1916–)** legendary long-time anchorman of the *CBS Evening News* (1962–81) known as "The Most Trusted Man in America" and "Uncle Walter"; signed off broadcasts with "And that's the way it is." [Am. Jour. and TV: *SJEPC*]

6. **crook** staff carried as a symbol of office and authority. [Western Culture: Misc.]

7. **crosier** bishop's staff signifying his ruling power. [Christian Symbolism: Appleton, 21]

8. **cross and ball** signifies that spiritual power is above temporal. [Heraldry: Jobes, 387]

9. **crown** headpiece worn as symbol of royal authority. [Western Culture: Misc.]

10. **double bar cross** signifies archbishops, cardinals, and patriarchs. [Christian Iconog.: Jobes, 386]

11. **eagle** attribute of Zeus, thus of authority. [Art: Hall, 109]

12. **fasces** rods bundled about ax; emblem of magistrates, Fascists. [Rom. Hist.: Hall, 119; Ital. Hist.: Brewer *Dictionary*, 399]

13. **gavel** small mallet used by judge or presiding officer to signal order. [Western Culture: Misc.]

14. **Gibbon, Edward (1737–1794)** English historian and authority on Roman Empire; author of *The History of the Decline and Fall of the Roman Empire* [Br. Hist.: *ODA*]

15. **globe** in Christ child's hands signifies power and dominion. [Christian Symbolism: de Bles, 25]

16. **Hoyle** authoritative rules for playing cards and other games. [Misc.: Barnhart, 590]

17. **key** symbol of authority, both spiritual and secular. [Symbolism: *CEOS&S*]

18. **keys** symbolic of St. Peter's spiritual authority. [Christian Symbolism: N.T.: Matthew 16:19]

19. **Lord's Anointed, the** Jewish or other king by divine right. [Judaism: O.T.: I Samuel 26:9]

20. **mace** ceremonial staff carried as a symbol of office and authority. [Western Culture: Misc.]

21. **miter** bishop's headdress signifying his authority. [Christian Symbolism: *EB*, VI]

22. **nimbus** cloud of light signifying might, divinely imparted. [Gk. Lit.: *Iliad*]

23. **Ozymandias** king of ancient Egypt, evoked by Shelley as an example of the perishability of power. [Br. Lit.: Benét, 749]

24. **pectoral cross** worn by prelates on chain around neck. [Christian Iconog.: Child, 255; Jobes, 386]

25. **Pope, The** presides at the Vatican and functions as leader of the Roman Catholic Church; considered by believers to be infallible in matters of faith and morals. [Rel.: *SJEPC*]

26. **purple** color worn by persons of high rank. [Western Culture: Misc.]

27. **Real McCoy, the** relating to the invention of the automatic lubricating cup by Elijah McCoy (1844–1929); something that is reliable, authoritative, and genuine. [Am. Hist.: *BBInv*]

28. **Robert's Rules of Order** the authority on parliamentary procedure, codified by U.S. Gen. Henry M. Roberts (1837–1923); still used by legislative bodies nationwide. [Am. Hist.: *EB*]

29. **rod** wand or staff carried as a symbol of office and authority. [Western Culture: Misc.]

30. **scepter** symbol of regal or imperial power and authority. [Western Culture: Misc.]

31. **Stone of Scone** coronation stone where kings of Scotland were crowned. [Br. Hist.: Brewer *Dictionary*, 970]

32. **throne** seat of political or religious authority. [Western Folklore: Jobes, 1567]

33. **triple cross** three upper arms; symbolizes authority of the pope. [Christian Iconog.: Jobes, 386]

Autobiography (See BIOGRAPHY and AUTOBIOGRAPHY.)

51. AUTOMOBILE

1. **Chitty-Chitty-Bang-Bang** magical flying car in 1960s series of stories for children by Ian Fleming. [Br. Children's Lit.: *OCCL*]

2. **Chrysler Building** glamorous, towering Art Deco-style corporate headquarters in New York City conveyed powerful image of Chrysler Motor Corporation before the Great Depression. [Am. Architecture: *SJEPC*]

3. **convertible** sporty car with retractable roof allows passengers to experience the freedom and romance of the open road. [Hist.: *SJEPC*]

4. **Corvette** sleek, European-style sports car produced by General Motors debuted in 1953. [Am. Business: *SJEPC*]

5. **drive-in theater** accelerating American car culture drove the popularity of watching movies on a large outdoor screen while sitting in one's vehicle, particularly in the 1940s-60s. [Am. Entertainment: *SJEPC*]

6. **Edsel** Ford Motor Company car with distinctive styling named after Henry Ford's son debuted in 1957 but neglected to win the market's heart during a sluggish economy; production ended after three model years, one of the industry's most spectacular failures. [Am. Business: *SJEPC*; Misc.]

7. **fast food** America's car culture contributed to emergence of convenient, quickly prepared, standardized foods found at ubiquitous franchises such as White Castle and McDonald's for people on the go. [Am. Cuisine: *SJEPC*]

8. **Ford Motor Company** automobile manufacturer founded in 1903 by Henry Ford found success in mass market with Model T (1908–27) and sporty Mustang (1964–); revolutionary assembly line (1913) and five-dollar day (1914) helped create America's middle class. [Am. Business: *SJEPC*]

9. **Ford, Henry (1863–1947)** icon of automotive industry established his own manufacturing company in 1903, introduced affordable Model T in 1908, revolutionized production process with assembly line in 1913, and offered generous five-dollar daily wage to laborers. [Am. Hist.: *SJEPC*]

10. **General Motors** automotive giant founded in 1908 by Billy Durant became one of the largest corporations in the world and included Cadillac, Chevrolet, Buick, Pontiac, and Saturn lines; promoter of America's car culture and harbinger of America's economic fortunes. [Am. Business: *SJEPC*]

11. **Iacocca, Lee (1924–)** auto executive who was mastermind behind the Ford Mustang; at Chrysler, he made himself the image of the company and attained celebrity status as its spokesman. [Am. Business: *SJEPC*]

12. **Jeep** originally all-terrain vehicle developed for U.S. troops in WWII; popular vehicle with many loyal owners and forerunner to larger, heavier SUVs. [Am. Business: *SJEPC*]

13. **Model T** Henry Ford's wildly successful mass-produced car (1908); a symbol of a basic, simple, inexpensive, and now, old-fashioned American product. [Am. Business: Misc.]

14. **Route 66** planned to meander, connecting the main streets of U.S. from Chicago to Los Angeles; came to symbolize the joys of the open road. [Am. Culture: *SJEPC*]

15. **SUVs (Sports Utility Vehicles)** favored by many baby boomers for their size, power, and handling in rough terrain or bad weather; denounced by enviornmentalists for copious use of gas and off-road impact on pristine areas. [Am. Pop. Culture: *SJEPC*]

16. **Volkswagen Beetle** two-door sedan of 1950s and 1960s with profile of scarab was immensely popular with young drivers; microbus model became the standard vehicle of rock bands and soon became associated with hippie culture. [Am. Pop. Culture: *SJEPC*]

52. AUTUMN

1. **Autumnus** personification of fall; portrayed as mature and manly. [Rom. Myth.: *LLEI*, I: 322]

2. **Bacchus** god of this season. [Rom. Myth.: Hall, 130]

3. **Carpo** goddess of the autumn and corn season. [Gk. Myth.: Kravitz, 53]

4. **chrysanthemum** in Western art, a symbol of autumn. [Symbolism: *CEOS&S*]

5. **cornucopia** conical receptacle full of the fruits of the harvest. [World Culture: Misc.]

6. **grapes and vine leaves** symbolize harvest of vineyards for wine. [Art: Hall, 130]

7. **Indian summer** a period of mild, dry weather occurring in U.S. and Canada in late autumn. [Am. Culture: Misc.]

53. AVIATION (See also BALLOONING, SPACE TRAVEL.)

1. *Airplane!* spoof on disaster films of the 1970s turned air travel concerns into humorous situations. [Am. Film: *SJEPC*]

2. **friendly skies** following World War II, airline industry boomed as mobile Americans chose flying as an efficient, routine form of travel; "Fly the friendly skies" became a promotional phrase in ads for United Air Lines. [Am. Business: *SJEPC*]

3. **Kitty Hawk** site of first powered, sustained controlled flight (1903). [Am. Hist.: Jameson, 563]

4. **Lafayette Escadrille** American aviators assisting Allies in WWI. [Am. Hist.: Jameson, 273]

5. **NASA (National Aeronautics and Space Administration)** established in 1958 by U.S. government to conduct aeronautical and space research and travel. [Am. Science: *SJEPC*]

6. *Night Flight* relates the harrowing experiences of early airmail pilots on South American routes. [Fr. Lit.: Magill III, 687]

7. **Red Baron** nickname give to Baron Richthofen, WWI flying ace. [Aviation: *EB*, VIII: 574]

8. **Smilin' Jack** comic strip pilot who solves crimes. [Comics: "Smilin' Jack" in Horn, 624–625]

9. **Snoopy** imagines himself as WWI flying ace; was adopted as official emblem of NASA in late 1960s. [Aviation: *SJEPC*]

10. *Spirit of St. Louis* Charles Lindbergh's plane. [Am. Hist.: Jameson, 287]

11. **Wright brothers** creators-aviators of first aircraft capable of powered, sustained, controlled flight (1903). [Am. Hist.: Jameson, 563]

12. **X-15** early test plane, set speed and altitude records from 1959–1968; data from its test flights led to the development of NASA space craft. [Am. Hist.: Misc.]

Award (See PRIZE.)

54. AWKWARDNESS (See also INEPTITUDE.)

1. **Clouseau, Inspector Jacques** bungling detective who inadvertently but always gets his man. [Am. Cinema: "The Pink Panther" in Halliwell, 565–566]

2. **Crane, Ichabod** lanky Yankee schoolmaster who loves Katrina. [Am. Lit.: *The Legend of Sleepy Hollow*]

3. **Dobbin, Captain William** tall, uncouth, awkward fellow with large feet. [Br. Lit.: *Vanity Fair*]

4. **Goofy** bumbling, awkward dog; originally named Dippy Dawg. [Comics: "Mickey Mouse" in Horn, 492]

5. **Gringoire** a penniless, stupid, and oafish poet. [Fr. Lit.: *The Hunchback of Notre Dame*]

6. **Li'l Abner** ungainly comic strip oaf with height of six foot three. [Comics: Horn, 450]

7. **nerd** brainy, but socially inept and physically awkward; sometimes wealthy computer-savvy entrepreneur. [Am. Culture: *SJEPC*]

8. **Small, Lennie** simple-minded, clumsy giant; parasite of George. [Am. Lit.: *Of Mice and Men*]

9. **White Knight** falls off his horse every time it stops. [Br. Lit.: Lewis Carroll *Through the Looking-Glass*]

B

55. BACHELOR

1. **bachelor's button** celibacy symbol. [Flower Symbolism: Jobes, 171]

2. **Dillon, Matt** bachelor U.S. marshal fights for law and order in Old West. [TV: "Gunsmoke" in Terrace, I 331–332]

3. **laurel** symbol of unmarried scholar; whence, *baccalaureate*. [Flower Symbolism: Emboden, 25]

4. **Mason, Perry** bachelor lawyer. [TV: Terrace, II, 199]

5. **Morgan, Rex** bachelor doctor stars in comic strip. [Comics: "Rex Morgan, M.D." in Horn, 580–581]

6. *Odd Couple, The* pair of bachelors living the good life in New York. [Am. Lit. and TV: Terrace, II, 160–161]

7. **Pumblechook** eminently "available" uncle of Joe Gargery. [Br. Lit.: *Great Expectations*]

Bachelorette (See SINGLE WOMAN.)

Badness (See EVIL.)

56. BALDNESS

1. **Aeschylus** mistaking his bald head for a rock, an eagle dropped a tortoise on it, thus killing him. [Gk. Legend: Brewer *Dictionary*, 13]

2. **bald eagle** U.S. national bird whose white head looks bald. [Am. Hist.: *EB*, I: 753]

3. **Brynner, Yul (1915–1985)** Russian-born Mongolian actor's bald head in *The King and I* (1951) became symbol of virility. [Musical: *SJEPC*]

4. **Kojak** character from popular TV show of same name; commander of detective squad in New York; tough-guy mannerisms, lollipop addiction, and trademark "Who loves ya, baby?" [Am. TV: *SJEPC*]

5. **Mowgli (the Frog)** name given infant by wolves for hairlessness from Rudyard Kipling's series for young readers, *The Jungle Books* (1894–1895). [Br. Children's Lit.: Jones]

6. **Savalas, Telly (1922–1994)** film and TV actor with forty-year career; well known for award-winning portrayal of tough cop Lt. Theo Kojak in 1970s TV drama and for his signature shaved head, which he adopted after his role as Pontius Pilate in biblical film *The Greatest Story Ever Told* . [Am. Film and TV: Misc.]

7. **Stewart, Patrick (1940–)** distinguished bald English actor of stage, screen, and TV who has laudable career in many Shake-

spearean productions, a one-man production of *A Christmas Carol*, and other outstanding roles; to many, however, he will always be Captain Jean-Luc Picard, of *Star Trek: The Next Generation*. [Br. and Am. Theater, Film, and TV: Misc.]

57. BALLOONING (See also AVIATION.)

1. *Balloon Hoax, The* 1844 news story falsely reports that eight men have crossed the Atlantic in a balloon. [Am. Lit.: *The Balloon Hoax* in Poe]

2. **Ferguson, Samuel** embarks with two others on air-borne journey over Africa. [Fr. Lit.: *Five Weeks in a Balloon*]

3. **Montgolfier, Joseph (1740–1810) and Jacques (1745–1799)** French brothers who invented the first practical balloon, making possible the first human flight (1783). [Fr. Hist.: *BBInv*]

4. **Wizard of Oz** reaches and departs from Oz in circus balloon. [Children's Lit.: *The Wonderful Wizard of Oz*]

58. BANISHMENT

1. **Acadians** America's lost tribe; suffered expulsion under British. [Am. Hist.: Jameson, 2; Am. Lit.: "Evangeline" in Hart, 263]

2. **Adam and Eve** banished from the Garden of Eden for eating forbidden fruit. [O.T.: Genesis 3:23–24]

3. **anemone** ordered from Flora's court. [Gk. Myth.: *Flora Symbolica*]

4. **blacklisting** alleged Communists in entertainment industry (1947–1960s) prevented from working in Hollywood. [Am. Hist.: *SJEPC*]

5. **Bolingbroke, Henry** banished, along with Mowbray, by King Richard. [Br. Lit.: Shakespeare *Richard II*]

6. **Bonnie Prince Charlie (1720–1788)** Charles Edward Stuart, pretender to the British throne; exiled to France after unsuccessful rebellion and defeat at Culloden. [Br. Hist: *ODA*]

7. **Cain** cast out from homeland for murdering Abel. [O.T.: Genesis 4:12]

8. **Devil's Island** former French penal colony off French Guiana. [Fr. Hist.: *NCE*, 754]

9. **diaspora** originally the banishment of the Jews from Jerusalem after the destruction of Solomon's temple (586 B.C.E.); now, any dispersion of refugees. [O.T.: Psalm 137; Hist. *FOF MOD*]

10. **Elba** site of Napoleon's first exile (1814). [Fr. Hist.: *NCE*, 854]

11. **fire and water** Roman symbol of exile. [Rom. Hist.: Brewer *Note-Book*, 451]

12. **Hagar and Ishmael** Sarah orders Abraham to drive them out. [O.T.: Genesis 21:9–13]

13. **Ivanhoe** disinherited by father, Cedric the Saxon. [Br. Lit.: *Ivanhoe*]

14. **Jackson, "Shoeless" Joe (1887–1951)** multifaceted talent as player; involved in 1919 Black Sox scandal and banned for life from the sport; at trial, allegedly confronted by child who pleaded "Say it ain't so, Joe." [Am. Sports: *SJEPC*]

15. **Jenik** banished by jealous stepmother. [Czech. Opera: Smetana, *Bartered Bride*, Westerman, 404]

16. **Nolan, Philip** treasonous man sentenced to live remainder of life at sea. [Am. Lit.: *Man Without a Country*]

17. **Oedipus** exiles himself for killing father and marrying mother. [Gk. Lit.: *Oedipus Rex*]

18. **Patmos** island of exile for St. John. [N.T.: Revelation 1:9]

19. **Posthumus** marries Cymbeline's daughter; Cymbeline banishes him. [Br. Lit. *Cymbeline*]

20. **Pride's Purge** Cromwell's ejection of royalist MPs (1648). [Br. Hist.: Brewer *Handbook*, 871]

21. **Rivers of Babylon** exile of the Jews to Babylon. [O.T.: Psalm 137]

22. **Rosalind** her sylvan exile sets scene for comedy. [Br. Lit. *As You Like It*]

23. **Rose, Pete (1941–)** known as a baseball player for competitive attitude and skill; controversy surrounding allegations of betting on games led to banishment from baseball. [Am. Sports: *SJEPC*]

24. **Saint Helena** place of Napoleon's second exile (1815). [Fr. Hist.: *NCE*, 2397]

25. **Siberia** place of banishment and exile. [Geography: *NCE*, 2509–2510]

26. **Swaggart, Jimmy (1935–)** after being discovered with a prositute, the televangelist was suspended from broadcasting for three months by a ruling from the governing body of the Assemblies of God; he returned before the suspension was up and was defrocked, losing his ministerial license and credentials. [Am. TV: Misc.]

27. **Trail of Tears** forced march of 18,000 Cherokees westward to Indian Territory (Oklahoma); 4000 die of disease and exposure (winter 1838–1839). [Am. Hist.: *EB*, 2: 808]

28. **Tristram** expelled from Cornwall by King Mark for ten years. [Br. Lit.: *Le Morte d'Arthur*]

29. **Untouchables** lowest caste in India; social outcasts. [Ind. Culture: Brewer *Dictionary*, 1118]

59. BANKRUPTCY (See also POVERTY.)

1. **Birotteau, Cèsar** ruined by bad speculations and dissipated life. [Fr. Lit.: *Greatness and Deciline of Cèsar Birotteau*, Walsh *Modern*, 58]

2. **Black Friday** day of financial panic (1869). [Am. Hist.: *RHDC*]

3. **Black Tuesday** day of stock market crash (1929). [Am. Hist.: Allen, 238]

4. **green cap** symbol of bankruptcy. [Eur. Hist.: Brewer *Note-Book*, 390–391]

5. **Harland, Joe** drunk who loses fortune on Wall Street. [Am. Lit.: *The Manhattan Transfer*]

6. **Hassan, Abu** pretends to be dead to avoid debts. [Ger. Opera: von Weber, *Abu Hassan*, Westerman, 138–139]

7. **Henchard, Michael** loses business and social standing through bad financial planning. [Br. Lit.: *Mayor of Casterbridge*]

8. **Lydgate, Tertius** driven deeper into debt on daily basis. [Br. Lit.: *Middlemarch*]

9. **Panic of 1873** bank failures led to extended depression. [Am. Hist.: Van Doren, 267–268]

10. **Queer Street** condition of financial insolvency. [Am. Usage: Misc.]

60. BAPTISM

1. **Aenon** where St. John performed rites. [N.T.: John 3:23]

2. **Cornelius** Roman centurion baptized by Peter. [N.T.: Acts 10, 11]

3. **John the Baptist** prophet who baptized crowds and preached Christ's coming. [N.T.: Matthew 3:1–13]

4. **scallop shell** vessel used for conferral of sacrament. [Christian Symbolism: Appleton, 88]

61. BARRENNESS

1. **Andermatt, Christiane** takes series of baths hoping to cure childlessness. [Fr. Lit.: *Mont-Oriol*, Magill I, 618–620]

2. *Barren Ground* novel portraying a woman's emotional sterility and her harsh labor on a farm. [Am. Lit.: *Barren Ground*]

3. **brown** symbol of unfruitfulness. [Color Symbolism: Jobes, 357]

4. **Death Valley** sterile, arid basin in Nevada and California. [Geography: *EB*, III: 417]

5. **Elizabeth** Virgin's kinswoman, blessed with pregnancy as old woman. [N.T.: Luke 1:5–25]

6. **Empty Quarter** vast desert in the Arabian penninsula. [Geography: *EB*, VIII: 703]

7. **Hannah** Elkanah's barren wife; prays to Lord who grants her a son, Samuel. [O.T.: I Samuel 1:6]

8. **Sahara** vast north African desert. [Geography: *EB*, VIII: 768]

9. **Sarah** Abraham's wife; unable to bear children. [O.T.: Genesis 11:30]

10. **"Waste Land, The"** portrays sterility and chaos of the contemporary world. [Br. Lit.: "The Waste Land" in Hart, 899–900]

62. BARRIER

1. **Berlin Wall** barrier erected by East Germany in 1961, dividing Berlin into East (Soviet) and West (free world); symbol of Cold War hostilities. [Western Hist.: *FOF, MOD*]

2. **Checkpoint Charlie** border point dividing East and West at the Berlin Wall; a symbol of Cold War hostilities. [Western Hist.: *FOF, MOD*]

3. **gated communities** residential areas surrounded by barriers such as walls and fences are often secured with staffed gatehouses and electronic systems to prevent outsiders from entering without permission. [Am. Hist.: *SJEPC*]

4. **iron curtain** Winston Churchill's phrase to describe countries under communist control after WW II. [Western Hist.: *FOF, MOD*]

63. BASEBALL

1. **Aaron, Hank (1934–)** Atlanta Braves outfielder broke all-time home run record (714) of Babe Ruth in 1974; finished career with 755 home runs and was inducted into Baseball Hall of Fame in 1982. [Am. Sports: *SJEPC*]

2. **Bench, Johnny (1947–)** baseball Hall of Famer and catcher for the Cincinnati Reds in the 1970s. [Am. Sports: *SJEPC*]

3. **Black Sox** nickname of the 1919 Chicago White Sox players, who threw the World Series that year, and were banned from baseball. [Am. Sports: *EB*]

4. **Brooklyn Dodgers** talented underdog team that broke racial barrier in 1947 captured America's heart in 1950s battling for World Series title with rival New York Yankees; beat Yankees in 1955 but moved to Los Angeles two years later. [Am. Sports: *SJEPC*]

5. **Caray, Harry (1919–1998)** beloved Major League Baseball radio and TV broadcaster for the St. Louis Cardinals, Chicago White Sox, and Chicago Cubs whose career spanned from 1945 to 1998; known for phrase "Holy Cow" and singing "Take Me Out to the Ballgame." [Am. Sports, Radio, and TV: *SJEPC*]

6. **Chicago Cubs** National League baseball team known fondly as the Lovable Losers; the Cubbies haven't won a World Series title in over 100 years. [Am. Sports: *SJEPC*]

7. **Clemente, Roberto (1934–1972)** Puerto Rican rightfielder and star batter for the Pittsburgh Pirates was National League's Most Valuable Player in 1966 and World Series MVP in 1971; smacked his 3,000th hit just before his untimely death. [Am. Sports: *SJEPC*]

8. **Cobb, Ty (1886–1961)** tempermental, cantankerous Southern-born baseball legend joined Detroit Tigers in 1905 and led the team to World Series (1907, 1908, 1909); batted over .300 in 23 consecutive seasons. [Am. Sports: *SJEPC*]

9. **Cooperstown, New York** considered the town where baseball originated in 1839; 100 years later, National Baseball Hall of Fame opened there. [Am. Sports: *SJEPC*]

10. **DiMaggio, Joe (1914–1999)** the famous "Yankee Clipper," slugger for the New York Yankees noted for his batting skills, team play, and gentlemanliness. [Am. Sports: *FOF, MOD*]

11. **double play** in baseball, fielding that leads to two outs in one play; in common usage, excellence in a group effort. [Am. Sports: *FOF, MOD*]

12. **Durocher, Leo (1905–1991)** controversial manager of cross-town rivals Brooklyn Dodgers and New York Giants in the 1940s-50s also known for his quote, "Nice guys finish last." [Am. Sports: *SJEPC*]

13. *Field of Dreams* ghost of Shoeless Joe Jackson and other baseball players from a bygone era emerge from cornfield to play on baseball diamond created by an Iowa farmer who has heeded a haunting voice; film based on W. P. Kinsella's 1982 novel *Shoeless Joe* (1989). [Am. Film: *SJPEC*]

14. **Garvey, Steve (1948–)** popular National League first baseman played with Los Angeles Dodgers and San Diego Padres in 1970s-80s; four-time World Series contender and eight-time All-Star team member. [Am. Sports: *SJEPC*]

15. **Gehrig, Lou (1903–1941)** phenomenal yet humble New York Yankees player known as the "Iron Horse" was a powerful hitter (batted over .300 for 12 straight years) and helped lead his team to six world championships; stricken with degenerative disease ALS, he retired in 1939. [Am. Sports: *SJEPC*]

16. **Gibson, Bob (1935–)** competitive, intimidating right-handed pitcher for St. Louis Cardinals (1959–75) dominated in three World Series; registered 3,000 career strikeouts. [Am. Sports: *SJEPC*]

17. **Greenberg, Hank (1911–1986)** first baseman "Hammerin' Hank" broke ground as first Jewish superstar in 1933 starting with Detroit Tigers; batting dynamo was inducted into Baseball Hall of Fame in 1956. [Am. Sports: *SJEPC*]

18. **ground rules** in baseball, the game rules for a particular venue; in common usage, the basic rules. [Am. Sports: *FOF, MOD*]

19. **Jackson, Reggie (1946–)** outfielder with great batting average; candy bar named after him; first player to hit five home runs in one World Series (1977). [Am. Sports: *SJEPC*]

20. **Jackson, "Shoeless" Joe (1887–1951)** multifaceted talent as player; involved in 1919 Black Sox scandal and banned for life from the sport; at trial, allegedly confronted by child who pleaded : "Say it ain't so, Joe." [Am. Sports: *SJEPC*]

21. **Koufax, Sandy (1935–)** southpaw sometimes called greatest pitcher of all times; twelve-year career ended with retirement at age 31 and induction into Baseball Hall of Fame. [Am. Sports: *SJEPC*]

22. **Kuhn, Bowie (1926–2007)** baseball commissioner from 1969–1984. [Am. Sports: *SJEPC*]

23. **Lardner, Ring (1885–1933)** leading satirist of 1920s know for use of slang and first-person epistolary baseball stories about fictitious Jack Keefe, dimwitted Chicago White Sox pitcher. [Am. Lit.: *SJEPC*]

24. **Lasorda, Tommy (1927–)** for two decades beginning in 1976, manager of Los Angeles Dodgers; his enthusiasm, loyalty, and ability to get his players to excel won him respect. [Am. Sports: *SJEPC*]

25. **Mantle, Mickey (1931–1995)** legendary switch-hitter who became symbol of America's heartland. [Am. Sports: *SJEPC*]

26. **Mays, Willie (1931–)** multidimensional talent made him a natural pick for the Baseball Hall of Fame. [Am. Sports: *SJEPC*]

27. **McGwire, Mark (1963–)** in 1998, broke Roger Maris's 37–year-old record for home runs; record tainted by accusations of steroid use. [Am. Sports: *SJEPC*]

28. **Negro Leagues** organized African-American teams before black players were allowed to play in the Major Leagues in the 1940s [Am. Sports: *SJEPC*]

29. **Paige, Satchel (1899?-1982)** outstanding pitcher for Negro Leagues and Major Leagues in remarkable three-decade career. [Am. Sports: *SJEPC*]

30. **Palmer, Jim (1945–)** successful pitcher for Baltimore Orioles; later fame as underwear model. [Am. Sports: *SJEPC*]

31. **Ripkin, Cal, Jr. (1960–)** good-natured, phenomenally talented shortstop; in 1995, broke Lou Gehrig's 1939 record for most consecutive games played; broke world record in 1996. [Am. Sports: *SJEPC*]

32. **Robinson, Frank (1935–)** impressive batting average and home run record and Major League's first African-American manager (Cleveland Indians, 1975). [Am. Sports: *SJEPC*]

33. **Robinson, Jackie (1919–1972)** first black player in Major League Baseball (1947); taunts and abuse followed, but his brilliant per-

formance quelled objetions; staunch supporter of civil rights. [Am. Sports: *SJEPC*]

34. **Rose, Pete (1941–)** known as a player for competitive attitude and skill; controversy surrounding allegations of betting on games led to banishment from baseball. [Am. Sports: *SJEPC*]

35. **Ryan, Nolan (1947–)** talented power pitcher with 100–plus-mile fastball. [Am. Sports: *SJEPC*]

36. **Sosa, Sammy (1968–)** outstanding outfielder; broke Roger Maris's home run record in 1998; acheivements tainted by accusations of steroid use. [Am. Sports: *SJEPC*]

37. **Spalding, Albert G. (1850–1915)** baseball player, manager, and owner; helped found National League in 1876; went on to found successful sporting goods chain. [Am. Sports: *SJEPC*]

38. *Sporting News, The* official newspaper of baseball in first half of 20th century; helped to expand popularity of the game. [Am. Jour.: *SJEPC*]

39. **Steinbrenner, George (1930–)** owner of the New York Yankees beginning in 1973; often in the news for making critical comments about his team and embroiled in arguments with his managers. [Am. Sports: *SJEPC*]

40. **Stengel, Casey (1890–1975)** known for practical jokes, fights, and colorful expressions, managed New York teams with mixed results. [Am. Sports: *SJEPC*]

41. **Strawberry, Darryl (1962–)** promising career marred by personal problems. [Am. Sports: *SJEPC*]

42. **Thorpe, Jim (1988–1953)** gold medal winner of both pentathlon and decathlon in 1912 Olympics; medals later confiscated because of brief professional baseball career; went on to play professional baseball and football with great skill, winning numerous awards, many posthumously. [Am. Sports: *SJEPC*]

43. **Valenzuela, Fernando (1960–)** successful pitcher for the Dodgers and other teams for 17 seasons (1980–1997) with a consistently impressive strike-out record. [Am. Sports: *SJEPC*]

44. **Wagner, Honus (1874–1955)** phenomenal Pittsburgh Pirates shortstop called "The Flying Dutchman"; one of the first players to be inducted into Baseball Hall of Fame. [Am. Sports: *SJEPC*]

45. **"Who's on First?"** Abbott and Costello's famous comedy routine merited inclusion in Baseball Hall of Fame. [Am. Entertainment: *SJEPC*]

46. **Williams, Ted (1918–2002)** one of best hitters of all times, even though less celebrated than other, more amicable players. [Am. Sports: *SJEPC*]

47. **World Series** the final competition at the end of every baseball season between the two top teams in the American and National League; also used to mean any great competition. [Am. Sports: *EB*]

48. **Yastrzemski, Carl (1939–)** left fielder and impressive batter for Boston Red Sox; upon retirement, had made more than 3000 hits and 400 home runs. [Am. Sports: *SJEPC*]

49. **Young, Cy (1867–1955)** extraordinary pitcher who won more Major League games than any other player; annual award given to best pitcher in each league is named after him. [Am. Sports: *SJEPC*]

Bashfulness (See TIMIDITY.)

64. BASKETBALL

1. **Abdul-Jabbar, Kareem (1947–)** one of the greatest players in basketball history, the 7–foot, 2–inch center for the Milwaukee Bucks and Los Angeles Lakers won six professional championships and was named NBA's most valuable player six times. [Am. Sports: *SJEPC*]

2. **Auerbach, Red (1917–2006)** innovative Boston Celtics coach led team to nine NBA championships. [Am. Sports: *SJEPC*]

3. **Bird, Larry (1956–)** Boston Celtics superstar of 1980s helped revive fans' interest in the professional game. [Am. Sports: *SJEPC*]

4. **Boston Celtics** professional basketball dynasty. [Am. Sports: *SJEPC*]

5. **Boston Garden** home court of the Boston Celtics until 1995, landmark arena boasted parquet basketball floor. [Am. Architecture: *SJEPC*]

6. **Chamberlain, Wilt (1936–1999)** dominant, imposing, 7–foot, 1–inch basketball player instrumental in sparking American interest in NBA games. [Am. Sports: *SJEPC*]

7. **Chicago Bulls** one of the NBA's dynasty teams. [Am. Sports: *SJEPC*]

8. **Dream Team** greatest U.S. Olympic basketball team in history won gold medal in 1992, boasted talents of top NBA players like Magic Johnson, Larry Bird, and Michael Jordan. [Am. Sports: *SJEPC*]

9. **Harlem Globetrotters** for more than 80 years, this team made up of former NBA greats has traveled the world, dazzling and entertaining audiences with their athletic ability and humor; also active in humanitarian concerns. [Am. Sports: *EB*]

10. **Havlicek, John (1940–)** NBA star forward for the Boston Celtics; first player to make 1,000 points in 16 consecutive seasons. [Am. Sports: *EB*]

11. **Johnson, Earvin (1959–)** nicknamed "Magic"; began in NBA in 1980 and dominated sport for decade; retired in 1991 and revealed he was HIV-positive to his shocked fans. [Am. Sports: *SJEPC*]

12. **Jordan, Michael (1963–)** one of highest paid and most acclaimed players in NBA; became not only sports legend but icon whose name made Nike Air Jordan shoe an astonishing sports marketing success; gained celebrity status even outside sports world. [Am. Sports: *SJEPC*]

13. **Knight, Bobby (1940–)** very successful coach of Indiana University basketball team (1971–2000); known for hot temper and strict demands on players; fired from Indiana in 2000, he coached Texas Tech 2001–2008). [Am. Sports: *SJPEPC*]

14. **Naismith, Dr. James (1861–1939)** credited with the invention of the game in 1891 in Springfield, Massacusetts. [Am. Sports: *SJEPC*]

15. **NBA (National Basketball Association)** US basketball league formed in 1949. [Am. Sports: *SJEPC*]

16. **O'Neal, Shaquille (1972–)** seven-foot, three-hundred pound star player and media sensation. [Am. Sports: *SJEPC*]

17. **Pippen, Scottie (1965–)** outstanding at defense; named one of greatest fifty players of all time. [Am. Sports: *SJEPC*]

18. **Rodman, Dennis (1961–)** star rebounder whose outlandish behavior and appearance made him a favorite with the media. [Am. Sports: *SJEPC*]

19. **Russell, Bill (1934–)** great defensive player for Boston Celtics known for being true team player; first African-American to become head coach of an NBA team (Celtics, 1966). [Am. Sports: *SJEPC*]

20. **Thomas, Isiah (1961–)** legendary point guard; captain and star of Detroit Pistons in 1980s and 1990s. [Am. Sports: *SJEPC*]

21. **Thompson, John (1941–)** first African-American to coach an NCAA championship team (Georgetown University Hoyas, 1984); encouraged academic achievement and wholesome social life as well as dedication to the game. [Am. Sports: *SJEPC*]

22. **Walton, Bill (1952–)** gifted center with great skill in rebounding and blocking shots playing in NBA with Portland Trailblazers in mid-1970s and Boston Celtics in mid-1980s. [Am. Sports: *SEJPC*]

23. **West, Jerry (1938–)** extremely talented guard in 1960s and 1970s and later general manager of Los Angeles Lakers whose likeness was used for silhouette in NBA logo. [Am. Sports: *SJEPC*]

65. BATTLE (See also WAR.)

1. **Actium** Octavian's naval defeat of Antony and Cleopatra (31 B.C.) [Rom. Hist.: *NCE*, 15]

2. **Agincourt** longbow helps British defeat French (1415). [Br. Lit.: *Henry V*; Br. Hist.: Harbottle *Battles*, 5]

3. **Alamo** fort at San Antonio that was site of Mexican massacre of Texans (1836). [Am. Hist.: Jameson, 8]

4. **Antietam** indecisive battle of the Civil War (1862). [Am. Hist.: Harbottle *Battles*, 15]

5. **Arbela** Alexander's rout of Darius (331 B.C.). [Classical Hist.: Harbottle *Battles*, 17]

6. **Armageddon** final battle between forces of good and evil. [N.T.: Revelation 16:16]

7. **Austerlitz** Napoleon's brilliant success over Austro-Russian coalition (1805). [Fr. Hist.: Harbottle *Battles*, 23–24]

8. **Balaclava** fought between Russians and British during Crimean War (1854). [Russ. Hist.: Harbottle *Battles*, 25–26]

9. **Battle of the Bulge** unsuccessful attempt by Germans to push Allies back from German territory (1944–1945). [Ger. Hist.: *EB*, II: 360–361]

10. **Belleau Wood** locale of significant American triumph in WWI (1918). [Am. Hist.: Jameson, 47]

11. **Bhagavad Gita** Sanskrit epic relates the great fratricidal battle between two noble families. [Hindu Lit.: *Bhagavad-Gita* in Benét, 103]

12. **Bull Run** site of two important battles of the Civil War (1861) (1862). [Am. Hist.: Jameson, 68]

13. **Bunker Hill** "Don't shoot until you see the whites of their eyes"; American Revolutionary battle (1775). [Am. Hist.: Worth, 22]

14. **Cannae** perhaps Hannibal's greatest victory (216 B.C.) [Rom. Hist.: Harbottle *Battles*, 48]

15. **Coral Sea** first naval engagement exclusively involving planes versus ships (1942). [Am. Hist.: Van Doren, 488]

16. **Crécy** English over French; preeminence of longbow established (1346). [Fr. Hist.: Bishop, 382–385]

17. **Desert Storm** decisive victory for allied forces fighting Iraq during the Gulf War (1990). [World Hist.: *EB*]

18. **Fort Sumter** site of opening blow of Civil War (1861). [Am. Hist.: Jameson, 486–487]

19. **Gettysburg** pivotal battle of the Civil War, fought in Gettysburg, PA, on July 3, 1863; commemorated in one of Abraham Lincoln's most famous speeches. [Am. Hist.: Harbottle *Battles*, 97]

20. **Guadalcanal** Marines triumphed in first major U.S. offensive of WWII (1942–1943). [Am. Hist.: Van Doren, 490]

21. **Hastings** battle that determined the Norman Conquest of England (1066). [Br. Hist.: Harbottle *Battles*, 107]

22. **Iwo Jima** inspiring American triumph in the Pacific (1945). [Am. Hist.: Leonard, 472–480]

23. **Jutland** established British WWI naval supremacy (1916). [Br. Hist.: *EB*, 19: 954–955]

24. **Lexington** opening engagement of the American Revolution (1775). [Am. Hist.: Jameson, 283]

25. **Lindisfarne** object of first major Viking raid in Britain (792). [Br. Hist.: Grun, 86]

26. **Lucknow** Indian mutiny put down by British (1858). [Ind. Hist.: Harbottle *Battles*, 143]

27. **Marathon** plain near Athens where Greeks defeated Persians in 490 B.C. [Gk. Hist.: Benét, 633]

28. **Midway** site of decisive battle between Japanese and Americans in WWII (1942). [Am. Hist.: *EB*, VI: 877–878]

29. **Mount Badon** here Arthur soundly defeated the Saxons (c. 520). [Arthurian Legend: Benét, 72]

30. **New Orleans** end of War of 1812; fought after treaty had been signed (1815). [Am. Hist.: Worth, 22]

31. **Normandy Invasion** Allied invasion of Europe during WWII; D-Day (June 6, 1944). [Eur. Hist.: *EB*, VII: 391]

32. **Okinawa** scene of American amphibian operations during WWII (1945). [Am. Hist.: *EB*, VII: 505]

33. **Orlèans** Joan of Arc's inspired triumph over English (1429). [Fr. Hist.: Bishop, 392]

34. **Pearl Harbor** site of Japanese surprise attack (December 7, 1941). [Am. Hist.: *EB*, VII: 822]

35. **Plains of Abraham** English victory decided last of French and Indian wars (1759). [Br. Hist.: *NCE*, 7]

36. **Ravenna** site of battle between Byzantines and an Italian force under Pope Gregory II. Byzantines were routed (729). [Gk. Hist.: Harbottle *Battles*, 207]

37. **Salamis** Xerxes' horde repulsed by numerically inferior Greek navy (480 B.C.). [Class. Hist.: Harbottle *Battles*, 219]

38. **Samarkand** Arabs defeated Chinese (751).; adopted some of Chinese technology and culture. [Chinese Hist.: Grun, 78]

39. **Saratoga (Stillwater)** fought between Americans and British during Revolution (1777). [Am. Hist.: Harbottle *Battles*, 237–238]

40. **Sedan** decisive battle of the Franco-German War (1870). [Fr. Hist.: Harbottle *Battles*, 225]

41. **Stalingrad** unsuccessful German assault on Stalingrad, Russia (1942–1943). [Ger. Hist.: *EB*, IX: 517]

42. **Tet Offensive** defining offensive launched in 1968 by Viet Cong and N. Vietnamese armies against the South during the Vietnam War; a turning point, as many Americans turned against the war policies of Lyndon B. Johnson, leading to his decision not to run for re-election. [Am. and Vietnamese Hist.: *EB*]

43. **Thermopylae** 300 Spartans hold off Xerxes' horde (480 B.C). [Classical Hist.: Harbottle *Battles*, 248]

44. **Trafalgar** defeat of French and Spanish; zenith of British naval history (1805). [Br. Hist.: Harbottle *Battles*, 252–253]

45. **Trenton** Washington's brilliant surprise attack galvanized American morale (1776). [Am. Hist.: Jameson, 508]

46. **Valmy** battle fought between French and Prussians (1792). [Eur. Hist.: Harbottle *Battles*, 259]

47. **Verdun** site of numerous battles. [Fr. Hist.: *EB*, X: 395]

48. **Vicksburg** city held by Confederates; besieged several times (1862, 1863). [Am. Hist.: Harbottle *Battles*, 261–262]

49. **Waterloo** site of Napoleon's defeat (1815). [Fr. Hist.: Harbottle *Battles*, 266]

50. **Yorktown** site of American victory over British, ending Revolutionary War (1781). [Am. Hist.: Harbottle *Battles*, 271]

66. BEAUTY

1. **Aglaia** one of the Graces; embodiment of comeliness. [Gk. Myth.: Brewer *Dictionary*, 481]

2. **Blodenwedd** created from oak flowers and meadowsweet. [Welsh Lit.: *Mabinogion*]

3. **cowslip** symbol of beauty. [Flower Symbolism: Jobes, 377]

4. **Euphrosyne** one of the Graces; epitome of beauty in joy. [Gk. Myth.: Brewer *Dictionary*, 481]

5. **Graces** three daughters of Zeus and Eurynome; goddesses of charm and beauty. [Gk. Myth.: Howe, 61]

6. **hibiscus** symbol of beauty. [Flower Symbolism: *Flora Symbolica*, 174]

7. **Hora Quirini** goddess of loveliness. [Rom. Myth.: Kravitz, 44]

8. **lilies of the field** more splendidly attired than Solomon. [N.T.: Matthew 6:28–29; Luke 12:27–31]

9. **Madonna** Mary, the mother of Jesus, depicted in art as a beatific woman. [Eur. Art: *ODA*]

10. **Monday's child** fair of face. [Nurs. Rhyme: Opie, 309]

11. **peri** beautiful fairylike creatures, guided way to heaven. [Pers. Myth.: Brewer *Dictionary*, 822]

12. **plastic surgery** procedures used to change one's looks, sometimes to adhere to societal image of beauty. [Culture: *SJEPC*]

13. **Thalia** one of the Graces; bestowed charm on others. [Gk. Myth.: Brewer *Dictionary*, 481]

14. **Ugly Duckling** scorned as unsightly, grows to be graceful swan. [Dan. Fairy Tale: *Andersen's Fairy Tales*]

15. **white camellia** symbol of beauty. [Flower Symbolism: Jobes, 281]

67. BEAUTY, FEMININE (See also BEAUTY, SENSUAL.)

1. **Amoret (Amoretta)** typical of female loveliness. [Br. Lit.: *Fairie Queene*, Brewer *Dictionary*, 30]

2. **Annabel Lee** poet's beautiful beloved. [Am. Lit.: "Annabel Lee" in *Portable Poe*]

3. **Aphrodite (Rom. Venus)** archetype of feminine beauty. [Gk. Myth.: Parrinder, 24]

4. **Astarte** beautiful goddess of fertility and sexual love. [Phoenician Myth.: Zimmerman, 33]

5. **Barbie doll** popular, shapely, plastic fashion doll "born" in 1959 has influenced and challenged female conventions of beauty. [Am. Culture: *SJEPC*]

6. **Bathsheba** king David killed to gain her. [O.T.: II Samuel 11]

7. **Beauty** beautiful woman married to an enchanted beast who turns into a prince. [Fr. Fairy Tale: "Beauty and the Beast" in Walsh *Classical*, 49]

8. **Bergman, Ingrid (1915–1982)** naturally beautiful, talented Swedish actress became Academy Award-winning Hollywood star, despite scandalous love affair with Italian director Roberto Rossellini in 1950. [Am. Film: *SJEPC*]

9. **Clairol** revolutionary do-it-yourself hair color introduced to American women in 1956 made changing one's image easier and more acceptable. [Culture: *SJEPC*]

10. **Cleopatra (69–30 B.C.)** beautiful queen of Egypt; wins Marc Antony's heart. [Br. Lit.: *Antony and Cleopatra*]

11. **crabapple blossom** traditional symbol. [Chinese Flower Symbolism: Jobes, 377]

12. **Crawford, Cindy (1966–)** fashion supermodel of the 1980s-90s with healthy, wholesome, girl-next-door looks. [Am. Culture: *SJEPC*]

13. **Deirdre** prophesied to become the most beautiful woman in Ireland. [Irish Legend: Benét, 259]

14. **Diana** Roman goddess associated with hunting, virginity, and the moon; related to the Greek Artemis. [Rom. Myth: *ODA*]

15. **Dietrich, Marlene (1901–1992)** beautiful German actress and star of such films as *The Blue Angel*. [Am. Film *FOF MOD*]

16. **Doone, Lorna** her good looks stir John Ridd and others. [Br. Lit.: *Lorna Doone*, Magill I, 524–526]

17. **Dorothy la Desiree** Jurgen's childhood sweetheart; when he finds her again in a magic garden she has retained the beauty he had praised in his poems. [Am. Lit.: *Jurgen* in Magill I, 464]

18. **Duchess of Alba** Goya's lover and model, immortalized on canvas. [Span. Art: Wallechinsky. 192]

19. **Etain** most beautiful woman in Ireland. [Irish Folklore: Briggs, 123–125]

20. **flappers** youthful, daring, sexually spirited women of 1920s symbolized modern post-World War I America; had athletic, flat-chested look and wore shorter skirts, bobbed hair, and plenty of make-up. [Am. Hist.: *SJEPC*]

21. **Frederick's of Hollywood** lingerie company founded by Frederick N. Mellinger in 1946 known for innovative, seductive undergarments that reproportion women's anatomy to produce curves, contours, and cleavage according to Frederick's concept of feminine beauty. [Am. Culture: *SJEPC*]

22. **Freya** goddess of love, beauty, and fecundity; beautiful, blue-eyed blonde. [Norse Myth.: Leach, 425]

23. **Galatea** statue so striking, Venus grants sculptor Pygmalion's wish that it live. [Gk. Myth.: *LLEI*, I: 286]

24. **Garbo, Greta (1905–1990)** beautiful Swedish actress known for her reclusive ways, and the phrase: "I vant to be alone." [Pop. Cult.: Misc.]

25. **Gibson girl** classic, comely woman of illustrations (1890s). [Am. Hist.: Flexner, 283]

26. **Golden Bells** epitome of the beautiful Chinese woman. [Irish Lit.: *Messer Marco Polo*, Magill I, 584–585]

27. **Hebe** beautiful cupbearer to the gods. [Gk. Myth.: Zimmerman, 117]

28. **Helen of Troy** beautiful woman kidnapped by smitten Paris, precipitating Trojan war. [Gk. Lit.: *Iliad*; *Trojan Women*; Euripides, *Helene*]

29. **Hepburn, Audrey (1929–1993)** beautiful actress often portrayed the lovely ingenue in such films as *Roman Holiday*, *Sabrina*, and

Breakfast at Tiffany's; spent her later years working for UNICEF. [Am. Film: *EB*]

30. **Hypatia (c. 370–415)** Greek philosopher, renowned for beauty and wit. [Gk. Hist.: *NCE*, 1302]

31. **Kelly, Grace (1928–1982)** popular film star of the 1950s; classic beauty who married into royalty, becoming Princess Grace of Monaco; died in auto accident. [Am. Film: *SJEPC*]

32. **knockout** from boxing, a woman overpoweringly beautiful. [Pop. Culture: *FOF, MOD*]

33. **Kriemhild** Burgundian princess's beauty known throughout Europe. [Ger. Lit.: *Nibelungenlied*]

34. **Lamarr, Hedy (1913–2000)** Austrian actress who came to Hollywood in 1930s and, despite relatively short-lived movie career, became known as one of most beautiful women on screen. [Am. Film: *SJEPC*]

35. **Marcella** farmer's daughter; every bachelor fancies her. [Span. Lit.: *Don Quixote*]

36. **Marie Antoinette (1755–1793)** beautiful queen consort of King Louis XVI of France. [Fr. Hist.: *EB*, VI: 620]

37. **Miss America** annually selected most beautiful young woman in America. [Am. Hist.: Allen, 56–57]

38. **Monroe, Marilyn (1926–1962)** voluptuous blonde screen star became perhaps the most famous sex symbol and icon of beauty in modern times. [Am. Film: *SJEPC*]

39. **Moss, Kate (1974–)** British waiflike supermodel best known for her work with Calvin Klein. [Culture: *SJEPC*]

40. **Nefertiti** Egyptian queen of the 14th century B.C.; symbol of beauty. [Egypt. Hist.: *ODA*]

41. **O'Hara, Scarlett** epitome of a beautiful Southern belle. [Am. Lit.: *Gone With the Wind*]

42. **Pre-Raphaelite** in the style of the Pre-Raphaelite painters of 19th-century England, especially Dante Gabriel Rosetti, featuring women with long dark hair and fair skin. [Br. Art.: *ODA*]

43. **Simonetta** Botticelli's hauntingly beautiful young model. [Ital. Art: Wallechinsky, 190]

44. **Snow White** snow-toned flesh, ebony hair, blood-red lips. [Ger. Fairy Tale: Grimm, 184]

45. **supermodels** in 1980s and 1990s models rose to star status in American consumers' eyes; marketed themselves and drew huge salaries. [Am. Pop. Culture: *SJEPC*]

46. **swan** romantic symbol of masculine light and feminine beauty in Western music and ballet. [Symbolism: *CEOS&S*]

47. **Taylor, Elizabeth (1932–)** extremely beautiful and talented actress who has had seven husbands, fabulous jewels, and tumultuous personal life; campaigned for several causes, notably AIDS research. [Am. Film: *SJEPC*]

48. **Teal Eye** "Her beauty remained forever in Boone's memory." [Am. Lit.: *The Big Sky*]

49. **Tehani** lovely Tahitian girl loved by Byam. [Br. Lit.: *Mutiny on the Bounty*]

50. **Turner, Lana (1920–1995)** nicknamed the "Sweater Girl" because of her full figure; popular sexy blonde actress best known for roles in *The Postman Always Rings Twice* (1946) and *Peyton Place* (1957). [Am. Film: *SJEPC*]

51. **Twiggy (1949–)** 1960s English fashion model who changed image from 1950s curvy sex symbols to more androgynous slenderness. [Pop. Culture: *SJEPC*]

52. **Van Tassel, Katrina** rich farmer's daughter, pursued by Ichabod Crane and Brom Bones. [Am. Lit.: *The Legend of Sleepy Hollow*]

53. *Venus de Milo* armless statue of pulchritudinous goddess. [Gk. Art: Brewer *Dictionary*, 1126]

68. BEAUTY, MASCULINE

1. **Absalom** flawlessly handsome. [O.T.: II Samuel 14:25]

2. **Adonis** beautiful youth. [Gk. Myth.: Brewer *Dictionary*, 11]

3. **Andrews, Joseph** handsome, virtuous man admired by many ladies. [Br. Lit.: *Joseph Andrews*]

4. **Apollo** god of manly beauty. [Gk. Myth.: Leach, 67]

5. **Arrow Collar Man** figure in advertisements for Arrow shirts from the 1920s on, handsome and debonaire. [Am. Cult.: *FOF, MOD*]

6. **Balder** god of light and joy; known for his beauty. [Norse Myth.: Leach, 106]

7. **Beatty, Warren (1937–)** handsome screen actor known for sexual charisma. [Am. Film: *SJEPC*]

8. **Chateaupers, Phoebus de** gallant, handsome horseman eternally loved by Esmeralda. [Fr. Lit.: *The Hunchback of Notre Dame*]

9. *David* sculpture by Michelangelo depicting figure epitomizing male beauty. [Art: Osborne, 718]

10. **Fabio (1961–)** bare-chested model with rippling muscles and long, straight, blond hair graced romance novel covers in 1980s; Italian-born sex symbol branched out into acting and writing. [Pop. Culture: *SJEPC*]

11. **Glaucus** handsome, wealthy young Greek pursued by various ladies. [Br. Lit.: *The Last Days of Pompeii*, Magill I, 490–492]

12. **Grimek, John (1910–1998)** bodybuilder with muscular physique (1930s-40s). [Am. Sports: *SJEPC*]

13. **Hasselhoff, David (1952–)** creator of TV show *Baywatch* played veteran lifeguard with perfect physique. [Am. TV: *SJEPC*]

14. **Hylas** Hercules' servant; so captivates Naiads, they abduct him. [Gk. Myth.: Hall, 158]

15. **Hyperion** one of the Titans; known for his beauty. [Gk. Myth.: Zimmerman, 132]

16. **Narcissus** beautiful youth who falls in love with his own reflection. [Gk. Myth.: Zimmerman, 171–172]

17. **Tadzio** handsome Polish boy exerts a fatal attraction for an elderly writer. [Ger. Lit.: Thomas Mann *Death in Venice*]

18. **Valentino, Rudolph (1895–1926)** sexy and suave actor of silent films, wildly popular with female fans, who mobbed him at appearances; *The Shiek* (1921) made him a star. [Am. Film: *SJEPC*]

19. **Washington, Denzel (1954–)** versatile, award-winning black actor who has coupled good looks with talent in the tradition of Sidney Poitier. [Am. Film: *SJEPC*]

69. BEAUTY, RUSTIC

1. **Amaryllis** a favorite subject of pastoral poets. [Rom. Lit.: *Eclogues*]

2. **Chloe** beautiful shepherdess beloved by Daphnis. [Rom. Lit.: "Daphnis and Chloe" in Brewer *Handbook*, 204]

3. **Dulcinea** beautiful peasant woman idealized by Don Quixote. [Span. Lit.: *Don Quixote*]

4. **Pocahontas** natural beauty embodied in an Indian maiden. [Am. Hist.: *EB*, VIII: 57]

5. **Ragmaid** no one but the prince sees through her dishevelment. [Br. Fairy Tale: "The Little Ragmaid" in Macleod, 39–44]

6. **Tess of the D'Urbervilles** beautiful country girl. [Br. Lit.: *Tess of the D'Urbervilles*]

7. **Thestylis** embodiment of peasant prettiness. [Br. Lit.: *L'Allegro*, Brewer*Dictionary*, 1074]

70. BEAUTY, SENSUAL (See also BEAUTY, FEMININE; BEAUTY, MASCULINE; SEX SYMBOL.)

1. **Angelica** infidel princess of exquisite grace and charm. [Ital. Lit.: *Orlando Innamorato; Orlando Furioso*]

2. *Baywatch* TV show featuring sexy, scantily clad male and female lifeguards of Los Angeles County Beach Patrol. [Am. TV: *SJEPC*]

3. **Borgia, Lucrezia (1480–1519)** her beauty was as legendary as her rumored vices and heartlessness. [Ital. Hist.: Plumb, 59]

4. **Bow, Clara (1905–1965)** "It Girl" a Jazz Age icon; Hollywood sex symbol epitomized bold, spirited flapper persona. [Am. Culture: *SJEPC*]

5. **Buchanan, Daisy** Jay Gatsby's femme fatale. [Am. Lit.: *The Great Gatsby*]

6. **Cleopatra (69–30 B.C.)** seductive queen of Egypt; beloved by Marc Antony. [Br. Lit.: *Antony and Cleopatra*]

7. **Dandridge, Dorothy (1922–1965)** beautiful, sensuous African-American actress was first black woman to appear on the cover of *Life* magazine. [Am. Film: *SJEPC*]

8. **Gypsy Rose Lee (1914–1970)** beautiful American striptease artist, immortalized in the musical *Gypsy* by Jule Styne, Steven Sondheim, and Arthur Laurents. [Am. Culture: *FOF, MOD*]

9. **Helen of Troy** Greek beauty, the "face that launched a thousand ships," abducted by Paris, taken to Troy; the Trojan War was fought to reclaim her. [Gk. Lit.: *The Iliad*]

10. **Jezebel** Phoenician princess; enemy of the prophets; name is a byword for wicked woman. [O.T.: I Kings 16:21, 31; II Kings 9:1–10, 30–37]

11. **Lolita** precociously seductive 12–year-old. [Am. Lit.: *Lolita*]

12. **Madeline** gazed at in awe by Porphyro. [Br. Lit.: "The Eve of St. Agnes" in Magill I, 263–264]

13. **Montez, Lola (c. 1818–1861)** Irish singer and dancer; mistress to famous men. [Irish Hist.: *NCE*, 1821]

14. **O'Keefe, Georgia (1887–1986)** American painter noted for her sensual flowers. [Am. Art: *FOF, MOD*]

15. **Phryne** courtesan, acquitted of charge by baring bosom. [Gk. Hist.: *Brewer Dictionary*, 830]

16. **Playmate of the Month** nude girl provocatively gracing *Playboy's* centerfold. [Am. Culture: *Flexner*, 285]

17. **Queen of Sheba** sultry Biblical queen who visits Solomon. [O.T.: I Kings 10]

18. **Salome** seductive dancer who obtains head of John the Baptist as reward. [N.T.: Matthew 14:3, 11]

19. **Vargas girl** drawn by Alberto Vargas; curvaceous women became favorite WWII pin-ups later appeared in *Esquire* magazine, then in *Playboy* as the Vargas girl. [Am. Pop. Culture: *SJEPC*]

20. **Victoria's Secret** began in the early 1980s; retail chain selling sexy lingerie for women in upscale boutique mall stores. [Am. Business: *SJEPC*]

21. **Vye, Eustacia** capricious, seductive, trouble-making heroine. [Br. Lit.: *Return of the Native*, Harvey, 690]

71. BESTIALITY (See also PERVERSION.)

1. **Asterius** Minotaur born to Pasiphae and Cretan Bull. [Gk. Myth.: Zimmerman, 34]

2. **Leda** raped by Zeus in form of swan. [Gk. Myth.: Zimmerman, 149]

3. **Lucius** transformed into ass, makes love with harlot. [Rom. Lit.: *The Golden Ass*]

4. **Pasiphae** positioned inside hollow cow, consummates lust for bull. [Gk. Myth.: Hall, 234; Gk. Lit.: *Imagines* 1:16]

5. **Zeus** in form of a swan, seduces and impregnates Leda. [Gk. Myth.: Zimmerman, 149]

72. BETRAYAL (See also TREACHERY, TREASON.)

1. **Arnold, Benedict (1741–1801)** American general in the Revolutionary War who plotted to betray the Americans to the British. [Am. Hist. *ODA*]

2. *Double Indemnity* after plotting together and committing the "perfect crime," ruthless insurance agent Walter Neff turns against lover Phyllis, murdering her (novel, 1935; film, 1944). [Am. Film and Lit.: *SJEPC*]

3. **Judas Iscariot** apostle who betrays Jesus. [N.T.: Matthew 26:15]

4. **Proteus** though engaged, steals his friend Valentine's beloved, reveals his plot and effects his banishment. [Br. Drama: Shakespeare *Two Gentlemen of Verona*]

73. BIGOTRY (See also ANTI-SEMITISM.)

1. *All in the Famiily* 1970s TV sitcom introduced social realism, discussing racism, sexism, religious bias, and politics. [Am. TV: *SJEPC*]

2. **Anderson, Marian (1897–1977)** world-renowned African-American contralto faced racial prejudice and segregation, paving the way for other black artists. [Am. Music: *SJEPC*]

3. **apartheid** system of government-enforced racial separation in South Africa from 1948–1992; also used to mean segregation. [Politics *FOF, MOD*]

4. **Beaumanoir, Sir Lucas de** prejudiced ascetic; Grand Master of Templars. [Br. Lit.: *Ivanhoe*]

5. *Birth of a Nation, The* film set during Reconstruction in the South depicts Ku Klux Klan as heroic and newly freed slaves as violent (1915). [Am. Film: *SJEPC*]

6. **blackface minstrelsy** entertainment style from 1820s to 1950s in which white performers blackened their faces to parody Southern blacks in song, speech, and dance. [Am. Entertainment: *SJEPC*]

7. **Bunker, Archie** middle-aged bigot in television series. [TV: "All in the Family" in Terrace, I, 47–48]

8. **Connor, Bull (1897–1973)** Birmingham, Alabama sherrif known for brutal tactics against Civil Rights workers; by extension, a brutal racist. [Am. Hist.: *EB*]

9. *Do the Right Thing* African-American filmmaker Spike Lee's 1989 film, set in a Brooklyn neighborhood one sweltering hot summer day, explores the complexities of racism in America. [Am. Film: *SJEPC*]

10. **fiery cross** used as symbolic threat by Ku Klux Klan. [Am. Hist.: Jobes, 387]

11. **Great White Hope** from the early 1900s, a term describing the hoped-for white boxer who could defeat Jack Johnson, the first black heavyweight champion; a film of the same title (1970) is a thinly veiled retelling of Johnson's story. [Am. Sports: Misc.]

12. **hate crimes** crimes motivated by hatred for a racial, ethnic, or religious group, or sexual orientation; now recognized in the U.S. and other nations as a separate criminal category. [Am. Hist.: *EB*]

13. **high-tech lynching** racially motivated smear campaign to discredit an African-American; term used by Clarence Thomas when Anita Hill accused him of sexual harrasment during his Supreme Court confirmation hearings. [Am. Law and Politics: *SJEPC*]

14. **Hitler, Adolf (1889–1945)** German dictator; his New Order excluded non-Aryans, e.g., Jews, Slavs. [Ger. Hist.: *Hitler*]

15. **Japanese-American Internment Camps** in 1942, West Coast residents of Japanese descent were sent to internment camps by U.S. government for duration of WWII; founded on belief that *issei* (first generation) and *Nisei* (second generation, American born) were implicated in Japanese attack on Pearl Harbor. [Am. Hist.: *SJEPC*]

16. **Jim Crow** legal, systematic racial discrimination, derived from the "separate but equal" concept, denying blacks basic civil rights in education, housing, employment, etc. [Am. Hist.: *BBAAL1*]

17. **John Birch Society** ultra-conservative, anti-Communist U.S. organization founded in 1958. [Am. Hist.: *NCE*, 1421]

18. **Ku Klux Klan** racist, terrorist organization, started in southern U.S., targeting African-Americans, Jews, Catholics, immigrants,

and others; a symbol of bigoted intolerance. [Am. Hist.: Allen, 46–49]

19. *Kung Fu* popular TV show of 1970s dealt with Shaolin priest in American West of 1800s, showing racism towards Chinese immigrants. [Am. TV: *SJEPC*]

20. **Lebenshorn** Himmler's adoption/breeding scheme to produce master race. [Ger. Hist.: *Hitler*, 1046]

21. *Light in August* study of race problem in South. [Am. Lit.: *Light in August*]

22. *Little Black Sambo* famous 1899 picture book by Helen Bannerman; story of black boy who loses his beautiful new clothes to threatening tigers; ferocious fight and subsequent chase turns tigers into pool of butter, and Sambo enjoys buttery pancakes for supper; beginning in 1970s, the book has been accused of racial stereotypes. [Scot. Children's Lit.: *OCCL*]

23. **Little Rock, Arkansas** required military intervention to desegregate schools (1957–1958). [Am. Hist.: Van Doren, 556–557]

24. **Magee, Maniac** protagonist of novel for young readers by Jerry Spinelli; orphaned runaway who finds acceptance for his athletic talents, but faces racism when a black family takes him in. [Am. Children's Lit.: Jones]

25. *Native Son* Richard Wright's searing indictment of racism. [Am. Lit.: *Native Son*, Magill I, 643–645]

26. **Nazi** *Nazionalsozialist*; rabid anti-Semite member of Hitler's party. [Ger. Hist.: Shirer]

27. **New Order** partially fulfilled Nazification of Europe. [Eur. Hist.: *Hitler*, 935, 1055]

28. **Oreo** a cookie that is chocolate, or black, on the outside, with white filling on the inside; a racial epithet for an African-American deemed by some to be too accomodating to whites: "white" on the inside. [Am. Culture: Misc.]

29. **Parks, Rosa (1913–2005)** civil rights activist whose refusal to give up her seat on a bus in the segregated South led to the Montgomery Bus Boycott, 1956. [Am. Hist.: *BBAAL2*]

30. **racial profiling** practice (especially by law enforcement) for determining whether a person is more likely to commit a certain crime based on their race. [Am. Culture: Misc.]

31. *Raisin in the Sun, A* Lorraine Hansberry's groundbreaking play (1959), the first play on Broadway with an all-black cast and director, was an unflinching look at the effect of racism on African-American life. [Am. Theater: *BBAAL2*]

32. **redneck** pejorative term used to describe a racist, reactionary, uneducated American. [Am. Culture: Misc.]

33. ***Roots*** novel by Alex Haley about several generations of his mother's family, brought to the US from Africa as slaves; drew wide audiences in 1977 as TV miniseries. [Am. Lit. and TV: *SJEPC*]

34. **Sneetches** protagonists of Dr. Seuss's comical fable for children (1961) about bigoted star-bellied Sneetches who disdain their plain-bellied counterparts; once the plain-bellied ones get stars, things become muddled and the discrimination ends. [Am. Children's Lit.: "The Sneetches"]

35. ***Sounder*** 1969 children's book about a lovable coon dog whose fate echoes treatment of the black patriarch who faces cruel racial bigotry in the South. [Am. Children's Lit.: Jones]

36. **stereotyping** preconceived set of notions held by one group of people about another specific group; often oversimplified generalizations. [Am. Culture: Misc.]

37. ***To Kill a Mockingbird*** both a Pultizer Prize-winning novel (1960) and Academy Award-winning film (1962); young Southern girl witnesses her ethical lawyer father defend a black man accused of a rape for which he is convicted despite evidence to the contrary. [Am. Lit.: *SJEPC*]

38. **Uncle Tom** pejorative term for an African-American who is submissive to whites; from Harriet Beecher Stowe's famous *Uncle Tom's Cabin*, whose titular character is an acquiescent slave. [Am. Lit.: Harriet Beecher Stowe *Uncle Tom's Cabin*]

39. **white flight** whites moving to new neighborhoods to avoid racial integration; usually from urban locations to suburbs. [Am. Culture: *SJEPC*]

40. **"White Man's Burden, The"** poem written by Rudyard Kipling in 1899; his intent debated, but poem used to promote imperialism as a noble endeavor; phrase came to mean reponsibility of whites to educate and change others to be more like those in West; often viewed as Eurocentric racism. [Br. Hist.: Brewer *Dictionary*, 1152]

41. **white supremacists** often fueled by fear, believe in superiority of whites over other races; the object of hatred and derision changes with historical conditions. [Culture: *SJEPC*]

74. BIOGRAPHY and AUTOBIOGRAPHY

1. **Boswell, James (1740–1793)** Scottish author and devoted biographer of Samuel Johnson. [Br. Hist.: *NCE*, 341]

2. **Cellini, Benevenuto (1500–1571)** Italian sculptor and author of important autobiography. [Ital. Lit.: *NCE*, 488]

3. ***Confessions*** Rousseau (1712–1778) reveals details of an erratic and rebellious life. [Fr.Lit.: Benét, 218]

4. *Confessions of St. Augustine, The* St. Augustine tells of his life and conversion. [Christian Hagiog.: Haydn & Fuller, 153]

5. **Driffield, Edward** novelist whose life story is examined by Kear and Ashenden. [Br. Lit.: Maugham *Cakes and Ale* in Magill I, 99]

6. *Education of Henry Adams, The* intellectual autobiography traces the thought processes and moral degeneration of modern man. [Am. Lit.: *The Education of Henry Adams*; Magill I, 238]

7. **Franklin, Benjamin (1706–1790)** American statesman; author of famous autobiography. [Am. Lit.: *NCE*, 1000]

8. *Lives of the Caesars* biographies by Suetonius of the first twelve Roman Emperors. [Rom. Hist.: Benét, 973]

9. *Memoirs of George Sherston, The* fictional autobiography of a poet as country gentleman, soldier, and pacifist. [Br. Lit.: Magill I, 575, 579]

10. *Naked Lunch* through the persona of William Lee, nightmarish satire of American life recounts author William S. Burroughs's 14–year addiction to morphine (1959). [Am. Lit.: Henderson, 37]

11. **Pepys, Samuel (1633–1703)** English public official; author of diary. [Br. Lit.: *NCE*, 2103]

12. **Plutarch (c. 46–c. 120)** Greek biographer known for his *Lives*, a collection of biographies of Greek and Roman leaders. [Gk. Lit.: *NCE*, 2170]

13. **Sandburg, Carl (1878–1967)** noted poet and famed biographer of Abraham Lincoln. [Am. Lit.: *SJEPC*]

14. **Stone, Irving (1903–1989)** his fictionalized biographies have entertained readers for decades; most notable are *Lust for Life: A Novel of Vincent Van Gogh,* (1934) and *The Agony and the Ecstasy: A Novel of Michelangelo,* (1961). [Am. Lit.: *SJEPC*]

15. *This Is Your Life* radio show in 1940s, TV show in 1950s hosted by Ralph Edwards; documentary-like biographies of notables with testimonials by people who knew them. [Am. Radio and TV: *SJEPC*]

16. **Toklas, Alice B.** *The Autobiography of Alice B. Toklas* was actually an autobiography by Gertrude Stein; Toklas was her long-time lover and companion. [Am. Lit.: *FOF, MOD*]

17. **Venerable Bede (c. 673–735)** Benedictine monk; wrote memorable biographies of English saints. [Br. Hist.: *NCE*, 257]

75. BIRD

1. **Audubon, John James (1785–1851)** his paintings of North American birds in their natural habitats made his name synonymous with bird watching and bird protection. [Hist.: *WB2*]

2. **Birdman of Alcatraz (Robert Stroud, 1890–1963)** from jailbird to famous ornithologist. [Am. Hist.: Worth, 28]

3. ***Birds, The*** Hitchcock film in which birds turn on the human race and terrorize a town. [Am. Cinema: Halliwell, 51]

4. **Blue Bird of Happiness** symbolizes the goal of the two children in Maeterlinck play. [Belg. Lit.: *The Blue Bird* in Haydn & Fuller, 94]

5. **Cloud-cuckoo-land (Nephelococcygia)** city in which all power is to be vested in the birds. [Gk. Drama: Aristophanes *Birds*]

6. **cranes of Ibycus** called on by the dying poet to bear witness against his murderers, they lead to the murderers' conviction. [Gk. Myth.: *NCE*, 1307]

7. **Gripp** talking raven, beloved pet of half-wit Barnaby Rudge. [Br. Lit.: Dickens *Barnaby Rudge*]

8. **Halitherses** Ithacan seer; ornithologist. [Gk. Myth.: Kravitz, 46]

9. **phoenix** fabulous Arabian bird; sings a dirge, burns itself to ashes, and rises to a new life. [Gk. Myth.: Brewer *Dictionary*, 699]

10. **Polynesia** wise old parrot who teaches Dr. Dolittle the languages of birds and animals. [Children's Lit.: Hugh Lofting *Dr. Dolittle*]

11. **raven** bird of ill omen visits the despairing poet. [Am. Lit.: Poe *The Raven*]

12. **Seagull, Jonathan Livingston** ambitious seagull is determined to improve its flying techniques and achieve greater speeds. [Am. Lit.: Richard Bach *Jonathan Livingston Seagull*]

13. **swallows of Capistrano** symbol of springtime, when they return to the mission of San Juan Capistrano from warmer climes. [Am. Culture: *EB*]

14. **Tweety Pie** part of Academy Award-winning cartoon duo with voices supplied by Mel Blanc; dimwitted Sylvester cat attempts unsuccessfully to catch big-eyed, baby-voiced Tweety bird in animated stories. [Am. TV: *SJEPC*]

Birth (See CHILDBIRTH).

76. BIRTHSTONE

1. **amethyst** February. [Am. Gem Symbolism: Kunz, 319–320]

2. **aquamarine** March alternate birthstone. [Am. Gem Symbolism: Kunz, 319]

3. **bloodstone** March. [Am. Gem Symbolism: Kunz, 319–320]

4. **diamond** April. [Am. Gem Symbolism: Kunz, 319–320]

5. **emerald** May. [Am. Gem Symbolism: Kunz, 319–320]

6. **garnet** January. [Am. Gem Symbolism: Kunz, 319–320]

7. **moonstone** June alternate birthstone. [Am. Gem Symbolism: Kunz, 319]

8. **opal** October. [Am. Gem Symbolism: Kunz, 319–320]

9. **pearl** June. [Am. Gem Symbolism: Kunz, 319–320]

10. **peridot** August alternate birthstone. [Am. Gem Symbolism: Kunz, 319]

11. **ruby** July. [Am. Gem Symbolism: Kunz, 319–320]

12. **sapphire** September. [Am. Gem Symbolism: Kunz, 319–320]

13. **sardonyx** August. [Am. Gem Symbolism: Kunz, 319–320]

14. **topaz** November. [Am. Gem Symbolism: Kunz, 319–320]

15. **tourmaline** October alternate birthstone. [Am. Gem Symbolism: Kunz, 320]

16. **turquoise** December. [Am. Gem Symbolism: Kunz, 319–320]

77. BLACKMAIL (See also BRIBERY.)

1. **Rigaud** adventurer and extortionist. [Br. Lit.: *Little Dorrit*]

2. **Rudge** extorts to achieve personal ends. [Br. Lit.: *Barnaby Rudge*]

3. **Sextus** threatens murder and dishonor to bed Lucretia. [Rom. Lit.: *Fasti*; *Livy*; Br. Lit.: *The Rape of Lucrece*]

4. **Wegg, Silas** attempts to blackmail Boffin. [Br. Lit.: *Our Mutual Friend*]

Blasphemy (See APOSTASY.)

78. BLINDNESS

1. **Agib** dervish who lost an eye. [Arab.Lit.: *Arabian Nights*]

2. **Anchises** blinded by lightning. [Gk. Myth.: Walsh *Classical*, 22]

3. **Blind Pew** David, the blind beggar. [Br. Lit.: *Treasure Island*]

4. **Braille, Louis (1809–1852)** teacher of blind; devised raised printing which is read by touch. [Fr. Hist.: *NCE*, 354]

5. **Charles, Ray (1930–2004)** overcame loss of sight to glaucoma at age six and continued his music studies, becoming legendary composer and performer of soul, blues, pop, jazz, and country music. [Am. Music: *SJEPC*]

6. **Cratus** Titan who blinded Prometheus. [Gk. Myth.: Kravitz, 67–68]

7. **Demodocus** blind bard rewarded by Odysseus. [Gk. Lit.: *Odyssey* VIII]

8. **Ephialtes** giant deprived of his left eye by Apollo and of his right eye by Hercules. [Gk. Myth.: Brewer *Dictionary*, 333]

9. **Feliciano, Jose (1945–)** blind since birth, Puerto Rican guitar virtuoso/singer learned music at an early age and achieved fame with classic hits "Light My Fire" (1968) and "Feliz Navidad" (1970). [Am. Music: *SJEPC*]

10. **Gloucester** cruelly blinded by those he served. [Br. Lit.: *King Lear*]

11. **Graeae, the** share one eye among them. [Gk. Myth.: Gayley, 208–210]

12. **Heldar, Dick** artist who gradually goes blind and is abandoned by his sweetheart. [Br. Lit.: *The Light that Failed* in Benét, 586]

13. **Homer** sightless writer of *Iliad* and *Odyssey*. [Gr. Hist.: Wallechinsky, 13]

14. **Justice** personified as a blindfolded goddess, token of impartiality. [Rom. Tradition: Jobes II, 898]

15. **Keller, Helen (1880–1968)** Achieved greatness despite blindess and deafness. [Am. Hist.: Wallechinsky, 13]

16. **Lucy, Saint** vision restored after gouging out of eyes. [Christian Hagiog.: Brewster, 20–21]

17. **Milton, John (1698–1674)** English poet who became blind in later life; dictated his masterpiece, *Paradise Lost*. [Br. Lit: FOF, MOD]

18. **mole** said to lack eyes. [Medieval Animal Symbolism: White, 95–96]

19. **Nydia** beautiful flower girl lacks vision but "sees" love. [Br. Lit.: *The Last Days of Pompeii*, Magill I, 490–492]

20. **Odilia, Saint** recovered vision; shrine, pilgrimage for visually afflicted. [Christian Hagiog.: Attwater, 257]

21. **Oedipus** blinded self on learning he had married his mother. [Gk. Lit.: *Oedipus Rex*]

22. **Paul, Saint** blinded by God on road to Damascus. [N.T.: Acts 9:1–19]

23. **Peeping Tom** stricken blind for peeping as the naked Lady Godiva rode by. [Br. Legend: Brewer *Dictionary*]

24. **Plutus** blind god of Wealth. [Gk. Lit.: *Plutus*]

25. **Polyphemus** Cyclops blinded by Odysseus. [Gk. Myth.: *Odyssey*]

26. **Rochester, Edward** blinded when his home burns down, depends on the care of Jane Eyre. [Br. Lit.: Charlotte Bronte *Jane Eyre*]

27. **Samson** Israelite hero treacherously blinded by Philistines. [O.T.: Judges 16:4–21]

28. **Stagg** sightless roomkeeper. [Br. Lit.: *Barnaby Rudge*]

29. **three blind mice** sightless rodents; lost tails to farmer's wife. [Nurs. Rhyme: Opie, 306]

30. **Tiresias** made sightless by Athena for viewing her nakedness. [Gk. Myth.: Brewer *Dictionary*, 1086]

31. **Tobit** sparrow guano falls into his eyes while sleeping. [Apocrypha: Tobit 2:10]

32. **Wonder, Stevie (1950–)** blind African-American songwriter and performer; tremendously talented and versatile; has worked in various genres with many instruments (most notably the synthesizer). [Am. Music: *SJEPC*]

33. **Zedekiah** eyes put out for revolting against Nebuchadnezzar. [O.T.: II Kings 25:7]

79. BOASTFULNESS (See also ARROGANCE, CONCEIT, EGOTISM.)

1. **Aglaonice** Thessalian who claimed power over moon. [Gk. Legend: Brewer *Dictionary*, 16]

2. **Ajax (the greater)** archetypal *Miles Gloriosus* [Br. Lit.: *Troilus and Cressida*]

3. **Anchises** Trojan prince; crippled for boasting of intimacy with Aphrodite. [Gk. Myth.: Zimmerman, 22]

4. **Armado** verbose braggart and pedant. [Br. Lit.: *Love's Labour Lost*]

5. **Basilisco** knight renowned for foolish bragging. [Br. Lit.: *Solomon and Persida*, Brewer *Dictionary*, 83]

6. **Bessus** braggart soldier in the *Miles Gloriosus* tradition. [Br. Lit.: Walsh, *Modern*, 55]

7. **Bluffe, Captain** blustering braggart and spurious war veteran. [Br. Lit.: *The Old Batchelour*]

8. **Bobadill, Captain** blustering braggadocio of yellow stripe. [Br. Lit.: *Every Man in His Humour*]

9. **Braggadocchio** empty braggart. [Br. Lit.: *Fairie Queene*]

10. **Capaneus** struck dead by a thunderbolt for boasting that not even Jove could stop him from scaling the wall of Thebes. [Gk. Myth.: Benét, 166]

11. **Drawcansir** blustering bully, known for his extravagantly boastful speeches. [Br. Lit.: *The Rehearsal*]

12. **Falstaff, Sir John** jovial knight and rascal of brazen braggadocio. [Br. Lit.: *Merry Wives of Windsor*; *I Henry IV*; *II Henry IV*]

13. **Gascon** inhabitant of Gascony, France; people noted for their bragging. [Fr. Hist.: *NCE*, 1049]

14. **Glendower, Owen** Welsh ally of the Percys; his boastfulness antagonizes Hotspur. [Br. Lit.: *I Henry IV*]

15. **Hàry, Jànos** peasant hero of fanciful adventures. [Hung. Lit. and Opera: Osborne *Opera*, 148]

16. **Kay, Sir** rude and vainglorious knight of the Round Table. [Br. Lit.: *Le Morte d'Arthur*; *Idylls of the King*]

17. **Mahon, Christopher** runaway boy tells stories with self as epitome of bravery. [Irish Lit.: *The Playboy of the Western World*, Magill I, 758–759]

18. **Parolles** cowardly braggart and wastrel. [Br. Lit.: *All's Well That Ends Well*]

19. **Pistol** knight of the "killing tongue and quiet sword." [Br. Lit.: *II Henry IV*]

20. **Rodomont** gallant but blustering Saracen leader. [Ital. Lit.: *Orlando Furioso; Orlando Innamorato*]

21. **Roister Doister, Ralph** well-to-do dolt brags loud and long of bravery. [Br. Lit.: *Ralph Roister Doister*]

22. **Sacripant** noisy braggart. [Ital. Lit.: *Sechia Rapita*, Brewer *Handbook*, 945]

23. **Scaramouche** talks a good fight; never does. [Ital. Lit.: Espy, 125]

24. **Tartarin** tells tall tales of his fantastic adventures. [Fr. Lit.: *Tartarin de Tarascon*]

25. **Texan** resident of second largest U.S. state; known for his tall tales. [Am. Culture: Misc.]

26. **Thraso** swaggering but foolish soldier. [Rom. Lit.: *The Eunuch*]

27. **Vicar of Bray** declared that he would retain his office regardless of the reigning king's religion. [Br. Balladry: Walsh *Classical*, 61]

80. BOHEMIANISM

1. *Autobiography of Alice B. Toklas, The* Gertrude Stein's memoir of Paris' Bohemia. [Am. Lit.: *The Autobiography of Alice B. Toklas* in Benét, 66]

2. **Beat Generation** 1950s movement in poetry and prose whose members rebelled against the strictures of middle-class society. [Am. Culture: Misc.]

3. **beatnik** an individual rebelling against conformist society, from the 1950s and associated with the Beat Generation. [Am. Culture: Misc.]

4. **Bloomsbury** section of London where, in the first half of the 20th century, a group of artists and intellectuals frequently congregated. [Br. Culture: Benét, 115]

5. **Greenwich Village** area of southern Manhattan long identified with artists and writers. [Am. Culture: Misc.]

6. **Haight-Ashbury** neighborhood in San Francisco associated with hippies and "flower people" in the 1960s. [Am. Culture: Misc.]

7. **hippies** from the word, "hip," hippies were young people, who, in the 1960s, rebelled against societal strictures to forge their own

culture; a symbol of disaffected, nontraditional, anti-capitalist, peace-loving youth. [Am. Culture: Misc.]

8. *La Bohème* Puccini's beloved masterpiece, depicts young love among struggling artists in Paris in the 1890s. [Ital. Opera: *EB*]

9. **Latin Quarter** section of Paris on left bank of the Seine; home of students, artists, and writers. [Fr. Culture: *EB*, VI: 71–72]

10. **Olenska, Countess Ellen** often considers divorce; likes "unacceptable" people. [Am. Lit.: *The Age of Innocence*]

11. **SoHo** once bohemian, now very hip, neighborhood So(uth of) Ho(uston Street), New York City. [Am. Culture: Misc.]

81. BOREDOM (See also DESPAIR, FUTILITY.)

1. **Aldegonde, Lord Saint** bored nobleman, empty of pursuits. [Br. Lit.: *Lothair*]

2. **assembly line** method of production made famous by Henry Ford; efficient, but boring for the worker. [Am. Business: Misc.]

3. **Bovary, Emma** housewife suffers from ennui. [Fr. Lit.: *Madame Bovary*]

4. **Des Esseintes, Jean** in dissipation and isolation, develops morbid ennui. [Fr. Lit.: *Against the Grain*]

5. **Harthouse, James** thorough gentleman, weary of everything. [Br. Lit.: *Hard Times*]

6. **Oblomov, Ilya** Russian landowner; emodiment of physical and mental sloth. [Russ. Lit.: *Oblomov*]

7. **Povey, Constance Baines** uneventful thoughts, marriage best described as routine. [Br. Lit.: *The Old Wives' Tale*, magill I, 684–686]

82. BORESOMENESS

1. **Bellenden, Lady Margaret** tiresomely repeats story of Charles II's visit. [Br. Lit.: *Old Mortality*]

2. **Bovary, Charles** "dull-witted husband reeked of medicine and drugs." [Fr. Lit.: *Madame Bovary*]

3. **Dryasdust, Rev.** imaginary preface writer with wooden style. [Br. Lit.: Wheeler, 108]

4. **Warburton, Lord** Isabel's kindly, thoughtful, but overly boring suitor. [Am. Lit.: *The Portrait of a Lady*, Magill I, 766–768]

5. **Welland, May** "correct buy unexciting personality." [Am. Lit.: *The Age of Innocence*]

83. BOXING

1. **Ali, Muhammad (1942–)** one of the greatest boxers of all time; born Cassius Clay, "The Greatest" won gold medal at 1960

Olympics and became three-time world heavyweight champion. [Am. Sports: *SJEPC*; *WB2*]

2. **Balboa, Rocky** lower-class Philadelphia boxer who wins golden opportunity to fight in prize bout in 1976 film. [Am. Film: *Rocky*]

3. **Corbett, James J. (1866–1933)** "Gentleman Jim's" scientific techniques in boxing beat out John L. Sullivan's brute force style after new rules took effect in 1892; won the heavyweight championship. [Am. Sports: *SJEPC*]

4. **Dares** one of Aeneas's companions; noted for his boxing skill. [Rom. Lit.: *Aeneid*]

5. **De La Hoya, Oscar (1973–)** popular Mexican-American pro boxer, alias Golden Boy, won a gold medal in 1992 Olympics. [Am. Sports: *SJEPC*]

6. **Dempsey, Jack (1895–1983)** tough boxing champion known as the "Manassa Mauler" held the heavyweight world title from 1919 to 1926. [Am. Sports: *SJEPC*]

7. **Duran, Roberto (1951–)** Panamanian boxing champion won world titles in lightweight, welterweight, junior middleweight, middleweight, and super middleweight divisions; nicknamed "Manos de Piedra" (Hands of Stone). [Sports: *SJEPC*]

8. **Entellus** powerful Sicilian boxer; won match for Anchises against Dares. [Rom. Lit.: *Aeneid*]

9. **Eryx** great boxer; killed at own game by challenger, Hercules. [Gk. Myth: Howe, 97]

10. **Foreman, George (1949–)** 1973 heavyweight champion retired to become minister, then returned to boxing and recaptured heavyweight title at age 45, the oldest man to do so (1994). [Am. Sports: *SJEPC*]

11. **Frazier, Joe (1944–)** in 1971, reigning heavyweight champion "Smokin' Joe" defeated former champ Muhammad Ali in the "Fight of the Century"; fought but lost two rematches with his tough rival in 1970s. [Am. Sports: *SJEPC*]

12. **Golden Boy** violinist turns boxer for fame, wealth. [Am. Lit.: *Golden Boy*]

13. **Great White Hope** 1910 personification of white people's aspirations for a white heavyweight champion. [Am. Hist.: Misc.]

14. **Johnson, Jack (1878–1946)** first African-American to be crowned heavyweight boxing champion of the world (1908). [Am. Sports: *SJEPC*]

15. **La Motta, Jake (1922–)** middleweight boxer known for win in 1943 during fight against the great Sugar Ray Robinson; his volatile temperament masterfully depicted by actor Robert De Niro in film *Raging Bull* (1980). [Am. Sports: *SJEPC*]

16. **Louis, Joe (1914–1981)** famous African-American boxer, known as the "Brown Bomber," heavyweight champion of the world. [Am. Sports: *FOF, MOD*]

17. **Palooka Joe** comicdom's great white hope. [Comics: Horn, 343–344]

18. **pull a punch** in boxing, not to strike with full force; in common speech, to back off, not act agressively. [Am. Sports: *FOF, MOD*]

19. **Queensberry, Marquis of** (Sir John Douglas, 1844–1900) established basic rules of boxing; a symbol of authority and following the rules. [Br. Hist.: *NCE*,2257]

20. **Robinson, Sugar Ray (1921–1989)** African-American powerhouse nicknamed for his sweet-as-sugar style of boxing; strength, skill, and good looks brought him fame and celebrity. [Am. Sports: *SJEPC*]

21. *Rocky* box-office hit of 1976; boxing film about blue-collar hero who wins bout against all odds because of determination and courage. [Am. Film: *SJEPC*]

22. **Sullivan, John L. (1858–1918)** Irish-American prizefighter who became early sports celebrity. [Am. Sports: *SJEPC*]

23. **Tyson, Mike (1966–)** boxing champ by age of 19; volatile personality spilled over into personal life, leading to brutality in and out of ring and imprisonment. [Am. Sports: *SJPEC*]

84. BRAVERY (See also FORTITUDE, HERO.)

1. **Achilles** foremost Greek hero of Trojan War; brave and formidable warrior. [Gk. Hist.: *NCE*, 12]

2. **Adrastus** courageous Indian prince; Rinaldo's enemy. [Ital. Lit.: *Jerusalem Delivered*]

3. **Agenor** Antenor's son; distinguished for his valor in battle. [Gk. Myth.: Zimmerman, 12]

4. **Aragorn** character in Tolkien's Lord of Rings trilogy (1954–1956); heir to throne of Gondor; wise and brave natural leader with knightly purity and fair treatment for all; after fall of Sauron, he becomes King of Gondor. [Br. Lit.: Gillespie and Naden]

5. **Bajazet** fierce, reckless, indomitable Sultan of Turkey; Tamerlane's captive. [Br. Lit.: *Tamerlane*, Walsh *Modern*, 39]

6. *Band of Brothers* book and TV series documenting the courageous 101st Airborne unit during WWII. [Am. Hist.: *Band of Brothers*]

7. **Beowulf** singlehandedly fights firebreathing dragon. [Br. Lit.: *Beowulf*]

8. **Birch, Harvey** at great risk spies on British. [Am. Lit.: *The Spy*]

9. **black agate** makes athletes brave and invincible. [Gem Symbolism: Jobes, 45]

10. **black poplar** symbol of bravery. [Plant Symbolism: *Flora Symbolica*, 176]

11. **Boadicea (Boudicca)** British queen and female warrior; slew 80,000 Romans. [Br. Hist.: Walsh, *Classical*, 58]

12. **Bold Beauchamp** 14th-century champion; British generic for *warrior*/ [Br. Hist.: Walsh, *Classical*, 49]

13. **Breck, Alan** while evading enemies, risks his life to save others. [Br. Lit.: *Kidnapped*]

14. **bull** heraldic symbol of courage. [Heraldry: Halberts, 21]

15. **carp** a pictorial symbol of bravery. [Chinese and Jap. Folklore: Jobes, 292]

16. **Clorinda** Amazonian, battles in armor. [Ital.Lit.: *Jerusalem Delivered*]

17. **Cowardly Lion** from L. Frank Baum's Oz series; because he confuses fear with cowardice, he wants the Wizard to make him brave; in truth, he fights courageously. [Br. Children's Lit.: Jones]

18. **David** audaciously stands before and slays Goliath. [O.T.: I Samuel 17:48–51]

19. **French willow** indicates courage. [Flower Symbolism: *Flora Symbolica*, 176]

20. **Fritchie, Barbara** her bravery impressed Stonewall Jackson. [Am. Lit.: "Barbara Fritchie" in Hart, 57]

21. **Gawain, Sir** bravery in the Castle of Wonders. [Arth. Legend: *Parsival*]

22. **Hale, Nathan (1755–1776)** Revolutionary war hero, calmly accepted fate. [Am. Hist.: Jameson, 215]

23. **Havelok** right makes might as gallant prince triumphs. [Dan. Lit.: *Havelok the Dane*]

24. **Hawkeye** scout and woodsman who risks his life to save English girls from hostile Indians. [Am. Lit.: Cooper *The Last of the Mohicans* in Magill I, 494]

25. **Hector** captain and chief hero of Trojan forces. [Rom. Lit.: *Aeneid*; *Metamorphoses*]

26. **Horatius** holds off Etruscan forces while Romans burn bridge. [Rom. Hist.: *Livy*]

27. **Iron Cross** German medal awarded for outstanding bravery in wartime. [Ger. Hist.: Misc.]

28. **Joan of Arc, Saint** peasant leader of French rout of British. [Christian Hagiog.: Attwater, 187]

29. **Kenobi, Obi-Wan** brave Jedi knight who trains Luke Skywalker in the *Star Wars* movies. [Am. Film: Misc.]

30. **larch** symbol of bravery. [Tree Symbolism: *Flora Symbolica*, 175]

31. **Little Dutch Boy** hero who uses his finger to plug a hole in a dyke, saving his town. [Am. Lit.: Dodge, Mary Mapes, *Hans Brinker or the Silver Skates*]

32. **Lochinvar** hero of Sir Walter Scott's poem *Marmion*, comes out of the west to claim his love. [Br. Lit.: *FOF, MOD*]

33. **Medal of Honor** highest American military decoration for wartime gallantry. [Am. Hist.: Misc.]

34. **Murphy, Audie (1924–1971)** one of the most decorated, and most famous war heroes in U.S. history; his exploits during WWII won him the Congressional Medal of Honor and a career as a film star. [Am. Hist.: *EB*]

35. **Nelson, Lord Horatio (1758–1805)** English admiral and hero of the Battle of Trafalgar. [Br. Hist.: Misc.]

36. **Nicephorus, Saint** layman voluntarily executed to prevent priest's apostasy. [Christian Hagiog.: Attwater, 249]

37. **Paul, Saint** as a missionary he fearlessly confronts the "perils of waters, of robbers, in the city, in the wilderness." [N.T. : II Corinthians 11:26]

38. **Pevensie, Lucy** protagonist of C.S. Lewis's Narnia series for young readers; young and innocent, she discovers Narnia and believes in it completely; compassionate and courageous, she grows up to be Queen Lucy the Valiant. [Br. Children's Lit.: Jones]

39. **Pitcher, Molly (1744–1832)** took husband's place in battle during American Revolution. [Am. Hist.: Jameson, 393]

40. *Profiles in Courage* John F. Kennedy's anthology of biographies of brave statesman. [Am. Hist.: *Profiles in Courage*]

41. **Purple Heart** U.S. medal awarded to those wounded in military action. [Am. Hist.: Misc.]

42. **red badge** symbol of the conquest of fear. [Am. Lit.: *Red Badge of Courage*]

43. **Red Cross Knight** brave hero of *The Faerie Queen*, slays dragon and rescues Princess Una. [Br. Lit.: Edmund Spenser *The Faerie Queen*]

44. **Richard the Lion-Hearted (1159–1199)** romantic warrior-king renowned for his bravery and prowess. [Br. Hist.: Bishop, 49]

45. **Roland** brave French hero of medieval chansons de geste. [Fr. Lit.: *NCE*, 2344]

46. **salmon** migration upstream has made it symbol of courage and wisdom. [Symbolism: *CEOS&S*]

47. **Samson** strong, brave judge of Israel; strength was in is hair. [O.T.: Judges 13–16]

48. **Theseus** displays bravery in facing Minotaur; agianst Procrustes. [Gk. Myth.: *Odyssey; Metamorphoses*]

49. **Victoria Cross** highest British military award for valor. [Br. Hist.: Brewer *Dictionary*, 1129]

50. **wolf** in some cultures, symbol of courage, victory, or nurturance. [Symbolism: *CEOS&S*]

85. BRAWNINESS (See also STRENGTH.)

1. **Atlas, Charles (1893–1972)** American muscleman; successful selling body-building by mail order. [Am. Culture: Misc.]

2. **Big John** brawny, strapping miner who saves others in mine collapse. [Am. Music: Jimmy Dean, "Big Bad John"]

3. **Browdie, John** big Yorkshireman. [Br. Lit.: *Nicholas Nickleby*]

4. **Bunyan, Paul** lumberjack performs mighty deeds. [Am. Folklore: *The Wonderful Adventures of Paul Bunyan*]

5. **Goliath** gigantic, sinewy Philistine killed by David's slingshot. [O.T.: I Samuel 17: 21:9, 22:10; II Samuel 21:19]

6. **Hulk, The Incredible** one of Marvel Comics' most popular superheroes; Dr. Banner—exposed to gamma radiation—turns into the super-strong Hulk when angry or under stress; made into popular TV show in late 1970s. [Am. Comics and TV: *SJEPC*]

7. **McTeague** brawn his chief asset; accompanied with little brains. [Am. Lit.: *McTeague*]

8. **Popeye** sailor who owes his incredible muscle-power to a diet of canned spinach. [Comics: Horn, 658]

9. **Schwarzenegger, Arnold (1947–)** Austrian-born body builder who rose to stardom as action-film hero; went on to become Governor of California. [Am. Film and Politics: *SJEPC*]

10. **Stallone, Sylvester (1946–)** action-film star whose strong but hardly eloquent heroes have won the hearts of fans; best known for roles as boxer Rocky Balboa and Vietnam vet John Rambo. [Am. Film: *SJEPC*]

11. **Tarzan** muscular English lord, reared by African apes, hero of novels and films. [Am. Lit.: *Tarzan of the Apes* (1914); Am. Cinema: Rovin, 105–106]

86. BREVITY

1. **Adonis' garden** of short life. [Br. Lit.: *I Henry IV*]

2. **bubbles** symbolic of transitoriness of life. [Art: Hall, 54]

3. **cherry fair** cherry orchards where fruit was briefly sold; symbolic of transcience. [Folklore: Brewer *Dictionary*, 217]

4. **Gettysburg Address** terse but famous speech given by President Lincoln at dedication of national cemetery. (Gettysburg, Penn., 1863). [Am. Hist.: *EB*, IV: 515]

5. **Grey, Lady Jane (1537–1554)** queen of England for nine days. [Br. Hist.: *NCE*, 1146]

6. **night-blooming cereus** symbol of fading loveliness; blooms briefly. [Flower Symbolism: *Flora Symbolica*, 176]

7. **Six-Day War** Arab-Israeli War (1967). [Near East. Hist.: *EB*, I: 470]

87. BRIBERY (See also BLACKMAIL.)

1. **Black Sox Scandal** star White Sox players were bribed to lose the World Series (1919). [Am. Sports: Turkin, 478]

2. **Frollo, Claude** offers to save Esmeralda if she will be his. [Fr. Lit.: *The Hunchback of Notre Dame*]

3. **Joel and Abiah** intent on gain, pervert justice as Israel judges. [O.T.: I Samuel 8:2–2]

4. **Judas Iscariot** betrays Jesus for a bribe of thirty pieces of silver. [N.T.: Matthew 26:15]

5. **Maltese Falcon, The** though he rejects large bribe, detective becomes involved in crime. [Am. Lit.: *The Maltese Falcon*]

6. **Menahem** pays off Assyrian king to avoid Israel. [O.T.: II Kings 15:20]

7. **mess of pottage** hungry Esau sells birthright for broth. [O.T.: Genesis 25:29–34]

8. **payola** record company practice of bribing disc jockeys to play their artists' songs on the radio was investigated by Congress in late 1950s and created a scandal. [Am. Music: *SJEPC*]

9. **Shemaiah** suborned to render false prophecy to Nehemiah. [O.T.: Nehemiah 6:10–14]

10. **Tweed Ring** bribery is their essential method for corrupting officials (1860–1871). [Am. Hist.: Jameson, 511]

88. BRIDGE

1. **Al Sirat** fine as razor's edge, over which all must pass to enter paradise. [Islam: *Koran*]

2. **Amaurote** Utopian crossing; means "faintly seen." [Br. Lit.: *Utopia*]

3. **Bifrost** rainbow of water and fire for gods' passage from Asgard to Midgard. [Norse Myth.: Leach, 139]

4. **Bridge of San Luis Rey** rope bridge in Andes which breaks, killing five people. [Am. Lit.: *Bridge of San Luis Rey*]

5. **Brooklyn Bridge** suspension bridge spanning the East River from Manhattan to Brooklyn. [Am. Hist.: *EB*, II: 301]

6. **Golden Gate Bridge** suspension bridge in San Francisco spanning the Golden Gate. [Am. Hist.: *EB*, IV: 607]

7. **London Bridge** a bridge spanning the Thames at London (not the Tower Bridge). [Br. Hist.: *EB*, VI: 311]

8. **River Kwai Bridge** bridge built by British POWs under Japanese orders. [Jap. Hist.: *Bridge Over the River Kwai*]

9. **Xerxes** constructed famed pontoon crossing of Hellespont. [Gk. Hist.: Brewer *Dictionary*, 1169]

89. BRIGHTNESS

1. **Alpha Centauri** brightest star in Centaurus constellation; closest star to Earth. [Astronomy: *NCE*, 74]

2. **diamond** April birthstone, most reflective of gems. [Gem Symbolism: Jobes, 440–441]

3. **North Star** bright star visible to naked eye and nearest to the north celestial pole. [Astronomy: *EB*, VIII: 79]

4. **Sirius** dog star; brightest star in the heavens. [Astronomy: *EB*, IX, 238]

5. **St. Elmo's fire** glow of electrical discharge appearing on towers and ships' masts. [Physics: *EB*, VIII: 780]

6. **Venus** bright planet, second from the Sun. [Astronomy: *EB*, X: 392]

90. BRITAIN

1. **Albion** poetic name for England. [Br. Lit.: Benét, 19]

2. **beefeater** yeoman of the English royal guard, esp. at the Tower of London; slang for Englishman. [Br. Culture: Misc.]

3. **Bull, John** personification of England. [Br. Folklore: Benét, 45]

4. **Camelot** castle of legendary King Arthur of Britain. [Br. Legend: *WB2*]

5. **Court of Saint James's** British royal court. [Br. Hist.: Misc.]

6. **Diana, Princess of Wales (1961–1997)** compassionate, internationally revered "People's Princess" joined the British royal family upon her marriage to Prince Charles in 1981; remained a beloved figure to Brits upon her divorce in 1996 and premature death a year later. [Br. Hist.: *SJEPC*]

7. **George, Saint** patron saint of Britain. [Br. Hist.: *Golden Legend*]

8. **God Save the Queen** British national anthem. [Br. Culture: Scholes, 408]

9. **Nation of Shopkeepers** name disdainfully given to Britain by Napoleon Bonaparte. [Fr. Hist.: Wheeler, 256]

10. **Rule Britannia!** patriotic song of Britian. [Br. Culture: Scholes, 897–898]

11. **10 Downing Street** the British government; refers to location of Prime Minister's residence. [Br. Culture: Benét, 286]

12. **Union Jack** British national flag. [Br. Culture: Misc.]

13. *Upstairs, Downstairs* first broadcast in 1974, international hit TV series follows the lives of servants and masters in London household from 1903–1929; depicts how British class system eroded during and after Edwardian era. [Br. TV: *SJEPC*]

14. **Whitehall** many government offices on this street; synonymous with government. [Br. Hist.: *NCE*, 2970]

91. BROADCASTING (See also JOURNALISM, TELEVISION.)

1. **Barber, Red (1908–1992)** pioneer radio and TV sports broadcaster. [Am. Radio and TV: *SJEPC*]

2. **Brinkley, David (1920–2003)** broadcast news icon coanchored the *Huntley-Brinkley Report* (NBC, 1956–70) and remained active in the field as anchor, reporter, and writer. [Am. TV and Jour.: *SJEPC*]

3. **Brokaw, Tom (1940–)** broadcast journalist with easygoing manner hosted NBC's *Today Show*, anchored *NBC Nightly News*; known for reporting news on site as major historic events unfold. [Am. Jour.: *SJEPC*]

4. **Caray, Harry (1919–1998)** beloved Major League Baseball radio and TV broadcaster for the St. Louis Cardinals, Chicago White Sox, and Chicago Cubs whose career spanned from 1945 to 1998; known for phrase "Holy Cow" and singing "Take Me Out to the Ballgame." [Am. Sports, Radio, and TV: *SJEPC*]

5. **Corwin, Norman (1910–)** well-known and popular voice during radio's Golden Age in the 1940s; painted vivid, dramatic pictures of World War II in prose and poetry. [Am. Radio: *SJEPC*]

6. **Cosell, Howard (1918–1995)** verbose, egotistical, nasal-voiced sportscaster covered boxing and football on television from the 1960s to 1980s. [Am. Sports and TV: *SJEPC*]

7. **Costas, Bob (1952–)** popular broadcast journalist began covering professional and college sports for NBC in 1980; anchored Olympics from 1992 to 2006, hosted *NFL Live* and *Later with Bob Costas*. [Am. Sports: *SJEPC*]

8. **Cronkite, Walter (1916–)** iconic anchorman of the *CBS Evening News* (1962–81) projected trustworthiness and steadfastness during turbulent times. [Am. Jour. and TV: *SJEPC*]

9. **Downs, Hugh (1921–)** trustworthy broadcasting icon with reassuring, gracious manner began career in radio (1930s) and moved

on to television, hosting such programs as *The Today Show* and *20/20*. [Am. Radio and TV: *SJEPC*]

10. **ESPN** Entertainment and Sports Programming Network; premier sports network has broadcast 24 hours a day all over the world since 1979; expanded to radio in 1992, Internet in 1995, and magazine publishing in 1998. [Am. TV and Radio: *SJEPC*]

11. **Fadiman, Clifton (1904–1999)** literary moderator/host of hit radio quiz show *Information, Please!* (1938–48) in which listeners posed questions to a panel of experts. [Am. Radio: *SJEPC*]

12. *Fibber McGee and Molly* extremely popular, beloved comedic radio program featuring vaudevillian couple Jim and Marian Jordan as a big-mouthed tale-spinner and his heart-of-gold wife with an Irish brogue who resided at 79 Wistful Vista (NBC, 1935–59). [Am. Radio: *SJEPC*]

13. **Gulf War** progress of multinational forces led by the U.S. to free Kuwait from Iraqi invasion during 6–week Operation Desert Storm was viewed by millions globally via satellite TV; dawn of the 24/7 news cycle (1991). [Hist.: *SJEPC*]

14. **Huntley, Chet (1911–1974)** evening news co-anchor with David Brinkley from 1956 to 1970 on popular Huntley-Brinkley Report. [Am. Jour. and TV: Misc.]

15. *Information, Please!* popular radio quiz show moderated by Clifton Fadiman posed questions to a panel of experts, with a set of *Encyclopedia Brittanica* the prize for stumping the panel (1938–48). [Am. Radio: *SJEPC*]

16. **Jennings, Peter (1938–2005)** after many years overseas doing international news, he became television nightly news anchor for ABC; drew viewer loyalty and trust, while garnering several awards. [Am. Jour. and TV: *SJEPC*]

17. **Keillor, Garrison (1942–)** humorist whose writings depict small-town Midwest living at its most charming and sentimental; a devotee of radio, his extremely successful *Prairie Home Companion* show (debut, 1974) combines music performances and take-offs of old radio shows and ads [Am. Radio: *SJEPC*]

18. **Murrow, Edward R. (1908–1965)** iconic American radio and television broadcaster, noted for World War II reporting and for news programs "Hear It Now" and "See It Now" on CBS; symbol of integrity and courage for confronting the witch-hunting tactics of Joseph McCarthy. [Am. TV and Radio: *EB*]

19. **O'Reilly, Bill (1949–)** right-wing author, columnist, and host of *The O'Reilly Factor* cable TV news show; opinionated and abrasive; maintains that he creates news reporting that exists in a "no spin zone." [Am. Jour. and TV: Misc.]

20. **Rather, Dan (1931–)** news anchor of *CBS Evening News* and *60 Minutes*; airing of information from questionable documents about President George W. Bush's National Guard record led to Rather's dismissal. [Am. Jour.: *SJEPC*]

21. **Rivera, Geraldo (1943–)** highly touted Hispanic journalist and TV personality who won several awards for distinguished broadcast journalism; later turned to sensationalism and lowbrow specials. [Am. TV and Jour.: *SJEPC*]

22. **Russert, Tim (1950–2008)** NCB News Washington bureau chief and moderator of *Meet the Press* from 1991 until his death; show was considered an important proving ground in career of national politicians. [Am. Jour. and TV: Misc.]

23. **Sarnoff, David (1891–1971)** created the National Broadcasting Company (NBC) in 1926, the first permanent network; commercial broadcasting was born. [Am. TV: *SJEPC*]

24. **satellites** a network of satellites receiving and relaying signals meant a leap forward in communications and media broadcasting. [Am. Science: *SJEPC*]

25. **Schlessinger, Dr. Laura (1947–)** firm believer in personal responsibility, blunt personality and strict definition of morality have made her controversial; millions listen to her radio show and read her syndicated newspaper columns and books. [Am. Radio: *SJPEC*]

26. **Shadow, The** character in radio program from 1937–1954 known for hypnotic powers and memorable lines ("Who knows what evil lurks in the hearts of men? The Shadow knows."); also character in popular crime-fighting pulp novels and comic books. [Am. Comics and Radio: *SJEPC*]

27. **Shirer, William L. (1904–1993)** acclaimed for his newcasts of world events preceding WWII; helped form the fundamental principles of international news broadcasting. [Am. Radio: *SJEPC*]

28. **Shock Radio** radio shows begun earlier but popularized in the 1970s; hosts engage in audacious, lewd, and often derogatory humor; considered by some the epitome of free speech, by others the epitome of decadence. [Am. Radio: *SJEPC*]

29. *60 Minutes* first broadcast in 1968, the first network prime-time news program with "magazine format"; mixture of hard news, investigative stories, personality profiles, and lighter pieces, interspersed with image of ticking stopwatch. [Am. TV: *SJEPC*]

30. **Stern, Howard (1954–)** master of shock radio whose program covers outrageous and often distasteful subjects; profanity and sexually explicit conversations are the norm. [Am. Radio: *SJEPC*]

31. **talk radio** became prominent in 1990s; callers can join discussions on various topics from serious to frivolous. [Am. Radio: *SJEPC*]

32. ***This Is Your Life*** radio show in 1940s, TV show in 1950s hosted by Ralph Edwards; documentary-like biographies of notables with testimonials by people who knew them. [Am. Radio and TV: *SJEPC*]

33. **Toyko Rose** name given to various female Japanese deejays by WWII military men; taunted Allied servicemen and made demoralizing statements and urged surrender; one (Iva Ikuko Toguri D'Aquino, 1916–2006) was tried and convicted, probably unjustly; later pardoned. [Am. Hist.: *SJEPC*]

34. **Trout, Robert (1908–2000)** radio's first anchorman; beginning in 1938 he mastered the job of introducing reporters, reading reports, and ad-libbing. [Am. Radio: *SJEPC*]

35. ***20/20*** premiered in 1978 as ABC Television's first news magazine with Hugh Downs and Barbara Walters as anchors; interesting topics and interviews with notables such as Fidel Castro. [Am. TV: *SJEPC*]

36. **von Kaltenborn, Hans (1878–1965)** beginning in 1920s, he added analysis to news broadcasts, paving the way for later news commentators; career spanned 30 years of extemporaneous conversational programs. [Am. Jour.: *SJEPC*]

37. **Walters, Barbara (1931–)** TV journalist became the first female to anchor the evening news when she worked with Harry Reasoner in 1976; co-hosted *20/20* and moved into career as insightful interviewer; however, has been criticized at times for blending news and entertainment [Am. Jour.: *SJEPC*]

38. ***War of the Worlds*** broadcast on radio on October 30, 1938; Orson Welles's story of Martian invasion sent thousands of Americans into a panic. [Am. Radio: *SJEPC*]

39. ***World News Roundup, The*** began in 1938 during growing tension in pre-WWII Europe; first show to bring voices of correspondents stationed around the world together for live broadcast; longest-running news broadcast in history. [Am. Radio: Misc.]

92. BRUTALITY (See also CRUELTY, GENOCIDE, MUTILATION, RUTHLESSNESS, TYRANNY.)

1. **Amin, Idi (1925–)** brutal dictator of Uganda. [Afr. Hist.: *ODA*]

2. **Apache Indians** once fierce fighting tribe of American West. [Am. Hist.: *NCE*, 123]

3. ***Apocalypse Now*** U.S. Captain Wilard's journey into the Vietnamese jungle to assassinate murderous Colonel Kurz; 1979 film directed by Francis Ford Coppola based on Joseph Conrad's *Heart of Darkness* (1902). [Am. Film: *SJEPC*]

4. **bandersnatch** imaginary wild animal of great ferocity. [Br. Lit.: "Jabberwocky" in *Through the Looking-Glass*]

5. **berserkers** ancient Norse warriors; assumed attributes of bears in battle. [Norse Myth.: Leach, 137]

6. **Black Prince** angered by Limoges' resistance, massacred three hundred inhabitants (1370). [Eur. Hist.: Bishop, 75]

7. **Caracalla** Roman emperor (211–217) massacred many thousands. [Rom. Hist.: *EB* (1963) IV, 825]

8. **Cenci, Count** he delighted in making people suffer. [Br. Lit.: "The Cenci" in Magill I, 131–133]

9. *Clockwork Orange, A* in the future totalitarian state depicted in Anthony Burgess's novel and Stanley Kubrick's 1971 film, techniques used to modify an individual's immoral behavior rival the cruelty and brutality of the crimes themselves. [Lit. and Film: *SJEPC*]

10. **Comanche Indians** warlike tribe of American West. [Am. Hist.: *NCE*, 607]

11. **Cossacks** calvary soldiers in Czarist Russia noted for their brutality; in modern usage, a cruel, brutal group. [Russ. Hist.: *FOF, MOD*]

12. **Crommyonian sow** ravager of the Corinthian countryside. [Gk. Myth.: Benét, 237]

13. **Crown** a stevedore who deals with people by physical force. [Am. Lit.: *Porgy*, Magill I, 764–766]

14. **Drancy** concentration camp; France's largest Jewish deporation center. [Jew. Hist.: Wigoder, 161]

15. **Eichmann, Adolph (1906–1962)** Nazi SS officer; directed "Final Solution" in Europe. [Jew. Hist.: Wigoder, 167]

16. **Enlil** ordered wholesale destruction of humanity by flood. [Babylonian Myth.: *Gilgamesh*]

17. **Erymanthian boar** ravaged Arcadian countryside until capture by Hercules. [Gk. Myth.: Jobes, 523]

18. **Genghis Khan (1162–1227)** Mongol emperor noted for savagery in conquering Asia and Eastern Europe. [Hist. *FOF, MOD*]

19. **Gestapo** German secret police under Nazi regime. [Ger. History: *RHD*, 595]

20. *GoodFellas* Martin Scorcese's starkly realistic 1990 film based on a true story exposes the brutality of gangsterism by tracing a mobster's life. [Am. Fim: *SJEPC*]

21. **Grimes, Peter** fisherman suspected of ill-treating his apprentices. [Br. Opera: *Peter Grimes* in Osborne *Opera*, 240]

22. **Herod Antipas** presents John the Baptist's head to Salome. [N.T.: Mark 6:17–28]

23. **Himmler, Heinrich (1900–1945)** architect of the "Final Solution" to exterminate Jews. [Ger. Hist.: *Hitler*]

24. **Hitler, Adolf (1889–1945)** Nazi dictator; universal symbol of brutality and race hatred. [Ger. Hist.: *Hitler*]

25. **Huns** Mongolian invaders of western Europe until 453. [Eur. Hist.: Espy, 167]

26. **Jael** drove tent-peg through skull of Sisera. [O.T.: Judges 4:19–21]

27. *Killing Fields, The* 1984 film cataloging the brutal genocide in Cambodia under Pol Pot in the 1970s; a term for genocide. [Asian Hist.: *FOF, MOD*]

28. **King, Rodney (1965–)** African American beaten by police in Los Angeles in 1991; their subsequent acquittal led to riots in the city in 1992; made a famous plea two days after verdicts: "Can we all get along?". [Am. Hist.: *SJEPC*]

29. **Koch, Ilse** "Bitch of Buchenwald"; had inmates skinned for lampshades (WWII). [Ger. Hist.: Shirer, 1280]

30. **Kramer, Josef** "Beast of Belsen"; camp exterminator (WWII). [Ger. Hist.: Shirer, 878]

31. *Lord of the Flies* 1954 novel by William Golding is sobering account of band of schoolboys stranded on an island who become primitive and savage. [Br. Lit.: *OCCL*]

32. **Magua** a renegade Huron who scalps white men. [Am. Lit.: *The Pathfinder*, Magill I, 715–717]

33. **mares of Diomedes** lived on human flesh; their capture was Hercules' eighth labor. [Gk. and Roman Myth.: Hall, 149]

34. **Mengele, Dr. Joseph** Auschwitz concentration camp doctor; experimented on inmates (WWII). [Ger. Hist.: Wallechinsky, 83]

35. **Nazi** Jew-baiting, murderous Aryan supremacist under Hitler. [Ger. Hist.: Shirer]

36. **Nero** coarse, conceited, brutal emperor of Rome (37–68). [Polish Lit.: *Quo Vadis*, Magill I, 797–799]

37. **Papa Doc** nickname of Francois Duvalier (1907–1971), tyrannical president of Haiti, who terrorized his people with his security force, the Tontons Macoutes. [Caribbean Hist.: *ODA*]

38. **Procrustes** robber; stretches or amputates limbs of victims to fit his bed. [Class. Myth.: Zimmerman, 221]

39. **Punch and Judy** traditional British puppet show in which Punch and Judy brutalize one another, with Punch beating Judy to death. [Br. Culture: *ODA*]

40. **Reign of Terror** all roads led to the guillotine (1793–1794). [Fr. Hist.: *EB*, IX: 904]

41. **roller derby** full-contact aggressive skating by men and women alike; colorful personalities of competitors drew fans. [Am. Sports and Entertainment: *SJEPC*]

42. **S.S.** ruthless corps implemented Nazi atrocities. [Ger. Hist.: Brewer *Dictionary*]

43. **SAVAK** Iranian secret police. [Iranian History: *Facts* (1979), 125]

44. **spaghetti westerns** low-budget European films (mostly Italian) produced between 1961 and 1977 graphically depicting Wild West and its brutality; gave Clint Eastwood his early tough-guy roles. [Film: *SJEPC*]

45. **St. Evremonde, Marquis** ruthless aristocrat deliberately killed two people and ran over a child. [Br. Lit.: Dickens *A Tale of Two Cities*]

46. **Stalin, Josef (1879–1953)** brutal dictator of Soviet Union, responsible for the deaths of millions of his own people; a symbol of savage authoritarianism. [Russ. Hist.: *ODA*]

47. **Taras Bulba** savage yet strangely devoted Cossack leader. [Russ. Lit.: *Taras Bulba*, Walsh *Modern*, 77]

48. **Tartars** 13th-century rapacious hordes of Genghis Khan. [Medieval Hist.: Brewer *Dictionary*, 1064]

49. **tiger** aims at annihilating mankind. [Animal Symbolism: Mercatante, 55]

50. **Tse-Tung, Mao (1893–1976)** Chinese communist leader whose brutal tactics cost millions of lives. [Chinese Hist.: Misc.]

51. **Vandals** 5th-century sackers of Rome and its art. [Ital. Hist.: Espy, 168]

93. BUDDHISM (See also ENLIGHTENMENT, RELIGION.)

1. **arhat** one who is revered for attaining highest state of perfection. [Buddhist Rel.: Bowker]

2. **atman** the true self which underlies human appearance. [Buddhist Rel.: Bowker]

3. **bali** offering of grain or rice to gods and spirits. [Buddhist Rel.: Bowker]

4. **bodhi** the stages of the path to perfection. [Buddhist Rel.: Bowker]

5. **Bodhi Tree** tree under which Buddha gained enlightenment; also called Bo Tree. [Buddhist Rel.: Bowker]

6. **bodhisattva** someone who has taken the vow to become a Buddha for the sake of all sentient beings. [Buddhist Rel.: Bowker]

7. **dukkha** roughly translated as suffering; basis of Four Noble Truths of Buddha—the universality of suffering. [Buddhist Rel.: Bowker]

8. **Eightfold Path** necessary elements in the process toward enlightment and nirvana. [Buddhist Rel.: Bowker]

9. **enlightenment** the state of having attained insight, wisdom, truth, etc. [Buddhist Rel.: Bowker]

10. **Four Noble Truths** foundation of the Buddha's insight and teaching, explaining the existence of suffering and the means to being released from it. [Buddhist Rel.: Bowker]

11. **koan** fundamental practice in Zen training, challenging the pupil through a question which presents a paradox or puzzle. [Buddhist Rel.: Bowker]

12. **lama** honorary title in Tibetan Buddhism for spiritual teacher, especially those who have finished scholastic and yogic training. [Buddhist Rel.: Bowker]

13. **mandala** pictorial symbol of several rings representing the universe; found especially in Tibetan Buddhism. [Buddhist Rel.: Bowker]

14. **mudra** sign of power, through the body, usually the hands. [Buddhist Rel.: Bowker]

15. **nirvana** the realization that there is no self; therefore, realization of nonexistence of self and complete lack of attachment. [Buddhist Rel.: Bowker]

16. **samsara** cycle of birth and death as a consequence of action (karma). [Buddhist Rel.: Bowker]

17. **Shambala** semi-mythical Tibetan Buddhist kingdom; only Pure Land that exists on earth. [Buddhist Rel.: Bowker]

18. **t'ai chi** supremely important in Chinese philosophy and religion; produces two energies from which arise the five elements of all existence. [Buddhist Rel.: Bowker]

94. BULL

1. **Apis** bull of Memphis, created in Osiris' image. [Egypt. Myth.: Benét, 41]

2. **Buchis** black bull worshiped as chief city god. [Egypt. Rel.: Parrinder, 52]

3. **Cretan bull** sacred to Poseidon; sent to Minos. [Gk. Myth.: Kravitz, 68]

4. **Ferdinand** loves to sit quietly and smell flowers instead of being in the bullfights in Madrid; from Munro Leaf's picture book about remaining true to one's own desires, *The Story of Ferdinand the Bull* (1936). [Am. Children's Lit.: Jones]

5. **Minotaur** fabulous monster of Crete, half-bull, half-man. [Gk. Myth.: *EB*, VI: 922]

6. **Taurus** constellation of the zodiac symbolized by the bull. [Astrology: *EB*, IX: 844]

95. BULLYING

1. **Chowne, Parson Stoyle** terrorizes parish; kidnaps children. [Br. Lit.: *The Maid of Sker*, Walsh *Modern*, 94–95]

2. **Claypole, Noah** bully; becomes thief in Fagin's gang. [Br. Lit.: *Oliver Twist*]

3. **Curley** he picks on feeble-minded Lennie. [Am. Lit.: *Of Mice and Men*]

4. **Flashman, Harry** unconscionably impudent and overbearing coward. [Br. Lit.: *Flashman; Tom Brown's Schooldays*]

5. **Hector** street gang member (early 1600s). [Br. Hist.: Espy, 40]

6. **Kowalski, Stanley** crude humor, animal maleness. [Am. Lit.: *A Streetcar Named Desire*]

7. **Malfoy, Draco** character from J.K. Rowling's Harry Potter series for young readers (1997–2007); nasty bully at Hogwarts school who immediately takes a dislike to Harry and envies his power. [Br. Children's Lit.: Misc.]

8. **McTeague** forbidden to practice dentistry, he becomes mean and surly. [Am. Lit.: *McTeague*]

9. **Potter, Mr.** bullying character tries to destroy George Bailey in Frank Capra's *It's a Wonderful Life*. [Am. Film: *Misc.*]

96. BUREAUCRACY

1. **Brid'oison, Judge** jurist who loves red tape. [Fr. Lit.: *Marriage of Figaro*]

2. *Catch-22* concerned with the frustration of red-tape mechanisms. [Am. Lit.: *Catch-22*]

3. **Circumlocution Office, the** department of efficient bureaucratic evasiveness. [Br. Lit. *Little Dorrit*]

4. *Dead Souls* Gogol's masterpiece shows the absurdity of a government bureaucracy in its treatment of serfs. [Russ. Lit.: *EB*]

5. *Inspector General, The* drama highlighting foibles of petty officialdom. [Russ. Lit.: *The Inspector General*]

6. *M*A*S*H* bitter farce on bungling bureaucracy in a Korean Army hospital. [Am. Cinema and TV: Halliwell, 474–475]

7. **red tape** excessive formality; bureaucratic paperwork. [Am. and Br. Usage: Misc.]

8. **Secretary, the** repeatedly refuses permission to see the Consul. [Am. Opera: Menotti, *The Consul*, Westerman, 552–553]

9. *Trial, The* novel of individual accused of crime by impersonal bureaucracy. [Ger. Lit.: *The Trial*]

97. BURIAL ALIVE

1. **Antigone** condemned to be buried alive, she thwarts Creon's order by killing herself. [Gk. Lit.: *Antigone*]

2. **Fortunato** walled up in a catacomb by the man he had wronged. [Am. Lit.: Poe "The Cask of Amontillado"]

3. **Lafourcade, Victorine** found alive in her tomb by her rejected suitor. [Am. Lit.: Poe "The Premature Burial"]

4. **Sindbad** entombed, by custom, upon his wife's death, he manages to escape. [Arab. Lit.: *Arabian Nights*; Magill II, 50]

5. **Usher, Madeline** breaks out of vault in which she had been buried alive. [Am. Lit.: Poe "The Fall of the House of Usher"]

98. BURIAL GROUND

1. **Aceldama** potter's field; burial place for strangers. [N.T.: Matthew 27:6–10; Acts 1:18–19]

2. **Alloway graveyard** where Tam O'shanter saw witches dancing among opened coffins. [Br. Lit.: Burns *Tam O'shanter* in Benét, 985]

3. **Arlington National Cemetery** final resting place for America's war heroes. [Am. Hist.: Flexner, 95]

4. **Boot Hill** Tombstone, Arizona's graveyard, where gunfighters are buried. [Am. Hist.: Flexner, 178]

5. **Campo Santo** famous cemetery in Pisa, with Gothic arcades and Renaissance frescoes. [Ital. Hist.: *Collier's*, XV, 433]

6. **Castel Sant'Angelo** built in Rome by Hadrian as an imperial mausoleum. [Rom. Hist.: *Collier's*, XVI, 539]

7. **Catacombs of Saint Calixtus** in Rome, one of the largest of subterranean burial places, with eleven miles of galleries. [Ital. Hist.: *Collier's*, IV, 458]

8. **Escorial** former monastery in central Spain; mausoleum of Spanish sovreigns. [Span. Hist.: *NCE*, 890]

9. **Flanders Field** immortalized in poem; cemetery for WWI dead. [Eur. Hist.; Jameson, 176]

10. **Gettysburg** site of Civil War battle; cemetery for war dead. [Am. Culture: *EB*, IV: 515]

11. **God's Acre** Moravian graveyard in Winston-Salem, N.C., with 3000 identical marble markers. [Am. Hist.: *Collier's*, XIX, 471]

12. **Grant's Tomb** New York City burial place of General Ulysses S. Grant. [Am. Culture: *EB*, IV: 680]

13. **Great Pyramid of Cheops** enormous Egyptian royal tomb. [World Hist.: Wallechinsky, 255]

14. **Holy Sepulcher** Jerusalem cave where body of Jesus is said to have lain. [Christ. Tradition: Brewer *Dictionary*, 814]

15. **Machpelah** cave where Abraham, Sarah, Isaac, Jacob are buried. [O.T.: Genesis 23:19, 25:9, 49:30, 50:13]

16. **potter's field** burial ground purchased with Judas's betrayal money. [N.T.: Matthew 27:6–8]

17. **Stoke Poges** village whose churchyard is thought to be the scene of Gray's "Elegy." [Br. Lit.: Benét, 966]

18. **Taj Mahal** fabulous tomb built by Shah Jahan for wife. [Ind. Hist.: Wallechinsky, 317]

19. **Tomb of Mausolus** Queen Artemisia's spectacular memorial to husband. [World Hist.: Wallechinsky, 256]

20. **Tomb of the Unknowns** in Arlington National Cemetery; commemorates nameless war dead. [Am. Hist.: Brewer *Dictionary*, 1118]

21. **Westminster Abbey** abbey filled with tombs and memorials of famous British subjects. [Br. Hist.: *EB*, X: 632–633]

99. BUSINESS

1. **bottom line** the final line on a profit and loss statement; also a catchword for the central point of an issue. [Business: Misc.]

2. **Buffett, Warren (1930–)** legendary American investor and philanthropist; heads Berkshire Hathaway, one of the most successful stocks in U.S. history. [Business: Misc.]

3. **Covey, Stephen (1932–)** self-help consultant rose to prominence in 1980s-90s corporate America with his common-sense philosophy as found in *The 7 Habits of Highly Effective People* (1989). [Am. Business: *SJEPC*]

4. *Dilbert* comic strip portrays a dysfunctional American company with clueless managers, unmotivated employees, dehumanizing corporate policies, and unproductive meetings. [Am. Comics: *SJEPC*]

5. **Dot-com** an Internet-based business; from the ".com" designation in a company's email and web site addresses. [Business: Misc.]

6. **Fed** nickname of the Federal Reserve, the government body that determines economic policy in the U.S. [Am. Hist.: *EB*]

7. *Fortune* highly respected, biweekly business magazine established in 1930 annually ranks the 500 top performing American companies. [Am. Jour.: *SJEPC*]

8. **Fortune 500** annual ranking of America's 500 largest corporations by revenue, published by *Fortune* magazine since 1955. [Am. Business and Jour.: *SJEPC*]

9. **Gates, Bill (1955–)** American billionaire and founder of Microsoft; a symbol for success in technology and business. [Business: Misc.]

10. **irrational exuberance** term used by Alan Greenspan of the Federal Reserve to describe overly optimistic investors (1996). [Business: Misc.]

11. *Wall Street Journal, The* began as a handwritten page of business news in 1882; a century later had become a national newspaper—conservative in tone and broad in scope—and had won more than 30 Pulitzer Prizes. [Am. Jour.: *SJEPC*]

100. BUTLER (See also SERVANT.)

1. **Balderstone, Caleb** archetypal faithful servant of the Ravenswoods. [Br. Lit.: *Bride of Lammermoor*]

2. **Bunter** Lord Peter Wimsey's foil and jack-of-all-trades. [Br. Lit. *The Nine Tailors*]

3. **Crichton** resourceful servant proves more than equal to his employers when household is marooned. [Br. Lit. *The Admirable Crichton*]

4. **Davy** Justice Shallow's varlet; assumes identity of master. [Br. Lit. *Henry IV*]

5. **Face** Lovewit's house servant; connives to make profit by alchemy. [Br. Lit. *The Alchemist*]

6. **French, Mr.** gentleman's gentleman for architect and motherless children. [TV: "Family Affair" in Terrace, I, 254]

7. **Godfrey** when the inpecunious socialite is hired as a butler, he and his mistress fall in love. [Am. Cinema: *My Man Godfrey* in Halliwell.]

8. **Hudson, Mr.** nostalgic, punctilious master of "downstairs." [Br. TV: *Upstairs, Downstairs*]

9. **Jeeves** manservant who frequently rescues his master. [Br. Lit.: novels of P.G. Wodehouse; Espy, 337]

10. **Lurch** Addams's zombielike, extremely tall butler. [TV: "The Addams Family" in Terrace, I, 29]

11. **Passepartout** bungling foil to the punctilious Fogg. [Fr. Lit.: *Around the World in Eighty Days*]

101. BUXOMNESS (See also SEX SYMBOL.)

1. **Anderson, Pamela (1967–)** well-endowed actress played "Tool Time girl" on *Home Improvement* and scantily clad lifeguard on *Baywatch*. [Am. TV: *SJEPC*]

2. **Barbie doll** popular, full-figured, plastic fashion doll with measurements equivalent to 39–18–33 in real life. [Am. Culture: *SJEPC*]

3. **Daisy Mae** Dogpatch beauty with enviable figure. [Comics: "Li'l Abner" in Horn, 450]

4. **Little Annie Fanny** buxom version of Little Orphan Annie. [Comics: *Playboy*, Horn, 442]

5. **Mansfield, Jayne (1933–1967)** well-documented hourglass figure and obsession with pink were part of her self-promotion as a sex symbol. [Am. Entertainment: *SJEPC*]

6. **Monroe, Marilyn (1926–1962)** voluptuous blonde screen star became perhaps the most famous sex symbol and icon of beauty in modern times. [Am. Film: *SJEPC*]

7. **Morpho** epithet of Aphrodite, meaning "shapely." [Gk. Myth.: Zimmerman, 25]

8. **Russell, Jane (1921–)** actress whose statuesque figure drew the attention of Howard Hughes, who made her a star; censors decried the amount of her cleavage displayed in 1941 film *The Outlaw*. [Am. Film: *SJEPC*]

9. **Turner, Lana (1920–1995)** popular sexy blonde actress nicknamed the "Sweater Girl" because of her full figure. [Am. Film: *SJEPC*]

10. **West, Mae (1893–1980)** her suggestive dialogue, vampy acting style, and voluptuous figure made her a legend; many of her quips have become famous. [Am. Film: Halliwell, 759–760]

11. **Wife of Bath** well-endowed, lusty teller of tales. [Br. Lit.: *Canterbury Tales*]

C

102. CANNIBALISM

1. *Alive* account of cannibalism among air crash survivors. [Am. Lit.: *Alive*]

2. **Antiphates** chieftain of Laestrygones, man-eating giants of Italy. [Gk. Lit.: *Odyssey*; Rom. Lit.: *Metamorphoses*]

3. **Beane, Sawney** highwayman who fed his gang on victims' flesh. [Br. Culture: Misc.]

4. **black giants** kill, roast, and devour Sindbad's companions. [Arab. Lit.: *Arabian Nights* in Magill II, 50]

5. **Caliban** his name is anagram of cannibal. [Br. Lit.: *The Tempest*]

6. **Clymenus** eats child who is product of incestuous union with daughter Harpalyce. [Gk. Myth.: Howe, 114]

7. **Cronos** swallowed his children at birth; they lived again when he was forced by Zeus to disgorge them. [Gk. Myth.: *EB* (1963) VI, 747]

8. **Dahmer, Jeffrey (1960–1994)** notorious serial killer murdered, then molested and cannibalized, 17 young men. [Am. Hist.: *SJEPC*]

9. **Donner Party** of 89 emigrants to California, 47 survive by eating others (1846–1847). [Am. Hist.: *EB*, III: 623]

10. **Hansel and Gretel** fattened up for child-eating witch. [Ger. Fairy Tale: Grimm, 56]

11. **Laestrygones** man-eating giants encountered by Odysseus. [Gk. Lit.: *Odyssey*]

12. **Lamia** female spirit in serpent form; devours children. [Gk. Myth.: Zimmerman, 146; Br. Lit.: "Lamia" in Benét, 563]

13. **Lycaon** turned to wolf for cannibalistic activities; whence, *lycanthropy* [Gk. Myth.: Espy, 37]

14. **"Modest Proposal, A"** Swift's satire suggesting that children of the poor be used as food for the rich (1729). [Br. Lit.: "A Modest Proposal" in Harvey, 793]

15. *Narrative of Arthur Gordon Pym* for four days, survivors feed on Parker's flesh. [Am. Lit.: Poe, "The Narrative of Arthur Gordon Pym" in Magill I, 640–643]

16. **Pelops** cut up and served as meal to gods. [Gk. Myth.: Brewer *Dictionary*, 817]

17. *Silence of the Lambs* award-winning 1991 film based on 1988 novel by Thomas Harris; portrays female FBI Academy student

drawn into battle of wits with cunning imprisoned serial killer and cannibal Dr. Hannibal Lecter as she tries to work with him to thwart another killer. [Am. Film: *SJEPC*]

18. **Tereus** wife Procne murders son Itys and serves him to Terseus. [Gk. Myth.: Howe, 144]

19. **Thyestean banquet** banquet where Atreus serves Thyestes' sons to him as food. [Gk. Myth.: Brewer *Dictionary*, 1081]

20. **Ugolino** when his children die of starvation in prison, he devours them. [Ital. Poetry: *Inferno*]

103. CARELESSNESS (See also FORGETFULNESS, IRRESPONSIBILITY, LAZINESS.)

1. **Little Bo-peep** lost her sheep; found them tailless. [Nurs. Rhyme: Baring-Gould, 93]

2. **Little Boy Blue** sleeps while the sheep's in the corn. [Nurs. Rhyme: Baring-Gould, 46]

3. **Locket, Lucy** misplaced her pocket. [Nurs. Rhyme: *Mother Goose*, 23]

4. **Prism, Miss** nursemaid who misplaces manuscript and infant in railroad station. [Br. Lit.: *The Importance of Being Earnest*]

5. **Theseus** neglects to hoist the sail to signal his safety to his father Aegeus, who despairingly throws himself into the sea. [Gk. Myth.: Brewer *Dictionary*, 12]

104. CARTOON

1. **Blanc, Mel (1908–1989)** "Man of a Thousand Voices" created and performed distinct voices of now-classic animated cartoon characters like Bugs Bunny. [Am. Entertainment: *SJEPC*]

2. **Felix the Cat** popular, personable cat of the silent movie era, and later TV, created by Otto Messmer and Pat Sullivan starred in approximately 150 short animated cartoons in the 1920s. [Am. Film: *SJEPC*]

3. **Gertie the Dinosaur** first substantial animated cartoon (1919). [Am. Hist.: Van Doren, 362]

4. **Groening, Matt (1954–)** creator of animated TV comedy series *The Simpsons* (Fox, 1989–) and *Futurama* (Fox, 1999–2003; Comedy Central, 2008–). [Am. TV: *SJEPC*]

5. **Hanna-Barbera** successful cartoon duo William Hanna and Joseph Barbera created some of the most memorable cartoons of the 20th century, including *The Flintstones, The Jetsons,* and *Huckleberry Hound.* [Am. Comics: *EB*]

6. **Popeye** comic-strip and cartoon sailor who owes his incredible muscle-power to a diet of canned spinach [Am. Comics: *SJEPC*]

7. **Road Runner** outran and outwitted the ill-fated Wylie E. Coyote and his inexhaustible supply of ineffectual Acme products. [Am. TV: *SJEPC*]

8. *Rocky and Bullwinkle* 1959 to 1964 TV show with serial story-lines; satire and wit appealed to adults and goofiness drew young audiences; influenced later edgy cartoon shows. [Am. TV: *SJEPC*]

9. *Simpsons, The* begun in 1989; Matt Groening's animated family sitcom mixed a wickedly satirical view of world issues with goofy humor; lovable bright-yellow characters muddle through the complexities of modern life. [Am. TV: *SJEPC*]

10. *South Park* premiered in 1997; animators Trey Parker and Matt Stone depict four male third-graders whose profanities and mis-behavior belie the supposed innocence of children while plot lines poke fun at popular culture with dead-on wit. [Am. TV: *SJEPC*]

11. **SpongeBob SquarePants** protagonist of animated TV show (pre-miered in 1999); living on the floor of the Pacific Ocean, sea sponge lives in city modeled after Seattle, works as a fry cook, and gets involved in quirky misadventures despite his good inten-tions. [Am. TV: Misc.]

12. *Steamboat Willie* 1928 animated Disney cartoon that launched Mickey Mouse's career was first animated film with sound. [Am. Film: *SJEPC*]

13. *Teenage Mutant Ninja Turtles* orginally a comic book; 1980s and 1990s TV cartoon show about mutated pet turtles with names of famous Renaissance artists and superhero powers. [Am. Comics and TV: *SJEPC*]

14. **Thurber, James (1894–1961)** through cartoon sketches and hu-morous prose, much for the *New Yorker* magazine, he depicted hu-mans' struggles and lack of practical wisdom. [Am. Lit.: *SJEPC*]

15. **Tom and Jerry** immortal cat and mouse cartoon characters, creat-ed by William Hanna and Joseph Barbera for MGM in the 1930s, still battling after 70 years. [Am. Comics: *EB*]

16. **Tweety Pie and Sylvester** Academy Award-winning cartoon duo with voices supplied by Mel Blanc; dimwitted Sylvester cat at-tempts unsuccessfully to catch big-eyed, baby-voiced Tweety bird in animated stories. [Am. TV: *SJEPC*]

105. CASTAWAY (See also SHIPWRECK.)

1. **Arden, Enoch** shipwrecked sailor; lost for eleven years. [Br. Lit.: "Enoch Arden" in Benét, 316]

2. **Bligh, Captain** commander of H.M.S. *Bounty* who was cast adrift by mutinous crew. [Am. Lit.: *Mutiny on the Bounty*]

3. **Byam, Roger** crew member of the *Bounty* cast onto South Sea is-land. [Am. Lit.: *Mutiny on the Bounty*]

4. *Cast Away* 2000 film featuring Tom Hanks as a workaholic who gets stranded on a deserted island for four years. [Am. Film: *Cast Away*]

5. **Crichton** resourceful butler who leads master and his family through difficulties on deserted island. [Br. Lit.: *Admirable Crichton*]

6. **Crusoe, Robinson** shipwreck victim who lives on desert island with savage he names Friday. [Br. Lit.: *Robinson Crusoe*]

7. **Gilligan's Island** comedy about a party shipwrecked on a South Pacific island. [TV: Terrace, I, 312–313]

8. **Gunn, Ben** marooned pirate, helps secure treasure hidden on island. [Br. Lit.: *Treasure Island*]

9. *Lost in Space* family is shipwrecked in space. [TV: Terrace, II, 38–39]

10. **Selkirk, Alexander** real-life prototype of *Robinson Crusoe* [Br. Hist.: *EB*, IX: 45]

11. **Smith, Cyrus** knowledgeable engineer makes life bearable for castaway party on deserted island. [Fr. Lit.: *Mysterious Island*]

12. *Swiss Family Robinson* family shipwrecked on a deserted island. [Br. Lit.: *Swiss Family Robinson*]

106. CASTRATION

1. **Abelard, Peter** castrated by irate father of lover, Hèloise. [Fr. Lit.: *Hèloise and Abelard*]

2. **Barnes, Jake** castrated journalist whom Brett Ashley loves. [Am. Lit.: *The Sun Also Rises*]

3. **Cybele** hermaphroditic goddess honored orgiastically, usually by emasculation. [Phrygian Myth.: Parrinder, 68]

107. CAT

1. **Dick Whittington's cat** sent to Morocco, its purchase by the king gives the future Lord Mayor his stake to success. [Br. Legend: Benét, 1088]

2. **Felix** lonely star-crossed fantasist, fights against fate in strange worlds. [Comics: "Felix the Cat" in Horn, 246]

3. **Garfield** lazy gourmand, impudent to its master. [Amer. Comics: *Garfield*]

4. **Grizabella** character in Andrew Lloyd Webber's long-running musical *Cats* (1981) who sings of her downfall from days of glory, now faded. [Musical: *SJEPC*]

5. **Heathcliff** aggressive cat, hoodwinks fishmongers and upsets milkmen. [Amer. Comics: *Heathcliff*]

6. **Krazy Kat** perennially involved in conflict with his friend Ignatz the mouse. [Comics: Horn, 436]

7. **Macavity** mysterious feline, "Napoleon of crime." [Br. Lit.: T. S. Eliot *Old Possum's Book of Practical Cats* in Drabble, 714]

8. **Mehitabel** unladylike cat; its motto, "toujours gai." [Am. Lit.: *archy and mehitabel* in Hart, 525]

9. **Old Deuteronomy** elderly cat whose comfort is seen to by the entire village. [Br. Lit.: T. S. Eliot *Old Possum's Book of Practical Cats* in Drabble, 714]

10. **Pluto** pet of a brutal alcoholic who mutilates and hangs it, with dire consequences to himself. [Am. Lit.: Poe, "The Black Cat"]

11. **Puss in Boots** cleverly secures a fortune for its penniless master. [Fr. Fairy Tale: "Puss in Boots" in Benét, 829]

12. **Sylvester** part of Academy Award-winning cartoon duo with voices supplied by Mel Blanc; dimwitted Sylvester cat attempts unsuccessfully to catch big-eyed, baby-voiced Tweety bird in animated stories. [Am. TV: *SJEPC*]

13. **Tobermory** taught to speak fluently, it proves insolent and catty. [Br. Lit.: *The Short Stories of Saki* in Magill IV, 1148]

108. CELEBRITY

1. **Capote, Truman (1924–1984)** sharply witty, social star on the American literary scene wrote such classics as *Breakfast at Tiffany's* (1958) and *In Cold Blood* (1965). [Am. Lit.: *SJEPC*; Henderson, 503–4]

2. **Diana, Princess of Wales (1961–1997)** intense media exposure fueled the fame of the idolized "People's Princess" during her life and even after her tragic death. [Br. Hist. *SJEPC*]

3. **Dionne Quintuplets** born in 1934, French-Canadian identical quintuplet sisters Annette, Cecile, Emilie, Marie, and Yvonne received international attention and were publicly exploited throughout their childhood. [Can. Hist.: *SJEPC*]

4. **Hirschfeld, Al (1903–2003)** American artist best known for his caricatures of celebrities that appeared in the*New York Times*, and for hiding the name of his daughter, Nina, in each one. [Am. Art: *EB*]

5. **Hollywood** home of the American movie and entertainment industry, and of film celebrities; symbol of ambition to succeed in entertainment field. [Am. Culture: Misc.]

6. **Iacocca, Lee (1924–)** auto executive who was mastermind behind the Ford Mustang; at Chrysler, he made himself the image of the company and attained celebrity status as its spokesman. [Am. Business: *SJEPC*]

7. **Jordan, Michael (1963–)** one of highest paid and most acclaimed players in NBA; became not only sports legend but icon whose

name made Nike Air Jordan shoe an astonishing sports marketing success; gained celebrity status even outside sports world. [Am. Sports: *SJEPC*]

8. *People* image-laden magazine featuring details about celebrities and stories about unusual events in the lives of ordinary people. [Am. Jour.: *SJEPC*]

9. *Photoplay* early movie fan magazine featuring celebrity photos and gossip. [Am. Jour.: *SJEPC*]

10. **Studio 54** New York nightclub of 1970s and 1980s known for the lewd behavior of its clientele and its biased policy of admission to celebrities and others deemed worthy. [Am. Pop. Culture: *SJEPC*]

11. *This Is Your Life* radio show in the 1940s, TV show in the 1950s hosted by Ralph Edwards; documentary-like biographies of notables with testimontials by people who knew them. [Am. TV: *SJEPC*]

12. **Warhol, Andy (1928–1987)** renowned Pop artist who used everday objects— most notably, Campbell soup cans—as inspiration; his outrageous behavior and pursuit of celebrity oftentimes overshadowed his work as an artist. [Am. Art: *SJEPC*]

Cemetery (See BURIAL GROUND.)

109. CENSORSHIP

1. **blue laws** restrict personal action to improve community morality. [Am. Hist.: Hart, 87]

2. **Boston** arbiter of Puritanical taste as reflected in phrase "banned in Boston." [Am. Usage: Misc.]

3. **Bowdler, Thomas (1754–1825)** expurgated Shakespeare and Gibbon for family editions. [Br. Hist.: Wallechinsky, 164]

4. **Caldwell, Erskine (1903–1987)** often at the forefront of writers' First Amendment rights fights due to censorship of his sexually explicit novels. [Am. Lit.: *SJEPC*]

5. **Carlin, George (1937–2008)** stand-up comic's "Seven Words You Can Never Use on Television" routine was cause for his arrest in 1972 and tested the First Amendment in Supreme Court case concerning the broadcasting of profanity. [Am. Entertainment: *SJEPC*]

6. *Catcher in the Rye* controversial coming-of-age novel by J. D. Salinger has appeared on lists of banned books since its publication in 1951. [Am. Lit.: *SJEPC*; Harris *Characters*, 347–48]

7. **Comstock, Anthony (1844–1915)** in *comstockery*, immortalized advocated of blue-nosed censorship [Am. Hist.: Espy, 135]

8. *Fahrenheit 451* describes a future America in which books are prohibited and burned. [Am. Lit.: Bradbury *Fahrenheit 451* in Weiss, 289]

9.   **Hays, Will (1879–1954)** clean-minded arbiter of 1930s Hollywood tastes. [Am. Cinema: Griffith, 182]

10. **"Howl"** foremost Beat poem (1955) by Allen Ginsberg contained shocking language, gritty images, and vivid sexual references, leading to censorship and an obscenity trial in 1957. [Am. Lit.: Henderson, 38; *SJEPC*]

11. **imprimatur** license given by Roman Catholic Church to publish a book. [Christian Hist.: Misc.]

12. **Index Librorum Prohibitorum** list of forbidden books compiled by Roman Catholic Church. [Christian Hist.: *NCE*, 1323]

13. **Miller, Henry (1891–1980)** his explicit novels were often censored in the United States and United Kingdom. [Am. Lit.: *SJEPC*]

14. *Naked Lunch* violent, profane stream-of-consciousness1959 novel by William S. Burroughs subject of 1965 censorship trial. [Am. Lit.: *SJEPC*; Henderson, 37]

15. **nihil obstat** Roman Catholic Church's inscription in books denoting no objection to literary content. [Christian Hist.: Misc.]

16. **Russell, Jane (1921–)** actress whose statuesque figure led to her discovery by Howard Hughes; censors decried the amount of her cleavage displayed in 1941 film *The Outlaw*. [Am. Film: *SJEPC*]

17. **Smothers Brothers, The [Tom Smothers (1937–) and Dick Smothers (1938–)]** musical duo who hosted influential comic variety TV show in late 1960s; their choice of anti-establishment satire and veiled references to sex and drugs brought confrontations with the network and eventual cancellation of the show. [Am. TV: *SJEPC*]

18. *Tropic of Cancer* novel noted for its sexual frankness and use of obscenity, long banned in the U.S. [Am. Lit.: Henry Miller *Tropic of Cancer*]

19. *Ulysses* Joyce novel long banned in U.S. for its sexual frankness. [Irish Lit.: Benét, 1037]

20. **Unigenitus** papal bull condemning Quesnel's Jansenist book (1713). [Christian Hist.: Brewer *Dictionary*, 1115]

110. CHAMPION

1.   **Ali, Muhammad (1942–)** three-time heavyweight champion of the world [Am. Sports: *WB2*]

2.   **Connors, Jimmy (1952–)** International Tennis Hall of Famer won eight Grand Slam singles championships and ranked number one in the world several times in his career. [Am. Sports: *SJEPC*]

3.   **Dream Team** greatest U.S. Olympic basketball team in history won gold medal in 1992, boasted talents of top NBA players like Magic Johnson, Larry Bird, and Michael Jordan. [Am. Sports: *SJEPC*]

4. **Duran, Roberto (1951–)** Panamanian boxing champion won world titles in lightweight, welterweight, junior middleweight, middleweight, and super middleweight divisions; nicknamed "Manos de Piedra" (Hands of Stone). [Am. Sports: *SJEPC*]

5. **Evert, Chris (1954–)** popular, disciplined tennis champion boasts the best singles record in the game (.900), with 18 Grand Slam titles (7 French Open, 6 U.S. Open, 3 Wimbledon, 2 Australian Open). [Am. Sports: *SJEPC*]

6. **Fischer, Bobby (1943–2008)** American who defeated Soviet Boris Spassky in World Chess Championship at height of Cold War in 1972; considered greatest chess player of all times; played and again defeated Spassky in rematch 20 years later. [Am. Hist.: *SJEPC*]

7. **Foreman, George (1949–)** at age 45 became oldest boxer to win heavyweight championship (1994), regaining title he held in 1973. [Am. Sports: *SJEPC*]

8. **Foyt, A. J. (1935–)** aggressive race-car driver known as "Supertex" won Indianapolis 500 four times, the first driver ever to do so. [Am. Sports: *SJEPC*]

9. **Gibson, Althea (1927–2003)** trailblazing African-American tennis champion won four grand slam tournaments in the 1950s; inducted into Tennis Hall of Fame in 1971. [Am. Sports: *SJEPC*]

10. **Joyner-Kersee, Jackie (1962–)** African-American athlete who won six Olympic medals in the heptathlon and long jump; named Greatest Female Athlete of the 20th Century. [Am. Sports: *BBAAL1*]

11. **Louis, Joe (1914–1981)** famous African-American boxer, known as the "Brown Bomber"; heavyweight champion of the world. [Am. Sports: *FOF, MOD*]

12. **Muldowney, Shirley (1940–)** "First Lady of Drag Racing" won three National Hot Rod Association and one American Hot Rod Association world championships. [Am. Sports: *SJEPC*; Misc.]

13. **Navratilova, Martina (1956–)** Czech-born powerful tennis player; winner of an unprecedented number of singles titles. [Am. Sports: *SJEPC*]

14. **Nicklaus, Jack (1940–)** eminently successful golfer; record-breaking winner of twenty major championships. [Am. Sports: *SJEPC*]

15. **Woods, Tiger (1975–)** first person of color and youngest person to win the Masters (1997, at age 21); amazingly talented golf pro; has been called the best ever to play the game by some. [Am. Sports: *SJEPC*]

111. CHANCE (See also FATE.)

1. **Bridoison, Taiel de** judge who casts dice to decide cases. [Fr. Lit.: *Pantagruel*]

2. **Fata Morgana** lake-dwelling sorceress and personification of chance. [Ital. Lit.: *Orlando Inammorato*]

3. **Fortuna** goddess of chance. [Rom. Myth.: Kravitz, 58]

4. **Jimmy the Greek** renowned American oddsmaker. [Am. Culture: Wallechinsky, 468]

5. **Russian roulette** suicidal gamble involving a six-shooter, loaded with one bullet. [Folklore: Payton, 590]

6. **Sors** god of chance. [Rom. Myth.: Espy, 42–43]

7. **Three Princes of Serendip** always make discoveries by accident. [Br. Lit.: *Three Princes of Serendip*]

8. **Urim and Thummin** oracular gems used for casting lots, set in Aaron's breastplate. [O.T.: Exodus 28:30; Leviticus 8:8]

Charity (See GENEROSITY.)

Charm (See PROTECTION.)

112. CHASTITY (See also MODESTY, PURITY, VIRGINITY.)

1. **Agnes, Saint** virgin saint and martyr. [Christian Hagiog.: Brewster, 76]

2. **Artemis (Rom. Diana)** moon goddess; virgin huntress. [Gk. Myth.: Kravitz, 36]

3. **Bona Dea** goddess; so chaste no one but husband sees her after marriage. [Rom. Myth.: Zimmerman, 43]

4. **Britomart** embodiment of purity. [Br. Lit.: *Faerie Queene*]

5. **Claudia** proves innocence by rescuing goddess's ship. [Rom. Myth.: Hall, 70]

6. **Cunegunda** proves innocence by walking unharmed on hot ploughshares. [Christian Hagiog.: Hall, 86]

7. **garden, enclosed** wherein grow the red roses of chastity. [Christian Symbolism: *De Virginibus*, Appleton, 41]

8. **Gawain, Sir** remained chaste despite the temptations offered him each night by his hostess. [Br. Lit.: *Sir Gawain and the Green Knight* in Benét, 934]

9. **Joseph** resisted the advances of Potiphar's wife. [O.T.: Genesis 39]

10. **lapis lazuli** emblem of sexual purity. [Gem Symbolism: Kunz, 370]

11. **Lygia** foreign princess remains chaste despite Roman orgies. [Polish Lit.: *Quo Vadis*, Magill I, 797–799]

12. **mirror of Alasnam** by clearness or opacity shows woman's purity. [Arab. Lit.: *Arabian Nights*, "The Tale of Zayn Alasnam"]

13. **orange blossoms** symbolic of chastity when used in wedding ceremonies. [Flower Symbolism: *Flora Symbolica*, 176]

14. **phoenix** in Middle Ages, attribute of chastity personified. [Art: Hall, 246]

15. **sapphire** emblem of sexual purity. [Gem Symbolism: Kunz, 370]

16. **tortoise** symbol of sexual purity. [Animal Symbolism: Mercatante, 21]

17. **unicorn** capturable only by virgins; thus, a test of chastity. [Christian Symbolism: Appleton, 105]

18. **Venus Verticordia** Venus invoked to make women pure once more. [Rom. Myth.: Brewer *Dictionary*, 1126]

113. CHAUVINISM (See also BIGOTRY, PATRIOTISM.)

1. **Chauvin, Nicolas** soldier who passionately admired Napoleon; whence, ultranationalism. [Fr. Hist.: *NCE*, 518]

2. **Helmer, Torvald** treats wife Nora as an inferior being. [Nor. Lit.: *A Doll's House*]

3. **Jingo** legendary second-century empress of Japan, victorious invader of Korea and hence the conjectural eponym of jingoism. [Jap. Hist.: *EB* (1963) XIII, 69]

4. **Jingoes** nickname of 19th-century English pro-war party. [Br. Hist.: *EB* (1963) XIII, 69]

5. **male chauvinist pig** denigrating designation for a man who treats women as inferiors. [Am. Pop. Culture: Misc.]

6. **Riggs, Bobby (1918–1995)** spectacular tennis player known mostly for his chauvinistic "Battle of the Sexes" match with victorious Billie Jean King in 1973. [Am. Sports: *SJEPC*]

Cheerfulness (See GAIETY, GOODNATUREDNESS, JOVIALITY, OPTIMISM.)

114. CHILDBIRTH

1. **Artemis (Rom. Diana)** goddess of childbirth. [Gk. Myth.: Kravitz, 59]

2. **Asclepius** saved by his father Apollo from the body of pregnant Coronis when Apollo slays her for infidelity. [Gk. Myth.: Benét, 57]

3. **Athena** spang from the head of Zeus when Hephaestus split it open with an axe. [Gk. Myth.: Benét, 60]

4. **Auge** Arcadian goddess of childbirth. [Arcadian Myth.: Kravitz, 59]

5. **Carmenta** one of Camenae; protectress of women in confinement. [Rom. Rel.: Zimmerman, 50]

6. **Dionysus** unborn god is saved from his dead mother and sewn into Zeus's thigh, from which he is later born. [Gk. Myth.: Benét, 273]

7. **dittany** symbol of childbirth. [Herb Symbolism: *Flora Symbolica*, 173]

8. **Egeria** goddess of childbirth; protectress of the unborn. [Rom. Myth.: Avery, 425–426]

9. **Eileithyia** ancient Greek goddess of childbirth. [Gk. Myth.: Zimmerman, 92]

10. **Hera (Rom. Juno)** goddess of childbirth. [Gk. Myth.: Kravitz, 59]

11. **Lilith** demon; dangerous to women in childbirth. [Jew. Trad.: Benét, 586]

12. **Lucina** goddess of childbirth. [Rom. Myth.: Kravitz, 59]

13. **Mater Matuta** goddess of childbirth. [Rom. Myth.: Howe, 160]

14. **Parca** ancient Greek goddess of childbirth. [Gk. Myth.: Kravitz, 59]

15. **stork** said to deliver babies to new parents in modern folklore. [Symbolism: *CEOS&S*]

16. **test-tube baby** Louise Brown; first successful fertilization outside the body (1978). [Br. Hist.: *Facts* (1978), 596–597]

17. **Themis** goddess of childbirth. [Gk. Myth.: Kravitz, 53]

Childlessness (See BARRENNESS.)

115. CHILDREN

1. **bad seed** play about an evil child; also a term used to describe a disturbingly cruel child. [Am. Lit.: Maxwell Anderson *The Bad Seed*]

2. **Barbie doll** popular plastic dress-up doll made first appearance in 1959; extremely shapely and feminine. [Am. Hist.: Sann, 179; *SJEPC*]

3. *Barney and Friends* big, friendly talking purple dinosaur introduced on PBS in 1992 along with sidekick Baby Bop and diverse group of children. [Am. TV: *SJEPC*]

4. **baseball cards** bubble gum cards traded by young fans in early- to mid-20th century has become serious collectible business for adults. [Am. Culture: *SJEPC*]

5. **Bazooka Joe** blonde boy with eye patch featured in comics accompanying every piece of Bazooka bubble gum; debuted in 1953. [Am. Culture: *SJEPC*]

6. **Beanie Babies** small plush beanbag toys created by the Ty Corporation caused frenzy among kids and collectors in the 1990s. [Am. Culture: *SJEPC*]

7. **Cabbage Patch Kids** children and parents went wild in the 1980s collecting homely, soft-bodied dolls, each with its unique birth certificate and adoption papers. [Am. Culture: *SJEPC*]

8. *Captain Kangaroo* children's TV show, starring Bob Keeshan as the kindly host, ran from 1955–1975. [Am. TV: *FOF, MOD*]

9. *Child's Garden of Verses* R. L. Stevenson's famous collection of charming poems for children about the experiences and sensations of the early years of life. [Scot. Children's Lit.: *OCCL*]

10. **Disney, Walt (1901–1966)** famous producer of animated and live-action films beginning in the 1920s; he produced scores of TV shows and films that became famous—*Mickey Mouse Club, Davy Crockett, Mary Poppins, Fantasia* are just a few; created commercially successful versions of countless classics of varying quality and fidelity to their sources. [Am. Film and TV: *OCCL*]

11. **erector sets** construction toy made of metal nuts, bolts, gears, girders, and other parts introduced by A. C. Gilbert in 1913 allowed children to build their own skyscrapers, trucks, bridges, and more; popular throughout 20th century. [Am. Hist.: *SJEPC*]

12. **Fisher-Price toys** American toy manufacturer established in 1931 best known for sturdy, inexpensive play toys that stimulate the imaginations of infants and preschoolers, from Little People to educational software. [Am. Business: *SJEPC*]

13. **GI Joe** first plastic action figure for boys, outfitted to resemble World War II combat soldier, debuted in 1964. [Am. Hist.: *SJEPC*]

14. **"Howdy Doody"** children's TV show created by Buffalo Bob Smith and featuring puppets Howdy Doody and Clarabell the clown. [Am. TV: *FOF, MOD*]

15. *Kukla, Fran, and Ollie* popular puppets on unscripted genial children's TV show: Fran visited with mild-mannered dragon Ollie and spirited bald man Kukla; eventually drew audiences of all ages. [Am. TV: *SJEPC*]

16. **olive branches** humorous appellation for children. [O.T.: Psalms 128:3]

17. **Pancras, Saint** boy saint, patron of young boys. [Christian Hagiog.: Brewer *Dictionary*, 799]

18. **Peter Pan** determined always to remain a little boy. [Br. Lit.: J.M. Barrie *Peter Pan*]

19. **Quiz Kids** popular radio quiz show of the 1940s with intelligent children answering questions. [Am. Pop. Culture: *FOF, MOD*]

20. *Sesame Street* began in 1968; winner of more than 100 awards; Jim Henson's muppets and actors in an urban neighborhood teach children concepts through song, repetition, and entertaining

images and sounds; influenced children's TV and teaching styles from that point on. [Am. TV: *SJEPC*]

21. **snaps, snails, and puppy-dogs' tails** "what little boys are made of." [Nurs. Rhyme: *Mother Goose*, 108]

22. **Spock, Dr. Benjamin (1903–1998)** his child rearing theories changed rigid attitudes about what was best for children; his *Common Sense Book of Baby and Child Care,* originally published in 1946, advised parents to trust their own judgment. [Am. Pop. Culture: *SJEPC*]

23. **sugar and spice** "what little girls are made of." [Nurs. Rhyme: *Mother Goose*, 108]

24. *Swallows and Amazons* first of twelve novels for young readers by Arthur Ransome published 1930–1947; Ransome is at his best depicting vacation locales and outdoor activities and his child characters have a dignity and independence that has made his work very appealing to the young. [Br. Chldren's Lit.: *OCCL*]

25. **teddy bears** originally named Teddy's bears in 1902 after a bear cub President Theodore Roosevelt refused to shoot; huggable stuffed toys are a staple of every American nursery. [Am. Pop. Culture: *SJEPC*]

26. **Temple, Shirley (1928–)** popular child film star during 1930s and 1940s; dimples, gold ringlets and charming singing/tap dancing made her the darling of the American public. [Am. Film: *SJEPC*]

27. **Webkinz** plush animals in late 2000s include secret access code to Web site so child can officially adopt and interact with pet. [Am. Culture: Misc.]

116. CHIVALRY

1. **Amadis of Gaul** personification of chivalrous ideals: valor, purity, fidelity. [Span. Lit.: Benét, 27]

2. **Arthur, King** king of the Britons; head of the Round Table. [Br. Lit.: *L'Morte d'Arthur*]

3. **Bevis** chivalrous medieval knight, righting wrongs in Europe. [Br. Lit.: *Bevis of Hampton*]

4. **Book of the Courtier** Castiglione's discussion of the manners of the perfect courtier (1528). [Ital. Lit.: *EB*, II: 622]

5. **Calidore, Sir** personification of courtesy and chivalrous actions. [Br. Lit.: *Faerie Queene*]

6. **Camelot** capital of King Arthur's realm, evokes the romance of knightly activity. [Br. Legend: *Collier's* IV, 224]

7. **Cid, El** Spanish military leader who becomes a national hero through chivalrous exploits. [Span. Lit.: *Song of the Cid*]

8. **Courtenay, Miles** dashing and chivalrous Irishman. [Br. Lit.: *King Noanett*, Walsh *Modern*, 108]

9. **Dantès, Edmond** chivalrous adventurer. [Fr. Lit.: *Count of Monte-Cristo*]

10. **D'Artagnan** Dumas's ever-popular chivalrous character. [Fr. Lit.: *The Three Musketeers*]

11. **de Coverley, Sir Roger** ideal, early 18th-century squire. [Br. Lit.: "Spectator" in Wheeler, 85]

12. **Edward III, King** when a countess dropped her garter, he put it on to reproach the sniggering courtiers, and instituted the Order of the Garter. [Br. Legend: Benét, 383]

13. **Eglamour, Sir** "a knight well-spoken, neat, and fine." [Br. Lit.: *Two Gentlemen of Verona*]

14. **Galahad, Sir** gallant, chivalrous knight of the Round Table. [Br. Lit.: *L'Morte d'Arthur*]

15. **Gareth** knight who, though Lynette scorns him as only a kitchen hand, successfully accomplishes rescuing her sister. [Br. Poetry: Tennyson *Idylls of the King*]

16. **Gawain, Sir** King Arthur's nephew; model of knightly perfection and chivalry. [Br. Lit.: *Sir Gawain and the Green Knight*]

17. **Ivanhoe** the epitome of chivalric knights. [Br. Lit.: *Ivanhoe*]

18. **Knights of the Round Table** chivalrous knights in King Arthur's reign. [Br. Lit.: *L'Morte d'Arthur*]

19. **Knights Templar** protected pilgrims to the Holy Land and fought the Saracens. [Medieval Hist.: *NCE*, 1490]

20. **Lancelot, Sir** knight in King Arthur's realm; model of chivalry. [Br. Lit.: *L'Morte d'Arthur*]

21. *Morte d'Arthur, Le* monumental work of chivalric romance. [Br. Lit.: *L'Morte d'Arthur*]

22. **Orlando** gallant and steadfast hero of medieval romance. [Ital. Lit.: *Orlando Furioso; Orlando Inammorato; Morgante Maggiore*]

23. **Quixote, Don** knight-errant ready to rescue distressed damsels. [Span. Lit.: *Don Quixote*]

24. **Raleigh, Sir Walter** drops his cloak over a puddle to save Queen Elizabeth from wetting her feet. [Br. Lit.: Scott *Kenilworth* in Magill I, 469]

25. **Richard the Lion-Hearted (1159–1199)** king known for his gallantry and prowess. [Br. Hist.: *EB*, 15:827]

26. **Roland** paragon of chivalry; unyielding warrior in Charlemagne legends. [Fr. Lit.: *Song of Roland*]

27. **sweet william** symbolizes chivalry. [Flower Symbolism: *Flora Symbolica*, 181]

28. **Valiant, Prince** comic strip character epitomizes chivalry. [Comics: Horn, 565]

117. CHRIST (See also NATIVITY, PASSION OF CHRIST, RESURRECTION.)

1. **Agnus Dei** lamb of god. [Christian Tradition: Brewer *Dictionary*, 17]

2. **Aslan** huge golden lion symbolic of Christ who appears in C.S. Lewis's Narnia tales, suffers as Christ did, and rises from the dead. [Br. Children's Lit.: Jones]

3. **bread** symbol of Christ's body in Eucharist. [Christian Tradition: Luke 22:19]

4. **chi rho** monogram of first two letters of Christ's name in Greek. [Christian Symbolism: Appleton, 111]

5. **Emmanuel** Jesus, especially as the Messiah. [N.T.: Matthew 1:23]

6. **fish** Greek acronym for Jesus Christ, Son of God, Saviour. [Christian Symbolism: Child, 210]

7. **Galilee** Jesus's area of activity. [Christianity: Wigoder, 203]

8. **Good Shepherd** the Lord as the keeper of his flock of believers [N.T.: John 10:11–14]

9. **I.N.R.I.** acronym of *Iesus Nazarenus, Rex Iudaeorum* 'Jesus of Nazareth, King of the Jews,' inscription affixed to Christ's cross as a mockery. [Christianity: Brewer *Note-Book*, 450]

10. **ichthys** Greek for 'fish'; early Christian symbol and mystical charm. [Christian Symbolism: Brewer *Dictionary*, 478]

11. **IHS (I.H.S.)** first three letters of Greek spelling of *Jesus*; also taken as acronym of *Iesus Hominum Salvator* 'Jesus, Savior of Mankind.' [Christian Symbolism: Brewer *Dictionary*, 480]

12. *Jesus Christ Superstar* rock opera by Andrew Lloyd Webber about Passion and death of Christ; first released as album because no financial backing could be found; opened in NY in 1971 and filmed in 1973; brought accusations of humanizing Christ too much, but audiences approved. [Br. and Am. Theater and Film: *SJEPC*]

13. **King of Kings** appellation for Jesus Christ. [N.T.: Revelation 17:14]

14. **lamb** the Lord as the sacrificial animal. [Christian Symbolism: O.T.: Isaiah 53:7; N.T.: John 1:29]

15. **lion** symbol expressing power and courage of Jesus. [Christian Symbolism: Revelation 5:5]

16. **Lord of the Dance** "At Bethlehem I had my birth." [Br. Folk Music: Carter, "Lord of the Dance" in Taylor, 128]

17. **Lord's Anointed, the** designation for Christ or the Messiah. [Christian Tradition: O.T.: I Samuel 26:9]

18. **Man of Sorrows** epithet for the prophesied Messiah. [O.T.: Isaiah 53:3]

19. **Messiah** expected leader who will deliver the Jews from their enemies; applied by Christians to Jesus. [O.T., N.T.: Brewer *Dictionary*, 602]

20. **pelican** medieval misconception that it tore open its breast to feed its young led to representation as a symbol for Christ. [Symbolism: *CEOS&S*]

21. **Piers the Plowman** English plowman who becomes allegorical figure of Christ incarnate. [Br. Lit.: *The Vision of William, Concerning Piers the Plowman*, Magill III, 1105–1107]

22. **Prince of Peace** designation for the Messiah, Jesus Christ. [O.T.: Isaiah 9:6]

23. **star** token of the Lord and his coming. [Christian Symbolism: O.T.: Numbers, 24:17; N.T.: Revelation 22:16]

24. **vine** gives nourishment to branches or followers. [Christian Symbolism: Appleton, 107; N.T.: John 15:5]

25. **wine** symbol of Christ's blood in Eucharist. [Christian Tradition: "Eucharist" in Cross, 468–469]

118. CHRISTIANITY (See also CHRIST, RELIGION.)

1. **Abraham** personage of great distinction in three major religions; Christians see him as example of exemplary faith in his willingness to sacrifice his son to God. [Christian Rel.: Bowker]

2. **Abraham's bosom** limbo, where unbaptized babies go after death. [Catholic Rel.: Bowker]

3. **Adam** first man; created by God on the final day of creation, according to Genesis book of Bible. [Christian Rel. Bowker]

4. **Advent** season preceding Christmas (the holy day to honor Christ's birth), used for preparation and meditation. [Christian Rel.: Bowker]

5. **agape** love without sexual associations; used in the New Testament of the Bible to mean love of God or Christ or true love of others. [Christian Rel.: Bowker]

6. **alleluia** Latin and Greek form of the Hebrew expression "hallelujah"; acclamation used in Christian worship. [Christian Rel.: Bowker]

7. **amen** Hebrew for "so be it"; used in response to a prayer or blessing. [Christian Rel.: Bowker]

8. **angel** messenger who functions as intermediary between heaven and earth. [Christian Rel.: Bowker]

9. **annunciation** announcement to Virgin Mary by angel that she would conceive son of God. [Christian Rel.: Bowker]

10. **apocalypse** in holy writings, a time of future reckoning; revelation of things that are not known in the present. [Christian Rel.: Bowker]

11. **armageddon** last battle between good and evil. [Christian Rel.: Bowker]

12. **ash** symbol of human mortality. [Christian Rel.: Bowker]

13. **Ave Maria** invocation to Mary, mother of Jesus. [Christian Rel.: Bowker]

14. **Bethlehem** city of Jesus's birth; figured prominently in Old Testament of Bible as well. [Christian Rel.: Bowker]

15. **Bible** sacred writings for Jews and Christians; Old Testament documents faith before Christ's birth and corresponds to the Hebrew Bible; New Testament relates Christ's life and teachings and the writings of his apostles. [Christian Rel.: Bowker]

16. **Bible Belt** refers to portions of the U.S. where the Christian conservative movement exerts political power. [Am. Politics: Misc.]

17. **Catechism** manual outlining Christian doctrine. [Christian Rel.: Bowker]

18. **Christian Science** Church of Christ, Scientist, a worldwide movement and church founded by Mary Baker Eddy based on her 1875 text on spirituality and healing, *Science and Health with Key to the Scriptures*; members profess belief in health as rooted in the mind. [Am. Rel.: *SJEPC*; Willis, 119]

19. **Contemporary Christian Music (CCM)** songs expressing faith in Jesus Christ and his teachings took root in the 1960s and gained favor with a wider audience by the 1980s. [Am. Music: *SJEPC*]

20. **crucifix** representation of cross on which Christ was executed. [Christian Rel.: Bowker]

21. **dove** symbol of Holy Spirit and peace. [Christian Rel.: Bowker]

22. **eucharist** part of non-Protestant Christian services reenacting the Last Supper of Christ. [Catholic Rel.: Bowker]

23. **fish** symbol of Christ. [Christian Rel.: Bowker]

24. **gospel** literally "good news"; the content of Christian preaching; also, a book with sayings and stories of Jesus. [Christian Rel.: Bowker]

25. **hosanna** acclamation meaning "save, we beseech you" used in Christian worship. [Christian Rel: Bowker]

26. **host** bread of Christian eucharist, especially the thin, round wafer. [Catholic Rel.: Bowker]

27. **Jesuit** member of the Society of Jesus, a Roman Catholic order; noted for their rigorous intellectual training and power in debate. [Rom Catholic Rel.: *FOF, MOD*]

28. **lamb** symbol of Christ. [Christian Rel.: Bowker]

29. **Last Supper** final meal of Jesus with his disciples before his death; he says the bread and wine are his body and blood and asks that the meal be repeated in his name. [Christian Rel.: Bowker]

30. **limbo** place for dead who have neither gained admission into heaven or deserved the punishment of hell. [Catholic Rel.: Bowker]

31. **Lourdes** in southwest France, a shrine to Mary because she appeared in visions in 1858 to a fourteen-year-old girl named Bernadette; a spring appeared and miraculous healings were reported; it has become a place of pilgrimage. [Rom. Catholic Rel.: Bowker]

32. **Madonna** Christian designation for Virgin Mary, mother of Christ. [Christian Rel.: Bowker]

33. **Magnificat** Virgin Mary's song of praise: "My soul doth magnify the Lord." [Christian Rel.: Bowker]

34. **mass** service with emphasis on scriptural readings and celebration of eucharist. [Catholic Rel.: Bowker]

35. **messiah** for Christians, Jesus fulfilled the Jewish prophecy of messiah/savior. [Christian Rel.: Bowker]

36. **penance** punishment of sins committed after baptism. [Christian Rel.: Bowker]

37. **Pietà** representation of Virgin Mary with dead body of Christ after his crucifixion. [Christian Rel.: Bowker]

38. **Pope, The** presides at the Vatican and functions as leader of the Roman Catholic Church; considered by believers to be infallible in matters of faith and morals. [Rom. Catholic Rel.: *SJEPC*]

39. **Promise Keepers** organization of conservative Christian men who vow to abide by certain standards meant to build strong families; outdoor rallies held in the 1990s. [Am. Pop. Culture: *SJEPC*]

40. **PTL Club** TV ministry founded by Jim and Tammy Faye Bakker investigated for suspicious fund-raising methods and fraudulent practices. [Am. Rel.: *SJEPC*]

41. **purgatory** place for the dead who were in state of grace, but had minor sins to expiate; afterwards, they are admitted into heaven. [Catholic Rel.: Bowker]

42. **rapture** believers will be raised up to meet Christ at his second coming. [Christian Rel.: Bowker]

43. **requiem** mass offered for the dead. [Catholic Rel.: Bowker]

44. **rosary** devotion of 15 groups (decades) of ten Hail Marys; each decade preceded by Lord's Prayer and followed by Gloria Patri; also, a string of beads used to count the prayers. [Catholic Rel.: Bowker]

45. **saint** title for exemplary Christian who is venerated and invoked in prayer. [Christian Rel.: Bowker]

46. **Shroud of Turin** Christian relic considered to be the burial shroud of Jesus on which his image has been miraculously transferred. [Christian Rel.: Bowker]

47. **stigmata** wounds of Jesus at crucifixion reproduced on body of an (often Roman Catholic) Christian. [Christian Rel.: Bowker]

48. **televangelism** evangelical Christians broadened their influence and drew new followers through televised preaching; scandals involving Jim Bakker and Jimmy Swaggart in the 1980s brought religious broadcasters under scrutiny. [Am. TV and Rel.: *SJEPC*]

49. **Trinity, The** belief in Godhead as Father, Son, and Holy Spirit, as three persons in one God. [Christian Rel.: Bowker]

50. **Vatican** city-state of 109 acres on west bank of Tiber in Rome; seat of Roman Catholic church and residence of pope, leader of Roman Catholic faith. [Rom. Catholic Rel.: Bowker]

51. **Via Dolorosa** Latin for "way of grief"; route in Jerusalem which Jesus followed to his crucifixion on Mount Calvary. [Christian Rel.: Bowker]

52. **Wandering Jew** legend of Jew who rejected Jesus as Messiah and Son of God and will never die, but be condemned to wander homeless through the world until the Second Coming of Christ or until his last descendant has died. [Christian Rel.: Bowker]

119. CHRISTMAS (See also NATIVITY.)

1. *Amahl and the Night Visitors* lame shepherd boy gives crutch as gift for Christ Child; first opera composed for television (1951). [Am. Opera: *EB*, VI: 792–793]

2. **Befana** fairy fills stockings with toys on Twelfth Night. [Ital. Legend: *LLEI*, Ii: 323]

3. **carols** custom originating in England of singing songs at Christmas. [Christian Tradition: *NCE*, 552]

4. *Charlie Brown Christmas, A* 1965 prime-time animated TV special based on *Peanuts* comic strip by Charles Schultz; pointing out the commercialization of Christmas, the story explores the religious and altruistic aspects of the season. [Am. TV: Misc.]

5. *Child's Christmas in Wales, A* nostalgic remembrance of Welsh Christmases. [Brit. Lit.: *A Child's Christmas in Wales*]

6. **Christmas** feast of the nativity of Jesus Christ (December 25). [Christian Tradition: *NCE*, 552]

7. *Christmas Carol, A* Dickens's joyous, magical telling of the redemption of Ebeneezer Scrooge [Br. Lit.: *A Christmas Carol*]

8. **Christmas tree** custom originating in medieval Germany of decorating an evergreen tree at Christmas. [Christian Tradition: *NCE*, 552]

9. **"Deck the Halls with Boughs of Holly"** traditional Christmas carol. [Western Culture: "Deck the Halls with Boughs of Holly" in Rockwell, 146–147]

10. **Father Christmas** legendary bringer of gifts; another name for Santa Claus. [Children's Lit.: *Father Christmas*]

11. **"Feliz Navidad"** Christmas standard sung by Jose Feliciano in both Spanish and English is perennial favorite (1970). [Am. Music: *SJEPC*; Misc.]

12. **"First Noel, The"** traditional Christmas carol. [Western Culture: "The First Noel" in Rockwell, 136–137]

13. **Frosty the Snowman** character in popular song (1950), children's book, and animated TV program has become a Christmas holiday icon; comes to life and plays with children, but melts in the sun. [Am. Culture: *SJEPC*]

14. *Gift of the Magi, The* O. Henry's Christmas story of love and self-sacrifice. [Am. Lit.: Rockwell, 77–80]

15. **gold, frankincense, and myrrh** given to the infant Jesus by the three Wise Men. [N.T.: Matthew 2:1–11]

16. **Grinch, The** Dr. Seuss character from children's literature; hating the delights of Yuletide, he steals Christmas presents but eventually relents and joins in the merriment. [Am. Children's Lit.: Jones]

17. **"Hark! the Herald Angels Sing"** traditional Christmas carol. [Western Culture: "Hark! the Herald Angels Sing" in Rockwell, 132–133]

18. **holly** symbol of Christmas. [Flower Symbolism: *Flora Symbolica*, 174; Kunz, 331]

19. *It's a Wonderful Life* 1946 Frank Capra film about man who doesn't appreciate the value of his life until an angel shows him what would have happened if he had never been born; takes place at Christmas time and is often viewed at that time. [Am. Film: *SJEPC*]

20. **"Jingle Bells"** yuletide song composed by J.S. Pierpont. [Pop. Music: Van Doren, 200]

21. **"Joy to the World!"** traditional Christmas carol. [Western Culture: "Joy to the World!" in Rockwell, 138]

22. **Kringle, Kris** Santa Claus in Germany. [Ger. Folklore: *LLEI*, I: 277]

23. **Lord of Misrule** from pagan times, person chosen to lead revels and games during Winter celebrations; now adapted to Christmas. [Br. Folklore: Misc.]

24. **Magi** the three kings who visit Jesus after his birth, bringing gold, frankincense, and myrrh. [N.T.: Matthew 2:1]

25. *Messiah* Handel's great oratorio, now traditionally performed at Christmas [Br. Music: *Messiah*]

26. *Miracle on 34th Street* film featuring benevolent old gentleman who believes he is Santa Claus. [Am. Cinema: Halliwell, 493]

27. **mistletoe** traditional yuletide sprig under which kissing is obligatory. [Br. and Am. Folklore: Leach, 731]

28. **Moore, Clement (1779–1863)** author of *A Visit from St. Nicholas* (also known as *The Night before Christmas*, 1823), the classic narrative poem that did much to establish the modern image of Santa Claus. [Am. Lit.: *OCCL*]

29. **"Night Before Christmas, The"** poem celebrating activities of Christmas Eve. [Am. Lit.: "The Night Before Christmas"]

30. *Nutcracker, The* first written by E.T.A. Hoffmann in 1816; adapted by Alexandre Dumas in 1845 and used as the basis of Tchaikovsky ballet which has become world famous; favorite with children and adults alike, especially during Christmas season. [Ger. Children's Lit.: *OCCL*]

31. **"O Come, All Ye Faithful"** traditional Christmas carol. [Western Culture: "O Come, All Ye Faithful" in Rockwell, 142–143]

32. **"O Little Town of Bethlehem"** traditional Christmas carol. [Western Culture: "O Little Town of Bethlehem" in Rockwell, 120–121]

33. *Polar Express* 1985 picture book by Chris Van Allsburg; young boy is taken to the North Pole by Santa Claus and witnesses the magic of the preparations for Christmas. [Am. Children's Lit.: Misc.]

34. **red and green** traditional colors of Christmas. [Christian Tradition: Misc.]

35. **reindeer** flight of Christmas reindeer probably originated with flight of Lapp shaman. [Symbolism: *CEOS&S*]

36. **Rudolph, the Red-Nosed Reindeer** his nose lights Santa on his way. [Am. Music: "Rudolph, the Red-Nosed Reindeer"]

37. **Santa Claus** jolly, gift-giving figure who visits children on Christmas Eve. [Christian Tradition: *NCE*, 1937]

38. **Scrooge, Ebenezer** the great miser during season of giving. [Br. Lit.: *A Christmas Carol*]

39. **"Silent Night"** traditional Christmas carol. [Western Culture: "Silent Night" in Rockwell, 130–131]

40. **Star of Bethlehem** announces birth of the Christ child. [Christianity: N.T.: Matthew 2:22]

41. **Twelfth Night** traditional festival commemorating the 12th day after Christ's birth and the arrival of the Magi; a time of revelry. [Christian Tradition: *EB*]

42. **"We Three Kings of Orient Are"** traditional Christmas carol. [Western Culture: "We Three Kings of Orient Are" in Rockwell, 122–123]

43. **"White Christmas"** wistful, best-selling Christmas song written by Irving Berlin during World War II and sung by Bing Crosby. [Am. Music: *SJEPC*]

44. **yule log** log burned at Christmas. [Western Tradition: *NCE*, 552]

120. CIRCUMCISION

1. **Abraham** initiated rite in covenant with God. [O.T.: Genesis 17:11–14]

2. **Berith** Jewish rite of circumcising male child eight days after birth. [Judaism: Misc.]

3. **Elijah** traditionally represented at ceremony by empty chair. [Judaism: Wigoder, 172]

4. **Gibeath-haaraloth** Hill of Foreskins; where Joshua circumcised Israelites. [O.T.: Joshua 5:3]

5. **Shandy, Tristram** accidentally circumcised by a loose window in a sash. [Br. Lit.: *Tristram Shandy* in Magill I, 1027]

121. CLEANLINESS (See also ORDERLINESS.)

1. **Berchta** unkempt herself, demands cleanliness from others, especially children. [Ger. Folklore: Leach, 137]

2. **cat** continually "washes" itself; considered clean, good, spiritual animals by Muslims. [Animal Symbolism: Jobes, 296; Islamic Trad.: *UIMT*, 232]

3. **Clean, Mr.** brand of household cleaner. [Trademarks: Crowley, *Trade*, 379]

4. **hyssop** Biblical herb used for ceremonial sprinkling. [Flower Symbolism: O.T.: Psalms 51:17]

5. **Mary Mouse** constantly sweeping and dusting. [Children's Lit.: *Mary Mouse and the Doll's House*, Fisher, 216]

6. **Spic and Span** brand of household cleaner. [Trademarks: Crowley, *Trade*, 546]

7. **Wag-at-the-Wa'** brownie who is strict about neatness of houses. [Br. Folklore: Briggs, 425–426]

8. **wudu** the less thorough form of washing required before formal prayer. [Islam: *UIMT*, 142–45, 440]

Cleverness (See CUNNING.)

122. CLOCK

1. **Big Ben** bell of Houses of Parliament clock in London keeps Britons punctual. [Br. Culture: Misc.]

2. **Nuremberg Egg** first watch; created by Peter Heinlein (1502). [Ger. Hist.: Grun, 223]

3. **Strasbourg Cathedral clock** famous clock in Strasbourg Cathedral. [Fr. Culture *NCE*, 581]

123. CLOWN

1. **Bardolph** "coney-catching rascal"; follower of Falstaff. [Br. Lit.: *Merry Wives of Windsor*]

2. **Bertoldo** medieval jester, butt, and buffoon. [Ital. Folklore: Walsh *Classical*, 54–55]

3. **Dagonet** fool at the court of King Arthur, who knighted him. [Br. Lit.: Barnhart, 303]

4. **Feste** playful fool. [Br. Lit.: *Twelfth Night*]

5. **Geddes** jester in the court of Mary Queen of Scots. [Scot. Hist.: Brewer *Handbook*, 380]

6. **Gobbo, Launcelot** a "wit-snapper," a "merry devil." [Br. Lit.: *Merchant of Venice*]

7. **harlequin** comic character in commedia dell'arte; dressed in multicolored tights in a diamond-shaped pattern. [Ital. Drama: *NCE*, 1194]

8. **Hop-Frog** deformed dwarf; court fool. [Am. Lit.: "Hop-Frog" in *Portable Poe*, 317–329]

9. **Jocus** Cupid's companion and fool. [Rom. Lit.: *Psychomachia*]

10. **Joey** after Joseph Grimaldi, famous 19th-century clown. [Am. Hist.: Espy, 45]

11. **Jupe** a clown in Sleary's circus. [Br. Lit.: *Hard Times*]

12. **Kelly, Emmett (1897–1979)** foremost silent, sad-faced circus clown. [Am. Hist.: Flexner, 83]

13. **McDonald, Ronald** hamburger chain's Pied Piper. [Am. Culture: *Grinding*]

14. **Merry-Andrew** Andrew Borde, Henry VIII's physician. [Br. Hist.: Wheeler, 241]

15. **Pagliacci** clown Canio stabs his unfaithful wife and her lover. [Ital. Opera: Osborne *Opera*, 233]

16. **Patch** court fool of Elizabeth, wife of Henry VII. [Br. Hist.: Brewer *Handbook*, 380]

17. **Touchstone** a "motley-minded, " "roynish" court jester. [Br. Lit.: *As You Like It*]

18. **Yorick** jester in the court of Denmark. [Br. Lit.: *Hamlet*]

Clumsiness (See AWKWARDNESS, INEPTITUDE.)

124. COARSENESS (See also UNSOPHISTICATION.)

1. *Beavis and Butthead* irreverent MTV show featuring two crude, hormone-driven male adolescents broke taboos in 1990s. [Am. TV: *SJEPC*]

2. **Billingsgate** site of a London fishmarket, known for foul and abusive language. [Br. Hist. Brewer *Dictionary*, 106]

3. **Branghtons, the** Evelina's rude, coarse cousins. [Br. Lit.: *Evelina*]

4. **Crawley, Sir Pitt** vulgar aristocrat. [Br. Lit.: *Vanity Fair*]

5. **Cro-Magnon man** prehistoric ancestor of humankind; used to describe brutish behavior. [Pop. Culture: *FOF, MOD*]

6. **Goops** naughty, balloon-headed children. [Am. Lit.: *Goops and How To Be Them*, Hart, 323]

7. **Graceland** home of rock-and-roll icon Elvis Presley became popular tourist destination after his untimely death in 1977; Tennessee mansion displays singer's wealth in kitschy, gaudy style. [Am. Music: *SJEPC*]

8. **Neanderthal Man** prehistoric human ancestor; now a pejorative term for a coarse, brutish individual. [Pop. Culture: *FOF, MOD*]

9. *Newlywed Game, The* crude double-entendres were commonplace on this game show featuring young marrieds answering intimate questions. [Am. TV: *SJEPC*]

10. **Ochs, Baron** vulgar, lecherous nobleman. [Aust. Opera: R. Strauss, *Rosenkavalier*, Westerman, 423–425]

11. **Pike** "he expectorates vehemently" [Am. Lit.: *At Home and Abroad*, Hart, 655]

12. **Rivera, Geraldo (1943–)** highly touted journalist and TV personality who won several awards for distinguished broadcast journalism; later turned to sensationalism and lowbrow specials. [Am. TV and Journ.: *SJEPC*]

13. **Tearsheet, Doll** prostitute with vitriolic vocabulary. [Br.Lit. *II Henry IV*]

14. **Troglodytes** race of uncivilized cave dwellers. [Gk. Hist.: Brewer *Dictionary*, 1103]

15. **xanthium** symbolizes bad manners and rudeness. [Flower Symbolism: *Flora Symbolica*, 178]

16. **Yahoos** loutish, abusive brutes in shape of men. [Br. Lit.: *Gulliver's Travels*]

125. COCKNEY

1. **Bow Bells** famous bell in East End of London; "only one who is born within the bell's sound is a true Cockney." [Br. Hist.: *NCE*, 347]

2. **Doolittle, Eliza** Cockney girl taught by professor to imitate aristocracy. [Br. Lit.: *Pygmalion*]

3. **Weller, Tony and Samuel** father and son, coachman and bootblack, with colorful lingo. [Br. Lit.: Dickens *Pickwick Papers*]

126. COLDNESS

1. **Acis** blood turned into a "river of ice." [Gk. Myth.: *Metamorphoses*] .

2. **Antarctica** continent of constant cold. [Geography: *WB*, A:495]

3. **Arctic** area of constant cold. [Geography: *WB*, A:600]

4. **Frost, Jack** personification of freezing cold. [Am. and Br. Folklore: Misc.]

5. **Hyperboreans** fabulous people living beyond North Wind, traditionally near North Pole. [Rom. Myth.: Zimmerman, 132]

6. **Lapland** northern region of Scandinavian penninsula, mostly within Arctic Circle. [Geography: Misc.]

7. **Lower Slobbovia** cartoon land of perpetual cold. [Comics: "Li'l Abner" in Horn, 450–451]

127. COLLECTING

1. **baseball cards** bubble gum cards traded by young fans in early- to mid-20th century has become serious collectible business for adults. [Am. Culture: *SJEPC*]

2. **Beanie Babies** small plush beanbag toys created by the Ty Corporation caused frenzy among kids and collectors in the 1990s. [Am. Culture: *SJEPC*]

3. **Cabbage Patch Kids** children and parents went wild in the 1980s collecting homely, soft-bodied dolls, each with its unique birth certificate and adoption papers. [Am. Culture: *SJEPC*]

4. **Smithsonian Institution** established by an Act of Congress in 1846 with the bequest of English scientist James Smithson; one hundred million artifacts and specimens are stored or displayed in sixteen museums and galleries in Washington, DC. [Am. Culture: *SJEPC*]

128. COLONIZATION

1. **Evander** Arcadian, founded settlement in Italy. [Gk. Myth.: Kravitz, 100]

2. **Jamestown, Virginia** first permanent English settlement in New World (1607). [Am. Hist.: Jameson, 255]

3. **Mayflower** ship which brought Pilgrims to New World (1620). [Am. Hist.: *NCE*, 1730]

4. **Plymouth Plantation** first English settlement in New England (1620). [Am. Hist.: *Major Bradford's Town*]

5. **thirteen original colonies** earliest settlements became first states in U.S. [Am. Hist.: *NCE*, 2733]

6. **Williamsburg** monument of American colonial period; settled in 1632. [Am. Hist.: Hart, 930]

129. COMEDY (See also COMEDY, SLAPSTICK; SATIRE; ZANINESS.)

1. **Benny, Jack (1894–1974)** American radio and TV star, noted for great comic timing, stingy persona, violin playing. [Am. TV: *FOF, MOD*]

2. **Berle, Milton (1908–2002)** American comic, known as "Uncle Miltie," host of a famed TV variety show, his humor was broad and rowdy. [Am. TV: *FOF, MOD*]

3. **Borge, Victor (1909–2000)** Danish-American pianist incorporated comedy routines into serious classical music. [Music and Entertainment: *SJEPC*]

4. **Brice, Fanny (1891–1951)** vaudeville star was subject of musical and film *Funny Girl*. [Am. Entertainment: *SJEPC*]

5. **Bruce, Lenny (1925–1966)** radical stand-up comic's vulgar material, use of profanity, and unique style and delivery challenged society in the conservative 1950s and 1960s and influenced future comedians' work. [Am. Entertainment: *SJEPC*]

6. **Burnett, Carol (1933–)** beloved American comedian introduced unforgettable characters and skits on her weekly television variety show (1967–78). [Am. TV: *SJEPC*]

7. **Burns and Allen** comedy duo George Burns (1896–1996) and Gracie Allen (1906–1964) whose zany comedy show entertained Americans in the 1950s. [Am. TV: *FOF, MOD*]

8. **Carlin, George (1937–2008)** stand-up comic wove social commentary and everday experiences into routines; famous for "Seven Words You Can Never Use on Television." [Am. Entertainment: *SJEPC*]

9. **Chaplin, Charlie (1889–1977)** English star of the silent screen; created "The Tramp," a character with bowler hat, baggy pants, and cane. [Am. Film: *ODA*]

10. **Cheech and Chong** drug culture formed the basis of this comedy team's routines and movies in the 1970s and early 1980s. [Entertainment: *SJEPC*]

11. **Cosby, Bill (1937–)** charming African-American comedian enter-tains diverse audiences with routines about everyday family life, from live performances to recordings and television shows. [Am. Entertainment: *SJEPC*]

12. **Crystal, Billy (1947–)** beloved funnyman appeared as gay char-acter on TV's *Soap* (1977–81) and Fernando on *Saturday Night Live* (1984–85), acted in popular films like *Analyze This!* (1999), and has hosted numerous Academy Awards ceremonies. [Am. Entertain-ment: *SJEPC*; Misc.]

13. **DeGeneres, Ellen (1958–)** popular comedian starred in own TV sitcom, hosts the daytime talk show *The Ellen DeGeneres Show* (2003–), and has hosted the Emmy Awards and Academy Awards. [Am. TV: *SJEPC*; Misc.]

14. **Diller, Phyllis (1917–)** zany, wild-haired stand-up comic known for frumpy housewife persona made her national debut on TV in 1959, paved the way for future female comedians. [Am. Entertain-ment: *SJEPC*]

15. **Firesign Theatre** since 1968, four-man comedy troupe—Peter Bergman, David Ossman, Phil Proctor, and Phil Austin—has recorded comedy concept albums using pop culture as material for routines. [Am. Entertainment: *SJEPC*]

16. **Foxx, Redd (1922–1991)** black stand-up comedian portrayed cur-mudgeonly widower and junk yard dealer Fred Sanford on *San-ford and Son* (NBC, 1972–77), whose bickering with ambitious son Lamont and feigned heart attacks provided laughs. [Am. TV: *SJEPC*]

17. **Gleason, Jackie (1916–1987)** heavy-set comedian and film actor known as "The Great One" hosted own TV variety show (1950s-70s) but was best known for role as bus driver Ralph Kramden in *The Honeymooners* (1955–56). [Am. TV: *SJEPC*]

18. **Goldberg, Whoopi (1955?–)** outspoken, amiable African-Ameri-can stand-up comic with distinctive hairstyle and expressive face created memorable characters for her act; became film actress, Academy Awards host, and TV personality. [Am. Entertainment and Film: *SJEPC*]

19. **Gregory, Dick (1932–)** trailblazing African-American comedian won national, mainstream acclaim using his humor to highlight social and political issues, such as racisim and the Vietnam War in 1960s; continues to advance progressive social agenda. [Am. En-tertainment: *SJEPC*]

20. **Hope, Bob (1903–2003)** actor and comic who entertained audi-ences worldwide for more than 70 years; star of comedic "Road" films with Bing Crosby; traveled the world to entertain U.S. troops for more than 40 years. [Am. Film and Entertainment: *EB*]

21. *I Love Lucy* popular 1950s TV comedy starring husband-and-wife team of Lucille Ball and Desi Arnaz that exaggerated situations familiar to typical American married couples. [Am. TV: *SJEPC*]

22. **Kaufman, Andy (1949–1984)** idiosyncratic comic best known for character of foreign car mechanic Latka Gavas on TV show *Taxi* and unusual stand-up routines and publicity stunts; died of lung cancer at age 34. [Am. TV and Entertainment: *SJEPC*]

23. **Kaye, Danny (1913–1987)** song-and-dance funnyman who often played shy, likable guy who wins heart of girl; role in *White Christmas* (1954) one of his most popular. [Am. Film: *SJEPC*]

24. **Keillor, Garrison (1942–)** humorist whose writings depict small-town Midwest living at its most charming and sentimental; a devotee of radio, his extremely successful *Prairie Home Companion* show (debut, 1974) combines music performances and take-offs of old radio shows and ads, and news from the mythical Lake Woebegone. [Am. Lit. and Radio: *SJEPC*]

25. **Kinison, Sam (1953–1992)** created "rage comedy" in which he inserted screams and rants into his routine. [Am. Entertainment: *SJEPC*]

26. **Kovacs, Ernie (1919–1962)** used video technology and special effects to the fullest to creat innovative form of humor, often featuring outrageous characters. [Am. TV: *SJEPC*]

27. *Laugh-In* top-rated comedy show in late 1960s; hosted by Dan Rowan and Dick Martin; youthful focus with emphasis on liberal politics, sexual liberation, and rapid succession of one-liners complemented by psychedelic visuals and frenetic editing. [Am. TV: *SJEPC*]

28. **Newhart, Bob (1929–)** mild-mannered, stuttering nice guy comedian who played the lead in two wildly successful TV shows [Am. TV: *SJEPC*]

29. **Paulsen, Pat (1928–1997)** TV comedian who ran mock campaigns for President five times between 1968 and 1996, satirically criticizing the opposition; claimed he ran for those who wanted to vote "none of the above." [Am. TV: *SJEPC*]

30. **Pryor, Richard (1940–2005)** famous African-American comedian who used his racial background to create material that was often raunchy but hilarious. [Am. Entertainment and Film: *SJEPC*]

31. **Rivers, Joan (1933–)** bold, somewhat raunchy humor and sassy stage persona; opened doors for many female comedians who followed. [Am. Entertainment: *SJEPC*]

32. **Rogers, Will (1879–1935)** naïve common man persona worked as counterpoint to his deceptively clever political satire. [Am. Entertainment: *SJEPC*]

33. *Roseanne* blue-collar family sitcom starring stand-up comedian Roseanne Barr; success resulted from smart writing, relevant subjects and lack of easy resolutions. [Am. TV: *SJEPC*]

34. **Sahl, Mort (1927–)** pioneer of political satire in stand-up comedy. [Am. Entertainment: *SJEPC*]

35. *Saturday Night Live* began in 1970s; late-night comedy variety show that spawned multitude of stars and classic skits; reinvented TV comedy with irreverent satire and boisterous nonsense. [Am. TV: *SJEPC*]

36. **Second City** theater company in Chicago that specializes in improvisational humor; opened in 1959 by a group of performers and writers from University of Chicago. [Am. Entertainment: *SJEPC*]

37. *Seinfeld* popular and applauded sitcom; in many ways "a TV show about nothing," it portrayed the life of stand-up comic Jerry Seinfeld and his group of oddball friends living in Manhattan; aired 1990–1998. [Am. TV: *SJEPC*]

38. **Simon, Neil (1927–)** considered one of the most successful playwrights in American theater history; his best-known works are comic gems that have won huge audiences and numerous awards. [Am. Theater: *SJEPC*]

39. **Sonny & Cher [Salvatore Bono (1935–1998) and Cher Sarkisian (1946–)]** mid-1960s pop music sensation; went on to host very popular comedy variety TV show where they engaged in good-natured arguments and put-downs. [Am. Music and TV: *SJEPC*]

40. **Tomlin, Lily (1939–)** began career with part on *Laugh-In* TV show (1969–1973); spirited five-year-old Edith Ann in huge rocking chair and nasally telephone operator Ernestine two popular characters she created. [Am. Entertainment: *SJEPC*]

41. **Van Dyke, Dick (1925–)** accomplished actor of TV and film; probably best known for *The Dick Van Dyke Show* (1961–1966), in which he played a comedy writer and regular guy with subtle mastery. [Am. TV and film: *SJEPC*]

42. **Williams, Robin (1952–)** as a comic, both ingenious and frenetic; as a dramatic film actor, subtle and geniune as in *Good Will Hunting* (1997) for which he won an Academy Award. [Am. Film and Entertainment: *SJEPC*]

43. **Wilson, Flip (1933–1998)** brought African-American perspective to white audiences through successful, award-winning network variety series *The Flip Wilson Show* (1970–1974); there he portrayed numerous memorable characters, including sassy Geraldine Jones—played in drag. [Am. TV: *SJEPC*]

44. **Youngman, Henny (1906–1998)** king of the one-liners; career that spanned seven decades with rapid-fire series of unprovocative gag lines. [Am. Entertainment: *SJEPC*]

45.   *Your Show of Shows* 1950s variety TV show featuring comic par-
       odies performed by Sid Caesar and Imogene Coca, backed by a
       stable of gifted writers. [Am. TV: *SJEPC*]

130.   COMEDY, SLAPSTICK (See also COMEDY, ZANINESS.)

1.   **Abbott, Bud (1895–1974), and Lou Costello (1906–1959)** improv-
      isational routines of tall, lanky Abbott and short, squat Costello
      amused burlesque, film, and TV audiences for decades. [Am. En-
      tertainment *SJEPC*]

2.   *Airplane!* spoof on disaster films of the 1970s full of sight gags
      and verbal comedy (1980). [Am. Film: *SJEPC*]

3.   **Brooks, Mel (1926–)** over-the-top Jewish American writer, actor,
      and director created numerous comedic TV shows, musicals,
      films, and genre spoofs, such as *Get Smart!* (1965), *The Producers*
      (1968), *Blazing Saddles* (1973), and *Space Balls* (1987). [Am. Film,
      Musical, and TV: *SJEPC*]

4.   **Chase, Chevy (1943–)** actor and writer portrayed President Ger-
      ald Ford as clumsy and stumbling on TV's *Saturday Night Live*
      (1975–76); acted in such comedies as *National Lampoon's Vacation*
      (1983). [Am. TV and Film: *SJEPC*]

5.   **Fields, W.C. (1879–1946)** American comic film actor famous for
      his curmudgeonly sense of humor. [Am. Film: *FOF, MOD*]

6.   **Hill, Benny (1924–1992)** ribald English comic hosted TV series
      popular worldwide (1950s-1980s). [Br. TV: *SJEPC*]

7.   **Keaton, Buster (1895–1966)** famous silent movie funnyman who
      played unsmiling characters buffeted about—physically and
      metaphorically—by natural elements and machines in often sur-
      realistic comedies. [Am. Film: *SJEPC*]

8.   **Keystone Kops, The** first appeared in silent films in 1912; inept
      policemen with handlebar mustaches falling over each other and
      everything else at frenetic pace; humor still bears influence of
      their antics. [Am. Film: *SJEPC*]

9.   **Laurel and Hardy [Stan Laurel (1890–1965), Oliver Hardy
      (1892–1957)]** segued from silent films into talkies; two rather dim,
      but loyal friends bumbling through one "swell predicament" after
      another; their physical appearance (Hardy fat, Laurel thin, both in
      derbies) was often parodied. [Am. Film: *SJEPC*]

10. **Marx Brothers, The** group of brothers with wacky slapstick
      humor that transferred very successfully from vaudeville stage to
      film and TV. [Am. Entertainment: *SJEPC*]

11. **Sales, Soupy (1926–)** signature prank was throwing pies; popu-
      lar TV show for children in mid-1960s. [Am. TV: *SJEPC*]

12. **Sellers, Peter (1925–1980)** preeminent British comic actor; best known in America for film role as bumbling Inspector Clouseau in Pink Panther movies. [Br. and Am. TV and Film: *SJEPC*]

13. **Sennett, Mack (1880–1960)** founder of Keystone studio; directed numerous silent gems starring Keystone Kops, Mabel Normand, and Charlie Chaplin, among others. [Am. Film: *SJEPC*]

14. **Three Stooges, The [Moe Howard (1897–1975), Larry Fine (1902–1975), and Shemp Howard (1895–1955), replaced by Curly Howard (1903–1952)]** comedians whose short films made from 1934–1958 featured slapstick humor with much physical violence; brought to TV to immense popularity. [Am. Film and TV: *SJEPC*]

Comeuppance (See LAST LAUGH.)

Comfort (See LUXURY.)

131. COMIC

1. *Blondie* comic strip featuring long-lasting marriage of flighty Blondie Boopadoop and befuddled Dagwood Bumstead debuted in 1930. [Am. Comics: *SJEPC*]

2. *Bloom County* Berkeley Breathed's comic strip ridiculed American culture, society, and politics in the 1980s; animal and human characters interacted as equals. [Am. Comics: *SJEPC*]

3. *Brenda Starr* beautiful, spunky red-haired reporter debuted in 1940. [Am. Comics: *SJEPC*]

4. *Buck Rogers in the 25th Century* launched in 1929, comic strip featuring superhero space adventurer helped popularize science fiction. [Am. Comics: *SJEPC*]

5. *Calvin and Hobbes* popular comic strip (1985–95) by Bill Watterson featuring an imaginative, mischievous boy, Calvin, and his philosophical stuffed tiger, Hobbes, who came alive only when other characters were absent. [Am. Comics: *SJECP*]

6. *Captain Marvel* comic book character with special powers granted by the wizard, Shazam, giving him courage, strength, speed, and wisdom. [Am. Comics: *FOF, MOD*]

7. **Crumb, Robert (1943–)** underground comic artist known for sexually explicit content and social satire; created Keep on Truckin' logo and Fritz the Cat. [Am. Comics: *SJEPC*]

8. **DC Comics** influential comic book publisher founded in 1930s helped define appearance of the genre; stable includes respected superheroes like Superman, Batman, and Wonder Woman. [Am. Comics: *SJEPC*]

9. *Dick Tracy* comic strip created by Chester Gould featuring honest, square-jawed detective in a trenchcoat and fedora debuted in 1931 during the Depression era; character has appeared in

movies, TV, books, cartoons, and other media over the years. [Am. Comics: *SJEPC*]

10. *Dilbert* comic strip about an American white-collar office, complete with inane corporate policies and infuriating coworkers, has its roots in creator Scott Adams's own personal work experiences (1990s-). [Am. Comics: *SJEPC*]

11. *Dykes to Watch Out For* syndicated cartoon strip about lesbian life debuted in the 1980s, is "half op-ed column and half endless Victorian novel," according to creator Alison Bechdel. [Am. Comics: *SJEPC*]

12. **EC Comics** publisher of controversial, sophisticated, satirical comic books in the early 1950s produced the grotesque *Tales from the Crypt* and irreverent *Mad* under leadership of William M. Gaines. [Am. Comics: *SJEPC*]

13. **Eisner Awards** American comic book industry annual awards for excellence named in honor of innovative comic artist Will Eisner. [Am. Comics: *SJEPC*; Misc.]

14. **Eisner, Will (1917–2005)** influential comic book artist internationally recognized as master of sequential art and father of the graphic novel. [Am. Comics: *SJEPC*; Misc.]

15. *Family Circus, The* popular single-panel comic strip finding humor in the everyday lives of a white, middle-class nuclear family based on creator-artist Bil Keane's own parenting experiences; debuted in 1960 and appears in 1,500 newspapers. [Am. Comics: *SJEPC*; Misc.]

16. *Fantastic Four, The* superhero team of Mr. Fantastic, the Invisible Woman, the Human Torch, and the Thing protects the public but has human faults; created by Stan Lee and Jack Kirby in 1961. [Am. Comics: *SJEPC*]

17. *Far Side, The* Gary Larson's extremely popular, single-panel comic strip (1980–95) featured anthropomorphic animals, nerdy humans, and bizarre and sometimes obscure humor; seen in 1,900 newspapers. [Am. Comics: *SJEPC*]

18. **Felix the Cat** popular, personable animated cat character who starred in silent cartoons of 1920s also featured in his own comic strip from 1923 until 1967. [Am. Comics: *SJEPC*]

19. *Flash Gordon* comic featuring adventures of space-traveling hero Flash and love interest Dale Arden was first drawn by Alex Raymond and written by Don Moore as Sunday strip in 1934; basis of three motion pictures by Universal (1936, 1938, 1940). [Am. Comics and Film: *SJEPC*]

20. **Goldberg, Rube (1883–1970)** comic strip artist known for bizarre, complex creations. [Am. Comics: *FOF, MOD*]

21. *Green Lantern* intergalactic crime fighter aided by special power ring first graced comic book pages in 1940 as the protector of common Americans against greedy special interests. [Am. Comics: *SJEPC*]

22. *Incredible Hulk, The* one of Marvel Comics' most popular superheroes; Dr. Banner—exposed to gamma radiation—turns into the super-strong Hulk when angry or under stress; made into popular TV show and film versions. [Am. Comics and TV: *SJEPC*]

23. **Kirby, Jack (1917–1994)** creator of Captain America and founder of Marvel Comics; originated action-packed panels of superhero comics. [Am. Comics: *SJEPC*]

24. *Peanuts* Charles Schultz's intelligent comic strip featuring child characters, most notably depressive, insecure Charlie Brown; characters in several TV specials [Am. Jour. and TV: *SJEPC*]

25. **Popeye** comic-strip and cartoon sailor who owes his incredible muscle power to a diet of canned spinach. [Am. Comics: *SJEPC*]

26. *Ripley's Believe It or Not* newspaper comics about oddities and curiosities led to later books, radio and TV spots, and museums. [Am. Entertainment and Comics: *SJEPC*]

27. *Sandman* adult themes and unusual superhero made it influential and successful; first published in 1989; only comic to win World Fantasy Award. [Am. Comics: *SJEPC*]

28. *Seduction of the Innocent* 1954 book by New York psychiatrist Frederic Wertham purporting that comic books contributed to juvenile delinquency; mass burnings of comics, Senate hearings, etc. ensued. [Am. Comics: *SJEPC*]

29. **Shadow, The** character from radio program from 1937–1954 known for hypnotic powers and memorable lines ("Who knows what evil lurks in the hearts of men? The Shadow knows."); also character in popular crime-fighting pulp novels and comic books. [Am. Comics and Radio: *SJEPC*]

30. **Silver Surfer, The** travels through space on a surfboard to fight for good; his philosophical commentaries drew college readers and influenced future comic book writers. [Am. Comics: *SJEPC*]

31. *Spawn* Todd McFarlane founded Image Comics and created this centerpiece comic; deceased Al Simmons becomes super-powered Hellspawn, leader of Hell's army, then repents; considered "wallpaper" comic, with fantastic graphics and little story. [Am. Comics: *SJEPC*]

32. **Spider-Man** character first appeared in Marvel Comics in 1962; shy teenaged Peter Parker gets powers after bite from radioactive spider; fed fantasies and anxieties of adolescent readers; successful film versions followed. [Am. Comics and Film: *SJEPC*]

33.   *Tales from the Crypt* brutal horror stories were the hallmark of popular comic book series of the 1950s. [Am. Comics: *SJEPC*]

34.   *Teenage Mutant Ninja Turtles* originally a comic book; 1980s and 1990s TV cartoon show about mutated pet turtles with names of famous Renaissance artists and superhero powers. [Am Comics and TV: *SJEPC*]

35.   **Wonder Woman** first female comic book superhero (1941); strong and agile, but somewhat less violent than her male counterparts; her goal to reform the enemies she pursued. [Am. Comics: *SJEPC*]

36.   *X-Men, The* popular team of superheroes; teenaged mutants with powers who were dedicated to helping the world that shunned them; spawned successful film versions. [Am. Comics: *SJEPC*]

37.   *Zap Comix* quintessential underground comic book of the 1960s; included classics with adult themes such as Fritz the Cat and Mr. Natural. [Am. Comics: *SJEPC*]

Commerce (See FINANCE.)

132.   COMMUNICATION

1.   **AT&T (American Telephone and Telegraph)** once the largest corporation in the world, its telephone system and subsequent inventions paved the way for the Information Age. [Am. Business: *SJEPC*]

2.   **Bell, Alexander Graham (1847–1922)** Scottish-born American scientist and inventor of the telephone; his devotion to communication extended to the study of speech and deafness. [Am. Business: *BBInv*]

3.   **Berners-Lee, Tim (1955–)** British computer scientist and inventor of the World Wide Web. [Technology: *BBInv*]

4.   **Braille, Louis (1809–1852)** French educator and inventor of the Braille system of printing and writing for the blind [Technology: *BBInv*]

5.   **CB Radio** Citizens Band (CB) Radio allowed truckers and other drivers to communicate with each other from their vehicles, creating sense of community and empowerment while providing anonymity via on-air nicknames; introduced in 1947. [Am. Radio: *SJEPC*]

6.   **Edison, Thomas (1847–1931)** American inventor of more than 1,000 items, including the phonograph and motion picture projector, and the foundation of the recording industry. [Technology: *BBInv*]

7.   **Farnsworth, Philo (1906–1971)** American scientist and inventor of electronic television. [Technology: *BBInv*]

8.   **Gutenberg, Johannes (1400?-1468)** German printer and inventor of the movable-type printing press, which made books affordable

and available to people of all backgrounds, helping to spread knowledge worldwide. [Technology: *BBInv*]

9. **Internet, The** most powerful communications network in history; worldwide link between people for communication and information. [Am. Technology: *SJEPC*]

10. **Marconi, Guglielmo (1874–1937)** Italian scientist and inventor of successful long-distance transmission of radio. [Technology: *BBInv*]

11. **McLuhan, Marshall (1911–1980)** his *Understanding Media* (1964) analyzed the effect of media and electronic technology on society [Can. Lit.: *SJEPC*]

12. **Morse, Samuel F.B. (1791–1872)** American inventor of Morse Code and first practical electric telegraph, which allowed for the accurate and immediate transmission of information worldwide; led to the development of time zones, and to communication inventions that relied on the transmission of electricity, including the telephone, television, and computers. [Technolgy: *BBInv*]

13. **radar** acronym for: radio detection and ranging; refers to device that uses radio waves to detect and locate an object; commonly used to mean ability to detect emotions, other interpersonal communications. [Science *FOF, MOD*]

14. **satellites** a netword of satellites receiving and relaying signals meant a leap forward in communications and media broadcasts. [Am. Science: *SJEPC*]

15. **World Wide Web** the "web," or system, invented by Tim Berners-Lee, that allows documents to be coded, linked, and identified making them searchable on the Internet; the "www" that preceeds each web address. [Technology: *BBInv*]

133. COMMUNISM

1. **Berlin Wall** wall erected after World War II in Berlin, dividing East (Soviet) and West (democratic) Germany; symbol of Cold War hostilities. [World Hist.: *FOF, MOD*]

2. **blacklisting** alleged Communists in entertainment industry (1947–1960s) prevented from working in Hollywood. [Am. Hist.: *SJEPC*]

3. **Cold War** tense, ideological stand-off between the Soviet Union the U.S., the two superpowers after WWII; their conflict determined world politics until the collapse of the Soviet Union in 1991. [World Hist.: *Misc.*]

4. *Crucible, The* Arthur Miller wrote about the McCarthy trials to uncover communist sympathizers in this play about the Salem witch trials [Am. Lit.: *SJEPC*]

5. **Hollywood Ten** writers blacklisted in Hollywood after WW II, accused of being Communists, unable to find work. [Am. Hist.: *FOF, MOD*]

6. **Marx, Karl (1818–1883) and Frederick Engels (1820–1895)** authors of *The Communist Manifesto*, single most important document defining communism. [World Econ.: Misc.]

7. **McCarthyism** scare tactics by Senator Joseph McCarthy led to blacklisting and several anti-communist laws in the 1960s [Am. Hist.: *SJEPC*]

8. **red** Communist. [Hist.: *SJEPC*]

9. **Rosenberg, Julius (1918–1953) and Ethel (1915–1953)** first Americans executed for allegedly giving information to Soviet agents; their guilt has been debated because of anticommunist paranoia of Cold War era. [Am. Hist.: *SJEPC*]

10. **Steffens, Lincoln (1866–1936)** journalist who tirelessly investigated corrupt city officials throughout the U.S.; disillusioned with capitalism, traveled to Soviet Union in 1917 and joined Communist Party. [Am. Jour.: *SJEPC*]

Companionship (See FRIENDSHIP.)

Compassion (See KINDNESS.)

Compromise (See PEACEMAKING.)

134. COMPUTING

1. **Apple Computer** computer company with an anticorporate image known for ground-breaking, user-friendly innovations. [Am. Business: *SJEPC*]

2. **Gates, Bill (1955–)** American computer software pioneer and co-founder of Microsoft; his name an allusion to computers, big business, and philanthropy. [Technology: *BBINv*]

3. **HAL 9000** computer in Stanley Kubrick's *2001: A Space Odyssey*, which famously tries to take over a spaceship; symbol for human fear of machines. [Am. Film: *FOF, MOD*]

4. **hardware** the mechanical parts of a computer, including the system unit (input-output, telecommunication, circuity), and peripherals (keyboard, screen, monitor, mouse, speakers). [Technology: Misc.]

5. **IBM (International Business Machines)** hugely successful mainframe computer company established in the 1950s; accused of monopoly in the late 1960s. [Am. Business: *SJEPC*]

6. **Internet, the** most powerful communications network in history; worldwide link between people for communication and information. [Am. Technology: *SJEPC*]

7. **Jobs, Steven (1955–)** cofounder of Apple Computer known for creativity and marketing savvy [Am. Business: *BBInv*]

8. **Mac** Macintosh personal computer preferred for high-end graphics work. [Am. Technology: *SJEPC*]

9. **Microsoft** mammoth software company whose operating system is used worldwide. [Am. Business: *SJEPC*]

10. **PC** personal computer: the term for a computer designed for private use, as opposed to large mainframe computers; often called "desktop" computers. [Technology: Misc.]

11. **Perot, Ross (1930–)** computer salesman and presidential candidate; founded Electronic Data Systems (EDS) [Am. Business: *SJEPC*]

12. **software** the programs that provide instructions that are read and executed by a computer's hardware. [Technology: Misc.]

13. **Wozniak, Steve (1950–)** American inventor of the personal computer, co-counder of Apple Computer, and creator of Apple II. [Am. Technology: *BBInv*]

14. **Y2K** shorthand for the year 2000; some believed that computers not designed to handle data assigned to the twenty-first century would shut down, leading to disastrous malfunctions in banking, transportation, etc. [Am. Technology: *SJEPC*]

15. **zines** magazines done on home computers and distributed by their creators, or circulated online. [Am. Technology: *SJEPC*]

135. CONCEALMENT (See also REFUGE.)

1. **Ali Baba** 40 thieves concealed in oil jars. [Arab. Lit.: *Arabian Nights*]

2. **ark of bulrushes** Moses hidden in basket to escape infanticide. [O.T.: Exodus 2:1–6]

3. **booby trap** originally used in WW II to describe a hidden explosive; now a description for something dangerous that is concealed. [Am. Culture: *FOF, MOD*]

4. **cloak** symbol of metamorphosis and concealment. [Symbolism: *CEOS&S*]

5. **Holgrave** hides his identity as the builder's descendant and finds the concealed deed to the land. [Am. Lit.: Hawthorne *The House of the Seven Gables*]

6. **Hooper, Parson** wears a black veil as a symbol of secret sorrow and sin. [Am. Lit.: Hawthorne "The Minister's Black Veil" in Benét, 672]

7. **Inigo and Gonsalve** Concepciòn's would-be lovers; hides them in her husband's clocks. [Fr. Opera: Ravel, *The Spanish Hour*, Westerman, 198]

8. **Man in the Iron Mask** forced to perpetually wear an iron mask to conceal his identity. [Br. Lit. and Fr. Hist.: Benét, 628]

9. **Mrs. Rochester** concealed in the attic of Thornfield, she escapes and burns the house to the ground. [Br. Lit.: Charlotte Bronte *Jane Eyre*]

10. **Polonius** Hamlet stabs him through the arras. [Br. Lit.: *Hamlet*]

11. **sealed book** symbolic of impenetrable secrets. [Christian Symbolism: Appleton, 13]

12. **veil of Isis** never lifted to reveal the face of the goddess. [Anc. Egypt. Myth.: Brewer *Dictionary*, 492]

13. **wilderness of Maon** where David sought refuge from Saul's pursuit. [O.T.: I Samuel 23:25–29]

14. **wilderness of Ziph** where David hid to escape Saul's search. [O.T.: I Samuel 23:14]

136. CONCEIT (See also ARROGANCE, BOASTFULNESS, EGOTISM, VANITY.)

1. **Ajax (the lesser)** boastful and insolent; drowns due to vanity. [Gk. Myth.: Kravitz, 14]

2. **Barnabas, Parson** conceited and weak clergyman. [Br. Lit.: *Joseph Andrews*]

3. **Bottom, Nick** self-important weaver. [Br. Lit.: *A Midsummer Night's Dream*]

4. **Bunthorne, Reginald** fleshly poet; "aesthetically" enchants the ladies. [Br. Lit.: *Patience*]

5. **Butler, Theodosius** thinks he is a wonderful person. [Br. Lit.: *Sketches by Boz*]

6. **Collins, Mr.** pompous, self-satisfied clergyman who proposes to Elizabeth Bennet. [Br. Lit.: Jane Austen *Pride and Prejudice*]

7. **Dalgetty, Rittmaster Dugald** self-aggrandizing, pedantic soldier-of-fortune. [Br. Lit.: *Legend of Montrose*]

8. **Dedlock, Sir Leicester** contemplates his own greatness. [Br. Lit.: *Bleak House*]

9. **Dogberry and Verges** ignorant and bloated constables. [Br. Lit.: *Much Ado About Nothing*]

10. **Grosvenor, Archibald** idyllic poet of no imperfections. [Br. Lit.: *Patience*]

11. **Henry VIII** inflated self-image parallels bloated body. [Br. Lit.: *Henry VIII*]

12. **Horner, Little Jack** pats his back with "What a good boy am I!" [Nurs. Rhyme: *Mother Goose*, 90]

13. **Keefe, Jack** baseball pitcher is a chronic braggart and self-excuser suffering from an exaggerated sense of importance. [Am. Lit.: Lardner *You Know Me Al* in Magil III, 1159]

14. **Lewis** self-important coxcomb full of hollow, ostentatious valor. [Br. Lit. *Henry V*]

15. **Malvolio** Olivia's grave, self-important steward; "an affectioned ass." [Br. Lit. *Twelfth Night*]

16. **Montespan, Marquis de** regards exile and wife's concubinage as honor. [Br. Opera: *The Duchess of la Vallière*, Brewer *Handbook*, 721]

17. **narcissus** flower of conceit. [Plant Symbolism: *Flora Symbolica*, 170; Gk. Myth.: Zimmerman, 171–172]

18. **nettle** symbol of vanity and pride. [Flower Symbolism: *Flora Symbolica*, 176]

19. **Orion** scorpion stung him to death for boasting. [Rom. Myth.: Brewer *Dictionary*, 971]

20. **Prigio, Prince** too clever prince; arrogance renders him unpopular. [Children's Lit.: *Prince Prigio*]

21. **Slurk, Mr.** had a "consciousness of immeasurable superiority" over others. [Br. Lit. *Pickwick Papers*]

22. **Tappertit, Simon** boasted he could subdue women with eyes. [Br. Lit. *Barnaby Rudge*]

23. **Toad of Toad Hall** from Kenneth Grahame's children's classic *Wind in the Willows* (1908); conceited and impulsive Toad does whatever he feels like doing, to the dismay of his friends. [Br. Children's Lit.: Jones]

24. **Turveydrop, Mr.** conceited father of Prince. [Br. Lit.: *Bleak House*]

137. CONDEMNATION

1. **bell, book, and candle** symbols of Catholic excommunication rite. [Christianity: Brewer *Note-Book*, 85]

2. **Bridge of Sighs** passage from Doge's court to execution chamber in Renaissance Venice. [Ital. Hist.: Brewer *Note-Book*, 121]

3. **Eurydice** doomed to eternal death when Orpheus disobeys Hades. [Gk. Myth.: Kravitz, 97]

4. **lions' mouths** Venetian receptacles for denunciations, character assassinations. [Ital. Hist.: Plumb, 259–260]

5. **Prometheus** a Titan condemned by Zeus for giving fire to mortals. [Gk. Lit.: *Prometheus Bound*, Magill I, 786–788]

138. CONFORMITY

1. **Archer, Newland** too bound by conventional mores to seek happiness with wife's cousin. [Am. Lit.: *The Age of Innocence*]

2. **Levittown** post WWII housing development on Long Island, NY, featuring almost identical houses; symbol of conformity. [Am. Hist.: *FOF, MOD*]

3. *Man in the Gray Flannel Suit, The* novel and film exposing the bland, conformist life of ad execs in 1950s America; a symbol of conformity. [Am. Pop. Culture: Sloan, Wilson *The Man in the Gray Flannel Suit*]

139. CONFUCIANISM (See also RELIGION.)

1. **ch'i** vital energy which is in all things; often closely associated with the breath. [Confucian Rel.: Bowker]

2. *Four Books* philosophical teachings of Confucius containing instruction for attainment of sainthood. [Confucian Rel.: Bowker]

3. *I Ching* classic book of great influence in Chinese thought, much of it written in China before the time of Confucius; originally a diviner's manual; Confucius was thought to have added more philosophical commentary to the book. [Confucian Rel.: Bowker]

4. **li** outwardly, behavior which brings harmony; inner meaning is the proper moral attitude or motivation when acting, without which all action is without meaning; also the power to transform people and bring cosmic harmony. [Confucian Rel.: Bowker]

5. **Mencius (c. 391–c. 308 BCE)** philosopher, moral and political teacher considered second only to Confucius, his writings teach of the four potentials of human nature—benevolence, propriety, wisdom, and duty—that bring aid to others and produce profound satisfaction. [Confucian Rel.: Bowker]

6. **t'ai chi** supremely important concept in Chinese philosophy and religion; produces two energies from which arise the five elements of all existence. [Confucian Rel.: Bowker]

140. CONFUSION

1. **Babel** where God confounded speech of mankind. [O.T.: Genesis 11:7–9]

2. **bedlam** from Hospital of St. Mary of Bethlehem, former English insane asylum. [Br. Folklore: Jobes, 193]

3. **Cia** amnesia victim whose identity becomes doubtful when the same identity is claimed by an insane woman. [Ital. Drama: Pirandello *As You Desire Me* in Sobel, 35]

4. *Comedy of Errors, The* two pairs of identical twins wreak social havoc in Ephesus. [Br. Drama: Shakespeare *The Comedy of Errors*]

5. **Corybantes** half-divine priests of Cybele; celebrated noisy festivals in her honor. [Gk. Myth.: Howe, 67]

6. **Jude** "the other Judas, not Iscariot." [N.T.: John 14:22]

7. **Labyrinth** maze at Knossos where Minotaur lived. [Gk. Myth.: Hall, 185]

8. **Pandemonium** Milton's capital of the devils. [Br. Lit.: *Paradise Lost*]

9. **Pantagruelian Law Case** not understanding the defense, judge gives incomprehensible verdict. [Br. Lit.: *Pantagruel*]

10. **Serbonian Bog** Egyptian morass, "where armies whole have sunk." [Br. Lit.: *Paradise Lost*]

11. **Star-Splitter, The** "We've looked and looked, but after all where are we?" [Am. Lit.: "The Star-Splitter" in Hart, 799]

141. CONQUEROR

1. **Agricola (40–93)** enlightened governor and general; subdued all Britain. [Rom. Hist.: *NCE*, 35]

2. **Alaric (c. 370–410)** Visigoth chief; sacked Rome. [Eur. Hist.: Bishop, 14]

3. **Alexander the Great (356–323 B.C.)** Macedonian king and conqueror of much of Asia. [Gk. Hist. *NCE*, 61]

4. **Attila (d. 453)** king of Huns. [Eur. Hist.: *NCE*, 182]

5. **Batu Khan (d. 1255)** Mongol conqueror of 13th century; grandson of Genghis Khan. [Asian Hist.: *NCE*, 248]

6. **Caesar, Julius (102–44 B.C.)** Roman statesman and general; reduced all of Gaul and Britain to Roman control. [Rom. Hist.: *NCE*, 416]

7. **Canute (995–1035)** Norseman; subjugator of Enlgand. [Br. Hist.: Bishop, 42]

8. **Charlemagne (742–814)** established the Carolingian empire. [Fr. Hist.: *NCE*, 507]

9. **Charles V (1500–1558)** Holy Roman Emperor; last to sack Rome (1527). [Ital. Hist.: Plumb, 43, 406–407]

10. **Cortés, Hernando (1485–1547)** annihilated Aztec culture, claiming Mexico for Spain. [Span. Hist.: *EB*, 5: 194–196]

11. **Cyrus II (the Great) (d. 529 B.C.)** creator of Persian empire (553–529). [Class. Hist.: Grun]

12. **Genghis Khan (1167–1227)** Mongol chieftain overran most of Asia and eastern Europe (1206–1227). [Asian Hist.: *EB*, 7: 1013–1016]

13. **Genseric (c. 390–477)** Vandal king; controlled large portion of Mediterranean. [Rom. Hist.: *NCE*, 1034]

14. **Golden Horde** 13th-century Mongol overlords of Russia. [Russ. Hist.: Grun, 170]

15. **Hitler, Adolf (1889–1945)** led Germany to conquer or destroy most of Europe. [Ger. Hist.: *Hitler*]

16. **Mohammed II (1429–1481)** Ottoman conqueror of Constantinople (1453). [Eur. Hist.: Plumb, 292–293]

17. **Napoleon (1769–1821)** vanquished most of Europe. [Fr. Hist.: Harvey, 570]

18. **Nebuchadnezzar (d. 562 B.C.)** subjugated Jews, initiating Babylonian captivity (597–5 B.C.). [O.T.: Daniel 1:1–2]

19. **Pizarro, Francisco (c. 1476–1541)** with small force, detroyed Incan empire. [Span. Hist.: *EB*, 14: 487–488]

20. **Tamerlane (1336–1405)** Tartar; vanquished Persia and India. [Asian Hist.: Brewer *Dictionary*, 1061]

21. **William the Conqueror (1027–1087)** commanded Normans in conquest of Britain; victor at Hastings (1066). [Br. Hist.: Bishop, 42–46]

142. CONSCIENCE

1. **Aidos** ancient Greek personification of conscience. [Gk. Myth.: Zimmerman, 14]

2. **Clamence** haunted by guilt because he failed to respond when aware that a girl had jumped or fallen into the Seine. [Fr. Lit.: Camus *The Fall*]

3. *Elder Statesman, The* Lord Claverton ponders the shame of his past, personifiied by ghosts of his victims. [Br. Drama: T.S. Eliot *The Elder Statesman* in Magill IV, 262]

4. **Godunov, Boris** Tsar suffers pangs of conscience for having murdered the Tsarevitch in order to seize the throne. [Russ. Drama and Opera: *Boris Godunov*]

5. **Hamlet** "conscience doth make cowards of us all." [Br. Lit.: Shakespeare *Hamlet*]

6. **Jiminy Cricket** dapper mite guides the callow Pinocchio. [Am. Cinema: *Pinocchio* in *Disney Films*, 32–37]

7. **Karamazov, Ivan** guilt for wishing his father's death culminates in hallucinatory conversations with the Devil. [Russ. Lit.: Dostoevsky *The Brothers Karamazov*]

8. **Solness, Halvard** plagued by awareness of his past ruthlessness and the guilt of defying God's will. [Nor. Drama: Ibsen *The Master Builer* in Magill II, 643]

9. **Valdes and Cornelius** Good Angel and Evil Angel; symbolize Faustus's inner conflict. [Br. Lit.: *Doctor Faustus*]

10. **Wilson, William** his Doppelganger irrupts at occasions of duplicity. [Am. Lit.: "William Wilson" in *Portable Poe*, 57–82]

143. CONSERVATISM

1.   **Apley, George** scion of an old Boston society family, he exemplifies its traditions and remains in old-fashioned mediocrity. [Am. Lit.: *The Late George Apley* in Magill I, 499]

2.   **Bible Belt** portion of the U.S. where the Christian conservative movement is influential in politics. [Am. Politics: Misc.]

3.   **Buckley, William F. Jr. (1925–2008)** American author and publisher noted for his witty Conservative writings and long-time editorship of the *National Review*. [Am. Politics: Misc.]

4.   **Conservative party** British political party, once called the Tory party. [Br. Hist.: NCE, 632]

5.   **Coulter, Ann (1961–)** author of best-selling books and syndicated news column; attorney with confrontational style; completely unapologetic for her conservative bias; called by *The Observer* "Rush Limbaugh in a miniskirt." [Am. Politics: Misc.]

6.   **Daughters of the American Revolution (D.A.R.)** conservative society of female descendants of Revolutionary War soldiers. [Am. Hist.: Jameson, 132]

7.   **elephant** symbol of the Republican party. [Am. Hist.: Misc.]

8.   **John Birch Society** ultraconservative, anti-Communist organization. [Am. Hist.: NCE, 1421]

9.   **laissez-faire** political doctrine that an economic system functions best without governmental interference. [Politics: Misc.]

10.   **Luddites** arch-conservative workmen; smashed labor-saving machinery (1779). [Br. Hist.: Espy, 107]

11.   **Moral Majority** primarily Christian conservative movement aimed at countering what they perceive as a powerful liberal bias in American politics [Am. Politics: *SJEPC*]

12.   **O'Reilly, Bill (1949–)** right-wing author, columnist, and host of *The O'Reilly Factor* cable TV news show; opinionated and abrasive; maintains that he creates news reporting that exists in a "no spin zone." [Am. Jour. and TV: Misc.]

13.   **Quayle, Dan (1947–)** US vice-president (1989–1993) who took strong conservative stance; frequent blunders made him appear unintelligent; became favorite target of pundits. [Am. Politics: *SJEPC*]

14.   **Reagan, Ronald (1911–2004)** US president from 1981–1989; influential conservative Republican with oratorical skills from former acting career. [Am. Politics: *SJEPC*]

15.   **Religious Right** coalition of individuals and organizations focused on electing social conservatives and recruiting voters for Republican party; also known as Christian Right. [Am. Politics: *SJEPC*]

16. **Republican Party** U.S. political party, generally espousing a conservative platform. [Am. Hist.: Jameson, 424]

17. **Robertson, Pat (1930–)** Southern Baptist minister and president of Christian Coalition; powerful leader of evangelical Christians, encouraging increasing participation in politics. [Am. Rel. and Politics: *SJEPC*]

18. *Saturday Evening Post, The* known as *The Post*; dominated American magazine readership for first thirty years of twentieth century; characterized by common-sense conservatism and middle-class values. [Am. Jour.: *SJEPC*]

19. *700 Club, The* show hosted by influential Southern Baptist minister Pat Robertson and aired on his Christian Broadcasting Network. [Am. Rel. and TV: *SJEPC*]

20. *Wall Street Journal, The* began as a handwritten page of business news in 1882; a century later had become a national newspaper— conservative in tone and broad in scope—and had won more than 30 Pulitzer Prizes. [Am. Jour.: *SJEPC*]

21. **Warbucks, Daddy** espouses a reactionary law-and-order society threatened by decadence, bureaucracy, and loss of Puritan virtues. [Comics: Berger, 84]

22. **Will, George F. (1941–)** syndicated columnist with *Washington Post* and frequent TV panelist, with conservative bent and incisive political commentary. [Am. Jour.: *SJEPC*]

144. CONSPIRACY (See also INTRIGUE.)

1. **Babington Plot** abortive plot to assassinate Elizabeth I; sealed Mary Stuart's fate (1586). [Br. Hist.: *NCE*, 202]

2. **Black Friday (September 24, 1869)** gold speculation led to financial panic. [Am. Hist.: Van Doren, 259]

3. **Brutus** plotted against Caesar with Cassius and Casca. [Br. Lit.: *Julius Caesar*]

4. **cabal** from the initials of conspirators (CABAL) during the reign of Charles II of England (1670s), meaning "conspirators." [Eng. Hist.: *FOF, MOD*]

5. **Cassius** intriguer and accomplice in plot against Caesar. [Br. Lit.: *Julius Caesar*]

6. **Cinq-Mars** conspires against Cardinal Richelieu. [Fr. Lit.: *Cinq-Mars*]

7. **Cointet brothers** use a corrupt lawyer to ruin a young printer and cheat him of his invention. [Fr. Lit.: Balzac *Lost Illusions* in Magill II. 595]

8. **Deep Throat** secret source for Bob Woodward and Carl Bernstein during the Watergate scandal; named derived from a porno-

graphic film; revealed to be Mark Felt, FBI official, in 2005. [Am. Hist. Misc.]

9. **Doctors' Plot** physicians falsely tried for trying to poison Stalin. [Jew. Hist.: Wigoder, 160]

10. **Duke of Buckingham** Richard III's "counsel's consistory"; assisted him to throne. [Br. Lit.: *Richard III*]

11. **Fawkes, Guy (1570–1606)** leader of Gunpowder Plot to blow up Houses of Parliament (1605). [Br. Hist.: *EB*, IV: 70, 801]

12. *JFK* 1991 film by Oliver Stone; contends there was conspiracy to assassinate President John F. Kennedy; some critics feels it is history rewritten, others laud thoughtful portrayal of volatile subject. [Am. Film: *SJEPC*]

13. **Joseph's brothers** sold him into slavery out of envy and hatred. [O.T.: Genesis 37:18–28]

14. **Kennedy assassination** on November 22, 1963, U.S. President John F. Kennedy was shot as his car drove in a motorcade through Dallas, Texas; suspected killer, Lee Harvey Oswald was murdered within days, leading some to suspect a conspiracy. [Am. Hist.: *SJEPC*]

15. **Pontiac (1720–1769)** brains behind widespread American Indian uprising (1762). [Am. Hist.: Jameson, 398]

16. **pumpkin papers** refers to evidence supposedly passed by Alger Hiss to former Communist spy Whitaker Chambers, hidden in a pumpkin on Chambers' farm; a symbol of questionable evidence. [Am. Hist.: *FOF, MOD*]

17. **Roswell Incident, The** U.S. government is accused of covering up existence of UFO debris found near Roswell, New Mexico in 1947. [Am. Hist.: *SJEPC*]

18. **Shallum** plots and successfully executes overthrow of Zechariah. [O.T.: II Kings 15:10]

19. **Watergate** political intrigue leading to resignation of Pres. Nixon. [Am. Hist.: *EB*, X: 568–569]

20. *Woman in White, The* Laura Fairlie is unjustly confined to an insane asylum in a plot to obtain her money. [Br. Lit.: Magill I, 1125]

Constancy (See LOYALTY.)

145. CONSUMERISM (See also MARKETING.)

1. *American Psycho* characters in Brett Easton Ellis's disturbing novel about a yuppie serial killer are preoccupied with wealth and appearances (1991). [Am. Lit.: *SJEPC*]

2. *Consumer Reports* independent periodical rates products and services used by average consumer, promoting informed choices. [Am. Jour.: *SJEPC*]

3. **credit cards** helped ignite and fuel a consumer society. [Culture: *SJEPC*]

4. **Kmart** early discount chain department store; name synonymous with deeply discounted merchandise; opened first store in 1962, competing with department stores for suburban shoppers; offered special sales in areas marked by blue light. [Am. Business. *FOF, MOD*; *SJEPC*]

5. **Macy's** gigantic Herald Square store epitomizes New York City shopping scene. [Am. Business: *SJEPC*]

6. **Mall of America** gargantuan shopping mall in Minnesota is top US tourist attraction. [Am. Pop. Culture: *SJEPC*]

7. **McDonald's** billions of hamburgers sold by this fast-food giant. [Am. Business: *SJEPC*]

8. **MTV** music cable channel whose videos and advertisements promote mindless consumerism. [Am. TV: *SJEPC*]

9. **Nike** using famous athletes as spokepeople and a distinctive "swoosh" logo, brought sports apparel into every home. [Am. Business: *SJEPC*]

10. *Price Is Right, The* longest-running TV game show, debuting in 1956; contestants win prizes by guessing the cost of various products [Am. TV: *SJEPC*]

11. **Saks Fifth Avenue** Manhattan store with classy merchandise and services opened in 1924, but outlet stores bore the Fifth Avenue appellation to capitalize on the distinction; name became synonymous with wealth and stylishness. [Am. Business: *SJEPC*]

12. **Thompson, J. Walter** redefined advertising industry and transformed the business of media in U.S. by adding ads to magazines, reshaping the appearance of ads, applying psychology to advertising, and using celebrity testimonials. [Am. Business: *SJEPC*]

13. **Wall Drugs** rest stop in South Dakota began as small store offering free ice water to travelers in 1936; now several blocks with arcades of shops, a chapel, and more. [Am. Pop. Culture: *SJEPC*]

14. **Wal-Mart** American shopping was changed beginning in the 1960s by retail giant; proliferation of huge discount stores (especially in small towns) offering variety and value; accused of unfair labor practices and environmental irresponsibiliy. [Am. Business: *SJEPC*]

15. **yuppies** Young Urban Professionals of the 1970s and 1980s; high-paying jobs and few responsibilities meant being able to buy the best of everything; sometimes linked to recreational drug use, particularly cocaine. [Am. Culture: *SJEPC*]

146. CONTEMPLATION

1. *Compleat Angler, The* Izaak Walton's classic treatise on the *Contemplative Man's Recreation*. [Br. Lit.: *The Compleat Angler*]

2. **Merton, Thomas (1915–1968)** Trappist monk whose autobiographical *The Seven Storey Mountain* relates his eventful life and religious conversion [Am. Religion: *SJEPC*]

3. *Thinker, The* sculpture by Rodin, depicting completative man. [Fr. Art: Osborne, 988]

147. CONTROVERSY (See also SCANDAL.)

1. *All in the Family* 1970s TV sitcom introduced social realism, discussing racism, sexism, relgious bias, and politics. [Am. TV: *SJEPC*]

2. *American Psycho* disturbing novel by Brett Easton Ellis, written from perspective of a yuppie serial killer, generated controversy even before its 1991 publication; criticized for graphically violent, misogynistic, and homophobic content. [Am. Lit.: *SJEPC*]

3. **Anita Hill - Clarence Thomas** Senate hearings on Thomas's nomination to Supreme Court uncovered sexual harassment claim by law professor Hill. [Am. Law and Politics: *SJEPC*]

4. **Avignon** location of alternate papacy (1309–1377). [Fr. Hist.: Bishop, 376]

5. **Baker, Josephine (1906–1975)** flamboyant, exotic African-American dancer shocked and delighted both French and American audiences in the 1920s. [Am. Entertainment: *SJEPC*]

6. *Birth of a Nation, The* controversial 1915 film depicts the Ku Klux Klan sympathetically. [Am. Cinema: Griffith, 36–39]

7. **Brown, Murphy** character on popular TV sitcom who was portrayed as unmarried and pregnant, causing accusations of rejecting traditional family values. [Am TV: *SJEPC*]

8. **Chicago 7 Trial** alleged ringleaders of Chicago riots tried in circus atmosphere (1969). [Am. Hist.: Van Doren, 630]

9. **Christian Science** church discourages medical treatment for physical ailments; especially controversial when treament is withheld from chldren. [Am. Rel. and Medicine: *SJEPC*; Willis, 121]

10. **Creationism** Biblically-centered doctrine that evolution is false, and that God alone created the world generates controversy when taught as scientific theory in public schools. [Rel.: *SJEPC*]

11. **Dred Scott decision** Supreme Court decision that blacks had "no rights that white men are bound to respect." [Am. Hist.: Jameson, 151–152]

12. **Dungeons and Dragons** fantasy role-playing game especially popular on college campuses in the 1980s-90s accused of being

too violent, Satanic, and addicting for adolescents and young adults. [Am. Culture: *SJEPC*]

13. **Imus, Don (1940–)** American radio host; syndicated ABC Radio Networks talk show began in 1979 and, like his rival Howard Stern, was known for crude humor and lack of reserve; in 2007, made offensive, racially-insensitive remarks about NCAA women's basketball players; he was briefly off the air. [Am. Radio: Misc.]

14. *Joy of Sex, The* 1972 "lovemaking manual" by British gerontologist Dr. Alex Comfort; paved way to more lighthearted approach to sex; faced controversy for frankness and disparagement of same-sex relations. [Pop. Culture: *SJEPC*]

15. **Kinsey, Dr. Alfred C. (1894–1956)** founder of Institute for Sex Research at Indiana Univeristy; published reports on all aspects of sex lives of human male (1948) and human female (1952), devoid of moral judgment; overt treatment of previously taboo topics was controversial. [Am. Culture.: *SJEPC*]

16. **Laetrile** Vitamin B17, which some believed was a potent healing agent, especially for use against cancer; others found it toxic and dangerous; court battles ensued. [Am. Medicine: *SJEPC*]

17. **Lake, Ricki (1968–)** tallk-show host with well-documented personal dramas; her 1993 show covered topics of appeal to young adults, but faced accusations of sensationalism and vacuity. [Am. TV: *SJEPC*]

18. *Little Black Sambo* famous 1899 picture book by Helen Bannerman; story of black boy who loses his beautiful new clothes to threatening tigers; ferocious fight and subsequent chase turns tigers into pool of butter, and Sambo enjoys buttery pancakes for supper; accusations of racial stereotyping raised in the 1970s. [Scot. Children's Lit.: *OCCL*]

19. **Mailer, Norman (1923–2007)** controversial personal life and feuds tainted his literary career. [Am. Lit.: *SJEPC*]

20. **Moore, Michael (1954–)** filmmaker whose documentaries are sometimes called left-wing propaganda. [Am. Film: *SJEPC*]

21. *NYPD Blue* adult police TV drama whose R-rated language and partial nudity did not prevent awards and critical acclaim. [Am. TV: *SJEPC*]

22. *On the Road* Jack Kerouac's autobiographical beat novel of road trip: noncomformist lifestyle depicted brought censure. [Am. Lit.: *SJEPC*]

23. *Origin of Species, The* once revolutionary theory of evolution and natural selection (1859). [Br. Science: *The Origin of Species*]

24. **Pentagon Papers, The** Defense Department's Vietnam policy papers leaked to press. [Am. Hist.: Flexner, 376]

25. **Rather, Dan (1931–)** news anchor of *CBS Evening News* and *60 Minutes*; airing of information from questionable documents about President George W. Bush's National Guard record led to Rather's dismissal. [Am. Jour.: *SJEPC*]

26. *Rite of Spring, The* Stravinsky's score caused riot at premiere (1913). [Music Hist.: Thompson, 1900]

27. **Rivera, Geraldo (1943–)** highly touted Hispanic journalist and TV personality who won several awards for distinguished broadcast journalism; later turned to sensationalism and lowbrow specials. [Am. TV and Journ.: *SJEPC*]

28. **Rose, Pete (1941–)** known as a baseball player for competitive attitude and skill; controversy surrounding allegations of betting on games led to banishment. [Am. Sports: *SJEPC*]

29. **Sacco and Vanzetti [Ferdinando Nicola Sacco (1891–1927) and Bartolomeo Vanzetti (1888–1927)]** Italian immigrants tried and executed for murder in witch-hunt for anarchists. [Am. Hist.: *Sacco-Vanzetti Case: A Transcript*]

30. **Schlessinger, Dr. Laura** firm belief in personal responsibility; blunt personality and strict definition of morality controversial; millions listen to her radio show and read her syndicated newspaper column and her books. [Am. Culture: *SJEPC*]

31. **Scopes trial** 1925 trial attempting to ban Darwinsim from being taught in public schools; considered a trial of religion v. science or evolution v. creationism. [Am. Hist.: Allen, 142–146]

32. **Scottsboro case** sensational series of trials in which nine African-American young men were accused of raping two white girls (1931). [Am. Hist.: Hart, 753]

33. **scrap of paper** pre-WWI Belgian neutrality; German disregard precipitated British involvement. [Am. Hist.: Jameson, 450]

34. *Sex and the Single Girl* Helen Gurley Brown's 1962 controversial book for women about decorating, fashion, dating, cooking, and—shockingly—the joys of being single and sexually active. [Am. Lit.: *SJEPC*]

35. **Simpson trial** football great O.J. Simpson accused of 1994 stabbing death of his ex-wife Nicole and her friend Ron Goldman; subsequent trial ended with controversial acquittal and mixed reactions, with many whites convinced of his guilt, many blacks of his innocence. [Am. Hist.: *SJEPC*]

36. **Smothers Brothers, The [Tom Smothers (1937–) and Dick Smothers (1938–)]** musical duo who hosted influential comic variety TV show in late 1960s; their choice of anti-establishment satire and veiled references to sex and drugs brought confrontations with the network and eventual cancellation of show. [Am. TV: *SJEPC*]

37. **Springer, Jerry (1944–)** guests on his TV talk show are encouraged to share intimate details of their often outlandish stories and engage in shouting matches and brawls; some have speculated that the fights are staged, with actors as guests. [Am. TV: *SJEPC*]

38. **Stern, Howard (1954–)** master of shock radio whose program covers outrageous and often distasteful subjects; profanity and sexually explicit conversations are the norm. [Am. Radio: *SJEPC*]

39. **Stone, Oliver (1946–)** director and screenwriter sometimes accused of rewriting history or pandering to the demands for violence in films, nonetheless respected for the depth and social import of his work. [Am. Film: *SJEPC*]

40. **Styron, William (1925–2006)** gifted writer of *Sophie's Choice* (1979) and *The Confessions of Nat Turner* (1967); the latter brought accusations of historical inaccuracy and audacity for attempting to portray another race's experiences; novel won Pulitzer Prize nonetheless. [Am. Lit.: *SJEPC*]

41. **Swaggart, Jimmy (1935–)** leading televangelist of the 1980s; his puritanical stance and judgmental opinions meant bitter reactions when his own voyeuristic acts with a prostitute and other transgressions were revealed. [Am. Rel.: *SJEPC*]

42. **Tonkin Gulf** disputed N. Vietnamese attacks escalated U.S. war effort (1964). [Am. Hist.: Van Doren, 595]

43. *True Story* hugely popular magazine in 1920s with first-hand accounts of sensational problems; sales were brisk, but many felt it depicted the worst in American society. [Am. Jour.: *SJEPC*]

44. **Tyson, Mike (1966–)** boxing champ by the age of 19; volatile personality spilled over into personal life, leading to brutality in and out of ring and imprisonment. [Am. Sports: *SJEPC*]

45. **Wal-Mart** American shopping was changed beginning in the 1960s by retail giant; proliferation of huge discount stores (especially in small towns) offering variety and value; accused of unfair labor practices and environmental irresponsibility. [Am. Business: *SJEPC*]

46. **Warren Report** government's much disputed conclusion that President Kennedy's assassin acted alone. [Am. Hist.: Van Doren, 594]

Conventionality (See CONFORMITY.)

148. COOPERATION

1. **Achaean League** federation of Greek cities formed in 280 B.C. to resist Macedonian domination. [Gk. Hist.: Brewer *Dictionary*, 6]

2. **Allies, the** in World War I, nations, initially Russia, France, and Great Britain, allied against the Central Powers. 2. In World War

II, those allied against the Axis, including Great Britain, Russia, and U.S. [Eur. Hist.: *Collier's*, VIII, 457]

3. **Axis** in World War II, the alliance of Germany, Italy, Japan, etc., opposing the Allies. [Eur. Hist.: *Collier's*, VIII, 457]

4. **Central Powers** in World War I, the alliance of Hungary, Germany, Bulgaria, and Turkey. [Eur. Hist.: *NCE*, 493]

5. **Common Market** association of western European countries designed to facilitate free trade among members. [Eur. Hist.: *EB*, III: 1001]

6. **Confederacy** the eleven Southern States that seceded from the U.S. and banded together. [Am. Hist.: *NCE*, 623]

7. **Entente Cordiale** agreement between Great Britain and France to settle their disagreements over colonies as diplomatic partners. [Eur. Hist.: *WB*, 21: 367]

8. **European Union** economic and political partnership of 27 European nations with its own legislative body, whose goal is "peace, prosperity, and freedom." [Eur. Hist.: Misc.]

9. **Helsinki Accord** agreement between Soviet bloc and the West for economic, commercial, and scientific cooperation and for respect of human rights and fundamental freedoms. [World Hist.: *News Directory* (1977), 177–179]

10. **League of Nations** world organization for international cooperation. [World Hist.: *EB*, 6: 102]

11. **NAFTA** North American Free Trade Agreement, this 1994 accord among the U.S., Canada, and Mexico, was created to reduce economic trade barriers and improve the economies of each nation. [World Hist.: Misc.]

12. **NATO** free-world mutual security pact, formerly against Soviet bloc, now seeking peace and providing security for member nations. [World Hist.: Van Doren, 520]

13. **Nazi-Soviet Pact** nonaggression treaty freed Hitler to invade Poland. [Ger. Hist.: Shirer, 685–705]

14. **OPEC** cartel of nations that controls the export of petroleum. [World Hist.: *WB*, 14: 646]

15. **Pact of Steel** German-Italian treaty established common cause in future undertakings. [Eur. Hist.: Shirer, 646–648]

16. **Potsdam Conference** unconditional Japanese surrender demanded; war crimes trials planned (July, 1945). [World Hist.: Van Doren, 507]

17. **SEATO** organization formed to assure protection against Communist expansion in Southeast Asia (1955–1976). [World Hist.: *EB*, IX: 377]

18. **Tinker to Evers to Chance** legendary basebal double-play combination (1902–1910). [Am. Sports: Turkin, 474]

19. **Triple Entente** association among Great Britain, France, and Russia; nucleus of the Allied Coalition in WWI. [World Hist.: *EB*, 10: 128]

20. **United Nations** world organization for international discussion and peacekeeping. [World Hist.: Brewer *Dictionary*, 1116]

21. **Yalta Conference** Allies developed plan for reconstruction of post-war Europe (February, 1945). [World Hist.: Van Doren, 504]

149. CORRUPTION

1. **Gilded Age** era in U.S. History (1870s) noted for the extravagance and corruption of a wealthy elite. [Am. Hist.: Mark Twain and Charles Dudley Warner. *The Gilded Age*]

2. **Steffens, Lincoln (1866–1936)** journalist who tirelessly investigated corrupt city officials throughout U.S.; disillusioned with Capitalism, traveled to Soviet Union in 1917 and joined Communist Party. [Am. Jour.: *SJEPC*]

150. COUNSEL (See also GUIDANCE, WISDOM.)

1. **Achitophel** sage adviser to David; subsequently to Absalom. [O.T.: II Samuel 16:23]

2. **Antenor** counselor; advised Priam to return Helen to Menelaus. [Gk. Myth.: Zimmerman, 23]

3. **Areopagus** hill near the Acropolis used for Athenian council deliberations. [Gk. Hist.: Benét, 46]

4. **Chesterfield, Lord (1694–1773)** wrote *Letters to His Son* to educate him in the ways of the world. [Br. Lit.: Magill III, 565]

5. **Consus** god of councils and advice; agricultural god. [Rom. Myth.: Kravitz, 65; Parrinder, 66]

6. **Egeria** wife, instructress, and advisor of emperor Numa. [Rom. Myth.: Jobes, 491; Avery, 426]

7. **Jeeves** wise valet to good-hearted but dim Bertie Wooster in stories by P.G. Wodehouse; often gives advice to Wooster and his equally bumbling friends; reference to him in name of Internet search site "Ask Jeeves." [Br. Lit.: *SJEPC*]

8. **Krishna** Hindu god acts as spiritual and military counselor to Arjuna and his family. [Hindu lit.: *Mahabharata*]

9. **Laurence, Friar** adviser to the lovers. [Br. Lit.: *Romeo and Juliet*]

10. **Mentor** Odysseus's adviser; entrusted with care and education of Telemachus. [Gk. Lit.: *Odyssey*]

11. **Nestor** a sage old counselor to the Greeks in the Trojan War. [Gk. Myth.: *Iliad*]

12. **Polonius** gives Laertes rules of conduct. [Br. Drama: Shakespeare *Hamlet*]

13. **Poseidon Hippios** god of counsel and councils. [Gk. Myth.: Kravitz, 67]

14. **Proverbs** precepts for living according to God's law and common sense. [O.T.: Proverbs]

15. *Way to Wealth, The* maxims intended to inculcate virtue and frugality. [Am. Lit.: Benjamin Franklin *Poor Richard's Almanack* in Benét, 803]

151. COUNTERCULTURE (See also DRUG CULTURE, PSYCHEDELIA.)

1. **Altamont** free 1969 Rolling Stones concert in San Francisco ended in chaos and death. [Am. Hist.: *SJEPC*]

2. **Baez, Joan (1941–)** folk singer committed to social and political causes from the 1960s into the 21st century. [Am. Music and Politics: *SJEPC*]

3. **Birkenstocks** comfortable sandal created in Germany associated with hippies and earth-conscious people in 1970s; popular with urban professionals in 1990s. [Culture: *SJEPC*]

4. **Bruce, Lenny (1925–1966)** radical stand-up comic's social commentary and use of profanity challenged societal norms in America during conservative 1950s and 1960s. [Am. Entertainment: *SJEPC*]

5. **Burroughs, William S. (1914–1997)** morphine-addicted writer inspired the Beat Generation and eschewed mainstream post-World War II American society. [Am. Lit.: *SJEPC*]

6. **cannabis leaf** in Western world, symbol of protest against white mainstream society; also symbol of drug culture. [Symbolism: *CEOS&S*]

7. **Castaneda, Carlos (1925–1998)** his ventures with Yaqui Indian shaman Don Juan to reach higher spiritual levels through ingestion of psychedelic plants helped define the counterculture movement of the 1960s. [Am. Culture: *SJEPC*]

8. **Cheech and Chong** drug culture formed the basis of this comedy team's routines and movies in the 1970s and early 1980s. [Entertainment: *SJEPC*]

9. **Chicago Seven** seven political radicals protested political system, social injustice, and the Vietnam War during 1968 Democratic Convention in Chicago. [Am. Hist. and Politics: *SJEPC*]

10. **City Lights Books** San Francisco bookstore owned by Beat poet Lawrence Ferlinghetti was center of 1950s-60s literary counterculture. [Am. Lit.: Henderson, 38, 665–66; *SJEPC*]

11. **commune** group of unrelated people living together who reject mainstream values, with vision of more ideal society. [Hist.: *SJEPC*]

12. **Crosby, Stills, Nash, and Young** supergroup with tight vocal harmonies and countercultural lyrics blew away Woodstock festivalgoers in 1969. [Am. Music: *SJEPC*]

13. **Crumb, Robert (1943–)** underground comic artist known for sexually explicit content and social satire; created Keep on Truckin' logo and Fritz the Cat. [Am. Comics: *SJEPC*]

14. **Donovan (1946–)** Scottish-born singer/songwriter/guitarist personified 1960s counterculture with his flower-child hippie looks and drug-referential songs. [Br. Music: *SJEPC*]

15. **Doors, The** rock band's dark music, onstage image, and offstage behavior steeped in sex, drugs, and mysticism. [Am. Music: *SJEPC*]

16. **Dylan, Bob (1941–)** a key voice of the 1960s counterculture, his songs called for monumental changes in the social and political structure. [Am. Music: *SJEPC*]

17. *Easy Rider* rejecting mainstream conformist values, bikers Wyatt and Billy sell and ingest drugs, spend time at a hippie commune while on the road to New Orleans for Mardi Gras (1969). [Am. Film: *SJEPC*]

18. **Ginsberg, Allen (1926–1997)** anti-establishment poet regarded as the "father of the Beat Generation" (1950s-60s) defied social, political, and sexual conventions in his literary works and life; originated term "flower power" while living in hippie district Haight-Ashbury in 1960s. [Am. Lit.: *SJEPC*]

19. **hippies** youths of the 1960s, who opposed the Vietnam War and espoused countercultural values [Am. Culture: Misc.]

20. **punk** movement among young people in 1970s; music meant to offend, extreme attire with colored hair and studs and pins, and belligergence toward anything conventional. [Br. and Am. Pop. Culture: *SJEPC*]

21. **Steppenwolf** coined the phrase "heavy metal music" and went on to embody its clamorous rebelliousness; their "Born to Be Wild" was featured in 1969 counterculture film *Easy Rider*. [Am. Music: *SJEPC*]

22. **Thompson, Hunter S. (1939–2005)** "gonzo journalist" of 1960s and 1970s; claimed to throw together obviously crafted, impressive work; his books and articles were incisive and irreverent, his personal life excessive and outrageous. [Am. Jour.: *SJEPC*]

23. **Velvet Underground, The** latter half of the 1960s saw this very influential avant-garde rock band influencing many soon-to-be-

famous musicians despite modest commerical success; Andy Warhol produced their first album in 1966, with lyrics that spoke of much grittier topics than most. [Am. Music: *SJEPC*]

24. **Volkswagen Beetle** two-door sedan of 1950s and 1960s with profile of scarab was immensely popular with young drivers; microbus model was standard vehicle of rock bands and soon became associated with hippie culture. [Am. Pop. Culture: *SJEPC*]

25. **Whisky a Go Go** Sunset Boulevard discotheque and performance venue for notables in cutting edge of rock industry beginning in 1964; females dancing in cages were called go-go girls. [Am. Music: *SJEPC*]

26. ***Whole Earth Catalogue, The*** first published in 1968, became handbook of counterculture for its mix of philosophy, metaphysics, environmentalism, and marketing of green products. [Am. Publishing: *SJEPC*]

27. **Woodstock** Woodstock, NY was the site of three-day music and arts festival in 1969; despite chaos, drug use, and bad weather, was peaceful assemblage of 500,000 young hippies and has, for some, come to symbolize the best of the counterculture movement. [Am. Pop. Culture: *SJEPC*]

28. **Yippies** members of the late 1960s' Youth International Party, which protested "the system" through theatrical street events; led by activists Abbie Hoffman and Jerry Rubin. [Am. Culture: *SJEPC*]

29. ***Zap Comix*** quintessential underground comic book of the 1960s; included classics with adult themes such as Fritz the Cat and Mr. Natural. [Am. Comics: *SJEPC*]

Courage (See BRAVERY.)

152. COURTESAN (See also MISTRESS, PROSTITUTE.)

1. **Aspasia** mistress of Pericles; byword for cultured courtesan. [Gk. Hist.: Benét, 58]

2. **Camille** beautiful courtesan, the toast of Paris. [Fr. Lit.: *Camille*]

3. **Lais** celebrated Thessalonian courtesan, so beautiful the townswomen kill her out of jealousy. [Gk. Hist.: Benét, 561]

4. **Lescaut, Manon** lives well by giving affections to noblemen. [Fr. Lit.: *Manon Lescaut*]

5. **Marneffe, Madame** as courtesan for barons, she obtains wealth. [Fr. Lit.: *Cousin Bette*, Magill I, 166–168]

6. **Phryne (4th century B.C.)** wealthy Athenian hetaera of surpassing beauty. [Gk. Hist.: Benét, 784]

7. **Rosette** D'Albert's pliable, versatile, talented, acknowledged bedmate. [Fr. Lit.: *Mademoiselle de Maupin*, Magill I, 543–543]

8. **Thaïs** Alexandrian courtesan, converts to Christianity. [Medieval Legend: Walsh *Classical*, 307]

9. **Vasantasena** lovely courtesan whose many adventures culminate in an edict freeing her from her courtesan status. [Sanskrit Lit.: *The Little Clay Cart* in Haydn & Fuller, 432]

10. **Violetta** prosperous courtesan in fashionable Paris. [Ital. Opera: Verdi *La Traviata* in Benét, 1022]

153. COURTESY (See also HOSPITALITY.)

1. **Boy Scouts** youth organization, ever ready to perform good deeds. [Am. Hist.: Jameson, 59]

2. **Castiglione, Baldassare (1478–1529)** author of *The Courtier*, Renaissance bible of etiquette. [Ital. Lit.: Plumb, 316–319]

3. **Dickon** one of "nature's gentlemen." [Children's Lit.: *The Secret Garden*]

4. **Post, Emily (1873–1960)** etiquette book author; preaches "consideration for others." [Am. Hist.: Flexner, 277]

5. **Shem and Japheth** cover father's nakedness without looking at him. [O.T.: Genesis 9:23–27]

154. COURTESY, EXCESSIVE

1. **Alphonse and Gaston** personifications of overdone politeness. [Comics: Horn, 77–78]

2. **Haskell, Eddie** hypocritical teenager, gracious toward adults, pugnacious toward children. [TV: "Leave it to Beaver" in Terrace, II, 18–19]

3. **Petruchio** his excessive courtesy a stratagem to break Katharina. [Br. Lit.: *The Taming of the Shrew*]

Covetousness (See GREED.)

155. COWARDICE (See also TIMIDITY.)

1. **Acres, Bob** a swaggerer lacking in courage. [Br. Lit.: *The Rivals*]

2. **Bobadill, Captain** vainglorious braggart, vaunts achievements while rationalizing faintheartedness. [Br. Lit.: *Every Man in His Humour*]

3. **chicken** slang insult used toward the timid. [Western Folklore: Jobes, 322]

4. **Conachar** pathetically lacks courage. [Br. Lit.: *The Fair Maid of Perth*]

5. **Coup de Jarnac** to hit a man while he is down. [Fr. Folklore: Espy, 62]

6. **Cowardly Lion** king of the forest has yellow streak up back. [Am. Lit.: *The Wonderful Wizard of Oz*]

7. **Duke of Plaza-Toro** always leads the retreat and is the first to hide from the enemy. [Br. Opera: Gilbert and Sullivan *The Gondoliers*]

8. **Falstaff, Sir John** "the better part of valor is discretion." [Br. Lit.: *I Henry IV*]

9. **Fleming, Henry** young recruit, in his first battle, runs away in terror. [Am. Lit.: Stephen Crane *The Red Badge of Courage*]

10. **Indiana Volunteers** during Mexican war, ran when action began. [Am. Hist.: Espy, 183]

11. **Martano** poltroon claiming credit for another's feat. [Ital. Lit.: *Orlando Furioso*]

12. **Panurge** rogue who in several adventures proves to be a great coward. [Fr. Lit.: Rabelais *Gargantua and Pantagruel*]

13. **Panza, Sancho** always removes himself a safe distance from his master's combats. [Span. Lit.: Cervantes *Don Quixote*]

14. **Parolles** cowardly braggart and wastrel. [Br. Lit.: *All's Well That Ends Well*]

15. **Police, The** homeloving and fearful of death, reluctant to combat the pirate band. [Br. Opera Gilbert and Sullivan *The Pirates of Penzance*]

16. **Queeg, Captain Philip** captain of the *Caine* who is relieved of command by mutineers, proves to be a cowardly, unstable tyrant at courtmartial. [Am. Lit.: Herman Wouk *The Caine Mutiny*]

17. **Rogue's March** played in British Army to expel dishonored soldier. [Br. Music: Scholes, 885]

18. **Roister Doister, Ralph** foolish suitor repulsed by widow with household utensil. [Br. Lit.: *Ralph Roister Doister*]

19. **Scaramouche** stock character in commedia dell'arte; boastful poltroon. [Ital. Drama: Brewer *Dictionary*, 967]

20. **yellow** color symbolizing cowardice. [Western Culture: Misc.]

156. CRAFTSMANSHIP

1. **Alcimedon** a first-rate carver in wood. [Rom. Lit.: Vergil *Eclogues*, iii. 37]

2. **Argus** skillful builder of Jason's Argo. [Gk. Myth.: Walsh *Classical*, 29]

3. **Athena (Rom. Minerva)** protector of craftsmen. [Gk. Myth.: Kravitz, 67]

4. **Bezalel and Oholiab** called to make tabernacle and accoutrements for Moses. [O.T.: Exodus 31:1–11]

5. **Cyclopes** one-eyed, unruly giants; excellent metals craftsmen. [Gk. Myth.: Parrinder, 68]

6. **Dactyls** fabulous smiths; discovered iron and how to work with it. [Gk. Myth.: Leach, 273]

7. **Daedalus** great craftsman; built Labyrinth and Pasiphae's cow. [Gk. Myth.: Leach, 273]

8. **Epeius** designer and builder of the Trojan Horse. [Rom. Lit.: *Aeneid*]

9. **Hephaestus (Rom. Vulcan)** god of fire and metalworkers. [Gk. Myth.: Zimmerman, 121]

10. **Hiram** expert brazier commissioned by Solomon for temple work. [O.T.: I Kings: 7:13–14]

11. **Joseph** storied carpenter and foster-father of Jesus. [N.T.: Matthew 1:18–25; Hall, 177]

12. **Pygmalion** sculpts beautiful image that comes to life. [Rom. Lit.: *Metamorphoses*]

13. **Sidonians** known for timber-felling skill. [O.T.: I Kings 5:6]

14. **Tubal-cain** master of copper and iron smiths. [O.T.: Genesis 4:22]

157. CREATION

1. **Adam and Eve** first man and woman. [O.T.: Genesis 1:26, 2:21–25]

2. **Allah** made man from flowing blood. [Islam: Koran, 96:2]

3. **Apsu** primeval waters, origin of all things. [Babyl. Myth.: Leach, 68]

4. **Aruru** goddess pinched man, Enkidu out of clay. [Assyrian Myth.: Gaster, 9; Babyl. Myth.: *Gilgamesh*]

5. **Askr** first man; created from ash tree. [Norse Myth.: Benét, 58]

6. **Big Bang** theory in physics that posits that the universe began from a huge cosmic explosion, 15 billion years ago. [Physics: Misc.]

7. **Creationism** Biblically-based doctrine that God created the earth, universe, and all living beings. [Rel.: *SJEPC*]

8. **Darwin, Charles (1809–1882)** English scientist, developed the theory of evolution by natural selection. [Science: *ODA*]

9. **Ea** made man from primordial ocean clay. [Babyl. Myth.: Gaster, 9]

10. **Embla** first woman on Earth. [Norse Myth.: Benét, 58]

11. **fire** masculine symbol of creation, destruction, purification, revelation, regeneration, and spiritual or sexual ardor. [Symbolism: *CEOS&S*]

12. **Frankenstein's monster** living man created by a physiology student from body parts. [Br. Lit.: Mary Shelley *Frankenstein*]

13. **Genesis** Old Testament book dealing with world's creation. [O.T.: Genesis]

14. **God** created the world in six days. [O.T.: Genesis 1]

15. **Hatchery** mass produces everything, including human beings. [Br. Lit.: *Brave New World*]

16. **Khnum** ram god, created man from clay on potter's wheel. [Egypt. Rel.: Parrinder, 155]

17. **Prometheus** molded man of clay, animated him with fire. [Gk. Myth.: Wheeler, 304]

18. **serpent** often part of creation myths; Vishnu, the Hindu creator god, rests on the coils of a great snake. [Symbolism: *CEOS&S*]

19. **Shiva** Lord of creation; danced to begin life. [Hinduism: Binder, 23]

20. **Star Maker, the** the creator and destroyer of the universe, depicted primarily as an artist detached from it. [Sci. Fi.: Stapledon *Star Maker* in Weiss, 248]

21. **Tocupacha** molded man from clay. [Aztec Myth.: Gaster, 18]

22. **tree of life** universal symbol of creation; roots in water or the underworld, trunk in earthly world, branches in the heavens. [Symbolism: *CEOS&S*]

Creativity (See INVENTIVENESS.)

158. CRIME FIGHTING (See also DETECTIVE.)

1. **Batman** devotes his life to fighting Gotham City's criminals. [Comics: Berger, 160]

2. **Canadian Mounties (Royal Canadian Mounted Police)** corps which gained a romantic reputation for daring exploits and persistence in trailing criminals. [Can. Hist.: *NCE*, 2367]

3. *CSI* "Crime Scene Investigation" one of the most popular TV shows of the modern era, on CBS (2000–) [Am. TV: Misc.]

4. *Dragnet* television show in which justice is always served. [Am. TV: Buxton, 73]

5. **Earp, Wyatt (1848–1929)** law officer and gunfighter of American West. [Am. Hist.: *NCE*, 819]

6. **FBI** Federal Bureau of Investigation; government agents fight organized crime, terrorism, espionage, illegal drug trafficking. [Am. Hist.: *SJEPC*]

7. *French Connection, The* gritty, realistic movie based on an actual narcotics investigation/bust in New York City stars Gene Hackman and Roy Scheider as hardnosed, aggressive cops Jimmy

"Popeye" Doyle and Buddy "Cloudy" Russo; features one of film's most exciting car chases. [Am. Film: *SJEPC*]

8. **Friday, Joe** crime-fighting hero of *Dragnet*, dedicated, loyal, and laconic. [Am. TV: *FOF, MOD*]

9. **G-man** FBI agent; U.S. "government" man who fights federal crimes. [Am. Hist.: *SJEPC*]

10. **Guardian Angels, The** volunteer, citizen-based group established in New York City by Curtis Sliwa in 1979 to protect the public from crime; red-bereted, unarmed protectors are now a presence in cities throughout the world. [Am. Hist.: *SJEPC*]

11. *Hill Street Blues* popular TV show of the 1980s, featured personal lives behind a hard-working police force. [Am. TV: *EB*]

12. **Hoover, J. Edgar (1895–1972)** headed the FBI from 1924 to 1972, increasing its powers to investigate organized crime, Communists, political dissenters, and civil rights leaders; became a controversial figure for his obsessiveness in going after anyone he deemed anti-American. [Am. Hist.: *EB*]

13. **INTERPOL** International Crime Police Organization, since 1923 fighting crime worldwide, now 180 member nations. [World Hist.: *EB*]

14. **Kojak** character from popular TV show of same name; commander of detective squad in New York; tough-guy mannerisms, lollipop addiction, and trademark "Who loves ya, baby?" [Am. TV: Terrace I, 445; *SJEPC*]

15. **Lone Ranger** arch foe of criminals in early west. [Radio: "The Lone Ranger" in Buxton, 143–144; Comics: Horn, 460; TV: Terrace, II, 34–35]

16. **McGarrett, Steve** implacable nemesis of Hawaiian wrongdoers. [TV: "Hawaii Five-O" in Terrace, I, 342]

17. **Neighborhood Watch** organized groups of citizens report suspicious behavior to local police stations. [Am. Culture: *SJEPC*]

18. **Ness, Eliot** G-man successfully subdues Prohibition gangsters. [TV: "The Untouchables" in Terrace, II, 402–403]

19. **Peel, Sir Robert (1788–1850)** reorganized British police; established Irish constabulary. [Br. Hist.: Flexner, 276]

20. **Purvis, Melvin** gunned down Dillinger outside Chicago theater (1934). [Am. Hist.: Wallechinsky, 464]

21. **Scotland Yard** Criminal Investigation Department of Metropolitan Police. [Br. Hist.: Brewer *Dictionary*, 97]

22. **Shadow, The** character in radio program from 1937–1954 known for hypnotic powers and memorable lines ("Who knows what evil lurks in the hearts of men? The Shadow knows."); also char-

acter in popular crime-fighting pulp novels and comic books. [Am. Comics and Radio: *SJEPC*]

23. ***Starsky & Hutch*** popular detective TV show of the 1970s; close relationship between two main characters and car chases characterized each episode; shoot-outs were considered excessive at the time. [Am. TV: *SJEPC*]

24. **Superman** invincible scourge of crime. [Comics: Horn, 642–643]

25. **Texas Rangers** 19th-century constabulary thwarting villains. [Am. Hist.: Brewer *Dictionary*, 1071]

26. **Tracy, Dick** comic book cop. [Comics: Horn, 206–207]

27. **Webb, Jack (1920–1982)** played Sgt. Joe Friday of the Los Angeles Police Dept. in TV series *Dragnet* with deadpan forthright, unambiguous demeanor and unemotional "Just the facts, ma'am." [Am. TV: *SJEPC*]

159. CRIMINAL (See also GANGSTERISM, OUTLAW.)

1. **Fowl, Artemis** criminal genius of fantasy novels for young readers written by Eoin Colfer; ruthless, aloof, yet charismatic, Artemis is mainly concerned with acquiring money; his character softens, however, as the series progresses. [Irish Children's Lit.: Misc.]

2. **Lanksy, Meyer (1902–1983)** powerful organized crime leader; a shrewd, intelligent, powerful criminal. [Am. Culture: *FOF, MOD*]

3. **Leopold and Loeb** infamous teenage murderers who killed a 14–yr. old friend in 1924, just to prove they could do it. [Am. Hist.: *FOF, MOD*]

4. **Murder, Inc.** organized crime's crew of professional hit men, organized in the 1930s; they killed only other criminals, carrying out the orders of such notorious gangsters as Bugsy Seigel and Meyer Lansky. [Am. Hist.: *FOF, MOD*]

5. **Murgatroyd, Sir Despard** baronet forced by his ancestors to perform a crime a day. [Br. Opera: Gilbert and Sullivan *Ruddigore*]

6. **public enemies** term coined by former FBI head J. Edgar Hoover, to describe the most dangerous professional criminals and mobsters. [Am. Culture: *FOF, MOD*]

160. CRITICISM

1. *Blackwood's Magazine* Scottish literary magazine founded in 1817, notorious for its Tory bias and vicious criticism. [Br. Lit.: Benét, 111]

2. **Bludyer, Mr.** a "slashing" book reviewer with savage humor. [Br. Lit.: *Pendennis*]

3. **Bolo, Miss** "looked a small armoury of daggers" at those who made mistakes. [Br. Lit.: *Pickwick Papers*]

4. **Dutch uncle** strict elder who scolds and moralizes. [Br. Slang: Lurie, 122–123]

5. *Edinburgh Review* influential literary and political review, founded in 1802, inaugurating new literary standards. [Br. Lit.: Barnhart, 375]

6. **Eliphaz, Bildad, and Zophar** rebuke Job for his complaints. [O.T.: Job 4–31]

7. *Essay on Criticism* didactic poem on rules by which a critic should be guided. [Br. Lit.: Pope *Essay on Criticism* in Magill IV, 287]

8. **flak** from a German acronym for anti-aircraft assault, current usage means criticism. [Pop. Cult.: *FOF, MOD*]

9. **Joab** admonishes David for ingratitude to troops and servants. [O.T.: II Samuel 9:1–8]

10. **Michal** David's wife; castigates him for boyish exulting. [O.T.: II Samuel 6:20]

11. **Monday morning quarterback** football spectator who, in hindsight, points out where team went wrong. [Am. Sports and Folklore: Misc.]

12. **Sanballat and Tobiah** jeered Jews' attempt to rebuild Jerusalem's walls. [O.T.: Nehemiah 4:1–3]

13. **Theon** satirical poet of trenchant wit. [Rom. Lit.: Brewer *Dictionary*, 1073]

14. **Zoilus** malicious and contentious rhetorician; "Homer's scourge." [Gk. Hist.: Brewer *Dictionary*, 1175]

161. CROSS-DRESSER

1. **Bates, Norman** homicidal protagonist of 1960 horror film by Alfred Hitchcock with famous, frightening shower murder and surprise ending— Bates has been impersonating his dead mother while attacking young women. [Am. Film: *SJEPC*]

2. **Berle, Milton (1908–2002)** American TV comic whose broad humor often included him in women's clothes. [Am. TV: *FOF, MOD*]

3. **drag queen** a male, typically homosexual, dressing as and impersonating a female, often exaggerated to extremes. [Culture: *SJEPC*]

4. **Klinger, Cpl. Maxwell** dresses in women's clothes to try to win discharge from the army [Am. TV: *M*A*S*H* in Terrace]

5. **RuPaul** African-American entertainer; stunning looks and self-confidence won him contract with major cosmetics company. [Am. Culture: *SJEPC*]

6. ***Tootsie*** 1982 comedy film about out-of-work actor who dresses as a woman to get a role in a successful soap opera; he learns the complications of being a woman in American culture. [Am. Film: *SJEPC*]

7. **Wilson, Flip (1933–1998)** brought African-American perspective to white audiences through successful, award-winning network variety series *The Flip Wilson Show* (1970–1974); there he portrayed numerous memorable characters, including sassy Geraldine Jones—played in drag. [Am. TV: *SJEPC*]

8. **Wood, Ed (1924–1978)** cross-dressing director of notably bad films whose works drew a cult following, especially after 1994 biopic about his life and work. [Am. Film: *SJEPC*]

162. CRUELTY (See also BRUTALITY, HEARTLESSNESS, MUTILATION, TYRANNY.)

1. **Achren** mean, spiteful enchantress of Spiral Castle. [Children's Lit.: "The Castle of Llyr*]*

2. **Allan, Barbara** spurned her dying sweetheart because of a fancied slight. [Br. Balladry: Benét, 78]

3. **Blackbeard** nickname of pirate, Edward Teach (d.1718). [Am. Hist.: Hart, 84]

4. **Bligh, Captain** tyrannical master of the ship *Bounty*. [Am. Lit.: *Mutiny on the Bounty*]

5. **bull** symbolizes cruelty in Picasso's *Guernica*. [Span. Art.: Mercatante, 99]

6. **Bumble, Mr.** abusive beadle, mistreats Oliver and other waifs. [Br. Lit.: *Oliver Twist*]

7. **Cipolla** magician who hypnotizes and brutally humiliates members of the audience. [Ger. Lit.: *Mario and the Magician* in Benét, 636]

8. **Conchis** his psychological experiments cause repeated emotional anguish among his subjects. [Br. Lit.: John Fowles *The Magus* in Weiss, 279]

9. **Creakle, Mr.** headmaster at Salem House; enjoys whipping boys. [Br. Lit.: *David Copperfield*]

10. **cuscuta** symbol of cruelty. [Flower Symbolism: Jobes, 399]

11. **Diocletian** Roman emperor (284–305); instituted general persecutions of Christians. [Rom. Hist.: *EB*, 5: 805–807]

12. **Guilbert, Brian de Bois** dissolute and cruel commander of the Knights Templars. [Br. Lit.: *Ivanhoe*]

13. **Job's comforters** maliciously torment Job while ostensibly attempting to comfort him. [Br. Lit.: Job]

14. **Legree, Simon** harsh taskmaster; slavetrader. [Am. Lit.: _Uncle Tom's Cabin_]

15. **leopard** represents meanness, sin, and the devil. [Animal Symbolism: Mercatante, 56]

16. **Margaret of Anjou** hard, vicious, strong-minded, imperious woman. [Br. Lit.: _II Henry IV_]

17. **Mezentius** Etrurian king put his subjects to death by binding them to dead men and letting them starve. [Rom. Legend: Benét, 664]

18. **Murdstone, Edward** harsh and cruel husband of widow Copperfield. [Br. Lit.: _David Copperfield_]

19. **Nurse Ratched** cruel nurse who runs the mental hospital and plays the nemesis of Randall Patrick McMurphy; symbol of rigidity, cruelty. [Am. Lit.: Ken Kesey _One Flew Over the Cuckoo's Nest_; Am. Film: Milos Forman _One Flew Over the Cuckoo's Nest_]

20. **painted bird, the** painted by peasants and released, it is rejected and killed by its original flock. [Pol. Tradition: Weiss, 345]

21. **Slout, Mr.** punished Oliver for asking for more gruel. [Br. Lit.: _Oliver Twist_]

22. **Squeers, Wackford** brutal, abusive pedagogue; starves and maltreats urchins. [Br. Lit.: _Nicholas Nickleby_]

23. **Totenkopfverbande** tough Death's Head units maintaining concentration camps in Nazi Germany. [Ger. Hist.: Shirer, 375]

24. **Vlad the Impaler (c. 980–1015)** prince of Walachia; called Dracula; ruled barbarously. [Eur. Hist.: _NCE_, 2907]

163. CRYING

1. **Bokim** Hebrew toponym; "Weepers"; Israelites bewail their wrongdoings. [O.T.: Judges 2:1–5]

2. **Heraclitus** the weeping philosopher; melancholic personality. [Gk. Phil.: Hall, 98]

3. **Mary Magdalene** tearfully washes Christ's feet. [N.T.: Luke 7:37–38]

4. **Niobe** weeps when her children are slain, even after Zeus turns her to stone. [Gk. Myth.: _RHDC_]

5. **Rachel weeping for her children** Israel, for children slain by order of Herod. [N.T.: Matthew 2:16–18]

6. **tears of Eros** dewdrops; teardrops shed for slain son. [Gk. Myth.: Brewer _Dictionary_, 1065]

164. CUCKOLDRY (See also ADULTERY, FAITHLESSNESS.)

1. **Actaeon's horns** symbol of cuckoldry. [Medieval and Ren. Folklore: Walsh _Classical_, 5]

2.   **antlers** metaphorical decoration for deceived husband. [Western Folklore: Jobes, 395]

3.   **Arveragus** delivers wife to adulterer to keep promise. [Br. Lit. *Canterbury Tales*, "The Franklin's Tale"]

4.   **Boylan, Blazes** cuckolds Leopold Bloom. [Irish Lit.: James Joyce *Ulysses* in Magill I, 1040]

5.   **Cabot, Ephraim** Abbie, his young wife, seduces his youngest son, Eben. [Am. Drama: Eugene O'Neill *Desire Under the Elms*]

6.   **Chatterley, Sir Clifford** cripple whose wife has a prolonged affair with his gamekeeper. [Br. Lit. D. H. Lawrence *Lady Chatterley's Lover* in Benét, 559]

7.   **cuckoo** symbolizes adulterous betrayal by wife. [Western Folklore: Jobes, 395; Mercante, 164]

8.   **del Sarto, Andrea** cuckolded Florentine painter; protagonist of Browning's poem. [Art. Hist.: Walsh, *Modern*, 19–20;; Br. Lit.: "Andrea del Sarto" in Norton, 778–783]

9.   **Hildebrand, Old** sent away while wife and preacher play. [Ger. Fairy Tale: Grimm, 333]

10.   **Mannon, Ezra** kindly general deceived by adulterous wife and murdered. [Am. Lit.: *Mourning Becomes Electra*]

11.   **Mark, King** by Tristan after May-December marriage to Isolde. [Ger. Opera: Wagner *Tristan and Isolde*, Westerman, 220]

12.   **Menelaus** his wife, Helen, was also Paris's lover. [Gk. Lit.: *Iliad*]

13.   **Rubin, Maximiliano** sickly pharmacist; wife's infidelities begin on wedding night. [Span. Lit.: *Fortunata and Jacinta*]

14.   **Trusotsky** learns from his dead wife's letters that she had numerous lovers and that he is not the father of his child. [Russ. Lit.: Dostoevsky *The Eternal Husband*]

15.   **Uriah the Hittite** while he is at war, his wife sleeps with David. [O.T.: II Samuel 11:16]

165.   CULTISM

1.   **cult films** mostly out-of-the-mainstream motion pictures with strong appeal to a specific audience segment are viewed repeatedly and may invite predictable audience participation, as with subculture cult film *The Rocky Horror Picture Show* (1975). [Film: *SJEPC*]

2.   **Koresh, David (1959–1993)** troubled child molester who claimed to have apocalyptic visions established a cult following (Branch Davidians) who lived in a compound in Waco, Texas; during a 1993 raid by federal agents, Koresh and 80 others were shot or died in the fire at the ranch, [Am. Hist.: *SJEPC*]

3.   **Manson, Charles (1934–)** runaways and displaced petty criminals joined his murderous "Family." [Am. Hist.: *SJEPC*]

4. **Moon, Reverend Sun Myung (1920–)** Korean-born self-pro-claimed leader of the suspect Unification Church [Am. Rel.: *SJEPC*]

5. **Moonies** youthful followers of Rev. Sun Myung Moon lived communally, sold flowers, and submitted to the church's strict control. [Am. Rel.: *SJEPC*]

6. **People's Temple** destructive cult founded by Jim Jones (1931–1978); he and 914 of his followers died in mass mur-der/suicide in Jonestown, Guyana, Nov. 1978. [Am. Hist.: *EB*]

7. *Rocky Horror Picture Show* since 1976 fans throng to midnight screenings; audiences participate with counterpoint dialogue and props to the outlandish plot of sexual exploits, transvestism, alien invasion, and cannibalism. [Am. Film: *SJEPC*]

8. *Star Trek* short-lived late 1960s science-fiction TV show written by Gene Roddenberry; became a phenomenon; movies, TV spin-offs, books, clubs, conventions, memorabilia, and a host of other offshoots followed. [Am. TV: *SJEPC*]

9. *Star Wars* influential 1977 George Lucas film employed unprece-dented computer animation to depict outer space landscapes and battles while plot adhered to classic conflict between good and evil; conventions and merchandise remain incredibly popular with loyal fans. [Am. Film: *SJEPC*]

10. **Trekkies** fans of *Star Trek* phenomenon, attend conventions, col-lect memorabilia, etc. [Am. Pop. Culture: *SJEPC*]

11. **Waters, John (1946–)** writer and filmmaker who calls his ap-proach "good bad taste"; profanity and scatalogical humor in large portions; incest, castration, etc. but also a touching affection for the outsider; *Pink Flamingoes* (1972) became a cult favorite and *Hairspray* (1988). [Am. Film and Theater: *SJEPC*]

12. **Wood, Ed (1924–1978)** cross-dressing director of notably bad films whose works drew a cult following, especially after 1994 biopic about his life and work. [Am. Music: *SJEPC*]

166. CUNNING (See also TRICKERY, UNSCRUPULOUSNESS.)

1. **Adler, Irene** cleverly foiled Sherlock Holmes and the King of Bo-hemia. [Br. Lit.: Doyle "A Scandal in Bohemia" in *Sherlock Holmes*]

2. **Artful Dodger** nickname for the sly pickpocket, John Dawkins. [Br. Lit.: *Oliver Twist*]

3. **Asmodeus** clever, hell-born hero. [Fr. Lit.: *Le Diable Boiteux*, Walsh *Modern*, 31]

4. **Autolycus** craftiest of thieves; stole neighbors' flocks by chang-ing marks. [Gk. Myth.: *NCE*, 192]

5. **Bamber, Jack** law clerk with "strange wild slyness." [Br. Lit.: *Pickwick Papers*]

6. **Bolingbroke, Henry** cleverness and timing bring him England's crown. [Br. Lit.: *Richard II*]

7. **Borgia, Cesare (1476–1507)** unscrupulously plotted against friend and foe. [Ital. Hist.: Plumb, 59–61]

8. **Brer Fox** sly trickster; outwits everyone. [Children's Lit.: *Uncle Remus*]

9. **Bugs Bunny** for whom no trap is too tricky. [Comics: Horn, 140]

10. **Bundy, Ted (1946–1989)** attractive, charming, and manipulative serial killer often targeted young college women. [Am. Hist.: *SJEPC*]

11. **cheetah** pounces without warning on prey. [Western Folklore: Jobes, 320]

12. **Cleopatra (69–30 B.C.)** manipulates Antony through her "infinite variety." [Br. Lit.: *Antony and Cleopatra*]

13. **crow** symbolizes one who lives by his wits. [Western Folklore: Jobes, 388]

14. **Dido** contracts for as much land as can be enclosed by an ox-hide; by cutting it into a strip she obtains enough to found a city. [Rom. Legend: *Collier's* VI, 259]

15. **Dolius** epithet of Hermes, meaning 'crafty.' [Gk. Myth.: Zimmerman, 124]

16. **Fabius** delayed meeting Hannibal's troops; wore them down; hence, *fabian*. [Rom. Hist.: Espy, 177]

17. **Figaro** ingeniously contrives means to his own ends. [Fr. Lit.: *Barber of Seville; Marriage of Figaro*]

18. **fox** symbol of cleverness and deceit. [Animal Symbolism: Mercatante, 84–85]

19. **Foxy Grandpa** shrewd old man always turns the table on mischievous kids. [Comics: Horn, 602]

20. **Helena** tricks husband into fulfilling marital duties. [Br. Lit.: *All's Well That Ends Well*]

21. **Hippomenes** beat the swift Atalanta in a race by distracting her with golden apples. [Gk. Myth.: Bullfinch]

22. **Isabella** frustrates captor while pretending compliance. [Ital. Opera: Rossini, *Italian Girl in Algeria*, Westerman, 118–119]

23. **jackal** outwits the tiger; imprisons him. [Hindu Folklore: Mercatante, 55]

24. **Little Claus** grows rich by tricks and extortions. [Dan. Lit.: *Andersen's Fairy Tales*]

25. **Malengin** carries net on back to "catch fools with." [Br. Lit.: *Faerie Queene*]

26. **Marion, Francis (1732–1795)** Revolutionary general, nicknamed the "Swamp Fox." [Am. Hist.: Jameson, 308]

27. **Morgiana** female slave cleverly dispatches 40 thieves. [Arab. Lit.: *Arabian Nights*, "Ali Baba and the Forty Thieves"]

28. **mouse** Celtic symbol of destructive, dark forces, stealth, and cunning. [Symbolism: *CEOS&S*]

29. **Odysseus** wily and noble hero of the *Odyssey*. [Gk. Lit.: *Odyssey*]

30. **Oriol, Father** shrewd landowner with admirable bargaining ability. [Fr. Lit.: *Mont-Oriol*, Magill I, 618–620]

31. **Panurge** "received answers in twelve known and unknown tongues." [Fr. Lit.: *Gargantua and Pantagruel*]

32. **Philadelphia lawyer** clever at finding fine points and technicalities. [Am. Usage: Misc.]

33. **Road Runner** thrives on outwitting Wile E. Coyote. [Comics: "Beep Beep the Road Runner" in Horn, 105]

34. **Sawyer, Tom** hoodwinks friends into painting fence. [Am. Lit.: *Tom Sawyer*]

35. **Scheherazade** escapes being put to death by telling stories for 1001 nights. [Arab. Lit.: *Arabian Nights*]

36. **serpent** subtly deceives Eve in the Garden. [O.T.: Genesis 3:1]

37. **Sharp, Becky** clever heroine of Thackery's famous satirical novel, who rises from poverty to wealth through her cunning. [Br. Lit.: William Thackeray *Vanity Fair*]

38. **Silver, Long John** character from R.L. Stevenson's *Treasure Island*; villanous and charming, he tricks Jim Hawkins into trusting him, then attempts to steal part of Jim's treasure. [Br. Children's Lit.: Jones]

39. **Sinon** induces Trojans to take in wooden horse. [Rom. Lit.: *Aeneid*]

40. **spider ophrys** indicates cleverness. [Flower Symbolism: *Flora Symbolica*, 177]

41. **third little pig** outwits Wolf; lures him into boiling water. [Children's Lit.: Bettelheim, 41–45]

42. **Weller, Samuel** ingeniously rescues his master, Mr. Pickwick, from many scrapes. [Br. Lit.: Dickens *Pickwick Papers*]

43. **Whipple, Molly** outwits ferocious giant and gains his talismanic possessions. [Br. Fairy Tale: "Molly Whipple" in Macleod, 58–64]

44. **wolf** symbol on coats of arms. [Heraldry: Halberts, 16]

167. CURIOSITY (See also EAVESDROPPING, VOYEURISM.)

1. **Alice** young girl whose curiosity draws her into fantastic—and sometimes disconcerting—adventures in Lewis Carroll's fantasy books. [Br. Children's Lit.: Jones]

2. **Anselmo** so assured of wife's fidelity, asks friend to try to corrupt her; friend is successful. [Span. Lit.: *Don Quixote*]

3. **Cupid and Psyche** her inquisitiveness almost drives him away forever. [Gk. Myth.: Espy, 27]

4. **Curious George** protagonist of series of children's books by H. A. Rey; lovable but very curious monkey gets into trouble and finds adventure only to be rescued and forgiven by surrogate parent Man with the Yellow Hat. [Am. Children's Lit.: Jones]

5. **Fatima** Bluebeard's 7th and last wife; her inquisitiveness uncovers his murders. [Fr. Fairy Tale: Harvey, 97–98]

6. **Faustus, Doctor** makes demonic compact to sate thirst for knowledge. [Br. Lit.: *Doctor Faustus*]

7. **Harker, Jonathan** uncovers vampiric and lycanthropic activities at Castle Dracula. [Br. Lit.: *Dracula*]

8. **Lot's wife** ignores God's command; turns to salt upon looking back. [O.T.: Genesis 19:26]

9. **Lucius** his insatiable curiosity involves him in magic and his accidental transformation into an ass. [Rom. Lit.: *The Golden Ass*]

10. **Nosy Parker** after a meddlesome Elizabethan Archbishop of Canterbury. [Br. Hist.: Espy, 169]

11. **Odysseus' companions** to determine its contents, they open the bag Aeolus had given Odysseus, thus releasing winds that blow the ship off course. [Gk. Lit.: *Odyssey*]

12. **Pandora** inquisitively opens box of plagues given by Zeus. [Gk. Myth.: Zimmerman, 191]

13. **Pry, Paul** overly inquisitive journalist. [Br. Lit.: *Paul Pry*, Espy, 135]

14. **sycamore** symbolizes inquisitiveness. [Flower Symbolism: *Flora Symbolica*, 177]

15. **Vathek** journeys to Istakhar where world's secrets are revealed. [Br. Lit.: *Vathek*]

168. CURMUDGEON

1. **Brown, Murphy** cranky, but principled TV journalist from program of same name [Am. TV: *SJEPC*]

2. **Grinch, The** Dr. Seuss character from children's literature; tries to destroy Christmas in Who-ville just because he hates to see the townsfolk happy. [Am. Chldren's Lit.: Jones]

3. **Mencken, H. L. (1880–1956)** acerbic writer known for talent and ruthless criticism. [Am. Jour.: *SJEPC*]

4. **Tortelli, Carla** surly, foul-mouthed waitress at bar on TV's *Cheers* (1982–93). [Am. TV: *SJEPC*]

169. CURSE

1. **Alberich's curse** on the Rhinegold ring: possessor will die. [Ger. Opera: Wagner, *Rhinegold*, Westerman, 233]

2. **Ancient Mariner** cursed by the crew because his slaying of the albatross is causing their deaths. [Br. Poetry: Coleridge *The Rime of the Ancient Mariner*]

3. **Andvari** king of the dwarfs; his malediction spurs many events in the *Nibelungenlied*. [Norse Myth.: Bullfinch]

4. **Atreus, house of** cursed by Thyestes, whose children Atreus had served him in a stew. [Gk. Legend: Benét, 61]

5. **Cain** cursed by God for murdering Abel. [O.T.: Genesis 4:11]

6. **Eriphyle** dying at the hand of her son Alcamaeon, she curses any land that would shelter him. [Gk. Myth.: Benét, 20]

7. *Family Reunion, The* the Eumenides haunt a decaying English family because the head of the house had plotted to kill his pregnant wife. [Br. Drama: Magill II, 321]

8. **Flying Dutchman** sea captain condemned to sail unceasingly because he had invoked the Devil's aid in a storm. [Maritime Legend: Brewer *Dictionary*]

9. **Harmonia's necklace** brought disaster to all who possessed it. [Gk. Myth.: Benét, 442]

10. *Holes* book for young readers written in 1999 by Louis Sacher; a curse on Stanley's family is blamed for his bad luck; falsely accused of a crime, he is sent to a bizarre, brutal detention camp where he must help dig countless holes for no apparent reason. [Am. Children's Lit.: Misc.]

11. **Maule, Matthew** about to be executed as a wizard, laid a bloody doom on the Pyncheons. [Am. Lit.: Hawthorne *The House of Seven Gables*]

12. **Melmoth the Wanderer** doomed by a curse to roam the earth for 150 years after his death. [Br. Lit.: *Melmoth the Wanderer*]

13. **moonstone** wrested by an English officer from Buddhist priests who place a curse on all who possess it. [Br. Lit.: Collins *The Moonstone* in Benét, 683]

14. **Murgatroyd, Sir Rupert** he and all future lords of Ruddigore are doomed by a witch to commit a crime a day forever. [Br. Opera: Gilbert and Sullivan *Ruddigore*]

15. **Thyestes** cursed the house of Atreus, who had served him his sons in a stew. [Gk. Myth. and Drama: "Atreus," in Benét, 61]

16. **Tutankhamen's tomb** its opening supposed to have brought a curse upon its excavators, some of whom died soon after. [Pop. Cult.: Misc.]

170. CUTENESS

1. **Bambi** adorable deer grows rhapsodically in beautiful forest. [Am. Cinema: *Bambi* in *Disney Films*, 53–56]

2. **teddy bear** cuddly commodity named after President Theodore Roosevelt. [Am. Hist.: Frank, 46]

3. **Thumper** Bambi's huggable rabbit sidekick. [Am. Cinema: *Bambi* in *Disney Films*, 53–56]

171. CYNICISM (See also PESSIMISM, SKEPTICISM.)

1. **Antisthenes (444–371 B.C.)** Greek philosopher and founder of Cynic school. [Gk. Hist.: *NCE*, 121]

2. **Apemantus** churlish, sarcastic advisor of Timon. [Br. Lit.: *Timon of Athens*]

3. **Backbite, Sir Benjamin** sarcastic would-be poet and wit. [Br. Lit.: *School for Scandal*]

4. **Bierce, Ambrose (1842–1914)** acerbic journalist for *San Francisco Examiner*; nicknamed "Bitter Bierce." [Am. Lit.: Hart, 77]

5. **bread and circuses** term from Roman satirist Juvenal, who thought that people wanted only them; term for spectacles created by government to distract people from reality. [Culture *FOF, MOD*]

6. **Diogenes (412–323 B.C.)** frustratedly looked everywhere for an honest man. [Gk. Hist.: Avery, 395]

7. **Ferdinand** rogue drifter views all his experiences with profound cynicism. [Fr. Lit.: *Journey to the End of the Night* in Magill I, 453]

8. **Lescaut** assured Geronte sister will succumb to his money. [Ital. Opera: Puccini, *Manon Lescaut*, Westerman, 346]

9. **Pandarus** jaded about good graces of women. [Br. Lit.: *Troilus and Cressida*]

D

172. DANCE

1. **Ailey, Alvin (1931–1989)** African-American dancer and choreographer whose interracial dance company, founded in 1958, achieved international status. [Am. Dance: *SJEPC*]

2. **Astaire, Fred (1899–1987)** elegant dancer, often paired with Ginger Rogers, in many MGM musicals. [Am. Dance: *ODA*]

3. **Balanchine, George (1904–1983)** Russian choreographer, founder of New York City Ballet, noted for neoclassical, plotless ballets. [Am. Dance: *FOF, MOD*]

4. *Ballet Shoes* classic book for young readers written by Noel Streatfeild in 1936; began the genre of career novel; depicts three sisters who study dance and acting, while describing their family life; book also chronicles their professional experiences and decisions. [Br. Children's Lit.: *OCCL*]

5. **Barishnikov, Mikhail (1948–)** Russian ballet star who defected to the U.S. to dance and choreograph. [Am. Dance: Misc.]

6. **Berkeley, Busby (1895–1976)** choreographer for such Hollywood musicals as *42nd Street*, with scores of beautiful girls dancing in intricate patterns. [Am. Film: *FOF, MOD*]

7. **Carmichael, Essie** untalented girl who goes into her ballet routine with little or no experience. [Am. Drama: Kaufman and Hart *You Can't Take It with You* in Hart, 955]

8. **Castle, Vernon (1887–1918) and Irene (1893–1969)** fashionable husband-and-wife ballroom dancing duo created national interest in dance styles such as the foxtrot and tango in pre-World War I America. [Am. Dance: *SJEPC*]

9. **Checker, Chubby (1941–)** his recording of "The Twist" (1960) and subsequent Twist songs boosted popularity of the dance. [Am. Music: *SJEPC*]

10. **Cunningham, Merce (1919–)** innovative choreographer/dancer defied tradition with company he created in 1953; in collaboration with music composer John Cage and visual artist Andy Warhol, used element of chance in dance performances. [Am. Dance: *SJEPC*]

11. **Degas, Edward (1834–1917)** French Impressionist painter and sculptor known for his depictions of dancers. [Fr. Art: *ODA*]

12. **DeMille, Agnes (1905–1993)** American modern dancer and choreographer of *Oklahoma* and other musicals. [Am. Dance: *FOF, MOD*]

13. **Diaghilev, Serge (1872–1929)** Russian impressario, founder of the Ballet Russe, discovered Nijinksy; promoted the work of Stravinksy, Balanchine, Picasso, other great artists of the 20th century. [Eur. Dance: *FOF, MOD*]

14. **Duncan, Isadora (1878–1927)** influential modern dancer and choreographer, died in tragic car accident. [Am. Dance: *ODA*]

15. **Esmeralda** gypsy girl whose street dancing captivates onlookers. [Fr. Lit.: Victor Hugo *The Hunchback of Notre Dame*]

16. **Fonteyn, Margot (1919–1991)** English star of the Royal Ballet and partner of Rudolph Nureyev (stage name of Margaret Hookham). [Br. Dance: *ODA*]

17. **Fosse, Bob (1927–1987)** visionary dancer/director/choreographer whose distinctive, sexually suggestive style earned him Tony Awards for such stage musicals as *The Pajama Game* (1954), *Sweet Charity* (1966), and *Pippin* (1972). [Am. Dance: *SJEPC*]

18. **Graham, Martha (1894–1991)** American choreographer and dancer, progenitor of the modern dance movement, creator of such classics as *Appalachian Spring*. [Am. Dance: Misc.]

19. **Kelly, Gene (1912–1996)** athletic dancer and choreographer who helped expand the range of dance in movies by bringing dance out of the ballroom and into real-life situations, notably in a downpour on a city street in *Singin' in the Rain* (1952). [Am. Dance and Film: *SJEPC*]

20. **Nijinsky, Vaslav (1890–1950)** Russian star of the Ballet Russe, famous for roles in *L'Apres-midi d'un Faune* and *Petrouchka*. [Russ. Dance: *ODA*]

21. **Nureyev, Rudolph (1939–1993)** Russian ballet star, legendary partner of Margot Fonteyn, defected from Soviet Union in 1961. [Russ. Dance: *ODA*]

22. **Pavlova, Anna (1881–1931)** legendary Russian ballerina, known for her role in "The Dying Swan." [Russ. Dance: *ODA*]

23. **Rand, Sally (1904–1979)** famous for fan and bubble dances with suggestive moves and lots of skin. [Am. Entertainment: *SJEPC*]

24. **"Red Shoes, The"** bewitched shoes force Karen to dance unceasingly. [Danish Lit.: Andersen "The Red Shoes" in Magill II, 27]

25. **Robinson, Bill "Bojangles" (1878–1949)** American tap dancer, star of Broadway and movies, known for rhythmically complex, creative tap style. [Am. Dance: *FOF, MOD*]

26. **Rockettes** precision dancers; a fixture at New York's Radio City Music Hall. [Am. Dance: Payton, 576]

27. **Rogers, Ginger (1911–1995)** dancer and actress, often paired with Fred Astaire, in many MGM musicals. [Am. Dance: *ODA*]

28. **Roseland Ballroom** New York dance hall. [Pop. Culture: Misc.]

29. **Salome** danced to obtain head of John the Baptist. [N.T.: Matthew 14:6–11]

30. **Salsa Music** native to the Caribbean but evolved in New York City; incorporates African rhythms and European harmony into hot Latin American dance sounds. [Am. Music: *SJEPC*]

31. *Saturday Night Fever* 1977 film that echoes disco craze of the period; John Travolta as disco king and soundtrack tunes by the Bee-Gees. [Am. Film: *SJEPC*]

32. **Savoy Ballroom** famous dance venue in Harlem from 1926–1956; countless dance crazes began there and many jazz bands of Swing Era performed. [Am. Music: *SJEPC*]

33. **Shawn, Ted (1891–1972)** considered the forefather of modern dance; established dance as a legitimate career for men in America. [Am. Dance: *SJEPC*]

34. *Singin' in the Rain* 1952 film musical about film musicals; portrays the sometimes rocky beginnings of talkie pictures; most notable scene is Gene Kelly's dance down a street in a downpour. [Am. Film: *SJEPC*]

35. **St. Denis, Ruth and Ted Shawn (1877–1968) (1891–1972)** husband-and-wife team, founders of Denishawn dance schools. [Am. Dance: *NCE*, 2395]

36. **Temple, Shirley (1928–)** popular child film star during 1930s and 1940s; dimples, gold ringlets, and charming singing/tap dancing made her the darling of the American public. [Am. Film: *SJEPC*]

37. **Terpischore** muse of dancing. [Gk. Myth.: Brewer *Dictionary*, 849]

38. **Tharp, Twyla (1941–)** prominent choreographer of modern dance and ballet whose career burgeoned in the 1960s and 1970s. [Am. Dance: *SJEPC*]

39. **Villella, Edward (1936–)** principal dancer with New York City Ballet in 1960s and 1970s who, by his athleticism, debunked belief that ballet was effeminate. [Am. Dance: *SJEPC*]

40. **Vitus, Saint** patron saint of dancers. [Christian Hagiog.: *Saints and Festivals*, 291]

41. **Ziegfield Follies** beautiful dancing girls highlighted annual musical revue on Broadway (1907–1931). [Am. Theater: *NCE*, 3045]

173. DANGER

1. **Cape Horn** the southernmost point of South America, known for its dangerous waters. [Geography *ODA*]

2. **Geiger counter** radiation detector named for inventor. [Am. Hist.: Flexner, 12]

3. **Mayday** international radiotelephone distress signal. [Maritime Hist.: Misc.]

4. *Perils of Pauline* cliff-hangers in which Pauline's life is recurrently in danger. [Am. Cinema: Halliwell, 559]

5. **red alert** final alert; attack believed imminent. [Military: Misc.]

6. **red flag** symbol of peril. [Folklore: Jobes, 413]

7. **rhododendron** symbol of approaching pitfalls. [Flower Symbolism: *Flora Symbolica*, 177]

8. **rhubarb** symbol of approaching pitfalls. [Flower Symbolism: *Flora Symbolica*, 177]

9. **Scylla and Charybdis** rocks and whirlpool, respectively, opposite each other in the Strait of Messina. [Classical Myth.: Zimmerman, 59, 235–236]

10. **skull and crossbones** alerts consumers to presence of poison; represents death. [Folklore: Misc.]

11. **SOS** Morse code distress signal. [World Culture: Flexner, 359]

12. **sword of Damocles** signifies impending peril; blade suspended over banqueter by a hair. [Gk. Myth.: Brewer *Dictionary*, 297]

13. **Symplegades** "Clashing Cliffs" at the entrance to the Black Sea, said to crush vessels. [Classical Myth.: *New Century*, 1043]

14. **Syrtes** quicksands off the coast of northern Africa; any part of the sea dangerous to ships because of natural phenomena. [Rom. Myth.: Zimmerman, 251]

15. **thin ice** univeral symbol of possible danger. [Folklore: Misc.]

16. **Yuck, Mr.** pictorial symbol denoting poison; grimacing face with tongue sticking out. [Am. Culture: Misc.]

Darkness (See NIGHT.)

174. DAWN

1. **Aarvark** one of the horses of the sun. [Norse Myth.: Leach, 1]

2. **Aurora** goddess of dawn whose tears provide dew. [Rom. Myth.: Kravitz, 42]

3. **Daphne** Apollo's attempted rape represents dawn fleeing daylight. [Gk. Myth.: Parrinder, 72; Jobes, 414]

4. **Eos** goddess of dawn; announces Helios each morning. [Gk. Myth.: Kravitz, 89]

5. **Heimdall** god of dawn and protector of rainbow bridge, Bifrost. [Norse Myth.: Leach, 488]

6. **laughing jackass** bird whose cry brings in daylight. [Euahlayi Legend: *How the People Sang the Mountains Up*, 119]

7. **Octa** mountain from which sun rises. [Rom. Folklore: Wheeler, 7]

8. **rays, garland of** emblem of Aurora, dawn goddess. [Gk. Myth.: Jobes, 374]

9. **rooster** its crowing heralds each new day. [Western Folklore: Leach, 329]

10. **rosy fingers of dawn** Homer's picturesque depiction of daybreak. [Gk. Lit.: *The Iliad*]

175. DEADLINESS

1. **anaconda** South American boa constrictor; longest and deadliest of its kind. [Zoology: *NCE*, 317]

2. **basilisk** monstrous reptile; has fatal breath and glance. [Gk. Folklore: Jobes, 184]

3. **black widow spider** poisonous spider; consumes her mate after mating. [Zoology: *NCE*, 308]

4. **boa constrictor** largest of all snakes; squeezes its victims in a deadly grip. [Zoology: *NCE*, 317]

5. **cobra** bite believed to mean certain death. [Folklore: Jobes, 352]

6. **copperhead** deadly pit viper in eastern U.S. [Zoology: *NCE*, 652]

7. **coral snake** its bite is deadly. [Zoology: *NCE*, 654]

8. **Gila monster** small but venomous lizard found in U.S. desert. [Zoology: *NCE*, 1084]

9. **Humbaba** one-eyed, fire- and plague-breathing monster whose eyes could strike men dead. [Babyl. Myth.: *Gilgamesh*; Benét, 485]

10. **Hydra's gall** deadly; Hercules dipped his arrows in it. [Gk. and Rom. Myth.: Hall, 149]

11. **piranha** South American carnivorous fish. [Zoology: *EB*, VIII: 1]

12. **Portuguese man-of-war** a long-tentacled jellyfish whose sting can be deadly. [Zoology: *NCE*, 1408]

13. **python** nonvenomous jungle snake crushes its victims. [Zoology: *NCE*, 2252]

14. **rattlesnake** venomous snake, often deadly. [Zoology: *NCE*, 2281]

15. **shark** large and ferocious fish, sometimes man-eating. [Zoology: *NCE*, 2493]

16. **tarantula** spider with a deadly venom. [Zoology: *NCE*, 2695]

17. **upas** Asian and East Indian tree juice, extremely poisonous. [Eur. Myth.: Brewer *Dictionary*, 926]

18. **viper (or adder)** poisonous snake family; puff adder is deadliest of all. [Zoology: *NCE*, 2898]

19. **water moccasin (also cottonmouth)** highly poisonous snake found in southern U.S. [Zoology: *NCE*, 2490]

176. DEAFNESS

1. **Aged P.** Wemmick's deaf father. [Br. Lit.: *Great Expectations*]

2. **Beethoven, Ludwig van (1770–1827)** German composer continued to write masterpieces of classical music even after he became deaf. [Ger. Music: *EB*]

3. **Bell, Alexander Graham (1847–1922)** telephone inventor; renowned for studies of deafness. [Am. Hist.: *NCE*, 265]

4. **Keller, Helen (1880–1968)** overcame handicap of deafness as well as blindness. [Am. Hist.: *NCE*, 1462]

5. **Quasimodo** rendered totally deaf by his occupation as bellringer at Notre Dame Cathedral. [Fr. Lit.: Victor Hugo *The Hunchback of Notre Dame*]

177. DEATH

1. **Ah Puch** deity of doom; represented as bloated corpse or skeleton. [Maya Myth.: Leach, 30]

2. **Angel of Death** personification of death, sometimes as a winged messenger, or the angels Asrael, Michael, or Apollyon. [Jewish and Islamic Myth: *ODA*]

3. **Ankou** gaunt driver of spectral cart; collects the dead. [Brittany Folklore: Leach, 62]

4. **Anubis** god and guardian of the dead. [Ancient Egyptian Rel.: Parrinder, 10]

5. **Arrow of Azrael** angel of death's way of summoning dead. [Islamic Myth.: Jobes, 129]

6. *As I Lay Dying* Bundren family ordeal after Addie's death. [Am. Lit.: Faulkner *As I Lay Dying*]

7. **asphodel flower** bloom growing in Hades. [Gk. Myth.: Kravitz, 37]

8. **Atropos** Fate who cuts thread of life. [Gk. and Roman Myth.: Hall, 302]

9. **Azrael** angel of death; separates soul from the body. [Islamic Myth.: Walsh *Classical*, 41]

10. **banshee** female specter, harbinger of death. [Irish and Welsh Myth.: Walsh *Classical*, 45]

11. **bat** symbol of death, fear, witchcraft, and occult in Western folklore. [Symbolism: *CEOS&S*]

12. **bees** symbol of death and otherworld in European folklore. [Symbolism: *CEOS&S*]

13. **bell** passing bell; rung to indicate demise. [Christian Tradition: Jobes, 198]

14. **black** Western color for mourning. [Christian Color Symbolism: Leach, 242; Jobes, 357]

15. **Bodach Glas** gray specter; equivalent to Irish banshee. [Scot. Myth.: Walsh *Classical*, 45]

16. **Bran** god whose cauldron restored dead to life. [Welsh Myth.: Jobes, 241]

17. *Bury the Dead* six dead soldiers cause a rebellion when they refuse to be buried. [Am. Drama: Haydn & Fuller, 768]

18. **Calvary (Golgotha)** where Christ was crucified. [N.T.: Luke 23:33]

19. **Cer** goddess of violent death. [Gk. Myth.: Kravitz, 75]

20. **Charun** god of death. [Etruscan Myth.: Jobes, 315]

21. **Conqueror Worm** the worm ultimately vanquishes man in grave. [Am. Lit.: "Ligeia" in *Tales of Terror*]

22. **cross** for Christians, symbol of Christ's death and the acceptance of suffering. [Christian Rel.: *IEOTS*, 46]

23. **crow** in Europe and India, symbol of bad luck and war; also death, solitude, and evil. [Symbolism: *CEOS&S*]

24. *Dance of Death* Holbein woodcut, one of many medieval examples of the death motif. [Eur. Culture: Bishop, 363–367]

25. **danse macabre** Dance of Death; procession of all on their way to the grave. [Art: Osborne, 299–300, 677]

26. **dust and ashes** "I am become like dust and ashes." [O.T.: Job 30:19]

27. *Endgame* blind and chair-bound, Hamm learns that nearly everybody has died; his own parents are dying in separate trash cans. [Irish Lit.: Beckett *Endgame* in Weiss, 143]

28. **Ereshkigal** goddess of death; consort of Nergal. [Sumerian and Akkadian Myth.: Parrinder, 93]

29. **extreme unction** Roman Catholic sacrament given to a person in danger of dying. [Christianity: *RHD*, 506]

30. **fly** symbol of sickness, death, and the devil. [Symbolism: *CEOS&S*]

31. **Gibbs, Emily** dying in childbirth, welcomed by the other spirits in the graveyard, she tries to relive her twelfth birthday. [Am. Drama: Thornton Wilder *Our Town* in Benét, 747]

32. **Grim Reaper** name given to personification of death. [Pop. Culture: Misc.]

33. **handful of earth** symbol of mortality. [Folklore: Jobes, 486]

34. **horse** symbol of agents of destruction. [Christian Tradition: N.T.: Revelation 6; Mercatante, 65]

35. **Ilyitch, Ivan** afflicted with cancer, he becomes irritable, visits many doctors, gradually disintegrates, and dies almost friendless. [Russ. Lit.: Tolstoy *The Death of Ivan Ilyitch* in Magill III, 256]

36. **Kali** Hindu goddess to whom Thug sacrificed victims. [Hinduism: Brewer *Dictionary*, 600]

37. **Kevorkian, Dr. Jack** controversial "Dr. Death," who helped many terminally-ill people to commit suicide in the 1990s. [Am. Hist.: Misc.]

38. **Krook** rag dealer dies spectacularly and horribly of "spontaneous combustion." [Br. Lit.: *Bleak House*]

39. **Lenore** "saintly soul floats on the Stygian river." [Am. Lit.: "Lenore" in Hart, 468]

40. **Lord of the Flies** showing man's innate savagery and fear of death. [Br. Lit.: *Lord of the Flies*]

41. **manes** spirits of the dead. [Rom. Rel.: Leach, 672]

42. **Mania** ancient Roman goddess of the dead. [Rom. Myth.: Zimmerman, 59]

43. **Marat, Jean Paul (1743–1793)** French revolutionary, murdered in his bath; immortalized in the painting *The Death of Marat* by David. [Fr. Hist.: *ODA*]

44. **Niflheim** dark, cold region to which were sent those who died of disease or old age. [Scand. Myth.: Brewer *Dictionary*, 642]

45. **nightingale** identified with mortality. [Animal Symbolism: Mercatante, 163]

46. *On Borrowed Time* an old man chases "Death" up a tree and keeps him there until the old man is ready to die. [Am. Drama: Sobel, 517]

47. **pale horse** fourth horse of the Apocalypse, ridden by Death personified. [N.T.: Revelation 7:7–8]

48. **panther** black panther is feminiine symbol of night, death, and rebirth. [Symbolism: *CEOS&S*]

49. *Pardoner's Tale, The* seeking to slay death, three rioters are told he is under a certain tree; there they find gold and kill each other over it. [Br. Lit.: Chaucer "The Pardoner's Tale" in *Canterbury Tales*]

50. **raven** symbol of loss, death, and war in Western Europe. [Symbolism: *CEOS&S*]

51. **reindeer** in the far north, reindeer are considered the conductors of dead souls. [Symbolism: *CEOS&S*]

52. **requiem** religious mass (music or spoken) for the dead. [Christianity: Payton, 568]

53. **"Rime of the Ancient Mariner, The"** when Death wins the toss of the dice, the two hundred crew members drop dead. [Br. Poetry: Coleridge "The Rime of the Ancient Mariner"]

54. **Sacco Benedetto** yellow robe worn going to the stake during Inquisition. [Span. Hist.: Brewer *Dictionary*, 948]

55. **scythe** carried by the personification of death, used to cut life short. [Art: Hall, 276]

56. **skeleton** visual representation of death. [Western Folklore: Cirlot, 298]

57. **skull** representation of body's dissolution. [Christian Symbolism: Appleton, 92]

58. **skull and crossbones** symbolizing mortality; sign on poison bottles. [World Culture: Brewer *Dictionary*, 1099]

59. **Styx** river which must be crossed to enter Hades. [Gk. Myth.: Howe, 259]

60. **Thanatos (Mors)** god of death; brother of Somnos (sleep). [Gk. Myth.: Gayley, 54]

61. **Thoth** record-keeper of the dead. [Egyptian Myth.: Leach, 1109]

62. **toad** symbol of death and witchcraft in Western tradition. [Symbolism: *CEOS&S*]

63. **Valdemar, M.** in hypnotic trance, recounts impressions from other side of death. [Am. Lit.: "The Facts in the Case of M. Valdemar" in *Portable Poe*, 268–280]

64. **viaticum** Eucharist given to one who is dying. [Christianity: Brewer *Dictionary*, 1128]

178.   DEATH, ACCIDENTAL (See also DEATH, PREMATURE.)

1. **Aeschylus** dramatist killed when eagle dropped a turtle on his bald head, thinking it a rock. [Gk. Legend: Brewer *Dictionary*, 13]

2. **Ahab, Captain** whipped out of his boat by a flying harpoon-line. [Am. Lit.: Melville *Moby Dick*]

3. **Bosinney, Philip** distraught by a revelation, is run over in a London fog. [Br. Lit.: *The Forsyte Saga*]

4. *Bridge of San Luis Rey* primitive bridge in Peru breaks, hurling five people to their deaths. [Am. Lit.: *Bridge of San Luis Rey*]

5. **Havisham, Miss** burned to death in her old house. [Br. Lit.: Dickens *Great Expectations*]

6. **Kelly, Grace (1928–1982)** popular film star of the 1950s; classic beauty who married into royalty, becoming Princess Grace of Monaco; died in auto accident. [Am. Film: *SJEPC*]

7. **Kinison, Sam (1953–1992)** created "rage comedy" in which he inserted screams and rants into his routine; killed by drunk driver. [Am. Entertainment: *SJEPC*]

8. **Kovacks, Ernie (1919–1962)** used video technology and special effects to the fullest to create innovative form of humor, often featuring outrageous characters; killed in automobile accident. [Am. TV: *SJEPC*]

9. **Mitchell, Margaret (1900–1949)** author of phenomenally successful Civil War-era novel *Gone with the Wind* (1936) was killed by a speeding car while crossing a street in Atlanta. [Am. Lit.: *SJEPC*]

10. **Sikes, Bill** fleeing pursuers, hangs himself with the rope he was using to escape. [Br. Lit.: Dickens *Oliver Twist*]

11. **Solness, Halvard** becomes dizzy on the tower of his new home and falls to his death. [Nor. Drama: Ibsen *The Master Builder* in Magill II, 643]

12. **Vaughan, Stevie Ray (1954–1990)** influential rock guitarist of the 1980s in blues tradition; cocaine abuse sent him into rehab, but his life ended in a helicopter crash. [Am. Music: *SJEPC*]

13. **Wilson, Myrtle** escaping from house where she has been locked up by her husband, she is killed by a speeding car. [Am. Lit.: Fitzgerald *The Great Gatsby*]

14. **Yeobright, Eustacia** falls into lake and drowns, as does Wildeve in an attempt to save her. [Br. Lit.: Hardy *The Return of the Native*]

179. DEATH, PREMATURE (See also DEATH, ACCIDENTAL; LOVE, TRAGIC; VICTIMS.)

1. **Adonis** beautiful youth beloved by Venus, killed by a boar. [Gk. Myth.: Benét, 10]

2. **Byron, Lord (1788–1824)** English poet died of fever at 36. [Br. Lit.: Harvey, 129]

3. **Carpenter, Karen (1950–1983)** popular singer died from anorexia nervosa complications at age 32 after battling the disorder for years. [Am. Music: *SJEPC*]

4. **Chopin, Frederic (1810–1849)** Polish composer of the Romantic era; died of tuberculosis at 39. [Fr. Music: Misc.]

5. **Clemente, Roberto (1934–1972)** Puerto Rican rightfielder and World Series MVP (1971) died in airplane crash at the age of 38 while transporting supplies to Nicaraguan earthquake victims. [Am. Sports: *SJEPC*]

6. **Cline, Patsy (1932–1963)** popular country music singer died in a plane crash at the age of 30. [Am. Music: *SJEPC*]

7. **Croce, Jim (1943–1973)** successful songwriter, guitarist, and performer lost his life in a plane crash just as his career began to blossom. [Am. Music: *SJEPC*]

8. **Dean, James (1931–1955)** young actor of promise, died in car crash. [Am. Cinema: *NCE*, 730]

9. **Diana, Princess of Wales (1961–1997)** in an attempt to escape the prying paparazzi in Paris, "The People's Princess" met her untimely death in a tragic car crash. [Br. Hist.: *SJEPC*]

10. **Dombey, Paul** dies at the age of seven, destroying the hopes of his merchant father. [Br. Lit.: Dickens *Dombey and Son*]

11. **Frank, Anne (1929–1945)** young Dutch diarist, died in Bergen-Belsen camp during WWII. [Jew. Hist.: Wigoder, 196]

12. **Grey, Lady Jane (1537–1554)** English queen at 15; died at 17. [Br. Hist.: *NCE*, 1146]

13. **Hope, Evelyn** died at sixteen, unaware how deeply she was loved by an older man who still mourns her. [Br. Poetry: Browning "Evelyn Hope"]

14. **Joplin, Janis (1943–1970)** considered greatest white female blues singer; highly passionate style and powerful, gritty voice; excessive in her performances and personal life; died young of heroin overdose. [Am. Music: *SJEPC*]

15. **Joyner, Florence Griffith (1959–1998)** nicknamed Flo Jo; Olympic track and field star with flamboyant style and six-inch fingernails; her early death followed a history of health problems. [Am. Sports: *SJEPC*]

16. **Kaufman, Andy (1949–1984)** idiosyncratic comic best known for character of foreign car mechanic Latka Gavas on TV show *Taxi* and unusual stand-up routines and publicity stunts; died of lung cancer at age 34. [Am. TV and Entertainment: *SJEPC*]

17. **Keats, John (1795–1821)** English poet died of consumption at 25. [Br. Lit.: Harvey, 243]

18. *L'Aiglon* Napoleon's son dies before he can rouse the French to follow him. [Fr. Drama: *l'Aiglon* in Magill II, 551]

19. **Little Father Time** despondent boy kills two babies and himself. [Br. Lit.: Hardy *Jude the Obscure*]

20. **March, Beth** dies young; sensitive girl. [Children's Lit.: *Little Women*]

21. **Marvellous Boy, The** Thomas Chatterton (1752–1770), English poetic genius killed himself at seventeen. [Br. Hist.: Bénét, 188]

22. **Mendelssohn, Felix (1809–1847)** great German composer of the Romantic era; died at 37. [Ger. Music: Misc.]

23. **Miller, Glenn (1904–1944)** talented trombonist, composer, arranger, and band leader during swing era; while travelling to entertain U.S. troops during WWII, his plane disappeared in bad weather and he was presumed dead at age 40. [Am. Music: Misc.]

24. **Morrison, Jim (1943–1971)** lead singer of heralded rock band The Doors died at age 27 of probable drug overdose. [Am. Music: *SJEPC*]

25. **Mozart, Wolfgang Amadeus (1756–1791)** one of the greatest composers of all time; the early death of this musical genius has spawned speculation of a murder plot perhaps carried out by rival, Salieri. [Eur. Music: *EB*]

26. **Romeo and Juliet** star-crossed lovers die as teenagers. [Br. Lit.: *Romeo and Juliet*]

27. **Schubert, Franz (1797–1828)** brilliant composer, died at 31. [Music Hist.: Thompson, 1968]

28. **Shelley, Percy Bysshe (1792–1822)** English poet drowned at 30. [Br. Lit.: Harvey, 748]

29. **SIDS (Sudden Infant Death Syndrome)** death during sleep of seemingly healthy babies under one year of age. [Am. Medicine: *SJEPC*]

30. **Valens, Ritchie (1941–1959)** Latino teen rock star best known for "La Bamba," his rock version of a Mexican ballad: career cut short when he died in plane crash along with rock legends Buddy Holly and the Big Bopper. [Am. Music; *SJEPC*]

31. **Valentino, Rudolph (1895–1926)** sexy and suave actor of silent films, wildly popular with famale fans who mobbed him at apprearances; his death caused several suicides. [Am. Cinema: Halliwell, 734]

32. **Williams, Hank, Sr. (1923–1953)** founder of contemporary country music; short but influential career marked by plaintive songs and mesmerizing performances; long-term substance abuse might have contributed to his early death. [Am. Music: *SJEPC*]

Debauchery (See DISSIPATION, LICENTIOUSNESS, PROMISCUITY.)

Debt (See BANKRUPTCY, POVERTY.)

180. DECADENCE

1. **Borgias** decadent Italian family of the Renaissance noted for ruthless, criminal pursuit of power. [Ital. Hist: *FOF, MOD*]

2. *Buddenbrooks* portrays the downfall of a materialistic society. [Ger. Lit.: *Buddenbrooks*]

3. **cherry orchard** focal point of the declining Ranevsky estate. [Russ. Drama: Chekhov *The Cherry Orchard*, in Magill II, 144]

4. **Diver, Dick** dissatisfied psychiatrist goes downhill on alcohol. [Am. Lit.: *Tender is the Night*]

5. **fin de siècle** French term meaning "end of the century," used in reference to a time of moral decadence. [Eur. Hist.: *FOF, MOD*]

6. **Gray, Dorian** beautiful youth whose hedonism leads to vice and depravity. [Br. Lit.: Oscar Wilde *The Picture of Dorian Gray*]

7. *Great Gatsby, The* 1925 novel by F. Scott Fitzgerald symbolizies corruption and decadence. [Am. Lit.: *The Great Gatsby*]

8. **House of Usher** eerie, decayed mansion collapses as master dies. [Am. Lit.: "Fall of the House of Usher" in *Tales of Terror*]

9. *In Search of Lost Time* Proust's multivalent masterpiece examines, among many themes, time, memory, and the decay of society. [Fr. Lit.: Haydn & Fuller, 630]

10. **Las Vegas** legalized gambling site in Nevada; synonymous with decadent behavior. [Am. Pop. Culture: Misc.]

11. **Lonigan, Studs** Chicago Irishman whose life is one of physical and moral deterioration. (1935). [Am. Lit.: *Studs Lonigan: A Trilogy*, Magill III, 1028–1030]

12. *Manhattan Transfer* novel portraying the teeming greed of the city's inhabitants. [Am. Lit.: *Manhattan Transfer*]

13. *Nana* indictment of social decay during Napoleon III's reign (1860s). [Fr. Lit.: *Nana*, Magill I, 638–640]

14. *Satyricon* novel by Petronius depicting social excesses in imperial Rome. [Rom. Lit.: Magill II, 938]

15. *Sound and the Fury, The* Faulkner novel about an old Southern family gone to seed; victims of lust, incest, suicide, and idiocy. [Am. Lit.: Magill I, 917]

16. *Sun Also Rises, The* moral collapse of expatriots. [Am. Lit.: *The Sun Also Rises*]

17. **Warren, The** Haredale's house, "mouldering to ruin." [Br. Lit.: *Barnaby Rudge*]

18. **Yoknapatawpha County** northern Mississippi; decadent setting for Faulkner's novels. [Am. Lit.: Hart, 955]

181. DECAPITATION (See also HEADLESSNESS.)

1. **Antoinette, Marie (1755–1793)** queen of France beheaded by revolutionists. [Fr. Hist.: *NCE*, 1697]

2. **Argus** lulled to sleep and beheaded by Hermes. [Gk. Myth.: *Metamorphoses*, I]

3. **Boleyn, Anne (1507–1536)** beheaded by husband, Henry VIII, for adultery and incest. [Br. Hist.: *NCE*, 325]

4. **Gawain, Sir** challenged by the Green Knight, Gawain cuts off his head. [Br. Lit.: *Sir Gawain and the Green Knight* in Benét, 934]

5. **Grey, Lady Jane (1537–1554)** English queen beheaded at 17. [Br. Hist.: *NCE*, 1146]

6. **Guillotin, Joseph (1738–1814)** physician; advocated humane method of capital punishment. [Fr. Hist.: Wallechinsky, 164]

7. **Holofernes** Assyrian commander-in-chief beheaded by Judith. [Apocrypha: Judith, 13:4–10]

8. **Hydra** nine-headed serpent beheaded by Heracles. [Gk. Myth.: Benét, 489]

9. **John the Baptist** head presented as a gift to Salome. [N.T.: Mark 6:25–28]

10. **Mansfield, Jayne (1933–1967)** well-documented hourglass figure and obsession with pink were part of her self-promotion as a sex

symbol; rumored to have died by decapitation in auto accident. [Am. Entertainment: *SJEPC*]

11. **Medusa** beheaded by Perseus. [Gk. Myth.: Hall, 206; Rom. Lit.: *Metamorphoses*]

12. **More, Sir Thomas (1478–1535)** English statesman beheaded by King Henry VIII. [Br. Hist.: *NCE*, 1830]

13. **Queen of Hearts** despite her suit, she is cruel and tempermental, with a penchant for beheadings; from Lewis Carroll's *Alice's Adventures in Wonderland*. [Br. Children's Lit.: Jones]

182. DECEIT (See also FRAUDULENCE, UNSCRUPULOUSNESS.)

1. **Aimwell** pretends to be titled to wed into wealth. [Br. Lit.: *The Beaux' Stratagem*]

2. **Ananias** lies about amount of money received for land. [N.T.: Acts 5:1–6]

3. **Ananias Club** all its members are liars. [Am. Lit.: Worth, 10]

4. **angel of light** false apostles are like Satan in masquerade. [N.T.: II Corinthians 11:14]

5. **Apaturia** epithet of Athena, meaning 'deceitful.' [Gk. Myth.: Zimmerman, 36]

6. **apples of Sodom** outwardly sound fruit; inwardly rotten. [Class. Myth.: Jobes, 114]

7. **Arbaces** priest who frames Glaucus. [Br. Lit.: *The Last Days of Pompeii*, Magill I, 490–492]

8. **Archimago** uses sorcery to deceive people. [Br. Lit.: *Faerie Queene*]

9. **Arnolphe** plans marriage to ward; maintains guardianship under alias. [Fr. Lit.: *L'Ecole des Femmes*]

10. **bilberry** symbol for falsehood. [Flower Symbolism: *Flora Symbolica*, 172]

11. **Brunhild** outdone in athletic competition by Gunther with invisible assistance. [Ger. Myth.: *Nibelungenlied*]

12. **Buttermilk, Little Johnny** fools witch by substituting china for self in sack. [Br. Fairy Tale: Macleod, 21–24]

13. **Camilla, Mrs.** practices deception on Pip. [Br. Lit.: *Great Expectations*]

14. **clematis** symbol of deception. [Flower Symbolism: Jobes, 347; *Flora Symbolica*, 173]

15. **Conchis** for his psychological experiments he baits subjects with apparently seducible young women. [Br. Lit.: John Fowles *The Magus* in Weiss, 279]

16. **dogbane** symbol for deceit. [Flower Symbolism: Jobes, 458]

17. **Goebbels, Joseph (1897–1945)** Hitler's infamous minister of propaganda; a symbol of lying and deceit. [Ger. Hist.: *ODA*]

18. **Gollum** deceives Frodo, delivering him to the giant spider Shelob, so that he may have the One Ring. [Br. Lit.: *The Lord of the Rings*]

19. **Hlestakov, Ivan Alexandrovich** dissimulating gentleman hoodwinks town dignitaries as tsar's inspector. [Russ. Lit.: *The Inspector General*]

20. **hocus-pocus** magician's parody of *Hoc Est Corpus Domini* [Western Folklore: Espy, 76]

21. **Jingle, Alfred** pretends to be person of influence and elopes with an old maid for her money. [Br. Lit.: Dickens *Pickwick Papers*]

22. **Judas goat** decoy for luring animals to slaughter. [Western Folklore: Espy, 80]

23. **Latch, William** Esther's betrayer; seduces her on marriage pretense. [Br. Lit.: *Esther Waters*, Magill I, 254–256]

24. **Mak** Falstaffian figure; categorically maintains his innocence. [Br. Lit.: *The Second Shepherds' Play*]

25. **Malengin** personification of craftiness. [Br. Lit.: *Faerie Queene*]

26. **mask** a disguise; hence, symbol of deception. [Art: Hall, 204]

27. **Moncrieff, Algernon, and Jack Worthing** both assume fictitious name "Ernest" in wooing belles. [Br. Lit.: *The Importance of Being Earnest*]

28. **Montoni, Signor** marries Emily's aunt to secure her property. [Br. Lit.: *The Mysteries of Udolpho*, Magill I, 635–638]

29. **nightshade** poisonous flower; symbol of falsehood. [Flower Symbolism: *Flora Symbolica*, 176]

30. **Nimue** cajoles Merlin to reveal secret of power. [Arth. Romance: *History of Prince Arthur*, Brewer *Handbook*, 756]

31. **Nixon, Richard M. (1913–1994)** 37th U.S. president (1969–1974); nicknamed "Tricky Dicky." [Am. Hist.: Kane, 523]

32. **Pinocchio** wooden nose lengthens when he lies; protagonist of C. Collodi's book for children *The Adventures of Pinocchio* (1883). [Ital. Children's Lit.: Jones]

33. **Psychic Friends Network** scorned by serious psychics; $3.99–a-minute fortune telling over the phone. [Am. Pop. Culture: *SJEPC*]

34. **Sinon** convinced Trojans to accept wooden horse. [Rom. Lit.: *Aeneid*]

35. **St. Pé, Mme.** feigns paralysis for seventeen years to keep her husband away from the woman he loves. [Fr. Drama: Jean Anouilh *The Waltz of the Toreadors* in *On Stage*. 383]

36. **Trojan Horse** hollow horse concealed soldiers, enabling them to enter and capture Troy. [Gk. Myth.: *Iliad*]

37. **white flytrap** lures insects with sweet odor. [Flower Symbolism: *Flora Symbolica*, 178]

38. **winter cherry** inedible fruit symbolizes falsehood. [Plant Symbolism: Jobes, 319]

183. DEFEAT

1. **Appomattox Courthouse** scene of Lee's surrender to Grant (1865). [Am. Hist.: Jameson, 22]

2. **Armada, Spanish** defeat by English fleet marked Spain's decline and England's rise as a world power (1588). [Eur. Hist.: *EB*, 1: 521–522]

3. **Austerlitz** defeat of Austro-Russian coalition by Napoleon (1805). [Fr. Hist.: Harbottle *Battles*, 23–24]

4. **Bataan** Philippine peninsula where U.S. troops surrendered to Japanese (1942). [Am. Hist.: *NCE*, 245]

5. **Battle of the Boyne** sealed Ireland's fate as England's vassal state (1690). [Br. Hist.: Harbottle *Battles*, 39]

6. **Battle of the Bulge** final, futile German WWII offensive (1944–1945). [Eur. Hist.: *Hitler*, 1148–1153, 1154–1155]

7. **Caudine Forks** mountain pass where Romans were humiliatingly defeated by the Samnites. [Rom. Hist.: Brewer *Dictionary*, 186]

8. **count out** in boxing, the referee gives a fallen boxer a 10–second count to recover; if he does not, he's "counted out," or defeated; by extension, any defeat. [Am. Cult.: *FOF, MOD*]

9. **Culloden** consolidated English supremacy; broke clan system (1746). [Br. Hist.: Harbottle *Battles*, 70]

10. **Dien Bein Phu** Vietnam rout of French paved way for partition of Vietnam (1954). [Fr. Hist.: Van Doren, 541]

11. **down for the count** from boxing, referring to the count given a boxer to recover and rejoin the match; by extension, to be near defeat. [Am. Cult.: *FOF, MOD*]

12. **Gallipoli** poorly conceived and conducted battle ending in British disaster (1915). [Br. Hist.: Fuller, III, 240–261]

13. **Little Bighorn** scene of General Custer's "last stand" (1876). [Am. Hist.: Van Doren, 274]

14. **on the ropes** from boxing, depicting a weakened fighter, leaning on the ropes of the ring; to be on the brink of defeat. [Am. Sports: *FOF, MOD*]

15. **Pearl Harbor** Japan's surprise attack destroys U.S. fleet (1941). [Am. Hist.: *NCE*, 2089]

16. **Pyrrihic victory** a too costly victory: "Another such victory and we are lost." [Rom. Hist.: "Asculum I" in Eggenburger, 30–31]

17. **Salt River** up which losing political parties travel to oblivion. [Am. Slang: *LLEI*, I: 312]

18. **Sedan** decisive German defeat of French (1870). [Fr. Hist.: Harbottle *Battles*, 225]

19. **Stalingrad** German army succumbs to massive Soviet pincer movement (1942–1943). [Ger. Hist.: Fuller, III, 531–538]

20. **Waterloo** British victory in Belgium signals end of Napoleon's domination (1815). [Fr. Hist.: Harbottle *Battles*, 266]

21. **white flag** a sign of surrender. [Western Folklore: Misc.]

184. DEFENDER

1. **Bryan, William Jennings (1860–1925)** defended Creationism in famous Scopes trial. [Am. Hist.: *NCE*, 383–384]

2. **Canisius, Saint Peter** Jesuit theologian; buttressed Catholic faith against Protestantism. [Christian Hagiog.: Attwater, 276]

3. **Daniel** halts Susanna's execution; gets her acquitted. [Apocrypha: Daniel and Susanna]

4. **Darrow, Clarence Seward (1857–1938)** lawyer; Bryan's nemesis in Scopes trial (1925). [Am. Hist.: Jameson, 131]

5. **Defender of the Faith** Henry VIII as defender of the papacy against Martin Luther (1521). [Br. Hist.: *EB*, 8: 769–772]

6. **Defenders, The** father-son lawyer team in early 1960s. [TV: Terrace, I, 197]

7. **Donatello** Miriam's ardent friend ever ready to defend her. [Am. Lit.: *The Marble Farm*]

8. **Finch, Atticus** from *To Kill a Mockingbird* (1960) by Harper Lee; fair and honest lawyer who agrees to defend Tom Robinson, young black man accused of raping white woman in Alabama of 1930s; Atticus proves Robinson innocent, but he is convicted, nonetheless. [Am. Lit.: Gillespie and Naden]

9. **Hector** bravely defended Troy against Greek siege for ten years. [Gk. Lit.: *Iliad*]

10. **Mason, Perry** detective novels and TV series feature courtroom drama by lawyer. [Am. Lit.: Gardner, Erle Stanley, in *EB* IV: 416; Radio: Buxton, 186–187; TV: Terrace, II, 199]

11. **Ridd, John** defender of the parish of Oare in Somerset. [Br. Lit.: *Lorna Doone*, Magill I, 524–526]

12. **Zola, Emile (1840–1902)** attacked Army cover-up of Dreyfus affair in *J'accuse* (1886). [Fr. Hist.: Wallechinsky, 60]

185. DEFIANCE (See also REBELLIOUSNESS.)

1. **Becket, Thomas à (c. 1118–1170)** uncompromisingly defended the rights of the Church against King Henry II. [Br. Hist.: *NCE*, 2735]

2. **Mahon, Christopher** defies his father twice, knocking him out with a blow to the head. [Irish Drama: J. M. Synge *The Playboy of the Western World* in Magill, I, 758]

3. *Man for All Seasons, A* Sir Thomas More (1478–1535) refuses to acknowledge Henry VIII as supreme head of the church. [Br. Hist.: Benét, 686; Br. Drama: Robert Bolt *A Man for All Seasons* in *On Stage*, 439]

4. **Tell, William** Swiss patriot refused to salute the Austrian governor's cap. [Swiss Legend: Brewer *Dictionary*, 885]

186. DEFORMITY

1. **Byron, Lord (1788–1824)** British Romantic poet, limped because of clubfoot. [Br. Lit.: *EB*]

2. **Calmady, Sir Richard** born without lower legs. [Br. Lit.: *Sir Richard Calmady*, Walsh, *Modern*, 84]

3. **Carey, Philip** embittered young man with club foot seeks fulfillment. [Br. Lit.: *Of Human Bondage*]

4. **Cyclopes** one-eyed monsters. [Gk. Lit.: *Odyssey*]

5. **Elephant Man, the** Joseph Merrick, whose deformed face was said to resemble an elephant's. [Br. Cinema: *The Elephant Man*]

6. *Freaks* 1930s macabre movie about sideshow people. [Am. Cinema: Halliwell, 278]

7. **Giles, Saint** patron saint of the disabled; accidently hobbled, refused cures. [Christian Hagiog.: Brewster, 392]

8. **Gwynplaine** his disfigured face had a perpetual horrible grin. [Fr. Lit.: Hugo *The Man Who Laughs* in Benét, 632]

9. **Hephaestus** blacksmith god; said to have been lamed when ejected from Olympus by Zeus. [Gk. Myth: Zimmerman, 121]

10. **Mayeux** deformed man, both brave and witty. [Fr. Folklore: Wheeler *Dictionary*, 237]

11. **Oedipus** lamed by Laius with a spike through his feet in infancy. [Gk. Myth: *EB*]

12. *Phantom of the Opera, The* composer disfigured by fire haunts the sewers beneath the Paris Opera House. [Fr. Lit., Film, and Theater: *SJEPC*]

13. **Porgy** crippled beggar of Catfish Row. [Am. Musical: *Porgy and Bess*]

14. **Priapus** son of Aphrodite and Dionysus; grotesque man with huge phallus. [Gk. Myth.: Howe, 233]

15. **Quasimodo** hunchbacked bell-ringer. [Fr. Lit.: *Hunchback of Notre Dame*]

16. **Richard III** crook-back king. [Br. Lit.: Shakespeare *Richard III*]

17. **Sarn, Prudence** harelipped girl is servant on brother's farm. [Br. Lit.: *Precious Bane*, Magill I, 778–780]

18. **Tamerlane (1366–1405)** Mongol conqueror; his name a corruption of Timur I Long (Timur the Lame). [Asian Hist.: *EB*]

19. **thalidomide** supposedly harmless sedative resulted in disfigured babies. [Am. Hist.: Van Doren, 582–583]

20. **Thersites** deformed Greek officer at the siege of Troy; famed for his malevolence. [Gk. Lit.: *Iliad*]

21. **Tiny Tim** crippled son of Bob Cratchit. [Br. Lit.: *A Christmas Carol*]

22. **Toulouse-Lautrec, Henri de (1864–1901)** crippled and stunted; became great artist. [Fr. Hist.: Wallechinsky, 13]

187. DELIVERANCE (See also FREEDOM.)

1. **Apesius** epithet of Zeus, meaning "releaser." [Gk. Myth.: Zimmerman, 292–293]

2. **Bolívar, Simón (1783–1830)** the great liberator of South America. [Am. Hist.: *NCE*, 325]

3. **Boru, Brian** freed Ireland from the Danes. [Irish Myth.: Walsh *Classical*, 61–62]

4. **Brown, John (1800–1859)** abolitionist; attempted to liberate slaves. [Am. Hist.: Jameson, 64]

5. **Ehud** freed Israelites from Moabites by murdering king. [O.T.: Judges 3:15]

6. **Emancipation Proclamation** Lincoln's declaration freeing the slaves (1863). [Am. Hist.: Jameson, 161]

7. **Gideon** with 300 men, saved Israel from Midianites. [O.T.: Judges 6:14, 7:19–21]

8. **Jephthah** routed the Ammonites to save Israelites. [O.T.: Judges 11:32]

9. **Lincoln, Abraham (1809–1865)** 16th U.S. president, the Great Emancipator. [Am. Hist.: Jameson, 286–287]

10. **Messiah** expected leader sent by God to exalt Israel. [Judaism: Brewer *Dictionary*]

11. **Moses** led his people out of bondage. [O.T.: Exodus]

12. **Othniel** freed Israelites from bondage of Cushan-rishathaim. [O.T.: Judges 3:9]

13. **Parsifal** deliverer of Amfortas and the Grail knights. [Ger. Opera: Wagner, *Parsifal*, Westerman, 250]

14. **Passover** festival commemorating Exodus. [O.T.: Exodus 12]

15. **Purim** Jewish festival commemorating salvation from Haman's destruction. [O.T. Esther 9:20–28]

188. DELUSION

1. **Borkman, John Gabriel** suffers from delusions of power. [Nor. Lit.: *John Gabriel Borkman*]

2. **Bowles, Sally** night-club entertainer thinks she has the makings of a great film actress. [Br. Lit.: Isherwood *Berlin Stories* in Drabble, 498]

3. **Clamence, Jean-Baptiste** living with his own good and evil. [Fr. Lit.: *The Fall*]

4. **Dubois, Blanche** felt she and Mitch were above others. [Am. Lit.: *A Streetcar Named Desire*]

5. **Jones, Brutus** self-styled island emperor experiences traumatic visions. [Am. Lit.: *Emperor Jones*]

6. **Lockit, Lucy** steals jailer-father's keys to free phony husband. [Br. Lit.: *The Beggar's Opera*]

7. **opium of the people** Marx's classic metaphor for religion. [Ger. Hist.: *Critique of Hegel's "Philosophy of Right"*]

8. **ostrich** hides head, thinking itself concealed. [Animal Symbolism: Brewer *Dictionary*]

9. **Pan, Peter** little boy, refuses to grow up; resides in Never Never Land. [Children's Lit.: *Peter Pan*]

189. DEMAGOGUERY

1. **doublethink** propaganda that twists the truth and keeps the people under the tyranny of Big Brother. [Br. Lit.: *FOF, MOD*]

2. **Hague, Frank (1876–1956)** corrupt mayor of Jersey City, N.J., for 30 years. [Am. Hist.: *NCE*, 1173]

3. **Long, Hucy P. (1893–1935)** infamous "Kingfish" of Louisiana politics. [Am. Hist.: *NCE*, 1607]

4. **Pendergast, Thomas J. (1872–1945)** political boss in Kansas City, Mo.; convicted of income tax evasion. [Am. Hist.: *NCE*, 2096]

5. **Savonarola (1452–1498)** rabble-rousing bane of Renaissance Florence. [Ital. Hist.: Plumb, 141–142, 166–167]

6. **Stark, Willie** rises to top as graft-dealing political boss. [Am. Lit.: *All the King's Men*]

7. **Tweed, "Boss" William (1823–1878)** powerful Tammany Hall leader in New York City. [Am. Hist.: *NCE*, 2810]

190. DEMON (See also DEVIL.)

1. **Aello** Harpy; demon carrying people away; personifying a whirlwind. [Gk. Myth.: Jobes, 40]

2. **afreet or afrit** gigantic jinn, powerful and malicious. [Islamic Myth.: Benét, 13]

3. **Apophis** the snake god; most important of demons. [Ancient Egypt. Rel.: Parrinder, 24]

4. **Ashmedai** king of fiends. [Hebrew Myth.: Leach, 83]

5. **Asmodius** king of the devils. [Talmudic Legend: Benét, 58]

6. **bat** creature that is the devil incarnate. [Western Folklore: Mercatante, 181]

7. **cat** evil being, demonic in nature. [Animal Symbolism: Mercatante, 46]

8. **crocodile** feared as spirit of evil. [African Folklore: Jobes, 382; Mercatante, 9]

9. **Demogorgon** mere mention of his name brings death and destruction. [Western Folklore: Benét, 263]

10. **Dives** ferocious spirits under sovreignty of Eblis. [Persian Myth.: *LLEI*, I:326]

11. **dybbuk** demonic spirit with the power to possess a mortal. [Jewish Folklore: *FOF, MOD*]

12. **Fideal** evil water spirit; dragged men under water. [Scot. Folklore: Briggs, 175]

13. **Great Giant of Henllys** ghost of dead man turned demon. [Br. Folklore: Briggs, 199–200]

14. **incubus** demon in the form of a man. [Western Folklore: Briggs, 232]

15. **jinn (genii)** class of demon assuming animal/human form. [Arab. Myth.: Benét, 13, 521]

16. **Old Bogy** nursery fiend invoked to frighten children. [Br. Folklore: Wheeler, 265]

17. **succubus** demon in the form of a woman. [Western Folklore: Briggs, 232]

18. **whale** former symbol of demonic evil. [Animal Symbolism: Mercatante, 26]

191. DESPAIR (See also BOREDOM, FUTILITY, SUICIDE.)

1. **Achitophel** hanged himself from despair when his advice went unheeded. [O.T.: II Samuel 17:23]

2. **Aram, Eugene** scholar murders from pressure of poverty. [Br. Lit.: *Eugene Aram*]

3. **"Attention must be paid."** desperate cry of Linda Loman, wife of Willy, on discovering his suicide plans. [Am. Lit: Arthur Miller *Death of a Salesman*]

4. **Baudelaire, Charles (1821–1867)** French poet whose dissipated lifestyle led to inner despair. [Fr. Lit.: *NCE*, 248]

5. **Bellamy, James** character who goes through phases "playboy, war hero" to suicide. [Br. TV: *Upstairs, Downstairs*]

6. **"best lack all conviction"** famous line from William Butler Yeats's "The Second Coming," a cry of despair at the state of the world. [Irish Lit.: William Butler Yeats "The Second Coming"]

7. **Bowery, the** Manhattan skid row for alcoholics. [Am. Hist.: Hart, 97]

8. **downer** a non-medical term for a depressant drug; also a term for a depressing action. [Pop. Cult.: *FOF, MOD*]

9. **Giant Despair** imprisons Christian and Hopeful in Doubting Castle. [Br. Lit.: *The Pilgrim's Progress*]

10. **Henry, Frederic** loses lover and child; nothing left. [Am. Lit.: *A Farewell to Arms*]

11. **"Hollow Men, The"** poem evoking the despair of the human condition: hopeless, faithless, and incapable of change. [Br. Lit.: T.S. Eliot "The Hollow Men"]

12. **"The horror! The horror!"** final words of Mr. Kurtz, showing his despair at the true, and savage, state of human nature, in himself and those he tried to civilize. [Br. Lit.: Joseph Conrad *Heart of Darkness*]

13. **Hrothgar** Danish king desperately distressed by warrior-killing monster. [Br. Lit.: *Beowulf*]

14. **Maurya** mother loses six sons in the sea. [Br. Lit.: *Riders to the Sea*]

15. **Melusina** fairy who despaired when husband discovered secret. [Fr. Folklore: Brewer *Handbook*, 695]

16. **Narcissus** wastes away yearning to kiss reflection of himself. [Gk. Myth.: Brewer *Handbook*, 745; Rom. Lit.: *Metamorphoses*]

17. **Slough of Despond** bog enmiring and discouraging Christian. [Br. Lit.: *The Pilgrim's Progress*]

18. **Sullivan brothers** mother despairs over losing her five sons in WWII (1942). [Am. Hist.: *Facts* (1943), 106]

19. **Tristram or Tristan** falsely told that Iseult is not coming to save him from fatal poisoning; he dies of despair. [Medieval Legend: Brewer *Dictionary*]

20. **Williams, Tennessee (1911–1983)** dark subjects, vivid characters, and fragile, complex relationships made his plays fertile ground for early method acting of 1940s; classic films have been made of his drama, notably *A Streetcar Named Desire* (1950). [Am. Theater: *SJEPC*]

Destiny (See FATE.)

192. DESTRUCTION

1. **Abaddon** angel of the abyss; king of locusts. [N.T.: Revelation 9:11]

2. **abomination of desolation** epithet for the destructive or hateful. [Western Folklore: Benét, 3]

3. **Apocalypse** from the Book of Revelation, describes the destruction of the world; also an event of total devastation. [N.T. Revelation 6: 12]

4. **Armageddon** final battle between forces of good and evil. [N.T.: Revelation 16:16]

5. **atomic bomb (A-bomb)** fission device of enormous destructive power. [Am. Sci.: *EB*, I: 628]

6. **Bikini and Eniwetok** Pacific atolls, sites of H-bomb testing. [Am. Hist.: Flexner, 12]

7. **blitzkreig** from the German, "lightning war," for the Nazis methods in WWII; a swift, destructive attack. [Eur. Hist.: Misc.]

8. **collateral damage** a military term for the unintentional destruction during war; in common parlance, loss that takes place as a secondary result of an action. [Am. Culture: Misc.]

9. **danse macabre** "dance of death," image from medieval art representing a skeleton dancing and leading mortals to their death. [Eur. Art: *FOF, MOD*]

10. **Doomsday device** superpower nuclear capability to destroy the world if attacked. [Brit. Cinema: *Dr. Strangelove*]

11. *Dr. Strangelove* film by Stanley Kubrick (1964), a dark satire of the nuclear age; metaphor for the dangers of nuclear destruction. [Br. Film: *FOF, MOD*]

12. **Dresden, bombing of** allied incendiary bombs reduced city to inferno (February 13, 1945). [Ger. Hist.: *Hitler*, 1165; Am. Lit.: *Slaughterhouse-Five*]

13. **Enlil** storm god responsible for deluge. [Babyl. Myth.: Parrinder, 91]

14. **Enola Gay** B-52 that dropped the Hiroshima A-bomb. [U.S. Hist.: *WB*, W:405]

15. **fire** masculine symbol of creation, destruction, purification, revelation, regeneration, and spiritual or sexual ardor. [Symbolism: *CEOS&S*]

16. **firebranded foxes** Samson unlooses them to scorch cornfields. [O.T.: Judges 15:3–6]

17. **Four Horsemen of the Apocalypse** allegorical figures representing pestilence, war, famine, death. [N.T.: Revelation 6:1–8]

18. **Goetterdammerung** great final battle between Teutonic pantheon and forces of evil. [Ger. Myth.: Leach, 461]

19. **Hiroshima** Japanese city destroyed by A-bomb (1945). [Am. Hist.: Fuller, III]

20. **Hormah** Judah and his men level this Canaanite city. [O.T.: Judges 1:17]

21. **Hundred Years War** reduced much of France to wasteland (1337–1453). [Eur. Hist.: Bishop, 382–395]

22. **hydrogen bomb (H-bomb)** thermonuclear device more destructive than A-bomb. [Am. Sci.: *EB*, IX: 949]

23. **jackal** in India, symbol of destructiveness and evil. [Symbolism: *CEOS&S*]

24. **Jericho, Walls of** razed on the seventh blowing of trumpets. [O.T.: Joshua 6]

25. **Jerusalem** destroyed in 586 B.C. by Nebuchadnezzar, and in A.D. 70 by Titus. [Jew Hist.: *Collier's* XI, 16, 17]

26. **Juggernaut (Jagannath)** huge idol of Krishna drawn through steets annually, occasionally rolling over devotees. [Hindu Rel.: *EB*, V: 499]

27. **Krakatoa** volcano in southwest Pacific which violently exploded in 1883, destroying this island. [Asian Hist.: *NCE*, 1500]

28. **Kristallnacht** Nazi rampage against property of German Jews (November 9–10, 1938). [Ger. Hist.: *Hitler*, 689–694]

29. **Lidice** Czech town obliterated by Nazis (June 10, 1942). [Eur. Hist.: Van Doren, 489]

30. **M.A.D.** acronym for "mutually assured destruction," term for the deterrent factor of superpowers equally able to destroy each other with their nuclear weapons. [Am. Politics: Misc.]

31. **Mt. Saint Helens** volcanic eruption that devastated huge area in 1980. [U.S. Hist.: *WB*, M:735]

32. **mushroom cloud** the shape of the cloud created by force of blast of atomic bomb; symbol of destruction. [Science: Misc.]

33. **Nagasaki** Japanese city destroyed by A-bomb (1945). [Am. Hist.: Fuller, III: 626]

34. **neutron bomb** causes limited havoc; kills people, preserves property. [World Hist.: *Facts* (1978), 103]

35. **nuke** verb formed from "nuclear," to destroy; also, humorously, to heat in a microwave oven. [Pop. Cult.: Misc.]

36. *On the Beach* describes search for survivors after entire population of North America has been wiped out by nuclear war. [Br. Lit.: Weiss, 332]

37. **Ragnarok** destruction of gods and all things in final battle with evil. [Norse Myth.: *NCE*, 1762]

38. **Rome, Sack of** destroyed in 410 C.E. by Alaric and the Visigoths; again by the German-Spanish army under Charles V (1527). [Ital. Hist.: Plumb, 43, 406–7407]

39. **Sherman's "March to the Sea"** Confederate heartland ravaged by marauding Union army (1864). [Am. Hist.: Jameson, 307]

40. **Shiva** god of destruction, whom Robert Oppenheimer famously quoted at the first nuclear bomb test (1945): "I am become Death, the destroyer of Worlds." [Ind. Myth: *Bhagavad Gita*]

41. **Sodom and Gomorroah** Biblical cities destroyed by fire for wicked ways. [O.T.: Genesis 10:19; 13; 14; 18; 19]

42. **Thirty Years War** world war prototype reduced Germany to wasteland (1618–1648). [Eur. Hist.: *EB*, 18: 333–334]

43. **Vandal** Germanic tribes who invaded and destroyed Roman settlements in Europe, 4th-5th centuries; a symbol of destruction. [Eur. Hist.: *ODA*]

44. **Vesuvius** volcano in Italy which erupted in A.D. 79, burying Pompeii and Herculaneum. [Rom. Hist.: *NCE*, 2187]

45. **Vials of Wrath** seven plagues precipitating end of world. [N.T.: Revelation 16:1–17]

46. **Vulcan** god of destruction, placated by gifts of captured weapons. [Rom. Myth.: Howe, 294]

47. **W.M.D.** acronym for "weapons of mass desstruction"; Bush administration claimed Iraq had them in the run-up to Iraq invasion (2003). [Am. Hist.: Misc.]

193. DETECTIVE (See also CRIME FIGHTING, MYSTERY.)

1. **Alleyn, Inspector** detective in Ngaio Marsh's many mystery stories. [New Zealand Lit.: Harvey, 520]

2. **Archer, Lew** tough solver of brutal crimes. [Am. Lit.: Herman, 94–96]

3. **Belden, Trixie** thirteen-year-old protagonist embarked on adventures, often solving crimes with her brothers and friends in series of well-loved mysteries for young readers published from 1948–1986. [Am. Children's Lit.: *SJEPC*]

4. **Brown, Encyclopedia** protagonist of novels for young readers by Donald J. Sobol; son of the police chief who charges 25 cents to solve crimes in his town. [Am. Children's Lit.: Jones]

5. **Brown, Father** Chesterton's priest and amateur detective. [Br. Lit.: Herman, 20–21]

6. **Bucket, Inspector** shrewd detective solves a murder and uncovers Lady Dedlock's past. [Br. Lit.: *Bleak House* in Benét, 144]

7. **Campion, Albert** unpretentious cerebral detective. [Br. Lit.: Herman, 31–33]

8. **Carrados, Max** blind detective in stories by Ernest Bramah. [Br. Lit.: Barnhart, 159]

9. **Carter, Nick** turn-of-the-century flatfoot. [Radio: "Nick Carter, Master Detective" in Buxton, 173–174]

10. **Chan, Charlie** imperturbable Asian gumshoe. [Am. Lit.: Herman, 36–37; Comics: Horn, 165–166]

11. **Charles, Nick** urbane and witty private detective. [Am. Lit.: *The Thin Man*]

12. **Clouseau, Inspector Jacques** bungling French detective; inexplicably and with great asininity gets his man. [Am. Cinema: "The Pink Panther"]

13. **Columbo** untidy, cigar-smoking mastermind. [TV: "NBC Mystery Movie" in Terrace, II, 141]

14. **Cuff, Sergeant** first detective in English fiction. [Br. Lit.: *The Moonstone* in Benét, 683]

15. **Doyle, Sir Arthur Conan (1859–1930)** Scottish novelist and creator of the master sleuth, Sherlock Holmes. [Br. Lit.: *ODA*]

16. **Drew, Nancy** blonde teenaged detective in series of Stratemeyer Syndicate books for young readers beginning in 1930; bravely solves cases often given to her by her father, a criminal lawyer. [Am. Children's Lit.: Jones]

17. **Drummond, Bulldog** patriotic Englishman, hero of stories by Sapper. [Br. Lit.: Payton, 108]

18. **Dupin, Auguste** ratiocinative solver of unsolvable crimes. [Am. Lit.: Poe "The Murders in the Rue Morgue"; "The Mystery of Marie Roget"; "The Purloined Letter"]

19. **Fell, Dr. Gideon** fat, astute detective in John Dickson Carr's mysteries. [Am. Lit.: Benét, 170]

20. **Fosdick, Fearless** square-jawed, low-paid detective of questionable expertise and unquestionable obtuseness. [Comics: "Li'l Abner" in Horn, 450]

21. **Hardy Boys** one of the most successful juvenile series in history, featuring two young sleuths, produced by the Stratemeyer Syndicate. [Am. Lit.: *EB*]

22. **Hawkshaw** implacable detective with photographic memory. [Br. Lit.: *The Ticket-of-Leave Man*, Barnhart, 546]

23. **Holmes, Sherlock** the great detective; famous for deductive reasoning. [Br. Lit.: Payton, 316]

24. **inverness** coat with cape; emblem of Sherlock Holmes. [Br. Costume and Lit.: Espy, 267]

25. **Lane, Drury** Barney Ross's deaf ex-actor and amateur detective. [Am. Lit.: Herman, 105]

26. **Lecoq, Monsieur** meticulous detective; pride of French Sureté. [Fr. Lit.: *Monsieur Lecoq*]

27. **Lestrade** bungling Scotland Yard foil to Sherlock Holmes. [Br. Lit.: Payton, 387]

28. **Lupin, Arsène** murderer turned detective. [Fr. Lit.: Herman, 20]

29. **magnifying glass** traditional detective equipment; from its use by Sherlock Holmes. [Br. Lit.: Payton, 473]

30. **Maigret, Inspector** studiously precise detective; bases his work solidly on police methods. [Fr. Lit.: Herman, 114]

31. **Mannix** private eye with unorthodox style. [TV: Terrace, II, 62]

32. **Marlowe, Philip** hard-boiled private detective, creation of Raymond Chandler, main character of *The Big Sleep, Farewell, My Lovely* and other novels. [Am. Lit.: *FOF, MOD*]

33. **Marple, Miss** sweet old lady, tougher than she seems. [Br. Lit.: Herman, 51–55]

34. **Mason, Perry** attorney busier with detection than law. [Am. Lit.: Herman, 71–74]

35. **Mayo, Asey** the "codfish Sherlock." [Am. Lit.: Herman, 122–124]

36. **McGee, Travis** tough private eye and tougher private avenger. [Am. Lit.: Herman, 92–94]

37. **Milhone, Kinsey** female private detective featured in Sue Grafton's alphabet mystery series, begun in 1982 with *"A" Is for Alibi*. [Am. Lit.: *SJEPC*]

38. **Moto, Mr.** clever Japanese detective. [Am. Cin.: Halliwell, 494]

39. **Pinkertons** famous detective agency; founded in 1850. [Am. Hist.: Jameson, 392]

40. **Poirot, Hercule** brainy, dandified genius in Christie mysteries. [Br. Lit.: Herman, 51–55]

41. **Pollifax, Mrs.** redoubtable widow joins the C.I.A. [Am. Lit.: *A Palm for Mrs. Pollifax*]

42. **Pudd'nhead Wilson** lawyer uses fingerprint evidence to win his client's acquittal and expose the true murderer. [Am. Lit.: Mark Twain *Pudd'nhead Wilson*, Benét, 824]

43. **Queen, Ellery** dilettantish private investigator. [Am. Lit.: Herman, 105]

44. **Rabbi, the** Rabbi David Small solves crimes using his Talmudic training. [Am. Lit.: *Friday the Rabbi Slept Late*]

45. **red herring** false clue that leads sleuths astray in mysteries; based on the use of smoked herring, which is red, to train tracking dogs, and misused by criminals to throw law enforcement off the scent; now, a symbol of any false lead. [Lit: *FOF, MOD*]

46. **Saint, the** dashing diviner of knotty puzzles. [Radio: Buxton, 206; TV: Terrace, II, 264]

47. **Spade, Sam** hard-boiled private eye, created by Dashiell Hammett. [Am. Lit.: Dashiell Hammett *The Maltese Falcon*]

48. **Spillane, Mickey (1918–2006)** author of hard-boiled novels featuring private eye Mike Hammer and spy Tiger Mann; criticized for use of violence as solution in his works. [Am. Lit.: *SJEPC*]

49. **Strangeways, Nigel** urbane solver of intricate crimes. [Br. Lit.: Herman, 37–38]

50. **Thatcher, John Putnam** charming, civilized, urbane detective. [Am. Lit.: Herman, 86–87]

51. **Tibbs, Virgil** California's brilliant, black detective. [Am. Lit.: *In the Heat of the Night*]

52. **Tracy, Dick** square-chinned detective of police comic strip. [Comics: Horn, 206]

53. *True Dectective* early pulp magazine that helped pioneer American crime story genre in 1920s; related true-life crimes. [Am. Jour.: *SJEPC*]

54. **Vance, Philo** impressively learned, polished, and urbane detective. [Am. Lit.: Herman, 22, 126–127]

55. **Warshawski, V. I.** feminist detective created in 1982 by Sara Paretsky; forerunner of other prominent women protagonists in mystery genre. [Am. Lit." *SJEPC*]

56. **Wimsey, Lord Peter** Shakespeare-quoting gentleman turned amateur detective. [Br. Lit.: Herman, 113–114]

57. **Wolfe, Nero** corpulent, lazy, but persevering crime-solver, created by Rex Stout (1886–1975). [Am. Lit.: Herman, 119–122]

194. DETERMINATION (See also PERSERVERANCE.)

1. **Agathocles (361–289 B.C.)** Syracusan king; "burned his ships behind him" in attacking Carthage. [Gk. Hist.: Walsh *Classical*, 9]

2. **Balboa, Rocky** blue-collar hero of 1976 film who wins bout against all odds because of determination and courage.. [Am. Film: *Rocky* in *EB* (1978), 552]

3. **bulldog** bred for doggedly refusing to let go. [Dog Breeding: Misc.]

4. **Dry Guillotine** book by French escapee from Devil's Island. [Fr. Lit.: *Dry Guillotine*]

5. **Ignatz** tenaciously refuses Krazy Kat's advances. [Comics: "Krazy Kat" in Horn, 436–437]

6. **Ingalls, Laura** centerpiece of autobiographical frontier "Little House" series by Laura Ingalls Wilder; robust girl who embodies independence and determination of pioneers of late 1800s. [Am. Children's Lit.: Jones]

7. **Jones, John Paul (1747–1792)** Revolutionary War naval hero; remembered for saying: "I have not yet begun to fight!" [Am. Hist.: Jameson, 260–261]

8. **Keller, Helen (1880–1968)** though blind and deaf, becomes noted author and lecturer. [Am. Hist.: Hart, 439–440]

9. **Little Engine That Could** succeeds when others refuse to help. [Children's Lit.: *The Little Engine That Could*]

10. *Message to Garcia, A* against great odds, American officer makes his way to Cuban general leading a revolt against Spain. [Am. Lit. and Hist.: Benét, 662]

11. **Papillon** wily prisoner endeavors repeatedly to escape from Devil's Island. [Fr. Lit.: *Papillon*]

12. **Santiago** struggles long and hard for great fish. [Am. Lit.: *Old Man and the Sea*]

13. **tortoise** slow and steady, it wins the race against the hare. [Animal Symbolism: Mercatante, 22; Gk. Lit.: Aesop, "The Tortoise and the Hare"]

14. **Tovesky, Marie** outgoing and friendly, despite husband's insane jealousy. [Am. Lit.: *O Pioneers!*, Magill I, 663–665]

195. DEVIL (See also DEMON.)

1. **Adramalech** leader of fallen angels. [Br. Lit.: *Paradise Lost*]

2. **adversary** traditional appellation of Satan. [O.T.: Job 1:16; N.T.: I Peter 5:8]

3. **Amaimon** king of eastern portion of hell. [Medieval Legend: Brewer *Dictionary*, 28]

4. **Apollyon** Biblical name for Satan. [N.T.: Revelation 9:11]

5. **Applegate, Mr.** devil to whom aging Joe Boyd sells his soul to become a youthful champion outfielder. [Am. Lit.: Wallop *The Year the Yankees Lost the Pennant; Damn Yankees*]

6. **Auld Hornie** Scottish appellation for the devil. [Scot. Folklore: Leach, 353]

7. **Aule Ane** literally, 'old one'; nickname for demons. [Scot. Folklore: Walsh *Modern*, 35]

211

8. **Azazel** Satan's standard bearer. [Br. Lit.: *Paradise Lost*]

9. **Beelzebub** prince of demons. [N.T.: Matthew 12:24]

10. **Belial** chief of fiends. [O.T.: I Samuel 2:12]

11. **Cathleen** sells her soul to the devil in exchange for the souls of starving Irish peasants. [Irish Drama: Yeats *Countess Cathleen* in Benét, 228]

12. **Clootie** Scottish appellation for the devil. [Scot. Folklore: Leach, 353]

13. **Darkness, Prince of** "The Prince of Darkness," alias the Devil. [Br. Lit.: *All's Well That Ends Well*]

14. **Deuce, the** New England appellation for the devil. [Am. Folklore: Leach, 353]

15. **Devils, Prince of the** biblical equivalent for Satan. [N.T.: Matthew 9:34]

16. **divis** devils shown as cat-headed men with horns and hooves. [Pers. Myth.: Barber & Riches]

17. **Eblis** devil and father of devils, called Azazel before his fall. [Islam: Brewer *Dictionary*, 319]

18. **evil one** a name for Satan. [Western Folklore: Misc.]

19. **Faust (Dr. Faustus)** sells his soul to the devil in order to comprehend all experience. [Ger. Lit.: Goethe *Faust*; Br. Drama: Marlowe *Doctor Faustus*]

20. **fly** symbol of sickness, death, and the devil. [Symbolism: *CEOS&S*]

21. **Iblis (Eblis)** Muslim prince of darkness; chief evil spirit. [Islam: Leach, 513]

22. **Johnson, Robert (1914?-1938)** created legend that he had sold his soul to the devil for his amazing talent as a blues guitarist. [Am. Music: *SJEPC*]

23. **Lucifer** a Biblical name for Satan. [O.T.: Isaiah 14:12]

24. **Master Leonard** grand-master of sabbats and orgies. [Medieval Demonology: Brewer *Handbook*, 684]

25. **Mephistopheles** fiend to whom Faust sells his soul. [Ger. Lit.: *Faust*]

26. **Milton, John (1608–1674)** British poet created one of the most compelling portraits of Satan in his masterpiece, *Paradise Lost*. [Br. Lit.: *Paradise Lost*]

27. *Mysterious Stranger, The* devil appears as a pleasant stranger, convinces a boy of the falseness of morals and the nonexistence of God. [Am. Lit.: Twain *Mysterious Stranger* in Benét, 697]

28. **Nickie-Ben** a Scottish name for Satan. [Scot. Folklore: Wheeler, 258]

29. **Old Nick** Satan himself. [Western Folklore: Brewer *Dictionary*, 755]

30. **Old Scratch** Satan. [Eng. Usage: Brewer *Dictionary*, 973; Am. Lit.: "The Devil and Daniel Webster"]

31. **Peter, Meister** German euphemism alluding to the devil. [Ger. Folklore: Leach, 353]

32. *Rosemary's Baby* devil impregnates young woman in occult novel by Ira Levin; eerie 1968 film by Roman Polanski. [Am. Lit. and Film: *SJEPC*]

33. **Satan** the devil himself, source of all evil. [O.T.: Job, 1–2]

Devotion (See FAITHLFULNESS.)

196. DICTION, FAULTY

1. **Ace, Jane (1905–1974)** radio personality, remembered for sayings such as "up at the crank of dawn." [Radio: "Easy Aces" in Buxton, 74–75]

2. **Amos and Andy** early radio buffoons who distorted language: "I'se regusted!" [Radio: Buxton, 13–14]

3. **Berra, Yogi (1925–)** legendary catcher for the New York Yankees, known for hilarious malaprops. [Am. Sports: *FOF, MOD*]

4. **Bottom, Nick** tradesman-actor who constantly misuses words. [Br. Drama: Shakespeare *A Midsummer Night's Dream*]

5. **Claudius** because he stammered, held in little esteem as emperor. [Br. Lit.: *I, Claudius*]

6. **Clouseau, Inspector Jacques** infamous, tongue-tripping French detective. [Am. Cinema: *The Pink Panther* in Halliwell, 565]

7. **Dean, Dizzy (1911–1974)** famous baseball pitcher turned sports announcer: "He slud inta t'ird." [Radio: Buxton, 223]

8. **Dean, James (1931–1955)** actor whose inarticulateness epitomized the anti-eloquence of American youth in the 1950s. [Am. Cinema: Griffith, 423]

9. **Demosthenes (384–322 B.C.)** learned proper diction by practicing with mouth full of pebbles. [Gk. Hist.: *NCE*, 744]

10. **Dogberry** constable who garbles every phrase he speaks. [Br. Drama: Benét, 277]

11. **Doolittle, Eliza** Cockney flower girl transformed from guttersnipe to lady via better English. [Br. Lit.: *Pygmalion*]

12. **Elmer Fudd** disgruntled little man, stammers out his frustration at impish rabbit. [TV: "The Bugs Bunny Show" in Terrace, I, 125]

13. **Ephraimites** identified as enemy by mispronunciation of "shibboleth." [O.T.: Judges 12:6]

14. **Malaprop, Mrs.** eponymous blunderer in word usage. [Br. Drama: Benét, 623]

15. **Partington, Mrs.** foolish old lady who constantly misuses words. [Am. Lit.: Brewer *Dictionary*, 681]

16. **Pip** how orphan Philip Pirrup says his name. [Br. Lit.: *Great Expectations*]

17. **Porky Pig** stuttering porcine character in film cartoons. [Comics: Horn, 562–563]

18. **Spooner, Rev. W. A. (1844–1930)** legendary for transposing initial sounds: "our queer dean Mary"; hence, *spoonerism*. [Br. Hist.: Brewer *Dictionary*, 1029]

19. **Sylvester** the lisping feline star of film cartoons [TV: "The Bugs Bunny Show" in Terrace, I, 125]

197. DIGNITY (See also NOBLEMINDEDNESS.)

1. **cherub** celestial being symbolizing dignity, glory, and honor. [Heraldry: Halberts, 23]

2. **cloves** symbolic of stateliness. [Plant Symbolism and Folklore: Jobes, 350]

3. **dahlia** symbol of dignity. [Flower Symbolism: Jobes, 406]

4. **ermine** fur which represents nobility. [Heraldry: Halberts, 13]

5. *Grapes of Wrath, The* the Joad family maintains human dignity despite near-starvation as migrant workers in California (1939). [Am. Lit.: Harris *Characters*, 381–82; *SJEPC*]

6. **strawberry** symbolizes esteem. [Flower Symbolism: *Flora Symbolica*, 177]

198. DILEMMA

1. **Buridan's ass** placed exactly between two equal haystacks, could not decide which to turn to in his hunger. [Fr. Philos.: Brewer *Dictionary*, 154]

2. **Conrad, Joseph (1857–1924)** Polish-born English novelist (*Lord Jim, Heart of Darkness*) who often depicts characters facing moral dilemmas. [Br. Lit.: *FOF, MOD*]

3. *Sophie's Choice* William Styron's 1979 novel depicting a Polish woman in a Nazi concentration camp, forced to choose which of her children will live, and which will die; a symbol for an impossible choice, a dilemma for which there is no resolution. [Am. Lit.: William Styron *Sophie's Choice*]

199. DIMWITTEDNESS (See also IGNORANCE, STUPIDITY.)

1. **Allen, Gracie (1906–1964)** American comedian who projected a scatterbrained image. [Radio, TV, Am. Cinema: Halliwell, 14]

2. **Bodine, Jethro** oafish mental midget of millionaire hillbilly family. [TV: "The Beverly Hillbillies" in Terrace, I, 93]

3. **Bullwinkle** dimwitted moose with penchant for pedantry. [TV: "Rocky and His Friends" in Terrace, II, 252–253]

4. **Bunker, Edith** Archie's lovable "dingbat." [TV: "All in the Family" in Terrace, I, 47–48]

5. **Compson, Benjy** 33–year-old idiot loved and protected by his sister and both calmed and distracted by pictures that flow through his mind. [Am. Lit.: Faulkner *The Sound and the Fury* in Magill I, 917]

6. **Costello, Lou (1906–1959)** dumpy American comedian; used dimwittedness to spark humor. [Am. Cinema: Halliwell, 171]

7. **Drummle, Bentley** "heavy in comprehension"; suspicious of new ideas. [Br. Lit.: *Great Expectations*]

8. **Elspeth** Flashman's air-headed but beguiling wife. [Br. Lit.: *Flashman*]

9. **Happy Hooligan** simple and harmless tramp, serene and optimistic despite constant bad luck. [Comics: Horn, 302]

10. **Jeff** boob who usually bungles Mutt's schemes. [Comics: Berger, 48]

11. **Laurel, Stan (1890–1965)** bumbling foil for Oliver Hardy. [Am. Cinema: Halliwell, 425]

12. **Lennie** big, strong, simple-minded ranch hand. [Am. Lit.: *Of Mice and Men*, Magill I, 672–674]

13. **Moose** the epitome of "the obtuse jock," or dimwitted athlete. [Comics: "Archie" in Horn, 87]

14. **Palooka, Joe** semi-literate boxer, wholesome and bungling. [Comics: Horn, 343–344]

15. **Quayle, Dan (1947–)** US vice-president (1989–1993) who took strong conservative stance; frequent blunders made him appear unintelligent; favorite target of pundits. [Am. Politics: *SJEPC*]

16. **Rudge, Barnaby** grotesquely dressed, retarded son of a murderer. [Br. Lit.: *Barnaby Rudge*]

17. **Zero** army private whose name and IQ are almost equivalent. [Comics: "Beetle Bailey" in Horn, 105–106]

200. DIRTINESS

1. **Augean stables** held 3000 oxen, uncleaned for 30 years, Hercules's fifth labor; washes out dung by diverting a river. [Gk. and Rom. Myth.: Hall, 149]

2. **Daw, Margery** sold her bed and slept on dirt. [Nurs. Rhyme: Opie, 297]

3. **dog** thought to be unclean by Muslims. [Islamic Trad.: *UIMT*, 231]

4. **hoopoe** filthy bird; lines nest with dung. [Medieval Animal Symbolism: White, 150]

5. *Jungle, The* portrays the lack of hygiene among Chicago meatpacking plants (1906) [Am. Lit.: *The Jungle*, Payton, 356]

6. **Lake Erie** Great Lake; once so polluted, referred to as Lake Eerie. [Am. Hist.: *NCE*, 887]

7. **Madison, Oscar** disheveled and sloppy sportswriter for *New York Herald*. [Am. Drama: *The Odd Couple*; TV: "The Odd Couple" in Terrace, II, 160]

8. **pig** considered unclean by Muslims and Jews, who are not permitted to eat pork. [Islam and Judaism: *UIMT*, 232]

9. **Pig Pen** "a walking dust storm." [Comics: "Peanuts" in Horn, 542–543]

201. DISAPPEARANCE (See also ABDUCTION.)

1. **Arden, Enoch** missing for many years after being shipwrecked, returns to find his wife remarried. [Br. Poetry: "Enoch Arden"]

2. **Atlantis** submerged legendary island kingdom; never located. [Classical Folklore: Walsh *Classical*, 37]

3. **Bermuda Triangle** area of mysterious disappearance of ships and planes at sea. [Am. Hist.: *The Bermuda Triangle*]

4. **Bierce, Ambrose (1842–1914?)** journalist and short story writer; disappeared into Mexico in 1913. [Am. Hist.: *NCE*, 294]

5. **Crater, Judge (Joseph Force Crater, 1889–1930?)** Judge of N.Y. Supreme Court; vanished August 6, 1930. [Am. Hist.: *RHD*]

6. **Drood, Edwin** nephew of John Jasper; mysteriously vanishes. [Br. Lit.: *Edwin Drood*]

7. **Earhart, Amelia (1897–1937?)** aviatrix vanished in 1937 amid speculation and gossip. [Am. Hist.: *NCE*, 819]

8. **Hoffa, Jimmy (1913–1975?)** Teamsters' boss kidnapped and presumed dead. [Am. Hist.: *Facts* (1975), 573]

9. **Louis XVII (1785–1795)** "lost dauphin"; heir to French kingship imprisoned and died in captivity. [Fr. Hist.: *NCE*, 1617]

10. **Mister Keen** tracer of lost persons. [Radio: "Keen" in Sharp, IV, 354]

11. **Prospero's banquet** vanishes after being shown to the hungry castaways. [Br. Drama: Shakespeare *The Tempest*]

12. **Roanoke** Carolina settlement that twice vanished, leaving no trace (1587). [Am. Hist.: Jameson, 430]

202. DISASTER (See also SHIPWRECK.)

1. **Amoco Cadiz** oil tanker broke up off Brittany coast; 1.6 million barrels spilled (1978). [Fr. Hist.: *Facts* (1978), 201, 202]

2. **Angur-boda** Utgard giantess, worker of disaster; literally, 'anguish-boding.' [Norse Myth.: Leach, 58]

3. **Bhopal** Indian city, site of environmental disaster in 1984, when lethal gas leaked from a Union Carbide chemical plant; 2,000 died. [Ind. Hist.: *FOF, MOD*]

4. **Challenger** U.S. space shuttle exploded during liftoff, Jan. 28, 1986; all seven astronauts died. [Am. Hist. Misc.]

5. **Chernobyl** nuclear power plant in Ukraine that exploded on April 26, 1986; the subsequent release of radiation contaminated the region, making it uninhabitable; considered the greatest industrial disaster in history. [Russ. Hist.: Misc.]

6. **Chicago fire** conflagration destroyed most of city (1871). [Am. Hist.: Jameson, 94]

7. **Columbia** U.S. space shuttle exploded during re-entry, Feb. 1, 2003; all seven astronauts died. [Am. Hist. Misc.]

8. **Deluge** earth-covering flood that destroyed all but Noah's family and animals in the ark. [O.T.: Genesis 6–8]

9. **Deucalion's Flood** the Deluge of Greek legend. [Gk. Myth.: Benét, 266]

10. **Evangeline** concerns peaceful village vacated and destroyed during war. [Am. Lit.: "Evangeline" in Magill I, 261–263]

11. **Exxon-Valdez** oil tanker that ran aground in Alaska, spilling 11 million gallons of oil and destroying wildlife (1989); an allusion for environmental disaster. [Am. Hist.: Misc.]

12. **fallout** refers to radiation released after a nuclear explosion; in common usage, the negative results of an event. [Am. Culture: *FOF, MOD*]

13. **Fatal Vespers** 2 Jesuits and 100 others killed in collapse of lecture hall. [Br. Hist.: Brewer *Dictionary*, 1127]

14. **Gilgamesh epic** Babylonian legend contains pre-Biblical account of Flood. [Near East. Myth.: *EB*, IV: 542]

15. **Hindenburg, the** German airship blew up upon mooring in New Jersey (1937). [Am. Hist.: *NCE*, 43]

16. **Hurricane Katrina** hurricane that destroyed part of New Orleans and surrounding area in Aug. 2005; symbol of natural disaster and government ineptitude. [Am. Hist.: Misc.]

17. **Johnstown Flood** Pennsylvania city destroyed by flood (May 31, 1889); 2200 lives lost. [Am. Hist.: *NCE*, 1427]

18. *Lusitania* British luxury liner sunk by German submarine in World War I. [Br. Hist.: *EB* (1963) XX, 518]

19. **meltdown** nuclear reactor disaster resulting in superheating of the reactor core and subsequent release of radiation; in common usage, a business, or personal, emotional collapse. [Am. Hist.: Misc.]

20. **Pompeii** Roman city buried by eruption of Mt. Vesuvius (79). [Rom. Hist.: *NCE*, 2187]

21. **red cloud** indicates disaster is impending. [Eastern Folklore: Jobes, 350]

22. **San Francisco earthquake** disaster claiming many lives and most of the city (1906). [Am. Hist.: Jameson, 443–444]

23. *Titanic* seemingly invincible British luxury ocean liner that astonished the world when it collided with an iceberg on its maiden voyage in 1912 and sank, killing over 1500 passengers and crew. [Br. Hist.: *NCE*, 2753]

24. **World Trade Center** until their destruction, Twin Towers were tallest buildings in New York City and hub of financial district; hit by two planes hijacked by al-Qaeda terrorists on September 11, 2001, causing the collapse of the buildings and the deaths of nearly 3000. [Am. Hist.: *SJEPC*]

25. **Y2K** shorthand for the year 2000; some believed that computers not designed to handle data assigned to the twenty-first century would shut down, leading to disastrous malfunctions in banking, transportation, etc. [Am. Technology: *SJEPC*]

203. DISCIPLINE (See also ASCETICISM.)

1. **chicken** indicates martinetish authority. [Military Slang: Wentworth, 98]

2. **draconian law** included severe punishments prescribed by Draco, their codifier. [Gr. Hist.: *NCE*, 791]

3. **Patton, General George (1855–1945)** U.S. Army general known for imposing rigid discipline on his troops. [Am. Hist.: *NCE*, 2083]

4. **Puritans** strictly religious and morally disciplined colonists. [Am. Hist.: Payton, 551]

5. **spare the rod and spoil the child** axiomatic admonition. [O.T.: Proverbs 13:24]

6. **Spartans** Doric people noted for bravery, fugality, and stern self-discipline. [Gk. Hist.: Payton, 640]

7. **West Point** U.S. Military Academy focusing on discipline as part of training. [Am. Hist.: Payton, 729]

204. DISCORD (See also CONFUSION.)

1. **Andras** demon of discord. [Occultism: Jobes, 93]

2. **apple of discord** caused conflict among goddesses; Trojan War ultimate result. [Gk. Myth.: Benét, 43]

3. **Discordia** goddess of strife and discord. [Gk. Myth.: Kravitz, 83]

4. **Eris** goddess of discord; threw apple of discord among Peleus's wedding guests. [Gk. Myth.: Howe, 95]

5. **54–40 or Fight!** slogan alluding to disputed borders of Oregon territory under joint British and U.S. occupation. [Am. Hist.: Payton, 241]

6. **Gaza Strip** small coastal desert on borders of Egypt and Israel, the control of which has been in continual dispute. [Middle East. Hist.: Payton, 264]

7. **Great Schism, the** Catholic Church divided over papal succession (1378–1417). [Eur. Hist.: Bishop, 376–379]

8. **onyx** provokes disagreement and separates lovers. [Gem Symbolism: Kunz, 98–99]

9. **West Bank** Palestinian territory and center of dispute between Palestinians and Israelis. [Middle East. Hist.: *EB*]

205. DISCOVERY

1. **Archimedes (287–212 B.C.)** Greek mathematician and inventor, whose logical, practical methods led to ground-breaking scientific theories; "the father of experimental science." [Gk. Hist.: *BBInv*]

2. **Blue Nile** its source discovered by James Bruce, c. 1773. [Br. Hist.: *NCE*]

3. **Curie, Marie (1867–1934)** Polish physicist who discovered radium, received Nobel Prize in 1911; a symbol of achievement for women. [Science: *EB*]

4. **Dead Sea scrolls** ancient manuscripts of Biblical commentaries found in cave, mid-20th century. [Jew Hist.: Wigoder, 152]

5. **Eureka!** Greek word meaning "I have found it!", credited to Archimedes, after he discovered the theory of "relative density." [Gk. Hist.: *BBInv*]

6. **Franklin, Benjamin (1706–1790)** used simple kite to identify lightning as electricity. [Science: *NCE*, 1000]

7. **Galileo (1564–1642)** Italian mathematician, physicist and astronomer; his discoveries in astronomy and gravity led to important scientific breakthroughs; "the father of the scientific method." [Science: *BBInv*]

8. **Kaldi** Arabian goatherd; alleged discoverer of coffee (850). [Arab. Hist.: Grun, 97]

9. **New World** Christopher Columbus's expeditions to Americas from 1492 led to further exploration and development. [Eur. Hist.: Jameson, 107–108]

10. **Newton, Sir Isaac (1642–1727)** English physicist and mathematician, formulated key laws of motion, gravity, developed calculus. [Science: *BBInv*]

11. **Pacific Ocean** its American coast discovered by Vasco Nuñez de Balboa in 1513. [Am. Hist.: *NCE*, 213]

12. **Philippines** discovered by Magellan during his attempted circumnavigation of the globe. [World Hist.: Benét, 618]

13. **Rosetta Stone** inscribed in three languages; key to hieroglyphics. [Fr. Hist.: Brewer *Dictionary*, 935]

14. **San Salvador** Bahamian island, Columbus's probable first landfall in his discovery of America. [Am.Hist.: Benét, 214]

15. **Sutter's Mill** where James Marshall discovered California gold (1848). [Am.Hist.: *NCE*, 2662]

16. **Tutankhamen's tomb** incredible archaeological find unlocks the past. [Egypt. Hist.: *NCE*, 2809]

Discrimination (See ANTI-SEMITISM, BIGOTRY, RACISM.)

206. DISEASE

1. **AIDS** often fatal condition that weakens the human immune system, leaving the body vulnerable to infectious and opportunistic diseases, is transmitted in infected blood; by 2004, an estimated 40 million people worldwide were living with HIV/AIDS. [Hist.: *SJEPC*]

2. **Black Death** killed at least one third of Europe's population (1348–1349). [Eur. Hist.: Bishop, 379–382]

3. **bubonic plague** ravages Oran, Algeria, where Dr. Rieux perserveres in his humanitarian endeavors. [Fr. Lit.: *The Plague*]

4. *Cancer Ward, The* novel set in cancer ward of a Russian hospital. [Russ. Lit.: *The Cancer Ward* in Weiss, 64]

5. **condoms** barrier method of contraception now also used to prevent transmission of HIV, the virus causing AIDS. [Medicine: *SJEPC*]

6. **Decameron, The** tales told by young people taking refuge from the black death ravaging Europe. [Ital. Lit.: Magill II, 231]

7. **Fiacre, Saint** intercession sought by sick. [Christian Hagiog.: Attwater, 130]

8. **influenza epidemic** caused 500,000 deaths in U.S. alone (1918–1919). [Am. Hist.: Van Doren, 403]

9. **Joram** suffered for abandoning God's way. [O.T.: II Chronicles 21:15, 19]

10. *Journal of the Plague Year* Defoe's famous account of bubonic plague in England in 1665. [Br. Lit.: Benét, 529]

11. **Lazarus** leper brought back to life by Christ. [N.T.: John 11:1–44]

12. **Legionnaire's disease** 28 American Legion conventioneers die of flu-like disease in Philadelphia (1976). [Am. Hist.: *Facts* (1976), 573, 656]

13. **Lou Gehrig's disease** degenerative disease amyotrophic lateral sclerosis (ALS) named after baseball great Lou Gehrig, star player for the New York Yankees, who was diagnosed in 1939 and died two years later. [Am. Hist.: *SJEPC*]

14. **Molokai** Hawaiian island; site of former government leper colony. [Am. Hist.: *NCE*, 1807]

15. **Naaman** leperous Syrian commander healed by Elisha. [O.T.: II Kings 5]

16. **red death, the** pestilence, embodied in a masque, fatally penetrates Prince Prospero's abbey. [Am. Lit.: Poe *The Masque of the Red Death*]

17. **Rock, Saint** legendary healer of plague victims. [Christian Hagiog.: Attwater, 299]

18. **Sennacherib, army of** besieging Jerusalem, Assyrian force must withdraw after an outbreak of plague. [O.T.: II Kings 19:35; Br. Lit.: Byron *The Destruction of Sennacherib* in Benét, 266]

19. **seven plagues, the** visited upon the earth to signify God's wrath. [N.T.: Revelation]

20. **St. Anthony's Fire** horrific 11th-century plague. [Eur. Hist.: Brewer *Note-Book*, 34]

21. *Syphilis* Fracastoro's epic concerning *Syphilis*, mythical first victim. [Ital. Lit.: *RHD*, 1443; Plumb, 342]

22. **ten plagues, the** inflicted upon Egypt when Pharaoh refuses to let the Israelites emigrate. [O.T.: Exodus 7–12]

23. **Typhoid Mary (Mary Mallon, 1870–1938)** unwitting carrier of typhus; suffered 23–year quarantine. [Am. Hist.: Van Doren, 354]

207. DISGUISE

1. **Abigail** enters nunnery as convert to retrieve money. [Br. Lit.: *The Jew of Malta*]

2. **Achilles** disguised as a woman to avoid conscription. [Gk. Legend: Brewer *Handbook*, 642 (Lycomedes)]

3. **Aspatia** disguised as a man, engages a nobleman in a duel and dies of her wounds. [Br. Drama: Beaumont and Fletcher *The Maid's Tragedy* in Sobel, 444]

4. **Athena** assumes Mentor's form to persuade Telemachus to search for his father. [Gk. Lit.: *Odyssey*]

5. **Babbie** a young lady of good blood runs about in the dress and manners of a gypsy. [Br. Lit.: Barrie *The Little Minister* in Magill I, 513]

6. **Batman** millionaire Bruce Wayne dresses in his batlike cape and cowl. [Comics: Horn, 101]

7. **Beaucaire, Monsieur** to escape marriage, nobleman pretends to be a barber. [Am. Lit.: *Monsieur Beaucaire*]

8. **Biron** masks self as Muscovite; woos wrong woman. [Br. Lit.: *Love's Labour's Lost*]

9. **Blakeney, Percy** outwits his opponents by his ingenious disguises. [Br. Lit.: *Scarlet Pimpernel*]

10. **Bones, Brom** impersonates Headless Horseman to scare off rival suitor. [Am. Lit.: *The Legend of Sleepy Hollow*]

11. **Brainworm** impersonates variety of characters in his trickery. [Br. Lit.: *Every Man in His Humour*]

12. **Burchell, Mr.** baronet passes himself off as a beggar. [Br. Lit.: *The Vicar of Wakefield*]

13. **Burlingame, Henry** man with a thousand faces. [Am. Lit.: *The Sot-weed Factor*]

14. ***Charley's Aunt*** man poses as a woman in order to get his pal out of a jam. [Br. Drama: Barnhart, 228]

15. **Cléonte** masquerades as a Grand Turk to win pretentious man's daughter. [Fr. Lit.: *Le Bourgeois Gentilhomme*]

16. **Cupid** diguised as Ascanius, son of Aeneas. [Gk. Myth.: *Aeneid*]

17. **de Hautdesert, Sir Bercilak** disguised as Green Knight, challenges Gawain's valor. [Br. Lit.: *Sir Gawain and the Green Knight*]

18. **Deadwood Dick** first masked rider of Western fiction, appearing in dime novels by Edward L. Wheeler beginning in 1877; desperado protagonist of rousing books named after gold-mining town of Deadwood, S. Dakota. [Am. Lit.: *OCCL*]

19. **Demara, Ferdinand, Jr.,** "Great Impostor"; posed in professional roles. [Am. Hist.: Wallechinsky, 484]

20. **Despina** disguised doctor who supposedly restores lovers to life. [Ger. Opera: Mozart, *Cosi fan tutte*, Westerman, 98]

21. **Elaine** disguises herself as Guinevere in order to seduce Lancelot. [Br. Lit.: Malory *Le Mort d'Arthur*]

22. **Eugenia, Saint** dressed as male, becomes abbot of Egyptian monastery. [Christian Hagiog.: Attwater, 120]

23. **Finn, Huckleberry** after his supposed death, he dons a girl's dress and goes into town to gain information. [Am. Lit.: Mark Twain *Huckleberry Finn*]

24. **Ford** assumes pseudonym to uncover adulterer. [Br. Lit.: *Merry Wives of Windsor*]

25. **Gareth** queen requires him to disguise himself as a kitchen hand before he may seek knighthood. [Br. Poetry: Tennyson *Idylls of the King*]

26. **Gustavus, King** he and his lover Amelia are in disguises when he is killed by her husband. [Ital. Opera: *Un Ballo in Maschera* in Osborne *Opera*]

27. **Hardcastle, Kate** wins her suitor by pretending to be a barmaid. [Br. Drama: Goldsmith *She Stoops to Conquer*]

28. **Helena** disguises herself as a pilgrim in order to follow her husband from France to Italy. [Br. Drama: Shakespeare *All's Well That Ends Well*]

29. **Holmes, Sherlock** returns in disguise after his supposed death to surprise his enemies. [Br. Lit.: Doyle *The Return of Sherlock Holmes* in *Sherlock Holmes*]

30. **Imogen** dresses in boy's clothes to escape her husband's murder plot. [Br. Drama: Shakespeare *Cymbeline*]

31. **Jacob** dressed as Esau to obtain father's blessing. [O.T.: Genesis 27:15–16]

32. **Joker, the** master of disguise confounds Batman. [Comics: "Batman" in Horn, 101]

33. **Julia** masks self as page. [Br. Lit.: *Two Gentlemen of Verona*]

34. **Kenneth, Sir** as Richard's slave, saves king from assassination. [Br. Lit.: *The Talisman*]

35. **KISS** rock and roll band with sustainable songs and influence; onstage theatrics, energetic choreography, elaborate makeup and costumes (worn all the time), and individual personas made for crowd appeal. [Am. Music: *SJEPC*]

36. **Kopenick** tailor disguised as a captain, takes over city. [Ger. Lit.: *Captain from Kopenick*, Espy, 173]

37. **Leonora** masks as Fidelio to save imprisoned husband. [Ger. Opera: Beethoven, *Fidelio*, Scholes, 352–353]

38. **Leonora** dressed as a man, elopes with Alvaro and takes refuge in a hermit's cave. [Ital. Opera: *La Forza del Destino* in Osborne *Opera*]

39. **Leucippus** youth disguised as girl to be near Daphne; killed upon discovery. [Gk. Myth.: Zimmerman, 150]

40. **Lone Ranger** masked crime fighter hides true identity. [Radio: Buxton, 143–144; Comics: Horn, 460; TV: Terrace, II, 34–35]

41. **Maupin, Madelaine de** dresses and acts like a man in order to go among men and see them as they really are. [Fr. Lit.: *Mademoiselle de Maupin* in Magill I, 542]

42. *Merry Wives of Windsor, The* Mr. Ford disguises himself in order to thwart Falstaff's designs on Mrs. Ford. [Br. Drama: Shakespeare *The Merry Wives of Windsor*]

43. **Nanki-Poo** emperor's son disguised as a minstrel. [Br. Opera: *The Mikado*, Magill I, 591–592]

44. **Octavian** to spare his mistress, dresses as a chambermaid; Baron Ochs flirts with "her". [Ger. Opera: Strauss *Der Rosenkavalier* in Benét, 877]

45. **Odysseus** changed by Athena into an old beggar to avoid his recognition by Penelope's suitors. [Gk. Lit.: *Odyssey*]

46. **Paolo, Don** political agitator dressed incognito as priest. [Ital. Lit.: *Bread and Wine*]

47. **Paris** disguised as priest of Venus to free Helen. [Fr. Operetta: Offenbach, *La Belle Hélène*, Westerman, 272–273]

48. **Pierre, Maitre** a French merchant; in reality, King Louis XI. [Br. Lit.: *Quentin Durward*, Magill I, 795–797]

49. **Portia** heiress disguises herself as a lawyer and wins a case for her fiancé's friend. [Br. Drama: Shakespeare *The Merchant of Venice*]

50. **Rodolph, Grand Duke** roams the streets in disguise, befriending the unfortunate. [Fr. Lit.: Sue *The Mysteries of Paris* in Magill I, 632]

51. **Rosalind** diguises herself as a male. [Br. Lit.: *As You Like It*]

52. **Saladin** Saracen leader, in doctor's garb, cures Richard's illness. [Br. Lit.: *The Talisman*]

53. **Scarlet Pimpernel, The** very popular protagonist from historical novel by Baroness Orczy in 1905; wimpish, affected Englishman who wins love of French wife when she learns he, in disguise, helps French aristocrats escape beheading during the Revolution. [Br. Lit.: *OCCL*]

54. **Serannes, Theodore de** "young man" in reality Mademoiselle de Maupin. [Fr. Lit.: *Mademoiselle de Maupin* in Magill I, 542–543]

55. **Siegfried** disguised as Gunther, steals gold ring from Brunhild. [Ger. Opera: Wagner, *Gotterdammerung*, Westerman, 244]

56. **Spina, Pietro** antifascist patriot disguises himself as a priest. [Ital. Lit.: *Bread and Wine*]

57. **Superman** superhero under guise of Clark Kent, mild-mannered reporter. [Comics: Horn, 642]

58. **Thousandfurs** king's daughter works anonymously, cloaked in manypelted coat. [Ger. Fairy Tale: Grimm, 245]

59. **Toinette** disguises herself as a doctor and prescribes radical treatment for a hypochondriac. [Fr. Drama: Molière *Le Malade Imaginaire* in Sobel, 445]

60. **Vicentio** masquerades as Friar Lodowick. [Br. Lit.: *Measure for Measure*]

61. **Viola** masquerades as Cesario. [Br. Lit.: *Twelfth Night*]

62. **Zeus** disguises himself as: satyr to lie with Antiope, Amphitryon with Alcmena, Artemis with Callisto, shower of gold with Danae, white bull with Europa, swan with Leda, flame of fire with Aegina, and cuckoo with Hera. [Gk. Myth.: Jobes, 1719; *New Century*, 1158; Zimmerman, 293]

63. **Zorro** sword-carrying, masked Hispanic hero originated in 1919 in pulp magazine; fights to protect the weak and innocent in nineteenth-century California. [Am. Pop. Culture: *SJEPC*; Am. Cinema: Halliwell, 794; TV: Terrace, II, 461–462]

Dishonesty (See DECEIT.)

208. DISILLUSIONMENT

1. **Adams, Nick** loses innocence through WWI experience. [Am. Lit.: "The Killers"]

2. **Angry Young Men** disillusioned postwar writers of Britain, such as Osborne and Amis. [Br. Lit.: Benét, 37]

3. **Blaine, Amory** world-weary youth, typical of the lost generation that finds life unfulfilling. [Am. Lit.: *This Side of Paradise*]

4. **Chardon, Lucien (de Rubemprè)** young poet realizes he is not destined for success. [Fr. Lit.: Balzac *Lost Illusions* in Magill II, 595]

5. **Chuzzlewit, Martin** swindled, becomes disillusioned with Americans. [Br. Lit.: *Martin Chuzzlewit*]

6. **de Lamare, Jeanne** heartbroken by her husband's neglect and the discovery of his infidelities. [Fr. Lit.: Maupassant *A Woman's Life* in Magill I, 1127]

7. *Death of a Salesman* deceit, lies, and failure, rather than the success of which he dreamed, mark the life of salesman Willy Loman in Arthur Miller's 1949 masterpiece. [Am. Theater: *SJEPC*; Harris *Characters*, 269]

8. **Dodsworth, Sam** disillusioned with wife, European tour, and American situation. [Am. Lit.: *Dodsworth*]

9. **Eden, Martin** attains success as a writer but loses desire to live when isolated from former friends and disenchanted with new ones. [Am. Lit.: *Martin Eden*]

10. **Gatsby, Jay** Midwesterner from humble roots acquires wealth to gain prominence in sophisticated, moneyed world of long-lost love Daisy; ultimately, his quest for respect and happiness fail (*The Great Gatsby*, 1925). [Am. Lit.: *SJEPC*; Harris *Characters*, 111–12]

11. *Great Gatsby, The* poor Midwesterner Jay Gatsby acquires wealth illegally to gain foothold in New York's upper class socie-

ty and garner attention of long-lost love Daisy; American dream of money and happiness ultimately fails in F. Scott Fitzgerald's novel (1925). [Am. Lit.: *SJEPC*; Harris *Characters*, 111–12; Henderson, 310–11]

12. *Journey to the End of the Night* exposing the philosophy of postwar disillusionment. [Fr. Lit.: *Journey to the End of the Night*, Magill I, 453–455]

13. **Kennaston, Felix** learns in middle age that his life of romantic dreams was baseless. [Am. Lit.: *The Cream of the Jest* in Magill I, 168]

14. **Krasov, Kuzma Ilich** frustrated writer considers life complete waste. [Russ. Lit.: *The Village*]

15. **Loman, Willy** salesman victimized by own and America's values. [Am. Lit.: *Death of a Salesman*]

16. **Lost Generation** intellectuals and aesthetes, rootless and disillusioned, who came to maturity during World War I. [Am. Lit.: Benét, 600]

17. **March, Augie** "everyone got bitterness in his chosen thing." [Am. Lit.: *The Adventures of Augie March*]

18. **Melody, Cornelius** a failing tavern-keeper, flamboyantly boasts of his past. [Am. Drama: Eugene O'Neill *A Touch of the Poet* in Benét, 737]

19. *Mysterious Stranger, The* naïve youth is convinced by the devil that morals are false, God doesn't exist, and there is no heaven or hell. [Am. Lit.: Benét, 697]

20. **O'Hanlon, Virginia (1890–1971)** *N.Y. Sun* editorial dispels her disillusionment about Santa Claus. (1897). [Am. Hist.: Rockwell, 188]

21. **Pococurante** wealthy count who has lost his taste for most literature, art, music, and women. [Fr. Lit.: *Candide*]

22. *Rasselas* prince and his companions search in vain for greater fulfillment than is possible in their Happy Valley. [Br. Lit.: *Rasselas* in Magill I, 804]

23. **Smith, Winston** clerk loses out in totalitarian world. [Br. Lit.: *1984*]

24. **Webber, George** finds his native Southern town has degenerated morally and that his idealized, romantic Germany is corrupted. [Am. Lit.: Thomas Wolfe *You Can't Go Home Again*]

209. DISOBEDIENCE

1. **Achan** defies God's ban on taking booty. [O.T.: Joshua 7:1]

2. **Adam and Eve** eat forbidden fruit of Tree of Knowledge. [O.T.: Genesis: 3:1–7; Br. Lit.: *Paradise Lost*]

3. **Antigone** despite Creon's order, she buries Polynices. [Gk. Lit.: *Antigone*]

4. **Bartleby** copyist in Wall Street office; refuses to do anything but copy documents. [Am. Lit.: "Bartleby the Scrivener"]

5. **Brunhild** disobeys father's order to let Siegmund die. [Ger. Opera: Wagner, *Valkyrie*, Westerman, 237]

6. **Saul** contravening God, takes spoils from conquered Amalekites. [O.T.: I Samuel 15:17–19]

7. **Vashti, Queen** loses queenship for not submitting to king's demands. [O.T.: Esther 1:10–22]

Disorder (See CONFUSION.)

210. DISSIPATION (See also LICENTIOUSNESS, PROMISCUITY.)

1. **Bacchus (Gk. Dionysus)** god of wine; honored by Bacchanalias. [Gk. Myth.: Howe, 83]

2. **Baudelaire, Charles (1821–1867)** French poet whose dissipated lifestyle led to inner despair. [Fr. Lit.: *NCE*, 248]

3. **Behan, Brendan (1923–1964)** uninhibited Irish playwright who lived wildly. [Irish Lit.: *NCE*, 261]

4. **Bowery** Manhattan district, once notorious for brothels and gambling halls. [Am. Hist.: Hart, 97]

5. **Breitmann, Hans** lax indulger. [Am. Lit.: *Hans Breitmann's Ballads*]

6. **Burley, John** wasteful ne'er-do-well. [Br. Lit.: *My Novel*, Walsh *Modern*, 79]

7. **Camors** leads selfish, shameless life. [Fr. Lit.: *M. de Camors*, Walsh, *Modern*, 84]

8. **Carton, Sydney** wasteful bohemian; does not use his talents. [Br. Lit.: *A Tale of Two Cities*]

9. **Castlewood, Francis Esmond** gambles away living. [Br. Lit.: *Henry Esmond*]

10. **Christian II** sybaritic king. [Fr. Lit.: *Kings in Exile*, Walsh *Modern*, 96]

11. **Chuzzlewit, Jonas** dissipated, wasteful person. [Br. Lit.: *Martin Chuzzlewit*]

12. **Clavering, Sir Francis** dissipated gambling baronet. [Br. Lit.: *Pendennis*]

13. **Dalgarno, Lord Malcolm of** wasteful and ruinous; destroys several people. [Br. Lit.: *Fortunes of Nigel*]

14. **Fitzgerald, F. Scott (1896–1940)** American novelist whose works reflect a life of dissipation. [Am. Lit.: *NCE*, 957]

15. *Great Gatsby, The* self-indulgent, lavish world of Jay Gatsby and neighbors Tom and Daisy Buchanan include extravagant parties with plenty of bootleg liquor and moral recklessness in F. Scott Fitzgerald's novel, set in the Roaring Twenties (1925). [Am. Lit.: *SJEPC*; Harris *Characters*, 111–12; Henderson, 310–11]

16. **Jeshurun** citizens abandon God; give themselves up to luxury. [O.T.: Deuteronomy 32:15]

17. **Mite, Sir Matthew** dissolute merchant; displays wealth ostentatiously. [Br. Lit.: *The Nabob*, Brewer *Handbook*, 713]

18. **Pheidippides** his extravagant bets ruin father's wealth. [Gk. Lit.: *The Clouds*]

19. **prodigal son** squanders share of money in reckless living. [N.T.: Luke 15:13]

20. *Satyricon* tales of vice and luxury in imperial Rome. [Rom. Lit.: *Satyricon*]

Divination (See OMEN.)

211. DOG

1. **Argos** Odysseus' pet, recognizes him after an absence of twenty years. [Gk. Lit.: *Odyssey*]

2. **Asta** Nick and Nora Charles's beloved dog. [Am. Lit.: *The Thin Man*]

3. **Balthasar** almost a Pomeranian, companion of Jolyon Forsyte at Robin Hill. [Br. Lit.: "Indian Summer of a Forsyte"]

4. **Balto** courageous husky who, in 1925, led team on life-or-death race to bring diptheria serum to the children of Nome, Alaska; the route, and Balto's achievement, are celebrated each year in the Iditarod sled race. [Am. Hist.: Misc.]

5. **barghest** monstrous goblin-dog, a nocturnal specter portending death. [Br. Folklore: *EB* (1963) III, 110]

6. **Boatswain** Byron's favorite dog. [Br. Hist.: Harvey, 239]

7. **Buck** after murder of his master, leads wolf pack. [Am. Lit.: *The Call of the Wild*]

8. **Bullet** Roy Rogers's dog. [TV: "The Roy Rogers Show" in Terrace, II, 260]

9. **Bull's-eye** Bill Sykes's dog. [Br. Lit.: *Oliver Twist*]

10. **Cerberus** three-headed beast guarding gates of hell. [Classical Myth.: Zimmerman, 55–56]

11. **Charley** elderly poodle that accompanied Steinbeck on trip across U.S. [Am. Lit.: John Steinbeck *Travels with Charley* in Weiss, 471]

12. **Checkers** Richard Nixon's cocker spaniel; used in his defense of slush fund (1952). [Am. Hist.: Wallechinsky, 126]

13. **Cujo** canine protagonist of 1981 horror novel by Stephen King; friendly St. Bernard mysteriously turns violent and terrorizes small New England town. [Am. Lit.: Gillespie and Naden]

14. **Diogenes** Dr. Blimber's clumsy dog. [Br. Lit.: *Dombey and Son*]

15. **Dominic** hound who travels widely. [Children's Lit.: *Dominic*]

16. **Fala** Franklin Roosevelt's dog. [Am. Hist.: Wallechinsky, 126]

17. **Flopit** small, majestically self-important, and smelling of violets. [Am. Lit.: Booth Tarkington *Seventeen* in Magill I, 882]

18. **Flush** Elizabeth Barrett Browning's spaniel, subject of a biography. [Br. Lit.: Woolf *Flush* in Barnhart, 446]

19. **Gelert** greyhound slain by its master for killing his baby; he discovers that Gelert had killed a wolf menacing the child, who is found safe. [Eng. Ballad: *Beddgelert* in Brewer *Dictionary*, 93]

20. **Hound of the Baskervilles** gigantic "fiend dog" of Sir Arthur Conan Doyle's tale. [Br. Lit.: *The Hound of the Baskervilles*]

21. **Jip** Dora's little pet, lives in a tiny pagoda. [Br. Lit.: Dickens *David Copperfield*]

22. **Lassie** brave collie of films from 1943–1951 and award-winning eponymous TV show from 1954–1974; often parodied for her barking warning that there was danger or need for help; show was, nonetheless, great favorite with families and critics. [Am. TV: Terrace, II, 13–15; Radio: Buxton, 135]

23. **Marmaduke** floppy, self-centered, playful Great Dane. [Comics: *Marmaduke*]

24. **Mauthe Doog** ghostly black spaniel that haunted Peel Castle. [Br. Folklore: Benét, 649]

25. **Montmorency** companion on Thames boat trip. [Br. Lit.: Jerome *Three Men in a Boat* in Magill II, 1018]

26. **Nana** Newfoundland, nurse to the children. [Br. Lit.: J.M. Barrie *Peter Pan*]

27. **Old Yeller** ugly dog whose cleverness and loyalty make his death tragic in *Old Yeller* (1956), Fred Gipson's children's book about the acceptance of difficult decisions. [Am. Children's Lit.: Jones]

28. ***One Hundred and One Dalmations, The*** 1956 novel by Dodie Smith, and subsequent movies, about Dalmatian puppies stolen by Cruella de Vil (who has passion for furs) and Baddun brothers, who run a Dalmation fur farm. [Br. Children's Lit.: *OCCL*; Am. Film: Misc.]

29. **Peritas** Alexander the Great's dog. [Gk. Hist.: Harvey, 239]

30. **Rin-Tin-Tin** early film hero; German shepherd. [Radio: Buxton, 200]

31. **Sandy** Little Orphan Annie's dog. [Comics: "Little Orphan Annie" in Horn, 459]

32. **Snoopy** world's most famous beagle. [Comics: "Peanuts" in Horn, 542]

33. **Sounder** coon dog in 1969 children's book of same name; his fate echoes treatment of the black patriarch who faced cruel racial bigotry in the South. [Am.. Children's Lit.: Jones]

34. **Spot** dog accompanying Sally, Dick, and Jane in primers. [Am. Cult.: Misc.]

35. **Toto** pet terrier who accompanies Dorothy to Oz. [Am. Lit.: *The Wonderful Wizard of Oz*]

36. **Wishbone** Jack Russell terrier protagonist of children's TV show premiering in 1995; in costume, he acts out his dream of being the main character in tales from classical literature. [Am. TV: Misc.]

212. DOMESTICITY (See also WIFE.)

1. **Barr, Roseanne (1952–)** calling herself "a domestic goddess," she made quips about her role as homemaker; her sitcom *Roseanne* (1988–1997) found her cast as a wisecracking wife and mother. [Am. TV and Entertainment: Misc.]

2. *Better Homes and Gardens* magazine has influenced and informed American home life since 1920s. [Am. Jour.: SJEPC]

3. **Bombeck, Erma (1927–1996)** newspaper columnist wrote about housework, motherhood, and family life in humorous, irreverent, yet respectful tone. [Am. Jour.: SJEPC]

4. **Cosby, Bill (1937–)** recognizable domestic experiences and home life form the basis of the comedian's routines. [Am. Entertainment: SJEPC]

5. **Crocker, Betty** leading brand of baking products; byword for one expert in homemaking skills. [Trademarks: Crowley, *Trade*, 56]

6. *Dick Van Dyke Show, The* series on the vicissitudes of middle-class living. [TV: Terrace, I, 208–209]

7. **Diller, Phyllis (1917–)** comedically portrayed a frumpy housewife with wild hair who poked fun at housework and railed a husband named Fang. [Am. Entertainment: SJEPC]

8. *Donna Reed Show, The* joys and sorrows of a pediatrician and his family. [TV: Terrace, I, 220]

9. *Family Circle* "world's largest women's magazine" reached audience of 21 million by end of 1980s, has featured articles on child rearing, family issues, homemaking, and education since 1932. [Am. Jour.: SJEPC]

10. *Father Knows Best* wholesome TV sitcom presented the Andersons as the ideal family of 1950s America, with a wise father, sup-

portive mother, and three children living in the suburbs. [Am. TV: *SJEPC*]

11. ***Flintstones, The*** family life in the Stone Age. [TV: Terrace, I, 271–273]

12. ***Good Housekeeping*** magazine aimed at middle- and upper middle-class women established in 1885 still focuses on cooking, child-rearing, and homemaking; its Seal of Approval certifies products. [Am. Jour.: *SJEPC*]

13. **hearth** symbol of home life. [Folklore: Jobes, 738]

14. ***Honeymooners, The*** iconic TV comedy featured Jackie Gleason and Audrey Meadows as working-class couple battling through life. [TV: Terrace, I, 365–366]

15. ***Joy of Cooking, The*** best-selling cookbook first published in 1931; considered the bible of American culinary arts; offers simple, straightforward instructions for preparing meals in a way that defied common belief that cooking was drudgery. [Am. Cuisine: *SJEPC*]

16. **"Keep the Home Fires Burning"** song of love of home popular during World War I. [Music: Scholes, 549]

17. ***Leave It To Beaver*** tranquil life in surburbia (1957–1963). [TV: Terrace, II, 18]

18. **March, Meg** devoted wife and mother. [Children's Lit.: *Little Women*]

19. **Martha, Saint** patroness of housewives and cooks. [Christian Hagiog.: Brewster, 345]

20. ***My Three Sons*** trials and tribulations of womanless household. [TV: Terrace, II, 131–132]

21. ***Ozzie and Harriet*** depicting home life, American style. [TV: "The Adventures of Ozzie and Harriet" in Terrace, I, 34–35]

22. **sage** symbolizes domestic virtue. [Flower Symbolism: *Flora Symbolica*, 177]

23. **silky** female spirit who does household chores. [Br. Folklore: Briggs, 364–365]

24. **Tupperware** in 1947, Earl S. Tupper created plastic storage containers with lids that could be "burped" to let out excess air; beginning in 1950, the revolutionary and useful products were distributed only through private home sales. [Am. Business: *SJEPC*]

25. ***Women's Day*** began in 1937, the inexpensive magazine focused on recipes and how-to articles; sold exclusively in A&P grocery stores until 1958. [Am. Jour.: *SJEPC*]

213. DOUBLES (See also TWINS.)

1. **Amphitryon and Jupiter** god assumes man's form to lie with his wife. [Rom. Lit.: *Amphitryon*]

2. **Darnay, Charles** physical duplicate of Carton. [Br. Lit.: *A Tale of Two Cities*]

3. **Dostoevsky, Fyodor (1821–1881)** Russian novelist whose works frequently dealt with the duality of human nature. [Russ. Lit.: *FOF, MOD*]

4. **fetch** a Doppelganger. [Irish Folklore: Leach, 376]

5. **Janus** Roman god of gates and doorways, depicted with two faces. [Rom. Myth: *ODA*]

6. *My Double and How He Undid Me* story of a lazy minister who has his look-alike impersonator do all his chores. [Am. Lit.: Haydn & Fuller, 456]

7. *Prince and the Pauper, The* 1881 novel by Mark Twain; young Prince Edward VI of England and peasant boy switch places for the safety of the king; commentary on arbitrariness of social status. [Am. Lit: Misc.]

8. **Prince of Wales** switches places with his double, poor boy Tom Canty. [Am. Lit.: Mark Twain *The Prince and the Pauper*]

9. **Sam and Eric** their identities merge as "Samneric." [Br. Lit.: *Lord of the Flies*]

10. **Sosia and Mercury** god assumes slave's identity. [Rom. Lit.: *Amphitryon*]

11. **Wilson, William** his Doppelganger ultimately kills him. [Am. Lit.: "William Wilson " in *Portable Poe*]

214. DRAMATIST

1. **Aeschylus (c. 524 B.C. - c. 455 B.C.)** called "the father of Greek tragedy," his masterpiece is his Oresteia trilogy, *Agammemnon, The Libation Bearers, The Eumenides*, which inaugurated new concepts in dramatic dialogue and action. [Gk. Theater: *EB*]

2. **Albee, Edward (1928–)** American playwright whose best-known works include *Who's Afraid of Virginia Woolf?* and *The Zoo Story*, considered one of the most important American dramatists of the 20th century. [Am. Theater: *EB*]

3. **Beckett, Samuel (1906–1989)** Irish dramatist who wrote in French; his modern masterpieces include *Waiting for Godot* and *Endgame*, revealing an Absurdist world that is at once menacing and meaningless. [Fr. Theater: *TCLM*]

4. **Brecht, Bertolt (1898–1956)** German playwright whose works, such as *Mother Courage*, reflect his theory of "epic theater," where actors seek to instruct, not to elicit sympathy from, the audience. [Ger. Theater: *FOF, MOD*]

5. **Chekhov, Anton (1860–1904)** Russian dramatist whose works reflect insights into the melancholy and longing of the human heart. [Rus. Lit.: Misc.]

6. **Congreve, William (1670–1729)** British playwright of the Restoration era, whose masterpiece, *The Way of the World*, is a bawdy satire of the social and political mores of his era. [Br. Theater: *EB*]

7. **Euripedes (c. 484 B.C. - 406 B.C.)** great Greek tragedian, who in such works as *Medea, Electra*, and *Iphigenia at Aulis* created characters with very human flaws, whose suffering is witnessed by indifferent gods. [Gk. Theater: *EB*]

8. **Garcia Lorca, Federico (1898–1936)** Spanish dramatist and poet, whose best-known plays are the tragedies *Blood Wedding, Yerma*, and *House of Bernarda Alba*, all dealing with passion, love, and ritual. [Span. Theater: *EB*]

9. **Gay, John (1685–1732)** British dramatist and poet, best known for *The Beggar's Opera*, a biting, satirical ballad opera and the source for *The Three Penny Opera* by Bertolt Brecht and Kurt Weill. [Br. Theater: *EB*]

10. **Genet, Jean (1910–1986)** French dramatist and novelist, best known for his plays *The Balcony* and *The Blacks*, which reveal his intent to shock his audience into recognition of society's failings. [Fr. Theater: *TCLM*]

11. **Goethe, Johann Wolfgang von (1749–1832)** great German poet, dramatist, novelist, and central figure of German Romanticism, his masterpiece, *Faust* influenced literature for generations. [Ger. Theater: *EB*]

12. **Ibsen, Henrik (1828–1906)** hugely influential Norwegian dramatists whose Realist masterpieces *A Doll's House, The Master Builder*, and *The Wild Duck* investigate the confrontation of self and society. [Nor. Theater: *TCLM*]

13. **Ionesco, Eugene (1912–1994)** Romanian-born French dramatist whose Absurdist dramas include *The Bald Soprano* and *Rhinoceros*, his works reveal a universe devoid of meaning, where communication is impossible. [Fr. Theater: *TCLM*]

14. **Jonson, Ben (1572–1637)** Elizabethan playwright, creator of *Volpone* and other biting satires; second only to Shakespeare in his stature as an outstanding dramatist of his era. [Br. Theater: *EB*]

15. **Marlowe, Christopher (1564–1593)** brilliant dramatist, who created such Elizabethan masterpieces as *Tamburlaine the Great* and *The Tragicall History of Doctor Faustus*; killed in a bar fight at age 29, he is a symbol of brilliant, if dissolute, youth. [Br. Theater: *EB*]

16. **Miller, Arthur (1915–2005)** famous American playwright whose career is defined by artistic integrity and brilliant, provocative plays, including *Death of a Salesman*. [Am. Lit.: *SJEPC*]

17. **Molière (1622–1673)** pseudonym of Jean-Baptiste Poquelin; considered the greatest French dramatist; he created vibrant, memorable characters in such plays as *Tartuffe, The Miser*, and *School for Wives*; his plays are noted for their witty dialogue and insight into human nature. [Fr. Theater: *EB*]

18. **O'Casey, Sean (1884–1964)** Irish playwright whose works, especially *The Plough and the Stars*, reflect the turbulent social and political history of Ireland in the early 20th century. [Irish Theater: *TCLM*]

19. **O'Neill, Eugene (1888–1953)** preeminent American playwright of the 20th century; works such as *Long Day's Journey into Night* often focus on family or societal concerns. [Am. Lit.: *SJEPC*]

20. **Osborne, John (1929–1994)** one of England's "Angry Young Men," Osborne wrote the landmark *Look Back in Anger*, whose themes of class conflict in post-war Britain influenced a generation of playwrights. [Br. Theater: *TCLM*]

21. **Pinter, Harold (1930–2008)** British dramatist and Nobel laureate whose works often have an ambigous, menacing tone. [Br. Theater: *FOF, MOD*]

22. **Pirandello, Luigi (1867–1936)** influential Italian dramatist and Nobel Laureate best known for *Six Characters in Search of an Author*, which takes place inside the mind of a playwright, recounting a struggle between actors and characters demanding to exist. [Ital. Theater: *TCLM*]

23. **Sartre, Jean-Paul (1905–1980)** French philosopher, playwright, and novelist; his play *No Exit* is considered a brilliant exposition of his existentialist philosophy. [Fr. Theater: *TCLM*]

24. **Schiller, Friedrich (1759–1805)** German dramatist, poet, and essayist, best known for his plays *Wallenstein* and *Mary Stuart*, explications of the theme of human freedom; Beethoven set his "Ode to Joy" as the finale to his Ninth Symphony. [Ger. Theater: *EB*]

25. **Shakespeare, William (1564–1616)** the greatest dramatist, and the greatest writer of all time; in works like *Hamlet, King Lear, Twelfth Night*, and *Henry IV, Parts I and II*, he created characters of depth, range, and complexity never before found in drama; to be "Shakespearean" is to express the widest range of human feeling, in the most eloquent and resonant language. [Br. Theater: *FOF, MOD*]

26. **Shaw, George Bernard (1856–1950)** Irish dramatist noted for the intellectual depth of his work; in plays like *Pygmalion, Major Barbara*, and *Saint Joan* he presents lively characters and brilliant dramatic language. [Irish Theater: *FOF, MOD*]

27. **Sheridan, Richard Brinsley (1751–1816)** British dramatist most famous for his comedy *The Rivals*, featuring the marvelous, mis-speaking Mrs. Malaprop. [Br. Theater: *EB*]

28. **Sophocles (c. 496 B.C. - 406 B.C.)** considered to be the greatest Greek tragedian, he wrote *Oedipus Rex, Oedipus at Colonus,* and *Antigone,* noted for their development of dramatic language and characterization. [Gk. Theater: *EB*]

29. **Strindberg, August (1849–1912)** Swedish dramatist whose major works, *A Dream Play* and *Miss Julie* reflect the influence of Expressionism. [Swed. Theater: *TCLM*]

30. **Wilde, Oscar (1854–1900)** Irish playwright, novelist, and essayist whose masterpieces, *The Importance of Being Earnest* and *Lady Windemere's Fan,* are witty satires on Victorian mores. [Br. Theater: *EB*]

31. **Wilder, Thornton (1897–1975)** several Pulitzer Prizes established his reputation as a leading American playwright of mid-twentieth century; his most famous play, *Our Town* is one of the most enduring in the American repertoire. [Am. Theater: *SJEPC*]

32. **Williams, Tennessee (1911–1983)** dark subjects, vivid characters, and fragile, complex relationships made his plays fertile ground for early method acting of 1940s; classic films have been made of his drama, notably *A Streetcar Named Desire* (1950). [Am. Theater: *SJEPC*]

215. DREAMING

1. **Alice** dreams of falling down a rabbit-hole and experiencing strange adventures. [Br. Lit.: Lewis Carroll *Alice's Adventures in Wonderland*]

2. **Caedmon** 7th-century English religious poet supposed to have heard his verses in a dream. [Br. Lit.: Benét, 156]

3. **Calpurnia** dreams that a statue of Julius Caesar is spouting blood from a hundred wounds. [Br. Drama: Shakespeare *Julius Caesar*]

4. **Dali, Salvador (1904–1989)** Spanish painter; creator of works imbued with fantastic, dreamlike images. [Eur. Art: *ODA*]

5. *Finnegans Wake* Joyce novel based around the dreams and nightmares of H.C. Earwicker. [Br. Lit.: Joyce *Finnegans Wake*]

6. **Ibbetson, Peter** learns how to "dream true" and return to the scenes of childhood and the times of his ancestors. [Br. Lit. and Am. Opera: G. duMaurier *Peter Ibbetson* in Magill I, 736]

7. **Jacob's ladder** from the Biblical story of Jacob, who dreamed of a ladder between earth and heaven, with angels ascending and descending. [O.T.: Genesis 28: 12]

8. **"Kubla Khan"** poem supposedly composed by Coleridge from an opium dream. [Br. Lit.: Benét, 555]

9. **Little Nemo** dreams every night of Slumberland, a place of storybook palaces and fairy-tale landscapes. [Comics: Horn, 458]

10. **lotus-eaters** from *The Odyssey*, people who eat the fruit of the lotus, lulled into a dream-like state. [Gk. Myth: *The Odyssey*]

11. **Morpheus** god of dreams. [Gk. Myth.: Benét, 688]

12. **Pharaoh** had dreams of cattle and corn by which Joseph was able to foretell the future. [O.T.: Genesis 41]

13. *Pilgrim's Progress, The* Bunyan dreamed this allegory of Christian's adventures while in prison. [Br. Lit.: Bunyan *The Pilgrim's Progress*]

14. **Quixote, Don** falls into a trance and has visions of Montesinos and other heroes. [Sp. Lit.: Cervantes *Don Quixote*]

15. *Under Milk Wood* the commonplace inhabitants of a Welsh village voice their dreams. [Br. Drama: Dylan Thomas *Under Milk Wood* in Magill IV, 1247]

216. DRUG CULTURE (See also COUNTERCULTURE, PSYCHEDELIA.)

1. **cannabis leaf** in Rastafarianism, considered a holy herb; it is a symbol of drug use and protest against white mainstream society in Western world. [Symbolism: *CEOS&S*]

2. **Castaneda, Carlos (1925–1998)** his books promote the ingestion and smoking of psychedelic plants as a way of attaining a higher spiritual reality. [Am. Culture: *SJEPC*]

3. **Cheech and Chong** comedy team with burned-out, dopehead personas humorously epitomized 1960s-70s drug culture. [Entertainment: *SJEPC*]

4. *Go Ask Alice* published anonymously in 1971; diary of a teenage girl's rocky experiences with drugs. [Am. Children's Lit.: Gillespie and Naden]

5. **Tompson, Hunter S. (1939–2005)** "gonzo journalist" of 1960s and 1970s; claimed to throw together obviously crafted, impressive work; his books and articles were incisive and irreverent, his personal life excessive and outrageous. [Am. Jour.: *SJEPC*]

6. **Warhol, Andy (1928–1987)** renowned Pop artist who used everyday objects— most notably, Campbell soup cans—as inspiration; his outrageous behavior and pursuit of celebrity oftentimes overshadowed his work as an artist. [Am. Art: *SJEPC*]

217. DRUNKENNESS (See also ALCOHOLISM.)

1. **Acrasia** self-indulgent in the pleasures of the senses. [Br. Lit.: *Faerie Queene*]

2. **Admiral of the red** a wine-bibber. [Br. Folklore: Brewer *Dictionary*, 11]

3. *Animal House* National Lampoon's comedy portraying college fraternity life as a wild, drunken party. [Am. Film: *SJEPC*]

4. **Bacchus, priest of** a toper, perhaps originally because of cermonial duties. [Western Folklore: Brewer *Dictionary*, 65]

5. **Barleycorn, John** humorous personification of intoxicating liquor. [Am. and British Folklore: Misc.]

6. **Blutarsky, Bluto** outrageous, binge-drinking "party animal" college student portrayed by John Belushi. [Am. Film: *SJEPC*]

7. **Booze** sold cheap whiskey in a log-cabin bottle. [Am. Hist.: Espy, 152–153]

8. **Capp, Andy** archetypal British working-class toper. [Comics: Horn, 82–83]

9. **Gamrinus** mythical Flemish king; reputed inventor of beer. [Flem. Myth.: *NCE*, 1041]

10. **Maenad** females who indulge in Bacchanalian rites, drunkenness. [Gk. Myth.: *ODA*]

11. **Magnifico, Don** appointed Prince's butler, oversamples his wines. [Ital. Opera: Rossini, *Cinderella*, Westerman, 120–121]

12. **Noah** inebriated from wine, sprawls naked in tent. [O.T.: Genesis 9:20–23]

13. **Peterson, Norm** beer-swilling customer on TV's *Cheers* (1982–93). [Am. TV: *SJEPC*]

14. **Silenus** one of Bachhus's retinue; fat, always inebriated. [Gk. Myth.: Hall, 283]

15. **Sly, Christopher** identity changes during drunken stupor. [Br. Lit.: *Taming of the Shrew*]

16. **Tam O'Shanter** stumbling home from the tavern sees witches dancing around open coffins in the graveyard. [Br. Lit.: Burns *Tam O'shanter* in Benét, 985]

17. **Vincent, Saint** patron saint of drunks. [Christian Hagiog.: Brewer *Dictionary*, 1129]

218. DUPERY (See also GULLIBILITY.)

1. **Blake, Franklin** doped with laudanum, he is an unconscious accessory to the theft of the moonstone. [Br. Lit.: *The Moonstone* in Magill I, 263]

2. **Bobchinsky and Dobchinsky** town squires bamboozled by inspector-impostor. [Russ. Lit.: *The Inspector General*]

3. **Buonafede** tricked into financing and approving daughters' marriages. [Ger. Opera: Haydn, *The World of the Moon*, Westerman, 68–69]

4. **Calandrino** duped by friends into believing heliotrope confers invisibility. [It. Lit.: *Decameron*, "Calandrino and the Heliotrope"]

5. **cat's paw** from legend, someone who is duped into doing a deed for other's benefit. [Trad. Folklore: *FOF, MOD*]

6. **Chicken Little** a chicken, hit with an acorn, declares "the sky is falling"; alarmist tendencies lead her to be duped and become the fox's dinner. [Nurs. Rhyme *FOF, MOD*]

7. **Dapper** lawyer's clerk; swindled into believing himself perfect gambler. [Br.Lit.: *The Alchemist*]

8. **Drugger, Abel** cozened by rogues in hopes of future riches. [Br.Lit.: *The Alchemist*]

9. **Fenella** mute beauty tricked, imprisoned, and abandoned by Alfonso. [Fr. Opera: Auber, *Dumb Girl of Portici*, Westerman, 163–164]

10. **Iago** dupes Othello, Cassio, et.al. [Br.Lit.: *Othello*]

11. **Little Red Riding Hood** naïve protagonist of story recorded by Charles Perrault in 1697; her innocence causes her to fail to identify wolf who has climbed into her grandmother's bed. [Fr. Children's Lit.: *OCCL*]

12. **Matthew, Master** "the town gull." [Br.Lit.: *Every Man in His Humour*]

13. **Pelleas** used by Ettarre; betrayed by Gawain. [Br.Lit.: *Idylls of the King*, "Pelleas and Ettarre"]

14. **Roderigo** foppish dupe and tool of Iago. [Br. Lit.: *Othello*]

15. **Sawyer, Tom** hoodwinks friends into white-washing fence by pretending chore is a reward, not a punishment. [Am. Children's Lit.: *CCL*]

16. **Skvoznik-Dmukhanovsky, Anton Antonovich** prefect kowtows to supposed inspector for good impression. [Russ. Lit.: *The Inspector General*]

219. DWARF (See also SMALLNESS.)

1. **Alberich** king of the dwarfs; lives in subterranean palace. [Norse Myth.: Leach, 33; Ger. Lit.: *Nibelungenlied*]

2. **Andvari** sometimes considered king of dwarfs; guarded Nibelung treasure. [Norse Myth.: Leach, 56]

3. **Dvalin** inventor of runes. [Norse Myth.: Leach, 330]

4. **Elbegast** king of dwarfs; dwelt in underground palace. [Norse Myth.: *LLEI*, I: 327]

5. **Gimli** character from Tolkien's Lord of the Rings trilogy (1954–1956); fierce, ax-wielding fighter who aids Frodo in his quest. [Br. Lit.: Gillespie and Naden]

6. **Hop-Frog** crippled, deformed court fool. [Am. Lit.: "Hop-Frog" in *Portable Poe*, 317–329]

7. **Matzerath, Oskar** deliberately remains at the age of three physically. [Ger. Lit.: Gunther Grass *The Tin Drum* in Magill IV, 1220]

8. **Munchkin** from the story and film, the little people of the land of Oz. [Am. Lit *The Wizard of Oz*; Am. Film: *The Wizard of Oz*]

9. **Nibelungs** race of dwarfs who possess a hoard of gold. [Norse Myth.: Payton, 477]

10. **Oakmen** squat, dwarfish people with red caps. [Br. Folklore: Briggs, 313–314]

11. **Rumpelstiltskin** homunculus spins gold in exchange for lass's first child. [Ger. Fairy Tale: Grimm, 196]

12. **Seven Dwarfs** Doc, Happy, Sleepy, Sneezy, Bashful, Grumpy, and Dopey. [Am. Cinema: *Snow White and the Seven Dwarfs* in *Disney Films*, 25–32]

220. DYSTOPIA

1. *Blade Runner* dark 1992 film depicts bleak vision of the future in Los Angeles, where humans are hired to hunt and kill genetically designed replicant slaves trying to escape their fate. [Am. Film: *SJEPC*]

2. *Brave New World* Aldous Huxley's grim picture of the future, where scientific and social developments have turned life into a tragic travesty. [Br. Lit.: Magill I, 79]

3. *Clockwork Orange, A* Stanley Kubrick's 1971 film based on Anthony Burgess's 1966 novel depicts a dystopian future state that seeks to crush free will and control individuals through torture and other cruel techniques. [Am. Film: *SJEPC*]

4. **Erewhon** inhabitants worship superficiality, unreason, inconsistency, and evasion: a lampoon of 19th-century society. [Br. Lit.: *Erewhon* in Haydn & Fuller, 239]

5. *Giver, The* 1993 novel for young readers by Lois Lowry follows 12–year-old Jonas who appears to live in a perfect society; when he learns the frightening truth, he runs away. [Am. Children's Lit.: Gillespie and Naden]

6. *1984* masterpiece of science fiction written in 1949 by George Orwell; set in future country of Oceania, ruled by Big Brother, leader of controlling Inner Party; protagonist Winston Smith is captured and brainwashed when he begins to nurture anti-party thoughts [Am. Lit.: Gillespie and Naden]

E

Eagerness (See ZEAL.)

221. EARTH

1. **Bona Dea** "goddess of earthly creatures." [Rom. Myth.: Parrinder, 49]

2. **Bona Mater** Fauna, goddess of wildlife. [Rom. Myth.: Kravitz, 24]

3. **Demogorgon** tyrant-genius of soil and life of plants. [Medieval Eur. Myth.: *LLEI*, I: 326]

4. **Dyava-Matar** Hindu earthmother, equivalent of Demeter. [Hindu Myth.: Jobes, 480]

5. **Frigga** Odin's wife; symbolizes the earth. [Norse Myth.: *LLEI*, I: 328]

6. **Gaea** goddess of the earth; mother of the mountains. [Gk. Myth.: Howe, 104]

7. **gnome** ground-dwelling spirit in Rosicrucian philosophy. [Medieval Hist.: Brewer *Dictionary*, 468]

8. **Midgard** region between heaven and hell where men live. [Norse Myth.: Wheeler, 242]

9. **Mother Nature** epitome of the earth, especially its more benevolent phenomena. [Pop. Cult.: Misc.]

10. **Tapio** Finnish woodland god; realm described in Sibelius' *Tapiola*. [Music Hist.: Thompson, 2239]

11. **Tellus Mater** in allegories of elements, personification of earth. [Art: Hall, 128]

12. **two circles linked** symbol of earth as bride of heaven. [Christian Tradition: Jobes, 343]

13. **Vertumnus** god of changing seasons. [Rom. Myth.: Kravitz, 58]

222. EASTER

1. **basket** filled with treats, representative of feast on Easter Sunday. [Folklore: Misc.]

2. **bonnet** usually worn along with new clothes on Easter Sunday. ("Oh, I could write a sonnet about your Easter bonnet.") [Christian Tradition: Misc.; Am. Music: Irving Berlin, "Easter Parade"]

3. **bunny** delivers chocolates, etc., to children; symbol of fertility, and Spring. [Western Folklore: Jobes, 487]

4. **daisy** a flower traditionally displayed in homes during Easter season. [Christian Tradition: Jobes, 487]

5. **egg** colored eggs as symbol of new life, adopted to reflect Resurrection. [Christian Tradition: Brewer *Dictionary*, 361]

6. **jelly beans** traditional treat for children on Easter Sunday. [Pop. Culture: Misc.]

7. **parade** of finery; most notable ones in New York and Atlantic City on Easter Sunday. [Pop. Culture: Misc.]

8. **purple and yellow** traditional colors seen in churches during Easter season. [Christian Color Symbolism: Jobes, 487]

9. **spring flowers** token of Christ's resurrection. [Christian Tradition: Jobes, 487]

10. **white and green** signifies color of Easter holidays. [Christian Color Symbolism: Jobes, 487]

11. **white lily** symbol of Resurrection. [Christian Tradition: Jobes, 487]

223. EAVESDROPPING

1. **Andret** eavesdrops through keyhole on Tristan and Isolde's conversation. [Arthurian Legend: Walsh *Classical*, 22]

2. **Polonius** lurking behind arras, he is killed accidentally by Hamlet. [Br. Lit.: *Hamlet*]

3. **Pry, Paul** inquisitive, meddlesome character who "eavesdrops on everyone." [Br. Drama: *Paul Pry*, Payton, 514]

4. **Rumpelstiltskin** his name overheard by queen's messenger, allowing spell to be broken. [Ger. Fairy Tale: Grimm, 19]

224. ECCENTRICITY

1. **Addams Family** weird family, presented in grotesque domesticity. [TV: Terrace, I, 29]

2. **Boynton, Nanny** travels with set of *Encyclopaedia Britannica* to settle disputes. [Am. Lit.: "Percy" in *Stories*, 634–644]

3. **Dick, Mr.** odd but harmless old gentleman. [Br. Lit.: *David Copperfield*]

4. **Doolittle, Dr.** veterinarian who talks to animals. [Children's Lit.: *Dr. Doolittle*]

5. **Flite, Miss** "ancient" ward in Chancery. [Br. Lit.: *Bleak House*]

6. **Great-Aunt Dymphna** outlandish dresser who pointedly doesn't eat meat. [Children's Lit.: *The Growing Summer*, Fisher 124–127]

7. **Hall, Annie** idiosyncratic, scatterbrained love interest in Woody Allen's quasi-autobiographical film of same name. [Am. Film: *SJEPC*]

8. **Havisham, Miss** jilted bride turns into witchlike old woman. [Br. Lit.: *Great Expectations*]

9. **Jackson, Michael (1958–)** brilliant pop composer and singer who began his career as a child of sensational talent; as an adult, eccentric lifestyle and dazzling stage performances kept him in the headlines. [Am. Music: *SJEPC*]

10. **Longstocking, Pippi** outrageous, rebellious, imaginative child. [Children's Lit.: *Pippi Longstocking*]

11. **Madeline** adventurous, charming character braves mice, lions, even appendicitis. [Children's Lit.: *Madeline*, Fisher, 196]

12. **Madwoman of Chaillot** delightfully pixilated old woman manages to exploit the Parisian exploiters. [Fr. Lit.: *The Madwoman of Chaillot*, Benét, 618]

13. **Pickwick, Mr. (Samuel)** jolly "conformist" who understands anything but the obvious. [Br. Lit.: *Pickwick Papers*]

14. **Poppins, Mary** P.L. Travers character from children's book of the same name; eccentric and competent nanny who takes the Banks children on magical adventures before she opens her umbrella and the west winds carry her away. [Br. Children's Lit.: Jones]

15. **Salus, Saint Simeon** behaved queerly to share outcasts' contempt. [Christian Hagiog.: Attwater, 311]

16. **Tiny Tim (1927?-1996)** falsetto voice, odd clothes and demeanor made him a curiosity and a celebrity; best known for his 1968 recording of old standard "Tiptoe thru the Tulips with Me." [Am. Music: *SJEPC*]

17. **UFOs (Unidentified Flying Objects)** since the 1940s, Americans have periodically claimed to have sighted saucer-like flying objects which they were convinced were extraterrestrial spaceships; some people have attested to abduction by aliens for observation. [Am. Hist.: *SJEPC*]

18. **Wonka, Willy** eccentric confectioner from Roald Dahl's *Charlie and the Chocolate Factory* (1964); a tour of his secret factory brings punishment to a group of badly-behaved children and reward to polite, honest Charlie Bucket. [Br. Children's Lit.: Jones]

225. ECONOMICS

1. **Gresham's Law** from the theories of Thomas Gresham (1519–1579) that "bad money drives out good." [Business: Misc.]

2. ***Kapital, Das*** Karl Marx's treatise outlining the flaws of capitalism (1867–1894). [Eur. Hist.: *EB*]

3. **Keynes, John Maynard (1883–1946)** English economist who advocated government involvement to stimulate the national economy. [Hist.: Misc.]

4. **perestroika** Russian word for "restructuring," referring to the former Soviet economy; associated with the economic reforms promoted by Mikhail Gorbachev. [Russ. Hist.: Misc.]

5. **Reaganomics** refering to the economic policies of Pres. Ronald Reagan, esp. to the "trickle-down" theory, that the benefit of tax cuts for the rich would trickle down to the poor. [Am. Politics: Misc.]

6. **Smith, Adam (1723–1790)** Scottish economist whose writings were among the first studies of the history of capital and commerce. [Business: *An Inquiry into the Nature and Causes of the Wealth of Nations*]

226. EDUCATION (See also TEACHING.)

1. **ABCs** the first letters of the alphabet, and basis of language and reading; also refers to the "basics" needed for a task or trade. [Am. Education: Misc.]

2. **Adademy, the** Plato's school in Athens. [Gk. Hist.: Benét, 5]

3. **Arthur** education, especially reading and writing, are often the focus of the books and TV episodes involving Marc Brown's bespectacled young aardvark, his family, and friends. [Amer. Children's Lit. and TV: McElmeel]

4. **Baby Einstein** first produced in 1997, a line of multimedia products and toys designed for children ages three months to three years; main emphasis on classical music, art, and poetry as a way of boosting child's cognitive development. [Am. Business: Misc.]

5. *Blue's Clues* groundbreaking, award-winning TV show for preschool children from 1996–2000; accolades from educators for its ability to teach problem-solving skills to the very young; viewer presented with a puzzle for which animated dog, Blue, leaves clues to the solution. [Am. TV: Misc.]

6. *Brown v. Board of Education of Topeka* Supreme Court decision in 1954 declared racial segregation in public schools unconstitutional. [Am. Hist.: WB2]

7. **Cadmus** introduced the alphabet to the Greeks. [Gk. Myth.: Brewer *Dictionary*, 161]

8. **Cambridge** one of two leading British universities (since 1231); consists of 24 colleges. [Br. Education: Payton, 116]

9. **Catherine of Alexandria, Saint** patroness of education. [Christian Hagiog.: Hall, 58]

10. **Chautauqua** a movement for general education in the arts and humanities, started in Chautauqua, New York, flourished from 1870s to 1920s. [Am. Hist.: *FOF, MOD*]

11. *Dick and Jane* **readers** series of books with limited vocabulary featuring siblings Dick, Jane, and Sally along with dog Spot and kitten Puff taught American schoolchildren to read from the 1930s to the 1960s. [Am. Education: *SJEPC*]

12. **Du Bois, W. E. B. (1868–1963)** prominent African-American educator, scholar, and leader was first black to earn a doctorate from Harvard; advocated higher education as a means of achieving racial progress. [Am. Hist.: *SJEPC*]

13. *Education of Henry Adams, The autobiography describing intellectial influences on the author. [Am.Lit.: Hart, 249]*

14. **Emile** Rousseau's treatise on education of children (1762). [Fr. Lit.: Emile, Magill III, 330–333]

15. **Fadiman, Clifton (1904–1999)** witty literary critic, editor, book reviewer, and writer promoted knowledge, reading, and great classic books to the general public; moderated radio quiz show *Information, Please!* (1938–48). [Am. Publishing: *SJEPC*]

16. **Feverel, Sir Austen** rears his son by a scientific system in which women were a minor factor. [Br. Lit.: Meredith *The Ordeal of Richard Feverel* in Magill I, 692]

17. **Gradgrind, Thomas** raises and educates children on materialistic principles. [Br. Lit.: *Hard Times*]

18. **Grand Tour, the** European tour as necessary part of education for British aristocrats. [Eur. Hist.: Plumb, 414]

19. **Instructions to a Son** papyrus document; one of earliest preserved writings (c. 2500 B.C.). [Classical Hist.: Grun, 2]

20. **Ivy League** term used to designate eight prestigious East coast universities: Brown, Columbia, Cornell, Dartmouth, Harvard, Pennsylvania, Princeton, Yale. [Am. Education: Payton, 343; *SJEPC*]

21. **Locke, John (1632–1704)** philosopher and educator who believed instruction should be coupled with entertainment, thereby influencing writing and publishing for children in the eighteenth century; his *Some Thoughts Concerning Education* (1693) includes points considered insightful to this day. [Br. Lit.: *OCCL*]

22. **Lyceum** a gymnasium where Aristotle taught in ancient Athens. [Gk. Hist.: Hart, 502]

23. **Magic Schoolbus, The** series of books written by Joanna Cole and animated TV show for children; Ms. Frizzle takes her class on fun field trips into the human body, the solar system, and other improbable destinations to learn about science concepts. [Am. Children's Lit. and TV: Misc.]

24. **McGuffey Eclectic Readers** first published in 1836 and became widely used in American schools for 75 years; named after compiler William Holmes McGuffey; a Calvinist, he wrote lessons that were didactic and moralistic, but introduced children to many classics through short reprinted excerpts. [Am. Hist.: Hart, 509; *OCCL*]

25. **mortarboard** closefitting cap with flat square piece and tassel; part of academic costume. [Am. and Br. Culture: Misc.]

26. **Oxford** one of two leading British universities (c. 1167); consists of 34 colleges. [Br. Education: Payton, 502]

27. **PBS (Public Broadcasting)** Corporation for Public Broadcasting created in 1967; soon after, noncommercial TV blossomed into full spectrum of quality documentaries, drama, sitcoms, and children's programs. [Am. TV: *SJEPC*]

28. **Phi Beta Kappa** honorary scholarship society. [Am. Hist.: Hart, 651]

29. **PTA/PTO (Parent Teacher Association/Organization)** voluntary groups that bring parents and public schools together to improve the quality of education and parenting as well as addressing social issues like drug abuse and violence. [Am. Education: *SJEPC*]

30. *Sesame Street* began in 1968; winner of more than 100 awards; Jim Henson's muppets and actors in an urban neighborhood teach children basic concepts through song, repetition, and entertaining images and sound; influenced children's TV and teaching styles. [Am. TV: *SJEPC*]

31. **Seven Sisters** select group of colleges originally for women: Barnard, Bryn Mawr, Mount Holyoke, Radcliffe, Smith, Vassar, Wellesley. [Am. Education: Payton, 615]

32. **Sorbonne** University of Paris; long esteemed as educational center. [Fr. Hist.: Brewer *Dictionary*, 1019]

33. **Wanderjahr** a year's absence from one's schooling as period to reflect on learning. [Eur. Hist.: Plumb, 414]

227. EGOTISM (See also ARROGANCE, BOASTFULNESS, CONCEIT, INDIVIDUALISM, VANITY.)

1. **Ali, Muhammad (1942–)** three-time heavyweight champion of the world; known for quote: "I am the greatest." [Am. Sports *ODA*]

2. **baby boomers** post-World War II generation (born 1946–1964) stereotyped as self-indulgent, suburban, and conventional. [Am. Culture: *SJEPC*]

3. **Baxter, Ted** TV anchorman who sees himself as most important news topic. [TV: "The Mary Tyler Moore Show" in Terrace, II, 70]

4. **cat** symbol of egotism because of its aloofness and independence. [Animal Symbolism: Mercatante, 49]

5. **Milvain, Jasper** sees himself as extremely important in literary world. [Br. Lit.: *New Grub Street*, Magill I, 647–649]

6. **Miss Piggy** vain, egotistical Muppet. [Am. TV: *ODA*]

7. **narcissus** symbol of self-centeredness. [Flower Symbolism: *Flora Symbolica*, 176]

8. **Narcissus** falls in love with his reflection in pond. [Gk. Myth.: Brewer *Handbook*, 745; Rom. Lit.: *Metamorphoses*]

9. *Number One* portraying politician Crawford; self-gain as tour de force. [Am. Lit.: *Number One*]

10. **Patterne, Sir Willoughby** epitome of vanity and self-centeredness, tries to dominate all around him. [Br. Lit.: *The Egoist* in Magill I, 241]

11. **Singer, Alvy** neurotic, self-absorbed character in *Annie Hall*, based on and played by Woody Allen himself. [Am. Film: *SJEPC*]

12. **Skimpole, Horace** egocentric, wily fraud. [Br. Lit.: *Bleak House*]

13. **Templeton** self-centered rat. [Children's Lit.: *Charlotte's Web*]

228. ELEGANCE (See also GLAMOUR, SOPHISTICATION.)

1. **After Six, Inc.** makers of men's formal wear and accessories. [Trademarks: Crowley *Trade*, 9]

2. **Archer, Isabel** American heiress undergoes process of refinement amid European culture. [Am. Lit.: *The Portrait of a Lady*]

3. **Ashley, Lady Brett** heroine "as charming when drunk as when sober." [Am. Lit.: *The Sun Also Rises*]

4. **Belle Epoque** era of elegance and artistic greatness for the European upper classes, c.1870–1914. [Eur. Hist.: *FOF, MOD*]

5. **dahlia** represents elegance. [Flower Symbolism: Jobes, 406]

6. **Darlington, Lord** epitome of London's man about town (1800s). [Br. Lit.: *Lady Windemere's Fan*, Magill I, 488–490]

7. **Delmonico's** famous New York restaurant noted for its elegance. [Am. Culture: *FOF, MOD*]

8. **Grant, Cary (1906–1986)** English-born American actor noted for debonaire roles. [Am. Film: *FOF, MOD*]

9. **locust** tree representing elegance. [Tree Symbolism: *Flora Symbolica*, 175]

10. **Petronius** called by Roman historian Tacitus "a man of refined luxury," and "the arbiter of elegance"; lived in the reign of the emperor Nero. [Rom. Hist.: *EB* (1963) XVII 681]

229. ELF

1. **cluricaune** small creature who appears as an old man; knows about hidden treasure. [Irish Folklore: Brewer *Dictionary*, 213]

2. **Elrond** character from Tolkien's Lord of the Rings trilogy (1954–1956); lord of the elven kingdom; benevolent and wise ruler; great healer and sage who initiates the Fellowship of the Ring. [Br. Lit.: Gillespie and Naden]

3. **Legolas** character from Tolkien's Lord of the Rings trilogy (1954–1956); although not the most powerful elf, he is chosen to assist Frodo because he is an excellent scout and archer, and exceptionally brave. [Br. Lit.: Gillespie and Naden]

230. ELOPEMENT

1. **Clarker, James** with Dombey's wife. [Br. Lit.: *Dombey and Son*]

2. **Leonora** with Alvaro, rejected as suitor by her father. [Ital. Opera: Verdi, *La Forza del Destino*, Westerman, 315–317]

3. **Little Emily** with Steerforth, although engaged to Ham. [Br. Lit.: *David Copperfield*]

4. **Madeline** with Porphyro, who appears in dream. [Br. Lit.: "The Eve of St. Agnes" in Magill I, 263–264]

5. **Wardle, Rachel** elopes with the imposter Alfred Jingle. [Br. Lit.: Dickens *Pickwick Papers*]

231. ELOQUENCE

1. **Ambrose, Saint** bees, prophetic of fluency, landed in his mouth. [Christian Hagiog.: Brewster, 177]

2. **Antony, Mark** gives famous speech against Caesar's assassins. [Br. Lit.: *Julius Caesar*]

3. **Arnall, Father** his sermons fill Stephen with the fear of hell-fire. [Br. Lit.: Joyce *Portrait of the Artist as a Young Man*]

4. **bees on the mouth** pictorial and verbal symbol of eloquence. [Folklore and Christian Iconog.: Brewster, 177]

5. **Bragi** god of poetry and fluent oration. [Norse Myth.: *LLEI*, I: 324]

6. **Calliope** chief muse of poetic inspiration and oratory. [Gk. Myth.: Brewer *Dictionary*, 177]

7. **Churchill, Winston (1874–1965)** statesman whose rousing oratory led the British in WWII. [Br. Hist.: *NCE*, 556]

8. **Cicero (106–43 B.C.)** orator whose forcefulness of presentation and melodious language is still imitated. [Rom. Hist.: *NCE*, 558]

9. **Demosthenes (382–322 B.C.)** generally considered the greatest of the Greek orators. [Gk. Hist.: *NCE*, 559]

10. **Gettysburg Address** Lincoln's brief, moving eulogy for war dead (1863). [Am. Hist.: Jameson, 286–287]

11. **King, Martin Luther, Jr. (1929–1968)** civil rights leader and clergyman whose pleas for justice won support of millions. [Am. Hist.: *NCE*, 1134; *SJEPC*]

12. **lotus** symbol of eloquence. [Plant Symbolism: *Flora Symbolica*, 175]

13. **Mapple, Father** preaches movingly and ominously on Jonah. [Am. Lit.: Melville *Moby Dick*]

14. **Paine, Thomas (1737–1809)** powerful voice of the colonies; wrote famous "Common Sense." [Am. Hist.: Jameson 369–370]

15. **Webster, Daniel (1782–1852)** noted 19th-century American orator-politician. [Am. Hist.: Jameson, 539]

232. ENCHANTMENT (See also FANTASY, MAGIC, WITCHCRAFT.)

1. **Alidoro** fairy godfather to Italian Cinderella. [Ital. Opera: Rossini, *Cinderella*, Westerman, 120–121]

2. **Bottom, Nick** under spell, grows ass's head. [Br. Lit.: *A Midsummer Night's Dream*]

3. **Cinderella** enchantment lasts only till midnight. [Fr. Fairy Tale: *Cinderella*]

4. **Circe** enchantress who changes Odysseus's men into swine. [Gk. Lit.: *Odyssey*; Rom. Lit.: *Aeneid*]

5. **Geraldine, Lady** evil spirit who, by casting a spell, induces Christabel to bring her into her father's castle. [Br. Lit.: S.T. Coleridge "Christabel" in Benét, 195]

6. **Grimm, Jacob (1785–1863) and Grimm, Wilhelm (1786–1859)** German philologists and folklorists; transcribed and published German folk tales. [Ger. Lit.: *Grimm's Fairy Tales*]

7. **Land of Oz** bewitching realm of magic and mystery. [Am. Lit.: *The Wonderful Wizard of Oz"]*

8. **Lorelei** water nymph of the Rhine; lured sailors to their doom with her singing. [Ger. Folklore: Leach, 645]

9. **Maugis** enchanter; one of Charlemagne's paladins. [Fr. Folklore: Harvey, 526]

10. **Miracle, Dr.** bewitches Antonia into singing despite doctor's orders. [Fr. Opera: Offenbach, *Tales of Hoffman*, Westerman, 275–276]

11. **Oberon** fairy king orders love charm placed on Titania, the fairy queen. [Br. Lit.: *A Midsummer Night's Dream*]

12. **Orpheus** his singing opens the gates of the underworld. [Ger. Opera: Gluck, *Orpheus and Euridyce*, Westerman, 72]

13. **Pied Piper** charms children of Hamelin with music. [Children's Lit.: "The Pied Piper of Hamelin" in *Dramatic Lyrics*, Fisher 279–281]

14. **pishogue** Irish fairy spell that distorts reality. [Irish Folklore: Briggs, 327–328]

15. **Quixote, Don** ascribes all his misfortunes to the machinations of enchanters. [Span. Lit.: Cervantes *Don Quixote*]

16. **Scheherazade** spins yarns for Sultan for 1001 nights. [Arab Lit.: *Arabian Nights*]

17. **Schwanda** Czech Orpheus; bagpipe music moves even Queen Iceheart. [Gk. Myth.: Weinberger, *Schwanda*, Westerman, 412]

18. **Sirens** with song, bird-women lure sailors to death. [Gk. Myth.: *Odyssey*]

19. **Sleeping Beauty** sleeps for 100 years. [Fr. Fairy Tale: *The Sleeping Beauty*]

20. **Titania** experiences sleep-induced fascination over Bottom. [Br. Lit.: *A Midsummer Night's Dream*]

21. **Van Winkle, Rip** returns to village after sleep of 20 years. [Am. Lit.: *The Sketch Book of Geoffrey Crayon, Gent.*]

22. **vervain** indicates bewitching powers. [Flower Symbolism: *Flora Symbolica*, 178]

23. **Vivian** the Lady of the Lake, enchantress and mistress of Merlin. [Br. Lit.: Barnhart, 1118]

233. END

1. **Armageddon** battleground of good and evil before Judgment Day. [N.T.: Revelation 16:16]

2. **checkmate** end of game in chess; folk-etymology of *Shah-mat*, 'the Shah is dead.' [Br. Folklore: Espy, 217]

3. **fatal raven** indicates defeat or victory by arranging its wings. [Norse Legend: *Volsung Saga*]

4. **Judgment Day** final trial of all mankind. [N.T.: Revelation]

5. **Last Supper** Passover dinner the night before Christ died. [N.T.: Matthew 26:26–29; Mark 14:22–25; Luke 22:14–20]

234. ENDURANCE (See also LONGEVITY, SURVIVAL.)

1. **Atalanta** feminine name denotes power of endurance. [Gk. Myth.: Jobes, 148]

2. **Badger** from Kenneth Grahame's children's classic *Wind in the Willows* (1908); his love of tradition and ability to maintain order in his community are seen as signs of enduring spirit. [Br. Children's Lit.: Jones]

3. **Boston Marathon** famous 26–mile race held annually for long-distance runners. [Am. Pop. Culture: Misc.]

4. **cedrala tree** symbol of longevity and endurance. [Eastern Folklore and Plant Symbolism: Jobes, 301]

5. **Denisovich, Ivan** prisoner persists through travails of Soviet camp. [Russ. Lit.: *One Day in the Life of Ivan Denisovich*]

6. **dromedary** able to cover a hundred miles in one day. [Medieval Animal Symbolism: White, 80–81]

7. ***Grapes of Wrath, The*** John Steinbeck's Pulitzer Prize-winning novel about the struggling Joad family, who leave their farm in Oklahoma's Dust Bowl during the Great Depression in search of greener pastures in California (1939). [Am. Lit.: Harris *Characters*, 381–82; *SJEPC*]

8. **ironman triathlon** event combines swimming, bicycling, marathon run. [Pop. Cult.: Misc.]

9. **marathon dancing** dance contest with endurance as chief factor. [Am. Hist.: Sann, 57–69]

10. **oak** symbol of nobility and endurance. [Symbolism: *CEOS&S*]

11. **Prometheus** epitome of stoic endurance. [Gk. Myth.: Gayley, 10–15]

12. **Steadfast Tin Soldier** one-legged toy survives multiple casualties; totally immolated. [Dan. Lit.: *Andersen's Fairy Tales*]

13. **Tevye** Russian Jewish peasant in musical *Fiddler on the Roof* (1964) endures despite revolutionary changes in the social and political structures of his world. [Am. Musical: *SJEPC*]

235. ENEMY

1. **Amalekites** Israel's hereditary foe and symbol of perpetual hatred. [Jew. Hist.: Wigoder, 24]

2. **Antichrist** principal antagonist of Christ. [Christianity: *NCE*, 117]

3. **Armilus** legendary name of anti-Messiah. [Judaism: Wigoder, 41]

4. **Satan** also called the Adversary or the Devil. [Christianity: Misc.]

236. ENERGY

1. **black hole** in physics, sections of the universe with intense gravity that pull in everything around them; in common usage, an inextricable difficulty. [Science: *FOF, MOD*]

2. **blackout** power loss due to overuse of electricity; first used to describe the practice in England of covering all light sources during bombing in WWII. [World History: Misc.]

3. **bull** in cave art, the bull is symbolic of vital energy; holds great significance in many cultures as a symbol of natural elements: moon, sun, sky, rain, etc. and his bellowing energy linked with thunder and earthquakes. [Symbolism: *CEOS&S*]

4. **chain reaction** a chemical or nuclear reaction that causes similar reactions to produce energy; broadly, an event that causes a ripple effect. [Science: *FOF, MOD*]

5. **Qi** according to acupuncture theory, a flowing energy force in the body whose disruption can cause ill health in both the physical and emotional realms. [Chinese Medicine: *SJEPC*]

237. ENLIGHTENMENT

1. **ball and cross** symbol of gradual universal evangelism. [Christian Tradition: Jobes, 176]

2. **Bodhisattva** "the enlightened one" deferring Nirvana to help others. [Buddhism: Parrinder, 48]

3. **Buddha** a mortal who's achieved Nirvana, particularly Gautama. [Buddhism: Parrinder, 53]

4. **Chloe** "fearful virgin" learns love's delights on wedding night. [Gk. Lit.: *Daphnis and Chloe*, Magill I, 184]

5. **consciousness raising** from social movements of the 1960s: an effort to enable an individual to achieve self-knowledge. [Am. Cult.: Misc.]

6. **cross** in Hindu faith, represents communion of higher state with earthly state, leading to expansion of being. [Hindu Religion: *IEOTS*, 46]

7. **Gautama** sees "everything" and has "eyes on his feet." [Buddhism: Parrinder, 110]

8. **guru** a Hindu spiritual leader; by extension, a wise leader. [Hinduism: *FOF, MOD*]

9. **lotus** in Egypt, India, China, and Japan, symbol of birth, cosmic life, the divine, and human spiritual growth. [Symbolism: *CEOS&S*]

10. **New Age Music** soothing music, often instrumental; a favorite for meditation and relaxation. [Music: *SJEP*]

11. **prajna (Sanskrit)** "wisdom," used in abstract sense or sometimes personified as a goddess. [Sanskrit: Parrinder, 222]

12. **Sanatana Dharma** "eternal truth." [Hinduism: Parrinder, 122]

13. **scales falling from eyes** vision restored, Saul is converted. [N.T.: Acts 9:17–19]

14. **Seagull, Jonathan Livingston** seagull's quest for perfection in flight. [Am. Lit: *SJEPC*]

15. **Sedona** thought to contain seven vortexes of psychic energy; New Age religions and businesses have flocked to this area in Arizona. [Am. Culture: *SJEPC*]

16. *Siddhartha* 1922 novel by Hermann Hesse describes life-long search for inner peace and true self-knowledge by a Brahmin youth; based on the early life of Buddha. [Ger. Lit.: Gillespie and Naden]

238. ENTRAPMENT

1. *Fear of Flying* metaphor for housewife Isadora Wing's temporary inability to achieve self-awareness. [Am. Lit.: *Fear of Flying*]

2. **Frome, Ethan** chained to detestable wife and unsalable farm. [Am. Lit.: *Ethan Frome*]

3. **Loman, Willy** despite dreams of success, he is condemned to failure. [Am. Drama: *Death of a Salesman*, Payton, 397]

4. **Nora** trapped in the domesticity demanded by her husband. [Nor. Lit.: Ibsen *A Doll's House*]

5. **Prufrock, J. Alfred** aware that his life is meaningless and empty, he struggles to rise above it, but cannot. [Br. Lit.: *The Love Song of J. Alfred Prufrock"* in Payton, 548]

6. **Rochester, Edward** tied to insane wife; cannot marry Jane Eyre. [Br. Lit.: *Jane Eyre*]

239. ENTREPRENEURSHIP

1. **Astor, John Jacob (1763–1848)** German-born American merchant, made his fortune in the fur trade. [Am. Business: Misc.]

2. **Bell, Alexander Graham (1847–1922)** Scottish-born American scientist and inventor of the telephone; founder of Bell Telephone. [Am. Business: *BBInv*]

3. **Carnegie, Andrew (1835–1919)** Scottish-born American industrialist and philanthropist, made his fortune in iron and steel. [Am. Business: Misc.]

4. **Deere, John (1804–1886)** American inventor of the steel plow, founder of John Deere Company. [Am. Business: *BBInv*]

5. **Edison, Thomas Alva (1847–1931)** American inventor of more than 1,000 items, including the incandescent light bulb, the phonograph, and motion pictures. [Am. Business: *BBInv*]

6. **Ford, Henry (1863–1947)** American industrialist, inventor, philanthropist; founder of Ford Motor Company who developed mass production methods. [Am. Business: *BBInv*]

7. **Gates, Bill (1955–)** American computer software pioneer and cofounder of Microsoft, now a philanthropist who has given billions to cure diseases worldwide. [Am. Buisness: *BBInv*]

8. **Gordy, Berry (1929–)** former auto assembly line worker from Detroit founded music production company Motown in 1959, building an immensely successful enterprise with a distinctive sound recognized around the world. [Am. Music: *BBAAL2*]

9. **Hewlett-Packard** technology company founded by William Hewitt (1913–2001) and David Packard (1912–1996) in 1939; grew to become one of the most innovative and successful computer and electronics companies in the world. [Am. Business: Misc.]

10. **Jobs, Steven (1955–)** American founder of Apple Computer who helped create the personal computer, known for creativity and

marketing savvy reaching the film, music, as well as the computer business. [Am. Business: *BBInv*]

11. **Land, Edwin (1909–1991)** American physicist and inventor of instant photography, founded Polaroid. [Am. Business: *BBInv*]

12. **McCormick Cyrus (1809–1884)** American inventor of the mechanical reaper and innovative businessman. [Am. Business: *BBInv*]

13. **Rockefeller, John D. (1839–1937)** billionaire American industrialist and founder of Standard Oil; success led to charges of monopolistic practices, lawsuits, and the breakup of his original company. [Am. Business: Misc.]

14. **Spalding, Albert G. (1850–1915)** baseball player, manager, and owner who helped form the National League in 1876 and went on to found successful sporting goods chain. [Am. Sports: *SJEPC*]

15. **Vanderbilt, Cornelius (1794–1877)** American industrialist made his fortune in shipping and railroads. [Am. Business: Misc.]

16. **Walker, Madame C. J. (1867–1919)** first African-American female millionaire; her formula to prevent hair loss led to line of hair care products marketed to African Americans; known as the "Walker System," it was said to effectively soften coarse hair. [Am. Business: *BBAAL2*]

240. ENVIRONMENTALISM

1. **Adams, Ansel (1902–1984)** famous photographer of the American Southwest was also member of the Sierra Club and involved in environmental causes. [Am. Art: *SJEPC*]

2. **Audubon Society, National** conservation organization named after naturalist/bird artist John James Audubon was established in 1905; maintains sanctuaries across the United States to preserve habitat for wildlife and endangered species. [Am. Hist.: *WB2*]

3. **Carson, Rachel (1907–1964)** biologist/writer helped ignite the modern environmental movement with her best-selling book *Silent Spring* (1962), which discussed the effects of pollution and pesticides like DDT on ecology of streams and subsequent harm to the food chain. [Am. Science: *SJEPC*]

4. **Earth Day** celebrated on April 22 to bring worldwide attention to environmental concerns and issues affecting the planet; first organized in 1970. [Science: *SJEPC*]

5. **Earth Shoes** natural-fitting shoe with higher toe than heel was a hit with Earth-conscious generation of the 1970s. [Am. Culture: *SJEPC*]

6. **eco-terrorism** sabotage committed to protect and defend natural resources, typically by radical environmentalists. [Hist.: *SJEPC*]

7. **green** environmentally conscious. [Usage: Misc.]

8. **Greenpeace** worldwide environmental organization founded in 1971 promotes peace alongside environmental causes; known for highly publicized, confrontational, but nonviolent protests and campaigns in its efforts. [Hist.: *SJEPC*]

9. **monkeywrenching** the practice by radical environmentalists of sabotaging the equipment used by developers to deforest and degrade natural landscapes; rooted in Edward Abbey's novel *The Monkey Wrench Gang*. [Am. Usage: *SJEPC*]

10. **recycling** reusing trash to reduce waste as a partial antidote to American mass consumption. [Am. Culture: *SJEPC*]

11. **Sierra Club** conservation organization founded in 1892 by naturalist John Muir advocates protection of wilderness areas, natural resources, and animal life in the United States and Canada. [Am. Hist.: *WB2*]

12. *Silent Spring* Rachel Carson's 1962 book warning about the use of pesticides helped ignite the environmental movement. [Am. Science: *SJEPC*]

13. **SUVs (Sports Utility Vehicles)** favored by many baby boomers for their size, power, and handling in rough terrain or bad weather; denounced by environmentalists for copious use of gas and off-road impact on pristine areas. [Am. Pop. Culture: *SJEPC*]

14. *Watership Down* Richard Adams's 1972 award-winning novel for young readers about journey of a group of rabbits, displaced by a housing development, who search for a safe place to live. [Br. Children's Lit.: Gillespie and Naden]

15. *Whole Earth Catalogue, The* first published in 1968, became handbook of counterculture for its mix of philosophy, metaphysics, environmentallism, and marketing of green products. [Am. Publishing: *SJEPC*]

16. **World Wildlife Fund (WWF)** global conservation organization founded in 1961 seeks to preserve natural habitats and protect endangered plants and animals such as the giant panda. [Hist.: *WB2*]

241. ENVY (See also JEALOUSY.)

1. **Amneris** envious of Aida. [Ital. Opera: Verdi, *Aida*, Westerman, 325]

2. **Anastasia and Orizella** Cinderella's two step-sisters; envious of her beauty, they treat her miserably. [Fr. Fairy Tale: *Cinderella*]

3. **Cory, Richard** subject of Edward Arlington Robinson's poem: envied by all, commits suicide out of despair. [Am. Lit.: E.A. Robinson "Richard Cory"]

4. **green** symbol of envy; "the green-eyed monster." [Color Symbolism: Jobes, 357; Br. Lit.: *Othello*]

5. **Iago** Othello's ensign who, from malevolence and envy, persuades Othello that Desdemona has been unfaithful. [Br. Lit.: *Othello*]

6. **Joseph's brothers** resented him for Jacob's love and gift. [O.T.: Genesis 37:4]

7. **Lensky** envy of Onegin leads to his death in a duel. [Russ. Opera: Tchaikovsky, *Eugene Onegin*, Westerman, 395–397]

8. **Lisa** envious of Amina; tries unsuccessful stratagems. [Ital. Opera: Bellini, *The Sleepwalker*, Westerman, 128–130]

9. **Snow White's stepmother** envious of her beauty, queen orders Snow White's death. [Ger. Fairy Tale: Grimm, 184]

242. EPIC

1. *Aeneid* Virgil's epic poem glorifying the origin of the Roman people. [Rom. Lit.: *Aeneid*]

2. *Beowulf* Old English epic poem tells of brave warrior slaying monster, Grendel. [Br. Lit.: *Beowulf*]

3. *Divine Comedy* Dante's epic poem in three sections: *Inferno*, *Purgatorio*, and *Paradiso*. [Ital. Lit.: *Divine Comedy*]

4. *Faerie Queene* allegorical epic poem by Edmund Spenser. [Br. Lit.: *Faerie Queene*]

5. *Frithiof's Saga* Esaias Tegnèr's poetic vision of the Norse Saga of Frithiof the Bold. [Nor. Lit.: Haydn & Fuller, 275]

6. *Gilgamesh* Babylonia epic of myth and folklore, centered on the king, Gilgamesh. [Babyl. Myth.: *Gilgamesh*]

7. *Gone with the Wind* David O. Selznick's epic Civil War film adapted from Margaret Mitchell's novel about the South follows the trials, loves, and triumphs of Southern belle Scarlett O'Hara; starred Vivien Leigh as Scarlett and Clark Gable as Rhett Butler; phenomenally successful film won 10 Academy Awards. [Am. Film: *SJEPC*]

8. *Gosta Berling's Saga* Selma Lagerlof's story of the legendary life of an early nineteenth-century character. [Swed. Lit.: *Gosta Berling's Saga* in Benét, 412]

9. *Heimskringla* medieval account of the kings of Norway from legendary times to the twelfth century. [Nor. Hist.: Haydn & Fuller, 322]

10. *Iliad* Homer's epic detailing a few days near the end of the Trojan War. [Gk. Lit.: *Iliad*]

11. *Jerusalem Delivered* Tasso's celebrated romantic epic written during Renaissance. [Ital. Lit.: *Jerusalem Delivered*]

12. *Kalevala* alliterative epic poem of Finland. [Finn. Lit.: *Kalevala*]

13. *Lawrence of Arabia* numerous awards were bestowed on visually lush, beautifully scripted 1962 biopic of British scholar and mil-

itary officer T.E. Lawrence whose exploits in Middle East are legendary. [Am. Film: *SJEPC*]

14. ***Laxdale Saga*** medieval account of two Icelandic families and their feud. [Icel. Lit.: Benét, 572]

15. ***Lord of the Rings, The*** J.R.R. Tolkien's epic trilogy of quest of hobbit Frodo Baggins to destroy magic ring that tempts its owner with immense power before evil lord Sauron can reclaim the ring to rule world of Middle Earth; made into award-winning series of films in 2001–2003. [Br. Lit. and Am. Film: *SJEPC*]

16. ***Lusiad, The*** celebrates Portuguese heroes and wars. [Port. Lit.: Magill II, 608]

17. ***Mahabharata*** Indian epic poem of the struggle between the Pandavas and the Kauravas. [Indian Lit.: *Mahabharata*]

18. ***Nibelungenlied*** medieval German epic poem of Siegfried and the Nibelung kings. [Ger. Lit.: *Nibelungenlied*]

19. ***Njál's Saga*** greatest of the Icelandic sagas, based on the historical adventures of two families. [Icel. Lit.: Haydn & Fuller, 524]

20. ***Odyssey*** Homer's long narrative peoem centered on Odysseus. [Gk. Lit.: *Odyssey*]

21. ***One Hundred Years of Solitude*** encompasses 100 years in the life of the Buendia family. [Lat. Am. Lit.: Gabriel Garcia Marquez *One Hundred Years of Solitude, in Weiss, 336]*

22. ***Orlando Furioso*** Ariosto's romantic epic; actually a continuation of Boiardo's plot. [Ital. Lit.: *Orlando Furioso*]

23. ***Orlando Innamorato*** Boiardo's epic combining Carolingian chivalry and Arthurian motifs. [Ital. Lit.: *Orlando Innamorato*]

24. ***Paradise Lost*** Milton's epic poem of man's first disobedience. [Br. Lit.: *Paradise Lost*]

25. ***Ramayana*** epic poem of ancient India. [Indian Lit.: *Ramayana*]

26. ***Song of Igor's Campaign*** Old Russian epic poem of 12th-century Prince Igor. [Russ. Lit.: *Song of Igor's Campaign*]

27. ***Song of Roland*** chanson de geste of Roland and Charlemagne. [Fr. Lit.: *Song of Roland*]

28. ***Song of the Cid*** epic poem of Spain by an anonymous author. [Span. Lit.: *Song of the Cid*]

29. ***Ten Commandments, The*** opulent 1956 film of Biblical story of Moses with unprecedented special effects and cast of thousands. [Am. Film: *SJEPC*]

30. ***Terra Nostra*** combines the myths and history of twenty centuries of Western civilization. [Lat. Am. Lit.: Carols Fuentes *Terra Nostra* in Weiss, 458]

31. ***Volsunga Saga*** cycle of Scandinavian legends, major source of *Nibelungenlied*. [Scand. Lit.: Benét, 1064]

243. EPICURE (See also FEAST.)

1. **Belshazzar** gave banquet unrivalled for sumptuousness. [O.T.: Daniel 5:1–4]
2. **Epicurus (341–271 B.C.)** Greek philosopher who believed that happiness was found in hedonism. [Gk. Phil.: *ODA*]
3. **Finches of the Grove** eating club established for expensive dining. [Br. Lit.: *Great Expectations*]
4. **Gatsby, Jay** modern Trimalchio, wines and dines the upper echelon. [Am. Lit.: *The Great Gatsby*]
5. **Lucullus, Lucius Licinius (110–57 B.C.)** gave luxurious banquets. [Rom. Hist.: *New Century*, 650]
6. **Marius** young pagan who follows the original philosophical tenets of Epucurus in his search for an answer to life. [Br. Lit.: Pater *Marius the Epicurean* in Magill II, 630]
7. **Trimalchio** vulgar freedman gives lavish feast for noble guests. [Rom. Lit.: *Satyricon*]

244. EPILEPSY

1. **Myshkin, Peter** suffered fits from early youth, affecting his physical and mental health. [Russ. Lit.: Dostoevsky *The Idiot*]
2. **Vitus, Saint** his chapel at Ulm famed for epileptic cures. [Christian Hagiog.: Brewster, 291]

245. EROTICISM

1. ***Aphrodite*** novel of Alexandrian manners by Pierre Louys. [Fr. Lit.: Benét, 783]
2. ***Ars Amatoria*** Ovid's treatise on lovemaking. [Rom. Lit.: Magill IV, 45]
3. **Barbarella** frequently semi-nude heroine of sexy French comicstrip. [Comics: Berger, 211]
4. **Daphnis and Chloë** their idyll reconciles naivetè and sexual fulfillment. [Gk. Lit.: Magill I, 184]
5. ***Delta of Venus*** stories of sexual adventure including incest, perversion, prostitution, etc. [Am. Lit.: Anais Nin *Delta of Venus* in Weiss, 124]
6. **Hill, Fanny** narrator of Cleland's 18th-century novel of erotic experiences. [Br. Lit.: Cleland *Memoirs of Fanny Hill*]
7. ***Kama-Sutra*** detailed Hindu account of the art of lovemaking. [Ind. Lit.: Benét, 538]
8. **Madonna (1958–)** overtly sexual performances, videos, and book played out her "Boy Toy" image. [Am. Music: *SJEPC*]

9. **Miller, Henry (1891–1980)** beginning with *Tropic of Cancer* (1934), wrote early sexually-explicit novels. [Am. Lit.: *SJEPC*]

10. **900 Numbers** phone sex numbers normally begin with this prefix rather than an area code. [Am. Culture: *SJEPC*]

11. **O** a beautiful woman willing to undergo every form of sexual manipulation at the bidding of her lover. [Fr. Lit.: Pauline Rèage *The Story of O* in Weiss, 445]

12. **pear** love symbol with erotic associations, probably due to its shape. [Symbolism: *CEOS&S*]

13. *Penthouse* Bob Guccione's sexually explicit magazine for those who found *Playboy* a bit too tame. [Br. and Amer. Jour.: *SJEPC*]

14. *Perfumed Garden, The* Arabian manual of sexual activity. [Arab. Lit.: *EB* (1963) IV, 448]

15. **Peyton Place** fictitious New England town rife with sex and vice. [Am. Lit., Film, and TV: *SJEPC*]

16. **Phone Sex** sexually stimulating phone calls for a price. [Am. Culture: *SJEPC*]

17. **Pin-Up, The** ranges from Hollywood posters to centerfolds, but most common reference is to depictions of girls in scanty outfits from the WWII era. [Am. Culture: *SJEPC*]

18. *Playboy* Hugh Hefner established the magazine in 1953; featured profiles of luxury items, interviews with famous people, fiction by notable writers, and photos of naked women. [Am. Jour.: *SJEPC*]

19. *Playgirl* established in 1973; first magazine that functioned as counterpart to *Playboy*; male nudity was sometimes featured. [Am. Jour.: *SJEPC*]

20. **Prince (1958–)** prolific songwriter and intriguing performer; has faced cricitism for sexual, sometimes sadomaschistic, themes. [Am. Music: *SJEPC*]

21. **Rand, Sally (1904–1979)** famous for fan and bubble dances with suggestive moves and lots of skin. [Am. Entertainment: *SJEPC*]

22. **Sheldon, Sidney (1917–2007)** frequently translated and immensely popular writer of steamy novels with fast-paced plots. [Am. Lit.: *SJEPC*]

23. **Summer, Donna (1948–)** queen of disco with breakthrough hit "Love to Love You Baby" in 1975; its frank sexuality was unheard of at the time. [Am. Music: *SJEPC*]

246. ERROR

1. **Breeches Bible, the** the Geneva Bible, so dubbed because it stated that Adam and Eve made themselves breeches. [Br. Hist.: Brewer *Dictionary*, 101]

2. **Cortez** alluded to in a poem by Keats, mistaken for Balboa, as discoverer of Pacific Ocean. [Br. Poetry.: "On First Looking into Chapman's Homer"]

3. **off base** term from baseball: to step off base, and be tagged out; in general usage, to be in error. [Am. Culture: *FOF, MOD*]

4. **seacoast of Bohemia** Shakespearean setting in a land with no seacoast. [Br. Drama Shakespeare *The Winter's Tale*, III, iii]

5. **Wicked Bible, the** misprinted a commandment as "Thou shalt commit adultery." [Br. Hist.: Brewer *Dictionary*, 102]

247. ESCAPE

1. **Abiathar** only son of Ahimelech to avoid Saul's daughter. [O.T.: I Samuel 22:20]

2. **Ariadne** Minos's daughter; gave Theseus thread by which to escape labyrinth. [Gk. Myth.: Zimmerman, 31]

3. **Cerambus** transformed into beetle in order to fly above Zeus's deluge. [Gk. Myth.: Zimmerman, 55]

4. **Christian** flees the City of Destruction. [Br. Lit.: *The Pilgrim's Progress*]

5. **Daedalus** escaped from Crete by flying on wings made of wax and feathers. [Gk. Myth.: Benét, 244]

6. **Dantès, Edmond** after fifteen years in the Chateau d'If he escapes by being thrown into the sea as another prisoner's corpse. [Fr. Lit.: Dumas *The Count of Monte Cristo*]

7. **Deucalion** on Prometheus' advice, survived flood in ark. [Gk. Myth.: Gaster, 84–85]

8. **Dunkirk** 340,000 British troops evacuated against long odds (1941). [Eur. Hist.: Van Doren, 475]

9. **Exodus** Jewish captives escape Pharaoh's bondage. [O.T.: Exodus]

10. **Florida vacation** warm, sunny winter getaway for northerners, especially families and the elderly; escape from cold and snowy climate ranges from a few days to an entire season. [Culture: *SJEPC*]

11. **Fugitive, The (Dr. Richard Kimble)** tale of wrongfully-accused man fleeing imprisonment. [TV: Terrace, I, 290–291; Film: Misc.]

12. **Hansel and Gretel** woodcutter's children barely escape witch. [Ger. Fairy Tale: Grimm, 56]

13. **Hegira (Hijrah)** Muhammad's flight from Mecca to Medina (622). [Islamic Hist.: EB, V: 39–40]

14. **Houdini, Harry (1874–1926)** shackled magician could extricate himself from any entrapment. [Am. Hist.: Wallechinsky, 196]

15. **Ishmael** the only one to escape when the *Pequod* is wrecked by the white whale. [Am. Lit.: Melville, *Moby Dick*]

16. **Jim** Miss Watson's runaway slave; Huck's traveling companion. [Am. Lit.: *Huckleberry Finn*]

17. **Jonah** delivered from fish's belly after three days. [O.T.: Jonah 1, 2]

18. **Noah** with family and animals, escapes the Deluge. [O.T.: Genesis 8:15–19]

19. **Papillon** one of the few to escape from Devil's Island. [Fr. Hist.: *Papillon*]

20. **parting of the Red Sea** God divides the waters for Israelites' flight. [O.T.: Exodus 14:21–29]

21. **Phyxios** epithet of Zeus as god of escape. [Gk. Myth.: Kravitz, 94]

22. **Robin, John, and Harold Hensman** run away from "petticoat government" to live in forest. [Children's Lit.: *Brendon Chase* Fisher, 306]

23. *Strange Cargo* prisoners escape by boat from Devil's Island, accompanied by mysterious stranger. [Am. Cinema: *Strange Cargo*]

24. **Theseus** escapes labyrinth with aid from Ariadne. [Gk. Myth.: Zimmerman, 31]

25. **Tyler, Toby** runs away from cruel Uncle Daniel to join circus. [Children's Lit.: *Toby Tyler*]

26. **Ziusudra** Sumerian Noah. [Sumerian Legend: Benét, 1116]

248. EVANGELISM

1. **Gantry, Elmer** fire and brimstone, fraudulent revivalist. [Am. Lit.: *Elmer Gantry*]

2. **Graham, Billy (1918–)** highly respected, internationally known, and media-savvy Evangelical Christian preacher called "America's Pastor" by President George H. W. Bush has spread the gospel of Jesus Christ across the globe via his crusades. [Am. Rel.: *SJEPC*]

3. **John** disciple closest to Jesus. [N.T.: John]

4. **Luke** early Christian; the "beloved physician." [N.T.: Luke]

5. **Mark** Christian apostle. [N.T.: Mark]

6. **Matthew** one of the twelve disciples. [N.T.: Matthew]

7. **Sunday, Billy (1862–1935)** itinerant preacher of early 1900s turned evangelism into carefully planned production of Fundamental religion and showmanship. [Am. Rel.: *SJPEC*]

8. **Swaggart, Jimmy (1935–)** leading televangelist of the 1980s; his puritanical stance and judgmental opinions meant bitter reactions when his own voyeuristic acts with a prostitute and other transgressions were revealed. [Am. Rel.: *SJEPC*]

9. **televangelism** evangelical Christians broadened their influence and drew new followers through televised preaching; scandals involving Jim Bakker and Jimmy Swaggart in the 1980s brought religious broadcasters under scrutiny. [Am. TV and Rel.: *SJEPC*]

10. **Warren, Dr. Rick (1954–)** vastly influential writer and evangelical leader; senior pastor of Saddleback Church in California, with 22,000–member congregation; author of best-selling *The Purpose Driven Life* (2002) about finding one's calling according to God's plan. [Am. Rel.: Misc.]

249. EVERYMAN (See also WHOLESOMENESS.)

1. **A. N. Other** British *John Doe* [Br. Usage: Misc.]

2. **Alda, Alan (1936–)** best known for his portrayal of Hawkeye Pierce in M*A*S*H (1972–83), actor/director has on- and off-screen persona as typical, all-around nice guy. [Am. TV and Film: *SJEPC*]

3. **Angstrom, Harry** protagonist of four "Rabbit" novels by John Updike; middle-class former athlete dealing with his own inadequacies, the elusiveness of the American dream, and an uncaring, often meaningless world. [Am. Lit.: *SJEPC*]

4. **Brother Jonathan** British slang for the typical American. [Br. Usage: Misc.]

5. **Dilbert** the engineer lead character of comic strip embodies the frustrated white-collar worker in corporate America. [Am. Comics: *SJEPC*]

6. **Douglas, Mike (1925–2006)** likeable daytime TV talk show host embodied mainstream Middle American values. [Am. TV: *SJEPC*]

7. **Ivanov Ivan Ivanovich** embodiment of ordinary Russian person. [Russ. Usage: *LLEI*, I: 292]

8. **Jane Doe** female counterpart of *John Doe*. [Am. Usage: Misc.]

9. **Jean Crapuad** personification of peculiarities of French people. [Fr. Usage: *LLEI*, I: 292]

10. **John a Noakes** fictitious, litigious character; used in legal proceedings. [Br. Legal Usage: Br. Legal Usage:]

11. **John a Styles** fictitious, litigious counterpart to John a Noakes. [Br. Legal Usage: Br. Legal Usage:]

12. **John Bull** any Englishman, or Englishmen collectively. [Br. Lit.: *History of John Bull*, Brewer *Dictionary*, 591]

13. **John Doe** formerly any plaintiff; now just anybody. [Am. Pop. Usage: Brewer *Dictionary*, 329]

14. **John Q. Citizen** fictitious average man on the street. [Am. Jour.: Mathews, 910]

15. **John Q. Public** fictitious typical citizen. [Am. Jour.: Mathews, 910]

16. **John Q. Voter** fictitious typical citizen. [Am. Jour.: Mathews, 910]

17. **Mertz, Ethel** neighbor of the Ricardos in *I Love Lucy* sitcom; she was the voice of commonsense. [Am. TV: *SJEPC*]

18. **Mertz, Fred** neighbor of the Ricardos in *I Love Lucy* sitcom; he was frugal and stuffy and often teamed with Ricky to teach the women a lesson. [Am. TV: *SJEPC*]

19. **Newhart, Bob (1929–)** mild-mannered, stuttering nice guy comedian who played the lead on two wildly successful TV sitcoms [Am. TV: *SJEPC*]

20. **Richard Roe** formerly, any defendant; now just anybody. [Am. Pop. Usage: Brewer *Dictionary*, 329]

21. **Stewart, Jimmy (1908–1997)** gangly, easygoing and likable, he endeared audiences to him no matter what role he played; especially beloved for his role in *It's a Wonderful Life*, his favorite film. [Am. Film: *SJEPC*]

22. **Terkel, Studs (1912–2008)** interviewer known for series of books that reflected lives of everyday people; considered his work oral histories of America. [Am. Lit.: *SJEPC*]

23. **Tevye** poor Russian Jewish dairyman in musical *Fiddler on the Roof* (1964) proclaims: "You might say every one of us is a fiddler on the roof, trying to scratch out a pleasant, simple tune without breaking his neck. It isn't easy." [Am. Musical: *SJEPC*]

24. **Tracy, Spencer (1900–1967)** his understated style graced comedy and drama; sheer talent got him leading roles without being handsome or suave; among other notable roles, as protagonist of film version of Hemingway's *The Old Man and the Sea*. [Am. Film: *SJEPC*]

25. **Van Dyke, Dick (1925–)** actor who masterfully played comedy writer Rob Petrie on 1960s TV sitcom *The Dick Van Dyke Show*, the quintessential regular guy. [Am. TV: *SJEPC*]

250. EVIL (See also DEMON, DEVIL, VILLAIN, WICKEDNESS.)

1. **Ahriman** represents principle of wickedness; will one day perish. [Persian Myth.: *LLEI*, I: 322; Zoroastrianism: Benét, 16]

2. **Apollyon** demon, personification of evil, vanquished by Christian's wholesomeness. [Br. Lit.: *The Pilgrim's Progress*]

3. **Badman, Mr.** from childhood to death, has committed every sin. [Br. Lit.: Bunya *The Life and Death of Mr. Badman* in Magill III, 575]

4. **black** symbol of sin and badness. [Color Symbolism: Jobes, 357]

5. **black dog** symbol of the devil. [Rom. Folklore: Brewer *Dictionary*, 329]

6. **black heart** symbol of a scoundrel. [Folklore: Jobes, 223]

7. **black poodle** a transformation of Mephistopheles. [Ger. Lit.: *Faust*]

8. **Chamber of Horrors** wax depictions of murderers, in Madame Tussaud's London waxworks. [Pop. Culture: *ODA*]

9. **crocodile** epitome of power of evil. [Medieval Animal Symbolism: White, 8–10]

10. **crow** in Europe and India, symbol of bad luck and war; also death, solitude, and evil. [Symbolism: *CEOS&S*]

11. **darkness** traditional association with evil in many dualistic religions. [Folklore: Cirlot, 76–77]

12. **dragon** archetypal symbol of Satan and wickedness. [Christian Symbolism: Appleton, 34]

13. **Drug** principle of evil. [Zoroastrianism: Leach, 325]

14. **Gestapo** Nazi secret police. [Ger. Hist.: *Hitler*, 453]

15. **Golden Calf** Mephisto's cynical and demoniacal tarantella. [Fr. Opera: Gounod, *Faust*, Westerman, 187]

16. **Iago** declaims "I believe in a cruel god." [Br. Lit.: *Othello*; Ital. Opera: Verdi, *Otello*, Westerman, 329]

17. **jackal** in India, symbol of destructiveness and evil. [Symbolism: *CEOS&S*]

18. **John, Don** plots against Claudio. [Br. Lit.: *Much Ado About Nothing*]

19. **Klingsor** enemy of Grail knights. [Ger. Opera: Wagner, *Parsifal*, Westerman, 248]

20. **Kurtz, Mr.** white trader in Africa, debased by savage natives into horrible practices. [Br. Lit.: Joseph Conrad *Heart of Darkness* in Magill III, 447]

21. **lizard** to Greco-Romans, Christians, and Maori, symbol of evil. [Symbolism: *CEOS&S*]

22. **lobelia** traditional symbol of evil. [Flower Symbolism: *Flora Symbolica*, 175]

23. **Loki** god of fire, evil, and strife who contrived the death of Balder. [Scand. Myth.: Brewer *Dictionary*, 560]

24. **Mephistopheles** the cynical, malicious devil to whom Faust sells his soul. [Ger. Lit.: *Faust*, Payton, 436]

25. **Miles and Flora** apparently sweet children assume wicked miens mysteriously. [Am. Lit.: *The Turn of the Screw*]

26. **Monterone** after humiliation, curses both Duke and Rigoletto. [Ital. Opera: Verdi, *Rigoletto*, Westerman, 299]

27. **o'Nell, Peg** wicked spirit claiming victim every seven years. [Br. Folklore: Briggs, 323]

28. **Pandora's box** contained all evils; opened up, evils escape to afflict world. [Rom. Myth.: Brewer *Dictionary*, 799]

29. **Popeye** degenerate gangster and murderer who rapes Temple Drake. [Am. Lit.: *Sanctuary*]

30. **Powler, Peg** wicked water-demon; lures children to death. [Br. Folklore: Briggs, 323–324]

31. **Queen of the Night** urges the murder of Sarastro, her husband, by their daughter. [Ger. Opera: Mozart *The Magic Flute* in Benét, 619]

32. **Quint, Peter** dead manservant who haunts James's story. [Am. Lit.: *The Turn of the Screw*]

33. **Rasputin** immoral person of tremendous power and seeming invulnerability. [Russ. Hist.: Espy, 339–340]

34. **Satan** the chief evil spirit; the great adversary of man. [Christianity and Judaism: Misc.]

35. **Sauron** from Tolkien's Lord of the Rings trilogy (1954–1956); known as the Dark Lord or Lord of Mordor; wants complete dominance over Middle Earth which leads to his determination to steal the powerful ring from Frodo; never appears in stories, except as monstrous. [Br. Lit.: Gillespie and Naden]

36. **Vader, Darth** fallen Jedi Knight has turned to evil. [Am. Film: *Star Wars*]

37. **Vandals** East German people known for their wanton destruction (533). [Ger. Hist.: Payton, 705]

38. **Voldemort, Lord** character from J.K. Rowling's Harry Potter series for young readers (1997–2007); murderer of Harry's parents; power-hungry lord of evil who is intent on overpowering and destroying Harry and all that he stands for. [Br. Children's Lit.: Misc.]

39. **Wicked Witch of the West** the terror of Oz. [Am. Lit.: *The Wonderful Wizard of Oz*]

40. **Wolf's Glen** scene of macabre uproar. [Ger. Opera: von Weber, *Der Freischutz*, Westerman, 139–140]

251. EXAGGERATION

1. **Bunyan, Paul** legendary giant, hero of tall tales of the logging camps. [Am. Folklore: *The Wonderful Adventures of Paul Bunyan*]

2. **federal case** in law, a federal case is usually more important than a state or local one; this term is used ironically, meaning to exaggerate the importance of something. [Am. Culture: Misc.]

3. **Jenkins' ear** trivial cause of a great quarrel. [Br. Hist.: Espy, 336]

4. **Madison Avenue** New York street; home of advertising companies. [Am. Culture: Misc.]

5. **Munchausen, Baron (1720–1797)** soldier, adventurer, and teller of tall tales. [Ger. Hist.: *EB*, VII: 99]

252. EXASPERATION (See also ANGER, FRUSTRATION, IRASCIBILITY, RANTING.)

1. **Carter, Sargeant** Marine Corps sargeant exasperated by Gomer's ceaseless stupidity. [TV: "Gomer Pyle, U.S.M.C." in Terrace, I, 319]

2. **Dagwood** comic strip character exasperated over Blondie's sale purchases. [Comics: "Blondie" in Horn, 118–119]

3. **Dithers, Mr.** Dagwood's boss; ever exasperated over Dagwood's sloppy work habits. [Comics: "Blondie" in Horn, 118–119]

4. **Gildersleeve, Throckmorton P.** comic character exasperated by nephew Leroy's antics. [Radio: "The Great Gildersleeve" in Buxton, 101]

5. **Kennedy, Edgar** film actor famous for "slow burn." [Am. Cinema: Halliwell]

6. **Kowalski, Stanley** exasperated by Blanche DuBois' affected refinement. [Am. Lit.: *A Streetcar Named Desire*]

7. **Kramden, Ralph** frustrated bus driver projects exasperation toward his wife and Ed Norton. [TV: "The Honeymooners" in Terrace, I, 365–366]

8. **Lodge, Mr.** Veronica's wealthy father driven to distraction by Archie. [Comics: Horn, 87]

9. **Mammy** outspoken motherly slave, then domestic servant, of Southern O'Hara family in Civil War-era film *Gone with the Wind* (1939) often exasperated by the foibles of her household. [Am. Film: *SJEPC*]

10. **Moe** continually exasperated at Larry and Curly for their mischievous pranks. [TV: "The Three Stooges" in Terrace, II, 366]

11. **Ricardo, Ricky** bandleader frustrated by Lucy's mischief. [TV: "I Love Lucy" in Terrace, I, 383–384]

12. **Smith, Ranger** park manager "driven bananas" by Yogi's incorrigibility. [TV: "Yogi Bear" in Terrace, II, 448–449]

253. EXCELLENCE

1. **Academy Awards** created by the Academy of Motion Picture Arts and Sciences to honor excellence in film; ceremony conferring the Oscar has taken place every year since 1929. [Am. Film: *SJEPC*]

2. **All-American** designation for outstanding college athletes. [Am. Sports: Misc.]

3. **Dream Team** greatest U.S. Olympic basketball team in history won gold medal in 1992, boasted talents of top NBA players like

Magic Johnson, Larry Bird, and Michael Jordan. [Am. Sports: *SJEPC*]

4. **first string** a term from sports referring to the best athletes on a team, by extension any first-rate performer. [Pop. Cult.: *FOF, MOD*]

5. **Good Housekeeping Seal of Approval** from *Good Housekeeping* magazine, which awarded its "seal" to outstanding products; by extension, a highly regarded product. [Am. Business *FOF, MOD*]

6. **major league** referring to the American or National Baseball Leagues; by extension, describing the best. [Pop. Cult.: *FOF, MOD*]

7. *New Yorker* dedicated editors and a host of acclaimed contributors made the magazine a favorite among the intelligent and wealthy. [Am. Jour.: *SJEPC*]

8. **Olympics (modern)** two-week competitions held every four years in which the world's greatest athletes vie for medals [Sports: *SJEPC*]

9. **PBS (Public Broadcasting)** Corporation for Public Broadcasting created in 1967; soon after, noncommercial TV blossomed into full spectrum of quality documentaries, drama, sitcoms, and children's programs. [Am. TV: *SJEPC*]

254. EXCESS

1. **Bakker, Jim (1940–), and Tammy Faye Bakker (1942–2007)** husband-and-wife televangelists with lavish lifestyle. [Am. Rel.: *SJEPC*]

2. **Belushi, John (1949–1982)** talented, energetic comedian and actor who pushed the envelope was addicted to drugs and died of an overdose. [Am. Entertainment: *SJEPC*]

3. *Dallas* prime time soap opera set in Texas, with family given to excess in all things. [Am. TV Misc.]

4. *Dynasty* prime time soap opera featuring characters obsessed with money and power. [Am. TV: *FOF, MOD*]

5. **fast lane** originally referring to the left, or passing lane of a freeway; now, a life of excess. [Pop. Cult.: Misc.]

6. **Jazz Age** the 1920s in America, named for jazz music, evokes a lifestyle of pursuit of pleasure. [Am. Hist.: *FOF, MOD*]

255. EXECUTION

1. **Budd, Billy** court-martialed and hanged for accidently killing a ship's officer. [Am. Lit.: Herman Melville *Billy Budd*]

2. **cigarette** final favor granted one about to die. [Pop. Cult.: Misc.]

3. **Deever, Danny** hanged by his regiment for shooting a comrade. [Br. Lit.: Kipling *Danny Deever* in Benét, 549]

4. **Derrick** famous hangman; eponym of modern hoisting apparatus. [Br. Hist.: Espy, 170]

5. **Doeg the Edomite** dispatches priests of Nob under Saul's order. [O.T.: I Samuel 22:18–19]

6. **Esmeralda** her hanging is triumphantly watched from a tower by Frollo, who is thereupon thrown from it by Quasimodo. [Fr. Lit.: Victor Hugo *The Hunchback of Notre Dame*]

7. **guillotine** invented during French Revolution as a humane method of capital punishment. [Fr. Hist.: Benét, 429]

8. **hangman's noose** characteristic knot for death by hanging. [Pop. Cult.: Misc.]

9. **Ko-Ko** appointed by the Mikado as Lord High Executioner. [Br. Opera: *The Mikado*]

10. **Lord of the Manor of Tyburn** nickname for ordinary hangman at Tyburn gallows. [Br. Hist.: Brewer *Dictionary*, 1110]

11. **Macheath, Capt.** swaggering highwayman sentenced to execution but reprieved at the last moment. [Br. Lit.: *The Beggar's Opera* in Magill I, 59; *The Threepenny Opera* in Benét, 90]

12. **Maximilian, Emperor of Mexico** executed in 1867; subject of painting by Manet. [Mex. Hist.: *NCE*, 1728; Fr. Art.: *EB*, 11:440]

13. **Savonarola (1452–1498)** reformer priest, hanged and burned at the stake as a heretic. [Ital. Hist.: Benét, 900]

14. *Seven That Were Hanged, The* describes the fears and actions of five men and two women before their deaths on the scaffold. [Russ. Lit.: Magill II, 957]

15. **Sorel, Julien** attempts to kill his employer's wife, (his mistress), is condemned to the guillotine. [Fr. Lit.: Stendhal *The Red and the Black* in Magill I, 808]

16. **"Third of May, 1808, The"** Goya painting of Napoleon's soldiers firing on Spanish rebels. [Sp. Art: *EB*, 8:260]

17. **Tyburn** site of gallows where criminals were publicly hanged. [Br. Hist.: Brewer *Dictionary*, 920]

256. EXISTENTIALISM

1. **Beckett, Samuel (1906–1989)** Irish dramatist who wrote in French; creator of such works as *Waiting for Godot*, noted for their bleak pessimism. [Irish Lit.: *ODA*]

2. **Camus, Albert (1913–1960)** French novelist, dramatist, and essayist whose works, including *The Stranger*, are linked to existentialism. [Fr. Lit.: *The Stranger*]

3. **Estragon** existentialist anti-hero of Beckett's *Waiting for Godot*. [Fr. Lit.: *Waiting for Godot*]

4. **Godot** character waited for who never appears: *Waiting for Godot*. [Fr. Lit.: *ODA*]

5. **Sartre, Jean-Paul (1905–1980)** French philosopher, dramatist, novelist, journalist and major theorist of existentialism. [Fr. Lit.: Misc.]

Expensiveness (See EXTRAVAGANCE.)

257. EXPLOITATION (See also OPPORTUNISM.)

1. **Barnum, P. T. (1810–1891)** circus impressario famous for his saying, "Never give a sucker an even break." [Am. Hist.: Van Doren, 825–826]

2. **carpetbaggers** Northerners who moved to the South during Reconstruction after Civil War in mid-1860s to 1870s; many reaped economic and political benefits from struggling Southern States. [Am. Hist.: Jameson, 84]

3. **Casby, Christopher** rack-renting proprietor of slum property. [Br. Lit.: *Little Dorrit*]

4. **Dionne Quintuplets** French-Canadian identical quintuplet sisters born in 1934 whose childhood appearances and images brought tremendous financial gain to adults in their lives. [Can. Hist.: *SJEPC*]

5. **Miss America Pageant** accustions of exploitation of women have tainted the popular beauty contest. [Am. Pop. Culture: *SJEPC*]

6. **Nike** allegations of sweatshop conditions at Asian factories have haunted the company. [Am. Business: *SJEPC*]

7. **Rivera, Geraldo (1943–)** highly touted Hispanic journalist and TV personality who won several awards for distinguished broadcast journalism; later turned to sensationalism and lowbrow specials. [Am. TV and Jour.: *SJEPC*]

8. **Stromboli** wicked puppetmaster enslaves Pinocchio aboard troupe caravan. [Am. Cinema: *Pinocchio* in *Disney Films*, 32–37]

9. **tabloid television** popular television shows with quasi-journalistic approach to sex, crime, and gossip. [Am. TV: *SJEPC*]

10. **tabloids** small-sized newspapers, often found in grocery store checkout aisles, that specialize in scandal and sensational stories. [Am. Jour.: *SJEPC*]

11. **Wal-Mart** American shopping was changed beginning in the 1960s by retail giant; proliferation of huge discount stores (especially in small towns) offering variety and value; accused of unfair labor practices and environmental irresponsibility. [Am. Business: *SJEPC*]

269

258. EXPLORATION

1. **Balboa, Vasco Nunez de (1475–1517)** discovered the Pacific Ocean. [Sp. Hist.: Benét, 75]

2. **Columbus, Christopher (1446–1506)** expeditions to West Indies, South and Central America; said to have discovered America in 1492. [Ital. Hist.: Jameson, 107–108]

3. **Conquistadores** Spanish explorers of North and South America, often employing brutal tactics against the native populations. [Am. Hist.: *BBWE*]

4. **Cook, James (1728–1779)** English navigator who explored the Pacific Ocean and its islands. [Br. Hist.: *BBWE*]

5. **Cortés, Hernando (1485–1547)** Spanish Conquistador who conquered Mexico. [Sp. Hist.: *BBWE*]

6. **Cousteau, Jacques (1910–1997)** pioneering French undersea explorer and commander of research ship *The Calypso* introduced the marine world to millions through his film documentaries, books, and TV programs. [Fr. Science: *SJEPC*]

7. **de Soto, Hernando (c. 1500–1542)** discovered the Mississippi River. [Sp. Hist.: Benét, 266]

8. **Dora the Explorer** protagonist of TV show for children which premiered in 2000; along with her monkey friend Boots, she goes on a trip to find something or help someone each episode; teaches children Spanish-language terms and how to read a map. [Am. TV: Misc.]

9. **Enterprise** starship whose missions to explore space are chronicled in TV and movies; also the name of one of the earliest space shuttles used by NASA. [TV: *Star Trek* in Terrace]

10. **Erikson, Leif (980?–1020?)** Norwegian Viking and first European to reach North America. [Am. Hist.: *BBWE*]

11. **Gama, Vasco da (c. 1460–1524)** navigator who discovered route around Africa to India. [Port. Hist.: *NCE*, 1040]

12. *Golden Hind* ship on which Sir Francis Drake (1540–1596) became the first Englishman to sail around the world. [Br. Hist.: *EB* (1963) VII, 575]

13. **Hudson, Henry** seeking a northwest passage to Asia, in 1609 he explored the river later named for him. [Am. Hist.: Benét, 482]

14. *Journey to the Center of the Earth* expedition through the core of a volcano to the earth's center. [Fr. Lit.: Verne *A Journey to the Center of the Earth* in Benét, 1055]

15. **Lewis and Clark Expedition** while looking for the Northwest Passage, proved feasibility of overland route to the Pacific. [Am. Hist.: Benét, 583]

16. **Livingstone, David (1813–1873)** Scottish missionary and explorer of Africa; rescued by Henry Stanley: "Dr. Livingstone, I presume?" [Br. Hist.: *BBWE*]

17. **Magellan, Ferdinand (1480–1521)** Portuguese navigator and explorer who led the first expedition to circumnavigate the world. [Eur. Hist.: *BBWE*]

18. **Mt. Everest** highest mountain in the world; first ascent in 1955 by Sir Edmund Hillary and Tenzing Norgay; symbol of human striving. [Hist.: *FOF, MOD*]

19. *National Geographic Magazine* venerable journal whose glossy pictures and articles enables armchair travel for millions of readers. [Am. Jour.: *SJEPC*]

20. **Northwest Passage** the elusive sea route linking Europe and Asia sought by many explorers of the New World. [Am. Hist.: *BBWE*]

21. **Pizarro, Francisco (1475?-1541)** Spanish Conquistador who explored Peru and conquered the Incas. [Eur. Hist.: *BBWE*]

22. **Polo, Marco (1254–1324)** Venetian traveler in China. [Ital. Hist.: *NCE*, 1695]

23. **Ponce de León, Juan (c. 1460–1521)** seeking the "fountain of youth," he discovered Florida and explored its coast. [Sp. Hist.: Benét, 802]

24. **Sacagawea (1778?-1812)** Shoshone guide and translator for the Lewis and Clark expedition. [Am. Hist.: *BBWE*]

25. **Scott, Robert Falcon (1868–1912)** English naval officer and explorer of Antarctica; perished on expedition to the South Pole. [Br. Hist.: *BBWE*]

26. **Stanley, Henry M. (1841–1904)** English-American explorer and journalist who rescued David Livingstone in Africa: "Dr. Livingstone, I presume?" [Br. Hist.: *BBWE*]

259. EXTINCTION

1. **bald eagle** once on verge of extinction, this bird is now protected but no longer an endangered species. [Ecology: Hammond, 290]

2. **dinosaur** dinosaurs died out, possibly due to an environmental catastrophe. [Ecology: Hammond, 290]

3. **dodo** large, flightless bird exterminated on Mauritius. [Ecology: Wallechinsky, 131]

4. **eight-track tape** promising audio technology of the 1960s-70s allowed people to listen to their own music while driving in the car; obsolete by 1980. [Am. Technology: *SJEPC*]

5. **great auk** hunters killed such large numbers, these birds became extinct in 1840s. [Ecology: Hammond, 290]

6. **heath hen** human settlement of U.S. Atlantic Coast contributed to the extinction of these birds. [Ecology: Hammond, 290]

7. *Last of the Barons, The* portrays England's brilliant aristocracy as dying breed (1470s). [Br. Lit.: *The Last of the Barons*, Magill I, 492–494]

8. *Last of the Mohicans, The* novel forseeing the extinction of various Indian tribes. [Am. Lit.: *The Last of the Mohicans*]

9. **mastodon** similar to the elephant, the mastodon is now extinct. [Ecology: Hammond, 290]

10. **moa** large ostrichlike bird, hunted chiefly for its food; it died out in 1914. [Ecology: Hammond, 290]

11. **passenger pigeon** hunted to extinction by 1914; vast numbers once darkened American skies during migratory flights. [Ecology: *EB*, VII: 786]

12. **saber-toothed tiger** wild cat that died out about 12,000 years ago. [Ecology: Hammond, 290]

13. **whale** many species in danger of extinction, owing to massive hunting. [Ecology: Hammond, 290]

260. EXTRAVAGANCE (See also LUXURY, SPECTACLE, SPLENDOR.)

1. **Berkeley, Busby (1895–1976)** American choreographer of extravagant dancing sequences in Hollywood films. [Am. Film: *FOF, MOD*]

2. **Bonfire of the Vanities** phrase originally coined by the religious reformer Savonarola, became a catchword for extravagant lifestyles in the 1980s, from a novel by Tom Wolfe. [Am. Lit.: Tom Wolfe, *Bonfire of the Vanities*]

3. **Bovary, Emma** spends money recklessly on jewelry and clothes. [Fr. Lit.: *Madame Bovary*, Magill I, 539–541]

4. **Cleopatra's pearl** dissolved in acid to symbolize luxury. [Rom. Hist.: Jobes, 348]

5. **De Mille, Cecil B. (1881–1959)** American film director of extravagant spectacles, including *The Ten Commandments*. [Am. Film: *FOF MOD*]

6. **Gilded Age** era in U.S. history (1870s) noted for the extravagance and corruption of the wealthy elite. [Am. Hist.: Mark Twain and Charles Dudley Warner *The Gilded Age*]

7. **Lais** charged Demosthenes 10,000 drachmas for night in bed. [Gk. Hist.: Wallechinsky, 328]

8. **Metro-Goldwyn-Mayer** often lavish productions came out of the motion picture studio with "more stars than there are in the heavens." [Am. Film: *SJEPC*]

9. **one thousand Philistine foreskins** price David paid to marry Saul's daughter. [O.T.: I Samuel 18: 25–27]

10. **Vincy, Rosamund** Lydgate's income did not meet her spendthrift habits. [Br. Lit.: *Middlemarch*, Magill, 588–591]

261. EXTREMISM (See also FANATICISM.)

1. **Al Qaeda** Islamic terrorist extremists, responsible for the 9/11 attacks on the U.S. [World Hist.: Misc.]

2. **drys** advocates Prohibition in America. [Am. Hist.: Allen, 41]

3. **Jacobins** rabidly radical faction; principal perpetrators of Reign of Terror. [Fr. Hist.: *EB*, V: 494]

4. **John Birch Society** rabid right-wing group ideologically similar to the Ku Klux Klan. [Am. Hist.: Van Doren, 576]

5. **Ku Klux Klan (KKK)** group espousing white supremacy takes law into its own hands. [Am. Hist.: *EB*, V: 935]

6. **McCarthy, Senator Joseph (1909–1957)** anti-Communist zeal frequently resulted in injustice. [Am. Hist.: Van Doren, 522]

7. **Mikado of Japan, the** demands Ko-Ko execute one person a month. [Br. Opera: *The Mikado*, Magill I, 591–592]

8. **Weathermen, The** in the late 1960s to mid-1970s, protested Vietnam War and social and political injustices, through bombings and other extreme methods. [Am. Hist.: *SJEPC*]

F

262. FAD (See also FASHION.)

1. **Barbie doll** popular dress-up doll; extremely conventional and feminine. [Am. Hist.: Sann, 179]

2. **baseball cards** bubble gum cards traded by young fans in early- to mid-20th century has become serious collectible business for adults. [Am. Culture: *SJEPC*]

3. **Beanie Babies** small plush beanbag toys created by the Ty Corporation caused frenzy among kids and collectors in the 1990s. [Am. Culture: *SJEPC*]

4. **Beatle cut** hairstyle with bangs, sides trimmed just below ears; banned by many school boards (1960s). [Am. Hist.: Sann, 251–254]

5. **bee-stung lips** in the 1920s, ruby red and puckered female mouth make-up; now, collagen-filled lips look similarly swollen, as if by a bee sting. [Pop. Culture: Misc.]

6. **bellbottoms** pants (particularly denim) with wide bottom cuffs associated with the 1960s and 1970s; fashion revived in the 1990s and 2000s. [Am. Culture: *SJEPC*]

7. **bobbed hair** short, curly boyish hairstyle caused shock (1920s). [Am. Hist.: Griffith, 198]

8. **bobby socks** female short socks that epitomized 1940s teen fashion. [Am. Cult.: Misc.]

9. **Cabbage Patch Kids** children and parents went wild in the 1980s collecting homely, soft-bodied dolls, each with its unique birth certificate and adoption papers. [Am. Culture: *SJEPC*]

10. **car-stuffing** one example: 23 people stuffed in a Volkswagen bug. (1950s-1960s). [Am. Hist.: Sann, 300]

11. **chain letters** at height in 1930s, craze crippled postal service. [Am. Hist.: Sann, 97–104]

12. **charm bracelets** charms representing a girl's hobbies, interests, and memories popular in 1930s-1960s. [Am. Culture: *SJEPC*]

13. **coonskin caps** raccoon cap with tail worn in recognition of Davy Crockett, Daniel Boone revival (1950s). [Am. Hist.: Sann, 30]

14. **disco** beyond the thumping bass and hypnotic rhythms, this style of dance music spawned its own fashions, such as form-fitting, glitzy clothing in synthetic fabrics and sparkling mirror balls on the dance floor during late 1970s craze. [Am. Culture and Music: *SJEPC*]

15. **erector sets** construction toy made of metal nuts, bolts, gears, girders, and other parts introduced by A. C. Gilbert in 1913 allowed children to build their own skyscrapers, trucks, bridges, and more; popular throughout 20th century. [Am. Hist.: *SJEPC*]

16. **flagpole sitting** sitting alone at the top of a flagpole; craze comes and goes. [Am. Hist.: Sann, 39–46]

17. **frisbees** tossing plastic disks still a favorite pastime, especially among collegians. [Am. Hist.: Sann, 178]

18. **GI Joe** first plastic action figure for boys, outfitted to resemble World War II combat soldier, debuted in 1964. [Am. History: *SJEPC*]

19. **gold fish-swallowing** collegiate craze in 1930s. [Am. Hist.: Sann, 289–292]

20. **hip-flask** liquor bottle designed to fit into back pockets; indispensable commodity during Prohibition. [Am. Hist.: Allen, 70]

21. **hula hoops** large plastic hoops revolved around body by hip action (1950s). [Am. Hist.: Sann, 145–149]

22. **Kewpie doll** designed by Rose O'Neill and modeled on her baby brother; millions were made (starting about 1910). [Am. Hist.: *WB*, 5: 240–241]

23. **marathon dancing** dance contests, the longest of which lasted 24 weeks and 5 days (1930s). [Am. Hist.: McWhirter, 461]

24. **marathon eating** contestants consume ridiculous quantities of food; craze comes and goes. [Am. Hist.: Sann, 77–78]

25. **miniskirt** skirts hemmed at mid-thigh or higher; heyday of the leg in fashion world (1960s). [Am. Hist.: Sann, 255–263]

26. **mud baths** warm mud applied on skin supposedly to retain fresh, young complexion. (1940s). [Am. Hist.: Griffith, 198]

27. **panty raids** collegiate craze in the 1940s and 1950s. [Am. Hist.: Misc.]

28. **Pet Rocks** a popular purchase in 1975; small rock in a carrying case with training manual [Am. Pop. Culture: *SJEPC*]

29. **raccoon coats** popular attire for collegians (1920s). [Am. Hist.: Sann, 175]

30. **rolled stockings** worn by flappers to achieve risquè effect (1920s). [Am. Hist.: Griffith, 198]

31. **Rubik's Cube** multicolored cube puzzle developed by Hungarian professor to challenge his students; became fad toy in U.S. during 1970s. [Am. Pop. Culture: *SJEPC*]

32. **saddle shoes** an oxford, usually white, with a saddle of contrasting color, usually brown; a favorite fad of the 1940s and 1950s. [Am. Pop. Cult.: Misc.]

33. **Silly Putty** synthetic clay; uses ranging from bouncing balls to false mustaches. [Am. Hist.: Sann, 165]

34. **skateboards** mini surfboard supported on roller-skate wheels; 1960s craze still enormously popular. [Am. Hist.: Misc.]

35. **telephone booth-stuffing** bodies piled on top of one another inside a telephone booth; 1950s and 1960s craze. [Am. Hist.: Sann, 297]

36. **tulipomania** tulip craze in Holland during which fortunes were lost. (1600s). [Eur. Hist.: *WB*, 19: 394]

37. **Webkinz** plush animals in late 2000s include secret access code to Web site so child can officially adopt and interact with pet. [Am. Culture: *SJEPC*]

38. **yo-yo** child's toy that periodically overwhelms public's fancy. [Am. Hist.: Sann, 173]

39. **zoot suits** popularized by hip young males in 1930s and 1940s; padded shoulders, baggy pants and wide-brimmed hat; believed to have originated in African-American community. [Am. Culture: *SJEPC*]

263. FAILURE

1. **Army Bomb Plot** attempted assassination of Hitler; his miraculous escape brought dreadful retaliation (1944). [Ger. Hist.: Van Doren, 500]

2. **Brown, Charlie** comic strip character for whom losing is a way of life. [Comics: "Peanuts" in Horn, 542–543]

3. **Bunion Derby** financially disastrous cross-country marathon. [Am. Hist.: Sann, 48–56]

4. **Carker, John** broken-spirited man occupying subordinate position. [Br. Lit.: *Dombey and Son*]

5. **Chicago Cubs** National League baseball team known fondly as the Lovable Losers hasn't won a World Series title in over 100 years. [Am. Sports: *SJEPC*]

6. *Death of a Salesman* deceit, lies, and failure, rather than the success of which he dreamed, mark the life of salesman Willy Loman in Arthur Miller's 1949 masterpiece. [Am. Theater: *SJEPC*; Harris *Characters*, 269]

7. **Edsel** much bruited automobile fails on market (1950s). [Am. Hist.: Flexner, 78]

8. **English, Julian** contentious and unloved salesman; commits suicide in despair. [Am. Lit.: *Appointment in Samarra*]

9. **Gunpowder Plot** attempt to blow up the Parliament building led to the execution of its leader, Guy Fawkes (1605). [Brit. Hist.: *EB*, IV: 70–71]

10. **lemon** symbol of bitterness, failure, and disappointment. [Symbolism: *CEOS&S*]

11. **Little Tramp** Chaplin's much-loved, much-imitated hapless, "I'm a failure" persona. [Am. Cinema: Griffith, 79]

12. **Loman, Willy** traveling salesman who gradually comes to realize that his life has been a complete failure; commits suicide. [Am. Lit.: *The Death of a Salesman*, Payton, 397]

13. **Mighty Casey** ignominiously strikes out in the clutch. [Am. Lit.: "Casey at the Bat" in Turkin, 642]

14. **Reardon, Edwin** very promising writer who, after unsuccessful publication, returns to clerical job. [Br. Lit.: *New Grub Street* Magill I, 647–649]

15. **skid row** district of down-and-outs and bums. [Am. Usage: Brewer *Dictionary*, 1008]

16. **WIN buttons** President Ford's scheme to reduce inflation: for the American public to wear shields stating "W.I.N." (Whip Inflation Now). [Am. Hist.: Misc.]

17. **World League** "ingenious" creation of a third professional league that never materialized. [Am. Sports: Misc.]

18. **Yank** steamship stoker vainly tries to climb the social ladder, then fails in attempt to avenge himself on society. [Am. Drama: O'Neill *The Hairy Ape* in Sobel, 339]

264. FAIRY

1. **Abonde, Dame** good fairy who brings children presents on New Year's Eve. [Fr. Folklore: Brewer *Dictionary*, 3]

2. **Ariel** sprite who confuses the castaways on Prospero's island. [Br. Drama: Shakespeare *The Tempest*]

3. **fairy godmother** fulfills Cinderella's wishes and helps her win the prince. [Fr. Fairy Tale: *Cinderella*]

4. **Grandmarina** fairy who provides everything for Princess Alicia's happiness. [Br. Lit.: Dickens "The Magic Fishbone"]

5. **leprechaun** small supernatural creature associated with shoemaking and hidden treasure. [Irish Folklore: Benét, 579]

6. **Mab, Queen** fairies' midwife delivers man's brain of dreams. [Br. Legend: Benét, 610]

7. **Oberon and Titania** King and Queen of the Fairies. [Br. Drama: Shakespeare *A Midsummer Night's Dream"*]

8. **Pigwiggin** his love for Queen Mab ruptures her harmony with Oberon. [Br. Poetry: *Nymphidia* in Barnhart, 824]

9. **Puck** the "shrewd and knavish sprite" who causes minor catastrophes and embarrassing situations. [Br. Drama: Shakespeare *A Midsummer Night's Dream"*]

10. **Tinker Bell** from J.M. Barrie's classic play *Peter Pan* (1904); poisoned by Captain Hook, she is saved by Peter, who gets all children who believe in fairies to clap their hands. [Scot. Theater.: Jones]

11. **tooth fairy** benevolent sprite leaves money under a child's pillow, in exchange for pulled teeth. [Am. Culture: Misc.]

265. FAITHFULNESS (See also LOYALTY.)

1. **Abdiel** seraph who refused to join Satan's rebellion. [Br. Lit.: *Paradise Lost*]

2. **Abigail** prostrates herself before David and vows devotion. [O.T.: I Samuel 25:40–41]

3. **Abraham** in obedience to God, would sacrifice his only son. [O.T.: Genesis 22:1–18]

4. **Akawi-ko** waits eighty years for lover to return. [Jap. Legend: Jobes, 59]

5. **Amelia** despite financial woes, remains faithful to Booth. [Br. Lit.: *Amelia*]

6. **Andromache** devoted wife of Hector. [Gk. Lit.: *Iliad*; *Trojan Women*; *Andromache*]

7. **Aramati** name of Vedic goddess means faithfulness. [Hindu Myth.: Jobes, 117]

8. **Arsinoe** Alcamaeon's wife; continues to love husband though he is unfaithful. [Gk. Myth.: Zimmerman, 32]

9. **Becket, Thomas à** (c.1118–70) uncompromisingly defended the rights of the Church against King Henry II. [Br. Hist.: *NCE*, 2735]

10. **Brandimante** loyal to lover and leader. [Ital. Lit.: *Orlando Innamorato*]

11. **Briseis** loved Achilles despite her capture by Agamemnon. [Gk. Myth.: Walsh *Classical*, 62]

12. **Britomart** waits many years for true love, Artegall. [Br. Lit.: *Faerie Queene*]

13. **Caleb** faithfully followed God in exploration of Canaan. [O.T.: Numbers 14:24–25]

14. **Candida** ever faithful to husband. [Br. Lit.: *Candida*]

15. **Canterbury bell** flower memorializing harness bells of Canterbury pilgrims. [Br. Hist.: Espy, 303]

16. **Charlotte** faithful to fiancé lost at sea. [Br. Lit.: *Fatal Curiosity*]

17. **China aster** symbol of fidelity. [Flower Symbolism: Jobes, 326]

18. **Clärchen** devoted to Egmont. [Ger. Lit.: *Egmont*]

19. **Cordelia** remains faithful to her father, even when he spurns her. [Br. Lit.: *King Lear*]

20. **crow** faithful; does not mate again for nine generations. [Animal Symbolism: Mercatante, 161]

21. **Cynara** woman to whom Dowson is faithful in his thoughts even when consorting with others. [Br. Poetry: Barnhart, 301]

22. **de Cleves, Princess** despite her love for another, remains faithful to her husband even after his death. [Fr. Lit.: Lafayette *The Princess*]

23. **doves** faithfulness reflected in their pairing for life. [Christian Symbolism: Child, 211]

24. **Dupre, Sally** Clay Wingates's fiancée quietly waits for his return. [Am. Lit.: "John Brown's Body" in Magill I, 445–448]

25. **Enid** though falsely accused of infidelity, nurses husband through wounds. [Br. Lit.: *Idylls of the King*]

26. **Evangeline** lifelong search for lover, Gabriel. [Am. Lit.: *Evangeline*]

27. **Gamgee, Samwise** Frodo's faithful servant to the end of the quest to destroy the One Ring. [Br. Lit.: *Lord of the Rings*]

28. **goose** symbol of home, fidelty, and married life. [Symbolism: CESO&S]

29. **heliotrope** symbol of lovers' faithfulness. [Flower Symbolism: *Flora Symbolica*, 174]

30. **Hezekiah** brings people of Judah back to God. [O.T.: II Chronicles 29:3–11; 31:20–21]

31. **Horton** elephant protagonist of Dr. Seuss books for children; trustworthy and diligent in his care of a neglected bird's egg and those who are weaker and unprotected. [Am. Children's Lit.: Jones]

32. **Hypermnestra** only one of Danaides who did not murder husband on wedding night. [Gk. Myth.: Howe, 136]

33. **Imogen** spurns the advances of Iachimo, who had wagered her husband that he could seduce her. [Br. Drama: Shakespeare *Cymbeline*]

34. **ivy** traditional symbol of faithfulness. [Plant Symbolism: *Flora Symbolica*, 175]

35. **Jehoshaphat** destroyed idols; adjured men to follow God. [O.T. II Chronicles 17:3–6, 19:9–11]

36. **Job** maintains his faith despite severe trials, is finally rewarded by God. [O.T.: Job]

37. **Josiah** tenaciously follows Moses' law; orders keeping of Passover. [O.T.: II Kings 23:21–24]

38. **key** attribute of the personified Fidelity. [Art: Hall, 184]

39. **Laodamia** commits suicide to join husband Protesilaus in underworld. [Gk. Lit.: *Iliad*; Rom Lit.: *Aeneid*]

40. **lemon** in Christian art, symbol of faithfulness. [Symbolism: *CEOS&S*]

41. **Leonore** disguises as Fidelio to save imprisoned husband. [Ger. Opera: Beethoven, *Fidelio*, Westerman, 109–110]

42. **Micawber, Mrs. Emma** swears she will never desert husband. [Br. Lit.: *David Copperfield*]

43. **Nanna** immolated herself on pyre with husband, Baldur. [Norse Myth.: Wheeler, 256]

44. **Noah** saved from flood because of his faith. [O.T.: Genesis: 6–10]

45. **Penelope** Odysseus' patient wife; faithful for 20 years while waiting for his return. [Gk. Lit.: *Iliad*; *Odyssey*]

46. **Perseus** ever devoted to wife, Andromeda. [Gk. Myth.: Zimmerman, 200]

47. **Pietas** goddess of faithfulness, respect, and affection. [Rom. Myth.: Kravitz, 192]

48. **plum** symbol of faithfulness. [Flower Symbolism: *Flora Symbolica*, 176]

49. **Portia** takes own life after husband, Brutus's, suicide. [Rom. Hist.: *Plutarch's Lives*]

50. **red on yellow** symbol of faithfulness. [Chinese Art.: Jobes, 357]

51. **Rodelinda** faithful to her deposed husband, Bertarido. [Br. Opera: Handel, *Rodelinda*, Westerman, 50–52]

52. **Roxy** tries to "save" immoral husband. [Am. Lit.: *Roxy*]

53. **Sita** princess abducted from her husband by the demon-king; she remains faithful throughout her captivity. [Indian Lit.: *Ramayana*]

54. **Sonia** reformed prostitute stays near prison to comfort Raskolnikov. [Russ. Lit.: *Crime and Punishment*]

55. **Valentine** a true friend and constant lover. [Br. Lit.: *Two Gentlemen of Verona*]

56. **veronica** symbol of faithfulness. [Flower Symbolism: *Flora Symbolica*, 178]

57. **violet** symbol of faithfulness. [Flower Symbolism: *Flora Symbolica*, 178; Kunz, 327]

58. **Zelda** shows devotion to Dobie, who manfully resists. [TV: "The Many Loves of Dobie Gillis" in Terrace, II, 64–66]

266. FAITHLESSNESS (See also ADULTERY, CUCKOLDRY.)

1. **Angelica** betrays Orlando by eloping with young soldier. [Ital. Lit.: *Orlando Furioso*]

2. **Camilla** falls to temptations of husband's friend. [Span. Lit.: *Don Quixote*]

3. **Carmen** throws over lover for another. [Fr. Lit.: *Carmen*; Fr. Opera: Bizet, *Carmen*, Westerman, 189–190]

4. **Coronis** princess killed by Apollo for being unfaithful to him. [Gk. Myth.: Howe, 66]

5. **Cressida** unfaithful mistress of Troilus; byword for unfaithfulness. [Br. Lit.: *Troilus and Cressida*]

6. **Dear John** letter from woman informing boyfriend that relationship is over. [Am. Usage: Misc.]

7. **Frankie and Johnnie** Johnnie, unfaithful to Frankie, is shot by her; there are nearly 500 versions of the song. [Am. Music: Misc.]

8. **Goneril and Regan** Lear's disloyal offspring; "tigers, not daughters." [Br. Lit.: *King Lear*]

9. **Manon** indifferently allows lover to be abducted. [Fr. Opera: Massenet, *Manon*, Westerman, 194–195]

10. **Shahriyar** convinced of female wantonness, marries a new wife each night, kills her in the morning. [Arab. Lit.: *Arabian Nights*]

267. FAME

1. **cardinal flower** traditional symbol of eminence. [Flower Symbolism: Jobes, 290]

2. **daphne** traditional symbol of fame. [Plant Symbolism: Jobes, 414]

3. **fifteen minutes of fame** the artist Andy Warhol (1928–1987) predicted that "in the future everyone will be famous for 15 minutes." [Am. Culture: Misc.]

4. **Grauman's Chinese Theater** famous for the imprints of movie stars' handprints in its forecourt. [Am. Cinema: Payton, 284]

5. **Halls of Fame** national shrines honoring outstanding individuals in a particular field (baseball, football, acting, Great Americans, etc.). [Am. Culture: *WB*, 9, 22–23]

6. **Lady Fame** capriciously distributes fame and slander. [Br. Lit.: Chaucer *The House of Fame* in Benét, 479]

7. **Madame Tussaud's Waxworks** representation by a wax figure in this London museum is a sure sign of notoriety. [Pop. Culture: *EB* (1963) XXII, 634]

8. **trumpet** attribute of fame personified. [Art: Hall, 119]

9. **trumpet flower** indicates notoriety. [Flower Symbolism: *Flora Symbolica*, 178]

10. *Who's Who* biographical dictionary of notable living people. [Am. Hist.: Hart, 922]

268. FAMILY

1. **Berenstain Bears, The** anthropomorphic bear family created by Stan and Jan Berenstain; in books and popular TV show, the family deals with typical life events in upbeat manner. [Am. Children's Lit. and TV: Misc.]

2. *Cosby Show, The* featured the everyday experiences of the Huxtables, an upper-middle-class black family of five children, obstetrician-father Cliff, and attorney-mother Claire. [Am. TV: *SJEPC*]

3. **drive-in theater** viewing movies outdoors from one's car provided inexpensive, family-friendly entertainment, especially in the 1940s-60s. [Am. Entertainment: *SJEPC*]

4. *Family Circle* "world's largest women's magazine" reached audience of 21 million by end of 1980s, has featured articles on child rearing, family issues, homemaking, and education since 1932. [Am. Jour.: *SJEPC*]

5. *Family Circus, The* popular single-panel comic strip finding humor in the everyday lives of a white, middle-class nuclear family—Daddy, Mommy, Billy, Dolly, Jeffy, and PJ—based on creator-artist Bil Keane's own parenting experiences. [Am. Comics: *SJEPC*]

6. *Family Ties* TV sitcom set during the Reagan era featured the Keaton family, where the idealistic, 1960s countercultural values of the parents often clashed with the materialistic, 1980s consumer culture values of the children (NBC, 1982–89). [Am. TV: *SJEPC*]

7. *Father Knows Best* wholesome TV sitcom presented the Andersons as the ideal family of 1950s America, with a wise father, supportive mother, and three children living in the suburbs. [Am. TV: *SJEPC*]

8. *Godfather, The* quintessential gangster film directed by Francis Ford Coppola based on Mario Puzo's novel about the Italian Mafia and rise of Corleone family in America won Academy Award for Best Picture in 1972; begat two sequels (1974, 1990). [Am. Film: *SJEPC*]

9. *Good Times* popular sitcom about a working class African-American family anchored by strong, responsible parents who lived in an inner city Chicago tenement and struggled to make ends meet; starred Esther Rolle and John Amos as Florida and James Evans (CBS, 1974–79). [Am. TV: *SJEPC*]

10. *Home Improvement* 1990s sitcom starring Tim Allen as a bumbling but loving father who hosts a local TV show devoted to home repair. [Am. TV: *BT1994*]

11. **minivan** seven-seat vehicle introduced in 1983 was perfect family transport. [Am. Culture: *SJEPC*]

12. *Ordinary People* 1976 novel by Judith Guest depicts dysfunctional, yet recognizable family. [Am. Lit.: Gillespie and Naden]

13. *Partridge Family, The* chaste 1970s sitcom loosely based on folk music family, the Cowsills. [Am. TV: *SJEPC*]

14. **Promise Keepers** organization of conservative Christian men who vow to abide by certain standards meant to build strong families; outdoor rallies held in the 1990s. [Am. Pop. Culture: *SJEPC*]

15. **PTA/PTO (Parent Teacher Association/Organization)** voluntary groups that bring parents and public schools together to improve the quality of education and parenting as well as addressing social issues like drug abuse and violence. [Am. Education: *SJEPC*]

16. *Sound of Music* Rodgers and Hammerstein musical and subsequent film based on story of famous singing Von Trapp family, who manage to escape Austria just before Nazi Germany annexes the country. [Am. Theater and Film: *SJEPC*]

17. *Waltons, The* TV show from 1972–1980 about wholesome devoted Depression-Era family who represent life in a bygone time; always signed off by saying "goodnight" to each other. [Am. TV: *SJEPC*]

269. FANATICISM (See also EXTREMISM.)

1. **Adamites** various sects preaching a return to life before the fall. [Christian Hist.: Brewer *Note-Book*, 8]

2. **assassins** Muslim murder teams used hashish as stimulus (11th and 12th centuries). [Islamic Hist.: Brewer *Note-Book*, 52]

3. **Fakirs** mendicant Indian sects bent on self-punishment for salvation. [Asian Hist.: Brewer *Note-Book*, 310]

4. **flagellants** various Christian sects practicing self-punishment. [Christian Hist.: Brewer *Note-Book*, 331–332]

5. **Harmony Society** Harmonists, also Rappites; subscribed to austere doctrines, such as celibacy, and therefore no longer exist (since 1960). [Am. Hist.: *NCE*, 910]

6. **Hitler, Adolf (1889–1945)** German dictator tried to conquer the world. [Ger. Hist.: *Hitler*]

7. **Jonestown** American religious zealots lived in Peoples Temple in Guyana under leadership of pastor Jim Jones; in 1978, U.S. officials investigated accusations of members being held against their will; there was violent reaction and subsequent mass suicide/murder of 914 members. [Am. Hist.: *SJEPC*]

8. **Shakers (or Alethians)** received their name from the trembling produced by excesses of religious emotion; because of doctrine of celibacy, Shakers are all but extinct. [Am. Hist.: *NCE*, 1938]

270. FANTASY (See also ENCHANTMENT, MAGIC, SCIENCE FICTION.)

1. **Aladdin's lamp** when rubbed, genie appears to do possessor's bidding. [Arab. Lit.: *Arabian Nights*, "Aladdin and the Wonderful Lamp"]

2. **Alice** undergoes fantastic adventures, such as dealing with the "real" Queen of Hearts. [Br. Lit.: *Alice's Adventures in Wonderland; Through the Looking Glass*]

3. **Alnaschar** dreams of the wealth he will realize from the sale of his glassware. [Arab. Lit.: Benét, 26]

4. *Arabian Nights* compilation of Middle and Far Eastern tales. [Arab. Lit.: Parrinder, 26]

5. *Back to Methuselah* England in the late twenty-second century is a bureaucracy administered by Chinese men and African women. [Br. Drama: Shaw *Back to Methuselah* in Magill III, 82]

6. **Bloom, Leopold** enlivens his uneventful life with amorous daydreams. [Irish Lit.: Joyce *Ulysses* in Magill I, 1040]

7. *Chitty Chitty Bang Bang* magical car helps track down criminals. [Children's Lit.: *Chitty Chitty Bang Bang*]

8. *Dark Is Rising* ominous novel by Susan Cooper and best known title from series of the same name; young Will Stanton experiences disconcerting events on his eleventh birthday; it is revealed that he is the last of the Old Ones and the only hope in the battle against the Dark. [Br. Children's Lit.: *OCCL*]

9. **Disney, Walt (1901–1966)** American producer of movies and cartoons, many on themes drawn from fairy tales and fantasy. [Am. Film: *FOF, MOD*]

10. **Dorothy** flies via tornado to Oz. [Am. Lit.: *The Wonderful Wizard of Oz*]

11. *Dream Children* in a reverie, Charles Lamb tells stories to his two imaginary children. [Br. Lit.: Benét, 287]

12. **Dungeons and Dragons** role-playing game based on fantasy literature in which players are characters adventuring together in an imaginary, mythical place created by the Dungeon Master. [Am. Culture: *SJEPC*]

13. *Fantasia* music comes to life in animated cartoon. [Am. Cinema: *Fantasia* in *Disney Films*, 38–45]

14. *Fantasy Island* TV drama in which dream-seekers arrived on the tropical island each week, where their fantasies would come true under the magical management of the mysterious white-suited Mr. Roarke and his dwarf sidekick Tatoo (ABC, 1978–84). [Am. TV: *SJEPC*]

15. **Grimm, Jacob (1785–1863) and Grimm, Wilhelm (1786–1859)** German philologists and folklorists; transcribed and published German folk tales. [Ger. Lit.: *Grimm's Fairy Tales*]

16. **Harvey** six-foot rabbit who appears only to a genial drunkard. [Am. Lit.: Benét, 444]

17. **Jurgen** regaining his lost youth, he has strange adventures with a host of mythical persons. [Am. Lit.: *Jurgen* in Magill I, 464]

18. **Land of the Giants** a *Gulliver's Travels* in outer space. [TV: Terrace, II, 10–11]

19. **LeGuin, Ursula K. (1929–)** renowned writer of science fiction and fantasy whose knowledge of anthropology influences her ability to create utterly believable alternate worlds; noteworthy titles include science-fiction classic *The Left Hand of Darkness* (1969) and Earthsea series (1968–2001.) [Am. Lit.: *SJEPC*]

20. *Little Prince, The* travels to Earth from his star; fable by Antoine de Saint-Exupèry (1943). [Fr. Lit.: Benét, 889]

21. *Lord of the Rings,The* epic trilogy of quest of hobbit Frodo Baggins to destroy magic ring that tempts its owner with immense power before evil lord Sauron can reclaim the ring to rule the world of Middle Earth; made into award-winnng series of films in 2001–2003. [Br. Lit. and Am. Film: *SJEPC*]

22. **Millionaire, The** mysterious Croesus bestows fortunes on unsuspecting individuals. [TV: Terrace, II, 97–98]

23. **Mitty, Walter** timid man who imagines himself a hero. [Am. Lit.: Benét, 1006; Am. Cinema and Drama: *The Secret Life of Walter Mitty*]

24. **Narnia** kingdom in which fantasy cycle of seven tales by C.S. Lewis takes place. [Children's Lit.: Fisher, 289–290]

25. **O'Gill, Darby** protagonist of Herminie Kavanagh books (1903 and 1926) and 1959 Disney film; befriends fairies and leprechauns. [Irish Lit.: *Darby O'Gill and the Little People* in *Disney Films*, 159–162]

26. *Once and Future King* four books by E.B. White, published as one volume in 1958, that tells the story of King Arthur; his early lessons in the ways of the world, through the use of enchantment, by Merlin, to his final days, mortally wounded and transported to the land of Avalon. [Br. Lit.: Gillespie and Naden]

27. **Pan, Peter** escapes to Never Never Land to avoid growing up. [Br. and Am. Drama: Benét, 778]

28. *Redwall* published in 1986 as first volume in Brian Jacques's series of fantasy novels set in Medieval times about the mice of Redwall Abbey; in this book, they defend their abbey against a group of dangerous bilge rats. [Br. Children's Lit.: Gillespie and Naden]

29. **Serling, Rod (1924–1975)** author of scripts that brought quality drama to early TV: created and hosted *The Twilight Zone,* eerie science-fiction/fantasy series with serious themes and name actors. [Am. TV: *SJEPC*]

30. ***Thirteen Clocks, The*** beautiful princess is won by a disguised prince who fulfills her guardian's task with the aid of laughter that turns to jewels. [Am. Lit.: Thurber *The Thirteen Clocks* in Weiss, 462]

31. **Tolkien, J. R. R. (1892–1973)** famous fantasy writer of *The Hobbit* (1937) and *The Lord of the Rings* trilogy set in imaginary world of Middle Earth; believed fantasy entailed creation of credible alternative world and elements of recovery, escape, and consolation. [Br. Lit.: *SJEPC*]

32. ***Twilight Zone, The*** influential TV series aired 1959–1964; employing outstanding writers and talented actors, creator Rod Serling used science fiction and fantasy format to pursue weighty themes. [Am. TV: *SJEPC*]

33. ***Wizard of Earthsea, A*** 1968 fantasy novel for young readers by Ursula K. LeGuin; first volume of her trilogy about the archipelago of Earthsea where magic abounded and her adolescent protagonist Ged searched for his identity. [Am. Children's Lit.: *OCCL*]

34. ***Wonderful Wizard of Oz, The*** adventures in land "somewhere over the rainbow." [Am. Lit.: *The Wonderful Wizard of Oz*]

271. FAREWELL

1. **Auld Lang Syne** closing song of New Year's Eve. [Music: Leach, 91]

2. **extreme unction (last rites)** anointing at the hour of death, sacrament of Orthodox Church and Roman Catholic Church. [Christianity: *NCE*, 689]

3. **gold watch** token of gratitude often bestowed on retiring employee after years of service. [Am. Pop. Culture: Misc.]

4. **golden handshake** token of gratitude bestowed on retiring employee after years of service. [Br. Pop. Culture: Misc.]

5. **kiss of death** gangsters' farewell ritual before murdering victim. [Am. Cult.: Misc.]

6. ***Last Hurrah, The*** portrays epitome of a politician's goodbye. [Am. Lit.: *The Last Hurrah*]

7. **Last Supper** Christ's final dinner with disciples before crucifixion. [N.T.: Matthew, 26:26–29; Mark 14:22–25; Luke 22:14–20]

8. **MacArthur's goodbye** "Old soldiers never die; they just fade away." [Am. Hist.: Van Doren, 528]

9. **Michaelmas daisy** traditional symbol of farewell. [Flower Symbolism: Jobes, 407]

272. FARMING

1. **Aristaeus** honored as inventor of beekeeping. [Gk. Myth.: *NCE*, 105]

2. **Ashman** goddess of grain. [Sumerian Myth.: Benét, 57]

3. *Barren Ground* Dorinda Oakley makes her father's poor farm prosperous. [Am. Lit.: Glasgow *Barren Ground* in Magill I, 57]

4. **Bergson, Alexandra** proves her ability above brothers' to run farm. [Am. Lit.: *O Pioneers!*, Magill I, 663–665]

5. **bread basket** an agricultural area, such as the U.S. Midwest, that provides large amounts of food to other areas. [Am. Hist.: Misc.]

6. **Ceres** goddess of agriculture. [Rom. Myth.: Kravitz, 13]

7. **Chávez, César (1927–1993)** farm labor activist spent early years working in the agricultural fields of Arizona and California. [Am. Hist.: *SJEPC*]

8. **Chicomecoatl** goddess of maize. [Aztec Myth.: Jobes, 322]

9. **cow college** an agricultural college. [Pop. Culture: Misc.]

10. **Dea Dia** ancient Roman goddess of agriculture. [Rom. Myth.: Howe, 77]

11. **Demeter** goddess of corn and agriculture. [Gk. Myth.: Jobes, 429–430]

12. **Dionysus** god of fertility; sometimes associated with feritlity of crops. [Gk. Myth.: *NCE*, 575]

13. **Farm Aid** organization spearheaded by country music legend Willie Nelson provides services and financial assistance to struggling American family farmers and lobbies for agricultural policy change; funded by concerts featuring popular artists (1985–). [Am. Music: *SJEPC*]

14. **Fiacre, Saint** extraordinary talent in raising vegetables; patron saint. [Christian Hagiog.: Attwater, 130]

15. **Freya** goddess of agriculture, peace, and plenty. [Norse Myth.: Payton, 257]

16. **Frome, Ethan** epitome of struggling New England farmer (1890s). [Am. Lit.: *Ethan Frome*]

17. **Gaea** goddess of earth. [Gk. Myth.: *NCE*, 785]

18. *Georgics* Roman Vergil's poetic statement set in context of agriculture. [Rom. Lit.: Benét, 389]

19. *Giants in the Earth* portrayal of man's struggle with the stubborn earth. [Am. Lit.: *Giants in the Earth*, Magill I, 303–304]

20. *Good Earth, The* portrayal of land as only sure means of survival. [Am. Lit.: *The Good Earth*]

21. *Grapes of Wrath, The* John Steinbeck's Pulitzer Prize-winning novel about the Joad family depicts the farmers' struggles first as

sharecroppers in the Dust Bowl of Oklahoma, then as agricultural migrant workers in California. [Am. Lit.: Harris *Characters*,
381–82; *SJEPC*]

22. **horn of plenty** cone-shaped bowl full of the bounty of the harvest, symbol of abundance. [Am. Culture: Misc.]

23. **Joad Family** impoverished farm family flees Oklahoma and the
Dust Bowl hoping to find a better life in California. [Am. Lit.: John
Steinbeck *The Grapes of Wrath*]

24. **King Cotton** term personifying the chief staple of the South.
[Am. Hist.: Hart, 445]

25. **Kore** name for Persephone as symbol of annual vegetation cycle.
[Gk. and Roman Myth.: *NCE*, 1637]

26. **Odin** god of farming. [Norse Myth.: Benét, 728]

27. **Persephone (Roman Proserpine)** goddess of fertility; often associated with crops. [Gk. and Roman Myth.: *NCE*, 1637]

28. **Shimerda, Antonia** "like wavering grass, a child of the prairie
and farm." [Am. Lit.: *My Antonia*, Magill I, 630–632]

29. **Silvanus** god of agriculture. [Rom. Myth.: Kravitz, 13]

30. **Triptolemus** an Eleusinian who learns from Demeter the art of
growing corn. [Gk. Myth.: *NCE*, 557]

31. **Walstan, Saint** English patron saint of husbandmen. [Christian
Hagiog.: Brewer *Dictionary*, 1138]

32. **wheat ears, garland of** to Demeter, goddess of grain. [Gk. Myth.:
Jobes, 374]

273. FASCISM

1. **Cipolla** brutal magician, symbol of fascist oppression. [Ger. Lit.:
Mario and the Magician; Haydn & Fuller, 636]

2. *Duce Il* title of Benito Mussolini (1883–1945), Italian Fascist
leader. [Ital. Hist.: Brewer *Dictionary*]

3. **Nazism** National Socialist party, German fascists who held
power from 1933–1945, began WWII. [Ger. Hist.: *EB*]

4. **Webley, Everard** sinister figure leads a growing Fascist movement. [Br. Lit.: Huxley *Point Counter Point* in Magill I, 760]

274. FASHION (See also FAD.)

1. **Adidas** distinctive footwear and clothing worn by athletes for
decades became fashionable in the 1970s and associated with rap
music in the late 1980s. [Culture: *SJEPC*]

2. **Armani, Giorgio (1934–)** men's fashionwear designer redefined
masculine silhouettes with stylish, expensive clothing lines. [Ital.
Culture: *SJEPC*]

3. **Blass, Bill (1922–2002)** among the first recognizable American "name" fashion designers; licensed brand name in products beyond clothing. [Am. Culture: *SJEPC*]

4. **Brummel, George B. (Beau Brummel) (1778–1840)** set styles for men's clothes and manners for a quarter century. [Western Fashion: *NCE*, 926]

5. **Campbell, Naomi (1971–)** British model with African heritage became a sensation in the United States; wide general appeal made her the first black supermodel. [Culture: *SJEPC*]

6. **Chanel, Gabrielle "Coco" (1886–1971)** French fashion designer noted for her classic styling. [Pop. Culture Misc.]

7. **Crawford, Cindy (1966–)** fashion supermodel of the 1980s-90s with healthy, wholesome, girl-next-door looks appeared in TV, film, fitness videos, and ads. [Am. Culture: *SJEPC*]

8. **disco** beyond the thumping bass and hypnotic rhythms, this style of dance music spawned its own fashions, such as form-fitting, glitzy clothing in synthetic fabrics and sparkling mirror balls on the dance floor during late 1970s craze. [Am. Culture and Music: *SJEPC*]

9. **Doc Martens** chunky boots first created in 1945 have made a fashion statement for years, popular with skinheads, punk rockers, grunge devotees, and others. [Culture: *SJEPC*]

10. **Earth Shoes** blocky, natural-fitting shoe with higher toe than heel was popular with Earth-conscious crowd of the 1970s. [Am. Culture: *SJEPC*]

11. **Ellis, Perry (1940–1986)** popular designer of luxurious women's and men's sportswear and fashions for the home. [Am. Culture: *SJEPC*]

12. **Factor, Max (1872–1938)** stage, screen, and street cosmetics pioneer created Pancake Makeup when Hollywood began making movies in Technicolor film. [Am. Culture: *SJEPC*]

13. **flappers** daring, sexually spirited young women of 1920s America had athletic, flatter chested look and wore shorter skirts, bobbed hair, and plenty of make-up. [Am. Hist.: *SJEPC*]

14. **Fu Manchu** style of mustache that extends downward past the mouth to the chin; named after Chinese villain created by English novelist Sax Rohmer in 1913. [Culture: *SJEPC*]

15. **Gucci** Italian fashion brand considered the height of luxury, status, and taste; designer of leather goods originated in Florence in 1906. [Ital. Culture: *SJEPC*]

16. **Halston (1932–1990)** American fashion designer Roy Halston Frowick created elegant fashions popular in the 1970s and 1980s. [Am. Culture: *EB*]

17. *Harper's Bazaar* leading fashion magazine. [Am. Culture: Misc.]

18. **hot pants** short-shorts fashionable in the 1970s; symbol of sexually alluring clothing. [Am. Culture: Misc.]

19. **Karan, Donna (1948–)** emerging from the Anne Klein company, her business was one of the first publicly traded fashion houses; her DKNY label reflects the New York sensibility. [Am. Culture: *SJEPC*]

20. **Klein, Calvin (1942–)** known for cutting-edge ads and sleek styles; name appears on everything from suits to underwear. [Am. Culture: *SJEPC*]

21. **Lacoste shirts** sports shirt of cotton pique with crocodile logo was named for its creator, tennis pro Jean Rene "The Crocodile" Lacoste; he designed shirt in 1929 for his personal use to replace stiff, long-sleeved Oxford shirts worn for tennis; popular item for preppy [Culture: *SJEPC*]

22. **Lauren, Ralph (1939–)** fabulously successful designer of clothing line whose designs are often described as reflecting monied, country club, upscale American West. [Am. Culture: *SJEPC*; Misc.]

23. *Miami Vice* Sonny Crockett's stubble and rumpled pastel linen clothes and Ricardo Tubb's casually elegant suits and diamond earring influenced men's fashions druing the 1980s. [Am. TV: *SJEPC*]

24. **Mod** fashion that began as social dissent in the working class in Britain, but the look was imitated in the U.S. by all classes. [Pop. Culture: *SJEPC*]

25. **polyester** fashionable in the 1960s and 1970s, the fabric's "wash and wear" property and its durability made it popular, but it soon became synonymous with bad taste. [Am. Pop. Culture: *SJEPC*]

26. **preppy** refers to someone who attends a college preparatory high school, specifically fashions worn by those of the upper class [Am. Culture: *SJEPC*]

27. **punk** movement among young people in 1970s; music meant to offend, extreme attire with colored hair and studs and pins, and belligerence toward anything conventional. [Br. and Amer. Pop. Culture: *SJEPC*]

28. **retro** the often playful revival of styles from the past. [Pop. Culture: *SJEPC*]

29. **Royal Ascot** annual horserace, occasion for great fashionable turnout. [Br. Cult.: Brewer *Dictionary*, 49]

30. **Sassoon, Vidal (1928–)** his free-flowing, geometric hairstyles of the 1960s revolutionized the industry and freed women from curlers and stiff, heavy hairdos. [Pop. Culture: *SJEPC*]

291

31. **Versace, Gianni (1946–1997)** colorful designer of fashion for men and women that often accentuated the body dramaticallly; killed outside his Miami mansion by serial killer Andrew Cunanan. [Am. Culture: *SJEPC*]

32. **Victoria's Secret** began in the early 1980s; retail chain selling sexy lingerie for women in upscale boutique mall stores. [Am. Business: *SJEPC*]

33. *Vogue* the first illustrated fashion magazine (1909); soon became legendary as the magazine for women wanting information on style, influential people, and cultural trends. [Fr. and Amer. Culture: Misc.]

34. **zoot suit** popularized by hip young males in 1930s and 1940s; padded shoulders, baggy pants and wide-brimmed hat; believed to have originated in African-American community. [Am. Culture: *SJEPC*]

275. FASTIDIOUSNESS (See also PUNCTUALITY.)

1. **Fogg, Phileas** entire life turned to precise schedule. [Fr. Lit.: *Around the World in Eighty Days*]

2. **Linkinwater, Tim** handles minutest details with order and precision. [Br. Lit.: *Nicholas Nickleby*]

3. **Morris the cat** finicky eater; eats only "9–Lives." [TV: Wallechinsky, 129]

4. **Steva** Jenufa's new scar cools his adulterous ardor. [Czech Opera: Janàcek, *Jenufa*, Westerman, 407]

5. **Unger, Felix** for him, godliness is next to cleanliness. [Am. Lit.: *The Odd Couple*; Am. Cinema: *The Odd Couple*; TV: "The Odd Couple" in Terrace II, 160–161]

276. FATE (See also CHANCE.)

1. **Adrastea** goddess of inevitable fate. [Gk. Myth.: Jobes, 35]

2. **Atropos, Clotho, and Lachesis** the three Fates; worked the thread of life. [Gk. and Roman Myth.: Bullfinch]

3. *Bridge of San Luis Rey, The* catastrophe as act of divine providence. [Am. Lit.: *The Bridge of San Luis Rey*]

4. **dance of death, the** recurring motif in medieval art. [Eur. Culture: Bishop, 363–367]

5. **Destiny** goddess of destiny of mankind. [Gk. Myth.: Kravitz, 78]

6. **Fates** three goddesses who spin, measure out, and cut the thread of each human's life. Also called *Lat.* Parcae, *Gk.* Moirai. [Gk. Myth.: Benét, 757]

7. *Jennie Gerhardt* novel of young girl trapped by life's circumstances (1911). [Am. Lit.: *Jennie Gerhardt*, Magill III, 526–528]

8. **karma** one's every action brings inevitable results. [Buddhist and Hindu Trad.: *EB* (1963), 13: 283; Pop. Culture: Misc.]

9. **kismet** Turkish word, meaning "portion, lot" hence, "fate." [Turk. Lang.: Misc.; Pop. Culture: Misc.]

10. **Leonora** cursed by father; stabbed by brother. [Ital. Opera: Verdi, *La Forza del Destino*, Westerman, 316–317]

11. **Meleager** death would come when firebrand burned up. [Gk. Myth.: Walsh *Classical*, 186]

12. **Necessitas** goddess of the destiny of mankind. [Gk. Myth.: Kravitz, 78, 162]

13. **Nemesis** goddess of vengeance and retribution, *nemesis* has come to mean that which one cannot achieve. [Gk. Myth.: *WB*, 14: 116; Pop. Culture: Misc.]

14. **Norns** wove the fabric of human destiny. [Norse Myth.: Benét, 720]

15. **wool and narcissi, garland of** emblem of the three Fates. [Gk. Myth.: Jobes, 374]

277. FATHERHOOD

1. **Abraham** progenitor of a host of nations. [O.T.: Genesis 17:3–6]

2. **Adam** first man and progenitor of humanity. [O.T.: Genesis 5:1–5]

3. **Cosby, Bill (1937–)** "America's Dad" played role of lovable obstetrician-father Cliff Huxtable on *The Cosby Show* (1984–92); wrote *Fatherhood* (1986). [Am. TV and Lit.: *SJEPC*; Misc.]

4. **Dag(h)da** great god of Celts; father of Danu. [Celtic Myth.: Parrinder, 68; Jobes, 405]

5. **Dombey, Mr.** embittered by the death of his young son, neglects his daughter. [Br. Lit.: *Dombey and Son*]

6. *Father Knows Best* ultimately wise dad Jim Anderson, played by Robert Young, managed to solve every family problem before end of the show in this TV sitcom of 1950s suburban life. [Am. TV: *SJEPC*]

7. **Goriot, Père** deprives himself of his wealth in order to ensure good marriages for his two daughters. [Fr. Lit.: Balzac *Père Goriot* in Magill I, 271]

8. **Liliom** dead for sixteen years, he is allowed to return from Heaven for a day, and attempts to please the daughter he had never seen. [Hung. Drama: Molnar *Liliom* in Magill I, 511]

9. **Priam, King of Troy** fathered fifty children, among them Hector, Paris, Troilus, and Cassandra. [Gk. Lit.: *Iliad*]

10. **Tevye** pious dairyman concerned with marrying off his seven beautiful daughters. [Yid. Lit.: *Tevye's Daughters*; Am. Musical: *Fiddler on the Roof* in *On Stage*, 468]

11. **Vatea** the first man; the father of mankind. [Polynesian Legend: *How the People Sang the Mountains Up*, 85]

12. **Zeus (Jupiter Jove)** "Father of the gods and men"; had many legitimate and illegitimate children. [Gk. and Rom. Myth.: Benét, 1115; Bullfinch, Ch. I]

278. FATNESS

1. **Bagstock, Major** corpulent army officer. [Br. Lit.: *Dombey and Son*]

2. **Challenger, Professor** amusing and opinionated scientist of notable rotundity. [Br. Lit.: *The Lost World*]

3. **Domino, Antoine "Fats" (1928–)** popular singer of the 1950s, nicknamed for his size and shape. [Am. Music: Misc.]

4. **Double, Edmund** loves to eat; represents the Fattipuffs. [Children's Lit.: *Fattipuffs and Thinifers*, Fisher, 100–101]

5. **Eglon** obese Moabite king; sword engulfed in adiposity. [O.T.: Judges 3:17–22]

6. **Falstaff** "that swoln parcel of dropsies." [Br. Drama: Benét, 339]

7. **Five by Five, Mr.** obese subject of song by Gene DePaul and Don Raye (1942). [Am. Pop. Music: Kinkle, 1, 379]

8. **Gleason, Jackie (1916–1987)** heavyweight TV comedian. [TV: "The Jackie Gleason Show," "The Honeymooners" in Terrace, I, 402]

9. **Hardy, Oliver (1892–1957)** portrayed—along with Stan Laurel—two rather dim, but loyal friends bumbling through one "swell predicament" after another; their physical appearance (Hardy fat, Laurel thin, both in derbies) was often parodied. [Am. Film: *FOF, MOD*]

10. **Humpty Dumpty** "egg" in Mother Goose who, among other things, alludes to fatness. [Children's Lit.: *Mother Goose*]

11. **Joe ("Fat Boy")** sole employment consists in alternately eating and sleeping. [Br. Lit.: *Pickwick Papers*]

12. **king and his ministers** "large, corpulent, oily men." [Am. Lit.: "Hop-Frog" in *Portable Poe*, 317–329]

13. **Limkins, Mr.** large gentleman with "a very round red face." [Br. Lit.: *Oliver Twist*]

14. **Minnesota Fats (Rudolph Walter Wanderone, Jr., 1903–1996)** world champion billiard player easily recognized by his fleshy physique. [Am. Sports: Misc.]

15. **Robbin and Bobbin** "eat more victuals than threescore men." [Nurs. Rhyme: Baring-Gould, 33]

16. **Rubens, Peter Paul (1577–1640)** Flemish painter noted for his voluptuous, full-figured nudes. [Flem. Art: *FOF, MOD*]

17. **Snuphanuph, Lady** obese visitor at Bath. [Br. Lit.: *Pickwick Papers*]

18. **Tweedledum and Tweedledee** two little fat men who quickly get out-of-breath. [Br. Lit.: Lewis Carroll *Through the Looking-Glass*]

19. **Welles, Orson (1915–1985)** rotund director of innovative theater and groundbreaking films. [Am. Film and Theater: *SJEPC*]

20. **Wolfe, Nero** detective whose obesity makes him reluctant to leave his office. [Am. Lit.: Herman, 119]

279. FEARSOMENESS

1. **Deimos** attendant of Ares; personification of fear. [Gk. Myth.: Howe, 77]

2. *Dracula* eerie tale of vampires and werewolves. [Br. Lit.: *Dracula*]

3. **Hitchcock, Alfred (1899–1980)** English film director and creator of suspenseful classics, including *The Birds* and *Psycho* [Film ODA]

4. **Iroquois** strongest, most feared of eastern confederacies. [Am. Hist.: Jameson, 250]

5. **Jaggers, Mr.** lawyer esteemed and feared by clients. [Br. Lit.: *Great Expectations*]

6. **Karloff, Boris (1887–1969)** British-born American actor noted for his performances in many horror films, including *Frankenstein* [Am. Film: ODA]

7. **Ko-Ko** holder of dread office of High Executioner. [Br. Opera: *The Mikado*, Magill I, 591–592]

8. *Native Son* portrays oppressor and oppressed as both filled with fear. [Am. Lit.: *Native Son*, Magill I, 643–645]

9. **Phobus** god of dread and alarm. [Gk. Myth.: Kravitz, 14, 84]

10. *Seven That Were Hanged, The* analyzes the fears of an official threatened with assassination and of seven condemned prisoners. [Russ. Lit.: Magill, II, 957]

11. **Shere Khan** lame tiger who wants to devour Mowgli; causes fear throughout story; from Rudyard Kipling's series for young readers, *The Jungle Books* (1894–1895). [Br. Children's Lit.: Jones]

12. *War of the Worlds* Orson Welles's broadcast; terrified a credulous America (1938). [Am. Hist.: Misc.]

280. FEAST (See also EPICURE.)

1. **Barmecide feast** a sham banquet, with empty plates, given to a beggar by wealthy Baghdad nobleman. [Arab. Lit.: *Arabian Nights*, "The Barmecide's Feast"]

2. **Belshazzar's Feast** lavish banquet, with vessels stolen from Jerusalem temple. [O.T.: Daniel, 5]

3. **Camacho's wedding** lavish feast prepared in vain, as Camacho's fiancée runs off with her love just before the ceremony. [Span. Lit.: Cervantes *Don Quixote*]

4. **Epicurus (341–271 B.C.)** Greek philosopher who believed that happiness was found in pleasure and indulgence. [Gk. Phil.: *ODA*]

5. **Hanukkah (Feast of Lights or Feast of Dedication)** Jewish festival lasting eight days; abundance of food is characteristic. [Judaism: *NCE*, 1190]

6. **Lucullan feast** a lavish banquet; after Lucullus, Roman general and gourmet. [Rom. Hist.: Espy, 236]

7. **Prospero's banquet** shown to the hungry castaways, then disappears. [Br. Drama: Shakespeare *The Tempest*]

8. **Thanksgiving** national holiday with luxurious dinner as chief ritual. [Am. Pop. Culture: Misc.]

9. **Thyestean banquet** at which Atreus served his brother Thyestes' sons to him as main course. [Gk. Myth.: Brewer *Dictionary*, 1081]

10. **Trimalchio's Feast** lavishly huge banquet given by wealthy vulgarian. [Rom. Lit.: *Satryricon*]

11. **Zeus** disguised as Amphitryon, gives a banquet at the latter's house. [Gk. Myth.: Benét, 32]

281. FEMALE POWER

1. **Boadicea** British warrior-queen who led a revolt against the Romans. [Br. Hist.: Brewer *Dictionary*, 116]

2. **Camilla** maiden-warrior who battles Aeneas' forces. [Rom. Lit.: Virgil *Aeneid*]

3. *Fatal Attraction* film about an extramarital fling portrays single, professional woman Alex Forrest as obsessed, psychopathic stalker whose power is destructive. [Am. Film: *SJEPC*]

4. **Hippolyta** queen of the Amazons; attacked Attica but was defeated by Theseus, who then married her. [Gk. Myth.: Benét, 468]

5. **Macbeth, Lady** goads Macbeth to murder Duncan and seize power. [Br. Drama: Shakespeare *Macbeth*]

6. **Pilar** strong-minded female leader of a group of guerillas in the Spanish Civil War. [Am. Lit.: Hemingway *For Whom the Bell Tolls*]

7. **Semiramis** warrior-queen founded Babylon; legendary conqueror, identified with the goddess Ishtar. [Asiatic Hist.: *EB* (1963) XX, 315]

8. **Valkyries** warlike virgins who ride into battle to select, from the heroes to be slain, those worthy of dining with Odin in Valhalla. [Scand. Myth.: Benét, 1046]

Feminism (See RIGHTS, WOMEN's.)

282. FERRYING

1. **Charon** ferries dead across the river Styx. [Gk. and Rom. Myth.: Hall, 147; Ital. Lit.: *Inferno*]
2. **Christopher, Saint** took the Christ child and the weak across river. [Christian Hagiog.: Hall, 68]
3. **Julian the Hospitaler** carries leper across river. [Christian Hagiog.: Hall, 181]
4. **Phlegyas** conveyed Dante and Virgil through Stygian marsh. [Ital. Lit.: *Inferno*]
5. **Siddhartha** "one who has attained goal," personified in ferryman role. [Ger. Lit.: *Siddhartha*]
6. **Tuck, Friar** jolly member of Robin Hood's gang; carries Robin over stream but dumps him coming back. [Br. Lit.: *Robin Hood*]

283. FERTILITY (See also ABUNDANCE.)

1. **ant** considered a symbol of fecundity in parts of Africa. [African Animal Symbolism: *CEOS&S*, 207]
2. **antelope** symbol of fecundity and the moon in Africa. [African Animal Symbolism: *CEOS&S*, 207]
3. **antler dance** archaic animal dance, preceding mating. [Br. Folklore: Brewer *Dictionary*, 1]
4. **Anu** Irish goddess of fecundity. [Irish Folklore: Briggs, 9]
5. **Aphrodite** goddess of fecundity. [Gk. Myth.: Parrinder, 24]
6. **Astarte** goddess of fecundity. [Phoenician Myth.: Jobes, 144]
7. **Astarte's dove** emblem of fecundity. [Phoenician Myth.: Jobes, 466]
8. **Atargatis' dove** emblem of fecundity. [Hittite Myth.: Jobes, 466]
9. **Athena** Athens' patroness; goddess of war and fecundity. [Gk. Myth.: Parrinder, 33; Kravitz, 40]
10. **Baal** chief male god of Phoenicians; the generative principle. [Phoenician Rel.: Parrinder, 38]
11. **Bacchus' cup** symbolizes fecundity. [Gk. Myth.: Jobes, 397]
12. **Bona Dea** goddess of fertility; counterpart of Faunus. [Rom. Myth.: Zimmerman, 43]
13. **breast** symbol of nourishment and fecundity. [Ren. Art: Hall, 52]

14. **Cernunnos** horned deity of fecundity, associated with snakes. [Celtic Myth.: Parrinder, 58]

15. **Cerridwen** nature goddess whose magical cauldron was misused. [Celtic Myth.: Parrinder, 58]

16. **Chloe** beloved maiden, goddess of new, green crops. [Gk. Myth.: Parrinder, 62]

17. **Clothru** Irish goddess of fertility. [Irish. Myth.: Jobes, 349]

18. **clover** symbolizes fecundity. [Folklore: Jobes, 350]

19. **coconut** presented to women who want to be mothers. [Ind. Folklore: Binder, 85]

20. **Cybele** nature's fruitfulness assured by orgiastic rites honoring her. [Phrygian Myth.: Parrinder, 68; Jobes, 400]

21. **Dag(h)da** god of abundance, war, healing. [Celtic Myth.: Parrinder, 68; Jobes, 405]

22. **Dagon (Dagan)** fish-corn god symbolizing fecundity and abundance. [Babyl. Myth.: Parrinder, 71; Jobes, 405]

23. **Demeter** goddess of fecundity. [Gk. Myth.: Jobes, 429–430]

24. **Don** goddess of fecundity; Welsh equivalent of Irish Danu. [Brythonic Myth.: Leach, 321; Jobes, 461]

25. **double ax** emblem of fecundity. [Folklore: Jobes, 163]

26. **figs, garland of** a traditional pictorial identification of Pan, pastoral god of fertility. [Gk. Myth.: Jobes, 373]

27. **fish** signifies fecundity. [Mexican Folklore: Binder, 17]

28. **flowers and fruit, garland of** traditional headdress of Pomona, goddess of fertility. [Rom. Myth.: Jobes, 373]

29. **flowers, garland of** traditional pictorial identification of Flora, goddess of flowers and fertility. [Rom. Myth.: Jobes, 373]

30. **Freya** goddess of agriculture, peace, and plenty. [Norse Myth.: Payton, 257]

31. **grape leaves, garland of** traditional headdress of Bona Dea, goddess of fertility. [Rom. Myth.: Jobes, 373]

32. **green** symbol of fruitfulness. [Color Symbolism: Jobes, 356]

33. **hippopotamus** in Ancient Egypt, female hippo was symbol of fertility and worshippped as an upright hippo goddess. [Symbolism: *CEOS&S*]

34. **horn** believed to promote fertility. [Art: Hall, 157]

35. **horse** symbolizes fecundity. [Bengali Folklore: Binder, 67]

36. **Ishtar** Babylonian goddess of fertility, sex, and love. [Babyl. Myth: *ODA*]

37. **Lavransdatter, Kristin** gives birth to eight sons in ten years. [Nor. Lit.: *Kristin Lavransdatter*, Magill I, 483–486]

38. **Mylitta** goddess of fertility. [Babyl. Myth.: Leach, 776]

39. **old woman who lived in a shoe** what to do with so many children? [Nurs. Rhyme: Opie, 434]

40. **Ops** Sabine goddess of fecundity. [Rom. Myth.: Brewer *Dictionary*, 782]

41. **orange** commonly held as symbol of fertility. [Symbolism: *CEOS&S*]

42. **orange blossoms** symbolic of bride's hope for fruitfulness. [Br. and Fr. Tradition: Brewer *Dictionary*, 784]

43. **peach** very important Chinese symbol with many meanings, including immortality, marriage, fertility. [Symbolism: *CEOS&S*]

44. **pomegranate** indicates abundance. [Heraldry: Halberts, 36]

45. **Pomona** goddess of gardens and fruit trees. [Rom. Myth.: Zimmerman, 218]

46. **rabbit** symbol of fecundity. [Animal Symbolism: Mercatante, 125–126]

47. **Rhea** worshiped orgy and fertility; mother of Zeus, Poseidon, Hera, Hades, Demeter, and Hestia. [Gk. Myth.: *NCE*, 1796]

48. **rhinoceros horn** in powdered form, considered powerful fertility agent. [Eastern Culture: Misc.]

49. **rice** emblem of growth, rebirth, and fertility, especially in India and China, where it is considered divine nourishment; also fecundity symbol at Indian weddings.. [Symbolism: *CEOS&S*]

50. **waxing moon** only effective time for sowing seeds. [Gardening Lore: Boland, 31]

51. **yellow** color of fecundity; relating to yellow sun and earth. [Eastern Color Symbolism: Binder, 78]

284. FESTIVAL

1. **Bayreuth** since 1876, international center for Wagner's operas. [Opera Hist.: Thompson, 165]

2. **Berkshire Music Festival (Tanglewood)** summer home of Boston Symphony since 1934. [Music Hist.: Thompson, 202–203]

3. **Cannes** founded after WWII, annual festival of Hollywood and independent films. [Cinema Hist.: *EB*, 12: 496]

4. **Edinburgh Festival** internationally famous arts celebration since 1947. [Music Hist.: Thompson, 617]

5. **Eisteddfod** ancient congress of bards, still held annually in Wales. [Music Hist.: Benét, 305]

6. **Festival of the Two Worlds (Spoleto Festival)** founded in 1958 by Gian-Carlo Menotti and held annually in Charleston, South Carolina, and Spoleto, Italy. [Music Hist.: *NCE*, 2599]

7. **Glyndebourne Festivals** annual operatic events held in Sussex, England since 1934. [Music Hist.: *NCE*, 1097]

8. **Marlboro Festival** founded by pianist Rudolf Serkin in 1949, a summer music festival held in Vermont. [Music Hist.: *EB*]

9. **Newport Jazz Festival** annual summer jazz celebration; moved to New York City in 1971. [Am. Hist.: *NCE*, 1927]

10. **Salzburg Festival** summer music festival held in Salzburg since 1920. [Music Hist.: *EB*]

11. **Sundance** Sundance Institute founded in 1981 by actor Robert Redford to support budding filmmakers; annual Utah festival has become showcase of American independent films. [Am. Film: *SJEPC*]

12. **Woodstock** Woodstock, NY was the site of three-day music and arts festival in 1969; despite chaos and bad weather, was peaceful assemblage of 500,000 young hippies and has, for some, come to symbolize the best of the counterculture movement. [Am Music Hist.: *EB*, X: 741]

Fierceness (See SAVAGERY.)

285. FILMMAKER

1. **Bergman, Ingmar (1918–2007)** Swedish filmmaker of iconic works of the 20th century, noted for their bleak, tragic worldview. [Swed. Film: *FOF, MOD*]

2. **Burns, Ken (1953–)** his documentary film style featuring primary materials and voiceovers captivated TV audiences and brought history to life in such award-winning films as *The Civil War* (1990) and *The War* (2007). [Am. Film: *SJEPC*]

3. **Chaplin, Charlie (1889–1977)** one of the greatest comedians of all times; writer/director/actor of numerous classic silent films; spent time in workhouses as a child; desperate poverty of his early years manifested in films, most notably in character of Little Tramp. [Am. Film: Misc.]

4. **Cukor, George (1899–1983)** prolific film director of such classics as *Little Women* (1933), *The Philadelphia Story* (1940), *A Star Is Born* (1954), and *My Fair Lady* (1964). [Am. Film: *SJEPC*]

5. **Fairbanks, Douglas, Sr. (1883–1939)** silent film actor famous for swashbuckler roles (1910s-20s) cofounded United Artists. [Am. Film: *SJEPC*]

6. **Fellini, Federico (1920–1993)** Italian filmmaker whose works are noted for their autobiographical themes and striking, often surrealistic imagery. [Ital. Film: *FOF, MOD*]

7. **Ford, John (1894–1973)** prolific, Academy Award-winning director's career spanned 50 years; best known for his movies in the

Western genre, like *Stagecoach* (1939) and *The Man Who Shot Liberty Valance* (1962) starring John Wayne. [Am. Film: *SJEPC*]

8. **Godard, Jean-Luc (1930–)** French filmmaker and part of the New Wave movement in French movies. [Fr. Film: *FOF, MOD*]

9. **Goldwyn, Samuel (1879–1974)** Polish immigrant became influential Hollywood film producer during the motion picture industry's formative years and heyday (1913–59); produced classic Academy Award winner *The Best Years of Our Lives* (1946). [Am. Film: *SJEPC*]

10. **Griffith, D. W. (1875–1948)** director known as the father of film pioneered innovative filmmaking techniques in his landmark feature-length motion picture, the epic *Birth of a Nation* (1915). [Am. Film: *SJEPC*]

11. **Kubrick, Stanley (1928–1999)** American filmmaker noted for wide variety of movies, including *2001: A Space Odyssey, Dr. Strangelove, The Shining*. [Am. Film: *FOF, MOD*]

12. **Lang, Fritz (1890–1976)** fled Nazi Germany in 1932, settling in Hollywood and making over 20 films, notably crime dramas which gave birth to film noir; fine example found in *M* (1931). [Am. Film: *SJEPC*]

13. **Pickford, Mary (1890–1979)** famous sweet-faced actor in early films; shrewd businesswoman who went on to become one of the founders of United Artists Studios. [Am. Film: *SJEPC*]

14. **Preminger, Otto** vehemently independent producer/director of famous noir films and grand-scale movies with serious themes [Am. Film: *SJEPC*]

15. **Renoir, Jean (1894–1979)** master of realistic films of great complexity and subtlety and mentor to the French New Wave directors for the late 1950s. [Fr. Film: *SJEPC*]

16. **Scorcese, Martin (1942–)** critically-acclaimed director whose provocative works often depict New York City thugs and criminals; the allusive Oscar came in 2007 for *The Departed*. [Am. Film: *SJEPC*]

17. **Selznick, David O. (1902–1965)** influential and successful film producer whose greatest work was done during the 1930s and 1940s; examples include *Gone with the Wind* and *Rebecca*. [Am. Film: *SJEPC*]

18. **Spielberg, Steven (1946–)** director of blockbuster adventure films and dramatic films with weighty themes; founder of DreamWorks SKG studio and Shoah Foundation to archive testimonies of Holocaust survivors. [Am. Films: *SJEPC*]

19. **Stone, Oliver (1946–)** director and screenwriter sometimes accused of rewriting history or pandering to the demands for vio-

lence in films, nonetheless respected for depth and social import of his work. [Am. Film: *SJEPC*]

20. **Tarantino, Quentin (1963–)** casual violence, sex, drugs, and other pulp genre elements are found in his witty, inventive films; probably best known for writing and directing acclaimed *Pulp Fiction* (1994). [Am. Film: *SJEPC*]

21. **Thalberg, Irving G. (1899–1936)** talented movie executive who was head of production for Metro Goldwyn Mayer; Thalberg Memorial Award given by Academy of Motion Picture Arts and Sciences for high production achievement is named after him. [Am. Film: *SJEPC*]

22. **Welles, Orson (1915–1985)** after an early career on Broadway, directing innovative productions, became one of most influential filmmakers of the 20th century; probably best known for his seminal film *Citizen Kane* (1941). [Am. Film and Theater: *SJEPC*]

Filth (See DIRTINESS.)

286. FINANCE (See also MONEY.)

1. **Bourse** the Paris stock exchange. [Fr. Commerce: Misc.]

2. **bubble** a time period in which an asset is overvalued, then loses money, as in "dot.com bubble" or "housing bubble." [Am. Business: Misc.]

3. **Dow Jones** the best known of several U.S. indexes of movements in price on Wall Street. [Am. Hist.: Payton, 202]

4. *Fortune* highly respected, biweekly business magazine established in 1930 annually ranks the 500 top performing American companies. [Am. Jour.: *SJEPC*]

5. **Fortune 500** annual ranking of America's 500 largest corporations by revenue, published by *Fortune* magazine since 1955. [Am. Business and Jour.: *SJEPC*]

6. **invisible hand** from Adam Smith's influential *The Wealth of Nations*, the theory that economies work best when unfettered by government interference. [Am. Business: Misc.]

7. **Keynes, John Maynard (1883–1946)** influential English economist who advocated government spending to stimulate a nation's economy. [Hist.: Misc.]

8. **Lombard Street** London bankers' row; named for 13th-century Italian moneylenders. [Br. Hist.: Plumb, 15]

9. **Morgan, J. P. (1837–1913)** American banker; he used his own money to stabilize the economy in 1895. [Am. Hist.: Misc.]

10. **Old Lady of Threadneedle Street** nickname for the Bank of England. [Br. Culture: Misc.]

11. **Ponzi scheme** named for Charles Ponzi (1877–1949), who swindled millions from unwitting investors in a "get rich quick" scheme in the 1920s. [Am. Business: *FOF, MOD*]

12. **Praxidice** goddess of commerce. [Gk. Myth.: Kravitz, 88]

13. **Rockefeller, John D(avison) (1839–1937)** multimillionaire oil tycoon and financier. [Am. Hist.: *EB*, VIII: 623]

14. **Throgmorton Street** location of British Stock Exchange; by extension, financial world. [Br. Hist.: Brewer *Dictionary*, 1079]

15. **Wall Street** N.Y.C. financial district; by extension, the business interests in the U.S. [Am. Hist.: Jameson, 530]

16. **World Trade Center** until their destruction, Twin Towers were tallest buildings in New York City and hub of financial district; hit by two planes hijacked by al-Qaeda terrorists on September 11, 2001, causing the collapse of the buildings and the deaths of nearly 3000. [Am. Hist.: *SJEPC*]

287. FIRE

1. **Agni** intermediary of the god through sacrificial fire. [Hindu Myth.: Parrinder, 12]

2. **Armida** sorceress sets fire to her own palace when it is threatened by the Crusaders. [Ital. Lit.: *Jerusalem Delivered (Gerusalemme Liberata)*; in Benét, 391]

3. **burning bush** form taken by Angel of the Lord to speak to Moses. [O.T.: Exodus 3:2–3]

4. **Caca** goddess of the hearth. [Rom. Myth.: Kravitz, 49]

5. **Dactyli** introduced fire to Crete. [Gk. Myth.: Kravitz, 74]

6. **Etticoat, Little Nancy** candle personified: longer she stands, shorter she grows. [Nurs. Rhyme: *Mother Goose*, 39]

7. *Fahrenheit 451* in an America of the future, the fireman's job is to burn all books that have been concealed from authorities. [Am. Lit.: Bradbury *Fahrenheit 451* in Weiss, 289]

8. **Florian** miraculously extinguished conflagration; popularly invoked against combustion. [Christian Hagiog.: Hall, 126]

9. **Great Chicago Fire** destroyed much of Chicago; it was supposedly started when Mrs. O'Leary's cow kicked over a lantern (1871). [Am. Hist.: Payton, 141]

10. **Hephaestus** Prometheus' kinsman and the god of fire. [Gk. Lit.: *Prometheus Bound*, Magill I, 786–788]

11. **Lucifer** kitchen match; from Lucifer, fallen archangel. [Br. Folklore: Espy, 66]

12. **Phlegethon** river of liquid fire in Hades. [Gk. Myth.: Brewer *Dictionary*, 699]

13. **phoenix** fabulous bird that consumes itself by fire every five hundred years and rises renewed from the ashes. [Arab. Myth.: Brewer *Dictionary*, 699]

14. **Polycarp, Saint** sentenced to immolation, flames unscathingly ensheathed him. [Christian Hagiog.: Attwater, 290]

15. **Prometheus** Titan who stole fire from Olympus and gave it to man. [Gk. Myth.: Payton, 546]

16. **salamander** flame-dwelling spirit in Rosicrucian philosophy. [Medieval Hist.: Brewer *Dictionary*, 956]

17. **Shadrach, Meshach, and Abednego** walk unscathed in the fire of the furnace into which Nebuchadnezzar has them thrown. [O.T.: Daniel 3:21–27]

18. **Smokey the Bear** warns "only you can prevent forest fires." [Am. Pop. Cult.: Misc.]

19. **Taberah** Israelite camp scorched by angry Jehovah. [O.T.: Numbers 11:1–3]

20. **Topheth** where parents immolated children to god, Moloch. [O.T.: II Kings 23:10; Jeremiah 7:31–32]

21. **Vesta** virgin goddess of hearth; custodian of sacred fire. [Rom. Myth.: Brewer *Dictionary*, 1127]

22. **Vulcan** blacksmith of gods; personification of fire. [Art: Hall, 128]

288. FIREARMS

1. **AK47** Soviet automatic assault rifle with banana clip often associated with rebellions, insurrections, and revolutionaries. [Am. Hist.: *SJEPC*]

2. **Colt .45** six-shot revolver invented by Samuel Colt and used throughout the West. [Am. Hist.: *WB*, 4: 684–85; *SJEPC*]

3. **M16** automatic or semi-automatic American military assault rifle adopted during the Vietnam War in 1960s also associated with urban American drug gang warfare. [Am. Hist.: *SJEPC*]

4. **Tommy gun** automatic Thompson sub-machine gun with rat-a-tat-tat sound associated with organized crime and Depression-era gangsters like John Dillinger. [Am. Hist.: *SJEPC*]

5. **Winchester** famous rifle, first cast in 1866, associated with the American West. [Am. Hist.: Misc.]

289. FIRSTS

1. **Adam** in the Bible, the first man. [O.T.: Genesis 1:26–5:5]

2. **Alalcomeneus** the first man. [Gk. Myth.: Zimmerman, 14]

3. **Aldine Classics** first standardized, comprehensive editions of the classics (16th century). [Ital. Hist.: Plumb, 267]

4. **Armstrong, Neil (1930–)** first person to set foot on the moon (July 20, 1969). [Am. Hist.: *NCE*, 172]

5. **Bannister, Roger (1929–)** first runner to break the four-minute mile. [Sports: *EB*, I: 795]

6. *Bay Psalm Book, The* first book published in U.S (1640). [Am. Hist.: Van Doren, 784]

7. **Brooks, Gwendolyn (1917–2000)** first African-American writer to receive Pulitzer Prize (1950). [Am. Lit.: *SJEPC*]

8. **Buck, Pearl S. (1892–1973)** first American woman to receive Nobel Prize in literature in 1938; author of *The Good Earth* (1931). [Am. Lit.: *SJEPC*]

9. **Cabrini, Saint Frances (1850–1917)** first U.S saint; tirelessly helped new Italian Americans. [Christian Hagiog.: Attwater, 135–136]

10. **Caedmon (b. 671)** earliest English Christian poet. [Br. Hist.: Grun]

11. **Cincinnati Red Stockings** first all-professional baseball team (1869). [Am. Hist.: Van Doren, 260]

12. **Clemente, Roberto (1934–1972)** Puerto Rican rightfielder was first Hispanic elected to baseball's Hall of Fame (1973). [Am. Sports: *SJEPC*]

13. *Dafue* first true opera (Florence, 1597). [Ital. Opera: Westerman, 17]

14. **Dandridge, Dorothy (1922–1965)** singer/entertainer/actress was first African-American woman to headline at the Waldorf-Astoria, to receive Academy Award nomination for Best Actress, and to appear on the cover of *Life* magazine. [Am. Hist. and Film: *SJEPC*]

15. **Dare, Virginia (b. 1587)** first English child born in the New World. [Am. Hist.: Jameson, 131]

16. **Delaware** first colony to ratify the Constitution; thus, "the first state." [Am. Hist.: *NCE*, 738]

17. **Eve** in the Bible, the first woman. [O.T.: Genesis 1–5]

18. **Franklin, Aretha (1942–)** first black woman on cover of *Time* magazine (1968); first female inductee into Rock and Roll Hall of Fame (1987). [Am. Music: *SJEPC*]

19. **Gagarin, Yury (1934–1968)** first man in space (1961). [Russ. Hist.: Wallechinsky, 116]

20. **Genesis** first book of the Old Testament. [O.T.: Genesis]

21. **Gertie the Dinosaur** first substantial animated cartoon. (1909). [Am. Hist.: Van Doren, 362]

22. **GI Joe** first plastic action figure for boys, outfitted to resemble World War II combat soldier, debuted in 1964. [Am. Hist.: *SJEPC*]

23. **Gibson, Althea (1927–2003)** trailblazing African-American tennis champion won four grand slam tournaments in the 1950s; inducted into Tennis Hall of Fame in 1971. [Am. Sports: *SJEPC*]

24. **Great Exhibition, The** the first industrial exhibition, promoted by Prince Albert and held in Hyde Park in Crystal Palace. [Br. Hist.: Payton, 285]

25. *Great Train Robbery, The* considered the first "real" movie. [Am. Cinema: Griffith, 10]

26. **Greenberg, Hank (1911–1986)** first major Jewish baseball player (Detroit Tigers, 1933); first Jewish owner/general manager in baseball (1954); first Jewish player inducted into Baseball Hall of Fame (1956). [Am. Sports: *SJEPC*; Misc.]

27. **Gutenberg, Johannes (1397–1468)** German printer, inventor of movable type. (c. 1436). [Ger. Hist.: *NCE*, 1166]

28. **Harvard** the first American college (1636). [Am. Hist.: *NCE*, 1200]

29. *I Spy* espionage TV show of mid-1960s; young Bill Cosby starred in first show to feature black and whlte protagonists of equal importance. [Am. TV: *SJEPC*]

30. *In Living Color* TV show from 1990–1994; first sketch comedy show to feature majority African-American cast. [Am. TV: *SJEPC*]

31. *Jazz Singer, The* first talking film (1927) featured Al Jolson. [Am. Cinema: Halliwell, 213]

32. **Johnson, Jack (1878–1946)** first African-American to be crowned heavyweight boxing champion of the world (1908). [Am. Sports: *SJEPC*]

33. **La Navidad** first European settlement in New World (1492). [Am. Hist.: Van Doren, 2]

34. **LaLanne, Jack (1914–)** jumpsuit-wearing fitness guru whose daily TV exercise program ran from 1959 to 1985; opened first fitness club in America in 1936 and was considered fanatic for doing so; also invented first weight machines and produced first fitness video. [Am. Culture: *SJEPC*]

35. **Laver, Rod (1938–)** Australian-born tennis player who was first two-time winner (1962, 1969) of Grand Slam; considered by some to be best player ever. [Am. Sports: *SJEPC*]

36. **Lindbergh, Charles (1902–1974)** U.S. aviator; made the first solo, nonstop transatlantic flight (1927). [Am. Hist.: *NCE*, 1586]

37. *Little Women* 1868 autobiographical novel by Louisa May Alcott chronicles few months in the lives of Alcott and her three sisters; was first children's novel written in America that became classic. [Am. Children's Lit.: *OCCL*]

38. **Macy's** prototype of the department store. [Am. Hist.: Van Doren, 217–218]

39. **Marshall, Thurgood (1908–1993)** first African-American justice of the Supreme Court (1967). [Am. Law: *WB2*]

40. **Montgolfier brothers (Joseph, 1740–1810) (Jacques, 1745–1799)** first to make practical, manned balloon flight (1783). [Fr. Hist.: *NCE*, 1821]

41. **Obama, Barack (1961–)** first African-American president. [*BBPrez3*]

42. **Oberlin College** first college to admit African-Americans and to give women degrees. [Am. Hist.: Hart, 612]

43. **Robinson, Frank (1935–)** major league baseball's first African-American manager (Cleveland Indians, 1975). [Am. Sports: *SJEPC*]

44. **Robinson, Jackie (1919–1972)** first black player in Major League baseball (1947); taunts and abuse followed, but his briliant performance quelled objections. [Am. Sports: *NCE*, 2335]

45. **Rodriguez, Chi Chi (1935–)** first Hispanic to become international champion in golf. [Am. Sports: *SJEPC*]

46. **Rosenberg, Julius (1918–1953) and Ethel (1915–1953)** first Americans executed for allegedly giving information to Soviet agents. [Am. Hist.: *SJEPC*]

47. **Russell, Bill (1934–)** great defensive player for Boston Celtics known for being true team player; first African American to become head coach of an NBA team (Celtics, 1966). [Am. Sports: *SJEPC*]

48. *Sandman* first comic to win World Fantasy Award. [Am. Comics: *SJEPC*]

49. *Seventeen* begun in 1944, first magazine totally devoted to teen girls. [Am. Jour.: *SJEPC*]

50. **Shula, Don (1930–)** first coach in National Football League history to have undefeated season (1972–1973). [Am. Sports: *SJEPC*]

51. **Simon, Paul (1941–)** first recipient of The Library of Congress Gershwin Prize for Popular Song in 2007. [Am. Music: Misc.]

52. *Soul Train* in 1970, first mainstream American TV show to feature soul and rhythm and blues artists. [Am. TV: *SJEPC*]

53. **Spitz, Mark (1950–)** world-class swimmer who was first athlete to win seven gold medals in a single Olympics (1972). [Am. Sports: *SJEPC*]

54. **"Steamboat Willie"** 1928 animated Disney cartoon that launched Mickey Mouse's career was first animated film with sound. [Am. Film: Van Doren, 431]

55. **Thompson, John (1941–)** first African American to coach an NCAA championship basketball team (Georgetown University Hoyas, 1984). [Am. Sports: *SJEPC*]

56. *Time* first mass-circulation digest of news and commentary organized into departments; also, first publication to use "Mr." when describing both white and black subjects. [Am. Jour.: *SJEPC*]

57. **Tom Thumb** first American steam locomotive. [Am. Hist.: Van Doren, 141]

58. *Toy Story* first fully computer animated feature-length film; the 1995 collaboration between Disney and Pixar studios which tells the adventures of animated toys was huge box-office success. [Am. Film: *SJEPC*]

59. *Treasure Island* first adventure story for young readers (published in 1883); written by R.L. Stevenson; set in mid-eighteenth century, rousing tale of buried treasure and a young boy's adventures with the pirates who are seaching for the loot. [Scot. Children's Lit.: *OCCL*]

60. **Trevino, Lee (1939–)** first Mexican American to win a major professional golf championship with 1968 U.S. Open victory. [Am. Sports: *SJEPC*]

61. **Trout, Robert (1908–2000)** radio's first anchorman; beginning in 1938, he mastered the job of introducing reporters, reading reports, and ad-libbing. [Am. Radio: *SJEPC*]

62. *Uncle Remus* first collection of African-American fables, rewritten by Joel Chandler Harris and published in 1881; although stories are sometimes humorous, Harris declared serious intention of documenting legends to perserve them as part of Sourthern history. [Am. Folktales: *OCCL*]

63. **Virginia** first of the Thirteen Colonies. [Am. Hist.: *NCE*, 289]

64. *Vogue* the first illustrated fashion magazine (1909); soon became legendary as the magazine for women wanting information on style, influential people, and cultural trends. [Fr. and Am. Jour.: *SJEPC*]

65. **Walker, Madame C. J. (1867–1919)** first African-American female millionaire; her formula to prevent hair loss led to line of hair care products marketed to African Americans; known as the "Walker System," it was said to effectively soften coarse hair. [Am. Business: *SJEPC*]

66. **Walters, Barbara (1931–)** TV journalist became the first female to anchor the evening news when she worked with Harry Reasoner in 1976; co-hosted *20/20* and moved into career as insightful interviewer; however, has been criticized at times for blending news and entertainment [Am. Jour.: *SJEPC*]

67. **Washington, George (1732–1799)** first United States president. [Am. Hist.: *NCE*, 3012]

68. **White Castle** three burger shops in 1921, when the name was coined; by 1931, 115 shops; first fast-food chain in the world, leading the way for countless others. [Am. Cuisine: *SJEPC*]

69. **Wonder Woman** first female comic book superhero (1941); strong and agile, but somewhat less violent than her male counterparts; her goal to reform the enemies she pursued. [Am. Comics: *SJEPC*]

70. **Woods, Tiger (1975–)** first person of color and youngest person to win the Masters (1997, at age 21); amazingly talented golf pro with racially diverse background has spurred interest in the sport among minorities. [Am. Sports: *SJEPC*]

71. *World News Roundup, The* began in 1938 during growing tension in pre-WWII Europe; first show to bring voices of correspondents stationed around the world together for live broadcast; longest-running news broadcast in history. [Am. Radio: Misc.]

72. **Wright Brothers (Wilbur, 1867–1912) (Orville, 1871–1948)** made the first controlled, sustained flight in a power-driven airplane (1903). [Am. Hist.: Misc.]

290. FLATTERY

1. **Adams, Jack** toady to his employer. [Br. Lit.: *Dombey and Son*]

2. **Amaziah** fawningly complains of Amos to King Jeroboam. [O.T.: Amos 7:10]

3. **bolton** one who flatters by pretending humility. [Br. Hist.: Espy, 343]

4. **Chanticleer** cajoled by fox into singing; thus captured. [Br. Lit.: *Canterbury Tales*, "Nun's Priest's Tale"]

5. **Clumsy, Sir Tunbelly** toadies towards aristocracy. [Br. Lit.: *The Relapse*, Walsh *Modern*, 102]

6. **Collins, Mr.** priggish, servile clergyman; toady to the great. [Br. Lit.: *Pride and Prejudice*]

7. **Damocles** for his sycophancy to Dionysus, seated under sword at banquet. [Gk. Myth.: *LLEI*, I: 278]

8. **Mutual Admiration Society** circle of mutual patters on the backs. [Br. Hist.: Wheeler, 254]

9. **Oreo** a cookie that is black on the outside, white on the inside; pejoratively refers to obsequious black person bent on pleasing whites. [Am. Culture: Flexner, 49]

10. **Ruach** island of people sustained by insincere praise. [Fr. Lit.: *Pantagruel*]

11. **Uncle Tom** Stowe character came to signify subservient Black. [Am. Lit.: *Uncle Tom's Cabin*]

12. **Wren, Jenny** wooed by Robin Redbreast with enticing presents. [Nurs. Rhyme: *Mother Goose*, 23]

291. FLIGHT, IMAGINARY

1. **Chitty Chitty Bang Bang** magical flying car in 1960s series of stories for children by Ian Fleming. [Br. Children's Lit.: *OCCL*]

2. **Daedalus** father of Icarus, escaped Minos by creating wings of wax and feathers. [Gk. Myth.: Bullfinch]

3. **Dolor** possesses magic cloak which permits flight. [Children's Lit.: *The Little Lame Prince*]

4. **Dumbo** little elephant's huge ears take him up and away. [Am. Cinema: *Dumbo* in *Disney Films*, 49–53]

5. **Houssain** rode upon magic carpet that could fly. [Arab. Lit.: *Arabian Nights*, "Ahmed and Paribanou"]

6. **Icarus** Daedalus's son whose wings disintegrated in flight when approaching the sun. [Gk. Myth.: Kravitz, 126]

7. **Pegasus** winged horse. [Class. Myth.: Zimmerman, 195]

8. **Peter Pan** teaches the Darling children to fly to Neverland in J.M. Barrie's classic play *Peter Pan; or, The Boy Who Wouldn't Grow Up* (1904). [Scot. Children's Lit.: Jones]

9. **Phaëthon** ill-fated driver of the chariot of sun. [Gk. Myth.: *Metamorphoses*]

10. **Seagull, Jonathan Livingston** seagull spends its time elaborating flying techniques. [Am. Lit.: Richard Bach *Jonathan Livingston Seagull*]

11. **Sindbad** a roc flies him to the Valley of Diamonds, and an eagle flies him to its nest. [Arab. Lit.: *Arabian Nights*]

12. **winged ram** bearer of the golden fleece, sent by Zeus to save the life of Phryxus, who crossed the sea on its back. [Gk. Myth.: Brewer *Dictionary*, 405]

292. FLIRTATION (See also SEDUCTION.)

1. **Boop, Betty** comic strip character who flirts to win over boys. [Comics: Horn, 110]

2. **can-can** boisterous and indecorous French dance designed to arouse audiences. [Fr. Hist.: Scholes, 151]

3. **Célimène** unabashed coquette wooed by Alceste. [Fr. Lit.: *The Misanthrope*]

4. **Columbine** light-hearted, flirtatious girl. [Ital. Lit.: Walsh *Classical*, 83]

5. **dandelion** traditional symbol of flirtation. [Flower Symbolism: Jobes, 413]

6. **daylily** traditional symbol of flirtation. [Flower Symbolism: *Flora Symbolica*, 175]

7. **fan** symbol of coquetry. [Folklore: Jobes, 370]

8. **Frasquita** woman character chiefly remembered for her flirtatiousness toward old Don Eugenio. [Ger. Opera: Wolf, *The Magistrate*, Westerman, 262]

9. **Habanera** Carmen's "love is a wild bird" provokes hearers. [Fr. Opera: Bizet, *Carmen*, Westerman, 189–190]

10. **Jimènez, Pepita** young widow coquettishly distracts seminarian; love unfolds. [Span. Lit.: *Pepita Jimènez*]

11. **Miss Julie** young gentlewoman high-handedly engages servant's love. [Swed. Lit.: *Miss Julie* in *Plays by August Strindberg*]

12. **Musetta** leads on Alcindoro while pursuing Marcello. [Ital. Opera: Puccini, *La Bohème*, Westerman, 349]

13. **O'Hara, Scarlett** hot-tempered heroine-coquette who wooed Southern Gentlemen. [Am. Lit.: *Gone With The Wind*]

14. **Varden, Dolly** Watteau-style colorful costume; broad-brimmed hat and dress with deep cleavage; honors Dickens character. [Br. Costume: Misc.; Br. Lit.: *Barnaby Rudge*, Espy, 272]

15. **West, Mae (1893–1980)** her suggestive dialogue, vampy acting style, and voluptuous figure made her a legend; many of her quips have become famous. [Am. Film: Halliwell, 759]

293. FLOWER

1. **Anthea** epithet of Hera, meaning "flowery." [Gk. Myth.: Zimmerman, 121]

2. **Anthesteria** ancient Athenian festival, celebrating flowers and new wine. [Gk. Hist.: Misc.]

3. *Black Tulip, The* Dumas romance involved with tulipomania of 17th-century Holland. [Fr. Lit.: Benét, 111]

4. **Chloris** goddess of flowers. [Gk. Myth.: Kravitz, 59]

5. **O'Keefe, Georgia (1887–1986)** American painter, noted for her sensuous flowers. [Am. Art: *FOF, MOD*]

6. **Tournament of Roses** New Year's Day flower festival and parade in Pasadena. [Am. Cult.: *WB*, C:45]

7. **Zephyr and Flora** wedded pair, scatter flowers from cornucopia. [Rom. Myth.: Hall, 125]

294. FLOWER or PLANT, NATIONAL (See also FLOWER, STATE.)

1. **almond blossom** of Israel. [Flower Symbolism: *WB*, 7: 264]

2. **blue anemone** of Norway. [Flower Symbolism: *WB*, 7: 264]

3. **blue cornflower** of West Germany. [Flower Symbolism: *WB*, 7: 264]

4. **cantua** of Bolivia. [Flower Symbolism: *WB*, 7: 264]
5. **carnation** of Egypt. [Flower Symbolism: *WB*, 7: 264]
6. **cattleya** of Brazil. [Flower Symbolism: *WB*, 7: 264]
7. **ceibo** of Argentina. [Flower Symbolism: *WB*, 7: 264]
8. **chrysanthemum** of Japan. [Flower Symbolism: *WB*, 7: 264]
9. **cinchona** of Ecuador. [Flower Symbolism: *WB*, 7: 264]
10. **dahlia** of Mexico. [Flower Symbolism: *WB*, 7: 264]
11. **edelweiss** of Switzerland. [Flower Symbolism: Jobes, 490]
12. **fern** of New Zealand. [Flower Symbolism: *WB*, 7: 264]
13. **flame lily** of Rhodesia. [Flower Symbolism: *WB*, 7: 264]
14. **fleur-de-lis** of France. [Flower Symbolism: Halberts, 28]
15. **frangipani** of Laos. [Flower Symbolism: *WB*, 7: 264]
16. **golden wattle** of Australia. [Flower Symbolism: *WB*, 7: 264]
17. **hibiscus** of Malaysia. [Flower Symbolism: *WB*, 7: 264]
18. **jasmine (also rose)** of Indonesia. [Flower Symbolism: *WB*, 7: 264]
19. **leek** of Wales. [Flower Symbolism: Brewer *Note-Book*, 334]
20. **lily** of then city-state Florence. [Flower Symbolism: Brewer *Note-Book*, 334]
21. **lily of the valley** of Finland. [Flower Symbolism: *WB*, 7: 264]
22. **linden** of former Prussia. [Flower Symbolism: Brewer *Note-Book*, 334]
23. **lotus** of India. [Flower Symbolism: *WB*, 7: 264]
24. **maple leaf** of Canada. [Flower Symbolism: Jobes, 283]
25. **mignonette** of the former Saxony. [Flower Symbolism: Brewer *Note-Book*, 334]
26. **orchid** of Venezuela. [Flower Symbolism: *WB*, 7: 264]
27. **poppy** of Greece. [Flower Symbolism: *WB*, 7: 264]
28. **protea** of South Africa. [Flower Symbolism: *WB*, 7: 264]
29. **red rose** of England. [Flower Symbolism: Brewer *Note-Book*, 334]
30. **rhododendron** of Nepal. [Flower Symbolism: *WB*, 7: 264]
31. **rose** of Honduras. [Flower Symbolism: *WB*, 7: 264]
32. **sampaguita** of Philippines. [Flower Symbolism: *WB*, 7: 264]
33. **shamrock** of Ireland. [Flower Symbolism: Brewer *Note-Book*, 334]
34. **thistle** of Scotland. [Flower Symbolism: Halberts, 38]
35. **tulip** of Netherlands. [Flower Symbolism: *WB*, 7: 264]
36. **violet** of then-state Athens. [Flower Symbolism: Brewer *Note-Book*, 334]
37. **white orchid** of Guatemala. [Flower Symbolism: *WB*, 7: 264]

295. FLOWER, STATE (See also FLOWER or PLANT, NATIONAL.)

1. **American pasque flower** of South Dakota. [Flower Symbolism: Golenpaul, 642]

2. **apple blossom** of Arkansas and Michigan. [Flower Symbolism: Golenpaul, 626]

3. **bitterroot** of Montana. [Flower Symbolism: Golenpaul, 636]

4. **black-eyed susan** of Maryland. [Flower Symbolism: Golenpaul, 633]

5. **bluebonnet** of Texas. [Flower Symbolism: Golenpaul, 643]

6. **camellia** of Alabama. [Flower Symbolism: Golenpaul, 625]

7. **Carolina yellow jessamine** of South Carolina. [Flower Symbolism: Golenpaul, 642]

8. **Cherokee rose** of Georgia. [Flower Symbolism: Golenpaul, 629]

9. **dogwood** of North Carolina and Virginia. [Flower Symbolism: Golenpaul, 639]

10. **flower of saguaro cactus** of Arizona. [Flower Symbolism: Golenpaul, 626]

11. **forget-me-not** of Alaska. [Flower Symbolism: Golenpaul, 625]

12. **golden poppy** of California. [Flower Symbolism: Golenpaul, 627]

13. **goldenrod** of Kentucky and Nevada. [Flower Symbolism: Golenpaul, 632]

14. **hawthorn** of Missouri. [Flower Symbolism: Golenpaul, 635]

15. **hibiscus** of Hawaii. [Flower Symbolism: Golenpaul, 629]

16. **Indian paintbrush** of Wyoming. [Flower Symbolism: Golenpaul, 646]

17. **iris** of Tennessee. [Flower Symbolism: Golenpaul, 642]

18. **magnolia** of Louisiana and Mississippi. [Flower Symbolism: Golenpaul, 632]

19. **mayflower** of Massachusetts. [Flower Symbolism: Golenpaul, 633]

20. **mistletoe** of Oklahoma. [Flower Symbolism: Golenpaul, 640]

21. **mountain laurel** of Connecticut and Pennsylvania. [Flower Symbolism: Golenpaul, 628]

22. **orange blossom** of Florida. [Flower Symbolism: Golenpaul, 628]

23. **Oregon grape** of Oregon. [Flower Symbolism: Golenpaul, 640]

24. **peach blossom** of Delaware. [Flower Symbolism: Golenpaul, 628]

25. **peony** of Indiana. [Flower Symbolism: Golenpaul, 631]

26. **purple lilac** of New Hampshire. [Flower Symbolism: Golenpaul, 637]

27. **red clover** of Vermont. [Flower Symbolism: Golenpaul, 644]

28. **rhododendron** of Washington and West Virginia. [Flower Symbolism: Golenpaul, 627]

29. **Rocky Mountain columbine** of Colorado. [Flower Symbolism: Golenpaul, 627]

30. **rose** of New York. [Flower Symbolism: Golenpaul, 638]

31. **sagebrush** of Nevada. [Flower Symbolism: Golenpaul, 636]

32. **scarlet carnation** of Ohio. [Flower Symbolism: Golenpaul, 639]

33. **sego lily** of Utah. [Flower Symbolism: Golenpaul, 643]

34. **showy lady slipper** of Minnesota. [Flower Symbolism: Golenpaul, 634]

35. **sunflower** of Kansas. [Flower Symbolism: Golenpaul, 631]

36. **syringa** of Idaho. [Flower Symbolism: Golenpaul, 630]

37. **violet** of Illinois, New Jersey, Rhode Island, and Wisconsin. [Flower Symbolism: Golenpaul, 630]

38. **white pine cone and tassel** of Maine. [Flower Symbolism: Golenpaul, 633]

39. **wild prairie rose** of North Dakota. [Flower Symbolism: Golenpaul, 639]

40. **wild rose** of Iowa. [Flower Symbolism: Golenpaul, 631]

41. **yucca** of New Mexico. [Flower Symbolism: Golenpaul, 638]

296. FOLLY

1. **Abu Jahl** "father of folly"; opposes Mohammed. [Muslim Tradition: Koran 22:8]

2. **Alnaschar's daydream** spends profits before selling his goods. [Arab. Lit.: *Arabian Nights*, "The Barber's Fifth Night"]

3. *Bateau, Le* Matisse's famous painting, displayed in the Museum of Modern Art for 47 days before someone discovered it was being shown upside down. [Am. Hist.: Wallechinsky, 472]

4. **Bay of Pigs, the** disastrous U.S.-backed invasion of Cuba (1961). [Am. Hist.: Van Doren, 577]

5. **Chamberlain, Arthur Nevil** British Prime Minister attempted to avert war by policy of appeasement. [Eur. Hist.: *Collier's*, IV, 552]

6. **columbine** traditional symbol of folly. [Plant Symbolism: *Flora Symbolica*]

7. **dog returning to his vomit** and so the fool to his foolishness. [O.T.: Proverbs 26:11]

8. **Fulton's Folly** the first profitable steamship, originally considered a failure. [Am. Hist.: *NCE*, 1025]

9. **Gotham** English village proverbially noted for the folly (sometimes wisely deliberate) of its residents. [Eng. Folklore: Brewer *Dictionary*, 410]

10. **Grand, Joseph** spends years writing novel; only finishes first sentence. [Fr. Lit.: *The Plague*]

11. **Hamburger Hill** bloody Viet Nam battle over strategically worthless ojective (1969). [Am. Hist.: Van Doren, 631]

12. **Howard Hotel** after completing construction, the contractors installed boilers and started fires before discovering they had forgotten to build a chimney. [Am. Hist.: Wallechinsky, 470]

13. **Laputa and Lagada** lands where wise men conduct themselves inanely. [Br. Lit.: *Gulliver's Travels*]

14. **monkey** its skill at mimicry make it symbol of human vanity and folly. [Symbolism: *CEOS&S*]

15. **Seward's Folly** Alaska, once seemingly valueless territory which William Henry Seward bought for only two cents an acre (1867), two years before the Klondike gold rush. [Am. Hist.: Payton, 610]

297. FOOD and DRINK

1. **Child, Julia (1912–2004)** American Cordon Bleu graduate introduced French cooking to the States in early 1960s and transformed American culinary culture. [Fr. and Am. Cuisine: *SJEPC*]

2. **Coca-Cola** spicy, reddish-brown-colored soft drink created by Georgia pharmacist in 1886 became popular worldwide. [Am. Business and Culture: *SJEPC*]

3. **cocktail parties** social gatheings featuring mixed alcoholic beverages and snacks became popular in 1950s suburban America. [Am. Culture: *SJEPC*]

4. **Coors** brewery established by German immigrant Adolph Coors in 1870s in Golden, Colorado; "pure Rocky Mountain spring water" touted as special ingredient in its beer. [Am. Business: *SJEPC*]

5. **diners** restaurants with long counters and booths originating in the 1930s served inexpensive, simple food and beverages such as meatloaf, mashed potatoes, hamburgers, pie, and soda fountain drinks. [Am. Cuisine: *SJEPC*; Misc.]

6. **Dunkin' Donuts** unpretentious coffee and doughnut shop with pink and orange sign founded in 1950 has expanded menu and locations, becoming large international chain. [Am. Cuisine: *SJEPC*]

7. **fast food** increased pace of American life created desire for convenient, quickly prepared, standardized foods that could be eaten on the go, such as the hamburgers and fries at ubiquitous franchises like White Castle and McDonald's. [Am. Cuisine: *SJEPC*]

8. **Foreman, George (1949–)** former heavyweight boxing champion with sparkly personality now a spokesman for his popular

George Foreman series of indoor and outdoor food grills. [Am. Cuisine: *SJEPC*; Misc.]

9. **French fries** crispy deep-fried, salted potato strips are fast food staple, an accompaniment to hamburgers and other sandwiches; a symbol of bad nutrition. [Cuisine: *SJEPC*]

10. **grits** regional breakfast food of the South made from ground corn can be served warm or cold, with milk and sugar or gravy and meat. [Am. Cuisine: *SJEPC*]

11. **Jell-O** ubiquitous inexpensive dessert of flavored, colored gelatin found everywhere from diners to school cafeterias, hospitals to potluck dinners; produced in 1902, making it one of first convenience foods. [Am. Cuisine: *SJEPC*]

12. *Joy of Cooking, The* 1931 best-selling cookbook; considered the bible of American culinary arts; offers simple, straightforward instructions for preparing meals in a way that defied common belief that cooking was drudgery. [Am. Cuisine: *SJEPC*]

13. **Kentucky Fried Chicken** later named KFC; mid-1950s chain of fast-food fried chicken franchises opened by "Colonel" Harland Sanders, whose likeness was used to promote the down-home, "finger lickin' good" food. [Am. Business: *SJEPC*]

14. **Starbucks** with origins in Seattle in 1971, by 1980s had broadened to European-style coffeehouse as meeting place; successful expansion worldwide. [Am. Business: *SJEPC*]

15. **Stuckey's** chain of turquoise-roofed buildings that housed restaurant, gas station, and souvenir store in the 1950s and 1960s; famous for their Pecan Log Rolls candy. [Am. Pop. Culture: *SJEPC*]

16. **Tang** vitamin-fortified orange drink powder chosen in 1960s by NASA to be drink of the astronauts; led to popularity among children. [Am. Cuisine: *SJEPC*]

17. **Trillin, Calvin (1935–)** many pieces written for the *New Yorker* focused on his love of food. [Am. Jour.: *SJEPC*]

18. **TV dinners** frozen dinners introduced by Swanson gained acceptance as pace of life accelerated, selling 70 million the first year (1955); aluminum trays holding meat, starch, vegetable, and dessert were often eaten while watching TV. [Am. Cuisine: *SJEPC*]

19. **White Castle** three burger shops in 1921, when the name was coined; by 1931, 115 shops; first fast-food chain in the world, leading the way for countless others. [Am. Cuisine: *SJEPC*]

Foolishness (See DIMWITTEDNESS, STUPIDITY.)

Fools (See CLOWNS.)

298. FOOTBALL

1. **Bradshaw, Terry (1948–)** quarterback Hall of Famer became NFL broadcaster. [Am. Sports: *SJEPC*]

2. **Brown, Jim (1936–)** spectacular running back played nine seasons with Cleveland Browns (1957–65), earned MVP title three times, and retired from football at his prime in 1965. [Am. Sports: *SJEPC*]

3. **Butkus, Dick (1942–)** intensely fierce, rough-and-tough linebacker for the Chicago Bears respected on and off the field; became football analyst and actor after retiring as player in 1973. [Am. Sports: *SJEPC*]

4. **Cosell, Howard (1918–1995)** witty, nasal-voiced sportscaster helped launch innovative prime-time show *Monday Night Football* in 1970. [Am. Sports and TV: *SJEPC*]

5. **Dallas Cowboys** consistently successful football franchise dubbed "America's Team"; five-time Super Bowl champs. [Am. Sports: *SJEPC*]

6. **Dallas Cowboys Cheerleaders** sexy cheerleading squad for America's Team has provided high-energy halftime entertainment since the mid-1970s. [Am. Sports: *SJEPC*]

7. **Ditka, Mike (1939–)** "Iron" Mike played tight end for professional teams (1961–72), then turned to coaching the Chicago Bears and New Orleans Saints; won Super Bowl championships as both player and coach. [Am. Sports: *SJEPC*]

8. **Elway, John (1960–)** Hall of Fame quarterback for the Denver Broncos led his team to five Super Bowls, winning the last two (1998, 1999) before retiring from a 16–year professional career. [Am. Sports: *SJEPC*]

9. **Halas, George (1895–1983)** founder, owner, and coach of the Chicago Bears, pioneer of the game, helped found the NFL, developed the offensive "T-Formation," still in use today. [Am. Sports: *EB*]

10. **Landry, Tom (1924–2000)** tremendously successful coach of Dallas Cowboys from 1960–1988, ranking third in wins for coaches in history of NFL; elected to Professional Football Hall of Fame in 1990. [Am. Sports: *SJEPC*]

11. *Monday Night Football* weekly prime-time telecast covered the game with technical dazzle and amusing commentary. [Am. TV: *SJEPC*]

12. **Montana, Joe (1956–)** among the best quarterbacks in National Football League history. [Am. Sports: *SJEPC*]

13. **Naismith, Dr. James (1861–1939)** credited with inventing the football helmet. [Am. Sports: *SJEPC*]

14. **Namath, Joe (1943–)** nicknamed "Broadway Joe"; fearless quarterback famous for his off-the-field antics. [Am. Sports: *SJEPC*]

15. **NFL (National Football League)** successful association of football teams formed in 1922. [Am. Sports: *SJEPC*]

16. **Payton, Walter (1954–1998)** great running back for Chicago Bears; sweet-tempered and altruistic, known for charitable work with Chicago inner-city youth. [Am. Sports: *SJEPC*]

17. **Rice, Jerry (1962–)** considered among the best wide-receivers in NFL history; most of career with the San Francisco 49ers. [Am. Sports: *SJECP*]

18. **Rockne, Knute (1888–1931)** innovative and spirited coach for Notre Dame; legendary for telling his team to "win one for the Gipper," repeating the dying words of star player George Gipp. [Am. Sports: *SJEPC*]

19. **Rose Bowl** considered college football's preeminent post-season game; held on New Year's Day in Pasadena, California, preceded by Tournament of Roses Parade. [Am. Sports: *SJEPC*]

20. **Sanders, Barry (1968–)** humble, gifted running back; averaged more than 100 rushing yards in every game he played. [Am. Sports: *SJEPC*]

21. **Shula, Don (1930–)** unprecedented number of wins; first coach in NFL history to have undefeated season (1972–1973). [Am. Sports: *SJEPC*]

22. **Simpson, O. J. (1947–)** top-notch running back and Heisman trophy winner in the late 1960s and 1970s; defendant in 1994 murder trial of his ex-wife; found not guilty. [Am. Sports: *SJPEC*]

23. **Stagg, Amos Alonzo (1862–1965)** coached college football for 57 years; innovator who organized the first scrimmage games, invented the tackling dummy, and added numbers to his players' jerseys; helped turn collegiate sport into a moneymaking industry. [Am. Sports: *SJEPC*]

24. **Starr, Bart (1934–)** retired from Green Bay Packers as winningest quarterback in professional football history. [Am. Sports: *SJEPC*]

25. **Staubach, Roger (1942–)** Heisman trophy-winning quarterback played eleven stellar years for Dallas Cowboys. [Am. Sports: *SJEPC*]

26. **Super Bowl** hundreds of millions of viewers in nearly 200 countries watch the televised game between the top teams; costly but lucrative advertising and promotions have become a central aspect of the game as well as revenue brought into the host city. [Am. Sports: *SJEPC*]

27. **Swann, Lynn (1952–)** wide receiver who excelled in making acrobatic, crucial catches. [Am. Sports: *SJEPC*]

28. **Thorpe, Jim (1888–1953)** gold medal winner of both pentathlon and decathlon in 1912 Olympics; medals later confiscated because of brief professional baseball career; went on to play professional baseball and football with great skill, winning numerous awards, many posthumously. [Am. Sports: *SJEPC*]

29. **Unitas, Johnny (1933–2002)** Baltimore Colts quarterback from 1956–1972; one of the premier, record-breaking quarterbacks of all times; called "The Golden Arm." [Am. Sports: *SJEPC*]

299. FOP

1. **Acres, Bob** affected, vain, cowardly, blustery country gentleman. [Br. Lit.: *The Rivals*]

2. **Aguecheek, Sir Andrew** silly old fop, believes himself young. [Br. Lit.: *Twelfth Night*]

3. **Blakeney, Percy** rescuer of French revolution victims disguises himself as a brainless fop. [Br. Lit.: *Scarlet Pimpernel*]

4. **Brummel, Beau (George B. Brummel, 1778–1840)** "prince of dandies." [Br. Hist.: *Century Cyclopedia*, 682]

5. **Flutter, Sir Fopling** witless dandy. [Br. Lit.: *The Man of Mode*]

6. **Foppington, Lord** a selfish coxcomb, most intent upon dress and fashion. [Br. Hist.: Brewer *Handbook*, 381]

7. **Malyneaux** epitome of the British dandy. [Am. Lit.: *Monsieur Beaucaire*, Magill I, 616–617]

8. **Yankee Doodle Dandy** feather-capped dandy; "handy" with the girls. [Nurs. Rhyme: Opie, 439]

300. FORGERY (See also FRAUDULENCE.)

1. **Acta Pilati (Acts of Pilate)** apocryphal account of Crucifixion. [Rom. Hist.: Brewer *Note-Book*, 7]

2. **Altamont, Col. Jack** convicted of forgery; banished; escapes. [Br. Lit.: *Pendennis*]

3. **Caloveglia, Count** creates a bronze statue of a Greek faun and sells it as an authentic antique. [Br. Lit.: *South Wind* in Magill II, 988]

4. **Chatterton** boy poet produced poems allegedly by 15th-century monk. [Br. Hist.: Brewer *Note-Book*, 164]

5. **Constitutum Constantini** so-called Donation of Constantine, a document in which Constantine gave Rome authority over his capital at least a decade before his capital was founded. [Rom. Hist.: Wallechinsky, 45]

6. **Mr. X** by definition, the identity of the greatest forger of all time. [Pop. Culture: Wallechinsky, 47]

7. ***Protocols of the Elders of Zion*** tract purporting to reveal a Jewish conspiracy to control the world. [Jew. Hist.: Wigoder, 170]

8. **Raspigliosi cup** masterpiece attributed to Cellini, discovered in 1984 to have been forged by Reinhold Vasters, 19th-century goldsmith. [Ital. Art: *N. Y. Times*, Feb. 12, 1984]

9. **Rowley poems** the work of Thomas Chatterton (1752–1770), who said they were written by a 15th-century priest. [Br. Hist.: Brewer *Dictionary*, 371]

10. **Vermeer** successful fakes of his paintings went undetected for many years. [Dutch Hist.: Brewer *Dictionary*, 371]

301. FORGETFULNESS (See also CARELESSNESS.)

1. **"Absent-Minded Beggar, The"** ballad of forgetful soldiers who fought in the Boer War. [Br. Lit.: "The Absent-Minded Beggar" in Payton, 3]

2. **absent-minded professor** personification of one too contemplative to execute practical tasks. [Pop. Culture: Misc.]

3. **jujube** causes loss of memory and desire to return home. [Classical Myth.: Leach, 561–562]

4. **Lethe** river of Hades which induced forgetfulness. [Gk. Myth.: Brewer *Dictionary*, 687; Br. Lit.: *Paradist Lost*; Rom. Lit.: *Aeneid*]

5. **limbo** place or condition of neglect and inattention (from Dante). [Western Folklore: Espy, 124]

6. **Lotophagi** African people, eaters of amnesia-inducing fruit. [Gk. Lit.: *Odyssey*; Br. Lit.: *The Lotus-Eaters* in Norton, 733–736]

7. **lotus-eaters** when Odysseus's men eat lotus fruit with the lotus-eaters, they are lulled into forgetfulness and no longer wish for home. [Gk. Myth: *Odyssey*]

8. **Madison, Percival Wemys** character who no longer remembers his name. [Br. Lit.: *Lord of the Flies*]

9. **soma** drug that induces forgetfulness. [Br. Lit.: *Brave New World*]

10. **Van Winkle, Rip** awakening from 20 years' of sleep, forgets how things have changed. [Am. Lit.: *Sketch Book*, Payton, 574]

302. FORGIVENESS

1. **Angelica, Suor** is forgiven by Virgin Mary for ill-considered suicide. [Ital. Opera: Puccini, *Suor Angelica*, Westerman, 364]

2. **Bishop of Digne** character who forgives Jean Valjean when latter steals the bishop's valuables. [Fr. Lit.: *Les Misèrables*]

3. **Christ** forgives man for his sins. [Christianity: Misc.]

4. **fatted calf** killed to celebrate return of prodigal son. [N.T.: Luke 15:23]

5. **Matthias** of his brother, for twenty years' false imprisonment. [Ger. Opera: Kienzl, *The Evangelist*, Westerman, 264]

6. **Melibee** shepherd who pardons his enemies. [Br. Lit.: *Canterbury Tales*, "Tale of Melibee"]

7. **Muhammad (c.570–632)** the Key of Mercy (Miftah ar-Rahmah); another name for the Islamic prophet. [Islam: *UIMT*, 180]

8. **Myriel, Bishop** saintly cleric befriends Jean Valjean after the latter steals his candlesticks. [Fr. Lit.: Victor Hugo *Les Misèrables*]

9. **Porgy** of Bess's promiscuity with Crown. [Am. Opera: Gershwin, *Porgy and Bess*, Westerman 555]

10. **prodigal son** received with open arms by loving father. [N.T.: Luke 15:20–21]

11. **Tannhäuser** unexpectedly absolved by the Pope for sinning in the Venusberg. [Ger. Myth.: Brewer *Dictionary*, 932]

12. **Timberlane, Cass** receives Jinny after her extramarital venture. [Am. Lit.: *Cass Timberlane*]

13. **Titus** Roman emperor pardons those attempting his destruction. [Ger. Opera: Mozart, *La Clemenza di Tito*, Westerman, 100–101]

303. FORTITUDE (See also BRAVERY.)

1. **Asia** despite torture, refuses to deny Moses. [Islam: Walsh *Classical*, 35]

2. **Brinker, Hans** character from Mary Mapes Dodge's story for children set in Holland, *Hans Brinker; or, The Silver Skates* (1865); hardworking boy who shows the rewards of fortitude. [Am. Children's Lit.: Jones]

3. **Calantha** fulfills wifely and queenly duties despite losses. [Br. Lit.: *The Broken Heart*]

4. **Corey, Giles** martyred without flinching. [Am. Lit.: *New England Tragedies*, Walsh *Modern*, 106]

5. **helmeted warrior** representation in painting of cardinal virtue. [Art.: Hall, 127]

6. **lion** personification of intrepidity. [Animal Symbolism: Hall, 193]

7. **Valley Forge** proving ground of American mettle. [Am. Hist.: Jameson, 519]

304. FOURTH OF JULY

1. **American flag** omnipresent on the day celebrating America's freedom; 13 red and white stripes represent original 13 colonies that fought for independence from Britain; five-point white stars represent each state in the union, on field of blue. [Am. Hist.: Thompson, 169]

2. **bald eagle** national bird of the United States whose image appears on U.S. currency, stamps, the Great Seal; decorates banners and floats during Fourth of July celebrations. [Am. Hist.: Thompson, 170]

3. **Declaration of Independence** document declaring the independence of the North American colonies approved by the Continental Congress on July 4, 1776. [Am. Hist.: Payton, 186; Thompson, 167]

4. **fireworks** elaborate displays are a favorite way of celebrating Independence Day all over the country, whether staged by experts in public parks or by amateurs in private backyards. [Am. Hist.: Thompson, 170–71]

5. **Liberty Bell** symbol of American freedom; at Independence Hall, Philadelphia. [Am. Hist.: Jameson, 284]

6. **parades** held in almost every city and town to celebrate Independence Day; typically include marching bands, military veterans, members of local organizations and government, and fife and drum corps, along with patriotically decorated floats and cars. [Am. Hist.: Thompson, 172]

7. **picnics** mid-nineteenth century, feasting outdoors became a traditional way to commemorate the Fourth of July; favorite foods include fried chicken and potato salad, and games include softball, races, and watermelon-eating contests. [Am. Hist.: Thompson, 172–73]

8. **Red, White, and Blue** colors of American flag are prominently displayed in July 4 celebrations; symbolically, colors stand for courage, liberty, and loyalty. [Am. Hist.: Thompson, 169]

9. **"Yankee Doodle"** unofficial anthem of the United States traditionally played by fife and drum corps in Fourth of July parades; sung at first Independence Day celebration in Philadelphia in 1777. [Am. Hist.: Thompson, 174–75]

Fratricide (See MURDER.)

305. FRAUDULENCE (See also DECEIT, FORGERY, HOAX.)

1. **Barnum, P. T. (1810–1891)** circus owner whose sideshows were sometimes fraudulent; wrote *Humbugs of the World*. [Am. Hist.: NCE, 234]

2. **Cagliostro** lecherous peasant posing as count. [Ital. Hist.: Espy, 335]

3. **The Confidence Man** an imposter gulls passengers on a Mississippi steamboat. [Am. Lit.: Melville *The Confidence Man* in Magill III, 221]

4. **Duke and the King, the** a pair of charlatans exposed by Huckleberry Finn. [Am. Lit.: *Huckleberry Finn*]

5. **Face** cunning butler, sets up scam in master's absence. [Br. Lit.: *The Alchemist*]

6. **Gantry, Elmer** personifies hypocrisy and corruption in America's religious practices. [Am. Lit.: *Elmer Gantry*]

7. *Inspector General, The* pretending to be a governmental inspector, Khlestakov takes bribes and woos the mayor's wife and daughter. [Russ. Lit.: *The Inspector General*]

8. **Krull, Felix** lives a double life, passing himself off under various identities. [Ger. Lit.: Mann *The Confessions of Felix Krull* in Magill III, 218]

9. *Medium, The* Menotti opera about a fraudulent medium haunted by her own hoax. [Am. Opera: Benét, 653]

10. **Milli Vanilli** attractive pop duo lip-synched to music of a studio band, conning audiences and Grammy judges alike. [Am. Music: *SJECP*]

11. **Mississippi Bubble, the** land speculation scam; ultimately backfired on creators. [Am. Hist.: Jameson, 326]

12. **Pathelin, Master** small-town lawyer cheats his draper, who cheats a shepherd, who hires Pathelin and then cheats him out of his fee. [Fr. Drama: Haydn & Fuller, 466]

13. **Peters, Jeff** made a career out of schemes for bamboozling the public. [Am. Lit.: O. Henry "The Gentle Grafter"]

14. **Sabbatai, Zevi** false messiah, head of Kabbalic movement in mid-1600s. [Jew. Hist.: Wigoder, 544]

15. **Schicchi, Gianni** effects a fraudulent will on the pretense that he is the testator. [Ital. Hist. and Opera: *Gianni Schicchi* in *Collier's*]

16. **Sludge, Mr.** medium pretends to greater powers and deceives many people. [Br.Lit.: Browning *Dramatis Personae* in Magill IV, 250]

17. **Subtle** charlatan, posing as alchemist, bilks hapless victims. [Br. Lit.: *The Alchemist*]

18. **Tchitchikov** attempts to make a fortune by buying up landlords' titles to dead serfs in order to mortgage them for capital. [Russ. Lit.: Gogol *Dead Souls*]

19. **Tichborne case** false claimant to the Tichborne baronetcy sentenced to fourteen years' imprisonment. [Br. Hist.: Brewer *Dictionary*, 898]

20. **Wizard of Oz** false wizard takes up residence in Emerald City. [Am. Lit.: *The Wonderful Wizard of Oz*]

21. **wooden nickel** cheap counterfeits circulating in 1850s America. [Am. Hist.: Brewer *Dictionary*, 1164]

22. **wooden nutmeg** sold by dishonest Connecticut peddlers as real thing. [Am. Hist.: Brewer *Dictionary*, 1164]

306. FREEDOM (See also DELIVERANCE.)

1. *Areopagitica* pamphlet supporting freedom of the press. [Br. Lit.: Benét, 46]

2. **Berihah** 1940s underground railroad for Jews out of East Europe. [Jew. Hist.: Wigoder, 80]

3. **Bill of Rights (1791)** term popularly applied to the first 10 Amendments of the U.S. Constitution. [Am. Hist.: Payton, 78]

4. **Declaration of Human Rights (1948)** declaration passed by the United Nations; the rights are the individual freedoms usually associated with Western democracy. [World. Hist.: Payton, 186]

5. **Declaration of Independence (1776)** document declaring the independence of the North American colonies. [Am. Hist.: Payton, 186]

6. **Declaration of Indulgence (1672)** Charles II's attempt to suspend discrimination against Nonconformists and Catholics. [Br. Hist.: Payton, 186]

7. **Declaration of the Rights of Man (1789)** proclaimed legal equality of man. [Fr. Hist.: Payton, 186]

8. **eagle** widely used as national symbol. [Animal Folklore: Jobes, 213]

9. *Easy Rider* bikers Wyatt and Billy reject mainstream conformist values in favor of individualism, independence, and the freedom of the open road (1969). [Am. Film: *SJEPC*]

10. **Eleutherius** epithet of Zeus, meaning "god of freedom." [Gk. Myth.: Zimmerman, 292]

11. **Ellis Island** island in New York Harbor, port of entry for millions of immigrants to the U.S. from 1892–1954; symbol of freedom. [Am. Hist.: *FOF, MOD*]

12. **Fourth of July** American independence day. [Am. Culture: Misc.]

13. **"free at last"** final words from Martin Luther King Jr's famous "I Have a Dream" speech, referring to the goal of racial equality. [Am. Hist.: *FOF, MOD*]

14. **glasnost** policy of greater freedom of expression, part of Mikhail Gorbachev's campaign to initiate political change in the Soviet Union in the 1980s. [Rus. Hist.: Misc.]

15. **Great Emancipator, The** sobriquet of Abraham Lincoln. [Am. Hist.: Hart, 329]

16. **Henry, Patrick (1736–1799)** famous American patriot known for his statement: "Give me liberty or give me death." [Am. Hist.: Hart, 367]

17. **Jubilee year** fiftieth year; liberty proclaimed for all inhabitants. [O.T.: Leviticus 25:8–13]

18. **Liberty Bell** symbol of American freedom; at Independence Hall, Philadelphia. [Am. Hist.: Jameson, 284]

19. **Magna Carta** symbol of British liberty. [Br. Hist.: Bishop, 49–52, 213]

20. **Minute Man** heroic citizen-soldier of the American Revolution helped defeat the British and secure independence and liberty for the people. [Am. Hist.: *SJEPC*]

21. **Mole** from Kenneth Grahame's children's classic *Wind in the Willows* (1908); leaves the confinement and drudgery of underground home and moves to River Bank to enjoy life more. [Br. Children's Lit.: Jones]

22. **Monroe Doctrine** consolidated South American independence; stonewalled European intervention. [Am. Hist.: Jameson, 329–330]

23. **Phrygian cap** presented to slaves upon manumission. [Rom. Hist.: Jobes, 287]

24. **Rienzi** liberator of Rome from warring Colonna and Orsini families. [Ger. Opera: Wagner *Rienzi*, Westerman, 203]

25. **Runnymede** site of Magna Charta signing (1215). [Br. Hist.: Bishop, 49–52, 213]

26. **Rutli Oath** legendary pact establishing independence of Swiss cantons (1307). [Swiss Hist.: *NCE*, 2384]

27. **Statue of Liberty** perhaps the most famous monument to independence. [Am. Hist.: Jameson, 284]

28. **Underground Railroad** effective means of escape for southern slaves. [Am. Hist.: Jameson, 514]

29. **water willow** indicates independence. [Flower Symbolism: *Flora Symbolica*, 178]

307. FRENZY

1. **Beatlemania** term referring to the Beatles' immense popularity; manifested by screaming fans in the 1960s. [Pop. Culture: Miller, 172–181]

2. **Big Bull Market** speculation craze precipitated stock market crash (1929). [Am. Hist.: Allen, 205–226]

3. *Crucible, The* 1953 Arthur Miller play of a Salem witchhunt depicted hysteria's tragic consequences. [Am. Drama: *SJEPC*]

4. **Gold Rush** lure of instant riches precipitated onslaught of prospectors (1848, 1886). [Am. Hist.: Jameson, 203]

5. **Klondike, the** scene of wild rush for riches (1886). [Am. Hist.: Jameson, 269]

6. **Old Woman of Surrey** "morn, noon, and night in a hurry." [Nurs. Rhyme: *Mother Goose*, 117]

7. **Valentino's funeral** overwhelmed with grief, fans rioted. [Am. Hist.: Sann, 317–327]

8. *War of the Worlds* broadcast on radio on October 30, 1938; Orson Welles's story of Martian invasion sent thousands of Americans into a panic. [Am. Radio: *SJEPC*]

9. **White Queen** in a perpetual dither. [Br. Lit.: *Through the Looking-Glass*]

10. **White Rabbit** agitated rabbit in a perpetual hurry. [Br. Lit.: *Alice's Adventures in Wonderland*]

308. FRIENDSHIP (See also LOYALTY.)

1. **acacia** traditional symbol of friendship. [Flower Symbolism: *Flora Symbolica*, 172]

2. **Achilles and Patroclus** beloved friends and constant companions, especially during the Trojan War. [Gk. Myth.: Zimmerman, 194]

3. **Amos and Andy** dim-witted Andy Brown and level-headed partner Amos Jones, owners of the Fresh Air Taxi Cab Company. [Radio and TV: "The Amos 'n' Andy Show" in Terrace , I, 54]

4. **Amys and Amylion** the Pylades and Orestes (q.v., below) of the feudal ages. [Medieval Lit.: *LLEI*, I: 269]

5. **Biddy and Pip** "friends for life." [Br. Lit.: *Great Expectations*]

6. **Castor and Pollux** twin brothers who lived and died together. [Gk. Myth.: Zimmerman, 52]

7. *Cheers* at the bar where everybody knows your name, staff and long-time customers form close bonds. [Am. TV: *SJEPC*]

8. **Chingachgook and Natty Bumppo** Chingachgook as Natty Bumppo's constant sidekick and advisor. [Am. Lit.: *The Pathfinder*, Magill I, 715–717]

9. *Corduroy* 1968 picture book by Don Freeman; stuffed bear who lives in department store is given home by loving girl, fulfilling their mutual wish for a friend. [Am. Children's Lit.: Jones]

10. **Damon and Pythias** each agreed to die to save the other. [Gk. Hist.: Espy, 48]

11. *Deer Hunter, The* three working-class friends from a small Pennsylvania mill town become soldiers together and vow loyalty to

one another; experience the horrors of the Vietnam War. [Am. Film: *SJEPC*]

12. **Diomedes and Sthenelus** Sthenelus was the companion and charioteer of Diomedes. [Gk. Myth.: Zimmerman, 248]

13. **E.T.** alien character forms friendship with young boy in Steven Spielberg's 1982 *E.T.* [Am. Film: *ODA*]

14. **Fannie and Edmund Bertram** while others ignored Fannie, he comforted her. [Br. Lit.:*Mansfield Park*, Magill I, 562–564]

15. **Fred and Ethel** the Ricardos' true-blue pals. [TV: "I Love Lucy" in Terrace, I, 383–384]

16. **Friday and Robinson Crusoe** Friday was Robinson Crusoe's sole companion on desert island. [Br. Lit.: *Robinson Crusoe*]

17. *Golden Girls, The* four widowed or divorced older women share a household in Florida, navigating their post-menopausal years with supportive friendship and humor (NBC, 1985–92). [Am. TV: *SJEPC*]

18. **ivy leaves** symbolic of strong and lasting companionship. [Heraldry: Halberts, 31]

19. **Jane Frances de Chantal and Francis de Sales, Saints** two of most celebrated in Christian annals. [Christian Hagiog.: Attwater, 183]

20. **Jonathan and David** swore compact of love and mutual protection. [O.T.: I Samuel 18:1–3, 20:17]

21. **Lennon, John (1940–1980), and Paul McCartney (1942–)** songwriting duo of The Beatles were close friends and creative rivals. [Br. Music: *SJEPC*]

22. **Lightfoot, Martin and Hereward** Hereward's companion during various wanderings. [Br. Lit.: *Hereward the Wake*, Magill I, 367–370]

23. **Nisus and Euryalus** fought bravely together; Nisus dies rescuing Euryalus. [Rom. Hist.: Wheeler, 259; Rom. Lit.: *Aeneid*]

24. **Peggotty, Clara, and David Copperfield** lifelong friends. [Br. Lit.: *David Copperfield*]

25. **Petronius and Nero** Petronius as nobleman and intimate friend of Nero. [Polish Lit.: *Quo Vadis*, Magill I, 797–799]

26. **Philadelphia** nicknamed "City of Brotherly Love." [Am. Hist.: *NCE*, 2127]

27. **Pylades and Orestes** Pylades willing to sacrifice life for Orestes. [Gk. Lit.: *Oresteia*, Kitto, 68–90]

28. **Standish, Miles and John Alden** best friends, despite their love for Priscilla. [Am. Lit.: "The Courtship of Miles Standish" in Magill I, 165–166]

29. **Theseus and Pirithous** Pirithous, King of Lapitae, was intimate friend of Theseus, Athenian hero. [Gk. Myth.: Zimmerman, 195]

30. **Three Musketeers, The** three comrades known by motto, "All for one, and one for all." [Fr. Lit.: *The Three Musketeers*]

31. **Tiberge and Chevalier** Tiberge as ever-assisting shadow of the chevalier. [Fr. Lit.: *Manon Lescaut*]

32. **Weasley, Ron** character from J.K. Rowling's Harry Potter series for young readers (1997–2007); loyal friend to Harry and companion in his fight against Lord Voldemort. [Br. Children's Lit.: Misc.]

33. **Wilbur and Charlotte** spider and pig as loyal companions. [Children's Lit.: *Charlotte's Web*]

34. *Wind in the Willows, The* Kenneth Grahame's 1908 book that is a classic of children's literature; tells of the friendship of four anthropomorphized animal characters, each with distinct personalities; Grahame denied any deep meaning, simply joy of life as lived by the simplest of creatures. [Br. Children's Lit.: OCCL]

35. *Winnie-the-Pooh* first of Christopher Robin stories by A.A. Milne, published in 1926; tells of young boy and his stuffed toys, who are portrayed as live animal friends living in the forest and enjoying quietly humorous adventures. [Br. Children's Lit.: OCCL]

309. FRIVOLITY

1. **Blondie** the gaffe-prone, frivolous wife of Dagwood Bumstead. [Comics: Horn, 118]

2. **Dobson, Zuleika** charming young lady who unconcernedly dazzles Oxford undergraduates. [Br. Lit.: Magill II, 1169]

3. **Golightly, Holly** madcap New York playgirl, indulges in wacky escapades. [Am. Lit.: Capote *Breakfast at Tiffany's*, in Hart, 133]

4. **grasshopper** sings instead of storing away food. [Animal Symbolism: Mercatante, 108]

5. **Lescaut, Manon** amorally chooses luxury above loyalty. [Ital. Opera: Puccini, *Manon Lescaut*, Westerman, 346]

6. **Merry Mount** colonists frolic around Maypole, causing Morton's arrest. [Am. Hist.: Hart, 543]

7. **Misanthrope** exposes frivilolity and inconsistency of French society (1600s). [Fr. Lit.: *Le Misanthrope*]

8. **Nickleby, Mrs.** forever introducing inapposite topics into conversations. [Br. Lit.: *Nicholas Nickleby*]

9. **Yorick, Mr.** traveling on the Continent, he and his servant engage in a series of casual love affairs. [Br. Lit.: Sterne *A Sentimental Journey* in Magill I, 879]

310. FRONTIER (See also WEST, THE.)

1. **Boone, Daniel (1734–1820)** American frontiersman in coonskin cap. [Am. Hist.: Hart, 90]

2. **Bowie, Jim (1799–1836)** frontiersman and U.S. soldier; developed large hunting knife named after him. [Am. Hist.: Payton, 95]

3. **Bumppo, Natty** also known as Leatherstocking, a tough backwoodsman. [Am. Lit.: *Deerslayer, Pathfinder*]

4. **California Joe (Moses Embree Milner, 1829–1876)** frontiersman and scout. [Am. Hist.: *NCE*, 424]

5. **Crockett, Davy (1786–1836)** iconic American frontiersman and legendary hero who died at the Alamo. [Am. Hist.: *FOF, MOD*]

6. **Ingalls, Laura** centerpiece of autobiographical frontier Little House series by Laura Ingalls Wilder; robust girl who embodies independence and determination of pioneers of late 1800s. [Am. Children's Lit.: Jones]

7. *Virginian, The* up-and-coming cowpuncher defends his honor, espouses justice, and gains responsibility and a bride. [Am. Lit.: *The Virginian* in Magill I, 1072]

8. **Woodlawn, Caddie** protagonist of 1935 novel for young readers by Carol Ryrie Brink; tomboy living in close, patriotic family in woods of western Wisconsin during pioneer days. [Am. Children's Lit.: *OCCL*]

311. FRUSTRATION (See also EXASPERATION, FUTILITY.)

1. **Akaki** poor government clerk saves to buy a new overcoat, only to have it stolen. [Russ. Lit.: Gogol *The Overcoat* in Magill II, 790]

2. **Angstrom, Harry "Rabbit"** former basketball star frustrated by demands of adult life. [Am. Lit.: *Rabbit, Run*, Magill IV, 1042–1044]

3. **Barataria** dishes removed before Sancho tasted them. [Span. Lit.: *Don Quixote*]

4. **Bundren, Addie** family continually thwarted in 9–day attempt to bury her. [Am. Lit.: *As I Lay Dying*]

5. *Catch-22* Air Force captain's appeal to be grounded for insanity not granted because desire to avoid combat proves sanity. [Am. Lit.: Joseph Heller *Catch-22*]

6. **coyote** foiled in attempts to enjoy prey. [Am. Ind. Folklore: Mercatante, 77–78]

7. *Dilbert* comic strip highlights white-collar employee frustration over recognizable work situations such as pointless meetings, uncooperative coworkers, clueless managers, and inane corporate policies. [Am. Comics: *SJEPC*]

8. **Henderson the Rain King** character's frustration shown by his continually saying, "I want, I want." [Am. Lit.: *Henderson the Rain King*]

9. **Josef K** accused of mysterious crime, fails in his attempts to seek exoneration, and is executed. [Ger. Lit.: Kafka *The Trial*]

10. **K.** continually hindered from gaining entrance to mysterious castle. [Ger. Lit.: *The Castle*]

11. **Old Mother Hubbard** foiled at all attempts to care for dog. [Nurs. Rhyme: Baring-Gould, 111–113]

12. **Raven, The** answer for quests of longing: "Nevermore." [Am. Lit.: "The Raven" in Hart, 656]

13. **Sharpless** frustrated in attempt to prepare Cio-Cio-San for disappointment. [Ital. Opera: Pucccini, *Madame Butterfly*, Westerman, 358]

14. **Tantalus** condemned in Hades to thirst after receding water. [Gk. Myth.: Brewer *Dictionary*, 1062]

15. ***Three Sisters, The*** sisters live dull, provincial lives, yearning to return to the gay life of Moscow. [Russ. Drama: Benét, 1005]

16. **Watty, Mr.** bankrupt; waits years for court action. [Br. Lit.: *Pickwick Papers*]

312. FUTILITY (See also BOREDOM, DESPAIR, FRUSTRATION.)

1. ***American Scene, The*** portrays Americans as having secured necessities; now looking for amenities. [Am. Lit.: *The American Scene*]

2. **Babio** performs the useless and superogatory. [Fr. Folklore: Walsh *Classical*, 42]

3. **Canute** king of England demonstrated the limits of his power by commanding waves to stand still in vain. [Eng. Legend: Benét, 165]

4. **Dada** artistic and literary movement of the early 20th century, rejected logical and beautiful in favor of absurd, illogical, despairing worldview. [Eur. Hist.: *ODA*]

5. **Danaides** fifty daughters, forty-nine of whom are condemned to Hades to collect water in sieves. [Rom. Myth.: *LLEI*, I: 326]

6. ***Fall, The*** tale of the monotonous life and indifference of modern man. [Fr. Lit.: *The Fall*]

7. **Grandet, Eugènie** lacking everything but wealth, she is indifferent to life. [Fr. Lit.: *Eugènie Grandet*, Magill I, 258–260]

8. **Moreau, Frederic** law student whose amatory attachments all come to nothing, concludes that existence is futile. [Fr. Lit.: Flaubert *A Sentimental Education* in Magill I, 876]

9. **"Necklace, The"** having lost a borrowed diamond necklace, M. and Mme. Loisel suffer ten years of privation to purchase a duplicate, then find that the original was paste. [Fr. Lit.: Maupassant "The Necklace"]

10. **Ocnus, the cord of** eaten by ass as quickly as it is made. [Gk. And Rom. Myth.: Wheeler, 767]

11. *Of Mice and Men* story of George Milton and Lennie Small's futile dream of having their own farm. [Am. Lit.: *Of Mice and Men*]

12. **Partington, Dame** tried to turn back tide with mop. [Br. Hist.: Brewer *Dictionary*, 807]

13. **pearls before swine** Jesus adjures one not to waste best efforts. [N.T.: Matthew 7:6]

14. **Pickett's Charge** during the battle of Gettysburg, July 3, 1863, Confederate General George Pickett began a futile attack on Union soldiers, his troops were decimated; a symbol of futile action. [Am. Hist.: *FOF, MOD*]

15. **Sisyphus** man condemned to roll up a hill a huge stone which always rolls back before he gets it to the top. [Gk. Myth.: Brewster *Dictionary*, 1006]

16. *Sun Also Rises, The* story of American expatriates living a futile existence in Europe. [Am. Lit.: *The Sun Also Rises*]

17. *Tobacco Road* tale of Jeeter Lester and other oppressed, degraded lives. [Am. Lit.: *Tobacco Road*]

18. **Tregeagle** condemned to bail out Dozmary Pool with leaky shell. [Br. Legend: Brewer *Dictionary*, 1099]

G

313. GAIETY (See also JOVIALITY, JOY.)

1. **butterfly orchis** symbol of gaiety. [Plant Symbolism: *Flora Symbolica*, 172]

2. **coreopsis** symbol of cheerfulness because of its bright yellow flowers. [Flower Symbolism: Jobes, 371]

3. **crocus** symbol of cheerfulness. [Flower Symbolism: Jobes, 383]

4. **Gay Nineties** the 1890s, a decade of carefree and exciting days in America. [Am. Hist.: Flexner, 162]

5. **"L'Allegro"** pastoral idyll celebrating gaiety and cheerfulness. [Br. Lit.: Milton "L'Allegro"]

6. **Mardi Gras** festive day celebrated at the close of the pre-Lenten season in France and in New Orleans. [Fr. and Am. Trad.: *EB*, VI, 608]

7. **Roaring Twenties** the 1920s decade of the Jazz Age and the boom years before the depression. [Am. Hist.: Payton, 515]

8. **Sabbath's (Sunday's) Child** bonny and blithe; good and gay. [Nurs. Rhyme: Opie, 309]

9. **shamrock** indicates light-heartedness. [Flower Symbolism: *Flora Symbolica*, 177]

Gallantry (See CHIVALRY.)

314. GAMBLING

1. **Atlantic City** New Jersey city has become the Las Vegas of the East. [Am. Hist.: Misc.]

2. **Bet-a-million Gates** wealthy American industrialist John Warne Gates (1855–1911). [Am. Culture: Misc.]

3. **Brady, "Diamond Jim" (1856–1917)** diamond-attired rail magnate and financier who loved to gamble. [Am. Hist.: Payton, 192]

4. **"Camptown Races"** Foster's ode to betting. [Pop. Music: Van Doren, 192]

5. **Cincinnati Kid, the** "one of the shrewdest gamblers east of the Mississippi." [Cinema: Halliwell, 462]

6. **Clonbrony, Lord** absentee landlord is compulsive gambler. [Br. Lit.: *The Absentee*]

7. **Consus** ancient Roman god of horse-racing and counsel. [Rom. Myth.: Zimmerman, 68]

8. **de Balibari, Chevalier** professional gambler and adventurer. [Br. Lit.: *Barry Lyndon*]

9. **de Beaujeu, Monsieur** known for his betting. [Br. Lit.: *Fortunes of Nigel*]

10. **devil's bones** epithet for dice. [Folklore: Jobes, 436]

11. **Google, Barney** hopelessly in love with the ponies. [Comics: Horn, 99–100]

12. **Ivanovich, Alexei** irrevocably drawn to betting tables. [Russ. Lit.: *The Gambler*]

13. **Jackson, "Shoeless" Joe (1887–1951)** multifaceted talent as player; part of the 1919 Black Sox scandal, in which 8 White Sox players were accused of throwing the World Series, and banned for life from the sport; at trial, allegedly confronted by child who pleaded : "Say it ain't so, Joe." [Am. Sports: *SJEPC*]

14. **Las Vegas** city in Nevada notorious for its gambling casinos since 1945. [Am. Hist.: Payton, 382]

15. **Lucky, Mr.** alias Joe Adams, gambler who owns the *Fortuna*, fancy supper club and gambling yacht. [TV: Terrace, II, 117]

16. **Maverick** family name of two brothers, Bret and Bart; self-centered and untrustworthy gentlemen gamblers. [TV: Terrace, II, 80]

17. **Minnie** plays poker to save Jack Johnson's life. [Ital. Opera: Puccini, *Girl of the Golden West*, Westerman, 361]

18. **Monte Carlo** town in Monaco principality, in southeast France; a famous gambling resort. [Fr. Hist.: *NCE*, 1819]

19. **Mutt and Jeff** hapless punters always looking for a quick buck. [Comics: Horn, 508–509]

20. **Nathan Detroit** his obsession with crap games so persistent that it even keeps him from getting married. [Musical Comedy: Damon Runyon *Guys and Dolls* in *On Stage*, 322]

21. **Pit, the** Board of Trade's cellar, where all bidding occurs. [Am. Lit.: *The Pit*, Magill I, 756–758]

22. **"Queen of Spades, The"** Aleksandr Pushkin's short story about the downfall of the gambler Germann. [Russ. Lit.: Benét, 833]

23. **Rose, Pete (1941–)** known as a baseball player for his competitive attitude and skill; controversy surrounding allegations of betting on games led to banishment from baseball. [Am. Sports: *SJEPC*]

24. **Siegel, Bugsy (1906–1947)** mobster who built the Flamingo hotel and casino in Las Vegas; mastermind behind the establishment of the city as mecca of legalized gambling. [Am. Culture: *SJEPC*]

25. **Smiley, Jim** bets his frog can outjump any other; loses by sabotage. [Am. Lit.: *The Celebrated Jumping Frog of Calaveras County*]

315. GAME

1. **bridge** four-person card game once viewed as leisure activity for the wealthy has become popular among college students and regular folks. [Entertainment: *SJEPC*]

2. **Dungeons and Dragons** role-playing game based on fantasy literature in which players are characters adventuring together in an imaginary, mythical place created by the Dungeon Master; popular in 1980s-90s. [Am. Culture: *SJEPC*]

3. **Griffin, Merv (1925–2007)** his production company created such TV game show favorites as *Jeopardy* and *Wheel of Fortune*. [Am. TV: *SJEPC*]

4. *Jeopardy!* began in 1964 and went on to become one of most popular prime-time TV shows ever; reversed question-and-answer format of most game shows: answers were supplied, contestants provided question that fit the answer. [Am. TV: *SJEPC*]

5. *Jumanji* 1981 picture book by Chris Van Allsburg; two bored children discover an abandoned board game and begin playing; they soon discover that they have unleashed fantastic occurrences. [Am. Children's Lit.: Misc.]

6. **Milton Bradley** successful manufacturer of board games and home versions of TV game shows. [Am. Culture: *SJEPC*]

7. **Monopoly** enormously popular real estate board game with Atlantic City, NJ street names. [Am. Culture: *SJEPC*]

8. **Parker Brothers** company produced popular games, including Monopoly, Clue, Trivial Pursuit. [Am. Culture: *SJEPC*]

9. *Price Is Right, The* longest-running TV game show, debuting in 1956; contestants win prizes by guessing the cost of various products [Am. TV: *SJEPC*]

10. *To Tell the Truth* panel quiz show of the 1950s and 1960s; celebrity panelists tried to determine which of three contestants was giving truthful account of unusual life event; at end "real" contestant stood and imposters introduced themselves in interesting postscript. [Am. TV: *SJEPC*]

11. **Trivial Pursuit** challenge of remembering minutiae from various categories made the game fascinating entertainment; first created in the 1980s, it has gone on to great success, with 40 variations sold in 33 countries. [Entertainment: *SJEPC*]

12. *What's My Line?* panelists tried to guess profession of contestants or identity of masked celebrities; wildly popular with a seventeen-year run beginning in 1950. [Am. TV: *SJEPC*]

13. *Wheel of Fortune* popular quiz show which began in 1998; Pat Sajak and Vanna White host contestants who spin wheel to win

chances to uncover letters until they can guess mystery phrase. [Am. TV: *SJEPC*]

316. GANGSTERISM (See also CRIMINAL, OUTLAW.)

1. **Apaches** name given to Parisian gangsters. [Fr. Hist.: Payton, 31]

2. **Black Hand, the** sobriquet for the Mafia. [Am. Hist.: *NCE*, 1657]

3. **Capone, Al "Scarface" (1899–1947)** Chicago mobster, famous gangland bootleg king. [Am. Hist.: Flexner, 73]

4. **Cosa Nostra** the Mafia. [Am. Hist.: Misc.]

5. **Crips and Bloods** two notorious L.A.-based gangs, responsible for murder and illegal activity for decades. [Am. Hist.: Misc.]

6. **FBI** Federal Bureau of Investigation; government agents gained special public respect during Prohibition and the Great Depression, when gangsters created violent crime wave (1920s-30s). [Am. Hist.: *SJEPC*]

7. **Godfather** the head of a group of Mafia families. [Am. Lit.: *The Godfather*; Am. Cinema: Halliwell, 297]

8. *Godfather, The* quintessential gangster film directed by Francis Ford Coppola based on Mario Puzo's novel about the Italian Mafia and rise of the Corleone family in America (1972). [Am. Film: *SJEPC*]

9. *GoodFellas* Martin Scorcese's starkly realistic 1990 film based on a true story exposes the brutality of gangsterism by tracing a mobster's life from his New York City childhood through his violent adulthood. [Am. Film: *SJEPC*]

10. **Gotti, John (1940–2002)** cocky organized crime antihero and leader of the Gambino family became media favorite in 1980s-90s; "Teflon Don" finally convicted of racketeeering and murder, sent to prison in 1992. [Am. Hist.: *SJEPC*]

11. **Krik, Benya** tough Jewish gangster of Odessa. [Russ. Lit.: *Benya Krik, the Gangster*]

12. **Lansky, Meyer (1902?-1983)** famous Jewish mobster who functioned as influential Godfather, moving organized crime into realms of legitimate business world. [Am. Culture: *SJEPC*]

13. *Little Caesar* archetypal gangster, brilliantly portrayed by Edward G. Robinson. [Am. Cinema: Griffith, 269]

14. *M* criminals are so revolted by the murder of several children that they search and capture the murderer. [Ger. Cinema: Halliwell, 256]

15. **M16** automatic or semi-automatic American military assault rifle adopted during the Vietnam War in 1960s also associated with urban American drug gang warfare. [Am. Hist.: *SJEPC*]

16. **Mafia** sinister crime syndicate promotes violence to achieve goals. [Am. Hist.: *NCE*, 1657]

17. *Mean Streets* Martin Scorsese's film captured small-time crime in Little Italy. [Am. Film: *SJEPC*]

18. **Purple Gang** Detroit gangster mob of the 1920s. [Am. Hist.: *NCE*, 2018]

19. **Robinson, Edward G. (1893–1973)** adroit portrayals of various snarling mobsters in gangster movies of the 1930s. [Am. Film: *SJEPC*]

20. **Runyon, Damon (1880–1946)** best known for *Guys and Dolls* and other fiction about the seamier side of New York during Prohibition. [Am. Lit.: *SJEPC*]

21. **Scorsese, Martin (1942–)** critically-acclaimed film director whose provocative works often depict New York City thugs and criminals. [Am. Film: *SJEPC*]

22. **Siegel, Bugsy (1906–1947)** mobster who built the Flamingo hotel and casino in Las Vegas; mastermind behild the establishment of the city as mecca of legalized gambling. [Am. Culture: *SJEPC*]

23. *Sopranos, The* influential and popular TV show created by David Chase, chronicles the life of prominent Mafia don Tony Soprano (1999–2007). [Am. TV: Misc.]

24. **Syndicate** organized crime groups throughout major cities of the United States. [Am. Hist.: *NCE*, 2018]

25. **Tommy gun** automatic Thompson sub-machine gun with rat-a-tat-tat sound associated with organized crime and Depression-era gangsters like John Dillinger. [Am. Hist.: *SJEPC*]

317. GENERATION GAP

1. *Family Ties* TV sitcom set during the Reagan era featured the Keaton family, where the idealistic, 1960s countercultural values of the parents often clashed with the materialistic, 1980s consumer culture values of the children (NBC, 1982–89). [Am. TV: *SJEPC*]

2. *Fathers and Sons* Turgenev novel depicts conflicts of politics and generations. [Russ. Lit.: Benét, 341]

3. *Graduate, The* aimless graduate Benjamin despises parents' upper-class lifestyle; has affair with father's partner's wife, Mrs. Robinson, then runs away with her daughter. [Am. Film: *SJEPC*]

4. **Pontifex, Theobald** domineering father disinherits his unworldly son. [Br. Lit.: Butler *The Way of All Flesh* in Magill I, 1097]

5. **Wynne, Hugh** never wins the understanding or favor of his stern Quaker father. [Am. Lit.: *Hugh Wynne, Free Quaker*, Magill I, 390]

318. GENEROSITY (See also AID, ORGANIZATIONAL; HELPFULNESS; KINDNESS; PHILANTHROPIST.)

1. **Amelia** takes interest in Paul. [Br. Lit.: *Dombey and Son*]

2. **Antonio** lends money gratis. [Br. Lit.: *Merchant of Venice*]

3. **ape** Hindu emblem of the monkey-god Hanuman and symbol of benevolence. [Hindu Animal Symbolism: *IEOTS*, 14]

4. **Appleseed, Johnny (John Chapman, 1774–1845)** gave settlers apple seeds and a helping hand. [Am.Hist.: Hart, 146]

5. **Baboushka** female Santa Claus on Feast of Epiphany. [Russ. Folklore: Walsh *Classical*, 50]

6. **Bartholomea Capitanio and Vincentia Gerosa, Saints** founded order to nurse sick, teach young. [Christian Hagiog.: Attwater, 58]

7. **Befana** female Santa Claus who comes at Epiphany. [Ital. Legend Walsh *Classical*, 50]

8. **Borromeo, Saint Charles (1538–1584)** Archbishop of Milan; lived thriftily; gave money to poor. [Ital. Hist.: Hall, 65]

9. **Bountiful Lady** benevolent, beneficent, but a bit overbearing. [Br. Lit.: *Beaux' Stratagem*, Espy, 129]

10. **buffalo** heraldic symbol of unselfishness. [Heraldry: Halberts, 21]

11. **bull** heraldic symbol of magnamity. [Heraldry: Halberts, 21]

12. **Burchell, Mr.** gave to the poor. [Br. Lit.: *Vicar of Wakefield*]

13. **Cinderella** feeds beggar whom sisters scorn. [Ital. Opera: Rossini, *Cinderella*, Westerman, 120–121]

14. **Clemente, Roberto (1934–1972)** Puerto Rican native and baseball World Series MVP (1971) died in airplane crash on New Year's Eve while transporting supplies to Nicaraguan earthquake victims. [Am. Sports: *SJEPC*]

15. **Constantin, Abbé** self-sacrificing priest; curé of Longueral. [Fr. Lit: *The Abbé Constantin*, Walsh *Modern*, 105]

16. **Dana** almsgiving to poor, giftgiving to priests. [Hindu Rel.: Parrinder, 72]

17. **Ephron** tried unsuccessfully to give Abraham free burial ground. [O.T.: Genesis 23:10–16]

18. **Goriot, Père** generosity to daughters caused his own poverty. [Fr. Lit.: *Père Goriot*]

19. **Maecenas** to poets, esp. Virgil, as a patron. [Rom. Hist.: Espy, 123]

20. **Nicholas, Saint** bringer of presents to children on Christmas. [Folklore: Wheeler, 327]

21. **Robin Hood** robbed rich to help poor. [Br. Lit.: *Robin Hood*]

22. **Rosie** could not deny love to anyone. [Br. Lit.: *Cakes and Ale*]

23. **Salvation Army** Christian religious organization devoted to evangelism and charity. [Am. Hist.: Misc.]

24. **Santa Claus** gives gifts to children on Christmas. [Folklore: Walsh *Classical*, 50]

25. **shmoo** ham-shaped beast that laid eggs, provided milk, and happily gave its flesh to the hungry. [Comics: *Li'l Abner*]

26. **Trot, Tommy** sold bed to buy wife a mirror. [Nurs. Rhyme: Opie, 416]

27. **Twelve Days of Christmas** presents increase with each day of Yuletide. [Am. Music: "Twelve Days of Christmas" in Rockwell.]

28. **Twm Shon Catti** Welsh Robin Hood. [Welsh Hist.: Brewer *Dictionary*, 1110]

29. **Unferth** offers Beowulf finest sword in kingdom. [Br. Lit.: *Beowulf*]

30. **Vincent de Paul, Saint** worked and gave prodigiously of himself to poor. [Christian Hagiog.: Attwater, 337]

31. **Water Rat** from Kenneth Grahame's children's classic *Wind in the Willows* (1908); generous Rat shares his love of the river and all its pleasures with his friends. [Br. Children's Lit.: Jones]

32. **widow's mite** poor woman's contribution of all she had. [N.T.: Mark 12:42–44; Luke 21"2–4]

33. **zakat** almsgiving; the third pillar of Islam requires adult Muslims to give 2.5 percent of their wealth (income and goods) to the poor each year. [Islamic Rel.: *UIMT*, 37, 440]

Genetics (See SCIENCE.)

Genius (See INTELLIGENCE.)

319. GENOCIDE (See also ANTI-SEMITISM, BRUTALITY, MASSACRE.)

1. **Auschwitz** largest Nazi exterminiation camp; more than 1,000,000 deaths there. [Ger. Hist.: *Hitler*, 958–959, 970, 1123]

2. **Babi Yar** ravine near Kiev where Nazis slaughtered 10,000 Jews. [Russ. Hist.: Wigoder, 56]

3. **Bergen-Belsen** Nazi slave labor and extermination camp. [Ger. Hist.: *Hitler*, 1187, 1188]

4. **Bosnia** site of the systematic murder, or "ethnic cleansing" of Bosnian Muslims by Bosnian Serbs, 1992–95. [Eur. Hist.: Misc.]

5. **Buchenwald** showcase of Nazi atrocities. [Ger. Hist.: *Hitler*, 1055]

6. **Dachau** primarily work camp, experienced share of Nazi horrors. [Ger. Hist.: *Hitler*, 1055]

7. **Darfur** section of western Sudan, site of ongoing ethnic and political conflict; more than 200,000 deaths and 4 million refugees. [African Hist.: Misc.]

8. **ethnic cleansing** term for the forcible displacement and extermination of a people; from a Serbo-Croatian term used during the Serbian wars in the Balkans (1990s). [Eur. Hist.: Misc.]

9. **Final Solution** Nazi plan decided fate of 6,000,000 Jews. [Ger. Hist.: *Hitler*, 1037–1061]

10. **Holocaust** Nazi attempt at extermination of European Jewry (1933–1945). [Jew. Hist.: Widogder, 266–267]

11. *Killing Fields, The* 1984 film cataloging the genocide in Cambodia under Pol Pot in the 1970s. [Asian Hist.: *FOF, MOD*]

12. **Lublin** Nazi extermination camp. [Ger. Hist.: *Hitler*, 970]

13. **Majdanek** Nazi extermination camp. [Ger. Hist.: Widogder, 113]

14. **Ravensbrueck** women's concentration camp in Germany. [Ger. Hist.: Shirer, 1275]

15. **Rwanda** conflict between the Tutsi minority and the Hutu majority in 1994 led to the deaths of 800,000 Tutsis, at the hands of Hutu extremists; a symbol of man's inhumanity to man, genocide, and the passivity of the international community. [African Hist.: Misc.]

16. **Sachsenhausen** Nazi concentration camp. [Ger. Hist.: Shirer, 375]

17. **Six Million Jews** their deaths a testimony to Nazi "Final Solution." [Eur. Hist.: *Hitler*, 1123]

18. **Treblinka** Nazi extermination camp. [Ger. Hist.: *Hitler*, 970]

19. **Wannsee Conference** "Final Solution" plotted and scheduled. [Ger. Hist.: Widogder, 619]

20. **Zyklon B** hydrogen cyanide; used by Nazis for mass extermination in concentration camps. [Ger. Hist.: *Hitler*, 970]

320. GENTLENESS

1. **Brown, Matilda** meek, mild heroine. [Br. Lit.: *Cranford*]

2. **Casper the Friendly Ghost** meek little ghost who desires only to make friends. [Comics: Horn, 162]

3. **Cordelia** gentle daughter of Lear. [Br. Lit.: *King Lear*]

4. **Eliante** her kind heart contrasted with Celimene's caustic wit. [Fr. Lit.: *Le Misanthrope*]

5. **Ferdinand** loves to sit quietly and smell flowers instead of being in the bullfights in Madrid; from Munro Leaf's picture book about remaining true to one's own desires, *The Story of Ferdinand the Bull* (1936). [Am. Children's Lit.: Jones]

6. **Gentle Ben** massive but extremely tame bear. [TV: Terrace, I, 302]

7. *Goodnight Moon* beloved picture book written in 1947 by Margaret Wise Brown; simple, very gentle bedtime story in which each familiar item in a little one's world is addressed: "Goodnight room. Goodnight moon.", etc. [Am. Children's Lit.: Misc.]

8. **mallow** traditional symbol of gentleness or mildness. [Plant Symbolism: *Flora Symbolica*, 175]

9. **March, Beth** the domestic, sensitive, sweater-knitting March daughter. [Am. Lit.: *Little Women*]

10. **Pevensie, Susan** protagonist from C.S. Lewis's Narnia series for young readers; her fears and doubts keep her from truly believing in Aslan; she eventually becomes Queen Susan the Gentle, but falls for the evil Rabadash and proves ineffectual in battle. [Br. Children's Lit.: Jones]

11. **Virgilia** meek, gentle wife of Coriolanus. [Br. Lit.: *Coriolanus*]

12. **Wilkes, Melanie** gentle, mild-mannered, dutiful Southern wife. [Am. Lit.: *Gone With the Wind*]

321. GENUINENESS

1. **acid test** test of genuineness for gold; not destructive of genuine metal. [Assaying: Brewer *Dictionary*, 7]

2. **Bible** name used for Scriptures; "the real source of truth." [Christianity: *NCE*, 291]

3. **Gospel** one of the four biographies of Jesus Christ that begin the New Testament; thus, "the real beginning of Christianity." [Christianity: *NCE*, 1112]

4. **Pure, Simon** young Quaker who Colonel Feighnwell impersonates to marry Pure's ward. [Am. Lit.: *A Bold Stroke for a Wife*, Brewer *Handbook*, 1008]

5. **Real McCoy, the** relating to the invention of the automatic lubricating cup by Elijah McCoy (1844–1929); something that is reliable, authoritative, genuine. [Am. Hist.: *BBAAL1*]

6. *To Tell the Truth* question-and-answer probe to determine which of three people is "the real McCoy." [TV: Terrace, II, 383]

322. GHOST

1. **Akakyevich, Akakii** his ghost steals coats off people's backs. [Russ. Lit.: Gogol *The Overcoat*]

2. **Alfonso** the murdered prince returns as a ghost to frustrate the usurper and proclaim the true heir. [Br. Lit.: Walpole *The Castle of Otranto* in Magill I, 124]

3. **Alonzo the Brave** appears as ghost to lover. [Br. Lit.: "Alonzo the Brave" in Walsh *Modern*, 14]

4. **Andrea** ghost returns to the Spanish court to learn of the events that followed his death. [Br. Drama: *The Spanish Tragedy* in Magill II, 990]

5. **Angels of Mons** a spectral army of angels that supposedly came between German and British forces (1914). [Br. and Fr. Hist.: Wallechinsky, 447]

6. **Banquo** his ghost appears to Macbeth at a banquet, sitting in Macbeth's own seat. [Br. Drama: Shakespeare *Macbeth*]

7. **Bhta** haunter of cemeteries; attendant of Shiva. [Hindu Myth.: Parrinder, 45]

8. *Blithe Spirit* ghost of witty first wife returns to mock her husband and his second wife. [Br. Drama: Noel Coward *Blithe Spirit* in *On Stage*, 236]

9. **Caesar's ghost** warns Brutus that he and Caesar will meet again at Philippi. [Br. Drama: Shakespeare *Julius Caesar*]

10. **Canterville ghost** after haunting an English house for three centuries, disappeared forever when new American owners refused to take him seriously. [Br. Lit.: Oscar Wilde "The Canterville Ghost"]

11. **Casper** meek little ghost who desires only to make friends. [Am. Comics: "Casper the Friendly Ghost" in Horn, 162]

12. *Devil and Daniel Webster, The* Webster defends his client before a jury of the ghosts of American villains. [Am. Lit.: Haydn & Fuller, 382]

13. **Drury Lane Theatre ghost** said to bring great acting success to those who see it. [Br. Folklore: Wallechinsky, 446]

14. **Epworth Poltergeist** supposedly invaded the house of Rev. Samuel Wesley. [Am. Folklore: Wallechinsky, 446]

15. *Field of Dreams* baseball-playing ghosts, including Shoeless Joe Jackson and others from the scandalized 1919 World Series Chicago White Sox team, emerge from an Iowa farmer's cornfield to take up the game on a specially created baseball diamond (1989). [Am. Film: *SJEPC*; Misc.]

16. *Flying Dutchman* ghost ship off Cape of Good Hope; sighting it forbodes disaster. [Folklore: Brewer *Note-Book*, 335]

17. *Ghost and Mrs. Muir, The* New England cottage haunted by the spirit of its 19th-century owner. [Am. TV: Terrace]

18. *Ghost Goes West, The* merry Scottish ghost follows his castle when it is moved to America. [Am. Cinema: Halliwell]

19. **Ghost of Charles Rosmer, the** itinerant peddler returns to the property where he was murdered. [Folklore: Wallechinsky, 446]

20. **Ghost of Christmas Past, the** Scrooge's first monitor; spirit presenting past. [Br. Lit.: *A Christmas Carol*]

21. **Ghost of Christmas Present, the** Scrooge's second monitor; spirit presenting present. [Br. Lit.: *A Christmas Carol*]

22. **Ghost of Christmas Yet to Come, the** Scrooge's third monitor; spirit presenting future. [Br. Lit.: *A Christmas Carol*]

23. **Ghost of Hamlet's Father, the** appears to the prince, states he was murdered by Claudius and demands revenge. [Br. Lit.: *Hamlet*]

24. **Ghost's Walk, the** spirit and step of Lady Morbury Dedlock. [Br. Lit.: *Bleak House*]

25. **Glas, Bodach** ghostly bearer of evil tidings. [Br. Lit.: *Waverley*]

26. **Headless Horseman** phantom who scares Ichabod Crane out of his wits. [Am. Lit.: *The Legend of Sleepy Hollow*]

27. **Homunculus** formless spirit of learning. [Ger. Lit.: *Faust*]

28. **Kirby, George and Marian** ghosts who occupy Topper's house. [TV: "Topper" in Terrace II, 381]

29. **Ligeia** months after her own death and the narrator's remarriage, she materializes upon the death of his second wife. [Am. Lit.: Poe *Ligeia*]

30. **Marley** the ghost of his former partner who helps Ebenezer Scrooge become more benevolent. [Br. Lit.: *A Christmas Carol*]

31. **Mauthe Doog** ghostly black spaniel that haunted Peel Castle. [Br. Folklore: Benét, 649]

32. **Morland, Catherine** terrified by imagined ghosts at the medieval abbey where she is a guest. [Br. Lit.: *Northanger Abbey* in Benét, 720]

33. **Nighe, Bean** ghost of a woman who died in childbirth. [Scot. Folklore: Briggs, 15–16]

34. *Phantom of the Opera, The* deformed man haunts opera house for vengeance. [Am. Film: Halliwell, 562]

35. **Phantom, The** mysterious, ghostlike foe of injustice in a mythical African-Asian country. [Am. Comics: Horn, 551]

36. **Quint, Peter and Miss Jessel** former lovers return to haunt house. [Am. Lit.: *The Turn of the Screw*]

37. **Richard III** visited by the ghosts of all his victims. [Br. Lit.: Shakespeare *Richard III*]

38. *Ruddigore* the ghosts of his ancestors confront the current baronet and change his life. [Br. Opera: Gilbert and Sullivan *Ruddigore*]

39. **Samuel** his spirit appears to Saul through the witch of Endor. [O.T.: I Samuel 28:24]

40. **Short Hoggers of Whittinghame** ghost of baby murdered by his mother cannot rest because he is "nameless." [Br. Folklore: Briggs, 363–364]

41. **Topper** house he purchases is haunted by the young couple who owned it previously and their dog. [Am. Lit.: *Topper* in Halliwell, 718; Cinema: ; TV:]

42. **Vermilion Phantom** ghost rumored to have appeared at various times in French history, such as before deaths of Henry IV and Napoleon. [Fr. History: Wallechinsky, 445]

43. **White House ghost** several people supposedly saw Abraham Lincoln's ghost there. [Am. Folklore: Wallechinsky, 447]

44. **White Lady** ghost seen in different castles and palaces belonging to Prussia's royal family. [Prussian Folklore: Brewer *Handbook*, 1207]

45. **White Lady of Avenel** "a tutelary spirit." [Br. Lit.: *The Monastery*, Brewer *Handbook*, 1208]

46. **White Lady of Ireland** the domestic spirit of a family; intimates approaching death with shrieks. [Irish Folklore: *The Monastery*, Brewer *Handbook*, 1208]

47. **Wild Huntsman** spectral hunter with dogs who frequents the Black Forest. [Ger. Folklore: *The Monastery*, Brewer *Handbook*, 1207]

323. GIANT (See also TALLNESS.)

1. **Albion** son of Neptune and ancestor of England. [Br. Lit.: *Faerie Queene*]

2. **Alcyoneus** one of the Titans. [Gk. Myth.: Kravitz, 17]

3. **Alice** drinking a magic potion, she grows so tall that she fills an entire room. [Br. Children's Lit.: Lewis Carroll *Alice's Adventures in Wonderland*]

4. **Aloeidae** name given to twins Otus and Ephialtes. [Gk. Myth.: Kravitz, 17]

5. **Anakim** race of tall men routed by Joshua. [O.T.: Numbers 13:32–33]

6. **Antaeus** colossal wrestler slain by Hercules. [Gk. Myth.: Brewer *Dictionary*, 38]

7. **Antigonus** giant nicknamed the Hand-Tosser. [Belgian Legend: Walsh *Classical*, 25]

8. **Ascapart** thirty feet tall; defeated by Sir Bevis. [Medieval Romance: Walsh *Classical*, 34]

9. **Atlas** Titan condemned to support world on his shoulders. [Gk. Myth.: Brewer *Handbook*, 13]

10. **Babe, the Blue Ox** Paul Bunyan's gigantic animal-of-all-work. [Am. Folklore: Spiller, 720]

11. **Balan** strong and courageous colossus. [Span. Lit.: *Amadis de Gaul*]

12. **Balor** Formorian giant with evil eye. [Irish Myth.: Benét, 76]

13. **Beaver, Tony** equals mythical exploits of Paul Bunyan. [Am. Lit.: *Up Eel River*]

14. **Bellerus** a Cornish giant. [Br. Lit.: Brewer *Handbook*, 108]

15. **Blunderbore** nursery tale giant killed by Jack. [Br. Lit.: Brewer *Dictionary*, 128]

16. **Brobdingnag** country of people twelve times the size of men. [Br. Lit.: *Gulliver's Travels*]

17. **Bunyan, Paul** legendary lumberjack who accomplished prodigious feats. [Am. Folklore: Brewer *Dictionary*, 163]

18. **Cardiff giant** a gypsum statue passed off as a petrified prehistoric man till revealed as a hoax (1869). [Am. Hist.: *EB* (1963), 9: 533]

19. **Clifford** house-sized red dog who first appeared in Norman Bridwell's *Clifford the Big Red Dog* (1963) and whose adventures have graced many popular picture books since. [Am. Children's Lit.: McElmeel]

20. **Clytius** son of Uranus and Gaea. [Gk. Myth.: Kravitz, 64]

21. **Colossos** a gigantic brazen statue126 ft. high executed by Chares for the harbor at Rhodes. [Gk. Hist.: Brewer *Handbook*, 226]

22. **Cormoran** nursery tale giant felled by Jack. [Br. Lit.: Brewer *Dictionary*, 262]

23. **Cyclopes** race of one-eyed, gigantic men. [Gk. Lit.: *Odyssey*]

24. **Egil** giant who watched over Thor's goats. [Norse Myth.: *LLEI*, I: 327]

25. **Enceladus** powerful giant whose hisses cause volcanic eruptions. [Gk. Myth.: Kravitz, 88]

26. **Ephialtes and Otus** nine fathoms tall; threatened to battle Olympian gods. [Gk. Myth.: Leach, 39; Gk. Lit.: *Iliad*]

27. **Ferragus** the Portuguese giant who took the empress Bellisant under his care. [Br. Lit.: "Valentine and Orson" in Brewer *Handbook*, 364]

28. **Foawr** stone-throwing slaughterer of cattle. [Br. Folklore: Briggs, 178]

29. **Galapos** giant slain by King Arthur. [Br. Lit.: *History of Arthur*, Brewer *Handbook*, 400]

30. **Gargantua** royal giant who required 17,913 cows for personal milk supply. [Fr. Lit.: *Gargantua and Pantagruel*]

31. **Glumdalca, Queen** captive giantess in love with Tom. [Br. Lit.: *Tom Thumb*]

32. **Gog and Magog** two Cornish giants taken captive by Brutus, legendary founder of Britain. [Br. Legend: Brewer *Dictionary*, 471]

33. **Goliath** towering Philistine giant slain by youthful David. [O.T.: I Samuel 17:49–51]

34. **Jack-in-Irons** gigantic figure that attacks lonely wayfarers. [Br. Folklore: Briggs, 237]

35. **Jolly Green Giant** trademark comes alive in animated commercials. [Am. Advertising: Misc.]

36. **Jotunn** race of giants frequently in conflict with gods. [Norse Myth.: Leach, 559]

37. **King Kong** giant ape brought to New York as "eighth wonder of world." [Am. Cinema: Payton, 367]

38. **Long Meg of Westminster** 16th-century giantess. [Br. Hist.: Espy, 337]

39. **Lubbard Fiend** brownie of gigantic size. [Br. Folklore: Briggs, 270–272]

40. **Miller, Maximilian Christopher** the Saxon giant. [Br. Hist.: Brewer *Handbook*, 706]

41. **Mimir** gigantic god of primeval ocean. [Norse Myth.: Leach, 728]

42. **Morgante** ferocious giant converted to Christianity. [Ital. Lit.: *Morgante Maggiore*, Wheeler, 248]

43. **Nephilim** race dwelling in Canaan before Israelites. [O.T.: Genesis 6:4]

44. **Og** giant who attacked Israelites. [O.T.: Deuteronomy 3:2]

45. **Orgoglio** a hideous giant, as tall as three men; son of Earth and Wind. [Gk. Myth.: Brewer *Handbook*, 780]

46. **Orion** colossus of great beauty and hunting skill. [Gk. and Roman Myth.: Wheeler, 271]

47. **Pantagruel** gigantic, virtuous king who needed 4,600 cows to nurse him. [Fr. Lit.: *Gargantua and Pantagruel*]

48. **Polyphemus** cruel monster; one of the Cyclopes. [Gk. Lit.: *Odyssey*; Rom. Lit.: *Aeneid*]

49. **Titans** lawless children of Uranus and Gaea. [Gk. Myth.: Brewer *Dictionary*, 1086]

50. **Tityus** son of Zeus; body covered nine acres. [Gk. and Roman Myth.: Wheeler, 368]

51. **Typhon** fire-breathing colossus. [Gk. and Roman Myth.: Wheeler, 373]

52. **Utgard** residence of colossi. [Norse Myth.: Brewer *Dictionary*, 1120]

53. **Ymir** father of the giant race. [Norse Myth.: Wheeler, 395]

Global Warming (See ENVIRONMENTALISM.)

324. GLUTTONY

1. **Belch, Sir Toby** gluttonous and lascivious fop. [Br. Lit.: *Twelfth Night*]

2. **Biggers, Jack** one of the best known "feeders" of eighteenth-century England. [Br. Hist.: Wallechinsky, 377]

3. **Ciacco** Florentine damned to the third circle of Hell for gluttony. [Ital. Lit.: Dante *Inferno*]

4. **Cookie Monster** Muppet character from *Sesame Street* TV show for children; voracious appetite, especially for cookies, but has been known to eat everything from telephones to trucks. [Am. TV: Misc.]

5. **crab** loves to devour oysters. [Medieval Animal Symbolism: White, 210–211]

6. **Dagwood** relieves tension by making and eating gargantuan sandwiches. [Comics: "Blondie" in Horn, 118]

7. **Fat Freddy** character who loves food more than anything else. [Comics: "The Fabulous Furry Freak Brothers" in Horn, 239–240]

8. **Gargantua** enormous eater who ate salad lettuces as big as walnut trees. [Fr. Lit.: Brewer *Handbook*, 406]

9. **Gastrolaters** people worshiped food in the form of Manduce. [Fr. Lit.: *Pantagruel*]

10. **hedgehog** attribute of gourmandism personified. [Animal Symbolism: Hall, 146]

11. **Johnson, Nicely-Nicely** Damon Runyon's Broadway glutton. [Am. Lit. and Drama: *Guys and Dolls*]

12. **Jughead** character renowned for his insatiable hankering for hamburgers. [Comics: "Archie" in Horn, 87]

13. **Laphystius** epithet of Zeus, meaning "gluttonous." [Gk. Myth.: Zimmerman, 292–293]

14. **Lucullus** Roman epicure chiefly remembered for his enormous consumption of food. [Rom. Hist.: Payton, 406]

15. **lupin** traditional symbol of voracity. [Plant Symbolism: *Flora Symbolica*, 175]

16. **Manduce** idol worshiped by the Gastrolaters. [Fr. Lit.: *Pantagruel*]

17. **Pantagruel** son of Gargantua noted for his continual thirst. [Fr. Lit.: Jobes, II, 1234]

18. **pig** symbol of both gluttony, lust, and selfishness as well as motherhood, prosperity, and happiness. [Symbolism: *CEOS&S*]

19. **Snorkel, Sergeant** character devoted to God, country, and belly. [Comics: "Beetle Bailey" in Horn, 106]

20. **Sobakevitch** huge, bearlike landowner astonishes banquet guests by devouring entire sturgeon. [Russ. Lit.: Gogol *Dead Souls*]

21. **Stivic, Michael "Meathead"** Archie's son-in-law; has insatiable appetite. [TV: "All in the Family" in Terrace, I, 47]

22. **Willey, Walter** servant who achieved fame through his public gluttony. [Br. Hist.: Wallechinsky, 378]

23. **Wimpy, J. Wellington** Popeye's companion, a corpulent dandy with a tremendous capacity for hamburgers. [Comics: "Thimble Theater" in Horn, 657–658]

24. **Wood, Nicholas** his gastronomic abilities inspired poems and songs; at one historic sitting, he consumed all the edible meat of a sheep. [Br. Hist.: Wallechinsky, 378]

25. **Wood, Willy** "ate up cream cheese, roast beef, piecrust"; incessant eater. [Nurs. Rhyme: Baring-Gould, 158]

26. **Yogi Bear** character with insatiable appetite; always stealing picnic baskets from visitors to Jellystone Park. [Am. Comics: Misc.; TV: Terrace, II, 448–449]

325. GOD

1. **Abba** title of reverence for God the Father. [N.T.: Mark 14:36; Romans 8:15]

2. **Adonai** spoken in place of the ineffable Yahweh. [Judaism: *NCE*, 22]

3. **Aesir** the Teutonic pantheon. [Norse Myth.: Leach, 17]

4. **Ahura Mazda (Ormuzd, Ormazd)** the spirit of good and creator of all things. [Zoroastrianism: Payton, 11]

5. **Allah** Arabic name of the Supreme Being. [Islam: Benét, 24]

6. **alpha** first letter of Greek alphabet, therefore, along with omega, associated with Judeo-Christian God, who is thought to be the beginning and the end. [Rel.: *CEOS&S*, 206]

7. **Amen-Ra** national and chief god of Egyptians. [Egypt. Myth.: Leach, 42]

8. **Ancient of Days** scriptural epithet for God. [O.T.: Daniel 7:9]

9. **Assur** principal god. [Assyrian Myth.: Benét, 59]

10. **Brahman** supreme soul of the universe. [Hindu Phil.: Parrinder, 50]

11. **Buddha** "the Enlightened One"; mystical supremacy. [Hinduism: Payton, 108]

12. **Creator, the** common sobriquet for God. [Pop. Usage: Misc.]

13. **El** rare Biblical appellation of the Lord. [Judaism: Wigoder, 169]

14. **Elohim** spoken in place of the ineffable Yahweh. [Judaism: *NCE*, 22]

15. **Huitzilopochtli** supreme war god of the Aztecs. [Aztec Religion: *NCE*, 1286]

16. **Jehovah** the ancient Hebrew name for God; anglicization of "Yahweh." [Heb. Lang.: *NCE*, 1407]

17. **Manitou** supreme deity of Algonquin and neighboring tribes. [Am. Indian Religion: *Collier's*, X, 91]

18. **Marduk** warrior god, chief of the Babylonian pantheon; creator of heaven, earth, and man. [Babylonian Myth.: Benét, 634]

19. **Ninety-Nine Names of Allah** reciting the 99 names is an important Muslim devotion; the names reflect Islam's view of God's qualities. [Islam: *UIMT*, 156–57]

20. **omega** last letter of Greek alphabet, therefore, along with alpha, associated with Judeo-Christian God, who is thought to be the beginning and the end. [Rel.: *CEOS&S*, 206, 236]

21. **Ormuzd** supreme deity and embodiment of good. [Persian Myth.: Wheeler, 272]

22. **Osiris** supreme deity and ruler of eternity. [Ancient Egyptian Myth.: Benét, 745]

23. **Pantheon** from the Greek meaning "all the gods," used to describe a group of exemplary people. [Am. Culture: *ODA*]

24. **Quetzalcoatl** god of the Toltecs. [Toltec Religion: *NCE*, 2258]

25. **rays, garland of** emblem of God the Father. [Christian Iconog.: Jobes, 374]

26. **Sat Nam** Sikh name for God; also a mantra. [Sikh Religion: Misc.]

27. **Shekinah** equivalent for Lord in Aramaic interpretation of Old Testament. [Targumic Lit.: Brewer *Dictionary*, 991]

28. **Tetragrammaton** Hebrew word for Lord: YHWH; pronunciation forbidden. [Judaism: Wigoder, 593]

29. **Yahweh** reconstruction of YHWH, from the Hebrew *Elohim* ("God") and *Adonai* ("My Lord"), ancient Hebrew name for God. [Heb. Lang.: *NCE*, 3019]

326. GOLF

1. **British Open** one of the four major tournaments in the PGA. [Am. Sports: *EB*]

2. **Didrikson, Babe (1911–1956)** aggressive, wisecracking golf champion was instrumental in establishing the Ladies Professional Golfers Association (LPGA) in 1949. [Am. Sports: *SJEPC*]

3. **Hogan, Ben (1912–1997)** one of the legends of the game, Hogan won nine major tournaments, and is remembered for his tenacity and accuracy. [Am. Sports: *EB*]

4. **Jones, Bobby (1902–1971)** winningest golfer of his era; won 62% of major championships he entered and competed for free, as an amateur; co-designed Augusta National Golf course. [Am. Sports: *SJEPC*]

5. **Masters, The** one of the four major tournaments in the PGA. [Am. Sports: *EB*]

6. **Nicklaus, Jack (1940–)** eminently successful golfer; record-breaking winner of twenty major championships. [Am. Sports: *SJEPC*]

7. **Palmer, Arnold (1929–)** popular and talented golfer who dominated the sport in the early 1960s. [Am. Sports: *SJEPC*]

8. **PGA** Professional Golfers' Association: the organization that sanctions professional golf. [Am. Sports: *EB*]

9. **PGA Championship** one of the four major tournaments in the PGA. [Am. Sports: *EB*]

10. **Rodriguez, Chi Chi (1935–)** first Hispanic to become international champion. [Am. Sports: *SJEPC*]

11. **Sorenstam, Annika (1970–)** Swedish pro golfer and Hall-of-Famer, considered the finest woman player of all time, with 88 career wins. [Am. Sports: *BTSportsv.6*]

12. **Trevino, Lee (1939–)** first Mexican American to win a major professional golf championship with 1968 U.S. Open victory; stellar career followed with 30 tournament wins. [Am. Sports: *SJEPC*]

13. **U.S. Open** one of the four major tournaments in the PGA. [Am. Sports: *EB*]

14. **Watson, Tom (1949–)** five-time winner of the British Open and two Masters victories highlighted his stellar career. [Am. Sports: *SJEPC*]

15. **Woods, Tiger (1975–)** first person of color and youngest person to win the Masters (1997, at age 21); one of the best golfers in history, with 65 PGA wins, and 14 major victories. [Am. Sports: *SJEPC*]

327. GOODNATUREDNESS (See also JOVIALITY.)

1. **Booth, Amelia** good-natured heroine. [Br. Lit.: *Amelia*]

2. **Boythorn, Laurence** amiable, pleasant character. [Br. Lit.: *Bleak House*]

3. **Cadwallader, Rev. Mr.** pleasant and cheery rector. [Br. Lit.: *Middlemarch*]

4. **Cheshire Cat** imperturbable cat with perpetual grin. [Br. Lit.: *Alice's Adventures in Wonderland*]

5. **de Coverley, Sir Roger** soul of amiability. [Br. Lit.: *The Spectator*, Walsh *Modern*, 108]

6. **Good Joe** personification for a good-hearted, obliging person. [Pop. Culture: Payton, 278]

7. **Herf, Jimmy** newspaper reporter as everybody's friend. [Am. Lit.: *The Manhattan Transfer*]

8. **jasmine** traditional representation of a pleasant nature. [Flower Symbolism: *Flora Symbolica*, 175]

9. **Raggedy Ann** goodnatured despite misadventures; doll with perpetual smile. [Children's Lit.: *Raggedy Ann Stories*]

10. **Silver, Mattie** Zeena's cousin-companion; brightens Frome's gloomy house. [Am. Lit.: *Ethan Frome*]

11. **white mullein** indicates amiability. [Flower Symbolism: *Flora Symbolica*, 178]

12. **xeranthemum** symbolizes goodnaturedness in adversity. [Flower Symbolism: *Flora Symbolica*, 178]

Goodness (See KINDNESS.)

328. GOSSIP (See also SLANDER.)

1. **assembly of women** symbolizes gossip in dream context. [Dream Lore: Jobes, 143]

2. **Blondie and Tootsie** two characters continually gossiping from morning to night. [Comics: "Blondie" in Horn, 118]

3. **Duchess of Berwick** rumor-jabbering woman upsets Lady Windermere. [Br. Lit.: *Lady Windermere's Fan*, Magill I, 488–490]

4. **Hopper, Hedda (1885–1966)** former actress-turned-Hollywood gossip columnist influenced careers both positively and negatively with her stories and scoops; archrival was Louella Parsons (1930s-60s). [Am. Jour.: *SJEPC*; Misc.]

5. **Norris, Mrs.** Fanny's aunt, the universal type of busybody. [Br. Lit.: *Mansfield Park*, Magill I, 562–564]

6. **Parsons, Louella (1881–1972)** powerful Hollywood gossip columnist broke scandalous news about the movie industry and its players, often harming careers; competing columnist Hedda Hopper was archrival (1920s-60s). [Am. Jour.: *SJEPC*; Misc.]

7. **Peyton Place** New Hampshire town where everyone knows everyone else's business. [Am. Lit.: *Peyton Place*, Payton, 523]

8. **Sneerwell, Lady** leader of a group that creates and spreads malicious gossip. [Br. Drama: Sheridan *The School for Scandal*]

9. **Winchell, Walter (1897–1972)** syndicated gossip columnist with weekly radio program who had millions of Americans enthralled by his unverified stories of the private lives of the rich and famous; led the way for the culture of celebrity. [Am. Jour. and Radio: *SJEPC*]

Gourmand (See EPICURE, GLUTTONY.)

Graciousness (See COURTESY, HOSPITALITY.)

329. **GRATITUDE**

1.   **agrimony** traditional symbol for gratitude. [Flower Symbolism: *Flora Symbolica*, 172]

2.   **Androcles** because he had once extracted a thorn from its paw, the lion refrained from attacking Androcles in the arena. [Rom Lit.: Brewer *Dictionary*, 33]

3.   **Canticle of the Sun, The** St. Francis of Assisi's pantheistic hymn of thanks. [Christian Hagiog.: Bishop, 296]

4.   **Hannah** jubilantly thankful to God for giving son. [O.T.: I Samuel 1:6]

5.   **Magwitch, Abel** amply repays Pip for having helped him when in desperate straits. [Br. Lit.: Dickens *Great Expectations*]

6.   **Noah's altar** built to thank God for safe landing. [O.T.: Genesis 8:20–21]

7.   **Thanksgiving Day** American holiday expressing gratitude for the material and spiritual blessings bestowed on the U.S.. [Am. Culture: *PatHols*]

330. **GREED (See also MISERLINESS.)**

1.   *Almayer's Folly* lust for gold leads to decline. [Br. Lit.: *Almayer's Folly*]

2.   **Alonso** Shakespearean symbol of avarice. [Br. Lit.: *The Tempest*]

3.   **Barak's wife** agrees to sell shadow, symbol of her fertility. [Aust. Opera: R. Strauss, *Woman Without a Shadow*, Westerman, 432]

4.   **Béline** fans husband's hypochondria to get his money. [Fr. Lit.: *Le Malade Imaginaire*]

5.   **Brown, Joe** turns in partner Joe Christmas for reward money. [Am. Lit.: *Light in August*]

6.   *Citizen Kane* classic 1941 film directed by and starring Orson Welles employed innovative film techniques to tell story of tyrannical millionaire publisher, who is destroyed by greed and hubris. [Am. Film: *SJEPC*]

7.   *Common Lot, The* the get-rich-quick club. [Am. Lit.: *The Common Lot*, Hart, 369]

8.   **Crawley, Pitt** inherits, marries, and hoards money. [Br. Lit.: *Vanity Fair*]

9.   **Eugénie Grandet** wealth as raison d'etre. [Fr. Lit.: *Eugènie Grandet*, Magill I, 258–260]

10. **Ewing, J. R.** central character in TV hit *Dallas*: greed personified. [Am. TV: Misc.]

11. ***Financier, The*** riches as raison d'etre. [Am. Lit.: *The Financier*, Magill I, 280–282]

12. **Gehazi** behind master's back, takes money he declined. [O.T.: II Kings 5:21–22]

13. **Griffiths, Clyde** insatiable desire for wealth causes his downfall. [Am. Lit.: *An American Tragedy*]

14. **Hoard, Walkadine** hastily marries courtesan posing as wealthy widow. [Br. Lit.: *A Trick to Catch the Old One*]

15. **Kibroth-hattaavah** Hebrew place name: where greedy were buried. [O.T.: Numbers 11:33–35]

16. **Las Vegas** legalized gambling has made this city in Nevada synonymous with greed. [Am. Pop. Culture: Misc.]

17. **Lucre, Pecunious** duped into succoring profligate nephew by lure of a fortune. [Br. Lit.: *A Trick to Catch the Old One*]

18. **Mammon** avaricious fallen angel. [Br. Lit.: *Paradise Lost*]

19. **Mammon, Sir Epicure** avaricious knight; seeks philosopher's stone for Midas touch. [Br. Lit.: *The Alchemist*]

20. ***Mansion, The*** shows material advantages of respectability winning over kinship. [Am. Lit.: *The Mansion*, Hart, 520]

21. **Midas** greedy king whose touch turned everything to gold. [Classical Myth.: Bullfinch, 42–44]

22. **Montgomery** mercenary chief proverbially kept for himself all the booty. [Fr. Hist.: Brewer *Dictionary*, 618]

23. **Naboth's Vineyard** another's possession gotten, by hook or crook. [O.T.: I Kings, 21]

24. ***New Grub Street*** place of ruthless contest among moneymongers. [Br. Lit.: *New Grub Street*, Magill I, 647–649]

25. **Osmond, Gilbert** marries Isabel Archer for her money. [Am. Lit.: *The Portrait of a Lady*, Magill I, 766–768]

26. **Overreach, Sir Giles** grasping usurer, unscrupulous and ambitious. [Br. Lit.: *A New Way to Pay Old Debts*, Wheeler, 275]

27. **"Pardoner's Tale, The"** three brothers kill each other for treasure. [Br. Lit.: *Canterbury Tales*, "Pardoner's Tales]

28. **pig** medieval symbol of avarice. [Art.: Hall, 247]

29. **Putnam, Abbie** marries old man in anticipation of inheritance. [Am. Lit.: *Desire Under the Elms*]

30. **Scrooge, Ebenezer** byword for greedy miser. [Br. Lit.: *A Christmas Carol*]

31. **Sisyphus** condemned to impossible task for his avarice. [Gk. Myth.: Wheeler, 1011]

331. GRIEF

1. **Adonais** Shelley's elegy for John Keats. [Br. Lit.: "Adonais" in Benét, 10]

2. **Aedon** changed to nightingale for murdering son; her song funereal. [Gk. Legend: *NCE*, 24]

3. **Aegiale (Aegle)** her tears of grief become amber. [Gk. Myth.: Kravitz, 6]

4. **All Souls' Day** holy day of prayer for repose of departed souls. [Christianity: Brewer *Dictionary*, 1021]

5. **arms reversed** visual symbol of grieving. [Heraldry: Jobes, 128]

6. **Artemisia (4th century B.C.)** built Mausoleum to commemorate husband. [Gk. Hist.: Walsh *Classical*, 32]

7. **Balder (Baldur)** when he was slain, all things on earth wept. [Scand. Myth.: Brewer *Dictionary*, 70]

8. **black** Islamic symbol of mourning; also Western color for mourning. [Islamic and Christian Symbolism: *UIMT*, 230; Leach, 242]

9. **Canens** Janus's daughter; cried herself to death over disappearance of husband, Picus. [Rom. Myth.: Zimmerman, 49]

10. **Ceres** grieving over the loss of her daughter Persephone, she withholds gifts from the earth, thus bringing on winter. [Gk. Myth.: Hamilton *Mythology*, 49]

11. **Clementine** forty-niner's drowned daughter; "lost and gone forever." [Am. Music: Leach, 236]

12. **cypress** symbol of mourning. [Flower Symbolism: Jobes, 402]

13. **dandelion** symbol of grief. [Flower Symbolism: Jobes, 413]

14. **Eos** inconsolably weeps for slain son, Memnon. [Gk. Myth.: Brewer *Dictionary*, 1065]

15. *Grief* Adams memorial by St.-Gaudens in Washington, D.C. [Am. Art: *EB*, VIII: 781]

16. **Hecuba** mourns the death of her children. [Gk. Drama: Benét, 450]

17. **Hyacinthus** beautiful youth, accidentally killed; from his blood sprang flower marked with letters AI, a lament. [Gk. Myth.: Howe, 134]

18. *In Memoriam* Tennyson's tribute to his friend, A.H. Hallam. [Br. Lit.: Harvey, 808]

19. **Kaddish** a prayer said after the death a close relative. [Judaism: Jobes, II, 901]

20. **Kinah** woeful dirge recited on Tishah b'Av. [Judaism: Wigoder, 342]

21. **Kumalo, Rev. Stephen** Zulu clergyman saddened by fate of his son, Absalom, and, by extension, the fate of the blacks of South Africa. [South African Lit.: *Cry, the Beloved Country*]

22. **Libbeus the Apostle** gentlest apostle, dies from despair at Christ's death. [Ger. Lit.: *The Messiah*]

23. *Lycidas* Milton's elegy for his friend, Edward King (1637). [Br. Lit.: *NCE*, 1781]

24. **marigold** symbol of grief. [Flower Symbolism: *Flora Symbolica*, 175]

25. **Mary Magdalene** follower of Jesus, often depicted weeping. [N.T.: Luke 8:2]

26. **Niobe** weeps unceasingly for her murdered children. [Gk. Myth.: Wheeler, 259]

27. *O Captain! My Captain!* Whitman's elegy commemorating Lincoln's death. [Am. Lit.: Benét, 726]

28. *On My First Son* Ben Jonson's short poem mourning the death of his first son. [Br. Lit.: Norton, 243]

29. **Pietà** representation of sorrowing Virgin with the dead Christ. [Art: Hall, 246]

30. **poppy** symbol of consolation. [Flower Symbolism: *Flora Symbolica*, 176; Kunz, 329]

31. **Rachel** massacre of innocents fulfills prophecy that she will weep. [N.T.: Matthew 2:18; Jeremiah 31:15]

32. **red on blue** symbol of death and mourning. [Chinese Art: Jobes, 357]

33. **Rivers of Babylon** representing the grief of the Jews when they were exiled in Babylon. [O.T.: Psalm 137]

34. **shivah** seven days of grieving following close relative's burial. [Judaism: Wigoder, 550]

35. **swallow** bird that cried "consolation" at Lord's crucifixion. [Animal Symbolism: Brewer *Dictionary*, 1050]

36. **Tishah be'Av (9th of Av)** Jewish day of lamentation for destruction of Temple. [Judaism: Wigoder, 51]

37. **Wailing Wall** called the Western Wall by Jews, the remnants of the Temple in Jerusalem and a sacred place of prayer for Jews; receives millions of visitors of all faiths every year. [Jewish Rel.: *EB*, X: 627]

38. **weeping willow** symbolizes grief at loss. [Flower Symbolism: *Flora Symbolica*, 178]

39. *When Lilacs Last in the Dooryard Bloom'd* Whitman poem mourns the death of Lincoln. [Am. Lit.: Benét, 1085]

40. **yew** tree symbolizes grief. [Flower Symbolism: *Flora Symbolica*, 178]

332. GROWTH

1. **acorn** used to symbolize the beginning of growth. [Pop. Culture: Misc.]

2. ***Jack and the Beanstalk*** magic seeds make beanstalk grow overnight, leads Jack to goose that lays the golden eggs. [Br. Folktale: Misc.]

3. **mustard seed** kingdom of Heaven thus likened; for phenomenal development. [N.T.: Matthew 13:31–32]

4. **rice** emblem of growth, rebirth, and fertility, especially in India and China, where it is considered divine nourishment. [Symbolism: *CEOS&S*]

333. GUARDIAN (See also PROTECTOR.)

1. **Argus** hundred-eyed giant guarding Io. [Gk. Myth.: Leach, 72]

2. **Argus Panoptes** all-seeing herdsman with one hundred eyes. [Gk. Myth.: Walsh *Classical*, 29]

3. **battle ax** symbol of wardship. [Western Folklore: Jobes, 163]

4. **beefeater** popular name for a Yeoman of the Guard or Yeoman Warder of the Tower of London. [Br. Hist.: Payton, 88]

5. **Bodhisattva** enlightened one deferring to Nirvana to help others. [Buddhism: Parrinder, 48]

6. **Cardea** protects children from witches. [Rom. Myth.: Leach, 191]

7. **Cerberus** three-headed dog, guards gate to Hades. [Gk. Myth.: Zimmerman, 55]

8. **cherubim** defended tree of life with flaming swords. [O.T.: Genesis 3:24]

9. **cock** watchful church-tower sitter. [Christian Symbolism: Appleton, 21]

10. **Cybele** protector of cities and mother-goddess. [Phrygian Myth.: Avery, 345]

11. **Delphyne** half-woman, half-beast; guarded Zeus while imprisoned by Typhon. [Gk. Myth.: Howe, 78]

12. **dog** in Japan and China, guardian symbol; in China, also linked to demons. [Animal Symbolism: *CEOS&S*]

13. **Egil** giant who watched over Thor's goats. [Norse Myth.: *LLEI*, I: 327]

14. **Erytheis** stood vigil over golden apples of Hesperides. [Gk. Myth.: *LLEI*, I: 327]

15. **eunuch** castrated guardian of Eastern harems. [Arab. Culture: Jobes, I, 530–531]

16. **Fafnir** dragon guarding the Nibelung's gold. [Ger. Opera: Wagner, *Siegfried*, Westerman, 240–241]

17. **fairy godmother** mythical being who guards children from danger and rewards them for good deeds. [Folklore: Misc.]

18. **Faithful Eckhardt** old man; warns people of death procession on Maundy Thursday. [Ger. Folklore: *LLEI*, I: 281]

19. **Ferohers** tutelary angels. [Persian Myth.: *LLEI*, I: 328]

20. **fiery swords** brandished by cherubim safeguarding tree of life. [O.T.: Genesis 33:24]

21. **Fisher King** guardian of the Grail. [Ger. Legend: *Parzival*; Arthurian Legend: Walsh *Classical*, 227]

22. **Fylgie** guardian spirit assigned to each human for life. [Norse Myth.: *LLEI*, I: 328]

23. **Garm** ferocious watchdog at gate of Hell. [Norse Myth.: *LLEI*, I: 328]

24. **guardian angel** term for angels who watches over the living. [Christianity: Misc.]

25. **Hemdall** guardian of Bifrost; distinguished for acute vision and hearing. [Norse Myth.: Leach, 488]

26. **Ladon** hundred-headed dragon; guarded apples of the Hesperides. [Rom. Myth.: Zimmerman, 145]

27. **lion** sleeps with eyes open. [Christian Symbolism: Appleton, 59]

28. **Mahub Ali** horse-dealer in charge of Kim. [Br. Lit.: *Kim*]

29. **Michael, Saint** guardian archangel. [O.T.: Daniel 10:13, 12:1]

30. **Nana** gentle old dog; guards the Darling children. [Br. Lit.: *Peter Pan*]

31. *Palace Guard, The* sobriquet for the zealous spokesmen-defenders of the Nixon Administration. [Am. Hist.: *The Palace Guard*]

32. **Palladium** a "safeguard"; Troy believed safe while statue of Pallas Athene remained. [Gk. Lit.: *Iliad*, Espy, 40]

33. **raven** guardian of the dead. [Christian Folklore: Mercatante, 159]

34. **Swiss Guards** papal praetorian guard instituted by Julius II. [Ital. Hist.: Plumb, 218, 254]

35. **wyvern** protector of treasure and wealth. [Heraldry: Halberts, 40]

334. GUIDANCE (See also COUNSEL, WISDOM.)

1. *Analects, The* emphasize human relationships, the golden rule, and usefulness to the state and society. [Chin. Lit.: *The Analects of Confucius* in Benét, 33]

2. **Anthony, Mr.** gave guidance to supplicants on radio show. [Am. Radio: "Ask Mr. Anthony" in Buxton, 99]

3. **Baloo** bear who teaches Mowgli jungle law; from Rudyard Kipling's series for young readers, *The Jungle Books* (1894–1895). [Br. Children's Lit.: Jones]

4. **Deborah** under her aegis, Barak routed the Canaanites. [O.T.: Judges 4:4–10]

5. **Dix, Dorothea (1870–1951)** syndicated columnist who gave advice to the lovelorn. [Am. Pop. Culture: Misc.]

6. **Dooley, Mr.** Irish saloonkeeper in Chicago who sagely and humorously dispenses folk philosophy. [Am. Humor: Hart, 240]

7. **Glinda** the "Good Witch" from L. Frank Baum's Oz series; takes all of Dorothy's companions to place where each will rule and helps Dorothy understand how to return home using her own powers. [Br. Children's Lit.: Jones]

8. **lamp** Word of God showing the way. [Christian Symbolism: O.T.: Psalms, 119:105]

9. **Landers, Ann (1918–2002)** syndicated columnist who gave advice on personal problems; twin sister of Abigail Van Buren ("Dear Abby" advice columnist). [Am. Pop. Culture: Misc.]

10. **Mentor** Odysseus's friend and advisor. [Gk. Lit.: *Odyssey*]

11. **Ten Commandments** God's precepts for man's life. [O.T.: Exodus 20:3–17; Deuteronomy 5:7–21]

12. **Van Buren, Abigail (1918–)** wrote syndicate advice column as Dear Abby; column now written by her daughter; twin sister of advice columnist Ann Landers. [Am. Pop. Culture: Misc.]

335. GUIDE

1. **Aleka** leader of wolfpack. [Br. Lit.: *The Jungle Books*]

2. **Anchises** Aeneas' guide in Elysium. [Rom. Lit.: *Aeneid*]

3. **Anubis** "Pathfinder"; conducted dead to judgment before Osiris. [Egyptian Myth.: Jobes, 105]

4. **Baedeker** series of guidebooks for travelers. [Travel: *NCE*, 207]

5. **Beatrice** Dante's beloved soul; directs him in Paradise. [Ital. Lit.: *Divine Comedy*, Magill I, 211–213]

6. **Cumaean sibyl** famous prophetess; leads Aeneas through underworld. [Rom. Lit.: *Aeneid*]

7. **dolphin** transported blessed souls to islands of dead. [Gk. and Roman Myth.: Appleton, 31]

8. **Jack the Porpoise** led ships through treacherous strait off New Zealand. [Br. Hist.: Wallechinsky, 128]

9. **Judas goat** a goat used to lead sheep to slaughter. [Eur. Culture: Misc.]

10. **lighthouse at Pharos** 400 ft. tall; beacon visible 300 miles at sea. [World. Hist.: Wallechinsky, 257]

11. **Palinurus** pilot of Aeneas. [Rom. Lit.: *Aeneid*]

12. **pillar of cloud, pillar of fire** Jehovah leads way to promised land. [O.T.: Exodus 13:21–22]

13. **raven** in Africa, raven is guide. [Symbolism: *CEOS&S*]

14. **star of Bethlehem** guiding light to Jesus for the Magi. [Christian Symbolism: N.T.: Matthew 2:9]

15. **Tiphys** pilot of the Argonauts. [Rom. Myth.: Brewer *Dictionary*, 1085]

16. **Vergil** Dante's guide in Hell and Purgatory. [Ital. Lit.: *Divine Comedy*, Magill I, 211–213]

336. GULLIBILITY (See also DUPERY.)

1. **Big Claus** foolishly falls for Little Claus's falsified get-rich-quick schemes. [Dan. Lit.: *Andersen's Fairy Tales*]

2. **Emperor** orders a new outfit from weavers who claim it will be invisible to anyone unworthy of his position. [Dan. Lit.: "The Emperor's New Clothes" in *Andersen's Fairy Tales*]

3. **Georgette** Mary Richards's coworker and Ted Baxter's wife; epitomizes gullibility. [TV: "The Mary Tyler Moore Show" in Terrace, II, 70]

4. **Oswald** believes Edmund's false charges against Edgar. [Br. Lit.: *King Lear*]

5. **Othello** "thinks men honest that but seem to be so." [Br. Lit.: *Othello*]

6. **Peachum, Polly** among others, believes she is Macheath's wife. [Br. Opera: *The Beggar's Opera*]

7. **Quixote, Don** completely taken in by all the tales and plans of his squire and others who humor his delusions. [Span. Lit.: Cervantes *Don Quixote*]

8. **Simple Simon** credulous booby. [Nurs. Rhyme: Opie, 387]

9. **Tenderfoot** told that cowpunching is a cinch, is badly hurt when he tries it and is tossed. [Am. Balladry: "The Tenderfoot"]

10. **Urfe, Nicholas** trusts in the specious sincerity of the actors in Conchis's psychological experiments on him. [Br. Lit.: John Fowles *The Magus* in Weiss, 279]

H

337. HAIR

1. **Absalom** hair entangled in branches, he was left dangling. [O.T.: II Samuel 18:9]

2. **Aslaug** used hair as cloak to meet king. [Norse Myth.: Walsh *Classical*, 35]

3. **Beatles** initially, their moplike haircuts were nearly as sensational as their music. [Br. Music: Misc.]

4. **Bes** shaggy-haired, shortlegged god with tail. [Egyptian Myth.: Leach, 138]

5. **Buffalo Bill (William F. Cody, 1846–1917)** American cowboy and showman whose image was fortified by his long blond hair. [Am. Hist.: *NCE*, 390]

6. **Clairol** revolutionary do-it-yourself hair color introduced to American women in 1956 made changing one's image easier and more acceptable. [Culture: *SJEPC*]

7. **Cousin Itt** Addams' relative; four feet tall and completely covered with blond hair. [TV: "The Addams Family" in Terrace, I, 29]

8. **Custer, General George (1839–1876)** American army officer whose image included long, yellowish hair. [Am. Hist.: *NCE*, 701]

9. **Enkidu** hirsute companion of Gilgamesh. [Babyl. Myth.: Gilgamesh*]*

10. **Fawcett, Farrah (1947–)** costar of TV's *Charlie's Angels* in late 1970s started American hairstyle trend with her full, tousled, feathered hair. [Am. TV and Culture: *SJEPC*]

11. **Godiva, Lady (d. 1057)** Leofric's wife who rode through Coventry clothed only in her long, golden hair. [Br. Hist.: Payton, 274]

12. **Gruagach** "the hairy one"; fairy lady. [Scot. Folklore: Briggs, 206–207]

13. *Hair* rock musical celebrating youthful exuberance as evidenced by growing long hair. [Am. Mus.: *On Stage*, 517]

14. **hippies** 1960s dropouts of American culture usually identified with very long hair adorned with flowers. [Pop. Cult.: Misc.]

15. **Mullach, Meg** long-haired and hairy-handed brownie. [Scot. Folklore: Briggs, 284–285]

16. **Rapunzel** her golden tresses provide access to tower loft. [Ger. Fairy Tale: *Rapunzel*]

17. **Samson** the Hercules of the Israelites; rendered powerless when Delilah cut off his hair. [O.T.: Judges 13–16]

Happiness (See JOY.)

338. HARMONY

1. **Andrews Sisters, The** popular music trio of the 1930s and 1940s known for their harmonic singing style and for entertaining American troops during World War II. [Am. Music: *SJEPC*]

2. **barbershop quartet** four-part, a cappella vocal music group known for close harmonies and improvisational style. [Am. Music: *SJEPC*]

3. **Beach Boys, The** band with close-harmony style vocals formed by Wilson brothers Brian, Dennis, and Carl; epitomized 1960s Southern California youth culture. [Am. Music: *SJEPC*]

4. **Concordia** goddess of harmony, peace, and unity. [Rom. Myth.: Kravitz, 65]

5. **cross** incorporates all states of being. [Islamic Rel.: *IEOTS*, 46]

6. **duck** in Japan and China, pair of mandarin ducks symbolizes marriage and domestic harmony. [Symbolism: *CEOS&S*]

7. **Harmony** child of ugly Hephaestus and lovely Aphrodite; union of opposites. [Gk. Myth.: Espy, 25]

8. **Polyhymnia** muse of lyric poetry; presided over singing. [Gk. Myth.: Brewer *Dictionary*, 849]

9. **yin-yang** complementary principles that make up all aspects of life. [Chinese Trad.: *EB*, X: 821]

339. HATRED

1. **Ahab, Captain** main character whose monomania is an expression of hatred. [Am. Lit.: *Moby Dick*]

2. **basil flower** flower representing hatred of the other sex. [Flower Symbolism: Jobes, 184]

3. **Claggart** dislikes Billy Budd so that he falsely accuses him of fomenting mutiny. [Am. Lit.: Herman Melville *Billy Budd*]

4. **Coughlin, Father Charles Edward (1891–1979)** American Catholic priest whose weekly radio programs provided the platform for his message of hatred, anti-semitism, and facism in the 1930s. [Am. Rel.: *FOF, MOD*]

5. **Esau** despised brother for stealing Isaac's blessing. [O.T.: Genesis 27:41–42]

6. **Eteocles and Polynices** their hatred extended to the funeral pyre where even their flames would not mingle. [Gk. Myth.: "The Seven Against Thebes" in Benét, 917]

7. **Feverel, Sir Austin** after wife left him, he became a woman-hater. [Br. Lit.: *The Ordeal of Richard Feverel* Magill I, 692–695]

8. **Frithiof** kills proud sea-kings, saves a king and queen from death, and defeats her brothers in battle. [Nor. Lit.: Haydn & Fuller, 275]

9. **Grimes, Peter** a community hounds a man to his death. [Br. Opera: Britten, *Peter Grimes*, Westerman, 536–539]

10. **Medea** legendery sorceress whose hatred came of jealousy. [Gk. Myth.: Payton, 433]

11. **St. John's wort** indicates animosity. [Flower Symbolism: *Flora Symbolica*, 177]

12. **Styx** river of aversion. [Br. Lit.: *Paradise Lost*]

13. **Thomas, Bigger** possesses a pathological hatred of white people. [Am. Lit.: *Native Son*, Magill I, 643–645]

14. **Tulliver, Mr.** instructs children to despise Mr. Wakem. [Br. Lit.: *The Mill on the Floss*, Magill I, 593–595]

340. HEADLESSNESS (See also DECAPITATION.)

1. **Acephali** fabled Libyan nation of men without heads. [Rom. Hist.: Leach, 6]

2. **Alban, Saint** carries his head in his hands. [Christian Hagiog.: Brewer *Dictionary*, 18]

3. **Denis of Paris, Saint** French patron; carried severed head to burial. [Christian Hagiog.: Attwater, 104–105]

4. **Headless Horseman** spectral figure haunts Ichabod Crane. [Am. Lit.: *The Legend of Sleepy Hollow*]

341. HEALING (See also HEALTH, MEDICINE.)

1. **Acesis** daughter of Asclepius; name means 'healing remedy.' [Gk. Myth.: Kravitz, 37]

2. **Achilles' spear** had power to heal whatever wound it made. [Gk. Lit.: *Iliad*]

3. **acupuncture** Chinese medical treatment used for pain relief and prevention gained greater acceptance in the United States by the 1990s; involves stimulation of pressure points in the body. [Chinese Medicine: *SJEPC*]

4. **Agamede** Augeas' daughter; noted for skill in using herbs for healing. [Gk. Myth.: Zimmerman, 11]

5. **Ahmed, Prince** possessed apple of Samarkand; cure for all diseases. [Arab Lit.: *Arabian Nights*]

6. **Amahl** cripple cured when he offers his only possession, his crutch, as a gift for the Christ child. [Am. Opera: *Amahl and the Night Visitors*, Benét, 28]

7. **Ananias** Lord's disciple restores Saul's vision. [N.T.: Acts 9:17–19]

8. **Angitia** goddess of healing. [Rom. Myth.: Kravitz, 24]

9. **Antony, Saint** invoked against venereal diseases and erysipelas (St. Antony fire). [Christian Hagiog.: Daniel, 28–29]

10. **Asclepius (Aesculapius)** god of healing. [Gk. Myth.: Kravitz, 37]

11. **balm in Gilead** metaphorical cure for sins of the Israelites. [O.T.: Jeremiah 8:22]

12. **Bethesda** Jerusalem pool, believed to have curative powers. [N.T.: John 5:2–4]

13. **Carmenta** goddess of healing. [Gk. Myth.: Kravitz, 53]

14. **Christian Science** church's philosophy based on mental and spiritual healing as cure for physical ailments discourages adherents from seeking medical treatment. [Am. Rel. and Medicine: *SJEPC*; Willis, 121]

15. **copper** Indian talisman to prevent cholera. [Ind. Myth.: Jobes, 369]

16. **coral** cures madness; stanches blood from wound. [Gem Symbolism: Kunz, 68]

17. **emerald** relieves diseases of the eye. [Gem Symbolism: Kunz, 370]

18. **Iaso** Asclepius's daughter; personification of his healing power. [Gk. Myth.: Kravitz, 37]

19. **Jesus' five cures** he makes blind beggars see. [N.T.: Matthew 9:27–31, 20:31–34; Mark 10:46–52; Luke 18:35–43]

20. **Panacea** daughter of Greek god of healing. [Gk. Myth.: Kravitz, 37]

21. **Roch, Saint (also Saint Rock)** invoked against infectious diseases; especially in the 15th century, against plague. [Christian Hagiog.: Daniel, 198]

22. **sweet fennel** said to remedy blindness and cataracts. [Herb Symbolism: *Flora Symbolica*, 164]

23. **Vitus, Saint** invoked against epilepsy and chorea (St. Vitus's dance). [Christian Hagiog.: Attwater, 338]

342. HEALTH (See also HEALING, MEDICINE.)

1. **aerobics** dance-based cardiovascular exercise became American trend by 1980s, with workouts popularized by actress and fitness guru Jane Fonda. [Misc.: *SJEPC*]

2. **agate** symbolizes health; supposed to relieve snake and scorpion bites. [Class. And Medieval Legend: Leach, 27]

3. **Asclepius' cup** symbolizes well-being. [Gk. Myth.: Jobes, 397]

4. **Carna** goddess of physical fitness. [Rom. Myth.: Leach, 192]

5. **Damia** goddess of health. [Gk. Myth.: Jobes, 409]

6. **Eddy, Mary Baker (1821–1910)** founder of the Christian Science movement, her beliefs as espoused in *Science and Health with Key to the Scriptures* (1875) held that health and healing are rooted in the mind. [Am. Rel. and Hist.: *SJEPC*; Willis, 119]

7. **holistic medicine** alternative approach to health care emphasizes the whole patient, incorporating the treament of physical, environmental, mental, social, spiritual ailments. [Am. Science: Misc.]

8. **Hygeia** goddess of health; daughter and personification of Asclepius. [Gk. Myth.: Kravitz, 123]

9. **Hygeia's cup** symbol of fertility and fitness. [Gk. Myth.: Jobes, 396–397]

10. **LaLanne, Jack (1914–)** jumpsuit-wearing fitness guru whose daily TV exercise program ran from 1959 to 1985; opened first fitness club in America in 1936 and was considered fanatic for doing so; also invented first weight machines and produced first fitness video. [Am. Culture: *SJEPC*]

11. **Muscle Beach** Southern California beach where fit athletes met and worked out. [Am. Culture: *SJEPC*]

12. **National Institutes of Health** the "steward of medical and behavioral research in the U.S.," it funds research in all areas of health and medicine. [Am. Science: Misc.]

13. **Spock, Dr. Benjamin (1903–1998)** his child rearing theories changed rigid attitudes about what was best for children; his *Common Sense Book of Baby and Child Care,* originally published in 1946, advised parents to trust their own judgment. [Am. Pop. Culture: *SJEPC*]

343. HEARTLESSNESS (See also CRUELTY, RUTHLESSNESS.)

1. **Chester, Sir John** towards son's love affair. [Br. Lit.: *Barnaby Rudge*]

2. **Clare, Angel** cannot forgive Tess's past. [Br. Lit.: *Tess of the D'Urbervilles*]

3. **Estella** trained by Miss Havisham to take advantage of men. [Br. Lit.: *Great Expectations*]

4. **Ettarre** encourages knight's love to gain his tournament prize. [Br. Lit.: *Idylls of the King*, "Pelleas and Ettarre"]

5. **Gabler, Hedda** ruthlessly debases and cruelly deceives a former lover, driving him to suicide. [Swed. Drama: Isben *Hedda Gabler*]

6. **Gerard, Lieutenant Philip** unfeeling in singleminded pursuit of Kimble. [TV: "The Fugitive" in Terrace, I, 290]

7. **Gessler** sentenced Tell to shoot apple off son's head. [Swiss Legend: Brewer *Dictionary*, 1066; Ital. Opera: Rossini, *Wilhelm Tell*]

8. **Hatto** for hardheartedness to poor during famine, eaten by mice. [Ger. Legend: *LLEI*, I: 290]

9. **Infanta** laughs at the death of the little Dwarf who can no longer dance for her. [Br. Lit.: Oscar Wilde, 'The Birthday of the Infanta"]

10. **Javert** coldhearted in his relentless pursuit of Valjean. [Fr. Lit.: *Les Misèrables*]

11. **La Belle Dame Sans Merci** cruel and heartless lady. [Br. Lit.: "La Belle Dame Sans Merci" in Walsh *Modern*, 51]

12. **Queen of Hearts** despite her suit, she is cruel and heartless, with a penchant for beheadings; from Lewis Carroll's *Alice's Adventures in Wonderland*. [Br. Children's Lit.: Jones]

13. **Sanine** has no pity for others' sufferings. [Russ. Lit.: Magill III, 921]

14. **Turandot** in revenge for dishonor to ancestor. [Ital. Opera: Puccini, *Turandot*, Westerman, 368]

344. HEAVEN (See also PARADISE.)

1. **Aaru** abode of blessed dead and gods. [Egyptian Myth.: Benét, 1]

2. **Abraham's bosom** reward for the righteous. [N.T.: Luke 16:23]

3. **animals in heaven** Jonah's whale and Balaam's ass are among the ten animals allowed to enter paradise. [Muslim Legend: Benét, 37]

4. **Anu (An)** Babylonian god of heaven. [Babyl. Myth.: Benét, 41]

5. **Asgard** abode of the gods. [Norse Myth.: Walsh, *Classical*, 34]

6. **Avalon** the blissful otherworld of the dead. [Celtic Myth.: *NCE*, 194]

7. **Beulah** allegorical name for Israel. [O.T.: Isaiah 62:4–5]

8. **Dilmun** dwelling of gods where sun rose. [Sumerian Myth.: Gaster, 24]

9. **Elysian Fields** home of the blessed after death. [Gk. Myth.: Kravitz, 88]

10. **Elysium** abode of the blessed after death. [Gk. Myth.: Zimmerman, 94; Gk. Lit.: *Odyssey*]

11. **Firdaws** paradise; Islamic heaven. [Islamic Rel.: *ODWR*, 418]

12. **Fortunate Isles (Happy Isles)** otherworld for heroes favored by gods. [Gk. Myth.: *NCE*, 861]

13. **garden of the Hesperides** in this garden grew a tree with golden apples. [Gk. Myth.: Zimmerman, 109]

14. **Happy Hunting Ground** concept found in several Native American tribes; a paradise where souls pass after death, to hunt and feast. [North Am. Indian Myth.: Misc.]

15. **Holy City** poetical name for heaven. [World Rel.: *NCE*, 1213]

16. **Jacob's ladder** from the Biblical story of Jacob, who dreamed of a ladder reaching from earth to heaven. [O.T.: Genesis 28: 12]

17. **Janna** garden; Islamic heaven. [Islamic Rel.: *ODWR*, 418]

18. **Kailasa** heavenly dwelling of the god Shiva; a peak of the Himalayas. [Hindu Rel.: *ODWR*, 523]

19. **Land of the Leal** abode of the blessed dead. [Scot. Myth.: Misc.]

20. **Mount Zion** celestial city. [Br. Lit.: *The Pilgrim's Progress*]

21. **New Jerusalem** new paradise; dwelling of God among men. [N.T.: Revelation 21:2]

22. **Olympus** abode of the chief gods. [Gk. Myth.: Espy, 22]

23. **Paradise** poetic name for heaven. [World Rel.: *NCE*, 1213]

24. **Pure Land** most pervasive concept of heaven among Buddhists; realm of exquisite beauty; anyone there will arrive at nirvana quickly. [Buddhist Rel.: *ODWR*, 776]

25. **Sach Khand** a type of heavenly state in Sikh faith; the final stage of spiritual ascent and union with God. [Sikh Rel.: *ODWR*, 831]

26. **San-ch'ing** the three Taoist heavens. [Taoist Rel.: *ODWR*, 853]

27. **seventh heaven** formed of indescribable divine light; inhabitants are supremely happy, all chanting of God. [Islamic Religion: Benét, 449]

28. **Sukhavati** for Pure Land Buddhists, Western Pure Land inhabited by the Buddha Amitabha; here one does not fall back into rebirth. [Buddhist Rel.: *ODWR*, 927]

29. **svarga** Hindu heaven found on one of the Himalayas; through sacrifice, the good can attain svarga. [Hindu Rel.: *ODWR*, 932]

30. **T'ien** Chinese concept of place where gods and other immortals live. [Chinese Rel.: *ODWR*, 975]

31. **tusita** Buddhist heaven where the "contented" gods live; the enlightened who have one more time on earth to work out their karma also abide there. [Buddhist Rel.: *ODWR*, 997]

32. **Vaikuntha (or Baikunth)** paradise of Hiindu diety Visnu; eternal, unlike heavens attained through rebirth. [Hindu Rel.: *ODWR*, 1011]

33. **Valhalla** celestial banquet hall for departed war heroes. [Norse Myth.: Brewer *Dictionary*, 1122]

Height (See GIANT, TALLNESS.)

345. HELL (See also UNDERWORLD.)

1. **Abaddon** place of destruction. [N.T.: Revelation 9:11; Br. Lit.: *Paradise Lost*]

2. **Abi** lowest realms of Buddhist hell; place where one suffers most intense pain, but not eternally. [Buddhist Rel.: *ODWR*, 8]

3. **al-nar** Islamic hell; the fire. [Islamic Rel.: *ODWR*, 418]

4. **bardo** in Tibetan Buddhism, the state after death and before re-birth. [Buddhist Rel.: *ODWR*, 127]

5. **Gehenna (or Gehinnom)** the valley of Hinnom, where children were sacrificed by fire to the god Moloch. [Judaism: Misc.]

6. **Hades** the great underworld. [Gk. Myth.: *NCE*, 1219]

7. **Hinnom** valley of ill repute that came to mean hell. [Judaism: *NCE*, 1244]

8. **Jahannam** Islamic hell where punishment is given according to the gravity of the sins. [Islamic Rel.: *ODWR*, 420]

9. **Jigoku** Japanese for Naraka; punishment and torment, but not everlasting. [Buddhist Rel: *ODWR*, 501]

10. **Naraka (or Niraya)** Hindu and Buddhist concept of punishment and torment, but not everlasting. [Hindu and Buddhist Rel.: *ODWR*, 684]

11. **Pandemonium** chief city of Hell. [Br. Lit.: *Paradise Lost*]

12. **Sheol (or Tophet)** gloomy place of departed, unhappy souls. [Judaism: *NCE*, 1219]

346. HELPFULNESS (See also AID, ORGANIZATIONAL; GENEROSITY; KINDNESS.)

1. **Bauchan** hobgoblin often helpful to man. [Scot. Folklore: Briggs, 19]

2. **Bodachan Sabhaill** barn brownie who threshed for old men. [Scot. Folklore: Briggs, 29]

3. **Boy Scouts** founded in Great Britain in 1908 by Lord Baden-Powell; young males dedicated to organized activities and community service. [Br. Hist.: *OCCL*]

4. **Brownie** elf-like creature that came out at night and finished housework left from the day; helpful children then called Brownies, which led to use of name for junior Girl Scouts. [Scot. and Br. Folklore and Hist.: *OCCL*]

5. **bwbachod** Welsh equivalent of brownies; helpful domestically. [Welsh Folkore: Briggs, 55–56]

6. **Dorcas** made garments for widows. [N.T.: Acts 9:39]

7. **Gal Friday** epitome of the helpful servant or employee; var. of "Man Friday," from D. Defoe's *Robinson Crusoe*. [Am. Cult.: *FOF, MOD*]

8. **Girl Guides/Scouts** Guides organized by Lord Baden-Powell and his sister Agnes in England by 1914; Girl Scouts formed in

U.S. in 1912 by Juliette Gordon Low; young females dedicated to organized activities and service to others. [Br. and Am. Hist.: *OCCL*]

9. **Good Samaritan** man who helped half-dead victim of thieves after a priest and a Levite had "passed by." [N.T.: Luke 10:33]

10. **Killmoulis** brownie that haunted mill, helping miller. [Br. Folklore: Briggs, 246–247]

11. **Phynnodderee** benevolent Manx brownie of great strength. [Manx Folklore: Brewer *Dictionary*, 830]

12. **Robin Round-cap** domestic spirit who helped with chores. [Br. Folklore: Briggs, 344]

13. **Simon the Cyrenian** made to help bear Christ's cross to Calvary. [N.T.: Matthew 27:32; Luke 23:26]

14. **Thomas the Tank Engine** character in series of books beginning in 1945 by Rev. W. Awdry; the little engine dislikes his lowly status at the Big Station; eventually he wins the respect of his fellow locomotives and becomes tremendously useful; stories adapted into very popular TV show. [Br. Chldren's Lit. and TV: *OCCL*]

347. HENPECKED HUSBAND

1. **Belphegor** fiend turned man; henpecked by wife. [Ital. Lit.: *Belphegor*]

2. **Dithers, Mr.** Dagwood's irascible boss; fears only his demanding wife. [Comics: "Blondie" in Horn, 118]

3. **Fondlewife** old banker, dotingly submissive to wife. [Br.Lit.: *The Old Bachelor*]

4. **Jiggs** nouveau riche; forever ducking nagging wife Maggie's rolling pin. [Comics: "Bringing Up Father" in Horn, 132]

5. **Mitty, Walter** daydreaming, henpecked husband. [Am. Lit.: "The Secret Life of Walter Mitty" in Cartwell, 606–610]

6. **Syntax, Doctor** harried and hectored clergyman takes off for the good life. [Br. Lit.: *Doctor Syntax, LLEI*, 1: 279]

7. **Tesman, George** Hedda's scholarly husband; jumps at her command. [Nor. Lit.: *Hedda Gabler*]

348. HERESY (See also APOSTASY, SACRILEGE.)

1. **Albigenses** heretical sect; advocated Manichaean dualism. [Fr. Hist.: *NCE*, 53]

2. **Arians** 4th-century heretical sect; denied Christ's divinity. [Christian Hist.: Brewer *Note-Book*, 43]

3. **Beaufort, Cardinal (1377–1447)** haughty churchman; dies execrating God. [Br. Lit.: *II Henry IV*]

4. **Big-endians** heretical group; always break eggs unlawfully at large end. [Br. Lit.: *Gulliver's Travels*]

5. **Cathari** heretical Christian sect in 12th and 13th centuries; professed a neo-Manichaean dualism. [Christian Hist.: *EB*, II: 639]

6. **Donatists** Christian group in North Africa who broke with Catholicism (312). [Christian Hist.: *EB*, III: 618]

7. **Ebionites** 2nd- and 3rd-century Christian ascetic sect that retained a Jewish emphasis. [Christian Hist.: *EB*, III: 768]

8. **Erastianism** doctrine declaring state is superior to the church in ecclesiastical affairs (1524–1543). [Christian Hist.: *EB*, III: 937]

9. **Fires of Smithfield** Marian martyrs burnt at stake as heretics. [Br. Hist.: Brewer *Dictionary*, 1013]

10. **Gnosticism** heretical theological movement in Greco-Roman world of 2nd century. [Christian Hist.: *EB*, IV: 587]

11. **Inquisition** Roman Catholic tribunal engaged in combating and suppressing heresy. [Christian Hist.: *NCE*, 1352]

12. **Lollards** in late medieval England, a name given to followers of unorthodox philosopher John Wycliffe. [Christian Hist.: *EB*, VI: 306]

13. **min** appellation of any heretic, Jew or non-Jew. [Judaism: Wigoder, 417]

14. **Monophysites** 2nd-century heretical Christian movement led by prophet Montanus. [Christian Hist.: *EB*, VI: 1012]

15. **Sabellianism** 3rd-century Christian heresy led by Sabellius. [Christian Hist.: *EB*, VIII: 747]

349. HERO (See also BRAVERY.)

1. **Achilles** Greek hero without whom Troy could not have been taken. [Gk. Lit.: *Iliad*]

2. **Aeneas** Trojan hero; legendary founder of Roman race. [Rom. Lit.: *Aeneid*]

3. **Argonauts** those accompanying Jason to fetch Golden Fleece. [Gk. Myth.: Parrinder, 26]

4. **Arjuna** hero of the civil war between two royal houses of ancient India. [Hindu Lit.: *Mahabharata*]

5. **Arthur** king and hero of Scotland, Wales, and England. [Arthurian Legend: Parrinder, 28]

6. **Baggins, Frodo** hero of J.R.R. Tolkien's Lord of Rings trilogy (1954–1956); travels to devastated land of Mordor to destroy magic ring with power to tempt all who possess it before it is used for evil by dark lord Sauron. [Br. Lit.: *SJEPC*; Gillespie and Naden]

7. **Bagradian, Gabriel** leads heroic defense by a group of Armenians against the besieging Turks; is killed by a Turkish bullet. [Ger. Lit.: *The Forty Days of Musa Dagh* in Magill I, 291]

8. **Balboa, Rocky** blue-collar hero of 1976 film who wins bout against all odds because of determination and courage. [Am. Film: *SJEPC*]

9. **Bellerophon** rider of Pegasus; conquered monsters and Amazons. [Gk. Myth.: Parrinder, 42; Kravitz, 43]

10. **Beowulf** saved Danes from monster Grendel. [Br. Lit.: *Beowulf*]

11. **Blaise, Modesty** heroine of comic strip by Peter O'Donnell; former gangster turned crime fighter. [Pop. Culture *FOF, MOD*]

12. **Caspian, Prince** in C.S. Lewis's Narnia chronicles, escapes death threat, rules Narnia, and—inspired by Aslan—heroically completes his quest. [Br. Children's Lit.: Jones]

13. **Cid** Spanish knight renowned for exploits against Moors. [Span. Hist.: *EB*, 4: 615–616]

14. **Cooper, Gary (1901–1961)** American movie star, hero of many Westerns, including *High Noon*. [Am. Film: *FOF, MOD*]

15. **Cuchulain** "the Achilles of the Gael." [Irish Myth.: Benét, 239–240]

16. **D'Artagnan** challenges horseman, rescues a lady, and earns fame as a doughty soldier. [Fr. Lit.: Dumas *The Three Musketeers*]

17. **David** boy who slew Goliath. [O.T.: Samuel 18:4–51]

18. **Do-Right, Dudley** brave mountie protagonist who fights evil in cartoon spoof of Nelson Eddy/Jeanette MacDonald movies; while courting his sweetheart Nell, Dudley faces life with a cheerful, rather naïve disposition and a determinedly cleft chin. [TV: "The Dudley Do-Right Show" in Terrace, I, 229–230]

19. **Durward, Quentin** seeking his fortune abroad, he saves the life of King Louis XI, wards off attacks by the king's enemies, and distinguishes himself in a seige. [Br. Lit.: *Quentin Durward*]

20. **Edricson, Alleyne** knighted for chivalry by the Black Prince. [Br. Lit.: *The White Company* in Magill I, 108]

21. *Fantastic Four, The* superhero team of Mr. Fantastic, the Invisible Woman, the Human Torch, and the Thing protects the public but has human faults. [Am. Comics: *SJEPC*]

22. **Frithiof** kills proud sea-kings, saves a king and queen from death, and defeats her brothers in battle. [Nor. Lit.: Haydn & Fuller, 275]

23. **Grettir the Strong** Viking adventurer whose exploits are related in *The Grettisaga*. [Icelandic Lit.: Magill I, 335]

24. **Hale, Nathan (1755–1776)** Revoluntionary War hero; calmly accepted fate. [Am. Hist.: Jameson, 215]

25. **Hancock, John (1736–1793)** American Revolutionary War hero and prominent signer of the Declaration of Independence; his name is synonymous with "signature." [Amer. Hist.: Misc.]

26. **Hanuman** monkey deity, conqueror of demons, builder of a stone bridge from India to Ceylon. [Hindu Myth.: *Collier's*, IX, 214]

27. **Harmodius** slew Hipparchus, brother of the tyrant Hippias. [Gk. Hist.: *EB* (1963) XI, 198]

28. **Hector** King Priam's son; dies fighting for Troy. [Gk. Lit.: *Iliad*]

29. **Hercules** completed tasks requiring great bravery, strength, and ingenuity. [Gk. Myth.: Brewer *Dictionary*, 448]

30. **Hereward the Wake** last of the English; dies defending homeland. [Br. Lit.: *Hereward the Wake*, Magill I. 367–370]

31. **Hornblower, Captain Horatio** victorious captain of HMS *Lydia* and HMS *Sutherland*. [Br. Lit.: *Captain Horatio Hornblower*]

32. **Jason** leader of the Argonauts. [Gk. Myth.: Payton, 347]

33. **Jones, Indiana** archeologist-turned-adventure hero of several films by Steven Spielberg, played by Harrison Ford. [Am. Film: *Raiders of the Lost Ark*]

34. **Judith** saved her city from the onslaught of Holofernes by beheading him during a drunken sleep. [Apocrypha: Judith 13:4–10]

35. **Lassie** brave collie of films from 1943–1951 and award-winning eponymous TV show from 1954–1974; often parodied for her barking warning that there was danger or need for help; show was, nonetheless, great favorite with families and critics. [Am. Film and TV: *SJEPC*]

36. **Leonidas** Spartan king held off thousands of Persians at Thermopylae with a few hundred men. [Gk. Hist.: Benét, 578]

37. **Marvel, Captain** teenage boy transforms into strong, invulnerable superhero upon uttering the word "Shazam." [Am. Comics: *SJEPC*]

38. **Mowgli** human intelligence allows him to aid the other animals in the jungle where he has been raised by wolves; from Rudyard Kipling's series for young readers, *The Jungle Books* (1894–1895). [Br. Children's Lit.: Jones]

39. **Pevensie, Peter** with shield and sword becomes heroic warrior and leader of army and Crowned King of Narnia in C.S. Lewis's classic series for young readers. [Br. Children's Lit.: Jones]

40. **Prometheus** stole divine fire for man's sake. [Gk. Myth.: Espy, 33]

41. **Rambo** macho protagonist of a series of films; plots involve dramatic use of guerilla warfare skills for survival and battle. [Am. Film: *SJEPC*]

42. **raven** in Native American cultures, raven is considered a hero. [Symbolism: *CEOS&S*]

43. **Richard the Lion-Hearted (1157–1199)** nicknamed the Black Knight; performer of valorous deeds. [Br. Hist.: *EB*, VIII: 566; Br. Lit.: *Ivanhoe*]

44. **Rogers, Buck** 25th-century adventurer who combats menacing aliens and other villains in order to save the world. [Comics: Berger, 93]

45. **Roland** chief paladin of Charlemagne; renowned for his prowess. [Fr. Lit.: *NCE*, 2344]

46. **Samson** hero of Israel. [O.T.: Judges 13–16]

47. **Schindler, Oskar** Catholic German industrialist who saved over 1000 Poles from Nazi camps; subject of renowned 1993 film by Steven Spielberg. [Ger. Hist.: *SJEPC*]

48. **Shaft, John** hero of early Blaxpoitation film, *Shaft*, starring Richard Roundtree as the defiant African-American detective. [Am. Film: *SJEPC*]

49. **Siegfried** killed many great heroes, won the fabulous hoard of the Nibelungs, and was made invisible by the blood of a dragon he had slain. [Ger. Myth.: *Nibelungenlied* in Magill I, 653]

50. **Stanton, Will** protagonist of Susan Cooper's *Dark Is Rising* fantasy series for young readers; on his eleventh birthday, finds his true identity as an Old One, immortals who fight against the Dark. [Br. Children's Lit.: Jones]

51. **Tancred** crusader renowned for his fighting helps capture Jerusalem from the infidels. [Ital. Lit.: *Jerusalem Delivered*; Ital. Opera: Rossini *Tancredi*]

52. **Theseus** hero of Attica who slew the Minotaur, conquered the Amazons, and helped drive off the Centaurs. [Gk. Myth.: Hamilton *Mythology*, 152]

53. **Wayne, John (1907–1979)** playing heroes and cowboys (sometimes at the same time) made him a Hollywood legend; millions of fans saw him as quintessentially American. [Am. Film: *SJEPC*]

54. **Willis, Bruce (1955–)** despite other roles, probably identified in minds of most for easygoing, wisecracking heroes like cop John McClane of *Die Hard* series of films. [Am. Film: *SEJPC*]

55. **Worthies, the Nine** nine heroes - three each from the Bible, from the classical period, and from medieval romance - who were frequently grouped together. [Pop. Culture: Brewer *Dictionary*, 694]

56. **York, Sargeant Alvin (1887–1964)** hero of WWI; captured hundreds of Germans. [Am. Hist.: Misc.]

57. **Zorro** dashing, sword-carrying, masked Hispanic hero originated in 1919 in pulp magazine; fights to protect the weak and innocent in nineteenth-century California. [Am. Pop. Culture: *SJEPC*]

350. HIGHSPIRITEDNESS (See also MISCHIEVOUSNESS.)

1. *Anne of Green Gables* very popular novel by L.M. Montgomery published in 1908 and set in fictitious town of Avonlea on Prince Edward Island; orphaned Anne is sent to help farmer and his wife who, while desiring a boy, soon learn to love the vivacious girl; followed by a number of sequels. [Can. Children's Lit.: *OCCL*]

2. **Brandybuck, Meriodac** character from Tolkien's Lord of the Rings trilogy (1954–1956); longtime friend of Frodo; jovial and carefree hobbit who learns to be reponsible and mature; also called Merry. [Br. Lit.: Gillespie and Naden]

3. **Gashouse Gang** boisterous Cardinals ballclub of the 1930s. [Am. Sports: Shankle, 167]

4. **Gay Nineties (Naughty Nineties)** the 1890s; the *fin-de-siècle* epoch when traditional Victorian religosity was flouted. [Am. and Br. Hist.: Payton, 264]

5. **Hal, Prince** led boisterous life in the company of Falstaff. [Br. Lit.: *I Henry IV*]

6. **Lilly** Kevin Henkes's spirited mouse character, whose good humor and spunk make for fun reading; she flaunts her fashion sense in *Lilly's Purple Plastic Purse* (1996). [Am. Children's Lit.: McElmeel]

7. **Nickleby, Nicholas** adventurous student facing adversities of life. [Br. Lit.: *Nicholas Nickleby*]

8. **Quimby, Ramona Geraldine** domineering, determined, and thoroughly engaging protagonist of series of books by Beverly Cleary. [Am. Children's Lit.: Jones]

9. **Roaring Twenties** decade of exuberance (1920s). [Am. Hist.: Flexner, 309]

10. **Shirley, Anne** protagonist of L.M. Montgomery's Anne of Green Gables series for young readers; orphaned Anne has vivid imagination and spirited personality; shakes up Prince Edward Island community she comes to. [Can. Children's Lit.: Jones]

351. HIGHWAYMAN (See also OUTLAW, THIEF.)

1. **Band of Merry Men** Robin Hood's brigands. [Br. Lit.: *Robin Hood*]

2. **Beane, Sawney** English highwayman whose gang slew and ate their victims. [Brit. Folklore: Misc.]

3. **Duval, Claude** 17th-century British highwayman; subject of ballads. [Br. Legend: Harvey, 256]

4. **Faggus, Tom** stole, especially from the Doone clan. [Br. Lit.: *Lorna Doone*, Magill I, 524–526]

5. **Highwayman, the** loves an innkeeper's daughter, who vainly tries to save him from capture. [Br. Poetry: Noyes "The Highwayman"]

6. **King, Tom** the "Gentleman Highwayman"; associate of Dick Turpin. [Br. Hist.: Brewer *Note-Book*, 363]

7. **Macheath, Captain** highwayman hero of the opera. [Br. Lit.: *Beggar's Opera*]

8. **Moon's men** highwaymen; worked their crimes by night. [Br. Lit.: *I Henry IV*]

9. **Rob Roy** Robin Hood of Scotland. [Br. Lit.: *Rob Roy*]

10. **Robin Hood** outlaw; stole from rich to give to poor. [Br. Lit.: *Robin Hood*]

11. **Turpin, Dick (1706–1739)** enjoyed short and brutal career as horsestealer and highwayman. [Br. Hist.: *NCE*, 2808]

12. **Twitcher, Jemmy** treacherous and crafty brigand. [Br. Lit.: *Beggar's Opera*]

352. HINDUISM (See also RELIGION.)

1. **atman** the real or true self. [Hindu Rel.: Bowker]

2. **bali** offering of grain or rice to gods and spirits. [Hindu Rel.: Bowker]

3. *Bhagavad Gita* fundamental text for Hindus. [Hindu Rel.: Bowker]

4. **bodhi** state of perfect knowledge. [Hindu Rel.: Bowker]

5. **braham** custodian; interpreter, teacher of religious knowledge; intermediary between humans and God. [Hindu Rel.: Bowker]

6. **dharma** order and custom which makes life possible; appropriateness, as in appropriate way to live so as to keep order maintained. [Hindu Rel.: Bowker]

7. **Ganga** river Ganges; sacred among Hindus. [Hindu Rel.: Bowker]

8. **guru** teacher, especially of religious knowledge or spiritual insight. [Hindu Rel.: Bowker]

9. **Hare Krishna** founded in the U.S. in 1965, this Hindu religious sect became popular with disaffected youth in the 1960s; they frequently proselytized at airports and other public places, chanting and asking for money. [Hindu Rel.: *EB*]

10. **hari** divine manifestation, especially in forms of Visnu and Krishna. [Hindu Rel.: Bowker]

11. **hatha-yoga** designed to locate and activate chakras (centers of energy) and raise the kundalini (dormant spiritual power); works through bodily postures and control of breath. [Hindu Rel.: Bowker]

12. **holi** important Hindu annual festival; held in spring, it is a fertility festival; also associated with gods Kama and Krishna. [Hindu Rel.: Bowker]

13. **jata** hair that is left matted or uncared for as a sign of mourning or asceticism. [Hindu Rel.: Bowker]

14. **jiva** the self that is alive in the world and identifies with the mind and body. [Hindu Rel.: Bowker]

15. **jivanmukti** one who has obtained enlightenment; is living in the world, but is beyond human fears, desires, etc. [Hindu Rel.: Bowker]

16. **karma** driving force behind cycle of reincarnation; every action has a consequence which will come to fruition in this, or a future, life. [Hindu Rel.: Bowker]

17. **Maharishi Mahesh Yogi** proponent of transcendental meditation who toured the world, lecturing and training TM teachers. [Hindu. Rel.: Bowker]

18. **Mahatma** one who has a great soul; exceptionally wise person. [Hindu Rel.: Bowker]

19. **mantra** verse, syllable, or series of syllables thought to be sacred; used in meditation or rituals. [Hindu Rel.: Bowker]

20. *Manusmrti* authoritative Sanskrit legal text with moral and ethical precepts; among other things, describes creation, nature of good and evil, dietary obligations, and social and caste systems. [Hindu Rel.: Bowker]

21. **mudra** sign of power, through the body, usually the hands. [Hindu Rel.: Bowker]

22. **nirvana** the loss of earthly desires so union with God is possible. [Hindu Rel.: Bowker]

23. **samsara** cycle of birth and death as a consequence of action (karma). [Hindu Rel.: Bowker]

24. **smrti** along with sruti, scripture; passed along orally, but recorded in wide range of written works. [Hindu Rel.: Bowker]

25. **soma** intoxicating or hallucinogenic substance offered to the gods and taken by the brahams in sacrificial rituals. [Hindu. Rel.: Bowker]

26. **sruti** sacred and eternal truth, revealed to people in the past and transmitted orally by brahams. [Hindu Rel.: Bowker]

27. **Veda** body of sacred knowledge; basis of true belief and practice. [Hindu Rel.: Bowker]

28. **yoga** means of transforming consciousness by focusing the mind. [Hindu Rel.: Bowker]

353. HOAX (See also FORGERY, FRAUDULENCE.)

1. *Balloon Hoax, The* news story in 1844, reporting the transatlantic crossing of a balloon with eight passengers. [Am. Lit.: *The Balloon Hoax* in Poe]

2. **Mandeville** supposed author of an exaggerated travelogue. [Br. Lit.: *Voyage of Sir John Mandeville*, Harvey, 511]

3. **Piltdown man** missing link turned out to be orangutan. [Br. Hist.: Wallechinsky, 46; *Time*, October 13, 1978, 82]

4. **Psychic Friends Network** scorned by serious psychics; $3.99–a-minute fortune telling over the phone. [Am. Pop. Culture: *SJEPC*]

5. *War of the Worlds* broadcast on radio on October 30, 1938; Orson Welles's story of Martian invasion sent thousands of Americans into a panic; whether this was the intention is still under debate. [Am. Radio: *SJEPC*]

354. HOCKEY

1. **Gretzky, Wayne (1961–)** Canadian pro hockey legend, called "the Great One"; with Gordie Howe, considered the best hockey player of all time; his NHL records include: 844 goals and 2857 points. [Am. And Can. Sports: *BT1992*]

2. **Howe, Gordy (1928–)** Canadian pro hockey legend widely regarded as the greatest in history; played his NHL career with the Detroit Red Wings, and was a six-time winner of the MVP award in the NHL; also played in the World Hockey Assoc. [Am. and Can. Sports: *BTSportsv.2*]

3. **Hull, Bobby (1939–)** Canadian pro hockey star who played for the Chicago Blackhawks from 1957–1972; scored 610 lifetime goals; later played in the WHA. [Am. and Can. Sports: *EB*]

4. **NHL (National Hockey League)** alliance of Canadian and US hockey teams formed in 1917. [Am. and Can. Sports: *SJEPC*]

5. **Orr, Bobby (1948–)** famous Boston Bruins player named to Hockey Hall of Fame in 1979 at age of 31, youngest player to win that honor. [Am. Sports: *SJEPC*]

6. **Stanley Cup** the finals of the NHL season, and the trophy awarded each year to the winning team. [Am. and Can. Sports: Misc.]

355. HOLY DAY and PERIOD

1. **ember days** certain days of fasting and prayer occurring in each of the four seasons. [Christian Tradition: *NCE*, 862]

2. **Friday** Yawm al-Juma in Arabic, the Day of Congregation; the Muslim day of communal worship, with midday prayers at a mosque. [Islam: *UIMT*, 371, 427]

3. **Ramadan** holy month of the Muslim year. [Islamic Religion: Brewer *Dictionary*, 747]

4. **Sabbath** the seventh day of the week, prescribed as a day of rest and worship. [Judaism: Brewer *Dictionary*, 788]

356. HOMECOMING

1. **E.T.** alien accidently abandoned on earth, longs for home, from 1982 film *E.T.* [Am. Film: *ODA*]

2. *Odyssey* concerning Odysseus's difficulties in getting home after war. [Gk. Myth.: *Odyssey*]

3. *You Can't Go Home Again* revisiting his home town, a writer is disillusioned by what he sees. [Am. Lit.: Thomas Wolfe in *You Can't Go Home Again*]

357. HOMOSEXUALITY (See also RIGHTS, GAY.)

1. *Advocate, The* magazine advocating for rights of the lesbian, gay, bisexual, and transgender community. [Am. Journalism: Misc.]

2. **AIDS** fatal disease first manifested in gay men in 1981, striking the homosexual community almost exclusively that decade; epidemic resulted in increased political activity and artistic expression, and altered sexual practices. [Hist.: *SJEPC*]

3. **Albertine** discovery of her promiscuous lesbianism breaks up her impending marriage to Marcel. [Fr. Lit.: Proust *In Search of Lost Time†*]

4. *Angels in America* Tony Kushner's powerful, award-winning play in two parts, described by the dramatist as "A Gay Fantasia on National Themes," explores the homosexual experience in the age of AIDS (1993). [Am. Theater: Berkowitz, 171]

5. **bathhouses** same-sex communal facilities popular with gay males until advent of AIDS in the 1980s. [Am. Culture: *SJEPC*]

6. **Bilitis** putative singer of Sapphic lyrics. [Fr. Lit.: *Les Chansons de Bilitis, NCE*, 1621]

7. **Castro, The** district in San Francisco is heart of gay community and symbol of gay liberation. [Am. Culture: *SJEPC*]

8. **Charlus, Baron de** fails to conceal his homosexual relations with a young tailor and a talented violinist. [Fr. Lit.: Proust *Remembrance of Things Past*]

9. *City and the Pillar, The* portraying a young gay man separated from "normal" people. [Am. Lit.: *The City and the Pillar*]

10. *Death in Venice* aging successful author loses his lifelong self-discipline in his love for a beautiful Polish boy. [Ger. Lit.: *Death in Venice*]

11. **DeGeneres, Ellen (1958–)** groundbreaking lesbian comedian came out on her TV show to become first gay main character (1997) and was first openly homosexual host of the Academy Awards (2007). [Am. TV: *SJEPC*; Misc.]

12. **drag queen** a male, typically homosexual, dressing as and impersonating a female, often exaggerated to extremes. [Culture: *SJEPC*]

13. ***Dykes to Watch Out For*** syndicated cartoon strip featuring a diverse group of lesbian friends and their community is "half op-ed column and half endless Victorian novel," according to creator Alison Bechdel. [Am. Comics: *SJEPC*]

14. **Edward II** weak English king whose love for Gaviston, Earl of Cornwall, so arouses the anger of the nobles that he loses the crown and is murdered. [Br. Drama: Marlowe *Edward II* in Magill II, 286]

15. **Fierstein, Harvey (1954–)** homosexual stage and screen actor, playwright, and gay rights activist wrote and starred in autobiographical Broadway play *Torch Song Trilogy* (1982); narrated documentary about assassinated gay San Francisco politician Harvey Milk. [Am. Theater and Film: *SJEPC*; Misc.]

16. **Ganymede** beautiful shepherd entrances Jupiter. [Rom. Lit.: *Metamorphoses*]

17. **Garland, Judy (1922–1969)** legendary singer and film actress with powerful, emotive voice and a vulnerable edge is a gay icon; revered by gay men and drag queens, in particular. [Am. Film and Music: *SJEPC*]

18. **gay liberation** organization that supports equal rights in jobs, housing, etc. for homosexuals. [Am. Pop. Culture: Misc.]

19. **Hudson, Rock (1925–1985)** popular actor's death from AIDS in 1985 led to wider acceptance and awareness of the disease. [Am. Film: *EB*]

20. **John, Elton (1947–)** flamboyant singer-songwriter whose career began in 1969 and whose onstage persona and intriguing costumes drew fans; after controversial announcement of bisexuality, eventually admitted to homosexuality and a history of substance abuse; became dedicated to fundraising for humanitarian causes. [Br. Music: *SJEPC*]

21. ***La Cage aux Folles*** farce, with serious overtones, about a nightclub owner and his homosexual lover and employee. [Fr. Cinema: *La Cage aux Folles*]

22. **lambda** Greek letter adopted as symbol by gay liberation movement. [Am. Pop. Culture: Misc.]

23. **lang, k.d. (1961–)** smooth, sophisticated voice with broad range; often thought to be a study in contradictions because of unusual and rather bristly cross-gender appearance; very open about her lesbiansim. [Am. Music: *SJEPC*]

24. **Lesbos** Greek island and home of Sappho, the poet of passionate love poems written to women; source of "Lesbian" [Gk. Hist.: *ODA*]

25. *Man without a Face* 1972 young adult novel by Isabelle Holland; touching story of a lonely 14–year-old boy who escapes his troubled home life through his relationship with his scarred, reclusive neighbor; they are able to reach out to each other through physical intimacy. [Am. Children's Lit.: Gillespie and Naden]

26. **Milk, Harvey (1930–1978)** openly gay San Francisco politician known as "the mayor of Castro Street" fought for human rights of homosexuals; assassinated at City Hall in 1978. [Am. Hist.: *SJEPC*]

27. **Molinier, Oliver** loved by two writers, his uncle Edouard and Count Robert de Passavant. [Fr. Lit.: Gide *The Counterfeiters* in Magill I, 160]

28. **Navratilova, Martina (1956–)** Czech-born tennis champion who stunned the world when she came out at the height of her career. [Am. Sports: *SJEPC*]

29. **O'Donnell, Rosie (1962–)** often outspoken lesbian comedian, actor, and talk-show host. [Am. TV: *SJEPC*]

30. **Oglethorpe, John** his sexual preference causes marital problems. [Am. Lit.: *The Manhattan Transfer*]

31. **outing** revealing someone as homosexual, usually against their will. [Culture: *SJEPC*]

32. **Queer Nation** founded in 1990, activist organization with focus on making homosexuality more prominent in American society; controversial for outing people whose sexual orientation had been previously undisclosed. [Am. Pop. Culture: *SJEPC*]

33. **rainbow** symbol of gay pride; different colors represent diversity within the lesbian, gay, bisexual, and transgendered community. [Culture: *SJEPC*; Misc.]

34. **Sappho** Greek poetess from Lesbos; hence, *lesbian*. [Gk. Hist.: Brewer *Dictionary*, 962]

35. **Sodomites** insisted on having sexual intercourse with angels disguised as men. [O.T.: Gen. 19]

36. **Stonewall Rebellion** 1969 resistance by patrons of Greenwich Village gay men's bar during police raid; annual Gay Pride parades and rallies held nationwide to commemorate the event; led to formation of Gay Liberation Front and others committed to civil rights for homosexuals. [Am. Pop. Culture: *SJEPC*]

37. *Torch Song Trilogy* autobiographical, Tony Award-winning Broadway play written by and starring Harvey Fierstein as Arnold Beckoff, a young gay man searching for love, as well as the acceptance of his disapproving mother (1982); adapted for film (1988). [Am. Theater and Film: *SJEPC*; Misc.]

38. **Venable, Sebastian** his homosexuality and morbid fascination with vice are revealed by a witness to his horrible death. [Am. Drama: Tennessee Williams *Suddenly Last Summer* in Weiss, 448]

39. *Well of Loneliness, The* novel about female homosexuality; once banned, but defended by eminent authors. [Br. Lit.: Barnhart, 530]

40. **Wilde, Oscar (1854–1900)** Irish dramatist, poet, and novelist; his homosexual relationship with Lord Alfred Douglas, led to his imprisonment and the composition of his famous "Ballad of Reading Gaol." [Irish Lit.: *EB*]

41. **Willard, Jim** his first homosexual fulfillment at seventeen. [Am. Lit.: Gore Vidal *The City and the Pillar*]

42. **Williams, Tennessee (1911–1983)** his homosexuality sometimes found in his plays (*Cat on a Hot Tin Roof*), along with dark subjects, vivid characters, and fragile, complex relationships. [Am. Theater: *SJEPC*]

358. HONESTY (See also NOBLEMINDEDNESS, RIGHTEOUSNESS, VIRTUOUSNESS.)

1. **Alethia** ancient Greek personification of truth. [Gk. Myth.: Zimmerman, 18]

2. **Better Business Bureau** nationwide system of organizations investigating dishonest business practices. [Am. Commerce: Misc.]

3. **bittersweet** traditional symbol of truth. [Plant Symbolism: *Flora Symbolica*, 172]

4. **Boffin, Nickodemus** despite personal loss, endows patron's son. [Br. Lit.: *Our Mutual Friend*]

5. **Bunker, Edith** her uprightness frequently conflicts with Archie's opportunism. [TV: "All in the Family" in Terrace, I, 47–48]

6. **cherry tree** young George Washington's admission of chopping it down was proof of his honesty. [Am. Legend: Misc.]

7. **chrysanthemum** symbol of truth. [Flower Symbolism: *Flora Symbolica*, 173; Kunz, 330]

8. **Cordelia** though it costs her an inheritance, she refuses to flatter her father with obsequious pledges of love. [Br. Drama: Shakespeare *King Lear*]

9. **Cranmer, Thomas** a meek, patient, honest churchman. [Br. Lit.: *Henry VIII*]

10. **Diogenes (c. 412–323 B.C.)** philosopher; fabled lantern-carrying searcher for an honest man. [Gk. Hist.: Hall, 104]

11. **Edgar** truthful, straightforward character; does no evil. [Br. Lit.: *King Lear*]

12. **John of Gaunt** overly blunt uncle of Richard II. [Br. Lit. *Richard II*]

13. **Lenox, John** his straightforward dealings with Harum's approval. [Am. Lit.: *David Harum*]

14. **Lincoln, Abraham (1809–1865)** 16th U.S. president; nicknamed "Honest Abe." [Am. Hist.: Kane, 525]

15. **Melantius** honest soldier; trusts everyone until shown otherwise. [Br. Lit.: *The Maid's Tragedy*]

16. **open book** signified spreading of truth by text and doctrine. [Christian Symbolism: Appleton, 13]

17. **Pericles (c.500–429 B.C.)** Greek ruler noted for his wisdom and integrity. [Gk. Hist.: *ODA*]

18. **Pure, Simon** character in Centlire play (1718). [Br. Lit.: *Bold Stroke for a Wife*]

19. **Trelawney, Squire** sincere, genuine ship owner; benevolent authority. [Br. Lit.: *Treasure Island*]

20. **Truman, Harry (1884–1972)** 33rd U.S. president who, despite much controversy over his policies, is remembered for impeccable honesty and plain speaking. [Am. Hist.: *NCE*, 2793]

21. **truth serum** drug inducing one to speak uninhibitedly. [Science: Brewer *Dictionary*, 1105]

22. **Una** personification of honesty; leads lamb and rides white ass. [Br. Lit.: *Faerie Queene*]

23. **Washington, George (1732–1799)** first U.S. president; reputed to have said, "Father, I cannot tell a lie." [Am. Hist.: *NCE*, 2933]

24. **white chrysanthemum** traditional symbol of truth. [Flower Symbolism: Jobes, 333]

359. HOPE (See also OPTIMISM.)

1. **cinquefoil** traditional representation of hope. [Flower Symbolism and Heraldry: Jobes, 341]

2. *Emigrants, The* shows Norwegians in Dakota wheatlands striving for better life. [Nor. Lit.: *The Emigrants*, Magill I, 244–246]

3. **flowering almond** symbol of spring; blooms in winter. [Flower Symbolism: Jobes, 71]

4. **Great Pumpkin, the** awaited each Halloween by Linus. [Comics: "Peanuts" in Horn, 542]

5. **green** color represents hope, peace, and paradise in Islam. [Islamic Symbolism: *UIMT*, 229]

6. **holly** symbol of hope. [Symbolism: *CEOS&S*]

7. *Iceman Cometh, The* "The lie of the pipe dream is what gives life." [Am. Lit.: *The Iceman Cometh*]

8. *Of Mice and Men* portrays a philosophy that humans are made of hopes and dreams. [Am. Lit.: *Of Mice and Men*]

9. **"Over the Rainbow"** Academy Award-winning song introduced by Judy Garland as Dorothy in *The Wizard of Oz* (1939) expressed hope for a happier future in a distant world and became the troubled Garland's signature song. [Am. Music: *SJEPC*]

10. **rainbow** God's assurance He would not send another great flood. [O.T.: Genesis 9:12–16]

360. HORROR

1. **Addams, Charles (1912–1988)** famed cartoonist of the macabre. [Am. Comics: *NCE*, 19]

2. *Alien* chilling drama featuring alien life forms aboard space ship. [Am. Film: *SJEPC*]

3. **Bhairava (m), Bhairav (f)** terrible forms of Shiva and spouse. [Hindu Myth.: Parrinder, 44]

4. **Black Death** plague whose unprecedented mortality was incomprehensible to medieval mind. [Eur. Hist.: Bishop, 379–382]

5. **Bosch, Hieronymus (c. 1450–1516)** paintings contain grotesque representations of evil and temptation. [Art Hist.: Osborne, 149]

6. *Cabinet of Dr. Caligari, The* thrilling horror story told by a madman. [Ger. Cinema: Halliwell, 119]

7. *Carrie* 1974 horror novel by Stephen King in which 17–year-old girl with telekinesis unleashes her power on her cruel classmates; bloodbath ensues. [Am. Lit.: Gillespie and Naden]

8. **Chaney, Lon (1883–1930)** American actor and star of many silent horror films, especially *The Hunchback of Notre Dame*. [Am. Film: *FOF, MOD*]

9. **Collins, Barnabas** tortured, love-cursed vampire in TV soap *Dark Shadows* (ABC, 1966–71). [Am. TV: *SJEPC*]

10. *Danse Macabre* Saint-Saens' musical depiction of a dance of the dead. [Music Hist.: Thompson, 1906]

11. *Dark Shadows* paranormal soap opera featured ghosts, vampires, curses, and family secrets (ABC, 1966–71). [Am. TV: *SJEPC*]

12. *Disasters of War* Goya's violent protest against French occupation of Spain. [Art Hist.: Osborne, 497]

13. **Dracula, Count** vampire terrifies Transylvanian peasants and London circle. [Br. Lit.: *Dracula*]

14. **dragonwort** traditional representation of horror. [Flower Symbolism: Jobes, 469]

15. *Exorcist, The* supernatural horror story about a girl possessed by the devil (1974). [Am. Cinema: Halliwell, 247]

16. *Freaks* disturbing film about deformed circus sideshow performers who take revenge on two conniving able-bodied performers

starred disabled actors; faced decades of censorship for its exploitive nature (1932). [Am. Film: *SJEPC*]

17. *Friday the 13th* psychopath Jason Voorhees stalks and murders adolescent victims in horror film and its many sequels (1980–). [Am. Film: *SJEPC*]

18. *Halloween* classic horror film that first appeared in 1978, and spawned numerous sequels, featuring fiendish slasher in a hockey mask. [Am. Film: *SJEPC*]

19. *Interview with a Vampire* Anne Rice's 1976 horror novel documents an interview with Louis, who became a vampire in 1791 at the age of 25; he tells of his life and his determination to destroy the powerful vampire Lestat. [Am. Lit.: Gillespie and Naden]

20. *Jaws* 1975 Steven Spielberg film based on Peter Benchley novel mixed fun with fright; three men attempt to kill great white shark terrorizing beaches of New England resort town; eerie, pulsating score by John Williams won Oscar. [Am. Film and Lit.: Halliwell, 380; *SJEPC*]

21. *Jurassic Park* best-selling novel by Michael Crichton published in 1990 and made into film in 1993 by Steven Spielberg; eccentric millionaire builds theme park on tropical island with live dinosaurs created out of fossilized DNA; terror ensues. [Am. Lit. and Film: *SJEPC*]

22. **Karloff, Boris (1887–1969)** British-born American actor and star of many famous horror films, including *Frankenstein*. [Am. Film: *ODA*]

23. *King Kong* 1933 classic monster film with groundbreaking special effects; most notably, giant ape Kong perched at top of Empire State Building while swatting at attack planes; wildly popular in its day and mimicked to the present. [Am. Film: *SJEPC*]

24. **King, Stephen (1948–)** prolific writer best known for his quality horror fiction; interesting narratives and insight into American culture characterizes his work; first best-seller *Salem's Lot* (1976); since then often has several best-sellers at a time. [Am. Lit.: *SJEPC*]

25. **mandrake** traditional representation of horror. [Plant Symbolism: *Flora Symbolica*, 175]

26. *Night of the Living Dead* 1968 low-budget zombie film; graphic depiction of cannibalism and gore won it a cult status and some critical acclaim. [Am. Film: *SJEPC*]

27. *Phantom of the Opera, The* story of an angry, disfigured composer who haunts the sewers beneath the Paris Opera House. [Am. Cinema: Halliwell, 562]

28. ***Pit and the Pendulum, The*** study in bone-chilling terror. [Am. Lit.: "The Pit and the Pendulum" in *Portable Poe*, 154–173]

29. **Price, Vincent (1911–1993)** best known for what he called "Gothic films" in which he played golden-voiced, somewhat ironical, creepy villians. [Am. Film: *SJEPC*]

30. ***Psycho*** 1960 horror film by Alfred Hitchcock with famous, frightening murder scene in shower and surprise ending. [Am. Cinema: *NCE*, 1249]

31. ***Rosemary's Baby*** devil impregnates young woman in occult novel by Ira Levin; eerie 1968 film by Roman Polanski. [Am. Lit. and Film: *SJEPC*]

32. ***Scream*** 1996 film that brought about a slew of "teenie kill" movies; all-out terror and spoofing brought huge box-office profits and spawned sequels. [Am. Film: *SJEPC*]

33. **snakesfoot** indicates shocking occurrence. [Flower Symbolism: *Flora Symbolica*, 177]

34. **Stine, R. L. (1943–)** convoluted, intriguing plots and blood-curdling horror engage young readers; his Goosebump series brought enormous success. [Am. Lit.: *SJEPC*]

35. ***Tales from the Crypt*** brutal horror stories were the hallmark of popular comic book series of the 1950s. [Am. Comics: *SJEPC*]

36. ***Tell-Tale Heart, The*** mad murderer dismembers victim, mistakes ticking watch for dead man's heart, and confesses. [Am. Lit.: Poe *The Tell-Tale Heart*]

37. ***Thing, The*** 1982 film about group of scientists in Antarctica stalked by alien that takes on its victim's identity; terrifying special effects and doom-laden plot have brought film loyal following. [Am. Film: *SJEPC*]

361. HORSE (See also RACING, HORSE.)

1. **Al Borak** white horse Muhammad rode to the seven heavens. [Islam: Leach, 172]

2. **Arion** fabulous winged horse; offspring of Demeter and Poseidon. [Gk. Myth.: Zimmerman, 31]

3. **Arundel** Bevis's incomparable steed. [Br. Lit.: *Bevis of Hampton*]

4. **Assault** famous horse in history of thoroughbred racing. [Am. Lit.: *NCE*, 1273]

5. **Balius** immortal steed of Achilles. [Gk. Myth.: Kravitz, 44]

6. **Bavieca** the Cid's horse. [Sp. Legend: Brewer *Dictionary*, 80]

7. **Black Beauty** his life with various owners is depicted in children's book by Anna Sewell; good breeding makes him pleasant and conscientious, but humane treatment brings out the best in

him and poor treatment brings him great suffering. [Br. Children's Lit.: Jones]

8. **Black Bess** belonged to the notorious highwayman, Dick Turpin. [Br. Hist.: Benét, 103]

9. **Bucephalus** wild steed, broken by Alexander to be his mount. [Gk. Hist.: Leach, 167]

10. **centaur** beast that is half-horse, half-man. [Gk. Myth.: Mercatante, 201–202]

11. **Citation** famous horse in history of thoroughbred racing. [Am. Hist.: *NCE*, 1273]

12. **Clavileño** legendary wooden horse on which Don Quixote and Sancho Panza think they are taking a journey through the air. [Span. Lit.: Benét, 205]

13. **Flicka** a paragon of horses. [TV: "My Friend Flicka" in Terrace, II, 125]

14. **Four Horsemen of the Apocalypse, The** they ride white, red, black, and pale horses, symbolizing, respectively, War, Pestilence, Famine, and Death. [N.T.: Revelation 6:1–8]

15. **Francis the Talking Mule** intelligent, wise-talking mule featured in seven films (1949–56) along with naïve human companion played by Donald O'Connor. [Am. Film: *SJEPC*]

16. **Gallant Fox** famous horse in history of thoroughbred racing. [Am. Hist.: *NCE*, 1273]

17. **Gilpin, John** his borrowed horse carrries him at a mad pace for miles to its owner's home, then turns and runs back. [Br. Poetry: *John Gilpin's Ride*]

18. **Grane** Brünhilde's war horse, presented to Siegfried. [Ger. Opera: Wagner, *Götterdämmerung*, Westerman, 244]

19. **Gringalet** Gawain's steed. [Br. Lit.: *Sir Gawain and the Green Knight*]

20. **Gunpowder** Ichabod Crane's favorite steed. [Am. Lit.: Washington Irving "The Legend of Sleepy Hollow"]

21. **Hambletonian** famous trotting horse after which race for three-year-old trotters is named. [Am. Culture: Mathews, 769]

22. **Harum, David** would rather trade horses than eat or sleep. [Am. Lit.: *David Harum* in Magill I, 192]

23. **Hippolytus, Saint** patron saint of horses. [Christian Hagiog.: Brewster, 367]

24. **Houyhnhnms** race of horses that represent nobility, virtue, and reason. [Br. Lit.: *Gulliver's Travels*]

25. **Man o' War ("Big Red")** famous racehorse foaled at Belmont Stables. [Am. Hist.: Payton, 421]

26. **Meg (Maggie)** Tam O'shanter's gray mare that lost her tail to the witch. [Scot. Poetry: Burns "Tam O'shanter"]

27. **Mr. Ed** the talking horse. [TV: Terrace, II, 116–117]

28. *National Velvet* very successful story written by Enid Bagnold in 1930; fourteen-year-old Velvet Brown acquires horse and wins the Grand National; book and film in 1944 helped establish pony story as popular genre for girl readers. [Br. Children's Lit.: *OCCL*]

29. **Native Dancer** famous horse in history of thoroughbred racing. [Am. Hist.: *NCE*, 1273]

30. **Pegasus** winged mount of Bellerophon. [Gk. Myth.: Hall, 238]

31. **roan stallion** tramples its owner to death and is shot by his wife, though she had been seduced by the stallion's beauty. [Am. Poetry: Robinson Jeffers *The Roan Stallion* in Magill I, 835]

32. **Rosinante** Don Quixote's mount. [Span. Lit.: *Don Quixote*]

33. **Scout** Tonto's horse. [TV: "The Lone Ranger" in Terrace, II, 34; Radio: "The Lone Ranger" in Buxton, 143]

34. **Seabiscuit** famous horse in history of thoroughbred racing. [Am. Hist.: *NCE*, 1273]

35. **Seattle Slew** famous horse in history of thoroughbred racing. [Am. Hist.: *NCE*, 1273]

36. **Secretariat** famous horse in history of thoroughbred racing. [Am. Hist.: *NCE*, 1273]

37. **Shadowfax** great horse of the wizard Gandalf. [Br. Lit.: J.R.R. Tolkein *Lord of the Rings*]

38. **Silver** the Lone Ranger's trusty steed. [Radio: "The Lone Ranger" in Buxton, 143–144; TV: "The Lone Ranger" in Terrace, II, 34–35]

39. **Sleipnir** Odin's eight-legged gray horse. [Norse Myth.: Benét, 937]

40. **Tony** Tom Mix's "Wonder Horse." [Radio: "Tom Mix" in Buxton, 241–242]

41. **Topper** Hopalong Cassidy's faithful horse. [Cinema and TV: "Hopalong Cassidy" in Terrace, I, 369]

42. **Trigger** Roy Roger's horse. [TV: "The Roy Rogers Show" in Terrace, II, 260]

43. **Whirlaway** famous horse in history of thoroughbred racing. [Am. Hist.: *NCE*, 1273]

362. HOSPITALITY (See also COURTESY.)

1. **Abigail** undoes husband's unneighborliness with fare for David's troops. [O.T.: I Samuel 25:23–27]

2. **Abraham** graciously receives and treats three wayfarers. [O.T.: Genesis 18:1–15]

3. **Acestes** Sicilian king; entertains Aeneas. [Rom. Lit.: *Aeneid*]

4. **Alcandre** Polybus' wife; entertains Helen and Menelaus on their way home from Troy. [Gk. Lit.: *Odyssey*]

5. **Bailley, Harry** "Mr. Congeniality." [Br. Lit.: *Canterbury Tales*]

6. **Boniface** jovial innkeeper; name became generic for restaurateur. [Br. Drama: *The Beaux' Stratagem*, Espy, 129]

7. **fatted calf** best calf killed for feast to celebrate return of prodigal son. [N.T.: Luke 15:13]

8. **friendly skies** after WWII, airline industry promoted comfort, safety, convenience, and friendly stewardesses on commercial flights; became slogan for United Airlines ads. [Am. Business: *SJEPC*]

9. **Gatsby, Jay** character who serves nothing but the best to his guests. [Am. Lit.: *The Great Gatsby*]

10. **Glorious Appollers, the** known for their cordiality and sociability. [Br. Lit.: *Old Curiosity Shop*]

11. **Julian the Hospitaler** set up famed hospice for weary travelers. [Medieval Romance: Hall, 181]

12. **Lot** treated and feted two disguised angels. [O.T.: Genesis 19:1–3]

13. **Lycus** by hospitably entertaining Hercules, earned his gratitude and military assistance. [Gk. Myth.: Zimmerman, 156]

14. **oak** symbol of graciousness. [Flower Symbolism: *Flora Symbolica*, 176]

15. **Phaeacians** island people befriend and aid both Odysseus and the Argonauts. [Gk. Myth.: Benét, 780]

16. **Philemon and Baucis** poor couple welcomes disguised gods refused by rich households. [Rom. Lit.: *Metamorphoses*]

363. HOUSE, FATEFUL

1. **Bates Motel** run by madman Norman Bates, the rundown motel is the scene of murder and insanity in Alfred Hitchcock's classic thriller *Psycho*. [Am. Film: *SJEPC*]

2. **Collinwood** cursed, gloomy estate of the Collins family, full of mysterious secrets (*Dark Shadows*, ABC, 1966–71)). [Am. TV: *SJEPC*]

3. **Manderley** place of Maxim de Winter's unhappy marriage, and of his happy one, goes up in flames. [Br. Lit.: D. duMaurier *Rebecca* in Magill I, 806]

4. **Northanger Abbey** medieval house where Catherine Morland imagines dungeons, ghosts, and mysterious events. [Br. Lit.: Austen *Northanger Abbey* in Magill II, 750]

5. **Satis House** scene of Miss Havisham's reclusive life and fiery death. [Br. Lit.: Dickens *Great Expectations*]

6. **Tara** plantation home of Scarlett O'Hara. [Am. Lit.: Margaret Mitchell *Gone With the Wind*]

7. **Thornfield Hall** home where Jane Eyre met Mr. Rochester and where his hidden first wife perishes in a fire. [Br. Lit.: Charlotte Brontë *Jane Eyre*]

8. **Wuthering Heights** remotely situated home where Heathcliff nurses his vengeful plans. [Br. Lit.: Emily Brontë *Wuthering Heights* in Magill I, 1137]

Hugeness (See GIANT.)

364. HUMILITY (See also MODESTY.)

1. **Bernadette Soubirous, Saint** humble girl to whom Virgin Mary appeared. [Christian Hagiog.: Attwater, 65–66]

2. **Bonaventura, Saint** washes dishes even though a cardinal. [Christian Hagiog.: Hall, 50]

3. **broom** traditional representation of humility. [Plant Symbolism: *Flora Symbolica*, 167]

4. **Bruno, Saint** pictured with head bent as sign of humbleness. [Christian Hagiog.: Hall, 53]

5. **camel** Christian symbol of humility and obedience. [Christian Symbolism: *CEOS&S*]

6. **cattail** used by da Vinci as symbol of humility. [Plant Symbolism: Embolden, 25]

7. **Elizabeth of Hungary, Saint** meek princess renounced world, cared for sick. [Christian Hagiog.: Attwater, 112]

8. **Job** abases self in awe of the Lord. [O.T.: Job 40:3–5, 42:1–6]

9. **John the Baptist** feels unworthy before Christ. [N.T.: Mark 1:7; Luke 3:16]

10. **small bindweed** traditional representation of humility. [Plant Symbolism: *Flora Symbolica*, 172]

Humorousness (See WITTINESS.)

365. HUNGER

1. **Bangladesh** suffered devastating famine in 1970s. [World Hist.: *NCE*, 224]

2. **Biafra** secessionist state of western Africa in which, during war with Nigeria, more than 1,000,000 people died of starvation (1968). [African Hist.: *NCE*, 290]

3. **Erysichthon** condemned by Demeter to perpetual insatiety. [Gk. Myth.: Kravitz, 93]

4. **Irish Potato Famine** over one million people died as the result of potato blight, 1845–1850. [Irish Hist.: *EB*]

5. **Lazarus** the beggar full of sores. [N.T.: Luke 16:19–31]

6. **Mother Hubbard** mother of the nursery rhyme whose cupboard is bare. [Nurs. Rhyme Misc.]

7. **Tantalus** punished with ceaseless hunger for food just beyond his reach. [Gk. Myth.: Hamilton, 346]

8. **Twist, Oliver** asks workhouse-master for more gruel. [Br. Lit.: *Oliver Twist*]

366. HUNTING

1. **Agraeus** epithet of Apollo, meaning "hunter." [Gk. Myth.: Zimmerman, 26]

2. **Agrotera** epithet of Artemis, meaning "huntress." [Gk. Myth.: Zimmerman, 32]

3. **Artemis** moon goddess; virgin huntress. [Gk. Myth.: Kravitz, 36]

4. **Atalanta** famous huntress; slew the Centaurs. [Gk. Myth.: Leach, 87]

5. **Britomartis** Cretan nymph; goddess of hunters and fishermen. [Gk. Myth.: Zimmerman, 43]

6. **Calydonian boar hunt** famed hunt of Greek legend. [Class. Myth.: *Metamorphoses*]

7. **Diana** Roman goddess, related to Artemis, associated with hunting, virginity, and the moon. [Rom. Myth: *ODA*]

8. *Field and Stream* quintessential outdoorsman's magazine aimed at America's middle-class hunters and anglers was introduced in 1895, advocates conservation measures for wildlife and fish populations. [Am. Jour.: *SJEPC*]

9. *Green Hills of Africa* portrays big game-hunting coupled with literary digressions. [Am. Lit.: *Green Hills of Africa*]

10. **Hubert, Saint** patron saint; encountered stag with cross in horns. [Christian Hagiog.: Brewster, 473–474]

11. **Jorrocks** irrepressible pseudo-aristocratic cockney huntsman. [Br. Lit.: *Jorrock's Jaunts and Jollies*]

12. **Nimrod** Biblical hunter of great prowess. [O.T.: Genesis 10:9; Br. Lit.: *Paradise Lost*]

13. **NRA (National Rifle Association of America)** organization that encourages use of firearms for hunting and protection. [Am. Pop. Culture: *NCE*, 1895]

14. **Orion** hunter who pursued the Pleiades. [Classical Myth.: Zimmerman, 184–185]

15. **Sagittarius** the Archer of the Zodiac; used occasionally to symbolize hunting. [Astrology: Payton, 594]

16. **Stymphalian birds** venomous Arcadian flock shot by Hercules; sixth Labor. [Gk. and Roman Myth.: Hall, 149]

17. **"tally ho"** traditional rallying cry in English fox hunts. [Pop. Cult.: Misc.]

367. HYPOCRISY (See also PRETENSION.)

1. **Alceste** judged most social behavior as hypocritical. [Fr. Lit.: *Le Misanthrope*]

2. **Ambrosio** self-righteous abbot of the Capuchins at Madrid. [Br. Lit.: *Ambrosio, or The Monk*]

3. **Angelo** externally austere but inwardly lecherous and hypocritical. [Br. Lit.: *Measure for Measure*]

4. **Archimago** enchanter, disguised as hermit, wins confidence of Knight. [Br. Lit.: *Faerie Queene*]

5. **Arsinoé** false prude. [Fr. Lit.: *The Misanthrope*]

6. **Atar Gul** trusted domestic; betrays those he serves. [Fr. Lit.: *Atar Gul*, Walsh *Modern*, 32]

7. **Bakker, Jim (1940–), and Tammy Faye Baker (1942–2007)** husband-and-wife televangelists with lavish lifestyle founded PTL ministry and were embroiled in financial and moral scandals in the 1980s. [Am. Rel.: *SJEPC*]

8. **Bigotes** 12th-century French order regarded as hypocritical. [Fr. Hist.: Espy, 99]

9. **Blifil** Allworthy's nephew; talebearer and consummate pietist. [Br. Lit.: *Tom Jones*]

10. **Blood, Col. Thomas (1628–1680)** false in honor and religion. [Br. Lit.: *Peveril of the Peak*, Walsh *Modern*, 61]

11. **Boulanger, Ralph** Emma's lover pretends repentance to avoid commitment. [Fr. Lit.: *Madame Bovary*]

12. **bourgeois** reflecting middle-class, and often hypocritical, values. [Am. Culture: *FOF, MOD*]

13. **Boynton, Egeria** religious charlatan. [Am. Lit.: *Undiscovered Country*]

14. **Buncombe County** insincere speeches made solely to please constituency by its representative, 1819–1821. [Am. Usage: Misc.]

15. **Cantwell, Dr.** lives luxuriously by religious cant. [Br. Lit.: *The Hypocrite*, Brewer *Handbook*, 175]

16. **Célimène** ridicules people when absent; flatters them when present. [Fr. Lit.: *Le Misanthrope*]

17. **Chadband, Rev.** pharisaic preacher; thinks he's edifying his hearers. [Br. Lit.: *Bleak House*]

18. **Christian, Edward** conspirator; false to everyone. [Br. Lit.: *Peveril of the Peak* Walsh *Modern*, 96]

19. **crocodile tears** crocodile said to weep after devouring prey. [Western Folklore: Jobes, 383; Mercatante, 9–10]

20. **Dimmesdale, Arthur** acted the humble minister for seven years while former amour suffered. [Am. Lit.: *The Scarlet Letter*]

21. **Gallanbiles, the** pretend piety on Sabbath but demand dinner. [Br. Lit.: *Nicholas Nickleby*]

22. **Gantry, Elmer** ranting preacher succumbs to alcohol, fornication, theft, and cowardice. [Am. Lit.: *Elmer Gantry*]

23. **Gashford** humble manner masks sly, shirking character. [Br. Lit.: *Barnaby Rudge*]

24. **Goneril and Regan** to inherit their father's possessions they falsely profess great love for him. [Br. Drama: Shakespeare *King Lear*]

25. **Haskell, Eddie** gentleman with adults, troublemaker behind their backs. [TV: "Leave it to Beaver" in Terrace, II, 18–19]

26. **Heep, Uriah** the essence of insincerity. [Br. Lit.: *David Copperfield*]

27. **Honeythunder, Luke** his philanthropy hid animosity. [Br. Lit.: *Edwin Drood*]

28. **Manders** self-righteous pastor agrees to blackmail. [Nor. Lit.: *Ghosts*]

29. **Martext, Sir Oliver** a "most vile" hedge-priest. [Br. Lit.: *As You Like It*]

30. **Mawworm** sanctimonious preacher. [Br. Lit.: *The Hypocrite*, Brewer *Handbook*, 687]

31. **Mr. By-ends** embraces religion when it is easy to practice and to his advantage. [Br. Lit.: Bunyan *The Pilgrim's Progress*]

32. **newspeak** official speech of Oceania; language of contradictions. [Br. Lit.: *1984*]

33. **Pecksniff** pretentious, unforgiving architect of double standards. [Br. Lit.: *Martin Chuzzlewit*]

34. **Pharisees** sanctimonious lawgivers do not practice what they preach. [N.T.: Matthew 3:7, 23:1–15; Luke 18:9–14]

35. **Potemkin village** false fronts constructed to deceive. [Russ. Lit.: Espy, 339]

36. **Sainte Nitouche** sanctimonious and pretentious person (Fr. n'y touche). [Fr. Usage: Brewer *Dictionary*, 760]

37. **Snawley** sanctimonious hypocrite; placed stepsons in Dotheboys Hall. [Br. Lit.: *Nicholas Nickleby*]

38. **Square, Mr.** Tom's tutor; spouts hypocritically about the beauty of virtue. [Br. Lit.: *Tom Jones*]

39. **Surface, Joseph** pays lip service to high principles while engaging in treacherous intrigues. [Br. Drama: Sheridan *The School for Scandal*]

40. **Tartuffe** swindles benefactor by pretending religious piety. [Fr. Lit.: *Tartuffe*]

41. **Vicar of Bray** changes religious affiliation to suit reigning monarch. [Br. Folklore: Walsh *Classical*, 61]

42. **Walrus** wept in sympathy for the oysters he and the Carpenter devoured. [Br. Lit.: Lewis Carroll *Through the Looking-Glass*]

43. **Whelp, the** nickname for hypocritical Tom Gradgrind. [Br. Lit.: *Hard Times*]

44. **whited sepulchres** analogy in Jesus' denunciation of Pharisees' sanctimony. [N.T.: Matthew 23:27]

I

368. IDEALISM

1. **American Dream** belief that America holds opportunity for all, regardless of background; sometimes used ironically to indicate the failure of that dream. [Am. Cult.: Misc.]

2. **Camelot** King Arthur's reign in this perfect kingdom, featured in Lerner and Loewe's Broadway musical of the 1960s, became a metaphor for president John F. Kennedy's idealistic administration (1961–63) before his assassination. [Am. Musical: *SJEPC*]

3. **Kildare, Dr.** character in film and TV, an idealistic young physician [Am. Film, TV: Misc.]

4. **Stockmann, Dr. Thomas** sacrifices his career to show that the public baths are a health menace. [Nor. Lit.: *An Enemy of the People*, Magill II, 292]

369. IDENTIFICATION

1. **Emmaus** where two disciples discover identity of Jesus. [N.T.: Luke 24:13–35]

2. **Euryclea** Ulysses' nurse; recognized him by scar on thigh. [Gk. Lit.: *Odyssey*]

3. **Longinus** centurion finally sees Christ as son of God. [N.T.: Matthew 27:54; Mark 15:39; Luke 23:47]

4. **Passover** Jewish festival; blood of sacrificed lambs placed on houses of the Israelites to prevent death of their firstborn. [O.T.: Exodus 12:3–13]

5. **recognition scene** theatrical device common in classical and renaissance comedy in which relatives at last recognize one another, usually at the moment of denoument. [World Lit.: Misc.]

6. **Sakuntala** recognized as queen on return of lost ring. [Sanskrit Lit.: *Abhijnanasakuntala*, Brewer *Dictionary*, 955]

7. **shibboleth** word used by Gileadites to identify Ephraimites who could not pronounce *sh*. [O.T.: Judges 12:4–6]

8. **Simeon** recognizes young Jesus as messiah. [N.T.: Luke 2:22–34]

9. **Stanley, Henry (1841–1904)** American journalist finds explorer, Dr. Livingstone, in Africa (1871). [Am. Hist.: Van Doren, 263]

10. **Ulysses' bow** Penelope recognizes husband by his ability to bend Ulysses' bow. [Gk. Lit.: *Ulysses*]

370. IDOLATRY

1. **Aaron** responsible for the golden calf. [O.T.: Exodus 32]

2. **Ashtaroth** Canaanite deities worshiped profanely by Israelites. [O.T.: Judges 2:12]

3. **Baalim** Canaanite deities worshiped profanely by Israelites. [O.T.: Judges 2:11]

4. **Baphomet** fabled image; allegedly a Templar fetish. [Medieval Legend: Walsh *Classical*, 46]

5. **David** King of Israel who was held in reverence after he slew Goliath. [O.T.: Samuel 17:4–51]

6. **golden calf** idol made by Aaron in Moses's absence. [O.T.: Exodus 32:2–4]

7. **Jehu** obliterates profane worship of Baal. [O.T.: II Kings 10:29]

8. **Jeroboam** forsook worship of God; made golden calves. [O.T.: I Kings 12:28–33]

9. **Moloch** deity to whom parents sacrificed their children. [O.T.: II Kings 23:10]

10. **Parsis** religious community of India; worship fire along with other aspects of nature. [Hindu Rel.: *NCE*, 2075]

371. IGNORANCE (See also DIMWITTEDNESS, STUPIDITY.)

1. **Am ha-Arez** those negligent in or unobservant of Torah study. [Judaism: Wigoder, 26]

2. **avidya** ignorance as cause of suffering through desire. [Hindu Phil.: Parrinder, 36]

3. **Dark Ages** used in reference to the early Middle Ages (4th—11th centuries); symbol of irrationality, ignorance. [Eur. Hist.: *ODA*]

4. **Deane, Lucy** unaware of fiancé Stephen's obvious relationship with Maggie. [Br. Lit.: *The Mill on the Floss*]

5. **Dunsmen** opposers of Renaissance learning (14th century); hence, *dunce*. [Br. Hist.: Espy, 116]

6. **Islayev, Arkady** so entrenched in work, oblivious to wife's infidelities. [Russ. Lit.: *A Month in the Country*]

7. **It Pays to Be Ignorant** panelists fail to answer such questions as "Which player on a baseball team wears a catcher's mask?" [Am. Radio: Buxton, 120]

8. **Neanderthal** prehistoric human ancestor; now, a term for a backward, stupid individual. [Pop. Culture: *FOF, MOD*]

9. **Newman, Alfred E.** cartoon character personifying ignorance as bliss: "What, me worry?" [Comics: "Mad" in Horn, 442]

10. **Parable of the Cave** cave dwellers see only the shadows of reality. [Gk. Phil.: *Republic*]

11. **Peppermint Patty** cartoon character habitually stumped by teacher and forever failing exams. [Comics: "Peanuts" in Horn, 543]

12. **Scarecrow** goes to Wizard of Oz to get brains. [Am. Lit.: *The Wonderful Wizard of Oz*]

13. **Schweik** cheerful, feeble-minded character; the antithesis of German militarism. [Czech Lit.: *The Good Soldier: Schweik*, Magill IV, 390–392]

14. **Sweat Hogs** class of incorrigible students majoring in remedial education. [TV: "Welcome Back, Kotter" in Terrace, II, 423]

372. ILLEGITIMACY

1. **bend sinister** supposed stigma of illegitimate birth. [Heraldry: Misc.]

2. **Clinker, Humphry** servant of Bramble family turns out to be illegitimate son of Mr. Bramble. [Br. Lit.: *Humphry Clinker*, Payton, 324]

3. **Edmund** illegitimate son of Earl of Gloucester; conspires against father. [Br. Hist.: *King Lear*]

4. **Jones, Tom** revealed to be Squire Allworthy's sister Bridget's illegitimate son. [Br. Lit.: Fielding *Tom Jones*]

373. ILLUSION (See also APPEARANCES, DECEIVING.)

1. **Barmecide feast** imaginary feast served to beggar by prince. [Arab. Lit.: *Arabian Nights*, "The Barmecide's Feast"]

2. *Breakfast at Tiffany's* classic 1961 film starring Audrey Hepburn portrays young woman's romantic illusions. [Am. Film: *SJEPC*]

3. *Calvin and Hobbes* popular comic strip (1985–95) by Bill Watterson featuring an imaginative, mischievous boy, Calvin, and his philosophical stuffed tiger, Hobbes, who came alive only when other characters were absent. [Am. Comics: *SJEPC*]

4. **Emperor's new clothes** supposedly invisible to unworthy people; in reality, nonexistent. [Dan. Lit.: *Andersen's Fairy Tales*]

5. **Escher, M.C. (1902–1972)** Dutch artist known for prints featuring complex, paradoxical forms and structures. [Art: *ODA*]

6. **Fata Morgana** esp. in the Straits of Messina: named for Morgan le Fay. [Ital. Folklore: Espy, 14]

7. *Field of Dreams* Iowa farmer fears he's only imagined the mysterious voice urging, "If you build it he will come" and his vision of creating a baseball diamond in the middle of his cornfield (1989). [Am. Film: *SJEPC*]

8. **George and Martha** as an imaginary compensation for their childlessness, pretend they have a son, who would now be twenty-one. [Am. Drama: Edward Albee *Who's Afraid of Virginia Woolf?* in *On Stage*, 447]

9. ***Glass Menagerie, The*** drama of St. Louis family escaping reality through illusion (1945). [Am. Lit.: *The Glass Menagerie*, Magill III, 418–420]

10. **Herbert, Niel** Mrs. Forrester's affairs destoyed his image of her. [Am. Lit.: *A Lost Lady*]

11. **Hudibras** English Don Quixote; opponent of repressive laws. [Br. Lit.: *Hudibras*, Espy, 204]

12. **Marshland, Jinny** saw philanderer Brad Criley as true lover. [Am. Lit.: *Cass Timberlane*]

13. **mirage** something illusory, such as an imaginary tree and pond in the midst of a desert. [Pop. Usage: Misc.]

14. **Mitty, Walter** imagines self in brilliant and heroic roles. [Am. Lit.: "The Secret Life of Walter Mitty" in Cartwell, 606–610]

15. **Quixote, Don** attacks windmills thinking them giants. [Span. Lit.: *Don Quixote*]

16. **Snoopy** imaginative dog. [Comics: "Peanuts" in Horn, 542–543]

17. **Xanadu** place appearing in Coleridge's dream; where Kubla Khan "did/A stately pleasure-dome decree." [Br. Lit.: "Kubla Khan" in Payton, 744]

374. IMAGINATION

1. ***Harold and the Purple Crayon*** picture book written in 1955 by Crockett Johnson; curious four-year-old uses a purple crayon to draw a world that comes alive as he creates it. [Am. Children's Lit.: Misc.]

2. **Little Bear** protagonist of four stories by Else Holmelund Minarik, illustrated by Maurice Sendak; childlike and very imaginative, he enjoys the security and love of his nurturing mother. [Am. Children's Lit.: Jones]

3. **Randall, Rebecca Rowena** protagonist of children's book *Rebecca of Sunnybrook Farm* by Kate Douglas Wiggin; iimaginative and sensitive child; gets into a fair share of trouble before maturing into a devoted, self-sacrificing young woman. [Am. Children's Lit.: Jones]

4. ***Where the Wild Things Are*** best-selling 1963 picture book by Maurice Sendak; Max, punished and sent to his room, imagines a world of monsters who make him their king, but he returns home to be where he is loved; although critics had their doubts, children were enthralled. [Am. Children's Lit.: OCCL]

375. IMMORTALITY (See also AGELESSNESS.)

1. **Admetus** granted everlasting life when wife Alcestis dies in his place. [Gk. Myth.: NCE, 54]

2. **amber axe** symbol of everlasting life. [Western Folklore: Jobes, 82]

3. **ambrosia** food of the gods; bestows immortality. [Gk. Myth.: Brewer *Dictionary*]

4. **amrita** beverage conferring immortality. [Hindu Myth.: Parrinder, 19]

5. **ankh** symbol of eternal life. [Egyptian Culture: *IEOTS*, 45]

6. **apples of perpetual youth** admit Norse gods to eternal life. [Norse Myth.: Benét, 43]

7. **Calypso** promises Odysseus eternal youth and immortality if he will stay with her forever. [Gk. Myth.: Brewer *Dictionary*, 166]

8. **cedar** symbol of everlasting life. [Western Folklore: Jobes, 301]

9. **Chiron** immortal centaur. [Gk. Myth.: Kravitz, 58]

10. **cicada** symbol of eternal life. [Chinese Folklore: Jobes, 338]

11. **cypress** symbol of eternal life. [Flower Symbolism: Jobes, 402]

12. **cypress coffin** symbolizes everlasting life; used for burials of heroes. [Gk. and Egyptian Folklore: Leach, 272]

13. **fan palm** emblem of eternal life among early Christians. [Plant Symbolism: Embolden, 25–29]

14. **globe amaranth** flower of immortality. [Flower Symbolism: *Flora Symbolica*, 172]

15. **greybeard-grow-young** magical lake plant; its scent conferred everlasting life. [Babyl. Myth.: *Gilgamesh*]

16. **ichor** flows through the veins of gods instead of blood. [Gk. Myth.: Brewer *Dictionary*]

17. **ivy** symbol of immortality and friendship. [Symbolism: *CEOS&S*]

18. **Luggnagg** imaginary island; inhabitants immortal but lack immortal health. [Br. Lit.: *Gulliver's Travels*]

19. **nectar** drink of the gods; bestows eternal life. [Gk. and Roman Myth.: Brewer *Dictionary*, 75]

20. **nightingale** immortal bird whose voice has been heard from time immemorial. [Br. Poetry: Keats "Ode to a Nightingale"]

21. **peach** very important Chinese symbol with many meanings, including immortality, marriage, fertility. [Symbolism: *CEOS&S*]

22. **scarab** dung-beetle; said to carry secret of eternal life. [Egyptian Legend: Brewer *Dictionary*, 967]

23. **serpent** sheds skin to renew its life. [Gk. Myth.: Gaster, 37]

24. **Struldbrugs** race "cursed" with gift of deathlessness. [Br. Lit.: *Gulliver's Travels*]

25. **Tithonus** given eternal life but not eternal youth. [Gk. Myth.: Brewer *Dictionary*, 1087]

26. **tree of life** eat of its fruit and live forever. [O.T.: Genesis 3:22]

27. **Utnaphishtim** blessed by Enlil with everlasting life. [Babyl. Myth.: *Gilgamesh*]

28. **Wandering Jew** doomed to live forever for scorning Jesus. [Gr. Lit.: *The Wandering Jew*]

29. **Xanthus and Balius** Achilles' divine horses. [Gk. Lit.: *Iliad*]

30. **yew** traditionally planted in churchyards; symbol of deathlessness. [Br. Legend: Brewer *Dictionary*, 1171]

376. IMPERIALISM

1. **White Man's Burden** imperialist's duty to educate the uncivilized. [Br. Hist.: Brewer *Dictionary*, 1152]

377. IMPERSONATION

1. **Patroclus** wore the armor of Achilles against the Trojans to encourage the disheartened Greeks. [Gk. Lit.: *Iliad*]

2. *Prisoner of Zenda, The* Englishman impersonating his distant relative King Rudolf is crowned in his stead. [Br. Lit.: *The Prisoner of Zenda*]

3. **Schicci, Gianni** dressed to resemble the dying testator in order to dictate a fraudulent will. [Ital. Hist. and Opera: *Gianni Schicci* in *Collier's*]

4. **Tichborne case** claimant to the Tichborne baronetcy impersonated the missing heir; proved a perjuror and imprisoned. [Br. Lit.: Brewer *Dictionary*, 898]

5. **Zeus** assumes the appearance of her husband Amphitryon in order to seduce Alcmene. [Fr. Drama: Molière *Amphitryon*]

378. IMPERTINENCE

1. **Bugs Bunny** cartoon character who is impertinent toward everyone. [Comics: Horn, 140]

2. **McCarthy, Charlie** dummy who is impertinent toward master, Edgar Bergen. [Radio: "The Edgar Bergen and Charlie McCarthy Show" in Buxton, 76–77]

3. **Pierce, Hawkeye** wisecracking medic with an insult for everyone. [TV: "M*A*S*H" in Terrace, II, 71–72]

4. **Squirrel Nutkin** protagonist of Beatrix Potter tale for children (1903); impertinent and disrespectful to Old Brown Owl, he nearly loses his life. [Br. Children's Lit.: *The Tale of Squirrel Nutkin*]

Impetuousness (See RASHNESS.)

Impossibility (See UNATTAINABILITY.)

379. **IMPRISONMENT (See also ISOLATION.)**

1. **Alcatraz Island** former federal maximum security penitentiary, near San Francisco; "escape proof." [Am. Hist.: Flexner, 218]

2. **Altmark, the** German prison ship in World War II. [Br. Hist.: Brewer *Dictionary*, 27]

3. **Andersonville** in southwest Georgia; imprisoned Union soldiers died under wretched conditions. [Am. Hist.: *NCE*, 99]

4. **Attica** well-known prison in Attica, New York; remembered for its riot (1971). [Am. Hist.: *NCE*, 182]

5. **Bajazeth** Turkish emperor confined to a cage by Tamburlaine. [Br. Drama: *Tamburlaine the Great* in Magill I, 950]

6. **ball and chain** originally penological, now generalized symbol. [Western Folklore: Jobes, 176]

7. **Bastille** Paris prison stormed on July 14, 1789. [Fr. Hist.: Worth, 21]

8. **Birdman of Alcatraz** Robert F. Stroud (1890–1963), convicted murderer, became ornithologist in prison. [Am. Culture: Misc.]

9. **Black Hole of Calcutta** Indian dungeon in which prisoners were kept in inhuman conditions. [Br. Hist.: Harbottle, 45–46]

10. **Bok, Yakov** held in prison for two years under dreadful conditions. [Am. Lit.: Bernard Malamud *The Fixer*]

11. **Cash, Johnny (1932–2003)** country music legend with outlaw persona often performed his songs for prisoners inside their confines, including "Folsom Prison Blues." [Am. Music: *SJEPC*]

12. **Cereno, Benito** captain held captive by mutinous slaves. [Am. Lit.: *Benito Cereno*]

13. **Count of Monte Cristo** Edmond Dantès; wrongly imprisoned in the dungeons of Château D'If. [Fr. Lit.: *The Count of Monte Cristo*, Magill I, 158–160]

14. **Denisovitch, Ivan** struggles to stay alive in a Soviet prison camp. [Russ. Lit.: Solzhenitzyn *One Day in the Life of Ivan Denisovitch*]

15. **Devil's Island** Guiana island penal colony (1852–1938); Alfred Dreyfus among famous prisoners there. [Fr. Hist.: *NCE*, 754]

16. **Droma** chain forged to fetter wolf, Fenris. [Norse Myth.: *LLEI*, I: 326]

17. *Enormous Room, The* portrays three months behind bars in France. [Am. Lit.: *The Enormous Room*]

18. **Falconer** prison where former professor Farragut, who had killed his brother, witnesses the torments and chaos of the penal system. [Am. Lit.: Cheever *Falconer* in Weiss, 151]

19. **Fortunato** walled up to die in catacomb niche. [Am. Lit.: "The Cask of Amontillado" in *Portable Poe*, 309–316]

20. **Fotheringay** Mary Stuart's final prison and place of execution (1587). [Br. Hist.: Grun, 260]

21. **Gulag Archipelago** system of slave labor camps in the Soviet Union; Alexsandr Solzhenitsyn's book of the same name describes the camps; a symbol of prison, and of Soviet brutality. [Russ. Hist.: *ODA*]

22. *Hogan's Heroes* incarcerated in Stalag 13, unlikeliest of POW camps. [TV: Terrace, I, 357–358]

23. *House of the Dead, The* account of four years in the fortress-prison of Omsk. [Russ. Lit.: *The House of the Dead* in Benét, 480]

24. **Ibbetson, Peter** imprisoned for life, spends all his nights in blissful dreams of existence with his beloved. [Br. Lit & Am. Opera: G. du Maurier *Peter Ibbetson* in Magill I, 736]

25. **Leadbelly (1885–1949)** blues guitarist and singer/songwriter; his chaotic, often brutal life was basis of his incredible songs; twice released from prison on basis of his musical talent. [Am. Music: *SJEPC*]

26. **Leavenworth** the oldest military prison (est. 1874); also the name of a state penitentiary. [Am. Hist.: *NCE*, 984]

27. **Little Dorrit** born and grew up in the prison where for twenty years her father is incarcerated. [Br. Lit.: Dickens *Little Dorrit*]

28. *Man in the Iron Mask* mystery prisoner; legendary contender for Louis XIV's throne. [Fr. Hist.: Brewer *Note-Book*, 460, 555]

29. **Manette, Dr.** lost memory during 18–year term in France. [Br. Lit.: *A Tale of Two Cities*]

30. **Marshalsea** ancient London prison, long used for incarcerating debtors. [Br. Hist.: Benét, 640]

31. **Newgate** famed jail of London in centuries past. [Br. Hist.: Brewer *Dictionary*, 754]

32. **Pickwick, Mr. (Samuel)** imprisoned for refusing to pay damages in a breach-of-promise suit. [Br. Lit.: Dickens *Pickwick Papers*]

33. *Prisoner of Chillon, The* poem by Lord Byron; based on imprisonment of FranÁois de Bonnivard. [Br. Lit.: Benét, 817]

34. **Reading Gaol** jail where Oscar Wilde served his sentence for homosexual offenses; source of his poem. [Br. Lit.: Oscar Wilde *Ballad of Reading Gaol*]

35. **Robben Island** prison on an island off the coast of South Africa where Nelson Mandela was imprisoned; symbol of the brutality of apartheid. [History *ODA*]

36. **Rubashov, Nicholas** political prisoner held in isolation and brutally questioned. [Br. Lit.: Arthur Koestler *Darness at Noon* in Magill I, 187]

37. **San Quentin** famous western California prison (established in 1852); the subject of many songs. [Am. Hist.: *NCE* 2419]

38. **Sing Sing** notoriously harsh state prison at Ossining, New York. [Am. Hist.: Flexner, 219]

39. **Torquilstone** Front de Boeuf's castle, where he imprisoned Rowena, Rebecca, and Isaac. [Br. Lit.: Walter Scott *Ivanhoe*]

40. **Tower of London** famed as jail. [Br. Hist.: Brewer *Dictionary*, 1094]

41. **Tyson, Mike (1966–)** boxing champ by the age of 19; volatile personality spilled over into personal life, leading to brutality in and out of ring and imprisonment. [Am. Sports: *SJEPC*]

42. **Ugolino** treacherous 13th-century count of Pisa, imprisoned and starved to death with his sons and grandsons. [Ital. Poetry: *Inferno*]

43. **Valjean, Jean** spent nineteen years in prison for stealing loaf of bread. [Fr. Lit.: *Les Misèrables*]

380. INCEST

1. **Amnon** ravishes his sister, Tamar. [O.T.: II Samuel 13:14]

2. **Antiochus** commits incest with daughter; their incestuous relationship becomes the center of the riddle that must be solved by her suitors, or they perish. [Br. Lit.: *Pericles*]

3. **Canace** Aeolus's daughter; committed suicide after relations with brother. [Gk. Myth.: Zimmerman, 49]

4. **Cenci, Count Francesco** old libertine ravishes his daughter Beatrice. [Br. Lit.: Shelley *The Cenci*, Magill I, 131]

5. **Clymenus** Arcadian who violated his daughter, Harpalyce. [Gk. Myth.: Zimmerman, 65]

6. **Compson, Quentin** his only passion is for his sister Candace. [Am. Lit.: Faulkner *The Sound and the Fury* in Magill I, 917]

7. **Electra** bore great, passionate love for father, Agamemnon. [Gk. Myth.: Zimmerman, 92; Gk. Lit.: *Electra*; *Orestes*]

8. **Engstrand, Regina** Oswald's half-sister and chosen lover. [Nor. Lit.: *Ghosts*]

9. **Giovanni and Annabella** brother-sister romance. [Br. Lit.: *'Tis Pity She's a Whore*]

10. **Harpalyce** bears child by father, Clymenus. [Gk. Myth.: Howe, 114]

11. **Jocasta** unknowingly marries her son, Oedipus. [Gk. Lit.: *Oedipus Rex*]

12. **Judah** unknowingly has relations with daughter-in-law. [O.T.: Genesis 38:15–18]

13. **Lot** impregnates his two daughters. [O.T.: Genesis 19:36]

14. **Myrrha** mother of Adonis; daughter of Adonis' father. [Gk. Myth.: Brewer *Dictionary*. 741]

15. **Niquee and Anasterax** sister and brother live together in incest. [Span. Lit.: *Amadis de Gaul*]

16. **Oedipus** unknowingly marries mother and fathers four sons. [Gk. Lit.: *Oedipus Rex*]

17. **Sieglinde and Siegmund** twin brother and sister passionately in love. [Ger. Lit.: Mann "The Blood of the Walsungs"]

18. **Tamar** seduces her brother and her father. [Am. Lit.: Robinson Jeffers *Tamar* in Magill I, 948]

19. **Tower, Cassandra (Cassie)** had relations with Dr. Tower, her father. [Am. Lit.: *King's Row*, Magill I, 478–480]

20. **Warren, Nicole** suffers after having had sexual relations with father. [Am. Lit.: *Tender Is the Night*]

Incompetence (See INEPTITUDE.)

381. INCOMPLETENESS

1. *Unfinished Symphony, The* Schubert's eighth symphony of two movements instead of the customary four. [Ger. Music: Thompson]

2. *Venus de Milo* classic sculpture, discovered in 1820 with arms missing. [Gk. Art.: Brewer *Dictionary*]

Incorruptibility (See HONESTY.)

382. INDECISION

1. **Braddock, Benjamin** college graduate with absolutely no direction. [Am. Lit. and Film: *The Graduate*]

2. **Buridan's ass** unable to decide between two haystacks, he would starve to death. [Fr. Phil.: Brewer *Dictionary*, 154]

3. **Cooke, Ebenezer** his irresolution usually leads to catatonia. [Am. Lit.: *The Sot-Weed Factor*]

4. **Hamlet** tragic hero who tarries and broods over revenge and suicide. [Br. Lit.: *Hamlet*]

5. **hung jury** cannot decide guilt or innocence. [Am. Hist.: Misc.]

6. **Libra** seventh constellation of the Zodiac; those born under Libra may be indecisive. [Astrology: Payton, 389]

7. **Panurge** unable to decide whether to marry, he consults many people and undertakes a long voyage to visit an oracle. [Fr. Lit.: Rabelais *Gargantua and Pantagruel*]

8. **Penelope** put off a decision on which suitor to marry by secretly unraveling the shroud she said she must first complete. [Gk. Lit.: *Odyssey*]

9. **Theramenes** shilly-shallying oligarch; nicknamed Cothurnus, i.e., ambipedal boot. [Gk. Hist.: Brewer *Dictionary*, 960]

10. *Waiting for Godot* tramps are torn between waiting for Godot to solve their problems and hanging themselves. [Irish Lit.: Samuel Beckett *Waiting for Godot* in Magill III, 1113]

11. **Whiffle, Peter** would-be writer, cursed with indecision, accomplishes nothing. [Am. Lit.: *Peter Whiffle*, Magill I, 739–741]

383. INDEPENDENCE

1. **Bastille Day** July 14; French national holiday celebrating the fall of the Bastille prison (1789). [Fr. Hist.: *NCE*, 245]

2. **Declaration of Independence** written by delegates of the American Thirteen Colonies announcing U.S. independence from Great Britain (1776). [Am. Hist.: *NCE*, 733]

3. **Garibaldi, Giuseppe (1807–1882)** Italian leader who unified Italy and led the movement for independence. [Ital. Hist.: *ODA*]

4. **Huggins, Henry** character in series of children's books by Beverly Cleary; self-reliant boy; earns money for toys. [Am. Children's Lit.: *Henry Huggins*]

5. **Independence Day** Fourth of July; U.S. patriotic holiday celebrating the Declaration of Independence. [Am. Hist.: *NCE*, 990]

6. **Longstocking, Pippi** nine-year-old orphaned protagonist of eleven episodic stories in Astrid Lindgren's children's book; odd appearance and behavior; alter-ego of every child— totally independent, outrageous, and fun loving. [Swed. Children's Lit.: Jones]

7. **Maine** often thought of as the state of "independent Yankees." [Pop. Culture: Misc.]

8. **March, Jo** talented writer and actress, the tempetuous and forthright character of beloved children's book *Little Women* (1868) is based on Louisa May Alcott herself. [Am. Chldren's Lit.: Jones]

9. **Mugwumps** Republican party members who voted independently. [Am. Hist.: Jameson, 337]

10. **Quebec** Canada's French-speaking province has often attempted to attain independence from rest of country. [Canadian Hist.: *NCE*, 2555]

11. **Tree of Liberty** symbolic post or tree hung with flags and other devices and crowned with the liberty cap. [Misc.: Brewer *Dictionary*, 911]

12. **white oak** indicates self-sufficiency. [Flower Symbolism: *Flora Symbolica*, 178]

384. INDIFFERENCE

1. **Antoinette, Marie (1755–1793)** queen of France to whom is attributed this statement on the solution to the bread famine: "Let them eat cake." [Fr. Hist.: *NCE*, 1696]

2. **Bastienne** unsuccessful ploy to win back Bastien. [Ger. Opera: Mozart, *Bastien and Bastienne*, Westerman, 83]

3. **"Belle Dame Sans Merci"** poem by John Keats featuring a young knight bewitched by a fairy indifferent to his affections; symbol for a cruel temptress [Br. Lit.: *FOF, MOD*]

4. **Defarge, Madame** feigned indifference; knitted while executions were taking place. [Br. Lit.: *A Tale of Two Cities*]

5. **Laodicean** inhabitant of ancient Greek city, Laeodicea; people noted for indifferent attitude toward religion. [Gk. Hist.: *NCE*, 1529]

6. **Nero (37–68)** Roman emperor who is reported to have fiddled while Rome burned. [Rom. Hist.: Misc.]

7. **New York City** often thought of as a metropolis of cold, uncaring people. [Pop. Culture: Misc.]

8. **Oblomov** passed life in torpor; symbolically, died sleeping. [Russ. Lit.: *Oblomov*]

9. **senvy** indicates apathy and noncaring. [Flower Symbolism: *Flora Symbolica*]

10. **Snow Queen** character in Hans Christian Andersen story unmoved by the plight of her captive, Kai, who has lost the ability to feel human emotions; a symbol of cruel indifference. [Dan. Fairy Tale: *ODA*]

385. INDIVIDUALISM (See also EGOTISM.)

1. **Abstract Expressionism** highly subjective American art form originating in mid-20th-century New York; focuses on painter's unique, individual creative experience and expression. [Am. Art: *SJEPC*]

2. *Atlas Shrugged* novel by Ayn Rand; based on her Objectivist philosophy. [Am. Lit.: *SJEPC*]

3. **Beaumont, Ned** gambler-detective solves murder case in unorthodox manner. [Am. Lit.: *The Glass Key*, Magill I, 307–308]

4. **different drummer** famous phrase from Thoreau's "Where I Lived and What I Lived For," on the inner freedom and individualistic character of man: "If a man does not keep pace with his companions, perhaps it is because he hears a different drummer. Let him step to the music which he hears, however measured or far away." [Am. Lit.: *NCE*, 2739]

5. *Fountainhead, The* novel by Ayn Rand; based on her Objectivist philosophy. [Am. Lit.: *SJEPC*]

6. **Higgins, Mayo Cornelius** protagonist of Virginia Hamilton's children's novel *M.C. Higgins the Great* (1974); unusual and imaginative, M.C. learns how to help his family and make his life better in concrete ways. [Am. Children's Lit.: Jones]

7. **i-** Apple's line of personal electronic products such as iMac, iPod, iPhone. [Am. Technology: Misc.]

8. **Krupnik, Anastasia** protagonist of series of children's books written from 1979–1991 by Lois Lowry; records feelings in notebook, revising as she gains more experience and insight; opinionated and sensitive, she moves through many instructive and funny episodes in her life. [Am. Children's Lit.: Jones]

9. **Longstocking, Pippi** eccentric young girl who sets her own standards. [Children's Lit.: *Pippi Longstocking*]

10. **Objectivism** political philosophy of Ayn Rand; calls for libertarian individualism and atheism. [Am. Phil.: *SJEPC*]

11. **Rand, Ayn (1905–1982)** famous writer of philosophical novels about individuals rejecting societal and governmental restrictions. [Am. Lit.: *SJEPC*]

12. **Thoreau, Henry David (1817–1862)** in *Walden* and other works, described his belief in the importance of being true to one's self. [Am. Lit.: *FOF, MOD*]

386. INDUCEMENT

1. **Electra** incited brother, Orestes, to kill their mother and her lover. [Gk. Myth.: Zimmerman, 92; Gk. Lit.: *Electra*; *Orestes*]

2. **Hezekiah** exhorts Judah to stand fast against Assyrians. [O.T.: II Chronicles 32:6–8]

3. **Lantier, Etienne** exhorts fellow miners to massive strike. [Fr. Lit.: *Germinal*]

4. **Mannon, Lavinia** 20th-century Electra in New England. [Am. Lit.: *Mourning Becomes Electra*]

5. **Salome** beguilingly prompts decapitation of John the Baptist. [N.T.: Mark 6:22–28]

6. **Tricoteuses** sobriquet of battle-exhorting women at French Convention. [Fr. Hist.: Brewer *Dictionary*, 1100]

7. **Tyrtaeus (fl. 7th century B.C.)** elegist; roused Spartans to Messenian triumph. [Gk. Hist.: Brewer *Dictionary*, 1111]

387. INDUSTRIOUSNESS

1. **ant** works hard to prepare for winter while grasshopper plays. [Gk. Lit.: *Aesop's Fables*, "The Ant and the Grasshopper"]

2. **beaver** perpetually and eagerly active. [Western Folklore: Jobes, 192]

3. **bee** proverbial busyness refers to ceaseless activity of worker bees. [Western Folklore: Jobes, 445]

4. **beehive** heraldic and verbal symbol. [Western Folklore: Jobes, 193]

5. **grindstone** or grind; common metaphor for industriousness. [Pop. Culture: Misc.]

6. **red clover** symbolic of diligence. [Flower Symbolism: Jobes, 193]

7. **Saturday's child** works hard for his living. [Nurs. Rhyme: Opie, 309]

8. **Stakhanov, Aleksey (1906–1977)** Russian worker who "over-achieved"; increased daily output enormously. [Russ. Hist.: *NCE*, 2606]

9. **third little pig** builds his house of bricks while his two brothers fritter away their time. [Children's Lit.: *The Three Little Pigs*]

388. INEPTITUDE

1. **Band-Aid** from the name of a bandage, it means to inadequately address a problem. [Pop. Cult.: Misc.]

2. **Bedelia, Amelia** confused protagonist of series of chldren's books by Peggy Parish; well-meaning maid follows order literal-ly, with comic—and sometimes disastrous—results. [Am. Chil-dren's Lit.: Jones]

3. **Brown, Charlie** meek hero unable to kick a football, fly a kite, or win a baseball game. [Comics: "Peanuts" in Horn, 543]

4. **Dogberry** officious, inept constable. [Br. Lit.: *Much Ado About Nothing*]

5. **Fife, Barney** deputy who can't be trusted with loaded gun. [TV: "The Andy Griffith Show" in Terrace, I, 55–56]

6. **George of the Jungle** bungling do-gooder. [TV: Terrace, I, 305–306]

7. **Gilligan** whose every action reeks of incompetence. [TV: "Gilli-gan's Island" in Terrace, I, 312–313]

8. **Gordon, Dr.** called a "butcher" for his needless and bungled op-erations. [Am. Lit.: *King's Row*, Magill I, 478]

9. **Hagar the Horrible** soft-hearted, unkempt Viking whose raids yield miniscule plunder. [Comics: Horn, 299]

10. **Halftrack, General** the ultimate in inept officers. [Comics: "Bee-tle Bailey" in Horn, 105–106]

11. **Hound, Huckleberry** bungler trying to find niche; always fails. [TV: "The Huckleberry Hound Show" in Terrace, I, 367–377]

12. **Klink, Colonel** naïve official in charge of prisoner-of-war camp. [TV: "Hogan's Heroes" in Terrace, I, 357–358]

13. **lightweight** from boxing, term describing a fighter weighing between 126 and 135 pounds; catchword for an inept individual. [Am. Pop. Culture: *FOF, MOD*]

14. **Longbottom, Neville** character from J.K. Rowling's Harry Potter series for young readers (1997–2007); bungling friend of Harry's who never seems to get his spells right. [Br. Children's Lit.: Misc.]

15. **Lucky Eddie** Hagar's chinless aide, bungles the simplest assignments. [Comics: *Hagar the Horrible* in Horn, 299]

16. **Marplot** actions are well-meant, but his continual interference ruins lovers' plans. [Br. Drama: *The Busybody* in Barnhart, 185]

17. **Orbaneja** obliged to label painted objects for identification. [Span. Lit.: *Don Quixote*]

18. **Paddington Bear** bear from Darkest Peru found sitting on suitcase in London's Paddington Station and so named by the family that adopts him; his bumbling brings a series of misadventures; from series of books by Michael Bond. [Br. Children's Lit.: Jones]

19. *Peter Principle, The* book stating, "in a Hierarchy, every employer tends to rise to the level of his incompetence." [Am. Lit.: *The Peter Principle*, Payton, 522]

20. **Queeg, Captain Philip** incompetent commander of the minesweeper *Caine*. [Am. Lit. and Film: *The Caine Mutiny* in Benét, 157]

21. **Sad Sack** can't do anything right. [Comics: "The Sad Sack" in Horn, 595–596]

22. **Scarecrow** can't live up to his name. [Am. Lit.: *The Wonderful Wizard of Oz*; Am. Film: Halliwell, 780]

23. **Schultz, Sergeant** bumbling assistant to Colonel Klink at Stalag 13. [TV: "Hogan's Heroes" in Terrace, I, 357–358]

24. **Slop, Dr.** country doctor attends Tristram Shandy's birth and crushes the infant's nose with his forceps. [Br. Lit.: *Tristram Shandy* in Magill I, 1027]

25. **Smart, Maxwell** bumbling spy in genre spoof *Get Smart* (1965–70). [Am. TV: *SJEPC*]

26. **three men in a boat** inexperience makes their trip on the Thames a series of misfortunes. [Br. Lit.: Jerome *Three Men in a Boat* in Magill II, 1018]

27. **Toody and Muldoon** twin antitheses of "New York's Finest." [TV: "Car 54 Where Are You?" in Terrace, I, 138–139]

28. **Tumbleweeds** world's most incompetent sheriff. [Comics: Horn, 673]

29. **White Knight** invents clever objects that never work. [Br. Lit.: Lewis Carroll *Through the Looking-Glass*]

30. ***WKRP in Cincinnati*** 1978–1982 TV show about a struggling small-time radio station run by an incompetent owner and manned by a group of odd-ball personalities. [Am. TV: *SJEPC*]

31. **Wooster, Bertram** good-natured but bumbling rich young protagonist in witty stories by P.G. Wodehouse; constantly rescued by his "gentleman's gentleman" Jeeves. [Br. Lit.: *SJEPC*]

389. INEXPENSIVENESS

1. **bargain basement** sale of old stock at highly discounted prices. [Pop. Culture: Misc.]

2. **Costco** largest chain of wholesale clubs by sales volume; sells food, furniture, and much more at a discount through bulk. [Am. Business: Misc.]

3. **dollar store** retail store in which all items are one dollar or less in cost; similar stores exist throughout the world (100–yen shop, 1–Euro-Shop, etc.). [Business: Misc.]

4. **Five and Ten** popular sobriquet for various department stores, which at one time sold no item for more than a dime. [Pop. Culture: Misc.]

5. **flea market** yard sale of used items at low prices. [Pop. Culture: Misc.]

6. **Louisiana Purchase** about one third the area of the U.S. bought from Napoleon for $15 million (1803). [Am. Hist.: Jameson, 293]

7. **Manhattan** Manhattan Indians sold the island to Dutch West India Company supposedly for about $24 worth of merchandise (1626). [Am. Hist.: Jameson, 305]

8. **Mickey Mouse** squeaky-voiced cartoon hero; the term is often used in alluding to things of minor significance or expense. [Am. Comics: *EB*, VI: 862; Am. Pop. Culture: Misc.]

9. **Sam's Club** chain of membership-only warehouse stores owned by Wal-Mart Stores, Inc.; sells in bulk at lower prices. [Am. Business: Misc.]

10. **Seward's Folly** Alaska, purchased from Russia by Henry Seward for 2 cents an acre (1867). [Am. Hist.: Payton, 610]

11. **tag sale** yard sale of used items, usually at very low prices. [Pop. Culture: Misc.]

12. **Wal-Mart** large chain of discount department stores; highly criticized for tactics used to keep prices low. [Am. Business: Misc.]

13. **Woolworth's** international five-and-dime store. [Am. Business: *NCE*, 3004]

390. INEXPERIENCE (See also INNOCENCE, NAÏVETÉ.)

1. **Bowes, Major Edward (1874–1946)** originator and master of ceremonies of the Amateur Hour on radio. [Am. Radio: Buxton, 149–150]

2. ***Gong Show, The*** variety show in which beginners try to prove their abilities. [Am. TV: Misc.]

3. **greenhorn** a raw, inexperienced person; especially a new cowboy. [Pop. Culture: Misc.]

4. **Mack, Ted (1904–1976)** host of a television show starring amateurs. [TV: "Ted Mack and the Original Amateur Hour" in Terrace, II, 347]

5. **Newcome, Johnny** any unpracticed youth, especially new military officers. [Br. Folklore: Wheeler, 258]

6. **plebe** also plebeian; first or lowest class, especially at U.S. Military and Naval Academies. [Pop. Culture: Misc.]

7. **rookie** a novice; often an athlete playing his first season as a member of a professional sports team. [Sports: Misc.]

391. INFANTICIDE

1. **Astyanax** Hector's infant son, thrown from the walls of Troy by the Greeks. [Gk. Myth.: Hamilton, 289]

2. **Cronos** warned that a son would dethrone him, swallowed all his children at birth. [Gk. Myth.: Benét, 237]

3. **Sorrel, Hetty** leaves her illegitimate infant to die. [Br. Lit.: Eliot *Adam Bede*]

4. **Yates, Andrea (1964–)** Texan mother of five who drowned her children in 2001; found not guilty by reason of insanity. [Am. Hist.: Misc.]

Infertility (See BARRENNESS.)

Infidelity (See ADULTERY, CUCKOLDRY, FAITHLESSNESS.)

392. INFORMER

1. **Battus** revealed theft by Mercury; turned to touchstone. [Gk. and Roman Myth.: Walsh *Classical*, 47]

2. **Cenci, Count Francesco** old libertine ravishes his daughter Beatrice. [Br.Lit.: Shelley *The Cenci*, Magill I, 131]

3. **Chambers, Whittaker (1901–1961)** chief witness in perjury trial of Alger Hiss (1949). [Am. Hist.: *NCE*, 501]

4. **Dean, John W., III (1938–)** chief witness and informer against Nixon in the Watergate hearings. [Am. Hist.: *NCE*, 2939]

5. **Judas Iscariot** led armed band to Gethsemane and showed them which one was Jesus. [N.T.: Matthew 26:46–50; Mark 14:42–45; Luke 22:47–48]

6. **Libby, Lewis "Scooter" (1950–)** former chief-of-staff to Vice-President Dick Cheney; convicted in 2007 of revealing the identity of CIA undercover agent Valerie Plame Wilson. [Am. Hist.: Misc.]

7. **Morgan le Fay** reveals Lancelot and Guinevere's affair to Arthur. [Arthurian Legend: Harvey, 559]

8. **Nolan, Gypo** betrays friend to police for subsistence money. [Irish Lit.: *The Informer*]

9. **Peachum, Mr.** informer and fence for stolen goods. [Br. Lit.: *The Beggar's Opera*]

10. **Teresa, Vincent (1930–1990)** wrote book in which he revealed inner workings of the Mafia. [Am. Lit.: *My Life in the Mafia*]

11. **Tripp, Linda (1949–)** former White House secretary; in 1997, taped coworker Monica Lewinsky's confessions about sexual relationship with then-president Bill Clinton; gave the tapes to independent counsel Kenneth Starr, sparking an investigation. [Am. Hist.: Misc.]

12. **Valachi, Joe (1903–1971)** New York gangster who revealed the inner operations of the Mafia. [Am. Hist.: *Facts* (1971), 436]

13. **Wigand, Jeffrey (1942–)** former Brown & Williamson executive; on *60 Minutes* TV show, spoke out about tobacco industry's knowing disregard for health and safety issues of tobacco use; 1999 film *The Insider* tells his story. [Am. Hist.: Misc.]

393. INGRATITUDE

1. **Anastasie and Delphine** ungrateful daughters do not attend father's funeral. [Fr. Lit.: *Père Goriot*]

2. **Glencoe, Massacre of** Campbell clan, having accepted hospitality of the MacDonalds for more than a week, attacked their hosts, killing 38. [Scot. Hist.: *EB*, IV: 573]

3. **Goneril and Regan** two evil daughters of King Lear; their monstrous ingratitude upon receiving his kingdom drives him mad. [Br. Lit.: *King Lear*]

4. **Lucius** enjoyed Timon's generosity; refuses him loan when poor. [Br. Lit.: *Timon of Athens*]

5. **Lucullus** Timon's false friend; forgets all too easily his generosity. [Br. Lit.: *Timon of Athens*]

6. **Sempronius** shared in Timon's bounty; denies him loan when poor. [Br. Lit.: *Timon of Athens*]

7. **ten lepers** of the ten lepers cleansed by Jesus, only one returned to thank him. [N.T.: Luke 11–19]

394. INJUSTICE

1. **American internment camps** 120,000 Japanese-Americans incarcerated during WWII. [Am. Hist.: Van Doren, 487]

2. **Bassianus** murdered after being falsely accused. [Br. Lit.: *Titus Andronicus*]

3. **Bean, Judge Roy (1825–1904)** his brand of justice was the only "law west of the Pecos." [Am. Hist.: *WB*, 2, 137]

4. **Ben Hur** wrongly accused of attempted murder. [Am. Lit.: *Ben Hur*, Hart, 72]

5. *Bleak House* a fortune is dissipated by the long legal battle of Jarndyce vs. Jarndyce, and the heir dies in misery. [Br. Lit.: Dickens *Bleak House*]

6. **Bligh, William (1754–1817)** naval officer accused of practicing unfair and illegal cruelties. [Br. Hist.: *EB*, II: 82; Am. Lit.: *Mutiny on the Bounty*]

7. **Bok, Yakov** Jew falsely accused of ritual murder in Russia. [Am. Lit.: *The Fixer*]

8. **Budd, Billy** courtmartialed and unjustly hanged as mutineer and murderer. [Am. Lit.: *Billy Budd*]

9. **Child of the Cord** defendants brought before the *Vehmgerichte*. [Ger. Hist.: Brewer *Note-Book*, 166]

10. **Dred Scott decision** majority ruling by Supreme Court that a slave is property and not a U.S. citizen (1857). [Am. Hist.: Payton, 203]

11. **Dreyfus, Capt. Albert (1859–1935)** imprisoned on Devil's Island on falsified espionage charges. [Fr. Hist.: Wallechinsky, 60]

12. **Eurydice** Orpheus's wife; taken to underworld before her time. [Gk. Myth.: Magill I, 700–701]

13. **Falder, Justice** law clerk commits forgery for an unselfish purpose, is imprisoned, barred from work, eventually commits suicide. [Br. Lit.: Galsworthy *Justice*, Magill I, 466]

14. **Furry Lawcats** name given to a rapacious breed in Rabelais's violent satire on the venality of the courts. [Fr. Lit.: Rabelais *Gargantua and Pantagruel*]

15. **Hippolytus** falsely accused by stepmother of rape after he rejected her advances. [Rom. Lit.: *Aeneid*; *Metamorphoses*]

16. **hops** symbol of injustice. [Flower Symbolism: *Flora Symbolica*, 174; Kunz, 330]

17. **Jedburgh Justice** Scottish version of lynch law. [Scot. Hist.: Brewer *Note-Book*, 468]

18. **Jim Crow laws** late 19th-century laws passed by legislators of Southern U.S. states creating racial caste system; especially notable were separate facilities for blacks and whites in virtually every aspect of society. [Am. Hist.: Van Doren, 485]

19. **Josef K** though innocent of any crime, he is arrested, condemned, and executed. [Ger. Lit.: Kafka *The Trial* in Benét, 1023]

20. **kangaroo court** moblike tribunal, usually disregarding principles of justice. [Pop. Culture: Misc.]

21. **King, Rodney (1965–)** African American beaten by police in Los Angeles in 1991; their subsequent acquittal led to riots in the city in 1992; made a famous plea two days after verdicts: "Can we all get along?". [Am. Hist.: *SJEPC*]

22. **Lydford law** "hang first; try later." [Br. Hist.: Espy, 160]

23. **Lynch, Judge (1736–1796)** personification of mob law; summary execution. [Am. Hist.: Leach, 561]

24. **Martius and Quintus** falsely accused of Bassianus' murder. [Br. Lit.: *Titus Andronicus*]

25. **Mohicans** Indian tribe driven off homeland. [Am. Hist.: Hart, 515]

26. *Ox-Bow Incident, The* in revenge for having supposedly rustled cattle and killed a man, three suspects are lynched. [Am. Lit.: *The Ox-Bow Incident*]

27. **Queen of Hearts** "first the sentence, then the evidence!" [Br. Children's Lit.: *Alice's Adventures in Wonderland*]

28. **Rubashov, Nicholas** punished for crimes he never committed. [Br. Lit.: *Darkness at Noon*]

29. **Sacco and Vanzetti** [Sacco, Nicola (1891–1927) and Vanzetti, Bartolmeo (1888–1927)] accused and executed for murder (1927); their guilt has been largely disputed. [Am. Hist.: Allen, 59–61]

30. **Stamp Act** unfair revenue law imposed upon American colonies by Britain (1765). [Am. Hist.: Jameson, 475]

31. **Valjean, Jean** imprisoned nineteen years for stealing loaf of bread. [Fr. Lit.: *Les Misèrables*]

32. **Vehmgerichte** medieval Westphalian tribunals; judges abused juridicial powers. [Ger. Hist.: Brewer *Dictionary*, 1124]

395. INNOCENCE (See also INEXPERIENCE, NAÏVETÉ.)

1. **Adam and Eve** naked in Eden; knew no shame. [O.T.: Genesis 2:25]

2. **American's Sweetheart** name for wholesome actress Mary Pickford; now used to describe a wholesome, innocent girl. [Am. Film: Misc.]

3. **Arjuna** Sanskrit name means sinless. [Hindu Myth.: Benét, 50]

4. *Babes in the Wood* innocent children are lost in the woods and die. [Br. Lit.: *Babes in the Wood*, Walsh, *Classical*, 42]

5. **basin and ewer** Pilate's guiltlessness signified by washing of hands. [N.T.: Matthew 27:24]

6. **beardlessness** traditional representation of innocence and inexperience. [Western Folklore: Jobes, 190]

7. **Big Bird** Muppet character from *Sesame Street* TV show for children; very childlike despite his huge size; eight-foot yellow bird is lovable and naïve, thereby helping children accept their own lack of knowledge. [Am. TV: Misc.]

8. **Budd, Billy** friendly sailor; held in warm affection by crew. [Am. Lit.: *Billy Budd*]

9. **Christabel** free of evil. [Br. Lit.: "Christabel" in Walsh *Modern*, 95]

10. **Cinderella** with fairy godmother's aid, poor maligned girl wins prince's heart. [Fr. Fairy Tale: *Cinderella*]

11. **Cio-Cio San** believes marriage to Pinkerton is real. [Ital. Opera: Puccini, *Madama Butterfly*, Westerman, 357]

12. **Curlylocks** nursery rhyme heroine exemplifies innocence. [Folklore: Jobes, 398]

13. **daisy** symbol of blamelessness. [Flower Symbolism: *Flora Symbolica*, 173; Kunz, 328]

14. **Desdemona** blamelessness martyred through slander. [Br. Lit.: *Othello*]

15. **Dondi** foster child; confronts world with wide-eyed innocence. [Comics: Horn, 217–218]

16. **Forrest Gump** title character from novel and movie; an innocent, idealistic man, simple but strong and kind. [Am. Film: *FOF, MOD*]

17. **Goldilocks** innocent but curious visitor to house of three bears. [Fairy Tale: "Goldilocks and the Three Bears"]

18. **Gretchen** innocent young girl who is seduced and abandoned by Faust; she goes mad and murders their child. [Ger. Lit.: Goethe *Faust* Part One]

19. **Hallyard, Saint** Norwegian martyred in defense of guiltless woman. [Christian Hagiog.: Attwater, 165]

20. **Heidi** protagonist of Johanna Spyri's 1880 novel for children; has instinct for goodness. [Swiss Children's Lit.: Jones]

21. **Imogen** chaste wife unjustly suspected by Postumus of unfaithfulness. [Br. Drama: Shakespeare *Cymbeline*]

22. **lamb** attribute of young woman; personification of guiltlessness. [Art.: Hall, 161]

23. **Minnie** female saloonkeeper in mining town; never been kissed. [Ital. Opera: Puccini, *Girl of the Golden West*, Westerman, 360–361]

24. **Myshkin, Prince** loved for his innocence and frankness, lack of sophistication, and kind heart. [Russ. Lit.: Dostoevsky *The Idiot*]

25. **Pedro** in marrying former mistress of enemy. [Ger. Opera: d'Albert, *Tiefland*, Westerman, 371–374]

26. **Peter Pan** protagonist of J.M. Barrie's 1904 play about "the boy who wouldn't grow up"; he displays both imaginative playfulness and immature self-centeredness. [Scot. Theater: Jones]

27. **Pevensie, Lucy** protagonist of C.S. Lewis's Narnia series for young readers; young and innocent, she discovers Narnia and believes in it completely; compassionate and courageous, she grows up to be Queen Lucy the Valiant. [Br. Children's Lit.: Jones]

28. **Pinch, Tom** guileless, with unbounded goodness of heart. [Br. Lit.: *Martin Chuzzlewit*]

29. **Rima** beautiful jungle girl, lover of birds and animals, knows neither evil nor guile. [Br. Lit.: Hudson *Green Mansions* in Magill I, 333]

30. **Schlemihl, Peter** archetypal innocent; sold soul to devil. [Ger. Lit.: *Peter Schlemihl*; Fr. Opera: Westerman, *Tales of Hoffman*, 274–277]

31. **Susanna** unjustly condemned for adultery; later acquitted. [Apocrypha: Daniel and Susanna]

396. INNOVATION (See also INVENTIVENESS.)

1. **Apple Computer** computer company with an anticorporate image founded by Steven Jobs and Steven Wozniak known for ground-breaking, user-friendly innovations. [Am. Business: *SJEPC*]

2. **IBM (International Business Machines)** hugely successful mainframe computer company established in the 1950s; accused of monopoly in the late 1960s. [Am. Technology: *SJEPC*]

3. **Kodak** Eastman Kodak Company was established in 1901; succeeded rapidly because of Eastman's use of dry plate technology; became worldwide purveyor of photographic products and innovator in field for decades. [Am. Business: *SJEPC*]

4. **Mac** Macintosh personal computer with slogan "Think Different" introduced Graphical User Interface system of icons to mass market. [Am. Technology: *SJEPC*]

5. **Thompson, J. Walter** redefined advertising industry and transformed the business of media in U.S. by adding ads to magazines, reshaping the appearance of ads, applying psychology to advertising, and using celebrity testimonials. [Am. Business: *SJEPC*]

Inquisitiveness (See CURIOSITY.)

Insanity (See MADNESS.)

397. INSECURITY (See also ANXIETY.)

1. **Brown, Charlie** insecure, unpopular progagonist of Charles Schultz's comic strip, *Peanuts*. [Am. Comics: *SJEPC*]

2. **Hamlet** introspective, vacillating Prince of Denmark. [Br. Lit.: *Hamlet*]

3. **Linus** cartoon character who is lost without his security blanket. [Am. Comics: "Peanuts" in Horn, 542–543]

4. **McBeal, Ally** young, single, insecure Ally desires both career and motherhood. [Am. TV: *SJEPC*]

5. **Singer, Alvy** neurotic, self-absorbed character in *Annie Hall*, based on and played by Woody Allen himself. [Am. Film: *SJEPC*]

Inseparability (See FRIENDSHIP.)

Insolence (See ARROGANCE.)

398. INSPIRATION

1. **Aganippe** fountain at foot of Mt. Helicon, consecrated to Muses. [Gk. Myth.: *LLEI*, I: 322]

2. **angelica** traditional representation of inspiration. [Herb Symbolism: *Flora Symbolica*, 164]

3. **Beatrice** Dante's muse, and his guide through Paradise. [Ital. Lit.: *The Divine Comedy*]

4. **Calliope** Muse of heroic poetry. [Gk. Myth.: Zimmerman, 47]

5. **Castalia** Parnassian spring; regarded as source of inspiration. [Gk. Myth.: Zimmerman, 52]

6. **Clio** Muse of history. [Gk. Myth.: Zimmerman, 64]

7. **dove** source of afflatus. [Art.: Hall, 161]

8. **Dulcinea (del Toboso)** country girl, whom Quixote apotheosizes as guiding light. [Span. Lit.: *Don Quixote*]

9. **Erato** Muse of lyric poetry, love poetry, and marriage songs. [Gk. Myth.: Zimmerman, 97]

10. **Euterpe** Muse of music and lyric poetry. [Gk. Myth.: Zimmerman, 105]

11. **Hippocrene** Mt. Helicon spring regarded as source of poetic inspiration. [Gk. Myth.: *NCE*, 1246]

12. **lactating breast** representation of poetic and musical impulse. [Art: Hall, 161]

13. **light bulb** symbol of an original, inspired idea because it was invented by creative genius Thomas Alva Edison. [Am. Science: *SJEPC*]

14. **Melpomene** Muse of tragedy (tragic drama). [Gk. Myth.: Zimmerman, 163]

15. **palm, garland of** traditional identification of a Muse. [Gk. Myth.: Jobes, 374]

16. **Peale, Normal Vincent (1898–1993)** "applied Christianity"; optimism and self-help techniques were the core of his ministry and his 1952 best-seller *The Power of Positive Thinking.*" [Am. Rel.: SJEPC]

17. **Pegasus** steed of the Muses; symbolizes poetic inspiration. [Gk. Myth.: Espy, 32]

18. **Pierian spring** fountain in Macedonia, sacred to the Muses; believed to communicate inspiration. [Gk. Myth.: Benét, 787]

19. **Polyhymnia** muse of sacred song, oratory, lyric, singing, and rhetoric. [Gk. Myth.: Zimmerman, 216]

20. **Stroeve, Blanche** her body inspired Strickland to paint nude portrait. [Br. Lit.: *The Moon and Sixpence*, Magill I, 621–623]

21. **Terpischore** Muse of choral song and dancing. [Gk. Myth.: Zimmerman, 260]

22. **Thalia** Muse of comedy. [Gk. Myth.: Zimmerman, 261]

23. **tongues of fire** manifestation of Holy Spirit's descent on Pentecost. [N.T.: Acts 2:1–4]

24. **Urania** Muse of astronomy. [Gk. Myth.: Zimmerman, 284]

399. INTELLIGENCE (See also WISDOM.)

1. **Alexander the Great** looses the Gordian knot by cutting it with his sword. [Gk. Legend: Brewer *Dictionary*, 409]

2. **Aquinas, Saint Thomas (1225–1274)** preeminent mind of medieval church. [Eur. Hist.: Bishop, 273–274]

3. **Aristotle (384–322 B.C.)** famous Greek philosopher of *a priori* reasoning. [Gk. Hist.: NCE, 147]

4. **brain trust** term describing Pres. Franklin Roosevelt's inner circle of intellectuals who helped define the New Deal; now a group of intelligent advisors in business, etc. [Am. Culture: FOF, MOD]

5. **Darwin, Charles (1809–1882)** English scientist, developed the theory of evolution by natural selection. [Br. Science: ODA]

6. **Einstein, Albert (1879–1955)** German-born American physicist; developed theory of relativity, received Nobel Prize (1921); symbol of prodigious intelligence. [Am. Science ODA]

7. **Granger, Hermoine** character from J.K. Rowling's Harry Potter series for young readers (1997–2007); brainy friend of Harry's; the most competent and conscientious student at Hogwarts; her spells and antidotes nearly always save the day. [Br. Children's Lit.: Misc.]

8. **Hawking, Stephen (1942–)** English theoretical physicist; developed theories of black holes; known for intellectual brilliance. [Br. Science: Misc.]

9. **Howser, Doogie** protagonist of TV show (1989–1993); brilliant physician at age of 14; perfect score on SAT at age 6, Princeton grad by 10. [Am. TV: Misc.]

10. **IQ (intelligence quotient)** controversial measurement of intelligence by formula which compares mental age with chronological age. [Western Education: *EB*, V: 376]

11. *Jeopardy!* television quiz show that tests contestants' knowledge on a variety of topics; considered by many to be the show of choice for intelligent viewers and contestants. [Am. TV: Misc.]

12. **Mensa International** organization founded in England in 1946; only qualification for membership is high IQ, that is, in top 2% of general population. [Am. Pop. Culture: *EB*, VI: 793]

13. **Mr. Spock** Vulcan character from TV's *Star Trek* series, known for his reliance on logic. [Am. TV: *ODA*]

14. **nerd** brainy, but socially inept and physically awkward; sometimes wealthy computer-savvy entrepreneur. [Am. Culture: *SJEPC*]

15. **nut** in the Jewish tradition, a symbol of the scholar. [Symbolism: *CEOS&S*]

16. **on the ball** from sports, to be smart, and in control. [Am. Culture: Misc.]

17. **Prometheus Society, The** established in 1982 to promote fellowship among those with extrememly high intelligence; open to those with IQ score in highest one thirty-thousandth of the general population. [Pop. Culture: Misc.]

18. **Quiz Kids** radio quiz show from the 1940s featuring very intelligent children. [Am. Pop. Culture *FOF, MOD*]

19. **Scarecrow** from L. Frank Baum's Oz series; convinced he has no brain until the Wizard explains that all he lacks is an education. [Br. Children's Lit.: Jones]

20. **Stanford-Binet Intelligence Scale** test used to measure IQ; designed to be used primarily with children. [Am. Education: *EB*, IX: 521]

21. **vos Savant, Marilyn (1946–)** according to *Guinness Book of World Records*, highest recorded IQ (228); writer, lecturer, and playwright; popular syndicated columnist who answers questions from a variety of fields. [Am. Pop. Culture: Misc.]

Intemperance (See DRUNKENNESS.)

400.   INTERNET

1. **Berners-Lee, Tim (1955–)** English computer scientist; created World Wide Web in 1989, but never patented it because he

thought it should be shared freely; later director of the World Wide Web Consortium. [Tech.: Misc.]

2. **chatroom** real-time group conferencing done over instant messaging or on-line forums. [Tech.: Misc.]

3. **cyberpunk** subgenre of science fiction featuring computer technology-driven, on-line networked worlds; originated in William Gibson's *Neuromancer* (1984). [Am. Lit.: *SJEPC*]

4. **cyberspace** term coined in early 1980s by science fiction writer William Gibson referring to a computer-networked world on-line where information can be exchanged; the Internet. [Am. Lit.: *SJEPC*]

5. **domain name** recognizable term used to replace a harder-to-remember numerical Internet Protocol (IP) address. [Tech.: Misc.]

6. **Dot-com** company which does most of its business on-line using a website; name refers to a period followed by a shortened form of the word "commercial." [Tech..: Misc.]

7. **email** electronic mail, delivered over the Internet; symbol of instant communication of the modern age. [Technology: Misc.]

8. **Facebook** largest on-line network; originally launched for Harvard students in 2004 by Mark Zuckerberg; opened to anyone with an email address in 2006; extremely profitable U.S. Internet company. [Tech.: Misc.]

9. **firewall** a protective device installed in computers that prevents viruses, malware, etc. from damaging a computer; a symbol for protection. [Technology: Misc.]

10. **Gibson, William (1948–)** novelist and short-story writer created cyberpunk subgenre of science fiction with *Neuromancer* in 1984; works deal with positive and negative aspects of technology and relationships on the Internet in cyberspace, a term he originated. [Am. Lit.: *SJEPC*]

11. **Google** began in 1996 as an on-line search engine; later started providing e-mail, maps, and video. [Tech.: Misc.]

12. **http** stands for hypertext transfer protocol; system for the request and response between a client and a server. [Tech.: Misc.]

13. **hyperlink** electronic tie providing direct access to another on-line document or a different section of the same document; usually embedded in a word or phrase. [Tech.: Misc.]

14. **i-** Apple's line of personal electronic products such as iMac, iPod, iPhone. [Am. Technology: Misc.]

15. **MySpace** on-line social network created in 2003; provides access to use profiles, blogs, videos, photos, and music. [Tech.: Misc.]

16. *Neuromancer* William Gibson's first novel (1984) defined cyberspace and created the cyberpunk subgenre of science fiction; story

about a dystopian world of the Sprawl won Hugo Award, Philip K. Dick Memorial Award, and Nebula Award. [Am. Lit.: *SJEPC*]

17. **Silicon Valley** area south of San Francisco, California, that became the center of the computer and high-tech industry; so called because silicon is one of the main materials used to make computer chips. [Am. Technology: *BBInv*]

18. **surfing** clicking quickly through websites and pop-up advertisements. [Usage: *SJEPC*]

19. **Toffler, Alvin (1928–)** *Future Shock* (1970) claimed that Americans felt confusion and denial about immense changes in technology and recommended knowledge and flexibility as preparation; predicted use of home computers and information superhighway. [Am. Lit.: *SJEPC*]

20. **www (World Wide Web)** created by Tim Berners-Lee in 1989; network of documents containing text, images, and other media accessed via the Internet. [Tech.: Misc.]

21. **Yahoo!** popular American Internet service company; provides various services such as e-mail, news, and search engines. [Tech.: Misc.; Am. Business: Misc.]

22. **YouTube** extremely popular website created in 2005 for video uploading, viewing, and sharing; created a phenomenon of viral videos. [Tech.: Misc.]

Intimidation (See BULLYING.)

Intoxication (See DRUNKENNESS.)

401. INTRIGUE (See also CONSPIRACY.)

1. **Borgias** fifteenth-century family who stopped at nothing to gain power. [Ital. Hist.: Plumb, 59]

2. **Ems dispatch** Bismarck's purposely provocative memo on Spanish succession; sparked Franco-Prussian war (1870). [Ger. Hist.: *NCE*, 866]

3. **Machiavelli, Nicoló (1469–1527)** author of book extolling political cunning. [Ital. Hist.: *The Prince*]

4. **Mannon, Lavinia** undoes adulterous mother by brainwashing brother. [Am. Lit.: *Mourning Becomes Electra*]

5. ***Mission Impossible*** TV show with team of investigators using Byzantine *modus operandi*. [Am. TV: "Mission Impossible" in Terrace, II, 100–101]

6. **Paolino** has cohort woo his covertly wed wife. [Ital. Opera: Cimarosa, *The Secret Marriage*, Westerman, 63]

7. **Phormio** slick lawyer finagles on behalf of two men. [Rom. Lit.: *Phormio*]

8. **Ruritania** imaginary pre-WWI kingdom, rife with political machinations. [Br. Lit.: *Prisoner of Zenda*]

9. **XYZ Affair** thinly disguised extortion aroused anti-French feelings (1797–1798). [Am. Hist.: Jameson, 564]

402.   INVENTIVENESS (See also INNOVATION.)

1. **Archimedes (287–212 B.C.)** invented military engine which saved Syracuse. [Gk. Hist.: Hall, 31]

2. **Bell, Alexander Graham (1847–1922)** inventor of telephone (1876). [Am. Hist.: Jameson, 46]

3. **Connecticut Yankee, the** made mechanical devices in the sixth century. [Am. Lit.: *A Connecticut Yankee in King Arthur's Court*]

4. **da Vinci, Leonardo (1452–1519)** created prototypes for parachutes, submarines, tanks, helicopters. [Ital. Hist.: Plumb, 185–200]

5. **Dictynna** invented fishermen's nets. [Gk. Myth.: Kravitz, 79]

6. **Edison, Thomas Alva (1847–1931)** creative genius; originated revolutionary products that have influenced life and culture worldwide, such as the incandescent light bulb, phonograph, and motion picture projector. [Am. Science and Hist.: *SJEPC*]

7. **Erechtheus** inventor of chariots. [Gk. Myth.: Kravitz, 91]

8. **Ford, Henry (1863–1947)** invented, developed, and refined automotive-related products and processes, most famously the Model T and assembly line. [Am. Hist.: *SJEPC*]

9. **Franklin, Benjamin (1706–1790)** gave us lightning rod, bifocals, efficient stove, etc. [Am. Hist.: Jameson, 836]

10. **Fuller, Buckminster (1895–1983)** visionary inventor of the Dymaxion house (1929), Dymaxion car (1933), and Geodistic Dome (1949) sought to create greater value using fewer resources. [Am. Architecture: *SJEPC*; Misc.]

11. **Goldberg, Rube (1883–1970)** designed elaborate contraptions to effect simple results. [Am. Hist.: Espy, 111]

12. **Gumbrill, Theodore, Jr.** designs trousers with built-in air-cushion seats. [Br. Lit.: Aldous Huxley *Antic Hay* in Benét, 39]

13. **Jobs, Steven (1956–)** cofounder of Apple Computer known for creativity and marketing savvy. [Am. Business: Misc.]

14. **Mac** Macintosh personal computer with slogan "Think Different" preferred for high-end graphics work. [Am. Technology: *SJEPC*]

15. **McVey, Hugh** invents and builds successful machines for farm and mine operators. [Am. Lit.: Anderson *Poor White* in Magill I, 762]

16. **Swift, Tom** young inventor protagonist of novels for young readers published between 1910 and 1941 by Stratemeyer syndicate;

uses technology and ingenuity to defeat his rivals. [Am.Children's Lit.: *SJEPC*]

403. INVISIBILITY

1. **Abaris** magic arrow made him invisible. [Gk. Myth.: Benét, 1]

2. **agate** confers this power. [Rom. Folklore: Brewer *Dictionary*, 15]

3. **Ariel** invisible spirit plays tricks on the castaways. [Br. Lit.: Shakespeare *The Tempest*]

4. **Cheshire Cat** vanishes at will; grin the last feature to go. [Br. Children's Lit.: *Alice's Adventures in Wonderland*]

5. **chrysoprase** put in mouth, renders bearer invisible. [Gem Symbolism: Kunz, 67–68]

6. **cloak** in Teutonic and Celtic legends, magic cloaks were used for invisibility and forgetfulness; often found in modern tales of fantasy. [Symbolism: *CEOS&S*]

7. **Emperor's new clothes** supposed to be invisible to anyone unworthy of his post. [Dan. Children's Lit.: Anderson "The Emperor's New Clothes" in *Andersen's Fairy Tales*]

8. **fern seed** makes bearer invisible. [Western Folklore: Brewer *Dictionary*, 406]

9. **glory, hand of** severed hand of hanged man renders bearer invisible. [Western Folklore: Leach, 477]

10. **Gyges's ring** confers this power. [Gk. Folklore: Brewer *Dictionary*, 497]

11. **Harvey** six-foot rabbit invisible to everyone but the play's protagonist. [Am. Lit.: Benét, 444]

12. **heliotrope** effective if drunk with proper invocations. [Medieval Folklore: Boland, 43]

13. *Invisible Man* novel by Ralph Ellison (1952); nameless young black man who is symbolically invisible to the white world. [Am. Lit.: Misc.]

14. *Invisible Man , The* novel by H.G. Wells (1897) in which mad scientist uses ability to become invisible for nefarious purposes, including murder. [Br. Lit.: Misc.]

15. **Mabrino's Helmet** golden helmet makes wearer invisible. [Span. Lit.: *Don Quixote*]

16. **Perseus's helmet** made him invisible when he killed Medusa. [Gk. Myth.: *Metamorphoses*]

17. **Reynard the Fox's ring** when ring becomes green, Reynard is invisible. [Medieval Lit.: *Reynard the Fox*]

18. **tarnhelm** golden helmet that allowed its wearer to assume any form or even become invisible. [Ger. Opera: Wagner *The Ring of the Nibelung*]

19. **tarnkappe** cloak taken from the Nibelungs by Siegfried; grants the wearer invisibility and strength. [Ger. Lit.: *Nibelungenlied*]

404. IRASCIBILITY (See also ANGER, EXASPERATION, SHREWISHNESS.)

1. **Caius, Dr.** irritable physician. [Br. Lit.: *Merry Wives of Windsor*]

2. **Connors, Jimmy (1952–)** competitive, intense tennis champion could be tempermental on the court. [Am. Sports: *SJEPC*]

3. **Donald Duck** cantankerousness itself. [Am. Comics: Horn, 216–217]

4. **Elisha** sics bears on boys for their jibing. [O.T.: II Kings 2:23–24]

5. **Findlay, Maude** outspoken, oft-married, liberated woman. [Am. TV: "Maude" in Terrace, II, 79–80]

6. **Granny** cantankerous matriarch of the Clampett family. [Am. TV: "The Beverly Hillbillies" in Terrace, I, 93–94]

7. **Hotspur, Sir Henry Percy** so named for his fiery character. [Br. Lit.: *I Henry IV*]

8. **Houlihan, Hot Lips** resident termagant of M*A*S*H 4077. [Am. TV: "M*A*S*H" in Terrace, II, 70–71]

9. **Knight, Bobby (1940–)** very successful coach of Indiana University basketball team; known for hot temper and strict demands on players. [Am. Sports: *SJEPC*]

10. **Nipper, Susan** sharp-tongued nurse of Florence Dombey. [Br. Lit.: *Dombey and Son*]

11. **Schlessinger, Dr. Laura (1947–)** psychologist and author with radio show and syndicated newspaper column; firm believer in personal responsibility; blunt personality and strict definition of morality. [Am. Pop. Culture: *SJEPC*]

12. **Tybalt** irascible foil to peacemaking Benvolio. [Br. Lit.: *Romeo and Juliet*]

13. **yellow bile** humor effecting temperament of irritability. [Medieval Physiology: Hall, 130]

405. IRONY (See also LAST LAUGH.)

1. **Alvaro** attempt to disarm accidentally causes opponent's death. [Ital. Opera: Verdi, *La Forza del Destino*, Westerman, 316]

2. **Arrigo** fight for freedom means opposing newfound father. [Ital. Opera: Verdi, *Sicilian Vespers*, Westerman, 308–309]

3. **Artemidorus** presents Caesar with scroll outlining conspiracy; it remains unopened. [Br. Lit.: *Julius Caesar*]

4. **Barabas** perishes in trap he set for Turks. [Br. Lit.: *The Jew of Malta*]

5. *Barnaby Rudge* Dennis, the public hangman, is sentenced to be hanged on his own scaffold. [Br. Lit.: Dickens *Barnaby Rudge*]

6. **Bazaroff** reformed radical; dies accidentally. [Russ. Lit.: *Fathers and Sons*]

7. **Bishop, the** dying in a delirium, he speaks of pomp and luxury rather than salvation. [Br. Poetry: Browning "The Bishop Orders His Tomb"]

8. **Carlos, Don** loves bride he procured for his father. [Ital. Opera: Verdi, *Don Carlos*, Westerman, 319]

9. **Cassandra** true prophet, doomed to go unbelieved. [Gk. Myth.: Espy, 40]

10. *Catch-22* pleading insanity to leave army indicates sanity. [Am. Lit.: *Catch-22*]

11. **Claudius** emperor-scholar in soldier-worshiping nation. [Br. Lit.: *I, Claudius*]

12. *Cosi fan tutte* illustrates comically some shortcomings of feminine fidelity. [Ger. Opera: Mozart *Cosi fan tutte*, Westerman, 97–98]

13. **Creon** victim of his own harsh tyranny. [Gk. Lit.: *Antigone*]

14. **Defender of the Faith** Henry VIII's pre-Reformation title, conferred by Leo X. [Br. Hist.: Benét, 258]

15. **Gaigern, Baron** attempts to rob ballerina; becomes her lover. [Ger. Lit.: *Grand Hotel*]

16. *Gift of the Magi, The* young couple sell their dearest possessions to buy Christmas gifts for one another; discover that the sacrifice made the gifts unusable. [Am. Lit.: O. Henry *The Gift of the Magi*, in Benét, 395]

17. **Harmony Society** embraced communism and celibacy; the latter caused their extinction. [Am. Hist.: Hart, 349]

18. **John of Balue** imprisoned in an iron cage he invented. [Br. Lit.: *Quentin Durward*]

19. *Magic Mountain, The* sanatorium as escape from "insane world." [Ger. Lit.: *The Magic Mountain*, Magill I, 571–573]

20. *Mayor of Casterbridge, The* Henchard dies in care of man he tyrannized. [Br. Lit.: *The Mayor of Casterbridge*, Magill I, 571–573]

21. *Modest Proposal, A* essay in which Swift advises the Irish to eat their babies or sell them in order to relieve famine and reduce overpopulation. [Br. Lit.: Benét, 677]

22. **Otternschlag, Dr.** attempting suicide, discovers will to live. [Ger. Lit.: *Grand Hotel*]

23. **Pagliaccio** clown forced to be funny despite breaking heart. [Ital. Opera: Leoncavallo, *Pagliacci*, Espy, 339]

24. **Patterne, Sir Willoughby** egoist's actions lead to self-defeat. [Br. Lit.: *The Egoist*, Magill I, 241–242]

25. **Point, Jack** jester who must be funny even when events break his heart. [Br. Opera: Gilbert & Sullivan *The Yeoman of the Guard*]

26. **Polycrates** tyrant of Athens who, renowned for his continual good fortune, is ignominiously trapped and crucified by envious ruler. [Gk. Myth.: Benét, 801]

27. **Popeye** murderer; hanged for murder he did not commit. [Am. Lit.: *Sanctuary*]

28. **R.U.R.** robots, manufactured for man's ease, revolt. [Czech Lit.: *R.U.R.*]

29. **Rachel** executed as Jewess; revealed to be Christian clergyman's daughter. [Fr. Opera: Halèvy, *The Jewess*, Westerman, 168]

30. **Rigoletto** arranges murder of daughter's seducer; she dies instead. [Ital. Opera: Verdi, *Rigoletto*, Westerman, 299–300]

31. **Sholem Aleichem (1859–1916)** Russian Jewish author of wry stories, written in Yiddish,about Jewish folkways in Eastern Europe. [Russ. Lit.: *FOF, MOD*]

32. **Sitzkrieg** "phony war"; lull between Polish conquest and invasion of France. [Eur. Hist.: *Hitler*, 815–819]

33. **Sohrab** unaware, engages in single combat with Rustum, the father he had been seeking, and is slain. [Br. Poetry: *Sohrab and Rustum*, in Benét, 943]

34. **Thomas, Bigger** finds freedom through killing and life's meaning through death. [Am. Lit.: *Native Son*, Magill I, 643–645]

35. **War of 1812** Jackson's New Orleans victory occurred after treaty was signed. [Am. Hist.: Hart, 893]

406. IRREPRESSIBILITY

1. *Bell for Adano, A* Joppolo's stress on democracy overcomes superior's arrogance. [Am. Lit.: *A Bell for Adano*]

2. **Joad Family** Ma Joad cries, "We ain' gonna die out." [Am. Lit.: *The Grapes of Wrath*]

3. **Little Orphan Annie** a most irrepressible waif. [am. Comics: Horn, 459]

4. **Madeline** from series of picturebooks by Ludwig Bemelmans; free spirit living in rigid world of French convent school. [Am. Children's Lit.: Jones]

5. **March, Augie** man's "refusal to lead a disappointed life." [Am. Lit.: *The Adventures of Augie March*]

Irresolution (See INDECISION.)

407. IRRESPONSIBILITY (See also CARELESSNESS, FORGETFULNESS.)

1. **Alectryon** changed to cock because he forgot to warn Mars of sun's rising. [Rom. Myth.: *LLEI*, I: 322]

2. **Belch, Sir Toby** Olivia's riotous, reckless uncle. [Br. Lit.: *Twelfth Night*]

3. **Bovary, Emma** irresponsible, careless character; betrays husband. [Fr. Lit.: *Madame Bovary*]

4. **Capp, Andy** negligent of marital obligations. [Am. Comics: Horn, 82–83]

5. **Falstaff, Sir John** misuses "the King's press damnably." [Br. Lit.: *II Henry IV*]

6. **Google, Barney** neglects wife for race horse. [Am. Comics: Horn, 99–100]

7. **Grasshopper** sings through summer, overlooking winter preparations. [Gk. Lit.: *Aesop's Fables*, "Ant and the Grasshopper"]

8. **Palinurus** sleeping helmsman, falls overboard. [Rom. Lit.: *Aeneid*]

9. **Paragon, Mary Anne** careless servant of David and Dora. [Br. Lit.: *David Copperfield*]

10. **Toad of Toad Hall** from Kenneth Grahame's children's classic *Wind in the Willows* (1908); conceited and impulsive, does whatever he feels like doing to dismay of his friends. [Br. Children's Lit.: Jones]

11. **Took, Peregrine** character from Tolkien's Lord of the Rings trilogy (1954–1956); hobbit friend of Frodo; silly and immature, he gets into trouble until he learns to appreciate the meaning of the quest and mature into a brave warrior; also called Pippin. [Br. Lit: Gillespie and Naden]

12. **Trulliber, Parson** satire on one who does not do his job. [Br. Hist.: *Joseph Andrews*, Espy, 131]

13. **Wimpy** sloppily dressed comic strip character; always "forgets" to pay for hamburgers. [Am. Comics: "Popeye" in Horn, 657–658]

408. IRREVERSIBILITY

1. **crossing the Rubicon** Caesar passes point of no return into Italy. [Rom. Hist.: Brewer *Dictionary*, 941]

2. **Humpty Dumpty** all the King's men failed to reassemble him. [Nurs. Rhyme: *Mother Goose*, 40]

409. ISLAM (See also RELIGION.)

1. **adhan** call to prayer, issued five times a day from mosques. [Islamic Rel.: *UIMT*, 141–42, 424]

2. **Allah** literally, "the God" in Arabic; belief in one God is central to Islam. [Islam: *UIMT*, 34–35, 424]

3. **Allahu akbar** Arabic phrase "God is greater than all" acknowledging power and majesty of God is used in Muslim prayers and throughout the day to express joy or approval, or to offer praise. [Islam: *UIMT*, 189]

4. **angel** messenger who functions as intermediary between heaven and earth. [Islamic Rel.: Bowker]

5. **arabesque** swirling designs found in Islamic art, based on stylized renditions of twining vines, leaves, and flowers. [Islamic Art: *UIMT*, 425]

6. **Ashura** holiday observed by Shia Muslims as a day of mourning for the murdered Imam Husayn, grandson of the Prophet Muhammad, in 680 at Karbala (in modern-day Iraq). [Islam: *UIMT*, 261–74, 425]

7. **as-salam alaykum** greeting offered from one Muslim to another means "Peace be upon you" in Arabic. [Islam: *UIMT*, 188, 425]

8. **basmallah** short version of the Arabic phrase meaning "In the name of God, the merciful, the compassionate"; opens nearly every chapter of the Quran and is said throughout the day by Muslims to bless everyday activities; also used as grace before meals. [Islam: *UIMT*, 188, 425]

9. **black** color associated with Shia Muslims, especially clergy; historically, symbolic of the Abbasid Caliphs. [Islamic Symbolism: *UIMT*, 230]

10. **crescent moon** symbol of Islam, often depicted with five- or six-pointed star between its horns. [Islamic Symbolism: *UIMT*, 227]

11. **da'wa** Islam call to prayer. [Islamic Rel.: Bowker]

12. **Dome of the Rock** Muslim holy shrine in Jerusalem built on the site where Muhammad was said to have risen into heaven. [Islam: *UIMT*, 124–25]

13. **Eben Shetiyyah** rock on which the world is founded. [Islamic Rel.: Bowker]

14. **Eid al-Adha** Festival of the Sacrifice; holiday commemorating Abraham's willingness to sacrifice his son Ishmael; takes place on tenth day of Islamic month of Dhu al-Hijjah; celebrated with prayer and animal sacrifice, offered according to Islamic law. [Islam: *UIMT*, 365–70]

15. **Eid al-Fitr** festival that occurs at end of Ramadan; joyful family and community holiday celebrated with special foods and sweets,

new clothing, entertainment, and greeting cards. [Islam: *UIMT*, 313–14, 427]

16. **faqih** one who possesses religious knowledge. [Islamic Rel.: Bowker]

17. **fasting** fourth pillar of Islam requires Muslims to fast during entire month of Ramadan by not eating or drinking during the daylight hours; *sawm* in Arabic. [Islamic Rel.: *UIMT*, 37, 437]

18. **fatwa** opinion given by religious authority who is an expert in Islamic law. [Islamic Law: *UIMT*, 427]

19. **five pillars** five most important religious beliefs and practices required of Muslims. [Islam: *UIMT*, 427]

20. **Friday** Yawm al-Juma in Arabic, the Day of Congregation; the Muslim day of communal worship, with midday prayers at a mosque. [Islam: *UIMT*, 371, 427]

21. **green** color symbolizes Prophet Muhammad and Islam itself; represents peace, hope, and paradise. [Islamic Symbolism: *UIMT*, 229]

22. **hadith** account, report, or speech concerning the words or deeds of the prophet Muhammad, often translated as tradition; second only to the Quran in importance and authority. [Islam: *UIMT*, 428]

23. **Hajj** pilgrimage to Mecca that every Muslim is expected to make at least once in a lifetime; fifth pillar of Islam. [Islam: *UIMT*, 345–62, 428]

24. **halal** Arabic word used most commonly to distinguish those foods permitted to Muslims from those foods fobidden to them. [Islam: *UIMT*, 428]

25. **hijab** large scarf worn by some Muslim women to cover their head, neck, and hair to meet requirements for female modesty. [Islamic Trad.: *UIMT*, 193]

26. **Ibrahim** Abraham as named in the Quran; he is considered the original Muslim, who worshipped Allah as a monotheist with perfect submission. [Islamic Rel.: Bowker]

27. **inshallah** Arabic phrase meaning "if God wills" often recited by Muslims when making plans for the future. [Islam: *UIMT*, 188, 430]

28. **Jerusalem** city in modern-day Israel is sacred to Muslims, who believe it to be the earthly destination of Muhammad's Night Journey and the site of his ascension into heaven. [Islam: *UIMT*, 124–25]

29. **jihad** Arabic for "struggle," but sometimes translated as "holy war"; describes Muslims' struggle against their own weaknesses but also used to refer to warfare against non-Muslims. [Islam: *UIMT*, 430]

30. **jinn** good and bad spirits, often attached to particular places in nature, with magical powers. [Islamic Folklore: *UIMT*, 184–85, 431]

31. **jum'a** assembly on Friday for midday prayer. [Islamic Rel.: Bowker]

32. **Kaba** cube-shaped building in center of Grand Mosque in Mecca is Islam's holiest shrine. [Islamic Rel.: *UIMT*, 119–20, 431]

33. **kafir** unbeliever; punished in hell forever. [Islamic Rel.: Bowker]

34. **Mecca** birthplace of Muhammad; city in modern-day Saudi Arabia; Muslims turn toward Mecca in prayer and make pilgrimages there. [Islamic Rel.: *UIMT*, 119–20, 433; Bowker]

35. **Medina** city in Saudi Arabia where first Muslim community was organized. [Islamic Rel.: *UIMT*, 122, 433]

36. **mosque** Islamic house of worship. [Islamic Rel.: *UIMT*, 161–69, 434]

37. **Muhammad (c.570–632)** prophet who delivered the Quran to humanity, laying the foundation for the Muslim religion. [Islam: *UIMT*, 434]

38. **new moon** Muslim months begin when it is visible in the sky. [Islam: *UIMT*, 298–300]

39. **Ninety-Nine Names of Allah** reciting the 99 names is an important Muslim devotion; the names reflect Islam's view of God's qualities. [Islam: *UIMT*, 156–57]

40. **peace be upon him** blessing that devout Muslims traditionally insert after each mention of Muhammad's name. [Islam: *UIMT*, 435]

41. **Quran** the sacred book of Islam. [Islam: *UIMT*, 171]

42. **Ramadan** ninth month of the Islamic calendar during which Muslims fast, refraining from eating and drinking during daylight hours. [Islamic Rel.: *UIMT*, 297–314]

43. **Red Crescent** international disaster and wartime relief organization in predominantly Muslim societies affiliated with the Red Cross. [Islamic Hist.: *UIMT*, 227]

44. **salat** formal, ritualized prayers praising God offered in Arabic by devout Muslims five times a day; second of five pillars of Islam. [Islamic Rel.: *UIMT*, 35–37, 436]

45. **shahada** from the Arabic for "testify" or "witness"; the Muslim declaration of faith serving as the first pillar of Islam; consists of proclaiming in public, "I witness that there is no God but God, and Muhammad is the messenger of God." [Islamic Rel.: *UIMT*, 34–35, 437]

46. **sharia** Islamic law; religious rules that govern personal behavior, from crimes to marriage, clothing, and dress. [Islamic Law: *UIMT*, 45–46, 437]

47. **Sufi** Muslim who follows a mystical path, seeking direct experiences of God through various spiritual disciplines. [Islam: *UIMT*, 50, 438]

48. **white** color has special significance in Islam; worn by pilgrims making the Hajj, and associated with angels. [Islamic Symbolism: *UIMT*, 229]

49. **White Nights** nights before, during, and after a full moon thought to be especially lucky in some Muslim countries. [Islamic Trad.: *UIMT*, 381]

50. **wudu** the less thorough form of washing required before formal prayer. [Islam: *UIMT*, 142–45, 440]

51. **zakat** almsgiving; the third pillar of Islam requires adult Muslims to give 2.5 percent of their wealth (income and goods) to the poor each year. [Islamic Rel.: *UIMT*, 37, 440]

410. ISOLATION (See also IMPRISONMENT, REMOTENESS.)

1. **Alcatraz Island** "The Rock"; former federal prison in San Francisco Bay. [Am. Hist.: Flexner, 218]

2. *Alison's House* reclusive woman guards secrets and poems of her dead sister. [Am. Lit.: Glaspel *Alison's House* in Sobel, 18]

3. **beyond the pale** outside of civilization, from the Latin "palum" a stake that defined the edge of civilization and protection. [Eng. Hist.: *FOF, MOD*]

4. **Count of Monte Cristo** Edmond Dantès imprisoned in the dungeons of Ch,teau D'If for 14 years. [Fr. Lit.: *The Count of Monte Cristo*, Magill I, 158–160]

5. **Crusoe, Robinson** man marooned on a desert island for 24 years. [Br. Lit.: *Robinson Crusoe*, Magill I, 839–841]

6. **Dickinson, Emily (1830–1886)** secluded within the walls of her father's house. [Am. Lit.: Hart, 224]

7. **Fischer, Bobby (1943–2008)** eccentric, controversial American chess champion retreated from public eye after capturing world title in 1972; after rematch with Soviet nemesis Boris Spassky 20 years later, returned to reclusive life in Iceland until his death. [Am. Hist.: *SJEPC*; Misc.]

8. **ghetto** originally an Italian term for the Jewish section of Venice, a section of a city isolated by race, poverty, or class. [Am. Hist.: *FOF, MOD*]

9. **Hermit Kingdom** Korea, when it alienated itself from all but China (c. 1637–c. 1876). [Korean Hist.: *NCE*, 1233]

10. **Iron Curtain** political and ideological barrier of secrecy concealing Eastern bloc. [Eur. Hist.: Brewer *Dictionary*, 490]

11. *Magic Mountain, The* suspended in time, which exists in flat world below. [Ger. Lit.: *The Magic Mountain*, Magill I, 545–547]

12. *Man without a Country, The* story of man exiled from homeland. [Am. Lit.: *The Man without a Country*, Magill I, 553–557]

13. *Miss Lonelyhearts* novel by Nathanael West (1933) about a male advice columnist; now, a catchword for advice to the lonely and loveless. [Pop. Cult. *FOF, MOD*]

14. **Olivia** "abjured the company and sight of men." [Br. Lit.: *Twelfth Night*]

15. **prisoner of Chillon** cast into a lightless dungeon and chained there for countless years. [Br. Lit.: Byron *The Prisoner of Chillon* in Benét, 817]

16. **Selkirk, Alexander (1676–1721)** marooned on Pacific island; thought to be prototype of Robinson Crusoe. [Scot. Hist.: *EB*, IX: 45]

17. **Sleepy Hollow** out-of-the-way, old-world village on Hudson. [Am. Lit.: "Legend of Sleepy Hollow" in Benét, 575]

18. **Stylites** medieval ascetics; resided atop pillars. [Christian Hist.: Brewer *Dictionary*, 1045]

19. **Stylites, Saint Simeon** lived 36 years on platform atop pillar. [Christian Hagiog.: Attwater, 309]

20. **von Aschenbach, Gustave** spiritual and emotional solitude combine in writer's deterioration. [Ger. Lit.: *Death in Venice*]

J

411. JEALOUSY (See also ENVY.)

1. **adder's tongue** flower symbolizes jealousy. [Western Folklore: Jobes, 31]

2. **Arnolphe** representative of jealous middle age. [Fr. Lit.: *L'Ecole des Femmes*]

3. **Bartolo, Dr.** jealous and suspicious tutor. [Fr. Lit.: *Barber of Seville*]

4. **Calchas** dies from grief on encountering even wiser soothsayer. [Gk. Myth.: *LLEI*, I: 325]

5. **Callirrhoë** demands of husband former wife's necklace and robe. [Gk. Legend: *NCE*, 55]

6. **Cephalus and Procris** young married couple plagued by jealousy. [Gk. Myth.: Hall, 62]

7. **coat of many colors** Jacob's gift to Joseph; object of jealousy. [O.T.: Genesis 37:3]

8. **Deianira** kills husband Hercules for suspected affair with Iole. [Gk. Myth.: Leach, 303]

9. **Dionyza** jealously plots Marina's murder. [Br. Lit.: *Pericles*]

10. **Donald Duck** frustrated character jealous of Mickey Mouse. [Am. Comics: Horn, 216–217]

11. **Ferrando** jealous of Manrico's influence on Leonora. [Ital. Opera: Verdi, *The Troubadour*, Westerman, 302]

12. **Golaud** jealousy leads to the murder of his brother, Pelléas. [Fr. Opera: Debussy, *Pelléas and Mélisande*, Westerman, 196]

13. **green-eyed monster** epithet. [Br. Lit.: *Othello*]

14. **Kitelys** man and wife each laughably suspicious of the other's fidelity. [Br. Lit.: *Every Man in His Humour*]

15. **Leontes** jealous of wife and Polixenes. [Br. Lit.: *The Winter's Tale*]

16. **Malbecco** seeing his wife living among satryrs, he is so mad with jealousy that he casts himself from a cliff. [Br. Lit.: Spenser *The Faerie Queene*; Brewer *Dictionary*, 336]

17. **Medea** sends husband Jason's new bride poisoned cloak. [Gk. Lit.: *Medea*; Fr. Lit.: *Médée*]

18. **Oberon** King of Fairies; jealous of wife's attachments. [Br. Lit.: *A Midsummer Night's Dream*]

19. **Othello** smothers Desdemona out of jealousy. [Br. Lit.: *Othello*]

20. **Polyphemus** crushes lover's lover. [Rom. Lit.: *Metamorphoses*]

21. **Pozdnishef, Vasyla** murders wife in fit of insane resentment. [Russ. Lit.: *The Kreutzer Sonata*, Magill I, 481–483]

22. **Shabata, Frank** mistrusted everyone who showed kindness to wife, Marie. [Am. Lit.: *O Pioneers!*, Magill I, 663–665]

23. **wild ass** signifies jealousy. [Animal Symbolism: Jobes, 142]

24. **yellow** color symbolizing jealousy. [Western Folklore: Jobes, 1704]

25. **yellow rose** indicates jealousy. [Flower Symbolism: *Flora Symbolica*, 177]

Jester (See CLOWN.)

412. JOKE, PRACTICAL (See also MISCHIEVOUSNESS.)

1. **April Fool's Day** April 1st; a day for playing practical jokes on the unsuspecting. [Western Folklore: Payton, 34]

2. **Barmecide feast** beggar given empty dishes, imaginary food. [Arab. Lit.: *Arabian Nights*, "The Barmecide's Feast"]

3. **Goodfellow, Robin** fairies' jester famous for his practical jokes. [Br. Folklore: Brewer *Dictionary*, 768]

4. **Hop-Frog's king** "had an especial admiration for *breadth* in a jest." [Am. Lit.: "Hop-Frog" in *Portable Poe*, 317–329]

5. **Merygreeke, Matthew** mischievously puts Ralph up to wooing widow. [Br. Lit.: *Ralph Roister Doister*]

6. **Old Jackanapes** fills Miss Pussy's apple pies with frogs. [Children's Lit.: *The Golden Hen*, Fisher, 232–233]

7. **Panurge** conniving scoundrel whose forte was practical joking. [Fr. Lit.: *Pantagruel*]

8. **Pulver, Ensign** devised mechanisms to needle skipper. [Am. Lit.: *Mister Roberts*, Magill I, 605–607]

413. JOURNALISM (See also BROADCASTING, TELEVISION.)

1. *Amazing Stories* science fiction magazine established the genre. [Am. Jour.: *SJEPC*]

2. *Atlantic Monthly* magazine catering to cultivated, well-informed readers. [Am. Jour.: *SJEPC*]

3. **Bernstein, Carl (1944–)** *Washington Post* won Pulitzer Prize (1973) for his coverage (with Bob Woodward) of Watergate break-in; also wrote best-selling *All the President's Men* about the investigation and other books and writings on music. [Am. Jour.: Misc.]

4. *Boston Globe* largest daily newspaper in Boston, Massachusetts; owned by the New York Times Company. [Am. Jour.: Misc.]

5. **Bradlee, Ben (1921–)** distinguished career as executive editor of *Washington Post* (1968–1991); famous for his editorial decisions

concerning Woodward and Bernstein's articles on Watergate scandal. [Am. Jour.: Misc.]

6. **Capote, Truman (1924–1984)** influenced the development of New Journalism, a literary genre combining conventional journalistic methods with fictional technique, exemplified by his nonfiction novel *In Cold Blood* (1965). [Am. Lit. and Jour.: *SJEPC*; Henderson, 503–504]

7. *Chicago Tribune* main daily newspaper of the Midwest; fifth largest circulation in the United States. [Am. Jour.: Misc.]

8. *Christian Science Monitor* well-respected international daily newspaper established in 1908 by Mary Baker Eddy, founder of the Christian Science movement. [Am. Jour.: *SJEPC*]

9. **Condé Nast** influential publishing empire named after its innovative founder, who created or reinvented specialized lifestyle publications such as *Vogue, Vanity Fair, Bon Appetit,* and *GQ*. [Am. Jour.: *SJEPC*]

10. *Consumer Reports* independent periodical's reporting on products and services has influenced consumers' purchase decisions since 1936. [Am. Jour.: *SJEPC*]

11. *Cosmopolitan* wildly successful women's magazine revamped by editor Helen Gurley Brown in 1965; emphasizes sexuality and dating issues; by late 1990s, published in 29 editions in several languages. [Am. Jour.: *SJEPC*]

12. *Crisis, The* monthly magazine of the NAACP (National Association for the Advancement of Colored People) founded in 1910 by editor W. E. B. Du Bois; has defended African-American civil rights and served as the voice of black America for a century. [Am. Jour.: *SJEPC*]

13. *Drudge Report* Matt Drudge's website best known for breaking political news and scandals was established in 1990s; scooped mainstream media in 1998 when it reported President Bill Clinton's affair with Monica Lewinsky. [Am. Jour.: *SJEPC*; Misc.]

14. *Ebony* first photographic magazine focusing on African-American life debuted in 1945; created by John H. Johnson. [Am. Jour.: *SJEPC*]

15. *Esquire* sophisticated monthly lifestyle magazine aimed at educated men; founded in 1933; known for literary excellence with contributions by prominent American writers; also covers social and political issues, the latest fashion, news, and sexuality. [Am. Jour.: *SJEPC*]

16. *Family Circle* "world's largest women's magazine" reached audience of 21 million by end of 1980s; articles on child rearing, family issues, homemaking, and education since 1932. [Am. Jour.: *SJEPC*]

17. *Field and Stream* quintessential outdoorsman's magazine aimed at America's middle-class hunters and anglers; introduced in 1895, advocates conservation measures for wildlife and fish populations. [Am. Jour.: *SJEPC*]

18. *Fortune* highly respected, biweekly business magazine established in 1930; annually ranks the 500 top performing American companies. [Am. Jour.: *SJEPC*]

19. *Globe and Mail, The* prominent English-language Canadian newspaper based in Toronto; considered the most significant daily in the country. [Can. Jour.: Misc.]

20. *Good Housekeeping* magazine aimed at middle- and upper-class women established in 1885; still focuses on cooking, child rearing, and homemaking; its Seal of Approval certifies products. [Am. Jour.: *SJEPC*]

21. **Graham, Katherine (1917–2001)** published of *Washington Post* upon death of her husband (1969–1979); won Pulitzer Prize in 1998 for her autobiography. [Am. Jour.: Misc.]

22. **Grizzard, Lewis (1946–1994)** witty syndicated newspaper columnist/humorist of 1980s and 1990s with southern "good old boy" image and storytelling abilities akin to Mark Twain. [Am. Jour.: *SJEPC*]

23. *Harvard Lampoon* undergraduate humor publication launched in 1876 at Harvard University; still in publication, making it the world's longest-running humor magazine. [Am. Jour.: Misc.]

24. **Hearst, William Randolph (1863–1951)** American newspaper and magazine publisher; his papers were known for their sensationalist content, and their "penny" price. [Am. Jour.: Misc.]

25. *International Herald Tribune* international English-language newspaper; based in Paris since 1887; sold in over 180 countries. [Jour.: Misc.]

26. **Johnson, John H. (1918–2005)** influential founder of Johnson Publishing Company, one of the top black-owned businesses in America; created and published *Ebony* and *Jet* magazines. [Am. Jour.: *SJEPC*]

27. **Lardner, Ring (1885–1933)** American sports writer and humorist noted for his sarcastic wit. [Am. Jour.: *FOF, MOD*]

28. *London Times* United Kingdom's well-known daily newspaper; the first of the "Times" newspapers, founded in 1785. [Br. Jour.: Misc.]

29. *Los Angeles Times* daily newspaper distributed in the western United States; second largest metropolitan newspaper in America. [Am. Jour.: Misc.]

30. **Mencken, H.L. (1880–1956)** acerbic writer known for talent and ruthless criticism. [Am. Jour.: *SJEPC*]

31. ***National Enquirer, The*** weekly supermarket tabloid specializing in sensationalism. [Am. Jour.: *SJEPC*]

32. ***New Republic*** mostly left-wing journalism intended for the intellectually elite. [Am. Jour.: *SJEPC*]

33. ***New York Times*** daily newspaper; largest metropolitan newspaper in the United States; known for extremely reliable reporting. [Am. Jour.: Misc.]

34. ***New Yorker*** dedicated editors and a host of acclaimed contributors made the magazine a favorite among the intelligent and wealthy. [Am. Jour.: *SJEPC*]

35. ***Newsweek*** popular weekly news magazine with international circulation. [Am. Jour.: *SJEPC*]

36. ***Onion, The*** "fake news" publication that features satirical articles; topics range from local to international, real to fake. [Am. Jour.: Misc.]

37. ***Penthouse*** Bob Guccione's sexually explicit magazine for those who found *Playboy* a bit too tame. [Am. Jour.: *SJEPC*]

38. ***People*** image-laden magazine featuring details about celebrities and stories about unusual events in the lives of ordinary people. [Am. Jour.: *SJEPC*]

39. ***Philadelphia Inquirer*** founded in 1829; third oldest surviving daily newspaper in U.S. [Am Jour.: Misc.]

40. ***Photoplay*** early movie fan magazine featuring celebrity photos and gossip. [Am. Jour.: *SJEPC*]

41. ***Playboy*** Hugh Hefner established the magazine in 1953; featured profiles of luxury items, interviews with famous people, fiction by notable writers, and photos of naked women. [Am. Jour.: *SJEPC*]

42. ***Playgirl*** established in 1973, first magazine that functioned as counterpart to *Playboy*; male nudity was sometimes featured. [Am. Jour.: *SJEPC*]

43. ***Reader's Digest*** excerpts from books and other periodicals were gathered along with original quotes and anecdotes to compile this popular mainstream magazine. [Am. Jour.: *SJEPC*]

44. ***Rolling Stone*** journal with serious coverage of rock music, culture, and politics; appearing on the cover became a sign of popular culture distinction. [Am. Jour.: *SJEPC*]

45. **Royko, Mark (1932–1997)** award-winning journalist who wrote investigative reports exposing injustices and witty commentary expressed by fictional characters. [Am. Jour.: *SJEPC*]

46. ***Sassy*** 1988 magazine that approached teenaged females with information about sexual activity, unlike other magazines of the time. [Am. Jour.: *SJEPC*]

47. *Saturday Evening Post, The* known as *The Post*; dominated American magazine readership for first thirty years of twentieth century; characterized by common-sense conservatism and middle-class values. [Am. Jour.: *SJPEC*]

48. *Scientific American* begun in 1845, features articles on innovations, noted scientists, and events in the field. [Am. Jour.: *SJEPC*]

49. *Seventeen* begun in 1944; first magazine totally devoted to teen girls; extremely successful at focusing on topics relevant to its audience. [Am. Jour.: *SJEPC*]

50. *Sporting News, The* official newspaper of baseball in first half of the 20th century; helped to expand popularity of the game. [Am. Jour.: *SJEPC*]

51. *Sports Illustrated* first weekly magazine devoted entirely to sports; launched in 1954, it helped turn sports into big business; known for insightful analysis and high-charged photographs. [Am. Jour.: *SJEPC*]

52. **Steffens, Lincoln (1866–1936)** tirelessly investigated corrupt city officials throughout U.S.; disillusioned with capitalism, traveled to Soviet Union in 1917 and joined Communist Party. [Am. Jour.: *SJEPC*]

53. **tabloids** small-sized newspapers, often found in grocery store checkout aisles; specialize in scandal and sensational stories. [Am. Jour.: *SJEPC*]

54. **Thompson, Hunter S. (1939–2005)** "gonzo journalist" of 1960s and 1970s; claimed to throw together obviously crafted, impressive work; his books and articles were incisive and irreverent, his personal life excessive and outrageous. [Am. Jour.: *SJEPC*]

55. *Time* published weekly since March 3, 1923; designed for readers to catch up on various current events effortlessly. [Am. Jour.: *SJEPC*]

56. *True Detective* early pulp magazine that helped pioneer American crime story genre in 1920s; related true-life crimes. [Am. Jour.: *SJEPC*]

57. *True Story* hugely popular magazine of 1920s with first-hand accounts of sensational problems; sales were brisk, but many felt it depicted the worst in American society. [Am. Jour.: *SJEPC*]

58. *TV Guide* first published in 1953; weekly national television magazine with articles, reviews, and photos; separate editions cover local listings. [Am. Jour.: *SJEPC*]

59. *USA Today* conceived to provide business travelers with a standard newspaper as they moved from one city to another; introduced in 1982. [Am. Jour.: *SJEPC*]

60. *Vanity Fair* from 1914 to the Depression, magazine written for urban leisure class; consisted of articles on innovators and inno-

vations in visual art, literature, sports, film, and performing arts; text and artwork by top-notch contributors and very talented hopefuls. [Am. Jour.: *SJEPC*]

61. *Variety* weekly newspaper with focus on theater and film; began in 1905; characterized by light style peppered with slang and jargon; became "must read" publicaton of entertainment industry. [Am. Jour.: *SJEPC*]

62. *Vogue* first illustrated fashion magazine (1909); soon became legendary as the magazine for women wanting information on style, influential people, and cultural trends. [Fr. and Am. Jour.: *SJEPC*]

63. *Wall Street Journal, The* began as a handwritten page of business news in 1882; a century later had become national newspaper—conservative in tone and broad in scope—and had won more than 30 Pulitzer Prizes. [Am. Jour.: *SJEPC*]

64. *Washington Post, The* first published in 1877, but transformed into a first-rate newpaper in 1963 by Katharine Graham, peaking with its 1972 coverage of the Watergate scandal. [Am. Jour.: *SJEPC*]

65. **Woodward, Bob (1943–)** *Washington Post* won Pulitzer Prize (1973) for his coverage (with Carl Bernstein) of Watergate break-in; also wrote best-selling *All the President's Men* about the investigation and several other popular books. [Am. Jour.: Misc.]

66. **zines** non-commercial publications; usually self-published work; typically on a specialized topic and with limited circulation. [Am. Jour.: Misc.]

414. JOURNEY (See also ADVENTUROUSNESS, EXPLORATION, QUEST, TRAVEL, WANDERING.)

1. *Beagle* name of the ship in which Charles Darwin made his five-year voyage. [Br. Hist.: *NCE*, 721–722]

2. *Canterbury Tales* pilgrimage from London to Canterbury during which tales are told. [Br. Lit.: *Canterbury Tales*]

3. **Childe Harold** makes pilgrimage throughout Europe for liberty and personal revelation. [Br. Lit.: "Childe Harold's Pilgrimage" in Magill IV, 127–129]

4. **Christian** travels to Celestial City with cumbrous burden on back. [Br. Lit.: *The Pilgrim's Progress*]

5. **Christopher, Saint** patron saint; aided wayfarers across river. [Christian Hagiog.: Attwater, 85]

6. **Conestoga wagon** famed covered wagon taking pioneers to West before railroads. [Am. Hist.: *NCE*, 623]

7. **Dante** travels through Hell, Purgatory, and Paradise. [Ital. Lit.: *Divine Comedy*, Magill I, 211–213]

8. **Everyman** makes pilgrimage to God, unaccompanied by erstwhile friends. [Br. Lit.: *Everyman*]

9. **Exodus** departure of Israelites from Egypt under Moses. [O.T.: Exodus]

10. **hajj** pilgrimage to Mecca that every Muslim is expected to make at least once in a lifetime; fifth pillar of Islam. [Islamic Rel.: *UIMT*, 345–62, 428; *WB*, 10: 374–376]

11. **Hakluyt, Richard (c.1552–1616)** English geographer and publisher of eyewitness accounts of more than 200 voyages of exploration. [Br. Hist.: *EB*, 8: 553–554]

12. *Heart of Darkness* adventure tale of journey into heart of the Belgian Congo and into depths of man's heart. [Br. Lit.: *Heart of Darkness*, Magill III, 447–449]

13. *Kon Tiki* tale of trip taken on primitive raft by Thor Heyerdahl to cross from Peru to the Tuamotu Islands (1947). [World Hist.: *Kon-Tiki*; *NCE*, 1238–1239]

14. **Mandeville, Sir John (fl. 1356)** English writer of travelers' voyages around the world. [Br. Hist.: *EB*, VI: 559]

15. **Mayflower** vessel of America's pilgrims (1620). [Am. Hist.: Hart, 530]

16. **Oregon Trail** long ride on horseback from St. Louis to Portland, Oregon. [Am. Hist.: *The Oregon Trail*, Magill I, 695–698]

17. **petasus** hat; emblem of ancient travelers and hunters. [Gk. Art.: Hall, 145]

18. *Pilgrim's Progress, The* Bunyan's allegory of life. [Br. Lit.: Eagle, 458]

19. **Polo, Marco (1254–1324)** 13th-century Venetian traveler in central Asia and China; brought wonders of Orient to Europe.. [World Hist.: *WB*, 15: 572–573; Ital Lit.: *Travels of Marco Polo*]

20. *Roughing It* portrays trip from St. Louis across Nevada plains to California. [Am. Lit.: Hart, 729]

21. **Santa Fe Trail** caravan route from Missouri to New Mexico. [Am. Hist.: Hart, 743]

22. **Santa Maria, Pinta, and Niña** ships under Columbus in journey to New World. [Span. Hist.: *NCE*, 606]

23. **Syntax, Doctor** leaves home in search of the picturesque. [Br. Lit.: *Doctor Syntax*]

24. *Time Machine, The* H.G. Wells novel published in 1895; tells adventures of inventor who travels into future; sees degeneration of life. [Br. Lit.: Magill I, 986–988]

25. **Wilderness Road** pioneer route from eastern Virginia to Kentucky. [Am. Hist.: Hart, 924]

415. JOVIALITY (See also GAIETY, GOODNATUREDNESS, JOY.)

1. **Bob, Captain** Tahititan jailor known for his easygoing merriment with prisoners. [Am. Lit.: *Omoo*]

2. **Costigan, Captain J.** Chesterfield jovial, good-humored man. [Br. Lit.: *Pendennis*]

3. **Old King Cole** merry old soul. [Nurs. Rhyme: Opie, 134]

4. **saffron crocus** indicates mirth and laughter. [Flower Symbolism: *Flora Symbolica*, 177]

5. **Santa Claus** ho-ho-hoing merry gift-giver at Christmas. [Am. Pop. Cult.: Misc.]

6. **Tapley, Mark** jolly chief hostler at the Blue Dragon. [Br. Lit.: *Martin Chuzzlewit*]

7. **Tuck, Friar** fat friar, jovial companion of Robin Hood. [Br. Legend: Benét, 371]

416. JOY (See also GAIETY, JOVIALITY.)

1. **Auteb** female personification of gladness. [Egypt. Myth.: Jobes, 159]

2. **blue bird, the** symbolizes happiness sought by two poor children. [Belg. Lit.: *The Blue Bird*; Haydn & Fuller, 94]

3. **chrysanthemum** in Japan, solar and imperial symbol, linked with longevity and joy. [Symbolism: *COES&S*]

4. **cinquefoil** indicates gladness. [Flower Symbolism and Heraldry: Jobes, 341]

5. **Euphrosyne** one of Graces; name means "festivity." [Gk. Myth.: Kravitz, 96]

6. **gold on red** symbol of felicity and joy. [Chinese Art: Jobes, 357]

7. **Hathor** cow-headed goddess of joy and love. [Egypt. Myth.: Leach, 484]

8. **holly** symbol of hope and joy. [Symbolism: *CEOS&S*]

9. **Hyperboreans** blissful race lived beyond the North Wind in a region of perpetual Spring. [Gk. Myth.: Brewer *Dictionary*, 476]

10. **myrrh** symbol of gladness. [Flower Symbolism: *Flora Symbolica*, 176]

11. **red on green** symbol of felicity and joy. [Chinese Art: Jobes, 357]

12. *Rubaiyat of Omar Khayyam* series of poems celebrating hedonism as a way of life. [Br. Poetry: Benét, 881]

13. **wood sorrel** indicates gladness. [Flower Symbolism: *Flora Symbolica*, 177]

417. JUDAISM (See also RELIGION.)

1. **Abraham** in biblical tradition, patriarch of the Jewish people. [Jewish Rel.: Bowker]

2. **Abraham's bosom** expression for where righteous souls will be held. [Jewish Rel.: Bowker]

3. **Adam** first man; created in the image of God on the final day of creation, according to Genesis book of the Bible. [Jewish Rel.: Bowker]

4. **Altneuland** Theodore Herzl's imaginative description of the future Zionist settlement in Palestine. [Jewish Hist.: *Collier's*, XIX, 79]

5. **amen** Hebrew for "so be it"; used in response to a prayer or blessing. [Jewish Rel.: Bowker]

6. **angel** messenger who functions as intermediary between heaven and earth. [Jewish Rel.: Bowker]

7. **apocalypse** a time of future reckoning; revelation of things that are not known in the present. [Jewish Rel.: Bowker]

8. **ark** container; Old Testament Bible story of Noah's rescue of family and animals from flood tells of his building and sailing of an ark; ark of covenant contained tablets of the Ten Commandments given to Moses by God; in synagogue, where Torah scrolls are kept. [Jewish Rel.: Bowker]

9. **ash** symbol of human mortality. [Jewish Rel.: Bowker]

10. **bar mitzvah** ceremony and status of attaining religious adulthood for young Jewish men (at age 13). [Jewish Rel.: Bowker]

11. **bat mitzvah** ceremony and status of attaining religious adulthood for young Jewish women (at age 12). [Jewish Rel.: Bowker]

12. **Bethlehem** figured prominently in Old Testament of the Bible; city where Jesus was born. [Jewish Rel.: Bowker]

13. **Bible** sacred writings; divided into three sections, Torah (law), Nevi'im (prophets), and Ketuvim (writings). [Jewish Rel.: Bowker]

14. **Borscht Belt** Jewish culture and entertainment thrived in New York Catskills vacation spot throughout the 20th century. [Jewish Culture: *SJEPC*]

15. **Eben Shetiyyah** rock on which the world is founded. [Jewish Rel.: Bowker]

16. **hallelujah** Hebrew expression of praise. [Jewish Rel.: Bowker]

17. **Hanukkah** eight-day festival of lights celebrating the rededication of the Second Temple in Jerusalem; commemorated by lighting of Hanukkah lamp or menorah; in State of Israel, holiday celebrates the survival of the Jewish people. [Jewish Rel.: Bowker]

18. **heder** traditional Jewish elementary school. [Jewish Rel.: Bowker]

19. **Jerusalem** city filled with significant Jewish sites iincluding the Temple built in the place where God commanded Abraham to sacrifice his son Isaac. [Jewish Trad.: *WB2*]

20. **kabbalah** teachings of Jewish mystics; esoteric teachings which evolved from time of Second Temple. [Jewish Rel.: Bowker]

21. **manna** food sent from God to the Jewish people. [Jewish Rel.: Bowker]

22. **mehizah** separation screen between men's and women's seating in Jewish synagogues. [Jewish Rel.: Bowker]

23. **menorah** seven-branched candlestick; in 1948 became official symbol of State of Israel. [Jewish Culture and Rel.: Bowker]

24. **Messiah** descendant of King David who will restore the Jewish kingdom. [Jewish Rel.: Bowker]

25. **mitzvah** commandment, ritual, or good deed. [Jewish Rel.: Bowker]

26. **mizrah** easterly direction Jews face during prayer; also, ornament in Orthodox homes to mark east wall. [Jewish Rel.: Bowker]

27. **Oppenheimer, Josef Süss** chooses Judaism even when renunciation would save him from execution. [Ger. Lit.: Feuchtwanger *Power*; Magill I, 773]

28. **Passover** celebrated for seven days in Israel and eight days in the diaspora; commemorates the exodus from Egypt and the sparing of Israelites from the tenth plague of Egypt. [Jewish Rel.: Bowker]

29. **Pharisees** members of a religious sect of the Second Temple period; scrupulous in their obedience to the oral law and the written Torah; although sometimes considered extremists in the New Testament, they undoubtedly set example of high moral standards. [Jewish Rel.: Bowker]

30. **rabbi** learned man who had received ordination. [Jewish Rel.: Bowker]

31. **Sadducees** sect of Second Temple period made up of affluent priests who dominated Temple worship and formed majority of Sanhedrin. [Jewish Rel.: Bowker]

32. **Samaritans** tribe descended from Israelites; considered heretics by Jews. [Jewish Rel.: Bowker]

33. **Singer, Isaac Bashevis (1904–1991)** considered by many to be greatest postwar writer of Yiddish literature; won Nobel Prize for Literature in 1978. [Am. Lit.: *SJEPC*]

34. **Talmud** body of teaching, commentary, and discussion of Jewish spokesmen on the oral law. [Jewish Rel.: Bowker]

35. **Ten Commandments** ten laws proclaimed by God to Moses as representative of the Jewish people. [Jewish Rel.: Bowker]

36. **Tevye** Jewish peasant dairyman in musical *Fiddler on the Roof* (1964); struggles to maintain religious and cultural traditions during transformative times in his small Russian Jewish village. [Am. Musical: *SJEPC*]

37. **Torah** teachings of Jewish religion. [Jewish Rel.: Bowker]

38. **Wailing Wall** western wall of the Jewish temple in Jerusalem; all that remained of the temple after it was destroyed by Romans in 70 A.D.; therefore, most holy place in Jewish world. [Jewish Rel.: Bowker]

39. **yarmulke** skull cap worn by Orthodox Jewish men as a symbol of humility before God. [Jewish Rel.: Bowker]

40. **yeshiva** institute of Jewish learning of the Talmud. [Jewish Rel.: Bowker]

41. **zaddik** model of Jewish behavior much praised in biblical literature. [Jewish Rel.: Bowker]

Judgment (See JUSTICE, WISDOM.)

418. JUSTICE (See also LAWGIVING.)

1. **Aeacus** a judge of the dead. [Rom Lit.: *Aeneid*]

2. **Ahasuerus (519–465 B.C.)** Persian king rectifies wrongs done to Jews. [O.T.: Esther 8:7–8]

3. **Arthur, King** trained by Merlin to become a just ruler, he endeavors all his life to establish a realm where justice prevails. [Br. Lit.: Malory *Le Morte d'Arthur*]

4. **Asha** in moral sphere, presides over righteousness. [Persian Religion: Jobes, 138]

5. **Astraea** goddess of justice. [Gk. Myth.: Benét, 59]

6. **Bailey, F. Lee (1933–)** brilliant defense attorney known for self-promotion and involvement in high-profile cases: O.J. Simpson, Boston Strangler, Patty Hearst, to name a few. [Am. Law: Misc.]

7. **Barataria** island-city where Sancho Panza, as governor, settles disputes equitably. [Span. Lit.: Cervantes *Don Quixote*]

8. **blindfold** worn by personification of justice. [Art: Hall, 183]

9. **blue** in American flag, symbolizes justice. [Color Symbolism: Leach, 242; Jobes, 356]

10. **Brown v. Board of Education** landmark Supreme Court decision barring segregation of schools (1954). [Am. Hist.: Van Doren, 544]

11. **Bryan, William Jennings (1860–1925)** noted American orator and stateman; religious fundamentalism led him to assist the prosecution against Darrow in Scopes trial, where he won case

against teacher who wanted to teach theory of evolution in public school. [Am. Law: *WB2*]

12. **Cambyses, Judgment of** corrupt judge's flayed flesh provides judicial throne. [Gk. Hist.: *Herodotus*]

13. **Carlos, Don** conscience piqued, tries to lift Spanish yoke from Flemish. [Ger. Lit.: *Don Carlos*]

14. **Cauchon, Bishop** presided impartially over the ecclesiastical trial of Joan of Arc. [Fr. Hist.: *EB*, (1963) V, 60]

15. **Cochran, Johnnie, Jr. (1937–2005)** known for defending celebrities (perhaps, most notably O.J. Simpson, Lenny Bruce) and other high-profile clients; flamboyant style often parodied by comics. [Am. Law: Misc.]

16. **Darrow, Clarence Seward (1857–1938)** famous criminal defense attorney; defender of Leopold and Loeb who kept the teenagers from receiving death penalty; also defended Scopes in famous 1925 trial for right to teach theory of evolution in public schools. [Am. Law: *WB2*]

17. **Dike** one of Horae; personification of natural law and justice. [Gk. Myth.: Zimmerman, 85]

18. **Gideon v. Wainwright** established right of all defendants to counsel (1963). [Am. Hist.: Van Doren, 585]

19. **Grisham, John (1955–)** lawyer-turned-novelist writes bestselling legal thrillers; *A Time to Kill*, *The Firm*, and others have been adapted to film. [Am. Lit.: *SJEPC*]

20. **Hatto** during a famine he saves food for the rich by burning the poor, whom he compares to mice; mice invade his tower and devour him. [Ger. Legend: Brewer *Dictionary*, 439]

21. **Henry VII (1457–1509)** deliverer of Richard III's just desserts. [Br. Lit.: *Richard III*]

22. **Holmes, Oliver Wendell, Jr. (1841–1935)** one of best-known American judges of 1900s; argued for judicial restraint, advising judges to avoid letting personal opinions color their decisions; promoted laws that developed with the society they served. [Am. Law: *WB2*]

23. **International Court of Justice** main judicial organ of U.N. [World Hist.: *NCE*, 1351]

24. **Kunstler, William M. (1919–1995)** considered a radical egoist or a stalwart advocate of those he called "the damned"; represented controversial clients including Stokely Carmichael, Jack Ruby, and Jerry Rubin; famous for defending Chicago Seven against charges of inciting a riot during 1968 Democratic National Convention. [Am. Law: Misc.]

25. ***L.A. Law*** prime-time TV drama with definite comic bent; from 1986 to 1994, ensemble series followed personal and professional lives of employees of fictional high-powered law firm and garnered many significant awards along the way. [Am. TV: *SJEPC*]

26. **Libra** sign of the balance, weighing of right and wrong. [Zodiac: Brewer *Dictionary*, 640]

27. **Marshall, Thurgood (1908–1993)** first African-American justice of the Supreme Court (1967); important voice for rights of minorities and freedom of expression; primary strategist in cases that ended with the decision of Brown v. Board of Education of Topeka, finding segregation of public schools unconstitutional. [Am. Law: *WB2*]

28. **Mason, Perry** upstanding criminal lawyer protagonist of Erle Stanley Gardner's novels and courtroom dramas. [Am. Lit., Radio, and TV: *SJEPC*]

29. **Minos** his justice approved even by the gods; became one of the three judges of the dead. [Gk. Myth.: Zimmerman, 168]

30. **Moran** equitable councilor to King Feredach. [Irish Hist.: Brewer *Dictionary*, 728]

31. **Moran's collar** strangled wearer if he judged unfairly. [Irish Folklore: Brewer *Dictionary*, 728]

32. **Nuremburg Trials** surviving Nazi leaders put on trial (1946). [Eur. Hist.: Van Doren, 512]

33. **Pevensie, Edmund** protagonist in C.S. Lewis's Narnia series for young readers; initially weak, he yields to temptations of White Witch; later changes and becomes compassionate King Edmund the Just. [Br. Children's Lit.: Jones]

34. **Portia** as a lawyer, ingeniously interprets to Shylock the terms of Antonio's bond. [Br. Lit.: Shakespeare *The Merchant of Venice*]

35. **pound of flesh** what Shylock demands as his "price" when Antonio cannot repay his loan; by extension, the terms of an agreement strictly adhered to no matter how harsh. [Br. Lit.: Shakespeare *The Merchant of Venice*]

36. **Prince Po** settles dispute over a stolen child by asking the two claimants to pull it out of a circle of chalk by its arms. [Chinese Lit.: *The Circle of Chalk* in Magill III, 193; cf. Brecht *The Caucasian Chalk Circle* in Weiss, 74]

37. **Rhadamanthus** made judge in lower world for earthly impartiality. [Gk. Myth.: Brewer *Handbook*, 911]

38. **rudbeckia** indicates fairness. [Flower Symbolism: *Flora Symbolica*, 177]

39. **scales** signify impartiality. [Art: Hall, 183]

40. **scepter** denotes fairness and righteousness. [Heraldry: Halberts, 37]

41. **Sheindlin, Judith (1942–)** known as Judge Judy; famous for her outspoken nature when presiding over a television courtroom; featured small claims cases are not staged or scripted. [Am. TV: Misc.]

42. **Solomon** perspicaciously resolves dilemma of baby's ownership. [O.T.: I Kings 16–28]

43. **Starr, Kenneth (1946–)** appointed to Office of Independent Counsel to investigate suicide death of deputy White House counsel Vince Foster; later submitted Starr Report about President Clinton's sexual relationship with White House aide Monica Lewinsky and subsequent denial under oath; criticized for graphic sexual details of report, which was available to readers of all ages on the Internet. [Am. Law: Misc.]

44. **stars, garland of** emblem of equity. [Western Folklore: Jobes, 374]

45. **sword and scales** attributes of St. Michael as devil-fighter and judge. [Christian Symbolism: Appleton, 98]

46. *Tale of Two Cities, A* barrister London Stryver gets Charles Darnay acquitted by showing his resemblance to Sydney Carton. [Br. Lit.: Dickens *A Tale of Two Cities*]

47. *To Kill a Mockingbird* 1960 novel by Harper Lee set in South of 1930s; young black man is falsely accused of rape and represented by brave and ethical white lawyer. [Am. Lit.: Gillespie and Naden]

48. **Turow, Scott (1949–)** attorney and author of best-selling novels and nonfiction, including *One L* (1977) about his experience as law student at Harvard. [Am. Lit.: Misc.]

49. **Valley of Jehosaphat** where men will be ultimately tried before God. [O.T.: Joel 3:2]

50. **Wapner, Joseph Albert (1919–)** Judge Wapner starred on *The People's Court*; first judge to preside over real cases on television. [Am. TV: Misc.]

51. **World Court** popular name for International Court of Justice which assumed functions of the World Court. [World Hist.: *NCE*, 3006–3007]

52. **Yves, Saint** equitable and incorruptible priest-lawyer. [Christian Hagiog.: Attwater, 347]

K

Kidnapping (See ABDUCTION.)

Killing (See ASSASSINATION, INFANTICIDE, MURDER, PATRICIDE.)

419. KINDNESS (See also GENEROSITY, HELPFULNESS.)

1. **Allworthy, Squire** Tom Jones's goodhearted foster father. [Br. Lit.: *Tom Jones*]

2. **Androcles** relieves lion of thorn in paw and is repaid in arena by lion's failure to attack him. [Rom. Lit.: *Noctes Atticae*, Leach, 55]

3. **Bachelor, the** "the universal mediator, comforter, and friend." [Br. Lit.: *Old Curiosity Shop*]

4. **Bishop of Digne** gave starving Valjean food, bed, and comfort. [Fr. Lit.: *Les Misèrables*]

5. **Boaz** took benevolent custody of Ruth. [O.T.: Ruth 2:8–16]

6. **Brown, Charlie** often rejected or ridiculed by the other *Peanuts* comic characters, yet he reacts benevolently. [Am. Comics and TV: *SJEPC*]

7. **Brownlow, Mr.** rescued Oliver Twist from arrest and adopted him. [Br. Lit.: Dickens *Oliver Twist*]

8. **calycanthus** symbol of compassion. [Plant Symbolism: Jobes, 279]

9. **Carey, Louisa** Philip's loving, sensitive aunt. [Br. Lit.: *Of Human Bondage*, Magill I, 670–672]

10. **Cuttle, Captain** kindly shelters runaway, Florence Dombey. [Br. Lit.: *Dombey and Son*]

11. **Doolittle, Dr. John** protagonist of Hugh Lofting's 1920 book for young readers*The Story of Dr. Doolittle*; compassionate physician abandoned by his human patients because he has so many pets; taught to talk to the animals by his parrot; becomes successful animal doctor. [Br. Children's Lit.: Jones]

12. **Evilmerodach** Babylonian king; kind to captive king, Jehoiachin. [O.T.: II Kings 25:27–29]

13. **Finn, Huckleberry** refuses to turn in Jim, the fugitive slave. [Am. Lit.: *Huckleberry Finn*]

14. **Francis of Assisi, Saint (1182–1226)** patron saint and benevolent protector of animals. [Christian Hagiog.: Hall, 132]

15. **Friday's child** loving and giving. [Nurs. Rhyme: Opie, 309]

16. **Glinda** the "Good Witch"; Dorothy's guardian angel. [Am. Lit.: *The Wonderful Wizard of Oz*; Am. Cinema: Halliwell, 780]

17. **Good Samaritan** helps out man victimized by thieves and neglected by other passersby. [N.T.: Luke 10:30–35]

18. **heart** symbol of kindness and benevolence. [Heraldry: Halberts, 30]

19. **Heidi** happy, loving orphan from children's book by Johanna Spyri; shows kindness for others, especially her gruff grandfather. [Swiss Children's Lit.: Jones]

20. **Jesus Christ** kind to the poor, forgiving to the sinful. [N.T.: Matthew, Mark, Luke, John]

21. **Joseph of Arimathaea** retrieved Christ's body, enshrouded and buried it. [N.T.: Matthew 27:57–61; John 19:38–42]

22. **Kangaroo, Captain** persona created by Bob Keeshan; kindly host of a children's TV show, 1955–1975. [Am. TV: *FOF, MOD*]

23. **Kuan Yin** goddess of mercy. [Buddhism: Binder, 42]

24. **La Creevy, Miss** spinster painter of miniatures who devoted herself to befriending the Nicklebys. [Br. Lit.: *Nicholas Nickleby*]

25. **lemon balm** symbol of compassion. [Herb Symbolism: *Flora Symbolica*, 164]

26. **Martin, Saint** in midwinter, he gave his cloak to a freezing beggar. [Christian Hagiog.: Brewer *Dictionary*]

27. **Merrick, Robert** doing good to others as *raison d'être*. [Am. Lit.: *The Magnificent Obsession*, Magill I, 547–549]

28. **Mother Teresa (1910–1997)** Roman Catholic missionary nun and Nobel laureate who ministered to the poor and dying of Calcutta for decades; a symbol of selfless giving. [Roman Catholic Rel.: *ODA*]

29. **Nereus** venerable sea god of great kindliness. [Gk. Myth.: *Century Classical*, 744–745]

30. **Old Woman of Leeds** "spent all her time in good deeds." [Nurs. Rhyme: *Mother Goose*, 97]

31. **ox** exhibits fellow-feeling for comrades. [Medieval Animal Symbolism: White, 77–78]

32. **Peggotty, Daniel** kindhearted bachelor who shelters niece and nephew. [Br. Lit.: *David Copperfield*]

33. **Philadelphia** "city of brotherly love." [Am. Hist.: Hart, 651]

34. **Rivers, Saint John** takes starving Jane Eyre into his home. [Br. Lit.: *Jane Eyre*]

35. **Robin Hood** helps the poor by plundering the rich. [Br. Lit.: *Robin Hood*]

36. **Rodolph, Grand Duke** helps criminals and the poor to a better life. [Fr. Lit.: Sue *The Mysteries of Paris* in Magill I, 632]

37. **Romola** cares lovingly for her blind father, provides for her husband's mistress and children, and is kind to all who suffer. [Br. Lit.: Eliot *Romola*]

38. **Schindler, Oskar (1908–1974)** German industrialist who hired, and saved, thousands of Jews from Nazi concentration camps in World War II. [Eur. Hist.: Thomas Keneally *Schindler's Ark*; Am. Film *Schindler's List*]

39. **Strong, Doctor** "the kindest of men." [Br. Lit.: *David Copperfield*]

40. **throatwort** indicates sympathy. [Flower Symbolism: *Flora Symbolica*, 178]

41. **Tin Woodsman** from L. Frank Baum's Oz series; wants a heart because he believes he has no feelings; unaware that he is already sentimental and caring. [Br. Children's Lit.: Jones]

42. **Tutu, Desmond (1931–)** South African Anglican bishop and Nobel laureate who has devoted his life to fighting injustice through non-violence and bringing peace to all nations. [South African Rel.: *ODA*]

43. **Veronica, Saint** from pity, offers Christ cloth to wipe face. [Christian Hagiog.: Attwater, 334]

44. **Vincent de Paul, Saint** French priest renowned for his charitable work. [Christian Hagiog.: *NCE*, 2896]

45. **Wenceslas, Saint** Bohemian prince noted for piety and generosity. [Eur. Hist.: Brewer *Dictionary*, 1147]

Knowledge (See INTELLIGENCE, WISDOM.)

L

420. LABOR

1. **A.F.L.-C.I.O. (American Federation of Labor-Congress of Industrial Organizations)** federation of autonomous labor unions in North America. [Am. Hist.: *NCE*, 84]

2. **Chávez, César (1927–1993)** labor activist fought against exploitation of Mexican American farm workers, founded first farm workers union in 1962. [Am. Hist.: *SJEPC*]

3. **Debs, Eugene V. (1855–1926)** prominent labor leader founded American Railway Union (1893); ran for U.S. president five times as Socialist Party candidate. [Am. Hist. and Politics: *SJEPC*]

4. **five-dollar day** 8–hour daily wage for assembly-line laborers at Ford Motor Company, instituted by Henry Ford in 1914; higher, doubled wage helped create middle class. [Am. Hist.: *SJEPC*]

5. **Gompers, Samuel (1850–1924)** labor leader; organizer of American Federation of Labor. [Am. Hist.: Jameson, 203]

6. **I.L.O. (International Labor Organization)** agency of the United Nations; aim is to improve labor and living conditions. [World Hist.: *EB*, V: 389–390]

7. **I.W.W. (Industrial Workers of the World)** revolutionary socialist industrial union formed in 1905 by Western Federation of Miners and several other labor organizations. [Am. Hist.: Hart, 400]

8. **Marx, Karl (1818–1883)** chief theorist of modern socialism; stimulated working class's consciousness. [Ger. Hist.: *NCE*, 1708]

9. **Meany, George (1894–1980)** former president of the A.F.L.-C.I.O. [Am. Hist.: *NCE*, 1733]

10. *On the Waterfront* classic film made in 1954 based on work conditions on New York docks: ex-prize fighter testifies about union's criminal activities despite dangers involved. [Am. Film: *SJEPC*]

11. **Seeger, Pete (1919–)** paved the way for singer/activists through devotion to many social cause, especially as voice of working class; wrote and recorded folk songs with intent of changing the status quo. [Am. Culture: *SJEPC*]

12. **Solidarity (Solidarnosc)** Polish labor union movement of the 1980s. [Pol. Hist.: *WB*, P: 541]

13. **Steinbeck, John (1902–1968)** writer of phenomenally transformative fiction, especially dealing with sorry plight of itinerant farm workers; *Grapes of Wrath* is his classic Depression-era novel on that theme. [Am. Lit.: *SJEPC*]

14. **Teamsters** large, powerful union of U.S. truckers. [Am. Hist.: *NCE*, 2703]

15. **U.A.W. (United Auto Workers)** large American auto workers union. [Am. Hist.: *WB*, U: 21]

16. **U.F.W. (United Farm Workers)** largest farm workers union founded in 1962 by César Chavez. [Am. Hist.: *SJEPC*]

17. **Wobblies** members of Industrial Workers of the World; radical labor union established in 1905 that believed in empowering non-skilled workers excluded from the American Federation of Labor; wanted "One Big Union" to fight the capitalist system. [Am. Hist.: Hart, 400; *SJEPC*]

Lamentation (See GRIEF.)

421. LAST LAUGH (See also IRONY.)

1. **Alcyoneus** giant who threw stone at Hercules; killed when Hercules batted it back. [Gk. Myth.: Zimmerman, 17]

2. **Diomedes** eaten by his own horses, which he had reared on human flesh. [Gk. and Roman Myth.: Hall, 149]

3. **Fulton's Folly** everybody scoffed at his 1807 steamboat, the "Clermont." [Am. Hist.: Jameson, 190]

4. **Hop-Frog** immolates king and court after repeated insults. [Am. Lit.: "Hop-Frog" in *Portable Poe*, 317–329]

5. ***Magnificent Ambersons, The*** Eugene acquires same position George fell from. [Am. Lit.: *The Magnificent Ambersons*]

6. **Mordecai and Haman** latter hanged on gallows he built for former. [O.T.: Esther 7:9–10]

7. **Palamon and Arcite** victorious jouster (Arcite) dies in fall; loser wins lady's hand. [Br. Lit.: *Canterbury Tales*, "Palamon and Arcite"]

8. **Pizarro, Don** illegally imprisons Florestan; is later imprisoned himself. [Ger. Opera: Beethoven, *Fidelio*, Westerman, 109–110]

9. **Seward's Folly** ridiculed purchase of Alaska proved wise buy (1867). [Am. Hist.: Van Doren, 254]

10. **Truman, Harry S. (1884–1972)** presidential winner; photographed with *Chicago Tribune* headline announcing Dewey's victory (1948). [Am. Hist.: *Plain Speaking*, 406]

11. **Tuck, Friar** cajoled to ferry Robin across stream; dumps him returning. [Br. Lit.: *Robin Hood*]

422. LAUGHTER

1. **Democritus (c.460–c. 370 B.C.)** the laughing philosopher. [Gk. Phil.: Jobes, 430]

2. **Diller, Phyllis (1917–)** comedian known for her harsh, screeching, crazy laugh. [Am. Entertainment: *SJEPC*]

3. **hyena** rapacious scavenger; known for its maniacal laughter. [Zoology: Misc.]

4. **laughing gas** nitrous oxide; sweet-smelling, colorless gas; produces feeling of euphoria. [Medicine: Misc.]

5. **Thalia** Muse of comedy. [Gk. Myth.: Brewer *Dictionary*, 1071]

423. LAWGIVING (See also JUSTICE.)

1. **Draco (fl. 621 B.C)** codified Athenian law. [Gk. Hist.: Benét, 286]

2. **fatwa** opinion given by religious authority who is an expert in Islamic law. [Islamic Law: *UIMT*, 427]

3. **hadith** account, report, or speech concerning the words or deeds of the prophet Muhammad, often translated as tradition;second only to the Quran in importance and authority. [Islam: *UIMT*, 428]

4. **Hammurabi** Babylonian king (c. 1800 B.C.); established first systematic legal code. [Classical Hist.: *EB*, 8: 598–599]

5. **Justinian (485–565)** ruler of eastern empire; codified Roman law. [Rom. Hist.: *EB*, 10: 362–365]

6. **Minos** scrupulous king and lawgiver of Crete. [Gk. Myth.: Wheeler, 244]

7. **Moses** presents God's ten commandments to Israelites. [O.T.: Exodus 20:1–12]

8. **Muhammad (c. 570–632)** prophet who delivered the Quran to humanity, laying the foundation for the Muslim religion. [Islam: *UIMT*, 434]

9. **sharia** Islamic law; religious rules that govern personal behavior, from crimes to marriage, clothing, and dress. [Islamic Law: *UIMT*, 45–46, 437]

10. **Solon (c. 639–c. 559 B.C.)** Athenian statesman and wise legislator. [Gk. Hist.: Brewer *Dictionary*, 1018]

11. **Talmud** great body of Jewish law and tradition, supplementing scripture. [Judaism: Haydn & Fuller, 725]

424. LAZINESS (See also CARELESSNESS.)

1. **automatic pilot** phrase describing someone who works without effort; from the automatic controls that guide a plane. [Pop. Cult. *FOF, MOD*]

2. **Bailey Junior** nonchalant, inefficient boardinghouse page. [Br. Lit.: *Martin Chuzzlewit*]

3. **Beetle Bailey** goldbricking army private. [Am. Comics: Horn, 105–106]

4. **Belacqua** too slothful in life, he repents after death. [Ital. Lit.: *Divine Comedy*]

5. **Bshyst** demon of sloth. [Zoroastrian Myth.: Leach, 175]

6. **Capp, Andy** deliberately jobless and shirks household duties. [Am. Comics: Horn, 82]

7. **Datchery, Dick** hotel resident with no occupation. [Br. Lit.: *Edwin Drood*]

8. **Jughead** terminally indolent, save when hunger dictates. [Am. Comics: "Archie" in Horn, 87]

9. **Krebs, Maynard G.** for whom "work" is a four-letter word. [Am. TV: "The Many Loves of Dobie Gillis" in Terrace, II, 64–66]

10. **Lake of Idleness** whoever drank therof, grew immediately "faint and weary." [Br. Lit.: *Faerie Queene*]

11. **La-Z-Boy loungers** first manufactured in 1927; easy chairs that reclined with built-in footrest; favorites for TV viewing; often viewed as epitome of relaxation and inactivity. [Am. Pop. Culture: *SJEPC*]

12. **"Lazybones"** popular song by Hoagy Carmichael (1933). [Am. Music: Kinkle, II, 268]

13. **Lester, Jeeter** hapless sharecropper too lazy to keep his large family from starving. [Am. Lit.: Caldwell *Tobacco Road*]

14. **Little Boy Blue** asleep under haystack while livestock roam. [Nurs. Rhyme: *Mother Goose*, 11]

15. **Oblomov** indolent landowner, always in robe and slippers. [Russ. Lit.: *Oblomov*]

16. **phlegm** humor effecting temperament of sluggishness. [Medieval Physiology: Hall, 130]

17. **sloth** arboreal mammal, always associated with sluggishness. [Zoology: Misc.]

18. **Speed** an "illiterate loiterer"; slow-moving servant. [Br. Lit.: *Two Gentleman of Verona*]

Lechery (See LUST.)

425. LEXICOGRAPHY

1. **Johnson, Samuel (1709–1784)** literary scholar, creator of first comprehensive lexicographical work of English. [Br. Hist.: *EB*, V: 591]

2. **Murray, James (1837–1915)** renowned editor of the *Oxford English Dictionary*. [Br. Hist.: *Caught in the Web of Words*]

3. *Oxford English Dictionary (OED)* great multi-volume historical dictionary of English. [Br. Hist.: *Caught in the Web of Words*]

4. **Webster, Noah (1758–1843)** philologist and compiler of popular comprehensive American dictionary. [Am. Hist.: Hart, 902]

5. **"Webster's"** now used generically, synonymous in U.S. with authoritativeness in a dictionary. [Am. Cult.: Misc.]

426. LIBERALISM

1. **ACLU (American Civil Liberties Union)** founded in 1920, it seeks to preserve civil liberties, including freedoms of speech, press, religion; equal protection; due process; and privacy. [Am. Politics. Misc.]

2. **blue states** states with generally liberal voting patterns favoring the Democrtic Party; from the colored maps used by TV journalists during elections. [Am. Politics: Misc.]

3. **Democratic Party** one of the two main political parties in the U.S., generally espousing a liberal platform. [Am. Politics: Misc.]

4. **donkey** symbol of the Democratic Party, and hence a symbol of liberalism. [Am. Hist.: Misc.]

5. **Emily's List** liberal American political network that raises money for female candidates, helps elect pro-choice women Democratic candidates. [Am. Politics: Misc.]

6. **Humphrey, Hubert (1911–1978)** liberal Democratic congressman, Vice President, and Presidential candidate from Minnesota; "The Happy Warrior," long associated with progressive causes. [Am. Politics: Misc.]

7. **Labor Party** a main political party in Britian, liberal political ideology. [Br. Politics: *EB*]

8. **MoveOn.org** Progressive political organization and on-line forum dedicated to education and advocacy of candidates holding mainly liberal political ideas. [Am. Politics: Misc.]

9. *Nation, The* magazine has been a liberal voice in American politics since 1865. [Am. Politics: Misc.]

10. **New Left** emerging in the 1960s as an international movement against ineffectual liberalism; in U.S. major opponent of Vietnam War. [Politics: *SJEPC*]

11. *New Republic, The* founded in 1914, one of the most influential politically liberal magazines in U.S.; among its former editors are Walter Lippman and Michael Kingsley. [Am. Jour.: Misc.]

12. **NOW (National Organization for Women)** founded in 1966, feminist organization dedicated to political and legislative action in support of equality, abortion and reproductive rights, and ending sexual discrimination. [Am. Politics: Misc.]

13. **People for the American Way** founded in 1983, progressive political organization that advocates anti-censorship, civil rights, individual rights, and social justice; co-founded by TV and film producer Norman Lear. [Am. Politics: Misc.]

14. **Progressive Party** name of several different political parties that have developed over the past century in the U.S., generally espousing liberal values. [Am. Politics: Misc.]

15. **Trilling, Lionel (1905–1975)** influential American literary critic and exponent of Progressive politics. [Am. Politics: Misc.]

427. LICENTIOUSNESS (See also DISSIPATION, PROMISCUITY, SEDUCTION.)

1. **Aeshma** fiend of evil passion. [Iranian Myth.: Leach, 17]

2. **Aholah and Aholibah** lusty whores; bedded from Egypt to Babylon. [O.T.: Ezekiel 23:1–21]

3. **Alcibiades** Athenian general known for his debauchery. [Gk. Myth.: *ODA*]

4. **Alcina** lusty fairy. [Ital. Lit.: *Orlando Furioso*]

5. **Alexander VI** Borgia pope infamous for licentiousness and debauchery. [Ital. Hist.: Plumb, 219–220]

6. **Ambrosio, Father** supposedly virtuous monk goatishly ravishes maiden. [Br. Lit.: *The Monk*]

7. **Angelo** asked by Isabella to cancel her brother's death sentence, Angelo agrees if she will yield herself to him. [Br. Lit.: Shakespeare *Measure for Measure*]

8. **ape** symbol of lust and vice in Christian tradition. [Christian Animal Symbolism: *IEOTS*, 14; *CEOS&S*, 207]

9. **Aphrodite Porne** patron of lust and prostitution. [Gk. Myth.: Espy, 16]

10. **Armida's Garden** symbol of the attractions of the senses. [Ital. Lit.: *Jerusalem Delivered*]

11. **Arrowsmith, Martin** simultaneously engaged to Maeline and Leona. [Am. Lit.: *Arrowsmith*]

12. **Aselges** personification of lasciviousness. [Br. Lit.: *The Purple Island*, Brewer *Handbook*, 67]

13. **Ashtoreth** goddess of sexual love. [Phoenician Myth.: Zimmerman, 32]

14. **Asmodeus** female spirit of lust. [Jew. Myth.: Jobes, 141]

15. **Balthazar B** shy gentleman afloat on sea of lasciviousness. [Am. Lit.: *The Beastly Beatitudes of Balthazar B*]

16. **Belial** demon of libidinousness and falsehood. [Br. Lit.: *Paradise Lost*]

17. **Bellaston, Lady** wealthy profligate; keeps Tom as gigolo. [Br. Lit.: *Tom Jones*]

18. **Bess** Porgy's "temporary" woman; she knew weakness of her will and flesh. [Am. Lit.: *Porgy*, Magill I, 764–766; Am. Opera: Gershwin *Porgy and Bess*]

19. **Booth, Captain** pleasure-loving prodigal; lacks discipline. [Br. Lit.: *Amelia*]

20. **Caro** loathsome hag; personification of fleshly lust. [Br. Lit.: *The Purple Island*, Brewer *Handbook*, 180]

21. **Casanova, Giovanni Jacopo (1725–1798)** myriad amours made his name synonymous with philanderer. [Ital. Hist.: Benét, 172]

22. **Cleopatra (69–30 B.C.)** Egyptian queen, used sex for power. [Egyptian Hist.: Wallechinsky, 323]

23. **Don Juan** internationally active profligate and seducer. [Span. Lit.: Benét, 279; Ger. Opera: Mozart, *Don Gionvanni*, Westerman, 93–95]

24. **elders of Babylon** condemn Susanna when carnal passion goes unrequited. [Apocrypha: Daniel and Susanna]

25. **Falstaff, Sir John** fancies himself a lady-killer. [Br. Lit.: *Merry Wives of Windsor*]

26. **Flashman, Harry** British soldier wenches his way around world. [Br. Lit.: *Flashman*]

27. **Fritz the Cat** a tomcat in every sense. [Comics: Horn, 266–267]

28. **Genji, Prince** Emperor's dashing and talented bastard woos many. [Jap. Lit.: *The Tale of Genji*]

29. **goat** lust incarnate. [Art: Hall, 139]

30. **hare** attribute of sexual desire incarnate. [Art: Hall, 144]

31. **Hartman, Rev. Curtis** lusts after a young woman viewed at her window, but turns the experience into a hysterical sense of redemption. [Am. Lit.: *Winesburg, Ohio*]

32. **Hell-fire Club** 18th-century British clique devoted to debauchery. [Br. Hist.: Brewer *Note-Book*, 411]

33. **horns** attribute of Pan and the satyr; symbolically, lust. [Rom. Myth.: Zimmerman, 190; Art: Hall, 157]

34. **Iachimo** scorns and craftily tests feminine virtue. [Br. Lit.: *Cymbeline*]

35. **John of the Funnels, Friar** monk advocating lust. [Fr. Lit.: *Gargantua and Pantagruel*]

36. **Jones, Tom** manly but all too human young man; has numerous amorous adventures. [Br. Lit.: *Tom Jones*]

37. **Karamazov, Dmitri** lusty and violent in most of his actions. [Russ. Lit.: Dostoevsky *The Brothers Karamazov*]

38. **long ears** symbol of licentiousness. [Indian Myth.: Leach, 333]

39. **Lothario** heartless libertine and active seducer. [Br. Lit.: *Fair Penitent*, Espy, 129]

40. **Lyndon, Barry** from bully to dissipative rake and cruel husband. [Br. Lit.: *Barry Lyndon*]

41. **Macheath, Captain** gambler and robber; has scores of illegitimate offspring. [Br. Opera: *The Beggar's Opera*]

42. **Maenad** females who indulged in Dionysian rites; also called the Bacchae. [Gk. Myth.: *ODA*]

43. **Malecasta** personification of wantoness. [Br. Lit.: *Faerie Queene*]

44. **Montez, Lola (1818–1861)** beguiling mistress to the eminent. [Br. Hist.: Wallechinsky, 325]

45. **Nero (A.D. 37–68)** hated as Roman emperor; led life of debauchery. [Rom. Hist.: *NCE*, 1909]

46. **Obidicut** fiend; provokes men to gratify their lust. [Br. Lit.: *King Lear*]

47. **Pan** man-goat of bawdy and lecherous ways. [Gk. Myth.: Brewer *Dictionary*, 798]

48. **Pandarus** a "honey-sweet lord"; go-between for lovers. [Br. Lit.: *Troilus and Cressida*]

49. **Paphnutius** monk converts a courtesan but cannot overcome his lust for her. [Fr. Lit.: Anatole France *Th‰ois* in Benét, 997]

50. **pig** attribute of lust personified. [Art: Hall, 247]

51. **Porneius** personification of fornication. [Br. Lit.: *The Purple Island*, Brewer *Handbook*, 865]

52. **Pornocracy** period of unparalleled papal decadence (early 10th century). [Christian Hist.: Grun, 106]

53. **Priapus** monstrous genitals led him on the wayward path. [Rom. Myth.: Hall, 252]

54. *Rake's Progress, A* Hogarth prints illustrating the headlong career and sorry end of a libertine. [Br. Art.: *EB* (1963) XI, 625]

55. **Rasputin (1871–1916)** debauchee who preached and practiced doctrine mixing religious fervor with sexual indulgence. [Russ. Hist.: *NCE*, 1770]

56. **Ridgeon, Sir Colenso** refrains from using his tuberculosis cure to save the life of a man whose wife he coveted. [Br. Lit.: Shaw *The Doctor's Dilemma* in Sobel, 173]

57. **Robinson, Mrs.** middle-aged lady lusts after young graduate. [Am. Lit. and Film: *The Graduate*; Am. Music: "Mrs. Robinson"]

58. **Salome** in her provocative Dance of the Seven Veils. [Aust. Opera: R. Strauss *Salome*, Westerman, 417]

59. **Santa Cruz, Juanito** loses his wife, lover, and esteem by philandering. [Span. Lit.: *Fortunata and Jacinta*]

60. **Saturnalia** licentious December 17th feast honoring Saturn. [Rom. Myth.: Espy, 19]

61. **satyr** mythical figure, half-man and half-goat; symbol of unbridled lust. [Gk. Myth.: *FOF Classical*]

62. **Satyricon** tales of vice and luxury in imperial Rome. [Rom. Lit.: *Satyricon*]

63. **Scales, Gerald** sales representative known for lavish living, gambling, amorality. [Br. Lit.: *The Old Wives' Tale*, Magill I, 684–686]

64. **Sergius III** instituted the Pornocracy. [Christian Hist.: Grun, 106]

65. **Sodom and Gomorrah** ancient cities destroyed by God because of their wickedness. [O.T.: Genesis 19:1–29]

66. **Spanish jasmine** flower symbolizing lust. [Flower Symbolism: *Flora Symbolica*, 175]

67. **Vathek** devotes his life to sexual and other sensuous indulgences. [Br. Lit.: Beckford *Vathek*]

68. **Venusberg** magic land of illicit pleasure where Venus keeps court. [Ger. Myth.: Brewer *Dictionary*, 932]

69. **Villiers, George** first Duke of Buckingham and libidinous dandy. [Br. Lit.: *Waverley*]

70. **widow of Ephesus** weeping over her husband's corpse, she is cheered by a compassionate sentry and they become ardent lovers in the burial vault. [Rom. Lit.: *Satyricon*]

71. **Zeus** the many loves of this god have made his name a byword for sexual lust. [Gk. Myth.: Howe, 297–301; Zimmerman, 292]

428. LIGHT (See also SUN.)

1. **Apollo** god of light. [Gk. Myth.: Espy, 28]

2. **Asvins** twin gods of light. [Hindu Myth.: Benét, 60]

3. **Balder** god of light and peace. [Norse Myth.: Leach, 106]

4. **Celestial City** Heaven, goal of allegorical Christian in *The Pilgrim's Progress*. [Br. Lit.: John Bunyan *The Pilgrim's Progress*]

5. **Jesus Christ** "I am the light of the world." [N.T.: John 8:12]

6. **Mithras** god of light. [Pers. Myth.: Wheeler, 246]

7. **patée cross** four spear-headed arms; symbolizes solar light. [Christian Iconog.: Brewer *Dictionary*, 280; Jobes, 386]

429. LIGHTNING (See also THUNDER.)

1. **Agni** god of fire and lightning. [Hindu Myth.: Benét, 15]

2. **double ax** variation of Jupiter's thunderbolt. [Rom. Myth.: Jobes, 163]

3. **Elicius** epithet of Jupiter as god of lightning. [Rom. Myth.: Kravitz, 87]

4. **Franklin, Benjamin (1706–1790)** flew kite in thunderstorm to prove electricity existed in lightning. [Am. Hist.: *NCE*, 1000]

5. **Jupiter Fulgurator** Jupiter as controller of weather and sender of lightning. [Rom. Myth.: Hower, 147]

6. **Thor** bravest of gods; protected man from lightning. [Norse Myth.: Brewer *Handbook*, 1099]

430. LITERATURE for CHILDREN and YOUNG ADULTS (See also WRITER for CHILDREN and YOUNG ADULTS.)

1. **Bettleheim, Bruno (1903–1990)** Viennese child psychologist who believed fairy tales spoke to children, offering solace and solutions to problems. [Aust. Science: *OCCL*]

2. **Caldecott, Randolph (1846–1886)** gifted illustrator said to be father of modern picture book; influenced artists from Beatrix Potter to Maurice Sendak; distinguished award for illustration named after him. [Br. Children's Lit.: *OCCL*]

3. **Crane, Walter (1845–1915)** famous illustrator of beautiful, colorful paintings for children's books of late nineteenth century; his illustrations filled the whole frame of the picture and integrated text and illustration, sometimes with calligraphed text as part of the painting. [Br. Children's Lit.: *OCCL*]

4. **Golden Books** familiar series of small, inexpensive, gold-spined children's picture books featuring tales by respected authors, Bible stories, and story lines based on favorite TV shows and movies; debuted in 1942 for 25 cents each. [Am. Children's Lit.: *SJEPC*; Misc.]

5. **Greenaway, Kate (1846–1901)** her pastel illustrations of sunlit gardens and children in modified eighteenth-century costumes inspired many imitators; children's book award is named after her. [Br. Children's Lit.: *OCCL*]

6. **Newbery, John (1713–1767)** first British publisher who took children's books seriously and attempted to make a market for them; children's book award named after him. [Br. Chldren's Lit.: *OCCL*]

7. **Rackham, Arthur (1867–1939)** famous illustrator of about 90 books; extremely versatile; used muted colors so that his paintings could be effectively and accurately reproduced. [Br. Children's Lit.: *OCCL*]

8. **Shepard, E. H. (1879–1976)** illustrator of many books, but probably best known for his charming drawings for A. A. Milne's Pooh books and Kenneth Grahame's *Wind in the Willows*. [Br. Children's Lit.: *OCCL*]

9. **Tenniel, John (1820–1914)** famous illustrator best known for his work on Lewis Carroll's *Alice's Adventure's in Wonderland* (1865); his illustrations are notable for their wittiness and effective use of line. [Br. Children's Lit.: *OCCL*]

10. **Wyeth, N. C. (1882–1945)** painter and world-famous illustrator of classic adventure books and stories in periodicals from early twentieth century. [Am. Children's Lit.: *SJEPC*]

Littleness (See DWARF, SMALLNESS.)

431. LONGEVITY (See also ENDURANCE.)

1. *Abie's Irish Rose* comedy by Anne Nichols ran for 2327 performances on Broadway. [Am. Lit.: Benét, 3]

2. *Back to Methuselah* by the end of the twenty-second century, mankind has extended the life span to nearly three hundred years. [Br. Drama: Shaw *Back to Methuselah* in Magill III, 82]

3. **carp** symbol of longevity, virility, and scholarly success. [Symbolism: *CEOS&S*]

4. **chrysanthemum** in Japan, a solar and imperial symbol, linked with longevity and joy. [Symbolism: *CEOS&S*]

5. **Iguarán, Úrsula** matriarch who holds the clan together and lives to be one hundred years old. [Lat. Am. Lit.: Gabriel Garcia Marquez *One Hundred Years of Solitude* in Weiss, 336]

6. **Long Parliament** sat from outbreak of Civil War to Charles II's accession (1640–1660). [Br. Hist.: *EB*, VI:; 319–320]

7. *Meet the Press* longest running television program; from 1947 to present. [Am. TV: McWhirter, 234]

8. **Methuselah** son of Enoch; patriarch said to have lived 969 years. [O.T.: Genesis 5:21–27]

9. *Mousetrap, The* London play by Agatha Christie, running since 1952. [Br. Lit.: McWhirter, 228]

10. **mushroom** in China, symbol of life arising from death, longevity, and happiness; in parts of central Europe and Africa, folklore links it with supernatural. [Symbolism: *CEOS&S*]

11. **pear** longevity symbol in China. [Symbolism: *CEOS&S*]

12. *Phantom of the Opera, The* by 2008, it had celebrated unprecedented 20–year run on Broadway. [Am. Musical: Misc.]

13. **Rolling Stones, The** wrote and performed blues-inspired rock music during the "British Invasion" of the 1960s and for many decades after. [Br. Music: *SJEPC*]

14. **Roosevelt, Franklin Delano (1182–1945)** 32nd U.S. President; elected to four terms. [Am. Hist.: Hart, 726]

15. **Shangri-La** hidden Tibetan lamasery where all enjoy long life provided they remain there. [Br. Lit.: *Lost Horizon*]

16. **She** beautiful African sorceress who has lived for 2000 years. [Br. Lit.: H. Rider Haggard *She* in Magill I, 886]

17. **stork** symbol of longevity and filial devotion. [Symbolism: *CEOS&S*]

18. **Victoria, Queen (1819–1901)** queen of Great Britain and Ireland (1837–1901). [Br. Hist.: *NCE*, 2886]

432. LONG-SUFFERING (See also PATIENCE, SUFFERING.)

1. **Aspasia** pathetic figure bearing fate with fortitude. [Br. Lit.: *The Maid's Tragedy*]

2. **Burns, Helen** long-suffering victim of school's cruel treatment. [Br. Lit.: *Jane Eyre*]

3. **Canio** must be funny despite rage over wife's unfaithfulness. [Ital. Opera: Leoncavallo, *Pagliacci*, Westerman, 341–342]

4. **Clayhanger, Edwin** makes concessions to wife's greed and irascibility. [Br. Lit.: *The Clayhanger Trilogy*]

5. **Dodsworth, Sam** patiently endures egotism of his childish wife until marriage dissolves. [Am. Lit.: *Dodsworth*]

6. **Griselda** endures husband's cruelty nobly. [Br. Lit.: *Canterbury Tales*, "Clerk's Tale; Ital. Lit.*: Decameron, "Dineo's Tale of Griselda"]

7. **Job** underwent trial by God at Satan's suggestion. [O.T.: Job]

8. **oxeye** symbol of long-suffering composure. [Flower Symbolism: *Flora Symbolica*, 176]

9. **Prynne, Hester** stoically endures the ostracism imposed on her for adultery. [Am. Lit.: *The Scarlet Letter*]

10. **Santa Cruz, Jacinta** passively tolerates husband's adultery; rears his bastard. [Span. Lit.: *Fortunata and Jacinta*]

Loquacity (See TALKATIVENESS.)

Loser (See FAILURE.)

433. LOUDNESS

1. **boiler factory** proverbial source of noise and confusion. [Am. Culture: Misc.]

2. **breaking of the sound barrier** boom of plane heard exceeding speed of about 750 m.p.h. or Mach 1. [Aviation: Misc.]

3. **Concorde** supersonic jet of British-French design. [Eur. Hist.: *EB*, III: 66]

4. **Joshua** Jericho walls razed by clamorous blasts from his troops' trumpets. [O.T.: Joshua 6]

5. **Krakatoa** volcanic explosion on this Indonesian island heard 3000 miles away (1883). [Asian Hist.: *NCE*, 1500]

6. **Olivant** Roland's horn, whose blast kills birds and is heard by Charlemagne, eight miles away. [Fr. Legend: Brewer *Dictionary*, 772]

7. **sonic boom** shock wave from plane breaking the speed of sound. [Aviation: Misc.]

8. **Stentor** Greek herald with voice of 50 men. [Gk. Myth.: Espy, 39]

434. LOVE

1. **Aengus** one of the Tuatha de Danaan; god of love. [Celtic Myth.: Jobes, 40]

2. **Amor** another name for Cupid. [Rom. Myth.: Kravitz, 19]

3. **Anacreon (563–478 B.C.)** Greek lyric poet who idealized the pleasures of love. [Gk. Lit.: Brewer *Dictionary*, 31]

4. **Aphrodite** goddess of love and beauty. [Gk. Myth.: Zimmerman, 25–26]

5. **Bast** cat-headed goddess of love and fashion. [Egyptian Myth.: Espy, 20]

6. **bees** symbol of romantic love in European, Chinese, and Hindu traditions. [Symbolism: *CEOS&S*]

7. **Biducht** goddess of love. [Persian Myth.: Jobes, 210]

8. **Cupid** god of love; known to the Greeks as Eros. [Rom. Myth.: Kravitz, 70]

9. **diamond** token of affection, e.g., for engagement. [Gem Symbolism: Jobes, 440–441]

10. **Frigg** Scandinavian goddess of love and fertility. [Norse Myth.: Parrinder, 101]

11. *Garden of Love, The* Rubens painting of ladies and gallants in an amorous mood. [Flem. Art.: *EB* (1963), III, 190]

12. **honeysuckle** symbol of affection. [Flower Symbolism: *Flora Symbolica*, 174; Kunz, 328]

13. **Hymen** Greek god of marriage, depicted bearing flowers and carrying a torch. [Gk. Myth: *ODA*]

14. **Ishtar** Babylonian goddess of love, sex, and fertility. [Babyl. Myth: *ODA*]

15. **Kama** god of love; Hindu equivalent of Eros. [Hindu Myth.: Brewer *Dictionary*, 661]

16. **Krishna** god who plays flute to enamored milkmaids. [Hindu Myth.: Binder, 23]

17. **myrtle** to Renaissance, its perpetual greenness symbolized everlasting love. [Art: Hall, 219]

18. **pear** symbol of love and tenderness. [Flower Symbolism: *Flora Symbolica*, 176]

19. **red chrysanthemum** symbol of love. [Flower Symbolism: Jobes, 333]

20. **ring** worn on fourth finger, left hand, symbolizes love. [Western Folklore: Brewer *Dictionary*, 919]

21. **Romance Novels** formulaic love stories with happy endings written mostly by women for women; account for half of all mass-produced paperback sales. [Am. Lit.: *SJEPC*]

22. **rose** traditional symbol of love. [Flower Symbolism: *Flora Symbolica*, 177]

23. *Rules of Courtly Love, The* dos and don'ts manual for medieval lovers. [Eur. Hist.: Bishop, 301]

24. *Seventeenth Summer* innocent, touching young adult romance novel by Maureen Daly that swept the U.S. when published in 1942; tells story of summer romance that ends when girl goes off to college, certain her first love has changed her forever. [Am. Children's Lit.: Gillespie and Naden]

25. *Sonnets from the Portuguese* Elizabeth Browning's famous poems celebrating love for her husband (1850). [Br. Lit.: Magill III, 1007–1009]

26. **sorrel** indicates love and tenderness. [Western Folklore: *Flora Symbolica*, 177]

27. **St. Valentine's Day** February 14; day of celebration of love. [Western Folklore: Leach, 1153]

28. **three circles** symbol indicates affection. [Western Folklore: Jobes, 343]

29. **Velveteen Rabbit, the** stuffed toy who becomes real through the love of a child; from picturebook of same name by Margery Williams. [Am. Children's Lit.: Jones]

30. **Venus** goddess of love and beauty. [Rom. Myth.: *Aeneid*]

31. **white lilacs** indicates initial feelings of love. [Western Folklore: *Flora Symbolica*, 175]

435. LOVE, MATERNAL

1. **asteria** symbol of motherly affection. [Gem Symbolism: Jobes, 144]

2. **cinquefoil** symbol of motherly love. [Flower Symbolism: Jobes, 341]

3. **Cornelia** indicates that two sons are her jewels. [Rom. Hist.: Hall, 75]

4. **de Lamare, Jeanne** adores and indulges her son Paul despite his escapades and excessive debts. [Fr. Lit.: Maupassant *A Woman's Life* in Magill I, 1127]

5. **Delphine, Madame** denies motherhood for daughter's marriage. [Am. Lit.: *Madame Delphine*, Hart, 513]

6. **Mary** the Madonna; beatific mother of Christ. [N.T.: Matthew, Mark, Luke, John; Christian Iconography: *NCE*, 1709]

7. **red carnation** clove pink, sprung from St. Mary's tears at Calvary. [Christian Legend: Embolden, 23]

8. *Silver Cord, The* Mrs. Phelps's love for sons becomes pathological. [Am. Lit.: Hart, 769]

9. **Venus** provided future protection for Aeneas, her son. [Rom. Myth.: *Aeneid*]

Love, Platonic (See LOVE, VIRTUOUS.)

436. LOVE, SPURNED

1. **Anaxarete** princess turned to stone for scorning commoner's love. [Gk. Myth.: Zimmerman, 21]

2. **Aoi, Princess** afflicted by husband's amours; declines and dies. [Jap. Lit.: *The Tale of Genji*]

3. **Butterfly, Madame** considered herself Pinkerton's wife; actually his mistress. [Am. Lit.: *Madame Butterfly*, Hart, 513; Ital. Opera: *Madama Butterfly*]

4. **Clavdia** thought Hans's proposal foolish and refused him. [Ger. Lit.: *The Magic Mountain*, Magill I, 545–547]

5. **Cloten** spurned but persistent lover of Imogen. [Br. Lit.: *Cymbeline*]

6. **Conchobar** spurned, the king murders intended's lover and his brothers. [Irish Legend: *LLEI*, I: 326]

7. **Courtly, Sir Hartley** rejected by heiress; she prefers his son. [Br. Lit.: *London Assurance*, Walsh, *Modern*, 108]

8. **De Nemours, Count** rejected by the Princess de Cleves, who will not betray her husband even after he dies. [Fr. Lit.: Countess de La Fayette *The Princess of Cleves* in Magill II, 856]

9. **Hermione** rejected by Pyrrhus, who weds Andromache. [Fr. Lit.: *Andromache*]

10. **Hudson, Roderick** sculptor loses Christina Light to rich prince. [Am. Lit.: *Roderick Hudson*]

11. **Hugon, George** rejected by Nana, he stabs himself. [Fr. Lit.: *Nana*, Magill I, 638–640]

12. **Jason** Medea's lover; leaves her for Glauce. [Gk. Lit.: *Medea*, Magill I, 573–575]

13. **Laurie** long in love with Jo March; he begs her to marry him and is rejected. [Am. Lit.: Louisa May Alcott *Little Women*]

14. **Litvinoff, Grigory** Irina dallies with him for years but never yields. [Russ. Lit.: *Smoke* in Magill I, 897]

15. **Maggie** rejected by brother, lover, mother, and neighbors. [Am. Lit.: *Maggie: A Girl of the Streets*, Magill I, 543–544]

16. **Mellefont** double-crossed by friend and rejected lover. [Br. Lit.: *The Double-Dealer*]

17. **Orestes** spurned suitor of Hermione. [Fr. Lit.: *Andromache*]

18. **Phaedra** feigns rape on being scorned. [Gk. Lit.: *Hippolytus*]

19. **Potiphar's wife** traduces Joseph when seduction of him fails. [O.T.: Genesis 39:7–18]

20. **Robin, Fanny** betrayed by Sergeant Troy, her betrothed. [Br. Lit.: *Far From the Madding Crowd*, Magill I, 266–268]

21. **Touchwood, Lady** dissolute matron rejected by nephew's love. [Br. Lit.: *The Double-Dealer*]

22. **Wiggins, Mahalah** her fiancé changed his mind on their wedding day. [Am. Lit.: *Peter Whiffle*, Magill I, 739–741]

23. **willow tree** emblem of rejected affection. [Plant Symbolism: "Tit-Willow," *Mikado*; "Willow Song," *Othello*]

24. **Wingfield, Laura** caller fails to reciprocate the love she secretly had for him since high school days. [Am. Lit.: *The Glass Menagerie* in Hart, 317]

437. LOVE, TRAGIC (See also DEATH, PREMATURE.)

1. **Abel and Rima** worldly Venezuelan falls passionately in love with girl who is killed by hostile Indians. [Br. Lit.: Hudson *Green Mansions* in Magill I, 333]

2. **Abélard, Pierre (1079–c.1144)** philosopher notorious for the tragic love affair with Héloïse. [Fr. Hist. Benét, 2]

3. **Alfredo and Violetta** his love for the courtesan is shattered by her renunciation and fatal illness. [Ital. Opera: Verdi *La Traviata* in Benét, 1022]

4. **Annabel Lee** a storm swept her away. [Am. Lit.: "Annabel Lee" in Hart, 35]

5. **Antony and Cleopatra** victims of conflict between political ambition and love. [Br. Lit.: *Antony and Cleopatra*]

6. **Archer, Newland** though attracted to his wife's cousin Ellen, he cannot act to win her. [Am. Lit.: *The Age of Innocence*]

7. ***Blessed Damozel, The*** Rossetti poem depicting the longing of a beatified maiden for her mortal lover. [Br. Poetry: *The Blessed Damozel* in Benét, 113]

8. **Cabot, Eben, and Abbie Putnam** after feuding, recognize love; each imprisoned thereafter. [Am. Lit.: *Desire Under the Elms*]

9. **Clärchen** commits suicide when beloved receives death sentence. [Ger. Lit.: *Egmont*]

10. **Deirdre** when Noisi is betrayed and slain, she kills herself. [Irish Legend: Benét, 259–260]

11. **Delphine and Leonce** she takes poison when he is shot as a traitor. [Fr. Lit.: Mme. De Staël *Delphine* in Benét, 262]

12. **Dido and Aeneas** with the gods demanding his departure, she commits suicide. [Rom. Lit.: *Aeneid*; Fr. Opera: Berlioz *The Trojans*, Westerman, 174–176]

13. **Elizabeth** dies when Tannhäuser vows return to Venus. [Ger. Opera: Wagner *Tannhäuser*, Westerman, 212]

14. **Elsa** loses Lohengrin on their wedding night when she disobeys his proviso that she never ask him to disclose his identity. [Ger. Legend: "Lohengrin" in Benét, 595]

15. **Evangeline and Gabriel** after years of searching, she finds him as he lay dying. [Am. Lit.: "Evangeline" in Hart, 263]

16. **Fabrizio and Clelia** archbishop and his mistress: she and their infant die, and he retires to a monastery. [Fr. Lit.: *The Charterhouse of Parma* in Magill I, 135]

17. **Fields of Mourning** place in underworld where lovers who committed suicide dwell. [Rom. Lit.: *Aeneid*]

18. **Forsyte, Fleur and Jon** their passion is foredoomed by the estrangement of her father and his mother. [Br. Lit.: *The Forsyte Saga*]

19. **Forsyte, Irene, and Philip Bosinney** she falls in love with him, her husband's architect; he dies in an accident. [Br. Lit.: *The Forsyte Saga*]

20. **Frankie and Johnnie** "sporting woman" shot her man for "doing her wrong." [Pop. Music: Leach, 415]

21. **Frome, Ethan** his twarted love for Mattie culminates in an attempted double suicide that leaves them both crippled. [Am. Lit.: *Ethan Frome* in Benét, 324]

22. **Galatea and Acis** love shattered by latter's death. [Rom. Lit.: *Metamorphoses*]

23. **Gerard and Margaret** their marriage forbidden, he is given a false report of her death, and enters a monastery. [Br. Lit.: *The Cloister and the Hearth* in Benét, 208]

24. **Ghismonda and Guiscardo** princess's and commoner's affair fatal upon discovery. [Ital. Lit.: *Decameron*]

25. **Gilliatt** his plan for wedding Déruchette foiled by her love for another; commits suicide by drowning. [Fr. Lit.: *Toilers of the Sea* in Magill II, 1037]

26. **Glaucus** loses love, Scylla, when she is made monster. [Rom. Lit.: *Metamorphoses*]

27. **Gráinne** second wife of Fionn, she elopes with Diarmiud; caught by Fionn, Diarmiud is killed. [Irish Legend: *Century Classical*, 509]

28. **Gretchen** innocent young girl seduced and abandoned by Faust; she goes mad and murders their child. [Ger. Lit.: Goethe *Faust*]

29. **Hero and Leander** latter drowns, former kills herself in grief. [Gk. Lit.: *Hero and Leander*; Br. Lit.: *Hero and Leander*]

30. **Hylonome** commits suicide after death of lover, Cyllarus. [Gk. Myth.: Kravitz, 72, 123]

31. *Iceland Fisherman, An* Breton fisherman and his girl marry just before fleet leaves; he is lost in a storm. [Fr. Lit.: *An Iceland Fisherman* in Magill I, 410]

32. **Karenina, Anna** her death destroys Count Vronsky's desire to live. [Russ. Lit.: *Anna Karenina*]

33. **Launcelot, Sir, and Queen Guinevere** exiled by King Arthur, he returns after the King's death to find Guinevere a nun. [Arthurian Legend: *Le Morte d'Arthur*]

34. **Le Sueur, Lucetta** her love for Henchard squelched by his degradation. [Br. Lit.: *The Mayor of Casterbridge*, Magill I, 571–573]

35. **Lenore** the lost love with whom the poet learns that he will nevermore be united. [Am. Poetry: Poe *The Raven*]

36. **Leonora and Alvaro** her brother must kill her for eloping with the man he mistakenly supposes has murdered their father. [Ital. Opera: *La Forza del Destino* in Osborne *Opera*]

37. **Liliom** ne'er-do-well adored by Julie, his young wife; caught in a robbery, he commits suicide, leaving her with child. [Hung. Drama: Molnar *Liliom* in Magill I, 511]

38. *Love Story* idyllic romance of a young couple that is shattered by the death of the woman. [Am. Lit.: Segal *Love Story*]

39. **Manrico and Leonora** supposed gypsy troubador loves the girl courted by his brother, the Count of Luna; she takes poison and he is executed. [Ital. Opera: Verdi *Il Trovatore* in Benét, 1028]

40. **Mimi** her love for Rodolfo ended by her early death. [Ital. Opera: Puccini *La Bohéme*, Westerman, 348–350]

41. **Norma and Pollio** die together as sacrifices to Druid war god. [Ital. Opera: Bellini, *Norma*, Westerman, 130–131]

42. **Olindo and Sophronia** latter condemned to stake; lover joins her. [Ital. Lit.: *Jerusalem Delivered*]

43. **Onegin, Eugene, and Tatyana** long hopelessly for each other after her marriage to another. [Russ. Lit.: *Eugene Onegin*]

44. **Orpheus and Eurydice** looking back to see if Eurydice was following him to earth, he lost her forever. [Gk. Myth.: Zimmerman, 103]

45. **Paolo and Francesca** slain by his jealous brother, her husbad, Giancotto. [Ital. Lit.: *Inferno*]

46. **Pelléas and Mélisande** she married the wrong brother; dies of disappointment. [Fr. Opera: Debussy,*Pelléas and Mélisande*, Westerman, 196]

47. **Pyramus and Thisbe** thinking lover mauled, Pyramus kills himself; upon discovery, Thisbe does likewise. [Rom. Lit.: *Metamorphoses*]

48. **Romeo and Juliet** archetypal star-crossed lovers. [Br. Lit.: *Romeo and Juliet*]

49. **Saint-Preux and Julie d'Etange** passion waxes, but class strictures block marriage. [Fr. Lit.: *The New Héloïse*]

50. ***Thornbirds, The*** love between Father Ralph and Meggie remains unfulfilled because of his priestly vows. [Australian Lit.: McCullough *The Thornbirds* in Weiss, 463]

51. **tin soldier** adores a cardboard dancer, but both are consumed in a fire. [Dan. Lit.: Andersen "The Steadfast Tin Soldier" in *Andersen's Fairy Tales*]

52. **Tony and Maria** from Broadway musical *West Side Story*; fated lovers from different cultures; modern Romeo and Juliet. [Am. Musical: *West Side Story*]

53. **Tosca and Cavaradossi** famous singer, witnessing her lover's execution, jumps to her death. [Ital. Opera: Puccini *Tosca* in Bénet, 1017]

54. **Tristan and Iseult** irrevocably enamored; die because of his wife's machinations. [Medieval Legend: *Tristan and Iseult*; Ger. Opera: *Tristan and Iseult*]

55. **Wray, Fay** innocent beauty drives giant gorilla, Kong, to his death. [Am. Film: *King Kong*]

56. ***Wuthering Heights*** Heathcliff's revenge for Catherine's supposed scorn leads to her marrying another and to his own lonely death. [Br. Lit.: Emily Brontë *Wuthering Heights* in Magill I, 1137]

57. **Zhivago, Dr. Yuri** has passionate but fleeting affair with Lara. [Russ. Lit.: *Doctor Zhivago* in Magill IV, 241]

438. LOVE, UNREQUITED

1. **Bashville** footman; has noble, unrequited love for heiress. [Br. Lit.: *Cashel Bryron's Profession*]

2. **Bede, Adam** thought only of Hetty; she loved another. [Br. Lit.: *Adam Bede*]

3. **Chastelard** died for love of Mary, Queen of Scots. [Br. Lit. *Chastelard*, Walsh *Modern*, 92]

4. **daffodil** symbol of unrequited love. [Flower Symbolism: Jobes, 405]

5. **de Clèves, Princess** secretly loves a man other than her husband. [Fr. Lit.: *La Princesse de Clèves*, Walsh *Modern*, 100]

6. **de Vargas, Luis** seminarian falls for father's fiancée. [Span. Lit.: *Pepita Jiménez*]

7. **Dobson, Zuleika** every Oxford undergraduate falls in love with and despairs over her. [Br. Lit.: *Zuleika Dobson*]

8. **Echo** pined for Narcissus till only voice remained. [Gk. Myth.: Brewer *Dictionary*, 363; Br. Lit.: *Comus*, in Bénet, 217]

9. **Elaine** nursing Lancelot, she falls in love with him, but he loves Guinevere; she dies of a broken heart. [Br. Poetry: Tennyson *Idylls of the King*]

10. **Goodwood, Casper** his suit thrice rejected by Isabel Archer. [Am. Lit.: *Portrait of a Lady* in Hart, 669]

11. **Hoffmann** thrice a loser when one girl turns out to be a mechanical doll, the second dies, and the third loves another. [Fr. Opera: *Tales of Hoffmann* in Scholes, 1005]

12. **Krazy Kat** fails to win Ignatz, despite his efforts to dissuade her. [Am. Comics: Horn, 436–437]

13. **Mignon** dies from hopelessness of love for Wilhelm. [Ger. Lit.: *Wilhelm Meister's Apprenticeship*, Walsh *Modern*, 266]

14. **Nureddin** lovesick for Margiana, the Caliph's daughter. [Ger. Opera: Cornelius, *Thief of Baghdad*, Westerman, 256]

15. **O'Hara, Scarlett** marriages to three other men fail to dim her love for Ashley Wilkes. [Am. Lit.: Margaret Mitchell *Gone with the Wind*]

16. **Orsino, Count** loved by Viola, disguised as Cesario; he loves Olivia, who loves the disguised Viola. [Br. Lit.: Shakespeare *Twelfth Night*]

17. **Porphyria** comes in a winter storm to show her devotion, and her lover strangles her with her own tresses. [Br. Poetry: Browning *Porphyria's Lover* in Magill IV, 247]

18. **Ray, Philip** locks deep within heart his love for Annie. [Br. Lit: "Enoch Arden" in Magill I, 249–250]

19. **Sasha** Russian princess hopelessly loved by Orlando. [Br. Lit.: *Orlando*, Magill I, 698–700]

20. **Standish, Miles (c. 1584–1656)** declared love for Priscilla; received no response. [Am. Lit.: "The Courtship of Miles Standish" in Magill I, 165–166]

21. **striped carnation** symbol of love's denial. [Flower Symbolism: Jobes, 291]

22. **Treplev, Konstantin** aspiring novelist; hopelessly enamored of actress, commits suicide. [Russ. Lit.: *The Seagull*]

23. **Zenobia** strong-minded woman; disappointed in love, drowns self. [Am. Lit.: *Blithedale Romance*]

439. LOVE, VICTORIOUS

1. **Ada and Arindal** mortal and fairy permitted to stay together. [Ger. Opera: Wagner *The Fairies*, Westerman, 202]

2. **Babbie** gypsy wins clergyman despite opposition of town. [Br. Lit.: *The Little Minister*]

3. **Beatrice and Benedick** witty rebels against love; become enamored. [Br. Lit.: *Much Ado About Nothing*]

4. ***Beauty and the Beast*** fairy story from France (written by Mme. De Beaumont and published in 1756) about beautiful young lady who learns to love ugly beast, thereby breaking an enchantment and revealing him to be handsome prince. [Fr. Children's Lit.: *OCCL*]

5. **Bell, Laura** wins Pendennis's love despite his slavish admiration for wealth. [Br. Lit.: *Pendennis*, Magill I, 726–728]

6. **Berling, Gosta, and Countess Elizabeth** marry after many years of misunderstanding and misadventure. [Swed. Lit.: Lagerlof *Gosta Berling's Saga* in Benét, 412]

7. **Bezuhov, Pierre** long in love with Natasha Rostov; united after the deaths of his wife and her lover. [Russ. Lit.: Tolstoy *War and Peace* in Magill I, 1085]

8. **Castlewood, Lady and Henry Esmond** both undergo many trials before he realizes their love and they marry. [Br. Lit.: *Henry Esmond*]

9. **Cellini and Teresa** their love prevails, despite jealous suitors and duels. [Fr. Opera: Berlioz, *Benvenuto Cellini*, Westerman, 169–170]

10. **di Ripafratta, Cavalier** avowed woman-hater falls to innkeeper's feminine charms. [Ital. Lit.: *The Mistress of the Inn*]

11. **Dodsworth, Sam** finally leaves hypocritical wife for true love. [Am. Lit.: *Dodsworth*]

12. **Doone, Lorna** John and Lorna's love wins over many obstacles. [Br. Lit.: *Lorna Doone*, Magill I, 524–526]

13. **Elliot, Anne** nine years after her family made her give up her fiancé, they meet again and are united. [Br. Lit.: *Persuasion* in Magill I, 734]

14. **Ernesto and Norina** their schemes permit love to conquer. [Ital. Opera: Donizetti, *Don Pasquale*, Westerman, 123–124]

15. **Frithiof and Ingeborg** childhood lovers separated for years by court intrigue, finally reunited. [Nor. Lit.: Haydn & Fuller, 275]

16. **Ione and Glaucus** though threatened by jealous rivals, a murder plot, and volcanic eruption, they eventually attain happiness. [Br. Lit.: *The Last Days of Pompeii*]

17. **Jones, Tom** eventually marries Sophia Western, his sweetheart from early childhood, after they have been kept apart by his adventurousness and unknown antecedents. [Br. Lit.: *Tom Jones*]

18. **Ladislaw, Will** finally marries Dorothea, despite her family's protests. [Br. Lit.: *Middlemarch*, Magill I, 588–591]

19. **Lavinia** after war, affianced to Aeneas. [Rom Lit.: *Aeneid*]

20. **Levin and Kitty** long kept apart by her early refusal, their pride, and misunderstanding, they are eventually reunited. [Russ. Lit.: Tolstoy *Anna Karenina*]

21. **Lochinvar and Ellen** lovers from Sir Walter Scott's *Marmion,,* united at last. [Br. Lit.: *ODA*]

22. **Lucia and Renzo** peasants whose marriage, long thwarted by the machinations of a local baron, is eventually consummated. [Ital. Lit.: Manzoni *The Betrothed* in Magill II, 88]

23. **Nanki-Poo** wins Yum-Yum despite his self-exile to defy his father's commands. [Br. Opera: Gilbert and Sullivan *The Mikado*]

24. **Nikulaussön, Erlend** despite social convention, he wins Kristin's hand. [Nor. Lit.: *Kristin Lavransdatter*, Magill I, 483–486]

25. *Peer Gynt* Solveig loves Peer Gynt, despite his life of wandering, and finally wins him. [Nor. Drama: Ibsen *Peer Gynt* in Sobel, 531]

26. **pierced heart** Renaissance emblem, with motto, "Love conquers all." [Art: Hall, 146]

27. **Pontmercy, Marius** despite grandfather's forbiddance, marries Cosette. [Fr. Lit.: *Les Misérables*]

28. *Pride and Prejudice* Jane Austen's classic novel published in 1813; willful Elizabeth Bennet and arrogant Fitzwilliam Darcy eventually fall in love despite their differences in social status and their initial hesitancies. [Br. Lit.: Gillespie and Naden]

29. **Prince Charming** handsome suitor fulfills a maiden's dreams. [Fr. Fairy Tale: *Cinderella*]

30. **Rowena** loved by Ivanhoe, who finally claims her hand. [Br. Lit.: *Ivanhoe*]

31. *Taming of the Shrew, The* Lucentio wins Bianca despite the machinations of his rivals and the objections of her father. [Br. Lit.: Shakespeare *The Taming of the Shrew*]

32. **Tamino and Pamina** undergo trials and confinement before being united. [Ger. Opera: Mozart *The Magic Flute* in Benét, 619]

33. **Western, Jasper** Bumppo relinquishes his claim on Mabel to Jasper, whom Mabel loves. [Am. Lit.: *The Pathfinder*, Magill I, 715–717]

34. **Wickfield, Agnes** her love for David, long concealed, is fulfilled after his first wife dies. [Br. Lit.: Dickens *David Copperfield*]

440. LOVE, VIRTUOUS

1. **Aphrodite Urania** patron of ideal, spiritual love. [Gk. Myth.: Espy, 16]

2. **Armande** loves Clitandre platonically; values mind over senses. [Fr. Lit.: *Les Femmes Savantes*]

3. **Athelny, Sally** loves and marries Philip, despite the latter's shortcomings. [Br. Lit.: *Of Human Bondage*, Magill I, 670–672]

4. **Beatrice** object of Dante's adoration, even after death. [Ital. Lit.: *La Vita Nuova*, Walsh *Classical*, 48; *Divine Comedy* Walsh *Classical*, 48]

5. **Camille** gives up Armand for his family's sake. [Fr. Lit.: *Camille*]

6. *Casablanca* set in French Morocco during World War II, stars Humphrey Bogart as nightclub owner Rick and Ingrid Bergman as long-lost love Ilsa, now married; he selflessly gives her up and they part in oft-parodied scene. [Am. Film: *SJEPC*]

7. **Cupid's golden arrow** symbolizes noble affection. [Rom. Myth.: Jobes, 397]

8. **de Bergerac, Cyrano** does not reveal his love for Roxanne. [Fr. Lit.: *Cyrano de Bergerac*]

9. **Diotima** prophetess, teacher of Socrates; speaks of an ideal love. [Gk. Lit.: Plato *Symposium* in Brewer *Handbook*]

10. **Dulcinea** Quioxote's ideal; now generic for "sweetheart" [Span. Lit.: *Don Quixote*, Espy, 128]

11. **Laura** Petrarch's perpetual, unattainable love. [Ital. Lit.: Plumb, 26–32]

12. **Murasaki** reared by future husband; causes his reform. [Jap. Lit.: *The Tale of Genji*]

13. **Oriana** faithful and fair beloved for Amadis. [Span. Lit.: *Amadis de Gaul*]

14. **Schouler, Marcus** sets aside love for Trina for McTeague's benefit. [Am. Lit.: *McTeague*, Magill I, 537–539]

441. LOVERS, FAMOUS

1. **Abélard, Pierre (1079–1142) and Héloïse (c. 1098–1164)** persecuted 12th-century lovers. [Fr. Hist.: *Century Cyclopedia, 14*]

2. **Addams, Gomez and Morticia** ghoulish married couple in Charles Addams's cartoon had obvious sexual spark in TV version. [Am. TV: *SJEPC*]

3. **Arnaz, Desi (1917–1986) and Lucille Ball (1911–1989)** Afro-Cuban music band leader Arnaz costarred with wife Lucille Ball in comedy series *I Love Lucy*, playing off Latin Lover and Dumb Blonde stereotypes. [Am. TV: *SJEPC*]

4. **Atala and Chactas** Indian lovers whose passion goes unconsumated. [Fr. Lit.: *Atala*]

5. **Aucassin and Nicolette** the love story of 12th-century France. [Fr. Lit.: *Aucassin and Nicolette*]

6. **Browning, Robert (1812–1889) and Elizabeth Barrett (1806–1861)** 19th-century love one of most celebrated of literary romances. [Br. Lit.: Benét, 139]

7. **Celadon and Astree** bywords for lovers in pastoral poetry. [Br. Lit.: *Celadon*, Walsh *Modern*, 91]

8. **Ceyx and Halcyone** to perpetuate love, changed into kingfishers after former's drowning. [Rom. Lit.: *Metamorphoses*]

9. **Daphnis and Chloë** innocent though passionate love of two children. [Gk. Lit.: *Daphnis and Chloë*, Magill I, 184]

10. **Darby and Joan** inseparable old-fashioned couple. [Br. Lit.: Espy, 335]

11. **David and Bathsheba** adulterous lovers of the Old Testament [O.T.: Samuel 2:11]

12. **Deirdre and Noisi** celebrated lovers of the Ulster Cycle. [Irish Legend: Benét, 259–260]

13. **Della and Jim** each sacrifices greatly for other's Christmas present. [Am. Lit.: "The Gift of the Magi" in Benét, 395]

14. **Eddy, Nelson (1901–1967) and Jeanette MacDonald (1903–1965)** singer stars of eight sentimental musical romance films of the 1930s and 1940s; known as "America's Singing Sweethearts." [Am. Film: *SJEPC*]

15. **Edward VIII (1894–1972) and Wallis Warfield Simpson (1896–1986)** British king abdicates throne to marry divorcee (1936). [Br. Hist.: *NCE*, 835]

16. **Eyre, Jane and Mr. Rochester** governess falls in love with her employer; their marriage plans are disrupted by a mad wife and a fire; all ends happily. [Br. Lit.: *Jane Eyre*]

17. **Fitzgerald, F. Scott (1896–1940) and Zelda (1900–1948)** celebrity literary couple with fast-paced lifestyle epitomized the Jazz Age. [Am. Lit.: *SJEPC*; Henderson, 310–11]

18. **Helen and Paris** their elopement caused the Trojan war. [Gk. Myth.: *Century Classical*, 525–528, 815–817]

19. **Hero and Leander** love affair on the Hellespont tragically ends with latter's drowning. [Gk. Lit.: *Hero and Leander*]

20. **Jacob and Rachel** he worked fourteen years to win her hand. [O.T.: Genesis 29:18]

21. **Lescaut, Manon and the Chevalier des Grieux** he accompanies Manon to Louisiana when she is exiled for prostitution. [Fr. Lit.: *Manon Lescaut*]

22. **lovebirds** small parrots, traditional symbol of affection. [Am. Culture: Misc.]

23. **O'Hara, Scarlett and Rhett Butler** scheming, spirited southern belle and the man who adores her, but finally rejects her when he realizes she will always love another. [Am. Lit.: Margaret Mitchell *Gone with the Wind*]

24. **Oliver and Jenny** rapturous college relationship leads to blissful marriage. [Am. Lit.: *Love Story*]

25. **Petrarch and Laura** lovers in spirit only. [Ital. Lit.: Plumb, 26–32]

26. **Ricardo, Ricky and Lucy** famous husband and wife in *I Love Lucy* sitcom; he is a struggling bandleader and she a housewife who yearns to be an actress. [Am. TV: *SJEPC*]

27. **Rinaldo and Armida** virgin witch seeks revenge but falls in love. [Ital. Lit.: *Jerusalem Delivered*]

28. **Romeo and Juliet** young love springs up amidst family feud. [Br. Lit.: *Romeo and Juliet*]

29. **Sonny & Cher** [Salvatore Bono (1935–1998) and Cher Sarkisian (1946–)] mid-1960s pop music sensation; went on to host very popular comedy variety TV show where they engaged in good-natured arguments and put-downs. [Am. Music and TV: *SJEPC*]

30. **Tristan and Iseult** their pact of undying love has tragic consequences. [Medieval Legend: *Tristan and Iseult*]

31. **Turner, Ike (1931–2007) and Tina (1938–)** with crossover music and energized performances, often backed by full orchestration, African-American husband and wife duo had unique R&B sound. [Am. Music: *SJEPC*]

32. **turtle doves** adoring couple, building their nest. [O.T.: Song of Songs 2:12]

33. **Zhivago, Yuri and Lara** passion stirs between idealistic doctor and nurse during Russian revolution. [Russ. Lit.: *Doctor Zhivago*]

442. LOYALTY (See also FAITHFULNESS, FRIENDSHIP, PATRIOTISM.)

1. **Achates** companion and faithful friend of Aeneas. [Rom. Lit.: *Aeneid*]

2. **Adam** family retainer; offers Orlando his savings. [Br. Lit.: *As You Like It*]

3. **Aeneas** carried his father Anchises from burning Troy. [Rom. Lit.: *Aeneid*]

4. **alexandrite** type of chrysoberyl typifying undying devotion. [Gem Symbolism: Jobes, 67]

5. **Antony, Mark** Caesar's beloved friend; turns public opinion against Caesar's assassins. [Br. Lit.: *Julius Caesar*]

6. **Argus** Odysseus' dog; overjoyed at Odysseus' return, he dies. [Gk. Lit.: *Odyssey*]

7. **Balderstone, Caleb** servant true to Ravenswoods despite poverty. [Br. Lit.: *The Bride of Lammermoor*]

8. **Bevis** mastiff who "saved his master by his fidelity." [Br. Lit.: *Woodstock*]

9. **Blondel** loyal troubadour to Richard the Lion-hearted; helps him escape. [Br. Lit.: *The Talisman*]

10. **bluebell** symbol of loyalty. [Plant Symbolism: *Flora Symbolica*, 172]

11. **Byam, Roger** remains faithful to Captain Bligh after mutiny. [Am. Lit.: *Mutiny on the Bounty*]

12. **Camillo** as counsellor, exemplifies constancy. [Br. Lit.: *The Winter's Tale*]

13. **Chauvin, Nicholas (fl. early 19th century)** he followed Napoleon through everything. [Fr. Hist.: Wallechinsky, 164]

14. **Chester** Matt Dillon's lame but game sidekick. [Am. TV: "Gunsmoke" in Terrace, I, 331–332]

15. **Chingachgook** ever-devoted to Hawkeye. [Am. Lit.: *The Last of the Mohicans*]

16. **Cordelia** faithful daughter of sea god Llyr. [Celtic Myth.: Parrinder, 67]

17. **Cordelia** loyal and loving daughter of King Lear. [Br. Lit.: *King Lear*]

18. **dog** ever pictured at feet of saints; "man's best friend." [Medieval Art: Brewer *Dictionary*, 332; Western Folklore: Misc.]

19. **Dolius** the loyal retainer of Odysseus and Penelope. [Gk. Lit.: *Odyssesy*]

20. **Eros** Antony's freed slave; kills himself rather than harm Antony. [Br. Lit.: *Antony and Cleopatra*]

21. **Eumaeus** loyal swineherd of Odysseus. [Gk. Lit.: *Odyssesy*]

22. **Faithful Johannes** loyal servant dies for king and is resurrected. [Ger. Fairy Tale: Grimm, 22]

23. **Flavius** loyal and upright steward of Timon. [Br. Lit.: *Timon of Athens*]

24. **Flipper** intelligent, friendly dolphin who starred in TV show and films in 1960s was loyal companion to humans, especially children. [Am. TV and Film: *SJEPC*]

25. **Gamgee, Samwise** character from Tolkien's Lord of the Rings trilogy (1954–1956); Frodo's hobbit gardener who becomes a loyal friend; without complaint, he protects Frodo and matures into a brave and honorable hero; also called Sam. [Br. Lit.: Gillespie and Naden]

26. **Gloucester** faithful to Lear, he tries to save the king from his daughters' cruelty. [Br. Lit.: Shakespeare *King Lear*]

27. **Gonzalo** Prospero's "true preserver and a loyal sir." [Br. Lit.: *The Tempest*]

28. **Good-Deeds** only companion who ultimately accompanies Everyman. [Medieval Lit.: *Everyman*]

29. **Hemingway, Ernest (1899–1961)** American novelist and creator of Hemingway Hero: loyal, courageous, having "grace under pressure." [Am. Lit.: *FOF, MOD*]

30. **Horatio** true-blue friend of Hamlet. [Br. Lit.: *Hamlet*]

31. **Iolaus** nephew and trusted companion of Hercules. [Gk. Myth.: Howe, 141]

32. **Jonathan** stalwartly defended David; aided him in escape. [O.T.: I Samuel 20:32–34, 42; 23:16]

33. **Kato** loyal servant of the Green Hornet. [Am. Radio: "The Green Hornet" in Buxton, 102–103]

34. **Kent** a "noble and true-hearted" courtier. [Br. Lit.: *King Lear*]

35. **Merrilies, Meg** Henry Bertram's Gypsy-nurse; thoroughly devoted and protective. [Br. Lit.: *Guy Mannering*]

36. **Moniplies, Richard** Nigel's servant; helps him out of imbroglio. [Br. Lit.: *Fortunes of Nigel*]

37. **Panza, Sancho** squire to Don Quixote. [Span. Lit.: *Don Quixote*]

38. **Passepartout** faithful valet of Phileas Fogg. [Fr. Lit.: *Around the World in Eighty Days*]

39. **Pilar** fiercely devoted leader of a loyalist guerilla group in the Spanish Civil War. [Am. Lit.: Hemingway *For Whom the Bell Tolls*]

40. **pirates of Penzance** surrender only when charged by the police to yield in the name of their beloved Queen Victoria. [Br. Opera: Gilbert and Sullivan *The Pirates of Penzance*]

41. **Ruth** devotedly follows mother-in-law to Bethlehem. [O.T.: Ruth 1:15–17]

42. **Scipio** Gil Blas's secretary; shares his imprisonment. [Fr. Lit.: *Gil Blas*]

43. **speedwell** indicates female faithfulness. [Flower Symbolism: *Flora Symbolica*, 177]

44. **Suzuki** ever faithful to her mistress, especially in sorrow. [Ital Opera: Puccini *Madama Butterfly*, Westerman, 358]

45. **Titinius** Cassius' loyal follower; follows him to death. [Br. Lit.: *Julius Caesar*]

46. **Tonto** the Lone Ranger's constant companion. [Am. Radio: "The Lone Ranger" in Buxton, 143–144; Comics: Horn, 460; TV: Terrace, II, 34–35]

47. **Uncle Tom** "noble, high-minded, devoutly Christian Negro slave." [Am. Lit.: *Uncle Tom's Cabin*]

48. **Weller, Samuel** servant helps imprisoned Mr. Pickwick by getting himself imprisoned with him. [Br. Lit.: Dickens *Pickwick Papers*]

49. **Wiglaf** stood by Beowulf to fight dragon while others fled. [Br. Lit.: *Beowulf*]

50. **Wynette, Tammy (1942–1998)** her 1969 hit proclaimed that a woman must "Stand by Your Man" to the consternation of feminists of the time. [Am. Music: *SJEPC*]

443. LUCK, BAD

1. **albatross** killing it brings bad luck. [Br. Lit.: "Rime of the Ancient Mariner" in Norton, 597–610]

2. **black cat** because of its demonic associations. [Animal Folklore: Jobes, 297]

3. **black ox** sacrificed to Pluto; symbolic of calamity. [Gk. Myth.: Brewer *Dictionary*, 790]

4. *Candide* the hero and his relatives and friends stoically undergo an endless series of misfortunes. [Fr. Lit.: *Candide*]

5. **crow** in Europe and India, symbol of bad luck and war; also death, solitude, and evil. [Symbolism: *CEOS&S*]

6. **dead man's hand** two aces, two eights; hand Wild Bill Hickok held when murdered. [Am. Pop. Culture: Leach, 299]

7. **eclipse** regarded as portent of misfortune. [World Folklore: Leach, 337]

8. **Fawley, Jude** lost everything his heart desired. [Br. Lit.: *Jude the Obscure*]

9. *Flying Dutchman* ominous spectral ship; seen in storms off Cape of Good Hope. [Marine Folklore: *LLEI*, I: 285]

10. **Friday the 13th** regarded as unlucky day. [Western Folklore: Misc.]

11. **Hope diamond** largest blue diamond known; believed to bring bad luck. [Western Culture: *EB* V: 126]

12. **Job** underwent trial by God at Satan's suggestion. [O.T.: Job]

13. **Jonah** trying to escape God, brought tempest to sea. [O.T.: Jonah 1:4–12]

14. **ladder** walking under one can bring only misfortune. [Western Folklore: Leach, 598]

15. **mirror** the breaking of one brings seven years of bad luck. [Western Folklore: Cirlot, 211]

16. **Mutt** compulsive gambler who always loses. [Am. Comics: Berger, 48]

17. **opal** unlucky stone; represents the Evil Eye. [Gem Symbolism: Kunz, 148, 320]

18. **Plornish** disaster was his specialty. [Br. Lit.: *Little Dorrit*]

19. **Ring of the Nibelungs** brought a curse on all who owned it. [Ger. Lit.: Benét, 860]

20. **Seian Horse** ownership fatal. [Rom. Legend: Brewer *Dictionary*, 978]

21. **shirt of Nessus** Centaur's bloodied shirt; give to Heracles as gift by unsuspecting wife, it caused his death. [Gk. Myth.: Benét, 708]

22. **spilt salt** courts evil. [Rom. Myth.: Brewer *Dictionary*, 958; Ital. Art: "Last Supper"]

23. **step on a crack** and break your mother's back; advice to avoid walking on cracks in pavement. [Am. Folklore: Misc.]

24. **thirteen** number attending Last Supper, including Judas; considered unlucky number. [Christian Hist.: Brewer *Dictionary*, 1075; Western Folklore: Misc.]

444. LUCK, GOOD

1. **albatross** its presence portends good luck. [Br. Lit.: "The Rime of the Ancient Mariner" in Norton, 597–610]

2. **bat** symbol of good fortune; bat flesh imparts felicity. [Eastern Folklore: Mercatante, 182]

3. **blue** color believed to help ward off the evil eye. [Islamic Folklore: *UIMT*, 230]

4. **carnelian** brings luck; drives away evil. [Gem Symbolism: Kunz, 62–63]

5. **cricket** in China, a symbol of death and resurrection; also symbol of good luck. [Symbolism: *CEOS&S*]

6. **crossed fingers** said to bring good luck to a person. [Western Folklore: Misc.]

7. **four-leaf clover** indicates good luck. [Plant Symbolism: Jobes, 350]

8. **frog** in Japan, a symbol of good luck. [Symbolism: *CEOS&S*]

9. **gypsum** in egg-shaped form, brings good fortune. [Gem Symbolism: Kunz, 80]

10. **horseshoe** protective talisman placed over doors of churches, stables, etc. [Western Folklore: Leach, 505]

11. **Irish sweepstakes** only lucky people win this famous lottery. [Irish Hist.: *NCE*, 1614]

12. **knock on wood** to bring good luck and ward off bad luck. [Am. Folklore: Misc.]

13. **moonstone** sacred stone; brings good fortune. [Gem Symbolism: Kunz, 97–98]

14. **new penny** placing new penny in gift of purse brings recipient good luck. [Western Folklore: Misc.]

15. **penny** finding one by chance in street brings good luck. [Western Folklore: Misc.]

16. **penny loafer** placing penny in slot at top of shoe brings good fortune. [Am. Folklore: Misc.]

17. **Polycrates** tyrant of Samos, known and feared for his proverbial good luck, though it is not permanent. [Gk. Hist.: Benét, 801]

18. **rabbit's foot** proverbial good luck charm. [Western Folklore: Misc.]

19. **red** life-granting color; worn by brides and babies. [Asian Color Symbolism: Binder, 78]

20. **seven** symbolizes good luck in ancient and modern societies. [World Culture: Jobes, 1421–1422]

21. **seventh son** always a lucky or gifted person. [Western Folklore: Leach, 999]

22. **swastika** ancient sign of good luck, often in the form of a charm or talisman. [Asiatic Culture: Brewer *Dictionary*, 1051]

23. **three** symbolizes good luck; most holy of all numbers. [World Culture: Jobes, 1563–1566]

24. *Three Princes of Serendip* adventures of three Ceylonese princes who continually discover things they are not looking for. [Persian Lit.: Benét, 915]

25. **toad** in China, good luck lunar symbol associated with rain and riches. [Symbolism: *CEOS&S*]

26. **White Nights** nights before, during, and after a full moon thought to be especially lucky in some Muslim countries. [Islamic Trad. *UIMT*, 381]

27. **white on red** symbolizes good fortune. [Chinese Art: Jobes, 357]

Lust (See DISSIPATION, LICENTIOUSNESS, PROMISCUITY.)

445. LUXURY (See also EXTRAVAGANCE, SOPHISTICATION, SPLENDOR, WEALTH.)

1. **angora cat** behavior suggests self-indulgence. [Animal Symbolism: Jobes, 96]

2. **Babylon** ancient city on Euphrates river; famed for its magnificence and culture. [Mid. East Hist.: *NCE*, 202]

3. **Cadillac** expensive automobile and status symbol. [Trademarks: Crowley *Trade*, 83]

4. **Cartier's** jewelry firm founded by Alfred and Louis Cartier in Paris (1898). [Fr. Hist.: *EB*, 10: 177]

5. **caviar** extremely expensive delicacy of sturgeon's roe; byword for luxurious living. [Western Culture: Misc.]

6. **chauffeur-driven car** sign of the high life. [Western Culture: Misc.]

7. **chinchilla** one of the costliest of furs, made into luxurious coats. [Western Culture: Misc.]

8. **Chivas Regal** expensive Scotch whisky. [Trademarks: Crowley *Trade*, 106]

9. **clover** indicates wealth and ease. [Western Folklore: Jobes, 350]

10. **Cockaigne** fabled land of luxury and idleness. [Medieval Legend: *NCE*, 589]

11. **Dom Perignon** renowned vintage French champagne. [Western Culture: Misc.]

12. **fat of the land** Pharaoh offers Joseph's family Egypt's plenty. [O.T.: Genesis 45:18]

13. **fleshpots of Egypt** where Israelites "did eat bread to the full." [O.T.: Exodus 16:3]

14. **Gucci** Italian fashion brand considered the height of luxury, status, and taste; interlocked G logo imprinted on accessories like leather handbags and luggage is a symbol of prestige. [Ital. Culture: *SJEPC*]

15. **land of milk and honey** promised by God to afflicted Israelites. [O.T.: Exodus 3:8, 13:5]

16. **life of Riley** easy and trouble-free existence. [Am. TV: "The Life of Riley" in Terrace, II, 26]

17. **Mercedes Benz** expensive automobile and status symbol. [Trademarks: Crowley *Trade*, 368]

18. **mink coat** highly prized fur apparel; traditionally associated with wealthy ladies. [Western Culture: Misc.]

19. **Park Avenue** street in New York City associated with great wealth and luxurious living. [Am. Culture Misc.]

20. **Pullman car** comfortable, well-appointed railroad sleeping car named for maker. [Am. Hist.: Flexner, 210]

21. **Ritz** elegant and luxurious hotel opened in Paris in 1898 by César Ritz; hence, "ritzy", "putting on the ritz." [Fr. Hist.: Wentworth, 429]

22. **Rolls Royce** the millionaire's vehicle. [Trademarks: Brewer *Dictionary*, 928]

23. **sable** fur of this mammal produces luxurious, soft fur coats. [Western Culture: Misc.]

24. **Savoy** sumptuous hotel in London; at the time of its opening, it set new standards of luxury. [Br. Hist.: *EB*, 8: 1118]

25. **Schlauraffenland** fantastic land of sumptuous pleasures and idleness. [Ger. Legend: Grimm "A Tale of Schlauraffenland"]

26. **silk** expensive fabric used in fine clothing. [Western Culture: Misc.]

27. **Tiffany and Company** jewelry firm founded by Charles Lewis Tiffany; store in New York caters to the wealthy. [Am. Hist.: *EB*, 10: 177]

M

446. MADNESS (See also SPLIT PERSONALITY.)

1. **Alcithoe** driven mad by Dionysus. [Gk. Myth.: Kravitz, 16]

2. **Alcmeon** driven mad by the Furies. [Gk. Myth.: Kravitz, 16]

3. *Apocalypse Now* U.S. Captain Willard's journey into the Vietnamese jungle to assassinate insane, murderous Colonel Kurz; 1979 film directed by Francis Ford Coppola based on Joseph Conrad's *Heart of Darkness* (1902). [Am. Film: *SJEPC*]

4. **Ashton, Lucy** goes mad upon marriage; stabs husband. [Br. Lit.: *Bride of Lammermoor*]

5. *Beautiful Mind, A* 2001 award-winning biopic of John Nash, brilliant mathematician who overcomes schizophrenia and goes on to win Nobel Prize. [Am. Film: Misc.]

6. **Bedlam** Hospital of St. Mary of Bethlehem; first asylum for the insane in England; noted for its brutal treatment of its patients. [Br. Hist.: *EB*, I" 924]

7. *Bell Jar, The* Sylvia Plath's 1971 novel; largely autobiographical account of nineteen-year-old Esther's slide into mental illness. [Am. Lit.: Gillespie and Naden]

8. **Belvidera** goes mad when husband dies. [Br. Lit.: *Venice Preserved*, Benét, 1052]

9. **Bess o' Bedlam** inmate of London's lunatic asylum; female counterpart of Tom o' Bedlam. [Br. Folklore: Walsh, *Modern*, 55]

10. **Broteas** angered Artemis; she drove him mad. [Gk. Myth.: Kravitz, 47]

11. **Butes** Dionysus drove him mad. [Gk. Myth.: Kravitz, 48]

12. **Clementina, Lady** mentally unbalanced; vacillates between love and religion. [Br. Lit.: *Sir Charles Grandison*, Walsh, *Modern*, 99]

13. **Dympna, Saint** curing of madness attributed to her intercession. [Christian Hagiog.: Attwater, 107]

14. **Elvira** great mad scene caused by betrayal of Arthur. [Ital. Opera: Bellini, *Puritani*, Westerman, 133–135]

15. **Erinyes** Furies; three sisters who tormented those guilty of blood crimes, driving them mad. [Gk. Myth.: Benét, 320]

16. **Furioso, Bombastes** goes mad upon loss of bethrothed. [Br. Opera: Rhodes, *Bombastes Furioso*, Walsh, *Modern*, 64–65]

17. **George III (1738–1820)** ruled England from 1760–1820; showed signs of madness beginning in 1780s. [Br. Hist.: *ODA*]

18. *Girl, Interrupted* 1999 film based on a young woman's account of her 18–month stay in a mental hospital in the 1960s; she becomes fascinated by a sociopathic, charismatic patient. [Am. Film: Misc.]

19. **Gunn, Ben** half-demented castaway. [Br. Lit.: *Treasure Island*]

20. **Hieronimo** Spanish general goes mad on seeing the body of his murdered son. [Br. Lit.: *The Spanish Tragedy* in Magill II, 990]

21. *I Never Promised You a Rose Garden* Joanne Greenberg wrote the novel in 1964 under the pseudonym of Hannah Green; documents teenaged Deborah's split from reality and her slow recovery in a mental hospital; based on author's own painful experiences with schizophrenia. [Am. Lit.: Gillespie and Naden]

22. **King Lear** goes mad as all desert him. [Br. Lit.: *King Lear*]

23. **Leverkühn, Adrian** brilliant musician attains pinnacle; rapidly deteriorates mentally. [Ger. Lit.: *Doctor Faustus*]

24. *Lisa, Bright and Dark* John Neufeld's 1969 young adult novel depicts the psychological problems of 16–year-old Lisa Shilling— long bouts of depression and self-destructive behavior. [Am. Children's Lit.: Gillespie and Naden]

25. **Lucia** frustration causes her to murder husband. [Ital. Opera: Donizetti, *Lucia di Lammermoor*, Westerman, 126–127]

26. **Mad Hatter** his loony behavior reflects the belief that hatters became insane from mercury used on the job; from Lewis Carroll's *Alice's Adventures in Wonderland*. [Br. Children's Lit.: Jones]

27. *Madwoman of Chaillot, The* four eccentric women foil capitalistic exploiters. [Fr. Lit.: Benét, 618]

28. **Mahony, Dr. Richard** tries in vain to stay the insanity that eventually overwhelms him. [Australian Lit.: *The Fortunes of Richard Mahony* in Magill II, 341]

29. **March Hare** crazy rabbit who co-hosts mad tea party in Lewis Carroll's *Alice's Adventures in Wonderland.*. [Br. Children's Lit.: Jones]

30. **McMurphy, Randall Patrick** protagonist of Ken Kesey's *One Flew over the Cuckoo's Nest*; lobotomized in asylum after attempts to oppose debilitating treatment of patients. [Am. Lit.: *One Flew Over the Cuckoo's Nest*]

31. **Myshkin, Prince** four years in sanitarium; thought mad, treated for epilepsy. [Russ. Lit.: *The Idiot*]

32. **o' Bedlam, Tom** an inmate of London's lunatic asylum. Cf. Bess o' Bedlam. [Br. Folklore: Benét, 3]

33. *One Flew Over the Cuckoo's Nest* novel by Ken Kesey and subsequent award-winning film; patients in mental hospital cruelly controlled by Nurse Ratched. [Am. Lit. and Film: *SJEPC*]

34. **Ophelia** goes mad after father's death. [Br. Lit.: *Hamlet*]

35. **Orlando** driven insane by lover's betrayal. [Ital. Lit.: *Orlando Furioso*]

36. **Rochester, Bertha** insane wife of Edward Rochester. [Br. Lit.: *Jane Eyre*]

37. *Snake Pit, The* film made in 1948 about woman who gets less-than-desirable treatment at a state insane asylum. [Am. Film: Misc.]

38. *Sunset Boulevard* 1950 film noir, narrated by dead man, who relates his strong entanglement with long-forgotten silent movie star he is using for her wealth and connections; her madness and obsessive love are powerful and destructive. [Am. Film: *SJEPC*]

39. *Sybil* book by Flora Rheta Schreiber about a psychiatrist who treats a patient for 11 years, during which it is revealed that patient has developed 16 personalities as result of extremely abusive treatment as a child; story filmed as a 1976 TV movie. [Am. Lit. and TV: Misc.]

40. *Taxi Driver* powerhouse 1976 film directed by Martin Scorcese; alienated Travis Bickle obsesses about corruption and decadence in New York; becomes increasingly deranged and ultimately plans assassination attempt on a Senator. [Am. Film: *SJEPC*]

41. *Three Faces of Eve, The* 1957 film loosely based on true story; quiet woman suffers from headaches and blackouts; when treated by psychiatrist, two new personalities emerge. [Am. Film: Misc.]

42. **Very, Jones** "monomaniac" or "profoundly insane"? [Am. Hist.: Hart, 883]

43. **Wozzeck** thought of blood drives him to murder and suicide. [Aust. Opera: Berg, *Wozzeck*, Westerman, 480–481]

447. MAGIC (See also ENCHANTMENT, FAIRY, FANTASY, WITCHCRAFT, WIZARD.)

1. **Aladdin's lamp** when rubbed, genie appears, grants possessor's wishes. [Arab. Lit.: *Arabian Nights*]

2. **Armida's girdle** enabled the enchantress to know and do whatever she willed. [Ital. Lit.: *Jerusalem Delivered*]

3. **Bleys** magician who taught Merlin arts of sorcery. [Arthurian Legend: Walsh *Classical*, 57]

4. **Copperfield, David (1956–)** master of grand illusion—walking through the Great Wall of China, making the Statue of Liberty disappear, etc. [Am. Entertainment: Misc.]

5. **Deptford Trilogy** three connected novels by Robertson Davies; revolves around the effect of one boy throwing a snowball at another and missing. [Can. Lit.: Misc.]

6. **frog** symbol of magic, evolution, water, and rain. [Symbolism: *CEOS&S*]

7. **hazel** in Northern Europe, hazel wand was the instrument of wizards and magicians. [Symbolism: *CEOS&S*]

8. **Hogwarts School of Witchcraft and Wizardry** from J.K. Rowling's Harry Potter series for young readers (1997–2007); school where Harry and his friends learn their trade; located somewhere in Scotland, it is full of staircases that lead nowhere, secret panels, ghosts, and other fantastical elements. [Br. Children's Lit.: Misc.]

9. **Houdini, Harry (1874–1926)** famous turn-of the-century American magician and escape artist. [Am. Hist.: *NCE*, 1275]

10. *I Dream of Jeannie* 1965–1970 sitcom about Air Force astronaut whose life is complicated when he becomes master to a lovely, mischievous female genie in a bottle he finds. [Am. TV: *SJEPC*]

11. **magic carpet** flew King Solomon and his court wherever he commanded the wind to take it. [Moslem Legend: Brewer *Dictionary*, 177]

12. *Magus, The* millionaire living on a Greek island magically manipulates an unhappy young Englishman through bewildering experiences into self-awareness. [Br. Lit.: Fowles *The Magus* in Weiss, 279]

13. *One Hundred Years of Solitude* 1967 novel by Gabriel García Márquez; combines history, fiction, and magic realism. [Columbian Lit.: Misc.]

14. **"Open, Sesame!"** formula that opens the door to the robber's cave. [Arab. Lit.: *Arabian Nights*]

15. **owl** in many traditions, associated with magic, the otherworld, wisdom, and prophecy. [Symbolism: *CEOS&S*]

16. **Prospero** uses magic to achieve ends. [Br. Lit.: *The Tempest*]

17. *Skidbladnir* ship large enough to hold all the gods and their possessions, yet so skillfully wrought by dwarves that it could be folded and pocketed. [Scand. Myth.: Bullfinch]

18. **sorcerer's apprentice** finds a spell that makes objects do the cleanup work. [Fr. Music: Dukas *The Sorcerer's Apprentice*]

19. **wild ass's skin** assures the fulfillment of its possessor's wishes, but with a fatal result. [Fr. Lit.: Balzac *The Wild Ass's Skin* in Magill II, 1133]

Magnificence (See SPLENDOR.)

448. MARKETING (See also CONSUMERISM.)

1. **Adidas** distinctive three-stripe logo seen on footwear and clothing sought by fashion-conscious consumers. [Business: *SJEPC*]

2. **Bazooka Joe** blonde boy with eye patch featured in comics accompanying every piece of Bazooka bubble gum; debuted in 1953. [Am. Culture: *SJEPC*]

3. **Book-of-the-Month Club** innovative marketing approach (1926) continues to bring current popular literature to readers through mail order. [Am. Publishing: *SJEPC*]

4. **brick and mortar** reference to a company located in a building, rather than Internet-only business. [Business: Misc.]

5. **Budweiser** popular beer has achieved greater name recognition with clever marketing campaigns such as the Bud Bowl, Budweiser Clydesdales, and "This Bud's for you." [Am. Business: *SJEPC*]

6. **Burma-Shave** unique and ubiquitous signs in comical verse advertised the shaving cream product along America's roadsides from 1925 to 1963. [Am. Business: *SJEPC*]

7. **Coca-Cola** soft drink's uniquely shaped, recognizable bottle, along with memorable marketing campaigns and giveaway products featuring the Coca-Cola image, made the brand an American icon. [Am. Business and Culture: *SJEPC*]

8. *Davy Crockett* popular 1950s Disney TV series about legendary 19th-century American frontiersman spawned industry of mass-marketed western- and Crockett-themed products, such as coonskin caps. [Am. TV: *SJEPC*]

9. **Dot-com** company which does most of its business on-line using a website; name refers to a period followed by a shortened form of the word "commercial." [Business: Misc.]

10. **Felix the Cat** image of widely recognized, personable animated cat character from cartoons and comics of the 1920s used to sell dolls, cigarettes, and other merchandise. [Am. Comics: *SJEPC*]

11. **Home Shopping Network** wildly successful cable TV network, advertising wide variety of merchandise purchased by home viewers. [Am. TV: Misc.]

12. **Joe Camel** cartoon-like character used to promote Camel cigarettes; recognized by 91 percent of six-year-olds in American Medical Association study (1991). [Am. Business: *SJEPC*]

13. **Marlboro Man** Philip Morris company ad campaign with cowboy model to convince men that cigarettes with filters were macho. [Am. Business: *SJEPC*]

14. **Nike** using famous athletes as spokepeople and a distinctive "swoosh" logo, brought sports apparel into every home. [Am. Business: *SJEPC*]

15. **Peanuts** Charles Schultz's comic strip was the first to be mass-marketed; Charlie Brown and his pals appeared on everything from clothing to the Broadway stage. [Am. Pop. Culture: *SJEPC*]

16. **Sears Roebuck Catalog** originated as mail-order merchandising for farming families; not the first of its kind, but the most successful and influential. [Am. Business: *SJEPC*]

17. **surfing** avoiding advertisements by changing TV channels via remote control or clicking to close website pop-ups. [Usage: *SJEPC*]

449. MARKSMANSHIP

1. **Buffalo Bill (1846–1917)** famed sharpshooter in Wild West show. [Am. Hist.: Flexner, 67]

2. **Crotus** son of Pan, companion to Muses; skilled in archery. [Gk. Myth.: Howe, 70]

3. **Deadeye Dick** sobriquet of 1880s cowboy-sharpshooter, Nat Love. [Am. Hist.: Flexner, 41]

4. **Egil** Norse god, famed archer; met the same challenge as William Tell. [Norse Myth.: Brewer *Dictionary*, 323]

5. **Hawkeye** sharpshooting frontier folk hero. [Am. Lit.: *The Last of the Mohicans*]

6. **Hickok, "Wild Bill" (1837–1876)** sharpshooting stage driver and marshal of U.S. West. [Am. Hist. Flexner, 387]

7. **Oakley, Annie (1860–1926)** renowned expert gunshooter of Buffalo Bill's Wild West show. [Am. Hist. Brewer *Dictionary*, 771]

8. **Robin Hood** famed throughout land for skill as archer. [Br. Lit.: *Robin Hood*]

9. **Robin-A-Bobbin** such a bad archer, killed crow while aiming for pigeon. [Nurs. Rhyme: *Mother Goose*, 33]

10. **Tell, William** shot apple off son's head with arrow. [Swiss Legend: Brewer *Dictionary*, 1066; Ital. Opera: Rossini, *William Tell*]

450. MARRIAGE

1. **American linden** symbol of marriage. [Plant Symbolism: *Flora Symbolica*, 182]

2. **Aphrodite Genetrix** patron of marriage and procreation. [Gk. Myth.: Espy, 16]

3. *As You Like It* its denouement has the marriages of four couples. [Br. Lit.: Shakespeare *As You Like It*]

4. **Benedick** nickname for groom; derived from Shakespeare's Benedick. [Br. Lit.: *Much Ado About Nothing*]

5. **Blondie and Dagwood** typify relationship between dominant wife and her inadequate mate. [Am. Comics: Berger, 108]

6. **"Bridal Chorus"** traditional wedding song; from Wagner's *Lohengrin*. [Ger. Music: Scholes, 1113]

7. **Cana** wedding feast where Christ made water into wine. [N.T.: John 2:1–11]

8. *Doll's House, A* after eight years of marriage, in which Torvald Helmer has treated Nora more like a doll than a human being, she declares her independence. [Nor. Drama: Ibsen *A Doll's House*]

9. **epithalamium** song or poem given in honor of a marriage, notably outside the bridal chamber. [Western Lit.: *LLEI*, 1: 283]

10. **Erato** Muse of bridal songs. [Gk. Myth.: Kravitz, 90]

11. **Frome, Ethan** his loveless and unhappy marriage to Zeena remains hopeless when his love affair with Mattie comes to a pitiful end. [Am. Lit.: *Ethan Frome* in Benét, 324]

12. **Gretna Green** place in Scotland, just across from the English border, where elopers could be married without formalities. [Br. Hist.: Brewer *Dictionary*, 418]

13. **Hulda** goddess of marriage and fecundity. [Ger. Myth.: Benét, 484]

14. **huppah** bridal canopy in Jewish weddings. [Judaism: Wigoder, 274]

15. **Hymen** Greek god of marriage, depicted with flowers and a torch. [Gk. Myth: *ODA*]

16. *I Love Lucy* popular 1950s TV comedy starring husband-and-wife team of Lucille Ball and Desi Arnaz that exaggerated situations familiar to typical American married couples. [Am. TV: *SJEPC*]

17. **knot** symbol of the power to bind and set free; also love and marriage. [Symbolism: *CEOS&S*]

18. *Marriage à la Mode* engravings in which Hogarth satrically depicts the daily lives of a countess and an earl. [Br. Art: *EB* (1963) XI, 625]

19. *Modern Love* dramatizes the feelings of a couple whose marriage is dying. [Br. Lit.: George Meredith *Modern Love* in Magill IV, 899]

20. *Newlywed Game, The* crude double entendres were commonplace on this game show featuring young marrieds answering intimate questions. [Am. TV: *SJEPC*]

21. **Niagara Falls** North America's greatest waterfall; favorite honeymoon destination. [Am. Geography: *SJEPC*]

22. **orange blossoms** traditional decoration for brides. [Br. and Fr. Tradition: Brewer *Dictionary*, 784]

23. **peach** very important Chinese symbol with many meanings, including immortality, marriage, fertility. [Symbolism: *CEOS&S*]

24. *Prothalamion* Spenser's poem celebrating the double marriage of the two daughters of the Earl of Worcester. [Br. Poetry: Haydn & Fuller, 615]

25. **quince** in portraits, traditionally held by woman in wedding. [Art: Hall, 257]

26. **rice** newly married couples pelted with rice for connubial good luck. [Western Folklore: Leach, 938]

27. **St. Agnes's Eve** when marriageable girls foresee their future husbands. [Br. Lit.: "The Eve of St. Agnes" in Norton, 686–693]

28. *These Twain* difficult marital adjustments of Edwin Clayhanger and Hilda Lessways. [Br. Lit.: Bennett *These Twain* in Magill I, 148]

29. **tin cans** put on car of newlyweds leaving ceremony. [Am. Cult.: Misc.]

30. *Way of the World, The* profound analysis of the marriage relation in which Mirabell and Millamant negoitate a marriage agreement. [Br. Lit.: Benét, 1077]

31. **"Wedding March"** popular bridal music from Mendelssohn's march in *Midsummer Night's Dream*. [Ger. Music: Scholes, 1113]

32. *Who's Afraid of Virginia Woolf?* marriage of George and Martha is a travesty, full of arguments, frustration, and hatred. [Am. Lit.: Edward Albee *Who's Afraid of Virginia Woolf?* in Magill IV, 1282]

33. **Wife of Bath** many marriages form theme of her tale. [Br. Lit.: *Canterbury Tales*, "Wife of Bath's Tale"]

451. MARTYRDOM (See also SACRIFICE, SELF-SACRIFICE.)

1. **Agatha, Saint** tortured for resisting advances of Quintianus. [Christian Hagiog.: Daniel, 21]

2. **Alban, Saint** traditionally, first British martyr. [Christian Hagiog.: *NCE*, 49]

3. **Andrew, Saint** apostle and missionary; condemned to be scourged and crucified. [Christian Hagiog.: Brewster, 4]

4. **arrow** Christian symbol of martyrdom. [Christianity: *CEOS&S*, 208]

5. **arrow and cross** symbol of martyrdom of St. Sebastian. [Christian Iconog.: Attwater, 304]

6. **Brown, John (1800–1859)** abolitionist leader; died for antislavery cause. [Am. Hist.: Hart, 111]

7. **Callista** beautiful Greek convert; executed and later canonized. [Br. Lit.: *Callista*]

8. **Campion, Edmund** harrassed and tortured by Anglicans, hanged on a false charge of treason. [Br. Lit.: *Edmund Campion* in Magill I, 237]

9. **carnelian** symbol of St. Sebastian. [Christian Hagiog.: Brewer *Handbook*, I, 411]

10. **Elmo, Saint** patron saint of sailors; intestines wound on windlass. [Christian Hagiog.: Attwater, 117]

11. **Golgotha** place of martyrdom or of torment; after site of Christ's crucifixion. [Western Folklore: Espy, 79]

12. **Holy Innocents** male infants slaughtered by Herod. [Christian Hagiog.: Attwater, 179; N.T.: Matthew 2:16–18]

13. **James Intercisus, Saint** cut to pieces for belief in Christianity. [Christian Hagiog.: Brewster, 2]

14. **Jesus Christ** crucified at demand of Jewish authorities. [N. T.: Matthew 27: 24–61; Mark 15:15–47; Luke 23:13–56]

15. **Joan of Arc, Saint (1412–1431)** burned at stake for witchcraft (1431). [Fr. Hist.: *NCE*, 1417; Br. Lit.: *I Henry IV*]

16. **John the Baptist, Saint** Jewish prophet; beheaded at instigation of Salome. [N.T.: Matthew 11:1–19; 17:11–13]

17. **More, Sir Thomas (1478–1535)** statesman and humanist; beheaded for opposition to Henry VIII's Act of Supremacy. [Br. Hist.: *NCE*, 1830]

18. **Nero's Torches** oil- and tar-smeared Christians implanted and set aflame. [Christian Hist.: Brewer *Note-Book*, 614]

19. **palm** appeared on martyrs' graves. [Christian Symbolism: Appleton, 73]

20. **Perpetua, Saint and Saint Felicity** gored by wild beasts; slain with swords. [Christian Hagiog.: Attwater, 273]

21. **Peter, Saint** apostle crucified upside down in Rome. [Christian Hagiog.: Brewster, 310]

22. **Sacco, Nicola (1891–1927) and Bartolomeo Vanzetti (1888–1927)** perhaps executed more for radicalism than murder (August 22, 1927). [Am. Hist.: Flexner, 311]

23. **Sebastian, Saint** Roman soldier; shot with arrows and struck with clubs. [Christian Hagiog.: Brewster, 75]

24. **Stephen, Saint** first martyr; stoned as blasphemer. [Christian Hagiog.: Attwater, 313]

25. **sword** instrument of decapitation of early saints. [Christian Symbolism: Appleton, 14]

26. **Thecla, Saint** first woman martyr. [Christian Hagiog.: Brewer *Dictionary*, 1072]

27. **Thomas à Becket, Saint (1118–1170)** brutally slain in Canterbury cathedral by king's knights. [Br. Hist.: *NCE*, 2735–2736]

452. MASCULINITY (See also BEAUTY, MASCULINE; HERO.)

1. **Bly, Robert (1926–)** founder of modern men's movement in 1990s; encouraged discovery of emotional and spiritual self. [Am. Culture: *SJEPC*]

2. **Bogart, Humphrey (1900–1957)** American actor known for roles in *Casablanca* playing the tough guy with a soft heart. [Am. Film: *FOF, MOD*]

3. **Bond, James** fictional character from Ian Fleming's novels and short stories; known for being a debonair womanizer and clever British secret agent. [Br. Lit.: Misc.; Am. Film: Misc.]

4. **Brosnan, Pierce (1953–)** known for his good looks and action-adventure roles; played suave secret agent and ladies man James Bond in four films. [Am. Film: Misc.]

5. **Cagney, Jimmy (1900–1986)** American actor, singer, dancer; roles ranged from tough guy gangster roles to song and dance man George M. Cohan. [Am. Film: *FOF, MOD*]

6. **Craig, Daniel (1968–)** sixth actor to play James Bond, the charming and daring secret agent. [Am. Film: Misc.]

7. **Dirty Harry** tough cop film character Harry Callaghan, played by Clint Eastwood; violent and prone to taking the law into his own hands. [Am. Film: *ODA*]

8. **Eastwood, Clint (1930–)** American movie actor who specializes in tough-guy roles in films like *Dirty Harry.* [Am. Film: *ODA*]

9. *Esquire* sophisticated monthly lifestyle magazine aimed at educated, literate men concerned not only with substance and social issues, but style, sex, and leisure pursuits (established 1933). [Am. Jour.: *SJEPC*]

10. **Flynn, Errol (1909–1959)** Australian film star who specialized in swashbuckling roles; also a notable ladies' man. [Am. Film." *FOF, MOD*]

11. **Ford, Harrison (1942–)** attractive, masculine action-hero actor; notable roles include Indiana Jones and Han Solo. [Am. Film: *SJEPC*; Misc.]

12. **Fury, Sergeant** archetypal he-man. [Comics: "Sergeant Fury and His Howling Commandos" in Horn, 607–608]

13. **Gable, Clark (1900–1960)** American actor, famous for playing manly roles, esp. Rhett Butler in *Gone with the Wind*. [Am. Film: *FOF, MOD*]

14. **Gibson, Mel (1956–)** charismatic actor/director/producer with rugged good looks; as action hero starred in *Mad Max* (1979), *Lethal Weapon* (1987), and *Braveheart* (1995). [Am. Film: *SJEPC*]

15. **Grant, Cary (1906–1986)** English-born American film star; a handsome, elegant, and debonaire leading man. [Am. Film: *FOF, MOD*]

16. **Hemingway, Ernest (1899–1961)** American novelist who lived a life devoted to "manly" pursuits: hunting, bullfighting, fishing, etc. [Am. Lit.: *ODA*]

17. **Henry, John** an African-American hero of legend. [Am. Lit.: Hart, 428]

18. **Heston, Charlton (1924–2008)** handsome, well-built actor starred in such Hollywood blockbusters as *The Ten Commandments* and *Ben-Hur*; his long-time association with the National Rifle Association made him a figure of conservative politics. [Am. Film: *EB*]

19. **Lancaster, Burt (1913–1994)** well-built American actor began as a circus acrobat, then established an acting career that lasted 40 years and encompassed broad range of types. [Am. Film: *SJEPC*]

20. **Macomber, Francis** Hemingway's hero assumes manhood by assertive act. [Am. Lit.: *The Short Happy Life of Francis Macomber*, in Magill IV, 1130–1133]

21. **Malone, Sam** good-looking, athletic owner of bar onTV's *Cheers* (1982–1993); exudes masculinity and attracts women. [Am. TV: *SJEPC*]

22. **Marlboro Man** cigarette advertising campaign established new symbol of virility. [Am. Pop. Culture: Misc.]

23. **McQueen, Steve (1930–1980)** rugged American actor best known for macho roles in quality action films. [Am. Film: *SJEPC*]

24. **Men's Movement** fought stereotyping of males beginning in the 1960s. [Am. Culture: *SJEPC*]

25. **Power, Tyrone (1914–1958)** known for swashbuckler and romantic lead roles in films due to his good looks and fancy swordplay. [Am. Film: Misc.]

26. **Priapus** male generative power personified. [Gk. Myth.: Espy, 27, 224]

27. **Rambo, John** macho protagonist of a series of films; plots involve dramatic use of his guerilla warfare skills for survival and battle. [Am. Film: *SJEPC*]

28. **Reynolds, Burt (1936–)** TV and film star whose machismo, good looks, and charm made him a favorite with male and female audiences alike. [Am. Film and TV: *SJEPC*]

29. **rooster** symbol of maleness. [Folklore: Binder, 85]

30. **Schwarzenegger, Arnold (1947–)** Austrian-born body builder who rose to stardom as action-film hero; went on to become Governor of California. [Am. Film and Politics: *SJEPC*]

31. **stag** symbol of maleness. [Animal Symbolism: Mercatante, 59–60]

32. **Stallone, Sylvester (1946–)** action-film star whose strong but hardly eloquent heroes have won the hearts of fans; best known for roles as boxer Rocky Balboa and Vietnam vet John Rambo. [Am. Film: *SJEPC*]

33. **Sweeney** in poems by T.S. Eliot, symbolizes the sensual, brutal, and materialistic 20th-century man. [Br. Poetry: Benét, 978]

34. **Vallella, Edward (1936–)** American principal dancer with New York City Ballet in 1960s and 1970s who, by his athleticism, debunked belief that ballet was effeminate. [Am. Dance: *SJEPC*]

35. **Viagra** first oral medication to treat male impotence; approved by FDA in 1998, setting off worldwide demand. [Am. Medicine: *SJEPC*]

36. **Wayne, John (1907–1979)** playing heroes and cowboys (sometimes at the same time) made him a Hollywood legend; millions of fans saw him as the epitome of male strength and vigor. [Am. Film: *SJEPC*]

37. **Willis, Bruce (1955–)** well known for his testosterone-fueled character John McClane in the Die Hard series. [Am. Film: Misc.]

Mass Hysteria (See FRENZY.)

453. MASSACRE (See also BRUTALITY, GENOCIDE.)

1. **Acre** after conquering city, Richard I executed 2700 Muslims (1191). [Eur. Hist.: Bishop, 83–84]

2. **Armenian Massacre** Turks decimated Armenian population, dispersed survivors (1896). [Eur. Hist.: *EB*, I: 525]

3. **Bloody Sunday** seeking audience with Czar, workers receive bullets instead (1905). [Russ. Hist.: *EB*, II: 93]

4. **Boston Massacre** skirmish between British troops and Boston crowd (1770). [Am. Hist.: *EB*, II: 180]

5. **Charge of the Light Brigade** Russians massacre English cavalry at Balaklava (1854). [Eur. Hist.: *NCE*, 212; Br. Lit.: Benét, 186]

6. **Columbine** Columbine High School, in Littleton, Colorado; site of school shooting deaths of 15 people by two students, April 20, 1997; symbol of violence in schools, culture, media. [Am. Hist.: Misc.]

7. **ethnic cleansing** Serbo-Croatian term used by the Serbs to describe their forcible displacement and destruction of non-Serbs in the Balkan wars (1990s). [Eur. Hist.: Misc.]

8. **Fetterman Massacre** party of 80 frontiersmen ambushed by Indians (1886). [Am. Hist.: *NCE*, 942]

9. **Goliad** 300 slain by Santa Ana in wake of Alamo (1836). [Am. Hist.: Van Doren, 155]

10. **Guernica** bombing of Guernica (1937); memorialized by Picasso's painting. [Span. Hist.: *NCE*, 1158; Art Hist.: Osborne, 867]

11. **Holy Innocents** infant boys massacred in Bethlehem under Herod. [O.T.: Matthew 2:16–18]

12. **jawbone of ass** with this, Samson kills 1000 men. [O.T.: Judges 15:15]

13. **Katyn Massacre** mass murder of 4250 Polish officers during WWII (c.1939). [Polish Hist.: *NCE*, 1457]

14. **Lawrence, Kansas** Union stronghold where Quantrill's Confederate band killed more than 150 people (1863). [Am. Hist.: *EB*, VIII: 338]

15. **Massacre of Glencoe** treated hospitably, king's men attempt annihilation of MacDonald clan (1692). [Br. Hist.: Brewer *Note-Book*, 567]

16. **Munich Olympics '72** Arab terrorists brutally killed 11 Israeli athletes. [Jew. Hist.: Wigoder, 462]

17. **My Lai Massacre** murder of over 300 Vietnamese villagers by American troops under Lt. William Calley, Jr. (1968). [Am. Hist.: *Facts* (1973), 145]

18. **ox-goad** using this weapon, Shamgar slew 600 Philistines. [O.T.: Judges 3:31]

19. **pogrom** massacre of Jewish villagers by Cossacks, late 19th and early 20th century; now an attack against a religious or ethnic group, especially one that is anti-Semitic. [Russ. Hist.: *FOF, MOD*]

20. **Sicilian Vespers** massacre of French (Angevins) Sicilian nationals (1282). [Ital. Hist.: *NCE*, 2511]

21. **St. Bartholomew's Day Massacre** thousands of French Huguenots murdered for their faith (1572). [Fr. Hist.: *EB*, VII: 775]

22. **St. Valentine's Day Massacre** murder of seven members of a gang of bootleggers in Chicago (1929). [Am. Hist.: *EB*, VII: 797]

23. **third of May (1808)** Murat's squads executed hundreds of Spanish citizens; memorialized in Goya's painting. [Sp. Hist. and Sp. Art: Daniel, 220]

24. **Tiananmen Square** seven-week demonstration for democratic reform by millions of unarmed protestors in Beijing; after warnings to disperse from government, several hundred shot dead. [Chinese Hist.: Misc.]

25. **Whitman Massacre** murder of missionary Marcus Whitman and family by Cayuse Indians (1847). [Am. Hist.: *NCE*, 2972]

26. **Wounded Knee** scene of the slaughter of 200 Sioux Indians (1890). [Am. Hist.: Van Doren, 306]

27. **Wyoming Massacre** colonial militia butchered by Tory-Indian force (1776). [Am. Hist.: Jameson, 564]

454. MATCHMAKING

1. **Kecal** marriage broker whose plans are foiled by a pair of lovers. [Czech Opera: Smetana *The Bartered Bride* in Osborne *Opera*, 32]

2. **Levi, Dolly** personable marriage broker who manages to make an excellent match for herself. [Am. Lit.: Thornton Wilder *The Matchmaker*; Am. Theater.: *Hello, Dolly!* in *On Stage*, 454]

3. **Woodhouse, Emma** mistakenly thinks she has a talent for finding mates for her young friends. [Br. Lit.: Jane Austen *Emma*]

455. MATHEMATICS

1. **Archimedes (c. 287–c. 212 B.C.)** Greek mathematician; formulated theory of"pi" and invented the Archimedean screw. [Gk. Science: *BBI*]

2. **Euclid (c.300 B.C.)** Greek mathematician; formulated theories in plane and solid geometry. [Gk. Science: *EB*]

3. **Fermat, Pierre (1601–1666)** French mathematician who developed an algebraic theorem ("Fermat's last theorem") that remained unsolved until 1995; an allusion to a particularly baffling problem. [Fr. Science: *EB*]

4. **Leibnitz, Gottfried Wilhelm (1646–1716)** German mathematician and philosopher; discovered the principles of calculus (independent of Newton). [Ger. Science: *EB*]

5. **Nash, John (1928–)** American mathematician and Nobel Prize-winning economist in game theory; subject of book and film *A Beautiful Mind*. [Amer. Science: *BTSci.v.7*]

6. **Newton, Sir Isaac (1642–1727)** English physicist and mathematician; formulated key laws of motion, developed calculus. [Br. Science: *BBI*]

7. **Pascal, Blaise (1623–1662)** French mathematician and philosopher; developed basic geometric theorem and invented first calculator. [Fr. Science: *EB*]

8. **Pythagorus (c. 582–c. 500 B.C.)** Greek philosopher and mathematician; developed fundamental theorems in geometry. [Gk. Science: *EB*]

Matricide (See MURDER.)

456. MEDDLESOMENESS

1. **Norris, Mrs.** interfering, spiteful, gossiping busybody. [Br. Lit.: Austen *Mansfield Park* in Magill I, 562]

2. **Werle, Gregers** interferes with the Ekdals' lives and brings about their daughter's suicide. [Nor. Lit.: Ibsen *The Wild Duck* in Magill I, 1113]

3. **Whiteside, Sheridan** meddles in his host's family affairs and insults the townspeople by interfering. [Am. Lit.: *The Man Who Came to Dinner* in Benét, 631]

Mediation (See PEACEMAKING.)

457. MEDICINE (See also HEALING, HEALTH.)

1. **Andromeda strain** biological agent in Michael Crichton novel of same name has become commonly used term for any newly discovered virulent strain. [Am. Usage: *SJEPC*]

2. **Apollo** patron of medicine. [Gk. Myth.: Kravitz, 28]

3. *Ben Casey* dramatic TV series of 1960s portrayed neurosurgeon main character as ideal doctor. [Am. TV: *SJEPC*]

4. **Benassis, Dr.** devotes himself to the poor and miserable inhabitants of a remote village. [Fr. Lit.: Balzac *The Country Doctor*; Magill II, 185]

5. **Bull, George** ignorant physician who cannot prevent an epidemic. [Am. Lit.: Cozzens *The Last Adam* Haydn & Fuller, 409]

6. **caduceus** snake-entwined staff; emblem of medical profession. [Gk. Myth.: Kravitz, 49]

7. **Cosmas, Saint and Saint Damian** patron saints; brothers, practiced medicine without charge. [Christian Hagiog.: Attwater, 94]

8. **Diver, Dick** failed psychiatrist becomes a small-town general practitioner. [Am. Lit.: *Tender Is the Night*]

9. *ER* realistic, fast-paced TV drama takes place in emergency room of inner-city Chicago hospital; features flawed but caring and competent characters in the medical profession. [Am. TV: *SJEPC*]

10. **Ferguson, George** young surgeon who goes to Vienna to become better qualified for a hospital job. [Am. Lit.: Kingsley *Men in White*; Haydn & Fuller, 183]

11. *Grey's Anatomy* primetime drama set in a Seattle, WA hospital; follows the work and lives of surgical interns, attending surgeons, and patients. [Am. TV: Misc.]

12. **Herriot, James (1916–1995)** pseudonym of James Wight; English veterinarian whose short stories evoke life in the Yorkshire countryside and his deep love of animals. [Br. Lit.: *All Creatures Great and Small*]

13. **Hippocrates (c. 460–c. 360 B.C.)** Greek physician and "Father of Medicine." [Gk. Hist.: *NCE*, 1246]

14. **Hippocratic oath** ethical code of medicine. [Western Culture: *EB*, 11: 827]

15. *House* medical drama centering on the bitter and cynical doctor Gregory House; despite his rough-around-the-edges personality, House brilliantly solves each medical mystery. [Am. TV: Misc.]

16. **Kildare, Dr.** character in film and TV; idealistic, caring young physician. [Am. Film, TV: Misc.]

17. **magic bullet** term for miracle cure, associated with the development of the drug Salvarsan to cure Syphilis by Paul Ehrlich. [Science: *FOF, MOD*]

18. ***Marcus Welby, M.D.*** TV show about avuncular doctor of impeccable ethics. [Am. TV: Terrace, II, 66]

19. **Mayo Clinic** voluntary association of more than 500 physicians in Rochester, Minnesota. [Am. Hist.: *EB*, 11: 723]

20. **Mitchell, Paris** studies medicine in the U.S. and abroad; returns as a physician at an insane asylum. [Am. Lit.: *King's Row*; Magill I, 478]

21. **Paean** physician to the gods. [Gk. Myth.: Espy, 29]

22. **Prince, Nan** becomes a successful physician like her foster father. [Am. Lit.: Jewett *A Country Doctor*; Magill II, 183]

23. **Rieux, Dr. Bernard** works unceasingly to relieve victims of a deadly epidemic. [Fr. Lit.: Camus *The Plague*]

24. ***Scrubs*** comedy-drama focusing on the lives of doctors and various employees at Sacred Heart Hospital; features fast-paced dialogue and slapstick comedy. [Am. TV: Misc.]

25. ***St. Elsewhere*** American drama about the goings-on at St. Eligius, a Boston hospital known for receiving patients no other hospital wants. [Am. TV: Misc.]

458. MEDIOCRITY

1. **B movie** second-rate, low-budget film. [Am. Film: *SJEPC*]

2. **bush league** from baseball's lower league, a term for inferior performance. [Am. Culture: *FOF, MOD*]

3. **Kmart** discount chain store noted for bargain prices, mediocre merchandise. [Am. Business: *FOF, MOD*]

4. **Made-for-Television Movies** lower budgets meant often mediocre plots and acting. [Am. TV: *SJEPC*]

5. **man in the street** term coined by Ralph Waldo Emerson to describe the average, not-too-intelligent American. [Am. Culture: *FOF, MOD*]

6. **Muzak** programmed background music piped into public places, often inferior and bland. [Am. Music: *SJEPC*]

7. **romance novels** formulaic love stories with happy endings written mostly by women for women; account for half of all mass-produced paperback sales. [Am. Lit.: *SJEPC*]

459. MELANCHOLY (See also GRIEF.)

1. **Acheron** river of woe in the underworld. [Gk. Myth.: Howe, 5]

2. ***Anatomy of Melancholy*** lists causes, symptoms, and characteristics of melancholy. [Br. Lit.: *Anatomy of Melancholy*]

3. **Barton, Amos** beset by woes. [Br. Lit.: "Sad Fortunes of Amos Barton" in Walsh *Modern*, 45]

4. **black bile** humor effecting temperament of gloominess. [Medieval Physiology: Hall, 130]

5. **blues** melancholy, bittersweet music born among African Americans. [Am. Music: Scholes, 113]

6. **Cargill, Rev. Josiah** serious, moody, melacholic minister. [Br. Lit.: *St. Ronan's Well*]

7. **Carstone, Richard** driven to gloom by collapse of expectations. [Br. Lit.: *Bleak House*]

8. **cave of Trophonius** oracle so awe-inspiring, consulters never smiled again. [Gk. Myth.: Brewer *Dictionary*, 1103]

9. **Eeyore** amusingly gloomy, morose donkey; character in A.A. Milne's Winnie-the-Pooh tales.. [Br. Children's Lit.: Jones]

10. *Elegy Written in a Country Churchyard* meditative poem of a melancholy mood. [Br. Lit.: Harvey, 266]

11. **Ellis Island** immigration center where many families were separated; "isle of tears." [Am. Hist.: Flexner, 193]

12. **Gummidge, Mrs.** "lone lorn creetur" with melancholy disposition. [Br. Lit.: *David Copperfield*]

13. **Hamlet** black mood dominates his consciousness. [Br. Lit.: Shakespeare *Hamlet*]

14. **hare** flesh brings melancholy to those who eat it. [Animal Symbolism: Mercatante, 125]

15. *Il Penseroso* poem celebrating the pleasures of melancholy and solitude. [Br. Lit.: Milton *Il Penseroso* in Magill IV, 577]

16. **Jaques** "can suck melancholy out of a song." [Br. Lit.: *As You Like It*]

17. **Mock Turtle** forever weeping and bemoaning his fate. [Br. Children's Lit.: *Alice's Adventures in Wonderland*]

18. **Mudville** no joy here when Casey struck out. [Am. Sports Lit.: "Casey at the Bat" in Turlin, 642]

19. **Orpheus** composed, sang many melancholic songs in memory of deceased Eurydice. [Gk. Myth.: *Orpheus and Eurydice*, Magill I, 700–701]

20. **Roquentin, Antoine** discomfited by his existence's purposelessness, solitarily despairs. [Fr. Lit.: *Nausea*]

21. **Sad Sack** hapless and helpless soldier; resigned to his fate. [Am. Comics: Horn, 595–596]

22. **Valley of the Shadow of Death** life's gloominess. [O.T.: Psalms 23:4]

23. **Wednesday's child** full of woe. [Nurs. Rhyme: Opie, 309]

501

460. MEMORY

1. **Aethalides** herald of the Argonauts; had perfect memory. [Gk. Myth.: Kravitz, 11]

2. **Balderstone, Thomas** knew all of Shakespeare by heart. [Br. Lit.: *Sketches by Boz*]

3. **Eunoe** river whose water sparks remembrance of kindnesses. [Ital. Lit.: *Purgatory*, 33]

4. *Fahrenheit 451* in a future America where books are prohibited, a group of people memorize texts in order to preserve their content. [Am. Lit.: Bradbury *Fahrenheit 451* in Weiss, 289]

5. **madeleine** cookie that awakened the stream of Marcel's recollections. [Fr. Lit.: Proust *Remembrance of Things Past*]

6. **Memory, Mr.** during his stage performance his feats of memory enable him to signal clues to a man trying to thwart England's enemies. [Am. Film: *The 39 Steps*]

7. **Mneme** Boeotian wellspring which whetted the memory. [Gk. Myth.: Wheeler, 713]

8. **Mnemosyne** goddess of memory; mother of Muses. [Gk. Myth.: Espy, 20]

9. **Munin** one of Odin's ravens; regarded as embodying memory. [Norse Myth.: Leach, 761]

10. **Nepenthe** Egyptian drug said to banish bad memories. [Gk. Myth.: *ODA*]

11. **Proust, Marcel (1871–1922)** author of the monumental *A la recherche du temps perdu* (*In Search of Lost Time*), an exploration of time and the transformation of memory into art. [Fr. Lit.: *ODA*]

Mercy (See FORGIVENESS.)

461. MESSENGER

1. **Aerthalides** herald of the Argonauts. [Gk. Myth.: Kravitz, 11]

2. **Alden, John (1599–1687)** speaks to Priscilla Mullins for Miles Standish. [Am. Lit.: "The Courtship of Miles Standish" in Hart, 188–189]

3. **caduceus** Mercury's staff; symbol of messengers. [Rom. Myth.: Jobes, 266–267]

4. **dove** sent by Noah to see if the waters were abated; returns with an olive leaf. [O.T.: Genesis 8:8–11]

5. **eagle** symbolic carrier of God's word to all. [Christian Symbolism: Appleton, 35]

6. **Gabriel** announces births of Jesus and John the Baptist. [N.T.: Luke 1:19, 26]

7. **Hermes** messenger of the gods; called Mercury by the Romans. [Gk. Myth.: Wheeler *Dictionary*, 240]

8. **Iris** messenger of the gods. [Gk. Myth.: Kravitz, 130; Gk. Lit.: *Iliad*]

9. **Irus** real name was Arunaeus; messenger of Penelope's suitors. [Gk. Lit.: *Odyssey*]

10. **Muhammad (c.570–632)** Islamic prophet called the Messenger (ar-Rasul). [Islam: *UIMT*, 180]

11. **Munin and Hugin** Odin's two ravens; brought him news from around world. [Norse Myth.: Leach, 761]

12. **Nasby** nickname for U.S. postmasters. [Am. Usage: Brewer *Dictionary*, 745–746]

13. **Pheidippides** ran 26 miles from Marathon to Athens to carry news of Greek defeat of Persians. [Gk. Legend: Zimmerman, 159]

14. **Pony Express** speedy relay mail-carrying system of 1860s. [Am. Hist.: Flexner, 276]

15. **Reuters** news agency; established as telegraphic and pigeon post bureau (1851). [Br. Hist.: Benét, 852]

16. **Revere, Paul (1735–1818)** warned colonials of British advance (1775). [Am. Hist.: 425–426]

17. **staff** symbolic of a courier on a mission. [Christian Symbolism: Appleton, 4]

18. **Stickles, Jeremy** messenger for the king of England (1880s). [Br. Lit.: *Lorna Doone*, Magill I, 524–526]

19. **Strogoff, Michael** courier of the czar. [Fr. Lit.: *Michael Strogoff*]

20. **thorn** according to Paul, a messenger of Satan sent to torment. [N.T.: II Corinthians 12:7]

21. **Western Union** company founded in 1851; provides telegraphic service in U.S. [Am. Hist.: *NCE*, 2958]

462. MIDDLE CLASS

1. **Babbitt** self-satisfied conformer to middle-class ideas and ideals. [Am. Lit.: *Babbitt*]

2. **baby boomers** post-World War II generation (born 1946–1964) stereotyped as self-indulgent, suburban, and conventional. [Am. Culture: *SJEPC*]

3. **bourgeois** reflecting middle-class values, especially materialism and conformity to social norms. [Am. Culture: *FOF, MOD*]

4. **bungalow** simple, functional, unpretentious house design rooted in the Arts and Crafts movement made home ownership affordable for America's middle class in the early to mid-20th century. [Am. Architecture: *SJEPC*]

5. **cocktail parties** social gatherings featuring mixed alcoholic beverages and snacks became popular in 1950s suburban America. [Am. Culture: *SJEPC*]

6. *Death of a Salesman* the American Dream eludes salesman Willy Loman, who longs for material success and middle-class status in Arthur Miller's 1949 masterpiece. [Am. Theater: *SJEPC*; Harris *Characters*, 269]

7. **minivan** utilitarian vehicle introduced in 1983; soon parked in nearly every middle-class garage in America. [Am. Culture: *SJEPC*]

8. *Saturday Evening Post, The* known as *The Post*; dominated American magazine readership for first thirty years of twentieth century; characterized by common-sense conservatism and middle-class values. [Am. Jour.: *SJEPC*]

9. **suburbia** American residential communities near cities peopled with middle-class residents, mostly families who had fled crowded, unsanitary urban centers. [Am. Pop. Culture: *SJEPC*]

463. MILITARY (See also BATTLE, MILITARY LEADER, WAR.)

1. **Atkins, Tommy** nickname for English soldiers. [Br. Folklore: Walsh *Modern*, 33]

2. **Beetle Bailey** hapless private who resists authority and seeks easy way out. [Comics: Horn, 105–106]

3. **Clancy, Tom (1947–)** bestselling author writes thrilling, technologically accurate, action-packed novels of political intrigue, espionage, and the military, such as *The Hunt for Red October* (1984) and *The Sum of All Fears* (1991). [Am. Lit.: *SJEPC*]

4. **Ellyat, Jack** from Connecticut; Union trooper undergoes many hardships. [Am. Lit.: "John Brown's Body" in Magill I, 445–448]

5. **Fuzzy-Wuzzy** name for bushy-haired Sudanese warriors celebrated in a Kipling ballad. [Br. Lit.: Kipling *Barrack-Room Ballads* in Benét, 81]

6. **G. I. Joe** any American soldier. [Am. Military Slang: Misc.]

7. **GI Joe action figure** first plastic action figure for boys, outfitted to resemble World War II combat soldier, debuted in 1964. [Am. Hist.: *SJEPC*]

8. **Good Soldier Schweik** simple, innocent Czech soldier in the Austrian army during World War I. [Czech Lit.: *The Good Soldier: Schweik*, Magill IV, 390–392]

9. **Gurkhas** Nepalese mercenaries, renowned for valor. [Nepalese Hist.: *NCE*, 1165]

10. **Hannibal (247–182 B.C.)** Carthiginian general who led soldiers, and elephants, over the Alps; battled Romans. [Ital. Hist.: *ODA*]

11. **Hessians** soldiers for hire, from Hesse-Cassel, Germany, many fought in the American Revolution; now, a term for a mercenary. [Am. Hist. *FOF, MOD*]

12. **Janissaries** elite Turkish infantry. [Turk. Hist.: Fuller, I, 499, 508]

13. **K.P.** initials of the Army's "kitchen police," refers to all work in the kitchen. [Am. Military Slang: Misc.]

14. **Minute Men** originally soldiers in the Revolutionary War, ready "at a minute's notice"; now a term used to describe a group who respond quickly to an incident; also an extra-military group defending the U.S. border with Mexico. [Am. Hist: Misc.]

15. **Sad Sack** whose travails reflect those of all soldiers. [Comics: Horn, 595–596]

16. **Sherston, George** involved in the heavy action of World War I. [Br. Lit.: *Memoirs of an Infantry Officer* in Magill I, 579]

17. **Spartans** residents of Greek city known for its stern dedication to militarism. [Gr. Hist.: *EB*, IX: 403]

18. **Uncle Toby and Corporal Trim** inarticulate ex-soldier and his loquacious orderly reconstruct campaigns on small bowling green. [Br. Lit.: *Tristram Shandy* in Magill I, 1027]

19. **Wingate, Clay** from Georgia; Confederate counterpart of Jack Ellyat. [Am. Lit.: "John Brown's Body" in Magill I, 445–448]

464. MILITARY LEADER

1. **Alexander the Great (356–323 B.C.)** considered by many one of the greatest military commanders in history; undefeated in battle and conqueror of Persian empire. [Gk. Hist.: Misc.]

2. **Bonaparte, Napolean (1769–1821)** French military leader, self-declared emperor, and conqueror of Europe; symbol of power and amibition [Fr. Hist.: *ODA*]

3. **Garibaldi, Giuseppe (1807–1882)** Italian leader who unified Italy and led the movement for independence. [Ital. Hist.: *ODA*]

4. **Hannibal (247–182 B.C.)** Carthaginian general who led soldiers, with elephants, over the Alps; battled the Roman army. [Ital. Hist.: *ODA*]

5. **MacArthur, Douglas (1880–1964)** preeminent general who received Medal of Honor (1942) for his service in the Philippines during WWII. [Am. Hist.: Misc.]

6. **Nelson, Lord Horatio (1758–1805)** English admiral, hero of Trafalgar, Britian's most famous naval leader. [Br. Hist.: Misc.]

7. **Patton, George S. (1885–1945)** leading U.S. Army combat general of WWII; outspoken, strict disciplinarian and brilliant strategist. [Am. Hist.: Misc.]

8. **Schwartzkoff, Norman, Jr. (1934–)** won three Silver Stars as a colonel in Vietnam; Commander in Chief of U.S. forces in Operation Desert Shield in 1988. [Am. Hist.: Misc.]

9. **Von Bismarck, Otto (1815–1898)** Prussian military commander and political leader; known as the "Iron Chancelor," unified Germany with "the iron fist in the velvet glove." [Ger. Hist.: *FOF, MOD*]

10. **von Clauswitz, Karl (1780–1831)** German general known for his idea of "total war": destruction of the enemy by destruction of population, resources, as a military goal. [Ger. Hist.: *FOF, MOD*]

465. MIMICRY

1. **chameleon** lizard able to change the color of its skin to match brown or green surroundings; has come to mean "inconstant person." [Western Culture: Misc.]

2. **Costard** apes Elizabethan courtly language. [Br. Lit.: *Love's Labour Lost*]

3. **Doolittle, Eliza** slum girl taught by professor to imitate upper class. [Br. Lit.: *Pygmalion*]

4. **lyrebird** Australian bird; one of the most famous mimic species. [Ornithology: Sparks, 116]

5. **mockingbird** noted for mimicking songs of other birds; one of the world's most noted singers. [Ornithology: Sparks, 116]

6. **monkey** known to copy human actions. [Western Culture: Misc.]

7. **myna** certain species are able to mimic human speech and other sounds. [Ornithology: Sparks]

8. **parrot** bird able to mimic human speech; hence, *parrot* "to repeat or imitate." [Western Culture: Misc.]

466. MIRACLE

1. **Aaron's rod** flowering rod proved him to be God's choice. [O.T.: Numbers 17:8]

2. **Agnes, Saint** hair grew to cover nakedness. [Christian Hagiog.: Brewster, 76–77]

3. **Anthony of Padua, Saint** believed to have preached effectively to school of fishes. [Christian Legend: Benét, 39]

4. **Cana** at wedding feast, Christ turns water into wine. [N.T.: John, 2:1–11]

5. **deus ex machina** improbable agent introduced to solve a dilemma. [Western Drama: *LLEI*, I: 279]

6. **Elais** produced olive oil from ground by touch. [Gk. Myth.: Kravitz, 86]

7. **Euphemus** Argonaut; could cross water without getting wet. [Gk. Myth.: Kravitz, 95]

8. **Geppetto** his wish fulfilled when marionette becomes real boy. [Ital. Children's Lit.: *Pinocchio*; Am. Film: *Pinocchio* in *Disney Films*, 32–37]

9. **Holy Grail** chalice enabled Sir Galahad to heal a cripple. [Br. Lit.: *Le Morte d'Arthur*]

10. **Jesus Christ** as son of God, performed countless miracles. [N.T.: Matthew, Mark, Luke, John]

11. **loaves and fishes** Jesus multiplies fare for his following. [N.T.: Matthew 14:15–21; John 6:5–14]

12. **Lourdes** underground spring revealed to Bernadette Soubirous in visions (1858); major pilgrimage site. [Fr. Hist.: *EB*, VI: 352; Am. Lit.: *Song of Bernadette*; Am. Cinema: *The Song of Bernadetter* in Halliwell, 670]

13. **Marah** undrinkably bitter waters, sweetened by Moses. [O.T.: Exodus 15:23–25]

14. **parting of the Pamphylean Sea** Alexander's hosts traverse sea in Persian march. [Class. Hist.: Gaster, 238]

15. **parting of the Red Sea** divinely aided, Moses parts the waters for an Israelite escape. [O.T.: Exodus 14:15–31]

16. **rod of Moses** transforms into serpent, then back again. [O.T.: Exodus 4:24]

17. **Tannhäuser** as a sign that the Pope should absolve him, the papal scepter suddenly sprouts green leaves. [Ger. Myth.: Brewer *Dictionary*, 932]

467. MIRROR

1. **Alasnam's mirror** indicates to Alasnam a girl's virtue. [Arab. Lit.: *Arabian Nights*, "Prince Zeyn Alasnam"]

2. **Alice's looking-glass** Alice passes through this into dreamland. [Br. Cjhildren's Lit.: *Through the Looking-Glass*]

3. **Cambuscan's mirror** warns of impending adversity; indicates another's love. [Br. Lit.: *Canterbury Tales*, "The Squire's Tale"]

4. **Lao's mirror** reflects the looker's mind and thoughts. [Br. Lit.: *Citizen of the World*]

5. **Merlin's magic mirror** allows king to see whatever concerns him. [Br. Lit.: *Faerie Queene*]

6. **Mirror, mirror** magically tells arrogant queen who is the most beautiful of all. [Ger. Fairy Tale: "Snow White" in Grimm, 184]

7. **Perseus's shield** he uses it as a mirror so that he will not have to look directly at Medusa. [Gk. Myth.: Howe, 214]

8. **Prester John's mirror** allows him to see happenings throughout his dominions. [Medieval Legend: Brewer *Handbook*, 710]

9. **Reynard's wonderful mirror** imaginary mirror; reflects doings a mile away. [Medieval Lit.: *Reynard the Fox*]

10. **Vulcan's mirror** showed past, present, and future to viewer. [Br. Lit.: *Orchestra*, Brewer *Handbook*, 710]

468. MISANTHROPY

1. **Ahab, Captain** consumed by hate, pursues whale that ripped off his leg. [Am. Lit.: *Moby Dick*]

2. **Alceste** antisocial hero. [Fr. Lit.: *Le Misanthrope*]

3. *Confidence Man, The* Melville's social satire castigating mankind. [Am. Lit.: *The Confidence Man*, Magill III, 221–223]

4. **Dryas** hated mankind; avoided public appearances. [Rom. Myth.: Kravitz, 84]

5. **Fuller's thistle** indicates hatred of mankind. [Flower Symbolism: *Flora Symbolica*, 178]

6. **Nemo, Captain** brilliant captain of submarine, "Nautilus"; bitter misanthropy the reason for his undersea seclusion. [Fr. Lit.: *Twenty Thousand Leagues Under the Sea*]

7. **Oscar the Grouch** Muppet character from *Sesame Street* TV show for children; lives in trash can; cynical and antisocial; revels in dirty, messy side of life. [Am. TV: Misc.]

8. **Sub-Mariner** friend of fish, scourge of man. [Comics: Horn, 640]

9. **teasel** indicates hatred of mankind. [Flower Symbolism: *Flora Symbolica*, 178]

10. **Timon** "undone by goodness," turns misanthropic. [Br. Lit.: *Timon of Athens*]

Misbehavior (See MISCHIEVOUSNESS.)

469. MISCHIEVOUSNESS (See also HIGHSPIRITEDNESS; JOKE, PRACTICAL.)

1. **Anansie** trickster spider from West African folklore [Afr. Folklore *ODA*, 259]

2. **Ate** goddess of evil and mischief. [Gk. Myth.: Parrinder, 33; Kravitz, 39]

3. **Beaver** mischievous ten-year-old beset by trivial troubles. [Am. TV: "Leave It to Beaver" in Terrace, II, 18–19]

4. **Beg, Little Callum** devilish page. [Br. Lit.: *Waverley*]

5. **Benjamin Bunny** cousin to Peter Rabbit; takes Peter back to Mr. McGregor's garden where they are trapped by a cat when Benjamin persuades Peter to help him steal vegetables. [Br. Children's Lit.: *The Tale of Benjamin Bunny*]

6. **Brer Rabbit** clever trickster. [Children's Lit.: *Uncle Remus*]

7. **Brown, Buster** turn-of-the-century *enfant terrible*, [Am. Comics: Horn, 145]

8. **Cat in the Hat** famous Dr. Seuss character from children's literature; talks children into breaking their parents' rules and creates total chaos in their home, which he magically cleans up just in time. [Am. Children's Lit.: Jones]

9. **Cercopes** apelike pygmies; tried to steal Hercules' weapons. [Gk. Myth.: Leach, 206]

10. **crocodile** symbolizes naughtiness and chicanery. [Jewish Tradition: Jobes, 382]

11. **Dennis the Menace** latter-day Buster Brown, complete with dog. [Am. Comics: Horn, 201]

12. **Devil's Night** October 30; night before Halloween is dedicated to playing pranks. [Am. Folklore: Misc.]

13. **Eulenspiegel, Till** legendary peasant known for his pranks. [Ger. Folklore: Benét, 325–326]

14. **Finn, Huckleberry** mischievous, sharp-witted boy has many adventures. [Am. Lit.: *Huckleberry Finn*]

15. **Georgie Porgie** kissed the girls and made them cry. [Nurs. Rhyme: Opie, 185]

16. **Junior** "the mean widdle kid," as portrayed by comic Red Skelton. [Am. Radio and TV: "The Red Skelton Show" in Buxton, 197]

17. **Katzenjammer Kids** twin Teutonic terrors. [Comics: "The Captain and the Kids" in Horn, 156–157]

18. **Lampwick** archetypal juvenile delinquent leads Pinocchio astray. [Am. Film: *Pinocchio* in *Disney Films*, 32–37]

19. **Little Rascals, The** scamps unite to terrorize adults. [Am. TV: Terrace, II, 31]

20. **Max** protagonist of children's book *Where the Wild Things Are* by Maurice Sendak; gets into mischief and runs away to the land of the Wild Things when he is sent to his room as punishment. [Am. Children's Lit.: Jones]

21. **Merop's Son** misguided do-gooder. [Gk. and Roman Myth.: Brewer *Dictionary*, 704]

22. **Moth** "handful of wit"; Armado's "pretty knavish page." [Br. Lit.: *Love's Labour's Lost*]

23. **Nicka-Nan Night** Shrove Tuesday eve when boys play tricks. [Br. Folklore: Brewer *Dictionary*, 756]

24. **otter** symbol of playfulness and mischievousness. [Symbolism: CEOS&S]

25. **Our Gang** group of children in comedy series; always into mischief. [Am. Film: Halliwell, 546; Am. TV: "The Little Rascals" in Terrace, II, 31]

26. **Peck's Bad Boy** mischievous boy plays pranks on his father. [Am. Lit.: *Peck's Bad Boy*, Hart, 642]

27. **Peter Rabbit** always ransacking Farmer MacGregor's patch. [Br. Children's Lit.: *The Tale of Peter Rabbit*]

28. **pixies** prank-playing fairies; mislead travelers. [Br. Folklore: Briggs, 328–330]

29. **pooka** wild shaggy colt that misled beknighted travelers. [Br. Folklore: Briggs]

30. **Puck** knavish hobgoblin who plays pranks. [Br. Folklore and Lit.: *A Midsummer Night's Dream*]

31. **Rooney, Andy** scatterbrained lad; makes trouble without trying. [Irish Lit.: *Handy Andy*]

32. **Sawyer, Tom** hookey-playing, imaginative lad of St. Petersburg, Missouri. [Am. Lit.: *Tom Sawyer*]

33. **Stalky** with his two friends, devises ingenious pranks that make life miserable for the masters of the school. [Br. Lit.: Kipling *Stalky and Company*]

34. **Wag, Charlie** school-skipping delinquent of penny dreadful. [Br. Lit.: *Charlie Wag, the Boy Burglar*, Opie, 117]

470. MISERLINESS (See also GREED.)

1. **Benny, Jack (1894–1974)** the king of penny pinchers. [Am. Radio and TV: "The Jack Benny Program" in Buxton, 122–123; TV: Terrace, 402]

2. **Carey, William** Philip's penny-pinching, smugly religious uncle. [Br. Lit.: Magill I, 670–672]

3. **Collyer, Homer (1882–1947) and Langley (1886–1947)** wealthy brothers who lived barren and secluded lives in junk-laden Harlem mansion. [Am. Hist.: *Facts* (1947) 116; Am. Lit.: *My Brother's Keeper*]

4. **Euclio** parsimonious and distrustful man hoards gold treasure. [Rom. Lit.: *The Pot of Gold*]

5. **Getty, John Paul (1892–1976)** American billionaire also known for miserliness [Am. Business *ODA*]

6. **Grandet, Monsieur** his loathsome miserliness and greed ruin the lives of his family. [Fr. Lit.: *Eugènie Grandet* in Magill I, 258]

7. **Green, Hetty (1834–1916)** "Witch of Wall Street"; financial wizard whose miserliness became legendary. [Am. Hist.: *The Day They Shook the Plum Tree*]

8. **Harpagon** his hoard of money means more to him than do his children. [Fr. Drama: Molière *The Miser*]

9. **Marner, Silas** cares only to amass gold; robbed of it, he finds new meaning in love for abandoned child. [Br. Lit.: Benét, 930]

10. **McTeague, Trina** loves to count her hoard of coins, is niggardly with her husband. [Am. Lit.: *McTeague*, Magill I, 537; Am. Cinema: *Greed*, Halliwell, 176]

11. **Mertz, Fred** neighbor to the Ricardos in *I Love Lucy* sitcom; many jokes made about his frugality. [Am. TV: *SJEPC*]

12. **Pitt, Crawley** inherits, marries, and hoards money. [Br. Lit.: *Vanity Fair*]

13. **Plyushkin** incredibly miserly landowner serves Tchitchikov a year-old Easter cake. [Russ. Lit.: Gogol *Dead Souls*]

14. **Scrooge, Ebenezer** "grasping old sinner" who learns that miserliness leads only to loneliness and pain. [Br. Lit.: "A Christmas Carol" in Benét, 196]

15. **Sieppe, Trina** begrudged every penny she spent. [Am. Lit.: *McTeague*]

471. MISSIONARY

1. **Aubrey, Father** converts savages to Christianity. [Fr. Lit.: *Atala*]

2. **Boniface, Saint** missionary to the German infidels in 8th century. [Christian Hagiog.: Brewster, 271]

3. **Buck, Pearl S. (1892–1973)** living in China as the daughter of missionaries informed her literature, but her criticism of "typical" missionaries as zealots upset the Presbyterian orthodoxy. [Am. Lit.: *SJEPC*]

4. **Davidson, Rev. Alfred** attempts to convert Sadie Thompson to religion but ends up seducing her. [Br. Lit.: "Miss Thompson" in Benét, 675; Am. Film: "Rain" in Halliwell, 593]

5. **Latour, Bishop and Fr. Vaillant** priests establish a diocese in New Mexico. [Am. Lit.: Cather *Death Comes for the Archbishop* in Magill I, 199]

6. **Livingstone, David (1813–1873)** explorer and missionary in Africa. [Br. Hist.: NCE, 1596]

7. **Patrick, Saint (c. 385–461)** early missionary to, and patron saint of, Ireland. [Christian Hagiog.: Brewster, 138]

8. **Salvation Army** international religious organization known for its charitable and missionary work. [Christian Rel.: NCE, 2408–2409]

9. **Society of Jesus** Roman Catholic order distinguished in foreign missions. [Christian Hist.: NCE, 1412]

10. **Xavier, Saint Francis** indefatigable pioneer converter of East Indies. [Christian Hagiog.: Attwater, 141–142]

472. MISTRESS (See also COURTESAN, PROSTITUTE.)

1. **Abra** favorite concubine of Solomon. [Br. Lit.: *Solomon on the Vanity of the World*, Benét, 3]

2. **Bains, Lulu** mistress of Elmer Gantry. [Am. Lit.: *Elmer Gantry*]

3. **Brangwen, Ursula** living with Anton Skrebensky without marriage license causes shock. [Br. Lit.: *The Rainbow*, Magill I, 800–802]

4. **Bridehead, Sue** mistress of Jude Fawley; two children by him. [Br. Lit.: *Jude the Obscure*]

5. **Burden, Joanna** mistress and benefactor to Joe Christmas. [Am. Lit.: *Light in August*]

6. **Chatterley, Lady** mistress of the gamekeeper Mellors. [Br. Lit.: Lawrence *Lady Chatterley's Lover* in Benét, 559]

7. **De Gournay, Mlle.** Montaigne's "adopted daughter." [Fr. Hist.: Brewer *Handbook*, 633]

8. **de Maintenon, Marquise** royal mistress and later wife of Louis XIV. [Fr. Hist.: Benét, 622]

9. **de Pompadour, Marquise (1721–1764)** official mistress of Louis XV of France; very influential—culturally, politically, intellectually—at French court. [Fr. Hist.: Benét, 802]

10. **Guinevere, Queen** King Arthur's wife; Sir Launcelot's mistress. [Br. Lit.: *Le Morte d'Arthur*]

11. **Merle, Mme.** Osmund's mistress, by whom he has a daughter, Pansy. [Am. Lit.: James *Portrait of a Lady* in Magill I, 766]

12. **Perdita** stage name of Mary Robinson, mistress of George IV when he was Prince of Wales. [Br. Hist.: Benét, 773]

13. **Roxana** mistress of many before marrying one of her lovers. [Br. Lit.: *Roxana*]

14. **Simonet, Albertine** paramour of narrator. [Fr. Lit.: *Remembrance of Things Past*]

473. MOCKERY

1. **Abas** changed into lizard for mocking Demeter. [Rom. Myth.: *Metamorphoses*, Zimmerman, 1]

2. **Beckmesser** pompous object of practical jokes. [Ger. Opera: Wagner, *Meistersinger*, Westerman, 226–227]

3. **crown of thorns** Christ thus ridiculed as king of Jews. [N.T.: Matthew 27:29; Mark 15:17; John 19:2–5]

4. **Ecce Homo** Pilate's presentation of Jesus to Jews. [N.T.: John 19:5]

5. **I.N.R.I.** inscription fastened upon Christ's cross as a mockery; stands for "Iesus Nazarenus, Rex Iudaeorum" or "Jesus of Nazareth, King of the Jews.". [Christianity: Brewer *Note-Book*, 450]

6. **Momus** god of blame and ridicule. [Gk. Myth.: Espy, 31]

474. MODESTY (See also CHASTITY, HUMILITY.)

1. **Bell, Laura** reserved, demure character. [Br. Lit.: *Pendennis*]

2. **Bianca** gentle, unassuming sister of Kate. [Br. Lit.: *The Taming of the Shrew*]

3. **fig leaves** used to cover Adam and Eve's nakedness. [O.T.: Genesis 3:7]

4. **hijab** large scarf worn by some Muslim women to cover their head, neck, and hair to meet requirements for female modesty. [Islamic Trad.: *UIMT*, 193]

5. **pearl** emblem of discreet shyness. [Gem Symbolism: Kunz, 69]

6. **sweet violet** indicates a modest temperament. [Flower Symbolism: *Flora Symbolica*, 178]

475. MONEY (See also FINANCE.)

1. **Brink's** Boston armored car service; carrying millions in currency. [Am. Business: *Facts* (1950), 24]

2. **Mammon** personification of money; one cannot serve him and God simultaneously. [N.T.: Matthew 6:24; Luke 16:9, 11, 13]

3. **Moneta** "monitress"; epithet of Juno; origin of *mint*. [Rom. Myth.: Espy, 20]

4. **Newland, Abraham** governor of Bank of England; eponymously, banknote. [Br. Hist.: Wheeler, 258]

476. MONOPOLY

1. **AT&T (American Telephone and Telegraph)** once the largest corporation in the world; telecommunications giant was government-regulated monopoly until early 1980s. [Am. Business: *SJEPC*]

2. **De Beers** price fixing charges in diamond trade brought by U.S. justice department in early 2000s. [Business: Misc.]

3. **IBM (International Business Machines)** hugely successful mainframe computer company beginning in the 1950s; accused of monopoly in the late 1960s. [Am. Business: *SJEPC*]

4. **Microsoft** behemoth faced antitrust charges in late 1990s for giving its Internet browser unfair advantage over others. [Am. Business: *SJEPC*]

5. **Monsanto** leading global provider of agricultural products and systems sold to farmers; international coalition of farmers led anti-trust, price fixing lawsuit against them in early 2000s. [Business: Misc.]

6. **Standard Oil** John D. Rockefeller's company; controlled nearly all of U.S. oil refineries until Supreme Court ruling of 1911. [Am. Business: Misc.]

7. **U.S. Steel** prosecuted unsuccessfully for anti-trust in 1911. [Am. Business: Misc.]

477. MONSTER

1. **Abominable Snowman** enigmatic yeti of the Himalayas. [Tibetan Lore: Wallechinsky, 443]

2. **Aegaeon** gigantic monster with 100 arms, 50 heads. [Gk.and Rom. Myth.: Wheeler, 5]

3. **Ahuizotl** small creature with monkey hands and feet, a hand at the end of its long tail. [Mex. Myth.: Leach]

4. **Ammit** part hippopotamus, part lion, with jaws like a crocodile's. [Egypt. Myth.: Leach]

5. **Amphisbaena** two-headed monster, either scaled like a snake or feathered; one head remains awake while the other sleeps. [Roman Myth.: White]

6. **Anubis** jackal-headed god. [Egypt. Myth.: Jobes, 105]

7. **Argus** hundred-eyed giant who guarded Io. [Gk. Myth.and Roman Lit.: *Metamorphoses*]

8. **banshee** spirit with one nostril, a large projecting front tooth, and webbed feet. [Irish Folklore: Briggs, 14]

9. **basilisk** lizard supposed to kill with its gaze. [Gk. Myth.: Brewer *Handbook*, 93]

10. **beasts of the Apocalypse** one has ten horns, seven heads, and ten crowns on the horns; the other has two horns and speaks like a dragon. [N.T.: Revelation 13:1, 11]

11. **bonnacon** Asian monster with bull's head and horse's body, and fatally incendiary excrement. [Gk.and Rom. Myth.: White]

12. **Briareus, Cottus, and Gyges** the three Hecatoncheires (or Centimani), giants each having 50 heads and 100 arms. [Gk. Myth.: Zimmerman, 118]

13. **Brontes** cruel thunder-maker of the three Cyclopes. [Gk. Myth.: Parrinder, 47; Jobes, 251, 400]

14. **cactus cat** has thorny hair and ears, knifelike leg bones, and a branched tail. [Am. Folklore: Botkin]

15. **Cacus** fire-breathing giant monster. [Rom. Myth.: Kravitz, 19]

16. **Caliban** misshapen "missing link." [Br. Lit.: *The Tempest*]

17. **capricornus** half goat, half fish. [Gk. Myth.: NCE, 450]

18. **Cecrops** the traditional founder of Athens was half man, half serpent. [Gk. Myth.: Hamilton, 393]

19. **Cerberus** three-headed watchdog of Hades. [Gk. Myth.: Avery, 270]

20. **Charybdis** Poseidon's daughter; monster of the deep. [Gk. Lit.: *Odyssey*; Rom. Lit.: *Aeneid*]

21. **chimera** mythical creature; goat-lion-dragon; vomited flames. [Classical Myth.: *LLEI*, I: 325]

22. **cockatrice** half-serpent, half-cock; kills with glance. [Heraldry: Brewer *Dictionary*, 243]

23. **Cyclopes** Poseidon's sons, each with one eye in the center of his forehead. [Gk. Lit.: *Odyssey*]

24. **divis** devils shown as cat-headed men with horns and hooves. [Pers. Myth.: Barber & Riches]

25. **Echidna** half nymph, half snake; never grew old. [Gk. Myth.: Kravitz, 85]

26. **Fenris** frightful wolf, grew sinisterly in size and strength. [Scand. Myth.: *LLEI*, I: 328]

27. **Frankenstein's monster** created from parts of corpses. [Br. Lit.: *Frankenstein*]

28. **Geryon** celebrated monster with three united bodies or three heads. [Rom. Lit.: *Aeneid*]

29. **Godzilla** monster star of many Japanese horror films; symbol of destruction of nuclear holocaust [Jpn. Film *ODA*]

30. **Gorgons** monsters with serpents for hair and brazen claws. [Gk. Myth.: Zimmerman, 114; Gk. Lit.: *Iliad*]

31. **Grendel** giant in human shape; lives in a murky pond. [Br. Lit.: *Beowulf*]

32. **griffin** fabulous animal, part eagle, part lion. [Gk. Myth. and Art: Hall, 143; Ital. Lit.: *Purgatory*]

33. **harpy** foul-smelling creature; half-vulture, half-woman. [Gk. Myth.: Mercatante, 212–213]

34. **hippocampus** fabulous marine creature; half fish, half horse. [Rom. Myth. and Art: Hall, 154]

35. **hippogriff** offspring of griffin and mare. [Ital. Lit.: *Orlando Furioso*]

36. **Hydra** seven-headed water snake; ravaged Lerna, near Argos. [Gk.and Rom. Myth.: Hall, 149]

37. **Jabberwock** frightful burbling monster with flaming eyes. [Br. Lit.: Carroll *Through the Looking-Glass*]

38. **King Kong** giant ape portrayed in 1933 classsic horror film; scene of him atop Empire State Building is reproduced in many forms to the present. [Am. Film: *SJEPC*]

39. **Kirtimukha** the Face of Glory, depicted as a lion's head, without body or limbs. [Hindu Myth.: Barber & Riches]

40. **Kraken** giant snakelike sea creature. [Dan. Folklore: Mercatante, 194–195]

41. **Ladon** dragon who guarded the Apples of the Hesperides. [Gk. Myth.: Zimmerman, 145]

42. **Lamia** scaly, four-legged, hermaphrodite creature. [Br. Folklore: Briggs, 260–262]

43. **Leviathan** frighteningly powerful sea serpent. [O.T.: Job 41; Psalms 74:14; 104:26; Isaiah 27:1]

44. **Loch Ness monster** "Nessie"; sea serpent said to inhabit Loch Ness. [Scot. Folklore: Wallechinsky, 443]

45. **Medusa** the only mortal Gorgon. [Gk. Myth.: Zimmerman, 161]

46. **Midgard serpent** monstrous serpent that encircles the earth. [Norse Myth.: Leach, 723]

47. **Minotaur** beast with bull's head and man's body. [Gk. Myth.: Brewer *Dictionary*, 714]

48. **Mock Turtle** turtle with a calf's head, hooves, and tail. [Br. Lit.: Lewis Carroll *Alice's Adventures in Wonderland*]

49. **Naga** semi-divine beings with serpent bodies and human heads of terrible and ferocious aspect. [Hindu Myth.: Leach]

50. **Nicor** Scandinavian sea monster; whence, "Old Nick." [Br. Folklore: Espy, 44]

51. **Nidhogg** terrible beast in Nastrond; gnaws ashtree, Yggdrasil. [Norse Myth.: Wheeler, 259]

52. **nix** also called nixie; siren-like water-sprite, sometimes fish-tailed, that lured men to drown. [Teutonic Myth.: Barber & Riches]

53. **opinicus** fabulous amalgam of dragon, camel, and lion. [Heraldry: Brewer *Dictionary*, 782]

54. **Orc** monstrous sea creature; devours human beings. [Ital. Lit.: *Orlando Furioso*]

55. **Orthos** two-headed dog; brother of Cerberus. [Gk. Myth.: Zimmerman, 186]

56. **python** huge serpent which sprang from stagnant waters after the Deluge. [Gk. Myth.: Zimemrman, 227]

57. **Questing Beast** serpent-headed leopard that emitted loud noises. [Br. Lit.: Malory *Le Morte d'Arthur*]

58. **roc** white bird of enormous size. [Arab. Lit.: *Arabian Nights*, "Second Voyage of Sindbad the Sailor"]

59. **Sagittary** half man, half beast with eyes of fire. [Gk. Myth.: Brewer *Handbook*, 947]

60. **Sasquatch** giant hairy hominid said to lurk about the Pacific Northwest. [Am. Hist.: Payton, 601]

61. **Scylla** half beautiful maiden, half hideous dog. [Gk. Lit.: *Odyssey*; Rom. Lit.: *Metamorphoses*]

62. **Siren** half-woman, half-bird, enticed seamen to their death with song. [Gk. Myth.: Benét, 934]

63. **666** number of the blasphemous beast with seven heads and ten horns. [N.T.: Revelation 13–14]

64. **Smaug** Tolkein's *The Hobbit* relates the battle to capture Lonely Mountain and its treasure from this fearful dragon, last of the great fire-drakes. [Br. Lit.: Misc.]

65. **Sphinx** head and breasts of a woman, body of a dog, and wings of a bird. [Gk. Myth.: Zimmerman, 246; Gk. Lit.: *Oedipus Rex*]

66. **Typhoeus** hundred-headed beast killed by Jovian thunderbolt. [Gk. Myth.: Brewer *Dictionary*, 1111]

67. **Typhon** tallest of the giants; his arms and legs ended in serpents. [Gk. Myth.: Benét, 1034]

68. **werewolf** a man transformed into a wolf, in some legends at full moon. [Eur. Folklore: Benét, 1082]

478. MOON

1. **Apollo missions** American space program in the 1960s and 1970s put the first man on the moon in 1969. [Am. Astronomy *SJEPC*]

2. **Artemis** goddess of the moon; called Diana by the Romans. [Gk. Myth.: Kravitz, 36; Brewer *Dictionary*, 727]

3. **Astarte** also called Ashtoreth; personification of moon in crescent stage. [Phoenician Myth.: Brewer *Dictionary*, 726–727]

4. **Bast** cat-headed goddess representing sun and moon. [Ancient Egyptian Rel.: Parrinder, 42]

5. **crescent moon** symbol of Islam, often depicted with five- or six-pointed star between its horns. [Islamic Symbolism: *UIMT*, 227]

6. **Cynthia** goddess of the moon. [Gk. Myth.: Kravitz, 72]

7. **Endymion** name of man in the moon. [Gk. Myth.: Brewer *Dictionary*, 376–377]

8. **Hecate** personification of the moon before rising and after setting. [Gk. Myth.: Brewer *Dictionary*, 726–727]

9. **Luna** ancient Roman goddess personifying the moon. [Rom. Myth.: Zimmerman, 153]

10. **new moon** Muslim months begin when it is visible in the sky. [Islam: *UIMT*, 298–300]

11. **Nokomis** daughter of the Moon and grandmother of Hiawatha. [Am. Lit.: Longfellow *The Song of Hiawatha* in Magill I, 905]

12. **otter** lunar symbol for its periodic habit of diving and rising in water. [Symbolism: *CEOS&S*]

13. **Petrus** caretaker of Heaven; makes sure moon shines on whole earth. [Ger. Opera: Orff, *The Moon*, Westerman, 115–116]

14. **Phoebe** moon as sister of sun (Phoebus). [Gk. Myth.: Brewer *Dictionary*, 726–727]

15. **Selene** the moon as lover of sleeping shepherd Endymion. [Gk. Myth.: Brewer *Dictionary*, 726–727]

16. **werewolf** man transformed into a wolf, in some legends at full moon. [Eur. Folklore: Benét, 1082]

17. **White Nights** nights before, during, and after a full moon thought to be especially lucky in some Muslim countries. [Islamic Trad. *UIMT*, 381]

479. MOTHERHOOD

1. **Asherah** mother of the gods; counterpart of Gaea. [Canaanite Myth.: Benét, 57]

2. **Baby M** name given to baby girl born in 1986 to surrogate mother; a symbol of the ethical issues surrounding modern reproduction. [Am. Science *FOF, MOD*]

3. **Crawford, Joan (1904–1977)** subject of expose autobiography, *Mommie Dearest*, written by daughter Christine, portraying her as a horrid mother. [Pop. Culture: *FOF, MOD*]

4. **Cybele** Great Mother; goddess of nature and reproduction. [Phrygian Myth.: Parrinder, 68; Jobes, 400]

5. **Cynosura** Idaean nymph; nursed the infant Zeus. [Gk. Myth.: Howe, 74]

6. **Danu** also Anu; divine procreator and guardian of gods and mortals. [Celtic Myth.: Parrinder, 72]

7. **Devaki** virgin mother of Krishna. [Hindu Myth.: Parrinder, 76]

8. **Devi** the "great goddess," wife of Shiva; "Mother." [Hindu Myth.: Parrinder, 77]

9. **Gaea** earth and mother goddess. [Gk. Myth.: Zimmerman, 108]

10. **Jewish mother** any overbearing, overprotective mother. [Pop. Culture: Misc.]

11. **kangaroo** traditional symbol of powerful mothering instincts and ancestor spirits. [Symbolism: *CEOS&S*]

12. **Madonna** another name for Mary, the mother of Christ. [Eur. Art: *ODA*]

13. **Mary** apotheosized as mother of Christ. [N.T.: Matthew, Mark, Luke, John]

14. **pig** symbol of both gluttony, lust, and selfishness as well as motherhood, prosperity, and happiness. [Symbolism: *CEOS&S*]

15. **Reed, Donna (1921–1986)** film actor probably best known for TV role as sweet-tempered housewife who epitomized motherhood in the 1950s in sitcom about clean-cut family, *The Donna Reed Show* (1958–1966). [Am. TV: *SJEPC*]

16. **Rhea** often titled Great Mother of the Gods. [Gk. Myth.: *NCE*, 1796]

17. ***Sophie's Choice*** 1979 novel by William Styron and 1982 film; concerns young writer who befriends tortured Holocaust survivor; learns that she was forced to make the most agonizing choice for any mother: which of her children would die. [Am. Lit. and Film: Misc.]

18. **Whistler's Mother** popular name for the painter's *Arrangement in Grey and Black, No. 1: The Artist's Mother.* [Am. Art: *EB*, 19: 814–815]

Motivation (See INDUCEMENT.)

Mourning (See GRIEF.)

480. **MOVIE STAR**

1. **Bergman, Ingrid (1915–1982)** Academy Award-winning Swedish actress was popular European film star before her American debut in 1939's *Intermezzo*; star of the beloved *Casablanca*. [Am. Film: *SJEPC*]

2. **Berry, Halle (1966–)** first African-American actress to win Academy Award for Best Actress, for *Monster's Ball* (2002). [Am. Film: *BBAAL2*]

3. **Bogart, Humphrey (1900–1957)** American actor known for roles in *Casablanca* playing the tough guy with a soft heart. [Am. Film: *SJEPC*]

4. **Brando, Marlon (1924–2004)** American actor, trained in the "method" technique, famous roles include *Streetcar Named Desire, On the Waterfront,* and *The Godather* [Am. Film: *SJEPC*]

5. **Cagney, Jimmy (1900–1986)** American actor, singer, dancer; roles ranged from tough guy gangster roles to song and dance man George M. Cohan. [Am. Film: *FOF, MOD*]

6. **Crosby, Bing (1903–1977)** popular singer/entertainer also starred in more than 50 movies, including "Road" pictures with Bob Hope; earned Academy Award for *Going My Way*. [Am. Film: *SJEPC*]

7. **Davis, Bette (1908–1989)** iconic actress of Hollywood's Golden Age, noted for her large eyes and assertive manner. [Am. Film: *FOF, MOD*]

8. **Day, Doris (1924–)** versatile, fresh-faced actress/singer starred in Hollywood musicals, comedies, and dramas from 1948 to 1968, including *The Pajama Game* (1957) and *Pillow Talk* (1959). [Am. Film: *SJEPC*]

9. **De Niro, Robert (1943–)** intense actor known for totally immersing himself in his roles using the Method technique; portrayed violent loner Travis Bickle in *Taxi Driver* (1976) and won an Academy Award for his portrayal of boxer Jake La Motta in *Raging Bull* (1980). [Am. Film: *EB*]

10. **Dean, James (1931–1955)** handsome, charismatic, enigmatic actor with tough yet vulnerable persona thrilled critics and audiences alike in *Rebel without a Cause* (1955) and *East of Eden* (1955). [Am. Film: *SJEPC*]

11. **Fairbanks, Douglas, Jr. (1909–2000)** debonair actor/producer and son of Douglas Fairbanks Sr. forged his own path in Hollywood; appeared in such movies as *Little Caesar* (1931) and *Gunga Din* (1939). [Am. Film: *SJEPC*]

12. **Flynn, Errol (1909–1959)** Australian film star who specialized in swashbuckling roles; also a notable ladies' man. [Am. Film: *SJEPC*]

13. **Fonda, Henry (1905–1982)** versatile screen and stage actor whose distinguished career spanned 46 years; often portrayed decent, honest characters such as Tom Joad in *The Grapes of Wrath* (1940); won first Best Actor Oscar for *On Golden Pond* a few months before his death. [Am. Film: *SJEPC*]

14. **Gable, Clark (1900–1960)** American actor, famous for playing manly roles, esp. Rhett Butler in *Gone with the Wind*. [Am. Film: *FOF MOD*]

15. **Garland, Judy (1922–1969)** legendary film actress and singer began Hollywood career as child of 13; role as Dorothy Gale in *The Wizard of Oz* (1939) catapulted her to fame; also known for Andy Hardy movies (1930s-40s) and musicals like *Meet Me in St. Louis* (1944). [Am. Film: *SJEPC*]

16. **Gish, Lillian (1893–1993)** pioneering screen actress from Hollywood's silent era had a career spanning eight decades; "the first lady of film" known for her fragile beauty, emotive performances, and strength of character. [Am. Film: *SJEPC*]

17. **Grant, Cary (1906–1986)** English-born American film star; a handsome, elegant, and debonaire leading man. [Am. Film: *SJEPC*]

18. **Hanks, Tom (1956–)** versatile, accomplished actor; winner of 2 Academy Awards (*Philadelphia* and *Forrest Gump*). [Am. Film: *EB*]

19. **Harlow, Jean (1911–1937)** blond bombshell and star of MGM's *Public Enemy* (1931) and *Dinner at Eight*. [Am. Film: *EB*]

20. **Hayworth, Rita (1918–1987)** beautiful actress and singer, sultry star of *Gilda* (1946) and *Lady from Shanghai* (1948). [Am. Film: *EB*]

21. **Hepburn, Audrey (1929–1993)** beautiful actress often portrayed lovely ingenue in such films as *Roman Holiday* and *Sabrina*; spent her later years working for UNICEF. [Am Film: *EB*]

22. **Hepburn, Katharine (1909–2003)** American actress who starred in such comedies as *Bringing up Baby* and *Adam's Rib*, often co-starring with Spencer Tracy. [Am. Film: *FOF, MOD*]

23. **Heston, Charlton (1924–2008)** handsome, well-built actor starred in such Hollywood blockbusters as *The Ten Commandments* and *Ben-Hur*; his long-time association with the National Rifle Association made him a figure of conservative politics. [Am. Film: *EB*]

24. **Hoffman, Dustin (1937–)** Academy-award winning actor praised for his broad range of roles, from *The Graduate* to *Rain Man*. [Am. Film *EB*]

25. **Holden, William (1918–1981)** suave, handsome actor starred in such films as *Sabrina, Sunset Boulevard,* and *Network*. [Am. Film: *EB*]

26. **Hudson, Rock (1925–1985)** handsome actor known for his romantic leading roles, often starring with Doris Day; his death from AIDS in 1985 led to greater awareness of the disease. [Am. Film: *EB*]

27. **Ladd, Alan (1913–1964)** extremely popular, gifted actor of 1930s and 1940s radio and film dramas; perhaps best known for starring role in 1953 Western *Shane*. [Am. Film and Radio: *SJEPC*]

28. **Lahr, Burt (1895–1967)** successful comedian from vaudeville whose expressive face and comic skills transferred to two memorable roles: on screen as the Cowardly Lion in *The Wizard of Oz* (1939) and on stage as Estragon in *Waiting for Godot* (1956). [Am. Film and Theater: *SJEPC*]

29. **Lancaster, Burt (1913–1994)** well-built American actor began as a circus acrobat, then established an acting career that lasted 40 years and encompassed broad range of types; produced films at time when actors rarely did and won Academy Award for lead role in *Elmer Gantry*. [Am. Film: *SJEPC*]

30. **Monroe, Marilyn (1926–1962)** blond bombshell and American sex symbol, whose personal life was marred with tragedies; she died of a drug overdose at 36. [Am. Film: *EB*]

31. **Nicholson, Jack (1937–)** three-time Academy Award winner and revered actor who often plays quirky, sometimes garrulous, characters with wit and charm. [Am. Film: Misc.]

32. **Pacino, Al (1940–)** many awards and demanding roles in *The Godfather, Scent of a Woman, Serpico,* etc.; often plays tough, yet sensitive characters. [Am. Film: Misc.]

33. **Pickford, Mary (1893–1979)** "America's Sweetheart," and the first female movie star; starred in such silent classics as *Rebecca of Sunnybrook Farm* (1917) and founded United Artists Studios with her husband, Douglas Fairbanks Jr. [Am. Film: *EB*]

34. **Roberts, Julia (1967–)** glamourous movie star and Academy Award winner for *Erin Brokovich* (2001); highly paid and influential actress of current era. [Am. Film: *EB*]

35. **Robinson, Edward G. (1893–1973)** adroit portrayals of various snarling mobsters in gangster movies of the 1930s. [Am. Film: *SJEPC*]

36. **Scott, George C. (1927–1999)** starred on stage, television, and in over forty films in commanding, difficult roles; notable portrayal of General George Patton in 1970 film. [Am. Film: *SJEPC*]

37. **Stewart, Jimmy (1908–1997)** lanky, easygoing and likable, he endeared audiences to him no matter what role he played; especially beloved for his role in *It's a Wonderful Life,* his favorite film. [Am. Film: *SJEPC*]

38. **Streep, Meryl (1948–)** considered by many one of the best actresses of the late twentieth century; Oscar for best actress for *Kramer vs. Kramer* (1979) and *Sophie's Choice* (1983); she has received 14 Academy Award nominations to date, more than any other actor. [Am. Film: *SJEPC*]

39. **Taylor, Elizabeth (1932–)** extremely beautiful and talented actress who has had seven husbands, fabulous jewels, and tumultuous personal life; campaigned for several causes, notably AIDS research. [Am. Film: *SJEPC*]

40. **Temple, Shirley (1928–)** popular child film star during 1930s and 1940s; dimples, gold ringlets and charming singing/tap dancing made her the darling of the American public. [Am. Film: *SJEPC*]

41. **Tovar, Lupita (1910–)** played a leading role in Spanish-language version of *Dracula*, filmed in 1931 using same sets as the English-language film; she also played in Mexico's first talkie film; a Mexican postage stamp was issued featuring Tovar. [Mex. Film: Misc.]

42. **Tracy, Spencer (1900–1967)** his understated style graced comedy and drama; sheer talent got him leading roles without being handsome or suave; often the co-star of Katharine Hepburn, in such films as *Adam's Rib*. [Am. Film: *SJEPC*]

43. **Valentino, Rudolph (1895–1926)** sexy and suave action of silent films, wildly popular with female fans, who mobbed him at appearances; *The Shiek* (1921) made him a star. [Am. Film: *SJEPC*]

44. **Washington, Denzel (1954–)** African-American actor and director, two-time Academy Award winner for *Glory* and *Training Day*. [Am. Film: *BBAAL2*]

45. **Wayne, John (1907–1979)** playing heroes and cowboys (sometimes at the same time) made him a Hollywood legend; millions of fans saw him as quintessentially American and the epitome of male strength and vigor. [Am. Film: *SJEPC*]

481. MURDER (See also ASSASSINATION, INFANTICIDE, PATRICIDE.)

1. **Abimelech** slew his 70 brothers to become ruler. [O.T.: Judges 9:5]

2. *American Psycho* disturbing novel by Brett Easton Ellis narrated in diary form by yuppie serial killer Pat Bateman, who describes his violent, murderous acts in graphic detail (1991). [Am. Lit.: *SJEPC*]

3. **Arbuckle, Fatty (1887–1933)** early Hollywood comic actor accused of actress's rape and murder during wild party in 1921. [Am. Hist.: *SJEPC*]

4. **Barnwell, George** noble motives cause him to murder uncle. [Br. Lit.: *The London Merchant*; Barnhart, 695]

5. **Beaumont, Jeremiah** kills the man who had seduced his wife; he is murdered by an enemy and his wife kills herself. [Am. Lit.: Warren *World Enough and Time* in Magill II, 1160]

6. **Berkowitz, David (1953–)** American serial killer also known as Son of Sam; arrested for shootings in New York City; claimed to be member of satanic cult. [Am. Hist.: Misc.]

7. **Bluebeard (1869–1922)** executed for murders of ten women (1915–18). [Fr. Hist.: *EB* (1972), XIII, 661]

8. **Borden, Lizzie (1860–1927)** woman accused of butchering father and stepmother with ax (1872). [Am. Hist.: Hart, 91]

9. **Boston Strangler (1932–)** strangled thirteen women between 1962 and 1964. [Am. Hist.: Misc.]

10. **Bundy, Ted (1946–1989)** charming, manipulative serial killer suspected of murdering up to 100 women across the United States; convicted of three murders and executed in Florida in 1989. [Am. Hist.: *SJEPC*]

11. **Busiris** murders predecessor to gain Egyptian throne. [Gk. Myth.: Avery, 231]

12. **Cain** jealous, slays Abel. [O.T.: Genesis 4:8]

13. **Cenci, Beatrice** with brothers, arranges murder of cruel father. [Br. Lit.: *The Cenci*]

14. **Claudius** murders brother to gain throne. [Br. Lit.: *Hamlet*]

15. **Dahmer, Jeffrey (1960–1994)** notorious serial killer; murdered, then molested and cannibalized, 17 young men. [Am. Hist.: *SJEPC*]

16. **Danaides** slew husbands on wedding night. [Gk. Myth.: Kravitz, 74]

17. **Donatello** throws Miriam's persecutor over cliff to death. [Am. Lit.: *The Marble Faun*]

18. **Donegild** killed by Alla for abandoning his wife and son at sea. [Br. Lit.: *Canterbury Tales*, "Man of Law's Tale"]

19. *Double Indemnity* ruthless insurance agent Walter Neff murders lover Phyllis as well as her husband to collect life insurance money (novel, 1935; film, 1944). [Am. Film and Lit.: *SJEPC*]

20. **Franceschini, Count** burtally murders his estranged young wife and her parents. [Br. Poetry: Browning *The Ring and the Book*]

21. **Gacy, John Wayne (1942–1994)** convicted and executed for the rape and murder of thirty-three boys and young men; also known as The Clown Killer. [Am. Hist.: Misc.]

22. **Gilligan, Amy Archer** poisons 48 elderly people in nursing homes. [Am. Hist.: Elizabeth S. Baxter *Newington*; Am. Drama: Kesselring *Arsenic and Old Lace*]

23. **Griffiths, Clyde** young social climber lets his pregnant mistress drown in a boating accident and is convicted of murder. [Am. Lit.: *An American Tragedy* in Hart, 30]

24. **Hagen** stabs Siegfried in back; kills Gunther. [Ger. Opera: Wagner, *Götterdämmerung*, Westerman, 245]

25. **Hines, Doc** kills Joe's father; lets mother die in childbirth. [Am. Lit.: *Light in August*]

26. **hired gun** someone hired to kill; by extension, someone hired to do a nasty job. [Am. Culture: *FOF, MOD*]

27. **hit list** from organized crime, a list of victims to be murdered; by extension, a list of people slated for firing, other bad news. [Am. Culture: *FOF, MOD*]

28. **Ibbetson, Peter** a confessed muderer, yet a sensitive, romantic man. [Br. Lit.: *Peter Ibbetson*, Magill I, 736–738]

29. *In Cold Blood* nonfiction novel about a brutal, senseless murder in Kansas. [Am. Lit.: *In Cold Blood*]

30. **Injun Joe** stabs town doctor to death. [Am. Lit.: *Tom Sawyer*]

31. **Ixion** first murderer of a relative in classical mythology. [Gk. Myth.: Zimmerman, 142; Rom. Lit.: *Aeneid*]

32. **Jack the Ripper** killed and disemboweled 9 London prostitutes (1888–1889). [Br. Hist.: Brewer *Note-Book*, 463]

33. **Julian, Saint** mistakenly kills his parents in their sleep. [Fr. Lit.: Flaubert "The Legend of St. Julian the Hospitaler"]

34. **Kaczynski, Theodore (1942–)** known as The Unabomber; responsible for mailing bombs to various universities and organizations; lived as hermit in isolated cabin in Montana. [Am. Hist.: Misc.]

35. *Kenilworth* intrigue in the court of Elizabeth I. [Br. Lit.: Scott *Kenilworth* in Magill I, 469]

36. **Leopold and Loeb** infamous teenage murderers who, in 1924, killed a 14–year- old friend, just to prove they could do it. [Am. Hist.: *FOF, MOD*]

37. *M* motion picture about a child-murderer hunted down by organized criminal element. [Ger. Cinema: Halliwell]

38. **Macbeth** became king of Scotland through a series of ruthless murders, but was ultimately slain by his enemy, Macduff. [Br. Lit.: Shakespeare *Macbeth*]

39. **Manson, Charles (1934–)** became leader of murderous cult in 1960s. [Am. Hist.: *SJEPC*]

40. **Medea** murdered her two children. [Gk. Lit.: *Century Classical*, 684–685]

41. **Michele** murders wife's lover; hides body under cloak. [Ital. Opera: Puccini, *The Cloak*, Westerman, 362–363]

42. **Modo** fiend presiding over homicide. [Br. Lit.: *King Lear*]

43. **Mordred, Sir** illegitimate son and treacherous killer of Arthur. [Br. Lit.: *Le Morte d'Arthur*]

44. **Orestes** commits matricide to avenge father's honor. [Gk. Lit.: *Electra*]

45. **Othello** believing false evidence of Desdemona's infidelity, he strangles her. [Br. Lit.: Shakespeare *Othello*]

46. **Ourang-Outang** brutally kills a mother and her daughter. [Am. Lit.: Poe *The Murders in the Rue Morgue*]

47. **Porgy** murders Crown, who tried to take Bess. [Am. Opera: Gershwin *Porgy and Bess*, Westerman, 556]

48. **Raskolnikov** plans and carries out the murder of an old woman pawnbroker. [Russ. Lit.: *Crime and Punishment*]

49. **Rogêt, Marie** girl assaulted and murdered, her corpse thrown into the Seine. [Am. Lit.: Poe *The Mystery of Marie Rogêt*]

50. **Rudge** murders master and gardener. [Br. Lit.: *Barnaby Rudge*]

51. **Sikes, Bill** hanged for killing of Nancy. [Br. Lit.: *Oliver Twist*]

52. **Simpson, O. J. (1947–)** top-notch running back and Heisman trophy winner in late 1960s and 1970s; defendant in 1994 murder trial of his ex-wife; verdict of innocence brought polarizing reactions, with many whites convinced of his guilt, many blacks of his innocence. [Am. Hist.: *SJEPC*]

53. **Smith, George Joseph** dispatched wives and lovers in bathtubs in 1910s. [Br. Hist.: Wallechinsky, 274]

54. **Spandrell** cynic opposed to fascist Everard Webley attacks and kills him, then commits suicide. [Br. Lit.: Huxley *Point Counter Point* in Magill I, 760]

55. **Sparafucile** his killing of Gilda fulfills curse against Rigoletto. [Ital. Opera: Verdi, *Rigoletto*, Westerman, 300]

56. **Thuggee** religious devotion to Kali involves human strangulation. [Indian Hist.: Brewer *Dictionary*, 1080]

57. **Todd, Sweeney** English barber who murders out of revenge with a straight razor and gives bodies to landlady to make meat pies;

legendary story made into musical in 1979 by Stephen Sondheim. [Br. Legend and Musical: Misc.]

58. **Tyrrel, James** at the kings behest, arranges the deaths of two young princes in the Tower. [Br. Drama: Shakespeare *Richard III*]

59. **Zodiac Killer** serial killer in California in the 1960s; known to have killed 5 victims thus far but identity is still a mystery; name derived from letters sent to the press, containing cryptograms. [Am. Hist.: Misc.]

482. MUSIC

1. **Amphion** his music so powerful that stones for a wall are moved into place. [Gk. Myth.: Benét, 32]

2. **Apollo** god of music and fine arts. [Gk. Myth.: Zimmrman, 26]

3. **Bragi** harpist-god; flowers bloomed, trees budded as he played. [Norse Myth.: Leach, 160]

4. **Cecilia, Saint** patron of music and legendary inventor of organ. [Christian Hagiog.: Thompson, 380]

5. **compact disc (CD)** flexibility offered by its digital technology and small size altered the music recording and retail industry after introduction to consumers in 1983. [Music and Technology: *SJEPC*]

6. **Corybantes** musicians; provided music for goddesses' orgiastic dances. [Gk. Myth.: Kravitz, 67]

7. **Daphnis** sheperd; invented pastoral music to console himself. [Gk. Myth.: Parrinder, 72; Jobes, 414]

8. **Demodocus** minstrel whom Odysseus hears singing the amours of Ares and Aphrodite. [Gk. Lit.: *Odyssey* VIII]

9. **eight-track tape** promising audio technology of the 1960s-70s allowed people to listen to their own music while driving in the car; obsolete by 1980. [Am. Technology: *SJEPC*]

10. **Euterpe** Muse of dramatic melody; patroness of flautists. [Gk. Myth.: Brewer *Dictionary*, 385]

11. **Grammy** award for musical achievement. [Am. Cult.: Misc.]

12. **Israfel** "none sing so wildly well." [Am. Lit.: "Israfel" in *Portable Poe*, 606]

13. **Jubal** forebear of all who play harp and pipe. [O.T.: Genesis 4:21]

14. **Linus** musician and poet; invented melody and rhythm. [Gk. Myth.: Zimmerman, 152]

15. **Muses** goddesses who presided over the arts; known to the Romans as Camanae. [Gk. Myth.: Howe, 172]

16. **Orpheus** musician, charmed even inanimate things with lyre-playing. [Gk. Myth.: Brewer *Dictionary*, 787]

17. **Polyhymnia** Muse of sacred song. [Gk. Myth.: Howe, 172]
18. **Syrinx** transformed into reeds which pursuing Pan made into pipe. [Gk. Myth.: Hall, 232; Rom. Lit.: *Metamorhphoses*]
19. **Tin Pan Alley** *lit.* 1650 Broadway, New York City; *fig.*, fount of American popular music. [Am. Music: Thompson, 1105]
20. **vinyl** long-playing records, recorded using analog technology. [Music and Technology: *SJEPC*]

483. MUSIC, CLASSICAL (See also SINGER.)

1. **Bach, Johann Sebastian (1685–1750)** great composer of the German baroque period, noted especially for developing the fugue form. [Ger. Music *ODA*]
2. **Bartók, Béla (1881–1945)** composer most recognized for the Hungarian flavor in his music. [Hungarian Music: Misc.]
3. **Beethoven, Ludwig van (1770–1827)** influential German composer of the classical and romantic periods; noted for powerful symphonic and chamber works. [Ger. Music *ODA*]
4. **Berlioz, Hector (1803–1869)** French composer and conductor of the Romantic period; famous for writing *Symphonie Fantastique*. [Fr. Music: Misc.]
5. **Bernstein, Leonard (1918–1990)** Jewish-American conductor of New York Philharmonic helped bring classical music to American mass audiences; composed *West Side Story*. [Am. Music: *SJEPC*]
6. **Borge, Victor (1909–2000)** Danish-American pianist incorporated comedy routines into serious classical music. [Dan. Music: *SJEPC*]
7. **Brahams, Johannes (1833–1897)** German composer and pianist; wrote in the Romantic period, but maintained traditional Classical ideas. [Ger. Music: Misc.]
8. **Chopin, Frédéric (1810–1849)** Polish-French composer of the Romantic period; wrote mainly piano pieces. [Fr. Music: Misc.]
9. **Copland, Aaron (1900–1990)** legendary American composer whose orchestral works tapped into American themes and folklore, such as *Rodeo* (1942); also composed film scores, operas, and jazz music. [Am. Music: *SJEPC*]
10. **Dvorak, Antonin (1841–1904)** Czech composer; known for bringing Bohemian folk music in the Romantic period. [Czech. Music: Misc.]
11. *Fantasia* generations of children introduced to classical music through Walt Disney's animated masterpiece, which features the music of Bach, Beethoven, and others under the baton of Leopold Stokowski (1940). [Am. Film: *SJEPC*]
12. **Gabrieli, Andrea (1532?-1585)** Italian composer of Renaissance organ music. [Ital. Music: Misc.]

527

13. **Gilbert and Sullivan [William Gilbert (1836–1911) and Arthur Sullivan (1842–1900)]** wrote popular, satirical operettas noted for their wit and humor. [Eng. Music: *FOF, MOD*]

14. **Handel, George Frideric (1685–1759)** German-born composer of late Baroque pieces such as *Messiah* and *Water Music*. [Ger. Music: Misc.]

15. **Mozart, Wolfgang Amadeus (1756–1791)** brilliant Austrian composer known for writing and excelling in all musical genres of the time; during his brief lifetime wrote what many consider the finest classical music ever composed. [Aust. Music: Misc.]

16. **Mendelssohn, Felix (1809–1847)** well-known German Romantic composer, pianist, and conductor; blended Classical models with Romantic feeling. [Ger. Music: Misc.]

17. **Puccini, Giacomo (1858–1924)** Italian opera composer known for his beautiful, memorable melodies such as "Nessun dorma"; wrote *La Bohème* and *Madama Butterfly*. [Ital. Music: Misc.]

18. **Schubert, Robert Alexander (1810–1856)** German composer of the Romantic period; mostly wrote pieces for the piano. [Ger. Music: Misc.]

19. **Schumann, Robert (1810–1856)** German romantic composer of remarkable range; mental instability profoundly affected his personal and professional life. [Ger. Music: Misc.]

20. **Stravinsky, Igor (1882–1971)** Russian composer; had significant influence on music before and after World War I. [Russ. Music: Misc.]

21. **Tchaikovsky, Pyotr Illyich (1840–1893)** famous Russian composer of Romantic period; well-known for composing lush, emotional works like *Swan Lake* and *The Nutcracker*. [Russ. Music: Misc.]

22. **Verdi, Giuseppe (1813–1901)** greatest Italian opera composer of the 19th century whose work is still considered some of the finest of the genre; wrote *La traviata* and *Aida*. [Ital. Music: Misc.]

23. **Vivaldi, Antonio (1678–1741)** influential Italian composer and violinist of the Baroque era. [Ital. Music: Misc.]

24. **Wagner, Richard (1813–1883)** German theorist and composer; his compositions strongly influenced the direction of Western music. [Ger. Music: Misc.]

484. MUSIC, JAZZ (See also SINGER.)

1. **Armstrong, Louis (1900–1917)** African-American jazz trumpeter and one of the most important figures in the development of jazz music; known as" Satchmo." [Am. Music: *BBAAL2*]

2. **Basie, Count (1904–1984)** influential pianist in the big band swing style of jazz. [Am. Music: *BBAAL2*]

3. **Beiderbecke, Bix (1903–1931)** American cornetist and composer; first major white jazz soloist. [Am. Music: *EB*]

4. **Brown, Les (1912–2001)** bandleader's swinging "Band of Renown" hit the heights in the 1930s-40s; "Sentimental Journey" was signature song. [Am. Music: *SJEPC*]

5. **Brubeck, Dave (1920–)** venerable jazz composer/pianist's quartet helped popularize the genre in the 1950s and 1960s with such classics as "Take Five." [Am. Music: *SJEPC*]

6. **Coltrane, John (1926–1967)** African-American influential, innovative jazz saxophonist of the 1950s and 1960s. [Am. Music: *SJEPC*]

7. **Davis, Miles (1926–1992)** African-American jazz trumpeter, composer, and band leader; developed the "cool" school of jazz and bebop. [Am. Music: *BBAAL2*]

8. **Dorsey Brothers** [Jimmy Dorsey (1904–1957) and Tommy Dorsey (1905–1956)] clarinetist and alto saxophonist Jimmy and trombonist Tommy formed and led their own highly acclaimed swing orchestra. [Am. Music: *SJEPC*]

9. **Ellington, Edward Kennedy "Duke" (1899–1974)** African-American jazz composer, band leader, and performer; popularized jazz music in the U.S.; symbol of sophistication and elegance. [Am. Music: *BBAAL2*]

10. **Fitzgerald, Ella (1917–1996)** African-American singer; "The First Lady of Song" and one of the greatest interpreters of some of the greatest songs of the 20th century. [Am. Music: *BBAAL2*]

11. **Gillespie, Dizzy (1917–1993)** African-American jazz trumpeter, composer, and pioneer of bebop and Afro-Cuban jazz. [Am. Music: *BBAAL2*]

12. **Goodman, Benny (1909–1986)** influential big band jazz clarinetist and bandleader renowned as the "King of Swing." [Am. Music: *SJEPC*]

13. **Guaraldi, Vince (1928–1976)** jazz pianist/composer famous for scoring animated Charlie Brown TV specials (1960s). [Am. Music: Misc.]

14. **Hancock, Herbie (1940–)** African-American jazz pianist, composer, band leader; worked with generations of musicians, from Miles Davis to Wynton Marsalis; a versatile, accomplished musician. [Am. Music: *EB*]

15. **Hawkins, Coleman (1904–1969)** African-American jazz saxophonist, called "The Bean"; improvisational genius, as heard in his masterpiece, "Body and Soul." [Am. Music: *EB*]

529

16. **Holiday, Billie (1915–1959)** African-American jazz and blues composer and vocalist, called "Lady Day," she was one of the most influential singers of the era. [Am. Music: *BBAAL2*]

17. **Krupa, Gene (1909–1973)** most famous Big Band drummer and, some say, best drummer ever; first drummer to become famous; his solo in Benny Goodman's "Sing, Sing, Sing" was first extended drum solo ever recorded. [Am. Music: *SJEPC*]

18. **Marsalis, Wynton (1961–)** African-American trumpeter, composer, and bandleader; major jazz and classical performer. [Am. Music: *EB*]

19. **Miller, Glenn (1904–1944)** talented trombonist, composer, arranger, and band leader during swing era; recordings of hits like "Little Brown Jug" and "In the Mood" rocketed him to fame. [Am. Music: Misc.]

20. **Monk, Thelonius (1917–1982)** African-American jazz composer and musician; one of the pioneers of bebop. [Am. Music: *BBAAL2*]

21. **Morton, Ferdinand "Jelly Roll" (1885?-1941)** first great composer and piano player of jazz; important transitional figure between ragtime and jazz piano styles in influential early jazz recordings with his Red Hot Peppers in late 1920s. [Am. Music: Misc.]

22. **Parker, Charlie (1920–1955)** African-American jazz saxophonist and one of the pioneers of bebop. [Am. Music: *BBAAL2*]

23. **Shaw, Artie (1910–2004)** big-band leader and clarinetist of renown. [Am. Music: *SJEPC*]

485. MUSIC, POPULAR (See also SINGER.)

1. **ABBA** Swedish quartet comprised of two couples; blazed onto the 1970s disco scene with hot singles like "Dancing Queen." [Swed. Music: *SJEPC*]

2. **AC/DC** Australian hard rock band popular from mid-1970s to present whose songs of sexual escapades harken back to the blues. [Australian Music: *SJEPC*]

3. **Aerosmith** 1970s rock band featuring charismatic vocalist Steven Tyler; still performing live in early 2000s. [Am. Music: *SJEPC*]

4. *American Bandstand* popular TV show hosted by Dick Clark from 1957 to 1989; introduced new rock music and dance styles; featured dancing teenagers who also rated songs. [Am. Music and TV: *SJEPC*]

5. *American Idol* extremely popular television reality show started in 2002; competition between singers across America to become the next big pop star. [Am. TV: Misc.]

6.　**Andrews Sisters, The** popular music trio of the 1930s and 1940s known for their harmonic singing style and for entertaining American troops during World War II. [Am. Music: *SJEPC*]

7.　**Band, The** band from the 1960s and 1970s drew from diversity of American musical styles, with some songs set in rural South. [Am. Music: *SJEPC*]

8.　**barbershop quartet** four-part, a cappella vocal music group known for close harmonies and improvisational style, rooted in early 20th-century America. [Am. Music: *SJEPC*]

9.　**Beach Boys, The** band with close-harmony style vocals formed by Wilson brothers Brian, Dennis, and Carl; epitomized 1960s Southern California youth culture. [Am. Music: *SJEPC*]

10.　**Beatles, The** often considered the best rock band of all times; John Lennon, Paul McCartney, George Harrison, and Ringo Starr disbanded in 1970 but the group continues to captivate listeners and influence musicians into the 21st century. [Br. Music: *SJEPC*]

11.　**Bee-Gees, The** [Barry Gibb (1947–), Robin Gibb (1949–), Maurice Gibb (1949–2003)] extraordinarily successful singers and composers with record sales of more than 200 million; three brothers best known for disco hits featured in film *Saturday Night Fever* and other hits like "How Can You Mend a Broken Heart." [Br. Music: Misc.]

12.　**Berlin, Irving (1888–1989)** Russian-born composer's popular and patriotic songs reflect 20th-century American life. [Am. Music: *SJEPC*]

13.　**Berry, Chuck (1926–)** groundbreaking rock 'n' roll songwriter, guitarist, and singer (1950s) influenced subsequent artists; wrote such classics as "Johnny B. Goode" and "Roll over Beethoven." [Am. Music: *SJEPC*]

14.　**British Invasion** British rock bands in the 1960s captured Americans' fancy following the Beatles' success. [Br. Music: *SJEPC*]

15.　**Brown, James (1933–2006)** "Godfather of Soul" with top hits in the 1960s; influenced rhythm and blues, hip-hop, and rap artists of later generations. [Am. Music: *SJEPC*]

16.　**bubblegum rock** commercial rock music marketed to preteens; arose in the 1960s with such bands as The Archies. [Am. Music: *SJEPC*]

17.　**Buffett, Jimmy (1946–)** singer with beach-bum image and signature hit "Margaritaville" spawned Parrot Head subculture of Hawaiian shirt-garbed concert audiences seeking escapism and a good party. [Am. Music: *SJEPC*]

18.　**Carmichael, Hoagy (1899–1981)** composer/pianist's most familiar tunes include "Heart and Soul" (1938), "Georgia on My Mind" (1931), and "Stardust" (1927). [Am. Music: *SJEPC*]

19. **Carpenters, The** internationally popular brother-and-sister duo Richard and Karen produced 19 top-10 singles in 1970s including "Close to You" and "For All We Know." [Am. Music: *SJEPC*]

20. **Charles, Ray (1930–2004)** legendary blind songwriter, pianist, and vocalist credited with inventing soul music in 1950s but mastered numerous genres, from jazz to country and western. [Am. Music: *SJEPC*]

21. **Checker, Chubby (1941–)** his recording of "The Twist" (1960) skyrocketed to #1 on the pop charts and fueled a dance craze. [Am. Music: *SJEPC*]

22. **Clapton, Eric (1945–)** extraordinary blues and rock guitarist played in numerous bands in the 1960s, including the Yardbirds, Cream, Blind Faith, and Derek and the Dominos, then went solo. [Br. Music: *SJEPC*]

23. **Clark, Dick (1929–)** legendary host of *American Bandstand* (1957–1989) introduced new styles of rock music on national television. [Am. Music and TV: *SJEPC*]

24. **Cohan, George M. (1878–1942)** American composer and performer, creator of patriotic songs including "I'm a Yankee Doodle Dandy." [Am. Music: Misc.]

25. **concept albums** long-playing records of the 1960s and 1970s containing songs with overall unifying theme, such as The Who's *Tommy* (1969). [Br. and Am. Music: *SJEPC*]

26. **Contemporary Christian Music (CCM)** songs focusing on Jesus and Christian themes took root in the 1960s; became a commercially successful genre by the 1980s. [Am. Music: *SJEPC*]

27. **Cooke, Sam (1935–1964)** groundbreaking soul music artist of 1950s-60s was rooted in gospel but branched off into secular realm; produced 31 popular hits before his untimely death. [Am. Music: *SJEPC*]

28. **Cooper, Alice (1948–)** hard rocker's star rose in the 1970s with energetic, theatrical stage shows. [Am. Music: *SJEPC*]

29. **Croce, Jim (1943–1973)** personable singer/guitarist's songs had storytelling quality; topped the charts even after his tragic death. [Am. Music: *SJEPC*]

30. **Crosby, Stills, Nash, and Young** supergroup with tight vocal harmonies and countercultural lyrics blew away Woodstock festivalgoers in 1969. [Am. Music: *SJEPC*]

31. **Dead Kennedys, The** hardcore rock band with politically controversial lyrics skewered big business, religious institutions, and flaws in 1980s American society. [Am. Music: *SJEPC*]

32. **Denver, John (1943–1997)** gentle, socially conscious singer and songwriter popular in the 1970s whose hits included "Take Me Home, Country Roads." [Am. Music: *SJEPC*]

33. **Devo** odd New Wave band of the 1970s-80s influenced by conceptual art and a de-evolution philosophy. [Am. Music: *SJEPC*]

34. **DJs** disc jockeys; radio hosts and record spinners were particularly influential in 1950s-60s, determining which new records and artists to play; in ensuing decades, have increasingly replaced live bands at celebrations like weddings and school dances. [Am. Music: *SJEPC*]

35. **Domino, Fats (1928–)** New Orleans native's boisterous piano playing style fed into emerging rock 'n' roll music in the 1950s. [Am. Music: *SJEPC*]

36. **Donovan (1946–)** Scottish-born singer/songwrite/guitarist's music was rooted in folk; branched out to embody 1960s psychedelia with songs such as "Mellow Yellow" (1966). [Br. Music: *SJEPC*]

37. **Doors, The** provocative, sexually charged rock band of the 1960s probed human nature with mystical lyrics; featured unpredictable, alluring lead singer Jim Morrison. [Am. Music: *SJEPC*]

38. **Dylan, Bob (1941–)** spanning folk, blues, and rock music in five decades, legendary songwriter/singer with nasal voice and poetic, profound lyrics; represented his generation during the period of monumental social change in the 1960s. [Am. Music: *SJEPC*]

39. **El Vez (1960–)** tongue-in-cheek "Mexican Elvis" Robert Lopez, with pencil-thin mustache and gelled hair; also performs traditional mariachi songs and sings alternate lyrics to popular music that address serious Chicano-related issues. [Am. Music: *SJEPC*]

40. **Eminem (1972–)** real name Marshall Mathers; one of the most popular rappers and rap lyricists of all time; first prominent white rapper. [Am. Music: Misc.]

41. **Ertegun, Ahmet (1923–2006)** Turkish-American iconic music executive cofounded Atlantic Records in 1947; with keen insight, recognized and signed such jazz, blues, and rock talents as John Coltrane, Ray Charles, and Led Zepplin. [Music: *SJEPC*]

42. **Feliciano, Jose (1945–)** blind, Puerto Rican-born guitar virtuoso/singer performs eclectic music in both Spanish and English; achieved fame in 1968 with his version of "Light My Fire" and unique, controversial performance of "The Star-Spangled Banner" at World Series game. [Am. Music: *SJEPC*; Misc.]

43. **Fleetwood Mac** popular during 1970s-80s; Stevie Nicks, Lindsey Buckingham, Christine McVie, John McVie, and Mick Fleetwood skyrocketed to top with album *Rumours* (1977), with songs that reflected turmoil in the band's personal relationships. [Am. Music: *SJEPC*]

44. **Franklin, Aretha (1942–)** singer/songwriter/pianist is undisputed "Queen of Soul," with "Respect" (1967) among her many hits;

first woman to be inducted into Rock and Roll Hall of Fame (1987). [Am. Music: *SJEPC*]

45. **Garland, Judy (1922–1969)** legendary singer and actress with powerful, emotive voice; introduced memorable songs such as "Over the Rainbow" (1939), "The Trolley Song" (1944), and "The Man that Got Away" (1954). [Am. Music and Film: *SJEPC*]

46. **Gaye, Marvin (1939–1984)** singer/songwriter of soul music was instrumental in Motown's distinct sound and success with such recordings as "I Heard It through the Grapevine" (1968) and "Ain't No Mountain High Enough" with Tammi Terrell (1967); tragically killed by his father. [Am. Music: *SJEPC*]

47. **Gillespie, Dizzy (1917–1993)** upbeat, charistmatic jazz trumpeter with signature bent horn and ballooned-out cheeks influenced jazz styles from the 1930s to the 1990s; instrumental in originating bebop and Afro-Cuban jazz. [Am. Music: *SJEPC*]

48. **Gordy, Berry (1929–)** founder of immensely successful music production company Motown, established in Detroit and named for the Motor City in 1959; responsible for distinctive Motown sound and for launching such acts as Diana Ross and the Supremes and Smoky Robinson and the Mi [Am. Music: *SJEPC*]

49. **Grand Ole Opry** iconic country music radio show in Nashville featuring live performances has been the hallmark of success for artists since 1925. [Am. Music: *SJEPC*]

50. **Grant, Amy (1960–)** singer/songwriter of Christian music transformed and popularized the genre with her emotional, personal style and a rock beat in early 1980s. [Am. Music: *SJEPC*]

51. **Grateful Dead, The** famous rock band who gained popularity in the late sixties; known for eclectic style; fiercely loyal Deadhead followers are numerous. [Am. Music: Misc.]

52. **Green, Al (1946–)** often called "the quintessential soul man"; Grammy award-winning reverend was most famous in the 1970s for songs such as "Let's Stay Together"; went on to produce highly successful gospel albums. [Am. Music: *SJEPC*]

53. **Guy, Buddy (1936–)** blues guitar virtuoso influenced other guitar greats like Stevie Ray Vaughan, Jimi Hendrix, and Eric Clapton. [Am. Music: *SJEPC*]

54. **Haley, Bill (1925–1983)** singer, guitarist, created one of the pioneering rock and roll groups, Bill Haley and the Comets, blending country and rock in such hits as "Rock around the Clock." [Am. Music: *EB*]

55. **Hendrix, Jimi (1942–1970)** guitar virtuoso and rock pioneer, especially in his influential *Are You Experienced?* (1967); died of an apparent drug overdose at age 27; a symbol of youthful talent and excess. [Am. Music: *EB*]

56. **hip-hop** rhythmic beat and chant-like singing grew out of an anti-gang movement in urban communities in the 1980s to celebrate African-American life. [Am. Music: *SJEPC*]

57. **Holly, Buddy (1936–1959)** legendary star of early rock whose hits include "Peggy Sue"; died in a plane crash at age of 22. [Am. Music: *EB*]

58. **Ink Spots, The** popular group during WWII and beyond; known for romantic ballads; influenced the "doo wop" groups of early rock 'n' roll. [Am. Music: *SJEPC*]

59. **Iron Maiden** quintessential heavy metal band with international appeal; music known for lyrics with roots in horror, mythology, wars, and history. [Br. Music: *SJEPC*]

60. **Jackson, Michael (1958–)** brilliant pop composer and singer who began his career as a child of sensational talent; as an adult, eccentric lifestyle and dazzlings stage performances kept him in the headlines. [Am. Music: *SJEPC*]

61. **Jefferson Airplane/Starship** formed in 1965; extremely popular band of West Coast Rock and typified underground, drug-infused culture of hippie generation. [Am. Music: *SJEPC*]

62. **John, Elton (1947–)** flamboyant singer-songwriter whose career began in 1969; onstage persona and intriguing costumes drew fans; controversial announcement of bisexuality, eventually admitted to homosexuality and a history of substance abuse. [Br. Music: *SJEPC*]

63. **Johnson, Robert (1914?-1938)** created legend that he had sold his soul to the devil for his amazing talent as a blues guitarist; his music featured interplay between instrument and voice and use of slide on guitar frets. [Am. Music: *SJEPC*]

64. **Joplin, Scott (1868–1917)** preeminent African-American composer of ragtime music at turn of twentieth century; best known for "Maple Leaf Rag" (1898). [Am. Music: *SJEPC*]

65. **Junior Walker and the All-Stars** talented rhythm-and-blues bank that released several hits for Motown in 1960s; their sound tougher than the typical songs produced there. [Am. Music: *SJEPC*]

66. **Kasem, Casey (1932–)** engaging host of radio and TV program *American Top 40* since 1970; played countdown of the week's top recordings and introduced the "teaser-bio" format, giving biographical information about the recording artist before playing the song. [Am. Radio and TV: *SJEPC*]

67. **Kern, Jerome (1885–1945)** Academy Award-winning composer of beautiful, timeless songs for Broadway musicals and films; "Ol' Man River" and "The Way You Look Tonight" are among the many. [Am. Theater and Film: *SJEPC*]

68. **King, Carole (1942–)** singer who started career as part of successful songwriting team writing Top Forty songs; in early 1970s recorded her own music to great acclaim. [Am. Music: *SJEPC*]

69. **KISS** rock and roll band with sustainable songs and influence; onstage theatrics, energetic choreography, elaborate makeup and costumes (worn all the time), and distinct individual personas made for crowd appeal. [Am. Music: *SJEPC*]

70. **Lauper, Cyndi (1953–)** vibrant 1980s pop star; her "Girls Just Wanna Have Fun" and other lyrics lauding women and her commitment to hiring women for all aspects of her music and video production earned her kudos and awards from *Ms. Magazine* and others. [Am. Music: *SJEPC*]

71. **Led Zepplin** English rock band; categorized as one the first and finest heavy metal bands; "Stairway to Heaven" is a classic of the genre. [Br. Music: Misc.]

72. **Lennon, John (1940–1980), and Paul McCartney (1942–)** songwriting duo of The Beatles were close friends and creative rivals. [Br. Music: *SJEPC*]

73. **Little Richard (1932–)** with wild falsetto, high pompadour, and frenetic performance style, embodies rebelliousness and free nature of rock 'n' roll; hits included "Tutti Frutti" and "Lucille." [Am. Music: Misc.]

74. **Marley, Bob (1945–1981)** his rebellious and socially conscious reggae songs found enthuiastic acceptance by audiences worldwide; often credited with bringing reggae to the world and setting the standard by which the subsequent music of the genre will be compared. [Jamaican Music: Misc.]

75. **McCartney, Paul (1942–)** singer/songwriter of melodic popular rock music; formerly of famous Beatles. [Br. Music: *SJEPC*]

76. **mosh pit** area in front of the stage at a rock concert that fills with dancing fans; can sometimes become violent and dangerous. [Pop. Culture: Misc.]

77. **Motown** legendary Detroit recording company for pop and rhythm and blues music by primarily African-American artists. [Am. Music: *SJEPC*]

78. **MTV** cable station of music videos, advertisements, and programs for youthful audiences. [Am. Music: *SJEPC*]

79. **Napster** on-line file-sharing program started in 1999 by Shawn Fanning; shut down for years because of the infringement on copyright laws, then re-opened for paying users. [Am. Business: Misc.]

80. **New Age Music** soothing music, often instrumental; a favorite for meditation and relaxation. [Music: *SJEPC*]

81. **New Kids on the Block** all-white teen singing group with innocent image and appeal to pre-adolescent females. [Am. Music: *SJEPC*]

82. **New Wave Music** arose as rejection of disco and arena-rock; eclectic mix of indie groups primarily recording in the 1980s. [Am. Music: *SJEPC*]

83. **Nirvana** famous grunge band whose "Seattle Sound" meant abrasive guitar rock and unpolished production. [Am. Music: *SJEPC*]

84. **Osbourne, Ozzy (1948–)** heavy metal vocalist who began with Black Sabbath; revelled in outrageous behavior onstage. [Br. Music: *SJEPC*]

85. **Paul, Les (1915–)** famous guitarist who devised multi-tracking recording techniques; solid body guitar model named after him. [Am. Music: *SJEPC*]

86. **Pearl Jam** popular grunge band, somewhat more accessible than others. [Am. Music: *SJEPC*]

87. **Peppermint Lounge, The** hangout of celebrities and music fans; birthplace of the *Peppermint Twist*. [Am. Music: *SJEPC*]

88. **Pink Floyd** quintessential psychedelic rock group; atmospheric music and special effects brought crowds to their concerts. [Am. Music: *SJEPC*]

89. **Porter, Cole (1891–1964)** prolific composer and lyricist of Broadway musicals and countless timeless songs; his lifestyle relected the essence of finesse [Am. Music: *SJEPC*]

90. **Presley, Elvis (1935–1977)** perhaps the most famous rock 'n' roll singer of all time, hence, called "The King"; his versatile voice, pioneering music, gyrations on stage, and tough-guy image made him a sensation world-wide [Am. Music: *SJEPC*]

91. **Prince (1958–)** prolific songwriter and intriguing performer; has undergone numerous permutations in his persona and music, at one time changing his name to a symbol; often faced criticism for sexually, sometimes sadomasochistic, themes. [Am. Music: *SJEPC*]

92. **Puente, Tito (1923–2000)** "King of Latin Music"; Grammy-winning musician, composer, and bandleader who brought Latin music to audiences worldwide. [Am. Music: *SJEPC*]

93. **punk** movement among young people in 1970s; music meant to offend, extreme attire with colored hair and studs and pins, and belligerence toward anything conventional. [Br. and Am. . Pop. Culture: *SJEPC*]

94. **Ramones, The** American rock band; considered forefathers of the rebellious punk movement. [Am. Music: *SJEPC*]

95. **rap** rhythmic beat and chant-like singing with graphic and sometimes controversial lyrics, especially the "gangsta" type; mainly performed by African-American artists. [Am. Music: *SJEPC*]

96. **Robinson, Smokey (1940–)** one of the premier singer/songwriters of pop music; love songs like "My Girl" and "The Tracks of My Tears" were recorded by Robinson and others and contributed greatly to the success of Motown Records; his sweet falsetto conveyed as much emotion as his lyrics. [Am. Music: Misc.]

97. *Rolling Stone* journal with serious coverage of rock music, culture, and politics; appearing on the cover became sign of popular culture distinction. [Am. Jour.: *SJEPC*]

98. **Rolling Stones, The** wrote and performed blues-inspired rock music and brought it to US audiences during the "British Invasion" of the 1960s; antithesis to attractive, well-groomed Beatles. [Br. Music: *SJEPC*]

99. **Santana** blending Latin and African sounds, Mexican Carlos Santana formed a monumentally successful band in America the 1960s; despite permutations in the band, their popularity persisted. [Am. Music: *SJEPC*]

100. **Savoy Ballroom** famous dance venue in Harlem from 1926–1956; countless dance crazes began there and many jazz bands of Swing Era performed. [Am. Music: *SJEPC*]

101. **Sex Pistols** their violent, raucous music and themes of anarchy brought punk to the forefront; led by Johnny Rotten and Sid Vicious; the latter's death by drugs symbolized the reckless punk lifestyle. [Br. Music: *SJEPC*]

102. **Shakur, Tupac (1971–1996)** also known as 2Pac; best-selling creator of rap songs about black culture, the brutality of police, and poverty; sometimes labeled a gangsta rapper for his controversial poetry; died of gunshot wounds. [Am. Music: *SJEPC*]

103. **Simon, Paul (1941–)** prolific songwriter who has experimented with a variety of styles since his early days in folk-rock music; poetic, meaningful lyrics and musically sound pop melodies characterize his influential work. [Am. Music: *SJEPC*]

104. **Simon and Garfunkel** [Paul Simon (1941–) and Art Garfunkel (1941–)] Simon's poetic lyrics with complex themes often reflecting social upheaval of the 1960s; songs with meld of folk acoustics, electric guitars, and drums and beautiful vocal harmonies. [Am. Music: *SJEPC*]

105. **Sinatra, Frank (1915–1988)** one of popular music's greatest icons; considered not only an incomparable singer, but a stylist; best known for emotional renditions of standards with masterfully arranged instrumental accompaniment. [Am. Music: *SJEPC*]

106. **Smith, Patti (1946–)** important punk songwriter/performer and poet. [Am. Music: *SJEPC*]

107. **Sonny & Cher** [Salvatore Bono (1935–1998) and Cher Sarkisian (1946–)] mid-1960s pop music sensation; went on to host very popular comedy variety TV show where they engaged in good-natured arguments and put-downs. [Am. Music and TV: *SJEPC*]

108. *Soul Train* in 1970, first mainstream American show to feature soul and rhythm and blues artists; the black *American Bandstand* showed teenaged guests decked out in the latest fashions dancing before the camera. [Am. TV: *SJEPC*]

109. **Sousa, John Philip (1854–1932)** composer of over 100 rousing marches and leader of world-renowned concert band; devoted to making people proud of America, bringing him great popularity and a host of honors. [Am. Music: *SJEPC*]

110. **Spector, Phil (1940–)** influential producer of pop music; created "the wall of sound" through arrangements of strings, horns, and percussion. [Am. Music: *SJEPC*]

111. **Spice Girls, The** British singing group of the 1990s with carefully chosen identities (Ginger, Scary, Posh, Sporty, Baby) who purported "girl power" and performed fun songs for young female audiences. [Br. Music: *SJEPC*]

112. **Springsteen, Bruce (1949–)** hugely successful rock and roll singer/songwriter whose blue-collar background informs his music, as does his political and social ideology. [Am. Music: *SJEPC*]

113. **Steppenwolf** coined the phrase "heavy metal music" and went on to embody its clamorous rebelliousness; their "Born to Be Wild" was featured in 1969 counterculture film *Easy Rider*. [Am. Music: *SJEPC*]

114. **Stewart, Rod (1945–)** singer and composer whose gritty voice and sexy stage persona brought fame; hits like "Da Ya Think I'm Sexy" reflected his fun-loving self-mockery, while those like "Maggie May" showed his more sensitive side. [Scot. Music: Misc.]

115. **Summer, Donna (1948–)** queen of disco with breakthrough hit "Love to Love You Baby" in 1975; its frank sexuality was unheard of at the time. [Am. Music: *SJEPC*]

116. **Sun Records** established in 1952 by Sam Phillips; greatly influenced popular music by recording Elvis Presley and other notable artists. [Am. Music: *SJEPC*]

117. **Supremes, The** early and prominent black Motown singing trio; glitzy look and outstanding songs brought success. [Am. Music: *SJEPC*]

118. **Talking Heads** ostensibly a punk band, their music was intellectual, emotional, and danceable; singer/songwriter David Bryne went on to work successfully in various musical forms. [Am. Music: *SJEPC*]

119. **Taylor, James (1948–)** major singer/songwriter with folk/ country blend, poetic lyrics, and angelic voice who rose to popularity in the 1970s. [Am. Music: *SJEPC*]

120. **Temptations, The** famous Motown group with smooth harmonies, slick choreography and flashy dress who recorded his songs in various genres. [Am. Music: *SJEPC*]

121. **Tiny Tim (1927?-1996)** falsetto voice, odd clothes and demeanor made him a curiosity and a celebrity; best known for his 1968 recording of old standard "Tiptoe thru the Tulips with Me." [Am. Music: *SJEPC*]

122. **Turner, Ike (1931–2007) and Tina (1938–)** with crossover music and energized performances, often backed by full orchestration African-American husband and wife duo had unique R&B sound; Tina went on to be one of the premier female singers of rock and pop. [Am. Music: *SJEPC*]

123. **Valens, Ritchie (1941–1959)** Latino teen rock star best known for "La Bamba," his rock version of a Mexican ballad; career cut short when he died in plane crash along with rock legends Buddy Holly and the Big Bopper. [Am. Music: *SJEPC*]

124. **Van Halen** blending experimentation with traditional rock 'n' roll and known for wild off-stage lifestyle; 1970s heavy-metal rock band (named after their guitarist Eddie Van Halen) continuously renovated their sound. [Am. Music: *SJEPC*]

125. **Vaughan, Stevie Ray (1954–1990)** influential rock guitarist of the 1980s in blues tradition; cocaine abuse sent him into rehab, but his life ended in a helicopter crash. [Am. Music: *SJEPC*]

126. **Velvet Underground, The** latter half of the 1960s saw this very influential avant-garde rock band reaching many soon-to-be-famous musicians despite modest commerical success; Andy Warhol produced their first gritty album in 1966. [Am. Music: *SJEPC*]

127. **Waits, Tom (1949–)** debut album released in 1973; gravelly voice and barfly stage persona linked with jazz/folk sound. [Am. Music: *SJEPC*]

128. **Walker, Aaron (1910–1975)** "T-Bone" Walker played both jazz and blues; father of electric blues; flamboyant stage act influenced Elvis Presley, Chuck Berry and more. [Am. Music: *SJEPC*]

129. **Welk, Lawrence (1903–1992)** bandleader whose phenomenal twenty-seven-year run as host of musical variety TV show attested to popularity of squeaky clean acts he featured. [Am. Music and TV: *SJEPC*]

130. **Whisky a-Go-Go** Sunset Boulevard discotheque and performance venue for notables in cutting edge of rock industry beginning in 1964; females dancing in cages were called go-go girls. [Am. Music: *SJEPC*]

131. **Who, The** led by composer/guitarist Peter Townsend; talented group of rock musicians known for exceptional music, flamboyant performances—often smashing their instruments at the end of show; their unique rock opera *Tommy* (1969) thrilled some and confused oth [Br. Music: *SJEPC*]

132. **Williams, John (1932–)** pianist, conductor, and award-winning composer; his famous scores are considered by many to be unparalleled in their emotional impact and perfect alignment with the intent of the films; include *Star Wars, E.T, Indiana Jones, Jaws*, etc. [Am. Music: Misc.]

133. **Wolfman Jack (1938–1995)** radio disc jockey with gravelly voice and signature growl who ruled the airwaves in the 1960s and brought rock 'n' roll (especially rhythm and blues music of black artists) into American homes. [Am. Music: *SJEPC*]

134. **Wonder, Stevie (1950–)** blind African-American songwriter and performer; tremendously talented and versatile; has worked in various genres with many instruments (most notably the synthesizer). [Am. Music: *SJEPC*]

135. **Young, Neil (1945–)** cited as inspiration of 1990s grunge movement; unusual and diverse music characterized by high-pitched voice and poetic, often socially-conscious lyrics. [Am. Music: *SJEPC*]

136. *Your Hit Parade* radio and TV show that ran primarily from 1935–1959; singers performed week's most popular songs with number one song revealed as determined by record sales, sheet music sales, jukebox play, etc. [Am. Music: *SJEPC*]

486. MUSIC, ROOTS (See also SINGER.)

1. **Baez, Joan (1941–)** folk singer committed to social and political causes from the 1960s into the 21st century. [Am. Music: *SJEPC*]

2. **Belafonte, Harry (1927–)** Jamaican-American singer launched calypso craze in the 1950s. [Am. Music: *SJEPC*]

3. **Brooks, Garth (1962–)** phenomenally popular country music artist brought the genre to a mass audience in the 1990s, successfully crossing over into pop music territory. [Am. Music: *SJEPC*]

4. **Carter Family** group recorded and performed traditional folk songs in the 1920s-1940s; laid the foundation of modern country music. [Am. Music: *SJEPC*]

5. **Cash, Johnny (1932–2003)** legendary country music songwriter, singer, and guitarist with rebellious image and deep baritone voice; career spanned from mid-1950s to his death. [Am. Music: *SJEPC*]

6. **Chenier, Clifton (1925–1987)** King of Zydeco; credited with creating the blend of Louisiana Creole dance music, blues, and soul known as zydeco. [Am. Music: *SJEPC*]

7. **Cline, Patsy (1932–1963)** helped bridge the gap between traditional country music and popular music, crossing over with her upbeat songs and smooth vocals. [Am. Music: *SJEPC*]

8. **Credence Clearwater Revival** under leader/songwriter John Fogarty, swamp rock band CCR climbed to top of the pop charts in the late 1960s and early 1970s with such protest songs as "Who'll Stop the Rain?" [Am. Music: *SJEPC*]

9. **Diddley, Bo (1928–2008)** guitarist/songwriter whose unique slap-and-stomp rhythm derived from a mixture of African and blues traditions in the 1950s later influenced rock 'n' roll and rap. [Am. Music: *SJEPC*]

10. **Dylan, Bob (1941–)** spanning folk, blues, and rock music in five decades, legendary songwriter/singer with nasal voice represented his generation during the period of monumental social change in the 1960s. [Am. Music: *SJEPC*]

11. **Elmore, James (1918–1965)** guitarist who was revolutionary in blues music; his opening riff on "Dust My Broom" is a classic blues sound, one found in many subsequent blues compositions; he influenced many others, most notably Jimi Hendrix. [Am. Music: *SJEPC*]

12. **Farm Aid** organization spearheaded by country music legend Willie Nelson to assist America's family farmers; funds its programs through mega-concerts featuring top artists. [Am. Music: *SJEPC*]

13. **Flatt, Lester (1914–1979)** bluegrass guitarist, singer, and composer; played with Bill Monroe, then formed the Foggy Mountain Boys with Earl Scruggs. [Am. Music: *EB*]

14. **Foggy Mountain Boys, The** classic bluegrass band formed by Lester Flatt and Earl Scruggs in 1948; recording of "The Ballad of Jed Clampett" (1962), theme for TV's "Beverly Hillbillies," brought mainstream audiences. [Am. Music: *SJEPC*]

15. **Folkways Records** independent label established in 1948 by Moe Asche recorded the music of American folk artists like Leadbelly and Woodie Guthrie to preserve the heritage; collection now housed at the Smithsonian Institution. [Am. Music: *SJEPC*]

16. **Ford, Tennessee Ernie (1919–1991)** country music singer popular in 1950s crossed over to mainstream with his "country boogie" style. [Am. Music: *SJEPC*]

17. **Guthrie, Arlo (1947–)** popular folksinger and activist associated with the 1960s antiwar movement through his song "Alice's Restaurant" learned the art of social protest music from famous father Woody Guthrie. [Am. Music: *SJEPC*]

18. **Guthrie, Woody (1912–1967)** iconic, influential American folksinger; his songs criticized social and economc inequities in

America and celebrated the irrepressible spirit of downtrodden men and women, particularly migrant farm workers during the Dust Bowl years (1930s). [Am. Music: *SJEPC*]

19. **Haggard, Merle (1937–)** influential country music singer and songwriter, known for blending of country and jazz stylings, duets with Willie Nelson and others. [Am. Music: *EB*]

20. **Handy, W. C. (1873–1958)** African-American composer who pioneered the blues, combining its stylings with those of ragtime; wrote "St. Louis Blues." [Am. Music: *EB*]

21. *Hee Haw* long-running TV show (1969–1993) featured co-hosts Buck Owens and Roy Clark; popularized bluegrass, country, gospel music. [Am. TV: Misc.]

22. **Hooker, John Lee (1917–2001)** African-American guitarist and singer, one of the most influential blues guitarist of his generation. [Am. Music: *EB*]

23. **Howlin' Wolf (1910–1976)** African-American singer and composer, one of the greatest of the Chicago blues men. [Am. Music: *EB*]

24. **Jennings, Waylon (1937–2002)** prominent and influential part of country western music's "Outlaw Movement" of 1970s, performing with road band and refusing slick honky-tonk sound of most Nashville music; became superstar and crossover pop star. [Am. Music: *SJEPC*]

25. **King, B. B. (1925–)** one of most influential and well known blues musicians ever; "King of the Blues" used fusion of acoustic country blues and jazz. [am. Music: *SJEPC*]

26. **Leadbelly (1885–1949)** blues guitarist and singer/songwriter; his chaotic, often brutal life was basis of his incredible songs; twice released from prison on basis of his musical talent. [Am. Music: *SJEPC*]

27. **Monroe, Bill (1911–1996)** father of bluegrass, originator of the "high lonesome" sound. [Am. Music: *BT*]

28. **Nelson, Willie (1933–)** one of the most successful and influential country music singer, songwriter, and composer of such classics as "Crazy"; organized Farm Aid. [Am. Music: *EB*]

29. **Peter, Paul, and Mary** folk trio known for beautiful harmonies and commitment to social activism. [Am. Music: *SJEPC*]

30. **reggae** music of Jamaica, blending Caribbean sounds with American rhythm and blues; sometimes uses political themes and often associated with Rastafarian religion. [Am. Music: *SJEPC*]

31. **Rodgers, Jimmie (1897–1933)** singer, songwriter, and musician who is considered the father of country music for themes of hardship, nasal vocals, yodeling, and guitar accompaniment. [Am. Music: *SJEPC*]

32. **Rogers, Roy (1912–1998)** singing cowboy; films featured horse Trigger, sidekick Gabby Hayes, and wife Dale Evans; successful TV show. [Am. Music: *SJEPC*]

33. **Salsa Music** native to Cuba, but evolved in New York City; incorporates African rhythms and European harmony into hot Latin American dance sound. [Am. Music: *SJEPC*]

34. **Scruggs, Earl (1924–)** virtuoso bluegrass banjo player and partner of Lester Flatt; three-finger method that he perfected bears his name. [Am. Music: *SJEPC*]

35. **Seeger, Pete (1919–)** quintessential folk musician who paved the way for singer/activists through his devotion to many social causes. [Am. Music: *SJEPC*]

36. **Selena (1971–1995)** award-winning Latino singer of Tejano, Tex-Mex fusion music; shot to death by employee at age 24. [Am. Music: *SJEPC*]

37. **Southern Rock** rock music with a country feel played by Southern bands such as the Allman Brothers, Charlie Daniels Band, and Little Feat; emerged as a genre in the 1970s. [Am. Music: *SJEPC*]

38. **Tejano Music** Mexican-American music reflecting both cultures; much originated in Texas. [Am. Music: *SJEPC*]

39. **Waters, Muddy (1915–1983)** well-known blues singer, guitarist, and songwriter; in the 1940s transformed southern blues into more gritty urban blues that greatly influenced rock 'n' roll. [Am. Music: *SJEPC*]

40. **Williams, Hank, Jr. (1949–)** country rock music artist whose biggest hits were autobiographical, reflecting his life as son of country music legend. [Am. Music: *SJEPC*]

41. **Williams, Hank, Sr. (1923–1953)** founder of contemporary country music; short but influential career marked by plaintive songs and mesmerizing performances. [Am. Music: *SJEPC*]

42. **Zydeco, Buckwheat (1947–)** according-playing ambassador of zydeco, the black Creole dance music originating in Louisiana. [Am. Music: *SJEPC*]

487. MUSICALS

1. *Annie* 1977 story of likable orphan Annie, who is taken in for a holiday weekend by billionaire "Daddy" Warbucks; most popular songs include "Tomorrow" and "Hard-Knock Life". [Am. Theater: Misc.]

2. *Bye, Bye Birdie* set in 1958; plot revolves around Elvis-inspired character Conrad Birdie whose performance on Ed Sullivan before he leaves for the army affects the lives of a songwriter and a member of his fan club. [Am. Theater: Misc.]

3. *Camelot* Lerner and Loewe's 1960 musical about King Arthur, Queen Guenevere, and Sir Lancelot featured top stars Richard Burton, Julie Andrews, and Robert Goulet, and famous songs "Camelot" and "If Ever I Would Leave You." [Am. Musical: *SJEPC*]

4. *Cats* Andrew Lloyd Webber's long-running musical based on T. S. Eliot's *Old Possum's Book of Practical Cats*; premiered in London in 1981, featured popular song "Memory." [Br. Musical: *SJEPC*]

5. *Chorus Line, A* Pulitzer Prize given to this 1975 portrayal of hopeful young dancers who reveal their personal stories as they audition for parts in the chorus line of a muscial. [Am. Theater: Misc.]

6. *Evita* famous 1979 Andrew Lloyd Webber musical; follows the life of Argentine president Juan Peron's controversial second wife, Eva. [Am. Theater: Misc.]

7. *Fantasticks, The* 1960 off-Broadway musical that went on to become a famous standard of theater; two children fall in love, learn it was part of their fathers' plan, and decide to separate and have their own experiences. [Am. Theater: Misc.]

8. *Fiddler on the Roof* cherished traditions and values in small Russian village of 1905 are difficult to maintain for poor Jewish peasant Tevye and his wife Golde as they raise five headstrong daughters in an ever-changing world (1964). [Am. Musical: *SJEPC*]

9. *42nd Street* musical motion picture about the drama behind the curtains of a Broadway musical's premiere ushered in a golden era for the genre in the depths of the Depression (1933); featured Busby Berkeley's kaleidoscopic choreography and starred Ruby Keeler. [Am. Film: *SJEPC*]

10. **Fosse, Bob (1927–1987)** visionary dancer/director/choreographer whose distinctive, sexually suggestive style earned him Tony Awards for such stage musicals as *The Pajama Game* (1954), *Sweet Charity* (1966), and *Pippin* (1972). [Am. Dance: *SJEPC*]

11. *Grease* 1972 musical based on the lives and loves of high school students in 1959. [Am. Theater: Misc.]

12. *Hair* 1967 musical about a group of antiwar hippies trying to create a Bohemian life in New York City. [Am. Theater: Misc.]

13. *Hairspray* features 1960s-style music; follows the mission of a high school student, Tracy Turnblad, to intergrate *The Corny Collins Show* while maintaining an upbeat attitude and having fun. [Am. Theater: Misc.]

14. *Hello, Dolly!* Broadway blockbuster, with lyrics by Jerry Herman, opened in 1964 and won 10 Tonys; stars in title role have included Carol Channing, Pearl Bailey, and, in the film version (1969) Barbra Streisand. [Am. Theater and Film: *EB*]

15. ***Jesus Christ Superstar*** rock opera by Andrew Lloyd Webber about Passion and death of Christ; first released as album because no financial backing could be found; opened in NY in 1971 and filmed in 1973; brought accusations of humanizing Christ too much, but audiences approved. [Br. and Am. Theater and Film: *SJEPC*]

16. ***Joseph and the Amazing Technicolor Dreamcoat*** early Andrew Lloyd Webber musical (1968); based on the Biblical story of Joseph and his coat of many colors. [Am. Theater: Misc.]

17. **Kern, Jerome (1885–1945)** Academy Award-winning composer of beautiful, timeless songs for Broadway musicals and films; "Ol' Man River" and "The Way You Look Tonight" are among the many. [Am. Theater and Film: *SJEPC*]

18. ***King and I, The*** classic musical by Rogers and Hammerstein; opened in 1951; Anna becomes the teacher of the King of Siam's children. [Am. Theater: Misc.]

19. ***Misérables, Les*** based on the classic novel by Victor Hugo; takes place during the Napoleonic wars in France; follows tragic hero Jean Valjean, haunted by a past he can't escape; also known as *Les Miz*. [Am. Theater: Misc.]

20. ***Music Man, The*** 1957 Broaday hit about a con man who plans on selling instruments and uniforms to small town residents and leaving town with the money until he falls in love. [Am. Theater: Misc.]

21. ***My Fair Lady*** 1956 musical by Lerner and Loewe based on George Bernard Shaw's *Pygmalion*; professor Henry Higgins gives speech lessons to a Cockney flower girl to transform her into a lady. [Am. Theater: Misc.]

22. ***On the Town*** music written by Leonard Bernstein; three American sailors fall in love with women and New York City during a 24–hour shore leave in 1944. [Am. Theater: Misc.]

23. ***Phantom of the Opera, The*** enormously successful Andrew Lloyd Webber musical about angry, disfigured composer who haunts the sewers beneath the Paris Opera House. [Theater: *SJEPC*]

24. **Prince, Hal (1928–)** director and producer of countless remarkable and successful Broadway musicals. [Am. Theater: *SJEPC*]

25. ***Rent*** rock musical based on Puccini's *La Bohème*; captures the lives of a group of artists and musicians in New York City, struggling with making ends meet and the effects of AIDS. [Am. Theater: Misc.]

26. **Robbins, Jerome (1918–1998)** preeminent choreographer and sometimes director of many major Broadway musicals, including

West Side Story (1957) and *Fiddler on the Roof* (1964). [Am. Theater: Misc.]

27. **Rodgers and Hammerstein** [Richard Rodgers (1902–1979) and Oscar Hammerstein II (1895–1960)] composer and lyricist; first collaborated in 1943 for *Oklahoma!*; other well-loved musicals followed. [Am. Music and Theater: *SJEPC*]

28. **Rodgers and Hart** [Richard Rodgers (1902–1979) and Lorenz Hart (1895–1943)] composer and lyricist duo for musical theater and films; many songs live on as cherished standards. [Am. Music: *SJEPC*]

29. *Show Boat* first produced in 1927; based on Edna Ferber novel with music and lyrics by Jerome Kern and Oscar Hammerstein II; tale of life on Mississippi River; probably best known song "Ol' Man River" which, along with others, became a standard. [Am. Theater: *SJEPC*]

30. *Singin' in the Rain* 1952 film musical about film musicals; portrays the sometimes rocky beginnings of talkie pictures; most notable scene is Gene Kelly's dance down a street in a downpour. [Am. Film: *SJEPC*]

31. **Sondheim, Stephen (1930–)** librettist for *West Side Story*; composer and lyricist of *Sweeney Todd* and many other notable productions. [Am Theater: *SJEPC*]

32. *Sound of Music, The* Rodgers and Hammerstein Broadway musical and subsequent film based on story of famous singing Von Trapp family, who manage to escape Austria just before Nazi Germany annexes the country. [Am. Theater and Film: *SJEPC*]

33. *South Pacific* opened in 1949; Rodgers and Hammerstein musical about social and racial issues during WWII based on two stories from James Michener's *Tales of the South Pacific*; songwriting team won Pulitzer Prize for their work. [Am. Theater: *SJEPC*]

34. *Spring Awakening* alt-rock musical based on a banned German play; focuses on German teenagers in the late 1800s dealing with issues such as masturbation, rape, abortion, and suicide. [Am. Theater: Misc.]

35. *Sweeney Todd* follows the life of a man who is wrongly convicted and sent away for fifteen years, then returns, using gruesome means to get revenge on the judge who wrongly accused him and caused his wife to commit suicide. [Am. Theater: Misc.]

36. *West Side Story* classic Broadway musical opened in 1957; reworking of *Romeo and Juliet* set in modern-day New York City, where rivalry between two gangs—white and Puerto Rican—dooms two lovers. [Am. Theater and Film: *SJEPC*]

37. *Wicked* based on the novel of the same name; debuted in 2003; tells a more complicated and personal version of the story of the

Wicked Witch of the West and Glinda the Good Witch, characters from *The Wizard of Oz*. [Am. Theater: Misc.]

488. MUTENESS

1. **Elops** dumb serpent; gives no warning of its approach. [Br. Lit.: *Paradise Lost*]

2. **Henry** bald-headed, pug-nosed and silent youngster of comic strip. [Comics: Sheridan, 200]

3. *Painted Bird, The* Kosinski novel about a foundling boy struck dumb by inhuman treatment. [Am. Lit.: Weiss, 345]

4. **Singer, Mr.** mute whose disability restricts his social contacts. [Am. Lit.: Carson McCullers *The Heart Is a Lonely Hunter* in Magill II, 416]

489. MUTILATION (See also BRUTALITY, CRUELTY.)

1. **Absyrtus** hacked to death; body pieces strewn about. [Gk. Myth.: Walsh *Classical*, 3]

2. **Agatha, Saint** had breasts cut off. [Christian Hagiog.: Attwater, 34]

3. **Amazons** female warriors cut or burnt off their right breasts to prevent interference when drawing the bow. [Gk. Myth.: Brewer *Dictionary*, 29]

4. **Atreus** slew his brother Thyeste's sons and served them to their father at banquet. [Gk. Myth.: Jobes, 153]

5. **Dagon** Philistine idol; falls, losing head and hands. [O.T.: I Samuel 5:1–4]

6. **ear and knife** at Christ's betrayal, Peter cut off soldier's ear. [Christain Symbolism: N.T.: John 18:10]

7. **Erasmus, Saint** disemboweled, windlass used to wind entrails out of his body. [Art.: Daniel, 95]

8. **harem, the** besieged, the starving Janissaries cut off and eat a buttock from each woman, including Cunegonde, beloved of Candide. [Fr. Lit.: Voltaire *Candide*]

9. **Jack the Ripper** killed and disemboweled 9 London prostitutes (1888–1889). [Br. Hist.: Brewer *Note-Book*, 463]

10. **Lavinia** her tongue is cut out to prevent her from testifying to the evil deeds she has witnessed. [Br. Lit.: Shakespeare *Titus Andronicus*]

11. **Monkey's Paw, The** short story in which mangled son is brought back to life *as is* to greedy, foolish old couple with three wishes. [Br. Lit.: Benét, 511]

12. **Philomela** violated by Terseus, king of Thrace; he cuts out her tongue to prevent her from revealing his conduct. [Gk. Myth.: Benét, 738]

13. **Procrustes** made travelers fit bed by stretching or lopping off their legs. [Gk. Myth.: Zimmerman, 221]

14. **Sinis** split victims by fastening them between two bent pines and then letting the pines spring upright. [Gk. Legend: Brewer *Dictionary*, 1005]

15. **Tereus** cuts off Philomela's tongue to prevent her telling he has raped her. [Gk. Myth.: Benét, 995]

Mutiny (See REBELLION.)

490. **MYSTERY (See also DETECTIVE.)**

1. **abominable snowmen** the yeti of Tibet; believed to exist, yet no sure knowledge concerning them. [Asian Hist.: Wallechinsky, 443–444]

2. **Bermuda Triangle** section of North America where many planes and ships have mysteriously disappeared. [Am. Hist.: *EB*, I: 1007]

3. **Big Foot** man ape similar to the yeti; reputed to have been seen in northwestern U.S. [Am. Hist.: "Yeti" in Wallechinsky, 443–444]

4. **Cain, James M. (1892–1977)** writer of hard-boiled crime fiction of high quality, including *The Postman Always Rings Twice* (1934) and *Double Indemnity* (1936). [Am. Lit.: Misc.]

5. **Chandler, Raymond (1888–1959)** creator of private detective Philip Marlowe; Los Angeles setting plays an important role in his books, many of which were made into films, including *The Big Sleep* and *Farewell, My Lovely*. [Am. Lit.: Misc.:]

6. **Christie, Agatha (1890–1976)** detective novelist who created memorable detectives Hercule Poirot and Miss Jane Marple; wrote fantastically successful books that were popular worldwide; her name is synonymous with mystery in the minds of most. [Br. Lit.: Misc.]

7. **Clark, Mary Higgins (1929?-)** "America's Queen of Suspense"; phenomenally best-selling novels with masterful plots and strong female characters; many have been adapted to film and TV. [Am. Lit.: Misc.]

8. **closed book** medieval symbolism for the unknown. [Christian Symbolism: Appleton, 13]

9. **Collins, Wilkie (1824–1889)** first English novelist to write mystery fiction; his *The Woman in White* (1860) and *The Moonstone* (1868) are classics of the genre. [Br. Lit.: Misc.]

10. ***Da Vinci Code, The*** phenomenally successful, controversial 2003 mystery novel by Dan Brown; symbologist investigates murder in Louvre which leads to discovery of plot to cover up possibility that Mary Magdalene was Jesus's wife and mother of his children;

hints found in the work of Renaissance painter Leonardo da Vinci. [Am. Lit.: Misc.]

11. **Dark Lady, The** mentioned in Shakespeare's later sonnets; she has never been positively identified. [Br. Lit.: *Century Cyclopedia*, I: 1191]

12. **Doyle, Sir Arthur Conan (1859–1930)** Scottish writer best known as the creator of Sherlock Holmes, detective extraordinaire. [Scot. Lit.: Misc.]

13. **du Maurier, Daphne (1907–1989)** best known for *Rebecca* (1938), Gothic suspense novel told by female protagonist who lives in shadow of husband's seemingly perfect late first wife. [Br. Lit.: Misc.]

14. **E=mc2** physical law of mass and energy; arcanum to layman. [Am. Hist.: Flexner, 298]

15. **Easter Island's statues** origin and meaning of more than two hundred statues remain unknown. [World. Hist.: Wallechinsky, 443]

16. **Eleusinian Mysteries** ancient religious rites; its secrets have never been discovered. [Gk. Myth.: Benét, 305]

17. **Forsyth, Frederick (1938–)** Edgar award-winning writer of suspenseful thrillers pays meticulous attention to detail, making his novels chillingly authentic, as in *The Day of the Jackal* (1971). [Br. Lit: *SJEPC*]

18. **Francis, Dick (1920–)** mystery writer of novels with realistic plots, often centering on sport of horse racing. [Br. Lit.: Misc.]

19. **gothic** a style of literature, prominent in the 19th century, featuring gloomy settings and mysterious characters. [Br. Lit.: *FOF, MOD*]

20. **Hammett, Dashiell (1894–1961)** helped develop hard-boiled school of detective fiction; created characters Sam Spade and detective couple Nick and Nora Charles; *The Maltese Falcon* (1930) is often considered his finest work. [Am. Lit.: Misc.]

21. **Hitchcock, Alfred (1899–1980)** British film director who created famous movie mysteries, including *Vertigo* and *Rear Window* [Film *ODA*]

22. *Inner Sanctum, The* radio program from 1941–1952 featuring mysteries introduced by an invitation to enter through a creaking door where sound effects produced a mix of horror and humor. [Am. Radio: *SJEPC*]

23. **James, Phyllis Dorothy (1920–)** well-respected author of intelligent and atmospheric mystery novels; creator of popular detectives Adam Dalgliesh and Cordelia Gray. [Br. Lit.: Misc.]

24. **"Lady or the Tiger, The"** Frank Stockton's 1882 tale never reveals which fate awaits the youth who dared fall in love with the king's daughter. [Am. Lit.: Benét, 559]

25. *Laura* cult classic; 1944 haunting murder mystery by Otto Preminger and starring a host of noteworthy actors; the score is one of the most famous ever. [Am. Film: *SJEPC*]

26. **Leonard, Elmore (1925–)** writer of crime novels often set in Detroit and Florida, marked by crafty dialogue and local color; films of his works have been well-received by audiences and critics alike. [Am. Lit.: Misc.]

27. **Loch Ness monster** supposed sea serpent dwelling in lake. [Scot. Hist.: Wallechinsky, 443]

28. **Man in the Iron Mask** mysterious prisoner in reign of Louis XIV, condemned to wear black mask at all times. [Fr. Hist.: Brewer *Note-Book*, 460]

29. *Mary Celeste* ship found in mid-Atlantic with sails set, crew missing (1872). [Br. Hist.: Espy, 337]

30. **Mona Lisa** enigmatic smile beguiles and bewilders. [Ital. Art.: Wallechinsky, 190]

31. **Queen, Ellery** [pseuodnym of Frederic Dannay (1905–1982) and Manfred B. Lee (1905–1971)] American cousins who coauthored series of more than 35 detective novels featuring sleuth Ellery Queen; also cofounded Mystery Writers of America. [Am. Lit.: Misc.]

32. **red herrring** false clue that leads sleuths astray in mysteries; based on the use of smoked herring, which is red, to train tracking dogs, and misused by criminals to throw law enforcement off the scent; now, a symbol of any false lead. [Lit.: FOF, MOD]

33. **Roanoke Island** fate of North Carolina colony has never been established (1580s). [Am. Hist.: Jameson 430]

34. **Roswell Incident, The** U.S. government is accused of covering up existence of UFO debris found near Roswell, New Mexico in 1947. [Am. Hist.: *SJEPC*]

35. **Sphinx** half woman, half lion; poser of almost unanswerable riddle. [Gk. Myth.: Howe, 258; Gk. Lit.: *Oedipus Rex*]

36. **Spillane, Mickey (1918–2006)** author of hard-boiled novels featuring private eye Mike Hammer and spy Tiger Mann; criticized for use of violence as solution in his works. [Am. Lit.: *SJEPC*]

37. **Stonehenge** huge monoliths with lintels in Wiltshire, England, have long confounded modern man as to purpose. [Br. Hist.: Wallechinsky, 442]

38. **U.F.O.** unexplained and unidentified flying object. [Science: Brewer *Dictionary*, 1112]

39. **Udolpho** sinister castle is the setting of Ann Radcliffe's *The Mysteries of Udolpho*, considered one of the first gothic mysteries. [Br. Lit.: Ann Radcliffe *Mysteries of Udolpho*]

40. *Vertigo* murder mystery often considered Hitchcock's most important film; the 1958 film employed techniques copied by others, most notably several filmmakers of the French New Wave. [Am. Film: *SJEPC*]

491. MYSTICISM

1. **cabala** Jewish oral traditions, originating with Moses. [Judaism: Benét, 154]

2. **Catherine of Siena, Saint** experienced visions from age seven. [Christian Hagiog.: Hall, 59]

3. **Druids** magical priests of Celtic religion; oak cult. [Celtic Rel.: Leach, 325; Jobes, 471]

4. **Hudson, Dr. Wayne** believed power obtained by good deeds and silence. [Am. Lit.: *The Magnificent Obsession*, Magill I, 547–549]

5. **mothers, the** keepers of the bodiless spirits of all who have lived; they supply Faust with an image of Helen of Troy. [Ger. Lit.: *Faust*]

6. **Ouija** letterboard reveals messages from spirits. [Am. Pop. Culture: Brewer *Dictionary*, 788]

7. **Sufi** Muslim who follows a mystical path, seeking direct experiences of God through various spiritual disciplines. [Islam: *UIMT*, 50, 438]

8. **Svengali** Hungarian hypnotist, mesmerizes artist's model who becomes famous singer under his influence. [Br. Lit.: *Trilby*]

9. **Teresa of Ávila, Saint** religious contemplation brought her spiritual ecstasy. [Christian Hagiog.: Attwater, 318]

10. **voodoo** religious beliefs and practices from the West Indies. [Am. Cult.: Brewer *Dictionary*]

11. **Zen** Buddhist sect; truth found in contemplation and self-mastery. [Buddhism: Brewer *Dictionary*, 1174]

12. *Zohar, The* cabalistic reinterpretation of the Bible. [Judaism: Haydn & Fuller, 812]

N

492. NAÏVETÉ (See also INEXPERIENCE, INNOCENCE, UNSOPHISTICATION.)

1. **Agnès** ignorant girl; unaware of world's and guardian's wiles. [Fr. Lit.: *L'Ecole des Femmes*]

2. **babes in the woods** applied to easily deceived or naïve persons. [Folklore: Jobes, 169]

3. **Boyd, Woody** ignorant bartender on TV's *Cheers* (1982–93) grew up on a farm in Indiana. [Am. TV: *SJEPC*]

4. **Carlisle, Lady Mary** couldn't determine true nobility. [Am. Lit.: *Monsieur Beaucaire*, Magill I, 616–617]

5. **Delano, Amasa** naïve, goodhearted captain rescues captive captain from mutineers. [Am. Lit.: *Benito Cereno*]

6. **Errol, Cedric** seven-year-old believes the best of everyone. [Am. Lit.: *Little Lord Fauntleroy*]

7. **Evelina** 17–year-old ingenously circulates through fashionable London. [Br. Lit.: *Evelina*]

8. **Georgette** Ted Baxter's pretty, ignorant wife. [Am. TV: "The Mary Tyler Moore Show" in Terrace, II, 70–71]

9. **Jemima Puddle-Duck** protagonist of tale for children by Beatrix Potter (1908); sets off to make nest in the woods, where she meets, but fails to identify, a wily fox who nearly has her for his supper. [Br. Children's Lit.: *The Tale of Jemima Puddle-Duck*]

10. **Little Nell** meek little girl reared by grandfather. [Br. Lit.: *The Old Curiosity Shop*]

11. **Miller, Daisy** innocent and ignorant American girl put in compromising European situations. [Am. Lit.: *Daisy Miller*]

12. **Miranda** innocent and noble-minded daughter of Prospero. [Br. Lit.: *The Tempest*]

13. **Shosha** narrator's mentally backward and utterly artless wife. [Am. Lit.: *Shosha*]

14. **Tessa** childlike young woman who thinks herself wedded to Tito and obeys his command to tell nobody of their supposed marriage. [Br. Lit.: George Eliot *Romola*]

15. **Topsy** young slave girl; completely naïve. [Am. Lit.: *Uncle Tom's Cabin*]

16. **white lilac** flowers indicative of naïveté, callowness. [Flower Symbolism: *Flora Symbolica*, 175]

493. NATIVITY (See also CHRISTMAS.)

1. **Bethlehem** birthplace of Jesus. [N.T.: Matthew 2:1]

2. **Caspar, Melchior, and Balthazar** Magi of the Orient pay homage to infant Jesus. [Christianity: Hall, 6]

3. **manger** cattle trough which served as crib for Christ. [N.T.: Luke 2:7]

4. **ox and ass** always present in pictures of Christ's birth. [Christian Art: de Bles, 29; O.T.: Habakkuk 3:4]

5. **shepherds** notified by angel of the birth of the Messiah. [N.T.: Luke 2:8–17]

6. **Star of Bethlehem** star in the east which directed the Magi and shepherds to the baby Jesus. [N.T.: Matthew 2:9]

7. **swaddling clothes** in which Mary wraps her newborn infant. [N.T.: Luke 2:7]

8. **three wise men** kings of the Orient, come to worship the baby Jesus. [N.T.: Matthew 2:1–2]

Neglectfulness (See CARELESSNESS.)

Nervousness (See INSECURITY.)

494. NEW YEAR'S EVE/DAY

1. **"Auld Lang Syne"** means "days gone by"; poem written by Robert Burns in Scottish in 1788; translated and set to music and sung in English-speaking countries at midnight on New Year's Eve. [Music: Misc.]

2. **Clark, Dick (1929–)** host of *New Year's Rockin' Eve* since 1972; counts down from New York's Times Square as the giant ball descends. [Am. Music and TV: *SJEPC*]

3. **Father Time and Baby New Year** personification of time, usually bearded old man in robe, and baby pictured together to symbolize passing of one year into next. [Am. Pop. Culture: Misc.]

4. **Lombardo, Guy (1902–1977)** band leader who led his orchestra, The Royal Canadians, in a rendition of "Auld Lang Syne" each New Year's Eve at midnight from 1929 until his death, first on radio, later on TV. [Am. Radio and TV: Misc.]

5. **Rose Bowl** considered college football's preeminent post-season game; held on New Year's Day in Pasadena, California, preceded by Tournament of Roses Parade. [Am. Sports: *SJEPC*]

6. **Times Square** named after *The New York Times* tower at 42nd and Broadway; intersection of Broadway and Seventh Avenue is site of annual New Year's Eve celebration with large crowds and huge ball lowered during countdown to midnight. [Am. Culture: *SJEPC*]

Newspapers (See JOURNALISM.)

495. NIGHT

1. **Apepi** leader of demons against sun god; always vanquished by morning. [Egyptian Myth.: Leach, 66]

2. **Apophis** opponent of sun god Ra. [Egyptian Myth.: Benét, 43]

3. **Ashtoreth** Moon goddess; Queen of night; equivalent of Greek Astarte. [Phoenician Myth.: Walsh *Classical*, 34–35]

4. **Cimmerians** half-mythical people dwelling in eternal gloom. [Gk. Lit.: *Odyssey*]

5. **Erebus** personification and god of darkness. [Gk. Myth.: Brewer *Dictionary*, 381]

6. **Fafnir** his slaying represents the destruction of night demon. [Norse Myth.: *LLEI*, I: 327]

7. **Niflheim** region of everlasting night and endless cold. [Scand. Myth.: Brewer *Dictionary*, 642]

8. **Nox** goddess of night. [Rom. Myth.: Wheeler, 261]

9. **owl** nocturnal bird; Night embodied. [Art: Hall, 231]

10. **panther** black panther is feminine symbol of night, death, and re-birth. [Symbolism: *CEOS&S*]

496. NOBLE SAVAGE

1. **Chactas** the "noble savage" of the Natchez Indians; beloved of Atala. [Fr. Lit.: *Atala*]

2. **Chingachgook** idealized noble Indian. [Am. Lit.: *The Deerslayer*]

3. **Daggoo** African savage and crew member of the *Pequod*. [Am. Lit.: *Moby Dick*]

4. **noble savage** concept of a simple, pure, and superior man, un-corrupted by civilization. [Western Culture: Benét, 718–719]

5. **Oroonoko** the noble savage enslaved; rebels against captors. [Br. Lit.: *Oroonoko*]

6. **Queequeg** Polynesian prince and Ishmael's comrade aboard whaling vessel, *Pequod*. [Am. Lit.: *Moby Dick*]

7. **Rousseau, Jean-Jacques (1712–1778)** French author and precursor of the Romantic movement; created the concept of the "Noble Savage" in works stressing the natural innocence of humans and the corruptibility of society. [Fr. Lit.: *FOF, MOD*]

497. NOBLEMINDEDNESS (See also DIGNITY, HONESTY, RIGHTEOUSNESS.)

1. **Andrews, Joseph** epitome of the virtuous male. [Br. Lit.: *Joseph Andrews*]

2. **Banquo** principled and noble compatriot of Macbeth. [Br. Lit.: *Macbeth*]

3. **Bede, Adam** accepts beloved even after illicit affair. [Br. Lit.: *Adam Bede*]

4. **Camiola** generously pays Bertoldo's ransom. [Br. Lit.: *The Maid of Honor*, Walsh *Modern*, 84]

5. **Cheeryble Brothers** noble, generous twins. [Br. Lit.: *Nicholas Nickleby*]

6. **Daphnis** afraid of causing pain, does not deflower Chloë. [Gk. Lit.: *Daphnis and Chloë*, Magill I, 184]

7. **Grandison, Sir Charles** magnanimous gentleman feels honor-bound to marry an acquaintance who loves him, despite his love for another. [Br. Lit.: *Sir Charles Grandison* in Magill III, 983]

8. **Levin, Konstantine** shows compassion in dealing with peasant laborers. [Russ. Lit.: *Anna Karenina*]

9. **Little Lord Fauntleroy** improverished boy inherits title and wealth and proves to be generous and charming; transforms his bitter, ailing grandfather; from book of same name by Frances Hodgson Burnette. [Am. Children's Lit.: Jones]

10. **Lohengrin** defeats Telramund in trial by combat; spares him. [Ger. Opera: Wagner, *Lohengrin*, Westerman, 215]

11. **Lord Jim** successful in lifelong efforts to regain honor lost in moment of cowardice. [Br. Lit.: *Lord Jim*]

12. **Newman, Christopher** destroys the evidence that could wreck the man who obstructed his marriage plans. [Am. Lit.: *The American*]

13. **pirates of Penzance** never attacked weaker parties; always freed orphans. [Br. Opera: *The Pirates of Penzance*]

14. **Rienzi** pardons his would-be murderer. [Ger. Opera: Wagner, *Rienzi*, Westerman, 203]

15. **Valjean, Jean** yields to the man who has harassed him unmercifully. [Fr. Lit.: *Les Misérables*]

16. **Wilkes, Ashley** sensitive Southerner who remains true to homeland and wife. [Am. Lit.: *Gone With the Wind*, Magill III, 424–426]

Noise (See LOUDNESS.)

Nonchalance (See INDIFFERENCE.)

498. NOSE

1. **Barabas** inventor of infernal machine; possessor of pachydermal snout. [Br. Lit.: *The Jew of Malta*]

2. **Bardolph** for red nose, known as "knight of the burning lamp." [Br. Lit.: *Merry Wives of Windsor*]

3. **de Bergerac, Cyrano** gallant Frenchman; mocked unceasingly for extremely large nose. [Fr. Lit.: *Cyrano de Bergerac*]

4. **Durante, Jimmy (1893–1980)** American pianist-comedian with huge nose; nicknamed "Schnozzola.". [Am. Entertainment: "The Jimmy Durante Show" in Buxton, 124–125; Am. Cinema: Halliwell, 232]

5. **Kovalëv, Major** loses social eminence when nose self-detaches. [Russ. Lit.: *The Nose*, Kent, 474–497]

6. **Pinocchio** wooden boy's nose grows longer with every lie; protagonist of C. Collodi's classic children's book *The Adventures of Pinocchio* (1883). [Ital. Children's Lit.: Jones]

7. **Rudolph** his red nose lit the way for Santa and his sleigh. [Am. Pop. Music: "Rudolph the Red-Nosed Reindeer"]

Nosiness (See GOSSIP.)

499. NOSTALGIA

1. *American Graffiti* George Lucas's 1973 movies captures 1950s youth culture. [Am. Film: *SJEPC*]

2. *Andy Griffith Show, The* popular 1960s TV show featuring wholesome character; set in small, Southern town of Mayberry, where life was slower, simpler, and friendlier. [Am. TV: *SJEPC*]

3. **Combray** village of narrator and family. [Fr. Lit.: *Remembrance of Things Past*]

4. **Currier and Ives** makers of mass-produced color lithographs of picturesque, idealized scenes from 19th-century America that evoke sense of nostalgia. [Am. Hist.: *SJEPC*]

5. *Dick and Jane* **readers** book series used to teach reading in American classrooms from the 1930s to the 1960s; featured a simpler, friendlier, more innocent world. [Am. Education: *SJEPC*]

6. **diners** shiny, boxcar-shaped food establishments with a long counter and booths; served basic, inexpensive meals; originated in 1930s as automobile travel became more common. [Am. Culture: *SJEPC*]

7. **doo-wop** tight harmonic singing style with roots in African-American rhythm and blues of the 1950s; evokes sense of nostalgia when used by contemporary popular music artists. [Am. Music: *SJEPC*]

8. *Happy Days* successful sitcom ran from 1974 to 1984; a celebration of 1950s life; starred Ron Howard and Henry Winkler. [Am. TV: *EB*]

9. **Keillor, Garrison (1942–)** humorist whose writings depict small-town Midwest living at its most charming and sentimental; a devotee of radio, his extremely successful *Prarie Home Companion*

show (debut, 1974) combines music performances and take-offs of old radio shows and ads. [Am. Lit. and Radio: *SJEPC*]

10. **Krapp** passes the time listening to tapes on which he had recorded his earlier experiences and reflections. [Br. Drama: Beckett *Krapp's Last Tape* in Weiss, 244]

11. *My Ántonia* book in which author recalls her precious childhood years. [Am. Lit.: Magill I, 630–632]

12. **"ou sont les neiges d'antan?"** "Where are the snows of yesteryear?" [Fr. Lit.: *Ballade des Dames du temps jadis*, "Villon" in Benét, 1061]

13. **retro** in fashion and other style trends, the often playful revival of sounds, designs, and styles from the past. [Pop. Culture: *SJEPC*]

14. **Rockwell, Norman (1894–1978)** best known for his illustrations for the cover of*Saturday Evening Post*; created folksy, traditional depictions of America. [Am. Art: *SJEPC*]

500. NOUVEAU RICHE

1. *Beverly Hillbillies, The* hillbillies transplanted by wealth to Beverly Hills. [Am. TV: Terrace, I, 93–94]

2. **Gatsby, Jay** nouveau riche entrepreneur displays wealth on Long Island. [Am. Lit.: *The Great Gatsby*]

3. **Jefferson, George** bumptious black who thinks money is everything. [Am. TV: "The Jeffersons" in Terrace, I, 409–410]

4. **Jiggs and Maggie** they flounder in seas of sudden wealth. [Comics: "Bringing up Father" in Horn, 132]

5. **Jourdain, Monsieur** elderly tradesman who spends wealth trying to raise his social status. [Fr. Lit.: *Le Bourgeois Gentilhomme*]

6. **Newman, Christopher** nouveau riche entrepreneur feels he deserves an aristocratic wife. [Am. Lit.: *The American*]

501. NOVELIST

1. **Austen, Jane (1775–1817)** masterful English prose stylist; depicted, with wit and elegance, the foibles of the English landed gentry in such novels as *Pride and Prejudice*, *Emma*, and *Persuasion*. [Br. Lit.: *EB*]

2. **Buck, Pearl S. (1892–1973)** author contributed to Western understanding of Chinese culture and was first American woman to receive Nobel Prize in literature in 1938; author of *The Good Earth* (1931). [Am. Lit.: *SJEPC*; Henderson, 504; Misc.]

3. **Conrad, Joseph (1857–1924)** Polish-born writer who often wrote of the sea and exotic places; masterful prose stylist known for *Lord Jim* (1900) and *Heart of Darkness* (1902). [Am. Lit.: Misc.]

4. **Cooper, James Fenimore (1789–1851)** considered the first major American novelist; created such adventure classics as *The Last of the Mohicans*. [Am. Lit.: *EB*]

5. **Defoe, Daniel (1660–1731)** prominent 18th-century English novelist and journalist; created such classic novels as *Robinson Crusoe* and *Moll Flanders*. [Br. Lit.: *EB*]

6. **Dickens, Charles (1812–1870)** one of the most prolific and popular novelists of all time; considered a master of prose and characterization, evidenced in such enduring classics as *Bleak House* and *David Copperfield*. [Br. Lit.: *TCLM*]

7. **Dostoevsky, Fyodor (1821–1881)** one of the greatest novelists of Russian realism; greatest works, *Crime and Punishment* and *The Brothers Karamazov* offer rich explications of themes of suffering and redemption, the nature of good and evil, and the duality of human nature. [Russ. Lit.: *TCLM*]

8. **Dreiser, Theodore (1871–1945)** deterministic nature of fate and the frustrated pursuit of success in a new urban capitalistic society figured prominently in Naturalistic author's works, including *Sister Carrie* (1900) and *An American Tragedy* (1925). [Am. Lit.: *SJEPC*; Harris *Characters*, 97–98; Henderson, 470–71]

9. **Dumas, Alexander (1802–1870)** French novelist; his best-known works, *The Count of Monte Cristo* and *The Three Musketeers* are still popular adventure tales. [Fr. Lit.: *EB*]

10. **Eliot, George (1819–1880)** pseudonym of Marian Evans; one of the most accomplished novelists of the Realist era; *Middlemarch* is a masterpiece of close psychological detail and rich descriptive prose. [Br. Lit.: *TCLM*]

11. **Ellison, Ralph (1914–1994)** African-American novelist; his *Invisible Man*, a powerful exploration of race in America, is considered one of the most important novels of the 20th century. [Am. Lit.: *BBAAL2*]

12. **Faulkner, William (1897–1962)** American novelist whose works are set in the South, in fictional Yoknapatawpha County and deal with enduring problems of racism, class, and history. [Am. Lit.: *ODA*]

13. **Fitzgerald, F. Scott (1896–1940)** American Jazz Age novelist, short-story writer, and essayist became voice of his generation; writing and personal life mirrored dissoluteness of Roaring Twenties, as represented in *The Great Gatsby* (1925), and the elusiveness of American Dream. [Am. Lit.: *SJEPC*; Harris *Characters*, 111–14; Henderson, 310–11, 349]

14. **Flaubert, Gustave (1821–1880)** one of the greatest novelists in literature; *Madame Bovary* is a masterpiece of realism, and one of the most influential novels ever written. [Fr. Lit.: *TCLM*]

15. **García-Márquez, Gabriel (1928–)** Colombian novelist and Nobel laureate best known for his *One Hundred Years of Solitude*, a masterful saga depicting several generations of the Buendia family, a work that brought the concept of "magic realism" to readers worldwide. [Colombian Lit.: *TCLM*]

16. **Golding, William (1911–1993)** British author and Nobel laureate best known for his *Lord of the Flies*, an examination of the inherent evil and savagery of the human condition, depicted in a group of young boys marooned on an island. [Br. Lit.: *EB*]

17. **Grass, Günter (1927–)** German novelist whose most famous work, *The Tin Drum*, is a scathing indictment of the Nazi regime and the corrosive effects of war. [Ger. Lit.: *EB*]

18. **Hawthorne, Nathaniel (1804–1864)** considered one of the greatest American novelists and short story writers; best known for *The Scarlet Letter*, an examination of the nature of good and evil, and guilt and redemption, set in Puritan New England. [Am. Lit.: *EB*]

19. **Hemingway, Ernest (1899–1961)** influential American novelist; best known for works written in a spare prose style that explore a code of manly conduct: in the bullring, big game hunting, always showing "grace under pressure." [Am. Lit.: *EB*]

20. **Hesse, Hermann (1877–1962)** German novelist and Nobel laureate; best known for *Siddhartha*, which reflects his fascination with Eastern mysticism. [Ger. Lit.: *EB*]

21. **Hugo, Victor (1802–1885)** French novelist whose Romantic masterpieces, *Les Misérables* and *The Hunchback of Notre Dame*, made him world famous; his characters have endured into the modern era as the basis of popular films and operas. [Fr. Lit.: *EB*]

22. **Huxley, Aldous (1894–1963)** British novelist best known for *Brave New World*, a dystopian work depicting a soulless future. [Br. Lit.: *EB*]

23. **James, Henry (1843–1916)** American novelist who explored the mores of upper-class American and European society in elegant, complex prose. [Am. Lit.: *EB*]

24. **Joyce, James (1882–1941)** Irish novelist and short story writer; one of the most influential writers of the modern era, noted for development of stream of consciousness and interior monologue in works like *Ulysses*. [Irish Lit.: *EB*]

25. **Mann, Thomas (1875–1955)** German novelist and novella writer; Nobel laureate whose finest works include *The Magic Mountain, Death in Venice*, and *Joseph and His Brothers*. [Ger. Lit.: *TCLM*]

26. **Melville, Herman (1819–1891)** American author who achieved modest success during his lifetime, but has attained greatness, primarily based on his masterpiece *Moby Dick* (1851). [Am. Lit.: Misc.]

27. **Morrison, Toni (1931–)** African-American novelist and first black woman to receive the Nobel Prize; praised for such powerful works as *Beloved*. [Am. Lit.: *BBAAL2*]

28. **Orwell, George (1903–1950)** pseudonym of Eric Arthur Blair; British novelist and journalist; his masterpiece, *1984*, has proved to be one of the most influential, and prescient, dystopian novels of all time. [Br. Lit.: *EB*]

29. **Proust, Marcel (1871–1922)** French novelist and creator of the monumental *À la recherche du temps perdu*, an exploration of time, and the transformation of memory into art. [Fr. Lit.: *ODA*]

30. **Shikibu, Lady Murasaki (c.973–c.1014)** pseudonym of a maid of honor in the imperial court whose real name is unknown; author of *The Tale of Genji* (written between 1000 and 1008), one of the earliest—if not *the* earliest— novel in human history. [Japanese Lit.: Misc.]

31. **Steinbeck, John (1902–1968)** writer of transformative fiction, especially dealing with sorry plight of itinerant farm workers; *Grapes of Wrath* is his classic Depression-era novel on that theme. [Am. Lit.: *SJEPC*]

32. **Stevenson, Robert Louis (1850–1894)** Scottish novelist, essayist, and poet whose novels *Treasure Island, Dr. Jekyll and Mr. Hyde,* as well as his *Child's Garden of Verses* make him one of the most popular writers of the past 100 years. [Scot. Lit.: *EB*]

33. **Styron, William (1925–2006)** gifted writer of *Sophie's Choice* (1979) and *The Confessions of Nat Turner* (1967); the latter won the Pulitzer Prize, but brought accusations of historical inaccuracy and audacity for attempting to portray another race's experiences. [Am. Lit.: *SJEPC*]

34. **Swift, Jonathan (1667–1745)** Irish-born writer considered England's finest prose satirist; *Gulliver's Travels* continues to be read for its insights into the human condition. [Br. Lit.: *EB*]

35. **Tolkien, J.R.R. (1892–1973)** English scholar and fantasy writer of *The Hobbit* (1937) and *The Lord of the Rings* trilogy (1985–55) set in imaginary world of Middle Earth. [Br. Lit.: *SJEPC*]

36. **Tolstoy, Leo (1828–1910)** considered one of the finest novelist in literature; best known for *War and Peace* and *Anna Karenina*, considered masterpieces of realist fiction. [Russ.Lit.: *TCLM*]

37. **Trollope, Anthony (1815–1882)** English novelist beloved for his "Barchester Chronicles," insightful, beautifully written depictions of Victorian life among the landed gentry of rural England. [Br. Lit.: *EB*]

38. **Turgenev, Ivan (1818–1883)** considered the father of Russian realism; best known for his greatest novel, *Fathers and Sons*. [Russ. Lit.: *TCLM*]

39. **Twain, Mark (1835–1910)** pseudonym of Samuel Clemens; considered one of the finest American novelists; created such classics as *The Adventures of Tom Sawyer* and *The Adventures of Huck Finn.* [Am. Lit.: *TCLM*]

40. **Updike, John (1932–)** prolific and materful novelist and winner of two Pulitzer Prizes for fiction; probably best known for four novels about Harry "Rabbit" Angstrom, middle-class protagonist dealing with his dysfunctional life in an uncaring world. [Am. Lit.: *SJEPC*]

41. **Vonnegut, Kurt, Jr. (1922–2007)** wit and philosophy coexist in his work; best known for *Slaughterhouse Five* (1969), ostensibly the experiences of a WWII P.O.W., but actually covering various time periods and topics. [Am. Lit.: *SJEPC*]

42. **Wharton, Edith (1862–1937)** prominent and successful American novelist of early 1900s who often explored upper-class mores during the Golden Age; her *Age of Innocence* won Pulitzer Prize in 1920. [Am. Lit.: *SJEPC*]

43. **Woolf, Virginia (1882–1941)** British novelist and essayist whose *Mrs. Dalloway* and *To the Lighthouse* are considered modernist masterpieces for their use of stream-of-consciousness narrative and poetic imagery. [Br. Lit.: *TCLM*]

502. NUDITY

1. **Adam and Eve** unashamed in Eden without clothes. [O.T.: Genesis 2:25]

2. **Agnes, Saint** hair grew to cover her nakedness. [Christian Hagiog.: Daniel, 21]

3. **burlesque show** stage entertainment to which was added striptease dancing. [Am. Hist.: *EB*, II: 383–384]

4. **Digambara** ascetic Jainist sect whose members went naked. [Jainism: *NCE*, 1392]

5. **Godiva, Lady (d. 1057)** rode naked through Coventry to secure tax reduction for the people. [Br. Legend: Brewer *Dictionary*, 471]

6. **Gymnosophists** ancient Indian philosophers forsook clothing. [Asian Hist.: Brewer *Note-Book*, 396]

7. **Lee, Gypsy Rose (1914–1970)** American burlesque artiste. [Am. Hist.: Halliwell, 429]

8. **Maja Desnuda** Goya's celebrated picture of woman in the nude. [Span. Art.: *Spain*, 246–247]

9. *Penthouse* Bob Guccione's sexually explicit magazine for those who found *Playboy* a bit too tame. [Br. And Am. Jour.: *SJEPC*]

10. *Playboy* Hugh Hefner established the magazine in 1953; featured, among other things, photos of naked women, most notably in the centerfold. [Am. Jour.: *SJEPC*]

11. *Playgirl* established in 1973, first magazine that functioned as counterpart to *Playboy*; male nudity was sometimes featured. [Am. Jour.: *SJEPC*]

12. **streaking** extremely popular in the 1970s; running naked through public gatherings, sometimes as a form of protest. [Am. Pop. Culture: *SJEPC*]

13. **Venus de Milo** half-naked marble Aphrodite. [Gk. Art.: Osborne, 1184]

14. **Wilberforce, Miss** English lady shocks the populace by publicly disrobing when drunk. [Br. Lit.: *South Wind* in Magill II, 988]

503. NURSING

1. **Barton, Clara (1821–1912)** American nurse whose efforts raised standards of American medicine; first president of the American Red Cross. [Am. Hist.: Misc.]

2. **de Lellis, Saint Camillus** improved hospitals; patroness of sick and nurses. [Christian Hagiog.: Attwater, 78–79]

3. **Eira** Frigga's attendant; taught science of nursing to women. [Norse Myth.: *LLEI*, I: 327]

4. **Irene (fl. 3rd century)** ministered to St. Sebastian, who was wounded by arrows. [Christian Hagiog.: Hall, 162]

5. **Nightingale, Florence (1820–1910)** English nurse; founder of modern nursing. [Br. Hist.: *NCE*, 1943]

504. NYMPH

1. **Atlantides** seven daughters of Atlas by Pleione. [Gk. Myth.: Zimmerman, 37]

2. **Camenae** fountain nymphs; identified with Greek Muses. [Rom. Myth.: Zimmerman, 49]

3. **dryads** divine maidens of the woods. [Gk. and Rom. Myth.: Wheeler, 108]

4. **hamadryads** wood nymphs. [Gk. Myth.: Howe, 113]

5. **Hyades** seven daughters of Atlas, entrusted with the care of the infant Dionysus. [Gk. Myth.: Howe, 134]

6. **limoniads** nymphs of meadows and flowers. [Gk. Myth.: Zimmerman, 152]

7. **naiads** divine maidens of lakes, streams, and fountains. [Gk. and Rom. Myth.: Wheeler, 256]

8. **Napaeae** nymphs of woodland glens and vales. [Rom. Myth.: Howe, 174]

9. **Nereids** sea nymphs of the Mediterranean. [Gk. and Rom. Myth.: Wheeler, 257]

10. **Oceanids** sea nymphs of the great oceans. [Gk. and Rom. Myth.: Wheeler, 263]

11. **oreads** divine maidens of the mountains. [Gk. and Rom. Myth.: Wheeler, 270]

O

Obesity (See FATNESS.)

505. OBSCENITY (See also RIBALDRY.)

1. **Bruce, Lenny (1925–1966)** radical stand-up comic was arrested, deported, and banned many times for using obscene language in routines; became defender of First Amendment rights. [Am. Entertainment: *SJEPC*]

2. **Carlin, George (1937–2008)** stand-up comic's "Seven Words You Can Never Use on Television" routine was cause for his arrest in 1972 and tested the First Amendment in Supreme Court case concerning the broadcasting of profanity. [Am. Entertainment: *SJEPC*]

3. *Lady Chatterley's Lover* written in the late 1920s but not published in full text until 1959; D.H. Lawrence's novel about passionate affair faced obscenity charges because of use of taboo sexual terms and graphic descriptions of intercourse. [Br. Lit.: Misc.]

4. **Mötley Crüe** rock music group faced obscenity charges against their lyrics by Tipper Gore's Parent's Music Resource Center. [Am. Music: *SJEPC*]

5. **Starr Report** Kenneth Starr's report in case against President Bill Clinton for obstruction of justice and perjury appeared on the Internet in 1998 and was criticized for its explicit details about Clinton's sexual relationship with White House aide Monica Lewinsky. [Am. Law and Hist.: *SJEPC*]

506. OBSESSIVENESS

1. **Ahab, Captain** obsessed with whale. [Am. Lit.: *Moby Dick*]

2. **Allmers, Mrs.** obsessed with crippled son. [Nor. Lit.: *Little Eyolf*]

3. *As Good as It Gets* 1997 film about obsessive-compulsive, misanthropic and bigoted romance novelist. [Am. Film: Misc.]

4. **Bounderby, Josiah** single-minded success addict. [Br. Lit.: *Hard Times*]

5. **Cardillac** goldsmith who murders to regain what he created. [Ger. Opera: Hindemith, *Cardillac*, Westerman, 487]

6. **Chillingworth, Roger** "very principle of his life [was] the systematic exercise of revenge." [Am. Lit.: *The Scarlet Letter*]

7. **Craig, Harriet** wrapped up in caring for her immaculate home, to the exclusion of all human relationships. [Am. Drama: *Craig's Wife* in Hart, 191]

8. **Defarge, Madame** "everlastingly knitting" before the guillotine as heads fell. [Br. Lit.: *A Tale of Two Cities*]

9. **Dick, Mr.** compulsively thinks, talks, and writes about King Charles's head. [Br. Lit.: Dickens *David Copperfield* in Brewer *Dictionary*, 520]

10. **Gollum** character from Tolkien's Lord of the Rings trilogy; killed his best friend to get the powerful ring; through its evil power, becomes a contemptible, half-crazed creature who keeps pursuing the ring. [Br. Lit.: Gillepsie and Naden]

11. **Herman** only goal in life becomes winning at cards. [Russ. Opera: Tchaikovsky, *Queen of Spades*, Westerman, 401]

12. **Javert** personification of law's inexorableness; relentlessly tracks down Valjean. [Fr. Lit.: *Les Misérables*]

13. **Melford, Lydia** could not think of anything but lover Wilson. [Br. Lit.: *Humphry Clinker*, Magill I, 394–397]

14. *Monk* TV series about obsessive-compulsive detective with gift for solving difficult cases. [Am. TV: Misc.]

15. **Nemo, Captain** mysterious submarine captain who attempts vengeance against society. [Fr. Lit.: *Twenty Thousand Leagues Under the Sea*]

16. **Séchard, David** neglects his business in unremitting effort to perfect a paper-making process. [Fr. Lit.: Balzac *Lost Illusions* in Magill I, 595]

17. **Tiberius** determined at any cost to become Emperor. [Br. Lit.: *I, Claudius*]

507. OBSTINACY

1. **Balmawhapple** bullheaded, blundering Scotch laird. [Br. Lit.: *Waverly*]

2. *Chocolate War, The* 1974 novel by Robert Cormier set in private Catholic boys' school where one student's obstinate refusal to sell fundraising candy brings brutal retaliation. [Am. Children's Lit.: OCCL]

3. **Deans, Davie** stern and righteous Presbyterian. [Br. Lit.: *The Heart of Midlothian*]

4. **Gradgrind, Thomas** rigid "man of realities." [Br. Lit.: *Hard Times*]

5. **Grant, Ulysses S. (1822–1885)** 18th U.S. president; nicknamed "Unconditional Surrender." [Am. Hist.: Kane, 523]

6. **Jorkins** intractable, unyielding lawyer. [Br. Lit.: *David Copperfield*]

7. **Mistress Mary** known for being "quite contrary." [Nurs. Rhyme: Baring-Gould, 31]

8. **mule** symbol of obstinacy: "stubborn as a mule." [Folklore: Jobes, 462]

9. **Pharaoh** refuses to heed Moses's mandate from God. [O.T.: Exodus 7:13, 22–23, 8:32, 9:7, 12]

10. **Zax** protagonists of cautionary tale for children by Dr. Seuss; two stubborn Zax meet head-on in the Prairie of Prax, refuse to budge, and are still there to this very day. [Am. Children's Lit.: "The Zax"]

Obtuseness (See DIMWITTEDNESS.)

Oddness (See ECCENTRICITY.)

Oldness (See AGE, OLD.)

508. OMEN (See also PROPHECY.)

1. **Amasis's ring** discarded ring turns up predicting Polycrates's death. [Gk. Hist.: Benét, 28]
2. **Guardian Black Dog** sinister omen of death. [Br. Folklore: Briggs, 207–208]
3. **handwriting on the wall** Daniel interprets supernatural sign as Belshazzar's doom. [O.T.: Daniel 5:25–28]
4. **huma** oriental bird; every head over which its shadow passes was believed destined to wear a crown. [Ind. Myth.: Brewer *Dictionary*, 472]
5. **Ides of March** 15 March; prophesied as fateful for Caesar. [Br. Lit.: *Julius Caesar*]
6. **merrow** Irish mermaid; her appearance signifies coming storms. [Irish Folklore: Briggs, 290–294]
7. **Mother Carey's chickens** stormy petrels; believed by sailors to be harbingers of storms. [Marine Folklore: Wheeler, 251]
8. **raven** often presages death or catastrophe. [Animal Folklore: Jobes, 213]
9. **waff** wraith whose appearance portends death. [Br. Folklore: Briggs, 425]
10. **white-winged crow** bird of evil omen. [Chinese Folklore: Jobes, 388]
11. **Wotan's ravens** of misfortune, usually fatal. [Ger. Opera: Wagner, Götterdämmerung, Westerman, 245]

509. OMNIPRESENCE (See also UBIQUITY.)

1. **Allah** supreme being and pervasive spirit of the universe. [Islam: Leach, 36]
2. **Big Brother** all-seeing leader watches every move. [Br. Lit.: *1984*]
3. **eye** God sees all things in all places. [Christian Symbolism: O.T.: Poverbs 15:3]
4. **God** transcendant over and immanent in the world. [Christianity and Judaism: *NCE*, 1098–1099]

510. OMNISCIENCE

1. **Ea** shrewd god; knew everything in advance. [Babylonian Myth.: *Gilgamesh*]

2. **God** knows all past, present, and future. [Christianity and Judaism: *NCE*, 1098–1099]

3. **Santa Claus** he knows who has been bad or good. [Western Folklore: Misc.]

4. **Sphinx** ancient Egyptian symbol of all-knowingness. [Heraldry: Halberts, 38]

511. OPPORTUNISM (See also EXPLOITATION.)

1. **Arabella, Lady** squire's wife matchmakes with money in mind. [Br. Lit.: *Doctor Thorne*]

2. **Ashkenazi, Simcha** shrewdly and unscrupulously becomes merchant prince. [Yiddish Lit.: *The Brothers Ashkenazi*]

3. **Butler, Rhett** southerner interested only in personal gain from Civil War. [Am. Lit.: *Gone With the Wind*]

4. **carpetbaggers** Northerners who moved to the South during Reconstruction after Civil War in mid-1860s to 1870s; many reaped economic and political benefits from struggling Southern States. [Am. Hist.: Jameson, 84]

5. **Cowperwood, Frank A.** capitalist involves politicians in shady dealings. [Am. Lit.: *The Financier*, Magill I, 280–282]

6. **de Ravenel, Gontran** weds peasant's plain daughter to obtain land. [Fr. Lit.: *Mont-Oriol*, Magill I, 618–620]

7. **Nostromo** entrusted with a cargo of silver, manages to conceal some for his own gain. [Br. Lit.: Conrad *Nostromo*]

8. **Peters, Ivy** shyster lawyer capitalizing in New Frontier territory. [Am. Lit.: *A Lost Lady*]

9. **Wallingford, "Get-Rich-Quick"** ingenious rascal of high finance; quasi-lawful. [Am. Lit.: *Get-Rich-Quick Wallingford*, Hart, 150]

10. **Wizard of Oz, The** from L. Frank Baum's Oz series; balloonist who drifts into the Land of Oz, then takes advantage of the assumption that he is a wizard; eventually leaves Oz because he tires of the charade. [Br. Children's Lit.: Jones]

Oppression (See ANTI-SEMITISM, BIGOTRY, EXPLOITATION, SUBJUGATION.)

512. OPTIMISM

1. **anchor** emblem of optimism; steadfastly secured the soul in adversity. [N.T.: Hebrews 6:18–19]

2. **blood** humor affecting temperament of sanguineness. [Medieval Physiology: Hall, 130]

3. **Bontemps, Roger** personification of cheery contentment. [Fr. Lit.: "Roger Bontemps" in Walsh *Modern*, 66]

4. **Candide** beset by inconceivable misfortunes, hero indifferently shrugs them off. [Fr. Lit.: *Candide*]

5. **Capra, Frank (1897–1991)** American filmmaker, creator of such films as *It's a Wonderful Life* known for their idealistic, wholesome themes. [Am. Film *ODA*]

6. **hawthorn** symbol of optimism. [Flower Symbolism: *Flora Symbolica*, 174; Kunz, 328]

7. **irrational exuberance** term used by Alan Greenspan of the Federal Reserve to indicate over-optimistic investors (1996) [Am. Business Misc.]

8. **Micawber, Mr.** sanguine gentleman, constantly "waiting for something to turn up." [Br. Lit.: *David Copperfield*]

9. **Neuman, Alfred E.** red-headed cover boy for *MAD Magazine* whose motto was "What, Me Worry?" [Am. Jour.: *SJEPC*]

10. **Pangloss, Dr.** Candide's incurably optimistic tutor. [Fr. Lit.: *Candide*]

11. **Pollyanna** protagonist of Eleanor H. Porter's 1939 novel for young readers; finds good in even the most dire situations, winning the hearts of everyone along the way. [Am. Children's Lit.: Jones; Am. Film: *Pollyanna* in *Disney Films*, 170–172]

12. **snowdrop** symbol of optimism. [Flower Symbolism: *Flora Symbolica*, 177; Kunz, 326]

513. ORDERLINESS (See also CLEANLINESS.)

1. **Barbara** maid exemplifying personal and domestic neatness. [Br. Lit.: *The Old Curiosity Shop*]

2. **Bertram, Sir Thomas** instructor and example of orderliness and moral conduct. [Br. Lit.: *Mansfield Park*, Magill I, 562–564]

3. **Eunomia** one of Horae; goddess of order and harmony. [Gk. Myth.: Kravitz, 95]

4. **Fogg, Phileas** British gentleman who regimented whole life minutely. [Fr. Lit.: *Around the World in Eighty Days*]

5. **Price, Fanny** appealing heroine keeps unstable house in order. [Br. Lit.: *Mansfield Park*, Magill I, 562–564]

6. **Robert's Rules of Order** manual of parliamentary procedure by General Robert. [Am. Hist.: Hart, 717]

7. **Unger, Felix** ultra-tidy roommate of the slovenly Oscar. [Am. Drama: *The Odd Couple*; Am. Film and TV: "The Odd Couple" in Terrace, II, 160–161]

514. ORPHAN (See also ABANDONMENT.)

1. **Adverse, Anthony** finally, at middle age, discovers origins. [Am. Lit.: *Anthony Adverse*]

2. **Babar** anthropomorhpic elephant who is adopted by kind old lady; matures and displays sophistication, generosity, and wisdom, especially in his role as king of his jungle home. [Fr. Children's Lit.: Jones]

3. **Bambi** young deer suffers loss of mother in a forest fire, matures, and falls in love. [Ger. Lit.: *OCCL*]

4. **Carey, Philip** brought up by stingy uncle and kindly aunt. [Br. Lit.: *Of Human Bondage*, Magill I, 670–672]

5. **Cass, Eppie** child found and brought up by Silas Marner. [Br. Lit.: Eliot *Silas Marner* in Benét, 903]

6. **Clickett** the "orfling" from St. Luke's workhouse; Mrs. Micawber's maid-of-all-work. [Br. Lit.: *David Copperfield*]

7. **Cosette** waif indentured to the cruel Thendardiers; saved by the honorable Valjean. [Fr. Lit.: *Les Misérables*]

8. **Dondi** Italian war baby taken in by Americans. [Comics: Horn, 217]

9. **Finn, Huckleberry** his mother dead; his father dies toward end of novel. [Am. Lit.: *Huckleberry Finn*]

10. **Gale, Dorothy** protagonist of L. Frank Baum's Oz series; sensitive orphan who improves all who come into contact with her; brave and self-sufficient, she finds it is by her own devices that she will find her way home from Oz. [Br. Children's Lit.: Jones]

11. **Heidi** happy, loving orphan from Johanna Spyri's chldren's book; shows kindness for others, especially her gruff grandfather. [Swiss Children's Lit.: Jones]

12. **King Arthur** legend says that King Arthur was a young orphan who was able to free the sword Excalibur and therefore meant to take the throne of England. [Arth. Legend: Misc.]

13. **Little Orphan Annie** feisty waif succored by paternal Daddy Warbucks. [Comics: Horn, 459]

14. **Longstocking, Pippi** nine-year-old orphaned protagonist of eleven episodic stories in Astrid Lindgren's children's book; odd appearance and behavior; alter-ego of every child— totally independent, outrageous, and fun loving. [Swed. Children's Lit.: Jones]

15. **Luck, Thomas** infant adopted by miners when his prostitute mother dies. [Am. Lit.: Bret Harte "The Luck of Roaring Camp" in Magill III, 597]

16. **Magee, Maniac** protagonist of novel for young readers by Jerry Spinelli; orphaned runaway who finds acceptance for his athletic

talents, but faces racism when a black family takes him in. [Am. Children's Lit.: Jones]

17. **Mowgli** infant lost in the Indian forest is brought up by a wolf pack; from Rudyard Kipling's series for young readers, *The Jungle Books* (1894–1895). [Br. Children's Lit.: Jones]

18. **Pip** Philip Pirrip, orphaned as an infant. [Br. Lit.: *Great Expectations*]

19. **Potter, Harry** hero of series (1997–2007) for young readers by J.K. Rowlings; scrawny, bespectled orphan learns that he is a powerful wizard on his eleventh birthday; his fate is tied to evil Lord Voldemort, who kiled his parents. [Br. Children's Lit.; Misc.]

20. **Shirley, Anne** protagonist of L.M. Montgomery's Anne of Green Gables series for young readers; orphaned Anne has vivid imagination and spirited personality; shakes up Prince Edward Island community she comes to. [Can. Children's Lit.: Jones]

21. **Twist, Oliver** foundling reared in school of hard knocks. [Br. Lit.: *Oliver Twist*]

22. **Whittier, Pollyanna** protagonist of Eleanor H. Porter's 1939 novel for young readers; finds good in even the most dire situations, winning the hearts of everyone along the way. [Am. Chldren's Lit.: Jones]

515. OUTLAW (See also CRIMINAL, GANGSTERISM, HIGHWAYMAN, PIRACY, THIEF.)

1. **Bass, Sam (1851–1878)** train robber and all-around desperado. [Am. Hist.: *NCE*, 244]

2. **Billy the Kid (1859–1881)** name given to William H. Bonney; infamous cold-blooded killer. [Am. Hist.: Flexner, 30]

3. **Bonnie and Clyde [Bonnie Parker (1910–1934) and Clyde Barrow (1909–1934)]** bank robbers and killers (1930s). [Am. Hist.: Worth, 35]

4. **Cassidy, Butch (1866–1908) and the Sundance Kid [Harry Longabaugh (1867–1908)]** Western outlaws made famous by popular film. [Am. Hist. and Am. Cinema: *Butch Cassidy and the Sundance Kid*, Halliwell, 116]

5. **Dalton gang** bank robbers of the late 1800s; killed in shootout (1892). [Am. Hist.: Flexner, 15–16]

6. **Dillinger, John (1902–1932)** murderous, gunslinging bank robber of 1930s. [Am. Hist.: Flexner, 290]

7. **Grettir** Viking adventurer, outlawed for his ruthless slayings. [Icelandic Lit.: *Grettir the Strong* in Magill I, 335]

8. **Holliday, "Doc" (fl. late 19th century)** outlaw who helped Wyatt Earp fight the Clanton gang (1881). [Am. Hist.: Misc.]

9. **James, Jesse (1847–1882)** romanticized train and bank robber. [Am. Hist.: Flexner, 219]

10. **Ringo, Johnny (fl. late 19th century)** notorious outlaw and gunfighter in the Southwest. [Am. Hist.: Misc.]

11. **Rob Roy (1671–1734)** Scottish Highland outlaw, Robert McGregor, remembered in Sir Walter Scott's novel *Rob Roy* (1818). [Scottish Hist.: *EB*, VIII: 619]

12. **Robin Hood (13th century)** legendary outlaw of England who robbed the rich to help the poor. [Br. Hist.: *EB*, VIII: 615–616]

13. **Turpin, Dick (1706–1739)** English outlaw who robbed travelers on the road from London to Oxford. [Br. Hist.: *WB*, 19: 425]

14. **Villa, Pancho (1878–1923)** notorious Mexican bandit and revolutionary. [Mex. Hist.: *EB*, X: 435–436]

15. *Wild One, The* 1954 film about motorcycle gang; Marlon Brando plays misunderstood outlaw whose demeanor and image (black leather) was mimicked by teenagers. [Am. Film: *SJEPC*]

516. OUTRAGEOUSNESS (See also OBSCENITY, REBELLION, ZANINESS.)

1. **Baker, Josephine (1906–1975)** flamboyant, exotic African-American dancer shocked and delighted both French and American audiences in the 1920s. [Am. Entertainment: *SJEPC*]

2. *Beavis and Butthead* irreverent MTV show featuring two crude, hormone-driven male adolescents broke taboos in 1990s. [Am. TV: *SJEPC*]

3. **Cooper, Alice (1948–)** rock star's live shows known for outrageous, theatrical stunts such as decapitation by guillotine and singing with a boa constrictor. [Am. Music: *SJEPC*]

4. **Divine (1945–1988)** outrageous, overweight actor dressed in tasteless women's clothing to play female roles in shocking cult films. [Am. Film: *SJEPC*]

5. **Hilton, Paris (1981–)** heiress to the Hilton hotel dynasty; known for bar-hopping and sex tape "A Night in Paris". [Pop. Culture: Misc.]

6. **Imus, Don (1940–)** American radio host; syndicated ABC Radio Networks talk show began in 1979; like his rival Howard Stern, known for crude humor and lack of reserve. [Am. Radio: Misc.]

7. **Jackson, Michael (1958–)** youngest member of the eccentric Jackson family; known for numerous plastic surgeries and public scandals. [Am. Music: Misc.]

8. **Madonna (1958–)** American pop singer known for taking on outrageous personas and giving unique, often risqué performances. [Am. Music: Misc.]

9. **Manson, Marilyn (1969–)** born Brian Hugh Warner; musician known for extremely bizarre persona and stage performances; name derives from Marilyn Monroe and mass murderer Charles Manson. [Am. Music: Misc.]

10. **Mötley Crüe** popular heavy metal group behaved badly onstage and off stage. [Am. Music: *SJEPC*]

11. **Osbourne, Ozzy (1948–)** heavy metal vocalist who began with Black Sabbath; revelled in outrageous behavior onstage. [Brit. Music: *SJEPC*]

12. **Rivers, Joan (1933–)** bold, somewhat raunchy humor and sassy stage persona; opened doors for many female comedians who followed. [Am. Entertainment: *SJEPC*]

13. *Rocky Horror Picture Show* since 1976, fans throng to midnight screenings; audiences participate with counterpoint dialogue and props to scenes in the outlandish plot of sexual exploits, transvestism, alien invasion, and cannibalism. [Am. Film: *SJEPC*]

14. **Rodman, Dennis (1961–)** star rebounder whose outlandish behavior and appearance made him a favorite with the media. [Am. Sports: *SJEPC*]

15. **Shock Radio** radio shows begun earlier, but popularized in the 1970s; hosts engage in audacious, lewd, and often derogatory humor; considered by some the epitome of free speech, by others the epitome of decadence. [Am. Radio: *SJEPC*]

16. *South Park* premiered in 1997; animators Trey Parker and Matt Stone depict four male third-graders; profanities and misbehavior belie the supposed innocence of children; plot lines poke fun at popular culture with dead-on wit. [Am. TV: *SJECP*]

17. **Spears, Britney (1981–)** American singer and performer; became a world-wide sex symbol after donning sexy outfits and giving raunchy performances. [Am. Music: Misc.]

18. **Springer, Jerry (1944–)** guests on his TV talk show are encouraged to share intimate details of their often outlandish stories and engage in shouting matches and brawls; some have speculated that the fights are staged, with actors as guests. [Am. TV: *SJEPC*]

19. **Stern, Howard (1954–)** master of shock radio; his program covers outrageous and often distastefjul subjects; profanity and sexually explicit conversations are the norm. [Am. Radio: *SJPEC*]

20. **Warhol, Andy (1928–1987)** renowned Pop artist who used everyday objects— most notably, Campbell soup cans—as inspiration; his outrageous behavior and pursuit of celebrity oftentimes overshadowed his work as an artist. [Am. Art: *SJEPC*]

21. **Waters, John (1946–)** writer and filmmaker who calls his approach "good bad taste"; profanity and scatalogical humor in

large portions; incest, castration, etc. but also touching affection for outsiders; *Pink Flamingoes* (1972) became a cult favorite and *Hairspray* a popular musical. [Am. Film and Theater: *SJEPC*]

22. **West, Mae (1893–1980)** her suggestive dialogue—unheard of at the time— vampy acting style, and voluptuous figure made her a legend; many of her quips have become famous. [Am. Film: *SJEPC*]

P

517. PACIFICATION

1. **Aegir** sea god, stiller of storms on the ocean. [Norse Myth.: Leach, 16]
2. **Feng** name taken by Odin in capacity of wave-stiller. [Norse Myth.: *LLEI*, I: 328]
3. **Saul and David** David plays his harp to mollify King Saul. [O.T.: I Samuel 16:16, 23]

Pain (See SUFFERING.)

518. PARADISE (See also HEAVEN, UTOPIA, WONDERLAND.)

1. **Bali** Indonesian island; thought of as garden of Eden. [Geography: *NCE*, 215–216]
2. **Brigadoon** magical Scottish village that materializes once every 100 years. [Am. Music: Payton, 100–101]
3. **Canaan** ancient region on Jordan river; promised by God to Abraham. [O.T.: Genesis 12:5–10]
4. **Earthly Paradise** place of beauty, peace, and immortality, believed in the Middle Ages to exist in some undiscovered land. [Eur. Legend: Benét, 298]
5. **Eden** earthly garden of luxury; abode of Adam and Eve. [O.T.: Genesis 2:8]
6. **Elysium** also Elysian Fields; abode of the blessed in afterlife. [Gk. & Rom. Myth.: Brewer *Dictionary*]
7. **Garden of the Hesperides** quiet garden of the gods where golden apples grew. [Gk. Lit.: *Hippolytus*; Gk. Myth.: Gaster, 25]
8. **green** color represents paradise, peace, and hope in Islam. [Islamic Symbolism: *UIMT*, 229]
9. **Happy Hunting Ground** paradise for American Indians. [Am. Culture: Jobes, 724]
10. **Happy Valley** beautiful spot in Kashmir's Jhelum Valley. [Indian Hist.: Payton, 300]
11. **hissu** where trees bear fruit of lapid lazuli. [Babylonian Lit.: *Gilgamesh*]
12. **land of milk and honey** proverbial ideal of plenty and happiness. [Western Cult.: Brewer *Dictionary*]
13. **Land of the Lotophagi** African land where eating lotos fruit produced amnesia and indolence. [Gk. Lit.: *Odyssey*; Br. Lit.: "The Lotos-Eaters" in Norton, 733–736]

14. **Nirvana** eternal bliss and the end of all earthly suffering. [Indian Religion: Jobes, 1175]

15. **Shangri-La** utopia hidden in the Himalayas. [Br. Lit.: *Lost Horizon*]

16. **Suhkavati** garden of jeweled trees and dulcet-voiced birds. [Buddhist Myth.: Gaster, 24]

17. **Timbuktu** fabled land of wealth and splendor. [Eur. Hist.: Brewer *Dictionary*, 1084]

18. **Tlapallan** land of luxuriance and red sunrise. [Aztec Myth.: Gaster, 25]

519. PARADOX

1. **Catch-22** claim of insanity to be relieved of military duty proves sanity. [Am. Lit.: Joseph Heller*Catch-22*]

2. **Zeno's paradoxes** four philosophical arguments purporting to show the impossibility of motion. [Gk. Phil.: *NCE*, 3043]

520. PASSION OF CHRIST

1. **agony in the garden** Christ confronts His imminent death. [N.T.: Matthew 26:36–45; Mark 14:32–41]

2. **cock** its crowing reminded Peter of his betrayal. [N.T.: John 18:27]

3. **Cross, the** upon which Christ was crucified. [N.T.: Matthew 27:31–50]

4. **crown of thorns** placed upon Christ's head after scourging. [N.T.: John 19:2]

5. **Deposition** Christ is taken from the cross and enshrouded. [N.T.: Matthew 27:57–60; Christian Art.: Appleton, 55]

6. **dice** cast by Roman guards for Christ's robe. [N.T.: Matthew 27:35]

7. **"Eloi, Eloi, lama sabachthani?"** "My God, my God, why hast thou forsaken me?"; Jesus's cry at the ninth hour. [N.T.: Mark 15:34]

8. **Entry into Jerusalem** first scene of Passion cycle in painting. [Art.: Hall, 114]

9. **gall** sponge soaked with it given to crucified Jesus. [N.T.: Matthew 26:48]

10. **Gethsemane** scene of Christ's agony over impending death. [N.T.: Matthew 26:36–45; Mark 14:32–41]

11. **Golgotha** site of Christ's crucifixion; also Calvary. [N.T.: Matthew 27:32]

12. **hammer** Christian symbol for martyrdom, crucifixion. [Christian Symbolism: Jobes, 391, 716]

13. **Jerusalem** city where significant events in Christ's life occurred, including the Last Supper and the Crucifixion. [Christianity: WB2]

14. **kiss** means by which Judas identified Jesus. [N.T.: Matthew 26:48–50]

15. **ladder** stood upon by Joseph to remove nails holding Christ to the cross. [Christian Symbolism: Appleton, 55]

16. **lantern** held by Judas, leading officers to Christ. [N.T.: John 18:3]

17. *Passion of Christ, The* 2003 film by Mel Gibson; graphic violence and dialogue in Aramaic, Latin, and Hebrew (with subtitles) kept some away; others flocked to see it, making it a big box-office success; controversy followed over whether its message was anti-Semitic. [Am. Film: Misc.]

18. **Passion Play** dramatic presentation of Christ's Passion, notably the production at Oberammergau. [Medieval Drama: Benét, 763]

19. **Peter's denial** Peter denies Christ three times. [N.T.: Matthew 26:67–75]

20. **pillar and cord** depicted Christ's scourging. [Christian Symbolism: Appleton, 76]

21. **scourges** instruments of Christ's flagellation. [Christian Symbolism: Matthew 27:26]

22. **seamless robe** Christ's garment, wagered for by Roman soldiers. [N.T.: John 19:23–24]

23. **Simon the Cyrenean** bystander compelled to carry Christ's cross. [N.T.: Matthew 27:32]

24. **spear** weapon plunged into Jesus's side during crucifixion. [N.T.: John 19:34]

25. **Stations of the Cross** depictions of episodes of Christ's death. [Christianity: Brewer *Dictionary*, 1035]

26. **stigmata** wounds of Christ appearing on others. [Christian Hagiog.: Attwater, 136, 146. 211]

27. **30 pieces of silver** price Judas was paid for identifying Christ. [N.T.: Matthew 26:15]

28. **three nails** used to crucify Jesus. [Christian Symbolism: Appleton, 67]

29. **vernicle** Veronica's veil with Jesus's facial image. [Christian Symbolism: Appleton, 107]

30. **Via Dolorosa** Christ's route to Calvary. [Christianity: Brewer *Dictionary*, 112]

31. **vinegar** given to Jesus to drink. [N.T.: Matthew 26:34, 48]

32. **whipping post** scene of Christ's scourging. [N.T.: Matthew 15:15]

521. PASSION, SENSUAL

1. *All My Children* daytime soap opera featuring Susan Lucci premiered in 1970 and emphasizes young love. [Am. TV: *SJEPC*]

2. *Another World* debuting in 1964, daytime soap opera was most popular in the 1970s and 1980s before cancellation in 1999. [Am. TV: *SJEPC*]

3. **Anteros** Eros's brother; avenger of unrequited love; god of passion. [Gk. Myth.: Zimmerman, 23]

4. *As the World Turns* long-running daytime soap opera set in Midwestern town of Oakdale popular with viewers since 1956. [Am. TV: *SJEPC*]

5. *Baywatch* sexy, scantily clad male and female lifeguards of Los Angeles County Beach Patrol became greater hit with audiences in post-network episodes of the 1990s. [Am. TV: *SJEPC*]

6. *Beverly Hills 90210* teen drama of 1990s set in posh Beverly Hills focused on group of fashion-conscious, upper-class high school students. [Am. TV: *SJEPC*]

7. **Blume, Judy (1938–)** her works for young readers covered previously taboo subjects like the onset of puberty, masturbation, and teenage sex; school library censors often placed her titles on their lists. [Am. Children's Lit.: Misc.]

8. **bodice rippers** historical romance novels so named because of sexually explicit plots and ever-present rape scenes. [Am. Lit.: *SJEPC*]

9. **Cleopatra (69–30 B.C.)** alluring and romantic queen of Egypt. [Egypt. Hist.: *NCE*, 577]

10. *Dallas* tremendously popular prime-time soap opera about wealthy Texan oil family premiered in 1978; described as "a series of dramatic feuds," it featured steamy romances, vengeance, greed, and a fair amount of glitz and glamour. [Am. TV: Misc.]

11. *Dark Shadows* popular daytime drama featured paranormal events and mysterious secrets at the Collins family estate (1966–1971). [Am. TV: *SJEPC*]

12. *Days of Our Lives* enduring NBC daytime drama (1965–) takes place in midwestern town of Salem; episodes begin with voice-over from original Tom Horton character, "Like sands through the hourglass, so are the days of our lives." [Am. TV: *SJEPC*]

13. *Dynasty* prime time soap opera featuring Joan Collins as a conniving villain and characters obsessed with money and power. [Am. TV: *FOF, MOD*]

14. *Edge of Night, The* daytime drama set in midwestern town of Monticello featuring detective Mike Karr and his criminal inves-

tigations often contained graphic violence (1956–1984). [Am. TV: *SJEPC*]

15. **Eros** called Cupid by the Romans; god of love; whence, word *erotic*. [Gk. Myth.: Zimmerman, 76]

16. *From Here to Eternity* emotionally powerful film about U.S. Army officers and enlisted men at Pearl Harbor just prior to Japanese attack featured memorable scenes, such as the passionate beach kiss between Burt Lancaster's Sgt. Warden and Deborah Kerr's Karen Holmes (1953). [Am. Film: *SJEPC*]

17. *General Hospital* venerable daytime drama set in a hospital centers on dynamics of coworker relationships, both professional and personal (1963–). [Am. TV: *SJEPC*]

18. *Guiding Light* longest-running soap opera began as radio program in 1937 and premiered on TV in 1952; like the familiar rotating lighthouse beacon, daytime drama storylines have shed light on six decades of social and cultural trends (1952–2009). [Am. TV: *SJEPC*]

19. **Himeros** god of erotic desire; attendant of Aphrodite. [Gk. Myth.: Howe, 131]

20. **Kama** god of erotic love. [Hindu Myth.: Leach, 569]

21. *Kiss, The* sculpture by French sculptor Rodin depicting passionate embrace. [Art.: Osborne, 988]

22. *Knots Landing* second longest running prime-time drama (14 seasons); spin-off of popular prime-time soap opera *Dallas*; featured often steamy adventures of neighboring married couples living on cul-de-sac in Southern California. [Am. TV: *SJEPC*]

23. *Lady Chatterley's Lover* written in the late 1920s but not published in full text until 1959; D.H. Lawrence's novel about passionate affair faced obscenity charges because of use of taboo sexual terms and graphic descriptions of intercourse. [Br. Lit.: Misc.]

24. *Lolita* twelve-year-old inspires lust in older man. [Am. Lit.: *Lolita*]

25. **Nixon, Agnes (1927–)** talented and influential TV writer of soap operas who added social issues and serious themes to her scripts; also introduced the bitch goddess to the genre. [Am. TV: *SJEPC*]

26. *Peyton Place* 1956 novel by Grace Metalious about fictional New England town rife with sex and vice; later a popular primetime series (1964–1969). [Am. Lit. and TV: Misc.]

27. **Roberts, Nora (1950–)** one of the most prolific novelists of the late 20th century; has penned over 100 romance novels. [Am. Lit.: *SJEPC*]

28. **romance novels** formulaic love stories with happy endings written mostly by women for women; account for half of all mass-produced paperback sales. [Am. Lit.: *SJEPC*]

29. **ruby** represents intensity of feeling; July birthstone. [Gem Symbolism: Kunz, 28, 319]

30. *Streetcar Named Desire, A* Tennessee Williams's Pulitzer Prize-winning 1947 play; passionate domestic drama about three people living in French Quarter of New Orleans. [Am. Theater and Film: *SJEPC*]

31. **White, Barry (1944–2003)** African-American pop music singer whose husky bass voice and sexy songs have made his name synonymous with romance to listeners. [Am. Music: *SJEPC*]

32. *Young and the Restless, The* long-running TV soap opera premiered in 1973; steamy plots were enhanced by new photographic techniques and edgy topics that set the standard for the genre. [Am. TV: *SJEPC*]

522. PASSOVER

1. **bitter herbs** part of the Seder feast: symbol of the hardship of the Jews during their bondage in Egypt. [Jewish Rel.: *HolSymb*]

2. **egg** part of the Seder feast: symbol of the spiritual strength of the Jewish people. [Jewish Rel.: *HolSymb*]

3. **Four Cups of Wine** part of the Seder feast, probably symbolizing the four phrases from Exodus describing how God will redeem Israel. [Jewish Rel.: *HolSymb*]

4. **Four Questions** part of the Seder feast, spoken by the youngest person; asks questions pertaining to the importance of the Seder. [Jewish Rel.: *HolSymb*]

5. **Haggadah** text read as part of the Seder, including Bible passages, hymns, prayers, and stories explaining the history and symbolism of Passover, the escape from bondage, and the Exodus. [Jewish Rel.: *HolSymb*]

6. **matzoh** part of the Seder feast: unleavened bread, symbolizing the haste with which the Jews fled Egypt. [Jewish Rel.: *HolSymb*]

7. **Seder** feast of Passover, in which symbolic foods are eaten in celebration of the Jews' flight from Egypt and slavery. [Jewish Rel.: *HolSymb*]

523. PASTORALISM

1. **Arcadia** mountainous region of ancient Greece; legendary for pastoral innocence of people. [Gk. Hist.: *NCE*, 136; Rom. Lit.: *Ecologues*; Span. Lit.: *Arcadia*]

2. **Chloë** Arcadian goddess; patronness of new, green crops. [Gk. Myth.: Parrinder, 62]

3. **Daphnis** Sicilian shepherd-flautist; invented bucolic poetry. [Rom. Myth.: *LLEI*, I: 326]

4. *Ecologues* short pieces by Roman poet Virgil. [Rom. Lit.: Benét, 1053]

5. **Granida and Daifilio** classic idyllic love between princess and shepherd. [Dutch Lit.: *Granida*, Hall, 141]

6. *Pastoral Symphony* Beethoven's Symphony No. 6 in F Major; hymn to nature. [Ger. Music: Thompson, 1634]

7. **Theocritus** poet; rhapsodized over charm of rustic life. [Gk. Lit.: Brewer *Dictionary*, 813]

8. *Walden* Thoreau's classic; advocates a return to nature. [Am. Lit.: Van Doren, 208]

9. *Works and Days* long poem by Hesiod, considered a farmers' almanac of ancient Greece. [Gk. Lit.: Benét, 1102]

524. PATIENCE (See also LONG-SUFFERING.)

1. **Amelia** idolized personification of patience and perserverance. [Br. Lit.: *Amelia*]

2. **dock bloom** symbolizes patience. [Flower Symbolism: Jobes, 454]

3. **Enid** constant and patient wife of Sir Geraint. [Welsh Lit.: *Mabinogion*; Br. Lit.: "Idylls of the King"]

4. **Griselda** lady immortalized for patience and wifely obedience. [Br. Lit.: *Canterbury Tales*, "Clerk of Oxenfords's Tale"]

5. **Hermione** bore Leontes's unfounded jealousy, thus gaining his love. [Br. Lit.: *The Winter's Tale*]

6. **Jacob** serves Laban for fourteen years before receiving permission to marry Rachel. [O.T.: Genesis 24:34]

7. **Penelope** Odysseus's wife; model of feminine virtue, waits twenty years for husband's return. [Gk. Lit.: *Odyssey*]

525. PATRICIDE

1. **Adrammelech and Sharezer** murder father, Sennacherib, for Assyrian throne. [O.T.: II Kings 19:37]

2. **Borden, Lizzie (1860–1927)** woman accused of butchering father and stepmother with ax (1872). [Am. Hist.: Hart, 91]

3. *Brothers Karamazov, The* Dostoevsky's masterpiece which depicts the search for faith, the meaning of truth, and forgiveness through the story of four sons brought together during the investigation into the murder of their despicable father. [Russ. Lit.: *The Brothers Karamazov*]

4. **Edward** killed his father at his mother's instigation. [Br. Balladry: *Edward* in Benét, 302]

5. **Menendez Brothers** [Joseph Lyle Menendez (1968–) and Erik Menendez (1971–)] sons of a rich Cuban-American business executive who shot and killed their parents in 1989 at their family

home, then spent the following months spending with abandon; convicted of first-degree murder and sentenced to life in prison. [Am. Hist.: Misc.]

6. **Oedipus** kills father in argument not knowing his identity. [Gk. Lit.: *Oedipus Rex*]

526. PATRIOTISM (See also CHAUVINISM, LOYALTY.)

1. **America, Captain** comic-strip character known as the "protector of the American way." [Comics: Horn, 155–156]

2. **American elm** traditional symbol of American patriotism. [Tree Symbolism: *Flora Symbolica*, 182]

3. **American Legion** patriotic service organization devoted to charitable causes. [Am. Cult.: Misc.]

4. **Berlin, Irving (1888–1989)** Russian-born composer wrote patriotic American songs during both world wars and donated proceeds to Army Relief Fund. [Am. Music: *SJEPC*]

5. **Boy Scouts** youth organization's values include service to God and country. [Am. Hist.: *SJEPC*]

6. **Cincinnatus** farmer-hero who defeated Rome's enemies, returned in triumph, went back to his farm. [Rom. Hist.: *EB* (1963) V, 712]

7. **Cohan, George M. (1878–1942)** American composer amd performer of patriotic classics such as "I'm a Yankee Doodle Dandy." [Am. Music: Misc.]

8. **Corwin, Norman (1910–)** wrote and broadcast poignant radio series and commentary during World War II such as *This Is War!* (1942) and "14 August" (1945) that promoted America's involvement yet pondered the price. [Am. Radio: *SJEPC*]

9. **flag clothing** wearing the American flag changed from subversive and disrespectful to mainstream and patriotic when flag was incorporated into sportswear designs by Ralph Lauren and Tommy Hilfiger in 1990s. [Am. Hist.: *SJEPC*]

10. **Fourth of July** "Independence Day"; day celebrating adoption of the Declaration of Independence. [Am. Hist.: Misc.]

11. **Hale, Nathan (1755–1776)** hero of American revolution; famous for "I regret I have but one life to give for my country." [Am. Hist.: Hart, 341]

12. **Joan of Arc, Saint (1412–14731)** heroically followed call to save France. [Christian Hagiog.: Attwater, 187]

13. **Marvel, Captain** muscular comic-book character popular in the 1940s promoted America's efforts during World War II. [Am. Comics: *SJEPC*]

14. ***Mr. Smith Goes to Washington*** 1939 Frank Capra film; naïve and moral US Senator stands up to political corruption. [Am. Film: *SJEPC*]

15. **nasturtium** symbolizes love of country. [Flower Symbolism: *Flora Symbolica*, 176]

16. **Nolan, Philip** long banished, he comes at last to passionately love the United States before his death. [Am. Lit.: Hale *The Man Without a Country* in Magill I, 553]

17. **Sousa, John Philip (1854–1932)** composer of over 100 rousing marches and leader of world-renowned concert band; devoted to making people proud of America, bringing him great popularity and a host of honors. [Am. Music: *SJEPC*]

18. **Tremain, Johnny** protagonist of historical novel for young readers written by Esther Forbes in 1943; in 18th-century Boston, fourteen-year-old silversmith's apprentice takes his place with the patriots in their fight against England. [Am. Children's Lit.: Gillespie and Naden]

19. **Uncle Sam** personification of U.S. government. [Am. Folklore: Misc.]

527. PATRON (See also PHILANTHROPIST.)

1. **Alidoro** fairy godfather to Italian Cinderella. [Ital. Opera: Rossini, *Cinderella*, Westerman, 120–121]

2. **Alphonso, Don** supports Blas in return for political favors. [Fr. Lit.: *Gil Blas*]

3. **Dionysus** inspired men through wine; considered a patron of the arts. [Gk. Myth.: *NCE*, 767]

4. **Fairy Godmother** maternal fairy abets Cinderella in ball preparations. [Fr. Fairy Tale: "Cinderella"]

5. **Medici** Italian family of the Renaissance powerful in politics and religion; noted patrons of Da Vinci and Michelangelo. [Ital. Art: *FOF, MOD*]

528. PEACE (See also ANTIWAR, PEACEMAKING.)

1. **arrow** when bundled or broken, symbol of peace in Native American lore. [Native Am. Folklore: *COES&S*, 208]

2. **"as-salam alaykum"** greeting offered from one Muslim to another means "Peace be upon you" in Arabic. [Islam: *UIMT*, 188, 425]

3. **Beulah, Land of** resting-place of pilgrims after crossing river of Death. [Br. Lit.: *The Pilgrim's Progress*]

4. **Chamberlain, Neville (1869–1940)** British statesman who signed peace agreement with Hitler in 1938, which failed to stop Hitler or the war. [Eur. Hist.: *ODA*]

5. **Concordia** ancient Roman goddess of peace and domestic harmony. [Rom. Myth.: Zimmerman, 68]

6. **dove** emblem of peace, tenderness, innocence, and gentleness. [Folklore: Brewer *Dictionary*, 340]

7. **Geneva** site of peace conferences (1955, 1960); seat of League of Nations (1920–1946). [Swiss Hist.: *NCE*, 1058]

8. **Goshen, Land of** place of peace and prosperity. [O.T.: Genesis 14:10]

9. **green** color represents peace, hope, and paradise in Islam. [Islamic Symbolism: *UIMT*, 229]

10. **Irene** goddess of peace and conciliation. [Gk. Myth.: Espy, 21]

11. **Jesus Christ** prince of peace in Christian beliefs. [N.T.: Matthew; Mark; Luke; John]

12. **laurel** traditional emblem of peace. [Plant Symbolism: Jobes, 374]

13. **olive branch** symbol of peace and serenity. [Gk. and Roman Myth.: Brewer *Handbook*; O.T.: Genesis 8:11]

14. **paper cranes** Japanese legend holds that 1000 origami paper cranes will make a wish come true; Sadako Sasaki folded paper cranes while dying of leukemia from the radiation of the bombing of Hiroshima during WWII; her friends erected a statue in Hiroshima Peace Park in 1958 in honor of all children killed by the bomb; from all over the globe, people continue to send paper cranes to the monument. [Jap. Culture: Misc.]

15. **Pax** goddess of peace. [Rom. Myth.: Zimmerman, 194]

16. **Pax Americana** term for U.S. foreign policy theory that, after WW II, as the sole nation with a nuclear bomb, the U.S. would become the sole arbiter of peace and war in the world. [Am. Hist.: *FOF, MOD*]

17. **peace pipe** pipe of North American Indians; smoked at conculsion of peace treaties. [Am. Hist.: *NCE*, 427]

18. **peace poles** over 200,000 have been erected in over 190 countries; started in Japan in 1955 and continued by World Peace Society, an NGO with the Department of Public Information at the United Nations; made from renewable material and display the message "May Peace Prevail on Earth" on each side. [Pop. Culture: Misc.]

19. **Peaceable Kingdom** from a Biblical passage, a vision of earthly peace, with animals and humans united in nonviolent accord. [O.T.: Isiah 11: 6–9]

20. **Quakers** nonmilitant, gentle, religious sect. [Am. Hist.: Jameson, 189]

529. PEACEMAKING (See also ANTIWAR, PEACE)

1. **Agrippa, Menenius** Coriolanus's witty friend; reasons with rioting mob. [Br. Lit.: *Coriolanus*]
2. **Antenor** percipiently urges peace with Greeks. [Gk. Lit.: *Iliad*]
3. **Benvolio** tries to stop Mercutio's fatal clash with Tybalt. [Br. Lit.: *Romeo and Juliet*]
4. **Lysistrata** leads women to use wifely continence to secure peace between countries. [Gk. Lit.: *Lysistrata*]

530. PEDANTRY

1. **Blimber, Cornelia** "dry and sandy with working in the graves of deceased languages." [Br. Lit.: *Dombey and Son*]
2. **Casaubon, Edward** dull pedant; dreary scholar who marries Dorothea. [Br. Lit.: *Middlemarch*]
3. **Caxton, Austin** erudite bookworm. [Br. Lit.: *The Caxtons*]
4. **Choakumchild, Mr.** pedantic master of Gradgrind's school. [Br. Lit.: *Hard Times*]
5. **Conseil** taxonomically talented servant of Prof. Aronnax. [Fr. Lit.: *Twenty Thousand Leagues Under the Sea*]
6. **Dalgetty, Rittmaster Dugald** garrulous pedant. [Br. Lit.: *A Legend of Montrose*]
7. **Fluellen** pedantic Welsh captain and know-it-all. [Br. Lit.: *Henry V*]
8. **Holofernes** shameless pedagogue-schoolmaster. [Br. Lit.: *Love's Labour's Lost*]
9. **Sampson, Dominie** old-fashioned, donnish scholar. [Br. Lit.: *Guy Mannering*]
10. **Scriblerus, Martinus** learned fool. [Br. Lit.: Benét, 909]
11. **Thwackum** selfish and ill-humored clerical pedagogue. [Br. Lit.: *Tom Jones*]

531. PENITENCE

1. **Act of Contrition** prayer of atonement said after making one's confession. [Christianity.: Misc.]
2. **Agnes, Sister** former Lady Laurentini; a penitent nun. [Br. Lit.: *The Mysteries of Udolpho*, Freeman, 4]
3. **Ancient Mariner** telling his tale is penance for his guilt. [Br. Poetry: Coleridge "The Rime of the Ancient Mariner"]
4. **Canossa** site of Henry IV's submission to Pope Gregory VII (1077). [Eur. Hist.: Grun, 140]
5. **Dimmesdale, Arthur** Puritan minister publicly atones for sin of adultery. [Am. Lit.: *The Scarlet Letter*]
6. **Dismas** in the Apocryphal gospels, the penitent thief; also Dysmas. [Christianity.: Benét, 274]

585

7. **Elul** sixth month of Jewish year; month of repentance. [Judaism: Wigoder, 174]

8. **flagellants** group of Christians who practiced public flagellation as penance. [Christian Hist.: *NCE*, 959]

9. **Henry IV (1050–1106)** Holy Roman Emperor who begged forgiveness from the Pope at Canossa. [Eur. Hist.: Benét, 456]

10. **Julian the Hospitaler, Saint** for having mistakenly killed his parents, atones by becoming a beggar and helping the wretched. [Christian Legend: Attwater]

11. **Mary Magdalene** abjectly cleans Jesus's feet with tears; dries them with her hair. [N.T.: Luke 7:37–50]

12. **Nineveh** townspeople repented for wickedness by fasting and donning sackcloth. [O.T.: Jonah 3:5–10]

13. **Pelagius the Repentant, Saint** dancing girl converts to solitary, saintly ways. [Christian Hagiog.: Attwater, 272]

14. **penance** Catholic sacrament, whereby the penitent is absolved of sins by the confessor. [Christianity.: *NCE*, 2096]

15. **sable** black fur represents repentance. [Heraldry: Halberts, 37]

16. **sackcloth and ashes** traditional garb of contrition. [O.T.: Jonah 3:6; Esther 4:1–3; N.T.: Matthew 11:21]

17. **scapegoat** sent into wilderness bearing sins of Israelites. [O.T.: Leviticus 16:8–22]

18. **Scarlet Sister Mary** seeks divine forgiveness in night of wild prayer. [Am. Lit.: *Scarlet Sister Mary*]

19. **skull** always present in pictures of Mary Magdalene repenting. [Christian Art.: de Bles, 29]

20. **Tannhäuser** seeking salvation, takes pilgrimage to Rome. [Ger. Opera: Wagner, *Tannhäuser*, Westerman, 211]

21. **Tenorio, Don Juan** after sinful lifetime, eleventh-hour repentance saves soul. [Span. Lit.: *Don Juan Tenorio*]

22. **Theodosius (346–395)** Roman Emperor; did public penance before St. Ambrose. [Rom. Hist.: *EB*, 18:272–273]

23. **Twelve Labors of Hercules** undertaken as penance for slaying his children. [Gk. and Roman Myth.: Hall, 148]

24. **violet** Christian liturgical color; worn during Lent and Advent. [Color Symbolism: Jobes, 357]

25. **Yom Kippur** most sacred Hebrew holy day; the day of atonement. [Judaism: *NCE*, 182]

532. PERFECTION

1. **Giotto's O** perfect circle drawn effortlessly by Giotto. [Ital. Hist.: Brewer *Dictionary*, 463]

2. **golden mean or section** a proportion between the length and width of a rectangle or two portions of a line; said to be ideal. [Fine Arts.: Misc.]

3. **Grosvenor, Archibald** poet who has no earthly rival in his claim to being quite perfect. [Br. Opera: Gilbert and Sullivan *Patience*]

4. **hole in one** source of one stroke for hole in golf. [Sports: *Webster's Sports*, 215]

5. **Jesus Christ** son of God; personification of human flawlessness. [Christian Hist.: *NCE*, 1412]

6. **perfect cadence** where the dominant passes into the harmony of the tonic chord. [Music: Thompson, 333]

7. **perfect contrition** sorrow for sin, coming from a love of God for His own perfections. [Christianity: Misc.]

8. **perfect game** baseball game in which all opposing batters are put out in succession. [Sports: *Webster's Sports*, 311]

9. **perfect number** equal in value to the sum of those natural numbers that are less than the given number but that also divide (with zero remainder) the given number. [Math: *EB*, VII: 872]

10. **rose** symbol of sacred, romantic, and sensual love, and perfection. [Symbolism: *CEOS&S*]

11. **royal flush** best possible hand in poker; one-suited hand from ten to ace. [Cards: Brewer *Dictionary*, 940]

12. **Superman** Nietzsche's ideal being, a type that would arise when man succeeds in surpassing himself. [Ger. Phil.: *Thus Spake Zarathustra* in Magill III, 1069]

13. **300 game** bowling game of twelve consecutive strikes, scoring maximum 300 points. [Sports: *Webster's Sports*, 311]

533. PERMANENCE

1. **law of the Medes and Persians** Darius's execution ordinance; an immutable law. [O.T.: Daniel 6:8–9]

2. **leopard's spots** there always, as evilness with evil men. [O.T.: Jeremiah 13:23; Br. Lit.: *Richard II*]

3. **Nubian's skin** permanently black, as evildoer is permanently evil. [O.T.: Jeremiah 13:23]

534. PERSECUTION

1. **Albigenses** medieval sect suppressed by a crusade, wars, and the Inquisition. [Fr. Hist.: *NCE*, 53]

2. **Camisards** uprising of Protestant peasantry after the revocation of Edict of Nantes in 1685 was brutally suppressed by the royal army. [Fr. Hist.: *NCE*, 434]

3. **Huguenots** Protestants of France, much persecuted from the 16th century onward. [Fr. Hist.: *NCE*, 1285]

4. *Quo Vadis* novel of Rome under Nero, describing the imprisonment, crucifixion, and burning of Christians. [Pol. Lit.: Magill I, 797]

5. **Spanish Inquisition** harsh tribunal established in 1478 to dispose of heretics, Protestants, and Jews. [Eur. Hist.: *Collier's*, X, 259]

535. PERSEVERANCE (See also DETERMINATION.)

1. **Ainsworth** redid dictionary manuscript burnt in fire. [Br. Hist.: Brewer *Handbook*, 752]

2. *Call of the Wild, The* dogs trail steadfastly through Alaska's tundra. [Am. Lit.: *The Call of the Wild*]

3. **canary grass** traditional symbol of perseverance. [Plant Symbolism: *Flora Symbolica*, 183]

4. **Cato the Elder (234–149 B.C.)** for his last eight years said in every Senate speech, "Carthage must be destroyed." [Rom. Hist.: *EB* (1963) V, 43]

5. **Deans, Jeanie** by resourcefulness and an arduous journey, manages eventually to obtain a pardon for her sister. [Br. Lit.: *The Heart of Midlothian*]

6. **Goodwood, Caspar** eternal American pursuer of Isabel Archer's hand. [Am. Lit.: *The Portrait of a Lady*, Magill I, 766–768]

7. *Little Engine That Could, The* pint-sized locomotive struggles long and hard to surmount hill before succeeding. [Children's Lit.: *Little Engine That Could*]

8. **Moses** Hebrew lawgiver; led his quarrelsome people out of bondage in Egypt. [O.T.: Exodus; Leviticus]

9. **Mutt** though usually thwarted in his schemes, he remains determined to triumph someday. [Comics: Berger, 48]

10. **Penelope** foils suitors for twenty years while awaiting return of Odysseus. [Gk. Myth.: Kravitz, 182]

11. **Santiago** stalwart in his attempt to subdue large fish through harshness of sea and weather. [Am. Lit.: *The Old Man and the Sea*]

12. **snail** symbol of deliberation and steadfastness. [Heraldry: Halbert's 38]

13. **tortoise** perseverance helps him succeed where those inclined to dawdle fail. [Folklore: Jobes, 1590]

14. **Zarechnaya, Nina** sacrifices everything to further career as actress. [Russ. Lit.: *The Seagull*]

536. PERVERSION (See also BESTIALITY.)

1. **bondage and domination (B&D)** practices with whips, chains, etc. for sexual pleasure. [Western Cult.: Misc.]

2. **Humbert, Humbert** middle-aged gentleman crisscrosses America staying in motels with 12–year-old "nymphet." [Am. Lit.: *Lolita*]

3. **Imp of the Perverse** perversity as motive for men's actions. [Am. Lit.: "Imp of the Perverse" in Hart, 402]

4. **Manson, Marilyn (1969–)** born Brian Hugh Warner; musician known for extremely bizarre persona and stage performances; name derives from Marilyn Monroe and mass murderer Charles Manson. [Am. Music: Misc.]

5. *Night of the Living Dead* 1968 low-budget zombie film; graphic depiction of cannibalism and gore won it cult status and some critical acclaim. [Am. Film: *SJEPC*]

6. **Sade, Marquis de (1740–1814)** jailed for sexual crimes; wrote of sexual cruelty. [Fr. Hist.: Wallechinsky, 165]

7. **sadism and masochism (S&M)** usually refers to sexual gratification by inflicting pain on others (sadism) or on oneself (masochism). [Pop. Culture: Misc.]

8. **von Sacher-Masoch, Leopold (1836–1895)** author who derived pleasure from being tortured. [Aust. Hist.: Wallechinsky, 165]

537.   PESSIMISM (See also CYNICISM, SKEPTICISM.)

1. **Beckett, Samuel (1906–1989)** Irish dramatist who wrote in French; creator of works noted for their bleak view of life. [Irish Lit.: *ODA*]

2. **Calamity Jane** [Martha Jane Canary or Martha Burke (1852–1903)] frontierswoman; mannish prophetess of doom. [Am. Hist.: Flexner, 71]

3. **Cassandra** no credence ever given to her truthful prophecies of doom. [Gk. Myth.: Zimmerman, 51]

4. *City of Dreadful Night, The* expresses a passionate faith in pessimism as the only sensible philosophy. [Br. Poetry: James Thomson *The City of Dreadful Night* in Benét, 202]

5. **Gerontion** old man who deplores aging, aridity, and spiritual decay and despairs of civilization. [Br. Poetry: Benét, 391]

6. **Gloomy Gus** one with a pessimistic outlook on the world. [Am. Usage: Misc.]

7. **Heraclitus (535–475 B.C.)** "Weeping Philosopher"; grieved over man's folly. [Gk. Hist.: Brewer *Dictionary*, 1146]

8. **Micaiah** always prophesied misfortune for King Ahab. [O.T.: I Kings 22:8]

9. **Murphy's Law** "If anything can go wrong, it will." [Am. Culture: Wallechinsky, 480]

10. **Schopenhauer, Arthur (1788–1860)** German philosopher known for philosophy of pessimism. [Ger. Hist.: *NCE*, 2447]

538. PHILANTHROPIST (See also PATRON.)

1. **Appleseed, Johnny** [John Chapman (c.1775–1847)] traveled through the Ohio Valley giving away apple seeds and caring for orchards. [Am. Hist.: *Collier's*, IV, 569]

2. **Branson, Richard (1950–)** successful businessman who helped form humanitarian group The Elders, which was designed to come up with solutions to global issues and conflicts objectively. [Br. Business: Misc.]

3. **Buffett, Warren (1930–)** American billionaire financier, founder of Berkshire Hathaway, philanthropist. [Am. Business: Misc.]

4. **Carnegie, Andrew (1835–1919)** steel magnate who believed the rich should administer wealth for public benefit. [Am. Hist.: Jameson, 83]

5. **Gates, Bill (1955–)** American billionaire, founder of Microsoft; has given billions to foundation for education and to end childhood disease. [Am. Business: Misc.]

6. **Guggenheim** 19th- and 20th-century family name of American industrialists and philanthropists. [Am. Hist.: *NCE*, 1159]

7. **Hughes, Howard (1905–1976)** started the Howard Hughes Medical Institute in 1953; largest institute dedicated to biomedical research. [Am. Hist.: Misc.]

8. **Ka-Shing, Li (1928–)** prominent and rich Chinese businessman; promised to donate a third of his fortune to charity, which is estimated to come to about $10 billion. [Chinese Business: Misc.]

9. **Mellon, Andrew (1855–1937)** financier and public official; left large sums for research and art. [Am. Hist.: *NCE*, 1743]

10. **Rhodes, Cecil (1853–1902)** British imperialist; left millions of pounds for public service; notably, the Rhodes scholarships. [Br. Hist.: *NCE*, 2316]

11. **Rockefeller, John D. (1839–1937)** American multimillionaire; endowed many institutions. [Am. Hist.: Jameson, 431]

12. **Soros, George (1930–)** well known for political philanthropic efforts; started various Soros Institutes to help post-Soviet states democratize. [Hungarian Hist.: Misc.]

13. **Turner, Ted (1938–)** innovator in TV broadcasting who has funded and supported numerous environmental and social causes and charities, including $1 billion to the United Nations. [Am. TV: *SJEPC*]

Piety (See RIGHTEOUSNESS.)

539. PIRACY

1. **Barbary Coast** Mediterranean coastline of former Barbary States; former pirate lair. [Afr. Hist.: *NCE*, 229]

2. **Blackbeard** [Edward Teach (1689?-1718)] colorful, albeit savage, corsair. [Br. Hist.: Jameson, 495]

3. **Conrad, Lord** proud, ascetic but successful buccaneer. [Br. Lit.: *The Corsair*, Walsh *Modern*, 104]

4. **Drake, Sir Francis (1540–1596)** British navigator and admiral; famed for marauding expeditions against Spanish. [Br. Hist.: *NCE*, 793]

5. **Fomorians** mythical, prehistoric, giant pirates who raided and pillaged Irish coast. [Irish Legend: Leach, 409]

6. **Hawkins, Sir John (1532–1595)** British admiral; led lucrative slave-trading expeditions. [Br. Hist.: *NCE*, 1206]

7. **Hook, Captain** treacherous pirate in Never-Never Land. [Scot. Lit.: *Peter Pan*]

8. **Jolly Roger** black pirate flag with white skull and crossbones. [World Hist.: Brewer *Dictionary*, 926]

9. **Jonsen, Captain** boards ship taking seven children to England, seizes its valuables, and sails off with the children, who have their own piratical plans. [Br. Lit.: *The Innocent Voyage (High Wind in Jamaica)* in Magill II, 488]

10. **Kidd, Captain William (1645–1701)** British captain; turned pirate. [Br. Hist.: *NCE*, 1476]

11. **Lafitte, Jean (1780–1826)** leader of Louisiana band of privateers and smugglers. [Am. Hist.: *NCE*, 1516]

12. **Morgan, Sir Henry (1635–1688)** Welsh buccaneer; took over privateer band after Mansfield's death. [Br. Hist.: *NCE*, 1832]

13. **Silver, Long John** character from R.L. Stevenson's *Treasure Island*; villanous and charming, he tricks Jim Hawkins into trusting him, then attempts to steal part of Jim's treasure. [Br. Children's Lit.: Jones]

14. **Singleton, Captain** buccaneer acquires great wealth depredating in West Indies and Indian Ocean. [Br. Lit.: *Captain Singleton*]

15. **Sparrow, Captain Jack** flamboyant pirate from Pirates of the Caribbean films; actor Johnny Depp has maintained his portrayal was inspired by rock star Keith Richards and cartoon character Pepé Le Pew; treacherous and conniving—and perhaps a bit crazy—he is nonetheless witty and engaging. [Am. Film: Misc.]

Pitilessness (See HEARTLESSNESS, RUTHLESSNESS.)

Plague (See DISEASE.)

540. POET

1. **al-Rumi, Julaluddin (1207–1273)** most famous poet of Islam, he is revered for his poems celebrating his deep Sufi faith, in visions

of the divine that impart profound spiritual wisdom, rendered in everyday language. [Islamic Lit.: UIMT]

2. **Baudelaire, Charles (1821–1867)** French poet whose *Flowers of Evil* is considered the first work of French Symbolism, reflecting his belief that poetry should connect the exterior world with the inner world of the artist. [Fr. Lit.: *TCLM*]

3. **Blake, William (1757–1827)** English poet and artist; works like *Songs of Innocence* combine his writing and painting. [Br. Lit.: *ODA*]

4. **Bragi** god of verse. [Norse Myth.: Parrinder, 50]

5. **Browning, Elizabeth Barrett (1806–1861)** English poet best known for her love poetry, especially *Love Sonnets from the Portuguese*. [Eng. Lit.: *EB*]

6. **Byron, (George) Lord (1788–1824)** the quintessential Romantic poet, this Englishman was best known for his *Don Juan*, as well as for his scandalous lifestyle, including many love affairs; he died at age 35, fighting for Greek independence. [Br. Lit.: *EB*]

7. **Calliope** muse of epic poetry. [Gk. Myth.: Kravitz, 159]

8. **Castalia** Parnassian fountain; endowed drinker with poetic creativity. [Gk. Myth.: *LLEI*, I: 325]

9. **Chaucer, Geoffrey (1343–1400)** English poet and creator of *The Canterbury Tales*. [Br. Lit.: *ODA*]

10. **Daphnis** creator of bucolic poetry. [Gk. Myth.: Kravitz, 75]

11. **Dickinson, Emily (1830–1886)** one of the greatest American poets, she created verse noted for its striking imagery and rich thematic treatment of love, nature, and death. [Am. Lit.: *EB*]

12. **Eliot, T. S. (1888–1965)** American-born English poet and one of the most influential writers of the 20th century; best known for *The Waste Land* and *Four Quartets*, which reveal his themes of faith, the nature of time and eternity, and metaphysical revelation. [Am. Lit. and Br. Lit.: *TCLM*]

13. **Erato** muse of love lyrics. [Gk. Myth.: Kravitz, 159]

14. **Euterpe** muse of lyric poetry. [Gk. Myth.: Kravitz, 159]

15. **Frost, Robert (1874–1963)** American Poet Laureate and four-time Pulitzer Prize winner; New England landscape and nature informed his work, presented in traditional metrical verse, as in "Stopping by Woods on a Snowy Evening" (1922). [Am. Lit.: *SJEPC*]

16. **Goethe, Johann Wolfgang von (1749–1832)** greatest German poet, best known for his elegant lyric style, inspired by nature and folk tales. [Ger. Lit.: *EB*]

17. **Homer** legendary author of the *Iliad* and the *Odyssey*. [Gk. Lit.: Benét, 474]

18. **Keats, John (1795–1821)** great English poet of the Romantic period; his greatest poems, including "Ode on a Grecian Urn," feature a vivid, senuous imagery. [Br. Lit.: *EB*]

19. **Khayyam, Omar (1048–1131)** Persian poet whose *Rubaiyat*, translated into English in 1859 by Edward FitzGerald, became a sensation; famous lines include: "A jug of wine, a loaf of bread, and thou." [Pers. Lit.: *EB*]

20. **Longfellow, Henry Wadsworth (1807–1882)** most famous American poet of the 19th century, he is best known for *Hiawatha* and other historical verse; his name is synonymous with "Poet." [Am. Lit.: *EB*]

21. **Milton, John (1608–1674)** English poet and creator of *Paradise Lost* [Br. Lit.: *ODA*]

22. **Parnassus** mountains sacred to Muses; hence, abode of poetry. [Gk. Myth.: Hall, 234]

23. **Plath, Sylvia (1932–1963)** American poet and novelist of the Confessional school; in such works as *Ariel* she delineated her personal suffering and tumultuous emotional state; she ended her own life at the age of 31. [Am. Lit.: *TCLM*]

24. **Pléiade, The** 16th century poets sought to revitalize French literature. [Fr. Hist.: Benét, 795]

25. **Poe, Edgar Allan (1809–1849)** American poet and short story writer whose poems, including "The Raven" and "The Bells" are American classics. [Am. Lit.: *TCLM*]

26. **Sandburg, Carl (1878–1967)** distinguished poet whose diction reflected ordinary speech and captured America's national identity. [Am. Lit.: *SJEPC*]

27. **Sappho (c. 620–c. 565 B.C.)** lyric poet from the island of Lesbos; wrote passionate love poetry for women; symbol of lesbianism. [Gk. Lit.: *ODA*]

28. **Shakespeare, William (1564–1616)** greatest writer of all time, best known for his plays, but was also a peerless poet; his sonnets, many written to a Dark Lady, speak of love, and often the ravages of time. [Br. Lit.: *EB*]

29. **Shelley, Percy Bysshe (1792–1822)** English Romantic poet and author of *Prometheus Unbound*, containing his famous "To a Skylark"; a symbol of Romantic love and fervor, and of early death. [Br. Lit.: *EB*]

30. **Stevens, Wallace (1879–1955)** American poet associated with Modernism, noted for his vivid imagery and elegant verse in such poems as "Sunday Morning." [Am. Lit.: *TCLM*]

31. **Tagore, Rabindranath (1861–1941)** greatest poet of India and Nobel laureate, best known for his religious verse; he introduced the West to Indian religion and culture. [Ind. Lit.: *EB*]

32. **Tennyson, Alfred Lord (1809–1892)** leading poet of Victorian England, he is best known for "The Charge of the Light Brigade" and *Idlylls of the King*, about King Arthur. [Br. Lit.: *EB*]

33. **White Goddess, the** goddess of ancient fertility and the moon whose worship is claimed by Robert Graves to be the origin of poetry. [Br. Lit.: Benét, 1087]

34. **Whitman, Walt (1819–1892)** American poet known for his earthy, naturalistic lyrics, especially in such works as *Leaves of Grass*. [Am. Lit.: *TCLM*]

35. **Yeats, William Butler (1865–1939)** Irish poet and dramatist, this Nobel laureate created poetry imbued with themes of Irish folk lore and is known for such visionary poems as "Sailing to Byzantium." [Irish Lit.: *TCLM*]

Politeness (See COURTESY.)

Politeness, Excessive (See COURTESY, EXCESSIVE.)

541. POLYGAMY

1. **David** had many wives. [O.T.: I Samuel 25:43–44; II Samuel 3:2–5]

2. **Draupadi** princess won by Arjuna, brings her home as the wife of all five brothers. [Hindu. Lit.: *Mahabharata*]

3. **Islam** religion permits four wives. [Islam: *WB*, A:549]

4. **Lamech** first man to have two wives. [O.T.: Genesis 4:19–20]

5. **Mongut of Siam, King** 9000 wives and concubines. [Thai. Hist.: Wallechinsky, 279]

6. **Mormons** religious sect; once advocated plural marriage. [Am. Hist.: *NCE*, 1833]

7. **Muhammad** had a total of ten wives and ten or fifteen concubines. [Islam: Brewer *Dictionary*, 614]

8. **Solomon** 700 wives, princesses, and 300 concubines. [O.T.: I Kings 11:1–8]

542. POMPOSITY

1. **Aldiborontephoscophornio** nickname from play by Carey, given by Scott to his pompous publisher, James Ballantyne. [Br. Lit.: Barnhart, 23]

2. **Chrononhotonthologos** bombastic, pompous king of Queerumania. [Br. Drama: Benét, 197]

3. **Crane, Frasier** vain, pompous, but lovable radio psychiatrist in sitcom *Frasier* has impeccable taste in clothing, furnishings, food, and drink. [Am. TV: *SJEPC*]

4. **Malvolio** pompous, conceited steward who aspires to his mistress's love. [Br. Drama: Shakespeare *Twelfth Night*]

543. POSSESSION (See also ENCHANTMENT.)

1. **Gadarene swine** Jesus sends demons from man to pigs. [N.T.: Matthew 8:28–32; Mark 5:1–13; Luke 8:26–33]

2. **Legion** man controlled by devils; exorcised by Jesus. [N.T.: Mark 5:9; Luke 8:30]

3. **Regan** young girl gruesomely infested with the devil. [Am. Lit.: *The Exorcist*]

544. POVERTY (See also BANKRUPTCY.)

1. **Aglaus** poorest man in Arcadia, but happier than king. [Gk. Myth.: Kravitz, 13]

2. **Appalachia** West Virginia coal mining region known for its abysmal poverty. [Am. Hist.: *NCE*, 160]

3. **Apple Annie** apple seller on street corners during Depression. [Am. Hist.: Flexner, 11]

4. **bare feet** symbol of impoverishment. [Folklore: Jobes, 181]

5. **Barnardo Home** one of many homes founded for destitute children. [Br. Hist.: *NCE*, 233]

6. **Bashmachkin, Akakii Akakiievich** poor clerk saves years for overcoat that is soon stolen. [Russ. Lit.: "The Overcoat" in *The Overcoat and Other Stories*]

7. **Bonhomme, Jacques** nickname for poor French peasants. [Fr. Folklore: Walsh *Classical*, 59]

8. **Booth, Captain** continually in and out of debtor's prison. [Br. Lit.: *Amelia*]

9. **Buddha** religious leader exchanges wealth for the robe of an ascetic mendicant. [Buddhism: *NCE*, 387]

10. **Bung** experiences modified and extreme levels of want. [Br. Lit.: *Sketches by Boz*]

11. **Chaplin, Charlie (1889–1977)** one of the greatest comedians of all times; writer/director/actor of numerous classic silent films; spent time in workhouses as a child; desperate poverty of his early years manifested in films, most notably in character of Little Tramp. [Br. Film: Misc.]

12. **Clare of Assisi, Saint** lived entirely on alms; founded "Poor Clares." [Christian Hagiog.: Attwater, 87]

13. **Cratchit, Bob** Scrooge's poorly paid clerk. [Br. Lit.: *A Christmas Carol*]

14. **Crawley, Rev. Josiah** debt-maddened clergyman. [Br. Lit.: *Last Chronicle of Barset*]

15. **Dickens, Charles (1812–1870)** great Victorian novelist whose childhood in poverty required him to work in a factory and inspired the many lost children who appear in his works like *Oliver Twist*. [Br. Lit.: Misc.]

16. **Francis, Saint (1182–1226)** renounced his worldly life and possessions, extolled the virtue of poverty. [Christian Hagiog.: Brewer *Dictionary*, 375]

17. **ghetto** from an Italian word referring to the Jewish section of Venice, now used to describe areas isolated by poverty and social decay. [Am. Hist.: Misc.]

18. *Grapes of Wrath, The* about the Joad family; jobless, facing starvation. [Am. Lit.: *The Grapes of Wrath*]

19. **Great Depression** economic crisis of 1929–1939, unprecedented in length and widespread poverty. [Am. Hist.: *NCE*, 1132]

20. **Grub Street** London street; home of indigent writers. [Br. Hist.: Brewer *Note-Book*, 394]

21. **Hell's Kitchen** section of midtown Manhattan; notorious for slums and high crime rate. [Am. Usage: Misc.]

22. **Hooverville** Depression shantytown arising during Hoover administration. [Am. Hist.: Flexner, 118]

23. **Hubbard, Old Mother** had not even a bone for her dog. [Nurs. Rhyme: Opie, 317]

24. **"If I Were a Rich Man"** monologue/song from musical *Fiddler on the Roof* (1964) in which hardworking dairyman in a small, turn-of-the-20th-century Russian village petitions God and dreams of a wealthy existence. [Am. Musical: *SJEPC*]

25. **Job** lost everything he owned to Satan. [O.T.: Job]

26. **Job's turkey** one-feathered bird even more destitute than its owner. [Can. and Am. Usage: Brewer *Dictionary*, 589]

27. **Lazarus** satisfied with table scraps; dogs licked sores. [N.T.: Luke 16:19–22]

28. **Micawber, Wilkins** optimistic, though chronically penniless and in debt. [Br. Lit.: *David Copperfield*]

29. **Okies** itinerant dust bowl farmers ((1930s). [Am. Hist.: Van Doren, 455; Am. Lit.: *The Grapes of Wrath*]

30. **War on Poverty** U.S. government program of 1960's to aid the needy. [Am. Hist.: *WB*, J:120]

31. **Yellow Kid, the** grotesque, unchildish slum-child, one of the impoverished inhabitants of Hogan's Alley. [Comics: Berger, 25]

545. POWER

1. **"Allahu akbar"** Arabic phrase "God is greater than all" acknowledges power of God. [Islam: *UIMT*, 189]

2. **axe** symbol of power and authority; linked with ancient sun and storm gods. [Symbolism: *CEOS&S*]

3. **big stick** from President Theodore Roosevelt's phrase, "speak softly and carry a big stick," referring to his foreign policy; the willingness to use force if necessary. [Am. Politics: Misc.]

4. **cross** for Native Americans, symbol of all human powers: intelligence, love. spirit, passion. [Native Am. Culture: *IEOTS*, 46]

5. **dybbuk** demon with the power to possess a mortal. [Jewish Folklore *FOF*]

6. **eagle** symbol of power (and imperial power), speed, and perception. [Symbolism: *CEOS&S*]

7. **elephant** in India and China, a symbol of sovereign power. [Symbolism: *CEOS&S*]

8. **eminence grise** in politics, "the power behind the throne," one who works behind the scenes. [Politics *FOF, MOD*]

9. **Force, The** mystical source of a Jedi Knight's righteous power. [Am. Film: *Star Wars* and sequels]

10. **Great White Father** of unknown origin, a term used ironically to refer to the U.S. President or other powerful white man. [Am. Politics: *FOF, MOD*]

11. **haymaker** term from boxing meaning a powerful punch that usually ends a match; by extension, a powerful action. [Am. Culture: *FOF, MOD*]

12. **heavy hitter** from baseball, meaning a slugger with the power to win games; by extension, any powerful person. [Am. Culture *FOF, MOD*]

13. **kitchen cabinet** non-elected, powerful and influential advisors to the president. [Am. Politics: Misc.]

14. **lizard** to Native Americans, associated with shamantic powers, vision quests, and strength. [Symbolism: *CEOS&S*]

15. **panther** common symbol of desire and power. [Symbolism: *CEOS&S*]

16. **push the envelope** to go beyond set limits; first used by test pilots of early supersonic aircraft as they approached, then broke, the sound barrier; now used to describe any attempt to break limits. [Am. Culture: Tom Wolfe *The Right Stuff*]

17. **Thought Police** from Orwell's iconic *1984*, refers to the surveillance of citizens, to silence all dissent through torture and brainwashing; now a metaphor for any political power that endeavors to control the thinking of a people. [Br. Lit.: George Orwell *1984*]

18. **tiger** in Asia and India replaces lion as symbol of all that is great and terrible in nature. [Symbolism: *CEOS&S*]

19. **Trump, Donald J. (1946–)** host of TV reality show *The Apprentice*, which premiered in 2004; wielded power to choose contestant who would be highly-paid president of one of his companies for a year or more. [Am. TV: Misc.]

546. PREDICAMENT

1. **behind the eight ball** from billiards, to be in a difficult situation. [Sports: *FOF, MOD*]

2. **Dancy, Captain Ronald** must persecute friend to save own skin. [Br. Lit.: *Loyalties*, Magill I, 533–534]

3. **Gordian knot** inextricable difficulty; Alexander cut the original. [Gk. Hist.: Espy, 49]

4. **"Lady or the Tiger, The"** hero must choose one of two doors. [Am. Lit.: Benét, 559]

5. **Marta** loves husband; forced into adultery by patron. [Ger. Opera: d'Albert, *Tiefland*, Westerman, 373]

6. **Scylla and Charybdis** two equally dangerous alternatives. [Gk. Lit.: *Odyssey*, Espy, 41]

7. **Symplegades** cliffs at Black Sea entrance; clashed together as ships passed through. [Gk. Myth.: Zimmerman, 251]

547. PRESTIGE (See also EXTRAVAGANCE, LUXURY, WEALTH.)

1. **Armani, Giorgio (1934–)** men's fashionwear designer of stylish, expensive clothing lines. [Ital. Culture: *SJEPC*]

2. **Gucci** Italian fashion brand considered the height of luxury, status, and taste; interlocked G logo imprinted on accessories like leather handbags and luggage is a symbol of prestige. [Ital. Culture: *SJEPC*]

3. *Masterpiece Theatre* quality literary adaptations and biographies for TV Public Broadcasting Stations. [Am. TV: *SJEPC*]

4. **Masters Golf Tournament** played at Augusta National Golf Club; winner gets coveted green jacket. [Am. Sports: *SJEPC*]

5. **Rolex** beautiful, very expensive watches from Switzerland; owning one is a sign of wealth and status. [Pop. Culture: Misc.]

6. **Rolls Royce** long, handsome British cars with signature "Spirit of Ecstasy" female-figure hood ornament; ownership signifies wealth and prestige. [Pop. Culture: Misc.]

7. **Saks Fifth Avenue** Manhattan store with classy merchandise and services opened in 1924, but outlets bore Fifth Avenue appellation to capitalize on the distinction; name became synonymous with wealth and stylishness. [Am. Business: *SJEPC*]

548. PRETENSION (See also HYPOCRISY.)

1. **Absolon** vain, officious parish clerk. [Br. Lit.: *Canterbury Tales*, "Miller's Tale"]

2. **Chambers, Diane** annoyingly intellectual graduate student waitress at working-class bar on TV's *Cheers* (1982–93). [Am. TV: *SJEPC*]

3. **Chrononhotonthologos** king whose pomposity provoked a fatal brawl with his general. [Br. Lit.: Walsh *Modern*, 96]

4. **Copper, Captain** pretends to great wealth; jewels are counterfeit. [Br. Lit.: *Rule a Wife and Have a Wife*, Walsh *Modern*, 105]

5. **Coriolanus** stiff-necked Roman aristocrat; contemptuous of the common people. [Br. Lit.: *Coriolanus*]

6. **Crane, Frasier** vain, pompous, but lovable radio psychiatrist in sitcom *Frasier* has impeccable taste in clothing, furnishings, food, and drink. [Am. TV: *SJEPC*]

7. **de Armado, Don Adriano** his language inordinately disproportionate to his thought. [Br. Lit.: *Love's Labour Lost*]

8. **Dodsworth, Fran** shallow industrialist's wife ostentatiously gallivants about Europe. [Am. Lit.: *Dodsworth*]

9. **Dogberry** ostentatiously and fastidiously examines prisoners. [Br. Lit.: *Much Ado About Nothing*]

10. **euphuism** style overly rich with alliteration, figures, and Latinisms. [Br. Lit.: *Euphues*, Espy, 127]

11. **Isle of Lanterns** inhabited by pretenders to knowledge. [Fr. Lit.: *Pantagruel*]

12. **Jourdain, Monsieur** parvenu grandiosely affects gentleman's mien. [Fr. Lit.: *The Bourgeois Gentilhomme*]

13. **Madelon and Cathos** their suitors had to be flamboyant. [Fr. Lit.: *Les Précieuses Ridicules*]

14. **Melody, Cornelius** self-deluded tavern-keeper boasts about his upper-class past to maintain a show of importance. [Am. Drama: Eugene O'Neill *A Touch of the Poet* in Benét, 737]

15. **morning glory** symbol of affection; flower of September. [Flower Symbolism: *Flora Symbolica*, 175; Kunz, 300]

16. **Parolles** boastful villain of affected sentiment and knowledge. [Br. Lit.: *All's Well That Ends Well*]

17. **Pendennis** enters university "posing as moneyed aristocrat." [Br. Lit.: *Pendennis*]

18. **Verdurin, M. & Mme.** nouveau-riche couple strive for social eminence. [Fr. Lit.: Proust *Remembrance of Things Past*]

19. **willow herb** indicates affection. [Flower Symbolism: *Flora Symbolica*, 178]

20. **Yvetot, King** affects grandeur; kingdom is but a village. [Fr. Legend: Brewer *Dictionary*. 1173]

Prey (See QUARRY.)

Pride (See BOASTFULNESS, EGOTISM, VANITY.)

549. PRIZE

1. **America's Cup** sailing trophy for regatta and match race winners; oldest trophy still used in international sport. [World Sports: Misc.]

2. **blue ribbon** denotes highest honor. [Western Folklore: Brewer *Dictionary*, 127]

3. **Bollingen** annual prize for highest achievement in American poetry. [Am. Lit.: Hart, 88]

4. **Booker Prize** also known as Man Booker Prize for Fiction; awarded each year for the best original English-language novel written by a citizen of the Commonwealth of Nations or the Republic of Ireland. [World Lit.: Misc.]

5. **Carnegie Medal Prize** award given anuallly since 1936; given to author of most exceptional book for young readers of previous year; began as British award, but since 1969 given to any book written in English and published in United Kingdom. [Children's Lit.: *OCCL*]

6. **Davis Cup** international men's team tennis award. [World Sports: Misc.]

7. **Edgar** award named after Edgar Allan Poe, presented annually by the Mystery Writers of America to recognize achievement in the mystery field. [Am. Lit.: *SJEPC*; Misc.]

8. **Eisner Awards** American comic book industry's annual awards for excellence, named in honor of innovative comic artist Will Eisner. [Am. Comics: *SJEPC*; Misc.]

9. **Emmy** awarded annually for best achievements in television programming and performance. [TV: Misc.]

10. **Enrico Fermi Award** given for "exceptional and altogether outstanding achievement" in atomic energy. [Am. Hist.: Misc.]

11. **FIFA World Cup** award for the winner of the World Cup Finals of soccer; there is a cup for men and women. [World Sports: Misc.]

12. **Gold Glove** annual award given to Major League Baseball players; one is awarded for each position and voted on by managers and coaches; also called Rawlings Gold Glove Award. [Am. Sports: Misc.]

13. **gold medal** traditional first prize. [Western Cult.: Misc.]

14. **Golden Globe** prestigious award given in the American film and television industry honoring the "best" in various categories; awards include best actress, director, and motion picture. [Am. Film: Misc.; Am. TV: Misc.]

15. **Goncourt** annual award for best French fiction. [Fr. Lit.: *NCE*, 1106]

16. **Grammy** awarded by the National Academy of Recording Arts and Sciences for the best in the recording field. [Am. Hist.: Misc.]

17. **Guggenheim** annual fellowships for creative work. [Am. Hist.: Hart, 337]

18. **Heisman Trophy** awarded to the outstanding college football player of the year by New York Athletic Club. [Am. Sports: Misc.]

19. **Kate Greenaway Medal** established in 1955 by Library Association of Great Britain; annually awards most distinguished illustrations in book published during previous year. [Br. Children's Lit.: *OCCL*]

20. **Kentucky Derby Trophy** given to the winner of the Kentucky Derby along with blanket of 554 red roses. [Am. Sports: Misc.]

21. **laurel wreath** ancient award for victory. [Western Cult.: Brewer *Dictionary*]

22. **Medal of Freedom** highest award given a U.S. citizen; established 1963. [Am. Hist.: Misc.]

23. **National Book Award** given by the American Academy and Institute of Arts and Letters to outstanding works. [Am. Hist.: Misc.]

24. **NCAA Championship** given to the college basketball team that wins the single-elimination tournament. [Am. Sports: Misc.]

25. **Newbery Medal** most pretigious American award for children's books; given annually to "the most distinguished contribution to American literature for children" during the previous year. [Am. Children's Lit.: *OCCL*]

26. **Nobel Prize** monetary awards for outstanding contributions benefiting mankind. [World Hist.: Wheeler, 718]

27. **Olympic Medal** given to athletes who place first, second, or third in a summer or winter Olympic game. [World Sports: Misc.]

28. **Oscar** gold statuette awarded to film actors, directors, writers, technicians, etc.; also called Academy Award. [Am. Film: Brewer *Dictionary*, 788]

29. **Pulitzer Prize** awards made in letters, music, and journalism. [Am. Hist.: Wheeler, 824]

30. **Randolph Caldecott Medal** awarded anually since 1938 to artist of most distinguished American picture book published in U.S. during preceding year. [Am. Children's Lit.: *OCCL*]

31. **Rock 'n' Roll Hall of Fame** induction is given to people or groups considered influential in music industry. [World Music: Misc.]

32. **Ryder Cup** golf trophy donated by Samuel Ryder; awarded to the winner of the Ryder Cup Matches; Americans and Europeans are matched to play together. [World Sports: Misc.]

33. **Stanley Cup** ice hockey championship trophy; given to National Hockey League playoff champions. [Am. Sports: Misc.]

34. **Tony** presented annually for outstanding work in the Broadway theater; also called Antoinette Perry Award. [Am. Hist.: Misc.]

35. **Vince Lombardi Trophy** awarded to winner of National Football League championship Super Bowl game. [Am. Sports: Misc.]

Prodigality (See DISSIPATION.)

Profligacy (See LICENTIOUSNESS, PROMISCUITY.)

550. PROLIFICNESS

1. **Abraham** promised countless descendants by God. [O.T.: Genesis 13:16]

2. **Aegyptus** fathered 50 sons, who married the daughters of his twin brother Danaus. [Gk. Myth.: Benét, 11]

3. **Danaus** fathered 50 daughters, who married the sons of his twin brother Aegyptus. [Gk. Myth.: Benét, 11]

4. **Flanders, Moll** adventuress bears a dozen children to various mates. [Br. Lit.: *Moll Flanders* in Magill I, 614]

5. **Lester, Jeeter and Ada** hapless sharecroppers with seventeen children. [Am. Lit.: Caldwell *Tobacco Road*]

6. **old woman who lived in a shoe** "had so many children she didn't know what to do." [Nursery Rhyme: Baring-Gould, 85]

7. **rabbit** progenitor of many offspring at short intervals. [Zoology: Misc.]

551. PROMISCUITY (See also DISSIPATION, LICENTIOUSNESS.)

1. **Anatol** constantly flits from one girl to another. [Aust. Drama: Schnitzler *Anatol* in Benét, 33]

2. **Aphrodite** promiscuous goddess of sensual love. [Gk. Myth.: Parrinder, 24]

3. **Ashley, Lady Brett** forever falling in love with young men. [Am. Lit.: *The Sun Also Rises*]

4. **Barbarella** scantily dressed, sex-loving, blonde astronaut. [Comics: Horn, 96]

5. **Camille** "a woman of Paris." [Fr. Lit.: *Camille*]

6. **Chamberlain, Wilt (1936–1999)** one of basketball's greatest players expounded on his off-court sexual activities, claiming to have slept with 20,000 women, in autobiography *A View from Above* (1991). [Am. Sports: *A View from Above*]

7. **Compson, Candace** gave herself freely to every man she met; her illegitimate daughter became equally promiscuous. [Am. Lit.: Faulkner *The Sound and the Fury in Magill I, 917*]

8. **Forrester, Mrs. Marian** traveling husband not enough to fulfill desires. [Am. Lit.: *A Lost Lady*]

9. **Ganconer** fairy who makes love with, then abandons, women. [Br. Folklore: Briggs, 183–184]

10. **Gomer** Hosea's wanton wife. [O.T.: Hosea 1:1–3]

11. *Looking for Mr. Goodbar* Theresa Dunn haunts singles bars in a compulsive quest for the ideal lover. [Am. Lit.: Weiss, 267]

12. **Messalina** wife of Emperor Claudius of Rome. [Rom. Hist.: Brewer *Handbook*, 701]

13. **Peyton Place** fictitious New England town rife with sex and vice.. [Am. Lit., Film, and TV: *SJEPC*]

14. **Pill, The** some feel that its use encourages promiscuity. [Am. Medicine: *SJEPC*]

15. **Rogers, Mildred** though a wanton, Philip loved her above all else. [Br. Lit.: *Of Human Bondage*; Magill I, 670–672]

552. PROPAGANDA

1. **Axis Sally** [Mildred Elizabeth Sisk (1900–) or Rita Louise Zucca, (1912–)] Nazi broadcaster who urged American withdrawal from WWII. [Am. Hist.: Flexner, 449]

2. **Big Lie** method used by Nazi propagandists to hide their true intent, especially in regards to the murder of 6 million Jews. [Eur. Hist.: *FOF, MOD*]

3. **Haw-Haw, Lord** [William Joyce (1906–1946)] British citizen becomes German propagandist in WWII. [Br. Hist.: *NCE*, 1435]

4. **Tokyo Rose** name given to various female Japanese deejays by WWII military men; taunted Allied servicemen and made demoralizing statemtents and urged surrender; one [Iva Ikuko Toguri D'Aquino(1916–2006)] was tried and convicted, probably unjustly; later pardoned. [Am. Hist.: Flexner, 449;; *SJEPC*]

553. PROPHECY (See also OMEN.)

1. **Ancaeus** prophecy that he would not live to taste the wine from his vineyards is fulfilled. [Gk. Myth.: Brewer *Dictionary*, 32]

2. **augurs** Roman officials who interpreted omens. [Rom. Hist.: Parrinder, 34]

3. **Balaam** vaticinally speaks with Jehovah's voice. [O.T.: Numbers 23:8–10; 24:18–24]

4. **banshee** Irish spirit who foretells death. [Irish Folklore: Briggs, 14–16]

5. **Belshazzar's Feast** disembodied hand foretells Belshazzar's death. [O.T.: Daniel 5]

6. **Brave New World** picture of world's condition 600 years from now. [Br. Lit.: *Brave New World*]

7. **Calamity Jane** [Martha Jane Canary or Martha Burke (1852–1903)] mannish prophetess of doom. [Am. Hist.: Flexner, 71]

8. **Calpurnia** sees bloody statue of Julius in dream. [Br. Lit.: *Julius Caesar*]

9. **Carmen** the cards repeatedly spell her death. [Fr. Opera: Bizet, *Carmen*, Westerman, 189–190]

10. **Cassandra** always accurate but fated to be disbelieved, predicts doom of Troy to brother, Hector. [Br. Lit.: *Troilus and Cressida*,; Gk. Myth.: Parrinder, 57]

11. **Clachas** declares that Iphigenia must be sacrificed to appease Artemis and ensure the Greeks' safe passage to Troy. [Gk. Myth.: Hamilton, 261]

12. **Cumaean sibyl** to discover future, leads Aeneas to Hades. [Gk. Lit.: *Aeneid*]

13. **Delphi** ancient oracular center near Mt. Parnassus. [Gk. Myth.: Parrinder, 74; Jobes, 428]

14. **Dodona** oldest oracle of Zeus in Greece. [Gk. Myth.: Kravitz, 83]

15. **Ezekiel** priest and prophet to the Jews during Babylonian captivity. [O.T.: Ezekiel]

16. **Golden Cockerel** its crowing predicts either peace or disaster. [Russ. Opera: Rimsky-Korsakov, *Coq d'Or*, Westerman, 392]

17. **haruspices** ancient Etruscan seers who divined the future from the entrails of animals. [Rom. Hist.: *EB*, IV: 933]

18. **Huldah** tells of impending disaster for the idolatrous. [O.T.: II Kings 22:14–19]

19. *I Ching* a book of divination and speculations. [Chinese Lit.: *I Ching*]

20. **Isaiah** foretells fall of Jerusalem; prophet of doom. [O.T.: Isaiah]

21. **Jeremiah** the Lord's herald. [O.T.: Jeremiah]

22. **John the Baptist** foretells the coming of Jesus. [N.T.: Luke 3:16]

23. **Joseph** predicted famine from Pharaoh's dreams. [O.T.: Genesis 41:25–36]

24. **Mopsus** seer who interpreted the words of the Argo's talking prow. [Gk. Myth: Benét, 684]

25. **Muhammad (570–632)** the prophet of Islam. [Islam. Hist.: *NCE*, 1854]

26. **Nostradamus (1503–1566)** startlingly accurate French astrologer and physician. [Fr. Hist.: *NCE*, 1969]

27. **pythoness** priestess of Apollo, the Delphic Oracle, endowed with prophetic powers. [Gk. Hist.: *Collier's*, VII, 682]

28. *Rocking-Horse Winner, The* a small boy predicts winners in horse races through the medium of a demonic rocking horse. [Br. Lit.: D.H. Lawrence *The Rocking-Horse Winner* in Benét, 866]

29. **Sibyllae** women endowed with prophetic powers who interceded with gods for men. [Gk. Myth.: Zimmerman, 239]

30. **Sibylline Books** nine tomes foretelling Rome's future. [Rom. Leg.: Brewer *Dictionary*]

31. **Smith, Joseph** Mormon prophet; professed visions of new faith. [Am. Hist.: Jameson, 467]

32. **Smith, Valentine Michael** messianic Martian shows earthlings the way. [Am. Lit.: *Stranger in a Strange Land*]

33. **sortes (Homericae, Virgilianae, Biblicae)** fortune-telling by taking random passages from a book (as *Iliad, Aeneid,* or the Bible). [Eur. Culture: *Collier's*, VII, 683]

34. **Sosostris, Madame** "the wisest woman in Europe," cleverly interprets the Tarot cards. [Br. Poetry: T.S. Eliot "The Waste Land"]

35. **Tarot cards** used to tell fortunes. [Magic: Brewer *Dictionary*, 1063]

36. **Tiresias** blind and greatest of all mythological prophets. [Gk. Myth.: Zimmerman, 255; Gk. Lit.: *Antigone; Odyssey*]

37. **Ulrica** foretells Gustavus's murder by his friend Anckarström. [Ital Opera: Verdi, *Masked Ball*, Westerman, 313–315]

38. **voice. . .crying in the wilderness** John the Baptist, in reference to his prophecy of the coming of Christ. [N.T.: Matthew 3:3]

39. **Weird Sisters** three witches who set Macbeth agog with prophecies of kingship. [Br. Lit.: *Macbeth*]

Prosperity (See SUCCESS.)

554. PROSTITUTE (See also COURTESAN, MISTRESS.)

1. **Adriana** comely girl becomes prostitute to support herself. [Ital. Lit.: *The Woman of Rome*]

2. **Brattle, Carrie** returns home reconciled after life in gutter. [Br. Lit.: *The Vicar of Bullhampton*]

3. **Celestina** old, evil procuress hired as go-between. [Span. Lit.: *Celestina*]

4. **Dolores and Faustine** provide Swinburne with masochistic pleasure. [Br. Poetry: *Poems and Ballads* in Magill IV, 704]

5. **Dupré, Ashley (1985–)** high-priced prostitute; when it was revealed in 2008 that one of her clients was New York govenor Eliot Spitzer, he resigned. [Am. Hist.: Misc.]

6. **Fleiss, Heidi (1965–)** madam of high-priced prostitution ring in Hollywood, servicing richest men in the world until her arrest in 1993. [Am. Hist.: Misc.]

7. **Hari, Mata (1876–1917)** stage name of Dutch dancer, Margaretha Geertruida Zelle; accused of spying for Germans in France during WWII; many Allied military officers as lovers from whom she supposedly gained valuable information. [Dutch Hist.: Misc.]

8. *Harlot's Progress, The* Hogarth engravings tracing a prostitute's miserable career to its degraded end. [Br. Art.: *EB* (1963) XI, 624]

9. **Hill, Fanny** frankly erotic heroine of frankly erotic novel. [Br. Lit.: *Memoirs of Fanny Hill*]

10. **Hollander, Xaviera (1943–)** author of *The Happy Hooker* (1971), best-selling memoir; frank account of her life as call girl and prominent madam in New York City. [Am. Hist.: Misc.]

11. **La Douce, Irma** leading French prostitute on Pigalle. [Am. Film: Halliwell, 460]

12. **Lulu** keeper of two others on her earnings. [Aust. Opera: Berg, *Lulu*, Westerman, 484]

13. **Maggie** innocent girl, corrupted by slum environment, becomes a prostitute. [Am. Lit.: *Maggie: A Girl of the Streets*, Hart, 514]

14. **Mary Magdalene** debatedly, the repentant prostitute who anointed Jesus's feet. [N.T.: Luke 7:36–50]

15. **Nana** beautiful lady who thrived on a troop of men. [Fr. Lit.: *Nana*, Magill I, 638–640]

16. **Overdone, Mistress** " a bawd of eleven years' continuance." [Br. Lit.: *Measure for Measure*]

17. **Rahab** harlot of Jericho who protected Joshua's two spies. [O.T.: Joshua 2]

18. **Tearsheet, Doll** violent-tempered prostitute, an acquaintance of Falstaff. [Br. Lit.: Shakespeare *II Henry IV*]

19. **Thaïs** notorious harlot in Malebolge, Hell's eighth circle. [Ital. Lit.: *Inferno*]

20. **Toast, Joan** a most saintly whore. [Am. Lit.: *The Sot-Weed Factor*]

21. **Warren, Mrs.** raises daughter in comfort and refinement on her bedside earnings. [Irish Lit.: *Mrs. Warren's Profession* in *Plays Unpleasant*]

555. PROTECTION

1. **Abracadabra** cabalistic charm used as an antidote for ague, toothache, etc. [Medieval Folklore: Brewer *Dictionary*, 3]

2. **aegis** protective mantle of Zeus given to Athena. [Gk. Myth.: Brewer *Dictionary*]

3. **alectoria** crystalline stone, having talismanic power, found in the stomach of cocks. [Gk. Myth.: Brewer *Dictionary*, 20]

4. **alum** charm against evil eye. [Egyptian Folklore: Leach, 40]

5. **amethyst** preserved soldiers from harm; gave them victory. [Gem Symbolism: Kunz, 58]

6. **bennet** excludes the devil; used on door frames. [Medieval Folklore: Boland, 56]

7. **blood of the lamb** used to mark houses of the Israelites so they could be passed over. [O.T.: Exodus 12:3–13]

8. **chrysoberyl** guards against evil spirits. [Gem Symbolism: Kunz, 65]

9. **condoms** ancient barrier method of contraception; now also recommended for use to prevent transmission of sexually-transmitted diseases, especially AIDS. [Medicine: *SJEPC*]

10. **cross** used to frighten away devils and protect from evil. [Christian Iconog.: Leach, 265]

11. **daisy** provides protection against fairies. [Flower Symbolism: Briggs, 87]

12. **firewall** a protective device installed in computers that prevents viruses, malware, etc. from damaging a computer; a symbol for protection. [Technology: Misc.]

13. **garlic** symbol of strength and protection from evil spirits. [Symbolism: *CEOS&S*]

14. **gated communities** residential areas surrounded by barriers such as walls and fences; often secured with staffed gatehouses and electronic systems to protect residents from outsiders, crime, and unnecessary traffic. [Am. Hist.: *SJEPC*]

15. **horseshoe** hung on buildings as defense against fairies. [Br. Folklore Briggs, 225]

16. **jacinth** guards against plague and wounds. [Gem Symbolism: Kunz, 81]

17. **kolem** rice designs drawn to attract guardianship of gods. [Hinduism: Binder, 61]

18. **magic flute** Tamino's guard against black magic. [Ger. Opera: Mozart, *Magic Flute*, Westerman, 102–104]

19. **malachite** guards wearer from evil spirits, enchantments. [Gem Symbolism: Kunz, 97]

20. **mark of Cain** God's safeguard for Cain for potential slayers. [O.T.: Genesis 4:15]

21. **mezuza** doorpost ornament; thought by primitive Jews to protect them from harm. [Judaism: Rosten, 239]

22. **moly** herb given by Hermes to Odysseus to ward off Circe's spells. [Gk. Myth.: *Odyssey*]

23. **rowan** ash tree which guards against fairies and witches. [Br. Folklore Briggs, 344]

24. **safe sex** sex that avoids risk of transmitting disease; especially vital since the discovery of the AIDS epidemic in the 1980s. [Am. Culture: *SJEPC*]

25. **sard** guards against incantations and sorcery. [Gem Symbolism: Kunz, 107]

26. **serpentine** guards against bites of venomous creatures. [Gem Symbolism: Kunz, 108]

27. **St. Benedict's cross** charm against disease and danger. [Christian Iconog.: Jobes, 386]

28. **St. Christopher medal** to protect travelers. [Christian Hist.: *NCE*, 552]

29. **St. John's wort** defense against fairies, evil spirits, the Devil. [Br. Folklore Briggs, 335–336]

30. **talisman** amulet with which Saladin cures Richard the Lion-Hearted. [Br. Lit.: *The Talisman*]

31. **wood** knocking on it averts dire consequences. [Western Culture: Misc.]

556. PROTECTOR (See also GUARDIAN.)

1. **Adams, Parson Abraham** bookish, unworldly protector of the weak and innocent. [Br. Lit.: *Joseph Andrews*]

2. **Darius (549?- 486 B.C.)** Persian king; permits and guarantees rebuilding of temple. [O.T.: Ezra 6:6–12]

3. **Douglas, the Widow** caretaker of Huck Finn. [Am. Lit.: *Huckleberry Finn*]

4. **Epona** goddess; watched over cattle and horses; also called Bubona. [Rom. Myth.: Kravitz, 90]

5. **Evelyn, Aunt** uses influence to keep nephew from war front. [Br. Lit.: *Memoirs of an Infantry Officer*, Magill I, 579–581]

6. **Genevieve, Saint** saved Paris from marauders by intercession. [Christian Hagiog.: Attwater, 147]

7. **Guardian Angels, The** volunteer, citizen-based group established in New York City by Curtis Sliwa in 1979 to protect the public from crime; red-bereted, unarmed protectors are now a presence in cities throughout the world. [Am. Hist.: *SJEPC*]

8. **Hendon, Miles** disinherited knight takes urchin-prince under wing. [Am. Lit.: *The Prince and the Pauper*]

9. **Ida** nymph who guarded infant Zeus from being eaten by father, Cronus. [Gk. Myth.: Zimmerman, 134]

10. **Jehosheba** secretes future king, Joash, from Athaliah's slaughter. [O.T.: II Kings 11:12; II Chronicles 22:11]

11. **Knights Templar** society formed to guard pilgrims to Jerusalem. [Medieval Hist.: Brewer *Dictionary*, 1066]

12. **Kuan Yin** protectress of fishermen and housemaids. [Buddhism: Binder, 42]

13. **lion** in China and Japan, symbol of protection. [Symbolism: *CEOS&S*]

14. **Magwitch, Abel** saved by Pip; dedicates himself to Pip's future. [Br. Lit.: *Great Expectations*]

15. **Man in the Yellow Hat, the** character from H.A. and Margret Rey's series of children's books; unflappable owner of Curious George the monkey; never fails to rescue George from whatever predicament he has gotten into. [Am. Children's Lit.: *OCCL*]

16. **Mannering, Guy** paternal helper of friend's daughter and tutor. [Br. Lit.: *Guy Mannering*]

17. **Nicholas, Saint** protector of sailors; patron saint of schoolboys. [Christian Hagiog.: Brewster, 12–13]

18. **Old Yeller** friend and watchdog assumes houndly nobility; from Fred Gipson's children's book *Old Yeller* (1968). [Am. Children's Lit.: Jones]

19. **Palladium** colossal statue whose presence ensured Troy's safety. [Rom. Legend: Brewer *Dictionary*, 796]

20. **Quasimodo** creature hides Esmeralda in sanctuary to save her. [Fr. Lit.: *The Hunchback of Notre Dame*]

21. **Rahab** conceals two Israelite spies from Jericho authorities. [O.T.: Joshua 2:2–6]

22. **ravens** during drought, Elijah is fed by them. [O.T.: I Kings 17:1–6]

23. **Secret Service** provides security for U.S. presidents. [Am. Hist.: *NCE*, 2466]

24. **Swiss Guard** traditional papal escort. [Rom. Cath. Hist.: Brewer *Dictionary*]

25. **Wells Fargo** armored carriers of bullion. [Am. Hist.: Brewer *Dictionary*, 1147]

557. PRUDENCE

1. **five wise virgins** brought lamp oil in case groom arrived late. [N.T.: Matthew 25:1–13]

2. **jacinth** endows owner with discretion. [Gem Symbolism: Kunz, 82]

3. **Metis** goddess of caution and discretion. [Rom. Myth.: Wheeler, 242]

4. **mountain ash** symbol of prudence. [Tree Symbolism: *Flora Symbolica*, 176]

558. PRUDERY

1. **Grundy, Mrs.** Ashfields' straitlaced neighbor whose propriety hinders them. [Br. Lit.: *Speed the Plough*]

2. **nice Nelly** excessively modest or prudish woman. [Am. Usage: Misc.]

3. **Quakers** pacifist religious sect, often associated with puritanical behavioral standards. [Am. Hist.: *NCE*, 1017]

4. **Shakers** sect believing in virgin purity. [Christian Hist.: Brewer *Note-Book*, 819]

5. **Victorian** one reflecting an unshaken confidence in piety and temperance, as during Queen Victoria's reign. [Am. and Br. Usage: Misc.]

559. PSYCHEDELIA (See also COUNTERCULTURE, DRUG CULTURE.)

1. **black light** lights that make fluorescent colors appear illuminated; many psychedelic posters were painted to offer full effect under black light. [Am. Pop. Culture: Misc.]

2. **Castaneda, Carlos (1925–1998)** ingested psychedelic plants like peyote in quest for higher spiritual reality as apprentice to Yaqui Indian shaman Don Juan. [Am. Culture: *SJEPC*]

3. **Dead Heads** fanatic followers of The Grateful Dead rock band. [Am. Music: *SJEPC*]

4. **Donovan (1946–)** Scottish-born singer/songwriter/guitarist personified 1960s counterculture with his flower-child hippie looks and drug-referential songs. [Br. Music: *SJEPC*]

5. ***Easy Rider*** countercultural bikers Wyatt and Billy sell drugs and get high at various stops on their road trip across the Southwest and South en route to New Orleans (1969). [Am. Film: *SJEPC*]

6. **Grateful Dead, The** San Francisco band was embodiment of psychedlic rock and retained intensely loyal fan base, known as Dead Heads, from 1960s to 1990s; named by charismatic cofounder Jerry Garcia. [Am. Music: *SJEPC*]

7. **incense** common in religious ceremonies worldwide; fragrant when burned, it was used to cover the smell of marijuana and became associated with drug use in the 1960s. [Am. Pop. Culture: Misc.]

8. **Jefferson Airplane** also Jefferson Starship; formed in 1965; extremely popular band of West Coast Rock; typify underground, drug-infused culture of hippie generation. [Am. Music: *SJEPC*]

9. **lava lamp** commonplace in college dorms of the 1960s; glass cylindar holds lighted colored liquid in which blobs of liquid wax float and change shape; more for decoration and amusement than for illumination, they became synonymous with hallucinations and recreational drug use. [Am. Pop. Culture: Misc.]

10. **Leary, Timothy (1920–1996)** psychologist who promoted study and use of psychedelic drugs (esp. LSD), which he believed had profound spiritual and therapeutic benefits; known for his motto: "Turn on, tune in, drop out." [Am. Pop. Culture: Misc.]

11. **Max, Peter (1937–)** his colorful psychedelic style influenced graphic art of the 1960s and beyond. [Art: *SJEPC*]

12. **Op Art** elements of artistic movement based on optical perception were incorporated into psychedelic images. [Art: *SJEPC*]

13. **Pink Floyd** quintessential psychedelic rock group; atmospheric music and special effects brought crowds to their concerts. [Am. Music: *SJEPC*]

14. **Volkswagen Beetle** two-door sedan of 1950s and 1960s with profile of scarab; immensely popular with young drivers; microbus model was standard vehicle of rock bands and soon became associated with hippie culture. [Am. Pop. Culture: *SJEPC*]

15. **Woodstock** New York site of three-day music and arts festival in 1969; despite chaos, drug use, and bad weather, was peaceful assemblage of 500,000 young hippies and has, for some, come to symbolize the best of the counterculture movement. [Am. Music: *SJEPC*]

560. PSYCHOLOGY (See also GUIDANCE, SELF-IMPROVEMENT.)

1. **Freud, Sigmund (1856–1939)** Austrian physician and founder of psychoanalysis; his theories stressed the importance of sex in interpreting human behavior. [Medicine: *ODA*]

2. **Jung, Karl (1875–1961)** Swiss psychiatrist who believed that humankind shared a "collective unconscious," expressed in archetypes and myths. [Medicine: *FOF, MOD*]

3. **Maslow, Abraham (1908–1970)** highly influential psychologist and founder of humanist psychology; belief in hierarchy of needs as motivation for behavior. [Am. Medicine: Misc.]

4. **Pavlov, Ivan (1849–1936)** Russian physiologist famous for conducting experiments on dogs in which they salivated in response to a sound associated with food, a symbol for conditioned response. [Medicine: *ODA*]

5. **psychopharmacology** refers to the increased practice of using drugs in addition to, or instead of, traditional psychotherapy. [Medicine: Misc.]

6. **Rorschach Test** Hermann Rorschach's 10 inkblots were first published in 1921; used to test patients by asking them to interpret form of the blot; psychological evaluation based on the responses. [Am. Culture: Misc.]

Public Interest (See ACTIVISM.)

561. PUNCTUALITY

1. **Fogg, Phileas** completes world circuit at exact minute he wagered he would. [Fr. Lit.: *Around the World in Eighty Days*]

2. **Gilbreths** disciplined family brought up to abide by strict, punctual standards. [Am. Lit.: *Cheaper by the Dozen*]

3. **Jones, Casey** legendary railroad engineer; crashes in attempt to arrive in "Frisco" on time. [Am. Folklore: Hart, 431]

4. **Linkinwater, Tim** "punctual as the Counting House Dial." [Br. Lit.: *Nicholas Nickleby*]

5. **Old Faithful** well-known geyser in Yellowstone Park; erupts every 64.5 minutes. [Am. Hist.: *NCE*, 3023]

562. PUNISHMENT (See also TRANSFORMATION.)

1. **Abijah** Jeroboam's child; taken by God for father's wickedness. [O.T.: I Kings 14:12]

2. **Adam** condemned to survive by sweat of brow. [O.T.: Genesis 3:19]

3. **Amfortas** sinful life led to perpetual suffering. [Arth. Legend: Walsh *Classical*, 20; Ger. Opera: *Parsifal*]

4. **Ammit** half-hippopotamus, half-lion monster of underworld; ate the sinful. [Egyptian Myth.: Leach, 50]

5. **Ashura** land of punishment for those who die angry. [Japn. Myth.: Jobes, 140]

6. **Atlas** Titan condemned to bear world on shoulders. [Gk. Myth.: Walsh *Classical*, 20]

7. **Cambyses** had a venal judge put to death and the body skinned as covering for his judgment seat. [Gk. Hist.: Herodotus in Magill III, 479]

8. ***Charlie and the Chocolate Factory*** 1964 children's book by Roald Dahl; young Charlie Bucket visits the crazy candy factory of Willy Wonka, where the owner and his small Oompa-Loompa workers teach nasty children about the consequences of misbehavior with bizarre punishments. [Br. Children's Lit.: *OCCL*]

9. **de Born, Bertrand** Dante has him carry his head as lantern. [Ital. Lit.: *Inferno*; Walsh,*Classical*, 55]

10. **Don Juan** for murder, devoured by fire. [Span. Lit.: Benét, 279; Ger. Opera: Mozart, *Don Giovanni*, Westerman, 95]

11. **Eve** for disobeying God, would suffer in childbirth. [O.T.: Genesis 3:16]

12. **flood** for his evilness, man perishes by inundation. [O.T.: Genesis 6:5–8; 7:4]

13. **Furies, the** also known as Dirae, or Erinyes to the Greeks; three sisters who pursue those guilty of crimes and avenge wrongs, usually by driving the perpetrators mad. [Rom. and Gk. Myth.: Benét, 320; Kravitz, 82, 91–92]

14. **Herod Agrippa I** was eaten by worms for playing god. [N.T.: Acts 12:23]

15. **Herodias** lived for nineteen centuries as punishment for her crime against John the Baptist. [Fr. Lit.: Eugène Sue *The Wandering Jew*]

16. **iron maiden** hollow iron figure in the shape of a woman, lined with spikes that impaled the enclosed victim. [Ger. Hist.: Brewer *Dictionary*, 491]

17. **Ixion** Thessalian king bound to fiery wheel by Zeus. [Gk.and Rom. Myth.: Zimmerman, 142; Rom. Lit.: *Metamorphoses*]

18. **Laocoön** Trojan priest offends Athena, is strangled to death by two sea serpents. [Gk. Myth.: Benét, 565]

19. **Nadab and Abihu** destroyed by God for offering Him "alien fire." [O.T.: Leviticus 10:1–3]

20. **Papageno** for lying, has mouth padlocked. [Ger. Opera: Mozart, *The Magic Flute*, Westerman, 102–104]

21. **Peeping Tom** struck blind for peeping at Lady Godiva. [Br. Legend: Brewer *Dictionary*, 403]

22. **plagues on Egypt** God visits Egypt with plagues and epidemics to show his power. [O.T.: Exodus 8, 12]

23. **Prometheus** for rebelliousness, chained to rock; vulture fed on his liver which grew back daily. [Rom. Myth.: Zimmerman, 221–222]

24. **Prynne, Hester** pilloried and sentenced to wear a scarlet "A" for her sin of adultery. [Am. Lit.: *The Scarlet Letter*]

25. **Sisyphus** condemned in Hades to roll boulder uphill which would immediately roll down again. [Gk. Myth.: Zimmerman, 244; Gk. Lit.: *Aeneid*]

26. *Struwwelpeter* immensely popular collection of cautionary tales in verse written and illustrated by Heinrich Hoffmann in 1845;

both hilarious and horrifying, it documents the dire consequences of misbehavior. [Ger. Children's Lit.: *OCCL*]

27. **Tantalus** for his crimes, sentenced to Hades to be within reach of water; he cannot drink. [Gk. Myth.: Zimmerman, 253; Gk. Lit.: *Odyssey*]

28. **Tell, William** ordered to shoot apple placed on son's head for refusing to salute governor's hat. [Ger. Lit.: *William Tell*; Ital. Opera: Rossini, *William Tell*, Westerman, 121–122]

29. **Thyestes** unknowingly eats sons served by vengeful brother. [Rom. Lit.: *Thyestes*]

30. **Tyburn tree** site of the London gibbet. [Br. Hist.: Espy, 169]

31. **Vale of Achor** site of lapidation of Achan, Israelite troublemaker. [O.T.: Joshua 7:24–26]

32. **Vathek** condemned to eternal flames for seeking forbidden knowledge. [Br. Lit.: Beckford *Vathek*]

563. PURITY (See also CHASTITY, VIRGINITY.)

1. **almond** pagan symbol of purity and Christian symbol of the Virgin Mary's innocence. [O.T. and Art: Numbers 17:1–11;; Hall, 14; *CEOS&S*, 206]

2. **America's Sweetheart** name for wholesome actress Mary Pickford; now used to describe a wholesome, innocent girl. [Am. Cult.: Misc.]

3. **crystal** its transparency symbolizes pureness. [Folklore: Jobes, 391]

4. **deer** symbol of dawn, light, purity, regeneration, creativity, and magic. [Symbolism: *CEOS&S*]

5. **Galahad, Sir** sole knight who could sit in siege perilous. [Br. Lit.: *Le Morte d'Arthur*; *Idylls of the King*]

6. **honey** linked with the gods; symbol of purity, inspiration, and plenty. [Symbolism: *CEOS&S*]

7. **Ivory soap** advertised as being "99.44% pure." [Trademarks: Crowley *Trade*, 289]

8. **Karamazov, Alyosha** pure at heart, with compassion for his erring and tortured family. [Russ. Lit.: Dostoevsky *The Brothers Karamazov*]

9. **lily** emblematic of the Blessed Virgin Mary. [Christian Symbolism: Appleton, 39]

10. **long unbound hair** custom for unmarried women, virgin saints, brides. [Art: Hall, 144]

11. **Lucretia** model of virtue; raped by son of Tarquin, she kills herself. [Rom. Legend: Daniel, 175]

12.   **sedge** used as symbol of purity in Leonardo Da Vinci paintings. [Plant Symbolism: Embolden, 25]

13.   **snow** "pure as the driven snow" used to denote purity. [Western Folklore: Misc.]

14.   **Star of Bethlehem** indicates pureness. [Flower Symbolism: *Flora Symbolica*, 183]

15.   **Virgin Mary** immaculately conceived; mother of Jesus Christ. [N.T.: Matthew 1:18–25; 12:46–50; Luke 1:26–56; 11:27–28; John 2; 19:25–27]

16.   **water** archetypal symbol. [Christian Symbolism: Appleton, 109]

17.   **water-lily** symbol of innocence of heart; flower of July. [Flower Symbolism: *Flora Symbolica*, 178; Kunz, 329]

18.   **white** symbol of virginity; in American flag, purity. [Color Symbolism: Leach, 242]

Q

564. QUACKERY

1. **barber-surgeon** inferior doctor; formerly a barber performing dentistry and surgery. [Medicine: Misc.]
2. **Dulcamara, Dr.** offered bad burgundy as panacea for lovelessness. [Ital. Opera: Donizetti, *Elixir of Love*; *EB*, 55: 953–954]
3. **Rezio, Dr.** Baratarian court physician; practically starves Sancho Panza in the interest of diet. [Span. Lit.: *Don Quixote*]
4. **Rock, Dr. Richard** fat, 18th-century quack; professed to cure every imaginable disease. [Br. Hist.: Brewer *Handbook*, 888]
5. **Sangrado, Dr.** ignorant physician; believed blood not necessary for life. [Fr. Lit.: *Gil Blas*]
6. **Walker, Dr.** great 18th-century quack, forever advising against disreputable doctors. [Br. Hist.: Brewer *Handbook*, 888]

565. QUARRY

1. **Cerynean stag** captured by Hercules as third Labor. [Gk. and Rom. Myth.: Hall, 149]
2. **Cretan bull** savage bull caught by Hercules as seventh Labor. [Gk. and Rom. Myth.: Hall, 149]
3. **Erymanthian boar** Hercules's fourth Labor; to take this ravaging beast alive. [Gk. and Rom. Myth.: Hall, 149]
4. **fetching Cerberus** Hercules's twelfth Labor; capture the Hadean watchdog. [Gk. and Rom. Myth.: Hall, 150]
5. **Moby Dick** pursued by Ahab and crew of *Pequod*. [Am. Lit.: *Moby Dicl*]
6. **Nemean lion** awesome beast strangled by Hercules as first Labor. [Gk. and Rom. Myth.: Hall, 148]
7. **Old Ben** great bear; subject of annual quest by mature men. [Am. Lit.: *The Bear* in *Six Modern Short Novels*]
8. **oxen of Geryon** captured after tremendous obstacles overcome; Hercules's tenth Labor. [Gk. and Rom. Myth.: Hall, 149]
9. **snark** elusive imaginary animal. [Br. Lit.: *The Hunting of the Snark*]
10. **Wolfman** metamorphosed man hunted down by armed men as wild beast. [Am. Lit.: *Wolfman*]

566. QUEST (See also ADVENTUROUSNESS, JOURNEY, WANDERING.)

1. **Ahab, Captain** pursues Moby Dick, the great white whale, even to the point of losing his own life. [Am. Lit.: Melville *Moby Dick*]

2. **Apollo missions** American space program in the 1960s and 1970s put the first man on the moon in 1969. [Am. Astronomy: *SJEPC*]

3. *Argo* Jason's galley, on which the Argonauts sailed in search of the Golden Fleece. [Gk. Myth.: Benét, 47]

4. **Baggins, Bilbo** hobbit protagonist of J.R.R. Tolkien's *The Hobbit*; reclaims treasures stolen by dragon and captures magic ring. [Br. Lit.: *SJEPC*]

5. **Baggins, Frodo** hobbit hero of J.R.R. Tolkien's trilogy *The Lord of the Rings*; travels to devastated land of Mordor to destroy magic ring—with power that tempts all who possess it—before it is used by dark lord Sauron. [Br. Lit.: *SJEPC*]

6. **Dorothy** young girl, lost in dream world, follows the Yellow Brick Road to find the Wizard of Oz. [Am. Children's Lit.: *OCCL*]

7. **El Dorado** mythical land of gold treasures, object of Spanish expeditions. [Am. Hist.: Jameson, 159]

8. **Fermat's Last Theorem** famously difficult mathematical theorem formulated by Pierre de Fermat in 1640; unsolved for years, in 1995 Andrew Wiles proved the theorem. [Mathematics *ODA*]

9. **Golden Fleece** pelt of winged ram sought by Jason and Argonauts. [Rom. Legend: Zimmerman, 113]

10. **grail** its pursuit is central theme of some Arthurian romances. [Br. Lit.: *Le Morte d'Arthur*]

11. **Hippolyta, girdle of** secured after fight with Amazon queen; Hercules's ninth Labor. [Gk. and Rom. Myth.: Hall, 149]

12. **Knights of the Round Table** set out to find the Holy Grail. [Br. Lit.: *Le Morte d'Arthur*]

13. **Little Prince** protagonist of book by Antoine de Saint-Exupéry beloved by young readers; sole inhabitant of Asteroid B-612 who leaves to gain knowledge and learn how to love. [Fr. Children's Lit.: Jones]

14. **paper chase** from the title of a 1970 novel and subsequent film; the pursuit of a degree as well as the pressures for academic success, especially at elite universities. [Am. Culture *The Paper Chase*]

15. **Pequod** ship in which Captain Ahab pursued the great white whale. [Am. Lit.: Melville *Moby Dick*]

16. **Ponce de León, Juan (c. 1460–1521)** Spanish explorer; sought the fountain of youth. [Span. Hist.: *NCE*, 2188]

17. **Santiago** old fisherman in search of marlin. [Am. Lit.: *The Old Man and the Sea*]

18. **Siege Perilous** a seat at King Arthur's Round Table for the knight destined to find the Holy Grail; it was fatal to any other occupant. [Br. Lit.: *Le Morte d'Arthur*]

19. **Sohrab** young warrior looks everywhere for the father he has never known. [Br. Poetry: Arnold "Sohrab and Rustum"]

20. **Telemachus** relentlessly searches for father, Odysseus. [Gk. Lit.: *Odyssey*]

R

567. RACIAL/ETHNIC IDENTITY

1. **Aaron, Hank (1934–)** African-American outfielder struggled with racial discrimination in the 1950s and 1960s as he helped integrate the South Atlantic League; faced racial animosity in the 1970s as he approached and then broke Babe Ruth's all-time home run record. [Am. Sports: *SJEPC*]

2. **Ailey, Alvin (1931–1989)** African-American dancer and choreographer whose interracial dance company, founded in 1958, achieved international status. [Am. Dance: *SJEPC*]

3. *Amos 'n' Andy Show* black characters in radio show and TV sitcom perpetuated racial stereotypes from the 1920s through the 1960s. [Am. Radio and TV: *SJEPC*]

4. **Apollo Theatre** famed Harlem venue for African-American entertainers, particularly during the Harlem Renaissance of the 1920s and 1930s. [Am. Hist.: *SJEPC*]

5. **Ashe, Arthur (1943–1993)** respected African-American tennis champion fought racism in America and South Africa. [Am. Sports: *SJEPC*]

6. *Autobiography of Miss Jane Putnam, The* 1971 novel by Ernest J. Gaines tells the fictional story of a strong African-American woman who witnesses, and often becomes involved in, events in American history from the Civil War to the Civil Rights Movement. [Am. Lit.: Gillespie and Naden]

7. **Baldwin, James (1924–1987)** African-American writer and activisit in the civil rights movement of the 1960s. [Am. Lit. and Politics: *SJEPC*]

8. **Belafonte, Harry (1927–)** Jamaican-American singer, actor, and activist fought for African and African-American civil rights. [Am. Music and Politics: *SJEPC*]

9. **Black Panthers** radical group of the 1960s sought empowerment for black America. [Am. Hist. *SJEPC*]

10. **blackface minstrelsy** entertainment style from 1820s to 1950s in which white performers blackened their faces to parody Southern blacks in song, speech, and dance. [Am. Entertainment: *SJEPC*]

11. **blaxploitation films** action-packed, low-budget films of 1970s featured all-black casts, excessive violence, and explicit sex. [Am. Film: *SJEPC*]

12. **Brooklyn Dodgers** team recruited and signed African-American player Jackie Robinson in 1947, breaking major league baseball's racial barrier. [Am. Sports: *SJEPC*]

13. **Brooks, Gwendolyn (1917–2000)** in 1950, poet was first African-American writer to receive Pulitzer Prize. [Am. Lit.: *SJEPC*]

14. **Brown, Jim (1936–)** spectacular football player retired in 1965 and went on to star in black action films and become activist for black community and black-owned businesses. [Am. Sports: *SJEPC*]

15. **Campbell, Naomi (1971–)** British model with African heritage became a sensation in the United States; wide general appeal made her the first black supermodel. [Culture: *SJEPC*]

16. **Chávez, César (1927–1993)** beloved Mexican-American farm labor leader; fought for Chicano rights and social justice. [Am. Hist.: *SJEPC*]

17. **Clemente, Roberto (1934–1972)** Puerto Rican rightfielder for the Pittsburgh Pirates took pride in his ethnicity, remained close to his homeland; died while helping Nicaraguan earthquake victims. [Am. Sports: *SJEPC*]

18. *Color Purple, The* 1982 novel by Alice Walker written as series of letters; documents 40 years in life of strong, determined Celie, who overcomes amazing cruelty and hardship to forge life for herself. [Am. Lit.: Gillespie and Naden]

19. **Cooke, Sam (1935–1964)** groundbreaking African-American soul and gospel star was one of the first black artists to establish his own record company; supported Civil Rights movement in the 1960s. [Am. Music: *SJEPC*]

20. **Cosby, Bill (1937–)** famous African-American comedian and actor; starred in *I Spy*, making him the first African-American star of a television drama; later *The Cosby Show* was acclaimed for its portrayal of an affluent, well-educated African-American family. [Am. TV: Misc.]

21. **Cotton Club** high-class nightclub owned by white gangsters during the Harlem Renaissance of the 1920s and 1930s; featured outstanding black performers but catered to exclusively white clientele. [Am. Hist.: *SJEPC*]

22. *Crisis, The* monthly magazine of the NAACP (National Association for the Advancement of Colored People); founded in 1910 by editor W. E. B. Du Bois; has defended African-American civil rights and served as the voice of black America for a century. [Am. Jour.: *SJEPC*]

23. *Dances with Wolves* film based on Michael Blake's novel defied western genre formula, gave voice to Native American perspective (1990). [Am. Film: *SJEPC*]

24. **Dandridge, Dorothy (1922–1965)** beautiful, sensuous African-American film actress starred in breakthrough Hollywood roles in the 1950s; first black woman featured on the cover of *Life* magazine. [Am. Film: *SJEPC*]

25. *Dragonwings* historical novel for young readers by Laurence Yep published in 1975; based on actual invention of flying machine flown by Chinese immigrant in 1909; tells of culture of immigrant community in turn-of-century San Francisco. [Am. Children's Lit.: Gillespie and Naden]

26. **Du Bois, W. E. B. (1868–1963)** prominent African-American leader and educator saw the "color-line" as the most significant problem of the 20th century; wrote *The Souls of Black Folk* (1903) and co-founded the NAACP (National Association for the Advancement of Colored People). [Am. Hist.: *SJEPC*]

27. *Ebony* first photographic magazine focused on African-American life debuted in 1945; created by John H. Johnson. [Am. Jour.: *SJEPC*]

28. **Edwards, James (1916?-1970)** African-American actor broke down film stereotypes in post-World War II Hollywood; starred in intelligent movies dealing with racial issues such as military desegregation and bigotry, including *Home of the Brave* (1949). [Am. Film: *SJEPC*]

29. **El Teatro Campesino** Mexican-American theater company founded in 1965 by actor/director Luis Valdez and farmworkers activist César Chávez; produces dramas from the Chicano perspective, exploring the Latino experience in America. [Am. Theater: *SJEPC*]

30. **El Vez (1960–)** tongue-in-cheek "Mexican Elvis" Robert Lopez; with pencil-thin mustache and gelled hair, also performs traditional mariachi songs and sings alternate lyrics to popular music that address serious Chicano-related issues. [Am. Music: *SJEPC*]

31. **Erdrich, Louise (1954–)** award-winning writer of Chippewa ancestry whose lyrical fiction and nonfiction deal with contemporary Native American life and culture. [Am. Lit.: *SJEPC*]

32. **Farrakhan, Louis (1933–)** Supreme Minister of the Nation of Islam and advocate for African-American issues; critical of American society; leader of Million Man March. [Am. Hist.: Misc.]

33. **Father Divine (18??-1965)** charismatic, controversial African-American founder of Universal Peace Mission Movement espoused racial equality; attracted large following of both blacks and whites during Great Depression. [Am. Rel.: *SJEPC*]

34. **Feliciano, Jose (1945–)** Puerto Rican-born guitar virtuoso/singer performs eclectic mix of traditional and popular Latin and American music in both Spanish and English, from salsa and flamenco

to folk and rock; paved the way for Latino artists in mainstream pop music scene. [Am. Music: *SJEPC*; Misc.]

35. **Fetchit, Stepin (1902–1984)** lanky African-American actor typically cast as grinning, dim-witted, comic servant in movies, particularly in the 1930s. [Am. Film: *SJEPC*]

36. **Garvey, Marcus (1887–1940)** black activist preached racial pride, unity, and importance of African heritage in early 20th century; founded United Negro Improvement Association (UNIA) in 1914 and inspired future generations of African-American leaders. [Am. Hist.: *SJEPC*]

37. *Go Tell It on the Mountain* 1953 novel by James Baldwin; groundbreaking story of African American experience without racial overtones; tells of a day in life of members of fundamentalist church in Harlem, especially young John, a preacher's son who agonizes over his future. [Am. Lit.: Gillespie and Naden]

38. *Good Times* popular 1970s sitcom about a working class African-American family anchored by strong, responsible parents who lived in an inner city Chicago tenement and struggled to make ends meet. [Am. TV: *SJEPC*]

39. *Goodbye, Columbus* Jewish-American writer Philip Roth's 1959 novella; a young Jewish man searches for identity in post-World War II New Jersey, dealing with religious, cultural, and moral issues. [Am. Lit.: Harris *Characters*, 343]

40. **gospel music** African-American religious music expressing faith in Jesus Christ; marked by blues and jazz rhythms, harmonic vocals, and emotional delivery. [Am. Music: *SJEPC*]

41. **Greenberg, Hank (1911–1986)** popular, respected Detroit Tigers first baseman; "Hammerin' Hank" paved way for future Jewish baseball players; a hero to fans of all backgrounds despite anti-Semitism in 1930s-1950s. [Am. Sports: *SJEPC*; Misc.]

42. **Gregory, Dick (1932–)** trailblazing African-American comedian won national, mainstream acclaim using his humor to highlight social and political issues such as racism and the Vietnam War in 1960s; continues to advance progressive social agenda. [Am. Entertainment: *SJEPC*]

43. **Grier, Pam (1949–)** African-American actress played strong, self-confident heroines in blaxploitation films of 1970s, such as *Foxy Brown* (1974). [Am. Film: *SJEPC*]

44. **Harlem** predominantly African-American area of New York City, center of black music, art, and culture. [Am. Hist.: *FOF, MOD*]

45. **Harlem Renaissance** group of African-American artists who, during the 1920s and 30s, created works celebrating the black experience. [Am. Culture: *BBAAL2*]

46. **hip-hop** rhythmic beat and chant-like singing that started in urban America as a means to fight gang violence; the distinction between hip-hop and rap has dwindled in recent years. [Am. Music: *SJEPC*]

47. **Homey D. Clown** character from sketch-comedy show, *In Living Color*; African-American ex-con who dresses up as a clown for community service; life mission is to get even with "The Man," the white men he thinks are holding him down. [Am. TV: Misc.]

48. **Hughes, Langston (1902–1967)** African-American poet and leading figure of the Harlem Renaissance. [Am. Lit.: *BBAAL2*]

49. **Hurston, Zora Neale (1891?-1960)** African-American anthropologist and writer, author of *Their Eyes Were Watching God*. [Am. Lit.: *BBAAL2*]

50. *Invisible Man, The* 1952 Ralph Ellison novel that challenged racial stereotypes of African Americans of the time; unnamed black narrator moves into adulthood through series of painful experiences. [Am. Lit.: *SJEPC*]

51. **Jackson, Jesse (1941–)** Baptist minister and civil rights leader who ran for President in the 1988 election; fought for economic justice of the poor; his fervor has sometimes brought accusations of grandstanding. [Am. Hist.: *SJEPC*]

52. *Jeffersons, The* 1975 sitcom about African-American family "movin' on up" in status when their dry cleaning business proves successful; scorned by some black audiences, was popular enough to last 10 seasons and led way for many other similar shows. [Am. TV: *SJPEC*]

53. **Jimenez, Jose** comic Mexican immigrant character with broken English created by TV writer/actor Bill Dana portrayed as clueless yet resourceful, a hard-working hotel bellhop supporting a large family back home. [Am. TV: *SJEPC*]

54. **Johnson, John H. (1918–2005)** influential founder of Johnson Publishing Company, one of the top black-owned businesses in America; created and published *Ebony* and *Jet* magazines. [Am. Jour.: *SJEPC*]

55. *Joy Luck Club, The* Amy Tan's 1989 novel chronicles the lives of four Chinese immigrants and their American-born daughters, examining life in modern-day San Francisco and China of pre-WWII era. [Am. Lit.: Gillespie and Naden]

56. **King, Martin Luther, Jr. (1929–1968)** preeminent leader of Civil Rights movement for African Americans; proposed nonviolent resistance as powerful weapon against discrimination; national holiday and various landmarks and buildings honor him. [Am. Hist.: *SJEPC*]

57. **Kingston, Maxine Hong (1940–)** American-born Chinese novelist whose work reflects the diversity of the American experience; her autobiography *The Woman Warrior* (1976) records her attempts to integrate her Chinese heritage with the culture of her homeland. [Am. Lit.: *SJEPC*]

58. **Kwanzaa** African-American cultural holiday created in 1966 by Ron Karenga honors African heritage and celebrates seven key principles over seven days (December 26–January 1). [Am. Culture: *SJEPC*; Thompson, 283–88]

59. **"La Bamba"** 1958 song that brought traditional Mexican music into the American rock 'n' roll scene, a trend later called Chicano Rock. [Am. Music: *SJEPC*]

60. **Lopez, George (1961–)** Mexican-American comedian; among first Mexican Americans to be prominent and well-recognized in American popular culture. [Am. Pop. Cult.: Misc.]

61. **Mandala, Nelson (1918–)** South African political leader who helped dismantle the racist regime and became the first black president of his country. [African History *FOF, MOD*]

62. **McDaniel, Hattie (1895–1952)** criticized for perpetuating racial stereotypes in portrayal of Mammy in film of *Gone with the Wind.* [Am. Film: *SJEPC*]

63. **McQueen, Butterfly (1911–1995)** portrayed simple slave in film of *Gone with the Wind.* [Am. Film: *SJECP*]

64. **Mencia, Carlos (1967–)** Honduran comedian known for addressing race, culture, and social class in his material. [Am. Pop. Cult.: Misc.]

65. **Million Man March** Louis Farrakhan, head of the Nation of Islam, called upon African-American men to reclaim and rebuild their communities. [Am. Hist.: *SJEPC*]

66. **Momaday, N. Scott (1934–)** first prominent author of modern Native-American literature. [Am. Lit.: *SJEPC*]

67. **Morrison, Toni (1931–)** in complex, artfully crafted novels, she voices the beliefs and desires of African-American characters. [Am. Lit.: *SJEPC*]

68. **Motown** legendary Detroit recording company for pop and rhythm and blues music by primarily African-American artists. [Am. Music: *SJEPC*]

69. **Negro Leagues** organized African-American baseball teams before black players were signed for the Major Leagues in the 1940s. [Am. Sports; *SJEPC*]

70. **Obama, Barack (1961–)** President of the United States; first African-American president, inaugurated in 2009; first African-American to be a major party's presidential nominee. [Am. Hist.: Misc.]

71. **Oreo** a cookie, chocolate, or black, on the outside, with white filling; a racial epithet, describing an African-American deemed too accomodating to whites: black on the outside, white on the inside. [Am. Culture: Misc.]

72. **Owens, Jesse (1913–1980)** black track and field superstar; won four gold medals in the 1936 Olympics in Berlin, thereby contradicting Hitler's doctrine of Aryan superiority. [Sports: *SJEPC*]

73. **Poitier, Sidney (1927–)** African-American actor who played strong characters in films with antiracist themes. [Am. Film: *SJEPC*]

74. **Powell, Colin (1937–)** first African American and Jamaican American to be United States Secretary of State. [Am. Hist.: Misc.]

75. **Puente, Tito (1923–2000)** "King of Latin Music"; Grammy-winning musician, composer, and bandleader who brought Latin music to audiences worldwide. [Am. Music: *SJEPC*]

76. **rap** rhythmic beat and chant-like singing with graphic and sometimes controversial lyrics; often celebrates "gangsta" lifestyle. [Am. Music: *SJEPC*]

77. **Rice, Condoleezza (1954–)** first African-American woman to be United States Secretary of State. [Am. Hist.: Misc.]

78. **Robinson, Jackie (1919–1973)** first black player in Major League baseball (1947); taunts and abuse followed, but his briliant performance quelled objections; staunch supporter of civil rights. [Am. Sports: *SJEPC*]

79. *Roll of Thunder, Hear My Cry* Mildred D. Taylor's 1976 novel for young readers set in Mississippi of mid-1930s; documents the discrimination and financial setbacks experienced by family of poor black landowners. [Am. Children's Lit.: Gillespie and Naden]

80. *Roots* novel by Alex Haley about several generations of his mother's family, brought to the US from Africa as slaves; drew wide audiences in 1977 as TV miniseries. [Am. Lit. and TV: *SJEPC*]

81. **Roundtree, Richard (1937–)** one of the first black action heroes; played gritty private eye John Shaft and other roles. [Am. Film: *SJEPC*]

82. **Sainte-Marie, Buffy (1941–)** Native American musician; member of the Red Power movement and spokesperson for rights of her race. [Can. Hist.: Misc.]

83. **Salsa Music** native to Cuba, but evolved in New York City; incorporates African rhythms and European harmony into hot Latin American dance sounds. [Am. Music: *SJEPC*]

84. **Santana** blending Latin and African sounds, Mexican Carlos Santana formed a monumentally successful band in America in the

1960s; despite permutations in the band, their popularity persisted. [Am. Music: *SJEPC*]

85. **Selena (1971–1995)** award-winning Latino singer of Tejano, Tex-Mex fusion music; shot to death by employee at age 24. [Am. Music: *SJEPC*]

86. *Shaft* early Blaxploitation film about tough, defiant African-American dectective John Shaft, portrayed by Richard Roundtree. [Am. Film: *SJEPC*]

87. **Smits, Jimmy (1945–)** prominent Hispanic actor; cofounder of the National Hispanic Foundation for the Arts to help Hispanics find jobs in entertainment. [Am. Entertainment: *SJEPC*]

88. *Snowy Day* 1962 picture book by white author/illustrator Ezra Jack Keats; the protagonist is black (almost unheard-of at the time), yet he is any boy enjoying a huge snowfal, making race irrelevant and subtly teaching that feelings are universal and color-blind. [Am. Children's Lit.: Jones]

89. *Soul Train* in 1970, first mainstream American TV show to feature soul and rhythm and blues artists; the black *American Bandstand* showed teenaged guests, decked out in the latest fashions, dancing before the camera. [Am. TV: *SJEPC*]

90. **Tan, Amy (1952–)** American writer of Chinese descent who often writes about Chinese-American women and their relationship with their immigrant parents, in particular the relationship between mother and daughter; probably best known for her novel *The Joy Luck Club* (19 [Am. Lit.: Misc.]

91. **Tejano Music** Mexican-American music reflecting both cultures; much originated in Texas. [Am. Music: *SJEPC*]

92. **Tovar, Lupita (1910–)** played a leading role in Spanish-language version of *Dracula*, filmed in 1931 using same sets as the English-language film; she also played in Mexico's first talkie film; a Mexican postage stamp was issued featuring Tovar. [Mex. Film: Misc.]

93. *Uncle Remus* first collection of African-American fables, rewritten by Joel Chandler Harris and published in 1881; although stories are sometimes humorous, Harris declared serious intention of documenting legends to perserve them as part of Southern history. [Am. Folktales: *OCCL*]

94. **Valdez, Luis (1940–)** "father of Chicano Theater" cofounded El Teatro Campesino in 1965 with farmworkers activist César Chávez, bringing attention to economic, political, and social concerns of Mexican Americans; wrote and directed movie *La Bamba* (1987). [Am. Theater and Film: *SJEPC*]

95. **Valens, Ritchie (1941–1959)** Mexican-American singer/songwriter most famous for "La Bamba," a traditional Mexican ballad done in rock 'n' roll style. [Am. Music: *SJEPC*]

96. **Van Vechten, Carl (1880–1964)** wrote articles supporting Harlem Renaissance of 1920s; best known novel, *Nigger Heaven* (1926), portrayed life in Harlem; book rejected by black critics because of its title. [Am. Lit.: *SJEPC*]

97. **Walker, Alice (1944–)** Pulitzer Prize-winning *The Color Purple* (1982) brought her international fame; although a story of abuse, it celebrates love and the triumph of spiritual survival; later a film and stage musical. [Am. Lit, Film, and Musical.: *SJEPC*]

98. **Walker, Madame C.J. (1867–1919)** first African-American female millionaire; her formula to prevent hair loss led to line of hair care products marketed to African Americans; known as the "Walker System," it was said to effectively soften coarse hair. [Am. Business: *SJEPC*]

99. **Wallace, Sippie (1898–1986)** influential blues singer whose risqué lyrics and themes related to being a woman of color had great appeal with her audiences. [Am. Music: *SJEPC*]

100. **Wilson, Flip (1933–1998)** brought African-American perspective to white audiences through successful, award-winning network variety series *The Flip Wilson Show* (1970–1974); there he portrayed memorable characters, including sassy Geraldine Jones, played in drag. [Am. TV: *SJEPC*]

101. **Woods, Tiger (1975–)** first person of color and youngest person to win the Masters (1997, at age 21); amazingly talented golf pro with racially diverse background has spurred interest in the sport among minorities. [Am. Sports: *SJEPC*]

102. **Wright, Richard (1908–1960)** controversial and internationally successful African-American writer known for his groundbreaking protest novel *Native Son* (1940) and his autobiographical *Black Boy* (1945). [Am. Lit.: Misc.]

103. *Zoot Suit* musical drama by Luis Valdez provided the Chicano perspective on the 1942 Zoot Suit riots in Los Angeles; first Chicano play on Broadway (1979) and also a film (1981). [Am. Theater and Film: *SJEPC*; Misc.]

568. RACING, AUTOMOBILE

1. **Andretti, Mario (1940–)** race car driver and Indianapolis 500 champion. [Am. Sports: *SJEPC*]

2. **Daytona 500** "The Greatest American Race" at Daytona International Speedway's tri-oval track in Florida in February is first stock car race of the season in NASCAR schedule; first run in 1959. [Am. Sports: *SJEPC*]

3. **drag racing** competition of acceleration between automobiles on a measured course, typically one-quarter mile. [Am. Sports: *SJEPC*]

4. **Earnhardt, Dale, Sr. (1951–2001)** nicknamed "The Intimidator"; NASCAR stock car racer with high reputation as bold and accomplished competitor and winner or numerous titles; died in crash at Daytona 500. [Am. Sports: Misc.]

5. **Foyt, A. J. (1935–)** patriarch of a race-car driving dynasty, "Supertex" dominated the sport during his four-decade career; four-time Indianapolis 500 victor also won Daytona 500, 24 Hours at Le Mans, and 24 Hours at Daytona, among others. [Am. Sports: *SJEPC*]

6. **Guthrie, Janet (1938–)** first woman to compete in Indianapolis 500 and Daytona 500 in 1977; her ninth-place finish in 1978 Indiananpolis 500 was undefeated by any other female driver until 2005. [Am. Sports: Misc.]

7. **Indianapolis 500** held on Memorial Day, the 200–lap race around Indianpolis Motor Speedway's two-and-a-half-mile track has long been considered the most important event in racing. [Am. Sports: *SJEPC*]

8. **Muldowney, Shirley (1940–)** "First Lady of Drag Racing" won three National Hot Rod Association and one American Hot Rod Association world championships. [Am. Sports: *SJEPC*; Misc.]

9. **NASCAR** National Association for Stock Car Auto Racing. [Am. Sports: *SJEPC*]

10. **Petty, Richard (1937–)** premier stock car race driver; winner of seven Winston Cup championships. [Am. Sports: *SJEPC*]

11. **Schumacher, Michael (1969–)** former Formula One driver; holds the best statistics of any race driver in history of the sport; World Champion from 2000–2004 with countless records by the time of his retirement in 2006. [Ger. Sports: Misc.]

12. **Unser, Al (1939–)** impressive Indianapolic 500 racer whose five-decade career includes four Indy wins and several other notable victories; brother of Bobby Unser. [Am. Sports: *SJEPC*]

13. **Unser, Bobby (1934–)** superb race car driver and color commentator for motor racing; brother of Al Unser. [Am. Sports: *SJEPC*]

569. RACING, HORSE (See also HORSE.)

1. **Belmont Stakes** annual American Grade 1 stakes race held at Belmont Park in June in Elmont, New York; 1.5 mile thoroughbred horse race. [Am. Cult.: Misc.]

2. **Derby** classic annual race at Epsom Downs. [Br. Cult.: Brewer *Dictionary*, 276]

3. **Francis, Dick (1920–)** mystery writer of novels with realistic plots, often centering on sport of horse racing. [Br. Lit.: Misc.]

4. **Kentucky Derby** classic annual race in Louisville. [Am. Cult.: Brewer *Dictionary*, 516]

5. **Palio, the** race with medieval trappings, held annually at Siena. [Ital. Hist.: *EB* (1963) XX, 620]

6. **Preakness Stakes** American Grade 1 stakes race held in Baltimore, Maryland every May; 13/16–mile race for three-year-old thoroughbreds. [Am. Cult.: Misc.]

7. **Royal Ascot** England's fashionable annual event. [Br. Cult.: Brewer *Dictionary*, 49]

8. **Triple Crown** premier achievement in U.S. racing, to win Kentucky Derby, Preakness, and Belmont Stakes. [Am. Cult.: *WB*, 16:59]

Racism (See BIGOTRY.)

570. RAMADAN

1. **Eid al-Fitr** festival that occurs at end of Ramadan is a joyful family and community holiday celebrated with special foods and sweets, new clothing, entertainment, and greeting cards. [Islam: *UIMT*, 313–14, 427]

2. **fasting** fourth pillar of Islam requires Muslims to fast during entire month of Ramadan by not eating or drinking during the daylight hours; *sawm* in Arabic. [Islamic Rel.: *UIMT*, 37, 437]

3. **iftar** the evening meal during Ramadan that breaks the daily fast often features special, rich foods. [Islam: *UIMT*, 305]

4. **new moon** its sighting signals the start of Ramadan, which ends when the next new moon appears. [Islam: *UIMT*, 298–300]

5. **suhur** the early morning meal during Ramadan must be eaten before dawn's light. [Islam: *UIMT*, 300–301]

6. **taraweeh** extra prayers offered during Ramadan. [Islam: *UIMT*, 306, 439]

7. **zakat** the payment to charity representing 2.5 percent of a Muslim's wealth, traditionally paid during Ramadan. [Islamic Rel.: *UIMT*, 308]

571. RAPE

1. **Amphissa** blinded by father Echetus for having been raped by Aechmodius. [Gk. Myth.: Howe, 23]

2. **Apemosyne** raped by Hermes; killed by brother for immorality. [Gk. Myth.: Zimmerman, 25]

3. *Are You in the House Alone?* Richard Peck's 1976 novel for young readers depicts Gail Osburne who is attacked and raped and bravely chooses to warn others about her rapist. [Am. Children's Lit.: Gillespie and Naden]

4. **Arne** blinded by stepfather Desmontes after he learned she had been raped and was pregnant. [Gk. Myth.: Howe, 39]

5. **Aziz, Dr.** accused of attempted rape but acquitted when his supposed victim realizes she must have been hallucinating. [Br. Lit.: Forster *Passage to India* in Magill I, 713]

6. **Belinda** violated tonsorially. [Br. Lit.: *The Rape of the Lock*]

7. **bodice rippers** historical romance novels so named because of sexually explicit plots and ever-present rape scenes. [Am. Lit.: *SJEPC*]

8. **Caenis** changed into a man by Poseidon after he raped her. [Gk. Myth.: Zimmerman, 46]

9. **Cassandra** raped by Ajax the Less on the night Troy fell. [Gk. Myth.: Brewer *Dictionary*, 17]

10. **Creusa** raped by Apollo; bore Janus. [Gk. Myth.: Kravitz, 68]

11. **Cunegonde** ravished in her father's castle by two Bulgarian soldiers. [Fr. Lit.: *Candide*]

12. **Danaë** Zeus raped her, posing as a golden shower. [Gk. Myth.: Kravitz, 74]

13. **Drake, Temple** provocative co-ed whose actions invite the rape she both fears and desires. [Am. Lit.: Faulkner *The Sanctuary*]

14. **Elvira** peasant girl raped by lusting nobleman. [Span. Lit.: *The King, the Greatest Alcalde*]

15. **Europa** seduced by Jupiter as bull; raped when he changes back. [Rom. Lit.: *Metamorphoses*; Gk. Myth.: Hall, 259]

16. **Lavinia** raped and mutilated by Demetrius and Chiron. [Br. Lit.: *Titus Andronicus*]

17. **Leda** raped by Zeus in form of swan. [Class. Myth.: Zimmerman, 149; Rom. Lit.: *Metamorphoses*; Br. Lit.: *Faerie Queene*]

18. **Lucretia** blackmailed into sex by despicable Sextus; commits suicide afterwards. [Rom. Lit.: *Fasti*; *Livy*; Br. Lit.: "The Rape of Lucrece"; Art.: Hall, 259]

19. **Philomela** raped by Tereus, who cut out her tongue to prevent her from revealing the act. [Gk. Myth.: Benét, 783]

20. *Streetcar Named Desire, A* Tennessee Williams's Pulitzer Prize-winning 1947 play; passionate domestic drama about three people living in French Quarter of New Orleans; culminates with powerful rape scene. [Am. Theater and Film: *SJEPC*]

21. **Tamar** raped by her half-brother, Amnon. [O.T.: II Samuel 13:11–14]

22. *To Kill a Mockingbird* both a Pulitzer Prize-winning novel (1960) and Academy Award-winning film (1962); young Southern girl witnesses her ethical lawyer father defend black man on accused of a rape for which he is convicted despite evidence to the contrary. [Am. Lit.: *SJEPC*]

572. RASHNESS

1. **Charge of the Light Brigade** ill-advised British assault at Balaklava, Crimea (1854). [Br. Hist.: Harbottle, 25]

2. **Gilpin, John** rides uncontrollably on fresh steed. [Br. Lit.: *John Gilpin's Ride*]

3. **Icarus** artificial wings destroyed by flying too close to sun. [Gk. Myth.: Kravitz, 126]

4. **Knievel, Evel (1938–2007)** famous motorcycle stuntman whose career peaked in late 1960s and 1970s; in red, white, and blue jumpsuit attempted (often unsuccessfully) to leap huge chasms, sometime incurring serious injuries. [Am. Entertainment: *SJEPC*]

5. **Lear** headstrong and "full of changes." [Br. Lit.: *King Lear*]

6. **Uzzah** rashly grabs for Ark of Covenant, a transgression. [O.T.: II Samuel 6:6–8]

573. REBELLION (See also RIOT.)

1. **Bastille Day** celebration of day Paris mob stormed prison; first outbreak of French Revolution (1789). [Fr. Hist.: *EB*, I: 866]

2. **Beer Hall Putsch** early, aborted Nazi coup (1923). [Ger. Hist.: *Hitler*, 198–241]

3. **Boston Tea Party** irate colonists, dressed as Indians, pillage three British ships (1773). [Am. Hist.: Jameson, 58, 495]

4. **Boxer Rebellion** xenophobic Chinese Taoist faction rebelled against foreign intruders (1900). [Chinese Hist.: Parrinder, 50]

5. *Caine Mutiny, The* sailors seize command from the pathological and incompetent Capt. Queeg. [Am. Lit.: Wouk *The Caine Mutiny* in Benét, 157]

6. **Christian, Fletcher (fl.late 18th century)** leader of mutinous sailors against Captain Bligh (1789). [Am. Lit.: *Mutiny on the Bounty*]

7. **Cromwell, Oliver (1599–1658)** English Puritan leader who led the rebellion against Charles I; later Lord Protector. [Br. Lit.: *ODA*]

8. **Easter Rising** unsuccessful Irish revolt against British (1916). [Irish Hist.: *EB*, III: 760–761]

9. **Gunpowder Plot** Guy Fawkes's aborted plan to blow up British House of Commons (1605). [Br. Hist.: *NCE*, 1165]

10. **Harper's Ferry** scene of Brown's aborted slave uprising. [Am. Hist.: John Jameson, 220]

11. **Hungarian Revolt** iron-curtain country futilely resisted Soviet domination (1956). [Eur. Hist.: Van Doren, 553]

12. **Jacquerie** French peasant revolt, brutally carried out and suppressed (1358). [Fr. Hist.: Bishop, 372–373]

13. **Jeroboam** with God's sanction, establishes hegemony over ten tribes of Israel. [O.T.: I Kings 11:31–35]

14. **Kralich, Ivan** fugitive from Turkish law; firebrand for Bulgarian independence of Ottoman rule. [Bulgarian Lit.: *Under the Yoke*]

15. *Mutiny on the Bounty* activities of mutineers, Captain Bligh, island wanderings (1789). [Am. Lit.: *Mutiny on the Bounty*]

16. **Peasants' Revolt, the** English villeins' attempt to improve their lot (1381). [Br. Hist.: Bishop, 220–221, 373–374]

17. **Pilot, the** Mr. Gray successfully carries out many assignments for the rebels and thwarts the British. [Am. Lit.: Cooper *The Pilot*]

18. **Sepoy Rebellion** Indian soldiers' uprising against British rule in India (1857–1858). [Br. Hist.: *NCE*, 1328]

19. **Sheba** led an aborted revolt against King David. [O.T.: II Samuel 20:1–2]

20. **Spina, Pietro** returns from exile disguised as a priest and engages in antifascist activities. [Ital. Lit.: *Bread and Wine*; 7]

574. REBELLIOUSNESS (See also DEFIANCE, OUTRAGEOUSNESS.)

1. **Absalom** conspires to overthrow father. [O.T.: II Samuel 15:10–18:33]

2. **Brando, Marlon (1924–2004)** American actor; in his early years, often played tough-guy characters with brooding effectiveness. [Am. Film: *SJEPC*]

3. **Cash, Johnny (1932–2003)** country music legend known as the Man in Black; had rebellious outlaw image and was often jailed for fighting and drunkenness. [Am. Music: *SJEPC*]

4. **Caulfield, Holden** schoolboy at odds with a "phoney" society. [Am. Lit.: *The Catcher in the Rye*]

5. **Chicago Seven** seven political radicals leading protest against Vietnam War during 1968 Democratic Convention in Chicago; clashed with police. [Am. Hist. and Politics: *SJEPC*]

6. **Dean, James (1931–1955)** star of *Rebel Without a Cause* (1955) and *East of Eden* (1955) with reckless, rebellious, tough-guy image both on and off screen. [Am. Film: *SJEPC*]

7. **Dedalus, Stephen** "heretical" youth rebels against Irish politics and religion. [Irish. Lit.: *Portrait of the Artist as a Young Man*]

8. **Finn, Huckleberry** unconventional and resourceful runaway boy. [Am. Lit.: *Huckleberry Finn*]

9. **Garfield, John (1913–1952)** virile actor who portrayed edgy, world-weary, rebellious characters; prototype for future film rebels like James Dean and Marlon Brando. [Am. Film: *SJEPC*]

10. **hip-hop** rhythmic beat and chant-like singing originated in urban centers to counter gang violence. [Am. Music: *SJEPC*]

11. **Hoffman, Abbie (1936–1989)** founder of the radical Yippie organization and one of the Chicago Seven; went underground after a drug conviction, surfacing later and devoting the remainder of his life to envionmentalism. [Am. Culture: *EB*]

12. **Korah** rose up against Moses; slain by Jehovah. [O.T.: Numbers 16:1–3]

13. **Maheu, Vincent** peaceful coalminer forced into striking for justice. [Fr. Lit.: *Germinal*]

14. **Morrison, Jim (1943–1971)** rebellious lead singer of The Doors pushed the envelope of accepted standards of decency on and off stage, often defying authorities (1960s). [Am. Music: *SJEPC*]

15. *One Flew over the Cuckoo's Nest* novel by Ken Kesey and subsequent award-winning film; patient in a mental hospital tries to strike out against the cruel control of Nurse Ratched. [Am. Lit. and Film: *SJEPC*]

16. **Presley, Elvis (1935–1977)** famous rock 'n' roll singer whose gyrations on stage, pioneering music, and tough-guy image made him a symbol of rebellious youth in the 1950s [Am Music: *SJEPC*]

17. **punk** movement among young people in 1970s; music meant to offend, extreme attire with colored hair and studs and pins, and belligerence toward anything conventional. [Br. and Am. Pop. Culture: *SJEPC*]

18. **Ramones, The** American rock band; considered forefathers of the rebellious punk movement. [Am. Music: *SJEPC*]

19. **rap** rhythmic beat and chant-like singing with graphic sometimes controversial lyrics, often celebrating "gangsta" lifestyle. [Am. Music: *SJEPC*]

20. *Rebel without a Cause* 1955 Nicholas Ray film starring James Dean as youth who is as sweet as he is troubled. [Am. Film: *SJEPC*]

21. **Satan** the Devil, or Lucifer; cast from heaven for rebelling against God. [O.T.: Isaiah 14:12; N.T.: Revelation 12:7–9; Br. Lit.: *Paradise Lost*]

22. **Scales, Sophia Baines** announcing her desire to be a teacher causes shock (1864). [Br. Lit.: *The Old Wives' Tale*, Magill I, 684–686]

23. **Sex Pistols** violent, raucous music and themes of anarchy that brought punk to the forefront; led by Johnny Rotten and Sid Vicious; the latter's death by drugs symbolized the reckless punk lifestyle. [Br. Music: *SJEPC*]

Recognition (See IDENTIFICATION.)

575. REDHEADEDNESS

1. **Ball, Lucille (1911–1989)** iconic redheaded comic who ruled the airwaves for 25 years with her immensely popular sitcom *I Love Lucy*; five Emmy awards and the first woman inducted into Television Academy Hall of Fame. [Am. TV: Misc.]

2. **Cortés, Hernanado (1485–1547)** conquistador received by Montezuma as god because of height and red hair. [Mex. Hist.: *NCE*, 662]

3. **Esau** Isaac's son. [O.T.: Genesis 25:25]

4. **Godfrey, Arthur (1903–1983)** affable, folksy redhead was TV pioneer in 1940s-50s. [Am. TV: *SJEPC*]

5. **Judas Isacariot** so depicted in art. [Christian Icon.: Gaster, 165]

6. **Little Orphan Annie** heroine of comic strip. [Comics: Horn, 459]

7. **Red-Headed League, the** non-existent club used to draw a redhead away from where he could interfere with a bank robbery. [Br. Lit.: "The Red-Headed League" in *Sherlock Holmes*]

8. **Shirley, Anne** protagonist of L.M. Montgomery's Anne of Green Gables series for young readers; orphaned Anne has vivid imagination and spirited personality; shakes up Prince Edward Island community; hates her red hair which, she believe, prevents her from being a beauty. [Can. Children's Lit.: Jones]

576. REFORMED, THE

1. **Arkadi** turns from the idea of obtaining power through wealth to a less materialistic goal. [Russ. Lit.: Benét, 843]

2. **Hal, Prince** transformation from rakish prince to responsible king. [Br. Lit.: *II Henry IV*]

3. **Knave of Hearts** vowed he'd steal no more tarts. [Nurs. Rhyme: Baring-Gould, 152]

4. **La Sacristaine** repents of sin and rejoins convent. [Medieval Legend: Walsh *Classical*, 48]

5. **Moses the Black, Saint** rascally thief; converted, became ordained priest. [Christian Hagiog.: Attwater, 247–248]

6. **Saul** becomes Christian proselytizer after Lord's visitation. [N.T.: Acts: 9:1–22]

7. **Scrooge, Ebenezer** Christmas becomes a merry affair when he abandons his miserliness. [Br. Lit.: *A Christmas Carol*]

8. **Thaïs** Alexandrian courtesan; converted to Christianity. [Medieval Legend: Walsh *Classical*, 307]

9. **Vinicus** lustful Roman becomes devout Christian. [Polish Lit.: *Quo Vadis*, Magill I, 797–799]

Reformer (See ACTIVISM.)

577. REFUGE (See also CONCEALMENT.)

1. **Adullam** cave where David hid from Saul. [O.T.: I Samuel 22:1]

2. **Alsatia** London Whitefriars monastery; former refuge for lawless characters. [Br. Hist.: Walsh *Modern*, 15]

3. **Bezer-in-the-wilderness** one of the appointed cities of sanctuary for unintentional murderers. [O.T.: Joshua 20:8]

4. **boat people** refugees who left Vietnam after the U.S. pullout in 1975; they fled in boats, seeking asylum. [Asian Hist.: *FOF, MOD*]

5. **Golan** appointed city of sanctuary for unintentional murderers. [O.T.: Joshua 20:8]

6. **Kedesh** city of sanctuary for unintentional murderers. [O.T.: Joshua 20:7]

7. **Kiriath-arba** city of sanctuary for unintentional murderers. [O.T.: Joshua 20:7]

8. **Noah's Ark** preserves Noah's family and animals from flood. [O.T.: Genesis 6:7–9]

9. **Ramoth** city of sanctuary for unintentional murderers. [O.T.: Joshua 20:8]

10. **Schechem** city of sanctuary for unintentional murderers. [O.T.: Joshua 20:7]

578. REGRET (See also REMORSE.)

1. **Epimetheus** Pandora's husband; regretted opening box. [Gk. Myth.: Kravitz, 90]

2. **Hale, Nathan (1755–1776)** American Revolutionary spy, hanged by British; regretted only having one life to give for country. [Am. Hist.: *NCE*, 1176]

3. **Moses** led his people to threshold of promised land but could not enter. [O.T.: Deuteronomy 34:1–4]

4. **Nebo, Mt.** from which Moses views promised land he cannot enter. [O.T.: Deuteronomy 34:1–4]

5. **raspberry** symbol of regret and grief. [Flower Symbolism: *Flora Symbolica*, 177]

6. *Separate Peace, A* in John Knowles young adult novel published in 1960, young Gene causes a devastating injury to his best friend, then reflects upon his misperceptions and regrets. [Am. Children's Lit.: Gillespie and Naden]

579. REJUVENATION (See also YOUTHFULNESS.)

1. **Aeson** in extreme old age, restored to youth by Medea. [Rom. Myth.: *LLEI*, I: 322]

2. **apples of perpetual youth** by tasting the golden apples kept by Idhunn, the gods preserved their youth. [Scand. Myth.: Brewer *Dictionary*, 41]

3. **Bimini** Bahamas island whose fountain conferred eternal youth. [Western Folklore: Brewer *Dictionary*, 373]

4. **Dithyrambus** epithet of Dionysus, in allusion to his double birth. [Gk. Myth.: Zimmerman, 88]

5. **Faust** rejuvenated by Mephistopheles at the price of his soul. [Ger. Lit.: Goethe *Faust*]

6. **Fountain of Youth** fabulous fountain believed to restore youth to the aged. [Western Folklore: Brewer *Handbook*, 389]

7. **Heidegger, Dr.** gives his aged friends water drawn form the Fountain of Youth, but its effects are temporary. [Am. Lit.: Hawthorne "Dr. Heidegger's Experiment" in Hart, 229]

8. **Ogier the Dane** hero at the age of 100 restored to ripe manhood by Morgan le Fay. [Medieval Romance: Brewer *Dictionary*, 656]

9. **sage** a rejuvenator; said to stop gray hair. [Herb Symbolism: *Flora Symbolica*, 165]

580. RELIGION (See also BUDDHISM; CHRISTIANITY; CONFUCIANISM; HINDUISM; ISLAM; JUDAISM; SACRED OBJECT; SACRED PLACE; SHINTO; SIKHISM; WRITINGS, SACRED.)

1. **afterlife** condition of existence after death or at the end of time. [Rel.: Bowker]

2. **almsgiving** work of merit—sometimes an obligation—in many religions. [Rel.: Bowker]

3. **altar** structure, usually flat on top, where offerings are made to god(s). [Rel.: Bowker]

4. **apocryphal** same form as scripture, but excluded from main scripture as doubtful. [Rel.: Bowker]

5. **Creationism** Biblically-based doctrine that God created the earth, universe, and all living beings. [Rel.: *SJEPC*]

6. **ephiphany** appearance of divine or superhuman being. [Rel.: Bowker]

7. **Hand of Fatima** decorated hand or palm; common in Islam as a symbol of power over disorder, but found in many other religions as well. [Rel.: Bowker]

8. **Just War** belief that war is sometimes just and must be conducted by certain standards; in every religion the propriety of war is sometimes admitted. [Rel.: Bowker]

9.   **omnipotence** characteristic of God in a theistic religions, especially in Islam, where everything that is or that happens is because of God's will. [Rel.: Bowker]

10.   **pilgrimage** literal or metaphorical journey to a condition or place of holiness or healing. [Rel.: Bowker]

11.   **Scopes trial** 1925 trial attempting to ban Darwinism from being taught in public schools; considered a trial of religion v. science or evolution v. creationism. [Am. Hist.: *SJEPC*]

581. REMORSE (See also REGRET, SUICIDE.)

1.   *Ayenbite of Inwit* Remorse of Conscience; Middle English version of medieval moral treatise, c. 1340. [Br. Lit.: Barnhart, 74]

2.   **Deianira** commits suicide out of remorse for unwittingly having killed husband, Hercules. [Gk. Myth.: Benét, 709]

3.   **Hermione** commits suicide upon the funeral pyre of her beloved Pyrrhus for having instigated his murder. [Fr. Drama: Racine *Andromaque*]

4.   **Jocasta** commits suicide when she realizes she has married son, Oedipus. [Gk. Lit.: *Oedipus Rex*]

5.   **Lord Jim** tormented by his memory of having saved himself from a sinking ship with 800 Muslims aboard. [Br. Lit.: Joseph Conrad *Lord Jim* in Magill I, 522]

6.   **Manfred** magician, living alone in an Alpine castle, broods on his alienation from mankind and on his destruction of the woman he loved. [Br. Poetry: Byron "Manfred"]

7.   **Mannon, Orin** crazed by guilt for inciting mother's suicide. [Am. Lit.: *Mourning Becomes Electra*]

8.   **Oedipus** blinds self upon learning of his crimes. [Gk. Lit.: *Oedipus Rex*]

9.   **Othello** commits suicide from guilt for wife's murder. [Br. Lit.: *Othello*]

582. REMOTENESS (See also ISOLATION.)

1.   **Antarctica** continent surrounding South Pole. [Geography: *NCE*, 113–115]

2.   **boondocks** originally a term for rough, backwoods country; now meaning an area far from civilization; unsophisticated. [Am. Culture: Misc.]

3.   **Dan to Beersheba** from one outermost extreme to another. [O.T.: Judges 20:1]

4.   **Darkest Africa** in European and American imaginations, a faraway land of no return. [Western Folklore: Misc.]

5. **end of the rainbow** the unreachable end of the earth. [Western Folklore: Misc.]

6. **Everest, Mt.** Nepalese peak; highest elevation in world (29,028 ft.). [Geography: *NCE*, 907]

7. **Great Divide** great ridge of Rocky Mountains; once thought of as epitome of faraway place. [Am. Folklore: Misc.]

8. **John O'Groat's House** traditionally thought of as the northern-most, remote point of Britain. [Geography: Misc.]

9. **Land's End** the southwestern tip of Britain. [Geography: Misc.]

10. **moon** earth's satellite; unreachable until 1969. [Astronomy: *NCE*, 1824]

11. **North and South Poles** figurative ends of the earth. [Geography: Misc.]

12. **Outer Mongolia** desert wasteland between Russia and China; figuratively and literally remote. [Geography: Misc.]

13. **Pago Pago** capital of American Samoa in South Pacific; thought of as a remote spot. [Geography: Misc.]

14. **Pillars of Hercules** promontories at the sides of Straits of Gibraltar; once the limit of man's travel. [Gk. Myth.: Zimmerman, 110]

15. **Siberia** frozen land in northeastern U.S.S.R.; place of banishment and exile. [Russ. Hist.: *NCE*, 2510]

16. **Tierra del Fuego** archipelago off the extreme southern tip of South America. [Geography: Misc.]

17. **Timbuktu** figuratively, the end of the earth. [Am. Usage: *NCE*, 2749]

18. **Ultima Thule** to Romans, extemity of the world, identified with Iceland. [Rom. Legend: *LLEI*, I: 318]

19. **Yukon** Northwestern Canadian territory touching on the Arctic Ocean. [Geography: Misc.]

Repentance (See PENITENCE.)

583. REPRODUCTION

1. **Baby M.** name given to infant girl born to a surrogate mother in 1986; now a symbol for the ethical issues surrounding reproduction. [Am. Science *FOF, MOD*]

2. **clone** to reproduce genetically identical cells and organisims by manipulating DNA; in common parlance, a close copy of something. [Science: *FOF, MOD*]

3. **Dionne Quintuplets** French-Canadian sisters—Annette, Cecile, Emilie, Marie, and Yvonne—born in 1934; were the first identical quintuplets known to survive infancy. [Can. Hist.: *SJEPC*]

4. **Malthusian** refers to the population theories of British economist Thomas Malthus; he believed that poverty, war, and disease acted as natural controls on populations. [Medicine and Politics: *FOF, MOD*]

5. **National Right to Life** pro-life organization desiring protection of human life in utero; supports constitutional amendment granting embryos and fetuses legal status as persons. [Am. Politics: *SJEPC*; Dudley, 166]

6. **Operation Rescue** pro-life organization founded in 1988 maintains abortion is murder at any stage of human development in utero. [Am. Politics: *SJEPC*]

7. **Pill, The** introduced in the 1960s, contraceptive that allows sexual activity without the fear of pregnancy. [Am. Medicine: *SJEPC*]

8. **Planned Parenthood** world's largest and oldest voluntary family planning organization is pro-choice and provides medical services and sexuality education; supports woman's right to decide when or whether to have a child. [Medicine and Politics: Keyzer, 475]

9. **Sanger, Margaret (1883–1966)** early 20th-century nurse and birth control advocate/educator founded International Planned Parenthood Federation in 1953. [Am. Hist.: *SJEPC*; Brakeman, 322]

Reproof (See CRITICISM.)

584. RESCUE (See also DELIVERANCE, HERO, SALVATION.)

1. **Abishai** saved David from death by Benob. [O.T.: II Samuel 21:17]

2. **Andromeda** saved by Perseus from sea monster. [Gk. Myth.: Hall, 239; Rom. Lit.: *Metamorphoses*]

3. **Ararat** traditional resting place of Noah's ark after the Flood. [O.T.: Genesis 8:4]

4. **Arion** thrown overboard; carried safely to land by dolphins. [Gk. Myth.: *LLEI*, I: 323; Br. Lit.: *Faerie Queene*]

5. **Barry** St. Bernard dog; saved over 40 snowbound people in Alps. [Swiss Hist.: Wallechinsky, 126]

6. *Charlotte's Web* 1952 children's book by E. B. White; Wilbur the pig is saved from slaughter through web messages woven by his spider friend Charlotte. [Am. Children's Lit.: *OCCL*]

7. **Deucalion** survived Zeus's flood in ark. [Gk. Myth.: Zimmerman, 85]

8. **Diana's statue** saved by Orestes from Scythian thieves. [Gk. Lit.: *Iphegenia in Tauris*]

9. **Do-Right, Dudley** Canadian Mountie constantly trying to rescue his beloved Nell, who prefers his horse. [Am. TV: "Dudley Do-Right of the Mounties"]

10. **Dunkirk** combined military-civilian operation rescued 340,000 British troops (1940). [Br. Hist.: Van Doren, 475]

11. **Entebbe** daring Israeli raid freed airline hostages at Ugandan airport (1977). [World Hist.: *Facts* (1977), 487]

12. **Flipper** loyal pet dolphin often rescued humans from danger in TV series *Flipper* (1964–68); also starred in two featurre films (1963, 1964). [Am. TV and Film: *SJEPC*]

13. **Hercules** rescues Alcestis from Hades after her self-sacrifice. [Gk. Lit.: *Alcestis*; Ger. Opera: Gluck, *Alcestis*, Westerman, 73–75]

14. **Iphigenia** rescued at the moment of her sacrificial stabbing,. [Gk. Myth.: Gayley, 80–81]

15. **Isaac** "saved" from being sacrificed by angel of the Lord. [O.T.: Genesis 22:2–13]

16. **Jonah** saved from drowning in belly of great fish. [O.T.: Jonah 1:17]

17. **Lassie** collie dog featured on TV show (1954–1973) where she regularly saved those in trouble; portrayed as highly intelligent and fiercely loyal. [Am. TV: Misc.]

18. **Macheath** saved from hanging by the king's reprieve. [Ger. Opera: Weill, *Threepenny Opera*, Westerman, 497]

19. **Mignon** rescued by Wilhelm Meister from gypsies. [Fr. Opera: Thomas, *Mignon*, Westerman, 187]

20. **Noah** with his sons, deemed by God worth saving from His destructive flood. [O.T.: Genesis 6–10]

21. **oak leaves** used in crown awarded to one who saves a life. [Rom. Tradition: Wheeler, 765]

22. **Rahab and family** spared from Jericho's destruction for aid rendered to Joshua's army. [O.T.: Joshua 6:25]

23. **Red Cross Knight** hero who bravely slays dragon and rescues Princess Una. [Br. Lit.: Edmund Spenser *The Faerie Queen*]

24. **Sanang** used magic powers to rescue Marco Polo. [Irish Lit.: *Messer Marco Polo*, Magill I, 584–585]

25. **Tinker Bell** fairy saved by the faith of the audience after she drinks a lethal poison. [Br. Drama: J.M. Barrie *Peter Pan* in Magill II, 820]

26. **U.S. Calvary** from the Western movie tradition, the Calvary is sent for and arrives in time to save the day; a symbol of ready rescue. [Am. Film: *ODA*]

585. RESOURCEFULNESS

1. **Aladdin** protagonist of *Aladdin, or the Wonderful Lamp* from the Arabian Nights collection; finds a magic lamp with a jinn inside and uses this newfound power to fulfilll all of his desires. [Children's Lit.: *OCCL*]

2. **Babe** brave and intelligent; saves himself from slaughter by becoming indispensable to farmer who owns him in Dick King-Smith's children's book *Babe: The Gallant Pig* (1985). [Br. Children's Lit.: Jones]

3. **Buck** clever and temerarious dog perseveres in the Klondike. [Am. Lit.: *Call of the Wild*]

4. **Cavatica, Charlotte A.** protagonist from E. B. White's children's book *Charlotte's Web*; very knowledgable large gray spider whose web words convince the humans not to slaughter her friend Wilbur the pig; after she has succeeded and has laid her eggs, she dies. [Am. Chldren's Lit.: Jones]

5. **Christopher Robin** based in part on A.A. Milne's son; protagonist of Winnie-the-Pooh tales for children; very much the child, yet has adult qualities that allow him to rescue others from trouble and offer gentle love and understanding. [Br. Children's Lit.: Jones]

6. **Crichton, Admirable** butler proves to be infinite resource for castaway family on island. [Br. Lit.: *The Admirable Crichton*]

7. **Crusoe, Robinson** inventive when shipwrecked on an island. [Br. Lit.: *Robinson Crusoe*]

8. **duck** from ingeniousness of duck in eluding enemies. [Heraldry: Halberts, 26]

9. **Fogg, Phileas** burns his boat's superstructure and decks for fuel and thus reaches London on time. [Fr. Lit.: Jules Verne *Around the World in Eighty Days*]

10. **Gale, Dorothy** protagonist of L. Frank Baum's Oz series; sensitive orphan who improves all who come into contact with her; brave and self-sufficient, she finds it is by her own devices that she will find her way home from Oz. [Br.Chidlren's Lit..: Jones]

11. **Little Black Sambo** protagonist of 1899 tale by Helen Bannerman; lives in India, but depicted in illustrations as African, Sambo outwits the tigers that threaten him and gorges himself on pancakes when the tigers are reduced to butter in their senseless chase. [Scot. Children's Lit.: OCCL]

12. **Swiss Family Robinson** shipwrecked family carves hospitable life from wilderness. [Swiss Children's Lit.: Jones]

13. **Thoreau, Henry David (1817–1862)** example of man's ability to build his own life in the wilderness. [Am. Hist.: NCE, 2738]

586. RESURRECTION

1. **Adonis** vegetation god, reborn each spring. [Gk. Myth.: Benét, 10]

2. **Alcestis** after dying in place of her husband, she is brought back from the dead by Heracles. [Gk. Drama: *Alcestis*]

3. **Amys and Amyloun** sacrificed children are restored to life. [Medieval Legend: Benét, 31]

4. **Ban** god whose cauldron restored the dead to life. [Welsh Myth.: Jobes, 241]

5. **butterfly** symbol of resurrection in many countries. [Symbolism: *CEOS&S*]

6. **Dorcas** raised from the dead by St. Peter. [N.T.: Acts 9:36–42]

7. **Drusiana** restored to life by John the Evangelist. [Christian Hagiog.: *Golden Legend*]

8. **Dumuzi** god of regeneration and resurrection. [Sumerian Myth.: Jobes, 476]

9. **egg** symbol of Christ's resurrection. [Art: Hall, 110]

10. **Elijah** breathes life back into child. [O.T.: I Kings 17:18]

11. **Fisher King** old, maimed king whose restoration symbolizes the return of spring vegetation. [Medieval Legend: T.S. Eliot *The Waste Land* in Norton *Literature*]

12. **Jarius's daughter** Christ raises her from the dead. [N.T.: Matthew 9:18–19; Mark 5:21–24; Luke 8:40–42]

13. **Jesus Christ** arose from the dead three days after His crucifixion. [N.T.: Matthew 28; Mark 16; Luke 24]

14. **Lazarus** Jesus calls him back to life from the tomb. [N.T.: John 11:43–44]

15. **McGee, Sam** Tennessee native freezes to death in Alaska but is brought back to life in the cremation furnace. [Am. Poetry: Service "The Cremation of Sam McGee"]

16. **mushroom** symbol of life arising from death, longevity, and happiness in China; in parts of central Europe and Africa, folklore links it with supernatural. [Symbolism: *CEOS&S*]

17. **phoenix** fabled bird, rises from its ashes. [Gk. Legend: Brewer *Dictionary*, 829; Christian Symbolism: Appleton, 76]

18. **pomegranate** bursting with seed, it symbolizes open tomb. [Christian Symbolism: Appleton, 77]

19. **scarab** symbol for Ra, sun-god; reborn each day. [Animal Symbolism: Mercatante, 180]

20. **Thammuz** god died annually and rose each spring. [Bably. Myth.: Brewer *Dictionary*, 1071]

21. **widow's son of Nain** touched by mother's grief, Christ brings him back to life. [N.T.: Luke 7:11–17]

587. REUNION

1. **Arafat, Mt.** Adam and Eve met here after 200 years. [Muslim Legend: Benét, 44]

2. **chickweed** flower symbolizing a rejoining. [Flower Symbolism: Jobes, 322]

3. **Esau and Jacob** after many years, they are reconciled. [O.T.: Genesis 33:1–4]

4. **Eurydice and Orpheus** reunited despite his backward look. [Ger. Opera: Gluck, *Orpheus and Eurydice*, Westerman, 72]

5. **Joachim and Anna** separated spouses joyfully meet at Jerusalem gate on news of her pregnancy. [Ital. Lit.: *Golden Legend*]

6. **Mary and Elizabeth** the two pregnant women meet after many years and rejoice. [N.T.: Luke 1:39–56]

7. **prodigal son and his father** repentant son returns home to a joyous welcome. [N.T.: Luke 15:11–32]

588. REVELRY

1. **Bacchanalia** festival in honor of Bacchus, god of wine. [Rom. Religion: *NCE*, 203]

2. **Boar's Head Tavern** scene of Falstaff's carousals. [Br. Lit.: *I Henry IV,*; *II Henry IV*]

3. **Buffett, Jimmy (1946–)** singer with beach-bum image; signature hit "Margaritaville" spawned Parrot Head subculture of Hawaiian shirt-garbed concert audiences seeking escapism and a good party. [Am. Music: *SJEPC*]

4. **Comus** hard-drinking god of festive mirth; whence, *comic*. [Gk. Myth.: Espy, 31]

5. **Dionysia** celebrations honoring the wine god, Dionysus. [Gk. Religion: Avery, 399, 404–408; Parrinder, 80]

6. **Dionysus** god of wine and revelry; Bacchus to the Romans. [Gk. Myth.: Parrinder, 39]

7. *Fête Champêtre* erotically tinged painting of picnic scene. [Fr. Art.: Daniel, 102]

8. **Goliards** wandering scholar-poets of satirical Latin verse celebrating sensual pleasure. [Medieval Hist.: *NCE*, 1105]

9. **grapes, garland of** traditional headdress of Dionysus (Bacchus). [Gk. and Roman Myth.: Jobes, 373]

10. **happy hour** created to draw in customers to bars, the practice of offering reduced prices on drinks during specific times. [Am. Culture: Misc.]

11. **Margaritaville** name of song and state of mind created by musician Jimmy Buffett, a metaphor for escapism, good times, and plentiful alcohol. [Am. Music: *SJEPC*]

Revenge (See VENGEANCE.)

Revolt (See REBELLION, REBELLIOUSNESS.)

Reward (See PRIZE.)

589. RIBALDRY (See also OBSCENITY.)

1. *Decameron, The* Boccaccio's bawdy panorama of medieval Italian life. [Ital. Lit.: Bishop, 314–315, 380]

2. *Droll Tales* Blazac's Rabelaisian stories, told in racy medieval style and frequently gross. [Fr. Lit.: *Contes Drolatiques* in Benét, 222]

3. **Fescennia** Etrurian town noted for jesting and scurrilous verse (Fescennine verse). [Rom. Hist.: *EB*, IV: 112]

4. *Gargantua and Pantagruel* Rabelais's farcical and obscene 16th-century novel. [Fr. Lit.: Magill I, 298]

5. *Golden Ass, The* tale of Lucius and his asininity, with a number of bawdy episodes. [Rom. Lit.: Apuleius *Metamorphoses* or *The Golden Ass* in Magill I, 309]

6. **Goliards** scholar-poets interested mainly in earthly delights. [Medieval Hist.: Bishop, 292–293]

7. **Iambe** girl who amused Demeter with bawdy stories. [Gk. Myth.: Howe, 136]

8. *LaFontaine, The Tales of* ribald stories in verse, adapted from Boccaccio and others. [Fr. Lit.: *Contes en Vers* in Benét, 222]

9. *Miller's Tale, The* lusty story told by the drunken Miller. [Br. Lit.: *Canterbury Tales* in Magill II, 131]

10. *Reeve's Tale, The* Oswald the Reeve retaliates in kind to *The Miller's Tale*. [Br. Lit.: *Canterbury Tales* in Benét, 919]

Ridicule (See MOCKERY.)

590. RIGHTEOUSNESS (See also HONESTY, NOBLEMINDEDNESS, VIRTUOUSNESS.)

1. **Amos** prophet of righteousness. [O.T.: Amos]

2. **Astraea** goddess of righteousness. [Gk. Myth.: Walsh *Classical*, 36]

3. **Benedetto, Don** Catholic teacher of moral precepts. [Ital. Lit.: *Bread and Wine*]

4. **dharma** multi-faceted concept of morality, truth, doctrine. [Hindu Rel.: Parrinder, 77]

5. **Enoch** traditionally seen as paragon of upright man. [O.T.: Genesis 5:21–24]

6. *Everyman* medieval play demonstrating man's salvation dependent on his righteousness. [Br. Lit.: *Everyman*]

7. **Josiah** virtuously reforms Jerusalem's evil ways. [O.T.: II Kings 23:1–20]

8. **Noah** only devout man of time; saved from flood. [O.T.: Genesis 6:9–22]

9. **Stockmann, Dr. Thomas** despite attempted bribery and intimidation, refuses to suppress evidence that the public baths are a health menace. [Norwegian Lit.: *An Enemy of the People*, Magill II, 292]

10. **Zosima** elder monk; preaches message of love and forbearance. [Russ. Lit.: *The Brothers Karamazov*]

591. RIGHTS, CIVIL

1. **Anderson, Marian (1897–1993)** her unabashed, flawless performance at the Lincoln Memorial in 1939 after she was denied use of Constitution Hall brought honor to her race; she received the Presidential Medal of Freedom in 1963. [Am. Music: *SJEPC*]

2. **Bakke decision** "reverse discrimination" victim; entered medical school with Supreme Court's help. [Am. Hist.: *Facts* (1978), 483]

3. **Baldwin, James (1924–1987)** African-American writer and activist in the civil rights movement of the 1960s. [Am. Lit. and Politics: *SJEPC*]

4. **Belafonte, Harry (1927–)** Jamaican-American singer, actor, and activist fought for African and African-American civil rights. [Am. Music and Politics: *SJEPC*]

5. **"Blowin' in the Wind"** Bob Dylan's 1963 protest song popularized by Peter, Paul and Mary; associated with civil rights movement. [Am. Music: *SJEPC*]

6. *Brown v. Board of Education of Topeka, Kansas* Supreme Court decision in 1954 declared racial segregation in public schools unconstitutional. [Am. Hist.: *SJEPC*; *WB2*]

7. **Charles, Ray (1930–2004)** African-American musical legend refused to allow promoter to segregate his audience, financially supported Martin Luther King's cause. [Am. Music: *SJEPC*]

8. **Chávez, César (1927–1993)** Mexican-American labor leader also championed the civil rights of women, gays, and African Americans. [Am. Hist.: *SJEPC*]

9. *Crisis, The* monthly magazine of the NAACP (National Association for the Advancement of Colored People) founded in 1910 by editor W. E. B. Du Bois; has defended African-American civil rights and served as the voice of black America for a century. [Am. Jour.: *SJEPC*]

10. **Dred Scott decision** conntroversial ruling stating that Negroes were not entitled to citizenship or "equal justice." [Am. Hist.: Payton, 203]

11. **Equal Employment Opportunity Commission** U.S. government agency appointed to promote the cause of equal opportunity for all U.S. citizens. [Am. Hist.: Payton, 224]

12. **"Freedom Rides"** nonviolent protest method to end racial segregation in interstate travel; in 1960s, black and white protesters together rode buses in South and requested service; were often beaten or arrested. [Am. Hist.: *SJEPC*]

13. **"I Have a Dream"** speech by Martin Luther King, Jr.; expresses longing for country with judgment not based on race, but on "content of character" [Am. Hist.: *SJEPC*]

14. **King, Martin Luther, Jr. (1929–1968)** considered the preeminent leader of Civil Rights movement for African Americans; proposed nonviolent resistance as powerful weapon against discrimination; national holiday and various landmarks and buildings honor him. [Am. Hist.: *SJEPC*]

15. **Malcolm X (1925–1965)** began by promoting separatism and violence, later preached against racism of all kinds. [Am. Hist.: *SJEPC*]

16. **March on Washington** 1963 Civil Rights march at which Martin Luther King, Jr. delivered his famous "I Have a Dream" speech. [Am. Hist.: *SJEPC*]

17. **Miranda Decision** Supreme Court decision (1966) requiring that suspected criminals be informed of their rights at time of arrest. [Am. Law: *SJEPC*]

18. **Montgomery Bus Boycott** boycott organized by M. L. King (1955) around the refusal of Rosa Parks to give up her seat on a Montgomery bus; led to the end of legal segregation in public transportation. [Am. Hist.: *BBAAL*]

19. **NAACP (National Association for the Advancement of Colored People)** vanguard of Negro fight for racial equality. [Am. Hist.: Van Doren, 548–549]

20. **Parks, Rosa (1913–2005)** her refusal to give her bus seat to a while man was just the beginning of her involvement in Civil Rights Movement [Am. Hist.: *SJEPC*]

21. **Seeger, Pete (1919–)** paved the way for singer/activists through devotion to many social causes; popularized "We Shall Overcome," which became the anthem of the civil rights movement of the 1960s. [Am. Culture: *SJPEC*]

22. **"We Shall Overcome"** anthem of civil rights movement, rallying song of black Americans. [Am. Pop. Culture: Misc.]

592. RIGHTS, GAY (See also HOMOSEXUALITY.)

1. **ACT-UP** AIDS Coalition to Unleash Power; committed to ending the AIDS crisis by demanding more financial support for AIDS research and education, and ending discrimination against HIV-positive people in housing and employment. [Am. Hist.: *SJEPC*]

2. **AIDS** fatal disease was considered a "gay issue" by conservative politicians in the 1980s, leading to increased political and social activism by homosexuals to educate the public and fund medical research. [Am. Hist.: *SJEPC*]

3. **Fierstein, Harvey (1954–)** homosexual actor/playwright is also active in supporting gay rights and AIDS research. [Am. Theater and Film: *SJEPC*]

4. **King, Billie Jean (1943–)** outstanding professional tennis player and outspoken proponent for equality for female athletes; instrumental in arranging first professional tennis tournament for women in 1970; forceful advocate for women's and gay rights. [Am. Sports: *SJEPC*]

5. **Milk, Harvey (1930–1978)** openly gay San Francisco politician known as "the mayor of Castro Street"; fought for human rights for homosexuals; assassinated at City Hall in 1978. [Am. Hist.: *SJEPC*]

6. **outing** revealing oneself or others as homosexual. [Culture: *SJEPC*]

7. **Queer Nation** founded in 1990; activist organization with focus on making homosexuality more prominent in American society; controversial for outing people whose sexual orientation had been previously undisclosed. [Am. Pop. Culture: *SJEPC*]

8. **Stonewall Rebellion** 1969 resistance by patrons of Greenwich Village gay men's bar during police raid; annual Gay Pride parade and rallies held nationwide to commemorate the event; led to formation of Gay Liberation Front and others committed to civil rights for homosexuals. [Am. Pop. Culture: *SJEPC*]

593. RIGHTS, WOMEN'S

1. **Addams, Jane (1860–1935)** social activist advocated women's suffrage and other feminist causes. [Am. Hist.: *SJEPC*]

2. **Alving, Mrs.** feminist; unconventional widow. [Nor. Lit.: *Ghosts*]

3. *Annie Get Your Gun* musical comedy's plot mirrored ambivalence in post-World War II America over women's equal rights in the workforce. [Am. Musical: *SJEPC*]

4. **Anthony, Susan B. (1820–1906)** along with Elizabeth Cady Stanton fought for women's legal rights and suffrage; also abolitionist. [Am. Politics: Schenken, 37]

5. **Bates, Belinda** intellectual and amiable advocate of women's rights. [Br. Lit.: "The Haunted House" in Fyfe, 16]

6. **Bloomer, Amelia (1818–1894)** dress reformer; designed bloomers. [Am. Hist.: Flexner, 391]

7. **blue-stocking** female intellectual; advocates nontraditional feminine talents. [Western Folklore: Brewer *Dictionary*, 127]

8. *Bostonians, The* suffagists for lost causes, vulnerable to romance. [Am. Lit.: *The Bostonians*]

9. **bra burner** in 1968, during a demonstration against the Miss America Pageant, 100 feminists were said to have burned their bras in protest; brought charges of being "anti-feminine." [Am. Culture: Tobias, 86]

10. **Buck, Pearl S. (1892–1973)** activist author advocated for women's rights in both China and America. [Am. Lit.: *SJEPC*]

11. **Chancellor, Olive** devotes her life to preaching women's rights. [Am. Lit.: Henry James *The Bostonians*]

12. **de Beauvoir, Simone (1908–1986)** author and philosopher whose 1949 essay *The Second Sex* is considered by many a foundational work of feminism; discusses treatment of women throughout history, role of women in modern world. [Fr. Lit.: *WB2*]

13. *Doll's House, A* drama on the theme of women's rights. [Nor. Lit.: *A Doll's House*]

14. **Equal Pay Act of 1963** bill that makes it illegal for private employers to pay women different amount for doing same work as male employees; first federal law to address sex discrimination. [Am. Law: Schenken, 236]

15. **Equal Rights Amendment (ERA)** to give women full equality; first introduced in Congress in 1923; never passed. [Am. Law: Schenken, 237]

16. **Equality State** nickname of Wyoming; first state to give women the right to vote. [Am. Hist.: Payton, 224]

17. *Fear of Flying* 1973 feminist novel by Erica Jong; explicit sex brought both acclaim and censure. [Am. Lit.: *SJEPC*]

18. *Female Eunuch, The* written in 1970 by Germaine Greer; encouraged women to recognize control by men and to live outside of traditional roles. [Australian Lit.: *WB2*, 387]

19. *Feminine Mystique, The* written by Betty Friedan and published in 1963; described the dissatisfaction of many American women; accused American society of discouraging women from pursuing careers outside the home. [Am. Lit.: *WB2*, 532]

20. **Findlay, Maude** militant, outspoken women's libber. [TV: "Maude" in Terrace, II, 79–80]

21. **Friedan, Betty (1921–)** considered founder of women's liberation movement in America; one of the founders of National Organization for Women (NOW). [Am. Politics: *WB2*, 532]

22. **glass ceiling** defined by federal commission as "artificial barriers based on attitudinal or organizational biases that prevent qualified women and minorities from advancing upward into management-level positions." [Am. Politics: Schenken, 294]

23. **Greer, Germaine (1939–)** writer whose *The Female Eunuch* (1970) encouraged women to leave traditional roles and control their own lives. [Australian Lit.: *WB2*, 387]

24. **Jong, Erica (1942–)** novelist who detailed women's sexual desires; sometimes criticized for promiscuous characters. [Am. Lit.: *SJEPC*]

25. **King, Billie Jean (1943–)** outstanding professional tennis player and outspoken proponent for equality for female athletes; defeated Bobby Riggs when he dared her to Battle of the Sexes match in 1973; instrumental in arranging first professional tennis tournament for women in 1970. [Am. Sports: *SJEPC*]

26. **Lucy Stoners** league of feminists. [Am. Hist.: *NCE*, 2628]

27. **Lysistrata** Athenian exhorts fellow women to continence for peace. [Gk. Lit.: *Lysistrata*]

28. **Mott, Lucretia Coffin (1793–1880)** leader of abolitionist and women's right movements in US; organized Seneca Falls Convention. [Am. Politics: *WB2*, 880]

29. *Ms. Magazine* started in 1962 by Gloria Steinem as a way to keep women apprised of feminist issues and guide them in grass-root activism. [Am. Jour.: Schenken, 456]

30. **National Organization for Women (NOW)** activist association begun in 1966 to promote women's "full participation in American society." [Am. Politics: *SJEPC*]

31. **Nineteenth Amendment** granted women the right to vote (1920). [Am. Hist.: Van Doren, 409]

32. **Nora** rebellious heroine; leaves stultifying marriage. [Nor. Lit.: *A Doll's House*]

33. **Pankhurst, Emmeline (1858–1928)** British suffragist who founded Women's Social and Political Union, using civil disobedience and vandalism to fight for suffrage. [Br. Politics: *WB2*, 131]

34. **Peel, Emma** early media manifestation of self-sufficient woman. [TV: "The Avengers" in Terrace, I, 71–73]

35. **Pill, The** introduced in the 1960s, it allows sexual activity without the fear of pregnancy. [Am. Medicine: *SJEPC*]

36. **Planned Parenthood** world's largest and oldest pro-choice organization advocates on behalf of women's reproductive rights, including the right to contraception and abortion. [Medicine and Politics: Keyzer, 475]

37. *Roe v. Wade* US Supreme Court declared state laws restricting abortion during the first three months of pregnancy were invalid; decision handed down in 1973. [Am. Law: Schenken, 581]

38. **Sanger, Margaret (1883–1966)** early 20th-century birth control activist fought for women's right to use contraception and terminate a pregnancy. [Am. Hist.: *SJEPC*; Brakeman, 316]

39. **Schlafly, Phyllis (1924–)** conservative leader opposed to state and federal Equal Rights Amendments; founder of Stop ERA and Eagle Forum. [Am. Politics: Schenken, 601]

40. **Stanton, Elizabeth Cady (1815–1902)** early women's rights advocate; also primary advocate for suffrage; organized Seneca Falls Convention. [Am. Politics: WB2, 839]

41. **Steinem, Gloria (1934–)** media celebrity and publicist for feminism; cofounded *Ms. Magazine* and campaigned for women's rights. [Am. Politics and Jour.: WB2, 886]

42. **Title IX** stated no one could be prevented from participating in any education program with federal funding; fight against it focused on equal funding of male and female sports programs. [Am. Law: Tobias, 122]

43. **Title VII** section of the 1964 Civil Rights Bill; prohibits discrimination in employment on the basis of race, religion, sex, or national origin. [Am. Law: Tobias, 81]

44. **Virginia Slims** cigarette trademark marketed to "independent women." "You've come a long way, baby," as slogan. [Trademarks: Crowley *Trad*, 630]

45. **Wisk, Miss** lady with a mission. [Br. Lit.: *Bleak House*]

46. **Women's Liberation Movement** appellation of modern day women's rights advocacy. [Am. Hist.: Flexner, 396]

47. **Wonder Woman** female comic strip heroine to offset Superman; she does everything a man can do and more. [Comics: Horn, 480]

594. RING, MAGIC

1. **Agramant's ring** given to dwarf, Brunello, and stolen. [Ital. Lit.: *Orlando Furioso*]

2. **Aladdin's ring** given him by the African magician to protect him from all harm. [Arab. Lit.: *Arabian Nights*: "Aladdin and the Wonderful Lamp"]

3. **Andvari's ring** he gave up magic ring to gain liberty. [Norse Myth.: Benét, 35]

4. **Draupnir** Odin's ring; symbol of fertility. [Norse Myth.: *LLEI*, I: 326]

5. **fairy rings** rings found in grassy meadows, once believed to have been produced by dancing fairies. [Br. Myth.: Brewer *Dictionary*, 345]

6. **Green Lantern's power ring** gives comic book superhero strength to perform mighty deeds. [Am. Comics: *SJEPC*]

7. **Gyges's ring** found in a chasm, it renders him invisible and thus able to gain Candaules's wife and kingdom. [Gk. Myth.: Brewer, 425]

8. **Luned's ring** rendered its wearer invisible. [Welsh Lit.: *Mabinogion*]

9. **One Ring, the** forged by the Dark Lord, it gave invisibility and long life but corrupted its users. [Br. Lit.: J.R.R. Tolkien *The Lord of the Rings* in Magill IV, 326]

10. **Polycrates's ring** thrown into the sea to ward off misfortune, it is miraculously returned in the belly of a fish, and tragedy ensues. [Gk. Myth.: Brewer *Dictionary*, 714]

11. **Reynard's wonderful ring** tricolored; each color performed different feat. [Medieval Lit.: *Reynard the Fox*]

12. **Ring of the Nibelungs** made from the Rhine gold, brought a curse on all who owned it. [Ger. Lit.: Benét, 860]

13. **steel ring** enabled wearer to read the secrets of another's heart. [Br. Lit.: Brewer *Handbook*, 916]

595. RIOT (See also REBELLION.)

1. **Attica** city in New York housing state prison; one of the worst prison riots in American history occurred there (1971). [Am. Hist.: NCE, 182]

2. **Birmingham riots** melee resulting from cilvil rights demonstrations (1963). [Am. Hist.: Van Doren, 585–586]

3. **Boston Massacre** civil uprising fueled revolutionary spirit (1770). [Am. Hist.: Jameson, 57]

4. **Boston Tea Party** colonists rioted against tea tax (1773). [Am. Hist.: NCE, 341]

5. **Chicago riots** "police riot" arguably cost Democrats election (1968). [Am. Hist.: Van Doren, 625]

6. **Donnybrook Fair** former annual Dublin county fair; famous for rioting and dissipation. [Irish Hist.: NCE, 784]

7. *Germinal* conflict of capital vs. labor; miners strike *en masse*. [Fr. Lit.: *Germinal*]

8. **Gordon, Lord George** leader of the anti-Catholic riots of 1780, in which the idiot Barnaby is caught up. [Br. Lit.: Dickens *Barnaby Rudge*]

9. **Haymarket Riot** Chicago labor dispute erupted into mob scene (1886). [Am. Hist.: Van Doren, 297]

10. **Kent State** Ohio university where antiwar demonstration led to riot, resulting in deaths of four students (1971). [Am. Hist.: NCE, 1466]

11. **Little Rock** capital of Arkansas; federal troops sent there to enforce ruling against segregation (1957). [Am. Hist.: NCE, 1594]

12. **Luddites** British workers riot to destroy labor-saving machines (1811–1816). [Br. Hist.: *NCE*, 1626]

13. **Molly Maguires** anti-landlord organization; used any means to combat mine owners. (1860s, 1870s). [Am. Hist.: Van Doren, 272]

14. **New York Draft Riots** anti-conscription feelings resulted in anarchy and bloodshed (1863). [Am. Hist.: Jameson, 429]

15. **Riot Act, the** reading it to unruly crowds, sheriffs under George I could force them to disperse or be jailed.; hence, "read him/her the riot act" means reprimanding someone. [Br. Hist.: Brewer *Dictionary*, 767]

16. **Shays' Rebellion** armed insurrection by Massachusetts farmers against the state government (1786). [Am. Hist.: *NCE*, 2495]

17. **Watts** district in Los Angeles where black Americans rioted over economic deprivation and socal injustices (1965). [Am. Hist.: *NCE*, 1612–1613]

18. **Whiskey Rebellion** uprising in Pennsylvania over high tax on whiskey and scotch products (1794). [Am. Hist.: *NCE*, 2967]

596. RIVALRY

1. **Brom Bones and Ichabod Crane** bully and show-off compete for Katrina's hand. [Am. Lit.: *The Legend of Sleepy Hollow*]

2. **Capulets and Montagues** bitter feud between these two houses leads to tragedy. [Br. Lit.: *Romeo and Juliet*]

3. **Diomedes and Troilus** rivals for hand of Cressida. [Br. Lit.: *Troilus and Cressida*]

4. **Esau and Jacob** struggled even in mother's womb. [O.T.: Genesis 25:22]

5. **Eteocles and Polynices** brothers battle for Theban throne. [Gk. Lit.: *Seven Against Thebes*]

6. **Gingham Dog and Calico Cat** stuffed animals eat each other up. [Am. Lit.: "The Duel" in Hollowell]

7. **Guelphs and Ghilbellines** perennial medieval Italian feuding political factions. [Ital. Hist.: Plumb, 42–43]

8. **Hatfields and McCoys** two warring families from West Virginia/Kentucky backcountry; longstanding (1878–1891) and bitter feud has made their names synonymous with animosity. [Am. Hist.: *NCE*, 942]

9. **Jets and Sharks** teenage gangs fight for supremacy amid the New York tenements. [Am. Lit. and Cinema: *West Side Story*]

10. **Kilkenny cats** contentious felines fight to the death. [Nurs. Rhyme: *Mother Goose*]

11. *Outsiders, The* 1967 novel by teenage author S.E. Hinton; violence erupts between members of two gangs; in the aftermath, three brothers are brought closer together. [Am. Children's Lit.: Gillespie and Naden]

12. **Percys and Douglases** the perennial Scottish border feud; recounted in famous ballad "Chevy Chase." [Scot. Hist.: Payton, 141]

13. **Proitus and Acrisius** fought in womb; contended for father's realm. [Gk. Myth.: Gaster, 164]

14. **Richard the Lion-Hearted and Saladin** Christian and Saracen leaders part friends after Crusade. [Br. Lit.: *The Talisman*]

15. **Sohrab and Rustum** champions of the Tartars and Persians, respectively, engage in mortal combat, unaware that one is the other's son. [Br. Poetry: Arnold *Sohrab and Rustum* in Magill III, 1002]

Robber (See THIEF.)

Romance (See LOVE; PASSION, SENSUAL.)

Rudeness (See COARSENESS.)

597. RUFFIAN

1. **Brown shirts (S.A.)** Nazi militia who terrorized citizens. [Ger. Hist.: *WB*, H:238]

2. **droogs** Alex's rough and tough band of hooligans. [Br. Lit.: *A Clockwork Orange*]

3. **Hawkubites** London toughs; terrorized old men, women, and children (1711–1714). [Br. Hist.: Brewer *Note-Book*, 406]

4. **Jackmen** medieval paramilitary thugs. [Br. Hist.: Brewer *Note-Book*, 463]

5. **Jets and Sharks** hostile street gangs. [Am. Lit. and Cinema: *West Side Story*]

6. **Mohocks** bullies terrorizing London streets in 18th century. [Br. Hist.: Brewer *Dictionary*, 720]

7. **Scowerers** London hooligans, at turn of the 18th century. [Br. Hist.: Brewer *Dictionary*, 972]

8. **Tityre Tus** young bullies in late 17th-century London. [Br. Hist.: Brewer *Dictionary*, 1087]

598. RUSTICITY (See also UNSOPHISTICATION.)

1. *American Gothic* Grant Wood's painting of stern Iowan farming couple. [Am. Art.: Osborne, 1215]

2. **Audrey** awkward rural wench who jilts a countryman for a clown. [Br. Lit.: Shakespeare *As You Like It*]

3. *Beverly Hillbillies, The* rural Clampett clan transported by wealth to Beverly Hills. [Am. TV: *SJEPC*]

4. **Claudill, Boone** epitome of the mountain man. [Am. Lit.: *The Big Sky*]

5. *Compleat Angler, The* fishing, hunting, and philosophizing in rural surroundings. [Br. Lit.: Izaac Walton *The Compleat Angler*]

6. **Currier and Ives** makers of colorful lithographs of scenes of nature and outdoor recreation. [Am. Hist.: *NCE*, 699]

7. *Dukes of Hazzard, The* 1979–1985 TV show set in the backwoods of Hazzard County down South featured the adventures of the Duke cousins, often involving car chases with bumbling lawmen. [Am. TV: *SJEPC*]

8. **North Woods** forest and lake region; setting for lumberjack legends. [Am. Lit.: Hart, 607]

9. *Petticoat Junction* farce set in rural America. [TV: Terrace, II, 205–206]

10. **Sears Roebuck Catalog** originated as mail-order merchandising for farming families; not the first of its kind, but the most successful and influential. [Am. Business: *SJEPC*]

11. **shtetl** any small-town Jewish settlement in East Europe. [Jewish Hist.: Wigoder, 552]

12. *Waltons, The* TV show from 1972–1980 about wholesome devoted Depression-Era farm famiily who represent life in a bygone time; always signed off by saying "goodnight" to each other. [Am. TV: *SJEPC*]

13. **Wyeth, Andrew (1917–2009)** austere new England subjects in earth tones and precise line, but tremendous depth of feeling; first living artist to have his work exhibited at National Gallery (1987) and first living artist to have retrospective at Metropolitan Museum of Art (1976). [Am. Art: *SJEPC*]

599. RUTHLESSNESS (See also BRUTALITY, CRUELTY, HEARTLESSNESS.)

1. **Borgia, Cesare (1476–1507)** prototype of Machiavelli's "Prince": intelligent and ruthlessly opportunistic. [Ital. Hist.: Plumb, 59]

2. **Caligula (12–41)** Roman emperor known for terror and cruel autocracy. [Rom. Hist.: *NCE*, 425]

3. **Citizen Kane** rich and powerful man drives away friends by use of power. [Am. Film: Misc.]

4. **Conquistadores** Spanish explorers of North and South America; noted for using brutal tactics against the native populations; a catchword for ruthless behavior. [Am. Hist.: Misc.]

5. **Hitler, Adolf (1889–1945)** Nazi dictator; universal symbol of brutality, race hatred, and ruthless genocide. [Ger. Hist.: *Hitler*]

6. **Ivan the Terrible (1533–1584)** his reign was characterized by murder and terror. [Russ. Hist.: *EB*, 9: 1179–1180]

7. **Larsen, Wolf** captain of the *Ghost*; terrorizes his crew. [Am. Lit.: London *The Sea-Wolf* in Magill I, 874]

8. **Nero (37–68)** demented Roman emperor; initiated persecutions against the Christians. [Rom. Hist.: *NCE*, 1909]

9. **play hardball** from baseball, to play with a "hardball" rather than a softball; an expression meaning to pursue a task with toughness, even ruthlessness. [Am. Culture: *FOF, MOD*]

10. **Robespierre, Maximilien Marie Isidore (1758–1794)** architect of the Reign of Terror (1793–1794) during the French Revolution. [Fr. Hist.: *EB*, 9: 907–910]

11. **Snopes** family of unscrupulous climbers, horse thieves, lechers, and murderers in Faulkner novels. [Am. Lit.: Benét, 940]

12. **Snopes, Flem** works his way up from obscurity to riches by ruining all his associates and relatives. [Am. Lit.: Faulkner *The Hamlet* in Magill II, 398; *The Town* in Magill III, 1074; *The Mansion* in Magill IV, 591]

13. **Vathek** sacrifices children, seduces a betrothed girl, and commits many other crimes to satisfy his desires. [Br. Lit.: *Vathek* in Magill II, 1095]

S

600. SACRED OBJECT

1. **Ark of the Covenant** gilded wooden chest in which God's presence dwelt when communicating with people. [O.T.: Exodus 25:10]

2. **baetyl** also baetylus; stone fallen from heaven, regarded as sacred. [Antiquity: *EB* (1963) II, 920]

3. **Black Stone, the** sacred stone at Mecca worshiped since ancient times. [Islamic Religion: Brewer *Dictionary*, 112]

4. **cow** to Hindus and Buddhists, its quiet, patient rhythms parallel holiness; to Hindus, it is sacred. [Symbolism: *CEOS&S*]

5. **Holy Grail** cups said to have been used by Jesus at the Last Supper and used to catch Christ's blood at his crucifixion. [Christian Tradition: Brewer *Dictionary*, 412; *CEOS&S*]

6. **zaïmph** mysterious veil of the Carthaginian moon-goddess Tanit. [Fr. Lit.: Flaubert *Salammbô* in Magill I, 860]

601. SACRED PLACE

1. **Alph** sacred river in Xanadu. [Br. Poetry: Coleridge "Kubla Khan"]

2. **Delphi** shrine sacred to Apollo and site of temple and oracle. [Gk. Myth.: Brewer *Dictionary*, 274]

3. **Dome of the Rock** Muslim holy shrine in Jerusalem built on the site where Muhammad was said to have risen into heaven. [Islam: *UIMT*, 124–25]

4. **Ganges** river sacred to the Hindus, who are freed from sin by bathing in it. [Hinduism: Brewer *Dictionary*, 385]

5. **Jerusalem** significant city in Judaism, Christianity, and Islam is home to numerous synagogues, churches, and mosques. [Rel.: *WB2*]

6. **Kaaba** central shrine at Mecca. [Islamic Religion: Brewer *Dictionary*, 513]

7. **Mecca** holy city where Muhammad was born. [Islamic Religion: Brewer *Dictionary*, 596]

8. **Medina** holy city to which Muhammad fled from Mecca. [Islamic Religion: Brewer *Dictionary*, 596]

9. **Nemi** lake in Italy, sacred to the cult of Diana and site of human sacrifices. [Rom. Myth.: *EB*, XVI, 211]

10. **Zem Zem** sacred well in Mecca where Hagar revived Ishmael. [Moslem Tradition: Brewer *Dictionary*, 969]

602. SACRIFICE (See also MARTYRDOM, SELF-SACRIFICE.)

1. **Adrammelech and Anammelech** Sepharvaite gods to whom children were immolated. [O.T.: II Kings 17:31]

2. **Akedah** biblical account of God commanding Abraham's offerings. [Jewish Hist.: Wigoder, 17]

3. **cross** traditional Christian symbol of acceptance of death or suffering and sacrifice. [Christianity: *IEOTS*, 46]

4. **Eid al-Adha** Festival of the Sacrifice; holiday commemorating Abraham's willingness to sacrifice his son Ishmael; takes place on the tenth day of Islamic month of Dhu al-Hijjah; celebrated with prayer and animal sacrifice, offered according to Islamic law. [Islam: *UIMT*, 365–70]

5. **Greatest Generation** ordinary Americans born in the 1920s who endured the Great Depression and made extraordinary sacrifices during World War II to serve the country, then returned to build modern America. [Am. Hist.: Brokaw *The Greatest Generation*; *SJEPC*]

6. **Idomeneus** Cretan king sacrifices his son to fulfill a vow. [Gk. Myth.: Benét, 492]

7. **Iphigenia** slain to appease Artemis's wrath. [Gk. Myth.: Walsh *Classical*, 156]

8. **lamb** in Islam and Judaism, important sacrificial and redemptive symbol. [Symbolism: *CEOS&S*]

9. **Moloch** god to whom idolatrous Israelites immolated children. [O.T.: II Kings: 23:10; Jeremiah 7:31–32, 32:35]

10. **Moriah** site intended for Abraham's offering up of Isaac. [O.T.: Genesis 22:2]

11. **ox** universal symbol of strength, submissiveness, and steady toil; Christians equate with sacrificial Christ; sacrificial animal in ancient world. [Symbolism: *CEOS&S*]

12. **suttee** former practice of self-immolation by widow on husband's pyre. [Hinduism: Brewer *Dictionary*, 1049]

13. **Tophet** site of propitiatory immolations to god, Moloch. [O.T.: II Kings: 23:10; Jeremiah 7:31–32]

14. *Yearling, The* 1938 novel by Marjorie Kinnan Rawlings; set in 1870s, it tells of young Jody, who tames a fawn and treasures it for years; when it begins eating their precious crops, Jody makes the difficult choice to sacrifice the fawn to save his family. [Am. Lit.: *OCCL*]

603. SACRILEGE (See also APOSTASY, HERESY.)

1. **abomination of desolation** epithet describing pagan idol in Jerusalem Temple. [O.T.: Daniel 9, 11, 12; N.T.: Mark 13:14; Matthew 24:15]

2. **Aepytus** Arcadian king; entering Poseidon's sanctuary forbidden to mortals, he is blinded. [Gk. Myth.: Zimmerman, 9]

3. **cleansing of the temple** sacrilegious money-changers driven out of temple by Christ. [N.T.: Matthew 21:12–13; Mark 11:15–18]

4. **Heliodorus** Syrian official attempted to loot Solomon's temple. [Apocrypha: II Maccabees 3]

5. **Hophni and Phinehas** contemptuously abused holiness of sacrifices. [O.T.: I Samuel 2:12–17]

6. **Simon Magus** tried to purchase apostolic powers; whence, *simony*. [N.T.: Acts 8:18–24]

Sadness (See MELANCHOLY.)

604. SALVATION (See also DELIVERANCE.)

1. **anchor** secret sign for cross in early Christianity; symbol of hope, salvation [Symbolism: *CEOS&S*]

2. **ark** symbol of salvation by cultures throughout the world. [Symbolism: *CEOS&S*, 208]

3. **cross** Christ's sacrifice by death on the cross saves all humans by promising life after death. [Christianity: *IEOTS*, 46]

4. **dolphin** in Christianity, symbol of Christ as savior; in Greek myth, considered and bearer of the gods, savior of heroes and carrier of souls to Islands of the Blessed. [Symbolism: *CEOS&S*]

5. **Esther, Queen** intercedes with king for cessation of extermination of Jews. [O.T.: Esther 7:8]

6. **Faerie Queene** gives a champion to people in trouble. [Br. Lit.: *Faerie Queene*]

7. **Jesus Christ** as savior of souls. [Christian Tradition: Jobes, 330]

8. **Moses** led his people out of bondage. [O.T.: Exodus]

9. **Noah** his ark was the vehicle for the salvation of all earthly creatures when God sent devastating flood. [O.T.: Genesis 6:14]

Sanctimony (See HYPOCRISY.)

Sanctuary (See REFUGE.)

605. SATIRE (See also COMEDY.)

1. *All in the Family* 1970s TV sitcom introduced social realism, discussing racism, sexism, religious bias, and politics. [Am. TV: *SJEPC*]

2. **Arbuthnot, Mr.** cliché expert who spoke exclusively in the clichés of each subject on which he was interviewed. [Am. Lit.: Frank Sullivan columns in *The New Yorker*]

3. **Barry, Dave (1947–)** humor writer of the Baby Boom generation provides contemporary social commentary. [Am. Lit.: *SJEPC*]

4. *Bloom County* Berkeley Breathed's comic strip ridiculed American culture, society, and politics in the 1980s; animal and human characters interacted as equals. [Am. Comics: *SJEPC*]

5. **Brooks, Mel (1926–)** over-the-top Jewish American writer, actor, and director created genre spoofs like *Blazing Saddles* (1973; westerns) and *History of the World, Part One* (1981; historical epics). [Am. Film: *SJEPC*]

6. *Clouds, The* attacks Socrates and his philosophy. [Gk. Drama: Haydn & Fuller, 144]

7. **Dickensian** like the novels of Charles Dickens (1812–1870), often satiric in depictions of human nature. [Br. Lit.: *ODA*]

8. *Doonesbury* comic strip by G.B. Trudeau; pokes fun at politics and the education system through the lives of various characters, including the President and Charles Doonesbury, a middle-aged, remarried father. [Am. Jour. Misc.; Comics Misc.]

9. *Frogs, The* lampoons the plays of Euripedes and his advanced thinking. [Gk. Drama: Haydn & Fuller, 276]

10. **Gilbert and Sullivan** [William Gilbert (1836–1911) and Arthur Sullivan (1842–1900)] wrote popular, satirical operettas noted for their wit and humor. [Br. Music: *FOF, MOD*]

11. *Joseph Andrews* satirizes the sentimentality of contemporary fiction. [Br. Lit.: Fielding *Joseph Andrews*]

12. *Knight of the Burning Pestle, The* play by Beaumont and Fletcher; burlesques the excesses of tales of chivalry. [Br. Drama: Haydn & Fuller, 399]

13. **Lardner, Ring (1885–1933)** leading satirist of 1920s; known for use of slang and first-person epistolary baseball stories about fictitious Jack Keefe, dimwitted Chicago White Sox pitcher. [Am. Lit.: *SJEPC*]

14. **M*A*S*H** medical farce on the horrors of war. [Am. Film and TV: Halliwell, 474]

15. *MAD* **magazine** take-offs on just about everything and exceptional graphic art. [Am. Jour.: *SJEPC*]

16. *Monty Python's Flying Circus* poked fun at institutions in skits like "the Ministry of Silly Walks;" British TV show of 1969–74 led the way for American late-night sketch comedy. [Br. TV: *SJEPC*]

17. *National Lampoon* Harvard humor magazine known for creativity and iconoclasm; spawned series of comedy films. [Am. Jour. and Film: *SJEPC*]

18. **Oliphant, Pat (1935–)** influential politcal cartoonist. [Am. Jour.: *SJEPC*]

19. **Paulsen, Pat (1928–1997)** TV comedian who ran mock campaigns for president five times between 1968 and 1996, satirically criticiz-

ing the opposition; claimed that he ran for those who wanted to vote "none of the above." [Am. TV: *SJEPC*]

20. *Pogo* comic strip rife with political satire. [Comics: Berger, 172]

21. *Praise of Folly, The* uses tongue-in-cheek praise to satirize contemporary customs, institutions, and beliefs. [Dutch Philos.: Erasmus *The Praise of Folly* in Haydn & Fuller, 607]

22. **Rabelais, Francois (c.1494–1553)** French satirist of the 16th century, whose bawdy comedy offended church and state. [Fr. Lit.: *Gargantua and Pantagruel*]

23. **Reed, Ishmael (1938–)** innovative satirist of many genres whose technique of Neo-HooDooism intermingles voodoo and other religious and cultural elements. [Am. Lit.: *SJEPC*]

24. **Sahl, Mort (1927–)** pioneer of political satire in stand-up comedy. [Am. Entertainment: *SJEPC*]

25. *Saturday Night Live* began in 1970s; late-night comedy variety show that spawned multitude of stars and classic skits; reinvented TV comedy with irreverent satire and boisterous nonsense. [Am. TV: *SJEPC*]

26. **Scourge of Princes** Pietro Aretino (1492–1556); wrote wicked satires on nobles and notables. [Ital. Lit.: Benét, 47]

27. *SCTV* Toronto company of Second City satirized television in TV show about a fictional television station, its staff and on-air talent; began in 1976 and ran for seven years. [Can.TV: *SJEPC*]

28. *Simpsons, The* begun in 1989; Matt Groening's animated family sitcom mixed wickedly satirical view of world issues with goofy humor; lovable bright-yellow characters muddle through the complexities of modern life. [Am. TV: *SJEPC*]

29. **Smothers Brothers, The** [Tom Smothers (1937–) and Dick Smothers (1938–)] musical duo who hosted influential comic variety TV show in late 1960s; their choice of anti-establishment satire and veiled references to sex and drugs brought confrontations with network and eventual cancellation of show. [Am. TV: *SJEPC*]

30. **Teufelsdröckh, Herr** fictitious professor, Carlyle's mouthpiece for criticism of Victorian life. [Br. Lit.: *Sartor Resartus*]

31. **Thurber, James (1894–1961)** through cartoon sketches and humorous prose, much for the *New Yorker* magazine, he depicted humans' struggles and lack of practical wisdom. [Am. Lit.: *SJEPC*]

32. *Troilus and Cressida* Homer's heroes are reduced in character and satirized. [Br. Drama: Shakespeare *Troilus and Cressida*]

33. *Ubu Roi* burlesques bourgeois values through outlandish political adventurism, including assassination, mock heroics, and buffoonery. [Fr. Drama: Alfred Jarry *Ubu Roi* in Benét, 1036]

34. **Yankovic, "Weird Al" (1959–)** using popular song melodies, creates tunes that closely resemble the originals and, with inventive, wacky lyrics, pokes fun at popular culture. [Am. Music: *SJEPC*]

35. **Zappa, Frank (1940–1993)** leader of 1960s freak band the Mothers of Invention and later solo career; inventive music, often irreverant satirical lyrics. [Am. Music: *SJEPC*]

36. *Zuleika Dobson* burlesques sentimental novels of the Edwardian era. [Br. Lit.: Magill II, 1169]

Savagery (See BRUTALITY.)

606. SCANDAL (See also CONTROVERSY.)

1. **Abelard, Peter (1079–c. 1144)** French theologian takes Hèloise, abbess, as lover; marries her in secret. [Fr. Hist.: *EB*, I: 18]

2. **Arbuckle, Fatty (1887–1933)** early Hollywood comic actor accused of actress's rape and murder during wild party in 1921. [Am. Hist.: *SJEPC*]

3. **Bakker, Jim (1940–), and Tammy Faye Bakker (1942–2007)** husband-and-wife televangelists with lavish lifestyle were involved in financial and moral scandals in the 1980s. [Am. Rel.: *SJEPC*]

4. **Black Sox Scandal** Chicago White Sox baseball players accused of taking bribes to lose the 1919 World Series. [Sports: *EB*, II: 66]

5. **Chappaquiddick** car driven by Senator Edward Kennedy plunges off bridge; woman companion dies (1969). [Am. Hist.: *Facts* (1969).]

6. **Edward VIII (1894–1972)** King of Britain whose decision to marry a divorcee forced him to abdicate throne (1936). [Br. Hist.: *NCE*, 835–836]

7. **Enron** American energy company; claimed huge revenues, which were later found to be bolstered by carefully planned accounting fraud. [Am. Business: Misc.]

8. **-gate** suffix that has become a term for a political scandal, from "Watergate." [Am. Hist. *FOF, MOD*]

9. **Iran Contra** despite an embargo and refusal by Congress to appropriate funds, President Ronald Reagan and his advisors sold arms to Iran in order to finance the Nicaraguan Contras, anticommunist insurgents. [Am. Hist.: *SJEPC*]

10. **Jackson, Michael (1958–)** brilliant pop composer and singer who began his career as a child of sensational talent; as an adult, eccentric lifestyle and dazzling stage performances kept him in the headlines; accusations of sexually molesting young boys disrupted his career. [Am. Music: *SJEPC*]

11. **Jackson, "Shoeless" Joe (1887–1951)** multifaceted talent as player; involved in 1919 Black Sox scandal and banned for life from

the sport; at trial, allegedly confronted by child who pleaded : "Say it ain't so, Joe." [Am. Sports: *SJEPC*]

12. **Lewinsky, Monica (1973–)** known for having affair while working in the White House with then-United States President Bill Clinton; resulted in a trial calling for Clinton's impeachment. [Am. Hist.: Misc.]

13. **McGwire, Mark (1963–)** allegations of muscle-building drugs tainted his home-run record of 1998. [Am. Sports: *SJEPC*]

14. **Milli Vanilli** 1989 Grammy award for Best New Artist was given to pop duo who lip-synched songs of a studio band. [Am. Music: *SJEPC*]

15. **Ponzi scheme** named for Charles Ponzi (1877–1949), American swindler who cheated unwitting investors looking to get rich quick out of millions; now a catchword for outrageous swindling. [Am. Business: *FOF, MOD*]

16. **PTL Club** TV ministry founded by Jim and Tammy Faye Bakker investigated for suspicious fund-raiding methods and fraudulent practices. [Am. Rel.: *SJEPC*]

17. **Savings and Loans Scandal** took place in 1980s and 1990s; created largest banking collapse since the Great Depression in 1929. [Am. Hist.: Misc.]

18. ***$64,000 Question, The*** game show discovered to be fixed (1958). [TV: Terrace, II, 295–296]

19. **South Sea Bubble** fraud is exposed in British South Sea Company (1720). [Br. Hist.: *EB*, IX: 383]

20. **Teapot Dome** government oil reserves fraudulently leased to private concerns (1922). [Am. Hist.: Flexner, 353]

21. **Watergate** scandals involving Nixon's administration (1972). [Am. Hist.: Kane, 460–462]

22. **Whitewater** real estate scandal involving Bill and Hilary Clinton that came out in 1993. [Am. Hist.: Misc.]

23. **WorldCom** American telecommunications company; doctored their books to make it seem that the company was growing and more profitable than it was. [Am. Business: Misc.]

Scapegoat (See DUPERY.)

607. SCIENCE FICTION (See also FANTASY, SPACE TRAVEL.)

1. *Alien* chilling drama featuring alien life forms aboard spaceship. [Am. Film: *SJEPC*]

2. *Amazing Stories* science fiction magazine established the genre. [Am. Jour.: *SJEPC*]

3. **Asimov, Isaac (1920–1992)** Russian-born author instrumental in establishing the genre of science fiction. [Am. Lit.: *SJEPC*]

4. *Blade Runner* dark 1982 film depicts bleak vision of the future in Los Angeles, where humans are hired to hunt and kill genetically designed replicant slaves trying to escape their fate. [Am. Film: *SJEPC*]

5. **Bradbury, Ray (1920–)** leading American science fiction writer with lyrical style; author of *The Martian Chronicles*, *The Illustrated Man*, and *Fahrenheit 451*. [Am. Lit.: *SJEPC*]

6. *Buck Rogers in the 25th Century* launched in 1929, comic strip featuring superhero space adventurer helped popularize science fiction. [Am. Comics: *SJEPC*]

7. **Clarke, Arthur C. (1917–2008)** venerable British science fiction writer's works emphasize scientific discovery, advanced technology, and human yearning to understand the universe; author of *2001: A Space Odyssey* (1968) and *Childhood's End* (1950). [Br. Lit.: *SJEPC*]

8. *Clockwork Orange, A* Stanley Kubrick's 1971 film based on Anthony Burgess's 1966 novel depicts a dystopian future state that seeks to crush free will and control individuals through behavior modification and other cruel techniques. [Am. Film: *SJEPC*]

9. **Crichton, Michael (1942–2009)** best-selling author with medical background; writes novels based on science and technology gone awry, such as *The Andromeda Strain* (1969), *The Terminal Man* (1972), and *Jurassic Park* (1990). [Am. Lit.: *SJEPC*]

10. **cyberpunk** subgenre of science fiction featuring computer technology-driven, online-networked worlds; originated in William Gibson's *Neuromancer* (1984). [Am. Lit.: *SJEPC*]

11. *Day the Earth Stood Still, The* early science fiction film about an alien (Klaatu) and his robot (Gort) visiting Earth with a warning and an ultimatum; influenced future movies in the genre (1951). [Am. Film: *SJEPC*]

12. **Dick, Philip K. (1928–1982)** novelist and short story writer's themes encompass artificial reality, authoritarian power, and dystopias; his novel *Do Androids Dream of Electric Sheep?* (1968) became the film *Bladerunner* (1982). [Am. Lit.: *SJEPC*]

13. *Doctor Who* long-running TV serial featuring time-traveling protagonist The Doctor has achieved cult status (original broadcasts, BBC, 1963–1989). [Br. TV: *SJEPC*]

14. **Ellison, Harlan (1934–)** contentious, prolific, award-winning short story writer of dark fantasies, including "Jeffty Is Five" (1977). [Am. Lit.: *SJEPC*]

15. **Gernsback, Hugo (1884–1967)** founded *Amazing Stories* (1926), the first magazine to feature science fiction; credited with establishing the science fiction genre. [Am. Lit.: *SJEPC*]

16. **Gibson, William (1948–)** novelist and short-story writer created cyberpunk subgenre of science fiction with *Neuromancer* in 1984; works deal with positive and negative aspects of technology and relationships on the Internet in cyberspace, a term he originated. [Am. Lit.: *SJEPC*]

17. **Heinlein, Robert (1907–1988)** influential American sci-fi writer whose best-known work is *Stranger in a Strange Land* (1961). [Am. Lit.: *EB*]

18. **Le Guin, Ursula K. (1929–)** renowned writer of science fiction and fantasy whose knowledge of anthropology influences her ability to create utterly believable alternate worlds; noteworthy titles include science-fiction classic *The Left Hand of Darkness* (1969). [Am. Lit.: *SJEPC*]

19. **Lucas, George (1944–)** American writer and film director; gained extraordinary fame when he created the science-fiction Star Wars saga. [Am. Film: Misc.]

20. *Neuromancer* William Gibson's first novel (1984); defined cyberspace and created the cyberpunk subgenre of science fiction; story about a dystopian world of the Sprawl; won Hugo Award, Philip K. Dick Memorial Award, and Nebula Award. [Am. Lit.: *SJEPC*]

21. *Outer Limits, The* mid-1960s television show, best known for imaginative monsters. [Am. TV: *SJEPC*]

22. *Planet of the Apes* science fiction film about futuristic Earth where humans are no longer dominant, but slaves of anthropomorphic apes. [Am. Film: *SJEPC*]

23. **Roddenberry, Gene (1921–1991)** creator of *Star Trek* television series; short, three-year run (1966–1969), but spawned host of TV shows, films, comics, books, conventions, and more. [Am. TV, , Pop. Culture: *SJEPC*]

24. **Serling, Rod (1924–1975)** author of scripts that brought quality drama to early TV; created and hosted *The Twilight Zone*, eerie science-fiction/fantasy series with serious themes and name actors. [Am. TV: *SJEPC*]

25. *Star Trek* short-lived late 1960s science-fiction television show depicting intergalactic travels of Spaceship Enterprise written by Gene Roddenberry; became a phenomenon; movies, books, clubs, conventions, memorabilia and a host of other offshoots followed. [Am. TV: *SJEPC*]

26. *Star Wars* influential 1977 George Lucas film employed unprecedented computer animation to depict outer space landscapes and battles while plot adhered to classic conflict between good and

evil; toys, games, books, etc. remain incredibly popular. [Am. Film: *SJEPC*]

27. ***Thing, The*** 1982 film about group of scientists in Antarctica stalked by alien that takes on its victim's identity; terrifying special effects and doom-laden plot have brought film a loyal following. [Am. Film: *SJEPC*]

28. **Trekkies** fans of *Star Trek* phenomenon; attend conventions, collect memorabilia, etc. [Am. Pop. Culture: *SJEPC*]

29. ***Twilight Zone, The*** influential TV series aired 1959–1964; employing outstanding writers and talented actors, creator Rod Serling used science fiction and fantasy format to pursue weighty themes otherwise ousted by TV executives and advertisers. [Am. TV: *SJEPC*]

30. ***2001: A Space Odyssey*** 1968 film by Stanley Kubrick based on story by Arthur C. Clarke; symbolic, without clear story line; confused many viewers, but stunned them with cinematic innovation and beauty, and visionary depiction of artificial intelligence. [Am. Film: *SJEPC*]

31. ***X-Files*** premiered in 1993; cashed in on America's fascination with the idea of alien encounters and government conspiracies to cover up extraterrestrial's sinister activities. [Am. TV: *SJEPC*]

608. SEA

1. **Aegir** god of the seas. [Norse Myth.: Brewer *Dictionary*, 12]

2. **Amphitrite** queen of the sea; Poseidon's wife. [Gk. Myth.: *NCE*, 94]

3. **Bowditch** standard navigational work, *American Practical Navigator*; so called form its compiler, Nathaniel Bowditch. [Am. Hist.: Hart, 97]

4. **Clement the First, Saint** drowned bound to anchor; invoked in marine dedications. [Christian Hagiog.: Attwater, 88]

5. **Cousteau, Jacques (1910–1997)** pioneering French undersea explorer and commander of research ship *The Calypso*; introduced the marine world to millions through his film documentaries, books, and TV programs. [Fr. Science: *SJEPC*]

6. **Cuchulain** mad with grief, he battles the sea. [Irish Myth.: Benét, 239]

7. **Dylan** god of waves, which continually mourn him. [Celtic Myth.: Leach, 332; Jobes, 480]

8. **Jones, Davy** personification of the ocean. [Br.and Am. Marine Slang: Leach, 298]

9. **Manannan** Irish god of the sea. [Irish Folklore: Briggs, 280]

10. **mermaid** half-woman, half-fish; seen by sailors. [Western Folklore: Misc.]

11. **Nereids** fifty daughters of Nereus; attendants of Poseidon. [Gk. Myth.: Zimmerman, 174]

12. **Nereus** son of Oceanus; father of the Nereids. [Gk. Myth.: Zimmerman, 174; Gk. Lit.: *Aeneid*]

13. **Njorthr** Scandinavian god; protector of sailors and ships. [Norse Myth.: Brewer *Dictionary*, 760]

14. **Oceanids** three thousand daughters of Oceanus and Tethys. [Gk. Myth.: Zimmerman, 178]

15. **Oceanus** Titan and father of the river gods and Oceanids. [Gk. Myth.: Zimmerman, 178]

16. **Poseidon** god of the oceans and all waters; Neptune to the Romans. [Gk. Myth.: Wheeler, 257]

17. **Salacia** consort of Neptune and goddess of springs. [Rom. Myth.: Kravitz, 208]

18. **Tethys** goddess-wife of Oceanus. [Gk. Myth.: Brewer *Dictionary*, 1070]

19. **Thetis** sea deity and mother of Achilles. [Gk. Myth.: Zimmerman, 269; Gk. Lit.: *Odyssey*]

20. **Tiamat** premieval sea represented as a dragon goddess, mother of all the gods. [Babylonian Myth.: Benét, 1007]

21. **trident** three-pronged fork; attribute of Poseidon. [Gk. Myth.: Hall, 309]

22. **Triton** gigantic sea deity; son and messenger of Poseidon. [Gk. Myth.: Zimmerman, 277]

23. **Varuna** god over the waters. [Vedic Myth.: Leach, 1155]

Season (See AUTUMN, SPRING, SUMMER, WINTER.)

609. SEDUCTION (See also FLIRTATION.)

1. **Armida** modern Circe; sorceress who seduces Rinaldo. [Ital. Lit.: *Jerusalem Delivered*]

2. **Aurelius** Dorigen's nobleminded would-be seducer. [Br. Lit.: *Canterbury Tales*, "The Franklin's Tale"]

3. **Bara, Theda (1885?-1955)** silent movie star vamp entrapped men with her exotic sex appeal. [Am. Film: *SJEPC*]

4. **Bathsheba** Uriah's wife, seduced by King David. [O.T.: II Samuel 11:4]

5. **Bond, James** suave, sophisticated, and virile secret agent 007 of Ian Fleming's spy novels seduced beautiful women. [Br. Lit.: *SJEPC*]

6. **Casanova, Giovanni Jacopo (1725–1798)** myriad amours made his name synonymous with philanderer. [Ital. Hist.: Benet, 172]

7. **Circe** enchantress who turned Odysseus's men into swine; byword for irresistibly fascinating woman. [Gk. Lit.: *Odyssey*; Rom. Lit.: *Aeneid*]

669

8. **de Hautdesert, Lady** tries to seduce Gawain to test his faithfulness. [Br. Lit.: *Sir Gawain and the Green Knight*]

9. **Delilah** fascinating and deceitful mistress of Samson. [O.T.: Judges 16]

10. **Dragon Lady** beautiful Chinese temptress. [Comics: "Terry and the Pirates" in Horn, 653]

11. **Europa** seduced by Zeus in form of a white bull. [Gk. Myth.: Kravitz, 96]

12. **Frederick's of Hollywood** lingerie company known for innovative, seductive undergarments that reproportion women's anatomy to produce curves, contours, and cleavage. [Am. Culture: *SJEPC*]

13. **Harlowe, Clarissa** seduced and raped by Lovelace. [Br. Lit.: Richardson *Clarissa Harlowe* in Benét, 203]

14. **Io** seduced by Jupiter in form of a cloud. [Rom. Myth.: *Metamorphoses*]

15. **Juan, Don** handsome Spanish lad seduces many women. [Eur. Legend: Benét, 279]

16. **Leucosia, Ligeia, and Parthenope** sirens; tried to lure Odysseus and his men to destruction. [Gk. Lit.: *Odyssey*]

17. **Little Em'ly** though engaged to Ham, is seduced and runs off with Steerforth. [Br. Lit.: Dickens *David Copperfield*]

18. **Lorelei** siren; lured ships to destruction with singing. [Ger. Folklore: Benét, 599]

19. **Mirandolina** innkeeper artfully seduces misogynist for sport. [Ital. Lit.: *The Mistress of the Inn*]

20. **Rustico** convinces Alibech that the way to serve God is by sexual intercourse. [Ital. Lit.: Boccaccio *Decameron*]

21. **Sorrel, Hetty** seduced by Arthur Donnithorne. [Br. Lit.: *Adam Bede*]

22. **Victoria's Secret** began in the early 1980s; retail chain selling sexy lingerie for women in upscale boutique mall stores. [Am. Business: *SJEPC*]

23. **White, Stanford (1853–1906)** famous architect killed by jealous husband of his mistress in 1906; seduced numerous women with invitation to "come up and see my etchings," the pick-up line he coined. [Am. Architecture: *SJEPC*]

610. SELF-IMPROVEMENT (See also GUIDANCE.)

1. **Brothers, Dr. Joyce (1928–)** media-savvy psychologist has dispensed advice on radio and television, and in newspapers and books, since the late 1950s; first gained fame through appearance

on TV quiz show *The $64,000 Question* (1955). [Am. Culture: *SJEPC*]

2. **Carnegie, Dale (1888–1955)** author of phenomenally popular *How to Win Friends and Influence People* and courses devoted to self-improvement. [Am. Culture: *FOF, MOD*]

3. **Covey, Stephen (1932–)** self-help consultant rose to prominence in 1980s-1990s corporate and mainstreet America with his common-sense philosophy as found in *The 7 Habits of Highly Effective People* (1989) and *The 7 Habits of Highly Effective Families* (1997). [Am. Business and Culture: *SJEPC*]

4. **Dyer, Wayne (1940–)** motivational speaker/author with positive "can-do" message wrote bestseller *Your Erroneous Zones* (1976. [Am. Culture: *SJEPC*]

5. **jihad** Arabic word for struggle; term used to decribe Muslims' struggle against their own weaknesses to improve themselves and their communities. [Islam: *UIMT*, 430]

6. **McGraw, Dr. Phil (1950–)** highly popular psychologist and TV personality; came into public view on *Oprah*; weekly appearances led to his own TV show; doling out advice with frankness and judgmental style that some have criticized as too simplistic and insulting; others are drawn to it. [Am. TV: Misc.]

7. ***Purpose Driven Life, The*** Dr. Rick Warren's 2002 best-selling motivational book which claims that God has 5 purposes for humans (Worship, Fellowship, Discipleship, Ministry, and Mission); reader is called to find own reason for existence according to God's plan. [Am. Lit.: Misc.]

8. **Schlessinger, Dr. Laura (1947–)** firm believer in personal responsibility; blunt personality and strict definition of morality has made her controversial; millions listen to her radio show and read her syndicated newspaper column and books. [Am. Culture: *SJEPC*]

9. ***7 Habits of Highly Effective People, The*** landmark self-help book by Stephen Covey used in corporate training seminars to improve the efficiency and morale of managers and employees (1989). [Am. Business: *SJEPC*]

10. **Warren, Dr. Rick (1954–)** vastly influential writer and evangelical leader; senior pastor of Saddleback Church in California with 22,000–member congregation; author of best-selling *The Purpose Driven Life* (2002) about finding one's calling according to God's plan. [Am. Rel.: Misc.]

11. **Winfrey, Oprah (1954–)** her TV talk show began in 1985; often focuses on well-being—physical, emotional, psychological, and spiritual. [Am. TV: *SJEPC*]

12. *Your Erroneous Zones* bestselling self-help book by Wayne Dyer based on his upbeat motivational lectures (1976). [Am. Publishing: *SJEPC*]

Selfishness (See CONCEIT, MISERLINESS.)

611. SELF-SACRIFICE (See also MARTYRDOM, SACRIFICE, SUICIDE.)

1. **Aïda** dies with her beloved Radames. [Ital. Opera: Verdi, *Aïda*, Westerman, 325]

2. **Alcestis** offered self up to die in the stead of Admetus. [Gk. Myth.: Leach, 11]

3. **Anderson, Parson** self-sacrificing captain of New England rebels. [Br. Lit.: Shaw *The Devil's Disciple* in Benét, 267]

4. **Arden, Enoch** returned castaway; keeps identity secret from wife to preserve her "new life" happiness. [Br. Lit.: *Enoch Arden*]

5. **Aslan** huge golden lion symbolic of Christ who appears in C.S. Lewis's Narnia tales; suffers as Christ did, and rises from the dead. [Br. Children's Lit.: Jones]

6. **Benedetto** monk gives up everything to serve others and reform the Church. [Ital. Lit.: *The Saint* in Magill II, 929]

7. **Brooke, Dorothea** gives up Casaubon's fortune for Ladislaw's affection. [Br. Lit.: *Middlemarch*, Magill I, 588–591]

8. **Burghers of Calais** they sacrificed themselves to save city from British siege after Battle of Crécy (1346). [Fr. Hist.: *EB*, II: 447]

9. **Camille** gives up Armand so as not to endanger his career. [Fr. Lit.: *La Dame aux Camélias]*

10. **Carton, Sydney** allows himself to be guillotined in place of Charles Darnay. [Br. Lit.: Dickens *A Tale of Two Cities*]

11. **Cavatica, Charlotte A.** protagonist from E. B. White's children's book *Charlotte's Web*; very knowledgable large gray spider whose web words convince the humans not to slaughter her friend Wilbur the pig; after she has succeeded and has laid her eggs, she dies. [Am. Children's Lit.: Jones]

12. **Colamartini, Christina** dies in wilderness attempting to help Paolo. [Ital. Lit.: *Bread and Wine*]

13. **Cratchit, Bob** ill-paid clerk; uncomplainingly supports large family. [Br. Lit.: *A Christmas Carol*]

14. **Damien, Father (1840–1889)** Belgian Catholic missionary who founded a leper colony on the Hawaiian island of Molokai; he contracted leprosy and died there. [Eur. Hist.: *ODA*]

15. **de Bergerac, Cyrano** composed eloquent love letters for another. [Fr. Lit.: *Cyrano de Bergerac*]

16. **de Posa, Marquis** clears prince's name in conspiracy by indicting himself. [Ger. Lit.: *Don Carlos*]

17. ***Deputy, The*** Father Fontana accompanies deported Jews to Auschwitz and dies with them in the gas chambers. [Ger. Drama: Weiss, 124]

18. **Din, Gunga** water-carrier killed as he rescues narrator of story. [Br. Lit.: "Gunga Din" in Benét, 430]

19. **Dounia** intends to marry Svidrigailov to relieve her brother's poverty. [Russ. Lit.: *Crime and Punishment*]

20. **Dudgeon, Dick** to save rebel leader Parson Anderson from the gallows, the reprobate Dudgeon allows himself to be arrested and sentenced to death. [Br. Drama: Shaw *The Devil's Disciple* in Benét, 267]

21. **Eponine** during fight, gives his life to save Marius. [Fr. Lit.: *Les Misèrables*]

22. **Fantine** woman becomes prostitute to support daughter. [Fr. Lit.: *Les Misèrables*]

23. **fasting** common practice in most religions as method of sacrifice and atonement, as in Christian Lent and Islamic Ramadan. [Religion: Bowker]

24. ***Gift of the Magi, The*** husband and wife each give up own treasure to buy the other's Christmas present. [Am. Lit.: "The Gift of the Magi" in Benét, 395]

25. **Gilda** sacrifices self to save her beloved Duke's life. [Ital. Opera: Verdi, *Rigoletto*, Westerman, 300]

26. **Grieux, des** accompanies banished Manon to exile in Louisiana. [Fr. Lit.: *Manon Lescaut*]

27. **Hansa, Per** dies in storm on errand of mercy. [Nor. Lit.: *Giants in the Earth*, Magill I, 303–304]

28. **innkeeper's daughter** Highwayman's sweetheart; shoots herself to help him avoid capture. [Br. Poetry: Noyes "The Highwayman"]

29. **Jephthah's daugher** accepts father's vow to God to die in exhange for his victory. [O.T.: Judges 11:30–40]

30. **Jesus Christ** died on cross to save mankind. [N.T.: Matthew 27:24–61]

31. **Jordan, Robert** young American teacher in Spain who gives his life helping the Loyalist guerillas. [Am. Lit.: Hemingway *For Whom the Bell Tolls*]

32. **Kamikaze** WWII Japanese suicide pilots; embodiment of "death before dishonor." [Jap. Hist.: Fuller, III, 618–619]

33. **little mermaid, the** sacrifices her own life to save her beloved prince. [Dan. Lit.: *Andersen's Fairy Tales*]

34. **Madeleine** executed her lover Andrea. [Ital. Opera: Girodano, *Andrea Chénier*, Westerman, 370–371]

35. **Mother Teresa (1910–1997)** Roman Catholic missionary, nun, and Nobel laureate; ministered to the poor and dying of Calcutta for decades; a symbol of selflessness and giving. [Religion: *ODA*]

36. **Myshkin, Prince** his desire for martyrdom makes him willing to marry a neurotic woman of easy virtue. [Russ. Lit.: Dostoevsky *The Idiot*]

37. **Norma** priestess betrays her vows and sacrifices herself in atonement. [Ital. Opera: Bellini *Norma* in Benét, 720]

38. **Oakhurst, John** kills himself so that three other outcasts may survive. [Am. Lit.: *The Outcasts of Poker Flat*]

39. **Ona** becomes a prostitute to support family. [Am. Lit.: *The Jungle*]

40. **pelican** tears open breast to feed young. [Christian Symbolism: de Bles, 29]

41. **Rieux, Dr. Bernard** remains in Algeria to care for plague victims and loses his wife to it. [Fr. Lit.: Albert Camus *The Plague*]

42. **Susanin, Ivan** leads Poles astray to safeguard tsar; executed. [Russ. Opera: Glinka, *A Life ofr the Tsar*, Westerman, 379]

43. **Violetta** courtesan renounces her lover in order to save his family from scandal. [Ital. Opera: Verdi *La Traviata* in Benét, 1022]

Sensuality (See BEAUTY, SENSUAL.)

612. SENTIMENTALITY

1. **"As Time Goes By"** signature song in *Casablanca* (1942); alludes to star-crossed love of Rick and Ilsa. [Am. Music: *SJEPC*]

2. *Bridges of Madison County, The* maudlin story of passion and regret featuring an illicit, discreet love affair between a middle-aged married mother and a world-travelling photographer in a small Iowa town (1992). [Am. Lit.: *SJEPC*]

3. **Checkers** dog given as gift to Nixon; used in his defense of political contributions during presidential campaign (1952). [Am. Hist.: Wallechinsky, 126]

4. *City Lights* Charlie Chaplin's finest silent film centers on the sentimental love story of a blind woman who sells flowers and mistakes the smitten Little Tramp for a millionaire (1931). [Am. Film: *SJEPC*]

5. **Dickensian** like the novels of Charles Dickens (1812–1870), often sentimental in tone and characterization [Br. Lit.: *ODA*]

6. **Disney, Walt (1901–1966)** American producer of films and cartoons, often sentimental in tone. [Pop. Cult. *FOF MOD*]

7. **Dondi** comic strip in which sentimentality is the main motif. [Comics: Horn, 217–218]

8.   **Fauntleroy, Little Lord** impossibly kind and unselfish child is loved by all and reforms selfish grandfather. [Am. Lit.: Benét, 591]

9.   *Five Little Peppers* saccharine story of five orphans. [Am. Lit.: Harriet Lothrop *Five Little Peppers and How They Grew* in Hart, 495]

10. **Goody Two Shoes** mawkish girl, overpleased to have two shoes, exclaims her fortune to all. [Nurs. Rhyme: "Little Goody Two Shoes" in Barnhart, 502]

11. **Hardy, Andy** protagonist of 1930s series of sentimental "family" movies. [Am. Cinema: Griffith, 300]

12. **Little Nell** death scene of sweet child epitomizes sentimentality. [Br. Lit.: *Old Curiosity Shop*]

13. **Mannilow, Barry (1946–)** singer/composer of melodic, romantic pop standards. [Am. Music: *SJEPC*]

14. **Mary Magdalene** portrayed traditionally in art as weeping; whence, *maudlin*. [Art.: Misc.]

15. **"Moon River"** sentimental theme song from *Breakfast at Tiffany's* (1961) written by Henry Mancini and Johnny Mercer. [Am. Music: *SJPEC*]

16. **Orsino** plays role of languishing lover. [Br. Lit.: *Twelfth Night*]

17. **Sentimental Tommy** forever playing the hero, he fails to be the faithful lover and husband of his adoring Grizel. [Br. Lit.: J.M. Barrie *Sentimental Tommy* in Benét, 914]

18. **sob sister** journalist who handles advice to lovelorn column. [Am. Journalism: Brewer *Dictionary*, 1016]

19. **"Sweet Adeline"** tune of a man's former romance, usually sung in barbershop harmony. [Am. Music: Hart, 823]

20. *Waltons, The* television show of depression-era America softened by nostalgia. [TV: Terrace, II, 418–419]

21. **Werther** artisitic young man whose ultra-romantic life is filled with hopeless passions. [Ger. Lit.: *The Sorrows of Young Werther* in Magil I, 915]

613. SERVANT (See also BUTLER.)

1.   **Abigail** helpmeet of King David; traditional name for handmaiden. [O.T.: I Samuel 25]

2.   **Albert** popular servant's name; assistant, manservant, page-boy. [Br. Lit.: *Loving*; *By the Pricking of My Thumbs*; *A Damsel in Distress*]

3.   **Brighella** prototype of interfering servant; meddles and gossips. [Ital. Drama: Walsh *Classical*, 62]

4.   **Despina** her stratagems control and resolve the plot. [Ital. Opera: Mozart, *Cosi fan tutte*, Scholes, 259]

5.   **Figaro** valet who outwits everyone by his cunning. [Fr. Lit.: *Marriage of Figaro*]

6. **Friday** young Indian rescued by Crusoe and kept as servant and companion. [Br. Lit.: *Robinson Crusoe*]

7. **Ganymede** mortal lad, taken by Zeus to be cupbearer to the gods. [Gk. Myth.: Howe, 106]

8. **golem** automaton homunculus performs duties not permissible for Jews. [Jew. Legend: Jobes, 674]

9. **Hazel** meddling maid in the Baxter house. [TV and Comics: Terrace, I, 343]

10. **Hebe** cupbearer to the gods; succeeded by Ganymede. [Gk. Myth.: Zimmerman, 117]

11. **Ithamore** purchased by Barabas to betray Governor of Malta. [Br. Drama: *The Jew of Malta*]

12. **Jeeves** loyal and brilliant English valet of Wodehouse stories. [Br. Lit.: *NCE*, 2997]

13. **Lichas** Hercules's attendant; unknowingly delivers poisoned robe to him. [Rom. Lit.: *Metamorphoses*]

14. **Notburga, Saint** Bavarian patroness of domestics; beneficent, though poor. [Christian Hagiog.: Attwater, 257]

15. **Passepartout** Phileas Fogg's rash valet. [Fr. Lit.: *Around the World in Eighty Days*]

16. **Thing** Addams family servant; a disembodied right hand. [TV: "The Addams Family" in Terrace, I, 29]

17. **Xanthias** carries Bacchus's heavy bundles. [Gk. Lit.: *The Frogs*]

18. **Zita, Saint** devout and generous domestic; patron saint. [Christian Hagiog.: Attwater, 348]

614. SEWING and WEAVING

1. **Arachne** skilled weaver; changed into spider for challenging Athena to weaving contest. [Gk. Myth.: Zimmerman, 27]

2. **Athena** goddess of spinning and weaving. [Gk. Myth.: Howe, 45]

3. **Marner, Silas** hand-loom weaver who comes, friendless, to Raveloe. [Br. Lit.: Benét, 930]

4. **Penelope** weaves shroud for 20 years, unraveling it each night. [Gk. Lit.: *Odyssey*]

5. **Prynne, Hester** ostracized, sewing becomes her daily preoccupation. [Am. Lit.: *The Scarlet Letter*]

6. **Rumpelstiltskin** dwarf who spun gold from straw to help imprisoned girl. [Ger. Fairy Tale: *Rumpelstiltskin*]

7. *Weavers, The* depicts plight of Silesian weavers. [Ger. Lit.: Benét, 1078]

615. SEX SYMBOL (See also BEAUTY, SENSUAL; BUXOMNESS.)

1. **Anderson, Pamela (1967–)** well-endowed actress played "Tool Time girl" on *Home Improvement* and scantily clad lifeguard on *Baywatch*. [Am. TV: *SJEPC*]

2. **Bow, Clara (1905–1965)** "It Girl"; Jazz Age icon and Hollywood sex symbol epitomized bold, spirited flapper persona. [Am. Culture: *SJEPC*]

3. *Charlie's Angels* 1970s TV show featured three sexy, often scantily clad, women detectives. [Am. TV: *SJEPC*]

4. **Conrad** dazzling, sexually irresistible pirate, typical Byronic hero. [Br. Lit.: Byron *The Corsair* in Benét, 226]

5. **Dallas Cowboys Cheerleaders** sexy cheerleading squad for America's Team has provided high-energy halftime entertainment since the mid-1970s. [Am. Sports: *SJEPC*]

6. **Dietrich, Marlene (1901–1922)** beautiful German actress, played the femme fatale in such films as *The Blue Angel*. [Am. Film: *FOF, MOD*]

7. **Duke, Daisy** sexy Southern backwoods character of *The Dukes of Hazzard* TV show (1979–85); wore tight denim cut-off shorts. [Am. TV: *SJEPC*]

8. **Fabio (1961–)** bare-chested model with rippling muscles and long, straight, blond hair graced romance novel covers in 1980s; Italian-born sex symbol branched out into acting and writing. [Pop. Culture: *SJEPC*]

9. **Fawcett, Farrah (1947–)** sexy blonde actress with tousled, feathered hair starred in TV's *Charlie's Angels*; became pin-up girl in late 1970s with best-selling poster featuring her swimsuited image and wide grin. [Am. TV and Culture: *SJEPC*]

10. **Gardner, Ava (1922–1990)** exotic, seductive brunette film actress known for passionate love affairs offscreen and high-profile marriages to actor Mickey Rooney, bandleader Artie Shaw, and singer Frank Sinatra. [Am. Film: *SJEPC*]

11. **Grable, Betty (1916–1973)** All-American pin-up girl graced the barracks of American GIs during World War II; gazed seductively over her shoulder, wearing a swimsuit and showing off her famous legs. [Am. Pop. Culture: *SJEPC*]

12. **Harlow, Jean (1911–1937)** American film actress of the 1930s; nicknamed the "Platinum Blonde" and "Blonde Bombshell" for her striking blonde hair. [Am. Film: Misc.]

13. **Hayworth, Rita (1918–1987)** beautiful actress and favorite pinup for World War II GIs; seductive role in *Gilda* (1946) made her known as "the Love Goddess." [Am. Film: *EB*]

14. **Jones, Tom (1940–)** Welsh singer with long and diverse career; known in 1960s for his sexy stage performances where female fans swooned and threw their underwear onstage. [Welsh Music: *SJEPC*]

15. **Lace, Miss** 1940s armed forces' pin-up girl from comic strip. [Comics: "Male Call" in Horn, 475]

16. **Mansfield, Jayne (1933–1967)** well-documented hourglass figure and obsession with pink were part of her self-promotion as a sex symbol. [Am. Entertainment: *SJEPC*]

17. **Monroe, Marilyn (1926–1962)** voluptuous blonde film star became perhaps the most famous sex-symbol and icon of beauty in modern times. [Am. Film: *SJEPC*]

18. **Morrison, Jim (1943–1971)** mystically alluring, sexually charged lead singer of The Doors (1960s). [Am. Music: *SJEPC*]

19. **Peel, Emma** capable, intelligent, sexy spy on British TV series *The Avengers*. [Br. TV: *SJEPC*]

20. **Petty girl** airbrushed beauty, scantily clad in *Esquire* magazine pages. [Am. Lit.: Misc.]

21. *Sports Illustrated* weekly magazine devoted entirely to sports whose mid-winter swimsuit issue with sexy models has brought admiration and condemnation. [Am. Jour.: *SJEPC*]

22. *10* fantasy of the ideal female sex object. [Am. Cinema: "10"]

23. **Turner, Lana (1920–1995)** nicknamed the "Sweater Girl" because of her full figure; popular sexy blonde actress best known for her roles in *The Postman Always Rings Twice* (1946) and *Peyton Place* (1957). [Am. Film: *SJEPC*]

24. **Valentino, Rudolph (1895–1926)** sexy and suave actor of silent films, wildly popular with female fans, who mobbed him at appearances; *The Shiek* (1921) made him a star. [Am. Film: *SJEPC*]

25. **Vargas girl** drawn by Alberto Vargas; curvaceous women became favorite WWII pin-ups; later appeared in *Esquire* magazine, then in *Playboy*. [Am. Pop. Culture: *SJEPC*]

26. **West, Mae (1893–1980)** her suggestive dialogue, vampy acting style, and voluptuous figure made her a legend; many of her quips have become famous. [Am. Film: *SJEPC*]

616. SEXUALITY

1. **Cosmo Girl** young, single, sexually liberated woman of independent means as portrayed in women's magazine *Cosmopolitan*. [Am. Jour. and Culture: *SJEPC*]

2. *Cosmopolitan* women's magazine rooted in sexual revolution of the 1960s; focuses on sexual issues and self-improvement; covers

feature vampy models wearing cleavage-revealing fashions. [Am. Jour.: *SJEPC*]

3. **drive-in theater** watching movies outdoors in the privacy of one's own car provided haven for teenage sexual activity, particularly in the 1940s-1970s. [Am. Entertainment: *SJEPC*]

4. *Flowers of Evil, The* thoroughly explores the possiblities of vice, depravity, and sin. [Fr. Poetry: Bauedelaire *The Flowers of Evil* in Magill III, 399]

5. **Freud, Sigmund (1856–1939)** Austrian physician and founder of psychoanalysis; his theories stressed the importance of sex on human behavior. [Science and Culture: Misc.]

6. **Freudian slip** an actionor verbal expression that is result of unconscious reasons; referring to the theories of Sigmund Freud. [Pop. Culture: Misc.]

7. **Hefner, Hugh (1926–)** American publisher and founder of *Playboy* magazine, which promoted permissive sexual behavior. [Pop. Culture: *FOF, MOD*]

8. **Hite Report** in several publications, Shere Hite published results of surveys documenting first women's, then men's, sexual attitudes and practices. [Am. Pop. Culture: Misc.]

9. **Hite, Shere (1942–)** social researcher and historian noted for her "Hite Report" series of books surveying sexual behavior. [Am. Culture: *EB*]

10. *Hustler* controversial sex magazine created by Larry Flynt; symbol of raunchiness, defiance of decency standards. [Am. Jour. And Culture: Misc.]

11. *Ideal Marriage* Van de Velde study of the physiology and technique of marital sex. [Pop. Culture: Misc.]

12. **Ishtar** Babylonian goddess of sexual love and fertility. [Babyl. Myth: *ODA*]

13. *Joy of Sex, The* 1972 "lovemaking manual" by British gerontologist Dr. Alex Comfort; paved way to more lighthearted approach to sex; faced controversy for frankness and disparagement of same-sex relations. [Pop. Culture: Dr. Alex Comfort *The Joy of Sex* in Weiss, 239; *SJEPC*]

14. **Kinsey reports** pioneer explorations of sexual behavior based on interviews with 10,000 men and women. [Am. Culture.: *SJEPC*]

15. **Kinsey, Dr. Alfred C. (1894–1956)** founder of Institute for Sex Research at Indiana Univeristy; published reports on all aspects of sex lives of human male (1948) and human female (1952), devoid of moral judgment; overt treatment of previously taboo topics was controversial. [Am. Culture: *SJEPC*]

16. *Lady Chatterley's Lover* written in the late 1920s but not published in full text until 1959; D.H. Lawrence's novel about passionate affair faced obscenity charges because of use of taboo sexual terms and graphic descriptions of intercourse. [Br. Lit.: Misc.]

17. **Lawrence, David Herbert (1885–1930)** poet and novelist known for works that are very sensual and passionate; controversy surrounded some of his work because of their sexual content, notably *Lady Chatterley's Lover*, which was the subject of legal battle over its publication. [Br. Lit.: Misc.]

18. **Madonna (1958–)** overtly sexual performances, videos, and book played out her "Boy Toy" image. [Am. Music: *SJEPC*]

19. **Masters and Johnson** published a study of sexual performance under laboratory conditions. [Sexology: Masters and Johnson *Human Sexual Response* in Weiss, 214]

20. **Miller, Henry (1891–1980)** beginning with *Tropic of Cancer* (1934), wrote early sexually-explicit novels. [Am. Lit.: *SJEPC*]

21. **Morel, Paul** his Oedipus complex makes erotic fulfillment impossible. [Br. Lit.: D.H. Lawrence *Sons and Lovers* in Magill I, 913]

22. **Portnoy** sex-obsessed, neurotic central character of Philip Roth's 1969 novel. [Am. Lit.: Philip Roth *Portnoy's Complaint*]

23. *Portnoy's Complaint* In Philip Roth's 1969 satiric novel, a Jewish man who presents a highly moral exterior uses obscenity and promiscuous sexual behavior in his private life to rebel against his upbringing and the gentile society in which he lives. [Am. Lit.: Harris *Characters*, 343–44]

24. *Psychology of Sex, The* seven-volume Ellis work revolutionized attitudes toward sex and sexual problems. [Pop. Culture: Misc.]

25. *Sassy* 1988 magazine that approached teenaged females with information about sexual acitivity unlike other magazines of the time. [Am. Jour.: *SJEPC*]

26. *Sex and the City* popular television show featuring modern sexual mores and relationships among four New York women. [Am. TV: Misc.]

27. *Sex and the Single Girl* Helen Gurley Brown's 1962 controversial book for women about decorating, fashion, dating, cooking, and—shockingly—the joys of being single and sexually active. [Am. Lit.: *SJEPC*]

617. SHEPHERD

1. **Corin** the faithful shepherdess; called "the Virgin of the Grove." [Br. Lit.: "The Faithful Shepherdess" in Brewer *Handbook*, 234]

2. **Daphnis** guards sheep; creator of bucolic poetry. [Gk. Myth.: Kravitz, 75]

3. **Jabal** father of herdsmen. [O.T.: Genesis 4:20]

4. **Jesus Christ** the Good Shepherd. [N.T.: John 10:11–14]

5. **Little Bo-peep** young shepherdess; searches everywhere for lost flock. [Nurs. Rhyme: Opie, 93]

6. **Little Boy Blue** asleep while his sheep are in the field. [Nurs. Rhyme: Baring-Gould, 46]

618. SHINTO (See also RELIGION.)

1. **haiden** front building of Shinto shrine complex; used as hall of worship or oratory. [Shinto Rel.: Bowker]

2. **hara-kiri** Shinto or Zen act of mastery over death by cutting into the body beneath the abdomen, which is thought to be the center of life and control. [Shinto Rel.: Bowker]

3. **kami** sacred life-powers venerated by Japanese and represented in Shinto shrines as objects of worship; any form of existence that has awe-inspiring quality. [Shinto Rel.: Bowker]

4. **kamidana** altar or high shelf for enshrining kami in house of Shintoist. [Shinto Rel.: Bowker]

5. **karma** driving force behind cycle of reincarnation; every action has a consequence which will come to fruition in this, or a future, life. [Shinto Rel.: Bowker]

6. **matsuri** Japanese festivals, often to serve the kami; in modern times, sometimes strictly commercial or civil celebrations. [Shinto Rel.: Bowker]

7. **norito** sacred words and prayers expressed in elegant ancient Japanese, addressing the kami in worship. [Shinto Rel.: Bowker]

8. **samsara** cycle of birth and death as a consequence of action (karma). [Shinto Rel.: Bowker]

9. **shinsen** food offerings made to kami as part of matsuri; offered as token of gratitude. [Shinto Rel.: Bowker]

10. **shintai** symbol of kami or object in which kami resides; used as object of worship in shrine; often a mirror. [Shinto Rel.: Bowker]

619. SHIPWRECK (See also CASTAWAY.)

1. *Edmund Fitzgerald* American lake freighter; on November 10, 1975 during a Lake Superior storm, the ship sank without sending out any distress signals; all of the crew died. [Am. Hist.: Misc.]

2. **Spens, Sir Patrick** sets sail in a deadly storm, his ship founders, and he is drowned with his crew. [Scot. Balladry: *Sir Patrick Spens* in Benét, 935]

3. *Tempest, The* ship bearing the King of Naples and his company is wrecked near Prospero's island. [Br. Drama: Shakespeare *The Tempest*]

4. *Titanic* seemingly invincible British luxury ocean liner astonished the world when it collided with an iceberg on its maiden voyage in 1912 and sank, killing over 1500 passengers and crew. [Br. Hist.: *SJEPC*]

620. SHREWISHNESS (See also IRASCIBILITY.)

1. **Caudle, Mrs. Margaret** nagging, complaining wife. [Br. Lit.: *The Curtain Lectures*, Walsh *Modern*, 90]

2. **Dollallolla, Queen** King Arthur's wife, and even he feared her; too much virago towards her husband. [Br. Lit.: *Tom Thumb the Great*]

3. **farmer's wife** makes hell too hot even for the devil, who sends her back home. [Am. Balladry: "The Devil and the Farmer's Wife"]

4. **Frome, Zenobia** Ethan Frome's hypochondriacal, nagging, belittling wife. [Am. Lit.: *Ethan Frome*]

5. **Galatea** 19th-century version: nags Pygmalion. [Aust. Operetta: von Suppé, *Beautiful Galatea*, Westerman, 285]

6. **Gargery, Mrs.** vixenish wife; keeps husband in thrall. [Br. Lit.: *Great Expectations*]

7. **Katherine** "intolerably crust and shrewd and forward." [Br. Lit.: *The Taming of the Shrew*]

8. **Lisa, Dame** Jurgen's petulant wife taken from him in gratitude by the Prince of Darkness. [Am. Lit.: *Jurgen* in Magill I, 464]

9. **MacStinger, Mrs.** widow; miserable to everyone. [Br. Lit.: *Dombey and Son*]

10. **Momus** personification of censoriousness, constantly carping, grumbling, and finding fault. [Gk. Myth.: *EB* (1963) XV, 685]

11. **Peninnah** continually harassed co-wife Hannah about her barrenness. [O.T.: I Samuel 1:6]

12. **Proudie, Mrs.** aggressive, domineering wife of Bishop Proudie. [Br. Lit.: Trollope *Barchester Towers* in Magill I, 75]

13. **Sofronia** Norina, disguised for mock marriage, pretends to be virago. [Ital. Opera: Donizetti, *Don Pasquale*, Westerman, 123–124]

14. **Tabitha** Mr. Bramble's virago sister; bent on matrimony. [Br. Lit.: *Humphry Clinker*]

15. **Termagant** tumultuous Muslim deity (male); today, a virago. [Medieval Lit.: Espy, 125]

16. **Xanthippe** Socrates's peevish, quarrelsome wife. [Gk. Hist.: Espy, 114]

Shyness (See TIMIDITY.)

621. SIKHISM (See also RELIGION.)

1. **Adi Granth** also called Guru Granth Sahib; scriptures, treated with same devotion as a human Guru; used in marriage, for daily advice, and on special occasions. [Sikh Rel.: Bowker]

2. **amrit** holy water with healing properties; metaphorically, immortality and sweetness as a result of meditation upon God's name. [Sikh Rel.: Bowker]

3. **gurmukh** pious Sikh who loses all self-centeredness, leads a life of serivce, and attains peace of ultimate union with God. [Sikh Rel.: Bowker]

4. **guru** teacher, especially of religious knowledge or spiritual insight; Sikhs believe there is God and ten Gurus in history and their sacred scripture, Guru Granth Sahib (or Adi Granth). [Sikh Rel.: Bowker]

5. **hukam** divine order; beyond human understanding; it is agent of creation, determining physical universe and one's status, joys, sorrows. [Sikh Rel.: Bowker]

6. **khalsa** body of initiated Sikhs; also any true Sikh. [Sikh Rel.: Bowker]

7. **kirtan** devotional singing that purifies the singer. [Sikh Rel.: Bowker]

8. **manmukh** self-willed, perverse person, controlled by impulses rather than by the dictates of God. [Sikh Rel.: Bowker]

9. **mantra** verse, syllable, or series of syllables thought to be sacred; used in mediation or rituals. [Sikh Rel.: Bowker]

10. **panth** religious community; those following a certain religious teacher or doctrine. [Sikh Rel.: Bowker]

11. **prasad** grace coming to the assistance of individuals. [Sikh Rel.: Bowker]

12. **rahit maryada** code of discipline; conduct expected of individual and the Panth. [Sikh Rel.: Bowker]

13. **seva** service rendered in accordance with God's will and without expectation of reward. [Sikh Rel.: Bowker]

Similarity (See TWINS.)

Sinfulness (See WICKEDNESS.)

622. SINGER

1. **Anderson, Marian (1897–1977)** world-renowned African-American contralto faced racial prejudice and segregation, paving the way for other black artists. [Am. Music: *SJEPC*]

2. **Bennett, Tony (1926–)** Italian-American singer of jazz and popular music began career in the 1950s but performs and records with current generation of musicians. [Am. Music: *SJEPC*]

3. **Bocelli, Andrea (1958–)** blind Italian operatic tenor. [Ital. Music: Misc.]

4. **Callas, Maria (1923–1977)** famous soprano opera singer in the 1950s. [Am. Music: Misc.]

5. **Caruso, Enrico (1873–1921)** most celebrated tenor of the early 20th century. [Opera Hist.: *NCE*, 469]

6. **Clooney, Rosemary (1928–2002)** popular female vocalist of the 1950s made her career in the concert circuit as well as in radio, television, and motion pictures. [Am. Music: *SJEPC*]

7. **Como, Perry (1912–2001)** Italian-American male vocalist with smooth tone gained popularity via nightclub, radio, TV, and film appearances in the 1940s and 1950s; continued performing and recording in his later years. [Am. Music: *SJEPC*]

8. **Crosby, Bing (1903–1977)** relaxed crooning style brought him worldwide fame from the 1930s on; recorded more than 1600 songs, including "White Christmas" (1942), and sold upwards of a billion records total. [Am. Music: *SJEPC*]

9. **Darin, Bobby (1936–1973)** famous American rock and roll teen idol; also sang jazz, folk, and country. [Am. Music Misc.]

10. **Day, Doris (1924–)** vocalist with wholesome looks sang with big bands in the 1940s, in Hollywood movies and musicals in the 1950s; "Que Sera Sera" (1956) a big hit. [Am. Music and Film: *SJEPC*]

11. **Eddy, Nelson (1901–1967)** handsome baritone sang with New York's Metropolitan Opera but gained greater fame as leading man in Hollywood musicals of the 1930s-40s, paired with Jeanette MacDonald. [Am. Music: *SJEPC*]

12. **Fisher, Eddie (1928–)** fast-living crooner and teen idol of 1950s saw career skyrocket and plummet; was married to actresses Debbie Reynolds, Elizabeth Taylor, and Connie Stevens. [Am. Music: *SJEPC*]

13. **Fitzgerald, Ella (1918–1996)** legendary jazz vocalist with smooth, clear voice, ability to scat in perfect pitch, and playful, lighthearted approach; known as "The First Lady of Song." [Am. Music: *SJEPC*]

14. **Fleming, Renée (1959–)** American soprano opera and lieder singer. [Am. Music: Misc.]

15. **Francis, Connie (1938–)** vocalist with "girl next door" image became a sensation after Dick Clark played her song "Who's Sorry Now?" in 1958; was top-selling artist throughout 1960s. [Am. Music: *SJEPC*]

16. **Franklin, Aretha (1942–)** undisputed "Queen of Soul" deeply rooted in gospel; passionate vocal delivery earned her numerous Grammy Awards and honor of being first female inductee into Rock and Roll Hall of Fame (1987). [Am. Music: *SJEPC*]

17. **Garland, Judy (1922–1969)** legendary singer and actress whose powerful, emotive voice and vulnerability resonated with millions of fans worldwide; "Over the Rainbow" (1939) her signature song; Carnegie Hall recording in 1962 won unprecedented five Grammy Awards. [Am. Music and Film: *SJEPC*]

18. **Groban, Josh (1981–)** American singer; known for pop ballads and classical music. [Am. Music: Misc.]

19. **Holliday, Billie (1915–1959)** African-American jazz and blues composer and vocalist; called "Lady Day," she was one of the most influential singers of the era. [Am. Music: *BBAAL2*]

20. **Horne, Lena (1917–)** singer and actress acclaimed for her vocal range and jazz stylings; one-woman show a huge success. [Am. Music: *EB*]

21. **Horne, Marilyn (1934–)** American mezzo-soprano; known mostly for Rossini and Handel. [Am. Music: Misc.]

22. **Ives, Burl (1909–1995)** versatile entertainer; best known as singer of grassroots folk songs. [Am. Music: *SJEPC*]

23. **Jackson, Mahalia (1912–1972)** often considered the best Gospel singer of all times; she appealed to audiences of all races with her powerful contralto voice; sang at the inauguration of John F. Kennedy and the funeral of Martin Luther King, Jr. [Am. Music: *SJEPC*]

24. **Jolson, Al (1886–1950)** called "The World's Greatest Entertainer"; comedian and blackface "Mammy" singer in vaudeville; introduced jazz, blues, and ragtime to white audiences; began film career with lead role in *The Jazz Singer* (1927). [Am. Entertainment: *SJEPC*]

25. **Jones, Tom (1940–)** Welsh singer with long and diverse career; known in 1960s for his sexy stage performances where female fans swooned and threw their underwear onstage. [Welsh Music: *SJEPC*]

26. **Joplin, Janice (1943–1970)** considered by many the greatest white female blues singer; highly passionate style and powerful, gritty voice; excessive in her performances and personal life; died young of heroin overdose. [Am. Music: *SJEPC*]

27. **lang, k.d. (1961–)** smooth, sophisticated voice with broad range; often thought to be a study in contradictions because of unusual and rather bristly cross-gender appearance; very open about her lesbiansim. [Am. Music: *SJEPC*]

28. **Lehmann, Lotte (1888–1976)** German soprano opera singer. [Ger. Music: Misc.]

29. **Lorelei** siren whose singing lured ships to their destruction. [Ger. Lit.: Benét, 599]

30. **MacDonald, Jeanette (1903–1965)** famous soprano film star of 1920s through 1940s best known for sentimental, romantic operetta movies with Nelson Eddy [Am. Miusic and Film: *SJEPC*]

31. **Pavarotti, Luciano (1935–2007)** beloved Italian tenor who introduced many to the glories of opera; one of the "Three Tenors" [Opera Hist.: Misc.]

32. **Presley, Elvis (1935–1877)** perhaps the most famous rock 'n' roll singer of all times; his versatile voice, pioneering music, gyrations on stage, and tough-guy image made him a sensation world-wide [Am. Music: *SPEPC*]

33. **Price, Leontyne (1927–)** African-American soprano opera singer. [Am. Music: Misc.]

34. **Sills, Beverly (1929–2007)** American soprano opera singer, famous in the 1960s and 1970s. [Am. Music: Misc.]

35. **Sinatra, Frank (1915–1988)** one of popular music's greatest icons; considered not just an incomparable singer, but a stylist; best known for emotional renditions of standards with masterfully arranged instrumental accompaniment. [Am. Music: *SJEPC*]

36. **Sirens** their singing so sweet, it lured sailors to their death. [Gk. Myth.: Hamilton, 48]

37. **Smith, Bessie (1894–1937)** American singer known as "Empress of the Blues." [Am. Music: Misc.]

38. **Streisand, Barbra (1942–)** career took off with portrayal of Fanny Brice in Broadway production of *Funny Girl* (1964) and blossomed into superstardom as a phenomenally popular singer and actress; writes, produces, directs fillms and supports social and political causes. [Am. Entertainment: *SJEPC*]

39. **Three Tenors** [Luciano Pavarotti (1935–2007), Placido Domingo (1941–), and José Carerras (1946–)] three opera stars who performed enormously popular televised concerts, bringing opera to millions. [Opera Hist.: Misc.]

40. **Tormé, Mel (1925–1999)** the "Velvet Fog" with long and varied career had smooth-as-silk voice and impressive style on stage. [Am. Entertainment: *SJEPC*]

41. **Vallee, Rudy (1901–1986)** very popular in the 1920s and 1930s; trademark using megaphone to amplify voice; later went on to do successful radio variety show and some film work. [Am. Music, Radio, and Film: *SJPEC*]

42. **Vaughan, Sarah (1924–1990)** jazz singer who recorded with the greats beginning with Earl Hines's big band in 1943; known for her improvisation and exceptional range. [Am. Music: *SJEPC*]

43. **Wallace, Sippie (1898–1986)** influential blues singer whose risqué lyrics and themes related to being a woman of color had great appeal with her audiences. [Am. Music: *SJEPC*]

44. **White, Barry (1944–2003)** African-American pop music singer whose husky bass voice and sexy songs have made his name synonymous with romance to listeners. [Am. Music: *SJPEC*]

45. **Williams, Andy (1930–)** smooth-as-silk voice and pleasant demeanor were perfectly suited to lovely ballads like "Moon River" (1961) and "The Days of Wine and Roses" (1963). [Am. Music: *SJEPC*]

46. **Wynette, Tammy (1942–1998)** country vocalist who was considered antifeminist for her 1969 hit "Stand by Your Man," but succeeded in a competitive male-dominated industry. [Am. Music: *SJEPC*]

623. SINGLE WOMAN

1. *Alice* no-nonsense widow and mother with singing career aspirations makes ends meet as waitress at Mel's Diner (1976–85). [Am. TV: *SJEPC*]

2. *Cathy* comic strip debuting in 1976 featured single career woman dealing with modern pressures and desire to have it all. [Am. Comics: *SJEPC*]

3. **Cosmo Girl** young, single, sexually liberated woman of independent means as portrayed in women's magazine *Cosmopolitan*. [Am. Jour. and Culture: *SJEPC*]

4. **Forsyte, June** jilted by her fiancé, never marries. [Br. Lit.: *The Forsyte Saga*]

5. **Grundy, Miss** prim and proper schoolteacher [Comics: "Archie" in Horn, 87]

6. **Havisham, Miss** old spinster; always wore her bridal dress though jilted on wedding day. [Br. Lit: *Great Expectations*]

7. **Lovell, Charlotte** rather than reveal that an orphan girl is her own child, she spends her life unmarried. [Am. Lit.: Edith Wharton *The Old Maid* in Magill I, 679]

8. **McBeal, Ally** young, single Ally desires both career and motherhood. [Am. TV: *SJEPC*]

9. **Richards, Mary** protagonist of *The Mary Tyler Moore Show*; single, independent career woman, unprecedented character on sitcoms of the time (1970s). [Am. TV: Misc.]

10. **Sloper, Catherine** remains single rather than marry a man interested in her inheritance. [Am. Lit.: *Washington Square* in Hart, 899]

11. **Throssel, Miss Phoebe** a spinster with marriage continually on her mind. [Br. Lit.: *Quality Street*, Magill I, 793–795]

624. SKATING

1. **Blair, Bonnie (1964–)** first U.S. woman to win five Olympic gold medals, which she did in speed skating; one of the greatest female athletes of the 20th century. [Am. Sports: *BB1995*]

2. **Boitano, Brian (1963–)** figure skater won many U.S., world titles, and an Olympic medal in 1988. [Am. Sports: *EB*]

3. **Brinker, Hans** character from Mary Mapes Dodge's story for children set in Holland, *Hans Brinker; or, The Silver Skates* (1865); hardworking boy who shows the rewards of fortitude. [Am.. Children's Lit.: Jones]

4. **Button, Dick (1929)** premier international male figure skater of the 1940s and 1950s; the only man to win the Olympic, World, European, N. American, and U.S. championships; now a TV commentator. [Am. Sports: *EB*]

5. **Fleming, Peggy (1948–)** graceful figure skater known for her layback spin, won Olympic gold for America in 1968; remained in the sport as respected, inspiring professional skater and TV commentator. [Am. Sports: *SJEPC*]

6. **Hamill, Dorothy (1956–)** graceful yet spunky skater won gold at the 1976 Olympics; her hairstyle became popular worldwide. [Am. Sports: *EB*]

7. **Harding, Tonya (1970–)** figure skater banned from the sport after her ex-husband and an accomplice arranged an attack on Nancy Kerrigan, her chief rival, prior to the 1994 Olympics; a symbol of tawdry scandal. [Am. Sports: *BT1994*]

8. **Kerrigan, Nancy (1969–)** 1993 U.S. figure skating champion; during the Olympic trials of 1994, she was attacked by associates of her rival, Tonya Harding in an ineffectual attempt to keep Kerrigan from competing. [Am. Sports: *SJEPC*]

9. **Kwan, Michelle (1980–)** popular and gifted skater with artistic style who won five World Championships and two Olympic medals. [Am. Sports: *SJEPC*]

10. **roller derby** full-contact aggressive skating by men and women alike; colorful personalities of competitors drew fans. [Am. Sports and Entertainment: *SJEPC*]

625. SKEPTICISM (See also CYNICISM, PESSIMISM.)

1. **Dawes, Jabez** mischievous brat ridicules Santa's existence. [Am. Lit.: "The Boy Who Laughed at Santa Claus" in Rockwell]

2. **mushroom** symbol of suspicion. [Plant Symbolism: *Flora Symbolica*, 310]

3. **Naaman** at first doubts efficacy of leprosy cure. [O.T.: II Kings 5:11–14]

4. **Thomas, Saint** wouldn't believe Christ's resurrection until he saw Him; hence, *Doubting Thomas*. [N.T.: John 20:24–25]

5. **Windemere, Lady** doesn't believe husband's "virutuous" generosity toward Mrs. Erlynne. [Br. Lit.: *Lady Windemere's Fan*, Magill I, 488–490]

6. **Zacharias** struck dumb for doubting Gabriel's birth annunciation. [N.T.: Luke 1:18–20]

Skinniness (See THINNESS.)

626. SLANDER (See also GOSSIP.)

1. **Basile** calumniating , niggardly bigot. [Fr. Lit.: *Barber of Seville*; *Marriage of Figaro*]

2. **Blatant Beast** monster with 100 tongues; calumnious voice of world. [Br. Lit.: *Faerie Queene*]

3. **Candour, Mrs.** the most energetic calumniator. [Br. Lit.: *School for Scandal*]

4. **cobaea vine** symbol of slander. [Flower Symbolism: *Flora Symbolica*, 173]

5. **hellebore** symbol of slander. [Flower Symbolism: *Flora Symbolica*, 174]

6. **Iago** malignant Venetian commander; slanders Cassio to Othello. [Br. Lit.: *Othello*]

7. **Kay, Sir** ill-mannered, mean-spirited, but above all, scurrilous. [Br. Lit.: *Le Morte d'Arthur*; *Idylls of the King*]

8. **Miriam** made leprous for maligning Moses's marriage to Cushite. [O.T.: Numbers 12:9–10]

9. **Shimei** villifies David, implying he stole Saul's throne. [O.T.: II Samuel 16:7–8]

10. **Thersites** dedicated to denigrating his betters. [Gk. Lit.: *Iliad*; Br. Lit.: *Troilus and Cressida*]

Slaughter (See MASSACRE.)

627. SLEEP

1. **Amina** in her sleep, walks on a dangerous bridge, complaining of her unhappiness. [Ital. Opera: *La Sonnambula* in Osborne *Opera*]

2. **Cupid** while sleeping, revealed by Psyche's lamp as her lover. [Gk. Myth.: Benét, 822]

3. **Deiphobus** while sleeping, he is betrayed by Helen and slain by Menelaus. [Rom. Lit.: *Aeneid VI*]

4. **dormouse** snoozes all through the mad tea-party. [Br. Lit.: *Alice's Adventures in Wonderland*]

5. **Endymion** man kept immortally youthful through eternal sleep. [Gk. Myth.: Howe, 91]

6. **Epimenides** philospher nods off for 57 years in a cave. [Gk. Legend: *LLEI*, I: 283]

7. **hypnale** asp which kills by inducing sleep. [Medieval Animal Symbolism: White, 174]

8. **Hypnos** god of slumber. [Gk. Myth.: Hall, 250]

9. **Lady Macbeth** while sleepwalking, discloses her terrible deeds. [Br. Drama: Shakespeare *Macbeth*]

10. **land of Nod** mythical land of sleep; humorous reference to biblical land in Genesis. [Am. and Br. Usage: O.T.: Genesis 4:16]

11. **Morpheus** Hypnos's son and god of dreams. [Gk. Myth.: Howe, 172]

12. **poppy** attribute of Hypnos, Greek god of sleep. [Art.: Hall, 250]

13. **Sandman** induces sleep by sprinkling sand in children's eyes. [Folklore: Brewer *Dictionary*, 966]

14. **Seven Sleepers** youths who fled Decian persecution; slept for more than 200 years. [Christian and Muslim Tradition: Bénét, 918]

15. **Sleeping Beauty** enchanted heroine awakened from century of slumber by prince's kiss. [Fairy Tale: Brewer *Dictionary*, 1011]

16. **Snow White** poisoned apple induces her sleep; prince awakens her. [Children's Lit.: Bettelheim, 213]

17. **Somnus** god of sleep; son of Nox. [Rom. Myth.: Wheeler, 349]

18. **Van Winkle, Rip** slept for 20 years, thereby missing war. [Am. Lit.: "Rip Van Winkle" in Hart, 714]

19. **Winkie, Wee Willie** made sure all the children were asleep. [Nurs. Rhyme: Opie, 424]

628. SMALLNESS (See also DWARF.)

1. **Alice** nibbles a magic cake to become a pygmy. [Br. Lit.: *Alice's Adventures in Wonderland*]

2. **Alphonse** petite page to Mr. Wititterly. [Br. Lit.: *Nicholas Nickleby*]

3. **Andorra** small state of 191 square miles, between France and Spain. [Eur. Hist.: *NCE*, 100]

4. **Anon, Mr.** a deformed and hunchbacked midget. [Br. Lit.: *Memoirs of a Midget*, Magill I, 577–579]

5. **Borrowers** characters from 1952 novel by Mary Norton; tiny family who live under floor of old mansion and use homeowners' things to survive. [Br. Children's Lit.: *OCCL*]

6. **hop-o'-my-thumb** generic term for a midget or dwarf. [Folklore: Brewer *Dictionary*, 544]

7. **Liechtenstein** central European principality, comprising 65 square miles. [Eur. Hist.: *NCE*, 1578]

8. **Lilliputians** race of pygmies living in fictitious kingdom of Lilliput. [Br. Lit.: *Gulliver's Travels*]

9. **Little Tich** midget music-hall comedian of late 1800s. [Br. Hist.: Brewer *Dictionary*, 1082]

10. **Luxembourg** duchy of 999 square miles in Western Europe. [Eur. Hist.: *NCE*, 1632]

11. **Miss M.** perfectly formed midget leads the pleasant social life of a young lady but disappears mysteriously. [Br. Lit.: Walter de la Mare *Memoirs of a Midget* in Magill I, 577]

12. **Mowcher, Miss** kindhearted hairdresser of small stature. [Br. Lit.: *David Copperfield*]

13. **Munchkin** little folk who people the land of Oz. [Br. Lit.: *The Wizard of Oz*; Am. Film: *The Wizard of Oz*]

14. **Pepin the Short** first Frankish king; progenitor of Carolingian dynasty. [Eur. Hist.: Bishop, 20, 25]

15. **Piglet** Pooh's close friend in A. A. Milne's Winnie-the-Pooh tales for children; tiny and timid, he also shows real courage at times. [Br. Children's Lit.: Jones]

16. **pygmy** an African and Asian tribe people who are small in stature; also refers to people who are small-minded. [African Culture: *FOF, MOD*; Am. Culture: *FOF, MOD*]

17. **Quilp, Daniel** small man with giant head and face. [Br. Lit.: *Old Curiosity Shop*]

18. **Rhode Island** smallest of the fifty states; nicknamed "Little Rhodie." [Am. Hist.: *NCE*, 2315]

19. **Stareleigh, Justice** "a most particularly short man." [Br. Lit.: *Pickwick Papers*]

20. **Stuart Little** mouselike tiny boy whose size forms the basis for stories in E.B. White's episodic book for young readers. [Am. Children's Lit.: Jones]

21. **Thumb, Tom (1838–1883)** stage name for the midget, Charles Sherwood Stratton. [Am. Hist.: Benét, 1016]

22. **Thumbelina** tiny girl, rescued by a swallow, marries the tiny king of the Angels of the Flowers. [Dan. Lit.: *Andersen's Fairy Tales*]

23. **Zacchaeus** little man took to tree to see Christ. [N.T.: Luke 19:3–4]

Snobbery (See ARROGANCE, PRETENSION.)

Soap Opera (See PASSION, SENSUAL.)

629. SOCCER

1. **Beckham, David (1975–)** English soccer star, one of the best in the world; now living and playing in the U.S. [Sports: *EB*]

2. **Donovan, Landon (1982–)** American soccer player, one of the finest of his generation. [Am. Sports: Misc.]

3. **Hamm, Mia (1972–)** American soccer player and Olmpic champion, now retired, perhaps the best soccer player in U.S. history. [Sports: *BTSportv.2*]

4. **Pele (1940–)** Brazilian soccer superstar; won three world cups. [Sports: *SJEPC*]

5. **Ronaldo (1976–)** Brazilian soccer star. [Eur. Sports: Misc.]

6. **World Cup** most popular sporting event in the world; held in different countries every four years since 1930 to determine best soccer team in the world. [Sports: *SJEPC*]

630. SOCIAL PROTEST (See also ACTIVISM; RIGHTS, CIVIL; RIGHTS, GAY; RIGHTS, WOMEN'S.)

1. **"Alice's Restaurant"** 1967 antiwar song written by folksinger Arlo Guthrie featured 18 minutes of storytelling to a blues beat and became basis of 1969 movie. [Am. Music: *SJEPC*]

2. **Birmingham, Alabama** effective 1963 protests and demonstrations to rid city of racially descriminatory policies; led by Martin Luther King, Jr.; citizens mostly used nonviolent tacits to protest unjust laws. [Am. Hist.: Misc.]

3. **"Blowin' in the Wind"** Bob Dylan's 1963 song protesting war and racial injustice in a series of questions was popularized by folk trio Peter, Paul and Mary. [Am. Music: *SJEPC*]

4. **Chávez, César (1927–1993)** Mexican-American labor activist led national, five-year campaign (La Huelga, 1966–1970) of hunger strikes, demonstrations, and a table grape boycott to make public aware of migrant workers' conditions. [Am. Hist.: *SJEPC*]

5. **Dead Kennedys, The** hardcore rock band with politically controversial lyrics skewered big business, religious institutions, and flaws in 1980s American society. [Am. Music: *SJEPC*]

6. **Dickensian** like the novels of Charles Dickens (1812–1870), which often drew attention to social injustice [Br. Lit.: *ODA*]

7. **Dylan, Bob (1941–)** legendary songwriter/singer's music protested racial inequality, social injustice, war, and nuclear armament. [Am. Music: *SJEPC*]

8. **flag burning** means of political protest protected by First Amendment elicits mixed feelings. [Am. Hist.: *SJEPC*]

9. *Germinal* portrays the sufferings of workers in the French mines. [Fr. Lit.: Zola *Germinal*]

10. **Ginsberg, Allen (1926–1997)** countercultural poet protested the Vietnam War, nuclear arms; actively supported environmental movement and gay rights. [Am. Lit.: *SJEPC*]

11. **Guthrie, Woody (1912–1967)** iconic American folksinger wrote songs that criticized social and economic inequities in America and celebrated the irrepressible spirit of downtrodden men and women, particularly migrant farm workers during the Dust Bowl years (1930s). [Am. Music: *SJEPC*]

12. **"Howl"** foremost Beat poem (1955) by Allen Ginsberg contained shocking language, gritty images, and vivid sexual references to protest contemporary society. [Am. Lit.: Henderson, 38; *SJEPC*]

13. *J'Accuse* Émile Zola's open letter to the president of the French Republic, defending Alfred Dreyfus, who had been charged with treason by the French army; Zola accused army of covering up false conviction of Dreyfus and brought huge public outcry (1898). [Fr. Lit.; Misc.]

14. *Jungle, The* novel exposed harrowing moral, economic, and hygienic conditions in the meat-packing industry. [Am. Lit.: Upton Sinclair *The Jungle*]

15. **Kent State** Ohio university where antiwar demonstration led to riot, resulting in deaths of four students (1971). [Am. Hist.: *NCE*, 1466]

16. **March on Washington** 1963 civil rights march at which Martin Luther King, Jr. delivered his "I Have a Dream" speech. [Am. Hist.: *SJEPC*]

17. **Seeger, Pete (1919–)** paved the way for singer/activists through his devotion to many social causes; wrote and recorded folk songs with intent of changing the status quo. [Am. Culture: *SJEPC*]

18. **Stonewall Rebellion** 1969 resistance by patrons of Greenwich Village gay men's bar during police raid; annual Gay Pride parade and ralles held nationwide to commemorate the event. [Am. Pop. Culture: *SJEPC*]

19. **Students for a Democratic Society (SDS)** one of largest and most militant groups opposing war in Vietnam in 1960s. [Am. Pol.: *SJEPC*]

20. **"The Times They Are a-Changin'"** folk song by Bob Dylan called for monumental changes in the social and political structure (1964). [Am. Music: *SJEPC*]

21. **Tiananmen Square** seven-week demonstration for democratic reform by millions of unarmed protestors in Beijing; after warnings to disperse from government, several hundred shot dead by Chinese army. [Chinese Hist.: Misc.]

22. *Tin Drum, The* Grass's surreal novel of 20th-century madness. [Ger. Lit.: Magill IV, 1220]

23. *Weavers, The* textile workers revolt against their employer and wreck the factory. [Ger. Drama: Haydn & Fuller, 792]

24. *What's Going On?* Motown and soul artist Marvin Gaye's best-selling album confronted and protested troubling social, political, and economic conditions of the day, including the Vietnam War (1971). [Am. Music: *SJEPC*]

Social Service (See AID, GOVERNMENTAL; AID, ORGANIZATIONAL.)

631. SONG, PATRIOTIC

1. **"America the Beautiful"** patriotic song by Katherine Bates glorifying national ideals (1893). [Am. Music: Scholes, 30]

2. **"Battle Hymn of the Republic"** Union's Civil War rallying song. [Am. Music: Van Doren, 228]

3. **"Deutschland über Alles"** German national anthem. [Ger. Music: Misc.]

4. **"Die Wacht am Rhein"** popular national song of Germany. [Ger. Music: Scholes, 1111]

5. **"God Bless America"** iconic patriotic song written by Irving Berlin during World War I; premiered by singer Kate Smith in 1938. [Am. Music: *SJEPC*]

6. **"God Save the Queen"** official national anthem of the British Commonwealth. [Br. Music: Scholes, 48]

7. **"John Brown's Body"** Union rallying hymn during Civil War. [Am. Music: Jameson, 257]

8. **"Maple Leaf Forever!"** Canadian national song (1867). [Can. Music: Scholes, 597]

9. **"Marseillaise"** French national anthem. [Fr. Music: Misc.]

10. **"Maryland, My Maryland"** song expressing sentiments of Southern cause during Civil War (1861). [Am. Music: Scholes, 602]

11. **"O Canada!"** national song of Canada, popular among French Canadians. [Can. Music: Scholes, 699]

12. **"O Deutschland, Hoch in Ehren!"** war song of the Germans in 1914. [Ger. Music Scholes, 700]

13. **"Over There"** George M. Cohan's song of American entry into WWI. [Am. Music: Flexner, 417]

14. **"Rule, Britannia!"** patriotic British song (1740). [Br. Music: Scholes, 897–898]

15. **"Star-Spangled Banner, The"** national anthem of the United States. [Am. Music: Scholes, 980]

16. **"This Land Is Your Land"** iconic American folk song by Woody Guthrie celebrates America from coast to coast (1940). [Am. Music: *SJEPC*; Misc.]

17. **"Tipperary"** war song popular in British Army in World War I. [Br. Music: Scholes, 1025]

18. **"Wearing of the Green, The"** patriotic song of Ireland (1797). [Irish Music: Scholes, 1111]

19. **"When Johnny Comes Marching Home"** Southern Civil War rallying song. [Am. Music: Van Doren, 228–229]

20. **"Yankee Doodle"** Revolutionary War paean of American glory. [Nurs. Rhyme: Opie, 439]

632. SOPHISTICATION (See also ELEGANCE, LUXURY, PRESTIGE.)

1. *Avengers, The* witty, sophisticated British TV spy series in the 1960s. [Br. TV: *SJEPC*]

2. **Bond, James** spy novelist Ian Fleming's suave secret agent 007 is at home in exotic locales, drinking the finest liquor, enjoying haute cuisine, and seducing beautiful women. [Br. Lit.: *SJEPC*]

3. **martini** gin and vermouth drink that epitomizes elegance and worldliness. [Am. Cuisine: *SJEPC*]

4. *New Yorker* dedicated editors and a host of acclaimed contributors made the magazine a favorite among the intelligent and wealthy. [Am. Jour.: *SJEPC*]

5. **Porter, Cole (1891–1964)** prolific composer and lyricist of Broadway musicals and countless timeless songs; his lifestyle reflected the essence of finesse [Am. Music: *SJEPC*]

6. **Short, Bobby (1924–2005)** singer and pianist who combined smooth performances of popular standards with deboniare style to entertain diners at Carlyle hotel in Manhattan. [Am. Music: Misc.]

7. **Tormé, Mel (1925–1999)** the "Velvet Fog" with long and varied career had smooth-as-silk voice and impressive style on stage. [Am. Entertainment: *SJEPC*]

Sorcery (See ENCHANTMENT, MAGIC, WITCHCRAFT.)

Sorrow (See GRIEF.)

633. SOUTHERN STATES (U.S.)

1. **Band, The** band from the 1960s and 1970s with some songs set in rural South. [Am. Music: *SJEPC*]

2. *Birth of a Nation, The* film set during Reconstruction in the South depicts Ku Klux Klan as heroic and newly freed slaves as violent (1915). [Am. Film: *SJEPC*]

3. **Caldwell, Erskine (1903–1987)** writer depicted Southern families as poverty-stricken, dysfunctional, ignorant, and sexually

promiscuous in his novels of the 1930s-1940s, such as *Tobacco Road* (1932). [Am. Lit.: *SJEPC*; Harris *Characters*, 54]

4. **Confederacy** government of 11 Southern states that left the Union in 1860. [Am. Hist.: *EB*, III: 73]

5. **Daisy Dukes** tight denim cut-off short shorts made famous by Southern backwoods character Daisy Duke in *The Dukes of Hazzard* (1979–1985). [Am. TV: *SJEPC*; Misc.]

6. **Dixie** popular name for Southern states in U.S. and for song. [Am. Hist.: *EB*, III: 587]

7. *Dukes of Hazzard, The* TV show set in the backwoods of Hazzard County down South featured the adventures of the Duke cousins, often involving car chases with bumbling lawmen (1979–1985). [Am. TV: *SJEPC*]

8. *Gone With the Wind* archetypal novel about the South (1936) by Margaret Mitchell, adapted for film in 1939; describes Southern life during the Civil War and Reconstruction through the eyes of Southern belle Scarlett O'Hara. [Am. Lit. and Film: *Gone With the Wind*; *SJEPC*]

9. **gray** color of the uniform of the Confederate soldier. [Am. Hist.: *NCE*, 566]

10. **grits** regional breakfast food of the South made from ground corn can be served warm or cold, with milk and sugar or gravy and meat. [Am. Cuisine: *SJEPC*]

11. **Grizzard, Lewis (1946–1994)** witty syndicated newpaper columnist/humorist of 1980s and 1990s with southern "good old boy" image and storytelling abilities akin to Mark Twain. [Am. Jour.: *SJEPC*]

12. **Johnny Reb** a Confederate soldier or a resident of the Confederate states. [Am. Usage: Misc.]

13. **Mason-Dixon Line** boundary between Pennsylvania and Maryland that came to divide the slave (southern) states from the free (northern) states. [Am. Hist.: *NCE*, 1714]

14. **Mitchell, Margaret (1900–1949)** Southern author wrote epic Civil War-era novel *Gone with the Wind* in her cramped Atlanta apartment nicknamed "The Dump"; former journalist won Pulitzer Prize in 1936. [Am. Lit.: *SJEPC*]

15. **Southern Rock** rock music with a country feel played by Southern bands such as the Allman Brothers, Charlie Daniels Band, and Little Feat emerged as a genre in the 1970s. [Am. Music: *SJEPC*]

16. **Spanish moss** silvery gray plant whose threadlike fronds hang from trees in the South. [Am. Culture: *EB*, IX: 400–401]

17. **Stars and Bars** flag of the Confederate States of the U.S. [Am. Hist.: *EB*, III: 73]

18. **wisteria** beautifully flowering, woody vine found in Southern gardens. [Am. Culture: *EB*, X: 716]

634. SPACE TRAVEL (See also AVIATION, SCIENCE FICTION.)

1. *Alien* chilling drama featuring alien life forms aboard space ship. [Am. Film: *SJEPC*]

2. **Apollo missions** American space program in the 1960s and 1970s put the first man on the moon in 1969. [Am. Astronomy: *SJEPC*]

3. **Clarke, Arthur C. (1917–2008)** venerable British science fiction writer's works emphasize scientific discovery, advanced technology, and human yearning to understand the universe; author of *2001: A Space Odyssey* (1968) and *Childhood's End* (1950). [Br. Lit.: *SJEPC*]

4. *Close Encounters of the Third Kind* director Steven Spielberg's 1977 film depicts humankind's first contact with friendly space-travelling aliens whose mothership lands in a remote region of Wyoming. [Am. Film: *SJEPC*]

5. *Day the Earth Stood Still, The* an alien and his robot descend to Earth in a spaceship to warn humans about their destructive behavior in this 1951 film. [Am. Film: *SJEPC*]

6. **Flash Gordon** space-traveling hero. [Am. Comics and Film: Halliwell]

7. *From the Earth to the Moon* Verne tale of a group who have a monster gun cast to shoot them to the moon. [Fr. Lit.: *WB*, 13:650]

8. **HAL 9000** computer from the Stanley Kubrick film *2001: A Space Odyssey*, which famously tries to take over a spaceship. [Am. Film: *FOF, MOD*]

9. **Kennedy Space Center** U.S. launch site for manned space missions. [Am.. Hist.: *WB*, So:562]

10. **Mercury missions** first U.S. space flight program, successfully launched manned capsules into space; served as preparation for the Apollo missions and landing on the moon. [Am. Hist.: *BBWE*]

11. **National Aeronautics and Space Administration (NASA)** established in 1958 by US government to conduct aeronautical and space research and travel. [Am. Govt.: *SJEPC*]

12. **Pfaal, Hans** to escape his creditors, constructs a balloon and travels to the moon. [Am. Lit.: *The Unparalleled Adventures of One Hans Pfaal* in Poe]

13. **Ransom, Dr. Elwin** kidnapped and taken to Malacandra (Mars), he escapes with the help of its wise inhabitants. [Br. Lit.: C. S. Lewis *Out of the Silent Planet* in Weiss, 437]

14. **right stuff** from a book by Tom Wolfe, the combination of flying ability, courage, and swagger found in the test pilots, and later,

the astronauts of the early U.S. space program. [Am. Hist.: Tom Wolfe *The Right Stuff*]

15. **Rogers, Buck** early spaceman in fantasy comics. [Comics: Horn, 137–138]

16. **Roswell Incident, The** U.S. government is accused of convering up existence of UFO debris found near Roswell, New Mexico in 1947. [Am. Hist.: *SJEPC*]

17. **Sagan, Carl (1934–1996)** his 1980 *COSMOS* and subsequent PBS broadcast made articulate scientist a household name; instrumental in choosing samples of Earth's culture sent with Voyager spacecraft into deep space. [Am. Science: *SJEPC*]

18. **space shuttle** U.S. spacecraft capable of reuse, making travel more practical. [Am. Hist.: *WB*, So:561]

19. **Sputnik** first artifical satellite; launched from Soviet Union in 1957; began space race that would pit U.S. and U.S.S.R. against one another in the Cold War era. [Science: *SJEPC*]

20. **Tang** vitamin-fortified orange drink powder chosen in 1960s by NASA to be drink of the astronauts; led to popularity among children. [Am. Cuisine: *SJEPC*]

21. ***2001: A Space Odyssey*** 1968 film by Stanley Kubrick based on story by Arthur C. Clarke; symbolic, without clear story line; confused many viewers, but stunned them with cinematic innovation and beauty, and visionary depiction of artificial intelligence. [Am. Film: *SJEPC*]

22. **Unidentified Flying Objects (UFOs)** since the 1940s, Americans have periodically claimed to have sighted saucer-like flying objects, which they were convinced were extraterrestrial spaceships; some people have attested to abduction by aliens for observation. [Am. Pop. Culture: *SJEPC*]

635. SPECTACLE (See also EXTRAVAGANCE.)

1. *Aïda* opera renowned for its scenic grandeur; sometimes played with on-stage elephants. [Ital. Opera: Verdi *Aïda* in Benét, 16]

2. ***Birth of a Nation, The*** D.W. Griffith's monumental Civil War film. [Am. Cinema: Halliwell, 51]

3. **De Mille, Cecil B. (1881–1959)** American film director famous for such spectacles as *The Ten Commandments*. [Am. Film: *ODA*]

4. **Folies Bergère** opulent musical show in Paris featuring dancers, rich costumes and scenery. [Fr. Theater: *EB* (1972 ed.), IX, 515]

5. **Las Vegas** setting for legalized gambling and outrageous behavior. [Am. Pop. Culture: Misc.]

6. **Ringling Bros., Barnum & Bailey Circus** Barnum's "Greatest Show on Earth," which combined circus acts, animals, and

sideshow freaks, morphed into the popular spectacles of the present after collaboration with Bailey and, later, the Ringling Brothers. [Am. Culture: *Collier's*, V, 110]

7. **Rockettes, The** precision dancers; a fixture at New York's Radio City Music Hall. [Am. Dance: Payton, 576]

8. *Ten Commandments, The* opulent 1956 film of Biblical story of Moses with unprecedented special effects and cast of thousands. [Am. Film: *SJEPC*]

9. **Ziegfield Follies** elaborate New York musical entertainment (1907–1931) with gorgeous settings and dancers. [Am. Theater: *NCE*, 3045]

Speed (See SWIFTNESS.)

636. SPLENDOR (See also EXTRAVAGANCE, LUXURY.)

1. **Aladdin's palace** built of marble, gold, silver, and jewels. [Arab. Lit.: *Arabian Nights*]

2. **Alhambra, the** palatial 13th-century Moorish citadel in Granada, noted for its lofty situation, beautiful courts, and fountains. [Span. Hist.: Benét, 24]

3. **baths of Caracalla and Diolcletian** massive public buildings of imperial Rome, the latter having accommodations for 3,200 bathers. [Rom. Arch.: *EB* (1963) XIX, 392]

4. **Biltmore Estate** chateau located in Asheville, North Carolina; built by George Washington Vanderbilt between 1888 and 1895; at 175,000 square feet, it is the largest privately owned home in America; still owned by Vandebilt descendents. [Am. Hist.: Misc.]

5. **Bucentaur** opulent Venetian ship of state. [Ital. Hist.: Plumb, 257]

6. **Crystal Palace** huge museum and concert hall made of iron and glass at Great Exhibition (1851). [Br. Hist.: *NCE*, 692]

7. **dahlia** symbol of splendor. [Plant Symbolism: *Flora Symbolica*, 168]

8. **Hanging Gardens of Babylon** Nebuchadnezzar's huge terraces, built to placate wife. [World Hist.: Wallechinsky, 255]

9. **Hearst Castle** estate located on 250,000 acres in San Simeon, California; constructed by newspaper tycoon William Randolph Hearst between 1919 and 1947; modeled after historical architecture such as Spanish cathedrals and Roman temples. [Am. Hist.: Misc.]

10. **Khan, Kubla (1215–1294)** splendors of imperial court dazzled Polo entourage. [Asian Hist.: *EB*, 10: 541–543]

11. **magnolia** symbol of magnificence. [Flower Symbolism: *Flora Symbolica*, 175]

12. **Mont-Saint-Michel** abbey, church, and fortress; one of the finest examples of medieval French architecture. [Fr. Hist.: *NCE*, 1824]

13. **Neuschwanstein Castle** 19th-century palace in Bavaria, Germany; commissioned by Ludwig II, who wanted to create a fairytale castle to embrace the German legend of the Swan Knight; prototype of the Disney castle. [Ger. Hist.: Misc.]

14. **Parthenon** magnificent temple of Athena, dominating the Acropolis of Athens. [Gk. Hist.: Benét, 761]

15. **Sainte-Chapelle, the** 13th-century chapel, called the most beautiful building in France for its architecture and stained glass. [Fr. Architecture: *NCE*, 2396]

16. **Taj Mahal** fabulous tomb of Shah Jahan's wife. [Indian Hist.: Wallechinsky, 317]

17. **Tutankhamen's tomb** full of treasures of Egyptian pharaoh (c. 1350 B.C.). [Egypt. Hist.: Osborne, 1164]

18. **Versailles** luxurious palace of French kings; outside Paris. [Fr. Hist.: Brewer *Dictionary*, 1127]

19. **Xanadu** site of Kubla Khan's "stately pleasure dome." [Br. Lit.: *Kubla Khan* in Payton, 744]

637. SPLIT PERSONALITY

1. **Haller, Harry** middle-aged man battles two selves. [Ger. Lit.: *Steppenwolf*]

2. **Jekyll, Dr., and Mr. Hyde** upright physician reduced to animality by potion. [Br. Lit.: *Dr. Jekyll and Mr. Hyde*]

3. *Sybil* book by Flora Rheta Schreiber about a psychiatrist who treats a patient for 11 years, during which it is revealed that patient has developed 16 personalities as result of extremely abusive treatment as a child; story filmed as a 1976 TV movie. [Am. Lit. and TV: Misc.]

4. *Three Faces of Eve, The* 1957 film loosely based on true story; quiet woman suffers from headaches and blackouts; when treated by psychiatrist, two new personalities emerge. [Am. Film: Bawden, 757 (Woodward, Joanne)]

638. SPRING

1. **Flora** goddess of this season. [Rom. Myth.: Hall, 130]

2. **flowers** represent this season. [Art: Hall, 129]

3. **garlanded girl** personification of spring. [Art: Hall, 130]

4. **peep frogs** their voices welcome the season. [Am. Culture: Misc.]

5. **Persephone** personification of spring. [Gk. Myth.: Cirlot, 252]

6. **ram** symbol of the return of feritlity and spring. [Symbolism: *CEOS&S*]

7. **robin** harbinger of spring. [Western Culture: Misc.]

8. **swallow** harbinger of the spring season. [Animal Symbolism: Mercatante, 164]

9. **turtle doves** "voice of the turtle is heard." [O.T.: Song of Songs 2:12]

10. **Venus** goddess of the season. [Rom. Myth.: Hall, 130]

11. **Ver** personification; portrayed as infantile and tender. [Rom. Myth.: *LLEI*, I: 322]

639. SPYING

1. *Avengers, The* witty, sophisticated British TV spy series in the 1960s. [Br. TV: *SJEPC*]

2. **Birch, Harvey** a double spy, secretly in the employ of George Washington. [Am. Lit.: Cooper *The Spy*]

3. **Bond, James** Agent 007; super spy, super hero. [Br. Lit.: Herman, 27]

4. **Central Intelligence Agency (CIA)** U.S. intelligence agency. [Am. Hist.: *NCE*, 492]

5. **Cheka** early Soviet secret police charged with guarding against counterrevolutionary activity. [Russ. Hist.: Benét, 190]

6. **Clancy, Tom (1947–)** bestselling author writes thrilling, technologically accurate, action-packed novels of political intrigue, espionage, and the military such as *The Hunt for Read October* (1984) and *The Sum of All Fears* (1991). [Am. Lit.: *SJEPC*]

7. **Cly, Roger** old servant of Darnay; became a spy. [Br. Lit.: *A Tale of Two Cities*]

8. **Fleming, Ian (1908–1964)** author of James Bond novels and short stories about a British secret agent. [Br. Lit.: Misc.]

9. **Follett, Ken (1949–)** internationally successful novelist best known for spy fiction, such as *Eye of the Needle* (1978), for which he won Edgar award, and *Lie Down with Lions* (1986). [Welsh Lit.: *SJEPC*]

10. **Forsyth, Frederick (1938–)** Edgar award-winning writer of suspenseful thrillers pays meticulous attention to detail, making his novels chillingly authentic, as in *The Day of the Jackal* (1971). [Br. Lit.: *SJEPC*]

11. **Hannay, Richard** opponent of foreign evil. [Br. Lit.: *The Thirty-Nine Steps*]

12. **Hushai the Archite** sent by David to inveigle Absalom's confidence. [O.T.: II Samuel 15:34]

13. *I Spy* espionage TV show of mid-1960s; young Bill Cosby starred in first show to feature black and whilte protagonists of equal importance. [Am. TV: *SJEPC*]

14. **KGB** the Committee of State Security, USSR agency (begun 1954) with responsibility for espionage and counter-espionage. [Russ. Hist.: *EB*, V: 780]

15. **Kuryakin, Illya** taciturn, blond partner of Solo form U.N.C.L.E. [TV: "The Man from U.N.C.L.E." in Terrace, II, 60]

16. **le Carré, John (1931–)** writer of numerous spy novels who very likely worked for British Secret Service; his novels blend conventions of whodunnit with those of spy thriller and carry serious themes about politics and human nature. [Br. Lit.: *SJEPC*]

17. **Leamas** British Secret Service agent torn between duty and the desire to give up espionage. [Br. Lit.: Le Carré *The Spy Who Came in from the Cold* in Weiss, 440]

18. **Mata Hari (1876–1917)** courtesan executed by French for German espionage (1917). [Ger. Hist.: *EB*, VI: 683]

19. **Muir, Lieutenant Davy** garrison quartermaster discovered to be French spy. [Am. Lit.: Magill, I, 715–717]

20. **NKVD** People's Commisariat of Internal Affairs, USSR police agency (1934–1943) that carried out purges of the 1930s. [Russ. Hist.: *EB*, VII: 366]

21. **OGPU** secret police agency, successor to the Cheka. [Russ. Hist.: Benét, 190]

22. **Palmer, Harry** anti-hero of *The Ipcress File*. [Am. Cinema: Herman, 28–29]

23. **Peel, Emma** capable, intelligent, sexy spy on British TV series *The Avengers*. [Br. TV: *SJEPC*]

24. **Polonius** spies on Hamlet and Gertrude. [Br. Drama: Shakespeare *Hamlet*]

25. **Rosenberg, Julius (1918–1953) and Ethel (1915–1953)** first Americans executed for allegedly giving information to Soviet agents; their guilt has been debated because of anticommunist paranoia of Cold War era. [Am. Hist.: *SJEPC*]

26. *Secret Agent, The* Conrad's novel of the intrigues of a foreign secret agent (1907). [Br. Lit.: Magill III, 949–951]

27. **Smart, Maxwell** bumbling spy in genre spoof *Get Smart* (1965–70). [Am. TV: *SJEPC*]

28. **Smersh** acronym for Smert Shpionam (Death to Spies), a section of the KGB. [Russ. Hist.: *EB*, IX: 283]

29. **Smiley, George** British Secret Service hero. [Br. Lit.: Le Carré in Drabble, 558]

30. **Solo, Napoleon** suave and debonair agent for U.N.C.L.E. [TV: "The Man from U.N.C.L.E." in Terrace, II, 60]

31. **Spillane, Mickey (1918–2006)** author of hard-boiled novels featuring private eye Mike Hammer and spy Tiger Mann; criticized for use of violence as solution in his works. [Am. Lit.: *SJEPC*]

640. STIGMA

1. **mark of Cain** God's mark on Cain, a sign of his shame for fratricide. [O.T.: Genesis 4:15]

2. **scarlet letter** the letter "A" for "adultery" sewn on Hester Prynne's garments. [Am. Lit.: Hawthorne *The Scarlet Letter*]

Stinginess (See GREED, MISERLINESS.)

Stoicism (See LONGSUFFERING.)

641. STORYTELLING

1. **Aesop** semi-legendary fabulist of ancient Greece. [Gk. Lit.: Harvey, 10]

2. **Boccaccio, Giovanni (1313–1375)** Italian author known for *The Decameron* in which aristocrats tell stories to pass the time during the Plague. [Ital. Lit.: *FOF MOD*]

3. **Chaucer, Geoffrey (1343–1400)** English poet, creator of *The Canterbury Tales*, which recounts the stories told by pilgrims on their way to Canterbury Cathedral. [Br. Lit.: *The Canterbury Tales*]

4. **Kipling, Rudyard (1865–1936)** British author of adventure tales, often set in India under British rule. [Br. Lit.: *FOF, MOD*]

5. **Michener, James (1907–1997)** prolific author of lengthy cultural sagas. [Am. Lit.: *SJEPC*]

6. **Mother Goose** originally a fictitious nursery rhyme spinner from Perrault, later a Bostonian authoress. [Fr. Lit.: Brewer *Handbook*, 732]

7. **Munchausen, Baron** traveler grossly embellishes his experiences. [Ger. Lit.: Harvey, 565]

8. **Odysseus** wily teller of tales. [Gk. Legend: *Odyssey*]

9. **Ovid (Publius Ovidius Naso, 43 B.C-A.D. 17)** great storyteller of classical mythology. [Rom. Lit.: Zimmerman, 187]

10. **Remus, Uncle** narrator of animal tales in Old South. [Am. Lit.: *Nights with Uncle Remus*]

11. **Sandy** told endless tales as she and Boss traveled. [Am. Lit.: *A Connecticut Yankee in King Arthur's Court*]

12. **Scheherazade** forestalls her execution with 1001 tales. [Arab. Lit.: *Arabian Nights*]

13. **Watson, Dr. John H.** chronicles Sherlock Holmes's cases. [Br. Lit.: Arthur Conan Doyle *Sherlock Holmes*]

642. STRENGTH (See also BRAWNINESS.)

1.   **acorn** heraldic symbol of strength. [Heraldry: Jobes, 27]

2.   **Atlas** Titan condemned to bear heavens on shoulders. [Gk. Myth.: Walsh *Classical*, 38]

3.   **Atlas, Charles (1892–1972)** 20th-century strongman; went from "98–pound weakling" to "world's strongest man." [Am. Sports: Amory, 38–39]

4.   **Babe** Paul Bunyan's blue ox; straightens roads by pulling them. [Am. Lit.: Fisher, 270]

5.   **Bionic Man** superman of the technological age. [TV: "The Six Million Dollar Man" in Terrace, II: 294–295]

6.   **buffalo** heraldic symbol of power. [Heraldry: Halberts, 21]

7.   **Bunyan, Paul** legendary woodsman of prodigious strength. [Am. Folklore: *Paul Bunyan*]

8.   **Cyclopes** one-eyed giants; builders of fortifications. [Gk. Myth.: Avery, 346]

9.   **Everson, Cory (1959–)** bodybuilder won Ms. Olympia title six years in a row (1984–89) before retirement. [Am. Sports: *SJEPC*]

10. **Gibraltar** British fortress on southern tip of Spain, gateway to the Mediterranean Sea; symbol of strength and an impregnable stronghold. [Br. Hist.: *FOF, MOD*]

11. **Grimek, John (1910–1998)** muscular yet flexible and graceful bodybuilder competed in weightlifting contests of 1930s-40s; known for his classic poses. [Am. Sports: *SJEPC*]

12. **Hercules** his twelve labors revealed his godlike powers. [Rom. Myth.: Howe, 122]

13. **Katinka, the Powerful** a female Man Mountain Dean. [Am. Comics: "Toonerville Folks" in Horn, 668]

14. **Little John** oak of a man in Robin Hood's band. [Br. Lit.: *Robin Hood*]

15. **Marciano, Rocky (1923–1969)** unbeaten heavyweight boxing champion in early 1950s. [Am. Sports: *SJEPC*]

16. **Marvel, Captain** teenage boy transforms into strong, invulnerable superhero upon uttering the word "Shazam." [Am. Comics: *SJEPC*]

17. **meginjardir** Thor's belt; doubled his power. [Norse Myth.: Brewer *Dictionary*, 1076]

18. **Milo of Croton** renowned athlete. [Gk. Myth.: Hall, 209]

19. **Polydamas** huge athlete who killed a fierce lion with his bare hands, stopped a rushing chariot, lifted a mad bull, and died attempting to stop a falling rock. [Gk. Myth.: Benét, 801]

20. **Samson** possessed extraordinary might which derived from hair. [O.T.: Judges 16:17]

21. **Superman** caped superhero and modern-day Hercules. [Comics: Horn, 642–643]

Strife (See DISCORD.)

Stubbornness (See OBSTINACY.)

643. STUPIDITY (See also DIMWITTEDNESS, IGNORANCE.)

1. **Abdera** maritime city whose inhabitants were known proverbially for their stupidity. [Gk. Folklore: Benét, 2]

2. **Boeotians** inhabitants of rural Greek district; considered by Athenians to be dolts. [Gk. Folklore: Brewer *Dictionary*, 124]

3. **Chelm** mythical place inhabited by amiable simpletons. [Jew. Folklore: Rosten, 84]

4. **donkey** chooses cuckoo's singing over nightingale's. [Ger. Folklore and Poetry: Brentano and Arnim, *Des Knaben Wunderhorn; NCE*, 363]

5. **Dull, Anthony** archexample of stupidity. [Br. Lit.: *Love's Labour's Lost*]

6. **Elbow** ignorant, blundering constable. [Br. Lit.: *Measure for Measure*]

7. **Gimpel** a baker, foolish to the point of saintliness, is cuckolded and mocked, becomes a Wandering Jew. [Jewish. Lit.: Singer *Gimpel the Fool* in Weiss, 174]

8. **Mendel, Menachem** hopeless schlemiel who devises impossible enterprises. [Yid. Lit.: Sholem Aleichem in Haydn & Fuller, 685]

9. **pomegranate** symbol of foolishness. [Flower Symbolism: *Flora Symbolica*, 176]

10. **Simple Simon** simpleton of bumptious ways. [Nurs. Rhyme: Opie, 385]

11. **Slender** "though well-landed, an idiot." [Br. Lit.: *Merry Wives of Windsor*]

12. **Smith, Knucklehead** dummy with self-referring name. [TV: "Winchell and Mahoney" in Terrace, II, 190–192]

13. **Snerd, Mortimer** a real dummy. [Radio: "The Edgar Bergen and Charlie McCarthy Show" in Buxton, 76–77]

14. **Stephen** simpleton; made gapingstock by all. [Br. Lit.: *Every Man in His Humour*]

15. **three wise men of Gotham** fools momentarily afloat in a light bowl. [Nurs. Rhyme: Opie, 193]

644. SUBJUGATION

1. **Cushan-rishathaim** Aram king to whom God sold Israelites. [O.T.: Judges 3:8]

2. **Gibeonites** consigned to servitude in retribution for trickery. [O.T.: Joshua 9:22–27]

3. **Ham** Noah curses him and progeny to servitude. [O.T.: Genesis 9:22–27]

4. **Higgins, Henry** in George Bernard Shaw's *Pygmalion*, he uses Eliza to prove a point about diction defining social classes; she becomes a pawn in his plot to convince others that she is member of upper class. [Irish Lit.: Misc.]

5. **Jabin** Canaanite king to whom God sold Israelites. [O.T.: Judges 4:1]

6. **Nebuchadnezzar** Babylonian king, plunders Jerusalem; carries people into exile. [O.T.: II Kings 24:10–16]

7. **Phantom of the Opera, The** deformed man haunts opera house for vengeance; subjects a young female singer to his will. [Musical: Misc.]

8. **Svengali** mesmerizes artist's model, making her a famous singer under his influence. [Br. Lit.: George DuMaurier *Trilby*]

645. SUBMISSION

1. **Islam** Arabic word meaning surrender, submission, or obedience; followers of Islam (Muslims) submit themselves to God. [Islam: *UIMT*, 33]

2. **ox** universal symbol of strength, submissiveness, and steady toil; Christians equate with sacrificial Christ; sacrificial animal in ancient world. [Symbolism: *CEOS&S*]

3. **sheep** symbol of meekness and helplessness, needing leadership and protection. [Symbolism: *CEOS&S*]

646. SUBSTITUTION

1. **Arsinoë** put her own son in place of Orestes; her son was killed and Orestes was saved. [Gk. Myth.: Zimmerman, 32]

2. **Barrabas** robber freed in Christ's stead. [N.T.: Matthew 27:15–18; Swed. Lit.: *Barrabas*]

3. **Canty, Tom** young beggar takes to throne in prince's stead. [Am. Lit.: *The Prince and the Pauper*]

4. **Carton, Sydney** substitutes self for Charles Darnay, at the guillontine. [Br. Lit.: Charles Dickens *A Tale of Two Cities*]

5. **Edward, Prince of Wales** kingling becomes urchin in clothing exchange. [Am. Lit.: *The Prince and the Pauper*]

6. **George, Tobey** after Marcus's death, replaces him in his family. [Am. Lit.: *The Human Comedy*]

7. **Hagar** thinking herself barren, Sarah offers slave to Abraham. [O.T.: Genesis 16:1–4]

8. **Leah** deceptively substituted for Rachel in Jacob's bed. [O.T.: Genesis 29:22–25]

9. *Parent Trap, The* 1961 Disney film remade in 1998; twins, separated as babies when their parents divorce meet by chance at summer camp; decide to switch places and devise plan to reunite their mom and dad. [Am. Film: Misc.]

10. **pinch hitter** in baseball, a substitute chosen to get the team out of a "pinch," and get a hit; also, anyone chosen to help achieve a goal. [Am. Culture: *FOF, MOD*]

11. *Prince and the Pauper, The* 1881 novel by Mark Twain; young Prince Edward VI of England and peasant boy switch places for safety of king; commentary on the arbitrariness of social status. [Am. Lit.: Misc.]

12. **whipping boy** surrogate sufferer for delinquent prince. [Eur. Hist.: Brewer *Note-Book*, 942]

647. SUCCESS

1. **Alger, Horatio (1834–1899)** writer of boys' stories where young me are instantly rewarded for honesty, perseverance, etc. [Am. Hist.: Hart, 19]

2. **Amway** network marketing company promising financial success to distributors was cofounded in rags-to-riches fashion. [Am. Business: *SJEPC*]

3. **batting average** from baseball, means a measure of success. [Pop. Cult.: Misc.]

4. **beat to the punch** from boxing, to gain the advantage and succeed. [Am. Culture: Misc.]

5. **Browndock, Miss** "made her fortune in no time at all." [Br. Lit.: *Nicholas Nickleby*]

6. **Carnegie Hall** performing at venerable concert hall is a measure of success. [Am. Culture: *SJEPC*]

7. **Grand Ole Opry** iconic country music radio show in Nashville featuring live performances has been the hallmark of success for artists since 1925. [Am. Music: *SJEPC*]

8. **McVey, Hugh** from poor white to leading manufacturer. [Am. Lit.: *Poor White*, Magill I, 762–764]

9. **O Pioneers!** realistic success story of those who fathered nation. [Am. Lit.: *O Pioneers!*, Magill I, 663–665]

10. **Porter, Sir Joseph** became First Lord of the Admiralty by sticking to desk jobs and never going to sea. [Br. Opera: Gilbert and Sullivan *H.M.S. Pinafore*]

11. **quantum leap** from physics, describing how electrons can "leap" within an atom; in common usage, describes a great breakthrough, or leap forward. [Physics: *WB*; Am. Culture: Misc.]

12. **Ragged Dick** hero of Alger's rags-to-riches epic. [Am. Lit.: Van Doren, 807]

13. **Wal-Mart** American shopping was changed beginning in the 1960s by retail giant; proliferation of huge discount stores (especially in small towns) offering variety and value; accusations of unfair labor practices and environmental irresponsibility followed. [Am. Business: *SJEPC*]

14. **white cloud** indicates high achievement. [Western Folklore: Jobes, 350]

15. **wolf** symbol of success on coats of arms. [Heraldry: Halberts, 16]

648. SUFFERING (See also LONG-SUFFERING.)

1. **aloe** symbol of suffering. [Flower Symbolism: Jobes, 71]

2. **Andersonville** horrible Civil War prison where 12,926 Union soldiers died. [Am. Hist.: Jameson, 18]

3. **avidya** cause of suffering through desire. [Hindu Phil.: Parrinder, 36]

4. **Bataan** site of U.S.-Filipino army "death march" (1943). [Am. Hist.: *EB*, I: 867–868]

5. **Black Beauty** his life with various owners is depicted in children's book by Anna Sewell; good breeding makes him pleasant and conscientious, but humane treatment brings out the best in him and poor treatment brings him great suffering. [Br. Children's Lit.: Jones]

6. **Black Hole of Calcutta** 146 Britishers imprisoned in small, stifling room (1756). [Br. Hist.: Harbottle, 45–46]

7. **Chiron** centaur, gave up his immortality in order to end the intolerable suffering accidentally inflicted by one of Heracles' poisoned arrows. [Gk. Myth.: Benét, 194]

8. **Concentration Camps** where millions of Jews were starved, experimented on, and exterminated by Nazis (1939–1945). [Eur. Hist.: Misc.]

9. **cross** for Christians, symbol of acceptance of suffering and death. [Christianity: *IEOTS*, 46]

10. **Gethsemane** garden east of Jerusalem where Jesus suffered in anguished fatigue. [N.T.: Matthew 26:36; Mark 14:32]

11. **Hiroshima** where the atomic bomb was dropped (August 6, 1945). [Am. Hist.: Fuller, III, 626]

12. **Io** having been changed into a heifer by Zeus, pestered by gadfly sent by Hera. [Gk. Myth.: Espy, 292]

13. ***J.B.*** Job's trials in modern setting and idiom. [Am. Lit.: *J.B.*]

14. **Job** beset with calamities. [O.T.: Job 1:13–22; 2:6–10]

15. **Mauperin, Renée** undergoes lingering and anguished death from guilt. [Fr. Lit.: *Renée Mauperin*]

16. **Orestes** persecuted and tormented by Furies. [Gk. Myth.: Wheeler, 271; Gk. Lit.: *The Eumenides*]

17. **Philoctetes** Greek hero, bitten by a serpent, suffers agonies for ten years. [Gk. Drama: Sophocles *Philoctetes* in Magill III, 741]

18. **prisoner of Chillon** chained for years in a damp, dark dungeon with his brothers, watches them die. [Br. Lit.: Byron *The Prisoner of Chillon*, in Benét, 817]

19. **Prometheus** chained to rock while vulture fed on his liver. [Gk. Myth.: Zimmerman, 221]

20. ***Raft of the Medusa, The*** realistically portrays anguished ship's crew. [Fr. Art.: Daniel, 166]

21. **Smith, Winston** beaten and tortured with rats for conspiring against the totalitarian regime. [Br. Lit.: George Orwell *1984*]

22. **Tantalus** condemned to Tartarus with food and water always just out of reach; hence, *tantalize*. [Gk. Myth.: Zimmerman, 253]

23. **Valley Forge** winter quarters of Washington's underfed, underclothed Continental army (1778). [Am. Hist.: Jameson, 519]

649. SUICIDE (See also DESPAIR, REMORSE, SELF-SACRIFICE.)

1. **Achitophel** hanged himself when his advice went unheeded. [O.T.: II Samuel 17:23]

2. **Aegeus** throws himself into the sea believing that his son, Theseus, has come to harm. [Gk. Myth.: Brewer *Dictionary*, 12]

3. **Ajax** kills himself in rage over loss of Achilles's armor. [Rom. Lit.: *Aeneid*]

4. **Antigone** imprisoned, kills herself in despair. [Gk. Lit.: *Antigone*]

5. **Antony, Mark** thinking Cleopatra is dead, he falls upon his sword. [Br. Lit.: Shakespeare *Antony and Cleopatra*]

6. **Bart, Lily** social climber takes poison when all her scheming comes to naught. [Am. Lit.: *The House of Mirth* in Hart, 385]

7. **Brand, Ethan** acknowledging "the unpardonable sin," throws himself into a lime kiln. [Am. Lit.: Hawthorne "Ethan Brand" in Hart, 261]

8. **Butterfly, Madame** stabs herself when her American lover returns with his lawful wife. [Ital. Opera: *Madama Butterfly* in Osborne *Opera*, 192]

9. **Calista** stabs herself on disclosure of adultery. [Br. Lit.: *The Fair Penitent*]

10. **Cassandra** commits suicide to escape the Athenians. [Fr. Opera: Berlioz, *The Trojans*, Westerman, 174]

11. **Charmian** kills herself after mistress Cleopatra's death. [Br. Lit.: *Antony and Cleopatra*]

12. **Chuzzlewit, Jonas** wicked murderer, found out, takes poison. [Br. Lit.: Dickens *Martin Chuzzlewit*]

13. **Cleopatra (69–30 B.C.)** kills herself rather than being led through Rome in defeat. [Br. Lit.: Shakespeare *Antony and Cleopatra*]

14. **Compson, Quentin** unable to prevent the marriage of his sister, he drowns himself on her wedding day. [Am. Lit.: Faulkner *The Sound and the Fury* in Magill I, 917]

15. **Deianira** accidentally kills husband, Hercules; kills herself out of guilt. [Gk. Myth.: Kravitz, 76]

16. **Dido** kills herself when Aeneas abandons her. [Rom. Myth.: Avery, 392–393; Rom. Lit.: *Aeneid*]

17. **Dobson, Zuleika** Oxford undergraduates commit suicide when she spurns them. [Br. Lit.: Magill II, 1169]

18. **Eden, Martin** disgusted by society snobbery, he drowns himself. [Am. Lit.: *Martin Eden*]

19. **Ekdal, Hedvig** heartbroken by her father's rejection, puts a bullet through her breast. [Nor. Drama: Ibsen *The Wild Duck* in Magill I, 1113]

20. **Enobarbus** kills himself for deserting Antony. [Br. Lit.: *Antony and Cleopatra*]

21. **Erigone** hangs himself in grief over father's murder. [Gk. Myth.: Kravitz, 91]

22. **Evadne** immolates herself on husband's funeral pyre. [Gk. Myth.: Kravitz, 100]

23. **Gabler, Hedda** shoots herself upon realizing that she is in the power of a man aware that she drove another man to suicide. [Swed. Drama: Ibsen *Hedda Gabler*]

24. **Goneril** stabs herself when her murder plot is discovered. [Br. Drama: Shakespeare *King Lear*]

25. **hara-kiri** Japanese ritual suicide; also a term to describe self-destructive decision or action. [Jap. Hist.: *FOF, MOD*; Am. Culture: Misc.]

26. **Hero** grief-stricken when her beloved Leander drowns while swimming the Hellespont, she drowns herself. [Gk. Myth.: Brewer *Dictionary*, 450]

27. **Iseult of Ireland** arriving too late to save Tristram (Tristan) from death, she kills herself; also called Yseult or Isolde. [Medieval Legend: Brewer *Dictionary*, 913]

28. **Javert** French inspector drowns himself to escape self-perpetuating torment. [Fr. Lit.: *Les Misèrables*]

29. **Jonestown** American religious zealots who lived in Peoples Temple in Guyana under leadership of pastor Jim Jones; in 1978 when U.S. officials investigated accusations of members being held against their will, there was violent reaction and subsequent mass suicide. [Am. Hist.: *Facts* (1978), 889–892; *SJEPC*]

30. **Juliet** stabs herself on seeing Romeo dead. [Br. Lit.: Shakespeare *Romeo and Juliet*]

31. **Kamikaze** WWII Japanese pilot corps plunge own planes into enemy ships in banzai attacks. [Jap. Hist.: Fuller, III, 618–619]

32. **Karenina, Anna** throws herself in front of approaching train. [Russ. Lit.: *Anna Karenina*]

33. **Kevorkian, Dr. Jack** controversial pathologist, called "Dr. Death," who assisted in the suicide of more than 130 terminally ill people in the 1990s. [Am. Hist.: Misc.]

34. **Little Father Time** solemn child hangs his foster-brothers and himself because of the family's misfortunes. [Br. Lit.: Hardy *Jude the Obscure*]

35. **Loman, Willy** crashes his car to bring insurance money to his family. [Am. Drama: Arthur Miller *Death of a Salesman*]

36. **Mannon, Christine** when her lover is killed she shoots herself. [Am. Drama: Eugene O'Neill *Mourning Becomes Electra*]

37. **Miss Julie** compromised by a clandestine affair and thwarted in her plans to run away, she decides to kill herself. [Swed. Drama: Strindberg *Miss Julie*]

38. **Nickleby, Ralph** learning that poor Smike is his own son, hangs himself. [Br. Lit.: Dickens *Nicholas Nickleby*]

39. **Ophelia** driven insane by Hamlet's actions, she drowns herself. [Br. Drama: Shakespeare *Hamlet*]

40. **Panthea** kills herself upon death of lover, Abradates. [Gk. Lit.: Walsh *Classical*, 3]

41. **Paul** deluded youth kills himself when his grandiose yearnings come to nothing. [Am. Lit.: Willa Cather "Paul's Case"]

42. **Phaedra** Athenian queen drinks poison after confessing guilt. [Fr. Lit.: *Phaedra*, Magill I, 741–742]

43. **"Richard Cory"** poem by Edward Arlington Robinson reveals the despair and suicide of a man who outwardly has everything. [Am. Lit.: E.A. Robinson "Richard Cory"]

44. **Romeo** thinking that Juliet's sleep is death, he drinks poison. [Br. Lit.: Shakespeare *Romeo and Juliet*]

45. **Saul** falls on sword to avoid humiliation of capture. [O.T.: I Samuel 31:4–6]

46. **Sophonisba** Carthaginian who took poison to avoid falling into Roman hands. [Rom. Hist.: Benét, 947]

47. **Suicide Club** members wishing to die are chosen by lot, as are those who are to effect their deaths. [Br. Lit.: Stevenson "The Suicide Club"]

48. **Vane, Sibyl** young actress kills herself after Dorian's betrayal. [Irish Lit.: *The Picture of Dorian Gray*, Magill I, 746–748]

650. SUMMER

1. **Aestas** personification of summer; portrayed as youthful and sprightly. [Rom. Myth.: *LLEI*, I: 322]

2. **Ceres** goddess of the season. [Rom. Myth.: Hall, 130]

3. **cricket** symbol of summer; weather prognosticator. [Insect Symbolism: Jobes, 382]

4. **naked girl with fruit** personification of summer. [Art: Hall, 130]

5. **sickle and sheaf of corn** representational of the season. [Art: Hall, 129]

651. SUN (See also LIGHT.)

1. **Apollo** sun god; his chariot ride spanned morning to night. [Gk. Myth.: Benét, 42]

2. **Aton** solar deity worshiped as the one god by Amenophis IV; also called Aten. [Egypt. Myth.: Parrinder, 33]

3. **Bast** cat-headed goddess representing sun and moon. [Egypt. Myth.: Parrinder, 41]

4. **Belenus** sun god. [Celtic Myth.: Parrinder, 42]

5. **Buto** goddess and mother of the sun and moon. [Egypt. Myth.: Kravitz, 48]

6. **cock** Helio's sacred bird; sacrificed to the sun in Mexico. [Rom. and Mex. Myth.: Leach, 239]

7. **Cuchulain** sun-figure and powerful fighter. [Irish Myth.: Parrinder, 68]

8. **double ax** symbol of the sun. [Hindu and Western Folklore: Cirlot, 22]

9. **eagle** symbol represents the sun. [Gk. Myth.: Brewer *Dictionary*, 358]

10. **fire** representation of the sun. [Western Symbolism: Cirlot, 105–106]

11. **gold** color of the sun's rays. [Color Symbolism: Jobes, 357]

12. **Helios** sun in its astronomic aspects; aspect of Apollo. [Gk. Myth.: Espy, 28]

13. **heron** emblem of the morning sun. [Symbolism: *CEOS&S*]

14. **Horus** solar deity; portrayed as a hawk-headed man. [Egypt. Myth.: Benét, 478]

15. **Hyperion** Titan and father of the sun. [Gk. Myth.: Zimmerman, 132]

16. **lion** symbol of the sun gods; corresponds to the sun. [Western Symbolism: Cirlot, 189–190]

17. **Mithra** god of sunlight; also called Mithras. [Persian Myth.: *EB*, VI: 944–945]

18. **Phaëthon** Apollo's son; foolishly attempted to drive sun chariot. [Gk. Myth.: Zimmerman, 202]

19. **Phoebus** epithet of Apollo as the sun god. [Gk. Myth.: Benét, 42]

20. **Ra** personification of the sun. [Egypt. Myth.: Parrinder, 235]

21. **Sol** the sun god. [Rom. Myth.: Zimmerman, 245]

652. SURPRISE

1. *Candid Camera* Allen Funt's tasteful but funny TV show secretly recorded ordinary people in humorous situations, then revealed "You're on Candid Camera!" (1950s-1990s). [Am. TV: *SJEPC*]

2. **Henry, O.** his plots characterized by unexpected dénouements. [Am. Lit.: Benét, 457]

3. **Operation Z** Japanese plan for Pearl Harbor attack. [Jap. Hist.: Toland, 177–178, 183–187]

4. **out of left field** from baseball, an unexpected occurance. [Am. Culture: *FOF, MOD*]

5. **Pearl Harbor** site of surprise attack on American fleet by the Japanese (December 7, 1941). [Am. Hist.: Fuller, III, 455–456]

6. **thief in the night** analogy to the Lord's unexpected coming. [N.T.: I Thessalonians 5:2]

7. **truffle** indicates the unexpected. [Flower Symbolism: *Flora Symbolica*, 178]

653. SURVIVAL (See also ENDURANCE.)

1. *Alive* story of the survivors of plane crash in the Andes. [Am. Lit.: *Alive*]

2. **Comanche** horse; sole survivor of Little Big Horn massacre (1876). [Am. Hist.: Wallechinsky, 126]

3. **Crusoe, Robinson** only survivor of shipwreck. [Br. Lit.: *Robinson Crusoe*]

4. **Deucalion** survives flood that destroys human race. [Gk. Myth.: Howe, 80]

5. **Donner Party** survivors of group of emigrants to California (1846–1847). [Am. Hist.: *NCE*, 783–784]

6. *Hatchet* 1987 novel for young readers by Gary Paulsen; thirteen-year-old Brian survives a plane crash; armed with only his Boy Scout hatchet, he must teach himself skills necessary to his survival. [Am. Children's Lit.: Gillespie and Naden]

7. *Island of the Blue Dolphins* 1961 novel for young readers by Scott O'Dell, based on the few facts known about the Lost Woman of San Nicholas; 12–year-old Karana lives on a Pacific island; when she is abandoned by her tribe in the early 1830s, she lives alone for nearly 20 years. [Am. Children's Lit.: Gillespie and Naden]

8. **Lot** allowed by God to escape the conflagration of Sodom and Gomorrah. [O.T.: Genesis 13:1–12]

9. **Mellitias, Saint** of "Forty Martyrs," the only one to survive icy ordeal. [Christian Hagiog.: Attwater, 133–134]

10. **Noah** chosen by God to escape the deluge. [O.T.: Genesis 5–9]

11. **Pilgrim, Billy** survives the fire-bombing of Dresden and is the only passenger to survive a domestic air crash. [Am. Lit.: Kurt Vonnegut *Slaughterhouse-Five*]

12. **Rambo** macho protagonist of a series of films; plots involve dramatic use of his guerilla warfare skills for survival and battle. [Am. Film: *SJEPC*]

13. **Robinsons** shipwrecked family learns to cope with nature on a desert island. [Children's Lit.: *Swiss Family Robinson*]

14. **Yossarian** always creating new ways to stay alive through long war. [Am. Lit.: *Catch-22*]

654. SUSTENANCE

1. **Amalthaea** goat who provided milk for baby Zeus. [Gk. Myth.: Leach, 41]

2. **ambrosia** food of the gods; bestowed immortal youthfulness. [Gk. Myth.: Kravitz, 19]

3. **locusts and wild honey** John the Baptist's meager fare in wilderness. [N.T.: Matthew 3:4; Mark 1:6]

4. **manna** given by the Lord to the Israelites. [O.T.: Exodus 16:14–15]

5. **Rose of Sharon** Joad sister who offers her breast to starving, dying man after giving birth to stillborn baby in John Steinbeck's novel *The Grapes of Wrath* (1939). [Am. Lit.: Harris *Characters*, 381–82; *SJEPC*]

655. SWIFTNESS

1. **Acestes** shoots an arrow with such force that it catches fire from friction with the air. [Rom. Lit.: *Aeneid* V, 525]

2. **Al Borak** horse who carried Muhammad from Mecca to Jerusalem overnight. [Muslim Tradition: Walsh *Classical*, 13–14]

3. **Andretti, Mario (1940–)** race car driver and Indianapolis 500 champion. [Am. Sports: *SJEPC*]

4. **Argo** swift, magic ship of the Argonauts. [Gk. Myth.: Avery, 145]

5. **Atalanta** heroine; fleet of foot; defeated by trickery. [Gk. Myth.: Walsh *Classical*, 36–37; Br. Lit.: *Atalanta*]

6. **Bayard** swiftest horse in the world. [Medieval and Renaissance Legend: Brewer *Dictionary*, 86]

7. **blitzkreig** German for "lightning war," refers to swift, sudden attack, as by Nazis in WW II. [Eur. Hist.: *FOF, MOD*]

8. **Camilla** Volscian queen; could run over cornfield without bending blades. [Rom. Lit.: *Aeneid*]

9. **cheetah** fastest four-footed animal alive; can reach 60 mph. [Zoology: Misc.]

10. *Cutty Sark* clipper ship, built in 1869; broke speed records in the tea trade. [Br. Hist.: *EB* (1963) V, 830]

11. **Hermes** messenger god; ran on the wings of the wind; Mercury to the Romans. [Gk. Myth.: Zimmerman, 124]

12. **Jehu** Israelite king noted for his rapid chariot driving. [O.T.: II Kings 9]

13. **Laelaps** hound so swift, it always overtook its quarry. [Gk. Myth.: Howe, 149]

14. **Pacolet's horse** enchanted steed of unparalleled quickness. [Fr. Lit.: *Valentine and Orson*; *LLEI*, I: 304]

15. **Pheidippides (fl. 490 B.C.)** ran 26 miles to Athens to announce Greek victory over Persians at Marathon. [Gk. Legend: Zimmerman, 159]

16. **Road Runner** foxy bird who continually zooms out of the coyote's reach. [TV: "The Road Runner Show" in Terrace, 247]

17. **Speedy Gonzalez** Mexican mouse who starred in many Warner Brothers cartoons; noted for his speed. [Am. TV: *ODA*]

18. **Superman** superhero; faster than a speeding bullet. [Comics: Horn, 642; TV: "Adventures of Superman" in Terrace, I, 37–38]

19. **winged petasus** Mercury's cap; symbolic of speed. [Gk. and Roman Myth.: 145]

656. SWIMMING

1. **Phelps, Michael (1985–)** American swimming phenomenon who won six gold medals at the 2004 Olympics and eight gold medals at the 2008 games. [Am. Sports: *BTSportv.13*]

2. **Spitz, Mark (1950–)** world-class swimmer who was first athlete to win seven gold medals in a single Olympics (1972). [Am. Sports: *SJEPC*]

3. **Van Dyken, Amy (1973–)** first American woman to win four gold medals in a single Olympics. [Am. Sports: *BTSportv.3*]

4. **Weissmuller, Johnny (1904?-1984)** Olympic gold medal swimmer who went on to play Tarzan, as an athletic, courageous man of few words in a series of movies during 1930s and 1940s. [Am. Sports: *SJEPC*]

5. **Williams, Esther (1922–)** American swimming champion who became a movie star, featured in many films performing intricate synchronized swimming routines; a symbol for a "bathing beauty." [Am. Films *EB*]

657. SWORD

1. **Almace** sabre of Turpin. [Fr. Lit.: *The Song of Roland*]

2. **Angurvadel** of Frithjof; blazed in war, gleamed dimly in peace. [Norse Myth.: *LLEI*, I: 323]

3. **Balisarda** made by sorceress for killing Orlando. [Ital. Lit.: *Orlando Furioso*, Benét, 75]

4. **Balmung** mighty sword belonging to Siegfried. [Ger. Lit.: *Nibelungenlied*]

5. **Barbamouche** Climborin's sabre. [Fr. Lit.: *The Song of Roland*]

6. **Colada** El Cid's two-hilted, solid gold sword. [Span. Lit.: *Song of the Cid*]

7. **Damocles, sword of** sword hung by a single hair over his head. [Rom. Lit.: Brewer *Handbook*, 257]

8. **Durnidana** Orlando's unbreakable sword; also called Durendal. [Ital. Lit.: *Morgante Maggiore*, Brewer *Handbook*, 309]

9. **Excalibur** Arthur's enchanted sword; extracting it from stone won him crown. [Br. Lit.: *Le Morte d'Arthur*]

10. **Fragarach** the "Answerer"; Lug's mighty blade could pierce any armor. [Irish Myth.: Leach, 415]

11. **Gram** belonged to Sigmund; broken by Odin. [Norse Lit.: *Volsung Saga*]

12. **Gramimond** Valdabrun's sabre. [Fr. Lit.: *The Song of Roland*]

13. **Hauteclaire** Oliver's trusty sabre. [Fr. Lit.: *The Song of Roland*]

14. **Joyeuse** Charlemagne's sword; buried with him. [Fr. Lit.: Brewer *Dictionary*, 594]

15. **Marmorie** Grandoyne's sabre. [Fr. Lit.: *The Song of Roland*]

16. **Merveilleuse** Doolin of Mayence's remarkably sharp sword. [Fr. Lit.: Wheeler, 241]

17. **Mimung** magic sword lent by Wittich to Siegfried. [Norse Myth.: Wheeler, 244]

18. **Mordure** Arthur's all-powerful sword, made by Merlin. [Br. Lit.: *Faerie Queene*]

19. **Morglay** Bevis's sword. [Br. Lit.: *Bevis of Hampton*]

20. **Murgleys** Ganelon's sabre. [Fr. Lit.: *The Song of Roland*]

21. **Notung** Sigmund's promised sword, found in ash tree; later, Siegfried's. [Ger. Opera: Wagner *Valkyrie*, Westerman, 236]

22. **Precieuse** sabre of the pagan, Baligant. [Fr. Lit.: *The Song of Roland*]

23. **Rosse** Alberich's gift to Otwit; frighteningly fine-edged. [Norse Myth.: Brewer *Dictionary*, 936]

24. **Sanglamore** Braggadocio's big, bloody glaive. [Br. Lit.: *Faerie Queene*]

25. **Sautuerdu** Malquiant's sabre. [Fr. Lit.: *The Song of Roland*]

26. **Sword of Justice** held by the personification of Justice. [Rom. Trad.: Jobes II, 898]

27. **Tizona** dazzling, golden-hilted sword of the Cid. [Span. Lit.: *Song of the Cid*]

28. **Zulfagar** sword of Ali, Muhammad's son. [Islamic Legend: Brewer *Handbook*, 1066]

Sycophancy (See FLATTERY.)

T

658. TACITURNITY

1. **Barkis** warmhearted but taciturn husband of Peggoty. [Br. Lit.: *David Copperfield*]

2. **Bartleby the Scrivener** "I prefer not to" was his constant refrain and all he ever said. [Am. Lit.: "Bartleby the Scrivener"]

3. **Bert and I** taciturn "down-Easterners." [Am. Culture: Misc.]

4. **Coolidge, Calvin (1872–1933)** 30th U.S. president; nicknamed "Silent Cal." [Am. Hist.: Frank, 99]

5. **Laconian** inhabitant of ancient country of Laconia; people noted for pauciloquy. [Gr. Hist.: *NCE*, 1514]

659. TALKATIVENESS

1. **Balwhidder** kind but loquacious Presbyterian clergyman. [Br. Lit.: *Annals of the Parish*]

2. **Bates, Miss** goodhearted purveyor of trivia and harmless gossip. [Br. Lit.: *Emma*]

3. **Bernstein, Baroness** loquaciously amusing, venomous, or coarse character. [Br. Lit.: *The Virginians*]

4. **blarney stone** whoever kisses the stone "will never want for words." [Irish Folklore: Leach, 147]

5. **Brigidda, Monna** unstoppable talker and gossiper. [Br. Lit.: George Eliot *Romola*]

6. **cicada** symbol of talkativeness because of its constant, strident noise. [Folklore: Jobes, 338]

7. **daisies** the flowers chatter incessantly at Alice. [Children's Lit.: *Through the Looking-Glass*]

8. **Echo** beautiful nymph who, by her constant talk, kept Hera away from Zeus. [Gk. Myth.: Howe, 89]

9. **Kenge, Mr.** garrulous soldier; nicknamed "conversation Kenge." [Br. Lit.: *Bleak House*]

10. **Old Woman of Gloucester** talkative woman displeased with her more talkative parrot. [Nurs. Rhyme: *Mother Goose*, 112]

11. **parrot** chattering bird; mimics human speech. [Animal Symbolism: Mercatante, 157]

12. **Polonius** wordy, "wretched, rash, intruding fool." [Br. Lit.: *Hamlet*]

13. **Trim, Corporal** dutiful attendant of Uncle Toby; distinguished for volubility. [Br. Lit.: *Tristram Shandy*]

660. TALLNESS (See also GIANT.)

1. **Burj Dubai** located in Dubai, United Arab Emirates; under construction as of 2008; when complete expected to be tallest building in the world at projected 693 meters. [Architecture: Misc.]

2. **Chrysler Building** tallest all-brick building in the world; 77 stories, 319 meters. [Architecture: Misc.]

3. **CITIC Plaza** one of the tallest buildings in the world; located in Guangzhou, China; 80 stories, 391 meters. [Architecture: Misc.]

4. **Colossus of Rhodes** statue of Apollo; wonder of ancient world. [Gk. Hist.: Osborne, 256]

5. **Eiffel Tower** built in 1889 in Paris; rises above city. [Architecture: *NCE*, 843]

6. **elevator shoe** shoe with insole designed to increase wearer's height. [Am. Pop. Culture: Misc.]

7. **Empire State Building** New York's famous skyscraper; first building to contain over 100 floors; 102 stories, 381 meters.. [Architecture: *NCE*, 865]

8. **giraffe** tallest of animals. [Zoology: *NCE*, 1088]

9. **Jin Mao Tower** one of tallest buildings in the world; located in Shaghai, China; 88 stories, 421 meters. [Architecture: Misc.]

10. **Petronas Towers** one of the tallest buildings in the world; located in Kuala Lampur, Malaysia; 88 stories, 452 meters. [Architecture: Misc.]

11. **redwoods** giant trees (sequoias) of Pacific Coast. [Botany: *NCE*, 2477]

12. **Sears Tower** in Chicago; America's tallest building; 108 stories, 442 meters.. [Architecture: Misc.]

13. **Shanghai World Financial** one of tallest buildings in the world; located in Shanghai, China; 101 stories, 492 meters. [Architecture: Misc.]

14. **Shun Hing Square** one of the tallest buildings in the world; located in Shenzhen, China; 69 stories, 384 meters. [Architecture: Misc.]

15. **Taipei 101 Tower** one of tallest buildings in the world; located in Taipei, Taiwan; 101 stories, 509 meters. [Architecture: Misc.]

16. **Two International Financial** one of the tallest buildings in the world; located in Hong Kong, China; 88 stories, 415 meters. [Architecture: Misc.]

17. **Woolworth Building** in New York City; erected by Frank Woolworth in 1913; tallest building until Empire State Building (1930–1931). [Architecture: *NCE*, 3004]

18. **World Trade Center** until their destruction, Twin Towers were tallest buildings in New York City and hub of financial district; hit

by two planes hijacked by al-Queda terrorists on September 11, 2001, causing the collapse of the buildings and the deaths of nearly 3000. [Am. Hist.: *SJEPC*]

Tastlessness (See COARSENESS.)

661. TEACHING (See also EDUCATION.)

1. **Aristotle (384–322 B.C.)** Greek philosopher who tutored Alexander the Great. [Gk. Hist.: *NCE*, 147]

2. **Arnold, Dr.** wise headmaster of Rugby shows his understanding of youth. [Br. Lit.: *Tom Brown's School Days*; Magill II, 1039]

3. **Auburn schoolmaster** learned and severe yet kind master of the village school. [Br. Poetry: Goldsmith *The Deserted Village* in Norton *Literature*]

4. **Bhaer, Professor** teaches writing to Jo; eventually marries her. [Am. Lit.: *Little Women*]

5. **blackboard jungle** from the title of a 1955 movie about teachers who struggle with race and class issues in inner-city school; phrase refers to the dangerous, violent atmosphere in U.S. schools. [Am. Hist.: *FOF, MOD*]

6. *Boston Public* American television series focusing on the teachers, administration, and students of a public school in Boston, Massachusetts; topics include affirmative action, teenage pregnancy, school violence, and drug abuse. [Am. TV: Misc.]

7. **Brodie, Miss Jean** dedicated teacher and heroine, creating "the crème de la crème" [Br. Lit.: Muriel Sparks *The Prime of Miss Jean Brodie*]

8. **Brooks, Miss Connie** popular TV show features a harried Miss Brooks as high school teacher. [TV: "Our Miss Brooks" in Terrace, II, 174]

9. **Chips, Mr.** lovable and didactic schoolteacher. [Br. Lit.: *Goodbye, Mr. Chips*]

10. **Chiron** knowledgeable Centaur; instructed Achilles, Jason, and Asclepius. [Gk. Myth.: Parrinder, 62]

11. **Confucius (c.551–479 B.C.)** classic Chinese sage. [Chinese Hist.: *NCE*, 625]

12. *Dead Poets Society* film set in a 1959 boys prep school; focuses on a teacher who uses poetry and literature to inspire his students. [Am. Film: Misc.]

13. **Grundy, Miss** Archie's grumpy high school teacher. [Am. Comics: "Archie" in Horn, 87]

14. **guru** Hindu spiritual leader and teacher; by extension, a wise teacher [Hindu Rel.: Bowker]

15. **Hartsook, Ralph** backwoods schoolteacher has severe problems with boisterous older pupils. [Am. Lit.: *The Hoosier Schoolmaster*; Magill I, 373]

16. **Hicks, Miss** history teacher, antiquated but wise, impassioned, and just to her pupils. [Am. Lit.: Saroyan *The Human Comedy* in Magill I, 392]

17. *Lean on Me* 1989 film based loosely on the inspirational story of Joe Clark, a principal who resuscitates an inner-city New Jersey school in danger of being taken over by the government due to low test scores. [Am. Film: Misc.]

18. **Leonowens, Mrs. Ann** young Welsh widow, tutors children and women of King of Siam. [Br. Lit.: Landon *Anna and the King of Siam*; Am. Musical: Rodgers and Hammerstein *The King and I* in *On Stage*, 333]

19. **Moffat, Miss** teacher in Welsh mining town. [Br. Lit.: *The Corn is Green*; NCE, 2982]

20. **Mr. Wizard** [Don Herbert (1917–2007)] made science lessons fun and interesting on his television show. [Am. TV: *SJEPC*]

21. **Pangloss** character who taught Candide "metaphysico-theologo-cosmolonigology." [Fr. Lit.: *Candide*]

22. **Phillotson, Mr.** Jude's former schoolmaster. [Br. Lit.: Thomas Hardy *Jude the Obscure*]

23. **Porpora** famous music master of Consuelo and Haydn. [Fr. Lit.: *Consuelo*, Magill I, 156–158]

24. **Silenus** knowledgeable tutor of Bacchus. [Rom. Myth.: Daniel, 213]

25. **Socrates (469–399 B.C.)** Greek philosopher; tutor of Plato. [Gk. Hist.: *NCE*, 2553]

26. **Squeers, Wackford** dismally ignorant schoolmaster; cruel to his charges. [Br. Lit.: Dickens *Nicholas Nickleby*]

27. *Stand and Deliver* film about a real-life Los Angeles high school mathematics teacher who uses humor and innovative teaching to motivate his students to pass their AP Calculus exam. [Am. Film: Misc.]

28. **Sullivan, Anne (1866–1936)** teacher famous for tutoring Helen Keller and opening the world to the blind, deaf and dumb young girl. [Am. Hist.: Misc.]

29. **Swift, Kate** stern schoolteacher; takes pains to encourage any signs of genius. [Am. Lit.: Anderson *Winesburg, Ohio* in Benét, 1095]

30. *To Sir, With Love* film addressing racial issues in an inner-city school; follows an idealistic black teacher starting a new teaching job at the school. [Am. Film: Misc.]

31. **village schoolmaster** stern yet kind; the rustics wondered "that one small head could carry all he knew." [Br. Poetry: Goldsmith *The Deserted Village* in Magill IV, 823]

32. ***Welcome Back, Kotter*** 1975–1979 sitcom about teacher who returns to his alma mater in Brooklyn; through humor and dedication, he inspires a group of unmotivated teenagers known as the Sweathogs. [Am. TV: *SJPEC*]

Technology (See INTERNET.)

Teenager (See ADOLESCENCE.)

662. **TELEVISION (See also BROADCASTING.)**

1. **Allen, Steve (1921–2000)** innovative TV personality and first host of NBC's *The Tonight Show*. [Am. TV: *ISJEPC*]

2. **Belushi, John (1949–1982)** talented, energetic comedian and actor who pushed the envelope was part of original *Saturday Night Live* cast. [Am. Entertainment: *SJEPC*]

3. **boob tube** in America and Canada, slang expression for a television set, referring to its mindless entertainment. [Am. and Can. TV: Misc.]

4. **Burnett, Carol (1933–)** queen of comedy a regular on television from 1960s on; hosted own variety show 1967–1978. [Am. TV: *SJEPC*]

5. **Carson, Johnny (1925–2005)** an institution in late-night TV; host of *The Tonight Show* for 30 years upon retirement in 1992; his self-effacing, dry wit made the show interesting and fun. [Am. TV: Misc.]

6. **Cavett, Dick (1936–)** witty talk show host (1968–1982) conducted lively, memorable interviews with his guests. [Am. TV: *SJEPC*]

7. **Child, Julia (1912–2004)** educated and delighted viewers on her public TV cooking show *The French Chef* (premiered 1962) with her unpretentious, often messy, style. [Fr. and Am. Cuisine: *SJEPC*]

8. **Clark, Dick (1929–)** legendary television veteran hosted dance show *American Bandstand* (1957–1989); continues to grace TV screens annually on *New Year's Rockin' Eve* (1972–). [Am. Music and TV: *SJEPC*]

9. **CNN (Cable News Network)** 24–hour cable network considered the world's premier source of international television news. [Am. TV: *SJEPC*]

10. **Cosby, Bill (1937–)** star of successful comedy series *The Cosby Show* (1984–92) about an upper middle-class black family; also appeared in *I Spy* (1965–68) and other TV series. [Am. TV: *SJEPC*]

11. **couch potato** slang name for someone who spends copious amounts of time on the couch; usually refers to excessive eatiing and TV viewing. [Am. TV: Misc.]

12. *CSI* stands for Crime Scene Investigation; popular drama series began in 2000; about team of police forensic evidence investigators in Las Vegas who solve mysteries behind unusual deaths; spin-offs about similar teams in Miami and New York. [Am. TV: Misc.]

13. *Dark Shadows* popular daytime drama featured paranormal events and mysterious secrets at the Collins family estate (1966–1971). [Am. TV: *SJEPC*]

14. *Dick Van Dyke Show, The* premiered in 1961; prime-time comedy series covered professional and personal life of affable TV writer Rob Petrie; Dick Van Dyke and a host of talented actors made the show a hit. [Am. TV: *SJEPC*]

15. **Ditka, Mike (1939–)** American professional football coach for the Chicago Bears; now a successful television commentator. [Am. TV: *SJEPC*]

16. **Donahue, Phil (1935–)** sensitive, charming originator of the daytime talk show tackled a range of controversial, serious, and silly topics, from feminist causes to the AIDS crisis to transvestite fashion, setting the course for the genre (1969–1996). [Am. TV: *SJEPC*]

17. **Douglas, Mike (1925–2006)** former big band singer hosted family-friendly daytime TV talk program *The Mike Douglas Show* (1961–1982), welcoming diverse guests from mainstream America to the counterculture. [Am. TV: *SJEPC*]

18. **Downs, Hugh (1921–)** longtime TV broadcasting giant with reassuring, gracious manner has appeared on the air more hours than any other network broadcaster, according to *The Guiness Book of World Records*. [Am. TV: *SJEPC*]

19. **Emmy** awarded annually for best achievements in television programming and performance. [Am. TV: *SJEPC*]

20. **Gleason, Jackie (1916–1987)** physically heavy comedian and film actor known as "The Great One" hosted own TV variety show (1950s-1970s) but was best known for role as bus driver Ralph Kramden in *The Honeymooners* (1955–1956). [Am. TV: *SJEPC*]

21. **Godfrey, Arthur (1903–1983)** affable, folksy redhead was TV pioneer, hosting popular variety show *Arthur Godfrey's Talent Scouts* and *Arthur Godfrey and His Friends* in late 1940s-1950s; "applause meter" allowed live audience to determine winner. [Am. TV: *SJEPC*]

22. **Goodson, Mark (1915–1992)** the "godfather of television game shows" produced such long-lived audience favorites as *What's My Line?* (1950–1974) and *To Tell the Truth* (1956–1977). [Am. TV: *SJEPC*]

23. **Griffin, Merv (1925–2007)** former big band singer was affable host of his popular namesake TV talk show from 1962 to 1986; formed Merv Griffin Productions, known for such TV game shows as *Jeopardy!*. [Am. TV: *SJEPC*]

24. *Hallmark Hall of Fame* series of fine arts performances to television, from opera to Shakespeare, to original films. [Am. TV: *EB*]

25. *I Love Lucy* popular 1950s TV comedy starring husband-and-wife team of Lucille Ball and Desi Arnaz; exaggerated situations familiar to typical American married couples. [Am. TV: *SJEPC*]

26. **King, Larry (1933–)** nationally prominent talk-show host with relaxed yet commanding interviewing style on his *Larry King Live* TV show; interesting guests and open phone lines for callers' questions and comments. [Am. TV: *SJEPC*]

27. **Kovacks, Ernie (1919–1962)** used video technology and special effects to the fullest to create innovative form of humor. [Am. TV: *SJEPC*]

28. *Kraft Television Theatre* from 1947 to 1958 show featured superior dramas by famous and soon-to-be-famous playwrights; many celebrated actors made early appearances as well. [Am. TV: *SJEPC*]

29. *Larry Sanders Show, The* 1992–1998 satire of the behind-the-scenes world of late-night TV starring comedian Garry Shandling as egotistical host of a late-night talk show; unique in its lack of laugh track and very edgy humor. [Am. TV: *SJEPC*]

30. *Law & Order* prime-time series began in 1990; follows crime (often taken from real cases); first half of show covers police investigation, second half of show covers prosecution of crime; spin-offs were *Law & Order: Special Victims Unit* and *Law & Order: Criminal Intent*. [Am. TV: Misc.]

31. **La-Z-Boy loungers** irst mfirst manufactured in 1927; easy chairs that reclined included built-in footrest; are favorites for TV viewing; often viewed as epitome of relaxation and inactivity. [Am. Pop. Culture: *SJEPC*]

32. **Leno, Jay (1950–)** stand-up comedian who took coveted spot of host of late-night talk show *The Tonight Show* in 1992 when Johnny Carson retired; likable and witty, he carried off the job with great success. [Am. TV: *SJEPC*]

33. **Letterman, David (1947–)** host of successful late night talk show for over 20 years; combination of interviews, wacky stunts, wisecracking, and Top Ten lists. [Am. TV: *SJEPC*]

34. **McGraw, Dr. Phil (1950–)** highly popular psychologist and TV personality; came into public view on *Oprah*; weekly appearances led to his own TV show; doling out advice with frankness and judgmental style that some have criticized as too simplistic and insulting; others are drawn to it. [Am. TV: Misc.]

35. **Muppets** with their quirky personalities and winsome humor, Jim Henson's charming puppets have won the hearts of TV viewers from the late 1950s to the present. [Am. TV: *SJEPC*]

36. **PBS (Public Broadcasting)** Corporation for Public Broadcasting created in 1967; soon after, noncommercial TV blossomed into full spectrum of quality documentaries, drama, sitcoms, and children's programs. [Am. TV: *SJEPC*]

37. **Reality Television** shows in which real-life events or situations are filmed; began in America in mid-1980s and rose to immense popularity. [Am. TV: *SJEPC*]

38. **Roddenberry, Gene (1921–1991)** creator of *Star Trek* science-fiction television series; short three-year run (1966–1969), but spawned host of TV shows, films, books, comice, conventions, and more. [Am. TV and Pop. Culture: *SJEPC*]

39. **Rogers, Roy (1912–1998)** singing cowboy; films featured horse Trigger, sidekick Gabby Hayes, and wife Dale Evans; successful TV show for children followed. [Am. Film and TV: *SJEPC*]

40. **Sarnoff, David (1891–1971)** created the National Broadcasting Company (NBC) in 1926, the first permanent network; commercial broadcasting was born. [Am. TV: *SJEPC*]

41. **satellites** a network of satellites receiving and relaying signals meant a leap forward in communications and media broadcasts. [Am. Science: *SJEPC*]

42. *Saturday Night Live* began in 1970s; late-night comedy variety show that spawned multitude of stars and classic skits; reinvented TV comedy with irreverent satire and boisterous nonsense. [Am. TV: *SJEPC*]

43. *SCTV* Toronto company of Second City satirize television in this TV show about a fictional television station, its staff and on-air talent; began in 1976 and ran for seven years. [Can. TV: *SJEPC*]

44. **Serling, Rod (1924–1975)** author of scripts that brought quality drama to early TV; created and hosted *The Twilight Zone*, eerie science-fiction/fantasy series with serious themes and name actors. [Am. TV: *SJEPC*]

45. *Sesame Street* began in 1968; winner of more than 100 awards; Jim Henson's muppets and actors in an urban neighborhood teach children basic concepts through song, repetition, and entertaining images and sounds; influenced children's TV and teaching styles. [Am. TV: *SJEPC*]

46. **Spelling, Aaron (1928–2006)** incredibly successful producer whose shows found great popular success, but little crical approval; from the 1960s on, his work often reflected Southern California lifestyle of glamour and wealth. [Am. TV: *SJEPC*]

47. **Sullivan, Ed (1902–1974)** host of variety show for 23 years begin-ning in 1948; stiff before the camera but genius at choosing acts to reflect best in performing arts. [Am. TV: *SJEPC*]

48. **surfing** using a remote control to skip from one TV channel to an-other, often to avoid advertisements. [Usage: *SJEPC*]

49. **Susskind, David (1923–1987)** host of TV talk show about wide range of topics; his confrontational approach and interesting guests led to a 19–year run. [Am. TV: *SJEPC*]

50. **tabloid television** popular television shows with quasi-journalis-tic approach to sex, crime, and gossip. [Am. TV: *SJEPC*]

51. **televangelism** evangelical Christians broadened their influence and drew new followers through televised preaching; scandals in-volving Jim Bakker and Jimmy Swaggart in the 1980s brought re-ligious broadcasters under scrutiny. [Am. TV and Rel.: *SJEPC*]

52. **Telstar** satellite launched in 1962 to relay images and telephone calls across the globe; name combines telecommunications and star. [Am. Science: *SJEPC*]

53. **Thomas, Danny (1912–1991)** comedian and star of popular sit-com about nightclub entertainer trying to have a normal family life; major fund raiser for St. Jude's Children's Hospital. [Am. TV: *SJEPC*]

54. *Today* long-running early morning live TV news magazine-style show, premiered in 1952; news, interviews, entertainment, and features on health, personal finances, etc.; crowds gather each day outside studio in New York, sometimes interviewed by hosts. [Am. TV: *SJEPC*]

55. *Tonight Show, The* beginning in 1954, top late-night talk show with monologue, series of conversations with guests, and spots for up-and-coming stand-up comics; began with host Steve Allen, followed by Jack Paar, Johnny Carson, and Jay Leno. [Am. TV: *SJEPC*]

56. **Turner, Ted (1938–)** using nonstop communications satellite, began world's first superstation, which became WTBS in 1979; created 24–hour cable news network (CNN) in 1980 and Turner Classic Movie channel in early 1990s. [Am. TV: *SJPEC*]

57. **TV dinners** frozen dinners introduced by Swanson; gained ac-ceptance as pace of life accelerated, selling 70 million the first year (1955); aluminum trays holding meat, starch, vegetable, and dessert were often eaten while watching TV. [Am. Cuisine: *SJEPC*]

58. *TV Guide* first published in 1953; weekly national television mag-azine with articles, reviews, and photos; separate editions cover local listings. [Am. Jour.: *SJEPC*]

59.   *Wide World of Sports* TV show that began in 1960s, covering variety of sports; opening narration about "the thrill of victory and the agony of defeat" became famous. [Am. TV: *SJEPC*]

60.   **Winfrey, Oprah (1954–)** African-American entrepreneur whose television show helped launch her media empire; one of the most successful people in modern American media. [Am. TV: *BBAL*]

663.   TEMPERANCE

1.   **Alcoholics Anonymous (AA)** organization founded to help alcoholics (1934). [Am. Culture: *EB*, I: 448]

2.   **amethyst** provides protection against drunkenness; February birthstone. [Gem Symbolism: Kunz, 58–59]

3.   **Anti-Saloon League** successfully led drive for Prohibition (1910s). [Am. Hist.: Flexner, 357]

4.   **Jonadab** enjoined his people to abstinence. [O.T.: Jeremiah 35:5–11]

5.   **Nation, Carry** [Amelia Moore (1846–1911)] hatchet-wielding saloon wrecker. [Am. Hist: Flexner, 253]

6.   **Prohibition** period from 1919–1933 when selling and consuming liquor was against the law. [Am. Hist.: *NCE*, 2710]

7.   **Rechabites** pastoral people who abstained from all wines. [O.T.: Jeremiah 35:5–19]

8.   **Samson** consecrated to God in abstinence. [O.T.: Judges 13:4–5]

9.   **Volstead Act** 18th Amendment, passed by Congress to enforce Prohibition (1919). [Am. Hist.: Flexner, 286]

10.   **Woman's Christian Temperance Union** society of militant housewives against drinking (20th century). [Am. Hist.: Flexner, 357]

664.   TEMPTATION

1.   **apple** as fruit of the tree of knowledge in Eden, has come to epitomize temptation. [O.T.: Genesis 3:1–7; Br. Lit.: *Paradise Lost*]

2.   **Baggins, Frodo** hero of J.R.R. Tolkien's trilogy *The Lord of the Rings*; travels to devastated land of Mordor to destroy magic ring with power to tempt all who possess it before it is used for evil by dark lord Sauron. [Br. Lit.: *SJEPC*]

3.   **evil one** name for Satan, the tempter [O.T. Genesis 3:1–7]

4.   **forbidden fruit** God prohibits eating from Tree of Knowledge. [O.T.: Genesis 2:16–17]

5.   **Potiphar's wife** tried to induce Joseph to lie with her. [O.T.: Genesis 39]

6.   **quince** symbol of temptation. [Flower Symbolism: *Flora Symbolica*, 176]

7. **Satan** offers world to Jesus in exchange for His obedience. [N.T.: Matthew 4:8–11]

8. **serpent** coaxes Eve to eat forbidden fruit. [O.T.: Genesis 3:1–5]

9. **Zuleika** name given in Arabian legend to Potiphar's wife, who vainly tempted Joseph. [Arab. Legend: Benét, 1117]

665. TENNIS

1. **Agassi, Andre (1970–)** high-profile tennis player won all four Grand Slam singles events during his career: Wimbledon, Australian Open, U.S. Open, and French Open. [Am. Sports: *SJEPC*]

2. **Ashe, Arthur (1943–1993)** respected African-American tennis champion also fought racism and the stigma of AIDS. [Am. Sports: *SJEPC*]

3. **Australian Open** played each year in January, beginning in 1905; only Grand Slam tournament with indoor play. [Aust. Sports: Misc.]

4. **Connors, Jimmy (1952–)** competitive, intense tennis player racked up eight Grand Slam singles championships and was number one in the world several times in his career; helped popularize the game in the 1970s. [Am. Sports: *SJEPC*]

5. **Evert, Chris (1954–)** known as "The Ice Maiden" for her composure and discipline on the court; ranks as one of the greatest and most popular female players in the game's history; boasts a .900 career winning percentage in singles. [Am. Sports: *SJEPC*]

6. **French Open** Grand Slam tournament held during two weeks in mid-May to early June in Paris; premier clay court tournament in the world. [Fr. Sports: Misc.]

7. **Gibson, Althea (1927–2003)** trailblazing African-American tennis champion won four grand slam tournaments in the 1950s; inducted into Tennis Hall of Fame in 1971. [Am. Sports: *SJEPC*]

8. **Graf, Steffi (1969–)** German tennis champ who won 22 Grand Slam titles, with her powerful, competitive play. [Ger. Sports: Misc.]

9. **King, Billie Jean (1943–)** outstanding professional tennis player and outspoken proponent for equality for female athletes; defeated Bobby Riggs when he dared her to Battle of the Sexes match in 1973; instrumental in arranging first professional tennis tournament for women in 1970. [Am. Sports: *SJEPC*]

10. **Lacoste, Jean René (1904–1996)** very talented French tennis pro who designed Lacoste piqué cotton shirt to replace stiff, long-sleeved Oxford shirts worn for tennis in the 1920s; also invented first tubular steel tennis racquet in 1963. [Fr. Sports: *SJEPC*]

11. **Laver, Rod (1938–)** Australian-born tennis player who was first two-time winner (1962, 1969) of Grand Slam; considered by some to be best player ever. [Am. Sports: *SJEPC*]

12. **McEnroe, John (1959–)** for several years in the 1980s, ranked number one tennis player in the world. [Am. Sports: *SJEPC*]

13. **Navratilova, Martina (1956–)** Czech-born powerful athlete; winner of an unprecedented number of single titles. [Sports: *SJEPC*]

14. **Riggs, Bobby (1918–1995)** spectacular tennis player known mostly for his chauvinistic "Battle of the Sexes" match with victorious Billie Jean King in 1973. [Am. Sports: *SJEPC*]

15. **Sampras, Pete (1971–)** one of the greatest tennis playes of all time; won a world-record 14 Grand Slam titles. [Am. Sports: *BT1997*]

16. **Seles, Monica (1973–)** was ranked number one at age 17; made a comeback after being stabbed by Steffi Graf fan. [Am. Sports: *SJEPC*]

17. **U.S. Open** Grand Slam tournament which began in 1881, making it one of the oldest tennis tournaments in the world; held in August and September over two weeks. [Am. Sports: Misc.]

18. **Williams, Serena (1981–)** African-American tennis champ, known for her powerful play; winner of several Grand Slam events, often against her sister, Venus. [Am. Sports: *BTSportsv.4*]

19. **Williams, Venus (1980–)** African-American tennis great, a powerful, dominant player, won several Grand Slam events, often against her sister, Serena. [Am. Sports: *BT1999*]

20. **Wimbledon** British tennis tournament begun in 1877; held in late June and early July; only one of four Grand Slam events still played on natural grass. [Br. Sports: *SJEPC*]

Terror (See HORROR.)

666. TERRORISM

1. **Achille Lauro** cruise ship hijacked on October 7, 1985 by four men from Palestinian Liberation Front, demanding release of 50 Palestinians in Israeli prisons. [Hist.: Miss.]

2. **Al Fata** Palestine Liberation movement's terrorist organization. [Arab. Hist.: Wigoder, 186]

3. **Al Qaeda** Islamic terrorist group, responsible for 9/11 attacks on U.S. [Am. Hist Misc.]

4. **Baader-Meinhof gang** German terrorists. [Ger. Hist.: *Facts* (1978), 114–115]

5. **Black Panthers** militant black revolutionists and civil-rightists. [Am. Hist.: Flexner, 46]

6. **Entebbe** Air France flight hijacked on June 21, 1976 by two Palestinian and two German extremists; plane landed at Entebbe Airport in Uganda where over 200 hostages were held. [Hist.: Misc.]

7. **Gestapo** Nazi secret police; executors of "Final Solution." [Ger. Hist.: Wigoder, 211]

8. **IRA** the Irish Republican Army; long history of terror and violence. [Irish Hist.: *NCE*, 1365–1366]

9. **Jewish Defense League** began in 1968 to protect Orthodox Jews in neighborhoods in Brooklyn; became terrorist organization, striking against Palestine Liberation Organization, Soviet officials, and others. [Am. Hist.: *SJEPC*]

10. **Ku Klux Klan** post-Civil War white supremacist organization used terrorist tactics against blacks. [Am. Hist.: *NCE*, 1505]

11. **militias** violent tactics by militia members in the 1990s have made these groups suspect in the minds of many. [Am. Culture: *SJEPC*]

12. **Nazis (National Socialism)** spread fear and terror throughout Hitler's Germany. [Ger. Hist.: *NCE*, 1894]

13. **9/11** the terrorist attack on the U.S. that took place on Sept. 11, 2001, in which nearly 3,000 people died in New York, Washington, D.C., and Pennsylvania. [Am. Hist.: Misc.]

14. **Red Brigade** Italian terrorist group; assassinated Aldo Moro (1978). [Ital. Hist.: *Facts* (1978), 133]

15. **Reign of Terror (1793–1794)** revolutionary government made terror its means of suppression, by edict (September 5, 1793). [Fr. Hist.: *EB*, IX: 904]

16. **Symbionese Liberation Army** small terrorist group that kidnapped Patty Hearst (1974–1975). [Am. Hist.: *Facts* (1974), 105]

17. **Weathermen, The** in the late 1960s to mid-1970s, protested Vietman Was and social and political injustices through bombings and other extreme methods. [Am. Hist.: *Facts* (1972), 384]

18. **World Trade Center** until their destruction, Twin Towers were tallest buildings in New York City and hub of financial district; hit by two planes hijacked by al-Queda terrorists on September 11, 2001, causing the collapse of the buildings and the deaths of nearly 3000. [Am. Hist.: Misc.]

667. TEST

1. **Abraham** his faith is tested when God demands the sacrifice of his son Isaac. [O.T.: Genesis 22:13]

2. **Arthur, King (c. 950–1000)** becomes King of England by pulling sword from stone. [Arth. Legend: *NCE*, 159]

3. **Carmel, Mt.** site of contest between Elijah and Baal priests. [O.T.: I Kings 18:19–40]

4. **Cuban missile crisis** President Kennedy called Krushchev's bluff, forcing dismantling of missile sites (1962). [Am. Hist.: Van Doren, 581–582]

5. ***J.B.*** testing of contemporary Job. [Am. Lit.: *J.B.*]

6. **Job** tormented to test devoutness. [O.T.: Job 1, 2]

7. **Judgment of God** medieval trial by combat or ordeal. [Eur. Hist.: Leach, 561]

8. **K'ung Fu** Confucian-based sect demands rigid tests for membership. [TV: Terrace, I , 448]

9. **litmus test** from science, a test that determines whether a solution is alkaline or acid; in common parlance a test to define a person's stance on a topic. [Pop. Culture: Misc.]

10. **ordeal by fire** noble accused of crime hold red-hot iron or walks blindfolded and barefoot over red-hot plowshares to proves his innocence. [Br. Hist.: Brewer *Handbook*, 779]

11. ***Turandot*** solver of riddles wins Turandot; failure brings death. [Ital. Opera: Puccini, *Turandot*, Westerman, 367–368]

668. THANKSGIVING

1. **cornucopia** traditional "horn of plenty," depicted as a horn-shaped basked filled with fruit, symbol of plenty and a bountiful harvest. [Am. Trad.: *HolSymb*]

2. **Macy's Thanksgiving Day Parade** held in New York City each year, featuring bands, floats, and mammoth balloon figures. [Am. Pop. Culture: *SJEPC*]

3. **Pilgrims** English immigrants arrived in New England in the early 1600s, fleeing religious persecution and supposedly held the first Thanksgiving feast, celebrating with local Indian tribes; a symbol of early America. [Am. Hist.: *HolSymb*]

4. **Plymouth Rock** the supposed site of the landing of the Pilgrims in Plymouth, Massachusetts; a symbol of America and the promise of freedom. [Am. Hist.: *HolSymb*]

5. **turkey** the center of the modern-day Thanksgiving feast, served with cranberries, stuffing, potatoes, and pumpkin pie, now all iconic elements of the meal. [Am. Trad.: *HolSymb*]

669. THEATER

1. **Abbey Theatre** home of famed Irish theatrical company. [Irish Hist.: *NCE*, 3]

2. **Apollo Theatre** famed Harlem venue for African-American entertainers, particularly during the Harlem Renaissance of the 1920s and 1930s. [Am. Hist.: *SJEPC*]

3. **Broadway** famous theatrical district at New York's Times Square. [Am. Hist.: Hart, 107]

4. **Carnegie Hall** New York's venerable theater for concert-goers. [Am. Hist.: *NCE*, 460]

5. **Comédie–Française** world's oldest established national theater; also Théâtre-Française . [Fr. Hist.: *EB*, III: 33]

6. **Drury Lane** London street famed for theaters; the theatrical district. [Br. Hist.: Herbert, 1321]

7. **Federal Theater** provided employment for actors, directors, writers, and scene designers (1935–1939). [Am. Hist.: *NCE*, 460]

8. **Garrick Theatre** famous London playhouse; named for David Garrick. [Br. Lit.: *NCE*, 1048]

9. **Globe Theatre** playhouse where Shakespeare's plays were performed. [Br. Lit.: *NCE*, 1094]

10. **Habima Theater** national theater of Israel; its troupe is famous for passionate acting style. [Israeli Hist.: *NCE*, 1170]

11. **La Scala** Teatro alla Scala, or "Theater at the Stairway"; Milan opera house; built 1776. [Ital. Hist.: *EB*, VI: 57]

12. **Lincoln Center** New York's modern theater complex. [Am. Hist.: *NCE*, 1586]

13. **Metropolitan Opera House** famous theater in New York City; opened in 1883. [Am. Hist.: *NCE*, 1761]

14. **Neil Simon Theatre, The** in 1983, the Alvin theater on Broadway was renamed The Neil Simon Theatre after the award-winning playwright of comic gems. [Am. Theater: *SJEPC*]

15. **Old Vic** London Shakespeare theater (1914–1963). [Br. Hist.: *NCE*, 1999]

16. **Radio City Music Hall** New York City's famous cinema; home of the Rockettes. [Am. Hist.: *NCE*, 2338]

17. **Shubert Theatre** well-known venue for many Broadway musicals, as well as other productions; built in 1913 by Lee and J.J. Shubert as tribute to brother Sam, who died in train crash. [Am. Theater: Misc.]

18. **Times Square** named after *The New York Times* tower at 42nd Street and Broadway; intersection of Broadway and Seventh Avenue in New York City, it is city's theater district and named "the great white way" for its brilliant lights. [Am. Culture: *SJEPC*]

19. **Tony** presented annually for outstanding work in the Broadway theater; also called Antoinette Perry Award. [Am. Hist.: Misc.]

20. *Variety* weekly newspaper with focus on theater and film; began in 1905 and characterized by a light style peppered with slang and

jargon; became "must read" publicaton of entertainment industry. [Am. Jour.: *SJEPC*]

21. **Winter Garden** a famous old theater in New York City. [Am. Hist.: Payton, 738]

670. THIEF (See also GANGSTERISM, HIGHWAYMAN, OUTLAW.)

1. **Alfarache, Guzmán de** picaresque, peripatetic thief; lived by unscupulous wits. [Span. Lit.: *The Life of Guzmán de Alfarache*]

2. **Armstrong, Johnnie** Scottish Robin Hood; robbed only the English. [Br. Hist.: Walsh *Classical*, 31–32]

3. **Artful Dodger** tricky thief; pupil of Fagin. [Br. Lit.: Dickens *Oliver Twist*]

4. **Autolycus** master robber. [Gk. Myth.: Leach, 96]

5. **Barabbas** thief released instead of Jesus to appease crowd. [N.T.: Matthew 27:16–26; Mark 15:7–15; John 18:40]

6. **Cacus** Vulcan's three-headed, thieving son. [Rom. Myth.: Benét, 154]

7. **Compeyson** accomplished criminal; swindles, forges, and steals. [Br. Lit.: *Great Expectations*]

8. **Crackit, Toby** a housebreaker; burglarizes Chertsey. [Br. Lit.: *Oliver Twist*]

9. **Dawkins, John** London pickpocket and thief. [Br. Lit.: *Oliver Twist*]

10. **Fagin** he trained young boys to become thieves. [Br. Lit.: *Oliver Twist*]

11. **Gradgrind, Tom** thief; robbed Bounderby's Bank. [Br. Lit.: *Hard Times*]

12. **Knave of Hearts** "stole the tarts" made by Queen of Hearts. [Nurs. Rhyme: Baring-Gould, 152]

13. **Lockhart, Jamie** a backwoods bandit with heroic qualities, chose by rich planter to be his daughter's husband. [Am. Lit.: Eudora Welty *The Robber Bridegroom* in Weiss, 124]

14. **Mak** sheep stealer succeeds by waiting till the shepherds fall asleep. [Br. Lit.: *The Second Shepherd's Play*]

15. **Mercury** god of thieves. [Gk. Myth.: Wheeler, 240]

16. **Nicholas's Clerks** slang for thieves. [Br. Usage: Brewer *Handbook*, 754; Br. Lit.: *I Henry IV*; *II Henry IV*]

17. **Nym** humorous thief and rogue. [Br. Lit.: *Merry Wives of Windsor*]

18. **Raffles** leading Victorian criminal-hero. [Br. Lit.: Herman, 19–20]

19. **Robin Hood** took from the rich and gave to the poor. [Br. Lit.: *Robin Hood*]

20. **Sikes, Bill** Fagin's thieving associate. [Br. Lit.: *Oliver Twist*]

21. **Taffy** Welshman who "stole a piece of beef." [Nurs. Rhyme: Baring-Gould, 72–73]

22. **Turpin, Dick (1706–1739)** English housebreaker and highwayman. [Br. Hist.: Brewer *Dictionary*, 1108]

23. **Valentine, Jimmy** a romanticized burglar. [Am. Lit.: *Alias Jimmy Valentine*, Espy, 337]

24. **Valjean, Jean** stole a loaf of bread; sentenced to 19 years in jail. [Fr. Lit.: *Les Misèrables*]

671. THINNESS

1. **Carpenter, Karen (1950–1983)** popular singer developed anorexia nervosa at the height of success in early 1970s; created public awareness of the disease upon her death in 1983. [Am. Music: *SJEPC*]

2. **Crane, Ichabod** Sleepy Hollow's gaunt schoolmaster. [Am. Lit.: *Legend of Sleepy Hollow*]

3. **Dartle, Rosa** Mrs. Steerforth's gaunt companion. [Br. Lit.: *David Copperfield*]

4. **Laurel, Stan (1890–1965)** played—along with Oliver Hardy— two rather dim, but loyal friends bumbling through one "swell predicament" after another; their physical appearance (Hardy fat, Laurel thin, both in derbies) was often parodied. [Am. Film: *SJEPC*]

5. **McBeal, Ally** petite character of TV show about young, single woman. [Am. TV: *SJEPC*]

6. **Moss, Kate (1974–)** British waiflike supermodel best known for her work with designer Calvin Klein. [Pop. Culture: *SJPEC*]

7. **Oyl, Olive** Popeye's skinny girlfriend. [Comics: "Thimble Theater" in Horn, 657–658]

8. **Sprat, Jack** "He could eat no fat." [Nurs. Rhyme: Opie, 238]

9. **supermodels** in 1980s and 1990s models rose to star status in American consumers' eyes; marketed themselves and drew huge salaries. [Am. Pop. Culture: *SJEPC*]

10. **Twiggy (1949–)** 1960s English fashion model who changed image from 1950s curvy sex symbols to more androgynous slenderness. [Pop. Culture: *SJEPC*]

672. THUNDER (See also LIGHTNING.)

1. **Bromius** epithet of Dionysus, meaning "thunder." [Gk. Myth.: Zimmerman, 43]

2. **Brontes** cruel Cyclops who controls the weather; able to cause great thunder. [Gk. Myth.: Parrinder, 47; Jobes, 241, 400]

3. **Donar** god of thunder; corresponds to Thor. [Ger. Myth.: Leach, 321]

4. **Indra** thunder god and controller of weather. [Vedic Myth.: Leach, 521]

5. **Mjolnir** Thor's hammer. [Norse Myth.: Brewer *Dictionary*, 1076]

6. **Thor** god of thunder. [Norse Myth.: Leach, 1109]

673. TIME

1. **Antevorta** goddess of the future. [Rom. Myth.: Kravitz, 24]

2. **countdown** just before a space launch, the count backward, from 10 to 1, or "blast off"; now a catchword for anticipation of any event. [Am. Cult.: Misc.]

3. **Cronos** Titan; god of the world and time; Saturn to the Romans. [Gk. and Rom. Myth.: Kravitz, 69]

4. **dance of Shiva** symbolizes the passage of time. [Hindu Tradition: Cirlot, 76]

5. **Father Time** classic personification of time with scythe and hourglass. [Art: Hall, 119]

6. **light year** in science, the distance light travels in one year; in common parlance, a long time. [Pop. Culture: Misc.]

7. **Marcel** the fast ebbing of time impels him to devote his life to recording it. [Fr. Lit.: *Remembrance of Things Past*]

8. **ring** represents the cyclical nature of time. [Pop. Culture: Cirlot, 273–274]

9. **river** represents the irreversible passage of time. [Pop. Culture: Cirlot, 274]

10. **Skulda** Norn of future time. [Norse Myth.: Wheeler, 260]

11. **Urda** Norn of time past. [Norse Myth.: Wheeler, 260]

12. **Verdandi** Norn of time present. [Norse Myth.: Wheeler, 260]

13. **white poplar** traditional symbol of time. [Flower Symbolism: *Flora Symbolica*, 178]

674. TIME TRAVEL

1. *Back to the Future* 1986 film featuring the time traveling adventures of Marty Mcfly in an old Delorean. [Am. Film: Misc.]

2. **Connecticut Yankee, the** struck on the head, he awakens to find himself in 6th-century England. [Am. Lit.: Mark Twain *A Connecticut Yankee in King Arthur's Court*]

3. *Dark Shadows* supernatural daytime drama's characters travelled between parallel time dimensions to understand the past and influence future events (1966–1971). [Am. TV: *SJEPC*]

4. *Doctor Who* long-running TV serial featuring time-travelling protagonist The Doctor has achieved cult status (original broadcasts, BBC, 1963–1989). [Br. TV: *SJEPC*]

5. *Looking Backward* Julian West awakens more than a century later to enjoy a new life in the Boston of A.D. 2000. [Am. Lit.: *Looking Backward* in Magill I, 520]

6. **Pilgrim, Billy** taught time-traveling by the Tralfamadorian space creatures. [Am. Lit.: Kurt Vonnegut *Slaugherhouse-Five*]

7. *Time Machine, The* Englishman voyages through millions of years to mankind's future. [Br. Lit.: Magill I, 980]

Timelessness (See AGELESSNESS, IMMORTALITY.)

675. TIMIDITY (See also COWARDICE,WEAKNESS.)

1. **Alden, John (c. 1599–1687)** too timid to ask for Priscilla's hand in marriage. [Am. Lit.: "The Courtship of Miles Standish" in Benét, 230]

2. **Bergson, Emil** could only express love for Marie in secret thoughts. [Am. Lit.: *O Pioneers!*, Magill I, 663–665]

3. **Blushington, Edward** upon taking marriage vows, he needs wine to say "I do." [Br. Lit.: *The Bashful Man*, Walsh *Modern*, 62–63]

4. **Cowardly Lion** timid king of beasts. [Am. Lit.: *The Wonderful Wizard of Oz*]

5. **Crane, Ichabod** timorous schoolteacher. [Am. Lit.: *The Legend of Sleepy Hollow*]

6. **cyclamen** traditional symbol of timidity. [Flower Symbolism: Jobes, 400]

7. **Florimel** feared "the smallest monstrous mouse that creeps on floor." [Br. Lit.: *Faerie Queene*]

8. **Kent, Clark** mild-mannered reporter whose dynamic alter ego is Superman. [Comics: Berger, 146]

9. **Little Dorrit** withdrawn, self-effacing seamstress. [Br. Lit.: *Little Dorrit*]

10. **Little Miss Muffet** frightened away by a spider. [Nurs. Rhyme: Opie, 323]

11. **Milquetoast, Casper** the timid soul; easily controlled by others. [Comics: *The Timid Soul*, Espy 141]

12. **Mitty, Walter** timid, henpecked husband. [Am. Lit.: Payton, 448]

13. **Peepers, Mr.** shy character in TV series. [TV: Terrace, II, 118–119]

14. **peony** symbol of shyness and timidity. [Flower Symbolism: *Flora Symbolica*, 176]

15. **Piglet** Pooh's close friend in A. A. Milne's Winnie-the-Pooh tales for children; tiny and timid, he also show real courage at times. [Br. Children's Lit.: Jones]

16. **Prufrock, J. Alfred** indecisive man, too shy and evasive to make a proposal. [Br. Poetry: T. S. Eliot *The Love Song of J. Alfred Prufrock*]

17. **rush** indicates docility and diffidence. [Flower Symbolism: *Flora Symbolica*, 177]

18. **Wingfield, Laura** crippled girl so shy that she has withdrawn into her own confined world. [Am. Drama: *The Glass Menagerie*]

676. TOTALITARIANISM

1. *Animal Farm* animals revolt against the depotism of Farmer Jones, but their leader sets up an equally totalitarian regime. [Br. Lit.: Orwell *Animal Farm*]

2. **Big Brother** ruler of Oceania, in George Orwell's *1984*; symbol for the invasion of privacy by government or other totalitarian power. [Br. Lit.: George Orwell *1984*; World History Misc.]

3. *Clockwork Orange, A* depicts a future state that enforces conformity and crushes all heresy and rebellion. [Br. Lit.: Anthony Burgess *A Clockwork Orange*]

4. *Darkness at Noon* Communists accused of having betrayed party principles are imprisoned, tortured, and executed. [Br. Lit.: Weiss, 117]

5. **doublethink** from George Orwell's *1984*, propaganda that twists the truth and keeps the people enslaved. [Br. Lit.: George Orwell *1984*]

6. **Ghengis Khan (1167–1227)** Mongol chieftain overran most of Asia and Eastern Europe (1206–1227). [Asian Hist.: Misc.]

7. *Gulag Archipelago, The* book by Alexsandr Solzhenitsyn (published 1973–1975) named after system of slave labor camps in the Soviet Union; symbol of prison and Soviet brutality. [Russ. Hist.: Aleksandr Solzhenitsyn *The Gulag Archipelago*]

8. **Hitler, Adolf (1889–1945)** ruled Germany from 1933–1945 with brutality and obsessive drive to create empire. [Ger. Hist.: Misc.]

9. **Kim Jong-il (1941–)** leader of Democratic People's Republic of Korea and commander of one of the largest armies in the world. [Korean Hist.: Misc.]

10. **Mussolini, Benito (1883–1945)** founder of Italian fascism; ruled as dictator beginning in 1925. [Ital. Hist.: Misc.]

11. *1984* George Orwell's 1949 dystopian novel depicting a totalitarian regime; a symbol of totalitarianism and its affects. [Br. Lit.: George Orwell *1984*]

12. **Oceania** totalitarian state dominated by Big Brother's omnipresence. [Br. Lit.: George Orwell *1984*]

13. **Pol Pot (1925–1998)** Prime Minister of Cambodia from 1976–1979, during which time almost 2 million of his countrymen perished from executions or brutal government impositions. [Cambodian Hist.: Misc.]

14. **Stalin, Josef (1879–1953)** ruthless socialist leader of U.S.S.R. from 1929 until his death; his was one of most brutal regimes in history. [Russ. Hist.: Misc.]

15. **Tse-Tung, Mao (1893–1976)** creator of the Chinese communist totalitarian state. [Chinese Hist.: Misc.]

677. TRANSFORMATION

1. **Actaeon** surprised Artemis bathing and was changed by her into a stag. [Gk. Myth.: Jobes, 28]

2. **Adonis** killed by a boar, he was changed into an anemone by Venus. [Gk. Lit.: *Metamorphoses*]

3. **Alectryon** changed into rooster by angry Ares for neglecting to warn against approach of the sun; doomed forever to announce its arrival. [Gk. Myth.: Zimmerman, 17]

4. **Alpheus** hunter pursuing Arethusa is turned into a river. [Gk. Myth.: Brewer *Dictionary*, 26]

5. **Arachne** won weaving contest against Athena, who then changed her into a spider. [Gk. Myth.: Jobes, 116]

6. **Arethusa** changed into stream by Artemas to save her from river god, Alpheus. [Gk. Myth.: Zimmerman, 29]

7. **Argus** hundred-eyed giant ordered slain by Zeus, changed by Hera into a peacock with a tail full of "eyes." [Gk. Myth.: Benét, 48]

8. **Ascalaphus** turned into an owl by Demeter. [Gk. Myth.: Kravitz, 37]

9. **Atys** beloved by Cybele, who changed him into a pine tree as he was about to commit suicide. [Gk. Myth.: Brewer *Dictionary*, 55]

10. **Battus** Arcadian shepherd who revealed Mercury's theft of sheep; he was punished by being turned to stone. [Rom. Myth.: Walsh *Classical*, 71]

11. ***Beauty and the Beast*** fairy story from France (written by Mme. De Beaumont and published in 1756) about beautiful young lady who learns to love ugly beast, thereby breaking an enchantment and revealing him to be handsome prince. [Fr. Children's Lit.: *OCCL*]

12. **Bottom, Nick** Puck turns his head into that of an ass. [Br. Drama: Shakespeare *A Midsummer Night's Dream*]

739

13. *Breast, The* literature professor transformed into a 155–pound breast topped by a football-size nipple. [Am. Lit.: Philip Roth *The Breast* in Weiss, 55]

14. **Cadmus** sows dragon's teeth that turn into armed men. [Gk. Myth.: Brewer *Dictionary*, 180]

15. **Callisto** nymph that Zeus transformed into a bear. [Gk. Myth.: Walsh *Classical*, 28]

16. **Ceyx and Halcyone** royal couple are changed into sea-birds. [Gk. Myth.: Bullfinch]

17. **Chelone** changed into tortoise for refusing to attend wedding of Zeus and Hera. [Gk. Myth.: Zimmerman, 59]

18. **Circe** seductive sorceress who turned Odysseus's companions into swine. [Gk. Myth.: Benét, 201]

19. **Clytie** ocean nymph, in love with Apollo, was changed into a heliotrope. [Gk. Myth.: Brewer *Dictionary*]

20. **Crocus** distressed by unrequited love, changed by Hermes into a saffron plant. [Gk. Myth.: Avery, 338]

21. **Cyane** turned by Hades into a fountain (or river). [Gk. Myth.: Kravitz, 70]

22. **Damascus, Road to** Saul of Tarsus, persecutor of Christians, is travelling to Damascus when he hears God's voice and is transformed into Paul, a Christian. [Christian Rel. N.T.: Acts 9:4]

23. **Daphne** turned into laurel tree to escape Apollo. [Gk. Myth.: Kravitz, 75]

24. **Derceto** nature deity; became mermaid when Mopsus pursued her. [Philistine Myth.: Jobes, 433; Avery, 389]

25. **Dirce** changed by gods into a fountain. [Gk. Myth.: Zimmmerman, 88]

26. **Doolittle, Eliza** Cockney flower-girl, trained by a professor, gains admission to polite society. [Br. Drama: G. B. Shaw *Pygmalion*; Am. Musical: *My Fair Lady* in *On Stage*, 373]

27. **Duchess's baby** ill-treated infant turns into a pig. [Br. Lit.: Lewis Carroll *Alice's Adventures in Wonderland*]

28. **Dylan, Bob (1941–)** legendary songwriter/singer has transformed himself numerous times throughout his five-decade career, from socially conscious folk guitar ballader to poetic rock star; 2007 film *I'm Not There* portrays the musician's various incarnations. [Am. Music: *SJEPC*; Misc.]

29. **Eurydice** transformed into a bacchante to suit enamored Zeus. [Fr. Operetta: Offenbach, *Orpheus in Hades*, Westerman, 271–272]

30. **frog prince** transformed by a witch, he is turned back into a prince by favor of a princess. [Ger. Fairy Tale: Grimm]

31. **Galatea** statue of a woman fashioned by Pygmalion and brought to life by Aphrodite. [Gk. Myth.: Jobes, 623]

32. **Hermine** her body is shrunk to figurine size. [Ger. Lit.: Herman Hesse *Steppenwolf*]

33. **Hippomenes and Atalanta** changed into a lion and a lioness for failing to honor Venus after their legendary race. [Gk. Myth.: Bullfinch]

34. **Hulk, The Incredible** one of Marvel Comics' most popular superheroes; Dr. Banner—exposed to gamma radiation—turns into the super-strong Hulk when angry or under stress; made into popular TV show in late 1970s. [Am. Comics and TV: *SJEPC*]

35. **Io** changed into heifer by Zeus because of Hera's jealousy. [Gk. Myth.: Zimmerman, 137]

36. **Jekyll, Dr. Henry** by means of a drug, changed himself into a repulsive, evil creature. [Br. Lit.: Stevenson *Dr. Jekyll and Mr. Hyde*]

37. **Jurgen** middle-aged pawnbroker turned into a young man ready for amorous adventure. [Am. Lit.: *Jurgen* in Magill I, 464]

38. **Lawford, Arthur** dozing in a graveyard, his body—but not his mind— is replaced by one of the dead. [Br. Lit.: Walter de la Mare *The Return* in Magill II, 896]

39. **Lot's wife** disobeyed God's order not to look back; she became a pillar of salt. [O.T.: Genesis 19:26]

40. **Lucius** metamorposed into an ass, has series of adventures. [Rom Lit.: Apuleius *Metamorphoses* or *The Golden Ass* in Magill I, 309]

41. **Lycaon** king turned into a wolf for having served human flesh. [Gk. Myth.: Brewer *Dictionary*, 570]

42. **Medusa** her face was so hideous that any who saw it were turned to stone. [Gk. Myth.: Brewer *Dictionary*, 596]

43. *Metamorphosis, The* Gregor Samsa turned into a huge insect. [Ger. Lit.: Kafka *The Metamorphosis*]

44. **Midas** everything he touched turned to gold. [Gk. Myth.: Zimmerman, 167]

45. **Myrmidons** orignally ants, turned into human beings by Zeus to populate the island of Oenone. [Gk. Myth.: Benét, 697]

46. **Narcissus** enamored of his own reflection in a pool, he pines away and is turned into a flower. [Gk. Myth.: Benét, 701]

47. **Niobe** her children slain, she is turned to stone by Zeus at her own request. [Gk. Myth.: Benét, 717]

48. **Odysseus's crew** turned into swine by Circe. [Gk. Lit.: *Odyssey*]

49. **Orion** slain by Diana, giant hunter becomes a constellation. [Gk. Myth.: Brewer *Dictionary*, 664]

50. **Orlando** born a man in 1588, dies a woman in 1928. [Br. Lit.: *Orlando*, Magill I, 698–700]

51. **Periclymenus** had the power to assume any form. [Gk. Myth.: Zimmerman, 199]

52. **Petrouchka** clown puppet that comes to life. [Russ. Ballet: *Petrouchka* in Thompson, 1657]

53. **Philemon and Baucis** couple turned into an oak and a linden so that they are together in death. [Gk. Myth.: Brewer *Dictionary*, 698]

54. **Philomela** changed by gods into nightingale; also Philomena. [Gk. Myth.: Zimmerman, 205–206]

55. **Phoulca** bogey-beast taking many forms; e.g., horse, bat, eagle. [Irish Folklore: Briggs, 326–327]

56. *Picture of Dorian Gray, The* while Gray himself stays youthful and attractive, his portrait becomes more hideous as he grows more vicious. [Br. Lit.: Oscar Wilde *The Picture of Dorian Gray*]

57. **Pinocchio** changed from mischievous puppet to loving boy; protagonist of C. Collodi's classic chidren's book *The Adventures of Pinocchio* (1883).. [Ital. Children's Lit.: Jones]

58. **Proteus** has ability to change shape. [Gk. Myth.: Kravitz, 201]

59. **pumpkin** turned into coach by Cinderella's fairy godmother. [Fr. Fairy Tale: *Cinderella*]

60. **Red Queen** shaken by Alice, she turns into kitten. [Br. Lit.: Lewis Carroll *Through the Looking-Glass*]

61. *Rhinoceros* Berenger discovers that Jean is turning into a rhinoceros like all the other townspeople. [Fr. Drama: Weiss, 394]

62. **Samsa, Gregor** young man wakes up one day to find that he has turned into an enormous insect. [Ger. Lit.: Kafka *The Metamorphosis* in Benét, 663]

63. *Secret Garden, The* novel for young readers by Frances Hodgson Burnett published in 1911; sickly, spoilt child blossoms and helps others through transforming neglected garden into beautiful refuge. [Am. Children's Lit.: OCCL]

64. **Syrinx** nymph, pursued by Pan, was changed into a reed, form which Pan made his pipes. [Gk. Myth.: Brewer *Dictionary*, 876]

65. **tarnhelm** golden helmet that allowed its wearer to assume any form or even become invisible. [Ger. Opera: Wagner *The Ring of the Nibelung*]

66. **Tebrick, Silvia Fox** changed from dignified woman into wild fox. [Am. Lit.: *Lady into Fox*, Magill I, 486]

67. **Tippetarius** boy changed into Ozma, Queen of Oz. [Children's Lit.: *The Land of Oz*]

68. **Tiresias** saw two snakes copulating and was changed into a woman. [Gk. Myth.: Jobes, 1576]

69. **Tithonus** unable to remove him from the earth because of his immortality, Eos changes him into a grasshopper. [Gk. Myth.: Brewer *Dictionary*, 901]

70. **transubstantiation** changing of bread to body of Christ. [Christian Theol.: Brewer *Dictionary*, 1097]

71. **Veretius** Welsh king changed into wolf by St. Patrick. [Br. Legend: Brewer *Dictionary*, 1148]

72. **Zeus** assumed many forms to indulge his passions. [Gk. Myth.: Zimmerman, 292–293]

678. TRAVEL (See also JOURNEY.)

1. **Amtrak** government-owned company that provides train transportation in the United States. [Am. Business: Misc.]

2. **Cracker Barrel** chain of over 500 "Old Country Stores" found off major highways across the United States; combination store and restaurant. [Am. Culture: Misc.]

3. *Expedition of Humphrey Clinker* describes Bramble family coach trip around 18th-century England. [Br. Lit.: Benét, 486]

4. **Greyhound buses** icon of American travel from coast to coast started serving travelers in 1914; slogan is "Go GreyhoundÖand leave the driving to us." [Am. Pop. Culture: *SJEPC*]

5. *Gulliver's Travels* Lemuel Gulliver visits fabulous lands. [Br. Lit.: *Gulliver's Travels*]

6. **Holiday Inns** national chain of reasonable motels, often found off major highways and used by traveling Americans. [Am. Culture: Misc.]

7. **Howard Johnson's** restaurant-motel chain throughout America; buildings recognized by their bright orange roofs. [Am. Culture: Crowley *Trade*, 274]

8. *Innocents Abroad, The* tour of Europe satirizes the pretentiousness of foreign culture. [Am. Lit.: Haydn & Fuller, 370]

9. *National Georgraphic Magazine* venerable journal whose articles and glossy pictures have enabled armchair travel for millions of readers. [Am. Jour.: *SJEPC*]

10. **Niagara Falls** the greatest waterfall in North America; immensely popular vacation destination. [Am. Geography: *SJEPC*]

11. *Old Patagonian Express* novelist Paul Theroux's 1979 account of his journey through North, Central, and South America. [Am. Lit.: Misc.]

12. *On the Road* classic best-selling beat autobiographical novel of road trip; nonconformist lifestyle depicted brought censure. [Am. Lit.: *SJEPC*]

13. **Recreational Vehicle (RV)** means of travel that puts the comforts of home on wheels; often favored by retirees. [Am. Culture: *SJEPC*]

14. **Red Roof Inn** United States budget hotel chain; over 300 properites nation-wide. [Am. Culture: Misc.]

15. **Route 66** planned to meander, connecting the main streets of U.S. from Chicago to Los Angeles; came to symbolize the joys of driving on the open road. [Am. Culture: *SJEPC*]

16. *Sentimental Journey, A* in a leisurely trip through 18th-century France, Mr. Yorick meets a variety of people and enjoys the company of the fair sex. [Br. Lit.: Sterne *A Sentimental Journey* in n Benet, 914]

17. **Stuckey's** chain of turquoise-roofed buildings that housed restaurant, gas station, and souvenir store in the 1950s and 1960s; famous for their Pecan Log Rolls candy. [Am. Pop. Culture: *SJEPC*]

18. **Transportation Security Association (TSA)** United States government agency; responsible for the security in transportation. [Am. Government: Misc.]

19. **traveler's checks** preprinted, fixed-amount check; convenient for travelers because they can easily be replaced if lost or stolen. [World Culture: Misc.]

20. *Travels with a Donkey* R. L. Stevenson's wanderings through the mountains of southern France, accompanied by a donkey. [Br. Lit.: Magill I, 1014]

21. *Travels with Charley* accompanied by his poodle, Steinbeck drives 10,000 miles through 40 states to discover America. [Am. Lit.: Steinbeck *Travels with Charley* in Benet, 961]

22. *Travels with My Aunt* 1969 English novel by Graham Greene; chronicles the European travels of a retired bank manager and his kooky aunt. [Br. Lit.: Misc.]

23. **U.S. One** labeled when federal highway numbering began as recognition for essential commerce and tourist uses of the road; stretching along the Atlantic seaboard, allows exploration of local color and roadside attractions. [Am. Pop. Culture: *SJEPC*]

24. **Wall Drugs** rest stop in South Dakota began as small store offering free ice water to travelers in 1936; now several blocks with arcades of shops, a chapel, and more. [Am. Pop. Culture: *SJEPC*]

679. TREACHERY (See also BETRAYAL, TREASON.)

1. **Aaron** plots downfall of Titus. [Br. Lit.: *Titus Andronicus*]

2. **Achitophel** traitorous Earl of Shaftesbury. [Br. Lit.: *Abalom and Achitophel*]

3. **Agravain, Sir** traitorous with Modred against Arthur. [Br. Lit.: *Le Morte d'Arthur*]

4. *Animal Farm* allegory in which the leader of the pigs turns their revolutionary cause of equality into a government of privilege for the "more equal." [Br. Lit.: George Orwell *Animal Farm*]

5. **Antenor** assigned to hell for actions defeating Troy. [Gk. Myth.: Avery, 106; Ital. Lit.: Dante, *Inferno*, Walsh *Classical*, 24]

6. **Antonio** schemes against his brother Prospero. [Br. Lit.: *The Tempest*]

7. **Ascalaphus** Hadean gardener; informs on Persephone, learning of her potential departure. [Gk. Myth.: Zimmerman, 33]

8. **Baanah and Rechab** Ishbosheth's captains decapitate him in bed. [O.T.: II Samuel 4:5–7]

9. **Bellerphon letter** letter, given in pretend friendship, denounces bearer. [Folklore: Walsh *Classical*, 52]

10. **Brutus, Decius** committed treachery against friend Caesar. [Br. Lit.: *Julius Caesar*]

11. **Cantwell, Dr.** treacherous towards Lady Lambert; arrested as swindler. [Br. Lit.: *The Hypocrite*, Walsh *Modern*, 85–86]

12. **Charrington, Mr.** antique-store keeper sets up lovers for captors. [Br. Lit.: *1984*]

13. **Chuzzlewit, Jonas** tries to poison father. [Br. Lit.: *Martin Chuzzlewit*]

14. **Claudius** plotted to kill Hamlet's father and marry his mother. [Br. Lit.: *Hamlet*]

15. **cock crow** before third crowing, Peter thrice denies Christ. [N.T.: Matthew 26:34, 74–75]

16. **Cortés, Hernando (1485–1547)** repaid Montezuma's courtesy by murdering him. [Span. Hist.: *EBN*, 5: 194–196]

17. **David** orders Uriah to be exposed in battle so he may marry Uriah's wife Bathsheba. [O.T.: II Samuel 11:16]

18. **Delilah** divulged secret of Samson's strength to Philistines. [O.T.: Judges 16:19–20]

19. **Ephialtes** Greek betrayer of Spartans at Thermopylae. [Gk. Hist.: Kravitz, 89]

20. **Ganelon** the Judas among Charlemagne's paladins. [Fr. Lit.: *Song of Roland*, LLEI, I: 286; Ital. Lit.: *Inferno*; Br. Lit.: *Canterbury Tales*, "Nun's Priest's Tale]

21. **Iago** soldier discredits Desdemona's fidelity. [Br. Lit.: *Othello*]

22. **Joab** murders two fellow commanders; sides with usurper, Adonijah. [O.T.: I Kings 2:32]

23. **Judas Iscariot** betrayer of Jesus. [N.T.: Matthew 26:14–16, 20–25, 47–56; 27:3–10]

24. **Maskwell** cunning doublecrosser; betrays friend and lover. [Br. Lit.: *The Double-Dealer*]

25. **Melema, Tito** betrays his foster father, his stepfather, and his political allies. [Br. Lit.: George Eliot *Romola*]

26. **Modred** revolted against King Arthur. [Arth. Legend: Brewer *Handbook*, 714–715; Br. Lit.: *Idylls of the King*]

27. **Morgan le Fay** tricks Accolon into stealing Excalibur. [Arth. Legend: *Le Morte d'Arthur*, Walsh *Classical*, 3]

28. **perfidious Albion** Napoleon's epithet for England, "perfide Albion." [Fr. Hist.: Misc.]

29. **Phaedra** in a letter written before her suicide, falsely accuses Hippolytus of attempting to ravish her. [Gk. Drama: *Hippolytus*]

30. **Polymestor** slays Priam's youngest son Polydorus, who had been entrusted to his care. [Gk. Drama: Euripedes *Hecuba* in Benét, 450]

31. **Potiphar's wife** spurned by Joseph, she falsely accuses him of trying to seduce her. [O.T.: Gen. 39]

32. **Ptolemy** captain of Jericho invites Simon Maccabeus and his sons to a banquet and then slays them. [O.T.: I Maccabees, 16:16]

33. **redheadedness** from Judas Iscariot; so depicted in art. [Christian Iconog.: Gaster, 165]

34. **Rosencrantz and Guildenstern** Hamlet's traitorous friends; "adders fang'd." [Br. Lit.: *Hamlet*]

35. **Saturninus** connives and plots politically; kills Titus. [Br. Lit.: *Titus Andronicus*]

36. **Schoolmaster of Falerii** Etruscan teacher, after delivering children to Romans, is rebuffed. [Rom. Hist.: Hall, 119]

37. **Sebastian** plots to murder Alonso and Gonzalo. [Br. Lit.: *The Tempest*]

38. **Thermopylae** shown the back door, Persians destroyed Spartans (480 B.C.) [Gk. Hist.: Harbottle, 248]

39. **30 pieces of silver** priced paid Judas to deliver Jesus. [Christian Symbolism: N.T.: Matthew 26:15]

40. **Ugolino** 13th-century count of Pisa who treacherously deserted his own party and then twice joined the enemies of his own city. [Ital. Hist.: Brewer *Dictionary*, 921]

41. **Uriah letter** Uriah carries David's letter ordering his own death. [O.T.: II Samuel 11:15]

42. **whale** lures fish to mouth with sweet breath. [Animal Symbolism: Mercatante, 27]

43. **woman in red** Dillinger's mysterious girlfriend; alerted FBI to his whereabouts. [Am. Hist.: Flexner, 291]

44. **yellow** color marking doors of convicted traitors. [Fr. Legend: Brewer *Dictionary*, 1171]

680. TREASON

1. **Antoinette, Marie (1755–1793)** queen of France; beheaded by revolutionists. [Fr. Hist.: *NCE*, 1697]

2. **Arnold, Benedict (1741–1801)** American Revolutionary general who plotted surrender of West Point to British. [Am. Hist.: Benét, 52]

3. **Boleyn, Anne (1501?-1536)** second wife of King Henry VIII of England; beheaded on charges of adultery, incest, and high treason, although it is assumed the real reason was her inability to produce a male heir. [Br. Hist.: Misc.]

4. **Burgundy, Duke of** fights for English, then joins French. [Br. Lit.: *I Henry VI*]

5. **Carne, Caryl** traitor to country. [Br. Lit.: *Springhaven*]

6. **Christian, Colonel William** executed for treason. [Br. Lit.: *Peveril of the Peak*, Walsh *Modern*, 96]

7. **Edmund** "a most toad-spotted traitor." [Br. Lit.: *King Lear*]

8. **Fawkes, Guy (1570–1606)** leader of Gunpowder Plot to blow up Houses of Parliament (1605). [Br. Hist.: *EB*, IV: 70, 801]

9. **Hitler, Adolf (1889–1945)** started a treasonous and violent putsch in Munich in 1923. [Ger. Hist.: Misc.]

10. **Howard, Catherine (1520?-1542)** fourth wife of King Henry VIII or England; beheaded after less than two years of marriage; charged with treason for committing adultery. [Br. Hist.: Misc.]

11. **Louis XVI (1754–1793)** reigned over France 1774–1792; arrested during the Insurrection on August 10, 1792; tried by the National Convention, found guilty of treason and executed. [Fr. Hist.: Misc.]

12. **Mary I of Scotland (1542–1587)** also known as Queen of Scots; tried and executed for treason because of her participation in plots to assassinate Elizabeth I of England to seize the throne. [Br. Hist.: Misc.]

13. **More, Sir Thomas (1478–1535)** English statesman beheaded by King Henry VIII. [Br. Hist.: *NCE*, 1830]

14. **Nolan, Philip** deserts the U.S. Army to join Burr's conspiracy. [Am. Lit.: Hale *The Man Without a Country* in Magill I, 553]

15. **Paine, Thomas (1737–1809)** powerful voice of the colonies; wrote famous "Common Sense." [Am. Hist.: Jameson, 369–370]

16. **Quisling, Vidkun (1887–1945)** Norwegian fascist leader; persuaded Hitler to attack Norway. [Nor. Hist.: Flexner, 444]

17. **Raleigh, Sir Walter (1552–1618)** English writer and explorer; imprisoned for supposed involvement in plot to kill King James I, who did not like Raleigh; finally had a show trial which led to his beheading. [Br. Hist.: Misc.]

18. **Vichy** seat of collaborationist government after German occupation (1941). [Fr. Hist.: Brewer *Dictionary*, 1128]

19. **Wallace, William (1272–1305)** Scottish knight heavily involved in the Wars of Scottish Indepedence against the English; executed for treason by Edward I of England. [Br. Hist.: Misc.]

20. **Wallenstein, Count** powerful German general in Thirty Years' War who corresponded with the Swedish enemy. [Ger. Drama: Schiller *Wallenstein* in Magill II, 1119]

681. TREASURE

1. **Ali Baba** uses magic to find thieves' storehouse of booty. [Arab. Lit.: *Arabian Nights*, "Ali Baba and the Forty Thieves"]

2. **Comstock Lode** richest silver vein in world. [Amer. Hist.: Flexner, 177]

3. **Dantès, Edmond** digs up the treasure revealed to him by a dying fellow prisoner. [Fr. Lit.: Dumas *The Count of Monte Cristo*]

4. **dragon** according to some legends, dragons protected hoards of treasures, usually kept in their den. [Legend: Misc.]

5. **El Dorado** legendary land of gold in South America. [Span. Myth.: *NCE*, 846]

6. **Fort Knox** U.S. depository of gold bullion. [Am. Hist.: *NCE*, 984]

7. **forty-niners** participants in California gold rush of 1849. [Am. Hist.: *LLEI*, I: 270]

8. **Golconda** fabled Indian city, meaning "source of great wealth." [Indian Hist.: *NCE*, 1101]

9. **gold bug** leads to finding Captain Kidd's buried treasure. [Am. Lit.: Poe "The Gold Bug"]

10. **Golden Fleece** fleece of pure gold from a winged ram, stolen from Colchis by Jason and the Argonauts. [Gk. Myth.: Benét, 406]

11. **Kidd, Captain (c. 1645–1701)** pirate captures prizes and buries treasure. [Am. Lit.: Hart, 444]

12. **King Solomon's mines** in Africa; search for legendary lost treasure of King Solomon. [Br. Lit.: *King Solomon's Mines*]

13. **Legrand, William** uncovers chest of gold by deciphering parchment. [Am. Lit.: Poe "The Gold Bug"]

14. **Mother Lode** name applied to gold-mining region of California. [Am. Hist.: Hart, 569]

15. **Nibelung, the** more gold, and jewels than wagons could carry. [Ger. Lit.: *Nibelungenlied*]

16. **Nostromo** inadvertently gains hoard of silver ingots. [Br. Lit.: *Nostromo*]

17. **Ophir** Red Sea area noted for gold. [O.T.: I Kings 9:28; 10:11: 22:48]

18. **Sutter's Mill** site of first strike precipitating Gold Rush. [Am. Hist.: Flexner, 175]

19. *Treasure Island* search for buried treasure ignited by discovery of ancient map. [Br. Lit.: *Treasure Island*]

20. *Treasure of the Sierra Madre, The* in Mexico, written by the reclusive, pseudonymous B. Traven. [Am and Mex. Lit.: *The Treasure of the Sierra Madre*]

682. TREE

1. **Birnam wood** apparently comes to Dunsinane, fulfilling a prophecy misinterpreted by Macbeth. [Br. Drama: Shakespeare *Macbeth*]

2. **Bo-tree** tree of perfect knowledge under which Gautama attained enlightenment and so became the Buddha. [Buddhism: Benét, 124]

3. **Chankiri Tree** tree in the Cambodia Killing Fields against which children and infants were beaten to kill them. [Am. Science: Misc.]

4. **Charter Oak** ancient white oak where the Connecticut charter was secreted in 1687 to avoid its seizure by the royal governor. [Am. Hist.: NCE, 515]

5. **Chestnuts, The** tree apartment, home of Owl. [Br. Lit.: A.A. Milne *Winnie-the-Pooh*]

6. **Druids** conducted their rites in oak groves and venerated the oak and the mistletoe. [Celtic Relig.: Benét, 289]

7. **Ents** treelike creatures who shelter and defend the friends of Frodo. [Br. Lit.: J.R.R. Tolkien *Lord of the Rings*]

8. **Great Banyan** located in the Indian Botanical Gardens; widest canopy in the world with thousands of aerial roots, giving it the appearance of a forest. [Am. Science: Misc.]

9. **laurel tree** sacred to Apollo; a wreath of laurel, or bay, protected the wearer from thunderstorms. [Roman Myth.: Brewer *Dictionary*, 81]

10. **oak** considered more likely to be struck by lightning, sacred to the god of thunder and venerated by the Druids. [Br. Legend: Brewer *Dictionary*, 652]

11. **Prometheus** bristlecone pine cut down in 1964; a reading of its growth rings revealed it to be about 4900 years old, making it oldest known tree. [Am. Science: Misc.]

12. **Redwood Forest** forest in Northern California with some of the tallest and oldest trees on earth. [Am. Geography: Misc.]

13. **upas** juice contains a poison used for tipping arrows; its vapor was believed capable of killing all who came within miles. [Eur. Myth.: Brewer *Dictionary*, 926]

14. **yew** symbol of immortality; hence, planted in churchyards and near Druid temples. [Br. Legend: Brewer *Dictionary*, 967]

15. **Ygdrasil** the great ash tree that supported the universe, having sprung from the body of the giant Ymir. [Norse Myth.: Benét, 111]

683. TRICKERY (See also CUNNING, DECEIT, UNSCRUPULOUSNESS.)

1. **Ananse** character from African and West Indian myths who is depicted as a spider and functions as a trickster. [Myth.: *OCCL*]

2. **Bilko, Sergeant** bunco artist extraordinaire. [TV: "You'll Never Get Rich" in Terrace II, 452–453]

3. **Bunsby, Captain Jack** trapped into marriage by landlady. [Br. Lit.: *Dombey and Son*]

4. **Camacho** cheated of bride after lavish wedding preparations. [Span. Lit.: *Don Quixote*]

5. *Captain Underpants* series of books for young readers by Dav Pilkey; two prankster fourth graders hypnotise the child-hating principal of their school into thinking he is a superhero. [Am. Children's Lit.: Misc.]

6. **Delilah** tricks Samson into revealing secret of his strength. [O.T.: Judges 16:6–21]

7. **gerrymander** political chicanery aimed at acquiring votes. [Am. Hist.: Jameson, 199]

8. **Gibeonites** obtained treaty with Joshua under false pretenses. [O.T.: Joshua, 9:3–15]

9. **Hippomenes** outraced Atalanta by tossing golden apples to distract her. [Gk. Myth.: Bullfinch]

10. **Jacob** through guile, obtained blessing intended for Esau. [O.T.: Genesis 27:18–29]

11. **Joseph's coat** dipped in the blood of a kid and shown to Jacob as proof of Joseph's death. [O.T.: Genesis 37:31–33]

12. **Laban** substitutes Leah for Rachel on Jacob's wedding night. [O.T.: Genesis 29:16–26]

13. **Loge** also Loki; enables Wotan to overpower Alberich, gain Rhinegold. [Ger. Opera: Wagner, *Das Rheingold*, Westerman, 232]

14. **Malatesta** schemes outwit mise,; enable young lovers to wed. [Ital. Opera: Donizetti, *Don Pasquale*, Westerman, 123–124]

15. **Rebekah** encouraged son Jacob to deceive father for blessing. [O.T.: Genesis 27:5–17]

16. **Serpina** dupes bachelor employer into marrying her. [Ital. Opera: Pergolesi, *La Serva Padrona*, Westerman, 61]

17. **Wile E. Coyote** untiring predator of Road Runner whose Acme contraptions inevitably backfire and leave him smoldering or plunging over a precipice. [Am. Comics: *SJEPC*]

684. TRINITY

1. **botonné cross** symbolizes Father, Son, and Holy Ghost. [Christian Iconog.: Jobes, 386]

2. **clover** trefoil; emblem of the Trinity. [Christian Symbolism: Cirlot, 50–51]

3. **equilateral triangle** perfect geometrical representation of triune God. [Christian Symbolism: Appleton, 102]

4. **fleur-de-lis** symbol of the trinity; resembles lily. [Christian Symbolism: *EB*, IV: 182]

5. **iris** emblem of the trinity in Leonardo da Vinci's "Madonna of the Rocks." [Plant Symbolism: Embolden, 26]

6. **shamrock** St. Patrick's legendary symbol of triune God. [Christian Symbolism: Appleton, 87]

7. **Sign of the Cross** signifying Father, Son, and Holy Ghost. [Christianity: *NCE*, 2786]

8. **Trimurti** Hindu triad of Brahma, Vishnu, and Siva. [Hinduism: Brewer *Dictionary*, 1101]

Truth (See HONESTY.)

685. TURNING POINT

1. **Alamogordo** site of first A-bomb explosion; heralded atomic age (1945). [Am. Hist.: Flexner, 11]

2. **Barbarossa** disastrous invasion of Russia; sealed Nazi fate (1941–1943). [Eur. Hist.: *Hitler*, 888–921, 922–955]

3. **Caesar crosses Rubicon** defying Roman law, Caesar moves to consolidate power (49 B.C.) [Rom. Hist.: *EB*, 3: 575–580]

4. **Cannonade of Valmy** dawn of modern warfare (1792). [Eur. Hist.: Fuller, II, 346–369]

5. **Crécy** first European use of gunpowder (by British) in battle (1346). [Eur. Hist.: Bishop, 382–385]

6. **D-Day** Allied invasion of France during WWII (June 6, 1944). [Eur. Hist.: Fuller, III, 562–567]

7. **El Alamein** "Desert Fox" outfoxed; Allies gained upper hand (1943). [Eur. Hist.: Fuller, III, 494–502]

8. **Fall of Constantinople** associated with the end of Middle Ages (1863). [Eur. Hist.: Bishop, 398]

9. **Gettysburg, Battle of** the deathblow of the Confederacy (1863). [Am. Hist.: Jameson, 199]

10. **Golden Spurs, Battle of** early victory of infantry over mounted knights (1302). [Eur. Hist.: *EB*, IV: 608]

11. **Hastings, Battle of** Norman conquest; last successful invasion of Britain (1066). [Br. Hist.: Harbottle, 107]

12. **Khe Sanh** savage siege marks turning point in Vietnam (1968). [Am. Hist.: Van Doren, 620]

13. **Magna Carta** beginning of British democratic system (1215). [Br. Hist.: Bishop, 49–52, 213]

14. **Marston Moor** deciding battle of British Civil War (1644). [Br. Hist.: Harbottle, 154]

15. **Midway** decisive American victory over Japanese in WWII (1942). [Am. Hist.: Fuller, III, 470–477]

16. **Moon Landing** astronauts Armstrong and Aldrin make history (1969). [Am. Hist.: *NCE*, 2579–2581]

17. **95 Theses** Martin Luther presented his theses at Wittenberg (1517). [Eur. Hist.: *EB*, 11: 188–196]

18. *Origin of Species, The* Darwin's revolutionary theory of human evolution (1859). [Science: *NCE*, 721–722]

19. **Spanish Armada** Britain supplanted Spain as master of the sea. [Br. Hist.: Harbottle, 19]

20. **theory of relativity** Einstein's contribution to the space-time relationship. [Science: *NCE*, 843–844]

21. **Tours** Arab onslaught halted by Franks under Charles Martel (732). [Eur. Hist.: Bishop, 19]

686. TWINS (See also DOUBLES.)

1. **Alcmena's sons** born in single delivery but conceived by two men. [Rom. Lit.: *Amphitryon*]

2.   **Antipholus** identically named sons of Aegeon and Emilia. [Br. Lit.: *Comedy of Errors*]

3.   **Apollo and Artemis** twin brother and sister; children of Leda and Zeus. [Gk. Myth.: *NCE*, 125–126]

4.   **Bobbsey Twins** protagonists of series of family stories written by Laura Lee Hope beginning in 1904; two sets of twins have adventures. [Am. Children's Lit.: *OCCL*]

5.   **Castor and Pollux** sons of Leda and Zeus, placed in heaven as constellation Gemini. [Gk. Myth.: Zimmerman, 52]

6.   *Comedy of Errors* based on Plautus's *Menaechmi*, with two sets of identical twins. [Br. Lit.: *Comedy of Errors*]

7.   **de Franchi, Lucien and Louis** one twin instinctively feels what happens to other. [Fr. Lit.: *The Corsican Brothers*]

8.   **Dioscuri** Castor and Pollux, twin sons of Leda and Zeus. [Gk. Myth.: Avery, 408; Leach, 314]

9.   **Donny, the Misses** twin principals of Greenleaf boarding school. [Br. Lit.: *Bleak House*]

10. **Dromio** Dromio of Ephesus; Dromio of Syracuse. [Br. Lit.: *Comedy of Errors*]

11. **Gemini** zodiacal twins; also Castor and Pollux. [Gk. Myth.: *NCE*, 1056]

12. **Gibb, Maurice (1949–2003) and Robin Gibb (1949–)** English musicians and songwriters of The Bee-Gees. [Br. Music: Misc.]

13. **Helen and Clytmnestra** Helen's abduction from her husband, the King of Sparta, led to the Trojan War; Clytmnestra was married to King Agamemnon of Argos. [Gk. Myth.: Misc.]

14. **Katzenjammer Kids** early comic strip featured incorrigible twins. [Comics: "The Captain and the Kids" in Horn, 421]

15. **Landers, Ann (1918–2002) and Abigail Van Buren (1918–)** twin sisters who both wrote syndicated advice columns for many decades. [Am. Pop. Culture: Misc.]

16. **Man in the Iron Mask** Bastille prisoner learns that he is the twin brother of Louis XIV; conspirators planned to substitute him for the king. [Fr. Hist.: Dumas *Vicomte de Bragellonne* in Magill I, 1063]

17. *Menaechmi* comedy by Plautus, about mistakes involving identical twins, Shakespeare's source for *Comedy of Errors* [Rom. Lit.: *Menaechmi*]

18. **Mike and Ike** short lookalike twins with derbies. [Comics: Horn, 492]

19. **Olsen, Mary-Kate and Ashley (1986–)** American actresses; famous for playing Michelle Tanner on the television show *Full*

House in 1987–1995 and later movies as young teens. [Am. TV: Misc.]

20. ***Parent Trap, The*** 1961 Disney film remade in 1998; twins, separated as babies when their parents divorce, meet by chance at summer camp; decide to switch places and devise plan to reunite their mom and dad. [Am. Film: Misc.]

21. **Perez and Zerah** born to Tamar; conceived by father-in-law, Judah. [O.T.: Genesis 38:29–30]

22. **Romulus and Remus** suckled by she-wolf; founded Rome. [Rom. Myth.: Wheeler, 320]

23. **Siamese twins** Eng and Chang (1814–1874), the original pair, were connected at the chest. [Medical Hist.: Brewer *Dictionary*, 828]

24. **Tweedledum and Tweedledee** identical characters in children's fantasy. [Br. Lit.: *Through the Looking-Glass*]

25. **two circles** symbol of twins; in particular, Castor and Pollux. [Gk. Myth.: Jobes, 343]

687. TYRANNY (See also BRUTALITY, CRUELTY.)

1. **Amin, Idi (1925–)** ruthless leader of Uganda [Afr. Politics *OAD*, 110]

2. **Big Brother** omnipresent leader of a totalitarian nightmare world. [Br. Lit.: *1984*]

3. **Caligula (12–41)** Roman emperor known for terror and cruel autocracy. [Rom. Hist.: *NCE*, 425]

4. **Creon** rules Thebes with cruel decrees. [Gk. Lit.: *Antigone*]

5. **Gessler** Austrian governor treats Swiss despotically; shot by Tell. [Ital Lit.: Rossini, *William Tell*, Westerman, 121–122]

6. **Hitler, Adolf (1889–1945)** Nazi dictator; universal symbol of brutality, race hatred, and ruthless genocide. [Ger. Hist.: *Hitler*]

7. **Hussein, Saddam (1937–2006)** took control over the various departments of Iraqi government during the 1970s; Prime Minister and President of Iraq from 1979–2003. [Iraqi Hist.: Misc.]

8. **Ivan the Terrible (1533–1584)** his reign was characterized by murder and terror. [Russ. Hist.: *EB*, 9: 1179–1180]

9. **Jones, Brutus** former porter sets himself up as dictator of a West Indies island and rules the natives with an iron hand. [Am. Drama: O'Neill *Emperor Jones*]

10. **Mussolini, Benito (1883–1945)** Italian dictator and facist leader; "Il Duce." [Ital. Hist.: Misc.]

11. **Necho, Pharaoh** oppresses Jerusalem by exaction of harsh taxes. [O.T.: II Kings 23:33–35]

12. **Papa Doc (1907–1971)** nickname of Francois Duvalier, tyrannical president of Haiti, who terrorized his people with his security force, the Tontons Macoutes. [Caribbean History: *ODA*]

13. **pig** mean, sadistic tyrant; epitome of human horridness. [Br. Lit.: *Animal Farm*]

14. **Pol Pot (1925–1998)** Prime Minister of Cambodia from 1976–1979, during which time almost 2 million of his countrymen perished from executions or brutal government impositions. [Cambodian Hist.: Misc.]

15. **Qaddafi, Muammar Al (1942–)** leader of Libya since coup in 1969, although he holds no offical office or position. [African Hist.: Misc.]

16. **Queeg, Captain Philip** captain of the *Caine* who is relieved of command by mutineers; proves to be a cowardly, unstable tyrant at courtmartial. [Am. Lit.: Herman Wouk *The Caine Mutiny*]

17. **Queen of Hearts** dictatorial ruler who orders subjects' heads chopped off. [Br. Lit.: *Alice's Adventures in Wonderland*]

18. **Rehoboam** bitterly repressed his people. [O.T.: I Kings 12:12–16]

19. **salamander** Francis I's symbol of absolute dictatorial power. [Animal Symbolism: Mercatante, 19]

20. **Stalin, Josef (1879–1953)** tyrannical dictator of the Soviet Union, responsible for the death of millions of his own people; a symbol of tyranny. [Russ. Hist.: *ODA*]

21. **Zedong, Mao (1893–1976)** also Mao Tse-tung; leader of the Communist Party of China and Chinese military; Mao's *Little Red Book* was required to be carried and studied in school. [Chinese Hist.: Misc.]

U

688. UBIQUITY (See also OMNIPRESENCE.)

1. **Burger King** fast-food chain featuring flame-broiled Whopper has restaurants around the world, is second to rival McDonald's. [Am. Business: *SJEPC*]

2. **Burma-Shave** their signs seen as "verses of the wayside througout America." [Am. Commerce and Folklore: Misc.]

3. **Coca-Cola** soft drink found throughout the world. [Trademarks: Crowley *Trade*, 115]

4. **Dunkin' Donuts** coffee and pastry shop with pink and orange signs founded in 1950 is the largest such chain in the world. [Am. Business and Culture: *SJEPC*]

5. **Gideon Bible** bible placed in hotel rooms and other establishments throughout the world. [Am. Hist.: *NCE*, 291]

6. **Howard Johnson's** restaurant-motel chain throughout America; buildings recognized by their bright orange roofs. [Am. Business: Crowley *Trade*, 274]

7. **Kilroy** fictitious American soldier; left inscription, "Kilroy was here," everywhere U.S. soldiers were stationed (1940s). [Am. Mil. Folklore: Misc.]

8. **McDonald's** fast-food restaurant chain throughout the world; recognized by golden arches. [Am. Culture: Misc.]

9. **Starbucks** with origins in Seattle in 1971, by 1980s had broadened to European-style coffeehouse as meeting place; expansion worldwide so successful, some cities boast shops across the street from one another. [Am. Business: *SJEPC*]

10. **Wal-Mart** American shopping was changed beginning in the 1960s by retail giant; proliferation of huge discount stores (especially in small towns) offering variety and value; accusations of unfair labor practices and environmental irresponsibility have arisen. [Am. Business: *SJEPC*]

689. UGLINESS

1. **Avagddu** ugly child of Tegid Voel and Cerridwen. [Celtic Folklore: Parrinder, 35]

2. **Balkis** hairy-legged type of Queen of Sheba. [Talmudic Legend: Walsh *Classical*, 45]

3. **Beast** enchanted prince of fairy tale, who wins the heart of Beauty [Fr. Fairy Tale: "Beauty and the Beast" in Walsh *Classical*, 49]

4. **Bendith Y Mamau** stunted, ugly fairies; kidnapped children. [Celtic Folklore: Briggs, 21]

5. **Berchta** beady-eyed, hook-nosed crone with clubfoot and stringy hair. [Ger. Folklore: Leach, 137]

6. **Black Annis** cannibalistic hag with blue face and iron claws. [Br. Folklore: Briggs, 24]

7. **Duessa** witch, stripped of lavish disguise, found to be hideous hag. [Br. Lit.: *Faerie Queene*]

8. **Ethel** buck-toothed, gangly teenager in love with idler, Jughead. [Comics: "Archie" in Horn, 37]

9. **Euryale and Stheno** the immortal Gorgons; had serpents for hair and brazen claws. [Gk. Myth.: Zimmerman, 114]

10. **Frankenstein's monster** ugly monster. [Br. Lit.: *Frankenstein*, Payton, 254]

11. **gargoyles** medieval European church waterspouts; made in form of grotesque creatures. [Architecture: *NCE*, 1046]

12. **Gorgons** snake-haired, winged creatures of frightful appearance. [Gk. Myth.: Howe, 108]

13. **Gross, Allison** repulsive witch "in the north country." [Scot. Ballad: *Childe Ballads*]

14. **Medusa** creature with fangs, snake-hair, and protruding tongue. [Gk. Myth.: Hall, 206]

15. **Quasimodo** The Hunchback of Notre Dame: "Nowhere on earth a more grotesque creature." [Fr. Lit.: *The Hunchback of Notre Dame*]

16. **Spriggans** grotesque fairies; "dourest and most ugly set of sprights." [Br. Folklore: Briggs, 380–381]

17. **Ugly Duchess** repulsive woman with pocket-shaped mouth. [Br. Lit.: *Alice's Adventures in Wonderland*]

18. **Ugly Duckling** ugly outcast until fully grown. [Fairy Tale: Misc.]

19. **Witch of Wookey** repulsive hag curses boys and girls. [Br. Legend: Brewer *Dictionary*, 1164]

690. UNATTAINABILITY

1. **belling the cat** mouse's proposal for warning of cat's approach; application fatal. [Gk. Lit.: *Aesop's Fables*]

2. **east and west** since one direction is relative to the other, "never the twain shall meet." [Pop. Usage: Misc.]

3. **Elixir of Life** fabulous potion conferring immortality. [Medieval Legend: Brewer *Dictionary*, 371]

4. **Fountain of Youth** legendary fountain of eternal youth. [World Legend: Brewer *Dictionary*, 432]

5. **leopard's spots** beast powerless to change them. [O.T.: Jeremiah 13:23]

6. **perpetual motion machine** machine operating of itself forever. [World Legend: Brewer *Dictionary*, 823]

7. **Philosopher's Stone** substance supposed to convert base metal to gold. [Medieval Legend: Brewer *Dictionary*, 829]

691. UNDERWORLD (See also HELL.)

1. **Aidoneus** epithet of Hades. [Gk. Myth.: Zimmerman, 14]

2. **Amenti** hidden world where the sun sets. [Egypt. Myth.: Leach, 42]

3. **Anunnaki** lesser Sumerian underworld deities. [Sumerian Myth.: Benét, 41]

4. **Aornum** entrance through which Orpheus descended to Hades. [Gk. Myth.: Zimmerman, 25]

5. **Aralu** desolate land of no return. [Babyl. Myth.: Leach, 69]

6. **Avernus, Lake** entrance to the maw. [Rom. Lit.: *Aeneid*; Art: Hall, 147]

7. **Dis** god of nether world; identifiied with Pluto. [Rom. Myth.: Leach, 315]

8. **Duat** one of the Egyptian abodes of the dead. [Egypt. Myth.: Benét, 290]

9. **Erebus** god of underground darkness. [Gk. Myth.: Benét, 319]

10. **Ereshkigal** queen of underworld; Persephone equivalent. [Sumerian Myth.: Benét, 319–320]

11. **Hades** realm of departed spirits. [Gk. Myth.: Brewer *Dictionary*, 499]

12. **Hel** ruled over world of the dead. [Norse Myth.: Leach, 488]

13. **Nergal** god ruling the world of dead. [Sumerian and Akkadian Myth.: Parrinder, 203]

14. **Niflheim** region of perpetual cold and darkness; afterworld. [Norse Myth.: Wheeler, 259]

15. **oak leaves, garland of** emblem of Hecate, goddess of the underworld. [Gk. Myth.: Jobes, 374]

16. **Orcus** nether world of the dead. [Rom. Myth.: Wheeler, 270]

17. **Pluto** god of the underworld. [Gk. Myth.: Howe, 224]

18. **Sheol** abode of the dead. [Hebrew Theology: Brewer *Dictionary*, 499]

19. **Styx** river of Hades across which souls of dead must travel. [Gk. Myth.: Howe, 259]

20. **Tartarus** infernal regions. [Gk. Myth.: Hall, 147]

Unfaithfulness (See FAITHLESSNESS.)

Ungratefulness (See INGRATITUDE.)

Unkindness (See CRUELTY.)

692. UNSCRUPULOUSNESS (See also CUNNING, DECEIT, FRAUDULENCE, TRICKERY.)

1. **Blas, Gil** educated rogue on warpath for self-gain. [Fr. Lit.: *Gil Blas*]

2. **Brass, Sampson** unprincipled attorney. [Br. Lit.: *Old Curiosity Shop*]

3. **Bray, Walter** to clear his debts to old Gride, arranges to have Gride marry his daughter. [Br. Lit.: *Nicholas Nickleby*]

4. **Butler, Rhett** war profiteer; morality not a concern. [Am. Lit.: *Gone With the Wind*]

5. **Claudio** asks sister to sacrifice her virtue to save his life. [Br. Lit.: *Measure for Measure*]

6. **Dodson and Fogg** unscrupulous lawyers who file breach-of-promise suit against Mr. Pickwick. [Br. Lit.: *Pickwick Papers*]

7. **Duroy, George** climbs to wealth by exploiting wife's disgrace. [Fr. Lit.: *Bel-Ami*]

8. **Hajji Baba** clever rogue travels around Persia taking glamorous jobs for illicit gain. [Fr. Lit.: *Hajji Baba of Ispahan* in Magill I, 343]

9. **Henchard, Michael** when drunk, offers wife and child for sale. [Br. Lit.: *The Mayor of Casterbridge*]

10. **Livia** she poisoned whoever interfered with her plans. [Br. Lit.: *I, Claudius*]

11. *Prince, The* practicality in power; end justifies means. [Ital. Lit.: *The Prince*]

12. **Steele, Lucy** jilts Edward for his brother Robert to take advantage of a switch of their inheritance. [Br. Lit.: *Sense and Sensibility*]

13. **Tweed, William Marcy "Boss" (1823–1878)** corrupt politico; controlled New York City government (1863–1871). [Am. Hist.: Jameson, 511]

14. **Winterset, Duke de** commonly described as "an English scoundrel." [Am. Lit.: *Monsieur Beaucaire*, Magill I, 616–617]

693. UNSOPHISTICATION (See also COARSENESS, NAÏVETÉ, RUSTICITY.)

1. **Adams, Parson** industrious curate; good-naturedly unsophisticated. [Br. Lit.: *Joseph Andrews*]

2. *Barefoot Boy* adventures of rural boyhood. [Am. Lit.: Hart, 57]

3. **Beverly Hillbillies** the rustication of California's wealthy Beverly Hills. [TV: Terrace, I, 93–94]

4. **brown ass** traditional symbol signifying lack of culture. [Animal Symbolism: Jobes, 142]

5. **Dogpatch** town of illiterate country folk. [Comics: "Li'l Abner" in Horn, 450]

6. **Donn, Arabella** Jude's wife; a vulgar country girl. [Br. Lit.: *Jude the Obscure*]

7. **Geese of Brother Philip** sheltered lad believes father's explanation of girls. [Ital. Lit.: *Decameron*, Hall, 135]

8. **Grand Fenwick, Duchy of** miniscule backward European kingdom that "bites the world's tail." [Am. Lit.: *The Mouse That Roared*]

9. **Grand Ole Opry** country-western music performance hall and radio show; "back-country" motif. [Radio: Buxton, 100–101]

10. **Green, Verdant** callow Oxford freshman; victim of practical jokes. [Br. Lit.: *The Adventures of Mr. Verdant Green*, Brewer *Dictionary*, 1126]

11. **Kadiddlehopper, Clem** character who epitomizes naïveness. [Radio: "The Red Skelton Show" in Buxton, 197]

12. **Li'l Abner** country-bred comic strip character. [Comics: Horn, 450–451]

13. **Miller, Daisy** her American ways caused scandal in Rome. [Am. Lit.: *Daisy Miller*]

14. **Okies** Californians' derogatory name for Oklahoma immigrants; meaning "ignorant tramps." [Am. Lit.: *The Grapes of Wrath*]

15. **polyester** fashionable in the 1960s and 1970s, the fabric's "wash and wear" property and its durability made it popular, but it soon became synonymous with bad taste [Am. Culture: *SJEPC*]

16. **Pyle, Gomer** innocent character in Marine Corps situation comedy. [TV: "Gomer Pyle, U.S.M.C." in Terrace, I, 319]

17. **Snerd, Mortimer** ventriloquist's dummy personifies unsophistication. [Radio: "The Edgar Bergen and Charlie McCarthy Show" in Buxton, 7–77]

Unworldliness (See ASCETICISM.)

Uselessness (See FUTILITY.)

694. USURPATION

1. **Adonijah** presumptuously assumed David's throne before Solomon's investiture. [O.T.: I Kings: 5–10]

2. **Anschluss** Nazi takeover of Austria (1938). [Eur. Hist.: *Hitler*, 590–627]

3. **Athalian** steals throne by killing all royal line. [O.T.: II Kings 11:1]

4. **Claudius** usurped throne of Hamlet's father. [Br. Lit.: *Hamlet*]

5. **Frederick** arrogated dominions of his brother. [Br. Lit.: *As You Like It*]

6. **Glorious Revolution** James II deposed; William and Mary dethroned (1688). [Br. Hist.: *EB*, 3: 248]

7. **Godunov, Boris (c. 1551–1605)** cunningly has tsarevich murdered; gallantly accepts throne. [Russ. Lit.: *Boris Godunov*; Russ. Opera: Moussorgsky, *Boris Godunov*]

8. **Menahem** murders Shallum and enthrones himself. [O.T.: II Kings 15:14]

9. **Otrepyev, Grigory** baseborn monk assumes dead tsarevich's identity and throne. [Russ. Lit.: *Boris Godunov*; Russ. Opera: Moussorgsky, *Boris Godunov*]

695. USURY

1. **Fledgeby** cowardly and deceitful moneylender. [Br. Lit.: *Our Mutual Friend*]

2. **Gride, Arthur** extorting moneylender. [Br. Lit.: *Nicholas Nickleby*]

3. **Milo** loaned gold for huge interest rates and sexual favors. [Gk. Lit.: *The Golden Ass*]

4. **Nickleby, Ralph** avaricious and ungentlemanly moneylender. [Br. Lit.: *Nicholas Nickleby*]

5. **Shylock** shrewd, avaricious moneylender. [Br. Lit.: *Merchant of Venice*]

696. UTOPIA (See also PARADISE, WONDERLAND.)

1. **Abbey of Telema** Rabelais's vision of the ideal society. [Fr. Lit.: *Garagantua*, Plumb, 394]

2. **Altneuland** future Jewish state; "if willed, no fairytale." [Hung. Lit.: *Altneuland*, Wigoder, 21]

3. **Altruria** equalitarian, socialist state founded on altruistic principles. [Am. Lit.: *A Traveler from Altruria* in Hart, 860]

4. **Amaurote** chief city in Utopia. [Br. Lit.: *Utopia*]

5. **Annfwn** land of perpetual beauty and happiness where death is unknown. [Welsh Myth.: Leach, 91]

6. **Arden** the forest setting of Shakespeare's *As You Like It*; an idealized, earthly paradise. [Br. Lit. *ODA*, 196]

7. **Atlantis** legendary island; inspired many Utopian myths. [Western Folklore: Misc.]

8. **Brook Farm** literary, socialist commune intended to be small utopia (1841–1846). [Am. Hist.: Jameson, 63]

9. **Castalia** founded by intellectuals to form a synthesis of arts and sciences, symbolized in the Glass Bead Game. [Ger. Lit.: Hesse *Magister Ludi* in Weiss, 278]

10. ***Coming Race, The*** depicts a classless society of highly civilized people living deep under the earth's surface. [Br. Lit.: Barnhart, 268]

11. **commune** group of unrelated people living together who reject mainstream values, with vision of more ideal society. [Hist.: *SJEPC*]

12. **Disneyland** amusement park created by Walt Disney (1955); symbol of magical land of wonder and fantasy. [Pop. Cult.: *FOF, MOD*]

13. **El Dorado** legendary place of fabulous wealth. [Am. Hist.: Espy, 335]

14. **Erewhon** utopia—anagram of "nowhere." [Br. Lit.: *Erewhon*]

15. **Golden Age** legendary period under the rule of Cronus when life was easy and blissful for all. [Gk. Myth.: *NCE*, 33]

16. **Helicon Home Colony** socialist community founded by Upton Sinclair. [Am. Hist.: *NCE*, 2524]

17. ***Looking Backward, 2000–1887*** utopian novel (1888). [Am. Lit.: Benét, 598]

18. **Nephelococcygia** ethereal wonderland of castle, secure from the gods; also Cloud Cuckooland. [Gk. Lit.: *The Birds*]

19. **Never Never Land** home of Peter Pan, where one never grows up. [Br. Lit.: *Peter Pan*, Espy 339]

20. ***New Atlantis, The*** Sir Francis Bacon's 1627 account of a visit to the island of Bensalem, which abounds in scientific discoveries. [Br. Lit.: Haydn & Fuller, 515]

21. **New Harmony** cooperative colony founded by Robert Owen in Indiana (1825). [Am. Hist.: *EB*, X: 315]

22. ***News from Nowhere*** account of a Socialist Utopia based on craftsmanship, love, and beauty. [Br. Lit.: Drabble, 695]

23. **Oneida** founded by John Humphrey Noyes in New York; based on extended family system. [Am. Hist.: *EB*, X: 315]

24. **Perelandra** used of the planet Venus, where life has been newly created, and the atmosphere has the innocent beauty of Eden. [Eng. Lit.: Lewis *Perelanda*; *The Space Trilogy* in Weiss, 437]

25. ***Republic, The*** Plato's dialogue describes the ideal state. [Gk. Lit.: Benét, 850]

26. **Saint-Simonism** sociopolitical theories advocating industrial socialism. [Fr. Hist.: Brewer *Dictionary*, 955]

27. **Seven Cities of Cibola** the land of the ZuÒis (New Mexico); great wealth sought by Coronado. [Mex. Myth.: Payton, 614]

763

28. **Shangri-La** earthly paradise in the Himalayas. [Br. Lit.: *Lost Horizon*]

29. ***Utopia*** More's humanistic treatise on the ideal state (1516). [Br. Lit.: *Utopia*]

V

Valor (See BRAVERY.)

697. VANITY (See also CONCEIT, EGOTISM.)

1. **Cassiopeia** claimed her beauty was greater than that of the Nereids. [Gk. Myth.: Leach, 196]

2. **Channing, Margot** vain and vicious actress played by Bette Davis in *All About Eve*. [Am. Film: *SJEPC*]

3. **Eglantine, Madame** distinguished by her feminine delicacy and seeming worldliness. [Br. Lit.: *Canterbury Tales*, "The Prioress's Tale"]

4. **Malone, Sam** good-looking owner of bar (on TV's *Cheers*, 1982–93); vain about his appearance, fancies himself a woman magnet. [Am. TV: *SJEPC*]

5. **March, Amy** beautiful, vain, spoiled girl. [Am. Lit.: *Little Women*]

6. **mirror** attribute of vainglory. [Art.: Hall, 211]

7. **Miss Piggy** vain, egotistical Muppet, noted for her arrogance. [Am. TV: *ODA*]

8. **monkey** its skill at mimicry make it symbol of human vanity and folly. [Symbolism: *CEOS&S*]

9. **Narcissus** fell in love with own image. [Gk. Myth.: Howe, 174]

10. **peacock** conceit personified. [Animal Symbolism: Hall, 239]

11. **Zion, Daughters of** Lord reacts harshly to their wanton finery. [O.T.: Isaiah 3:16–26]

698. VENGEANCE

1. **Absalom** kills half-brother, Amnon, for raping sister, Tamar. [O.T.: II Samuel 13:28–29]

2. **Acamas** Aeneas's companion; kills Promachus to avenge brother's murder. [Gk. Lit.: *Iliad*]

3. **Acarnan and Amphoterus** enabled by Zeus to grow to manhood in single day to avenge father's murder. [Gk. Myth.: Zimmerman, 2]

4. **Achilles** avenges Patroclus's death by brutally killing Hector. [Gk. Lit.: *Iliad*]

5. **Agag** mutilated by Samuel to requite Israelite slaughter. [O.T.: I Samuel 15:33]

6. **Ahab, Captain** seeks revenge on whale. [Am. Lit.: *Moby Dick*]

7. **Alastor** epithet applied to Zeus and others as avenger. [Gk. Myth.: *NCE*, 49]

8. **Alfio** takes vengeance on Turiddu for adultery with his wife. [Ital. Opera: Mascagni, *Cavilleia Rusticana*, Westerman, 338–339]

9. **Atreus** cuckolded by brother, serves him his sons for dinner. [Rom. Lit.: *Thyestes*, Brewer *Dictionary*, 1081]

10. **Balfour, Ebenezer** takes vengeance on David, whose father stole Ebenezer's woman. [Br. Lit.: *Kidnapped*]

11. **Barabas** his house and riches seized by the governor, murders the governor's son and others, and betrays the city to the Turks. [Br. Drama: *The Jew of Malta* in Benét, 521]

12. **Calvo, Baldasare** Tito's aged benefactor; robbed and betrayed by Tito, eventually denounces and strangles him. [Br. Lit.: George Eliot *Romola*]

13. **Chillingworth, Roger** tortures Dimmesdale for adultery. [Am. Lit.: *The Scarlet Letter*]

14. **clover** traditional symbol of vengeance. [Flower Symbolism: *Flora Symbolica*, 178]

15. **Colomba** will not rest until father's murder is avenged. [Fr. Lit.: *Columba*]

16. **Coppelius** destroys Olympia because of bad check. [Fr. Opera: Offenbach, *Tales of Hoffman*, Westerman, 275]

17. **Cousin Bette** deprived of her lover by Baron Hulot, she eventually manages to ruin the family. [Fr. Lit.: Balzac *Cousin Bette* in Magill I, 166]

18. **cry of blood** innocent victim's blood calls for justice. [O.T.: Genesis 4:10; Br. Lit.: *Richard II*]

19. **Dantès, Edmond** uses his wealth to punish those who betrayed him. [Fr. Lit.: Dumas *The Count of Monte Cristo*]

20. **Dirae** avenging goddesses or Furies. [Rom. Myth.: *LLEI*, I: 326]

21. **Don Carlos** takes vengeance upon Alvaro, alleged murderer of his father. [Ital. Opera: Verdi, *La Forza del Destino*, Westerman, 316–317]

22. **Electra** wreaks vengeance on her father's murderers. [Gk. Lit.: *Electra*]

23. **Epigoni, the** sons of the chiefs killed in the siege of Thebes avenge their fathers' deaths by razing the city. [Gk. Myth.: Benét, 318]

24. **eye for an eye** Moses's *lex talionis*. [O.T.: Exodus 21:23–25; Leviticus 24:20; Deuteronomy 19:21]

25. **Falke, Dr.** avenges his public humiliation by Eisenstein. [Aust. Operetta: J. Strauss, *Die Fledermaus*, Westerman, 278]

26. **Furies, the** horrible avengers of crimes. [Gk. Myth.: Brewer *Dictionary*, 381]

27. **golden cockerel, the** warns the king whenever enemies approach, but kills him when he breaks his promise of a reward. [Russ. Ballet: *Coq d'Or* in Goode, 78]

28. **Hamlet** spurred on by his father's ghost, avenges murder of his father. [Br. Lit.: *Hamlet*]

29. **Hecuba** kills Polymestor's children and blinds him for his treacherous murder of her son Polydorus. [Gk. Drama: Euripedes *Hecuba* in Benét, 450]

30. **Herodias** spitefully effects decapitation of John the Baptist. [N.T.: Mark 6:19–26]

31. **Hiawatha** adventurous avenger of his father's wickedness to his mother. [Am. Lit.: Longfellow *Song of Hiawatha* in Magill I, 905]

32. **Hieronimo** stages a play that gives him the opportunity to kill his son's murderers. [Br. Drama: *The Spanish Tragedy* in Magill II, 990]

33. **Hope, Jefferson** to avenge the murder of his sweetheart by two Mormons, trails them from Utah to London and kills both. [Br. Lit.: Doyle *A Study in Scarlet* in *Sherlock Holmes*]

34. **Joab** kills Abner, murderer of his brother. [O.T.: II Samuel 3:27]

35. **Kentucky Tragedy** noted tale of retribution, inspired many works. [Am. Hist.: Benét, 544]

36. *Malta, The Jew of* Christian-hating merchant's betrayal of Malta. [Br. Lit.: *The Jew of Malta*]

37. **Medea** uses poisoned nightgown to kill Jason's new wife. [Fr. Opera: Cherubini, *Medea*, Westerman, 81]

38. **Montresor** redresses insult by entombing insulter in catacomb niche. [Am. Lit.: Poe "The Cask of Amontillado"]

39. **Nemesis** daughter of Night; brought retribution upon haughty. [Gk. Myth.: Hall, 221]

40. **Orestes** killed his mother and her lover for having murdered his father. [Gk. Myth.: Benét, 741]

41. **Pied Piper** refused his promised reward for ridding Hamelin of rats, he lures the children away. [Ger. Legend: Benét, 787]

42. **Rigoletto** wreaks vengeance on daughter-seducing Duke of Mantua. [Ital. Opera: Verdi, *Rigoletto*, Westerman, 300]

43. **Samson** brings down the temple of the Philistines to avenge their blinding of him and dies in the process. [O.T.: Judges 16:28–30]

44. **Sextus** kills Ptolemy for the murder of Pompey. [Br. Opera: *Julius Caesar in Egypt*, Westerman, 52–53]

45. **Tamora** plots to avenge son by murdering the Andronicus family. [Br. Lit.: *Titus Andronicus*]

46. **Titus Andronicus** exacts revenge for crimes against his family. [Br. Lit.: *Titus Andronicus*]

47. **Todd, Sweeney** barber returns to England; takes revenge for false conviction by slitting throats of customers. [Br. Folklore: Misc.; Br. Lit.: *Sweeney Todd*; Am. Musical Theater: *Sweeney Todd, the Demon Barber of Fleet Street*]

48. **Zachanassian, Claire** a multi-millionairess, she bribes the villagers to execute the man who was responsible for her shame. [Swiss Drama: Duerrenmatt *The Visit* in Benét, 1063]

699. VICTIM (See also ASSASSINATION.)

1. **Cooke, Sam (1935–1964)** groundbreaking soul music artist of 1950s-1960s was rooted in gospel but branched off into secular realm; produced 31 popular hits before his untimely death. [Am. Music: *SJEPC*]

2. **Gaye, Marvin (1939–1984)** singer/songwriter of soul music instrumental in Motown's distinct sound in 1960s-1970s was tragically killed by his abusive father shortly after making a comeback. [Am. Music: *SJEPC*]

3. **John Paul II, Pope (1920–2005)** Roman Catholic pope shot and critically wounded by Turkish gunman on May 13, 1981 in St. Peter's Square. [Ital. Hist.: Misc.]

4. **Johnson, Robert (1914?-1938)** created legend that he had sold his soul to the devil for his amazing talent as a blues guitarist; his music featured interplay between instrument and voice and use of slide on guitar frets; killed by husband of a lover. [Am. Music: *SJEPC*]

5. **Kerrigan, Nancy (1969–)** 1993 U.S. figure skating champion; during the Olympic trials of 1994, she was attacked by associates of her rival, Tonya Harding in an ineffectual attempt to keep Kerrigan from competing. [Am. Sports: *SJEPC*]

6. **King, Rodney (1965–)** African American beaten by police in Los Angeles in 1991; their subsequent acquittal led to riots in the city in 1992; made a famous plea two days after verdicts: "Can we all get along?". [Am. Hist.: *SJEPC*]

7. **Lennon, John (1940–1980)** famous singer/songwriter who started with The Beatles, then moved on to career of his own; shot dead in 1980. [Am. Music: *SJEPC*]

8. **Pearl, Daniel (1963–2002)** United States journalist; kidnapped and murdered in Pakistan where he was investigating links between Al Qaeda and Pakistan's Inter-Services Intelligences. [Am. Jour.: Misc.]

9. **Reagan, Ronald (1911–2004)** victim of assassination attempt 69 days into his presidency (March 30, 1981). [Am. Hist.: Misc.]

10. **Selena (1971–1995)** award-winning Latino singer of Tejano, Tex-Mex fusion music; shot to death by employee at age 24. [Am. Music: *SJEPC*]

11. **Seles, Monica (1973–)** was ranked number one at age 17; made a comeback after being stabbed by Steffi Graf fan. [Am. Sports: *SJEPC*]

12. **Shakur, Tupac (1971–1995)** also known as 2Pac; creator of rap songs about black culture, the brutality of police, and poverty; sometimes labelled a gangsta rapper for his controversial poetry; died of gunshot wounds. [Am. Music: *SJEPC*]

13. **Versace, Gianni (1946–1997)** colorful designer of fashion for men and women that often accentuated the body dramatically; killed outside his Miami mansion by serial killer Andrew Cunanan. [Am. Culture: *SJEPC*]

14. **White, Stanford (1853–1906)** famous architect killed by jealous husband of his mistress in 1906; seduced numerous women with invitation to "come up and see my etchings," the pick-up line he coined. [Am. Architecture: *SJEPC*]

700. VICTORY

1. **Arc de Triomphe** arch built in Paris by Napoleon to celebrate his conquests (1806–1836). [Fr. Hist.: Misc.]
2. **arch** symbol of triumph. [Misc.: *CEOS&S*, 208]
3. **Arch of Trajan** triumphal monument by emperor (c. 100). [Rom. Hist.: Misc.]
4. **bay leaves** wreath used as victor's crown. [Heraldry: Halberts, 20]
5. **Beethoven's 5th** symphony's first four notes sound like Morse code for *V*, so the work has come to symbolize victory to many. [Western Culture: Misc.]
6. **Greek cross** symbol of Christ's triumph over death. [Christian Iconog.: Jobes, 386]
7. **laurel** leaves were, to Greco-Roman world, symbol of victory. [Symbolism: *CEOS&S*]
8. **laurel wreath** traditional symbol of victory, recognition, and reward. [Gk. and Roman Hist.: Jobes, 374]
9. **Nike** winged goddess of triumph; also called Victoria. [Gk. Myth.: Brewer *Dictionary*, 757]
10. **palm** sign of triumph. [N.T.: Revelation 7:9]
11. **V-E Day** Allies accept Gemany's surrender in WWII (May 8, 1945). [World Hist.: Van Doren, 506]
12. **V-J Day** Allies accept Japan's surrender in WWII (August 15, 1945). [World Hist.: Van Doren, 507]
13. **wolf** in some cultures, symbol of courage, victory, or nurturance. [Symbolism: *CEOS&S*]

701. VILLAIN (See also EVIL, WICKEDNESS.)

1. **Bligh, Captain (1754–1817)** sadistic, heavy-handed captain of the *Bounty*. [Am. Lit.: *Mutiny on the Bounty*]

2. **Bluto** Popeye's archenemy; also called Brutus. [Comics: "Thimble Theater" in Horn, 657–658]

3. **Boris and Natasha** duo of dirty dealers. [TV: "Rocky and His Friends" in Terrace, II, 252–253]

4. **d'Acunha, Teresa** portrait of devilish Spanish servant and kidnapper. [Br. Lit.: *The Antiquary*]

5. **Dalgarno, Lord** young profligate nobleman; betrays Lady Hermione, slanders Nigel. [Br. Lit.: *Fortunes of Nigel*]

6. **Dastardly, Dick** popular personification of a villain. [TV: "Dastardly and Mutley" in Terrace I, 185]

7. **deVille, Cruella** witchlike rich lady dognaps 99 dalmatians for coat-making. [Am. Cinema: *101 Dalmatians* in *Disney Films*, 181–184]

8. **Fagin** iniquitous old man; employs youngsters as thieves. [Br. Lit.: *Oliver Twist*]

9. **Foulfellow, J. Worthington** sly fox cajoles Pinocchio onto stage. [Ital. Children's Lit.: *Pinocchio* in *Disney Films*, 32–37]

10. **Fu Manchu** evil Chinese villain created by English novelist Sax Rohmer in 1913; depicted in comic books, film, and television with thin face, long skinny down-turned mustache, and goatee. [Br. Lit.: *SJEPC*]

11. **Hook, Captain James** from J.M. Barrie's classic play *Peter Pan* (1904); clever opponent of Peter whose hand has been eaten by a crocodile and now sports a hook; eventually killed by the croc. [Scot. Theater: Jones]

12. **Iago** slanders Desdemona; precipitates tragedy. [Br. Lit.: *Othello*]

13. **Joker** enemy of Batman in DC Comics; portrayals range from murderous sociopath to thieving prankster. [Am. Comics: Misc.]

14. **Legree, Simon** cruel slavemaster of Uncle Tom. [Am. Lit.: *Uncle Tom's Cabin*]

15. **Lovelace, Robert** nefariously seduces the honorable, virtuous Clarissa. [Br. Lit.: Richardson *Clarissa Harlowe* in Magill I, 143]

16. **Luthor, Lex** Superman's archenemy from the comic books by DC Comics; white collar criminal. [Am. Comics: Misc.]

17. **Mime** tries to poison Siegfried and get Nibleung treasure. [Ger. Opera: Wagner *Siegfried*, Westerman, 241]

18. **Montoni, Signor** imprisons and mistreats his wife, tries to force his niece into marriage, and terrorizes the area. [Br. Lit.: Radcliffe *The Mysteries of Udolpho* in Magill I, 635]

19. **Montserrat, Conrade de** attempts to assassinate king; detected by Kenneth's hound. [Br. Lit.: *The Talisman*]

20. **Moriarty, Professor** arch-criminal, foe of Sherlock Holmes. [Br. Lit.: Doyle *Sherlock Holmes*]

21. **Mother Saint Agatha** prioress abets lustful monk's plot to punish runaway. [Br. Lit.: *The Monk*]

22. **Murdour** reprehensible scoundrel; cuckolds and kills Bevis's father. [Br. Lit.: *Bevis of Hampton*]

23. **Oil Can Harry** a study in dastardliness. [Comics: "Mighty Mouse" in Horn, 492; TV: "The Mighty Mouse Playhouse" in Terrace, II, 96]

24. **Pizarro, Don** illegally imprisons and starves Florestan; plans murder. [Ger. Opera: Beethoven *Fidelio*, Westerman, 109–110]

25. **Plantagenet, Richard** murders Somerset. [Br. Lit.: *II Henry VI*]

26. **Queen, the** "a crafty devil"; "hourly coining plots." [Br. Lit.: *Cymbeline*]

27. **Sauron** from Tolkien's Lord of the Rings trilogy (1954–1956); known as the Dark Lord or Lord of Mordor; wants complete dominance over Middle Earth which leads to his determination to steal the powerful ring from Frodo; never appears, except as monstrous presence. [Br. Lit.: Gillespie and Naden]

28. **Scarpia** offers mock execution for Tosca's affections. [Ital. Opera: Puccini, *Tosca*, Westerman, 352–354]

29. **Sheriff of Nottingham** traditional badman; thwarted in attempts to capture Robin Hood. [Br. Lit.: *Robin Hood*]

30. **Tello, Don** lustful nobleman; sates his passion on Elvira. [Span. Lit.: *The King, the Greatest Alcalde*]

31. **Vader, Darth** fallen Jedi Knight has turned to evil. [Am. Film: *Star Wars*]

32. **Voldemort, Lord** character from J.K. Rowling's Harry Potter series for young readers (1997–2007); murderer of Harry's parents; power-hungry lord of evil who is intent on overpowering and destroying Harry and all that he stands for. [Br. Children's Lit.: Misc.]

33. **Wild, Jonathan** ambitious knave, schemer, and robber, whose "greatness" is satirized. [Br. Lit.: Fielding *Jonathan Wild the Great* in Magill II, 516]

Vindictiveness (See VENGEANCE.)

702.   VIOLENCE (See also BRUTALITY, CRUELTY.)

1. **AK47** deadly Soviet automatic assault rifle with banana clip; associated with violent rebellions and murderous revolutionaries. [Am. Hist.: *SJEPC*]

2. **Altamont** free 1969 Rolling Stones concert in San Francisco ended in chaos and death. [Am. Hist.: *SJEPC*]

3. *American Psycho* disturbing novel by Brett Easton Ellis narrated in diary form by yuppie serial killer Pat Bateman, who describes his violent, murderous acts in graphic detail (1991). [Am. Lit.: *SJEPC*]

4. *Blue Velvet* David Lynch film set in idyllic small town exposes disturbing, violent behavior of residents (1986). [Am. Film: *SJEPC*]

5. **Hell's Angels** motorcycle group considered violent criminals by law enforcement, while they claim otherwise. [Am. Culture: Misc.]

6. **McCarthy, Cormac (1933–)** writer of critcally-acclaimed novels often set in American southwest and marked by violence and bleakness. [Am. Lit.: Misc.]

7. **pogrom** violent massacre of Jewish villagers by Russian Cossacks in late 19th century; now used to describe violence against a group, especially by anti-Semites. [Russ. Hist.: *FOF, MOD*]

8. **postal, to go** refers to the massacre of fellow postal workers by disgruntled employees in the 1990s; now, to become violently enraged. [Am. Culture: Misc.]

9. *Pulp Fiction* Quentin Tarantino's 1994 film about criminals inn Los Angeles; original and effective blend of brutality and absurdity. [Am. Film: *SJEPC*]

10. **Punch and Judy** London street performances of puppet theater—mainly by Italians—recorded as early as eighteenth century; Punch resembled court jester or clown; comedy mixed with violence, not mild but rather murder, beatings, etc. [Br. Entertainment: *OCCL*]

11. **road rage** violence in response to driving violations and faux pas; blamed by some on maddening traffic congestion. [Am. Pop. Culture: *SJEPC*]

12. **slasher films** horror films with psychopathic killer brutally murdering; many have been done as serials: *Halloween, Friday the 13th, A Nightmare on Elm Street*. [Am. Film: Misc.]

13. **Spillane, Mickey (1918–2006)** author of hard-boiled novels featuring private eye Mike Hammer and spy Tiger Mann; criticized for use of violence as solution in his works. [Am. Lit.: *SJEPC*]

14. **Tarantino, Quentin (1963–)** casual violence, sex, drugs, and other pulp genre elements are found in his witty, inventive films; probably best known for writing and directing acclaimed *Pulp Fiction* (1994). [Am. Film: *SJEPC*]

15. **Tyson, Mike (1966–)** boxing champ by age of 19; volatile personality spilled over into personal ilfe, leading to brutality in and out of ring and imprisonment. [Am. Sports: *SJEPC*]

16. *Wild Bunch, The* director Sam Peckinpah set new standards in the blood-and-guts realism of violence depicted in this 1969 Western. [Am. Film: *SJEPC*]

703. VIRGINITY (See also CHASTITY, PURITY.)

1. **Agnes, Saint** patron saint of virgins. [Christian Hagiog.: Brewer *Dictionary*, 16]

2. **Atala** Indian maiden learns too late she can be released from her vow to remain a virgin. [Fr. Lit.: *Atala*]

3. **Ayhena** goddess who had no love affairs and never married, called Parthenos, "the Virgin." [Gk. Myth: Benét, 60]

4. **Cecilia, Saint** consecrated herself to God; bridegroom followed suit. [Christian Hagiog.: Attwater, 81–82]

5. **Chrysanthus and Daria, Saints** sexless marriage for glory of God. [Christian Hagiog.: Attwater, 86]

6. **Drake, Temple** chastity makes her the objects of attacks. [Am. Lit: *Sanctuary*]

7. **Josyan** steadfastly retains virginity for future husband. [Br. Lit.: *Bevis of Hampton*]

8. **lily** symbol of Blessed Virgin; by extension, chastity. [Christian Symbolism: Appleton, 57–58]

9. **ostrich egg** symbolic of virgin birth. [Art: Hall, 110]

10. **red and white roses, garland of** emblem of virginity, especially of the Virgin Mary. [Christian Iconog.: Jobes, 374]

11. **Vestals** six pure girls; tended fire sacred to Vesta. [Rom. Hist.: Brewer *Dictionary*, 1127]

12. **Virgin Mary, Blessed** mother of Jesus. [Christianity: *NCE*, 1709]

Virility (See MASCULINITY.)

704. VIRTUOUSNESS (See also DIGNITY, HONESTY, NOBLEMINDEDNESS, RIGHTEOUSNESS.)

1. **Amelia** faithful wife of William Booth, often in debtors' prison, saved by her purity from the men who prey upon her. [Br. Lit.: *Amelia*]

2. **Andrews, Pamela** servant who, despite threats, attempted seduction, and imprisonment by her master, remains chaste until their marriage. [Br. Lit.: Richardson *Pamela*]

3. **Andromache** thinks only of family; rejects king's advances. [Fr. Lit.: *Andromache*]

4. **Apostrophia** epithet of Aphrodite, meaning "rejector of sinful passion." [Gk. Myth.: Misc.]

5. **Christian** John Bunyan's virtuous, well-traveled hero. [Br. Lit.: *The Pilgrim's Progress*]

6. **Erlynne, Mrs.** gains socially admirable title of "good woman." [Br. Lit.: *Lady Windemere's Fan*, Magill I, 488–490]

7. **Galahad, Sir** noblest and purest knight of the Round Table. [Br. Lit.: *Le Morter d'Arthur*]

8. **Guyon, Sir** embodiment of virtuous self-control. [Br. Lit.: *Faerie Queene*]

9. **Marina** "a piece of virtue." [Br. Lit.: *Pericles*]

10. **Nickleby, Kate** pure-minded sister of Nicholas; repulses all advances. [Br. Lit.: *Nicholas Nickleby*]

11. **nut** in Jewish tradition, considered a symbol of virtue because in the beginning and end, fruit and nut are one and the same. [Symbolism: *CEOS&S*]

12. **Pamela** sweet maidservant who chastely repels disgraceful advances, marries her aristocratic pursuer, and attempts to reform him. [Br. Lit.: Richardson *Pamela*]

13. **Susanna** rejects advances of elderly men. [Apocrypha: Susanna]

14. **Thirty-Six Righteous Men** the minimum number of anonymous individuals in each generation believed to have the virtues and humility to which the world owes its continued existence. [Jew. Legend: *Encyclopedia Judaica*, X, 1367]

15. **Tuesday's child** full of grace. [Nurs. Rhyme: Opie, 309]

16. **Wilkes, Melanie** virtuous, long-suffering wife of Ashley. [Am. Lit.: *Gone With the Wind*]

Voluptuousness (See BEAUTY, FEMININE; BUXOMNESS; SEX SYMBOLS.)

Voracity (See GLUTTONY.)

705. VOYEURISM

1. **Actacon** turned into stag for watching Artemis bathe. [Gk. Myth.: Leach, 8]

2. *Candid Camera* Allen Funt's tasteful but funny TV show secretly recorded ordinary people in humorous situations, then revealed "You're on Candid Camera!" (1950s-1990s). [Am. TV: *SJEPC*]

3. **elders of Babylon** watch Susanna bathe. [Apocrypha: Susanna; Art: Daniel, 217]

4. **Gyges** king's bodyguard requested secretly to view queen undressing. [Gk. Lit.: Avery, 507–508]

5. *National Enquirer, The* weekly supermarket tabloid specializing in sensationalism. [Am. Jour.: *SJEPC*]

6. **Peeping Tom** illicitly glanced at the naked Godiva. [Br. Legend: Brewer *Dictionary*, 815]

7. **reality television** shows in which real-life events or situations are filmed; began in America in mid-1980s and rose to immense popularity. [Am. TV: *SJEPC*]

8. *Rear Window* classic Alfred Hitchcock film of 1954; wheelchair-bound photographer spends time watching the lives of others from his apartment window and believes he has witnessed a murder. [Am. Film: *SJEPC*]

9. **Roberts, Mr.** takes advantage of unshaded hospital window to watch nurses taking baths. [Am. Lit.: Heggen *Mister Roberts* in Sobel, 479]

10. **Swaggart, Jimmy (1935–)** leading televangelist of the 1980s; his puritanical stance and judgmental opinions meant bitter reactions when his own voyeuristic acts with a prostitute and other transgressions were revealed. [Am. Rel.: *SJEPC*]

Vulgarity (See COARSENESS.)

706. VULNERABILITY (See also WEAKNESS.)

1. **Achilles** warrior vulnerable only in his heel. [Gk. Myth.: Zimmerman, 4]

2. **Antaeus** only vulnerable if not touching ground. [Gk. and Roman Myth.: Hall, 151]

3. **Balder** conquerable only with mistletoe. [Norse Myth.: Walsh *Classical*, 43]

4. **Diarmuid** Irish Achilles; killed through cunning Fionn's deceit. [Irish Myth.: Jobes, 443; Parrinder, 79]

5. **Maginot Line** French fortification zone along German border; thought impregnable before WWII. [Fr. Hist.: *NCE*, 1658]

6. **Samson** strength derived from his hair; betrayed by Delilah. [O.T.: Judges 16]

7. **Siegfried** vulnerable only in one spot on his back. [Ger. Opera: Wagner, *Götterdämmerung*, Westerman, 245]

8. **Siegfried Line** German fortification zone opposite the Maginot Line between Germany and France. [Ger. Hist.: *WB*, 17: 370]

9. **Superman** invulnerable except for Kryptonite. [TV: "The Adventures of Superman" in Terrace, I, 38; Comics: Horn, 642]

10. *Titanic* seemingly invincible British luxury ocean liner astonished the world when it collided with an iceberg on maiden voyage in 1912 and sank, killing over 1500 passengers and crew; many saw it as sign of vulnerability of humans despite technogical progress. [Br. Hist.: *SJEPC*]

W

707. WANDERING (See also ADVENTUROUSNESS, JOURNEY, QUEST, TRAVEL.)

1. **Ahasuerus** German name for the Wandering Jew. [Ger. Lit.: Benét, 1071]

2. **Ancient Mariner** Coleridge's wandering sailor. [Br. Lit.: "The Rime of the Ancient Mariner" in Norton, 597–610]

3. **Aniara** spaceship condemned to perpetual earth orbit. [Swed. Opera: Blomdahl, *Aniara*, Westerman, 652]

4. **Argonauts** sailed with Jason in search of Golden Fleece. [Gk. Myth.: Howe, 36]

5. **Bedouin** a nomadic desert Arab. [Br. Folklore: Espy. 98]

6. **Bloom, Leopold** Jewish advertising salesman whose wanderings around Dublin are ironic parallels of Ulysses's voyages. [Irish Lit.: James Joyce *Ulysses*]

7. **Cain** punished by God to life of vagrancy. [O.T.: Genesis 4:12]

8. **Candide** a wanderer in search of best of all possible worlds. [Fr. Lit.: *Candide*]

9. **Cocytus** Hadean river where unburied were doomed to roam for 100 years. [Gk. Myth.: Benét, 210]

10. **Cook's Tour** named for Thomas Cook (1808–1892), English travel agent and founder of guided tours; a busy, if brief, tour of a place. [Pop. Cult.: *ODA*]

11. **Eulenspiegel, Till** roams Low Countries as soldier and deliverer. [Ger. Folklore: Benét, 325–326]

12. *Flying Dutchman* spectral ship doomed to eternal wandering. [Marine Folklore: Benét, 355]

13. *Fugitive, The* tale of wrongfully-accused man fleeing imprisonment. [Am. TV: Terrace, I, 290–291]

14. **Goedzak, Lamme** accompanies Eulenspiegel on his circumambulations. [Ger. Folklore: Benét, 325–326]

15. **Goliards** wandering scholar-poets of 12th-century Europe. [Medieval Hist.: *NCE*, 1105]

16. **Gynt, Peer** Norwegian farmer drifts around without purpose. [Nor. Lit.: *Peer Gynt*, Magill I, 722–724]

17. **Gypsy** member of nomadic people who usually travel in small caravans. [Eur. Hist.: *NCE*, 1168]

18. **Harold, Childe** seeking an end to disappointment in love, he wanders about Europe. [Br. Poetry: Byron *Childe Harold's Pilgrimage* in Magill IV, 127]

19. **Herodias** condemned to wander the world for centuries for her part in the execution of John the Baptist. [Fr. Lit.: Eugènie Sue *The Wandering Jew*]

20. **Ishmael** "the wanderer" aboard Ahab's ship. [Am. Lit.: *Moby Dick*]

21. **Kwai Chang Caine** Shaolin priest wanders throughout America. [TV: "Kung Fu" in Terrace I, 449]

22. **Labre, Saint Benedict** itinerant holy beggar. [Christian Hagiog.: Attwater, 64]

23. **land of Nod** condemned to vagabondage, Cain settles here. [O.T.: Genesis 4:16]

24. **Meaulnes, Augustine** dreamer with a lifelong fondness for wandering into romantic adventures. [Fr. Lit.: *The Wanderer* in Magill I, 1081]

25. **Melmoth the Wanderer** to win souls, he is cursed to roam earth after death. [Br. Lit.: *Melmoth the Wanderer*]

26. **Moses** led his people through the wilderness for forty years. [O.T.: Pentateuch]

27. **Mother Courage** shrewd old woman who makes her living by following the armies of the Thirty Years' War selling her wares to the soldiers. [Ger. Drama: Brecht *Mother Courage and Her Children* in Benet, 690]

28. **Nolan, Philip** transferred from ship to ship; never lands. [Am. Lit.: "The Man Without a Country" in Benet, 632]

29. **Odysseus** hero of the Trojan war wanders for seven years before returning home. [Gk. Lit.: *Odyssey*]

30. **Omoo** Polynesian word for an island rover. [Am. Lit.: *Omoo*]

31. **Ossian** a legendary, wandering Irish bard. [Irish Lit.: Harvey, 603]

32. ***Route 66*** adventure series of two young men wandering along highway Route 66. [TV: Terrace, II, 259]

33. **Rugg, Peter** wanders on horseback for fifty years, trying to find his way home. [Am. Lit.: Austin "Peter Rugg, the Missing Man" in Hart, 48]

34. **Siddhartha** character who wanders in search of "inner truth." [Ger. Lit.: Hesse *Siddhartha*]

35. **Wandering Jew** condemned to eternal wandering for mocking Christ. [Christian Legend: NCE, 2926; Fr. Lit.: *Wandering Jew*]

708. WAR (See also BATTLE, MILITARY, MILITARY LEADER.)

1. *All Quiet on the Western Front* youth Paul Baumer suffers the miseries of the first World War. [Ger. Lit.: Remarque *All Quiet on the Western Front*]

2. **Amazons** race of female warriors. [Gk. Myth.: Zimmerman, 19]

3. *Apocalypse Now* U.S. Captain Willard's journey into the Vietnamese jungle to assassinate murderous Colonel Kurz; 1979 film directed by Francis Ford Coppola based on Joseph Conrad's *Heart of Darkness* (1902). [Am. Film: *SJEPC*]

4. **Athena** goddess of war; called Minerva by the Romans. [Gk. Myth.: Howe, 44]

5. *Band of Brothers* book and TV series documenting the courageous 101st Ariborne unit during WWII. [Am. Hist.: Misc.]

6. **battle ax** symbol of military conflict. [Western Folklore: Jobes, 163]

7. **Bellona** Mars's charioteer and sister. [Rom. Myth.: Leach, 135]

8. *Best Years of Our Lives, The* film portrays struggle of three American World War II veterans as they readjust to civilian life (1946). [Am. Film: *SJEPC*]

9. *Bridge on the River Kwai* 1957 award-winning film loosely based on real-life event in WWII; in P.O.W. camp, British colonel and his men construct bridge for their Japanese captors; battle of wills between two officers. [Am. Film: Misc.]

10. **brinkmanship** cold war policy of going to the "brink" of war, created by Sec. of State John Foster Dulles. [Am. Politics: *FOF, MOD*]

11. **Burns, Ken (1953–)** documentary filmmaker brought history to life in *The Civil War* (1990) and *The War* (2007). [Am. Film: *SJEPC*]

12. **Cold War** hostilities between the Western powers and the Soviet Union that lasted from 1946 to the collapse of the Soviet Union in 1990. [Western Hist.: *FOF, MOD*]

13. **Corwin, Norman (1910–)** wrote and broadcast poignant radio series and commentary during World War II such as *This Is War!* (1942) and "14 August" (1945) that promoted America's involvement yet pondered the price. [Am. Radio: *SJEPC*]

14. *Deer Hunter, The* first film to deal with the brutality and emotional impact of Vietnam War; contrasts the home lives of three soldier friends with their traumatic wartime experiences. [Am. Film: *SJEPC*]

15. **doves and hawks** those that favor peace, and those that favor a more aggressive approach in foreign policy. [Am. Politics: Misc.]

16. *Dr. Strangelove* film by Stanley Kubrick (1964); dark satire and metaphor for the dangers of the nuclear age. [Br. Film *FOF, MOD*]

17. **Durga** malignant goddess of war. [Hinduism: Leach, 330]

18. **Enyo** goddess of battle and attendant of Ares. [Gk. Myth.: Howe, 91]

19. **fail-safe** originally, a signal to prevent a retaliatory strike in a nuclear attack launched by accident; now, a safeguard, or foolproof method [Am. Hist.: Misc.]

20. **friendly fire** battle casualties caused by one's own, nonenemy combat fire; in common speech, an unintended, damaging mistake. [Am. Cult.: *FOF, MOD*]

21. *From Here to Eternity* emotionally powerful, sexually frank novel by James Jones explored military corruption at Pearl Harbor's U.S. Army base just prior to Japanese attack; portrayed uncaring and manipulative officers, camaraderie of oppressed enlisted men (1951; film, 1953). [Am. Lit. and Film: *SJEPC*]

22. *Gone with the Wind* epic Civil War novel (1936) and film (1939) set in the South describes the War Between the States from the Confederate point of view. [Am. Lit. and Film: *SJEPC*]

23. **Greatest Generation** ordinary Americans born in the 1920s who made extraordinary sacrifices during World War II to serve the country, then returned to buiild modern America. [Am. Hist.: Brokaw, *The Greatest Generation*; *SJEPC*]

24. **guerilla warfare** style of warfare involving smaller groups of civilian combattants, surprise attacks; by extension, unconventional business tactics. [Am. Hist.: Misc.]

25. *Guernica* painting by Picasso depicting horror of war. [Art: Osborne, 866–867]

26. **Hersey, John (1914–1993)** novelist and journalist best known for *A Bell for Adano* (1944) and *Hiroshima*, works that depict WW II and its affects on humanity. [Am. Lit.: *EB*]

27. **Huitzilopochtli** war god of ancient Mexicans. [Mex. Myth.: Harvey, 403]

28. *Iliad* Homer's poetic account set during the legendary Trojan war. [Gk. Poetry: *The Iliad*]

29. **jihad** holy war; term used by some Muslims to refer to warfare against non-Muslims. [Islam: *UIMT*, 430]

30. *Longest Day, The* events of D-Day are related from both Allied and German perspective in 1962 WWII film. [Span. Art: Misc.]

31. **M.A.D.** acronym for "mutually assured destruction," term indicating the deterrent factor of equal nuclear arsenals held by two powers. [Am. Politics: Misc.]

32. *Mahabharata* lengthy narrative poem about the great war supposed to have taken place in India about 1400 B.C. [Sanskrit Lit.: Haydn & Fuller, 451]

33. **Manhattan Project** the name of the effort to build the first atomic bomb, dropped on Japan in World War II. [Science and History: Misc.]

34. **Mars** god of war; also called Ares. [Gk. Myth.: Kravitz, 31]

35. *Midway* made in 1976, film dramatizes battle that was turning point in Pacific theater of WWII. [Am. Film: Misc.]

36. **Molotov cocktail** easily assembled grenade, named for Russian minister; symbol of simple weapon of deadly power. [History *FOF, MOD*]

37. **Myrmidon** one of the fierce Thessalonians who fought in the Trojan War under their king, Achilles. [Gk. Myth.: *The Iliad*]

38. **Neman** form of Irish war goddess, Badb; also Morrigan or Macha. [Irish Folklore: Briggs, 308]

39. **no-man's-land** from World War I, the area between the trenches of the Allies and the Germans; refers to a disputed area that belongs to no one. [Western Hist.: *FOF, MOD*]

40. **Odin** god who presided over feasts of slain warriors. [Norse Myth.: Brewer *Dictionary*, 774]

41. *Platoon* Oliver Stone's somewhat autobiographical 1986 film of the Vietnam War and the brutality of combat. [Am. Fillm: *SJEPC*]

42. **preemptive strike** from the early years of nuclear weapon capabilities, the ability to strike the first, crippling blow to one's enemies in a war; now, an attempt to take control, as in a hostile takeover of a company. [Am. Hist.: Misc.]

43. *Red Badge of Courage, The* young Civil War recruit Henry Fleming receives his baptism of fire. [Am. Lit.: Stephen Crane *The Red Badge of Courage*]

44. **red cloud** indicates military conflict. [Eastern Folklore: Jobes, 350]

45. *Stalag 17* 1953 film set in German P.O.W. camp during WWII; all attempts to escape end in failure because of an informant; leading suspect determines to find the real spy. [Am. Film: Misc.]

46. *Tora, Tora, Tora* costly 1970 film about attack on Pearl Harbor during WWII; recounts the events from both American and Japanese sides, with Japanese scenes directed by Akira Kurosawa. [Am. Film: *SJEPC*]

47. **Tyr** god of victory in war. [Norse Myth.: Leach, 1147]

48. **Valkyries** Wotan's/Odin's warrior maidens. [Norse Myth.: Leach, 1154]

709. WARNING

1. **Canterbury bells** fairies' church bells; relied on for vigilance. [Flower Symbolism: *Flora Symbolica*, 167]

2. **Capitoline geese** squawked obstreperously at sight of invader mounting rampart. [Rom. Hist.: Benét, 166]

3. **cock** crows at trespassers; morning call routs evil spirits. [Folklore: White, 150; Mercatante, 173–175]

4. **crow's cry** warning of death or illness. [Western Folklore: Jobes, 388]

5. **fiery cross** traditional Highlands call to arms. [Scot. Hist.: Brewer *Note-Book*, 324–325]

6. **Laocoön** Trojan priest warns citizens not to accept wooden horse. [Rom. Lit.: *Aeneid*]

7. **Olivant** Roland's ivory horn; sounded to summon Charlemagne. [Fr. Lit.: *The Song of Roland*]

8. **Revere, Paul (1735–1818)** famous American patriot who warned, "The British are coming" (1775). [Am. Hist.: Jameson, 425–426]

710. WATER

1. **Adad** storm god; helped cause the Flood. [Babyl. Myth.: Benét, 7]

2. **Adam's ale** water; only drink in Paradise. [Folklore: Brewer *Dictionary*, 9]

3. **Alpheus** river god. [Gk. Myth.: Zimmerman, 18]

4. **Apsu** personification of fresh water. [Babyl. Myth.: Benét, 4]

5. **Arethusa** changed into stream by Artemis to save her from Alpheus. [Gk. Myth.: Zimmerman, 29]

6. **Cyane** turned into a fountain by Hades. [Gk. Myth.: Kravitz, 70]

7. **Dirce** turned into a fountain at death. [Gk. Myth.: Kravitz, 82–83]

8. **Galatea** grieving, turned into a fountain. [Gk. Myth.: *Metamorphoses*]

9. **Jupiter Pluvius** dispenser of rain. [Rom. Myth.: Espy, 22]

10. **Neptune** in allegories of the elements, personification of water. [Art: Hall, 128]

11. **undine** female water spirit. [Medieval Hist.: Brewer *Dictionary*, 1115]

711. WEAKNESS (See also TIMIDITY, VULNERABILITY.)

1. **Gertrude** "Frailty, thy name is woman!" [Br. Lit.: *Hamlet*]

2. **Henry VI** dominated by queen and vassal; shirks responsibilities. [Br. Lit.: *Henry VI*]

3. **John, King** without grandeur, strength, or any regal quality. [Br. Lit.: *King John*]

4. **Milquetoast, Casper** the original "Timid Soul"; afraid of calling soul his own. [Comics: Horn, 663]

5. **Mitty, Walter** epitome of weak-spirited man. [Am. Lit.: "The Secret Life of Walter Mitty" in Payton, 448]

6. **musk** traditional symbol of weakness. [Plant Symbolism: *Flora Symbolica*, 176]

7. **paper tiger** term originated by Mao Zedong to describe the United States, now any entity whose apparent strength masks weakness. [Hist. and Politics: Misc.]

8. **Pilate, Pontius** yields to clamoring of Jews, hands Jesus over. [N.T.: Matthew 27:24–26; Luke 23:16–25; John 19:1–16]

9. **Warren, Nicole** relies on Dick for stability and identity. [Am. Lit.: *Tender is the Night*]

712. WEALTH (See also LUXURY, TREASURE.)

1. **Abu Dhabi** Persian Gulf sheikdom overflowing with petrodollars. [Mid-East Hist.: *NCE*, 9]

2. **Astor, John Jacob (1763–1848)** American multimillionaire who made his money in fur trading and real estate; at his death he was the richest man in the U.S. [Am. Business: Misc.]

3. **Big Daddy** wealthy Mississippi landowner of humble origins. [Am. Lit.: *Cat on a Hot Tin Roof*]

4. **black and gold** symbol of financial prosperity. [Heraldry: Jobes, 222]

5. **blue chip** stocks of traditional high value; symbol of high quality. [Am. Business: Misc.]

6. **bridge** four-person card game used to be popular leisure activity for wealthy Americans. [Entertainment: *SJEPC*]

7. **Buffett, Warren (1930–)** American billionaire financier and founder of Berkshire Hathaway investments. [Am. Business: Misc.]

8. **buttercup** traditional symbol of wealth. [Plant Symbolism: *Flora Symbolica*, 167]

9. **camel** symbol of wealth and status in Middle East. [Symbolism: *CEOS&S*]

10. **Cave of Mammon** abode of god of riches. [Br. Lit.: *Faerie Queene*]

11. **Corinth** ancient Greek city; one of wealthiest and most powerful. [Gk. Hist. and Myth.: Zimmerman, 69]

12. **Croesus** Lydian king; name became synonymous with riches. [Gk. Myth.: Kravitz, 69]

13. **Dives** rich man who ignored poor man's plight; sent to Hell. [N.T.: Luke 16:19–31]

14. **Erichthonius** world's richest man in classical times. [Gk. Myth.: Kravitz, 91]

15. **Fifth Avenue** street in New York City associated with expensive, fashionable shops. [Pop. Cult.: Misc.]

16. **Forunatus's purse** luckless man receives gift of inexhaustible purse. [Ital. Fairy Tale: *LLEI*, I: 286]

17. **fox** in China and Japan, considered bringer of wealth. [Symbolism: *CEOS&S*]

18. **Fuggers** 16th-century German financiers. [Ger. Hist.: *NCE*, 1023–1024]

19. **Gates, Bill (1955–)** American billionaire and founder of Microsoft; one of the wealthiest men in the world. [Business: Misc.]

20. **Getty, John Paul (1892–1976)** American billionaire, wealthy but stingy. [Am. Business: *ODA*]

21. *Great Gatsby, The* F. Scott Fitzgerald's 1925 novel features the self-indulgent, wretched excess and moral emptiness of wealthy Jazz Age society with moneyed characters Tom and Daisy Buchanan and Jay Gatsby. [Am. Lit.: *SJEPC*; Harris *Characters*, 111–14; Henderson, 310–11]

22. **Hearst, William Randolph (1863–1951)** American newspaper publisher; built huge estate at San Simeon, with vast art collection. [Am. Business: Misc.]

23. **hedgehog** in China and Japan, a symbol of wealth. [Symbolism: *CEOS&S*]

24. **Hughes, Howard (1905–1976)** eccentric millionaire; lived as recluse. [Am. Hist.: *NCE*, 1284]

25. **Midas** Phrygian king; whatever he touched became gold. [Gk. and Roman Myth.: Wheeler, 24]

26. **Morgan, J. P. (1837–1913)** American banker, railroad, and steel tycoon; one of the wealthiest and most powerful men of his era. [Am. Hist.: Misc.]

27. **Onassis, Aristotle (1906–1975)** Greek shipping tycoon who married Jacqueline Kennedy; his name is synonymous with wealth. [Business *ODA*]

28. **Park Avenue** street in New York City associated with wealth and luxury. [Am. Culture: Misc.]

29. **Plutus** god of wealth; blind (indiscriminate); lame (slow to accumulate); and winged (quick to disappear). [Gk. Lit.: *Plutus*]

30. **preppy** refers to someone who attends a college preparatory high school; often refers to fashions of the upper class. [Am. Culture: *SJEPC*]

31. **Rockefeller, John D. (1839–1937)** oil magnate; name has become synonymous with "rich." [Am. Hist.: Jameson, 431]

32. **Rothschild** influential family of European bankers; a catchword for wealth. [Eur. Hist.: *FOF, MOD*]

33. **Saks Fifth Avenue** Manhattan store with classy merchandise and services opened in 1924 but outlets bore Fifth Avenue appellation to capitalize on the distinction; name became synonymous with wealth and stylishness. [Am. Business: *SJEPC*]

34. **Silicon Valley** area south of San Francisco, California, where technology companies like Cicso have made fortunes; name derives from the silicon used to make computer chips. [Am. Technology: *BBInv*]

35. **Solomon** fabulous riches garnered from gifts and tolls. [O.T.: I Kings 10:14–25]

36. **Spelling, Aaron (1928–2006)** incredibly successful TV producer whose shows found great popular success, but little critical approval; from the 1960s on, his work often reflected Southern California lifestyle of glamour and wealth. [Am. TV: *SJEPC*]

37. **Sun King** Louis XIV (1638–1715), called the Sun King, was one of the wealthiest monarchs of his time; his palace, Versailles, has always been associated with the outward trappings of wealth and an opulent lifestyle. [Fr. Hist.: *ODA*]

38. **Tiffany and Company** founded by Charles Lewis Tiffany in 1853 to produce beautiful jewelry and home furnishings; son Louis Comfort Tiffany designed exquisite glass items and succeeded his father as head of the company. [Am. Business: *SJEPC*]

39. **Timon** rich Athenian; ruined by his prodigal generosity to friends. [Br. Lit.: *Timon of Athens*]

40. **turquoise** seeing turquoise after a new moon brings wealth. [Gem Symbolism: Kunz, 345]

41. **Vanderbilt, Cornelius (1794–1877)** American financeer and philanthropist who made millions from railroad and shipping businesses; a symbol of great wealth. [Am. Hist.: *ODA*]

42. **Walton family** often cited as world's wealthiest family with a fortune in excess of $100 billion; inherited from Bud and Sam Walton, founders of Wal-Mart. [Am. Business: Misc.]

43. **Warbucks, Daddy** adventurous soldier of fortune and richest man in world. [Comics: "Little Orphan Annie" in Horn, 459]

44. **wheat stalk** traditional symbol of wealth. [Flower Symbolism: *Flora Symbolica*, 178]

45. **Winfrey, Oprah (1954–)** her TV talk show began in 1985 and her personal style and emotional connection with her audience brought great success—and made her the world's first black billionaire. [Am. TV: *SJEPC*]

Weaving (See SEWING and WEAVING.)

713. WEST, THE (See also FRONTIER.)

1. **Apache** North American Indians of Southwest who fought against frontiersman. [Am. Hist.: *NCE*, 123]

2. **Arapaho** North American Plains Indians living along the Platte and Arkansas rivers. [Am. Hist.: *EB*, I: 477–478]

3. **Autry, Gene (1907–1998)** virtuous singing cowboy. [Am. Entertainment: *SJEPC*]

4. **Bass, Sam (1851–1878)** desperado whose career inspired ballads. [Am. Hist.: *NCE*, 244]

5. **Bean, Judge Roy (c. 1825–1903)** legendary frontier judge who ruled by one law book and a six-shooter. [Am. Hist.: *NCE*, 252]

6. *Big Valley, The* portraying cattle-owning aristocrats of the Wild West. [TV: Terrace, I, 99–100]

7. **Billy the Kid** [William H. Bonney (1859–1881)] Brooklyn-born gunman of the Wild West. [Am. Hist.: Wlorth, 27]

8. *Bonanza* saga of the Cartwright family. [TV: Terrace, I, 111–112]

9. **Boom Town** originally, a western town that prospered suddenly, usually because of gold mines nearby. [Am. Hist.: Misc.]

10. **boot hill** typical graveyard of gunfighters and their victims. [Am. Folklore: Misc.]

11. **Bowie knife** throwing weapon invented by James or Rezin Bowie, frontiersmen in Texas. [Am. Folklore: *EB*, II: 207]

12. *Broken Arrow* a series depicting Indian-white man exploits. [TV: Terrace, I, 122]

13. **Calamity Jane** [Martha Jane Canary Burke (c. 1852–1903)] extraordinary markswoman and pony express rider. [Am. Hist.: *NCE*, 418]

14. **California Trail** route used by pioneers, extending from Wyoming to Sacramento. [Am. Hist.: *WB*, 21: 440f]

15. **Carson, Kit (1809–1868)** frontiersman, guide, and Indian fighter in the West and Southwest. [Am. Hist.: *NCE*, 466]

16. **Cassidy, Hopalong** cowboy character from the stories of Clarence Mulford, became a wildly successful movie character, called "the epitome of gallantry and fair play." [Am. Film: Misc.]

17. **Cather, Willa (1873–1947)** many of writer's novels set on Nebraska plains or American West, such as *O, Pioneers!* (1913) and *Death Comes for the Archbishop* (1927). [Am. Lit.: *SJEPC*; Harris *Characters*, 62–63]

18. **Cheyenne** North American Indians who made up part of the Wild West scene. [Am. Hist.: *NCE*, 562]

19. *Cheyenne* 1950s TV series about cowboy of the strong, silent type. [TV: Terrace, I, 153–154]

20. **Chisholm Trail** route used by traders and drovers bringing cattle from Texas to Kansas. [Am. Hist.: *NCE*, 543]

21. **circuit rider** frontier Methodist preacher who served "appointments" (services) in cabins, schoolhouses, and even taverns. [Am. Hist.: *NCE*, 561]

22. **Cochise (c. 1815–1874)** Apache Indian chief who led the fight against white men in the Southwest. [Am. Hist.: *NCE*, 589]

23. **Cody, "Buffalo Bill" (1846–1917)** ex-Army scout who joined and led a famous Wild West show. [Am. Hist.: *NCE*, 390]

24. **Colt .45** six-shot revolver invented by Samuel Colt and used throughout the West. [Am. Hist.: *WB*, 4: 684–685]

25. **Comanche** North American Indian tribe; often figured in Wild West stories. [Am. Hist.: *NCE*, 607]

26. **Comstock Lode** richest silver deposit in U.S.; famous during frontier days. [Am. Hist.: *NCE*, 418]

27. **Conestoga wagon** horse-drawn freight wagon; originated in the Conestoga Creek region in Pennsylvania. [Am. Hist.: *EB*, III: 72]

28. **Crazy Horse (1842–1877)** Indian chief who led Sioux against the white men in the northern plains. [Am. Hist.: *EB*, III: 225–226]

29. **Custer's Last Stand** U.S. troops led by Col. Custer are massacred by the Indians at Little Big Horn, Montana (1877). [Am. Hist.: *NCE*, 701]

30. *Dances with Wolves* Kevin Costner's Academy Award-winning film based on Michael Blake's novel defied western genre formula, gave voice to Native American perspective (1990). [Am. Film: *SJEPC*]

31. *Davy Crockett* early 19th-century American frontiersman and folk hero David Crockett immortalized in this popular weekly Walt Disney TV production of the 1950s. [Am. TV: *SJEPC*]

32. **Deadwood Gulch** Wild West city in South Dakota where graves of Hickok and Annie Oakley are located. [Am. Hist.: *NCE*, 729]

33. *Death Valley Days* vignettes depicting frontier life. [TV: Terrace, I, 195]

34. **Dillon, Matt** frontier marshal of Dodge City. [TV: "Gunsmoke" in Terrace, I, 331]

35. **Dodge City** onetime rowdy cowboy town under supervision of Bat Masterson and Wyatt Earp. [Am. Hist.: *NCE*, 776]

36. **Earp, Wyatt (1848–1929)** U.S. cowboy, lawman, and gunfigher. [Am. Hist.: *NCE*, 819]

37. **Ford, John (1894–1973)** prolific director's Westerns painted an idealized vision of America's Old West, from the wide-open frontier landscape to the people's enduring spirit. [Am. Film: *SJEPC*]

38. **Geronimo (1829–1909)** renegade Indian of the Wild West. [Am. Hist.: *NCE*, 1076]

39. **ghost town** town left vacant after gold strike; common during frontier days. [Am. Hist.: *NCE*, 1080]

40. *Good, the Bad, and the Ugly, The* spaghetti western directed by Sergio Leone depicted American West of the Civil War era as a violent, lawless, and chaotic place (1966). [Ital. Film: *SJEPC*]

41. **Grey, Zane (1875–1939)** his Western novels painted a vivid, idealized vision of the mythical Old West, in both the physical landscape and the frontier values of his characters. [Am. Lit.: *SJEPC*]

42. *Gunsmoke* Wild West television epic with Dodge City setting. [TV: Terrace, I, 331–332]

43. **Hickok, "Wild Bill" (1837–1876)** famous marshal of the West. [Am. Hist.: Hart, 371]

44. *High Noon* western film in which time is of the essence. [Am. Cinema: Griffith, 396–397]

45. **Holliday, "Doc" (fl. late 19th century)** outlaw who helped Wyatt Earp fight the Clanton gang at O.K. Corral. [Am. Hist.: Misc.]

46. **"Home on the Range"** popular song about the West "where the buffalo roam" and "the deer and the antelope play." [Am. Culture: Misc.]

47. *How the West Was Won* popular film of 1962, filmed in "Cinerama"; epic featuring four generations of a family that settles in the Western U.S. [Am. Film: Misc.]

48. **Indian Territory** area set aside for the Indians by the U.S. government. [Am. Hist.: *NCE*, 1331]

49. **James, Jesse (1847–1882)** American outlaw of the Wild West. [Am. Hist.: *NCE*, 1395]

50. **L'Amour, Louis (1908–1988)** American author known for writing numerous popular Western novels. [Am. Lit.: Misc.]

51. *Lone Ranger, The* masked hero of the Wild West. [TV: Terrace, II, 34–35; Radio: Buxton, 143–144]

52. *Lonesome Dove* 1989 television miniseries; about retired Texas Rangers herding cattle from Texas to Montana. [Am. TV: Misc.]

53. *McCabe and Mrs. Miller* McCabe opens a brothel and Mrs. Miller serves as its madam in Robert Altman's acclaimed 1971 Western film. [Am. Film: Misc.]

54. **McMurtry, Larry (1936–)** American writer known for 1985 novel set in the West, *Lonsome Dove*. [Am. Lit.: Misc.]

55. **O.K. Corral** scene of famous gunfight between Wyatt Earp and the Clanton gang (1881). [Am. Hist.: *WB*, 6: 9]

56. **Oakley, Annie (1860–1926)** sharpshooter; major attraction of Buffalo Bill's show. [Am. Hist.: *NCE*, 1982]

57. **"Oh Bury Me Not on the Lone Prairie"** popular song about life in the West. [Am. Culture: Misc.]

58. **Oregon Trail** wagon-train route used by pioneers, extending from Missouri to the Oregon Territory. [Am. Hist.: *NCE*, 2016]

59. **Paladin** archetypal gunman who leaves a calling card. [TV: *Have Gun, Will Travel* in Terrace, I, 341]

60. **Pecos Bill** giant folk hero famed for cowboy exploits. [Am. Lit.: Hart, 643]

61. **Pony Express** relay mail service during frontier days. [Am. Hist.: *NCE*, 2190]

62. **prairie schooner** horse-drawn wagon used by pioneers; its white canvas top resembled a schooner sailing on the prairie. [Am. Hist.: *NCE*, 2209]

63. *Rawhide* series depicting cowboys as cattle-punchers along the Santa Fe trail. [TV: Terrace, II, 235]

64. **Remington, Frederic (1861–1909)** his drawings, paintings, and bronze sculptures are energetic depictions of cowboys and Native Americans of the Western frontier. [Am. Art: *SJEPC*]

65. **Ringo, Johnny (fl. late 19th century)** notorious outlaw who fought many gun battles in the Southwest. [Am. Hist.: Misc.]

66. **rodeo** competition involving roping, riding, and bronco busting. [Am. Entertainment: *SJEPC*]

67. **Rogers, Roy (1912–1998)** singing cowboy; films featured horse Trigger, sidekick Gabby Hayes, and wife Dale Evans; successful TV show for children followed. [Am. Film, TV: *SJEPC*]

68. **Rogers, Will (1879–1935)** naïve common man persona worked as counterpoint to his deceptively clever political satire. [Am. Entertainment: *SJEPC*]

69. **Santa Fe Trail** wagon-train route extending from Independence, Missouri to Santa Fe, New Mexico. [Am. Hist.: *NCE*, 2421]

70. *Shane* a classic, serious western film about a pioneer family protected by a mysterious stranger. [Am. Cinema: Halliwell, 651]

71. **Sioux** confederation of North American Indian tribes; last battle fought at Wounded Knee. [Am. Hist.: *NCE*, 2527]

72. **Sitting Bull (1831–1890)** Indian chief who united the Sioux tribes against the white men. [Am. Hist.: *EB*, IX: 243–244]

73. **Slade the Terrible** stagecoach agent and desperado known for shooting his enemies dead at the drop of a hat. [Am. Lit.: Mark Twain *Roughing It* in Magill I, 858]

74. **spaghetti westerns** low-budget European films (mostly Italian) produced between 1961 and 1977; graphically depicted Wild West and its brutality; gave Clint Eastwood his early tough-guy roles. [Film: *SJEPC*]

75. *Stagecoach* John Ford's classic 1939 film helped bring Westerns into popularity as feature films. [Am. Film: *SJEPC*]

76. **Texas Rangers** established in 1835, a mounted fighting force to maintain law and order in the West. [Am. Hist.: *NCE*, 2723]

77. **Tombstone** Arizona town known for its outlaws, prospectors, and gun battles (1800s). [Am. Hist.: *EB*, X: 36]

78. *Unforgiven, The* Clint Eastwood directed award-winning 1992 Western; wildly successful and critically acclaimed as a modern revitalization of the genre. [Am. Film: *SJEPC*]

79. **Wayne, John (1907–1979)** playing heroes and cowboys (sometimes at the same time) made him a Hollywood legend; millions of fans saw him as quintessentially American. [Am. Film: *SJEPC*]

80. **Wells Fargo** company that handled express service to western states; often robbed. [Am. Hist.: *NCE*, 2953]

81. *Wild Wild West* American television series from 1965–1969; two secret-service agents who travel west on a mission during the 1800s. [Am. TV: Misc.]

82. **Winchester 73** repeating rifle manufactured by Oliver Winchester and widely used by the settlers of the West. [Am. Hist.: *EB*, X: 699]

714. WHITENESS

1. **ermine** winter stoat; said to die if whiteness is soiled. [Art: Hall, 115]

2. **Moby Dick** white whale pursued relentlessly by Captain Ahab; "It was the whiteness of the whale that above all things appalled me." [Am. Lit.: *Moby Dick*]

3. **pale horse** ridden by Death. [N.T.: Revelation 6:8]

4. **Silver** flashing white steed of the Lone Ranger. [Radio: Buxton, 143–144]

5. **white belt of wampum** giving one was giving the deepest pledge of honor. [Am. Indian Trad. Misc.]

6. **white forked flame** holiest flame on the altar. [Persian Folklore: Misc.]

7. **White Steed of the Prairies** charger who led the wild horses before the West was tamed. [Am. Indian Legend: Misc]

8. **white stone** marked a joyful day. [Rom. Trad.: Misc.]

715. WHOLESOMENESS (See also EVERYMAN.)

1. **Armstrong, Jack** "the all-American boy." [Radio: Buxton, 121–122]

2. **Autry, Gene (1907–1998)** virtuous singing cowboy. [Am. Entertainment: *SJEPC*]

3. **Avalon, Frankie (1939–)** clean-cut teen idol of the 1950s and 1960s starred in beach party films with Annette Funicello. [Am. Entertainment: *SJEPC*]

4. **Bobbsey Twins** two sets of twins in book series live in "perfect" fictional world. [Children's Lit.: *SJEPC*]

5. **Boone, Pat (1934–)** singer/actor with family-oriented image and unabashed religious beliefs. [Am. Entertainment: *SJEPC*]

6. **Boy Scouts** youth organization's values include service to God and country. [Am. Hist.: *SJEPC*]

7. **Brady Bunch, The** widower and widow marry, producing an instant, wholesome family of eight. [TV: Terrace, I, 115]

8. **Capra, Frank (1897–1991)** American filmmaker, creator of such movies as *It's a Wonderful Life* that celebrate idealism and wholesomeness. [Am. Film: *ODA*]

9. **Carpenters, The** brother-and-sister pop music duo of the 1970s with wholesome image. [Am. Music: *SJEPC*]

10. **Day, Doris (1924–)** fresh-faced, effervescent film actress and singer exuded wholesome, all-American girl appeal in 1950s. [Am. Film and Music: *SJEPC*]

11. **Funicello, Annette (1942–)** sweet, wholesome actress became pioneering member of Disney's Mickey Mouse Club (1955–59) at age of 12; starred in beach movies with fellow teen idol Frankie Avalon in 1960s. [Am. TV and Film: *SJEPC*]

12. **Grandma Moses (1860–1961)** American painter who began her career in her 70s; her works, primitive in style, are wholesome evocations of rural life. [Am. Art: *FOF, MOD*]

13. **Landon, Michael (1936–1991)** actor/producer, and sometimes writer/director of TV show *Little House on the Prarie* (1974–1982); heartfelt look at life in pioneer times; in 1984 created *Highway to Heaven*, then worked as actor/producer/writer/director for the series. [Am. TV: *SJEPC*]

14. *Mickey Mouse Club, The* clean-cut young people romped through educational program produced by Walt Disney. [Am. TV: *SJEPC*]

15. **Miss America** annual beauty contest features wholesome contestants. [Am. Hist.: Allen, 56–57]

16. *Mr. Rogers' Neighborhood* calm, approachable Fred Rogers charmed children with his brand of laid-back educational programming. [Am. TV: *SJEPC*]

17. **New Kids on the Block** all-white teen singing group with innocent image and appeal to pre-adolescent females. [Am. Music: *SJEPC*]

18. **Opie** fresh-faced young son of Sheriff Andy Taylor played by Ron Howard. [Am. TV: *SJEPC*]

19. *Our Town* Thornton Wilder's 1938 play celebrating the wholesomeness of small town life. [Am. Theater: Thornton Wilder, *Our Town*]

20. **Ozzie and Harriet** series portraying the wholesome, American family. [TV: "The Adventures of Ozzie and Harriet" in Terrace, I, 34]

21. **Reed, Donna (1921–1986)** film actor probably best known for TV role as sweet-tempered housewife in sitcom about clean-cut family, *The Donna Reed Show* (1958–1966). [Am. TV: *SJEPC*]

22. **Rogers, Roy (1912–1998)** singing cowboy; films featured horse Trigger, sidekick Gabby Hayes, and wife Dale Evans; successful TV show for children followed. [Am. Film and TV: *SJEPC*]

23. **Taylor, Sheriff Andy** likeable, slow-talking sheriff of small North Carolina town of Mayberry. [Am. TV: *SJEPC*]

24. *Waltons, The* TV show about poor rural family in the 1930s; they extol chastity, honesty, family unity, and love. [TV: Terrace, II, 418–419]

25. **Welk, Lawrence (1903–1992)** bandleader whose phenomenal twenty-seven-year run as host of musical variety TV show attested to popularity of squeaky clean acts he featured. [Am. Music and TV: *SJEPC*]

716. WICKEDNESS (See also EVIL, VILLAIN.)

1. **Admah and Zeboyim** cities destroyed by God for citizens' sinfulness. [O.T.: Deuteronomy 19:23]

2. **Ahab** honored false gods, usurped others' land; byword for baseness. [O.T.: I Kings 17:29–34; 21:25]

3. **Archimago** enchanter epitomizing wickedness. [Br. Lit.: *Faerie Queene*]

4. **Ate** goddess fo wickedness, mischief, and infatuation. [Gk. Myth.: Parrinder, 32]

5. **Bluebeard** murders six wives; a personification of wickedness. [Fr. Lit.: Walsh *Classical*, 58]

6. **de Winter, Rebecca** taunts her husband with her promiscuity and plots to have him accused of her murder. [Br. Lit.: D. du Maurier *Rebecca* in Magill I, 806]

7. **Jezebel** urged husband, Ahab, to evildoing. [O.T.: I Kings 21:25]

8. **Manasseh** idolatrously and murderously leads Jerusalem astray. [O.T.: II Kings 21:2–4, 9]

9. **Sodom and Gomorrah** cities of iniquity destroyed by God's wrath. [O.T.: Genesis 19:24]

10. **Thornhill, Squire** abducts a young woman and has her kind father jailed for debt. [Br. Lit.: Goldsmith *The Vicar of Wakefield*]

11. **Wicked Witch of the West** from L. Frank Baum's Oz series; evil and sadistic, she tries to destroy Dorothy and her companions; ultimately killed by water, symbol of life and purity. [Br. Children's Lit.: Jones]

717. WIDOWHOOD

1. **Douglas, the Widow** adopted Huck Finn and took care of him. [Am. Lit.: Mark Twain *Huckleberry Finn*]

2. **Gummidge, Mrs.** "a lone lorn creetur," the Pegotty's housekeeper. [Br. Lit.: Dickens *David Copperfield*]

3. *Old Wives' Tale, The* novel of two sisters widowed young, one by death, the other by desertion. [Br. Lit.: Magill I, 684]

4. **Onassis, Jacqueline Lee Bouvier Kennedy (1929–1994)** remarkable poise after witnessing the assassination of her husband, President John F. Kennedy in 1963 made her a favorite with the American public and a symbol of dignified widowhood. [Am. Culture: *SJEPC*]

5. **Wadman, Widow** romantic neighbor who unsuccessfully lays siege to Uncle Toby's affections. [Br. Lit.: *Tristram Shandy*; Magill I, 1027]

6. **widow of Ephesus** weeping over her husband's corpse, she is cheered by a compassionate sentry and they become ardent lovers in the burial vault. [Rom. Lit.: *Satyricon*]

7. **Wife of Bath, the** kept her five successive husbands under her thumb by trickery. [Br. Lit.: Chaucer *Canterbury Tales*]

718. WIFE (See also DOMESTICITY.)

1. **Amoret** Sir Scudamore's wife; loving and ever-devoted. [Br. Lit.: *Faerie Queene*]

2. **Arundhati** example of the ideal Hindu wife. [Hindu Legend: Benét, 56]

3. **Billy Boy** question-and answer ballad pointing up merits of possible bride. [Br. and Am. Folklore: Leach, 139]

4. **Martha** personification of the busy housekeeper. [N.T.: Luke 10:39]

5. **Penelope** a model of wifely virtue. [Gk. Lit.: *Odyssey*]

719. WIND

1. **Aeolian harp** musical instrument activated by winds. [Gk. Myth.: Jobes, 40]

2. **Aeolus** steward of winds; gives bag of winds to Odysseus. [Gk. Myth.: Kravitz, 10; Gk. Lit.: *Odyssey*]

3. **Afer** southwest wind; also known as Africus. [Gk. Myth.: Kravitz, 11]

4. **Apeliotes** east or southeast wind; also known as Lips. [Gk. Myth.: Kravitz, 27]

5. **Aquilo** equivalent of Boreas, the Greek north wind. [Rom. Myth.: Kravitz, 30]

6. **Argestes** name of the east wind. [Gk. Myth.: Kravitz, 32]

7. **Aura** goddess of breezes. [Gk. Myth.: Kravitz, 42]

8. **Auster** the southwest wind. [Gk. Myth.: Kravitz, 42]

9. **Boreas** god of the north wind. [Gk. Myth.: Parrinder, 49]

10. **Caicas** the northeast wind. [Gk. Myth.: Kravitz, 50]

11. **Corus** god of the north or northwest wind. [Rom. Myth.: Jobes, 374]

12. **Eurus** the southeast wind; also known as Volturnus. [Gk. Myth.: Kravitz, 97, 238]

13. **Favonius** ancient Roman personification of west wind. [Rom. Myth.: Howe, 103]

14. **Gentle Annis** weather spirit; controls gales on Firth of Cromarty. [Scot. Folklore: Briggs, 185]

15. **gregale** cold, northeast wind over the central Mediterranean; also known as Euroclydon. [Meteorology: *EB*, IV: 724; N.T.: Acts 27:14]

16. **Keewaydin** the Northwest Wind, to whose regions Hiawatha ultimately departed. [Am. Lit.: Longfellow *The Song of Hiawatha* in Magill I, 905]

17. **Mudjekeewis** Indian chief; held dominion over all winds. [Am. Lit.: "Hiawatha" in Benét, 466]

18. **Njord** god of the north wind. [Norse Myth.: Wheeler, 260]

19. **Ruach** isle of winds. [Fr. Lit.: *Pantagruel*]

20. **Sleipnir** Odin's eight-legged horse; symbolizes the wind that blows from eight points. [Norse Myth.: Benét, 937]

21. **Zephyrus** the west wind. [Gk. Myth.: Kravitz, 38, 242]

720. WINE

1. **Anacreon (563–478 B.C.)** Greek lyric poet who praised the effects of wine. [Gk. Lit.: Brewer *Dictionary*, 31]

2. **Andros** center for worship of Bacchus, wine god. [Rom. Myth.: Hall, 16]

3. **Bacchus** god of wine. [Rom. Myth.: Hall, 37, 142]

4. **Beaujolais** a wine-growing region in France; often a medium-dry, fruity burgundy. [Fr. Hist.: *NCE*, 2990]

5. **Bordeaux** French city whose wines (especially Médoc, Graves, Sauternes, Saint Émilion) are world-known. [Fr. Hist.: *EB*, II: 162]

6. **Burgundy** region of France that produces fine wines. [Fr. Hist.: *NCE*, 2989]

7. **Catawba** grape grown in the eastern U.S, producing a medium-dry white wine. [Am. Hist.: Misc.]

8. **Chablis** village in central France known for the white wine which bears its name. [Fr. Hist.: *NCE*, 497]

9. **chalice** cup holding wine at Eucharist. [Christian Tradition: N.T.: Mark 14:23]

10. **Champagne** province in northeastern France renowned for its sparkling wine. [Fr. Hist.: *EB*, II: 724]

11. **Chianti** well-known Italian wine. [Ital. Hist.: *NCE*, 2990]

12. **Dionysus** god of the vine and its enlightening powers. [Gk. Myth.: Avery, 404–408; Parrinder, 80]

13. **Epicurus (341–271 B.C.)** Greek philosopher who believed that happiness was found in pleasure and indulgence. [Gk. Phil.: *ODA*]

14. **Finger Lakes** the region in New York state where many eastern wines are made. [Am. Geography: *NCE*, 2990]

15. **Liber and Libera** ancient Italian god and goddess of wine and vine cultivation. [Rom. Myth.: Howe, 154]

16. **Liebfraumilch** well-known Rhine wine. [Ger. Cuisine: *NCE*, 2990]

17. **Marsala** a sweet, amber wine made in Sicily. [Ital. Cuisine: *NCE*, 2990]

18. **Médoc** a red Bordeaux wine. [Fr. Cuisine: *NCE*, 2990]

19. **Napa Valley** greatest wine-producing region of the United States. [Am. Geography: *NCE*, 2990]

20. **Naxian Groves** vineyards celebrated for fine vintages. [Gk. Geography: Brewer *Handbook*, 747]

21. **Oeneus** Calydonian king; first to cultivate grapes. [Rom. Myth.: Hall, 142]

22. **pinot noir** one of the oldest varities of grapes cultivated for the pupose of making wine; grown by ancient Romans as early as first century A.D; chiefly grown in Burgundy region of France,

produces red wine considered by many to be finest available. [Fr. Cuisine: Misc.]

23. **port** fortified sweet wine made from grapes grown in the Douro valley in Portugal. [Port. Cuisine: *NCE*, 2194]

24. **Rhine valley** region of Germany that produces fine wines. [Ger. Geography: *NCE*, 2990]

25. **Riesling** grape grown in Germany and California, producing a dry or sweet white wine. [Ger. Cuisine: Misc.]

26. **Rioja** Spain's most widely exported wine. [Span. Cuisine: *NCE*, 2990]

27. **Rothschild** fine wines from the family of European financers and bankers. [Fr. Cuisine: Misc.]

28. **sherry** dry fortified wine, originally made from grapes grown in Andalusia, Spain. [Span. Cuisine: *NCE*, 2501]

29. *Sideways* 2004 film about two male friends who embark on week-long road trip through California wine country, learning some things about themselves, and each other, in the process. [Am. Film: Misc.]

30. **Tokay** region of Hungary that produces wines. [Hung. Geography: *NCE*, 2889]

31. **Valpolicella** a dark, rich red wine from Veneto. [Ital. Cuisine: *NCE*, 2990]

32. **Vouvray** village in central France known for its medium-dry white wine. [Fr. Geography: Misc.]

721. WINTER

1. **Boreas** the north wind; associated with winter. [Rom. Myth.: Hall, 130]

2. **crane** pictorial emblem in Buddhist tradition. [Animal Symbolism: Jobes, 378]

3. **Ded Moroz** personification of winter; "Grandfather Frost." [Russ. Folklore: Misc.]

4. **goat** zodiacally belongs to December; hence, winter. [Astrology: Hall, 139]

5. **Hiems** personification; portrayed as old and decrepit. [Rom. Myth.: *LLEI*, I: 322]

6. **Jack Frost** personification of winter. [Pop. Culture: Misc.]

7. **Old Man Winter** personification of winter. [Pop. Culture: Misc.]

8. **old man wrapped in cloak** personification of winter. [Art: Hall, 130]

9. **Persephone** the period of her stay (winter) with Hades. [Gk. Myth.: Espy, 28]

722. WISDOM (See also COUNSEL, GUIDANCE, INTELLIGENCE.)

1. **Amenhotep (fl. 14th century B.C.)** pictured as bearded man holding papyrus roll. [Ancient Egypt. Art: Parrinder, 18]

2. **ankh** symbolizes the key to knowledge. [Egyptian Symbolism: *IEOTS*, 45]

3. **Aragorn** character in Tolkien's Lord of Rings trilogy (1954–1956); heir to throne of Gondor; wise and brave natural leader with knightly purity and fair treatment for all; after fall of Sauron, he becomes King of Gondor. [Br. Lit.: Gillespie and Naden]

4. **Athena** goddess of wisdom; Minerva to the Romans. [Gk. and Roman Myth.: Brewer *Dictionary* 713]

5. **Augustine, Saint (354–430)** patron saint of scholars; voluminous theological author. [Christian Hagiog.: Brewster, 384–385]

6. **Babar** protagonist in series of books for children by Jean and Laurent de Brunhoff beginning in 1931; anthropomorhpic elephant who matures and displays sophistication, generosity, and wisdom, especially in his role as king of his jungle home. [Fr. Children's Lit.: Jones]

7. **Balder** most beautiful, luminescent, and wise god. [Norse Myth.: Parrinder, 40]

8. **blue salvia** traditional symbol of wisdom; indicates mature judgment. [Flower Symbolism: *Flora Symbolica*, 177]

9. **Bodhi** knowledge by which one attains Nirvana. [Buddhism: Parrinder, 48]

10. **Bragi** god of wisdom, poetry, and eloquence. [Norse Myth.: Parrinder, 50]

11. **Chiron** knowlegeable Centaur; instructed Achilles, Jason, and Asclepius. [Gk. Myth.: Parrinder, 62]

12. **Confucius (551–479 B.C.)** Chinese philosopher and writer. [Chinese Hist.: Parrinder, 65]

13. **Enki** god of wisdom; counterpart of Akkadian Ea. [Sumerian Myth.: Parrinder, 90]

14. **Fudo** Japanese god of wisdom. [Jpn. Myth.: Leach, 427]

15. **Ganesha** wisdom god having a human body and an elephant head. [Hindu Myth.: Leach, 440]

16. **gold** symbol of sagacity. [Color Symbolism: Jobes, 356]

17. **hazel** symbol of divinity, wisdom, fertility, and rain. [Symbolism: *CEOS&S*]

18. **Hiawatha** "wise man"; legendary founder of Iroquois Confederacy. [Am. Hist.: Jameson, 229; Am. Lit.: "Hiawatha" in Benét, 466]

19. **Jerome, Saint** Latin doctor of Church; preeminent biblical scholar. [Christian Hagiog.: Attwater, 185]

20. **Kenobi, Obi-Wan** wise Jedi knight who trains Luke Skywalker in the *Star Wars* movies. [Am. Film: Misc.]

21. **Magi** the three wise men who visit Jesus after his birth; the Kings Caspar, Melchior, and Balthazar. [N.T.: Matthew 2:1]

22. **Mimir** guardian of well of wit and wisdom. [Norse Myth.: Wheeler, 244]

23. **Nebo** god of sagacity; inventor of writing. [Babyl. Myth.: Brewer *Dictionary* 749]

24. **Nestor** sage counselor and just king of Pylos. [Gk. Hist.: Wheeler, 257; Gk. Lit.: *Iliad*]

25. **Odin** god; drank from fountain, became all-knowing. [Norse Myth.: Brewer *Dictionary* 774]

26. **owl** associated with Athena, goddess of wisdom. [Gk. Myth.: Hall, 231]

27. **ox** Taoists and Buddhists consider ox symbol of the sage. [Symbolism: *CEOS&S*]

28. **Pericles (c.500–429 B.C.)** Greek ruler known for his wisdom and integrity. [Gk. Hist.: *ODA*]

29. **Plato (427–347 B.C.)** Greek philosopher revered for wisdom. [Gk. Hist.: *NCE*, 2165]

30. *Poor Richard's Almanac* Benjamin Franklin's almanac, published from 1733 to 1787; full of data relevant to everyday life, as well as practical wisdom and humor. [Am. Hist. Misc.]

31. **rat** in Asian traditions, associated with gods of wisdom, success, and prosperity. [Symbolism: *CEOS&S*]

32. **Sarastro** High Priest represents benevolent guidance. [Ger. Opera: Mozart *The Magic Flute* in Benét, 619]

33. **scroll** early form of manuscript; symbolic of learning. [Christian Symbolism: Appleton, 85]

34. **Socrates (469–399 B.C.)** wise and respected teacher adept at developing latent ideas. [Gk. Hist.: *EB*, 16: 1001–1005]

35. **Solomon** invested by God with unprecedented sagacity. [O.T.: I Kings 3:7–13; 4:29–34]

36. **tree of knowledge of good and evil** eat of its fruit and know all. [O.T.: 2:9; 3:6]

37. **white mulberry** traditional symbol of wisdom. [Tree Symbolism: *Flora Symbolica*, 176]

38. **Yoda** from the Star Wars films, teacher of the Jedi knights; gives Luke Skywalker instruction on combat techniques and philosophy of the Jedi. [Am. Film: Misc.]

723. WITCHCRAFT (See also ENCHANTMENT, MAGIC.)

1. **Alcina** Circelike spellmaker; defeated by good magic. [Br. Opera: Handel, *Alcina*, Westerman, 54–55]

2. **Baba Yaga** cannibalistic crone; stone-breasted companion of devil. [Russ. Folklore: Leach, 100]

3. **bat** symbol of death, fear, witchcraft, and occult in Western folklore [Symbolism: *CEOS&S*]

4. ***Blair Witch Project, The*** 1999 American horror film shot with a very limited budget; three fictional filmmakers investigate the legend of Blair Witch. [Am. Film: Misc.]

5. **Brocken** Harz peak; rendezvous for the Sabbat on Walpurgis Night. [Ger. Folklore: Leach, 165]

6. **Broom Hilda** witch as cigar-smoking, love-starved crone. [Comics: Horn, 134]

7. ***Charmed*** American television series about three sisters who are powerful good witches. [Am. TV: Misc.]

8. **Circe** turns Odysseus's men into animals. [Gk. Myth.: *Odyssey*]

9. **Cutty Sark** witch who pulls off the tail of Tam O'shanter's mare before it has fully escaped from her power. [Scot. Poetry: Benét, 242]

10. **Elphaba** name given to the Wicked Witch of the West in the novel *Wicked*; name derived from shortened form of L. Frank Baum, writer of the Oz series. [Am. Lit.: Misc.]

11. **Esmerelda** gypsy trains a goat to dance to her tambourine, is convicted of sorcery. [Fr. Lit.: Victor Hugo *The Hunchback of Notre Dame*]

12. **Glinda** the "Good Witch" of Oz; from 1900 novel *The Wonderful Wizard of Oz*. [Am. Lit.: Misc.]

13. **Hecate** mysterious goddess of Hades; associated with sorcery. [Gk. Myth.: Howe, 115]

14. **Kundry** sorceress; ugly messenger of the Grail castle. [Ger. Legend: *Parzival*; Ger. Opera: *Parsifal*]

15. **Morgan le Fay** sorceress of Arthurian legend. [Medieval Romance: Brewer *Dictionary*, 620]

16. **Pamphile** applies ointment to change into eagle. [Rom. Lit.: *The Golden Ass*]

17. ***Rosemary's Baby*** through witchcraft, child born with horns and tail. [Am. Lit.: *Rosemary's Baby*]

18. ***Sabrina, the Teenage Witch*** American sitcom; teeenager discovers and learns to use her magic powers. [Am. TV: Misc.]

19. **Salem, Massachusetts** locale of frenzied assault on supposed witches (1692). [Am. Hist.: Jameson, 442; Am. Lit.: *The Crucible*]

20. **Samantha** good witch married to a mortal. [TV: "Bewitched" in Terrace, I, 94–95]

21. **Strega Nona** good witch from series of picture books by Tomie dePaola; lives in Calabria and helps others, especially Big Anthony who needs her to rescue him from calamities. [Am. Children's Lit.: Jones]

22. **toad** symbol of death and witchcraft in Western tradition. [Symbolism: *CEOS&S*]

23. **Walpurgis Night** traditional German witches' sabbath. [Ger. Folklore: *NCE*, 2918]

24. **Weird Sisters** demon-women; predict Macbeth's fate. [Br. Lit.: *Macbeth*]

25. **White Witch** in C.S. Lewis's Narnia chronicles, calls herself Queen of Narnia and imposes her will on others, acting maliciously and coldly toward all. [Br. Children's Lit.: Jones]

26. **Wicked Witch of the West** uses her powers to upset the plans of Dorothy and her friends. [Am. Lit. and Cinema: *The Wonderful Wizard of Oz*]

27. **Witch of Endor** conjures up Samuel for distressed Saul. [O.T.: I Samuel 28:3–25]

28. **Witches' Hammer** manual for recognizing telltale marks of witches (15th century). [Eur. Hist.: Brewer *Note-Book*, 952]

29. *Witches of Eastwick, The* 1984 novel by John Updike; three women acquire powers after being left by their husbands. [Am. Lit.: Misc.]

724. WITTINESS

1. **Arkansas Traveler** clever traveler who disguises his wit by acting like a country hick. [Am. Folklore *FOF, MOD*]

2. **Bennet, Elizabeth** lively and clever character. [Br. Lit.: *Pride and Prejudice*]

3. **Boyet** "wit's pedler" and "an ape of form." [Br. Lit.: *Love's Labour's Lost*]

4. **Buckley, William F., Jr. (1925–2008)** witty conservative writer and long-time editor of the *National Review*. [Am. PoliticsL *FOF, MOD*]

5. **Carson, Johnny (1925–2005)** witty, urban host of *The Tonight Show* from 1962–1992. [Am. TV: *FOF, MOD*]

6. **Mercutio** clever, comic foil to Romeo. [Br. Lit.: *Romeo and Juliet*]

7. **Parker, Dorothy (1893–1967)** sarcastic wit colored her writings and conversation, especially at the Algonquin Round Table. [Am. Lit.: *SJEPC*]

8. **Wilde, Oscar (1854–1900)** Irish writer of comic masterpieces and other works; known for his witticisms. [Irish Lit.: Misc.]

725. WIZARD (See also MAGIC.)

1. **Dumbledore, Albus** character from J.K. Rowling's Harry Potter series; headmaster of Hogwarts School of Witchcraft and Wizardry; protector and teacher of Harry; wise and just, he functions as a father-figure in many ways to the orphaned boy. [Br. Children's Lit.: Misc.]

2. **Gandalf** character from Tolkien's Lord of the Rings trilogy (1954–1956); helps in the plan to destroy the powerful ring and functions as a source of information about ancient lore; courageous warrior and strong support for Frodo. [Br. Lit.: Gillespie and Naden]

3. **Ged** protagonist of Ursula K. LeGuin's Earthsea trilogy for young readers; sorcerer's apprentice living on an island in archipelago of Earthsea; yearning for full knowledge and use of his impressive powers brings about unleashing of a frightening evil power. [Am. Children's Lit.: *OCCL*]

4. **Gryffindor, Godric** founder of the Hogwart's house that Harry Potter belongs to; known for courage and strength of heart. [Br. Lit.: Misc.]

5. **Hufflepuff, Helga** from Harry Potter series; witch who valued loyalty and honesty; Hogwart's house named after her. [Br. Lit.: Misc.]

6. **Magus, Simon** appears in the Acts of the Apostles; regarded by some as the first heretic; said to have been able to levitate and fly. [N.T.: Misc.]

7. **Mandrake the Magician** character from US comic strip from 1934; illusionist who fought villains in his spare time. [Am. Comics: Misc.]

8. **Merlin** various legends surround him; most famously known as wizard and advisor to King Arthur. [Arth. Legend: Misc.]

9. **Potter, Harry** hero of series of books (1997–2007)by J.K. Rowlings; scrawny, bespectled orphan learns he is a powerful wizard on his eleventh birthday and is sent to Hogwarts school to learn magic; fate tied to evil Lord Voldemort, who killed Harry's parents. [Br. Children's Lit.: Misc.]

10. **Prospero** uses magic to achieve ends. [Br. Lit.: *The Tempest*]

11. **Ravenclaw, Rowena** founder of house at Hogwarts in Harry Potter series; witch known for cleverness and creativity. [Br. Lit.: Misc.]

12. **Saruman** character from Tolkien's Lord of the Rings trilogy (1954–1956); white wizard who was once revered, but has turned wicked because of his love of power; under Sauron's control, he is evil until his death. [Br. Lit.: Gillespie and Naden]

13. **Sauron** anatagonist from fantasy novel *The Lord of the Rings* by J.R.R. Tolkien. [Br. Lit.: Misc.]

14. **Slytherin, Salazar** founder of Hogwart's house in Harry Potter series; described as power-hungry. [Br. Lit.: Misc.]

15. **Snape, Severus** professor in Harry Potter series; teaches Potions but covets the job of Defense against the Dark Arts. [Br. Lit.: Misc.]

16. **Voldemort, Lord** born Tom Riddle; fictional character from Harry Potter series; most powerful dark wizard in the world. [Br. Lit.: Misc.]

17. **Wizard of Oz, The** from L. Frank Baum's Oz series; balloonist who drifts into the Land of Oz, then takes advantage of the assumption that he is a wizard; eventually leaves Oz because he tires of the charade. [Am. Children's Lit.: Jones]

726. WONDER, ARCHITECTURAL

1. **Acropolis, The** temple located in Greece; situated on highest hill. [Gk. Arch.: Misc.]

2. **Chichen Itza** Mayan architectural site in modern-day Mexico; displays Mexican styles, showing cultural diffusion through the area. [Mayan Arch.: Misc.]

3. **Colosseum** elliptical amphitheatre in Rome, Italy; great display of Roman architecture; now in partial ruins. [Gk. Arch.: Misc.]

4. **Great Pyramid, the** Cheops's tomb, built 4600 years ago, nearly 500 feet high, with bases 755 feet long. [Egypt. Arch.: Brewer *Dictionary*, 735]

5. **Great Wall of China** runs for 1400 miles along China's north and northwest borders. [Chin. Hist.: *NCE*, 538]

6. **Hagia Sophia** supreme achievement of Byzantine architecture, noted for its great size and rising succession of domes. [Turkish Arch.: *NCE*, 1172]

7. **Hoover Dam** constructed from 1930 to 1936 to harness the power of the Colorado River, it is the highest concrete arch dam in the U.S.; a major tourist destination. [Am. Arch.: *EB*]

8. **Kiyomizu Temple** Buddhist temple in Kyoto, Japan; recognizable by its large veranda and hundreds of pillars. [Jpn. Arch.: Misc.]

9. **Kremlin, The** located in Moscow, Russia; residence of the President of Russia; includes four castles, four cathedrals, the Kremlin Wall, and the Kremlin Towers. [Russ. Arch.: Misc.]

10. **Leaning Tower of Pisa** belltower has stood for eight centuries despite tilt. [Ital. Arch.: Brewer *Dictionary*, 539]

11. **Machu Picchu** Incan architectural site in Peru; example of traditional polished dry-stone walls. [Incan Arch.: Misc.]

12. **Pagoda of Nanking, the** unique octagonal stone structure, demolished c. 1860. [Chinese Arch.: *EB*, 12: 822]

13. **Stonehenge** prehistoric group of huge standing stones arranged in a circle 300 feet in diameter. [Br. Hist.: *NCE*, 2682]

14. **Temple of Artemis** in Ephesus, Asia Minor; one of the seven wonders of the world. [Gk. Arch.: Benét, 918]

727. WONDERLAND (See also HEAVEN, PARADISE, UTOPIA.)

1. **Annwn** land of joy and beauty without disease or death. [Welsh Lit.: *Mabinogion*]

2. **Atlantis** fabulous and prosperous island; legendarily in Atlantic Ocean. [Gk. Myth.: Leach, 89]

3. **Avalon** island where dead King Arthur was carried. [Arth. Legend and Br. Lit.: *Le Morte d'Arthur; Idylls of the King; The Once and Future King*]

4. **Camelot** King Arthur's kingdom; one in which the ideals of chivalry, justice, integrity, and bravery were found. [Br. Legend: Misc.]

5. **Disneyland** amusement park created by Walt Disney (1955); symbol of land of wonder and fantasy. [Pop. Cult.: *ODA*]

6. **Istakhar, mountains of** lair of Eblis; beautiful treasure land. [Br. Lit.: *Vathek*]

7. **Middle-earth** scene of J.R.R. Tolkien's fantasies. [Br. Lit.: *The Hobbit; The Lord of the Rings*]

8. **Munchkinland** domain of little people in Oz. [Am. Lit.: *The Wonderful Wizard of Oz*]

9. **Narnia** scene of fantasies by C. S. Lewis. [Br. Lit.: *Prince Caspian*]

10. **Never Never Land** magic land of lost boys and Indians. [Br. Lit.: *Peter Pan*]

11. **Oz** fabulous kingdom over the rainbow. [Am. Lit.: *The Wonderful Wizard of Oz*]

12. **Xanadu** site of Kubla Khan's "pleasure dome." [Br. Lit.: "Kubla Khan" in Benét, 555]

728. WORKING CLASS

1. *Alice* widow with singing career aspirations finds pink-collar work as waitress at Mel's Diner (1976–85). [Am. TV: *SJEPC*]

2. *All in the Family* 1970s TV sitcom featuring working class family introduced social realism, discussing racism, sexism, religious bias, and politics. [Am. TV: *SJEPC*]

3. **Balboa, Rocky** blue-collar hero of 1976 film who wins bout against all odds because of determination and courage. [Am. Film: *SJEPC*]

4. **bowling** "everyman's" sport of knocking over pins with a heavy ball has a working class image. [Am. Sports: *SJEPC*]

5. **Budweiser** extremely popular, mass produced King of Beers positions itself as the alcoholic beverage of choice among average, hard-working Americans and sports fans. [Am. Business: *SJEPC*]

6. **Cash, Johnny (1932–2003)** country music legend with rural, working-class background never lost touch with everyday folks. [Am. Music: *SJEPC*]

7. **Chávez, César (1927–1993)** international champion of farm workers' rights and dignity remained close to his roots as son of migrant workers. [Am. Hist.: *SJEPC*]

8. *Good Times* popular sitcom about a working class African-American family anchored by strong, responsible parents who lived in an inner city Chicago tenement and struggled to make ends meet (1974–1979). [Am. TV: *SJEPC*]

9. **hard hat** from the helmet-like hat worn by construction workers, a symbol of the working class. [Am. Culture: Misc.]

10. **Joe six-pack** symbol of the working class: a working-class everyman who drinks his beer in a six-pack. [Am. Culture: Misc.]

11. **Kelly Girls** Kelly Services founded in 1946 to provide temporary office workers (mostly female) to businesses; name later became synonymous with flexible temps of both sexes. [Am. Business: *SJEPC*]

12. **labor unions** historically, a dynamic force for social change and the rights of workers in America; workers have found individual and collective identity through association with their union, esp. as unions split into highly-defined groups along racial and ethnic lines. [Am. Hist. and Business: *SJEPC*]

13. *Laverne and Shirley* hit TV sitcom which premiered in 1976; story of two single women who worked as bottle cappers at Shotz Brewery and constantly involved in madcap situations. [Am. TV: *SJEPC*]

14. **Mod** fashion that began as social dissent in the working class in Britain, but the look was imiatated by all classes in the US. [Pop. Culture: *SJEPC*]

15. *Roseanne* blue-collar family sitcom starring stand-up comedian Roseanne Barr; success resulted from smart writing, relevant subjects, and lack of easy resolutions. [Am. TV: *SJEPC*]

16. **Springsteen, Bruce (1949–)** hugely successful rock and roll singer/songwriter whose blue-collar background informs his music. [Am. Music: *SJEPC*]

17. **Terkel, Studs (1912–)** interviewer known for series of books that reflected lives of everyday people; considered his work oral histories of America. [Am. Lit.: *SJEPC*]

18. **trailer parks** neighborhoods comprised of mobile homes began as a way for young couples to use as temorary dwelling while saving for surburban home; evolved into permanent residences for some working-class families. [Am. Pop. Culture: *SJEPC*]

19. **Wal-Mart** American shopping was changed beginning in the 1960s by retail giant; proliferation of huge discount stores (especially in small towns) offering variety and value; popular with working class shoppers. [Am. Business: *SJEPC*]

729. WRITER for CHILDREN and YOUNG ADULTS

1. **Alcott, Louisa May (1832–1888)** author of classic novels for young readers; notably the rather autobiographical *Little Women* (1868), which relates the experiences of the four March sisters— their illnesses, loves, successes; inspired many family story novels that followed. [Am. Children's Lit.: *OCCL*]

2. **Andersen, Hans Christian (1805–1875)** author of over 150 fairy tales and other stories, some original, some based on folk themes; internationally acclaimed writer whose works have been translated and published worldwide; notable tales include *The Nightingale* and *The Ugly Duckling* [Dan. Children's Lit.: *OCCL*]

3. **Barrie, J. M. (1860–1937)** author of drama *Peter Pan* (1904) about motherless, somewhat magical boy who teaches Darling children to fly and takes them to Neverland for adventures galore. [Scot. Theater: *OCCL*]

4. **Baum, L. Frank (1856–1919)** author of Oz series, beginning with *The Wonderful Wizard of Oz* (1900) about a young girl's quest for the way home when she is swept into a strange land by a tornado. [Am. Children's Lit.: *OCCL*]

5. **Blume, Judy (1938–)** popular writer well known for her explicit teenage fiction; in *Are You There God? It's Me, Margaret* (1970), an 11–year-old girl awaits onset of puberty. [Am. Children's Lit.: *OCCL*]

6. **Bond, Michael (1926–)** creator of Paddington Bear series which originated in 1958; tells of bear from Darkest Peru, dressed in duffle-coat, hat, and wellington boots, found abandoned in Paddington Station and adopted by loving Brown family. [Br. Children's Lit.: *OCCL*]

7. **Boston, L. M. (1892–1990)** among other fantasy books, wrote several titles about Green Knowe, English manor house occupied by Mrs. Oldknow and her great-grandson Tolly, who meets young residents from past centuries and befriends them. [Br. Children's Lit.: *OCCL*]

8. **Burton, Virginia Lee (1909–1968)** author/illustrator of several picture books, most notably classic *The Little House* (1942); simple,

subtle, but deeply emotional representation of home. [Am. Children's Lit.: McElmeel]

9. **Carle, Eric (1929–)** robust, simple collage illustration with surprise elements (pages with holes, flaps, etc.) characterize author/illustrator's work; *The Very Hungry Caterpillar* (1969), a perennial favorite, is a fine example. [Am. Children's Lit.: McElmeel]

10. **Carroll, Lewis (1832–1898)** author of *Alice's Adventures in Wonderland* (1865) and *Through the Looking Glass* (1871) and other classics; surrealism and humor pervade his tale of a young girl's journey to a fantastical land. [Br. Children's Lit.: OCCL]

11. **Cleary, Beverly (1916–)** best known for her Henry Huggins and Ramona books, humorously capturing elementary-school minor crises and adventures. [Am. Children's Lit.: OCCL]

12. **Cole, Joanna (1944–)** author of the Magic School Bus series among other books; slightly eccentric Ms. Frizzle takes her students on highly instructional and entertaining field trips; a popular animated TV show follwed. [Am. Children's Lit. and TV: McElmeel]

13. **Collodi, Carlo (1826–1890)** author of *Pinocchio* (1883), story of a lying and disobedient puppet who wants to become a real boy; does so when he becomes a loving son to carpenter who made him. [Ital. Children's Lit.: OCCL]

14. **Cooper, Susan (1935–)** author of fantasy; her five-volume Dark Is Rising series depicts struggle of Dark and Light set in modern world; characterized by sophisticated, atmospheric descriptions of setting. [Br. Children's Lit.: OCCL]

15. **Dahl, Roald (1916–1990)** writer of often fantastical, darkly humorous stories beloved by young readers if not by their parents; among better known works, *Charlie and the Chocolate Factory* (1964) and *The B.F.G.* (1982). [Br. Children's Lit.: OCCL]

16. **de Brunhoff, Jean (1899–1937) and Laurent (1925–)** father and son who wrote a series of beloved books about Babar the elephant and his family and friends beginning in 1931; Babar runs away to the city when his mother is killed, where he is adopted by a rich old lady. [Fr. Children's Lit.: OCCL]

17. **Gág, Wanda (1893–1946)** illustrator of books she wrote or stories she retold; her *Millions of Cats* (1928) helped revolutionize children's books with its double-page spreads and text flowing along with illustrations. [Am. Children's Lit.: McElmeel]

18. **Geisel, Theodor Seuss (1904–1991)** innovative approach faced tough resistance, but when *And to Think I Saw It on Mulberry Street* was published in 1937, children fell in love with his wacky poetry and highly original illustrations; Horton, Cat in the Hat, Grinch and others followed. [Am. Children's Lit.: McElmeel]

19. **Grimm, Jacob Ludwig Carl (1785–1863) and Wilhelm Carl (1786–1859)** famous philologists and folklorists; their versions of over 200 fairy tales became known the world over; the list includes *Rapunzel, Hanzel and Gretel, Snow White and the Seven Dwarfs*. [Ger. Children's Lit.: OCCL]

20. **Hinton, S. E. (1950–)** author of teenage novels who began her career at age 17 with publication of *The Outsiders* in 1967; set in the Tulsa area, her books deal with juvenile deliquency, rebellion, high school gangs and cliques, and other topics at the heart of adolescence. [Am. Children's Lit.: OCCL]

21. **Irving, Washington (1783–1859)** author of two books considered classics and beloved by young readers: *The Legend of Sleepy Hollow* (1820), story of schoolmaster Ichabod Crane, frightened by a headless horseman; also *Rip Van Winkle* (1819). [Am. Lit.: OCCL]

22. **Jacques, Brian (1939–)** author of Redwall fantasy series about anthropomorphic mice of medieval abbey and other animal inhabitants of the surrounding area, with stories of adventure and intrigue. [Br. Children's Lit.: Gillespie and Naden]

23. **Keats, Ezra Jack (1916–1983)** author/illustrator who created charming paint and collage illustrations in stories about typical childhood experiences; his use of black protagonist for *The Snowy Day* (1962) was rare for its time. [Am. Children's Lit.: McElmeel]

24. **Keene, Carolyn** pseudonym used by group of writers who worked for the Edward Stratemeyer Syndicate writing Nancy Drew mysteries for young readers beginning in 1930. [Am. Children's Lit.: Gillespie and Naden]

25. **Kipling, Rudyard (1865–1936)** poet and novelist who wrote many imaginative and adventure-filled books for young readers; among them *The Jungle Book* (1894) and *Captains Courageous* (1897). [Br. Children's Lit.: OCCL]

26. **Le Guin, Ursula K. (1929–)** renowned writer of science fiction and fantasy whose knowledge of anthropology influences her ability to create utterly believable alternate worlds; noteworthy titles include *The Left Hand of Darkness* (1969) and Earthsea series. [Am. Children's Lit.: SJEPC]

27. **Lear, Edward (1812–1888)** poet whose nonsense verse for the young was often imitated, but rarely matched; his *The Owl and the Pussycat* (1867) is an example of his endearing work. [Br. Children's Lit.: OCCL]

28. **L'Engle, Madeline (1918–2007)** probably best known for her fantasy books beginning with *A Wrinkle in Time* (1962), a story of family love and loyalty coupled with an appealing time travel adventure. [Am. Children's Lit.: OCCL]

29. **Lewis, C. S. (1898–1963)** author of Narnia chronicles, fantasy series about young siblings who journey through a wardrobe into a world where fate of kingly lion Aslan parallels Christ's death and resurrection; often considered greatest 20th-century achievement in children's fantasy. [Br. Children's Lit.: *OCCL*]

30. **Lindgren, Astrid (1907–2002)** author of Pippi Longstocking stories about eccentric and rambunctious redheaded girl; wrote over 50 books for young readers, many translated into a number of languages. [Swed. Children's Lit.: *OCCL*]

31. **Lobel, Arnold (1933–1987)** author/illustrator of the popular Frog and Toad easy readers in which the anthropomorphic characters share a warm and loving friendship. [Am. Children's Lit.: McElmeel]

32. **Lofting, Hugh (1886–1947)** author/illustrator of Dr. Doolittle books begun in 1920; created unusual children's book hero, an unconventional pacifist; when his menagerie causes his human patients to desert him, he becomes champion of animals, learning to talk to them. [Am. Chldren's Lit.: *OCCL*]

33. **Macaulay, David (1946–)** architect who began writing and illustrating for young readers in 1973 with *Cathedral*, an architectural history on construction of a Gothic church; other similar books followed as well as imaginative fiction and nonfiction. [Am. Children's Lit.: McElmeel]

34. **Mayne, William (1928–)** author of unconventional novels written during the 1950s and 1960s; many are tales of treasure hunts for something of great value; beautifully depicted settings and notable descriptions of the world as seen through eyes of young. [Br. Children's Lit.: *OCCL*]

35. **Milne, A. A. (1882–1956)** acclaimed children's author, even though he wrote only four books for the young; his tales of Christopher Robin and his stuffed animal friends brought to life as real animals gave birth to several of the most beloved characters in children's literature. [Br. Children's Lit.; *OCCL*]

36. **Nesbit, E. (185801924)** author of several works for children, including series about Oswald Bastable and his family, humorous chronicles of how the children try to raise money to help their struggling father and, through a magic amulet, begin time traveling. [Br. Children's Lit.: *OCCL*]

37. **Perrault, Charles (1628–1703) and Pierre (1678–1700)** talented French father and son author team who did commendable retellings of many fairy stories, including Cinderella, Puss in Boots, Little Riding Hood; it is uncertain whether father or son was primary writer. [Fr. Chlidren's Lit.: *OCCL*]

38. **Potter, Beatrix (1866–1943)** beloved author/illustrator of 23 simple tales with animals and landscapes from Scotland and England; Peter Rabbit, Squirrel Nutkin, Benjamin Bunny, Jemima Puddle-Duck and others have become favorites with children worldwide for over a century. [Br. Children's Lit.: McElmeel]

39. **Pullman, Philip (1946–)** best known as author of fantasy trilogy beginning with *The Golden Compass* (1995); his works involve young protagnists facing tough moral choices in a world of talking animals, mystery, and magic. [Br. Children's Lit.: Gillespie and Naden]

40. **Pyle, Howard (1853–1911)** author/illustrator whose career was established in 1883 with publication of *The Merry Adventures of Robin Hood*; in his Arthurian legends (1903), his book of pirates (1921), and others, he created masterful illustrations. [Am. Children's Lit.: OCCL]

41. **Ransome, Arthur (1884–1967)** author of Swallows and Amazons series of books, which established an accepted notion that children take pleasure in stories about the vacation adventures of other children, when told in engaging, non-condescending manner. [Br. Children's Lit.: OCCL]

42. **Rey, H. A. (1989–1977) and Margaret (1906–1996)** team with Margaret usually creating texts, H.A. illustrations; renowned for their Curious George series in which a rambunctious little monkey constantly gets himself into trouble from which he is always rescued by sensible, forgiving Man in the Yellow Hat. [Am. Children's Lit.: McElmeel]

43. **Rowling, J. K. (1965–)** author of immensely successful Harry Potter fantasy series about an insecure boy who grows into a wizard of magnificent powers and exceptional integrity; Rowling's ingeniously creates an alternate world where common things take on a magical twist. [Br. Children's Lit.; Misc.]

44. **Scarry, Richard (1919–1994)** his picture books have little plot, but rather vignettes of objects, or humans and/or anthropomorphic animals engaged in activities; each image is labeled and accompanied by simple text, encouraging young readers to learn word identification. [Am. Children's Lit.: OCCL]

45. **Sendak, Maurice (1928–)** venerated illustrator whose pastel, almost old-fashioned pictures have illuminated many books; author/illustrator of inimitable picture books including *Where the Wild Things Are* (1963) and *In the Night Kitchen* (1970). [Am. Children's Lit.: McElmeel]

46. **Snicket, Lemony** [Daniel Handler (1970–)] in 13–book *Series of Unfortunate Events*, Snicket narrates the absurd adventures of

three rich orphans, with satirical asides and frequently outrageous details about his own life. [Am. Children's Lit.: Misc.]

47. **Stevenson, Robert Louis (1850–1894)** never intended to be an author of adventure tales, but his *Kidnapped* and *Treasure Island* assured that he would be credited with raising the genre to a high level; his works for young readers were never condescending as many were at that time. [Scot. Children's Lit.: *OCCL*]

48. **Stratemeyer, Edward (1862–1930)** his syndicate hired ghost writers who used his outlines to create titles for popular children's series: Bobbsey Twins, Tom Swift, Hardy Boys, Nancy Drew; educators and critics disapproved of mass-produced fiction, but this did little to quell sales. [Am. Chidlren's Lit.: *SJEPC*]

49. **Tolkien, J. R. R. (1892–1973)** famous author of *The Hobbit* (1937) and the Lord of the Rings trilogy (1954–1956), beloved by young readers; unassuming hobbits become keepers of a magical, poweful ring; leads to daunting quest to destroy ring before it can be used for evil. [Br. Lit.: *OCCL*]

50. **Travers, P. L. (1906–1996)** best known for her series of books about nanny Mary Poppins, who combines magic and common sense to entertain and teach her charges. [Br. Children's Lit.: *OCCL*]

51. **Van Allsburg, Chris (1949–)** highly-touted author/illustrator whose sometimes eerie, otherworldly, and detailed pictures complement surrealistic texts, often quests or mysteries; examples of his beautiful, haunting work include *Jumanji* (1981) and *The Polar Express* (1985). [Am. Children's Lit: McElmeel]

52. **White, E. B. (1899–1985)** writer of classic children's books *Charlotte's Web* (1952), a story of friendship and self-sacrifice set in a barnyard and *Stuart Little* (1945) about a mouse-like child whose family doesn't quite know what to do with him. [Am. Children's Lit.: *OCCL*]

53. **White, T. H. (1906–1964)** author of highly imaginative retelling of Malory's King Arthur stories; although not intended for young audience, his *Once and Future King* (1958) became a favorite with children and adolescents. [Br. Children's Lit.: *OCCL*]

54. **Wilder, Laura Ingalls (1867–1957)** her Little House books relate a third-person account of her close-knit family, and the happy times and hardships they experienced as pioneers in the midwestern U.S. [Am. Children's Lit.: *OCCL*]

730. WRITINGS, SACRED

1. **Adi Granth** bible of the Sikhs; also called Guru Granth Sahib. [Indian Religion: *Collier's*, XVII, 304]

2. **Avesta** book of teachings of Zoroaster. [Zoroastrianism: Leach, 97]

3. **Bhagavad Gita** part of *Mahabharata*: most important Hindu scripture. [Hindu Rel.: Parrinder, 43]

4. **Bible, The** sacred writings for Jews and Christians; Old Testament documents faith before Christ's birth and corresponds to the Hebrew Bible; New Testament relates Christ's life and teachings and the writings of his apostles. [Judaism and Christiantiy: Bowker]

5. **Book of Mormon** supplementary bible of the Latter-Day Saints. [Am. Hist.: Payton, 455]

6. **Book of the Dead** instructions for the Art of Dying. [Ancient Egypt. Rel.: Parrinder, 49]

7. **Dead Sea Scrolls** papyrus scrolls containing texts of Old Testament, found in 1947. [Mid-East Hist.: NCE, 729]

8. **Eddas** bible of ancient Scandinavian religion; two separate collections. [Norse Lit.: Jobes, 490; Parrinder, 87]

9. **hadith** account, report, or speech concerning the words or deeds of the prophet Muhammad, often translated as tradition; second only to Quran in importance and authority. [Islam: *UIMT*, 428]

10. **Holy Bible** name for book containing the Christian Scriptures. [Christianity: *NCE*, 291]

11. *Mahabharata* long Sanskrit epic poem on theology and morals. [Indian Lit.: *Mahabharata*]

12. **Popul Vuh** "Book of the People"; sacred book of certain Mayan tribes. [Mayan Religion: *NCE*, 2191]

13. **Quran** the sacred book of Islam; also called Koran. [Islam: *NCE*, 1496]

14. **Talmud** Jewish civil and religious law, including the Mishna. [Judaism: Payton, 661]

15. **Torah** the Penteteuch, especially in the form of the handwritten scroll always present in the synagogue. [Jew. Hist.: Benét, 1017]

16. **Tripitaka** the ethical and doctrinal teachings of Buddha. [Buddhism: Haydn & Fuller, 759]

17. **Vedas, the** oldest scriptures of Hinduism. [Hinduism: *NCE*, 2870]

Y

731. YOUTHFULNESS (See also REJUVENATION.)

1. **Agni** Vedic light god; embodies eternal youth. [Vedic Myth.: *LLEI*, I: 322]

2. **Fountain of Youth** fabulous fountain believed to restore youth to the aged. [Western Folklore: Brewer *Handbook*, 389]

3. **Freya** goddess of eternal youth. [Ger. Myth. and Opera: Wagner *Rheingold*, Westerman, 232]

4. **grail** in European tradition, sacred object whose wondrous powers confer elixir of life and eternal youth. [Symbolism: *CEOS&S*]

5. **Hebe** goddess of the young; also called Juventas. [Gk. and Roman Myth.: Hall, 146]

6. *Peter Pan, or the Boy Who Wouldn't Grow Up* play by J.M. Barrie first performed in 1904; story of ever-youthful boy who lives in Neverland with his fairy Tinker Bell, preyed upon by evil Captain Hook; Peter is victorious in the end and lives on to charm young children for generations. [Scot. Theater: *OCCL*]

7. **primrose** symbol of early youth. [Flower Symbolism: *Flora Symbolica*, 327]

Z

732. ZANINESS (See also COMEDY; COMEDY, SLAPSTICK.)

1. **Allen, Gracie (1902–1964)** actress who played scatterbrained wife of George Burns. [TV: "The George Burns and Gracie Allen Show" in Terrace, I, 303–304]

2. **Ball, Lucille (1910–1989)** American comedienne; "unchallenged queen of scatterbrains." [TV: "I Love Lucy" in Terrace, I, 383]

3. **Caesar, Sid (1922–)** pillar of zany 1950s comedy. [TV: "Your Show of Shows" in Terrace, II, 290–291]

4. *Harvard Lampoon* mocking, satirical periodical. [Am. Pop. Culture: Misc.]

5. *Hellzapoppin* Olsen and Johnson's "screamlined revue" described by one drama critic as "demented vaudeville brawl." [Am. Theater: Misc.]

6. *I Love Lucy* famous TV comedy debuted in 1950 and continues to be popular in reruns; wacky redhead whose desire to break into show business was frequent motivation for her zany antics. [Am. TV: *SJEPC*]

7. **Keystone Kops, the** first appeared in silent films in 1912; inept policemen with handlebar mustaches falling over each other and everything else at frenetic pace; visual humor still bears resemblance to their antics. [Am. Film: Halliwell, 399; *SJEPC*]

8. **Krazy Kat** tremendously zany, popular comic character that delighted Jazz Age intellectuals. [Comics: Payton, 372; "Krazy Kat" in Horn, 436]

9. *MAD* **magazine** popular publication featuring zany approach to life. [Am. Pop. Culture: Misc.]

10. **Martin, Steve (1945–)** comedian whose white-suited decorous appearance belied wackky stand-up banter. [Am. Entertainment: *SJEPC*]

11. **Marx Brothers, The** group of brothers with wacky slapstick humor that transferred very successfully from vaudeville stage to film and TV. [Am. Entertainment: *SJEPC*]

12. *Monty Python's Flying Circus* poking fun at institutions in skits like "The Ministry of Silly Walks," the British TV show of 1969–1974 led the way for many American late-night sketch comedy. [Br. TV: *SJEPC*]

13. **Pee-Wee Herman** androgynous smart-aleck alter ego of comedian Paul Reubens. [Am. TV: *SJEPC*]

14. *Pee-Wee's Playhouse* wacky TV show for children (and adults) with androgynous smart-aleck host and human and puppet co-horts. [Am. TV: *SJEPC*]

15. **Sales, Soupy (1926–)** signature prank was throwing pies; popular TV show for children in mid-1960s. [Am. TV: "The Soupy Sales Show" in Terrace, II, 305; *SJEPC*]

16. *Seinfeld* popular and applauded sitcom; in many ways "a TV show about nothing," it portrayed the life of stand-up comic Jerry Seinfeld and his group of oddball friends living in Manhattan; aired 1990–1998. [Am. TV: *SJEPC*]

17. **Skelton, Red (1910–1997)** comedian with zaniness personified in characters such as Freddie the Freeloader and Clem Kadiddlehopper. [TV: "The Red Skelton Show" in Terrace, II, 238]

18. **Three Stooges, The** comedians whose short films made from 1934–1958 featured slapstick humor with much physical violence; brought to TV to immense popularity. [Am. Film and TV: Terrace, II, 366;; *SJEPC*]

19. **Williams, Robin (1952–)** early career as Mork from Ork on TV show *Mork and Mindy* showed his ability to be frenetic, yet ingenious, characteristics later found in his stand-up routines and comic film roles, as in his portrayal of the genie in Disney's *Alladin*. [Am. Film and Entertainment: *SJEPC*]

733. ZEAL

1. **Bows, Mr.** crippled fiddler with intense feelings. [Br. Lit.: *Pendennis*]

2. **Cedric of Rotherwood** zealous about restoring Saxon independence. [Br. Lit.: *Ivanhoe*]

3. **Faustus, Doctor** zealous for universal knowledge; sells soul to Lucifer. [Medieval Legend and Ger. Lit.: *Faust*; Br. Lit.: *Doctor Faustus*]

4. **flaming heart** attribute of St. Augustine; symbol of religious fervor. [Art: Hall, 123]

5. **Merridew, Jack** boy with lust for authority and killing.` [Br. Lit.: *Lord of the Flies*]

6. **Olsen, Jimmy** eager-beaver cub reporter and Superman's friend. [Comics: "Superman" in Horn, 341]

7. **Palace Guard** term used in alluding to Richard Nixon's zealous, ardent staff, with reference to Watergate and cover-up. [Am. Pop. Culture: Misc.]

8. **white dittany** traditional symbol of zeal. [Flower Symbolism: *Flora Symbolica*, 173]

734. ZODIAC (See also ASTROLOGY.)

1. **Aquarius** water-bearer (Jan. 20–Feb. 18). [Astrology: Hall, 314]
2. **Aries** ram (Mar. 21–Apr. 19). [Astrology: Hall, 314]
3. **Cancer** crab (June 21–July 22). [Astrology: Hall, 314]
4. **Capricorn** goat (Dec. 22–Jan. 19). [Astrology: Hall, 314]
5. **Gemini** twins (May 21–June 20). [Astrology: Hall, 314]
6. **Leo** lion (July 23–Aug. 22). [Astrology: Hall, 315]
7. **Libra** balance (Sept. 23–Oct. 22). [Astrology: Hall, 315]
8. **Pisces** fishes (Feb. 19–Mar. 20). [Astrology: Hall, 314]
9. **Sagittarius** archer (Nov. 22–Dec. 21). [Astrology: Hall, 315]
10. **Scorpio** scorpion (Oct. 23–Nov. 21). [Astrology: Hall, 315]
11. **Taurus** bull (Apr. 20–May 20). [Astrology: Hall, 314]
12. **Virgo** virgin (Aug. 23–Sept. 22). [Astrology: Hall, 315]

Bibliography

Bibliography

The Abbot
Scott, Sir Walter. *The Abbot.* Dutton, 1969.

Absalom and Achitophel
Dryden, John. *Absalom and Achitophel,* ed. James and Helen Kinsley. Oxford University Press, 1961.

The Absentee
Edgeworth, Maria. *The Absentee* in *Castle Rackrent.* Dutton, 1960.

Ackerman
Ackerman, A.S.E. *Popular Fallacies.* Gale, 1970.

Adam Bede
Eliot, George. *Adam Bede.* Washington Square Press, 1971.

The Admirable Crichton
Barrie, James M. *The Admirable Crichton in English Drama in Transition, 1880-1920,* ed. Henry F. Salerno. Pegasus, 1968.

Adonais
Shelley, Percy B. *Adonais, an Elegy on the Death of John Keats,* ed. Thomas J. Wise. AMS Press, 1886.

The Adventures of Augie March
Bellow, Saul. *The Adventures of Augie March.* Fawcett World, 1973.

The Adventures of Pinocchio
Collodi, Carlo. *The Adventures of Pinocchio.* Macmillan, 1972.

Adventures of the Little Wooden Horse
Williams, Ursula. *The Adventures of the Little Wooden Horse.* Penguin, 1975.

Aeneid
Vergil. *Aeneid,* 2nd ed., tr. and ed. Frank Copley. Bobbs-Merrill, 1975.

Aesop's Fables
Aesop. *Aesop's Fables,* tr. Samuel Croxall and Roger L'Estrange. Brownlow, 1969.

Against the Grain
Huysmans, Joris Karl. *Against the Grain.* Dover, 1969.

The Age of Innocence
Wharton, Edith. *The Age of Innocence.* Scribner, 1968.

Ah Sin
Harte, Bret and Mark Twain. *Ah Sin* in *The Complete Works of Bret Harte.* Chatto and Windus, 1880-1912.

Alastor
Shelley, Percy B. *Alastor: Or the Spirit of Solitude, and Other Poems,* ed. Bertram Dobell. AMS Press, n.d.

Alcestis
Euripedes. *Alcestis,* tr. William Arrowsmith. Oxford University Press, 1915.

The Alchemist
Jonson, Ben. *The Alchemist.* Hill and Wang, 1966.

Alice's Adventures in Wonderland
Carroll, Lewis. *Alice's Adventures in Wonderland.* Viking Press, 1975.

Alive
Read, Piers P. *Alive.* Avon, 1975.

All for Love
Dryden, John. *All for Love,* ed. John J. Enck. Crofts, 1966.

All Quiet on the Western Front
Remarque, Erich Maria. *All Quiet on the Western Front.* Fawcett World, 1969.

All the King's Men
Warren, Robert Penn. *All the King's Men*. Random House, 1960.

L' Allegro
Milton, John. "L'Allegro" in *L'Allegro and Il Penseroso*. Southwest Book Services, 1976.

Allen
Allen, Frederick Lewis. *Only Yesterday*. Bantam, 1959.

All's Well That Ends Well
Shakespeare, William. *All's Well That Ends Well*, ed. G. K. Hunter. Barnes & Noble, 1966.

Almayer's Folly
Conrad, Joseph. *Almayer's Folly*. Bentley, 1971.

Amadis de Gaul
Amadis de Gaul, tr. Edwin Place and Herbert Behm. University Press of Kentucky, 1974.

Ambrosio
Lewis, Matthew G. *Ambrosio, or The Monk*. Avon, 1975.

Amelia
Fielding, Henry. *Amelia*. Dutton, 1978.

The American
James, Henry. *The American*, ed. Joseph Beach and Quentin Anderson. Holt, Rhinehart, and Winston, 1949.

The American Dream
Albee, Edward. *The American Dream*. Coward, 1961.

The American Scene
James, Henry. *The American Scene*. Indiana University Press, 1968.

Amory
International Celebrity Register, ed. Cleveland Amory. Celebrity Register Ltd., 1959.

Amphitryon
Dryden, John. *Amphitryon* in *The Dramatic Works*, ed. M. Summers, 6 vols. Gordian, 1968.

Amphitryon
Molière, Jean B. *Amphitryon*, tr. Oscar Mandel. Spectrum, 1977.

Amphitryon
Plautus. *Amphitryon: Three Plays in New Verse Translation*. University of North Carolina Press, 1974.

Amphitryon 38
Giraudoux, Jean. *Amphitryon 38* in *Giraudoux: Three Plays*, tr. La Farge and Judd. Hill and Wang, 1964.

Anatole
Titus, Eve. *Anatole*. McGraw-Hill, 1956.

Anatomy of Melancholy
Burton, Robert. *Anatomy of Melancholy*. R. West, 1923.

Andersen's Fairy Tales
Andersen, Hans Christian. *Andersen's Fairy Tales*. Macmillan, 1963.

Androcles and the Lion
Shaw, George Bernard. *Androcles and the Lion*. Penguin, 1951.

Andromache
Euripedes. *Andromache*, ed. P.T. Stevens. Oxford University Press, 1971.

Andromaque
Racine, Jean B. *Andromaque*, ed. Philip Koch. Prentice-Hall, 1969.

Animal Farm
Orwell, George. *Animal Farm*. Harcourt, 1954.

Anna Karenina
Tolstoy, Leo. *Anna Karenina*. Bantam, 1977.

Annals
Tacitus. *Annals*, ed. F.R. Goodyear. Cambridge University Press, 1972.

Annals of the Parish
Galt, John. *Annals of the Parish: Or the Chronicles of Dalmailing During the Ministry of Reverend Micah Balwhidder Written by Himself,* ed. James Kinsley. Oxford University Press, 1967.

Anne Frank
Frank, Anne. *Anne Frank: Diary of a Young Girl.* Doubleday, 1967.

Anne of Green Gables
Montgomery, L.M. *Anne of Green Gables.* Bantam, 1976.

Ant and Bee
Banner, Angela. *Ant and Bee.* Franklin Watts, 1958.

Anthony Adverse
Allen, Hervey. *Anthony Adverse.* Holt, 1958.

Antigone
Anouilh, Jean. *Antigone.* Larousse, 1966.

Antigone
Sophocles. *Antigone,* tr. Richard Braun. Oxford University Press, 1973.

The Antiquary
Scott, Sir Walter. *The Antiquary.* Dutton, 1955.

Antony and Cleopatra
Shakespeare, William. *Antony and Cleopatra,* ed. C.J. Gianakaris. William C. Brown, 1969.

Apocrypha
Apocrypha. New English Bible. Oxford University Press, 1970.

Appleton
Appleton, Leroy, and Stephen Bridges. *Symbolism in Liturgical Art.* Scribner, 1959.

Appointment in Samarra
O'Hara, John. *Appointment in Samarra.* Popular Library, 1976.

Arabel's Raven
Aiken, Joan. *Arabel's Raven.* Dell, 1975.

Arabian Nights
Book of a Thousand Nights and One Night, tr. Powys Mathers. St. Martin's Press, 1972.

Arcadia
Greene, Robert. *Arcadia* in *The Life and Complete Works in Prose and Verse of Robert Greene.* Printed for private circulation, 1881-86.

La Arcadia
Lope de Vega, Felix. *La Arcadia,* ed. E.S. Morby. Castalia, c. 1975.

Arcadia
Sannazaro, Jacopo. *Arcadia and Piscatorial Eclogues,* tr. Ralph Nash. Wayne State University Press, 1966.

Arcadia
Sidney, Philip. *Arcadia.* Penguin, 1977.

archy and mehitabel
Marquis, Don. *archy and mehitabel.* Doubleday, 1970.

The Ark
Benary-Isbert, Margot. *The Ark.* Harcourt, 1953.

Arms and the Man
Shaw, George Bernard. *Arms and the Man.* Bantam, 1968.

Around the World in Eighty Days
Verne, Jules. *Around the World in Eighty Days.* Oxford University Press, 1959.

Arrowsmith
Lewis, Sinclair. *Arrowsmith.* Harcourt, 1949.

Ars Poetica
Horace. *Ars Poetica* in *Collected Works of Horace,* tr. Dunsany and Oakley. Dutton, 1961.

Arthur Mervyn
Brown, Charles Brockton. *Arthur Mervyn,* ed. W. Bertho ff. Holt, 1966.

As I Lay Dying
Faulkner, William. *As I Lay Dying.* Random House, 1964.

As You Like It
Shakespeare, William. *As You Like It,* ed. Agnes Latham. Barnes & Noble, 1975.

Ash Wednesday
Eliot, T.S. *Ash Wednesday* in *The Complete Poetry and Plays, 1909-1950.* Harcourt, 1952.

L' Assommoir
Zola, Emile. *L'Assommoir.* Penguin, 1970.

Atala
de Chateaubriand, René. *Atala.* Prentice-Hall, 1965.

Atalanta
Swinburne, A.C. *Atalanta in Calydon.* Scholarly Press, reprint of 1923 ed.

The Atheist's Tragedy
Tourneur, Cyril. *The Atheist's Tragedy,* ed. Brian Morris and Roma Gill. Norton, 1976.

Atlas Shrugged
Rand, Ayn. *Atlas Shrugged.* New American Library, 1970.

Attwater
Attwater, Donald. *Penguin Dictionary of Saints.* Penguin, 1965.

Aucassin and Nicolette
Aucassin and Nicolette & Other Medieval Romances & Legends, ed. Eugene Mason. Dutton, 1958.

Auden
Replogle, Justin. *Auden's Poetry.* University of Washington Press, 1971.

Ausubel
Ausubel, Nathan. *The Book of Jewish Knowledge.* Crown, 1964.

Avery
Avery, Catherine B. *The New Century Handbook of Greek Mythology and Legend.* Appleton-Century-Crofts, 1972.

The Awkward Age
James, Henry. *The Awkward Age.* Penguin, 1974.

Babbitt
Lewis, Sinclair. *Babbitt.* Harcourt, 1949.

Bailey
Bailey, Nathaniel. *Universal Etymological English Dictionary.* Alfred Adler Institute, 1969.

Balchin
Balchin, Nigel. "Guy Fawkes" in *British History Illustrated.* October 1975, pp. 2-13.

Ballet Shoes
Streatfeild, Noel. *Ballet Shoes.* Random House, 1950.

Balthazar B
Donleavy, J.P. *The Beastly Beatitudes of Balthazar B..* Dell, 1968.

Bambi
Salten, Felix. *Bambi.* Grosset and Dunlap, 1969.

The Barber of Seville
Beaumarchais, Pierre A. *The Barber of Seville,* tr. B.P. Ellis. AHM, 1966.

Baring-Gould
Baring-Gould, William S., and Ceil Baring-Gould. *The Annotated Mother Goose.* Bramhall House, 1962.

Barnaby Rudge
Dickens, Charles. *Barnaby Rudge.* Dutton, 1972.

Barnhart
New Century Handbook of English Literature, ed. Clarence Barnhart. Appleton-Century-Crofts, 1967.

Baron Münchh‰usen
Baron Münchh‰usen: Fifteen Truly Tall Tales, Retold by Doris Orgel. Addison Wesley, 1971.

Baron Münchh‰usen's Narrative
Raspe, Rudolph Erich. *Baron Münchh‰usen's Narrative.* Brentano's, 1907.

Barrabas
Lagerkvist, P‰r. *Barrabas.* Bantam, 1968.

Barren Ground
Glasgow, Ellen. *Barren Ground.* Hill and Wang, 1957.

Barry Lyndon
Thackeray, William Makepeace. *Memoirs of Barry Lyndon, Esq..* University of Nebraska Press, 1962.

Bartleby
Melville, Herman. "Bartleby the Scrivener" in *Complete Works*, ed. Howard Vincent. Hendricks House, 1947.

Bartlett
Bartlett's Familiar Quotations, 14th ed., revised E.M. Beck. Little, Brown, 1968.

Baxter
Baxter, John. *Sixty Years of Hollywood.* A.S. Barnes, 1973.

Baydo
Baydo, A. *Topical History of the United States.* Prentice-Hall, 1974.

BBAAL1
Harris, Laurie Lanzen. *Biography for Beginners: African-American Leaders, Vol. 1.* Favorable Impressions, 2007.

BBAAL2
Harris, Laurie Lanzen. *Biography for Beginners: African-American Leaders, Vol. 2.* Favorable Impressions, 2008.

BBInv
Harris, Laurie Lanzen. *Biography for Beginners: Inventors.* Favorable Impressions, 2006.

BBPrez3
Harris, Laurie Lanzen. *Biography for Beginners: Presidents of the U.S..* Favorable Impressions, 2009.

BBWE
Harris, Laurie Lanzen. *Biography for Beginners: World Explorers.* Favorable Impressions, 2003.

A Bear Called Paddington
Bond, Michael. *A Bear Called Paddington.* Dell, 1968.

Beau James
Fowler, Gene. *Beau James.* Viking Press, 1949.

The Beauties of English Poesy
Goldsmith, Oliver. *The Beauties of English Poesy.* W. Griffin, 1767.

The Beaux' Stratagem
Farquhar, George. *The Beaux' Stratagem.* British Book Centre, 1975.

Beggar on Horseback
Kaufmann, George, and Marc Connelly. *Beggar on Horseback.* Scholarly Press, 1925.

Beggar's Opera
Gay, John. *The Beggar's Opera*, ed. Peter Lewis. Barnes & Noble, 1973.

Bel Ami
de Maupassant, Guy. *Bel Ami*, tr. Douglas Parmee. Penguin, 1975.

A Bell for Adano
Hersey, John. *A Bell for Adano.* Bantam, 1970.

Benét
William Rose Benét. *The Reader's Encylopedia*, 2nd edition, Thomas Y. Crowell, 1965.

Benito Cereno
Melville, Herman. *Benito Cereno* in *Eight Short Novels*, ed. Dean Flower. Fawcett World, 1970.

Benvenuto Cellini
Cellini, Benvenuto. *The Autobiography of Benvenuto Cellini*, tr. John Symonds. Doubleday, 1960.

Benya Kirk, the Gangster
Babel, Isaac. *Benya Kirk, the Gangster and Other Stories*, ed. Avrahm Yarmolinsky. Schocken Books, 1969.

Beowulf
Beowulf, tr. Burton Raffel. New American Library, 1963.

Berger
Berger, Arthur Asa. *The Comic-Stripped American*. Walker & Co., 1973.

Berkowitz
Berkowitz, Gerald M. *New Broadways: Theater Across America Approaching the Millennium*. Applause, 1997.

The Bermuda Triangle
Berlitz, Charles. *The Bermuda Triangle*. Avon, 1977.

Bettelheim
Bettelheim, Bruno. *The Uses of Enchantment*. Vintage Books, 1977.

Bevis of Hampton
Unknown. *Bevis of Hampton*. Penguin, 1974.

The Big Sky
Guthrie, A.B., Jr. *The Big Sky*. Bantam, 1972.

The Big Sleep
Chandler, Raymond. *The Big Sleep*. Random House, 1976.

Billy Budd
Melville, Herman. *Billy Budd*. Doubleday, 1970.

Binder
Binder, Pearl. *Magic Symbols of the World*. Hamlyn, 1972.

Birds
Aristophanes. *Birds*. Chandler, 1968.

Birth of Tragedy
Nietzsche, Friedrich. *The Birth of Tragedy*, tr. Francis Gollffing. Doubleday, 1956.

Bishop
Bishop, Morris. *The Horizon Book of the Middle Ages*, ed. Norman Kotker, et. Al. American Heritage, 1968.

Black Beauty
Sewell, Anna. *Black Beauty*. Macmillan, 1962.

The Black Cauldron
Alexander, Lloyd. *The Black Cauldron*. Dell, 1969.

Black Oxen
Atherton, Gertrude. *Black Oxen*. Folcroft Library, 1923.

Blanchard
Blanchard, R. H. *Handbook of Egyptian Gods and Mummy Amulets*. Attic Books, 1974.

Bleak House
Dickens, Charles. *Bleak House*. Holt, 1970.

Blue Willow
Gates, Doris. *Blue Willow*. Viking Press, 1969.

Blunt
Blunt, Rev. John Henry. *Dictionary of Sects, Heresies, Ecclesiastical Parties, and Schools of Religious Thought*. Gale, 1974.

The Blythedale Romance
Hawthorne, Nathaniel. *The Blythedale Romance* in *Works*, vol. 5. Houghton Mifflin, 1882-91.

Bobbsey Twins
Hope, Laura Lee. *Bobbsey Twins' Mystery at Meadowbrook*. Grosset and Dunlap, 1963.

Boland
Boland, Bridget. *Gardener's Magic and Other Old Wives' Lore*. Farrar, 1977.

Bold Stroke for a Wife
Centlivre, Susannah. *Bold Stroke for a Wife*, ed. Thalia Stathas. University of Nebraska Press, 1968.

Bombaugh
Bombaugh, Charles C. *Gleanings for the Curious from the Harvest Fields of Literature*. Gale, 1970.

Bombaugh Facts
Bombaugh, Charles C. *Facts and Fancies for the Curious*. Gale, 1968.

The Book of Three
Alexander, Lloyd. *The Book of Three*. Holt, 1964.

Boris Godunov
Pushkin, Alexandre. *Boris Godunov*, tr. Philip Barbour. Greenwood Press, 1976.

The Borrowers
Norton, Mary. *The Borrowers*. Harcourt, 1965.

The Bostonians
James, Henry. *The Bostonians*. Penguin, 1974.

Le Bourgeois Gentilhomme
Molière, Jean P. *Le Bourgeois Gentilhomme* in *Oeuvres Complètes*. Gallimard, 1971.

Brakeman
Brakeman, Lynne and Susan Gall. *Chronology of Women Worldwide: People, Places, and Events That Shaped Women's History*. Gale, 1997.

Brand
Ibsen, Henrik. *Brand*. Dutton, 1959.

Brave New World
Huxley, Aldous. *Brave New World*. Harper & Row, 1969.

Bray
Bray, Frank Chapin. *Bray's University Dictionary of Mythology*. Apollo Editions, 1964.

Bread and Wine
Silone, Ignazio. *Bread and Wine*. Harper, 1937.

Breakfast of Champions
Vonnegut, Kurt. *Breakfast of Champions*. Dell, 1974.

Brewer Dictionary
Brewer, E. Cobham. *Brewer's Dictionary of Phrase and Fable*, ed. Ivor H. Evans. Harper, 1971.

Brewer Handbook
Brewer, E. Cobham. *The Reader's Handbook*. Gale, 1966.

Brewer Miracles
Brewer, E. Cobham. *A Dictionary of Miracles*. Gale, 1966.

Brewer Note-Book
Brewer, E. Cobham. *The Historic Note-Book*. Gale, 1966.

Brewster
Brewster, H. Pomeroy. *Saints and Festivals of the Christian Church*. Gale, 1974.

Brewton
Brewton, John E. and Sara W. *Index to Children's Poetry*. H.W. Wilson, 1965.

The Bride of Lammermoor
Scott, Sir Walter. *The Bride of Lammermoor*. Dutton, 1972.

The Bridge of San Luis Rey
Wilder, Thornton. *The Bridge of San Luis Rey*. Harper, 1967.

The Bridge Over the River Kwai
Boulle, Pierre. *The Bridge Over the River Kwai*. Bantam, 1970.

Brief Lives
Aubrey, John. *Brief Lives or Minutes of Lives*, ed. Edward G. McGehee. Oxford University Press, 1972.

Briggs
Briggs, Katherine. *An Encyclopedia of Fairies: Hobgoblins, Brownies, Bogies,*

and Other Supernatural Creatures. Pantheon, 1977.

The Broken Heart
Ford, John. *The Broken Heart*, ed. Brian Morris. Hill and Wang, 1966.

The Bronze Bow
Speare, Elizabeth. *The Bronze Bow.* Houghton Mifflin, 1972.

Brothers Ashkenazi
Singer, Israel Joshua. *The Brothers Ashkenazi.* Knopf, 1936.

The Brothers Karamazov
Dostoevski, Fyodor. *The Brothers Karamazov.* Bantam, 1971.

Browne
Browne, Ray B., and Marshall Fishwick, eds. *Icons of America.* Popular Press, 1978.

BT
Biography Today, Abbey, Cherie D. Omnigraphics, 1992-.

BTSPORTS
Biography Today, Abbey, Cherie D. Omnigraphics, 1995-.

Bullfinch
Bullfinch, Thomas. *Age of Fable.* Dutton, 1969.

Bungalow Mystery
Keene, Carolyn. *The Bungalow Mystery.* Grosset and Dunlap, 1930.

Bussy D'Ambois
Chapman, George. *Bussy D'Ambois*, ed. Maurice Evans. Hill and Wang, 1966.

Buxton
Buxton, Frank, and Bill Owen. *The Big Broadcast: 1920-1950.* Avon, 1973.

By Love Possessed
Cozzens, James Gould. *By Love Possessed.* Fawcett World, 1973.

By the Pricking of My Thumbs
Christie, Agatha. *By the Pricking of My Thumbs.* Pocket Books, 1975.

The Cabala
Wilder, Thornton. *The Cabala.* Avon, 1975.

Cain
Byron, George. *Cain* in *Byron: Poetical Works*, ed. Frederick Page and John Jump. Oxford University Press, 1970.

Call of the Wild
London, Jack. *The Call of the Wild.* AMSCO School Publications, 1969.

Callista
Newman, John H. *Loss and Gain: The Story of a Convert, 1848*, ed. Robert L. Wolff. Garland, 1975.

Camille
Dumas, Alexandre, fils. *Camille*, tr. Matilde Heron. Books for Libraries, 1976.

Campbell *Creative*
Campbell, Joseph. *The Masks of God: Creative Mythology.* Viking Press, 1964.

Campbell *Encyclopedia*
Campbell, Oscar J. *A Shakespeare Encyclopedia.* Methuen, 1966.

Campbell *Hero*
Campbell, Joseph. *Hero With a Thousand Faces.* Princeton University Press, 1968.

Campbell *Occidental*
Campbell, Joseph. *The Masks of God: Occidental Mythology.* Viking Press, 1964.

Campbell *Oriental*
Campbell, Joseph. *The Masks of God: Oriental Mythology.* Viking Press, 1962.

Campbell *Primitive*
Campbell, Joseph. *The Masks of God: Primitive Mythology.* Viking Press, 1959.

Candida
Shaw, George Bernard. *Candida.* Penguin, 1974.

Candide
Voltaire. *Candide*, ed. G.R. Havens. Holt, 1969.

Cannery Row
Steinbeck, John. *Cannery Row*. Viking Press, 1945.

Canterbury Tales
Chaucer, Geoffrey. *The Canterbury Tales*, tr. David Wright. Random House, 1965.

Captain Brassbound's Conversion
Shaw, George Bernard. *Captain Brassbound's Conversion* in *Four Plays by Shaw*. Dell, 1957.

Captain Hatteras
Verne, Jules. *At the North Pole: The Adventures of Captain Hatteras*. Aeonian Press, 1976.

Captain Horatio Hornblower
Forester, C.S. *Captain Horatio Hornblower*. Little, Brown, 1939.

Captain Singleton
Defoe, Daniel. *Captain Singleton: The Life, Adventures & Pyracies of the Famous Captain Singleton*. Oxford University Press, 1973.

Carmen
Mérimée, Prosper. *Carmen*, ed. Pierre de Beaumont. Odyssey, 1969.

Cartwell
Cartwell, Van. H., and Charles Grayson. *The Golden Argosy*. Dial, 1955.

Carved Lions
Molesworth, Mary. *The Carved Lions*. Dutton, 1964.

Case
Case, Brian, and Stan Britt. *The Illustrated Encyclopedia of Jazz*. Harmony, 1978.

Cashel Byron's Profession
Shaw, George Bernard. *Cashel Byron's Profession*, ed. Stanley Weintraub. Southern Illinois University Press, 1968.

Cass Timberlane
Lewis, Sinclair. *Cass Timberlane*. Random House, 1945.

The Castle
Kafka, Franz. *The Castle*. Random House, 1974.

Castle of Llyr
Alexander, Lloyd. *Castle of Llyr*. Holt, 1966.

Cat on a Hot Tin Roof
Williams, Tennessee. *Cat on a Hot Tin Roof*. New Directions, 1975.

Catch-22
Heller, Joseph. *Catch-22*. Simon and Schuster, 1961.

The Catcher in the Rye
Salinger, J.D. *The Catcher in the Rye*. Bantam, 1970.

Caught in the Web of Words
Murray, K.M. *Caught in the Web of Words*. Yale University Press, 1977.

The Caxtons
Bulwer-Lytton, Edward. *The Caxtons: A Family Picture*. Scholarly Press, 1971.

The Celebrated Jumping Frog of Calaveras County
Twain, Mark. *The Celebrated Jumping Frog of Calaveras County,*. Gregg, 1969.

Celestina
Riojas, Fernando. *Celestina*. Dutton, 1959.

The Cenci
Shelley, Percy B. *The Cenci*, ed. Roland A Duerksen. Bobbs-Merrill, 1970.

Century Classical
New Century Classical Handbook, ed. C.B. Avery and J. Johnson. Appleton-Century-Crofts, 1962.

Century Cyclopedia
New Century Cyclopedia of Names, ed. Clarence L. Barnhart and William D.

Halsey. Appleton-Century-Crofts, 1954.

Century English
Barnhart, Clarence L. *New Century Handbook of English Literature*, rev. ed. Appleton-Century-Crofts, 1967.

CEOS&S
O'Connell, Mark and Raje Airey. *The Complete Encyclopedia of Signs and Symbols*. Hermes House, 2006.

Chambers
Chambers, Robert. *The Book of Days*. Gale, 1967.

Charlotte's Web
White, E.B. *Charlotte's Web*. Harper, 1952.

Cheaper By the Dozen
Gilbreth, Frank, and Ernestine Carey. *Cheaper By the Dozen*. Crowell, 1963.

Child
Child, Heather, and Dorothy Colles. *Christian Symbols: Ancient and Modern*. Scribner, 1971.

Childe Harold
Traditional Tunes of the Childe Ballads, ed. Bertrand H. Bronson, 4 vols. Princeton University Press, 1959 (Vol. 1), 1962 (Vol. 2), 1966 (Vol. 3), 1972 (Vol. 4).

Children of Green Knowe
Boston, Lucy M. *The Children of Green Knowe*. Harcourt, 1967.

A Child's Christmas in Wales
Thomas, Dylan. *A Child's Christmas in Wales*. New Directions, 1959.

Chitty-Chitty-Bang-Bang
Fleming, Ian. *Chitty-Chitty-Bang-Bang*. Random House, 1964.

A Christmas Carol
Dickens, Charles. *A Christmas Carol*. Dutton, 1972.

Christmas Stories
Dickens, Charles. *Christmas Stories* in *New Oxford Illustrated Dickens*. Oxford University Press, 1956.

Cinderella
Perrault, Charles. *Cinderella*. Henry Walck, 1971.

Cinq-Mars
de Vigny, Alfred. *Cinq-Mars; or, a Conspiracy under Louis XIII*. Howard Fertig, 1978.

Cirlot
Cirlot, J.E. *Dictionary of Symbols*, 2nd ed. Philosophical Library, 1972.

Citizen of the World
Goldsmith, Oliver. *Citizen of the World*. Dutton, Everyman, n.d.

The City and the Pillar
Vidal, Gore. *The City and the Pillar*. Dutton, 1965.

Clockwork Orange
Burgess, Anthony. *A Clockwork Orange*. Ballantine, 1976.

The Clouds
Aristophanes. *The Clouds*, ed. William Arrowsmith. New American Library, 1970.

Clue in the Embers
Dixon, Franklin W. *The Clue in the Embers*. Grosset and Dunlap, 1956.

A Cold Wind Blowing
Willard, Barbara. *A Cold Wind Blowing*. Dutton, 1973.

Collier's
Collier's Encyclopedia. Collier, 1949-51.

Colomba
Mérimée, Prosper. *Colomba*. French and European Publication, 1963.

Colonel Sheperton's Clock
Turner, Philip. *Colonel Sheperton's Clock*. Collins, 1966.

Comedy of Errors
Shakespeare, William. *Comedy of Errors*, ed. R.A. Foakes. Barnes & Noble, 1968.

Common Sense
Paine, Thomas. *Common Sense*. Penguin, 1976.

Communist Manifesto
Marx, Karl, and Friedrich Engels. *The Communist Manifesto*. Penguin, 1968.

The Compleat Angler
Walton, Izaak. *The Compleat Angler*. Dutton, Everyman, n.d.

Confessions
De Quincey, Thomas. *Confessions of an English Opium Eater*. New American Library, 1966.

Coningsby
Disraeli, Benjamin. *Coningsby: or The New Generation*. Scholarly Press, 1976.

A Connecticut Yankee in King Arthur's Court
Twain, Mark. *A Connecticut Yankee in King Arthur's Court*. Harper & Row, n.d.

The Conquest of Granada
Dryden, John. *The Conquest of Granada, or Almanzor and Almahide* in *Dryden: Three Plays*, ed. George Saintsbury. Hill and Wang, 1957.

Cooper
Cooper, J.C. *An Illustrated Encyclopedia of Traditional Symbols*. Thames and Hudson, 1978.

Coriolanus
Shakespeare, William. *Coriolanus*, ed. B.H. Kemball-Cook. Oxford University Press, 1954.

Corpus Delicti
Herman, Linda, and Beth Stiel. *Corpus Delicti of Mystery Fiction*. Scarecrow Press, 1974.

Corsican Brothers
Dumas, Alexandre, père. *The Corsican Brothers*. Methuen, 1904.

Corson
Corson, Hiram. *Index of Proper Names and Subjects to Chaucer's Canterbury Tales*. Folcroft Library Editions, 1973.

Cott
Cott, Ted. *Victor Book of Musical Fun*. Simon and Schuster, 1945.

The Count of Monte-Cristo
Dumas, Alexandre, père. *The Count of Monte Cristo*. Hart, 1975.

Cousin Pons
Balzac, Honoré de. *Cousin Pons*. French and European Publication, 1962.

Cranford
Gaskell, Elizabeth. *Cranford*, ed. Elizabeth P. Watson. Oxford University Press, 1972.

Cricket on the Hearth
Dickens, Charles. *Cricket on the Hearth*. Frederick Warne, 1956.

Crime and Punishment
Dostoyevsky, Fyodor. *Crime and Punishment*, tr. Constance Garnett. Random House, Vintage, 1955.

Critique of Hegel's "Philosophy of Right"
Marx, Karl. *Critique of Hegel's "Philosophy of Right"*, ed. J. O'Malley. Cambridge University Press, 1970.

Crowley
Ellen, T. *Acronyms, Initialisms, and Abbreviations Dictionary*, 5th ed. Gale, 1976; annual supplements.

Crowley Trade
Crowley, Ellen. *Trade Names Dictionary*. Gale, 1974.

The Crucible
Miller, Arthur. *The Crucible: Text & Criticism*, ed. Gerald Weales. Viking Press, 1971.

Cry, The Beloved Country
Paton, Alan. *Cry, The Beloved Country*. Scribner, 1948.

Curious George
Rey, Hans A. *Curious George*. Houghton, Mifflin, 1951.

Cyclops
Cyclops in *Euripedes: The Complete Greek Tragedies*, ed. D. Grene and R. Lattimore, 3 vols. University of Chicago Press, 1955.

Cymbeline
Shakespeare, William. *Cymbeline*. Oxford University Press, 1972.

Cyrano
Rostand, Edmond. *Cyrano de Bergerac*, tr. Anthony Burgess. Knopf, 1971.

Daisy Miller
James, Henry. *Daisy Miller and Other Stories*. Airmont, 1968.

La Dame aux Camélias
Dumas, Alexandre, fils. *La Dame aux Camélias*. French and European Publication, 1955.

A Damsel in Distress
Wodehouse, P.G. *A Damsel in Distress*. British Book Centre, 1956.

Daniel
Daniel, Howard. *Encyclopaedia of Themes and Subjects in Painting*. Thames and Hudson, 1971.

Darrel of the Blessed Iles
Bacheller, Irving A. *Darrel of the Blessed Iles*. Grosset, 1903.

Davenport
Davenport, Adams W. *Dictionary of English Literature*. Gale, 1966.

David Copperfield
Dickens, Charles. *David Copperfield*. Dutton, 1953.

Davidson
Davidson, H.R. Ellis. *Gods and Myths of Northern Europe*. Penguin, 1964.

Dawson
Dawson, Lawrence H. *Nicknames and Pseudonyms*. Gale, 1974.

The Day They Shook The Plum Tree
Lewis, Arthur H. *The Day They Shook The Plum Tree*. Pocket Books, 1975.

de Bles
de Bles, Arthur. *How to Distinguish the Saints in Art*. Art Culture Publication, 1925.

de Mille
de Mille, Agnes. *The Book of the Dance*. Golden Press, 1963.

de Purucker
de Purucker, G. *Occult Glossary*. Theosophical University Press, 1956.

Dead Souls
Gogol, Nikolai. *Dead Souls*, tr. Andrew MacAndrew. New American Library, Signet, 1961.

Death in the Afternoon
Hemingway, Ernest. *Death in the Afternoon*. Scribner, 1932.

Death in Venice
Mann, Thomas. *Death in Venice*. Knopf, 1965.

Death of a Salesman
Miller, Arthur. *Death of a Salesman*. Viking Press, 1967.

Decameron
Boccaccio, Giovanni. *The Decameron*, tr. G.H. McWilliam. Penguin, 1972.

The Deerslayer
Cooper, James Fennimore. *The Deerslayer*. Macmillan, 1962.

Desire Under the Elms
O'Neill, Eugene. *Desire Under the Elms* in *Three Plays*. Random House, 1959.

Dictionary of Facts
The Standard Dictionary of Facts. Frontier Press, 1924.

Disney Films
Maltin, Leonard. *The Disney Films.* Bonanza Books, 1973.

Divine Comedy
Alighieri, Dante. *The Divine Comedy.* Random House, 1955.

Doctor Faustus
Mann, Thomas. *Doctor Faustus.* New American Library, 1969.

Doctor Syntax
Hamilton, Harlan W. *Dr. Syntax.* Kent State University Press, 1969.

Doctor Thorne
Trollope, Anthony. *Doctor Thorne.* Harcourt, 1962.

Dodsworth
Lewis, Sinclair. *Dodsworth.* New American Library, 1971.

A Doll's House
Ibsen, Henrik. *A Doll's House.* Dutton, 1954.

Dombey and Son
Dickens, Charles. *Dombey and Son.* Penguin, 1975.

Dominic
Steig, William. *Dominic.* Farrar, 1972.

Don Carlos
Schiller, Friedrich. *Don Carlos,* tr. Charles E. Passage. Ungar, 1959.

Don Juan Tenorio
Zorilla y Moral, José. *Don Juan Tenorio,* ed. Nicholson B. Adams. Prentice-Hall, 1971.

Don Quixote
Cervantes, Miguel de. *Don Quixote.* Airmont, 1967.

Don Segundo Sombra
Guiraldes, Ricardo. *Don Segundo Sombra,* tr. Angela B. Dellepiane. Prentice-Hall, 1974.

The Double-Dealer
Congreve, William. *The Double-Dealer.* British Book Centre, 1974.

Down to Earth
Wrightson, Patricia. *Down to Earth.* Harcourt, 1965.

Dr. Breen's Practice
Howells, William D. *Doctor Breen's Practice.* Scholarly Press, 1970.

Dr. Doolittle
Lofting, Hugh. *The Story of Dr. Doolittle.* Lippincott, 1920.

Dr. Jekyll and Mr. Hyde
Stevenson, Robert L. *Dr. Jekyll and Mr. Hyde.* Dutton, Everyman, 1962.

Dracula
Stoker, Bram. *Dracula.* Doubleday, 1959.

Dry Guillotine
Belbenoit, René. *Dry Guillotine.* Dutton, 1938.

Dudley
Dudley, William. *Issues on Trial: Reproductive Rights.* Greenhaven Press, 2006.

Dunkling
Dunkling, Leslie. *The Guinness Book of Names.* Guinness Superlatives, 1974.

Eagle
The Concise Oxford Dictionary of English Literature, 2nd ed., ed. Dorothy Eagle. Oxford University Press, 1970.

Eastman
Eastman, Mary H. *Index to Fairy Tales, Myths, and Legends.* F.W. Faxon, 1926.

EB
Encyclopaedia Britannica. Encyclopaedia Britannica, 2008.

EB (1963)
Encyclopaedia Britannica. Encyclopaedia Britannica, 1963.

EB (1978)
1978 Book of the Year: Events of 1977.
Encyclopaedia Britannica, 1978.

Eclogues
Virgil. *Eclogues,* ed. H.E. Gould. St.
Martin's Press, 1967.

L' Ecole des Femmes
Molière, Jean P. *L'Ecole des Femmes.*
French and European Publication,
1964.

Edgar
Treasury of Verse for Little Children,
ed. M.G. Edgar. Crowell, 1946.

Edwin Drood
Dickens, Charles. *Edwin Drood and
Master Humphrey's Clock.* Dutton,
1970.

Eggenberger
Eggenberger, David. *A Dictionary of
Battles From 1479 B.C. to the Present.*
Thomas Y.Crowell, 1967.

Egmont
Goethe, Johann W. Von. *Egmont,* tr.
Willard Trask. Barron's, 1960.

The Egoist
Meredith, George. *The Egoist.* Penguin, 1979.

Electra
Euripedes. *Electra,* tr. Gilbert Murray. Oxford University Press, 1905.

Eliot
A Choice of Kipling's Verse, ed. T.S.
Eliot. Faber and Faber, 1963.

Elmer Gantry
Lewis, Sinclair. *Elmer Gantry.* American Library, Signet, 1971.

Emboden
Emboden, W.A. *A Renaissance
Botanist: Leonardo da Vinci, Hortulus
Aliquando.* Winter 1975-76, pp. 13-
30.

Emma
Austen, Jane. *Emma.* New American
Library, 1964.

Emperor Jones
O'Neill, Eugene. *Emperor Jones.*
Prentice-Hall, 1960.

Encyclopedia Judaica
Encyclopedia Judaica. Macmillan,
1972.

Enoch Arden
"Enoch Arden" in *Tennyson,* ed.
Kingsley Amis. Penguin, 1973.

The Epicurean
Moore, Thomas. *The Epicurean.*
Miller, 1875.

Espy
Espy, Willard R. *O Thou Improper,
Thou Uncommon Noun.* Clarkson N.
Potter, 1978.

Eugene Aram
Bulwer-Lytton, Edward. *Eugene
Aram* in *Works.* Wanamaker, n.d.

Eugene Onegin
Pushkin, Alexander. *Eugene Onegin,*
ed. Avrahm Yarmolinsky, tr. Babette
Deutsch. Penguin, 1965.

The Eunuch
Terence. *The Eunuch,* tr. Frank O.
Copley. Bobbs-Merrill, 1965.

Evans
Evans, Bergen. *Dictionary of Mythology, Mainly Classical.* Centennial
Press, 1970.

Evelina
Burney, Fanny. *Evelina.* W.W. Norton, 1965.

Every Man in His Humour
Jonson, Ben. *Every Man in His Humour.* British Book Centre, 1974.

Everyman
Everyman, ed. A.C. Cawley. Barnes
& Noble, 1970.

The Exorcist
Blatty, William P. *The Exorcist.* Harper & Row, 1971.

Faber
Faber Book of English Verse, ed. John Hayward. Faber & Faber, 1958.

Fables
Fontaine, Jean de la. *Fables*, tr. Edward Marsh. Dutton, 1966.

Facts
Facts on File. Facts on File, various years.

Faerie Queene
Spenser, Edmund. *Faerie Queene*, ed. P.C. Bayley. Oxford University Press, 1965-66.

Fair Maid of Perth
Scott, Sir Walter. *The Fair Maid of Perth* in *Complete Works*. Houghton, 1923.

The Fair Penitent
Rowe, Nicholas. *The Fair Penitent*, ed. Malcolm Goldstein. University of Nebraska Press, 1969.

The Fall
Camus, Albert. *The Fall*. Knopf, 1957.

Family from One End Street
Garnett, Eve. *Family from One End Street*. Vanguard, 1960.

Far Out the Long Canal
De Jong, Meindert. *Far Out the Long Canal*. Harper, 1964.

Farewell, My Lovely
Chandler, Raymond. *Farewell, My Lovely*. Random House, 1976.

A Farewell to Arms
Hemingway, Ernest. *A Farewell to Arms*. Scribner, 1967.

Fasti
Ovid. *Fasti*, ed. Cyril Bailey. Oxford University Press, 1921.

Fatal Curiosity
Lillo, George. *Fatal Curiosity*, ed. William H. McBurney. University of Nebraska, 1967.

Father Christmas
Briggs, Raymond. *Father Christmas*. Coward, 1973.

Fathers and Sons
Turgenev, Ivan. *Fathers and Sons*, tr. R. Edmonds. Penguin, 1975.

Faust
Goethe, Johann W. von. *Faust*, tr. Walter Kaufmann. Doubleday, 1961.

Feminine Mystique
Friedan, Betty. *The Feminine Mystique*. Norton, 1974.

Les Femmes Savantes
Molière, Jean B. *Les Femmes Savantes*, ed. H. Gaston Hall. Oxford University Press, 1974.

Fentress
Fentress, Calvin. "Ram Dass, Nobody Special" in *New Times*. September 4, 1978, pp.37-47.

Ferguson
Ferguson, George. *Signs and Symbols in Christian Art*. Oxford University Press, 1954.

Fifteen
Cleary, Beverly. *Fifteen*. William Morrow, 1956.

Finn Family Moomintroll
Jansson, Tove. *Finn Family Moomintroll*. Henry Walck, 1965.

Finnegans Wake
Joyce, James. *Finnegans Wake*. Viking Press, 1959.

Fisher
Fisher, Margery. *Who's Who in Children's Books*. Holt, 1975.

The Five Hundred Hats of Bartholomew Cubbins
Seuss, Dr. *The Five Hundred Hats of Bartholomew Cubbins*. E.M. Hale, 1938.

Five on a Treasure Island
Blyton, Enid. *Five on a Treasure Island*. Atheneum, 1972.

Five Weeks in a Balloon
Verne, Jules. *Five Weeks in a Balloon*. Aeonian Press, reprint of 1869 ed.

The Fixer
Malamud, Bernard. *The Fixer*. Dell, 1966.

Flashman
Fraser, George. *Flashman*. New American Library, 1969.

Flexner
Flexner, Stuart Berg. *I Hear America Talking*. Van Nostrand, 1976.

Flight of the Doves
Macken, Walter. *The Flight of the Doves*. Macmillan, 1970.

Flora Symbolica
Flora Symbolica, reprinted in *Sex in the Garden*, ed. Tom Riker. Morrow, 1976.

Foerster
American Poetry and Prose, ed. Norman Foerster. Houghton Mifflin, 1970.

FOF, MOD
Cole, Sylvia, and Abraham Lass. *The Facts on File Dictionary of Modern Allusions*, Facts on File, 2000.

Follow My Back Plume
Trease, Geoffrey. *Follow My Back Plume*. Vanguard Press, 1963.

For Whom the Bell Tolls
Hemingway, Ernest. *For Whom the Bell Tolls*. Scribner, 1940.

Fordin
Fordin, Hugh. *The World of Entertainment! Hollywood's Greatest Musicals*. Doubleday, 1975.

The Forsyte Saga
Galsworthy, John. *The Forsyte Saga*. Scribner, 1933.

Fortunata and Jacinta
Galdos, Benito Perez. *Fortunata and Jacinta*, tr. Lester Clark. Penguin, 1975.

Fortunes of Nigel
Scott, Sir Walter. *Fortunes of Nigel*. Dutton, 1965.

Four Major Plays
Ibsen, Henrik. *Four Major Plays, vol. 2*, tr. Rolf Fjelde. New American Library, 1970.

Frank
Frank, Sid. *The Presidents: Tidbits & Trivia*. Hammond, 1975.

Frankenstein
Shelley, Mary W. *Frankenstein: Or, the Modern Prometheus*, ed. James H. Rieger. Bobbs-Merrill, 1974.

Franny and Zooey
Salinger, J.D. *Franny and Zooey*. Bantam, 1969.

Freeman
Freeman, William. *Dictionary of Fictional Characters*, rev. Fred Urquhart. The Writer, 1974.

Friar Bacon
Greene, Robert. *Friar Bacon and Friar Bungay*. British Book Centre, 1975.

Friday the Rabbi Slept Late
Kemelman, Harry. *Friday the Rabbi Slept Late*. Crown, 1964.

The Frogs
Aristophanes. *The Frogs and Other Plays*, tr. David Barrett. Penguin, 1964.

Fuller
Fuller, J.F.C. *A Military History of the Western World*, 3 vols. Funk & Wagnalls, 1956.

Fyfe
Fyfe, Thomas Alexander. *Who's Who in Dickens*. Gryphon Books, 1971.

The Gambler
Dostoevsky, Fyodor. *The Gambler*, ed. Edward Wasiolek, tr. Victor Terras. University of Chicago Press, 1972.

A Game of Dark
Mayne, William. *A Game of Dark.* Dutton, 1971.

Gardener's Dog
Lope de Vega, Felix. *The Gardener's Dog* in *Four Plays of Lope de Vega.* Hyperion Press, 1978.

Gargantua and Pantagruel
Rabelais, FranÁois. *Gargantua and Pantagruel,* tr. John M. Cohen. Penguin, 1955.

Gaster
Myth, Legend, and Custom in the Old Testament, ed. Theodore Gaster. Harper, 1969.

Gayley
Gayley, Charles Mills. *The Classic Myths in English Literature and Art.* Milford House, 1974.

Gemini
Kipling, Rudyard. *Gemini* in *Soldiers Three.* Doubleday, 1909.

Gentleman's Agreement
Hobson, Laura Z. *Gentleman's Agreement.* Simon and Schuster, 1947.

Gentlemen Prefer Blondes
Loos, Anita. *Gentlemen Prefer Blondes.* Boni and Liveright, 1925.

George
Trumbull, Agnes. *George.* E.M. Hale, 1965.

Germinal
Zola, Emile. *Germinal.* New American Library, 1970.

Ghost of Thomas Kempe
Lively, Penelope. *The Ghost of Thomas Kempe.* Dutton, 1973.

Ghosts
Ibsen, Henrik. *Ghosts.* Avon, 1965.

Gil Blas
Le Sage, Alain René. *The Adventures of Gil Blas of Santillane.* Hyperion, 1977.

Giles Goat-Boy
Barth, John. *Giles Goat-Boy.* Fawcett Crest, 1966.

Gilgamesh
Gilgamesh: A Verse Narrative, ed. Herbert Mason. New American Library, 1972.

Gillespie and Naden
Gillespie, John T., and Corinne J. Naden. *Characters in Young Adult Literature,* Gale Research, 1997.

Ginger Pye
Estes, Eleanor. *Ginger Pye.* Harcourt, 1972.

Go Down, Moses
Faulkner, William. *Go Down, Moses.* Random House, 1973.

God Bless You, Mr. Rosewater
Vonnegut, Kurt. *God Bless You, Mr. Rosewater.* Dell, 1974.

God's Little Acre
Caldwell, Erskine. *God's Little Acre.* Viking Press, 1933.

The Golden Ass
Apuleius, Lucius. *The Golden Ass,* tr. Jack Lindsay. Indiana University Press, 1962.

Golden Boy
Odets, Clifford, and William Gibson. *Golden Boy.* Atheneum, 1965.

Golden Legend
De Voragine, Jacobus. *Golden Legend.* Arno Press, 1941.

Golden Mary
Dickens, Charles. "The Wreck of the 'Golden Mary'" in *Christmas Stories* in *New Oxford Illustrated Dickens.* New Oxford University Press, 1956.

Golden Treasury
Golden Treasury of Poetry, ed. Louis Untermeyer. Golden Press, 1959.

Goldfinger
Fleming, Ian. *Goldfinger.* Macmillan, 1966.

Golenpaul
Golenpaul, Ann. _Information Please Almanac: Atlas and Yearbook, 1975._ Information Please Almanac, 1975.

The Gondoliers
The Gondoliers in _The Complete Plays of Gilbert and Sullivan._ Norton, 1976.

Gone With the Wind
Mitchell, Margaret. _Gone With the Wind._ Avon, 1974.

The Good Earth
Buck, Pearl. _The Good Earth._ Pocket Books, 1975.

The Graduate
Webb, Charles. _The Graduate._ New American Library, 1971.

Granger
Granger, Edith. _Granger's Index to Poetry and Recitation._ Books for Libraries, 1974.

Grapes of Wrath
Steinbeck, John. _The Grapes of Wrath._ Bantam Books, 1970.

Great Expectations
Dickens, Charles. _Great Expectations,_ ed. Angus Calder. Penguin, 1965.

The Great Gatsby
Fitzgerald, F. Scott. _The Great Gatsby._ Scribner, 1920.

The Green Carnation
Hichens, Robert. _The Green Carnation,_ ed. Stanley Weintraub. University of Nebraska Press, 1970.

The Green Hills of Africa
Hemingway, Ernest. _The Green Hills of Africa._ Scribner, 1935.

Grendel
Gardner, John. _Grendel._ G.K. Hall, 1972.

Griffith
Griffith, Richard, and Arthur Mayer. _The Movies._ Simon and Schuster, 1957.

Grimm
Grimms' Tales for Young and Old, tr. Ralph Manheim. Doubleday, 1977.

Grinding It Out
Kroc, Ray, and Robert Anderson. _Grinding It Out: The Making of McDonald's._ Contemporary Publishing, 1977.

Grove
Grove's Dictionary of Music and Musicians, 5th ed. St. Martin's Press, 1954.

Grun
Grun, Bernard. _The Timetables of History._ Simon and Schuster, 1975.

Guirand
Guirand, Felix. _New Larousse Encyclopedia of Mythology._ Putnam, 1973.

Gulliver's Travels
Swift, Jonathan. _Gulliver's Travels,_ ed. L.A. Landa. Houghton Mifflin, 1960.

The Guns of August
Tuchman, Barbara. _The Guns of August._ Bantam, 1976.

Guy Mannering
Scott, Sir Walter. _Guy Mannering._ Dutton, 1954.

Guzmán de Alfarache
Aleman, Mateo. _The Life of Guzmán de Alfarache._ Knopf, 1924.

Hall
Hall, James. _Dictionary of Subjects and Symbols in Art._ Harper, 1974.

Halliwell
Halliwell, Leslie. _The Filmgoer's Companion._ Hill and Wang, 1977.

Hamlet
Shakespeare, William. _Hamlet,_ ed. George Rylands. Oxford University Press, 1947.

Handy Andy
Lover, Samuel. _Handy Andy: A Tale of Irish Life._ Appleton, 1904.

Hans Breitman's Ballads
Leland, Charles G. *Hans Breitman's Ballads*. Dover, 1914.

The Happy Hooker
Hollander, Xaviera. *The Happy Hooker*. Dell, 1972.

The Happy Lion
Duvoisin, Roger. *The Happy Lion*. McGraw-Hill, 1954.

Harbottle *Battles*
Harbottle, Thomas Benfield. *Dictionary of Battles*. Gale, 1966.

Hard Times
Dickens, Charles. *Hard Times*, ed. David Craig. Penguin, 1969.

Harding's Luck
Nesbit, Edith. *Harding's Luck*. British Book Centre, 1974.

Hardwick
Hardwick, Michael. *A Literary Atlas and Gazetteer of the British Isles*. Gale, 1973.

Harris
Restoration Plays, ed. Brice Harris. Modern Library, 1966.

Harris *Characters*
Harris, Laurie Lanzen. *Characters in 20th-Century Literature*. Gale, 1990.

Hart
The Oxford Companion to English Literature, 4th ed., ed. James D. Hart. Oxford University Press, 1965.

Harvey
The Oxford Companion to English Literature, 4th ed. rev. Dorothy Eagle, ed. Sir Paul Harvey. Oxford University Press, 1967.

The Haunted House
Dickens, Charles. *The Haunted House* in *Christmas Stories from Household Words and All the Year Round*. n.d.

Havelok the Dane
Havelok the Dane, ed. Ean Serraillier. Walck, 1967.

Haydn & Fuller
Haydn, Hiram, and Fuller, Edmund. *Thesaurus of Book Digests*. Crown, 1949.

The Heart Is a Lonely Hunter
McCullers, Carson. *The Heart Is a Lonely Hunter*. Bantam, 1970.

The Heart of Midlothian
Scott, Sir Walter. *The Heart of Midlothian*. Dutton, 1956.

The Heathen Chinee
Harte, Bret. "The Heathen Chinee," usually known as "Plain Language from Truthful James" in *The Complete Works of Bret Harte*. Chatto and Windus, 1880-1912.

Hedda Gabler
Ibsen, Henrik. *Hedda Gabler and Other Plays*, tr. Eva LaGallienne and Norman Ginsbury. Dutton, Everyman, 1976.

Heidi
Spyri, Johanna. *Heidi*. Penguin, 1971.

Helen
Euripedes. *Helen*, ed. A.M. Dale. Oxford University Press, 1967.

Héloïse and Abelard
Moore, George. *Héloïse and Abelard*. Liveright, 1945.

Hemingway
Hemingway, Ernest. *Short Stories of Ernest Hemingway*. Scribner, 1938.

Henderson
Henderson, Helene and Jay P. Pederson.*Twentieth-Century Literary Movements Dictionary*. Omnigraphics, Inc., 2000.

Henderson the Rain King
Bellow, Saul. *Henderson the Rain King*. Fawcett World, 1974.

Henry and Beezus
Cleary, Beverly. *Henry and Beezus*. William Morrow, 1952.

Henry Edmond
Thackeray, William M. *Henry Edmond*. Dutton, 1972.

Henry Huggins
Cleary, Beverly. *Henry Huggins*. William Morrow, 1950.

I Henry IV
Shakespeare, William. *I Henry IV*, ed. George L. Kittredge and Irving Ribner. John Wiley, 1966.

II Henry IV
Shakespeare, William. *II Henry IV*. Oxford University Press, 1970.

Henry V
Shakespeare, William. *Henry V*. Oxford University Press, 1971.

I Henry VI
Shakespeare, William. *I Henry VI*. Oxford University Press, 1970.

II Henry VI
Shakespeare, William. *II Henry VI*. Oxford University Press, 1970.

III Henry VI
Shakespeare, William. *III Henry VI*, ed. George Kittredge and Irving Ribner. John Wiley, 1969.

Henry VIII
Shakespeare, William. *Henry VIII*. Oxford University Press, 1971.

Herbert
Herbert, Ian. *Who's Who in the Theatre*. Gale, 1977.

A Herd of Deer
Dillon, Eilis. *A Herd of Deer*. Funk & Wagnalls, 1970.

Herman
Herman, Linda, and Beth Stiel. *Corpus Delicti of Mystery Fiction*. Scarecrow Press, 1974.

Hero and Leander
Marlowe, Christopher. *Hero and Leander*. Johnson Reprint, 1972.

Hero and Leander
Musaeus. *Hero and Leander*, tr. F.L Lucas. Golden Cockerel Press, 1977.

Herzog
Bellow, Saul. *Herzog*. Fawcett World, 1974.

Hiawatha
Longfellow, Henry Wadsworth. *The Song of Hiawatha*. Tuttle, 1975.

The Hidden Staircase
Keene, Carolyn. *The Hidden Staircase*. Grosset and Dunlap, 1930.

Hippolytus
Euripides. *Hippolytus*, tr. Robert Bagg. Oxford University Press, 1973.

History of John Bull
Arbuthnot, John. *History of John Bull*. Oxford University Press, 1976.

Hitler
Toland, John. *Adolf Hitler*. Ballantine Books, 1976.

H.M.S. Pinafore
Gilbert, W.S. "H.M.S. Pinafore" in *The Complete Works of Gilbert and Sullivan*. Norton, 1976.

The Hobbit
Tolkien, J.R.R. *The Hobbit*. Houghton Mifflin, 1973.

HolFestDict
Henderson, Helene. *Holidays, Festivals, and Celebrations of the World Dictionary, 3rd ed.*. Omnigraphics, 2005.

Hollowell
Hollowell, Lillian. *A Book of Children's Literature*. Rinehart, 1950.

HolSymb
Henderson, Helene. *Holiday Symbols and Customs*, 4th ed. Omnigraphics, 2008.

Hone
Hone, William. *The Table Book*. Gale, 1966.

Hone *Everyday*
Hone, William. *The Everyday Book*. Gordon, 1967.

The Hope of the Katzekopfs
Paget, Frances E., and William Churne. *The Hope of the Katzekopfs: A Fairy Tale*. Johnson Reprints, 1968.

Horn
Horn, Maurice. *The World Encyclopedia of Comics*. Chelsea House, 1976.

Horton Hatches the Egg
Seuss, Dr. *Horton Hatches the Egg*. Random House, 1940.

The Hound of the Baskervilles
Doyle, A. Conan. *The Hound of the Baskervilles*. Dell, 1959.

House of Arden
Nesbit, Edith. *House of Ardon*. Dutton, 1968.

The House of Sixty Fathers
de Jong, Meindert. *The House of Sixty Fathers*. Harper, 1956.

The House of the Seven Gables
Hawthorne, Nathaniel. *The House of the Seven Gables*. Harcourt, 1970.

How the People Sang the Mountains Up
Leach, Maria. *How the People Sang the Mountains Up*. Viking Press, 1967.

Howe
Howe, George, and Harrer, G.A. *A Handbook of Classical Mythology*. Gale, 1970.

Huckleberry Finn
Twain, Mark. *The Adventures of Huckleberry Finn*. Holt, 1948.

Hugo and Josephine
Gripe, Maria. *Hugo and Josephine*. Dell, 1971.

Humphrey Clinker
Smollett, Tobias. *The Expedition of Humphrey Clinker*, ed. Lewis M.

Knapp. Oxford University Press, 1966.

The Hunchback of Notre Dame
Hugo, Victor. *The Hunchback of Notre Dame*. Dutton, 1953.

The Hunting of the Snark
Carroll, Lewis. *The Hunting of the Snark*. Clarkson N. Potter, 1975.

I Ching
I Ching or the Book of Changes, tr. Petter Legge. Citadel Press, 1971.

I, Claudius
Graves, Robert. *I, Claudius*. Random House, Vintage, 1961.

The Iceman Cometh
O'Neill, Eugene. *The Iceman Cometh*. Random House, 1957.

The Idiot
Dostoyevsky, Fyodor. *The Idiot*. New American Library, Signet, 1969.

Idylls
Theocritus. *Idylls of Theocritus*. Purdue University Studies, 1963.

Idylls of the King
Tennyson, Alfred, Lord. *Idylls of the King*. St. Martin's Press, 1930.

Iliad
Homer. *Iliad*, tr. Robert Fizgerald. Doubleday, 1975.

Imagines
Philostratrus. *Imagines*. Harvard University Press, 1972.

The Importance of Being Earnest
Wilde, Oscar. *The Importance of Being Earnest*. New York Public Library, 1968.

In Cold Blood
Capote, Truman. *In Cold Blood*. New American Library, 1971.

In Dubious Battle
Steinbeck, John. *In Dubious Battle*. Bantam, 1970.

In the Heat of the Night
Ball, John. *In the Heat of the Night*. Harper & Row, 1965.

Indian Summer
Howells, William Dean. *Indian Summer*. Indiana University Press, 1972.

Inferno
Dante Alighieri. *Inferno*. Dutton, 1965.

The Informer
O'Flaherty, Liam. *The Informer*. Triangle Books, 1943.

Ingleby
Ingleby, C.M., et al. *Shakspere AllusionBook: A Collection of Allusions to Shakspere from 1591 to 1700*. Books for Libraries, 1970.

The Injustice Collectors
Auchincloss, Louis. *The Injustice Collectors*. Avon, 1974.

The Inspector General
Gogol, Nikolai. *The Inspector General*. Avon, 1976.

The Invisible Man
Wells, H.G. *The Invisible Man*. Popular Library, 1972.

Iphigenia in Tauris
Euripedes. *Iphigenia in Tauris*, tr. Gilbert Murray. Oxford University Press, 1910.

Iron Giant
Hughes, Ted. *Iron Giant: A Story in Five Nights*. Harper, 1968.

The Iron Lily
Willard, Barbara. *The Iron Lily*. Dutton, 1974.

Ivanhoe
Scott, Sir Walter. *Ivanhoe*. Macmillan, 1962.

J.B.
MacLeish, Archibald. *J.B.*. Houghton Mifflin, 1958.

Jack
Jack, Alex. *The New Age Dictionary*. Kathanka Press, 1976.

Jack Sheppard
Ainsworth, William. *Jack Sheppard*. Century, 1909.

Jacobowsky & Der Oberst
Werfel, Franz. *Jacobowsky & Der Oberst*. Irvington, 1961.

Jameson
Jameson, J. Franklin. *Dictionary of United States History*. Gale, 1971.

Jane Eyre
Bronte, Charlotte. *Jane Eyre*. Dutton, 1963.

Jerusalem Delivered
Tasso, Torquato. *Jerusalem Delivered*. Putnam, 1963.

Jew of Malta
Marlowe, Christopher. *The Jew of Malta* in *Marlowe: Five Plays*, ed. Havelock Ellis. Hill and Wang, 1956.

Jobes
Jobes, Gertrude. *Dictionary of Mythology, Folklore, and Symbols, Parts 1 & 2*. Scarecrow Press, 1962.

John Brent
Winthrop, Theodore. *John Brent*, ed. H. Dean Propst. College and University Press, 1970.

John Gabriel Borkman
Ibsen, Henrik. *John Gabriel Borkman* in *Four Major Plays*, tr. Rolf Fjelde, vol. 2. New American Library, 1970.

John Gilpin's Ride
Cowper, William. *John Gilpin's Ride*. Watts, 1967.

Johnny Tremain
Forbes, Esther. *Johnny Tremain*. Dell, 1969.

Johnson
Johnson, Rossiter. *Dictionary of Famous Names in Fiction, Drama, Poetry, History, and Art*. Gale, 1974.

Jonathan Livingston Seagull
Bach, Richard. *Jonathan Livingston Seagull*. Macmillan, 1970.

Jones
Jones, Raymond E. *Characters in Children's Literature*. Gale Research, 1997.

Jorrock's Jaunts & Jollieties
Surtees, Robert S. *Jorrock's Jaunts & Jollieties*, ed. Herbert Van Thal. Dufour, 1969.

Joseph Andrews
Fielding, Henry. *Joseph Andrews*. Norton, 1958.

Josh
Southall, Ivan. *Josh*. Macmillan, 1972.

Joy
Joy, Charles Rhind. *Harper's Topical Concordance*, rev. ed. Harper, 1962.

Jude the Obscure
Hardy, Thomas. *Jude the Obscure*. St. Martin's Press, 1977.

Judgment Day
Farrell, James T. *Judgment Day*. Avon, 1973.

Julius Caesar
Shakespeare, William. *Julius Caesar*, ed. T.S. Dorsch. Barnes & Noble, 1964.

The Jungle
Sinclair, Upton. *The Jungle*. New American Library, 1973.

The Jungle Books
Kipling, Rudyard. *The Jungle Books*. Grosset and Dunlap, 1950.

Jurgi
Jurgi, E.J. *Great Religions of the Modern World*. Princeton University Press, 1946.

Kaganoff
Kaganoff, Benzion C. *A Dictionary of Jewish Names and Their History*. Schocken Books, 1977.

Kalevala
Loenrot, Elias. *Kalevala*, tr. Francis P. Magoun. Harvard University Press, 1963.

Kane
Kane, Joseph Nathan. *Facts About the Presidents*. Ace Books, 1976.

Karst
Karst, Gene, and Martin J. Jones, Jr. *Who's Who in Professional Baseball*. Arlington House, 1973.

Keddie
Keddie, William. *Cyclopaedia of Literary and Scientific Anecdote*. Gryphon, 1971.

Kent
Kent, Leonard J. *The Collected Tales and Plays of Nikolai Gogol*. Pantheon, 1964.

Keyzer
Keyzer, Amy Marcaccio. *Family Planning Sourcebook*. Omnigraphics, 2001.

Kidnapped
Stevenson, Robert L. *Kidnapped*. New American Library, 1959.

Killikelly
Killikelly, Sarah H. *Curious Questions*. Gale, 1968.

The King, the Greatest Alcalde
Lope de Vega, Felix. *The King, the Greatest Alcalde*, in *Poet Lore* 29 (1918): 379-446.

King John
Shakespeare, William. *King John*, ed. E.A. Honingmann. Barnes & Noble, 1965.

King Lear
Shakespeare, William. *King Lear* in *William Shakespeare: The Complete Works*, ed. Peter Alexander. Collins, 1951.

King of the Golden River
Ruskin, John. *King of the Golden River*. Dover, 1974.

King *Quotations*
King, William F. *Classical and Foreign Quotations*. Gale, 1968.

King *Things*
King, Edmund F. *Ten Thousand Wonderful Things*. Gale, 1970.

Kinkle
Roger, D. *The Complete Encyclopedia of Popular Music and Jazz, 1900-1950*, 4 vols. Arlington House, 1974.

Kipps
Wells, H.G. *Kipps*. Dell, 1968.

Kitto
Kitto, H.D.F. *Greek Tragedy: A Literary Study*. Doubleday, 1954.

Kon-Tiki
Heyerdahl, Thor. *Kon-Tiki*. Washington Square Press, 1973.

Koran
Koran, tr. N.J. Dawood. Penguin, 1964.

Kravitz
Kravitz, David. *Who's Who in Greek and Roman Mythology*. Clarkson N. Potter, 1975.

Kubla Khan
Coleridge, Samuel Taylor. "Kubla Khan, A Vision in a Dream" in *Collected Works of Samuel T. Coleridge*. Princeton University Press, 1972.

Kunz
Kunz, George Frederick. *The Curious Lore of Precious Stones*. Dover, 1971.

La Vita Nuova
Dante's *Vita Nuova*, tr. Mark Musa. Indian State University, 1973.

The Lady or the Tiger
Stockton, Frank. *The Lady or the Tiger and Other Stories*. MSS Information Co., 1972.

Lahue
Lahue, Kalton C. *World of Laughter: The Motion Picture Comedy Short,* *1910-1930*. University of Oklahoma Press, 1972.

The Land of Oz
Baum, L. Frank. *The Land of Oz*. Airmont, 1968.

The Lark and the Laurel
Willard, Barbara. *The Lark and the Laurel*. Harcourt, Brace, Jovanovich, 1970.

The Last Chronicle of Barset
Trollope, Anthony. *The Last Chronicle of Barset*, ed. Arthur Mizener. Houghton Mifflin, 1964.

The Last Days of Pompeii
Bulwer-Lytton, Edward. *The Last Days of Pompeii* in *Works*. Wanamaker, n.d.

Latham
Latham, Edward. *Dictionary of Names, Nicknames, and Surnames*. Gale, 1966.

Laughlin
Laughlin, William H. *Laughlin's Fact Finder—People, Places, Things, Events*. Parker, 1969.

Le Malade Imaginaire
Molière, Jean B. *Le Malade Imaginaire*. French and European Publication, 1964.

Leach
Funk & Wagnalls Standard Dictionary of Folklore, Mythology, and Legend, ed. Maria Leach. Funk & Wagnalls, 1972.

Leaves of Grass
Whitman, Walt. *Leaves of Grass*. Norton, 1968.

A Legend of Montrose
Scott, Walter. *A Legend of Montrose* in *Complete Works*. Houghton, 1923.

The Legend of Sleepy Hollow
Irving, Washington. *The Legend of Sleepy Hollow and Other Stories*. Airmont, 1964.

Leonard
Leonard, Thomas M. *Day by Day: the Forties*. Facts on File, 1977.

Lie Down in Darkness
Styron, William. *Lie Down in Darkness*. Viking Press, 1957.

The Life of John Buncle
Amory, Thomas. *The Life of John Buncle, Esq., 1756-1766*, ed. Michael F. Shurgrue. Garland, 1974.

Light in August
Faulkner, William. *Light in August*. Random House, 1967.

The Lion, the Witch, and the Wardrobe
Lewis, C.S. *The Lion, the Witch, and the Wardrobe*. Macmillan, 1970.

Little
Little, Charles. *Historical Lights: 6000 Quotations*. Gale, 1968.

Little Blue and Little Yellow
Lionni, Leo. *Little Blue and Little Yellow*. Astor-Honor, 1959.

Little Dorrit
Dickens, Charles. *Little Dorrit*, ed. John Holloway. Penguin, 1967.

The Little Engine That Could
Piper, Watty. *The Little Engine That Could*. Platt, 1976.

Little Eyolf
Ibsen, Henrik. *Little Eyolf* in *Ibsen: The Complete Major Prose Plays*. Farrar, Straus, and Giroux, 1978.

The Little House
Burton, Virginia. *The Little House*. Houghton Mifflin, 1943.

Little House in the Big Woods
Wilder, Laura Ingalls. *Little House in the Big Woods*. Harper & Row, 1953.

The Little Lame Prince
Mulock, Dinah. *The Little Lame Prince and his Travelling Cloak*. Hale, 1909.

Little Lord Fauntleroy
Burnett, Frances H. *Little Lord Fauntleroy*. Biblio Distribution Centre, 1975.

The Little Minister
Barrie, J.M. *The Little Minister*. Airmont, 1968.

Little Old Mrs. Pepperpot
Proysen, Alf. *Little Old Mrs. Pepperpot*. Astor-Honor, 1960.

Little Red Fox
Uttley, Allison. *Little Red Fox and the Wicked Uncle*. Bobbs-Merrill, 1963.

The Little Steam Roller
Greene, Grahame. *The Little Steam Roller*. Doubleday, 1975.

Little Tim
Ardizzone, Edward. *Little Tim and the Brave Sea Captain*. Henry Walck, 1955.

Little Women
Alcott, Louisa May. *Little Women*. Grosset and Dunlap, 1947.

Livy
Livy. *Livy*, ed. T.A. Dorey. University of Toronto Press, 1971.

LLEI
The Lincoln Library of Essential Information, 2 vols. The Frontier Company, 1972.

Lolita
Nabokov, Vladimir. *Lolita*. Berkeley Publishing Company, 1975.

The Long Goodbye
Chandler, Raymond. *The Long Goodbye*. Ballantine, 1977.

The Long Voyage
Dickens, Charles. "The Long Voyage" in *Reprinted Pieces*. Dutton, 1970.

Look Homeward, Angel
Wolfe, Thomas. *Look Homeward, Angel*. Scribner, 1929.

Lord Jim
Conrad, Joseph. *Lord Jim*. Double-day, 1927.

Lord of Burleigh
Tennyson, Alfred, Lord. "Lord of Burleigh" in *Poems of Tennyson*, ed. Christopher Ricks. Norton, 1972.

Lord of the Flies
Golding, William. *Lord of the Flies*. Putnam, 1959.

Lord of the Rings
Tolkien, J.R.R. *Lord of the Rings*. Houghton Mifflin, 1974.

Lost Horizon
Hilton, James. *Lost Horizon*. Washington Square Press, 1972.

A Lost Lady
Cather, Willa. *A Lost Lady*. Random House, Vintage, 1972.

The Lost World
Doyle, Arthur Conan. *The Lost World*. Random House, 1959.

Lothair
Disraeli, Benjamin. *Lothair*, ed. Vernon Bogdanor. Oxford University Press, 1975.

Louie's Lot
Hildrick, E.W. *Louie's Lot*. D. White, 1968.

Love Story
Segal, Erich. *Love Story*. Harper & Row, 1970.

Love's Labour's Lost
Shakespeare, William. *Love's Labour's Lost*, ed. Richard W. David. Barnes & Noble, 1966.

Loving
Green, Henry. *Loving*. Dufour, 1949.

Lucy Brown and Mr. Grimes
Ardizzone, Edward. *Lucy Brown and Mr. Grimes*. Henry Walck, 1971.

Lurie
Lurie, Charles N. *Everyday Sayings*. Gale, 1968.

Lusiads
Camoes, Luis de. *Lusiads*. Southern Illinois University Press, 1963.

Lysistrata
Aristophanes. *Lysistrata*, tr. Douglass Parker. New American Library, 1970.

Mabinogion
The Mabinogion, tr. Jeffrey Gantz. Penguin, 1976.

Macbeth
Shakespeare, William. *Macbeth*, ed. R.W. Dent. William C. Brown, 1969.

Macleod
Macleod, Ann, adapt. *English Fairy Tales*. Paul Hamlyn, 1965.

Madame Bovary
Flaubert, Gustave. *Madame Bovary*, ed. Charles I. Wieir. Holt, 1948.

Maggie: A Girl of the Streets
Crane, Stephen. *Maggie: A Girl of the Streets*. Fawcett World, 1978.

The Magician's Nephew
Lewis, C.S. *The Magician's Nephew*. Macmillan, 1970.

Magill
Magill, Frank. *Masterpieces of World Literature in Digest Form*, 4 vols. Harper & Row, 1960.

The Magnificent Ambersons
Tarkington, Booth. *The Magnificent Ambersons*. Avon, 1973.

Mahaˉbhaˉrata
Mahaˉbhaˉrata, tr. Chakravarthi V. Nasrasimhan. Columbia University Press, 1973.

The Maid's Tragedy
Beaumont, Francis, and John Fletcher. *The Maid's Tragedy*, ed. Andrew J. Gurr. University of California Press, 1969.

Main Street
Lewis, Sinclair. *Main Street*. Signet Classics, 1971.

Major Bradford's Town
Melville, Doris Johnson. *Major Brad-ford's Town: A History of Kingston*. Town of Kingston, Massachusetts, 1976.

The Maldonado Miracle
Taylor, Theodore. *The Maldonado Miracle*. Doubleday, 1973.

The Maltese Falcon
Hammett, Dashiell. *The Maltese Falcon*. Random House, 1972.

Manhattan Transfer
Dos Passos, John. *Manhattan Transfer*. Houghton Mifflin, 1963.

Manon Lescaut
Prevost, Antoine. *Manon Lescaut*, tr. Helen Waddell. Hyperion, 1977.

Manxmouse
Gallico, Paul. *Manxmouse*. Coward, McCann, and Geohegan, 1968.

The Marble Faun
Hawthorne, Nathaniel. *The Marble Faun*. Ohio State University Press, 1968.

Marianne Dreams
Storr, Catherine. *Marianne Dreams*. Penguin, 1975.

The Marriage of Figaro
Beaumarchais, P.A. *The Marriage of Figaro*, tr. B.P. Ellis. AHM Publishing, 1966.

Martin Chuzzlewit
Dickens, Charles. *Martin Chuzzlewit*, ed. P.N. Furbank. Penguin, 1975.

Martin Eden
London, Jack. *Martin Eden*. Macmillan, 1957.

Martin Pippin
Farjeon, Eleanor. *Martin Pippin in the Apple Orchard*. Lippincott, 1961.

Martinus Scriblerus
Pope, Alexander, et al. *Memoirs of Martinus Scriblerus* in *The Works of Alexander Pope*, ed. J.W. Croker, vol. 10. Gordian Press, 1967.

Marvin
Marvin, Frederic Rowland. *The Last Words of Distinguished Men and Women*. Gale, 1970.

Mary Poppins
Travers, Pamela L. *Mary Poppins*. Harcourt Brace Jovanovich, 1972.

Master of Ballantrae
Stevenson, Robert L. *Master of Ballantrae*. Dutton, 1972.

Mathews
Dictionary of Americanisms on Historical Principles, ed. Mitford Mathews. University of Chicago Press, 1951.

Mayers
Mayers, William F. *Chinese Reader's Manual*. Gale, 1968.

The Mayor of Casterbridge
Hardy, Thomas. *The Mayor of Casterbridge*. Norton, 1977.

McElmeel
McElmeel, Sharon L. *100 Most Popular Book Authors and Illustators*. Libraries Unlimited, 2000.

McWhirter
McWhirter, Norris, and Ross McWhirter. *Guinness Book of World Records*. Bantam, 1975.

Measure for Measure
Shakespeare, William. *Measure for Measure*, ed. R.E. Houghton. Oxford University Press, 1970.

Medea
Euripides. *Medea*, ed. Alan Elliott. Oxford University Press, 1969.

Médée
Anouilh, Jean. *Médée*. French and European Publication, 1953.

Meg and Mog
Nicoll, Helen. *Meg and Mog*. Atheneum, 1973.

Mein Kampf
Hitler, Adolf. *Mein Kampf*, tr. Ralph Manheim. Houghton Mifflin, 1962.

Melmoth the Wanderer
Maturin, Charles R. *Melmoth the Wanderer*. University of Nebraska Press, 1961.

Memoirs of Fanny Hill
Cleland, John. *Memoirs of Fanny Hill*. New American Library, Signet, n.d.

Menaechmi
Plautus. *Menaechmi*, tr. Frank O. Copley. Bobbs-Merrill, 1956.

Mencken
Mencken, H.L. *The American Language*, abridged R.I. McDavid. Knopf, 1963.

Mercatante
Mercatante, Anthony S. *The Zoo of the Gods: Animals in Myth, Legend, and Fable*. Harper & Row, 1974.

The Merchant of Venice
Shakespeare, William. *The Merchant of Venice*, ed., John R. Brown. Barnes & Noble, 1964.

The Merry Wives of Windsor
Shakespeare, William. *The Merry Wives of Windsor*, ed. H.J. Oliver. Barnes & Noble, 1971.

Messiah
Klopstock, F.G. *Messiah*. Collyer, 1769-71.

Metamorphoses
Ovid. *Metamorphoses*, tr. Rolfe Humphries. Indiana University Press, 1955.

Michael Strogoff
Verne, Jules. *Michael Strogoff*. Airmont, 1964.

Middlemarch
Eliot, George. *Middlemarch*. Macmillan, 1966.

Midshipman Quinn
Styles, Showell. *Midshipman Quinn*. Vanguard, 1958.

A Midsummer Night's Dream
Shakespeare, William. *A Midsummer Night's Dream*, ed. Sally Freeman. Gordon and Breach, 1975.

The Mikado
Gilbert, W.S., and Arthur Sullivan. *The Mikado* in *The Complete Plays of Gilbert and Sullivan*. Norton, 1976.

Mike Mulligan
Burton, Virginia Lee. *Mike Mulligan and His Steam Shovel*. Houghton Mifflin, 1977.

Miller
The Rolling Stone Illustrated History of Rock & Roll, ed. Sim Miller. Random House, 1976.

The Misanthrope
Molière, Jean B. *The Misanthrope*, tr. Wallace Fowlie. Barron's, 1965.

Misc.
Includes items of a proverbial nature and/or common knowledge.

Les Misèrables
Hugo, Victor. *Les Misèrables*. French and European Publication, 1951.

Mistress Masham's Repose
White, Terence H. *Mistress Masham's Repose*. Putnam, 1960.

The Mistress of the Inn
Goldoni, Carlo. *The Mistress of the Inn*. Moscow Art Theater series of Russian plays, 1923.

Moby Dick
Melville, Herman. *Moby Dick*, ed. Harold Beaver. Penguin, 1975.

A Modern Midas
Jókai, Mór. *A Modern Midas*. J.W. Lovell, 1886.

The Moffats
Estes, Eleanor. *The Moffats*. Harcourt Brace Jovanovich, 1968.

The Monastery
Scott, Sir Walter. *The Monastery.* Dutton, 1969.

The Monk
Lewis, Matthew. *The Monk.* Avon, 1975.

Monmouth
Geoffrey of Monmouth. *History of the Kings of Britain,* ed. Charles Dunn. Dutton, 1965.

Monsieur Boncaire
Tarkington, Booth. *Monsieur Boncaire.* McClure, Phillips, 1900.

Monsieur Lecoq
Gaboriau, Emile. *Monsieur Lecoq,* ed. E.F. Bleuler. Dover, 1975.

A Month in the Country
Turgenev, Ivan. *A Month in the Country.* French, 1957.

Moody
Moody, Sophy. *What Is Your Name.* Gale, 1976.

Mopsa, The Fairy
Ingleow, Jean. *Mopsa, The Fairy.* Dutton, 1964.

Le Morte d'Arthur
Malory, Thomas. *Le Morte d'Arthur,* ed. Janet Cowen. Penguin, 1975.

Mostly Mary
Rae, Gwynneth. *Mostly Mary.* Avon, 1972.

Mother Goose
The Real Mother Goose. Rand McNally, 1955.

Mourning Becomes Electra
O'Neill, Eugene. *Mourning Becomes Electra.* Random House, 1931.

The Mourning Bride
Congreve, William. *The Mourning Bride, Poems, and Miscellanies.* Somerset Publication, n.d.

The Mouse That Roared
Wibberley, Leonard. *The Mouse That Roared.* Little, Brown, 1955.

Mr. Polly
Wells, H.G. *The History of Mr. Polly,* ed. Gordon Ray. Houghton Mifflin, 1961.

Mrs. Easter's Parasol
Drummond, V.H. *Mrs. Easter's Parasol.* Faber and Faber, 1944.

Mrs. Frisby
O'Brien, Robert C. *Mrs. Frisby and the Rats of NIMH.* Atheneum, 1975.

Much Ado About Nothing
Shakespeare, William. *Much Ado About Nothing,* ed. Charles Hinman. Oxford University Press, 1972.

Mulberry Street
Seuss, Dr. *And to Think That I Saw It on Mulberry Street.* E.M. Hale, 1937.

Murder in the Cathedral
Eliot, T.S. *Murder in the Cathedral.* Harcourt Brace Jovanovich, 1964.

Mutiny on the Bounty
Nordhoff, Charles B. *Mutiny on the Bounty.* Washington Square Press, 1975.

My Brother's Keeper
Davenport, Marcia. *My Brother's Keeper.* Scribner, 1954.

My Father's Dragon
Gannett, Ruth. *My Father's Dragon.* Random House, 1948.

My Friend Flicka
O'Hara, Mary. *My Friend Flicka.* Lippincott, 1973.

My Life in the Mafia
Teresa, Vincent C., with Thomas C. Renner. *My Life in the Mafia.* Doubleday, 1973.

My Side of the Mountain
George, Jean. *My Side of the Mountain.* Dutton, 1967.

Mysterious Island
Verne, Jules. *Mysterious Island.* Pendulum Press, 1974.

Mythology
Hamilton, Edith. *Mythology*. Little, Brown, 1942.

The Namesake
Hodges, C. Walter. *The Namesake: A Story of King Alfred*. Coward, McCann and Geohegan, 1964.

Nares
Nares, Robert. *Glossary of Words, Phrases, Names, and Allusions in the Works of English Authors*. Gale, 1966.

Native Son
Wright, Richard. *Native Son*. Harper & Row, 1940.

Nausea
Sartre, Jean-Paul. *Nausea*, tr. Lloyd Alexander. New Directions, 1959.

NCE
The New Columbia Encyclopedia, ed. William H. Harris and Judith S. Levey. Columbia University Press, 1975.

A Nest of Simple Folk
O'Faolain, Sean. *A Nest of Simple Folk*. Viking Press, 1934.

New Héloïse
Rousseau, Jean-Jacques. *La Nouvelle Héloïse*. Pennsylvania State University Press, 1968.

The Newcomes
Thackeray, William Makepeace. *The Newcomes*. Bradbury and Evans, 1854.

Nibelungenlied
Nibelungenlied, tr. Frank G. Ryder. Wayne State University Press, 1962.

Nicholas Nickleby
Dickens, Charles. *Nicholas Nickleby*. Dutton, 1957.

Nigger of the Narcissus
Conrad, Joseph. *The Nigger of the Narcissus*. Macmillan, 1962.

The Night Before Christmas
Moore, Clement. *The Night Before Christmas*. Grosset and Dunlap, 1970.

Nine Tailors
Sayers, Dorothy. *Nine Tailors*. Harcourt Brace Jovanovich, 1966.

1984
Orwell, George. *1984*. New American Library, 1971.

Noctes Atticae
Gellius. *Noctes Atticae*, ed. P.K. Marshall. Oxford University Press, 1968.

Noddy and His Car
Blyton, Enid. *Noddy and His Car*. British Book Centre, 1974.

Norton
Eastman et al. *The Norton Anthology of Poetry*. Norton, 1970.

Norton *Literature*
Norton Anthology of English Literature, 3rd ed. 2 vols. Norton, 1974.

Norton *Modern*
Norton Anthology of Modern Poetry, ed. Richard Ellmann and Robert O'-Clair. Norton, 1973.

Nostromo
Conrad, Joseph. *Nostromo*. Modern Library, 1951.

N.T.
New Testament. *New English Bible*. Oxford University Press, 1970.

Number One
Dos Passos, John. *Number One*. Queens House, 1977.

Oblomov
Goncharov, Ivan. *Oblomov*, tr. Natalie Duddington. Dutton, 1972.

OCCL
Carpenter, Humphrey. *The Oxford Companion to Children's Literature*, Prichard, Mary. Oxford University Press, 1984.

ODA
Delahunty, Andrew, Sheila Dignen, and Penny Stock. *Oxford Dictionary of Allusions*. Oxford University Press, 2003.

The Odd Couple
Simon, Neil. *The Odd Couple*. Random House, 1966.

ODWR
Bowker, John, ed. *The Oxford Dictionary of World Religions*, Oxford University Press, 1997.

Odyssey
Homer. *Odyssey*, tr. Robert Fitzgerald. Doubleday, 1974.

Oedipus Rex
Sophocles. *Oedipus Rex*, tr. Gilbert Murray. Oxford University Press, 1948.

Oedipus Tyrannus
Sophocles. *Oedipus Tyrannus*. Norton, 1970.

Of Mice and Men
Steinbeck, John. *Of Mice and Men*. Bantam, 1970.

The Old Batchelour
Congreve, William. *The Old Batchelour*. British Book Centre, 1974.

The Old Curiosity Shop
Dickens, Charles. *The Old Curiosity Shop*, ed. A. Easson. Penguin, 1972.

The Old Man and the Sea
Hemingway, Ernest. *The Old Man and the Sea*. Scribner, 1961.

Old Mortality
Scott, Sir Walter. *Old Mortality*, ed. Angus Calder. Penguin, 1975.

Oliver Twist
Dickens, Charles. *Oliver Twist*, ed. Kathleen Tillotson. Oxford University Press, 1966.

Omoo
Melville, Herman. *Omoo*. Northwestern University Press, 1968.

On Stage
Beckerman, Bernard, and Howard Siegman. *On Stage: Selected Theater Reviews from* The New York Times. Arno Press, 1970.

On the Road
Kerouac, Jack. *On the Road*. Viking Press, 1978.

The Once and Future King
White, T.H. *The Once and Future King*. Putnam, 1958.

One Day in the Life of Ivan Denisovich
Solzhenitzyn, Alexandr. *One Day in the Life of Ivan Denisovich*, tr. Aitken Gillon. Farrar, 1971.

One Flew Over the Cuckoo's Nest
Kesey, Ken. *One Flew Over the Cuckoo's Nest*. New American Library, 1975.

Opie
Opie, Iona and Peter. *Oxford Dictionary of Nursery Rhymes*. Oxford University Press, 1951.

Orestes
Aeschylus. *Oresteia*, tr. Robert Fagles. Bantam, 1977.

Origin of Species
Darwin, Charles. *Origin of Species*. Macmillan, 1962.

Orlando Furioso
Ariosto, Ludovico. *Orlando Furioso*, tr. John Harrington. Oxford University Press, 1970.

Orlando Innamorato
Bojardo, Matteo Maria. *Orlando Innamorato*. Sansoni, 1892.

Oroonoko
Behn, Aphra. *Oroonoko: Or, The Royal Slave*. Norton, 1973.

Osborne
The Oxford Companion to Art, ed. Harold Osborne. Oxford University Press, 1970.

Osborne *Opera*
Osborne, Charles. *The Dictionary of the Opera*. Simon and Schuster, 1983.

O.T.
Old Testament. *New English Bible*. Oxford University Press, 1970.

Othello
Shakespeare, William. *Othello*, ed. J. Leeds Barroll. William C. Brown, 1971.

Our Mutual Friend
Dickens, Charles. *Our Mutual Friend*, ed. Stephen Gill. Penguin, 1971.

The Outcasts of Poker Flat
Harte, Bret. *The Outcasts of Poker Flat and Other Tales*. New American Library, Signet, 1961.

The Overcoat
Gogol, Nikolai. *The Overcoat and Other Stories*. Knopf, 1950.

Overland Launch
Hodges, C. Walter. *The Overland Launch*. Coward, McCann and Geohegan, 1969.

The Owl Service
Garner, Alan. *The Owl Service*. Henry Walck, 1968.

The Ox-Bow Incident
Clark, Walter van Tilberg. *The Ox-Bow Incident*. New American Library, 1943.

Oxford English Dictionary
The Oxford English Dictionary, ed. J.A. Murray, et al. Oxford University Press, 1943.

Paddle-to-the-Sea
Holling, Holling C. *Paddle-to-the-Sea*. Houghton Mifflin, 1941.

The Palace Guard
Rather, Dan, and Gary P. Gates. *The Palace Guard*. Harper & Row, 1975.

A Palm for Mrs. Pollifax
Gilman, Dorothy. *A Palm for Mrs. Pollifax*. Doubleday, 1973.

Pamela
Richardson, Samuel. *Pamela*. Norton, 1958.

Pansies
Lawrence, D.H. *Pansies*. P.R. Stephensen, 1929.

Pantagruel
Rabelais, FranÁois. *Pantagruel*. French and European Publication, 1964.

Papillon
Charrière, Henri. *Papillon*. Pocket Books, 1973.

Paradise Lost
Milton, John. *Paradise Lost*, ed. Scott Elledge. Norton, 1975.

Parish
Parish, James Robert. *Actors' Television Credits, 1950-1972*. Scarecrow Press, 1973.

Parrinder
Parrinder, Geoffrey. *Dictionary of Non-Christian Religions*. Westminster Press, 1971.

Parzival
Von Eschenbach, Wolfram. *Parzival*. Random House, 1961.

PatHols
Henderson, Helene. *Patriotic Holidays of the United States*. Omnigraphics, 2006.

Patience
Gilbert, W.S., and Arthur Sullivan. *Patience* in *The Complete Plays of Gilbert and Sullivan*. Norton, 1976.

A Pattern of Roses
Peyton, K.M. *A Pattern of Roses*. Thomas Y. Crowell, 1973.

852

Payton
Payton, Geoffrey. *Webster's Dictionary of Proper Names*. G & C Merriam, 1970.

Pendennis
Thackeray, William M. *The History of Pendennis*. Harper, 1864.

Pensées
Pascal, Blaise. *Pensées*, tr. A.J. Krailsheimer. Penguin, 1966.

Pepita Jimenez
Valera, Juan. *Pepita Jimenez*, tr. Harriet De Onis. Barron's, 1965.

Perceval
de Troyes, Chrétien. *Le Roman de Perceval*. Droz, 1959.

Père Goriot
Balzac, Honoré de. *Père Goriot*. Modern Library, 1950.

Pericles
Shakespeare, William. *Pericles*, ed. F.D. Hoeniger. Barnes & Noble, 1963.

Peter Churchmouse
Austin, Margo. *Peter Churchmouse*. Dutton, 1941.

Peter Pan
Barrie, James M. *Peter Pan*. Grosset and Dunlap, 1970.

Peter Schlemihl
Chamisso, Adelbert von. *Peter Schlemihl's Remarkable Story*, ed. Fred Honig. Arc Books, 1964.

The Peterkin Papers
Hale, Lucretia. *The Peterkin Papers*. Dover, 1960.

Phormio
Terence. *Phormio*, tr. Frank O. Copley. Bobbs-Merrill, 1958.

Phyfe
Phyfe, William Henry P. *5000 Facts and Fancies*. Gale, 1966.

Pickwick Papers
Dickens, Charles. *Pickwick Papers*, ed. Robert L. Patten. Penguin, 1975.

The Picture of Dorian Gray
Wilde, Oscar. *The Picture of Dorian Gray*. Dell, 1956.

Pierce
Pierce, Gilbert Ashville. *The Dickens Dictionary*. Haskell House, reprint of 1878 ed.

The Pilgrim's Progress
Bunyan, John. *Pilgrim's Progress*. Holt, 1949.

The Pilot
Cooper, James Fennimore. *The Pilot*. Townsend, 1859.

Pinky Pye
Estes, Eleanor. *Pinky Pye*. Harcourt, 1958.

Pinocchio
Collodi, Carlo. *Pinocchio*, tr. E. Harden. Penguin, Puffin, 1972.

Pippi Longstocking
Lindgren, Astrid. *Pippi Longstocking*. Viking Press, 1950.

The Pirates of Penzance
Gilbert, W.S., and Arthur Sullivan. *The Pirates of Penzance* in *The Complete Plays of Gilbert and Sullivan*. Norton, 1976.

The Pit
Norris, Frank. *The Pit: A Story of Chicago*. Bentley, 1971.

The Plague
Camus, Albert. *The Plague*. Random House, 1972.

Plain Speaking
Miller, Merle. *Plain Speaking*. Berkley, 1974.

Plays of Strindberg
Strindberg, August. *Plays of Strindberg*, tr. Michael Meyer, 2 vols. Random House, 1976.

Plays Unpleasant
Shaw, George Bernard. *Plays Unpleasant*. Penguin, 1950.

Pliny
Pliny. *Natural History*, 11 vols. Harvard University Press, 1962.

Plumb
Plumb, J.H. *The Horizon Book of the Renaissance*, ed. Richard Ketchum, et al. American Heritage, 1961.

Plutarch's Lives
Plutarch. *Plutarch's Lives*, ed. Edmund Fuller. Dell, 1968.

Plutus
Aristophanes. *Plutus*. W.B. Clive, 1889.

Poe
Poe, Edgar A. *Collected Works of Edgar Allan Poe, vol. 1: Poems*, ed. Thomas O. Mabbott. Harvard University Press, 1969.

Pollyanna
Porter, Eleanor. *Pollyanna*. A.L. Burt, 1913.

Pope
Pope, Alexander. *Poems of Alexander Pope*, ed. John Butt. Yale University Press, 1963.

Portable Poe
Poe, Edgar Allan. *The Portable Edgar Allan Poe*, ed. Philip Van Doren Stern. Viking Press, 1972.

Portrait of the Artist as a Young Man
Joyce, James. *Portrait of the Artist as a Young Man*. Penguin, 1977.

Pot of Gold
Plautus. *The Pot of Gold and Other Plays*, tr. E.F. Watling. Penguin, 1965.

Potiphar Papers
Curtis, George W. *The Potiphar Papers*. AMS Press, 1970.

Les Précieuses Ridicules
Molière, Jean P. *Les Précieuses Ridicules*. French and European Publication, 1965.

Pride and Prejudice
Austen, Jane. *Pride and Prejudice*. Oxford University Press, 1975.

The Prince
Machiavelli, Niccolo. *The Prince*. St. Martin's Press, 1964.

The Prince and the Pauper
Twain, Mark. *The Prince and the Pauper*. Macmillan, 1962.

Prince Caspian
Lewis, C.S. *Prince Caspian*. Macmillan, 1951.

Prince Prigio
Lang, Andrew. *Prince Prigio and Prince Ricardo*. Dutton, 1961.

The Prisoner of Zenda
Hope, Anthony. *The Prisoner of Zenda*. New American Library, 1971.

Private Lives
Coward, Noel. *Private Lives*. Doubleday, 1930.

Profiles in Courage
Kennedy, John F. *Profiles in Courage*. Harper & Row, 1964.

Psychomachia
Prudentius. "Psychomachia" in *Works*. Harvard University Press, 1942.

Puck of Pook's Hill
Kipling, Rudyard. *Puck of Pook's Hill*. Dover, 1968.

Pumping Iron
Gaines, Charles, and George Butler. *Pumping Iron*. Simon and Schuster, 1974.

Pygmalion
Shaw, George Bernard. *Pygmalion*. New American Library, 1975.

Queenie Peavy
Burch, Robert. *Queenie Peavy*. Viking Press, 1966.

Quennell
Quennell, Peter, and Hamish Johnson. *Who's Who in Shakespeare*. Weidenfeld and Nicholson, 1973.

Quentin Durward
Scott, Sir Walter. *Quentin Durward*. Dutton, 1965.

R.U.R.
C̆apek, Karel. *R.U.R.*. Oxford University Press, 1961.

Rabbit Hill
Lawson, Robert. *Rabbit Hill*. Dell, 1968.

Racketty Packetty House
Burnett, Frances Hodgson. *Racketty Packetty House*. Lippincott, 1975.

Radford
Radford, Edwin. *Unusual Words and How They Came About*. Philosophical Library, 1946.

Ragan
Ragan, David. *Who's Who in Hollywood*. Arlington House, 1970.

Ragged Dick
Alger, Horatio. *Ragged Dick and Mark the Match Boy*. Macmillan, 1962.

Raggedy Ann Stories
Gruelle, John B. *Raggedy Ann Stories*. Volland, 1918.

The Railway Children
Nesbit, Edith. *The Railway Children*. British Book Centre, 1974.

Ralph Roister Doister
Udall, Nicholas. *Ralph Roister Doister*. J.M. Dent, 1901.

Ramage *French*
Ramage, Crauford Tait. *Familiar Quotations from French and Italian Authors*. Gale, 1968.

Ramage *German*
Ramage, Crauford Tait. *Familiar Quotations from German and Spanish Authors*. Gale, 1968.

Ramage *Greek*
Ramage, Crauford Tait. *Familiar Quotations from Greek Authors*. Gale, 1968.

Ramayana
Almiki. *Ramayana*, tr. Chakravarti Rajagopalachari. InterCulture, 1974.

The Rape of Lucrece
Shakespeare, William. *The Rape of Lucrece*. British Book Centre, 1974.

Rape of the Lock
Pope, Alexander. *The Rape of the Lock*, ed. J.S. Cunningham. Oxford University Press, 1966.

Rapunzel
Grimm Brothers. *Rapunzel*. Crowell, 1975.

Rebecca of Sunnybrook Farm
Wiggin, Kate Douglas. *Rebecca of Sunnybrook Farm*. Macmillan, 1962.

The Red Badge of Courage
Crane, Stephen. *The Red Badge of Courage*. Macmillan, 1966.

The Red Pony
Steinbeck, John. *The Red Pony*. Viking Press, 1959.

Redburn
Melville, Herman. *Redburn*. Northwestern University Press, 1969.

The Rehearsal
Villiers, George. *The Rehearsal*. Folcroft, 1976.

The Relapse
Vanbrugh, John. *The Relapse*, ed. Curt Zimansky. University of Nebraska Press, 1970.

Reliques
Percy, Thomas. *Reliques of Ancient English Poesy*, ed. Henry B. Wheatley. Dover, 1966.

Remembrance of Things Past
Proust, Marcel. *Remembrance of Things Past*. Random House, 1934.

Renée Mauperin
de Goncourt, Edmond and Jules. *Renée Mauperin*. Fasquelle, 1920.

The Republic
Plato. *The Republic*, ed. Allan Bloom. Basic Books, 1968.

The Rescuers
Sharp, Margery. *The Rescuers*. Dell, 1974.

The Return of the Native
Hardy, Thomas. *The Return of the Native*. New American Library, Signet, 1973.

Reynard the Fox
Reynard the Fox, ed. Roy Brown. Abelard-Schuman, 1969.

RHD
The Random House Dictionary of the English Language, ed. Jess Stein, et al. Random House, 1973.

Richard II
Shakespeare, William. *Richard II*. Oxford University Press, 1966.

Richard III
Shakespeare, William. *Richard III*, ed. R.E. Houghton. Oxford University Press, 1965.

Riders to the Sea
Synge, John Millington. *Riders to the Sea*. Irish Academic Press, 1972.

The Rime of the Ancient Mariner
Colderidge, Samuel Taylor. "The Rime of the Ancient Mariner" in *The Oxford Book of English Verse*, ed. A. Quiller-Couch. Oxford University Press, 1939.

The Ring and the Book
Browning, Robert. *The Ring and the Book*. Dutton, 1962.

The Ring of the Nibelung
Wagner, Richard. *The Ring of the Nibelung*. Dutton, 1962.

The Rise of Silas Lapham
Howells, William Dean. *The Rise of Silas Lapham*. Indiana University Press, 1971.

The Rivals
Sheridan, Richard B. *The Rivals*. Oxford University Press, 1968.

Rob Roy
Scott, Sir Walter. *Rob Roy*. Dutton, 1973.

Robin Hood
Robin Hood, ed. J. Ritson. Rowman, 1972.

Robinson Crusoe
Defoe, Daniel. *Robinson Crusoe*, ed. J. Donald Crowley. Oxford University Press, 1972.

Rockwell
Norman Rockwell's Christmas Book, ed. Lena Tabori Fried and Ruth Eisenstein. Abrams, 1977.

Roderick Hudson
James, Henry. *Roderick Hudson*. Houghton Mifflin, 1977.

Roderick Random
Smollett, Tobias. *Roderick Random*. New American Library, 1964.

Rogers
Rogers, May. *The Waverly Dictionary*. Gale, 1967.

Roller Skates
Sawyer, Ruth. *Roller Skates*. Dell, 1969.

Romeo and Juliet
Shakespeare, William. *Romeo and Juliet*, ed. Maynard Mack and Robert Boynton. Hayden, 1975.

Romola
Eliot, George. *Romola* in *The Complete Works of George Eliot*. Harper, n.d.

The Rose and the Ring
Thackeray, William Makepeace. *The Rose and the Ring*. Pierpont Morgan Library, 1947.

Rosemary's Baby
Levin, Ira. *Rosemary's Baby*. Random House, 1967.

Rosie's Walk
Hutchins, Pat. *Rosie's Walk*. Macmillan, 1968.

Rosten
Rosten, Leo. *The Joys of Yiddish*. McGraw-Hill, 1968.

Rovin
Rovin, Jeff. *The Great Television Series*. A.S. Barnes, 1977.

Roxana, the Fortunate Mistress
Defoe, Daniel. *Roxana, the Fortunate Mistress*. Oxford University Press, 1964.

Roxy
Eggleston, Edward. *Roxy*. Gregg Press, 1968.

The Royal Family
Kaufmann, George S., and Edna Ferber. *The Royal Family*. French, 1929.

Ruddigore
Gilbert, W.S., and Arthur Sullivan *Ruddigore* in *The Complete Plays of Gilbert and Sullivan*. Norton, 1976.

Rumpelstiltskin
Grimm Brothers. *Rumpelstiltskin*. Scholastic Book Service, 1974.

Ryland
Ryland, Frederick. *Chronological Outlines of English Literature*. Gale, 1968.

Sacco-Vanzetti Case: A Transcript
Sacco-Vanzetti Case: A Transcript of the Trial of Nicola Sacco and Batolomeo Vanzetti in the Courts of Massachusetts and Subsequent Proceedings, 1920-27, 2nd ed., ed. Paul P. Appel. Appel, 1969.

Saints and Festivals
Brewster, H. Pomeroy. *Saints and Festivals of the Christian Church*. Gale, 1974.

Samson Agonistes
Milton, John. "Samson Agonistes" in *Compact Milton*, ed. H.S. Taylor. Barron's, 1967.

Sanctuary
Faulkner, William. *Sanctuary*. New American Library, 1968.

Sann
Sann, Paul. *Fads, Follies and Delusions of the American People*. Crown Publishers, 1967.

Sartor Resartus
Carlyle, Thomas. *Sartor Resartus*. Scholarly Press, 1977.

Sartoris
Faulkner, William. *Sartoris*. Random House, 1966.

The Saturdays
Enright, Elizabeth. *The Saturdays*. Dell, 1966.

Satyricon
Petronius. *Satyricon*. New American Library, 1960.

The Scarlet Letter
Hawthorne, Nathaniel. *The Scarlett Letter: A Romance*. Oxford University Press, 1965.

The Scarlet Pimpernel
Orczy, Emmuska. *The Scarlet Pimpernel*. New American Library, 1974.

Scarlet Sister Mary
Peterkin, Julie. *Scarlet Sister Mary*. Berg, 1929.

Schenken
Schenken, Suzanne O'Dea. *From Suffrage to Senate*. ABC-CLIO, 1999.

Scholes
Scholes, Percy A., ed. *The Oxford Companion to Music*, 10th ed., rev.

John Owen Ward. Oxford University Press, 1972.

The School for Scandal
Sheridan, Richard B. *The School for Scandal*, ed. C.J.Price. Oxford University Press, 1971.

The School for Wives
Molière, Jean P. *The School for Wives*, tr. Richard Wilbur. Harcourt, Brace, Jovanovich, 1972.

The Seagull
Chekhov, Anton. *The Seagull*, tr. Jean-Claude Van Itallie. Harper & Row, 1977.

Second Shepherds' Play
Second Shepherds' Play in *Specimens of Pre-Shakespearean Drama*, ed. J.M. Manly, vol. 1. Dover, 1967.

The Secret Garden
Burnett, Frances H. *The Secret Garden*. Lippincott, 1962.

The Secret Language
Nordstrom, Ursula. *The Secret Language*. Harper, 1960.

Sense and Sensibility
Austen, Jane. *Sense and Sensibility*. Oxford University Press, 1975.

Septimus and the Danedyke Mystery
Chance, Stephen. *Septimus and the Danedyke Mystery*. Nelson, 1973.

Seraphina
Harris, Mary K. *Seraphina*. Faber, 1960.

Seven Against Thebes
Aeschylus. *Seven Against Thebes*, ed. Christopher Dawson. Prentice-Hall, 1970.

Sexual Politics
Millett, Kate. *Sexual Politics*. Avon, 1973.

Shamela Andrews
Baker, Sheridan. *Shamela and Joseph Andrews*. Thomas Y. Crowell, 1972.

Sharp
Sharp, Harold and Marjorie Z. *Index to Characters in the Performing Arts*. 4 vols: Part 1- Non-Musical Plays, 1966; Part 2 - Opera & Musical Productions, 1969; Part 3 - Ballets A to Z and Symbols, 1972; Part 4 - Radio and Television, 1973. Scarecrow Press.

Shepard
Shepard, Leslie. *History of Street Literature*. Gale, 1973.

Sheridan
Sheridan, Martin. *Comics and Their Creators*. Hyperion Press, 1971.

Sherlock Holmes
Baring-Gould, William S. *The Annotated Sherlock Holmes*. Clarkson N. Potter, 1967.

Ship of Fools
Porter, Katherine Anne. *Ship of Fools*. Norton, 1972.

Shirer
Shirer, William L. *The Rise and Fall of the Third Reich*. Fawcett World, 1972.

Short Friday
Singer, Isaac Bashevis. *Short Friday*. Fawcett Crest, 1964.

Shosha
Singer, Isaac Bashevis. *Shosha*. Farrar, Straus & Giroux, 1978.

Siddhartha
Hesse, Hermann. *Siddhartha*, tr. Hilda Rosner. New Directions, 1951.

The Silver Chair
Lewis, C.S. *The Silver Chair*. Macmillan, 1970.

Simon
Simon, George T. *Simon Says: The Sights and Sounds of the Swing Era 1935-1955*. Galahad Books, 1971.

Simplicissimus
von Grimmelshausen, H.J.C. *Simplicissimus the Vagabond*, tr. A.T. Goodrich. Folcroft, 1978.

858

Sir Gawain and the Green Knight
Sir Gawain and the Green Knight in *The Age of Chaucer [Vol. I, Penguin Guide to English Literature]*. Penguin, 1954.

Sir Launcelot Greaves
Smollett, Tobias. *Sir Launcelot Greaves*, ed. David Evans. Oxford University Press, 1973.

Sirga
Guillot, Rene. *Sirga*. S.G. Phillips, 1959.

Six Modern Short Novels
Six Modern Short Novels. Dell, 1964.

SJEPC
St. James Encyclopedia of Popular Culture. St. James Press, 2003.

The Sketch Book of Geoffrey Crayon, Gendleman
Irving, Washington. *The Sketch Book of Geoffrey Crayon, Gentleman*. Twayne, 1978.

Sketches by Boz
Dickens, Charles. *Sketches by Boz*. Dutton, 1968.

Slaughterhouse-Five
Vonnegut, Kurt. *Slaughterhouse-Five*. Dell, 1971.

The Small House at Allington
Trollope, Anthony. *The Small House at Allington*. Dutton, 1972.

Smith
Garfield, Leon. *Smith*. Pantheon, 1967.

Smithsonian
Smithsonian. November 1977.

Snark
Carroll, Lewis. *The Hunting of the Snark*. Clarkson N. Potter, 1975.

The Snowy Day
Keats, Ezra Jack. *The Snowy Day*. Viking Press, 1962.

Sobel
Sobel, Bernard. *The New Theatre Handbook and Digest of Plays*. Crown, 1959.

Soldiers of Fortune
Davis, Richard Harding. *Soldiers of Fortune*. Scholarly Press, 1975.

Song of Igor's Campaign
Song of Igor's Campaign, tr. Vladimir Nabokov. McGraw-Hill, 1975.

Song of Roland
The Song of Roland, tr. Dorothy Sayers. Penguin, 1957.

Song of the Cid
Song of the Cid, tr. J. G. Markley. Bobbs-Merrill, 1961.

Sophocles Two
Sophocles Two, tr. David Grene and Richmond Lattimore. University of Chicago Press, 1957.

Sordello
Browning, Robert. "Sordello" in *Poems of Robert Browning*, ed. Donald Smalley. Houghton Mifflin, 1956.

The Sot-Weed Factor
Barth, John. *The Sot-Weed Factor*. Bantam, 1969.

Southwick Quizzism
Southwick, Albert P. *Quizzism and Its Key*. Gale, 1968.

Southwick Wisps
Southwick, Albert P. *Wisps of Wit and Wisdom*. Gale, 1968.

Spain
Spain: A History in Art, ed. Bradley Smith. Doubleday, 1971.

Sparks
Sparks, John. *Bird Behavior*. Bantam, 1971.

Spevack
Harvard Concordance to Shakespeare, ed. Marvin Spevack. Belknap, 1974.

Spiller
Spiller, Robert, et al. *Literary History of the United States*, 3rd ed. Macmillan, 1963.

Spoon River Anthology
Masters, Edgar Lee. *Spoon River Anthology*. Macmillan, 1968.

Sports Illustrated
"Inside the Eagle's Nest" in *Sports Illustrated*. February 15, 1979, pp.142-143.

Springhaven
Blackmore, Richard. *Springhaven*. Harper, 1887.

The Spy
Cooper, James Fennimore. *The Spy*. Popular Library, 1971.

St. Ronan's Well
Scott, Sir Walter. *St. Ronan's Well* in *Complete Works*. Houghton, 1923.

Stalky and Company
Kipling, Rudyard. *Stalky and Company*. Dell, 1968.

Stauffer
Stauffer, Francis H. *The Queer, the Quaint, and the Quizzical*. Gale, 1968.

Stefansson
Stefansson, Vilhjalmur. *Adventures in Error*. Gale, 1970.

Steppenwolf
Hesse, Hermann. *Steppenwolf*. Holt, Rinehart, Winston, 1970.

Stimpson
Stimpson, George W. *Nuggets and Knowledge*. Gale, 1970.

Stimpson *Questions*
Stimpson, George W. *Popular Questions Answered*. Gale, 1970.

The Stone-Faced Boy
Fox, Paula. *The Stone-Faced Boy*. Scholastic Book Service, 1972.

Stories
Cheever, John. *The Stories of John Cheever*. Knopf, 1978.

The Story About Ping
Flack, Marjorie. *The Story About Ping*. Viking, 1970.

The Story of Ferdinand
Leaf, Munro. *The Story of Ferdinand*. Viking Press, 1969.

Stranger in a Strange Land
Heinlein, Robert. *Stranger in a Strange Land*. Putnam, 1972.

Strawberry Girl
Lenski, Lois. *Strawberry Girl*. Lippincott, 1945.

A Streetcar Named Desire
Williams, Tennessee. *A Streetcar Named Desire*. New Directions, 1947.

The Sun Also Rises
Hemingway, Ernest. *The Sun Also Rises*. Scribner, 1926.

Swiss Family Robinson
Wyss, Johann. *Swiss Family Robinson*. Grosset and Dunlap, 1970.

Sylvester and the Magic Pebble
Steig, William. *Sylvester and the Magic Pebble*. Dutton, 1973.

Sylvestre Bonnard
France, Anatole. *The Crime of Sylvestre Bonnard*. Dodd Mead, 1924.

The Tale of Benjamin Bunny
Potter, Beatrix. *The Tale of Benjamin Bunny*. Dover, 1974.

The Tale of Genji
Murasaki, Lady Shikibu. *The Tale of Genji*. Modern Library, 1960.

The Tale of Peter Rabbit
Potter, Beatrix. *The Tale of Peter Rabbit*. Dover, 1972.

A Tale of Two Cities
Dickens, Charles. *A Tale of Two Cities*, ed. George Woodcock. Penguin, 1970.

Tales of Hoffmann
Hoffmann, E.T.A. *Tales of Hoffmann*, ed. Michael Bullock. Frederick Ungar, 1963.

Tales of Terror
Poe, Edgar Allan. *Tales of Terror and Fantasy*. Dutton, 1972.

Tales of the Genii
Tales of the Genii, tr. James Ridley. Harrap, 1919.

The Talisman
Scott, Sir Walter. *The Talisman*. Dutton, 1972.

The Taming of the Shrew
Shakespeare, William. *The Taming of the Shrew*, ed. George L. Kittredge and Irving Ribner. John Wiley, 1966.

Tartarin de Tarascon
Daudet, Alphonse. *Tatarin de Tarascon*. French and European Publication, 1965.

Tartuffe
Molière, Jean P. *Tartuffe*, ed. Hallam Walker. Prentice-Hall, 1969.

Tarzan of the Apes
Burroughs, Edgar Rice. *Tarzan of the Apes*. Grosset and Dunlap, 1973.

Taylor
Taylor, Margaret Fisk. *A Time to Dance*. United Church Press, 1967.

TCLM
Henderson, Helene and Jay P. Pederson. *Twentieth-Century Literary Movements Dictionary*. Omnigraphics, 2000.

The Tempest
Shakespeare, William. *The Tempest*, ed. Leonard Natanson. William C. Brown, 1969.

Tender Is the Night
Fitzgerald, F. Scott. *Tender Is the Night*. Scribner, 1960.

Terrace
Terrace, Vincent. *The Complete Encyclopedia of Television Programs, 1947-1976*, 2 vols. A.S. Barnes, 1976.

Tess of the D'Urbervilles
Hardy, Thomas. *Tess of the D'Urbervilles*, ed. Scott Elledge. Norton, 1966.

Thebaid
Statius. *The Thebaid*. Adolt M. Hakkert, 1968.

The Thin Man
Hammett, Dashiell. *The Thin Man*. Random House, 1972.

This Side of Paradise
Fitzgerald, F. Scott. *This Side of Paradise*. Scribner, 1920.

Thompson
Thompson, Oscar. *International Cyclopedia of Music and Musicians*, 10th rev. ed. Dodd, 1975.

Thorne *Facts*
Thorne, Robert. *Fugitive Facts*. Gale, 1969.

The Three Musketeers
Dumas, Alexandre père. *The Three Musketeers*. Hart, 1975.

Three Princes of Serendip
Hodges, Elizabeth J. *Three Princes of Serendip*. Atheneum, 1964.

The Three Royal Monkeys
de la Mare, Walter. *The Three Royal Monkeys*. Knopf, 1948.

The Three Toymakers
Williams, Ursula Moray. *The Three Toymakers*. Hamish Hamilton, 1945.

Through the Looking-glass
Carroll, Lewis. *Through the Looking-glass*. Random House, 1946.

Thyestes
Seneca. *Thyestes*, tr. Moses Hadas. Bobbs-Merrill, 1957.

Tiger at the Gates
Giraudoux, Jean. *Tiger at the Gates*. Oxford University Press, 1955.

Till Eulenspiegel
DeCoster, Charles T. *The Legend of the Glorious Adventures of Till Eulen-*

861

spiegel in the Land of Flanders and Elsewhere. Hyperion Press, 1978.

Timbs
Timbs, John. *Historic Ninepins*. Gale, 1969.

The Time Machine
Wells, H.G. *The Time Machine*. Bantam, 1968.

Time of Trial
Burton, Hester. *Time of Trial*. Dell, 1970.

Timon of Athens
Shakespeare, William. *Timon of Athens*, ed. H.J. Oliver. Barnes & Noble, 1958.

'Tis Pity She's A Whore
Ford, John. *'Tis Pity She's A Whore*. Hill and Wang, 1969.

Titus Andronicus
Shakespeare, William. *Titus Andronicus*, ed. J.C. Maxwell. Barnes & Noble, 1968.

To Have and Have Not
Hemingway, Ernest. *To Have and Have Not*. Scribner, 1937.

Tobacco Road
Caldwell, Erskine. *Tobacco Road*. New American Library, Signet, 1970.

Tobias
Tobias, Sheila. *Faces of Feminism: An Activist's Reflections*. Westview Press, 1997.

Toby Tyler
Otis, James. *Toby Tyler*. Scholastic Book Service, 1972.

Toland
Toland, John. *The Rising Sun*. Bantam Books, 1971.

Tom Brown's School Days
Hughes, Thomas. *Tom Brown's School Days*. Airmont, 1968.

Tom Jones
Fielding, Henry. *Tom Jones*, ed. W. Somerset Maugham. Fawcett World, 1969.

Tom Sawyer
Twain, Mark. *Tom Sawyer*. Washington Square Press, 1972.

Tom Thumb the Great
Fielding, Henry. *Tom Thumb and the Tragedy of Tragedies*. University of California Press, 1970.

Tom's Midnight Garden
Pearce, Philippa. *Tom's Midnight Garden*. Lippincott, 1959.

Torrie
Johnson, Annabel and Edgar. *Torrie*. Harper & Row, 1960.

Tortilla Flat
Steinbeck, John. *Tortilla Flat*. Viking Press, 1935.

The Tower Treasure
Dixon, Franklin W. *The Tower Treasure*. Grosset and Dunlap, 1927.

Traveller
Goldsmith, Oliver. *Traveller, Or, a Prospect of Society*. British Book Centre, 1975.

Travels of Marco Polo
Polo, Marco. *Travels of Marco Polo*. Dutton, Everyman, 1954.

Treasure Island
Stevenson, Robert Louis. *Treasure Island*. Macmillan, 1962.

Treat
Treat, Roger. *The Encyclopedia of Football*. A.S.Barnes, 1977.

The Trial
Kafka, Franz. *The Trial*. Random House, 1969.

Trial by Jury
Gilbert, W.S., and Arthur Sullivan. *Trial by Jury* in *The Complete Plays of Gilbert and Sullivan*. Norton, 1976.

A Trick to Catch the Old One
Middleton, Thomas. *A Trick to Catch the Old One*. University fo California Press, 1968.

Trilby
DuMaurier, George. *Trilby*. Dutton, 1953.

Tristan
Von Strassburg, Gottfried. *Tristan*, tr. Arthur T. Hatto. Penguin, 1960.

Tristan and Isolde
Wagner, Richard. *Tristan and Isolde: Complete Orchestral Score*. Dover, 1973.

Troilus and Cressida
Shakespeare, William. *Troilus and Cressida*, ed. Arthur Quiller-Crouch, et al. Cambridge University Press, 1969.

The Trojan Women
Euripides. *The Trojan Women*, tr. Gilbert Murray. Oxford University Press, 1915.

Tropic of Cancer
Miller, Henry. *Tropic of Cancer*. Ballantine, 1975.

Turkin
Turkin, Hy, and S.C. Thompson. *The Official Encyclopedia of Baseball*, 9th ed. A.S. Barnes, 1977.

The Turn of the Screw
James, Henry. *The Turn of the Screw*. Dell, 1956.

Turner
The Parlour Song Book, eds. Michael R. Turner and Anthomny Miall. Viking Press, 1972.

Twelfth Night
Shakespeare, William. *Twelfth Night*, ed. T.H. Howard-Hill. William C. Brown, 1969.

Twelve Famous Plays
Twelve Famous Plays of the Restoration and Eighteenth Century. Modern Library, 1933.

Twenty Thousand Leagues Under the Sea
Verne, Jules. *Twenty Thousand Leagues Under the Sea*, tr. Mendor Brunetti. New American Library, Signet, 1969.

The Twenty-One Balloons
DuBois, William Péne. *The Twenty-One Balloons*. Dell, 1969.

The Twisted Claw
Dixon, Franklin D. *The Twisted Claw*. Grosset and Dunlap, 1939.

Two Gentlemen of Verona
Shakespeare, William. *Two Gentlemen of Verona*, ed. George L. Kittredge and Irving Ribner. John Wiley, 1969.

Tyler, Wilkin, and Skee
Burch, Robert. *Tyler, Wilkin, and Skee*. Dell, 1971.

UIMT
Gulevich, Tanya. *Understanding Islam and Muslim Traditions*. Omnigraphics, 2004.

Uncle Remus
Harris, Joel C. *Uncle Remus: His Songs and Sayings*. Grosset and Dunlap, 1974.

Uncle Tom's Cabin
Stowe, Harriet Beecher. *Uncle Tom's Cabin*. Dutton, 1961.

Uncle Vanya
Chekhov, Anton. *Uncle Vanya*. Avon, 1974.

The Uncommercial Traveller
Dickens, Charles. *The Uncommercial Traveller*. Dutton, 1970.

Under the Yoke
Vazov, Ivan. *Under the Yoke*. Heinemann, 1912.

Understood Betsy
Fisher, Dorothy. *Understood Betsy*. Grosset and Dunlap, 1970.

The Undiscovered Country
Howells, William D. *The Undiscovered Country*. Scholarly Press, 1971.

Universal Dictionary
Bailey, Nathan. *Universal Etymological English Dictionary*. Adler's Foreign Books, 1969.

Up Eel River
Montague, Margaret P. *Up Eel River*. Arno, facsimile of 1928 ed.

Upstairs, Downstairs
Hawkesworth, John. *Upstairs, Downstairs*. Ulverscroft, 1976.

Utopia
More, St. Thomas. *Utopia*, ed. Edward Surtz. Yale University Press, 1964.

V.
Pynchon, Thomas. *V.*. Lippincott, 1961.

Van Doren
Webster's Guide to American History, eds. Van Doren, Charles, et al. G. & C. Merriam, 1971.

Vanity Fair
Thackeray, William M. *Vanity Fair*. Dutton, 1972.

Vargas
Austin, Reid, and Alberto Vargas. *Vargas*. Crown, 1980.

Vathek
Beckford, William. *Vathek*. Oxford University Press, 1970.

The Velveteen Rabbit
Williams, Margery. *The Velveteen Rabbit*. Doubleday, 1958.

The Vicar of Bullhampton
Trollope, Anthony. *The Vicar of Bullhampton*. Oxford University Press, 1975.

The Vicar of Wakefield
Goldsmith, Oliver. *The Vicar of Wakefield*. Dutton, 1956.

The Village
Bunin, Ivan. *The Village*, tr. I. Hapgood. Fertig, 1975.

Villon
Villon. *Poems*, tr. Peter Dale. St. Martin's Press, 1973.

The Virginians
Thackeray, William M. *The Virginians*. Smith, Elder, 1886.

Vizetelly
Vizetelly, Frank H., and Leander J DeBekker. *Desk-Book of Idioms and Idiomatic Phrases in English Speech and Literature*. Gale, 1970.

Volsung Saga
Volsung Saga, tr. William Morris. Macmillan, 1962.

Voyage of the 'Dawn Treader'
Lewis, C.S. *The Voyage of the 'Dawn Treader'*. Macmillan, 1970.

Voyage to the Moon
Verne, Jules. *Voyage to the Moon*. Harmony Books, 1977.

Walden
Thoreau, Henry David. *Walden*. Macmillan, 1966.

Wallechinsky
Wallechinsky, David, et al. *The Book of Lists*. William Morrow, 1977.

Walsh Classical
Walsh, William S. *Heroes and Heroines of Fiction: Classical, Medieval, Legendary*. Gale, 1966.

Walsh Curiosities
Walsh, William S. *A Handy Book of Literary Curiosities*. Gale, 1966.

Walsh Information
Walsh, William S. *A Handy Book of Curious Information*. Gale, 1970.

Walsh Modern
Walsh, William S. *Heroes and Heroines of Fiction: Modern Prose and Poetry*. Gale, 1966.

The Wandering Jew
Sue, Eugènie. *The Wandering Jew*. Modern Library, n.d.

The Water Babies
Kingsley, Charles. *The Water Babies*. Hart, 1977.

Watership Down
Adams, Richard. *Watership Down*. Macmillan, 1974.

Waverley
Scott, Sir Walter. *Waverley*. Dutton, 1969.

Webster's Sports
Webster's Sports Dictionary. G. &. C. Merriam, 1976.

Weiss
Weiss, Irving and Anne D. *Thesaurus of Book Digests 1950-1980*. Crown, 1981.

Wells
Wells, Carolyn. *A Whimsey Anthology*. Gale, 1976.

Wentworth
Wentworth, Harold, and S.B. Flexner. *Dictionary of American Slang*, 2nd supplemented ed. Thomas Y. Crowell, 1975.

Werner Bischof
Capa, Cornell. *Werner Bischof*. Grossman, 1974.

West Side Story
Bernstein, Leonard, et al. *West Side Story*. Random House, 1958.

Westerman
Westerman, Gerhart von. *Opera Guide*. Dutton, 1968.

What Makes Sammy Run
Schulberg, Budd. *What Makes Sammy Run*. Random House, 1941.

Wheeler
Wheeler, William A. *A Dictionary of the Noted Names of Fiction*. Gale, 1966.

Wheeler *Allusions*
Wheeler, William A. *Familiar Allusions*. Gale, 1966.

Where the Wild Things Are
Sendak, Maurice. *Where the Wild Things Are*. Harper & Row, 1963.

White
White, T.H. *The Book of Beasts*. Jonathan Cape, 1954.

The White Archer
Houston, James. *The White Archer: An Eskimo Legend*. Harcourt Brace Jovanovich, 1967.

The White Devil
Webster, John. *The White Devil*. Chandler, 1961.

White Fang
London, Jack. *White Fang*. Macmillan, 1935.

White Jacket
Melville, Herman. *White Jacket*. Holt, 1967.

Wieland
Brown, Charles Brockden. *Wieland*. Harcourt Brace Jovanovich, 1969.

Wigoder
Encyclopedic Dictionary of Judaica, ed. Geoffrey Wigoder. Leon Amiel, 1974.

Wild Jack
Christopher, John. *Wild Jack*. Macmillan, 1974.

William Tell
Schiller, Friedrich Von. *William Tell*, tr. Sidney E. Kaplan. Barron's, 1954.

William the Dragon
Donnison, Polly. *William the Dragon*. Coward, McCann and Geoghegan, 1973.

Willis
Willis, Jim. *The Religion Book: Places, Prophets, Saints, and Seers*. Visible Ink Press, 2004.

The Wind in the Willows
Grahame, Kenneth. *The Wind in the Willows*. Dell, 1969.

Wind, Sand, and Stars
De Saint-Exupèry, Antoine. *Wind, Sand, and Stars*. Harcourt Brace Jovanovich, 1967.

Winesburg, Ohio
Anderson, Sherwood. *Winesburg, Ohio*. Viking Press, 1960.

Winnie-the-Pooh
Milne, A.A. *Winnie-the-Pooh*. Dell, 1974.

The Winter's Tale
Shakespeare, William. *The Winter's Tale* in *William Shakespeare: The Complete Works*, ed. Peter Alexander. Collins, 1951.

The Witch's Daughter
Bawden, Nina. *The Witch's Daughter*. Lippincott, 1966.

A Wizard of Earthsea
LeGuin, Ursula. *A Wizard of Earthsea*. Bantam, 1975.

The Wolfman
Dreadstone, Carl. *The Wolfman*. Berkley, 1977.

The Woman of Rome
Moravia, Alberto. *The Woman of Rome*, tr. Lydia Holland. Manor Books, 1948.

The Wonderful Adventures of Nils
Lagerlof, Selma. *The Wonderful Adventures of Nils*. Pantheon, 1947.

The Wonderful Adventures of Paul Bunyan
The Wonderful Adventures of Paul Bunyan, retold by Louis Untermeyer. Heritage, c. 1945.

The Wonderful Wizard of Oz
Baum, L. Frank. *The Wonderful Wizard of Oz*. Random House, 1972.

The Wondrous Tale of Alroy
Disraeli, Benjamin. *The Wondrous Tale of Alroy*. Carey, Lea, and Blanchard, 1933.

Woods
Poetry of the Victorian Period, eds. George Benjamin Woods and Jerome Buckley. Scott Foresman, 1955.

Woodstock
Scott, Sir Walter. *Woodstock*. Dutton, 1969.

WB
World Book Encyclopedia. World Book-Childcraft International, 1979.

WB2
World Book Encylopedia. World Book, 2006.

Yankee Thunder
Shapiro, Irwin. *Yankee Thunder: The Legendary Life of Davy Crockett*. Julian Messner, 1944.

The Yearling
Rawlings, Marjorie K. *The Yearling*. Scribner, 1962.

The Yeoman of the Guard
Gilbert, W.S., and Arthur Sullivan *The Yeoman of the Guard* in *The Complete Plays of Gilbert and Sullivan*. Norton, 1976.

You Can't Go Home Again
Wolfe, Thomas. *You Can't Go Home Again*. Harper, 1940.

The Young Manhood of Studs Lonigan
Farrell, James T. *The Young Manhood of Studs Lonigan* in *Studs Lonigan: A Trilogy*. Vanguard, 1932-35.

Zeely
Hamilton, Virginia. *Zeely*. Macmillan, 1971.

Zimmerman
Zimmerman, J.E. *Dictionary of Classical Mythology*. Harper & Row, 1964.

Index

Index

A

A. N. Other, 249.1
A.F.L.-C.I.O., 420.1
Aaron, 370.1, 679.1
Aaron, Hank, 63.1,
567.1
Aaron's rod, 466.1
AARP (American Association of Retired
Persons), 5.1, 10.1
Aaru, 344.1
Aarvark, 174.1
Abaddon, 23.1, 192.1,
345.1
Abaris, 403.1
Abas, 473.1
Abba, 325.1
ABBA, 485.1
Abbey of Telema,
696.1
Abbey Theatre, 669.1
Abbott, Bud and Lou
Costello, 130.1
ABCs, 226.1
Abdera, 643.1
Abdiel, 23.2, 265.1
Abdul-Jabbar,
Kareem, 64.1
Abel and Rima, 437.1
Abelard, Peter, 106.1,
606.1
Abélard, Pierre, 437.2
Abélard, Pierre and
Héloïse, 441.1
Abi, 345.2
Abiathar, 247.1
Abie's Irish Rose, 431.1
Abigail, 207.1, 265.2,
362.1, 613.1

Abijah, 562.1
Abimelech, 481.1
Abishai, 584.1
Abolitionists, 29.1
Abominable Snowman, 477.1
abominable snowmen,
490.1
abomination of desolation, 192.2, 603.1
Abonde, Dame, 264.1
Abra, 472.1
Abracadabra, 555.1
Abraham, 118.1, 120.1,
265.3, 277.1, 362.2,
417.1, 550.1, 667.1
Abraham's bosom,
118.2, 344.2, 417.2
Absalom, 68.1, 337.1,
574.1, 698.1
"Absent-Minded Beggar, The", 301.1
absent-minded professor, 301.2
Absolon, 548.1
Absolute, Sir
Anthony, 38.1
Abstract Expressionism, 41.1, 385.1
Absyrtus, 489.1
Abu Dhabi, 712.1
Abu Jahl, 296.1
AC/DC, 485.2
acacia, 308.1
Academy, the, 226.2
Academy Awards,
253.1
See also Oscar
Acadians, 58.1
Acamas, 698.2

Acarnan and Amphoterus, 698.3
Ace, Jane, 196.1
Aceldama, 98.1
Acephali, 340.1
Acesis, 341.1
Acestes, 362.3, 655.1
Achaean League, 148.1
Achan, 209.1
Achates, 442.1
Acheron, 459.1
Achille Lauro, 666.1
Achilles, 24.1, 84.1,
207.2, 349.1, 698.4,
706.1
Achilles and
Patroclus, 308.2
Achilles' spear, 341.2
Achitophel, 150.1,
191.1, 649.1, 679.2
Achren, 162.1
acid test, 321.1
Acis, 126.1
ACLU (American Civil
Liberties Union),
426.1
acorn, 332.1, 642.1
Acrasia, 217.1
Acre, 453.1
Acres, Bob, 155.1, 299.1
Acropolis, The, 726.1
Act of Contrition,
531.1
Acta Pilati (Acts of Pilate), 300.1
Actaeon, 677.1, 705.1
Actaeon's horns, 164.1
Actium, 65.1
ACT-UP, 592.1
acupuncture, 341.3

Cobb, Ty, 63.8
cobra, 175.5
Coca-Cola, 20.9, 297.2, 448.7, 688.3
Cochise, 713.22
Cochran, Johnnie, Jr., 418.15
cock, 333.9, 520.2, 651.6, 709.3
cock crow, 679.15
Cockaigne, 445.10
cockatrice, 477.22
cocktail parties, 297.3, 462.5
coconut, 283.19
Cocytus, 707.9
Cody, "Buffalo Bill", 713.23
Cohan, George M., 485.24, 526.7
Cointet brothers, 144.7
Colada, 657.6
Colamartini, Christina, 611.12
Cold War, 133.3, 708.12
Cole, Joanna, 729.12
collateral damage, 192.8
Collins, Barnabas, 360.9
Collins, Mr., 136.6, 290.6
Collins, Wilkie, 490.9
Collinwood, 363.2
Collodi, Carlo, 729.13
Collyer, Homer and Langley, 470.3
Colomba, 698.15
Color Purple, The, 567.18
Colosseum, 726.3
Colossos, 323.21
Colossus of Rhodes, 660.4
Colt .45, 288.2, 713.24
Coltrane, John, 484.6

Columbia, 202.7
columbine, 296.6
Columbine, 292.4, 453.6
Columbo, 193.13
Columbus, Christopher, 258.2
Comanche, 653.2, 713.25
Comanche Indians, 92.10
Combray, 499.3
Comédie–Française, 669.5
Comedy of Errors, The, 140.4, 686.6
Coming Race, The, 696.10
Common Lot, The, 330.7
Common Market, 148.5
commune, 151.11, 696.11
Como, Perry, 622.7
compact disc (CD), 482.5
Compeyson, 670.7
Compleat Angler, The, 146.1, 598.5
Compson, Benjy, 199.5
Compson, Candace, 551.7
Compson, Quentin, 380.6, 649.14
Comstock Lode, 681.2, 713.26
Comstock, Anthony, 109.7
Comus, 588.4
Conachar, 155.4
Concentrations Camps, 648.8
concept albums, 485.25
conceptual art, 41.11
Conchis, 162.8, 182.15

Conchobar, 436.6
Concorde, 433.3
Concordia, 338.4, 528.5
Condé Nast, 413.9
condoms, 206.5, 555.9
Conestoga wagon, 414.6, 713.27
Confederacy, 148.6, 633.4
Confessions, 74.3
Confessions of an English Opium-Eater, 6.4
Confessions of St. Augustine, The, 74.4
Confidence Man, The, 305.3, 468.3
Confucius, 661.11, 722.12
Congreve, William, 214.6
Connecticut Yankee, the, 402.3, 674.2
Connor, Bull, 73.8
Connors, Jimmy, 110.2, 404.2, 665.4
Conqueror Worm, 177.21
Conquistadores, 258.3, 599.4
Conrad, 615.4
Conrad, Joseph, 198.2, 501.3
Conrad, Lord, 539.3
consciousness raising, 237.5
Conseil, 530.5
Conservative party, 143.4
Constance, 19.5
Constantin, Abbé, 318.15
Constitutum Constantini, 300.5
Consumer Reports, 5.11, 50.4, 145.2, 413.10

Drury Lane, 669.6
Drury Lane Theatre Ghost, 322.13
Drusiana, 586.7
Dry Guillotine, 194.4
dryads, 504.3
Dryas, 468.4
Dryasdust, Rev., 82.3
drys, 261.2
Du Bois, W. E. B., 5.13, 226.12, 567.26
du Maurier, Daphne, 490.13
Duat, 691.8
Dubois, Blanche, 188.4
Duce II, 273.2
Duchess of Alba, 67.18
Duchess of Berwick, 328.3
Duchess's baby, 677.27
duck, 338.6, 585.8
Dudgeon, Dick, 611.20
Duessa, 689.7
Duke and the King, the, 305.4
Duke of Buckingham, 144.10
Duke of Plaza-Toro, 155.7
Duke, Daisy, 615.7
Dukes of Hazzard, The, 598.7, 633.7
dukkha, 93.7
Dulcamara, Dr., 564.2
Dulcinea (del Toboso), 69.3, 398.8, 440.10
Dull, Anthony, 643.5
Dumas, Alexander, 501.9
Dumbledore, Albus, 725.1
Dumbo, 291.4
Dumuzi, 586.8
Duncan, Isadora, 172.14
Dundreary, Lord, 40.8

Dungeons and Dragons, 147.12, 270.12, 315.2
Dunkin' Donuts, 297.6, 688.4
Dunkirk, 247.8, 584.10
Dunsmen, 371.5
Dupin, Auguste, 193.18
Dupré, Ashley, 554.5
Dupre, Sally, 265.24
Duran, Roberto, 83.7, 110.4
Durante, Jimmy, 498.4
Durga, 708.17
Durnidana, 657.8
Durocher, Leo, 63.12
Duroy, George, 692.7
Durward, Quentin, 349.19
dust and ashes, 177.26
Dutch uncle, 160.4
Duval, Claude, 351.3
Dvalin, 219.3
Dvorak, Antonin, 483.10
Dyava-Matar, 221.4
dybbuk, 190.11, 545.5
Dyer, Wayne, 610.4
Dykes to Watch Out For, 131.11, 357.13
Dylan, 608.7
Dylan, Bob, 151.16, 485.38, 486.10, 630.7, 677.28
Dymaxion house, 37.10
Dympna, Saint, 446.13
Dynasty, 254.4, 521.13

E

e pluribus unum, 20.11
E.T., 1.4, 308.13, 356.1
E=mc2, 490.14
Ea, 157.9, 510.1

eagle, 50.11, 306.8, 461.5, 545.6, 651.9
ear and knife, 489.6
Earhart, Amelia, 201.7
Earnhardt, Dale, Sr., 568.4
Earp, Wyatt, 158.5, 713.36
Earth Day, 240.4
Earth Shoes, 240.5, 274.10
Earthly Paradise, 518.4
east and west, 690.2
Easter Island's statues, 490.15
Easter Rising, 573.8
Eastwood, Clint, 452.8
Easy Rider, 151.17, 306.9, 559.5
Eben Shetiyyah, 409.13, 417.15
Ebionites, 348.7
Eblis, 195.17
Ebony, 413.14, 567.27
EC Comics, 131.12
Ecce Homo, 473.4
Ecclitico, 46.2
Echidna, 477.25
Echo, 438.8, 659.8
eclipse, 443.7
Ecologues, 523.4
eco-terrorism, 240.6
Eddas, 730.8
Eddy, Mary Baker, 342.6
Eddy, Nelson, 622.11
Eddy, Nelson and Jeanette MacDonald, 441.14
edelweiss, 294.11
Eden, 518.5
Eden, Martin, 208.9, 649.18
Edgar, 358.11, 549.7
Edge of Night, The, 521.14

Golden Gate Bridge,
88.6

Golden Girls, The,
10.10, 308.17

Golden Globe, 549.14

golden handshake,
271.4

Golden Hind, 258.12

Golden Horde, 141.14

golden mean or sec-
tion, 532.2

golden poppy, 295.12

Golden Spurs, Battle
of, 685.10

golden wattle, 294.16

goldenrod, 295.13

Goldilocks, 395.17

Golding, William,
501.16

Goldwyn, Samuel,
285.9

golem, 613.8

Golgotha, 451.11,
520.11

Goliad, 453.9

Goliards, 588.8, 589.6,
707.15

Goliath, 85.5, 323.33

Golightly, Holly, 309.3

Gollum, 182.18, 506.10

Gomer, 551.10

Gompers, Samuel,
420.5

Goncourt, 549.15

Gone with the Wind,
242.7, 633.8, 708.22

Goneril, 649.24

Goneril and Regan,
266.8, 367.24, 393.3

Gong Show, The, 390.2

Gonzalo, 442.27

Good Earth, The,
272.20

Good Housekeeping,
212.12, 413.20

Good Housekeeping
Seal of Approval,
253.5

Good Joe, 327.6

Good Samaritan,
346.9, 419.17

Good Shepherd, 117.8

Good Soldier
Schweik, 463.8

Good Times, 268.9,
567.38, 728.8

*Good, the Bad, and the
Ugly, The,* 713.40

Goodbye, Columbus,
567.39

Good-Deeds, 442.28

GoodFellas, 92.20,
316.9

Goodfellow, Robin,
412.3

Goodman, Benny,
484.12

Goodnight Moon, 320.7

Goodson, Mark, 662.22

Goodwood, Caspar,
438.10, 535.6

Goody Two Shoes,
612.10

Goofy, 54.4

Google, 400.11

Google, Barney,
314.11, 407.6

Goops, 124.6

goose, 265.28

Gorboduc, 45.6

Gordian knot, 546.3

Gordon, Dr., 388.8

Gordon, Flash, 9.17

Gordon, Lord George,
595.8

Gordy, Berry, 239.8,
485.48

Gorgons, 477.30, 689.12

Goriot, Père, 277.7,
318.18

Goshen, 3.9

Goshen, Land of, 528.8

gospel, 118.24

Gospel, 321.3

gospel music, 567.40

Gosta Berling's Saga,
242.8

Gotham, 296.9

gothic, 37.15, 490.19

Gotti, John, 316.10

Grable, Betty, 615.11

Graceland, 124.7

Graces, 66.5

Gradgrind, Thomas,
226.17, 507.4, 670.11

Graduate, The, 317.3

Graeae, the, 78.11

Graf, Steffi, 665.8

Graham, Billy, 248.2

Graham, Katherine,
413.21

Graham, Martha,
172.18

grail, 566.10, 731.4

Gráinne, 437.27

Gram, 657.11

Gramimond, 657.12

Grammy, 482.11,
549.16

Grand Fenwick,
Duchy of, 693.8

Grand Ole Opry,
485.49, 647.7, 693.9

Grand Tour, the,
226.18

Grand, Joseph, 296.10

Grandet, Eugènie,
312.7

Grandet, Monsieur,
470.6

Grandison, Sir
Charles, 497.7

Grandma Moses,
715.12

Grandmarina, 264.4

Grane, 361.18

Mania, 177.42

Manichaean Sabbath, 43.17

Manitou, 325.17

manmukh, 621.8

Mann, Thomas, 501.25

manna, 417.21, 654.4

Mannering, Guy, 46.3, 556.16

Manilow, Barry, 612.13

Mannix, 193.31

Mannon, Christine, 8.24, 649.36

Mannon, Ezra, 164.10

Mannon, Lavinia, 386.4, 401.4

Mannon, Orin, 581.7

Manon, 266.9

Manrico and Leonora, 437.39

Mansfield, Jayne, 101.5, 181.10, 615.16

Mansion, The, 330.20

Manson, Charles, 165.3, 481.39

Manson, Marilyn, 516.9, 536.4

Mantle, Mickey, 63.25

mantra, 352.19, 621.9

Manusmrti, 352.20

maple leaf, 294.24

"Maple Leaf Forever!", 631.8

Mapple, Father, 231.13

Marah, 466.13

Marat, Jean Paul, 177.43

marathon, 49.9

Marathon, 65.27

marathon dancing, 234.9, 262.23

marathon eating, 262.24

Marcel, 673.7

Marcella, 67.35

March Hare, 446.29

March on Washington, 591.16, 630.16

March, Amy, 697.5

March, Augie, 208.17, 406.5

March, Beth, 179.20, 320.9

March, Jo, 383.8

March, Meg, 212.18

Marciano, Rocky, 642.15

Marconi, Guglielmo, 132.10

Marcus Welby, M.D., 457.18

Mardi Gras, 313.6

Marduk, 325.18

mares of Diomedes, 92.33

Margaret of Anjou, 162.16

Margaritaville, 588.11

Marguerite, 42.7

Marie Antoinette, 67.36

marigold, 331.24

Marina, 704.9

Marion, Francis, 166.26

Marius, 243.6

marjoram, 32.5

Mark, 248.5

mark of Cain, 555.20, 640.1

Mark, King, 164.11

Marlboro Festival, 284.8

Marlboro Man, 448.13, 452.22

Marley, 322.30

Marley, Bob, 485.74

Marlowe, Christopher, 214.15

Marlowe, Philip, 193.32

Marmaduke, 211.23

Marmorie, 657.15

Marneffe, Madame, 152.5

Marner, Silas, 470.9, 614.3

Marple, Miss, 193.33

Marplot, 388.16

Marriage à la Mode, 450.18

Mars, 708.34

Marsala, 720.17

Marsalis, Wynton, 484.18

"Marseillaise", 631.9

Marshall Plan, 12.6

Marshall, Thurgood, 5.25, 289.39, 418.27

Marshalsea, 379.30

Marshland, Jinny, 373.12

Marston Moor, 685.14

Marta, 546.5

Martano, 155.11

Martext, Sir Oliver, 367.29

Martha, 718.4

Martha, Saint, 212.19

Martin, Saint, 419.26

Martin, Steve, 732.10

martini, 632.3

Martius and Quintus, 394.24

Marvel, Captain, 349.37, 526.13, 642.16

Marvellous Boy, The, 179.21

Marx Brothers, The, 130.10, 732.11

Marx, Karl, 133.6, 420.8

Mary, 435.6, 479.13

Mary and Elizabeth, 587.6

Mary Celeste, 1.8, 490.29

Mary I of Scotland, 680.12

Norma, 611.37

Norma and Pollio, 437.41

Normandy Invasion, 65.31

Norns, 276.14

Norris, Mrs., 328.5, 456.1

North and South Poles, 582.11

North Star, 29.9

North Star, 89.3

North Woods, 598.8

Northanger Abbey, 363.4

Northwest Passage, 258.20

Nostradamus, 46.4, 553.26

Nostromo, 511.7, 681.16

Nosy Parker, 167.10

Notburga, Saint, 613.14

Notung, 657.21

NOW (National Organization for Women), 5.33, 426.12, 593.30

Nox, 495.8

NRA (National Rifle Association), 366.13

Nubian's skin, 533.3

nuke, 192.35

Number One, 227.9

Nureddin, 438.14

Nuremberg Egg, 122.2

Nuremberg Laws, 28.25

Nuremburg Trials, 418.32

Nureyev, Rudolph, 172.21

Nurse Ratched, 162.19

nut, 399.15, 704.11

Nutcracker, The, 119.30

Nydia, 78.19

Nym, 670.17

NYPD Blue, 147.21

O

O, 245.11

o' Bedlam, Tom, 446.32

"O Canada!", 631.11

O Captain! My Captain!, 331.27

"O Come, All Ye Faithful", 119.31

"O Deutschland, Hoch in Ehren!", 631.12

"O Little Town of Bethlehem", 119.32

O Pioneers!, 647.9

O.K. Corral, 713.55

oak, 234.10, 362.14, 682.10

oak leaves, 584.21

oak leaves, garland of, 691.15

Oakhurst, John, 611.38

Oakley, Annie, 449.7, 713.56

Oakmen, 219.10

Obama, Barack, 289.41, 567.70

Oberlin College, 289.42

Oberon, 232.11, 411.18

Oberon and Titania, 264.7

Obidicut, 427.46

Objectivism, 48.4, 385.10

Oblomov, Ilya, 81.6, 384.8, 424.15

O'Casey, Sean, 214.18

Oceania, 676.12

Oceanids, 504.10, 608.14

Oceanus, 608.15

Ochs, Baron, 124.10

Ocnus, the cord of, 312.10

Octa, 174.7

Octavian, 207.44

Odd Couple, The, 55.6

Odilia, Saint, 78.20

Odin, 272.26, 708.40, 722.25

O'Donnell, Rosie, 357.29

Odysseus, 9.40, 166.29, 207.45, 641.8, 707.29
See also Ulysses

Odysseus' companions, 167.11

Odysseus's crew, 677.48

Odyssey, 242.20, 356.2

Oedipus, 58.17, 78.21, 186.11, 380.16, 525.6, 581.8

Oeneus, 720.21

Of Mice and Men, 312.11, 359.8

off base, 246.3

Og, 323.44

Ogier the Dane, 579.8

O'Gill, Darby, 270.25

Oglethorpe, John, 357.30

OGPU, 639.21

"Oh Bury Me Not on the Lone Prairie", 713.57

O'Hanlon, Virginia, 208.20

O'Hara, Scarlett, 67.41, 292.13, 438.15

O'Hara, Scarlett and Rhett Butler, 441.23

Oil Can Harry, 701.23

O'Keefe, Georgia, 70.14, 293.5

Okies, 544.29, 693.14

Okinawa, 65.32

Old Ben, 565.7

940

Poseidon Hippios, 150.13

Post, Emily, 153.4

postal, to go, 702.8

Posthumus, 58.19

Potemkin village, 367.35

Potiphar's wife, 436.19, 664.5, 679.31

Potsdam Conference, 148.16

Potter, Beatrix, 729.38

Potter, Harry, 514.19, 725.9

Potter, Mr., 95.9

potter's field, 98.16

pound of flesh, 418.35

Povey, Constance Baines, 81.7

Powell, Colin, 567.74

Power, Tyrone, 452.25

Powler, Peg, 250.30

Pozdnishef, Madame, 8.26

Pozdnishef, Vasyla, 411.21

prairie schooner, 713.62

Praise of Folly, The, 605.21

prajna, 237.11

prasad, 621.11

Praxidice, 286.12

Preakness Stakes, 569.6

Precieuse, 657.22

preemptive strike, 708.42

Preminger, Otto, 285.14

preppy, 274.26, 712.30

Pre-Raphaelite, 41.37, 67.42

Presley, Elvis, 6.13, 485.90, 574.16, 622.32

Prester John's mirror, 467.8

Priam, King of Troy, 277.9

Priapus, 186.14, 427.53, 452.26

Price Is Right, The, 145.10, 315.9

Price, Fanny, 513.5

Price, Homer, 21.7

Price, Leontyne, 622.33

Price, Vincent, 360.29

Pride and Prejudice, 439.28

Pride's Purge, 58.20

Prigio, Prince, 136.20

prima donna, 40.16

primrose, 731.7

Prince, 245.20, 485.91

Prince and the Pauper, The, 213.7, 646.11

Prince Charming, 439.29

Prince of Peace, 117.22

Prince of Wales, 213.8

Prince Po, 418.36

Prince, Hal, 487.24

Prince, Nan, 457.22

Prince, The, 692.11

Priscillianism, 43.19

Prism, Miss, 103.4

prisoner of Chillon, 410.15, 648.18

Prisoner of Chillon, The, 379.33

Prisoner of Zenda, The, 2.13, 377.2

Procrustes, 92.38, 489.13

prodigal son, 210.19, 302.10

prodigal son and his father, 587.7

Profiles in Courage, 84.40

Progressive Party, 426.14

Prohibition, 15.13, 663.6

Proitus and Acrisius, 596.13

prom, 7.32

Prometheus, 137.5, 157.17, 234.11, 287.15, 349.40, 562.23, 648.19, 682.11

Prometheus Society, The, 399.17

Promise Keepers, 118.39, 268.14

Proserpina (Gk. Persephone), 2.14

Prospero, 447.16, 725.10

Prospero's banquet, 201.11, 280.7

protea, 294.28

Proteus, 72.4, 677.58

Prothalamion, 450.24

Protocols of the Elders of Zion, 28.26, 300.7

Proudie, Mrs., 620.12

Proust, Marcel, 460.11, 501.29

Proverbs, 150.14

Prozac, 31.4

Prufrock, J. Alfred, 238.5, 675.16

Pry, Paul, 167.13, 223.3

Prynne, Hester, 8.27, 432.9, 562.24, 614.5

Pryor, Richard, 6.14, 129.30

Psychic Friends Network, 182.33, 353.4

Psycho, 360.30

Psychology of Sex, The, 616.24

psychopharmacology, 560.5

952

U

Volstead Act, 663.9
Volsunga Saga, 242.31
Volumnia, 24.21, 40.22
von Aschenbach, Gus-
  tave, 410.20
Von Bismarck, Otto,
  464.9
von Clauswitz, Karl,
  464.10
von Kaltenborn, Hans,
  91.36
von Sacher-Masoch,
  Leopold, 536.8
Vonnegut, Kurt, Jr.,
  501.41
voodoo, 491.10
vos Savant, Marilyn,
  399.21
Vouvray, 720.32
Vulcan, 192.46, 287.22
Vulcan's mirror, 467.10
Vye, Eustacia, 70.21

W

W.M.D., 192.47
Wadman, Widow,
  717.5
waff, 508.9
Wag, Charlie, 469.34
Wag-at-the-Wa', 121.7
Wagner, Honus, 63.44
Wagner, Richard,
  483.24
Wailing Wall, 331.37,
  417.38
Waiting for Godot,
  382.10
Waits, Tom, 485.127
Walden, 523.8
Waldenses, 43.26
Walesa, Lech, 5.49
Walker, Aaron, 485.128
Walker, Alice, 567.97
Walker, Dr., 564.6
Walker, Madame C. J.,
  239.16, 289.65, 567.98

Wall Drugs, 145.13,
  678.24
Wall Street, 286.15
*Wall Street Journal,
  The*, 99.11, 143.20,
  413.63
Wallace, Sippie,
  567.99, 622.43
Wallace, William,
  680.19
Wallenstein, Count,
  680.20
Wallingford, "Get-
  Rich-Quick", 511.9
Wal-Mart, 145.14,
  147.45, 257.11, 389.12,
  647.13, 688.10, 728.19
Walpurgis Night,
  723.23
Walrus, 367.42
Walstan, Saint, 272.31
Walters, Barbara,
  91.37, 289.66
Walton family, 712.42
Walton, Bill, 64.22
Waltons, The, 268.17,
  598.12, 612.20, 715.24
Wandering Jew,
  118.52, 375.28, 707.35
Wanderjahr, 226.33
Wannsee Conference,
  319.19
Wapner, Joseph
  Albert, 418.50
War of 1812, 405.35
War of the Worlds,
  91.38, 279.12, 307.8,
  353.5
War on Poverty, 544.30
Warbucks, Daddy,
  143.21, 712.43
Warburton, Lord, 82.4
Wardle, Rachel, 230.5
Warhol, Andy, 41.47,
  108.12, 216.6, 516.20
Warren Report, 147.46

Warren, Dr. Rick,
  248.10, 610.10
Warren, Mrs., 554.21
Warren, Nicole, 380.20,
  711.9
Warren, The, 180.17
Warshawski, V. I.,
  193.55
Washington Post, The,
  413.64
Washington, Booker
  T., 5.50
Washington, D.C.,
  20.40
Washington, Denzel,
  68.19, 480.44
Washington, George,
  20.41, 289.67, 358.23
Waste Land, The, 61.10
water, 563.16
water moccasin, 175.19
Water Rat, 318.31
water willow, 306.29
Watergate, 144.19,
  606.21
water-lily, 563.17
Waterloo, 65.49, 183.20
Waters, John, 165.11,
  516.21
Waters, Muddy, 486.39
Watership Down,
  240.14
Watson, Dr. John H.,
  641.13
Watson, Tom, 326.14
Watts, 595.17
Watty, Mr., 311.16
waxing moon, 283.50
Way of the World, The,
  450.30
Way to Wealth, The,
  150.15
Wayne, John, 349.53,
  452.36, 480.45, 713.79
"We Shall Overcome",
  591.22

How to Use This Book

Ruffner's Allusions is a thematic dictionary, with almost 13,000 allusion entries organized under more than 730 thematic categories. These thematic categories are presented in the text in alphabetical order by the name of the category heading, for example, AMBITION, FRIENDSHIP, SLANDER. (A complete list, including cross references, is given in the Table of Thematic Categories, page xvii.) Under each thematic category, one or more—sometimes many more—appropriate entries for allusions are listed.

When seeking a set of allusions that deal with a particular theme, say ANGER, the reader will find it in the text as thematic category no. 24. Under that category number and name will be a list of allusions arranged alphabetically and numbered, as in the following example, which shows just a few of the listings under this category:

24	ANGER	(See also EXASPERATION,
The thematic category number, used for ease of reference in the Index.	The thematic category, listed in alphabetical order, with more than 730 throughout the book.	IRASCIBILITY, RANTING.) Cross references point to other related thematic terms.

24. ANGER (See also EXASPERATION, IRASCIBILITY, RANTING.)

1. **Achilles** Greek warrior whose ire is noted in the opening line of *The Iliad*: "Sing, goddess, of the anger of Achilles." [Gk. Myth: ODA]

arrow
Each allusion is given in alphabetical order in bold face type.

5. **arrow** Islamic symbol for Allah's rage. [Islam: *CEOS&S*, 208]
7. **Bernardo** enraged that member of a rival street-gang is making advances to his sister. [Am. Musical: *West Side Story*]
9. **Elmer Fudd** hapless man seethes over Bugs Bunny's antics. [Comics: "Bugs Bunny" in Horn, 140]
11. **Fawlty, Basil** temperamental proprietor of Fawlty Towers, from the TV show of the same name, hilariously acted by John Cleese. [Br. TV: *ODA*]

Islamic symbol for Allah's rage
A brief definition of the allusion is given after its name.

13. **Herod** angry at Wise Men's disobedience, orders slaughter of male infants. [N.T.: Matthew 2:16–17]
14. **Hulk, The Incredible** one of Marvel Comics' most popular super-heroes; Dr. Banner—exposed to gamma radiation—turns into the super-strong Hulk when angry or under stress; made into popular TV show and films. [Am. Comics and TV: *SJEPC*]
18. **Othello** smothers wife, Desdemona, in paroxysm of rage over her suspected adultery. [Br. Lit.: *Othello*]
19. **Rumpelstiltskin** stamps ground in rage over lass's discovery of his name. [Ger. Fairy Tale: *Rumpelstiltskin*]

Ger. Fairy Tale	Rumpelstiltskin
Descriptive categories (here, German Fairy Tale) provide more information about the origin of the allusion, generally nationality and genre (see the Table of Descriptive Categories on the adjoining page).	Source references (a primary or secondary source) provide further information about the background of the allusion; sources are identified in the Bibliography (see the Bibliography, page 819).